杨良宜 | 著

损失赔偿与救济

DAMAGES AND REMEDIES

法律出版社
LAW PRESS · CHINA
——北京——

序

在西方法治国家经常听到一些老生常谈的说法,其中有法律是一套“有组织的常识”(organized common sense),这表示如果任何人想在一个法治国家或者法治的环境中生存甚至兴旺,不掌握法律的知识就代表没有做人或者办事的常识。这里所讲的法律也不是任何国家的法律,某一个国家的法律代表了该国家或者民族的思维水平。而无可疑议的是,在今天的国际商业环境中,英美的普通法或商法代表了一套相对而言最完整、最实用、最符合商业人士的本性、和现实接轨且不断改善的法律。不论是国际公约、个别国家立法、个别的商业合约、国际商业人士处理事情的习惯做法、思维方式等,英美法的理念都占据了主导地位。国际商业无疑是在一个法治的环境里运行,如出了争议,就往往通过约定以仲裁或者法院根据适用的法律(往往是英国法)解决。这表示不了解英美商法的理念就投身国际商业是会处于非常不利与危险的地位,这些人士在西方商业人士的眼中也是没有常识或是“不可理喻”(irrational)。

其中最主要掌握的英美法律就是合约法,因为在国际商业的活动中每一个环节都是以一个个不同的合约串起来的。了解英美商法,除了能订立可以自我保护的合约,更加可以在履行的过程中占据有利地位。另外很重要的是,学好英美的合约法,除了能够建立一套有组织的常识外,也能够帮助建立一个有逻辑性、不相互矛盾与完整的思维。这在今天越来越复杂的国际商业环境是一件十分重要的事,没有这种思维的人士也是无法长期在国际商业环境中生存,更谈不上壮大了。

笔者十几年前所著的《国际商务游戏规则——英国合约法》(中国政法大学出版社2000年版)一书早已脱销。后来找人录入放在笔者的个人网站,不时看到有读者反映读了这本书很有收获,并感觉到思维的提高且能解决实际问题。也曾经听说过,如果这本书能够在中国年轻一代中推广,可能会对中国青年思维水平的提高有一定帮助,但这种推广不是仅靠笔者自己的力量可以做到的事。笔者目前只是想如何更新此书,原因是英国法与时俱进,不少内容已经有了很大改变。但笔者再也没有勇气重写一本全面的英国合约法的书籍,因为这一工程实在太大,耗费时间与精力太多。即使英国这方面的权威书籍,如《Chitty on Contract》,也需要好几个作者分别撰写才能成书。所以,笔者就改变了策略,转而针对中国商业人士相对薄弱或缺乏理念的合约法课题分别出书。第一本就是《合约的解释》(法律出版社 2007 年版),而本书是第二本。

本书是探讨合约法中最复杂也是最重要的课题——损失计算。这一课题的重要性在于,任何商业决定与发生纠纷后的和解或诉讼都免不了涉及,而最终赔偿的金额也就是各种商业决定的底线。例如,是否签订一个利润很高但同时要面对高昂赔偿风险的商业合约?如果签订,是否可以在合约中加入限制责任条文或者是否需要以"单项目公司"(Special Purpose Vehicle)的形式签订合约与承担责任?至于发生纠纷后的决定,底线是不会有人为了索赔或抗辩一个 1000 美元甚至 1 万美元的损失而花费庞大的律师费用。但现实中笔者见过外国公司把一个按照英国法律严格计算下实际只值 1 万美元的索赔案件变成 100 万美元的案件。这种漫天开价的索赔在英美法体系或者国际仲裁中是常见,原因是提高索赔金额不会给外国公司带来不良后果或是费用的增加(除了在一些机构仲裁可能会带来微小差别)。如果遇上不懂英国法律下损失计算原则的中国公司,往往是没有办法有板有眼地做出抗辩。这一来,双方在诉讼的半途可能以一人一半做出庭外和解,而中国公司还以为是省了不少钱。这种情况对中国公司而言特别重要,因为其在大部分案件中责任方面往往很难成功抗辩。原因也是在于不熟悉英美或国际上的合约法与理念,导致合约经常订得不好或者是在履行过程中粗暴地终断合约或违约或放弃自己的合约权利。中国公司的案件还值得花大量律师费用做出抗辩的是在损失计算方面,因为往往有水平的代表律师有可能把索赔的金额大幅度减少,如在上述的例子中把 100 万美元的索赔减到 1、2 万美元。即使双方在诉讼中途达成和解,中国公司所付出的钱恐怕也是 3、5 万美元。更重要的是,如果外国公司看到中国公司抗辩减少索赔金额,加上中国公司在其他程序上的刁难如要求外国公司提供费用担保,很有可能外国公司就会消失。

本书就是希望系统地告诉读者有关英国法律下计算损失的一些大小原则,内容十分丰富,这可以从本书的厚度上看出来。总体而言,第一章先介绍英国合约法下对违约损失计算的基本大原则就是"尽量用金钱来令受害方回到一个合约被履行的地位(*restitutio in integrum*)"(简称复原大原则)。第二章会介绍在复原大原则下,损失赔偿最常见的就是根据或找出违约受害方的"预期利益"(expectation interest),也可以称为"履行利益"(performance interest)或"交易损失"(loss of bargain)到底是多少钱。可以看到,找出如果合约获得履行,受害方能够预期得到什么利润或获得什么利益,作为违约方要支付的赔偿,正是符合复原大原则。该章同时介绍的就是寻找预期或履行利益,也不代表英国法律下所有不同类别的损失项目都可以索赔,其中包括了"非金钱的损失"(non – pecuniary losses)。

此外,英国法律下对损失计算也有其他重要的局限,如"损失遥远性"(remoteness

of damages)。遥远性包括在两个方面，订约的时候可否"合理预见"(reasonably foreseeable)与"因果关系"(causation)。而第三个重要局限是受害方必须"合理减少损失"(reasonable mitigation of damages)。这三个重要局限分别在第三、四、五章介绍。

损失计算应该是以哪一天为准也是一个非常重要与富争议性的课题，其中以"违约/毁约一天为准"(breach date rule)被普遍接受，特别是在一些损失计算适用"市场规则"(market rule)如在货物买卖的情况下。毕竟1979年英国《货物销售法》是立法规定货物买卖赔偿的表面规则就是市场规则。但另一个计算损失的日期也获得一定的案例支持，就是以"审理或判决一天为准"(judgment day rule)。以这一天计算损失的好处就是审理往往是在违约/毁约后的一段较长时间，有许多违约/毁约所导致的损失不需要做出估计，而是事实摆在眼前。但根据 breach date rule 或是 market rule 都需要对将来的损失有一定程度的估计或臆猜。这一重要与富争议性的课题在贵族院的先例 The "Golden Victory" (2007) 2 Lloyd's Rep 164 有了全面针对，但结果是三比二的多数做出判决是以审理或判决一天为准。看来这一方面的争议虽然出现了先例，但还是不断会有争议与不同的看法。

英国法律对损失赔偿的计算在最近十几年来还是有大量的先例与重要改变，这都会在本书提到。可以说是这方面的发展之快是其他领域的法律都跟不上的。其中一些重要的先例如 Allied Maples Group Ltd v. Simmons & Simmons (a firm) (1995) 1 WLR 1602，Ruxley Electronics & Construction Ltd v. Forsyth (1995) All ER 1936，Attorney General v. Blake (2001) 1 AC 268，The "Dynamic" (2003) 2 Lloyd's Rep 693，The "Achilleas" (2008) 2 Lloyd's Rep. 275 等，都会在本书有介绍。

有不少国际上的批评，特别是来自欧洲大陆法体系的国家，指英国合约法对保护预期或履行利益力度不足，导致受害方不能获得完全或充分的赔偿。这保护不足显示在英国法院不愿意轻易做出"履约指令"(specific performance)，毕竟强制违约方必须履行合约，否则面对刑事责任，会是最完美的保护预期或履行利益，这一方面会在本书第十二章详谈。

英国法律保护不足的批评也包括了复原大原则下只针对受害方的预期或履行利益，而不理会违约方可能通过违约可以获得的庞大利益并不公平。但这方面看来英国法律也在改变，这主要是在本书第一章所介绍的近十年发展起来的在合约的关系下也做出"返还性损失赔偿"(restitutionary damages)，也包括了对议定赔偿的尊重而不会太轻易以"惩罚性赔偿"(punitive damages)作为否定、对非金钱赔偿在一些类别的合约(特别是在一些涉及休闲娱乐的合约)中放宽、承认与放宽一些十分不肯定的损失类别并引进了"机会损失"(loss of chance)等。这些课题都在第一章、第二章、第六章中有详述。

最后,本书也针对各种主要与不同的商业活动所带来的损失赔偿计算的独特问题。包括:(1)本书第十五章与第十六章介绍的十分重要与普遍的市场规则计算办法,适用在所有有市场进行买卖的商业活动,包括货物买卖、航运、船舶买卖或造船合约、股票买卖等。(2)本书第十八章介绍的“投资仲裁”(investment arbitration),这会是将来中国作为主权国家并吸引大量外国投资可能会面对的大问题。(3)本书第十九章介绍的“衍生工具”(derivative)方面的损失计算。

这里要一提的是,笔者对第十九章所针对的课题完全是外行,这一章是由杨大志律师撰写的。该章本准备以中英文对照的形式出现,但出于出版要求的考虑,权衡之后决定保留英文原版。读者如果感兴趣,可以在笔者的个人网站(www. yangliangyee. com)下载中英文对照版本。杨大志律师是笔者的小儿子,笔者很高兴他能像哥哥杨大明律师一样,为营造中国健康环境作出贡献,并踏出了第一步。

最后笔者要感谢的是一批助手,包括许多读者已经熟悉的司嘉女士,另有王可心女士与贡航先生。他们通过参与这本书的撰写,对损失计算这一复杂的课题会比一般的英国律师还知道的多,希望他们将来能够为中国涉及国际商业活动作出实质的贡献。

杨良宜

2013. 2. 6

目　录

第一章　损失赔偿大原则

1. 对侵权或违约受害方做出赔偿性复原的大原则

英国法律针对损失赔偿的起点非常之简单，在合约与侵权，都是一个所谓的“复原”大原则。目的是补偿受害方或是受害方因为对方违反合约或造成侵权所带来的损失。这个损失一般是用金钱作出计算，在合约的说法是“尽量用金钱来令受害方回到一个合约被履行的地位”（as far as money can do it, to be placed, in the same position as if the contract had been performed），这也是著名拉丁文一词的“*restitutio in integrum*”的真意，英文是“compensatory principle”（复原或赔偿大原则）。这里著名的说法是在先例 Livingstone v. Rawyards Coal Co. (1880) 5 App. Cas. 25，Blackburn 勋爵说：“that sum of money which will put the party who has been injured, or who has suffered, in the same position as he would have been in if he had not sustained the wrong for which he is now getting his compensation or reparation.”在合约关系的说法是“尽量用金钱来令受害方回到一个合约被履行的地位”（as far as money can do it, to be placed, in the same position as if the contract had been performed）。也有说法是合约方有两个合约责任，第一个就是履行他所作出的合约承诺，第二个或是替代的合约责任就是赔偿对方因为没有履行而蒙受的损失。

这个大原则在理念上是很容易理解的，特别是商业合约，本来订立的目标就是赚钱。这些合约里面每一个条文中所作出的承诺在绝大多数情况下都可以量化为金钱，导致了违反承诺的一方就要对这笔金钱损失作出赔偿。但针对侵权，就会遇到不少情况是不容易复原的。例如，因为被告的疏忽造成原告的身体伤害，完美的复原应该就是还给被告失去的健康或健全。但这是不可能的事，法律所能做的只是尽量把他身体的伤害以及其他的损失以金钱量化，然后作出赔偿。但本质上，侵权的赔偿也是为了复原大原则。

另一种侵权会带来更加“不可捉摸”（intangible）的损失，就是“诽谤”（defamation）。但法院还是要尽其努力计算原告因为诽谤所造成的名誉损失并量化为金钱。显然，不同的原告会有不同的名誉损失。而且被告在诽谤后的言行举止也会导致金钱损失赔偿的高低。例如，被告在诽谤后很快就作出了道歉，特别是公开的道歉，这就等于是“减损”（mitigation），也减少了对原告的伤害，金钱上的赔偿就相应减低了。

但如果被告坚持他的诽谤,最后败诉所要作出的金钱赔偿就应该相应提高,因为对原告造成的名誉损失程度上更严重且时间上更长了。但本质上这种金钱上的赔偿还是必须符合复原大原则。

“侵犯土地/侵占财产”(trespass)也是一个很好的例子。从一个角度看,原告的土地(比如空置的房子或土地)被别人非法占用了,是没有对原告带来任何金钱上的损失。这不像是原告,把空置的房子出租给第三者,但由于被告的非法占用而导致了租金的损失,这就很容易计算。这种问题早在 Watson, Laidlaw & Co Ltd v. Pott, Cassels and Williamson(1914)31 PRC 104,119 先例中已有提到,如果有一个人骑了一匹从被告处侵占过来(如偷来)的马,这造成了什么损失?只要这马匹是安全的物归原主,可以说这匹马的主人是没有办法证明有任何损失的,甚至会有情况是该匹马因为有了这次经历而状态变得更好。但作出金钱上的赔偿从另一个角度就是原告如果同意被告或任何第三人借用这匹马(即使在个别案件原告不会这样做),他会收取合理市场租金。但由于被告的非法占用,就剥夺了原告赚取这笔金钱的机会。这表示要求被告对原告作出这笔租金作为赔偿,就是符合复原的大原则。这就表示法院就要尽其努力计算这笔估计的租金是多少,然后作出判决。

这种计算损失赔偿的做法,现在经常用在某些类别的案件里,如违反“专利”(patent)或“版权”(copyright)的案件。损失的计算是根据原告如果出售专利或版权可以收到的专利费或版权费,这就符合了复原的大原则。

这类案例比较著名的有贵族院的 Wrotham Park Estate Co Ltd v. Parkside Homes Ltd(1974)1 WLR 798 与 Attorney General v. Blake(2001)1 AC 268。

在 Attorney General v. Blake 一案中,涉及 George Blake 是前苏联潜伏在英国情报局 MI6 为期最长与对英国情报造成最大损害的间谍。他的身份在苏联解体之后被暴露,并且被英国法院定为叛国罪并判终身监禁。但他事后潜逃离开英国去了俄罗斯并获得庇护。而后他在俄罗斯出版了其间谍生涯自传并成了一本畅销书。这导致他在英国出版商中有一笔 9 万英镑的稿费,而英国政府则想没收这笔钱。英国政府曾经试图以 Blake 对政府有“受信义务”(fiduciary duty)关系,因为情报属于英国政府。但这个理由没有被法院接受,因为时间隔了很长,Blake 再已没有这一受信义务而且书中披露的资料也谈不上是机密。这导致英国政府以另一个诉因成功把这笔钱要回来,就是 Blake 这本书违反了他与 MI6 聘用合约中的保密条文。至于在损失赔偿的方面,贵族院多数意见认为 Blake 剥夺了英国政府可以赚取这笔金钱的机会(即使英国政府不会这样做),判 Blake 要赔这笔稿费。这种计算损失的办法也被称为“account for the profit”,本质上也是符合“赔偿性的复原”(compensatory damage)大原则,虽然这里有争议是属于“返还性损失”(restitutionary damages)。赔偿性的复原与复原损失赔偿主要分别是前者只针对受害方蒙受的损失,但后者针对被告从违约或是侵权所获得的利益,要求被告把利益交出给受害方,即使受害方根本没有蒙受损失。这一方面的争议涉及英国法下对损失赔偿的基本理念,稍后再进一步探讨。

Scott 勋爵在 2008 年的 Chancery Bar Association 的关于损失的发言中，有提到他是认为 A – G v. Blake 先例应该属于复原大原则说："In Blake the Crown had been deprived by Blake's breach of contract of the ability to forbid or to licence on its own terms the publication of the book. This was a loss created by the breach of contract. It was a loss capable of being attributed a monetary value. The correct analysis of the case, in my opinion, is that the royalties due from the publisher to Blake constituted, in the majority's view, the due measure of compensation to the Crown for being deprived of the ability to control the publication by Blake of his experiences as an MI6 officer. On the same principle, all awards of restitutionary damages should be justified, if they are justifiable at all, as compensatory damages..."

2. 复原大原则下赔不足损失的情况

有说法是受害方经常没有办法向侵权方或者违约方取回所有的损失，做不到完全的复原。例如，要求侵权方或违约方承担一些不可预见的损失会太苛刻。在 Victoria Laundry v. Newman (1949) 2 KB 528，上诉庭的 Asquith 大法官是这样说："This purpose, if relentlessly pursued, would provide the plaintiff with a complete indemnity for all losses *de facto* resulting from a particular breach, however improbable, however unpredictable."

总结而言，复原大原则有许多例外令受害方索赔的金额有所减少。这些例外包括：(1) 在合约关系中，违约方在订约的时候没有办法合理预见会产生这种损失，这方面在本书第三章有详论；(2) 在侵权（但也会发生在合约关系），受害方自己有部分的过错，这方面在本书第八章有详论；(3) 一些损失并非是侵权方或者违约方的行为所直接造成，这会是因果关系被中断，这方面在本书第四章有详论；(4) 受害方自己没有合理减少损失，这方面在本书第五章有详论；(5) 损失不肯定与没有办法量化，这方面在本书第六章有详论等。

以上的例外之(1)与(3)通常被称为"损失索赔的遥远性"（remoteness of damages），这些对受害方索赔损失的限制会在本书第三章与第四章分别探讨。

3. 复原大原则下赔偿超过损失的情况

会有情况是受害方获得的赔偿比他真正蒙受的损失还要多，这也是本章要重点探讨的方面，包括"加大损失"（aggravated damages）、"惩罚性赔偿"（punitive damages）、"返还性损失赔偿"（restitutionary damages）与"名义损失"（nominal damages）。

在正常情况下，让受害方"获利"不应该发生，英国法律也不允许偏离复原大原则。在复原大原则下是不理会侵权方或违约方是否通过这种错误行为而赚到利润，只理会赔偿受害方的损失。这是 Megarry V. C. 大法官在 Tito v. Waddell(No. 2)(1977) Ch. 106 所说的："It is fundamental to all questions of damages that they are to compensate the plaintiff for his loss or injury... The question is not one of making the defendant disgorge what he has saved by committing the wrong, but one of compensating the plaintiff."

但现实中还是经常会遇到这种情况，最常见的情况之一就是"惩罚性赔偿"(punitive damage)，这只会在合约关系中出现，就是约定一条惩罚性条文来阻吓对方，防止对方违约，这笔赔偿可能与损失毫无关系，而是具有惩罚性的味道。另是在近年来出了不少先例的"返还性损失赔偿"(restitutionary damages)，这包括介绍 A - G v. Blake(2001)1 AC 268 先例。严格说，英国政府没有因为 Blake 的违反雇佣合约中的保密条文而蒙受实质的损失，但还是可以把 Blake 所赚取的 9 万英镑稿费"没收"，而且 Scott 勋爵的说法还是认为没有偏离复原大原则。

本章接下去会探讨这一方面的问题，首先介绍同是属于普通法体系的英国与美国在这一个方面有不同看法。

3.1　英国法律不理会侵权方或违约方在其错误行为中获利的原因

英国法律不愿意对侵权方或违约方作出惩罚让无辜方获利，认为作出惩罚只是属于刑法的范畴，与民事诉讼无关。而刑事与民事之间有许多不同，如在举证责任方面，不应该混淆。

一般的说法是，英国法律在侵权与违约一般都不准索赔惩罚性损失。英国认为惩罚性损失不妥之处是：(1)给受害方一个发大财的机会，经常脱离了复原的"赔偿损失"(compensation)精神。(2)惩罚性损失与民事诉讼没有关系，这是刑事诉讼的范畴。(3)惩罚在刑事诉讼是需要举证至认定"没有任何合理的怀疑"(beyond reasonable doubt)，越严重的刑事罪名，经常见到检察官无法成功举证令被告入罪，有任何疑点都会把利益归被告所有。但民事诉讼只需要举证以"衡量可能性"(balance of probability)为尺度，等于是法院或仲裁员认为有 51% 的可能性该争议的事实是正确，就可以认定。换言之，举证尺度宽松得多，但也常会在现实中带来判错的情况，这在刑事诉讼不能接受。如果再加上金额庞大的惩罚性损失赔偿，但只要求相对低得多的举证责任，就会造成混乱、轻率、不公的情况。(4)如果在一个不法的行为中，侵权方的被告要面对两次惩罚，包括刑事诉讼与民事诉讼，这是违反基本的公正大原则 AB v. South West Water Services(1993) QB507 CA; Devenish Nutrition Ltd v. Sanofi - Aventis SA(2008)2 WLR 637"。(5)带来不肯定、和解困难与鼓励诉讼。毕竟，这惩罚性损失完全要靠"臆猜"，在陪审团作出赔偿金额判决的情况下特别危险。

英国法院不承认惩罚性条文涉及公共政策的考虑，而公共政策也是唯一可以漠视双方约定的合约条文或协议的理由。这可节录 Chadwick 勋爵在 Euro London Appointment Ltd v. Claessens International Ltd(2006) EWCA Civ 385 中说："the ordinary rule which the courts apply is that contracts should be enforce, *pacta sunt servanda*, unless they can be brought within that limited category of cases in which, for reasons of public policy, the court refuses to give effect to the agreement of the parties... One limited and well-known class is the... penalty."

3.2 美国法律的不同地位

美国虽然也是一个普通法的国家,在1760年开始就依从当时英国法院作出惩罚性损失赔偿的先例。但英国在60年代的 Rookes v. Barnard (1964) AC 1129 和 Broome v. Cassell & Co (1971) 2 QB 354 CA 的贵族院先例后对惩罚性损失赔偿大幅度收紧,而美国却没有继续依从。在美国,不论是在普通法或者是在不同的立法,都会允许作出惩罚性损失赔偿。例如1951年的 RICO 法案(Racketteer Influenced and Corrupt Organizations Act)已有好几次延展到航运的租约纠纷,令受害方获得真正损失的三倍"赔偿",以惩罚违约方:Octonia Trading Ltd v. Sinnes Interoil GmbH, Society of Maritime Arbitrators, No. 2424, 1987(船东盗取运载的燃油作为船舶之用,被仲裁庭惩罚10万美元);Triumph Tankers Ltd. v. Kerr McGee Ref. Corp, Society of Maritime Arbitrators, No. 2642 1990(案情也是一样,被惩罚368,495美元)。惩罚性赔偿也出现在其他的仲裁,如涉及证券买卖的 National Association of Securities Dealers,一个2003年的仲裁案件名为 Sawtelle v. Waddell & Reed, Inc., N. Y. App. Div. 1st Dept. Feb. 13, 2003 就涉及仲裁庭给予180万美元的赔偿损失,但另加上2500万美元的惩罚性赔偿。针对仲裁庭能否作出惩罚性赔偿,美国法院曾经持不同看法。在 Garrity v. Lyle Stuart, Inc. (353 N. E. 2ND 793 N. Y. 1976),纽约州的上诉庭认为只有法院才能作出。但也有看法是仲裁庭可以作出惩罚性赔偿,这看来也是《联邦仲裁法》(Federal Arbitration Act,简称 FAA)的地位,只要仲裁协议写的够广泛。在1995年的最高院 Mastrobuono v. Shearson Lehman Hutton, Inc 115 S. CT. pp 1215-19 先例,判是当事人可以在仲裁协议自由约定仲裁庭可以作出惩罚性赔偿,即使美国个别州不允许仲裁庭作出惩罚性赔偿,也会被 FAA 超越。双方当事人也可以自由约定仲裁庭不能作出惩罚性赔偿,而事实上去美国仲裁的有关仲裁协议或条文,也经常有约定是仲裁庭不能作出这一类的赔偿,看来完全有效。最高院也认为仲裁协议或条文如果没有针对这一问题,就假设是仲裁庭有权作出惩罚性赔偿。

美国法院作出这种惩罚性损失赔偿常有所闻。如在 North American Free Trade Agreement (NAFTA) 的投资仲裁中,就提到一个密西西比州法院的案例,涉及一家加拿大公司的商业争议,金额只是400万美元,但由于在审理的时候涉及人身攻击与不当行为,被陪审团判赔偿5亿美元,其中包括4亿美元的惩罚性赔偿。香港公司也有这方面惨痛的经验,如在1990年后期的香港九仓公司在其有线电视业务上被"罚"要赔上亿美元给一家美国公司,只为了一个口头协议有否被破坏之争,这种争议本来就是"罗生门",法官可随意相信任何一方证人。难怪外国人对美国法院的管辖权闻虎色变,视之为合法"抢劫"。

所以在美国的民事诉讼中经常会涉及惩罚性损失赔偿,美国的最高院先例 State Farm Mutual Automobile Insurance Co v. Campbell(2003)538 U. S. 408,Kennedy 大法官说“惩罚性损失赔偿是为了针对阻吓与报应”(punitive damages are aimed at deterrence and retribution)。但英国法律就很难接受这一说法,因为针对侵权方或违约方,作出阻吓并不让其继续或重复这一个错误的行为,在私人的范畴,受害方是完全可以去法院尽快申请禁令。而对于公众的范畴,政府也可以代表公众去法院申请禁令。这样完全只是个人权利的民事诉讼,就没有理由混淆这一个阻吓与报应的理念,为了希望被告以后不要再重复这种侵权或者违约,这样做混淆了公法与私法之间的区别。Scott 勋爵在 2008 年的 Chancery Bar Association 的关于损失的发言中提到了这一点,说:“... The law will have become incoherent. That may well have become the case in the US. But it must not be allowed to become the case here. The way to make sure it does not awarded. If deterrence is the purpose, whose are the rights that are being protected? If protection of the rights of the public at large is the purpose, or if punishment of the wrongdoer is the purpose, are those legitimate purposes to be pursued by a civil court in a private action brought on account of the infringement of the claimant's personal rights?”

在美国,这一惩罚性损失赔偿也带来了很多不肯定及压力。美国最高院也有不少尝试改善这一情况,如限制惩罚性损失赔偿的金额。在 State Farm Mutual Automobile Insurance Co v. Campbell(2003)538 U. S. 408 先例,案情涉及一个交通事故中,保险公司恶意拒绝赔偿。第一审的陪审团判保险公司要赔付 260 万美元的赔偿性损失加 1.45 亿美元的惩罚性赔偿。但这被法官减为 100 万美元加 2500 万美元。上诉去了犹他州的最高院,将惩罚性损失赔偿重新提高为陪审团判的 1.45 亿美元。最后在美国最高院,多数意见判是 1.45 亿美元的惩罚性损失赔偿实在太高,这样判也违反了美国宪法的“正当程序”(due process)。

这一先例与著名作家 John Grisham 的一本畅销书《The Rainmaker》的情节也差不多,涉及一个保险公司故意拒赔的案件。在书中,提到了原告的律师如何在开庭前培训证人(原告)应对盘问(这种做法在英国法院是不容许的),其中最重要的是不要让陪审团感觉到原告索赔惩罚性损失赔偿是为了贪心。在正式开庭时,果然代表保险公司的律师提出这一盘问,但原告的律师所指导的回应是“我对你的臭钱一毛钱也不想要,我将会把所有的惩罚性损失赔偿捐给白血病研究(I don't want a dime of your goddam money, I'm going to give the whole sum to leukaemia research)”。果然陪审团判保险公司要赔付这 4000 万美元的惩罚性损失赔偿。

《The Rainmaker》出版后不久,在俄亥俄州有另一个名为 Moore v. Conrail(1997)863 F. 2d 45 案例,原告的孩子被火车撞死,原告向被告索赔 1 千万美元的惩罚性损失赔偿并声称这笔钱会捐给一个针对改善道路安全的慈善机构,并获得胜诉。不久后,在另一个名为 Dardinger v. Anthem(2002)781 NE 2d 121 的先例,在同类的案件中,俄亥俄州的最高院自己把原告胜诉的部分惩罚性损失赔偿判给慈善机构而不是给原告。这看来是为了防止原告在开庭时讲这种好听的话,但获得赔偿后就根本不履行。但这在另一个俄勒冈州(Oregon)最高院的 Honeywell v. Sterling Furniture Co (1990)797 P 2d 1019 案例,判是原告即使是有意图把惩罚性损失赔偿捐作慈善性用途,也不准告诉陪审团。此外,法院也没有权力把判给原告的惩罚性损失赔偿部分转给任何其他机构包括慈善性机构。看来统一判法还是要看美国最高院的最后决定。

最后一提的是航运业十分熟悉的名为"Exxon Valdez"的油轮在阿拉斯加水域搁浅后的漏油事件。在 Exxon Shipping Company v. Baker(2008)128 SCt 先例,美国最高院判赔偿的金额是5亿美元左右。这看来金额庞大的赔偿比起第一审与上诉庭的判决实际上微不足道,在第一审判的赔偿金额是45亿美元,在上诉庭被减为25亿美元,但到了最高院更是大幅度被减为5亿美元左右。

4. 有惩罚性意味的损失类别的区分

在进一步探讨这一方面的问题之前,先把稍微区分以下容易混淆的概念:"加大损失"(aggravated damages)、"示范性损失"(exemplary damages)、"报复性损失"(vindictive damages)、"报应性损失"(retributory damages)与"惩罚性损失"(punitive damages)。可以说在 Rookes v. Barnard(1964)AC 1129 的贵族院先例之前,上述概念都是混为一谈。但在该先例后,就把加大损失区分出来,视为是符合"复原大原则"(compensatory principle),只是为了针对"无形损失"(intangible losses),就免不了要在一定程度上对赔偿的金额作出臆猜。但如果在一个涉及疏忽的交通事故中,无辜的行人如果身体受到实际伤害可以获得赔偿(如医疗费用或经济损失),就没有理由说是因为难核算,对他受到其他无形或非金钱的损失如"疼痛和苦难"(pain and suffering)和"心理创伤"(psychological injury)等不作出赔偿。这在 Scott 勋爵 2008 年的 Chancery Bar Association 的关于损失的发言中是这样说:"It is in this context that reference to 'aggravated' damages is often made. Aggravated damages are awarded for the purpose of providing compensation for conduct which has increased the seriousness of the wrong inflicted on the victim and, accordingly, increased the degree of the result for which compensation must be paid. The function of so-called 'aggravated' damages remains compensatory. Aggravated damages are not-repeat not-extra-compensatory damages. The purpose of the award should be compensation for what has happened."

至于"示范损失"(exemplary damages),以前曾经被视为与加大损失同一解释,但现在应该相对明确它与惩罚性损失一样,不属于复原大原则。在《McGregor on Damages》(18th edn,2009 年)一书就是这样称呼的。但也有一个说法是,示范损失可以视为复原大原则下的赔偿性损失与惩罚性损失之间的一种损失,特别适合针对违反了一些宪法或是法律的权益。例如在 1998 年《英国人权法》之 section 8 授权法院在公共机构如果违反有关条文,法院应该作出一个"合理的满足"(just satisfaction),这是从国际公约照搬过来的概念,应该也是这种示范损失,与复原无关。反正在这种情况下,往往依赖复原不足够,但英国法律不允许在民事诉讼中给予惩罚性赔偿,就适合给予这种类型的损失。针对这种示范损失,在 Merson v. Cartwright(2005)UKPC 38,英国枢密院的 Scott 勋爵是这样说:"If the case is one for an award of damages by way of constitutional redress... the nature of the damages awarded may be compensatory but should always be vindicatory and, accordingly, the damages may, in an appropriate case, exceed a purely compensatory amount. The purpose of a vindicatory award is not punitive purpose. It is not to teach the executive not to misbehave. The executive interference, mistreatment or oppression... in some cases a suitable declaration may suffice to vindicate the right; in other cases an award of damages, including substantial damages, may seem to be necessary."

在 Merson v. Cartwright 先例中,判是被告要赔偿原告 100,000 巴哈马元(相等于 100,000 美元),而这一笔钱既不视为赔偿性,也不属于惩罚性。

其余的概念如"报复性损失"(vindictive damages)、"报应性损失"(retributory damages)与"惩罚性损失"(punitive damages),还是同样,这些类别的损失赔偿都偏离了复原大原则。

5. 符合复原大原则的加大损失

5.1 加大损失适用的侵权案件类别

加大损失被视为赔偿性,符合民事诉讼中损失计算的复原大原则,虽然它是用来针对一些受害方的一些"无形伤害"(intangible injury),如"侮辱"(insult)、"羞辱"(humiliation)、"降级"(degradation)、"气愤"(indignation)、"激怒"(outrage)、"痛苦"(distress)、"伤害情感"(hurt feelings)、"歧视"(discrimination)等。此外,加大损失也适用在其他的侵权,并且有明确的先例,如:

(i)"诽谤"(defamation):Ley v. Hamilton(1935)153 LT 384;McCarey v. Associated Newspapers Ltd. (No. 2)(1965)2 QB 86;Broome v. Cassell(1972)AC 1027;

(ii)"殴打"(battery):Ansell v. Thomas, The Times, 23 May 1973;Flavius v. Metropolitan Police Commissioner(1982)132 NLJ 532;Ballard v. Metropolitan Police Commissioner(1983)133 NLJ 1133;W v. Meah(1986)1 All ER 935;

(iii)"非法禁锢"(false imprisonment):Smith v. Metropolitan Police Commissioner (1982)CLY 899;Warby v. Cascarina, The Times, 27 October 1989;Barnes v. Metropolitan Police Commissioner(July 1992)Legal Action 14;White v. Metropolitan Police Commissioner, The Times, 24 April 1982;

(iv)“恶意起诉”(malicious prosecution):White v. Metropolitan Police Commissioner,The Times,24 April 1982;Marks v. Chief Constable of Greater Manchester(1992) TLR 23;

(v)“恐吓”(intimidation):Messenger Newspapers Group Ltd. v. National Graphical Association(1984)IRLR 397;Godwin v. Uzoigwe(1992)TLR 300;

(vi)“歧视”(discrimination):Alexander v. Home Office(1988)1 WLR 968;Morris v. Higgs & Hill Building Ltd. (Jan/Feb 1992)41 Equal Opportunities Review,30;Duffy v. Eastern Health & Social Services Board(1992)IRLR 251;Hynes v. Warner Howard Ltd. (March 1993)Legal Action 18;

(vii)“侵入土地”(trespass to land):Merest v. Harvey(1814)5 Taunt. 442;Sears v. Lyons(1818)2 Stark. 317;Williams v. Currie(1845)1 CB 841;Emblen v. Myers(1860)6 H. & N. 54;Drane v. Evangelou(1978)1 WLR 455;

(viii)“欺骗”(deceit):Mafo v. Adams(1970)1 QB 548;Archer v. Brown(1985) QB 401;

(ix)“滋扰”(nuisance):Thompson v. Hill(1870)LR 5 CP 564;

(x)“非法干预商业活动”(unlawful interference with business):Messenger Newspapers Group Ltd v. National Graphical Association(1984)IRLR 397。

5.2 估计加大损失的难处

涉及这种无形伤害,要量化为金钱的赔偿,免不了有很大困难。主要的困难来自每一个不同的案例都“不能比较”(incommensurability),这导致判决的不肯定与无法让当事人预测结果。另一个困难是“主观与受害方难以证明”(subjectivity or difficulties of proof)。这在一定程度上与人身伤亡一并带来“非金钱损害”(non-pecuniary harm),如“疼痛和苦难”(pain and suffering)、“失去欢乐”(loss of amenity)和“心理创伤”(psychological injury)等。但后者的程度比前者的加大损失好得多,因为后者案件已经在《Administration of Justice(Miscellaneous Provisions)Act 1933》之 section 6 与之后的《Supreme Court Act 1981》之 section 69 规定不再由陪审团审理人身伤亡的案件,而是交由法院,而法院已经发展出来一个量刑标准针对各种不同人身伤亡会带来的疼痛和苦难或心理创伤。

5.3 加大损失不适用在合约

加大损失不适用在违约,因为合约是严格适用金钱赔偿作为“复原”(compensatory)大原则,合约也只是关心“金钱损失”(pecuniary damages):Addis v. Gramophone Co. Ltd(1909)AC 488;Kralj v. McGrath(1986)1 All ER 54;Levi v. Gordon,12 November 1992(Unreported,CA)。就算是违约同时涉及被告对受害方原告的“侮辱”或“羞辱”,也不能适用加大损失的救济。至于在违约的受害方因此而感觉到失望、受挫与压力等,都属于双方在订约时可以想象得到违约会带来的后果,都不能索赔加大损失:Bliss v. SE Thames RHA(1987)ICR 700;Hayes v. James & Charles Dodd(1990)2 All ER

815；Branchett v. Beaney(1992)3 All ER 910。在 Watts v. Morrow(1991)1 WLR 1421 先例，上诉庭的 Bingham 大法官说："(1) A contract – breaker is not in general liable for any distress, frustration, anxiety, displeasure, vexation, tension or aggravation which his breach of contract may cause to the innocent party. This rule is not, I think, founded on the assumption that such reactions are not foreseeable, which they surely are or may be, but on considerations of policy. (2) But the rule is not absolute. Where the very object of a contract is to provide pleasure(如度假、游轮等合约), relaxation, peace of mind or freedom from molestation, damages will be awarded if the fruit of the contract is not provided or if the contrary result is procured instead. If the law did not cater for this exceptional category of case it would be defective. A contract to survey the condition of a house for a prospective purchaser does not, however, fall within this exceptional category."

唯一的特殊例外是原告可以以侵权作为替代诉因向被告索赔加大损失，因为涉及侮辱性的违约，这尤其在房屋的租客与业主之间的诉讼，涉及业主延误修理导致租客的日子难过：Calabar Properties Ltd v. Stitcher(1984)1 WLR 287。或是租客得不到"安静的享用"(quiet enjoyment)，导致业主犯了"侵入"(trespass)或"滋扰"(nuisance)的侵权行为。

5.4　加大损失也不适用在侵权的疏忽

另外，在涉及"疏忽"(negligence)的侵权案件，也不适用加大损失的救济：Kralj v. McGrath(1986)1 All ER 54；AB v. South West Water Services Ltd(1993)QB 507。这是因为加大损失只适用在侵权方被告的"不正常行为"(exceptional conduct)，而显然被告仅是疏忽没有什么太不正常之处。

5.5　加大损失与惩罚性损失的区分不明显

加大损失不违反复原大原则，但在现实中加大损失还是经常与惩罚性损失分不开，而惩罚性赔偿明显偏离了复原大原则。只节录 Morris v. Higgs and Hill Building Ltd. (Jan/Feb 1992)41 Equal Opportunities Review, 30, 33 有关非法解雇的先例。该先例的"感情伤害"(injury to feelings)赔偿是4000英镑，另加大损失是2000英镑，而裁判庭对加大损失的原因如下："The factors which have led us to make this increased award are firstly, that the respondents advertised the job behind her back, something which she found out about. This is an extremely insulting and high – handed and oppressive thing to do. Secondly, there is the manner of her dismissal, sending her a letter whilst she was away on holiday to await her return, which was bound to cause the maximum amount of shock and distress. Thirdly, since the application was made the respondents have persisted in various untrue allegations, both about her work and about her conduct, and fourthly, the company as a whole... have failed to acknowledge the wider problems which have been exposed by this case in their lack of fair procedures and by the absence of any equal opportunities policy and have taken no steps to try and install such a policy."

在上述计算加大损失的四个原因中，只有一个是有关受害方原告的伤害。显然，其他原因就有很强的惩罚性味道。这也是在许多说法中被接受的现实，如有关最高院对诽谤的一个报告《Supreme Court Procedure Committee's Report on Practice and Procedure in Defamation(1991)》，就说道："We think that in those cases where a defendant's behaviour particularly merits disapproval the jury can adequately deal with this by an award of aggravated damages without stepping outside the notion of compensation."

难怪是在 Rookes v. Barnard(1964) AC 1129 和 Broome v. Cassell(1972) AC 1027 两个先例之前的两百年，有许多侵权诉讼（但没有违约方面）被认为是判惩罚性损失赔偿的先例都被这两个贵族院先例所推翻。认为英国法律下民事诉讼是不能作出惩罚性损失赔偿，惩罚只是刑事诉讼的范畴。但实际上上述两个先例也没有推翻许多以前的先例，只是对损失的叫法有不同。以前被称为是惩罚性损失的先例，实际上是加大损失，属于复原大原则，在一定程度上是"换汤不换药"。

6. 非复原性损失赔偿之一：惩罚性损失赔偿

6.1 Rookes v. Barnard 先例后允许的三种例外情况可导致惩罚性损失赔偿

在 Rookes v. Barnard(1964) AC 1129 先例，贵族院全面检讨了有关刑事诉讼后认为不应该允许在英国的民事诉讼继续作出惩罚性损失赔偿的决定，而主要原因就是这会给民事诉讼与刑事诉讼的区分造成混乱。但贵族院也认为有例外情况，并说明有三种情况可以判惩罚性损失赔偿，原因是 Devlin 大法官所说的能起到一定的作用："in which an award of exemplary damages can serve a useful purpose in vindicating the strength of the law and thus affording a practical justification for admitting into the civil law a principle which ought logically to belong to the criminal."

Rookes v. Barnard 的判决稍后在 Broome v. Cassell 先例的上诉庭审判中受到质疑，但这被贵族院改正，并明确支持 Rookes v. Barnard 说："not prepared to follow the Court of Appeal in its criticisms of Rookes v. Barnard, which... imposed valuable limits on the doctrine of exemplary damages as they had hitherto been understood in English law and clarified important questions which had previously been undiscussed or left confused."

这一来，英国法律在这两个贵族院先例是明确了不允许在民事诉讼中支持惩罚性损失赔偿。至于 Rookes v. Barnard 先例认为三种例外情况是允许惩罚性损失赔偿是：(1)政府官员的压迫性、随意性或违反宪法的行为(oppressive, arbitrary or unconstitutional conduct by government servants)；(2)侵权行为是侵权方计算过好处大过坏处，也就是侵权会带来更大的经济利益(conduct calculated to result in profit)；(3)立法明示允许作出惩罚性损失赔偿(express authorization by statute)。这三种例外情况与商务合约的关系都是没有或不大，但可以简单作出介绍。

6.1.1　例外情况之一:政府官员的压迫性、随意性或违反宪法的行为

在第一种例外情况,认为要保留惩罚性损失赔偿的原因主要是防止政府官员的独行独断,保护普通市民。Devlin 勋爵是这样说:"where one man is more powerful than another,it is inevitable that he will try to use his power to gain his ends;and if his power is much greater than the other's,he might,perhaps,be said to be using it oppressively. If he uses his power illegally,he must of course pay for his illegality in the ordinary way;but he is not to be punished simply because he is the more powerful. In the case of the government it is different,for the servants of the government are also the servants of the people and the use of their power must always be subordinate to their duty of service."在这一种例外情况,是要看两个方面。一是有关的行为是否压迫性或是随意性或是违反宪法。如果政府官员仅是疏忽,这不足够:Barbara v. Home Office(1984)134 NLJ 888;AB v. South West Water Services Ltd(1993)QB 507。二是指针对公职人员如政府官员或最容易与普通市民发生摩擦的警察(也是在英国法院最常见涉及惩罚性损失赔偿的被告),但看来不包括根据立法或者政府部门通过私有化达致商业目标所成立的企业或机构,如供应水、电的企业:AB v. South West Water Services Ltd.。与商业活动有关的政府官员是在"民间搜查令"(Anton Piller order)下的申请人代表律师,因为他在执行时是被视为法院的官员:Columbia Picture Industries Inc. v. Robinson(1987)Ch 38。

上述所讲也带来了困难,第一种困难是许多大公司如警卫,会作出与警察一样的行动而且是同样的压迫性与偶然性,如非法禁锢或非法搜身,但向他们索赔损失就会不一样:加拿大 Mckinnon v. FW Woolworth Co. Ltd(1968)70 DLR(2d)280 先例。第二种困难是判政府官员或警察要作出惩罚性损失赔偿,但该笔钱是要政府掏出来,变成是广大市民所交的税最后承担。这有一点说不通,在 Weldon v. Home Office(1992)1 AC 58 和 Racz v. Home Office(1992)TLR 624 先例,判是政府官员如果是明知故犯或恶意的情况下,要自己承担赔偿责任。

6.1.2　例外情况之二:侵权行为是侵权方计算过好处大过坏处

在第二种例外情况,是侵权方估计侵权会带来更大的经济利益,但根据复原大原则的赔偿会是有限,所以刻意作出侵权行为。这种行动法律要作出阻吓就要作出惩罚性损失赔偿,正如 Devlin 勋爵在 Rookes v. Barnard 先例中所说:"Exemplary damages can properly be awarded whenever it is necessary to teach a wrongdoer that tort does not pay"。Delvin 勋爵在 Rookes v. Barnard 也有以下进一步的解释:"with a cynical disregard for a plaintiff's rights has calculated that the money to be made out of his wrongdoing will probably exceed the damages at risk,it is necessary for the law to show that it cannot be broken with impunity. This category is not confined to money making in the strict sense. It extends to cases in which the defendant is seeking to gain at the expense of the plaintiff some object – perhaps some property which he covets – which he either could not obtain at all or not obtained except at a price greater than he wants to put down."

这种案件涉及报纸、杂志看来是有不少,就是刊登一些很可能造成诽谤的"内幕消息",为了刺激销量,估计好处会大大超出了将来要对受害方支付的赔偿:McCarey v. Associated Newspapers (1965) 2 QB 86 CA; Broadway Approvals v. Odhams Press (1965) 1 WLR 805 CA; Manson v. Associated Newspapers (1965) 1 WLR 1038; Broome v. Cassell & Co. (1972) AC 1027; Riches v. News Group Newspapers (1986) QB 256 CA; John v. MGN (1997) QB 586 CA。这种情况,在香港的娱乐杂志也经常会见到。

这种例子令笔者记得80年代著名的福特汽车厂明知故犯,知道某型号汽车的气缸有问题,会爆炸带来伤亡,但仔细计算过将来面对起诉要作出赔偿,经济上仍比马上收回所有出售的车来改装划算。注意是个别车主与汽车厂应有分销商夹在当中,所以他们之间关系不会是根据合约。遇上这种情形,不要说美国会肯定有惩罚性损失赔偿,连英国也会逃不掉,法律以此来表达对这种做法的极度不满。

但在做法上,目前对惩罚性损失赔偿的判决通常是不会考虑侵权方的利润,也没有这方面的证据。如在 Mcmillan v. Singh (1984) 17 HLR 120 先例,上诉庭判惩罚性损失赔偿是250英镑,但被告的利润只是在60~70英镑内。

6.1.3 例外情况之三:立法规定

在第三种例外情况的立法包括有:《Landlord and Tenant Act 1730》、《Distress for Rent Act 1737》、《Reserve and Auxiliary Forces (Protection of Civil Interests) Act 1951》和比较近期的《Copyright, Designs and Patents Act 1988》。其中在1988年针对版权与专利的立法,Section 97(2)说:"The court may in action for infringement of copyright having regard to all the circumstances, and in particular to – (a) the flagrancy of the infringement, and (b) any benefit accruing to the defendant by reason of the infringement, award such additional damages as the justice of the case may require."

上述立法的"额外损失"(additional damages)是否可以针对惩罚性损失很有争议,看来立法的用词不够明确。这些争议在《McGregor on Damages》(18th edn, 2009年)一书11-032段有介绍,笔者不节录,因为与中国大陆的读者关系很小。

另在1998年《英国人权法》之 section 8 授权法院说到公共机构如果违反有关条文,法院应该作出一个"合理的满足"(just satisfaction)。这是从国际公约照搬过来的名称,应该也是这种惩戒性损失,与复原大原则无关。反正在这种情况下,往往依赖复原大原则解释是不足够。

在较早有介绍过的 Merson v. Cartwright (2005) UKPC 38 先例,判要赔偿原告的100,000巴哈马元也应该属于这一类别的例外情况。

6.1.4 上述惩罚性赔偿的例外情况是否应该保留

有关惩罚性损失赔偿是否应该保留或是扩大适用范围,在英国是一个相当有争议的话题。如法律委员会在1997年的报告《Report on Aggravated, Exemplary and Restitutionary Damages, Law Commission No. 247》,就显示了持相反意见的各半。另在 Kuddus v. Chief Constable of Leicestershire (2002) 2 AC 122 先例,Scott 勋爵认为第一种

例外情况的惩罚性损失赔偿已经有了“加大损失”(aggravated damages)的替代,而第二种例外情况已经有了“返还性损失”(restitutionary damages)的替代。所以,英国的“民事法再也不需要惩罚性损失赔偿”(no longer any need for punitive damages in the civil law)。但贵族院的 Nicholls 勋爵与 Hutton 勋爵认为还是需要保留第一种例外情况的惩罚性损失赔偿。另 Slynn 勋爵与 Mackay 勋爵认为这不是双方争议的问题,不必作出决定。

也有说法是第二种例外情况实际上与“返还性损失”(restitutionary damages)一样,没有必要存在。这可节录《McGregor on Damages》(18th edn,2009 年)一书 11-029 段:“It is true that the awarding of exemplary damages is a somewhat makeshift and arbitrary method of preventing a tortfeasor's unjust enrichment, especially as it is dependent on the motivation of profit rather than its achievement. It may be that the emergence of restitutionary damages, particularly since Attorney General v. Blake(2001)1 AC 268, will take us beyond waiver of tort and account of profits to allow claimants a more direct recovery without the need to resort to, in this context, the rather clumsy device of exemplary damages.”

6.2 核算惩罚性损失应考虑的因素

惩罚性损失虽然是臆猜,但还是有一些案例针对应该考虑的因素给了指引。Devlin 勋爵在 Rookes v. Barnard(1964)AC 1129 先例就提到了三个必须要考虑的因素:(1)被告应该受到惩罚的侵权行为的真正受害方作为原告(the claimant to be the victim of the punishable behaviour);(2)适度的赔偿(moderation in awards);(3)当事人的财力(means of the parties)。还有一些其他考虑因素,以下分段作出进一步的探讨。

6.2.1 考虑因素之一:真正受害方作为原告

看来这一个考虑因素在现实中很少会适用,原因是侵权的诉因是不能转让,所以在侵权能够作为原告一定是受害方。唯一例外的是受害方在侵权的行为中死亡,变成他的遗属作为原告。这已经有立法针对并在 1934 年的《Law Reform(Miscellaneous Provisions)Act》之 Section 1(2)(a)规定遗属作为原告的索赔不能包括惩罚性损失赔偿。这样的立法规定倒是带来了质疑,如在《McGregor on Damages》(18th edn,2009 年)一书 11-034 段。例如,警察把疑犯打伤就会面对惩罚性损失赔偿,但如果把疑犯打死就会面对疑犯的遗属提出的索赔反而可避免作出惩罚性损失赔偿,这有点说不通。

6.2.2 考虑因素之二:适度的赔偿

在 Rookes v. Barnard(1964)AC 1129 先例,Devlin 勋爵看来是认为在过去先例中陪审团作出惩罚性损失赔偿的判决金额太高,说:“to amount to a greater punishment that would be likely to be incurred if the conduct were criminal; and, moreover, a punishment imposed without the safeguard which the criminal law gives to an offender. I should not allow the respect which is traditionally paid to an assessment of damages by a jury to prevent me from seeing that the weapon is used with restraint. It may even be that the House may find it necessary to follow the precedent it set for itself in Benham v. Gambling(1941) AC 157 and place some arbitrary limit on awards of damages that are made by way of punishment. Exhortations to be moderate may not be enough."

在较近期的 Thompson v. Commissioner of Police of the Metropolis and Hsu v. Commissioner of Police of the Metropolis(1998) QB 498 CA 先例,案情涉及"非法禁锢"(false imprisonment)与"恶意起诉"(malicious prosecution),上诉庭把陪审团估计的惩罚性损失在第一个先例中从200,000英镑减为15,000英镑,而第二个先例从50,000英镑减到25,000英镑。上诉庭的Woolf勋爵说:"Where exemplary damages are appropriate they are unlikely to be less than £ 5,000. Otherwise the case is probably not one which justifies an award of exemplary damages at all. In this class of action the conduct must be particularly deserving of punishment for an award of as much as £ 25,000 to be justified and the figure of £ 50,000 should be regarded as the absolute maximum, involving directly officers of at least the rank of superintendent."

6.2.3 考虑因素之三:当事人的财力

针对这一个考虑,当事人应该只是指被告。显然如果被告非常富有,一个小金额的惩罚性损失赔偿根本就起不到惩罚的作用。所以在 Benson v. Frederick(1766) 3 Burr 1845 和 John v. MGN(1997) QB 586 CA 先例,有说明被告的财力是一个考虑因素。

6.2.4 考虑因素之四:避免与刑事诉讼作出重复的惩罚

已经提到过,为同样的罪名或理由作出两次重复的惩罚是违反基本的公平大原则。所以在这种情况下,不仅是作出适度的赔偿或是小金额的惩罚,而是应该在民事诉讼中避免作出任何惩罚性损失赔偿。所以在 Archer v. Brown(1985) Q. B. 401 先例,涉及欺诈行为,但由于被告已经因为欺诈本身是刑事罪行而受到了起诉与定罪,并曾经被监禁,所以民事诉讼再为同一行为作出惩罚有严重不妥之处。

这在近期的 Devenish Nutrition Ltd v. Sanofi – Aventis SA(2008)2 WLR 637 先例,也有同样的考虑。

6.2.5 考虑因素之五:当事人的行为

这里所涉及的就是原告与被告的行为,如原告是否曾经做一些事情引发了被告的侵权行为。这在 Lane v. Holloway(1968)1 QB 379 CA 先例有提到过原告的"provocation would be relevant to the question of whether or not exemplary damages should be awarded, and, if so, how much."另在 Thompson v. Commissioner of Police of the Metropolis and Hsu v. Commissioner of Police of the Metropolis(1998) QB 498 CA 先例,Woolf 勋爵也有说是原告对被告(警察)的行为如果有不妥当,陪审团也应该考虑是否给予或减少惩罚性损失赔偿。

除了原告的行为外,被告的行为也是考虑因素。例如,被告在审理时对原告作出道歉就会减少惩罚性损失赔偿的考虑因素,但相反如果被告坚持自己的做法正确就会提高惩罚性损失赔偿的金额:Loudon v. Ryder(1953)2 QB 202 CA。

6.2.6 考虑因素之六:复原赔偿的金额

损失赔偿有两个部分:一是根据复原大原则的损失赔偿,二是惩罚性损失。后者永远不应该影响前者金额的高低,因为根据复原大原则计算出来的损失应该不会任意增加或减少。但前者会影响后者金额的高低,因为后者惩罚性损失是一个不肯定的金额,可以增加或减少。例如,法院认为根据复原大原则计算的损失已经很足够惩罚被告,就会减少甚至避免对被告作出惩罚性损失赔偿。相反,如果法院认为复原大原则下根本不足教训被告,就会需要提升惩罚性损失赔偿的金额。这方面可节录《McGregor on Damages》(18th edn,2009年)一书11-041段所说如下:"While the assessment of compensation can never be affected by the amount awarded by way of exemplary damages, the converse is not true. The size of an exemplary award may indeed be influenced by the size of the compensatory one, even to the extent of being eliminated. Lord Devlin in Rookes v. Barnard indicated that, in a case where exemplary damages were appropriate, 'a jury should be directed that if, but only if, the sum which they have in mind to award as compensation (which may, of course, be a sum aggravated by the way in which the defendant has behaved to the plaintiff) is inadequate to punish him for his outrageous conduct, to mark their disapproval of such conduct and to deter him from repeating it, then it can award some larger sum."

6.2.7 考虑因素之七:多位被告

如果在一个侵权诉讼,有多位被告被一并起诉,就会有情况只有一位被告的侵权行为可作出惩罚性损失赔偿的判决。这一来作出一个判决就不能作出惩罚性损失赔偿,因为这会影响其他不应该被惩罚的被告:Clark v. Newsam(1847)1 Ex. 131;Broome v. Cassell & Co(1972)AC 1027。

6.2.8 考虑因素之八:多位原告

在AB v. South West Water Services(1993)QB507 CA先例,案情涉及被告的供水受到污染,饮用了这些食水的受害方有接近200人之多,他们作为多位与共同原告向被告提出起诉,要求惩罚性损失赔偿。上诉庭的Stuart Smith大法官认为有太多原告所以不适合作出惩罚性损失赔偿,因为判多少金额与该笔钱怎样在受害方的原告中分摊会带来困难。同样的案例也有Devenish Nutrition Ltd v. Sanofi - Aventis SA(2008)2 WLR 637,涉及一个药厂非法在全球提高维他命药价格。这带来了非法抬高价格的集体诉讼,多位原告要求惩罚性损失赔偿。但这被法院拒绝,认为并不是所有原告都受到抬高价格的影响,其中不少住在欧洲大陆,他们所在的国家是没有这种惩罚性赔偿的救济。

6.3 合约下的惩罚性损失赔偿:英国法律地位

一般而言,英国法院是不准在合约纠纷作出任何惩罚性损失或加大损失(本章第5段)赔偿的:Addis v. Gramophone Co Ltd(1909)AC 488;Dunlop Pneumatic Tyre Co

Ltd v. New Garage & Motor Co Ltd(1915)AC 79;Watts,Watts & Co. Ltd v. Mitsui & Co. Ltd(1917)AC 227;Paris Oldham & Gustra v. Staffordshire B. G. (1988)2 E. G. L. R. 39; Reed v. Madon(1989)Ch. 408;Jobson v. Johnson(1989)1 WLR 1026,CA 等。可能只有一种例外是解除婚约。但与惩罚性损失赔偿有一点分不开的是,将"精神痛苦"(mental distress)、"不适"(discomfort)等"非金钱损失"(non - pecuniary losses)在部分类别的合约以金钱作出赔偿,令英国合约法针对损失赔偿不允许惩罚性赔偿的地位有所动摇。有关合约下能否做出惩罚性赔偿的方面可以节录 Ewan Mckendrick 教授在《Contract Law —— Text,Cases and Materials》(4th edn,2010 年)一书中 918 页所讲如下:

"The pressure to recognize that a breach of contract can, in principle, give rise to a claim for punitive damages is building. The Supreme Court of Canada has now recognized that punitive damages may be awarded in respect of a breach of contract upon proof of an independent actionable wrong arising out of the same facts as the breach(see Royal Bank of Canada v. W Got & Associates Electric Ltd(2000)178 DLR(4th)385 and Whiten v. Pilot Insurance Co (2002) SCC 18 and, more generally, J Edelman, 'Exemplary Damages for Breach of Contract'(2001)117 LQR 539.) Will the English courts eventually reach this conclusion? They have not done so yet (Devenish Nutrition Ltd v. Sanofi - Aventis SA (2008)EWCA Civ 1086;(2009)3 WLR 198,(143) but it may be that in time they will. If torts and equitable wrongs can generate a claim for punitive damages, why should a breach of contract never give rise to such a claim? As Lord Nicholls stated in A v. Bottrill(2002) UKPC 44; in recognizing that punitive damages can, in principle, be recovered in a case where the wrong committed by the defendant was neither intentional nor reckless, 'never say never is a sound judicial admonition'. A refusal to recognize that a breach of contract can give rise to punitive damages will simply encourage claimants to characterize the beach as some other cause of action for the purpose of seeking punitive damages. This subterfuge will bring little credit to the law. The logic behind the abolition of the 'cause of action' test will eventually bring down the rule that a breach of contract can never give rise to a claim for punitive damages.

This leads us on to the second question. When will punitive damages be available in a breach of contract case? The answer, it is suggested, will be**very rarely.** There are essentially two reasons for this. The first is that, as both Lord Nicholls and Lord Scott pointed out in Kuddus the effect of Attorney - General v. Blake(1998)Ch 439 may well be to undermine Lord Devlin's second category in Rookes v. Barnard(1964)AC 1129 on the basis that 'the profit made by a wrongdoer can be extracted from him without the need to rely on... exemplary damages'. This being the case, punitive damages are only likely to be available where the breach of contract by the defendant is 'so outrageous, his disregard of the plaintiff's rights so contumelious, that something more is needed to show that the law will not tolerate such behaviour'. Such cases are likely to be few and far between. In particular, the mere fact that the defendant has broken his contract with the claimant in order to pursue a more profitable relationship with another party will not suffice to entitle the claimant to punitive damages. Much more will be required before a finding is made that a defendant has behaved in an 'outrageous' fashion."

6.3.1 什么是惩罚性损失赔偿条文

6.3.1.1 惩罚性损失赔偿条文是为了阻吓

惩罚性损失赔偿条文可以以不同形式出现,因为有订约自由。可以说草拟一条没有任何惩罚性味道的条文面对将来千变万化的情况也不是一件容易的事。所以,不断有新的案例出现。在不同写法的条文找出是否是无效的惩罚性条文,就是通过条文的解释来看看在订约时,是否是为了阻吓一方合约方不得违约,否则会面对严重的惩罚性后果。这惩罚性后果可以是支付一笔庞大以及与估计的真正损失无关的金钱,或是要承担大幅度提高的对价,或是要面对更苛刻的条件等。最后的目的是可以客观看到是为了阻吓对方不得违约。这方面可节录 Colman 大法官在 Lordsvale Finance plc v. Bank of Zambia(1996)QB 752 先例中说:"whether a provision is to be treated as a penalty is a matter of construction to be resolved by asking whether at the time the contract was entered into the predominant contractual function of the provision was to deter a party from breaking the contract or to compensate the innocent party for breach. That the contractual function is deterrent rather than compensatory can be deduced by comparing the amount that would be payable on breach with the loss that might be sustained if breach occurred."

另一个著名的说法是 Clarke 大法官在 Murray v. Leisurepaly(2005)EWCA Civ 963 先例,说是考虑议定赔偿金额与真正的损失相比是否是夸大的、不诚实与不是一个真正对损失的估计(extravagant, unconscionable and not a genuine pre - estimate of loss)。另 Clarke 大法官也提到了是找出议定赔偿金额是否是"阻吓性或是赔偿性"(deterrent or compensation)。

6.3.1.2 不涉及金钱赔偿而是针对违约会带来更苛刻条件或更高昂对价也是惩罚性条文

最常见的惩罚性损失赔偿条文是涉及违约时要求违约方支付一笔远超出预计的真正损失作为赔偿,或是允许无辜方没收违约方所支付的金钱(如定金、押金),而该笔钱远超出预计的真正损失。但已经提到,会有情况是对违约方十分严厉的条文,即使不涉及金钱,也会有危险被视为惩罚性损失赔偿条文,但这就会涉及非常复杂的分析与解释。在许多的案例中先挑一个来介绍,在 Euro London Appointments Ltd v. Claessens International Ltd(2006)2 Lloyd's Rep 436 先例,涉及的合约是猎头公司与雇主的合约关系。猎头公司是收取费用为雇主寻找适合的员工,其中合约中有条文针对找到的员工如果上班后不久就辞职，在这种情况下猎头公司必须退还部分的收费。第4.1条文说明这一退还收费的权利只有雇主准时在中介公司开出发票的7天内支付，才有权享受。该条文是这样说："4.1 In order to qualify for the following refund, the Client must pay the Agency's fee within 7 days of the date of invoice and must notify the Agency in writing of the termination of the Engagement within 7 days of its termination."

问题是这一根本不涉及金钱的条文是否是惩罚性损失赔偿条文？它显然是针对雇主不准时支付费用的违约。而条文约定的雇主丧失退费的后果是与中介公司真正的损失很不一样并且会大大超出该损失，因为不准时支付通常的损失只是利息，而7天或多几天的利息损失很有限。这导致了在该先例的第一审，该条文被视为是一条"伪装"(disguised)的惩罚性损失赔偿条文，所以无效。但去了上诉庭该判决被推翻，上诉庭认为第4.1条文只是一条先决条件的条文，就是如果雇主希望享有退还收费的好处，就必须先遵守这一先决条件。这与惩罚性损失赔偿没有关系。上诉庭举例说是有关支付费用给中介公司的期限是在另一条文的第3.1(c)条文，要求是收到发票后的7天内支付费用。但这与第4.1条文没有必然的关系，所以在订约自由下，如果把第3.1(c)条文改为14天也是完全可以的。这表示雇主如果没有按照第4.1条文在发票作出后7天内支付，就会失去退还收费的好处，但他还没有任何的违约，因为第3.1(c)条文是变成允许他有14天才支付。这样看，第4.1条文根本就不是针对违约，也表示不是惩罚性损失赔偿条文。在该先例，只是第3.1(c)与第4.1条文碰巧都写的是7天。但他们之间没有必然关系，也可以有不同天数的规定，就显示了第4.1条文并非是惩罚性损失赔偿条文。

下一个先例是可节录上诉庭的Mance大法官在Cine Bes Filmcilik ve Yapimcilik v. United International Pictures(2003) EWCA Civ 1669先例中提到Colman大法官所说的有关条文是在对方违约时大幅度提高对价也可以是惩罚性，说："In the case before him, Colman J was concerned with a provision for prospective increase in the interest rate payable by a borrower, following the borrower's default. He said that, although the payment of liquidated damages is 'the most prevalent purpose' for which an additional payment on breach might be required under a contract" '... the jurisdiction in relation to penalty clauses is concerned not primarily with the enforcement of inoffensive liquidated damages clauses but rather with protection against the effect of penalty clauses. There would therefore seem to be no reason in principle why a contractual provision the effect of which was to increase the consideration payable under an executory contract upon the happening of a default should be struck down as a penalty if the increase could in the circumstances be explained as commercially justifiable, provided always that its dominant purpose was not to deter the other party from breach.'"

该先例是针对一种情况，就是在贷款合约中有条文针对贷款人如果违约，他在接下去的贷款就要支付大幅度提高的利息作为对价。这种条文不针对违约要支付一笔钱,但原则上还是可以被视为惩罚性条文。

6.3.1.3 不为了阻吓合约对方违约的条文不属于惩罚性损失赔偿条文

不容易拟定与区分条文是否属于惩罚性损失赔偿而无效其中一个微妙的分别是它有否针对违约时的赔偿或支付。如果不是,就不属于这一类别,也不会无效。这方面可介绍 Alder v. Moore(1961)2 QB 57 CA 先例,案情涉及一个球会为球员投保,其中有条文针对保险人对一位受伤并且不能再专业踢球的球员要赔付 500 英镑。案例中的被告是一位球员,踢球时眼睛受伤并被证明为残疾。他被支付了 500 英镑并签署了一份宣言说明以后再也不会专业踢球,否则将支付保险人罚金 500 英镑。但在 4 个月后,被告重新兼职专业踢球,这应该是违反了承诺。保险人向被告提出起诉要求归还这 500 英镑,但被告以该承诺为惩罚性损失赔偿条文为抗拒的理由。法院判是这一说法不适用,因为它不是针对阻吓被告违约,退还这 500 英镑也与被告有否真正损失没有关系。

再接下去介绍 Export Credits Guarantee Department v. Universal Oil Products Co(1983)1 WLR 399 HL 先例,案情涉及被告为一家第三人的纽芬兰公司建造炼油厂,而建造涉及一个银团的融资。银团的担保是由该纽芬兰公司作出的"本票"(promissory notes),并且由原告作出保证。而原告与被告的合约中有条文说明原告如果因为被告在建造合约中的违约导致了要在保证中作出任何的支付给银团,被告必须向原告作出补偿。事后发生违约,纽芬兰公司没有在本票下向银团作出支付,这导致原告需要支付银团高达约 4000 万英镑。原告事后向被告请求补偿,但被告的抗辩是指该有关条文属于惩罚性而无效。但贵族院判这不是属于惩罚性损失赔偿条文,因为它所针对的并非是原告与被告之间的违约,它所针对的是被告与第三人的纽芬兰公司之间的违约。

6.3.1.4 议定赔偿金额低过真正损失的估计不属于惩罚性损失赔偿条文

如果议定赔偿是低过真正损失的估计,就不存在有惩罚性条文的争议,这也可作为一种责任限制的做法。在 Widnes Foundry v. Cellulose Acetate(1931)2 KB 393 先例中,案情涉及一个建造丙酮回收的工厂,双方约定是完工日期如果被延误,承建商就要每周赔偿 20 英镑。建造慢了 30 周,而承建商也在责任上被判是违约,但损失只限制在 600 英镑而不是原告真正与更大高达 5850 英镑的损失。上诉庭的 Scrutton 大法官说:"I find great difficulty in saying that an estimate less than the actual loss can ever be a penalty *in terrorem*."

所以在现实中,程租合约的谈判中经常会见到承租人大力压低滞期费意图减轻他将来违约的赔偿责任,但船东大力提高,特别是面对航次中估计会遇上港口拥挤的情况。最后双方同意的滞期费金额则是要取决于双方谈判的力量、地位与知识水平等。同样在造船合约下,将来要作出支付议定赔偿的船厂应该在谈判时与程租合约下的承租人有同样的心态,要大力争取减低延误交船每天的赔偿金额。而且,为了防止一些船厂不能控制的严重延误(这种延误也不一定可以根据不可抗力事件条文而得到允许,从而延后交船日期,因为这是要看该不可抗力条文是否写得对船厂有利,够广泛),导致船厂要支付完全不能接受的巨额议定赔偿(如船价的一半甚至是全部),通常还会来一个“封顶”(cap),就是说明在延误的议定赔偿金额到了150万美元或者其他金额,或每天的议定赔偿累计到180日后,船厂就再也不必赔偿。至于这严重延误下船东可否中断造船合约,这是要看其他的条文怎样规定以及当时的船价市场,是另外一个问题。

约定金额较低的议定赔偿还可以取巧,只要懂得灵活使用。笔者可以在此举一个实际发生的例子,一家中国船厂与欧洲船东大约在2004年签订的造船合约中,船价为2000万美元。由于船价不高,因为订约时的航运市场仍是低迷,所以延误交船的议定赔偿也只是约定在9000美元一天,并且有一个150万美元总赔偿金额的封顶。接下来的两年内,航运市场大涨,到了临近交船日期之时,市场船价已经达到了5000万美元。欧洲船东非常想准时甚至提早接收船舶投入营运,可在高涨的市场大赚一笔。但中国船厂就因为钢材价格上涨所带来的造价上涨而会损失惨重。结果在笔者的建议下,船厂准备延误交船(但绝不是拒绝交船,因为这是违约/毁约,一被欧洲船东接受终断合约,就会带来庞大与比较市场船舶价格差价的索赔),并向欧洲船东承诺一定愿意承担这9000美元一天的议定赔偿,甚至是封顶的150万美元。字里行间给船东一个信号就是会延误交船很长时间,这导致欧洲船东的恐慌,毕竟航运市场会好多久是没人知道的。结果是很快就帮助中国船厂与欧洲船东达成协议,把造船合约约定的船价提高至船厂满意的一个金额,船厂会尽快与准时交船给船东。笔者听说之后中国船厂有不少在用同样的技巧迫使船东提高造船合约的价格,甚至知悉在中国法院也有类似的官司。

在这一说法下,表示议定赔偿的金额也就是违约方唯一要支付的赔偿。但由于是不足赔偿受害方真正蒙受的损失,所以经常会有争议是受害方试图打破这一偏低的议定赔偿。有关这一方面的问题,在笔者的《装卸时间与滞期费》一书之第十八章有十分详尽的针对,请参阅。这方面也可看贵族院的重要先例:Suisse Atlantique Societe d' Armement S. A. v. N. V. Rotterdamsche Kolen Centrale(1966)1 Lloyd's Rep. 529。

6.3.1.5 惩罚性损失赔偿条文不影响受害方索赔真正蒙受的损失

即使一条条文被视为是惩罚性而变为无效,其效果只是被视为该条文从来不存在,受害方还是可以向违约方索赔其真正的损失(金额会少一点),失去的只是惩罚性损失赔偿条文中比真正损失多出来的部分就再不能向违约方索赔。这方面可先举Wall v. Rederiaktiebolaget Luggude(1915)3 KB 66先例,其中Baihache大法官说:“This being the state of the law as I understand it, one easily sees why in charterparty cases no one sues on the penalty clause now. You cannot under it recover more than the proved damages, and if the proved damages exceed the penal sum you are restricted to the lower amount. As the penalty clause may be disregarded it always is disregarded and has become a dead letter, or from another point of view a '*brutum fulmen*' ..."

另在 Campbell Discount Co Ltd v. Bridge(1962) AC 600 先例中有说:"... Although in practice a penalty clause in a contract as described above is effectively a dead letter, it is important in the present case to note that, contrary to the submissions of [counsel for the defendants], the strict legal position is not that such a clause is simply struck out of the contract, as though with a blue pencil, so that the contract takes effect as if it had never been included therein. Strictly, the legal position is that the clause remains in the contract and can be sued upon, but it will not be enforced by the court beyond the sum which represents, in the events which have happened, the actual loss of the party seeking payment ..."

6.3.1.6 举证责任与其他考虑

举证责任是在声称议定赔偿属于惩罚性条文的一方,毕竟,法院通常是不会警觉如议定赔偿与惩罚性条文的分别:Robophone Facilities v. Blank(1966) 1 WLR 1428。

另在 Murray v. Leisureplay plc(2005) EWCA Civ 963 先例,案情涉及一个雇佣合约中的第 17 条规定,如果作为被告的公司没有向原告的雇员作出提前 1 年通知就解雇,被告就要赔偿原告 1 年的薪资总额。而被告在解雇原告时,只提前作出了 7.5 个星期的通知。根据该第 17 条文,被告的行为构成非法解雇,而原告有权获得 1 年的薪资总额。一审法院判是这个雇佣合约中的第 17 条是一个惩罚性条文而无效。而上诉庭驳回一审的判决。上诉庭认为要证明一个违约损失赔偿条文是惩罚性条文的举证责任是在声称该条文为惩罚性而免责的一方当事人,在本案毫无疑问要由被告举证。然而被告不能举证证明该第 17 条文不是对损失的合理预计,因为被告是在律师、财务顾问、董事等专业人士的同意下自愿与原告签署该合约,提前终断该雇佣合约对被告有潜在的好处而对原告也有潜在的损失,在商业环境中 1 年的解雇通知期也是合理的。因此被告不能证明第 17 条文具有阻吓性而应被判为惩罚性条文。仅仅因为这 1 年薪资总额的赔偿超出原告的损失不能使该条文无效。上诉庭的 Arden 大法官说:"The burden of showing that a clause for the payment of damages on breach is a penalty clause is on the party who seeks to escape liability under it, not on the party who seeks to enforce it. I have already made the point that there is no direct evidence as to why the parties agreed to clause 17 rather than (say) a clause making some allowance for mitigation. As explained above, this issue has to be judged as at the date of the agreement. In this case, there is no question of MFC showing that clause 17 was imposed *in terrorem*."

其他针对惩罚性损失赔偿条文的考虑可一提的是针对双方当事人都是有水平与有平等谈判力量所达成的协议,特别是商业合约,英国法院在许多重要的先例中都有重复尽量不干预。例如在 Philips Hong Kong Ltd v. Attorney General of Hong Kong (1993) 61 BLR 41 PC 先例中 Woolf 勋爵说:"Likewise the fact that two parties who should be well capable of protecting their respective commercial interests agreed the allegedly penal provision suggest that the formula for calculating liquidated damages is unlikely to be oppressive ..."

Woolf勋爵在同一先例中也提到不要太严格针对这方面，否则会带来商业合约的不肯定，说："... the court has to be careful not to set too high a standard and bear in mind that what the parties have agreed should normally be upheld. Any other approach will lead to undesirable uncertainty especially in commercial contracts."

此外，在Steria Ltd v. Sigma Wireless Communications Ltd.（2008）BLR 79先例也提到了把一个双方都是有水平的人士约定的商业合约中的有关条文判是惩罚性条文而无效，这是法院尽量要避免的（in commercial contracts the courts should exercise great caution before striking down a clause as penal）。

6.3.2　议定赔偿条文的好处

先谈谈"议定赔偿"（liquidated damages）条文在很多商业合约中都会有，它也是最常见会涉及与惩罚性损失赔偿的争议。议定赔偿条文在很多的商业合约中都会出现，就是在订立合约时，合约双方就某一特定的违约/毁约约定违约方向受害方做出的确定数额的赔偿。在造船合约中，它通常是针对两种经常发生的违约：（1）超过约定交船的日期，这就会约定每一天的延误要支付多少议定赔偿。（2）针对船厂对所造船舶的一些主要规范说明达不到约定的标准，如船速、耗油量、载重量、船舱容积等。这种约定是如船速慢了半节，船价要扣减5%。与造船合约本质相同的工程合约，也是对超期完成工程约定每一天延误要支付的议定赔偿。

在造船合约（或工程合约），交船延误如果是根据船东真正损失，就会给船厂带来相当大的不肯定。有可能在交船时，航运市场低迷，加上船东还没有找到下一个租约，反正准时接收了船舶也是要去抛老锚或待命，就表示船厂的延误交船也没有对船东造成任何真正的损失。但也会是另一个极端，就是交船时航运市场高涨，早日交船可以替船东带来很大的利润。这延误损失计算起来就难免有争议与昂贵的诉讼，好像贵族院的The "Achilleas"（2008）2 Lloyd's Rep 275先例。

本来在普通法，受害方可向违约方索赔损失是默示的地位，根本不必说明。但怎样计算或是证明真正损失在有一些违约十分不容易，而且经常会导致昂贵的诉讼。这种真正的损失说不准是多少，大原则是只要违约引起的损失类别不是在订约时不可以合理预见：Hadley v. Baxendale（1854）9 Exch 341，违约与造成损失类别之间的"因果关系"（causation）没有中断，都可以计算在内，谋求将受害方复原到一个合约没有被违反的地位，这也是所谓的"复原大原则"（compensatory principle）。所以，真正损失计算可被称为是"非议定赔偿"（unliquidated damage）。

一般在违约中，针对一些计算真正损失不容易与经常发生昂贵的争议与诉讼，所以在经常会发生的违约类别，订约双方就会为了省事，先约定议定赔偿。这样将来就算出了争议也可以局限在责任方面而不必在真正损失计算与证明方面添加麻烦。反之，针对一些不经常发生的违约，甚至加上了计算损失相对容易的因素，就不存在要在订约时约定议定赔偿了，毕竟这也涉及需要的延长谈判的额外工作。

以“程租合约”(voyage charter)或国际货物买卖合约为例,议定赔偿的做法就是“滞期费”(demurrage),因为承租人或非派船方(CIF 的买方或 FOB 的卖方)超出了固定的装卸时间导致违约是经常发生的事情。滞期费在早期是被视为“额外运费”(supplementary freight)或额外装卸时间:Lily v. Stevenson(1895)22 R 278。换言之,滞期费的支付与违约无关,如果承租人或非派船方欠下这笔钱,只涉及债务的追偿。但后来的看法认为是违约,而滞期费就是议定赔偿金额。这方面可节录 Brandon 勋爵在 The “Lips”(1987)2 Lloyd's Rep 311 所说如下:“Ideal first with that demurrage is not. It is not money payable by the charterer as the consideration for the exercise by him of the right to detain a chartered ship beyond the stipulated lay days. If demurrage were that, it would be a liability sounding in debt. I deal next with what demurrage is. It is a liability in damages to which a charterer becomes subject because, by detaining the chartered ship beyond the stipulated lay days, he is in breach of contract.”至于程租合约其他的违约,如船东超期交船或疏忽造成货损货差,或是承租人短装了货物等,就会以个别不同的违约计算与证明真正损失。毕竟在这种千变万化的违约下,订约时即使估计会发生也难以估计违约程度的严重性,难以预先约定一笔议定赔偿。

总结而言,在合约中约定议定赔偿的好处有以下几种:(1)可以很大程度上减少计算与证明真正损失的麻烦与费用,进而节省诉讼费用与时间。特别是一些非常复杂、困难与经常发生的违约,更是适合约定议定赔偿的金额:Clydebank Engineering & Shipbuilding Co. v. Don Jose Yzquierdo y Castaneda(1905)AC 6(HL);Philips Hong Kong v. Attorney General of Hong Kong(1993)61 BLR 41, PC。(2)可以让违约方知道如果发生违约事件,他面对的赔偿责任是多少,甚至可以对某一些风险作出投保。在 Widnes Foundry v. Cellulose Acetate(1931)2 KB 393, CA 中,Scrutton 大法官说:“In many cases a man before entering in contract wishes to know for what he is to be liable if he breaks it, and he agrees a sum payable by him in that event. That obviously has nothing to do with figures fixed *in terrorem*.”(3)在一定程度上,议定赔偿还可以作为一种责任限制,这在本章 6.3.1.4 段已经有提到。

6.3.3 议定赔偿条文是否是惩罚性损失赔偿条文

议定赔偿虽然有以上所讲的好处,但仍会面对各种抗辩或争议,而最主要与常见的抗辩就是争议它是一条惩罚性条文因而无效,损失要以真正损失计算与证明。一种经常会出现的情况,就是要赔偿的一方声称议定赔偿定得太高,属于惩罚性条文,法律不应该承认或执行:Watts, Watts & Co. Ltd v. Mitsui & Co. Ltd(1917)AC 227;Jobson v. Johnson(1989)1 WLR 1026, CA。

会造成这种情况就是在订约时,双方所约定的议定赔偿金额并非是真正损失的估计。更明显的是,有证据显示一方为了阻吓另一方不违约,而迫使另一方接受天文数字的议定赔偿,该数字大大超出真正损失的估计。在这方面权威的说法是贵族院的 Scandinavian Trading v. Flota Ecuatoriana(1983)2 AC 694 中 Diplock 勋爵所说的:

"The classic form of penalty clause is one which provides that upon breach of a primary obligation under the contract a secondary obligation shall arise on the part of the party in breach which does not represent a genuine pre – estimate of any loss likely to be sustained by him as the result of the breach of primary obligation but is substantially in excess of that sum."

这方面的争议有大量先例，如：Re Newman(1876)4 Ch. D. 724，CA；Public Works Commissioner v. Hills(1906) AC 368，PC；Euro London Appointments Ltd v. Claessens International Ltd(2006)2 Lloyd's Rep 436；M & J Polymers Ltd v. Imerys Minerals Ltd (2008)1 Lloyd's Rep 541 等。

6.3.4　怎样区分合约的一般议定赔偿条文与惩罚性条文

至于它们之间怎样区分，一些大原则有在著名的贵族院先例 Dunlop Ltd. v. New Garage Co. Ltd. (1915) AC 79 中涉及。该著名先例的案情是著名的轮胎公司 Dunlop 与分销商订立合约，其中规定了分销商不得以低于某一价格出售轮胎，以免造成恶性竞争，而其中有第 5 条文说明如果有违反，分销商就必须为每一个低价出售的轮胎支付一笔钱（名义上称为议定赔偿），条文如下："We(分销商) agree to pay to the Dunlop Pneumatic Tyre Co Ltd，the sum of(某一个金额) for each and every tyre，cover or tube sold or offered in breach of this agreement，as and by way of liquidated damages and not as penalty，but without prejudice to any other rights or remedies you or the Dunlop Pneumatic Tyre Co Ltd，may have hereunder."之后发生了分销商的违约，这就导致了双方之间的诉讼，而分销商作为被告的抗辩是指第 5 条文属于惩罚性条文。从不同法院的判法也可以看到这是不容易掌握的：一审的法院判第 5 条文是有法律效力的议定赔偿条文，但上诉庭改判是一条惩罚性条文，最后在贵族院又被改为是议定赔偿条文。

在贵族院，Dunedin 勋爵有说明如何区分议定赔偿与惩罚性损失赔偿条文，以下可作其中的一些介绍。

6.3.4.1　区分原则之一：条文的标题并不重要

Though the parties to a contract who use the words "penalty" or "liquidated damages" may *prima facie* be supposed to mean what they say，yet the expression used is not conclusive. The court must find out whether the payment stipulated is in truth a penalty or liquidated damages ...

这里也体现了英国法一贯的精神，也就是重视实质内容而非标题，这与我们中国人重视标题或名称有所不同。在英国法下一条条文可以写作是"议定损失赔偿条文"，但实质内容却被判是一条惩罚性条文：Re Newman(1876)4 Ch. D. 724，CA；Public Works Commissioner v. Hills(1906) AC 368，PC。反之，也可能是一条条文写作"惩罚性条文"，但被判为仅仅是对违约损失合理估计的"议定损失赔偿条文"：Ranger v. G. W. Railway(1854)5 HLC 72，HL；Crux v. Aldred(1866)14 WR 656；Re White(1901) 17 TLR 461，DC；Clydebank，etc.，Co. v. Yzquierdo，etc. (1905) AC 6，HL。

6.3.4.2 区分原则之二:约定的金额比真正损失大为阻吓一方当事人不敢违约

The essence of a penalty is payment of money(or other non - monetary rights) stipulated as*in terroem* of the offending party; the essence of liquidated damages is a genuine convenanted pre - estimate of damage.

这一大原则已经解释过,不必再重复。只多提一句就是作为惩罚性条文而导致不被法律所承认,主要就是金钱上大大超出订约时估计的真正损失,毕竟商业合约都是针对金钱。但如果是那些非金钱的约定,有这种惩罚的意味,也会有同样的后果。例如在 Jobson v. Johnson(1989)1 WLR 1026,涉及违约要把财产转让作为惩罚。但这种情况千变万化,有时候法院也要现实。例如贷款合约经常就会涉及了一条条文是如果贷款人违约,借款人或银行会有合约上的救济。而这违约的定义可以是很广泛的,如贷款人迟延定期还款,但也可以是许多其他方面。例如,贷款合约中针对贷款人哪些行为属于违约,如违反一些规定,或是被其他债权人在法院申请要将其清盘,又或是对船舶作为抵押品作出伤害(如不进行维修保养,这会导致抵押品的价值下降或者不投保)等。这方面可以参阅在一般船舶贷款合约内的"保证契约"内的多种违约事件,在笔者的《船舶融资与抵押》一书第五章 4.2.1 段有详细介绍。这时作为融资的银行其中的一个权力就可以要求马上把所有的贷款全部归还。这种所谓的"加速还款条文"(accelerated payment)也曾经被贷款方指称为惩罚性条文。

在 The "Angelic Star"(1988)1 Lloyd's Rep. 122,涉及船厂对船东作出的贷款,这些情况在今天好像是不可思议,但在 20 世纪 70、80 年代是非常普遍的现象。因为航运低迷而令造船业非常不景气,而一些造船国家不论是老牌的西方国家或是新兴的造船国家,如韩国、日本或巴西面对激烈的竞争都对自己国家的造船业作出庞大的经济援助。它们各有各的理由,包括保护造船工业对国防很重要,或是保护劳工市场,又或是带起自己国家其他的工业等。The "Angelic Star"先例就是一个典型的例子,船东只需要支付船价的 20% 就可以接船去航运市场营运,而余下的 80% 就在接船后分 8 年,每半年共 16 期来摊还,其中摊还的利率也是固定的。显然,没有国家的资助,船厂是无法承担这种做法的,因为造船期间船厂是需要大量的资金。这样一来,造船合约就好像船舶融资合约一样,需要各种担保,如要船东作出个人的担保或是集团公司作出担保,对船舶要登记抵押权等。其中亦包括一条针对船东违约情况下的"加速还款条文"。在该 The "Angelic Star"先例,该条文如下:"13. The loan together with all other monies due to the Lenders by the Owners shall immediately become payable and the Lender shall forthwith be put in funds to cover all existing and future liability under any outstanding bills drawn in connection with the loan, and the security for the loan and such monies shall become enforceable... if ... (a) The Owners fail to make payments of capital or interest... on due dates."

由于船东违约,船厂向船东本人(作为担保人)提出诉讼,船东作出的抗辩就是说上述条文是惩罚性条文,但这不被法院接受,上诉庭的 Donaldson 大法官这样说:

"Whatever the merits or demerits of this argument viewed as a whole, it depends upon the proposition that loan condition 13 is a penalty clause. This I do not accept. Clearly a clause which provided that in the event of any breach of contract a long term loan would immediately become repayable and that interest thereon for the full term would not only be still payable but would be payable at once would constitute a penalty as being 'a payment of money stipulated as *in terrorem* of the offending party' (proposition 2 in the speech of Lord Dunedin in *Dunlop Ltd. v. New Garage Co. Ltd.* (1915) AC 79.) But I do not so read condition 13. 'The loan' is the capital sum. 'All other monies due to the lenders by the owners' cannot be construed as 'all other monies which would otherwise become due by the owners in the future.' It means 'all other monies due at the time of the happening of an event of default'. The mere fact that the capital sum becomes immediately repayable upon a failure to comply with the conditions upon which credit was extended cannot constitute a penalty. The provision that the lenders shall forthwith be put under any outstanding bills drawn in connection with the loan is intended to safeguard the shipbuilders against their potential liability as drawers should the bills have been negotiated and the purchaser, as acceptor, fails to honour the bills upon maturity. This again is not a penalty provision."

在笔者看来,英国法院的这种现实的做法与长远的考虑,建立起一套对银行与金融机构非常有利的法律环境,从而给自己带来很大的经济利益。就拿上述例子来说,如果这样的"加速还款条文"被判为是惩罚性条文,除了这一期未支付的款项,很有可能是银行再也无法向贷款人拿到剩余但未到期的款项。因为贷款人可能面对清盘,而其届时对银行的违约责任仅限于当时到期未付的一期款项。而有了这"加速还款条文",就可以因为贷款人违约而令全部剩余的款项一并到期需要支付,而贷款人不支付就导致对这些所有剩余款项的违约,从而给了银行理由与诉因来追讨这些款项,趁手中还有担保时一次把欠款全数取回来。

6.3.4.3 区分原则之三:判断是否惩罚性条文是看订约时的情况

The question whether a sum stipulated is penalty or liquidated damages is a question of construction to be decided upon the terms and inherent circumstances of each particular contract, judged of as at the time of the making of the contract, not as at the time of the breach.

这方面也已经说过,一条条文是属于议定赔偿还是惩罚性条文,是要看在订约时其是否是对将来会发生的违约损失的合理估计,而不是在真正违约时看是否合理。因为到了真正违约时,可能已经是订了合约的几年后,市场可能已经发生了很大的变化,导致赔偿议定损失的金额相比当时的市场看来是太高与太不合理。以上的一段英文是 Dunedin 勋爵在 Dunlop Ltd. v. New Garage Co. Ltd. (1915) AC 79 先例中所讲的区分原则之一。

当然发生了违约事后看是否在订约时是一个对真正损失合理的估计也不是完全

没有作用。因为在一些违约,导致复杂的真正损失类别,就可以出了事才回头看订约时这种损失类别是否可以合理预见,会否是在考虑之中,从而得出议定赔偿是否有惩罚性意味。这可以节录在 Philips Hong Kong v. Attorney - General of Hong Kong(1993) 61 BLR 41 中所讲的:"The fact that the issue has to be determined objectively, judged at the date the contract was made, does not mean what happens subsequently is irrelevant. On the contrary it can provide valuable evidence as to what could reasonably be expected to be the loss at the time the contract was made . . . "

通常挑出可能有其中一种情况是议定损失会比真正损失高是并不足够,除非有其他客观的因素如强势的订约一方迫使弱势方非要接受该议定赔偿条文。这也是在 Philips Hong Kong v. Attorney - General of Hong Kong 一案所说的:"Except possibly in the case of situation where one of the parties to the contract is able to dominate the other as to the choice of the terms of a contract, it will normally be insufficient to establish that a provision is objectionably penal to identify situations where the application of the provision could result in a large sum being recovered by the injured party than his actual loss."

6.3.4.4 区分原则之四:其他帮助区分的考虑

6.3.4.4.1 将来可能发生的违约最大的损失也低于约定的金额

It will be held to be a penalty if the sum stipulated for isextravagant and unconscionable in amount in comparison with the greatest loss that could conceivably be proved to have followed from the breach.

这里介绍一些大原则考验哪些情况属于惩罚性条文,而其中第一个考验也是最重要的,就是议定赔偿的金额是非常夸大与过度的。这里又可以举 Clydebank Engineering & Shipbuilding Co. v. Don Jose Yzquierdo y Castaneda(1905) AC 6(HL)的先例,Halsbury 勋爵曾经举例说双方约定以 50 英镑造房子,1 年内完工,如果做不到就要支付 100 万英镑作为惩罚,这就是明显的惩罚性条文。他说:"if you agreed to build a house in a year, and agreed that if you did not build the house for £ 50, you were to pay a million of money as a penalty, the extravagance of that would become at once apparent. Between such an extreme case as I have supposed and other cases, a great deal must depend on the nature of the transaction—the thing to be done, the loss likely to accrue to the person who is endeavouring to enforce the performance of the contract, and so forth."

上述是一个极端的例子,很容易看到是惩罚性条文,但遇上模棱两可的例子就不这么容易掌握,而且判法也不会肯定。在上述的例子也要说明是合约的标的或对价与议定赔偿的金额也不是有必然关系,甚至是没有关系。因为对价只是名义上的,如一块钱,但这种合约如果双方作出承诺并约定在违约时要作出议定赔偿,这是完全不会受只有一块钱对价的影响。又例如,一个收费十分廉宜的工程建造一个展览场地,而且时间上非常急迫,如果不能准时完工就会带来很大的真正损失。这一来,双方针对工程延误约定了一个高昂的议定赔偿,而相对的工程费用并不高。结果因为工程延误了一段很短的时间,议定赔偿超出了工程的费用,但这并不表示这议定赔偿是一条惩罚性条文。

6.3.4.4.2 对纯金钱债务约定比债务更高的赔偿金额

It will be held to be a penalty if the breach consists only in not paying a sum of money, and the sum stipulated is a sum greater than the sum which ought to have been paid.

这是另一个有关议定赔偿是否惩罚性条文的考验,它是针对一种违约就是延期支付一笔钱。认为这种条文无效是因为这种违约的真正损失是完全知道,就是该付的这笔钱。所以再约定另一个金额更高的议定赔偿就很明显是惩罚性条文了。

另一方面,银行为了避免贷款人延迟还钱,可以与贷款人在合约中约定迟付款的利息为"伦敦同业拆放利率"(London Interbank Offered Rate,简称 LIBOR)或"最优惠利率"(prime rate) +3%(为例),这种条文不能说是惩罚性条文。虽然它比一般仲裁或者法院判的利率为高(一般是 prime +1%),毕竟每个人的融资成本或机会成本都不一样,以较高利息向银行、母公司或者是其他第三者借贷的情况经常发生,但是到了一个程度是如果该约定的利息百分比订得太高就会变成是惩罚性条文,当然分水线并不容易掌握。一个明显的例子是有传言说香港甘泉航空公司在 2008 年 4 月发生经济困难与在清盘之前曾向一位香港首富借贷,其中规定要支付的利息高达 40%,这就有很大可能是惩罚性条文了。

较近期有关高利息的案例有 Jeancharm Ltd v. Barnet Football Club Ltd(2003) EWCA Civ 58,92 Con LR 26,它涉及一个球会与供应商的合约中有关前者延期支付要赔偿每周 5% 的利息,这等于年利率的 260%。在后来的诉讼中,球会抗辩说这么高的利率是惩罚性。供应商的回应是应该看整个合约,包括他要承担的风险与其他条文针对延期供应要作出高额的赔偿。但上诉庭不认为这是改变了针对议定赔偿是否是惩罚性的基本看法,就是这议定赔偿金额是否是一个对将来的损失真正的估计,而 260% 显然不是,所以有关的高利息条文无效。

6.3.4.4.3 对于大小及严重程度不一的多种违约约定单一的赔偿金额

There is a presumption (but no more) that it is penalty when "a single lump sum is made payable by way of compensation, on the occurrence of one or more or all of several events, some of which may occasion serious and others but trifling damage." (Lord Elphinstone v. Monkland Iron and Coal Co. [1886] 11 App. Cas 332, HL)

举一个例子是在一个建造合约中,除了约定一般的延误一星期要赔偿的一笔金额外,还有一条文规定如果该承包商不能按时履行所有的合约规定项目就要给雇主一笔 1 万英镑的议定赔偿金额,这后面的规定被判是一条惩罚性条文:Re Newman, ex p. Capper(1876) 4 Ch. D 724; Cooden Engineering Co. Ltd v. Stanford(1953) 1 QB 86, CA。这等于在该条文下不能按时履行的合约规定项目即使只是一粒螺丝,承包商也要赔偿雇主 10,000 英镑。换言之,不能按时履行的所有项目会有很多,有大有小,都要承包商在许多小的项目支付 10,000 英镑就会是惩罚性了。加上大小事项不论严重与否，都约定要违约的承包商赔偿10,000英镑，本身就显示了双方没有在订约时估计或者想过不同事项下的违约会带来不同的真正损失。所以，就有了这种条文本质上是惩罚性的假设。此外，如果同一个建造合约其条文约定为当承包商不能在约定的日期前履行合约，要支付雇主200英镑加上延误一星期要支付5英镑，这被判是议定赔偿条文，因为这些金额是基于同一件事情（工程延误）而支付的：Law v. Redditch Local Board（1892）1 QB 127，CA；Pye v. British Automobile Commercial Syndicate（1906）1 KB. 425；Robophone Facilities Ltd v. Blank（1966）1 WLR 1428，CA。

这里也可以举一个造船合约的上诉庭先例 Cenargo Ltd v. Empresa Nacional Bazan de Construcciones Navales Militares SA（2002）EWCA Civ 524，案情部分是关系到一个船厂（Astilleros）的保证就是该建造的滚装渡轮可容纳146辆长13米的拖车，但所交的船舶由于甲板内的局限导致船东（Cenargo）声称少了6辆拖车的空间。该造船合约针对这一个船厂的担保如果受到破坏有一条文针对就是每少一辆拖车空间要支付150,000美元。该条文是如下："If the actual trailer carrying capacity of the Vessel is less than 146 Units of 13 metres each the Builder shall pay to the Buyer as liquidated damages One hundred and fifty thousand United States Dollars（ $ 150,000）for each trailer unit by which the Vessel is deficient but excluding the first one（1）in respect of which deficiency no liquidated damages shall be payable. If the deficiency in trailer carrying capacity is ten（10）or more the Buyer as an alternative to receiving the aforementioned liquidated damages may rescind the Contract. "

问题出在针对这6个减少了的拖车空间，可以很容易作出一些调整就可以解决问题，如搬走备用螺旋桨的桨翼与在龙骨上作结构上的调整等。反正是双方专家估计的调整费用由欧洲船厂进行也只不过是11,000美元，但如果允许船东向船厂根据造船合约索赔议定赔偿，6个拖车空间乘150,000美元就变成是900,000美元了。这里就带来争议是议定赔偿能否用在一些很轻微的违约还是只能用于较为严重或者是不能补救的违约。或会问，如果是这么廉宜就可以作出调整，船厂为什么不自己作出？这里可以有几种情况，一种情况是船厂自己不小心错失了这个机会；另一种情况可以是作出调整需要时间，而交船的"死亡日期"（drop dead date）已经届临导致船厂要硬着头皮马上交船。在该先例，又更是另一个原因，就是在造船合约约定了的拖车空间数目，这与其他船舶的特征不一样，如船速与耗油不符合造船合约规定。这些都可以在交船前的试航时被确定下来，如果船厂花很少金钱就可以把一些找到的缺陷解决，船厂肯定会这样做。顶多解决问题后再来一次试航才交船。但在本案例，涉及装运拖车的空间，这一船舶特征不存在有试航，所以有了数目不足的情况会是很容易看漏。这导致船东在事后经营船舶的时候才会发觉这6个减少了的拖车空间。而被发觉后，船东认为他可以向船厂要求支付一大笔的议定赔偿。

船厂其中一个争议是议定赔偿是要在最后一期船价的支付中扣减，所以在接船以后就不再适用。这抗辩看来不被接受，另主要的争议就是议定赔偿是否适用。

在该先例中，上诉庭推翻了高院的判决，认为该造船合约的议定赔偿条文只是针对重大的违约（违反船厂担保），因为双方在订约时的意图应该是这样想的，而没有想到适用在一些轻微与容易补救的违约。否则，这条文在大小违约都可以适用同一笔议定赔偿就会变成是一条惩罚性条文而无效。Longmore 大法官是这样说：

"27 If there was a breach of art. 1. 4, I would, for my part, conclude that the true loss of the buyers cannot have been intended to be covered by the liquidated damages clause. There is a danger that, if a liquidated damages clause is held to apply to trifling breaches of contract or breaches of contract which result in a trifling loss, the whole clause might be struck down as a penalty clause. In the court below Mr. Kendrick（船厂代表大律师）did indeed make that submission in relation to art. III. 5, but he did not wish to repeat that submission to this court; that was, no doubt, because liquidated damages clauses of the kind used in the present case have a genuinely useful function in pre – estimating damage which is likely to result. But it is important that such contracts should be construed, if possible, to avoid the result that breaches of contract resulting in minor losses will be covered by such clauses. As Lord Woolf said in Philips Hong Kong Ltd v. Attorney General of Hong Kong (1993) 61 BLR 41 at p. 59: 'So long as the sum payable in the event of non – compliance with a contract is not extravagant, having regard to the range of losses that it could be reasonably anticipated it [the relevant clause] would have to cover at the time the contract was made, it can still be a genuine pre – estimate of the loss that would be suffered and so a perfectly valid liquidated damage provision.'

28 That shows that it is important to have in mind the range of losses the parties would anticipate the clause would cover when they made their contract. I do not consider that the parties in this case, when agreeing liquidated damages in relation to trailer carrying capacity, could have had in mind defects in design or workmanship which could be rectified without incurring major expense, even if it could be said that until such defects were rectified the vessel's spaces were, in breach of contract, not fully available.

29 This approach to construction of a liquidated damages clause is similar to that of the Privy Council in Webster v. Bosanquet [1912] AC 394, where it was held that a potentially penal clause did not apply to every sale contrary to a right of pre – emption clause (for breach of which liquidated damages were agreed to be payable) but only to sales in the sort of commercial quantity which the parties must have had in mind when they made their contract.

30 Mr. Kendrick（船厂代表大律师）relied on a passage in Professor Sir Guenther Treitel's book on the《Law of Contract》(10th edn, 1999), at p. 932 as follows: 'A sum may, therefore, be regarded as penal if it might have become due on a trifling breach, even though the breach which actually occurred was quite a serious one, and one for which the sum

could be regarded as a genuine pre – estimate. In this way, the rule can invalidate perfectly fair bargains. The courts will do their best to avoid such results by construing the contract so as to make the sum payable only on major breaches, for which it is a valid pre – estimate.'

31 For this proposition Webster v. Bosanquet is cited. Mr. Eder(船东代表大律师) attacked the passage, firstly, as not justified by Webster v. Bosanquet and, secondly, as being difficult to justify in principle since a distinction between major breaches and minor breaches of contract would give rise to uncertainty and unnecessary argument.

32 For my part, I think the passage correctly states the law, for the reasons that I have given, so long as one understands the phrase 'major breaches' as referring to breaches of contract giving rise to substantial loss of the kind contemplated by the liquidated damages clause.

33 For these reasons I would hold that, even if there was a breach of art. 1.4 of the contract to the extent of an inability on the part of the vessel to provide six required slots, the loss resulting from that breach was not intended to be covered by the liquidated damages clause. I would therefore allow the builders' appeal by setting aside the judgment ..."

6.3.4.4.4 真正损失很难估计的情况

It is no obstacle to the sum stipulated being a genuine pre – estimate of damage, that the consequences of the breach are such as to make precise pre – estimation almost an impossibility. On the contrary, that is just the situation when it is probable that pre – estimated damage was the true bargain between the parties.

如果一种违约是明显会导致很大程度的损失而真正损失是多少却很难预先估计的情况下，就存在一个假设是议定赔偿条文不是惩罚性条文：Philips Hong Kong v. Attorney General of Hong Kong(1993)61 BLR 41, PC。

在 Dunlop Ltd. v. New Garage Co. Ltd. (1915) AC 79 这一贵族院先例中，主要也是这一原因议定赔偿条文被贵族院认为是可以接受的，所以订下一个金额作为估计赔偿并无不合理之处，除非该金额是高到完全不合理的数额。Dunedin 勋爵是这样说："Turning now to the facts of the case, it is evident that the damage apprehended by the appellants owing to the breaking of the agreement was an indirect and not a direct damage. So long as they got their price from the respondents for each article sold, it could not matter to them directly what the respondents did with it. Indirectly it did. Accordingly, the agreement is headed 'Price Maintenance Agreement', and the way in which the appellants would be damaged if prices were cut is clearly explained in evidence by Mr. Baisley (the appellants' manager), and successful attempt is made to controvert that evidence. But though damage as a whole from such a practice would be certain, yet damage from any one sale would be impossible to forecast. It is just, therefore, one of those cases where it seems quite reasonable for parties to contract that they should estimate that damage at a certain figure, and provided that figure is not extravagant there would seem no reason to suspect that it is not truly a bargain to assess damages, but rather a penalty to be held *in terrorem*."

6.3.4.4.5 一连串合约中的中间方(party in between)

在一连串的合约,如果对一位夹在中间的合约方而言,前后合约如果都有约定不同议定赔偿的金额针对某一些违约(如前后租约下不同的滞期费率),这会导致中间方会在有些情况下可以赚取一些差价。例如,中间方与原船东的租约约定滞期费是25,000美元/天,但转租给分承租人是35,000美元/天。但显然在同样的违约下(超出装卸时间),中间方的损失只是需要支付给原船东25,000美元/天,变为他可赚10,000美元/天的差价。问题是分承租人能否争辩这是惩罚性条文?笔者认为是不可以,因为中间方赚取差价也不表示这35,000美元/天的滞期费条文是阻吓分承租人别违约延误船舶,再说两个租约订立的时间不一样,市场也不一样,谈判手段与强弱也不一样,不可能是要求滞期费金额都要一致或是十分接近才不算是惩罚性条文。

在 Steria Ltd v. Sigma Wireless Communications Ltd. (2008) BLR 79 先例也有同样的争议。该先例的总承包商 Sigma 与雇主的主合约内有一条针对整个工程完工日期延误的议定赔偿条文。Sigma 把有关的电脑工程给了分包商 Steria。在分包合约中,也有一条议定赔偿条文,但条文内容与主合约中的条文内容不同,因为它分别针对了四个不同工程的延误。这一来,就会造成在分包合约出现了延误,但整个工程完工日期没有受到延误的情况下,就会导致 Sigma 根本没有损失也可以向分包商 Steria 收取议定赔偿。所以该条文被分包商指称在本质上是惩罚性条文。但 Stephen Davies 大法官不同意,说:"In such circumstances, in my judgment: (i) there is no substantial discrepancy between the liquidated damages provision of the subcontract and the level of damages likely to be suffered by Sigma; (ii) on the facts of this case I am unable to conclude that the clause was - objectively considered as at the date the contract was entered into - intended to be deterrent rather than compensatory. Overall, this being a commercial contract entered into between two substantial and experienced companies with knowledge of the difficulties which can occur where after the event one party seeks to recover general damages from the other for delay, I am not prepared to strike down the clause as penal."

6.3.4.4.6 针对同一种违约有不同金额的议定赔偿

会有情况是针对同一个违约有不同金额的议定赔偿,这包括在造船合约。例如在著名的 Pacific Ocean Shipping Corp v. Sembawang Corp Ltd (No. 1) (1998) Commercial Court 4 June 1998,该造船/改装合约针对工程的延误有以下的条文针对:

"33.4 If the BUILDER should fail to deliver the VESSEL by the DELIVERY DATE or any extension thereof granted in accordance with the CONTRACT, the BUILDER shall pay LIQUIDATED DAMAGES to the OWNERS for such default at the rates shown below ...

... first four weeks 70,000 Singapore dollars per week; next four weeks 140,000 Singapore dollars per week. For any delay in excess of the first eight weeks 200,000 Singapore dollars a week.

Delay for the purposes of this article shall mean the period which may elapse between the DELIVERY DATE and the actual date of the DELIVERY of the VESSEL.

33.5 The rates of LIQUIDATED DAMAGES to which the BUILDER may become liable represent a genuine pre – estimate of the loss which the OWNERS would sustain in the event of delay and is not to be construed as a penalty."

该先例没有争论这是否惩罚性损失赔偿的条文,但完全可以理解。因为很容易解释就是随着工程的延误加剧,后果会更严重,也代表损失会是更大。毕竟,该合约中有一条文说明工程的"时间是条件条文"(time is of the essence of the contract)。

6.4 定金与预付

在许多商业合约中,经常会有定金(deposit)的规定,主要目的是担保合约的履行。定金有另一种看来是非常接近的做法,可称为"部分支付或预付"(part payment or pre – payment)。预付也有同样的目的,加上可能有其他的目的,如在一些涉及机器的买卖合约中要求买方作出预付,就为了资助机器的制造。定金与预付最大的分别就是在支付方没有履行合约的情况下,定金会被"没收"(forfeit)。但预付的法律地位还未完全明确,通常就要退还给支付方。例如,在合约明确收款人是要产生一些因为依赖该合约而花费的钱时,这就有可能被视为是订约意图,特别是针对收款人而言,是在对方没有履行合约时可以没收:Hyundai Shipbuilding and Heavy Industries Ltd v. Papadopoulos(1980)1 WLR 1129。这一来,就可以看到定金是会涉及惩罚性条文的问题的,但预付就通常不会有这个危险。

在订约自由下,会有情况是条文写的不清不楚,难以区分定金或预付。例如,一方面把它称呼为预付,但另有条文说明对方不履行合约时可以没收。这里就涉及根据合约条文的解释原则,希望找出一个答案。只说英国法律在难以作出区分时通常会倾向解释为预付的条文:Dies v. British and International Mining and Finance Co (1939)1 KB 715。

定金与预付条文的分别可以举船舶买卖作为例子。在二手船买卖中,世界上主要使用的标准格式就是"1993 年挪威格式"(NSF' 93)。其第 2 条文就是要求买方在合约订立的规定时间内支付船价 10% 到一个共同账户,以作为买方买船的担保。另在第 13 条文,说明如果买方没有按时支付船价,卖方有权取消合约并没收定金:"Should the Purchase Price not be paid in accordance with Clause 3, the Sellers have the right to cancel the Agreement, in which case the deposit together with interest earned shall be released to the Sellers."

但如果涉及新船买卖,也就是造船,在做法上就不是定金而是预付条文了。这在一些著名的标准格式,如日本造船格式 SAJ 与 BIMCO 的 Newbuildcon 格式都这样规定。在 SAJ, Article II 是针对了船价的分期付款以及预付,在时间上是配合造船的进度。而针对船厂交不了船(不论是否涉及违约),就涉及船厂作为卖方需要退还预付给买方。造船合约也通常有其他条文针对买方会退还预付的船价,包括要求船厂在造船合约生效前提供"还款担保"(refund guarantee),就是为了在船厂交不出船舶或者有其他违约/毁约时,可以保证买方取回预付的船价。在造船合约下退还预付,非但不存在没收部分或者全部的预付金额,还往往要加上沉重的利息,这都是在合约关系下才可以做到。撇开合约条文,船厂交不出船舶需要退还预付的船价在英国法律的地位下也有其他的依据。一个是预付与定金的分别,另一个是船厂完全交不出对价,所以买方也可以收回他支付的部分对价,所谓的"total failure of consideration"说法。

6.4.1 定金会有危险被视为是惩罚性损失赔偿

定金涉及惩罚性损失赔偿的危险与议定赔偿一致,就是它只能作为一个双方在谈判时对一方不履行可能造成的损失一个真实与预先的估计,如果脱离了而且金额定的过高(也就是指高额定金),就会有惩罚性损失赔偿的危险。但凡事都有例外,这里就涉及定金这一课题的悠久历史。在罗马时代就已经有这种习惯做法,就是合约的一方交出一笔钱或一样实物(如一只戒指)表示履行合约的诚意。如果他在后来没有履行,定金或这一实物就会被没收。这些历史在 Howe v. Smith(1884)27 Ch D 89 先例有提到。在这种情况下,定金不一定是与双方估计将来违约/毁约会产生的损失有关系。在涉及土地的买卖,一直以来的惯例是以约10%的合约价格作为定金,而英国的衡平法院也是从不干预,把这种做法视为一种例外。

涉及定金与惩罚性条文可以介绍四个先例。

6.4.2 有关先例之一:Stockloser v. Johnson

在 Stockloser v. Johnson(1954)1 QB 476 先例,Denning 勋爵在该案的上诉庭说:"Again, suppose that a vendor of property, in lieu of the usual 10 per cent, deposit, stipulates for an initial payment of 50 per cent of the prices as a deposit and part payment; and later, when the purchaser fails to complete, the vendor resells the property at a profit and in addition claims to forfeit the 50 per cent deposit. Surely the court will relieve against the forfeiture. The vendor cannot forestall this equity by describing an extravagant sum as a deposit, any more than he can recover a penalty by calling it liquidated damages."(Denning 勋爵是说假设在土地买卖,双方约定不是10%的定金而是高达50%,之后买方没有及时完成交易,卖方转售有关的土地并赚了钱。但卖方没收这50%的定金,大赚特赚。这一来,法院不会认同,会把这种情况视为等同议定赔偿条文实是惩罚性损失赔偿而无效,并作出救济不允许卖方没收定金,因为卖方根本没有蒙受实际损失)。

6.4.3 有关先例之二:Linggi Plantations Ltd v. Jagatheesan

在 Linggi Plantations Ltd v. Jagatheesan(1972)1 MLJ 89 先例,判是卖方可以没收普遍的做法的10%定金,虽然卖方没有蒙受真正损失。Hailsham 勋爵是这样说:"It is also no doubt possible that in a particular contract the parties may use language normally appropriate to deposits properly so – called even to forfeit which turn out on investigation to be purely colourable and that in such a case the real nature of the transaction might turn out to be the imposition of a penalty, by purporting to render forfeit something which is in truth part payment. This no doubt explains why in some cases the irrecoverable nature of a deposit is qualified by the insertion of the adjective 'reasonable' before the noun. But the truth is that a reasonable deposit has always been regarded as a guarantee of performance as well as a payment on account, and its forfeiture has never been regarded as a penalty in English law or common English usage."

6.4.4 有关先例之三:Workers Trust and Merchant Bank Ltd v. Dojap Investments Ltd

在 Workers Trust and Merchant Bank Ltd v. Dojap Investments Ltd(1993)AC 573 先例,案情涉及 Jamaica 的土地买卖的一笔占合约价格 25% 的定金。买方比完成交易一天晚了一个星期才支付其余的合约价格,这是明显的违约,特别合约中有说明"时间是条件条文"(time is of the essence of the contract)。贵族院不接受这是一个没有惩罚性味道的定金,虽然卖方证明了 Jamaica 的土地买卖经常会发生买方要提供15% ~ 50% 的定金,这与英国的习惯做法不一样。但贵族院不认为有部分买卖把这个百分比的定金视为合理不影响其判断这一定金是否是惩罚性损失赔偿。Browne Wilkinson 勋爵是这样说:

"Since a true deposit may take effect as penalty, albeit one permitted by law, it is hard to draw a line between a reasonable, permissible amount of penalty and an unreasonable, impermissible penalty. In their Lordships' view the correct approach is to start from the position that, without logic but by long continued usage both in the United Kingdom and formerly in Jamaica, the customary deposit has been 10 percent. A vendor who seeks to obtain a larger amount by way of forfeiture deposit must show special circumstances which justify such a deposit.

... In the view of their Lordships, since the 25 percent deposit was not a true deposit by way of earnest, the provision for its forfeiture was a plain penalty. There is clear authority that in a case of a sum paid by one party to another under the contract as security for the performance of that contract, a provision for its forfeiture in the event of non – performance is a penalty from which the court will give relief by ordering repayment of the sum so paid, less any damage actually proved to have been suffered as a result of non completion: Commission of Public Works v. Hills (1906) AC 368. Accordingly, there is jurisdiction in the court to order repayment of the 25 percent deposit...

Finally, it appears that the bank may have suffered some damage as a result of the purchaser's failure to complete. If so, the bank is entitled to deduct the amount of such damages from the 'deposit' of 25 percent. Such damage has not been quantified in the judgment below but appears to be small in amount. It would not be right to keep the purchaser out of all its money to await the outcome of the necessary inquiry as to damages. The bank ought accordingly to make immediate repayment of a substantial amount of the deposit, leaving a fund out of which the bank's damages, if any, can be satisfied."

6.4.5 有关先例之四:Union Eagle Ltd v. Golden Achievement Ltd

在 Union Eagle Ltd v. Golden Achievement Ltd(1997) AC 514 PC 先例,是香港在1997年回归祖国之前上诉去英国枢密院(也就是贵族院同一批大法官)的房子买卖先例。案情涉及买方比约定完成交易的最后时间晚了10分钟,结果合约被卖方终断并没收10%的定金。因为有关合约写明"时间是条件条文"(time is of the essence of the contract),所以晚了10分钟也是违反了条件条文。买方向香港法院申请"履约指令"(specific performance),但在高院与上诉庭都不成功。在贵族院,买方也是败诉,其中 Hoffman 勋爵是这样说:

"... When a vendor exercises his right to rescind, he terminates the contract. The purchaser's loss of the right to specific performance may be said to amount to a forfeiture of the equitable interest which the contract gave him in the land. But this forfeiture is different in its nature from, for example, the vendor's right to retain a deposit or part payments of the purchase price. So far as these retentions exceed a genuine pre-estimate of damage or a reasonable deposit they will constitute a penalty which can be said to be essentially to provide security for payment of the full price. No objectionable uncertainty is created by the existence of a restitutonary form of relief against forfeiture, which gives the court a discretion to order repayment of all or part of the retained money. But the right to rescind the contract, though it involves termination of the purchaser's equitable interest, stands upon a rather different footing. Its purpose is, upon breach of an essential term, to restore to the vendor his freedom to deal with his land as he pleases. In a rising market, such a right may be valuable but volatile. Their Lordships think that in such circumstances a vendor should be able to know with reasonable certainty whether he may resell the land or not.

It is for this reason that, for the past 80 years, the courts inEngland although ready to grant restitutionary relief against penalties, have been unwilling to grant relief by way of specific performance against breach of an essential condition as to time. In Steedman v. Drinkle(1916)1 AC 275, 279 Viscount Haldane said: 'Courts of Equity, which look at the substance as distinguished from the letter of agreements, no doubt exercise an extensive jurisdiction which enables them to decree specific performance in cases where justice requires it, even though literal terms of stipulations as to time have not been observed. But they never exercise this jurisdiction where the parties have expressly intimated in their agreement that it is not to apply by providing that time is to be of the essence of their bargain'."

表面看来,如果房价在上涨,卖方借这个机会终断买卖合约并以更高的价格转售,但同时又可以把可怜买方的10%定金没收,好像很不合理。至少,应该把这10%

定金退还给买方。但仔细分析应该不能这样做,首先卖方向法院申请的是作出履约指令。但如果法院作出履约指令,就等于改变了双方约定的合约条文,也就是强制延长完成交易的期限10分钟。而且,也会带来法律的不肯定,因为卖方有可能一终断后随即把该层房子转售。但如果事后法院作出履约指令,卖方就会夹在当中。所以,法院是不会作出这种履约指令的。但如果买方向法院同时申请衡平法下的"禁止没收"(relief against forfeiture),也就是要卖方退还这10%,也是问题。在本章6.4.3段所介绍的Linggi Plantations Ltd v. Jagatheesan(1972)1 MLJ 89先例就显示了这一做法不可行。只会在定金约定是太高,如20%或30%,法院才会作出这一种的救济。

6.5 英国法院近期对惩罚性条文的放宽

较早时候已经说过,英国法院对美国法院针对惩罚性损失赔偿的做法不以为然,但在近期的一些先例看来,英国法院也在这方面放宽。这里的原因是惩罚性条文被视为干预商业合约的订约自由,所以有一个说法是只要该条文有一个"商业合理性"(commercial justification),英国法院就不愿再否定有关的条文。

首先,不干预订约自由的说法,是Philips Hong Kong v. Attorney General of Hong Kong(1993)61 BLR 41,PC先例中,Woolf勋爵认同加拿大最高院的Elsey v. J G Collins Insurance Agencies Ltd(1978)83 DLR 1与澳大利亚高院的Esanda Finance Corporation Ltd v. Plessnig(1989)ALJ 238,说:"It is now evident that the power to strike down a penalty clause is a blatant interference with freedom of contract and is designed for the sole purpose of providing relief against oppression for the party having to pay the stipulated sum. It has no place where there is no oppression."

其次,在接下去的Lordsvale Finance Plc v. Bank of Zambia(1996)QB 752先例,Colman大法官就提到了条文如果有"商业合理性"(commercial justification)的解释,就不应该干预,说:"The speeches in Dunlop... show that whether a provision is to be treated as a penalty is a matter of construction to be resolved by asking whether at the time the contract was entered into the predominant contractual function of the provision was to deter a party from breaking the contract or to compensate the innocent party for breach... The question that has always had to be addressed is therefore whether the alleged penalty clause can pass muster as a genuine pre - estimate of loss... However the jurisdiction in relation to penalty clauses is concerned not primary with the enforcement of inoffensive liquidated damages clauses but rather with protection against the effect of penalty clauses. There would therefore seem to be no reason in principle why a contractual provision the effect of which was to increase the consideration payable under an executory contract upon the happening of a default should be struck down as a penalty **if the increase could in the circumstances be explained as commercially justifiable**, provided always that its dominant purpose was not to deter the other party from breach."

再次，在接下去的 Alfred McAlpine Capital Projects Ltd v. Tilebox Ltd(2005)BLR 271 先例中，Jackson 大法官有类似的说法针对双方有同等谈判力量时订立的商业合约，说："Because the rule about penalties is an anomaly within the law of contract, the courts are predisposed, where possible, to uphold contractual terms which fix the level of damages for breach. This predisposition is even stronger in the case of commercial contracts freely entered into between parties of comparable bargaining power."

最后，要介绍的就是 M & J Polymers Ltd v. Imerys Minerals Ltd(2008)1 Lloyd's Rep 541 先例，涉及一条有争议是否属于惩罚性条文的"Take or Pay"(这种条文在商业合约经常会有，就是要求买方必须在一个期间内购买一定数量的货物，如果数量不足仍然必须支付一个最低限额的货价)，英国法院就非常重视双方在谈判时是如何达成这方面的协议的。其中 Burton 大法官这样解释：

"On the facts of this case, I am entirely satisfied that the take or pay clause was commercially justifiable, did not amount to oppression, was negotiated and freely entered into between parties of comparable bargaining power, and did not have the predominant purpose of deterring a breach of contract nor amount to provision *in terrorem*. The evidence was wholly clear. The negotiations took place between extremely well qualified, able and savvy commercial men against a very significant commercial background, including a background of previous dealings. At the time when they were negotiating there was, on the one hand, an extreme scarcity of acrylic acid(买卖的货物), a willingness on the part of the claimant to commit supply to the defendant, notwithstanding the requirements of their other customers, but in return expecting an absolute commitment to take a minimum quantity of the product to be manufactured with that acid, and, on the other hand, a clear recognition of the difficult commercial position in which the defendant found itself, a desperate need to secure supplies of the product and a desire to keep the contract as short as possible; with the result that there was give and take on both sides, a shorter term than the defendant desired, but so far as the defendant was concerned, the significant advantage, as it then saw it, of a get out clause via the meet or release provision in article 5.6...

There is more of the same. I am entirely satisfied that the take or pay provision does not offend against the rule against penalties and that the claimant is entitled to recover the price of the shortfall pursuant to article 5.5. This enables me to be satisfied that I can uphold and enforce a clause which might be described in similar terms to those used by Millett LJ in Jervis v. Harris(1996)Ch 195 at page 207. 'where the Court(was)asked for the first time to strike down (as a penalty)a standard claim which has been familiar to...lawyers for generation'."

6.6 近期部分有关惩罚性条文先例的介绍

6.6.1 先例之一：General Trading Company v. Richmond Corp Ltd

在 General Trading Company v. Richmond Corp Ltd(2008)2 Lloyd's Rep 475 先例，

涉及原告向被告购买一家英国的名店,名为"GTC Mayfair"。在双方谈判时,该名店正在严重的亏损,高达每月10万英镑。原告作为买方计划与相信可以把该名店的状况扭转,但估计会欠缺流动现金进货,特别是为圣诞节准备充足的存货。这一来,就在合约中要求被告的卖方通过向银行保证在两年内提供给买方20万英镑的资金。而如果被告没有这样做,原告就可以取消作为购买名店的54万英镑的"票据抵押贷款"(Loan Notes)。有关的条文可部分节录一下:

"17.11 The Seller shall procure the provision of the Loan Guarantees within 30 days of receiving notice in writing from the Company to such effect which the Company may give to the Seller(in accordance with the notice provisions in Clause 15) at any time from 60 days after the Completion Date.

17.15 If the Seller fails to procure the provision the Loan Guarantees as required under clauses 17.10 and 17.11(time being of the essence), the Loan Notes shall be cancelled with immediate effect and the Buyer shall be under noobligation to make any payments of any kind under the Loan Notes."

从表面看来,违约(没有提供20万英镑的资金)与后果(取消54万英镑的票据抵押贷款)并不相称,有很重的惩罚性味道。但Beatson大法官最后接受有关条文并非是惩罚性,认为不能仅看议定赔偿的金额与真正的损失相比是否相称,而是要全面考虑。在该先例,就考虑到双方都是有水平的商业人士,原告得不到这20万英镑的流动资金就会有要把该名店关门的风险,令他的投资化为乌有等方面。Beatson大法官是这样说:"At the outset of the hearing I inclined to the view that this clause inserted, at the very end to the negotiations, was penal because of the size of the difference between the amount of the loan to be guaranteed and the amount of the loan notes that would be cancelled. In the light of the evidence, however, and the broader approach of Buxton and Clarke LJJ in Murray v. Leisureplay plc(2005)EWCA Civ 963, I am satisfied that it is not. In the circumstances of the contract, judged on 4 May when it was made, the clause was commercially justifiable, did not amount to oppression, and was negotiated and freely entered into parties who were of comparable bargaining power. Most significantly, on the evidence the clause did not have the predominant purpose of deterring a breach of contract and did not thus amount to what in the older cases is referred to as a provision *in terrorem*. The evidence shows the following. First, as to the bargaining power of each side, although Richmond at that time was in a poor financial position, it was supported by offshore companies and trusts controlled by the Weston family and the financial, commercial and professional resources available to them, including two experienced business consultants, Messers Rodriguez and Barnett. Messers Gould and Middlemiss also had significant commercial experience in the retail business ..."

6.6.2 先例之二:The "Paragon"

在The "Paragon"(2009)2 Lloyd's Rep 688先例,涉及有关的3~5个月+/-15

天的租期的期租合约中有一条第101条文针对延误还船需要调整租约租金，内容说："The Charterers hereby undertake the obligation/responsibility to make thorough investigations and every arrangement in order to ensure that the last voyage of this Charter will in no way exceed the maximum period under this Charter Party. If, however, Charterers fail to comply with this obligation and the last voyage will exceed the maximum period, should the market rise above the Charter Party rate in the meantime, it is hereby agreed that the charter hire will be adjusted to reflect the prevailing market level from the 30th day prior to the maximum period date until actual redelivery of the vessel to the Owners."

该条文是要求承租人承诺最后航次不超出最长的租期，也就是5个月加上15天的最后一天，在2007年5月14日。如果承租人没有准时还船，而当时市场租金超出了租约的租金（事后的情况也正是如此），双方同意调整租约租金，就是在最后还船一天之前的30天，每天的租约的租金要作出调整从29,500美元一天提高至当时市场租金，也就是46,083美元一天。后来，承租人的确是延期还船，共达6.166天。承租人要支付这6.166天的市场租金差价没有异议，金额是89,560.87美元，承租人也的确支付了。但双方的争议是之前30天租约租金的调整，如果双方约定的有效，就会要求承租人多支付30天×（46,083美元－29,500美元）再扣取佣金相等于约471,603.32美元的一笔额外"赔偿"。光从这笔庞大金额要作出赔付，特别是承租人已经赔付了89,560.87美元，看来是惩罚与阻吓承租人不得行走会延误还船日期的最后航次。但问题是第101条文写的很技巧，它没有针对违约要支付的额外金额，而只是针对调整原来租约要支付的租金。船东的争辩是说该船舶通常的航次长度是60天，所以最后航次如果是非法，也就是估计会超出最后还船的一天，就有必要调整，而调整只是30天，这显示了双方在约定时曾经小心估计真正会蒙受的损失。但仲裁庭、高院与上诉庭都不接受船东的说法。认为承租人如果作出非法最后航次的命令，船东所能抗拒的就是要求承租人命令一个合法的最后航次。船东是不能假设承租人会坚持，这构成了"毁约"（repudiation）可让船东接受并终断租约。这种假设是不现实的，也不会事前知道承租人是否会坚持非法的最后航次，而不撤回另指定一个合法的最后航次。而在合法的最后航次在履行时，即使遇上延误而错过了最后还船日期，违约的损失计算也只能局限在延误的实际日期的市场租金差价。所以这101条文第2句的"调整"（adjust）租金并非是订约时估计违约会带来的真正损失，而是一条惩罚性损失赔偿条文。

6.6.3　先例之三：Tandrin Aviation Holdings Ltd v. Aero Toy Store

在Tandrin Aviation Holdings Ltd v. Aero Toy Store（2010）2 Lloyd's Rep 668先例，涉及飞机买卖合约，价格是3.175千万美元。而在订合约时，买方就需要支付300万美元的定金，并交给第三人（在本案例是列为第二被告）作为托管人。但之后的2009年1月（注意这是在2008年金融海啸后不久），卖方交付飞机但买方拒绝接收，也不支付飞机价款。这导致卖方要向英国法院申请下令第二被告把这笔定金交出给卖方作为议定赔偿。而买方的一个抗辩是指有关把定金充公的条文是属于惩罚性条文，该条文如下："In the event Purchaser fails to accept delivery of the Aircraft and pay the Purchase Price to Seller in violation of the terms and conditions of this Agreement, and provided Seller is not then in breach or default in timely performing its written obligations hereunder, Seller shall have the right, after ten (10) Business Days' prior written notice from Seller of such breach or default and Purchaser's failure to cure (or commence curing) the same with such 10 - day period, to terminate this Agreement by written notice to Purchaser and the Escrow Agent. If Seller elects to terminate this Agreement pursuant to this Section 7. 4. 2, the Escrow Agent shall pay the Deposit to Seller as liquidated damages (and Seller and Purchaser shall promptly give written instructions to the Escrow Agent to that effect), and this Agreement shall be of no further force or effect. Seller acknowledges and represents that the liquidated damages amount provided for in this Section 7. 4. 2 is a reasonable estimate of the damages that would be incurred by Seller in the event Purchaser defaults on Purchaser's obligations under this Agreement. Seller's right to receive the Deposit as liquidated damages, shall be cumulative and not alternative, and shall be the sole remedy available to Seller in the event Purchaser defaults on Purchaser's obligations under this Agreement (other than a default under this Article 7. 4. 2); and Seller waives any other remedies that may be available to Seller, at law or in equity, as a consequence thereof."

Hamblen 大法官判该条文不是惩罚性损失赔偿条文，说："The sum stipulated was not extravagant or unconscionable in amount in comparison with the greatest loss which could have followed from the breach. ATS's breach did not consist only in not paying a sum of money, but instead comprised the failure to accept delivery of the aircraft and pay for it. The deposit could be treated as liquidated damages only in the event of ATS's breach in failing to accept delivery of the aircraft and pay the balance of the purchase price, so this was not a case where the liquidated damages were payable by way of compensation on the occurrence of several events, some of which might occasion only trifling damage. The consequences of the breach were such as to make precise pre - estimation of damage almost an impossibility. In the circumstances, the pre - estimated damage was, and should be taken to be, the true bargain between the parties."

6.7　违约的疏忽/过错程度对损失计算没有影响

由于英国法律是不承认惩罚性损失赔偿，也解释了违约的疏忽与过错的程度是否轻微或严重对损失计算没有影响。只要是违约，被告有了责任，就要按照复原大原则计算损失赔偿，让受害方的原告恢复到合约被履行的经济地位。不论这违约是涉及"轻微疏忽"(simple negligence)、"严重疏忽"(gross negligence)、"故意疏忽"(intentional negligence)甚至是"恶意或欺诈性行为"(bad faith or fraudulent conduct)，损失赔偿的金额都是一样。所以，这会带来一些笔者难以理解的地方。例如，有部分大陆律师在香港或伦敦仲裁中，指控对方的违约有恶意或欺诈性质，好像这样就能增加胜诉的机会。但这种严重的指控会有很高的举证要求，甚至会达到刑事的举证程度，因为任何疑点利益都会被归于被告。所以反而增加了败诉的风险。对于违约来说，只要证明对方有轻微疏忽并构成违约，就可以获得与欺诈性违约（如果能够证明）一样金额的损失赔偿，这证明只需要是达到平衡性可能的标准，会是简单得多。

至于需要区分轻微疏忽、严重疏忽或欺诈性行为是在其他领域。例如，轻微疏忽是不能构成刑事犯罪，但欺诈行为显然可以构成。所以有必要做出区分。至于有必要在合约区分轻微疏忽与严重疏忽是因为其中经常会有免责或责任限制条文说明不适用在严重或故意疏忽，表示条文只是保护轻微疏忽。例如在 ICDL Saudi Arabia v. The European Computer Driving Licence Foundation Ltd（2011）IEHC 343 先例中有条文说："25.1　The Licensee's exclusive remedy and the total liability of ECDL – F in respect of any cause of action relating to or arising out of this Contract will, **to the extent that it is not caused by a wilful act or gross negligence** by ECDL – F, **not exceed 10 per cent** of the total amounts paid to ECDL – F by the Licensee **or 50,000.00, whichever is the lesser amount.**"（加黑是笔者的强调）

但英国普通法一直以来把轻微疏忽与严重疏忽视为是同一码事，例如在 Hilton v. Dibber（1842）2 Q. B. 646 先例，Denman 勋爵说："it may well be doubted whether between gross negligence, and negligence merely, any intelligible distinction exists"。另在 Grill v. General Iron Screw Collier Company（1866）LR 1 CP 612 先例，Wills 大法官说："gross...is a word of description, and not a definition, and it would have been only introducing a source of confusion to use the expression gross negligence, instead of the equivalent, a want of due care and skill."

在比较近期的 Tradigrain v. Intertek Testing Services（2007）EWCA Civ 154 先例，上诉庭说："the term 'gross negligence', although often found in commercial documents, has never been accepted by English civil law as a concept distinct from simple negligence"。而在更近期的 Sucden Financial Ltd v. Fluxo – Cane Overseas Ltd（2010）EWHC 2133（Comm），Blair 大法官说："gross negligence is not a term of art at common law, and... such a standard may amount to little more in practice than simple negligence."

在这方面英国法律的地位与大陆法并不一致，但英国法院也开始有一些改变。其中在一些近期的先例有所显示：Red Sea Tankers v. Papachristidis（1997）2 Lloyds Rep 547；Great Scottish & Western Railway v. British Railways Board（CA），10 February 2000，unreported；Camarata Property Inc v. Credit Suisse Securities（Europe）Ltd（2011）EWHC 479（Comm）；ICDL Saudi Arabia v. The European Computer Driving Licence Foundation Ltd（2011）IEHC 343 等。

在 Camarata Property Inc v. Credit Suisse Securities（Europe）Ltd 先例，Andrew Smith 大法官说是指控对方严重违约，就必须提供更多的证明"说明对方不仅是疏忽"

(show more than mere negligence)。他也有说到区分严重疏忽并不是英国法律的问题,而是看当事人的订约意图:"... is not whether generally gross negligence is a familiar concept in English civil law, but the meaning of the express in the contract terms in question."

另在 ICDL Saudi Arabia v. The European Computer Driving Licence Foundation Ltd 先例,Clarke 大法官说:"One would expect persons to mean something different by the use of the term ' gross negligence ' rather than the use of the term ' negligence '. Why else would be used?"他也指出严重疏忽是指"a degree of negligence where whatever duty of care may be involved has not been met by a significant margin."

6.8 大陆法与国际私法对惩罚性与议定赔偿的立场

大陆法看来对这方面的立场是与英国普通法很不一样,被认为是这种条文带来肯定与可预测性,所以完全可以获得承认与执行。但有许多国家法律强制规定如果议定赔偿金额相比真正损失太大,法院有权减少议定赔偿,这方面可看《法国民法典》之 Article 1152.2 和《意大利民法典》之 Article 1384。反过来如果认为是议定赔偿金额相比真正损失太低,法院有权增加议定赔偿,如《法国民法典》之 Article 1152.2。显然,这与英国普通法认为不应该干预双方的订约自由而改变他们之间约定的议定赔偿金额的地位很不一样,虽然英国法院不承认惩罚性条文本身已经是一种对订约自由的干预。

在国际上,做出过不少希望统一这方面法律的努力,而这些努力在较大程度上反映了大陆法的看法,其中包括法院可以减少议定赔偿。这方面可以先介绍在 1983 年 12 月"联合国国际贸易法委员会"(UNCITRAL)的《Uniform Rules on Contract Clauses for an Agreed Sum Due upon Failure of Performance》,建议以示范法或者公约的形式统一这一问题。

另介绍的是 UNIDROIT Principles,它在 Article 7.4.13 说:"(1) Where the contract provides that a party who does not perform is to pay a specified sum to the aggrieved party for such non – performance, the aggrieved party is entitled to that sum irrespective of its actual harm. (2) However, notwithstanding any agreement to the contrary the specified sum may be reduced to a reasonable amount where it is grossly excessive in relation to the harm resulting from the non – performance and to the other circumstances."

再接下去介绍的是 European Principles 之 Article 9:509:"(1) Where the contract provides that a party who fails to perform is to pay a specified sum to the aggrieved party for such non – performance, the aggrieved party shall be awarded that sum irrespective of its actual harm. (2) However, despite any agreement to the contrary the specified sum may be reduced to a reasonable amount where it is grossly excessive in relation to the loss resulting from the non – performance and the other circumstances."

最后介绍的是已经提到过的 UNCITRAL Uniform Rules,它在 Article 1 说:"These

Rules apply to international contracts in which the parties have agreed that, upon a failure of performance by one party (the obligor), the other party (the obligee) is entitled to an agreed sum from the obligor, **whether as a penalty or as compensation**."(加黑是笔者的强调)。另在 Article 8 是说:"The agreed sum shall not be reduced by a court or arbitral tribunal unless the agreed sum is substantially disproportionate in relation to the loss that has been suffered by the obligee."

但看来面对这些国际上的努力,个别国家包括英国并没有受到影响。所以,针对惩罚性与议定赔偿还是比较法一个很热门的话题。在国际仲裁包括像 ICC 仲裁,这也是一个经常要面对的课题,仲裁庭通常会根据有关合约的适用法针对。其中不少的仲裁案件是针对国际货物买卖,但也有在其他类别的合约,如少量拣几个有:

(1) ICC Case No. 7585/1992——案件涉及意大利卖方与芬兰买方,买卖合约中有关惩罚性的条文说:"if the agreement is terminated by fault or request of the purchaser-including force majeure-the seller is entitled to a compensation fee of 30% of the price."由于买方没有作出第三期的预付与开出信用证,卖方提出仲裁。仲裁庭判是卖方可以成功索赔这货价的 30% 作为赔偿金额,认为条文针对不可抗力,表示不必针对违约也需要作出的赔付作为买方终断合约的代价,说:"the wording 'compensation fee' has to be interpreted as an amount of money payable in a consideration of the termination of the contract independently of any damages suffered by Seller. It has to be paid independently of any contractual liability on behalf of Buyer. It is expressly stated in Article 19.3 of the contract that the compensation fee is due even in a 'force majeure' situation. According to Article 79 of the CISG, a party has not to pay damages 'if he proves that the failure was to due to an impediment beyond his control'. The mere fact that the compensation fee has to be paid in such a situation evidence that it has a nature different from damages in compensation of a loss. The conclusion is that Defendant has to pay the provided 'compensation fee' (30% of the price) added to the damages."

(2) Arbitral Award in Case No. 40/1995 of January 22, 1996 of the International Arbitration Court of Commerce and Industry of the Russian Federation——案件涉及俄罗斯卖方与英国买方,买卖合约有关惩罚性条文是第 7 条说:"if the terms of the contract as to payment agreed upon in advance are not performed, then the buyer will pay the seller damages which were estimated and agreed, in the amount of 0.1% of the whole price of the contract for each day of delay of the payment, but not exceeding 10% of the whole price of the contract."卖方在交货后,买方没有作出支付。这被仲裁庭判是根据《联合国国际货物销售公约》(这也是俄罗斯的实体法)卖方可以成功索赔欠下的货价再加上 10%。

(3) Arbitral Award in Case No. 229/1996 of June 5, 1997 of the International Arbitration Court of the Chamber of Commerce and Industry of the Russian Federation——涉及的买卖合约有一条文说明买方如果延迟支付货款就要每天赔偿货价的 0.5%,这条文

被指是惩罚性条文。合约双方是俄罗斯与保加利亚的买卖双方,合约是适用 CISG,而 CISG 并没有针对这一问题。所以,仲裁庭采用了 UNIDROIT Principles 并认定该条文计算出来的议定赔偿实在是太高,最后裁定卖方只能索赔 50% 金额。

(4) Arbitral Award in Case No. 134/2002 of April 4, 2003 of the International Arbitration Court of the Chamber of Commerce and Industry of the Russian Federation——案件涉及俄罗斯与德国买卖合约中的有关惩罚性条文,说明买方延误支付货款要赔偿卖方每天 0.5% 的货价。由于在该案件中,延误期涉及两年半之久。所以在两个裁决书中,第一个涉及买方要赔偿额外的 42% 货价,而第二个裁决书更是 487% 货价。仲裁庭考虑 UNIDROIT Principles,认为这一笔赔偿或惩罚的金额实在太高,需要减少。

(5) ICC Case No. 4462/1987 (Yearbook of Commercial Arbitration (1991) p. 54 and Collection of ICC Arbitral Awards, Vol. III, p. 3)——这不涉及国际货物买卖,而是一个有关钻探与生产石油的合约,适用法是利比亚法律。有关被指是惩罚性条文说:"In the event that any part of the Exploration Program for any Area is not properly completed by the end of the Exploration Period applicable to such Area, [合约方之 Sun Oil] shall immediately pay to [合约方之 NOC] the costs of such uncompleted part at the end of such Exploration Period."

仲裁庭根据《利比亚民法典》之 Article 227. 2 认为该条文针对的赔偿金额大大超出了估计的真正损失(因为原告 NOC 拒绝提供真正损失的证据),所以减少 Sun Oil 要赔偿的金额之 2000 万美元,说:"in fixing such an amount, which it considers fair and equitable, the Arbitral Tribunal is exercising its authority to make findings of fact based upon evidence and submission presented by the Parties, noting that despite repeated requests, NOC chooses not to produce any evidence as to its actual proven losses."

7. 非复原损失赔偿之二:"返还性损失"

这种"损失"(restitutionary damages)是指受害方的原告受到侵权方或违约方的被告的错误行为,虽然没有因此而受到任何实际损失,但被告却得到了利益。这一来,为了不希望让被告取得这种"不当得利"(unjust enrichment),判他们必须赔付一笔返还性损失。但这与英国法律针对民事诉讼的赔偿是根据"复原"大原则(*restitutio in integrum* 或 compensatory principle)有冲突之处,正如 Megarry V. C. 大法官在 Tito v. Waddell (No. 2) (1977) Ch. 106 所说的:"It is fundamental to all questions of damages that they are to compensate the plaintiff for his loss or injury... The question is not one of making the defendant disgorge what he has saved by committing the wrong, but one of compensating the plaintiff."

这笔损失也与其他已经在许多侵权案件(特别是涉及财产的侵权)存在的救济

办法,如“返还”(restitution)、“返还性救济”(restitutionary remedy)、“交出利润”(account for profits)或被告因为侵权或违约而节省的费用交出给原告有雷同或重叠之处。“返还性损失”(restitutionary damages)只是在 Attorney General v. Blake(2001)1 AC 268 先例之后才有的名称。

这种救济都是主要看被告得到的利益(如果有)是什么,要求把这些利益“吐出来”,而不是追究原告自己有什么真正的损失。也是这一个原因,有不少人认为返还型损失的名称有一点别扭,因为“返还”与“损失”不同,前者是“返还”(restitution),后者是“赔偿”(compensation),前者属于衡平法,后者属于普通法。

7.1　作出“返还性损失”赔偿的理由

这可先节录 Diplock 大法官在 McCarey v. Associated Newspapers Ltd(No. 2)(1965)2 QB 86 所说:“The law is mocked if it enables a man to make a profit from his own wrong - doing. This is not punishment; it is merely preventing the defendant from obtaining a reward for his wrong - doing. But equally it is not compensation; the plaintiff is the accidental beneficiary of a rule of law based on public policy rather than on the reparation of private wrongs.”

另在 My Kinda Town v. Soll(1983)RPC 15 中有说:“The purpose of awarding an account of profits... is not to prevent an unjust enrichment of the defendant ...”

接下去是节录 Nicholls 勋爵在 Attorney General v. Blake(2001)1 AC 268 先例中所说:“Even when awarding damages, the law does not adhere slavishly to the concept of compensation for financially measurable loss. When the circumstances require, damages are measured by reference to the benefit obtained by the wrongdoer... Further, in certain circumstances an account of profits is ordered in preference to an award of damages.”

适用返还性损失或交出利润的赔偿的情况很多,这主要是在侵权,包括有关“财产侵权”(proprietary torts)、“土地侵入”(trespass to land)、“侵占或非法干预货物”(conversion, wrongful interference or trespass to goods)、“知识产权的侵犯”(infringement of intellectual property rights)、“受信义务”(fiduciary duty)等。

7.2　早期有关返还性救济的部分侵权案例或说法

这方面可看一些先例的说法。首先可节录 Shaw 勋爵在 Watson, Laidlaw & Co Ltd v. Pott, Cassels and Williamson(1914)31 RPC 104 HL 中所举的例子,是有关一匹马在主人没有允许的情况下被一个陌生人(被告)私自短暂骑走。这种财产侵权没有对主人造成任何真正损失,因为在这期间该匹马只在马槽内等待,被告还可以说是短暂骑走让马匹做运动,对该匹马是好事。Shaw 勋爵是这样说:“If A, being a liveryman, keeps his hose standing idle in the stable, and B, against his wish or without his knowledge, rides or drives it out, it is no answer to A for B to say: ‘Against what loss do you want to be restored? I restore the horse. There is no loss. The horse is none the worse; it is better for the exercise.”

在 Strand Electric Co v. Brisford Entertainments(1952)2 QB 246 CA 先例涉及第三人的被告在没有受害方原告的的授权下私自使用了他的电子仪器,上诉庭是判被告要赔偿给原告这一段时间的市场租金。虽然在现实中,原告是不会出租这些电子仪器,所以所谓的损失赔偿有一点勉强。在该先例,Denning 大法官说相比一个侵权的赔偿,这是更接近返还性救济:"It is an action against him because he has had the benefit of the goods. It resembles therefore an action for restitution rather than an action of tort."

这种案件在土地侵入的先例就更多了:Martin v. Porter(1839)5 M. & W. 351; Whitwham v. Westminster Brymbo Coal Co(1896)2 Ch. 538 CA;Penarth Dock Engineering Co v. Pounds(1963)1 Lloyd's Rep. 359;Swordheath Properties v. Tabet(1979)1 WLR 285 CA;Ministry of Defence v. Ashman(1993)25 HLR 513 CA;Ministry of Defence v. Thompson(1993)24 HLR 552 CA;Inverugie Investments v. Hackett(1995)1 WLR 713 PC;Severn Trent Water Ltd v. Barnes(2004)2 EGLR 95 CA;Sinclair v. Gavaghan(2007) EWHC 2256 Ch;Field Common Ltd v. Elmbridge Borough Council(2008)EWHC 2079 Ch。

举例说,在 Penarth Dock Company v. Pounds(1963)1 Lloyd's Rep 359 先例,涉及一个二手"浮动干坞"(floating dock)的买卖,合约要求买方尽快把该浮动干坞移走,但没有规定时间。买方却迟迟没有把浮动干坞从卖方已经废置了的船厂移走,虽然卖方多次督促。这导致诉讼,卖方指买方违约与"侵占"(trespass)了他的地方长达大半年,而买方的抗辩是合约没有规定把浮动干坞移走的时间。而且,即使是违约,卖方并没有任何损失。在上诉庭,判是买方违约,即使没有时间上的规定,默示地位也是要求买方在合理时间内必须移走,而这一个合理时间已经过去。而针对卖方的损失,的确是卖方无法证明。但被告侵占了卖方的地方,被告如果不这样做而移走去其他地方需要交付租金。这是被告省下的费用,可以作为原告的救济。Denning 勋爵是这样说:"The question which remains is, what are the damages? True it is that the Penarth company themselves would not seem to have suffered any damage to speak of. They have not to pay any extra rent to the British Transport Commission. The dock is no use to them; they would not have made any money out of it. But, nevertheless, in a case of this kind, as I read the law, starting with Whitwham v. Westminster Brymbo Coal and Coke Company, (1896)2 Ch. 538, on which I commented myself in the case of Strand Electric and Engineering Company, Ltd v. Brisford Entertainments Ltd(1952)2 QB 246, at pp. 253 to 254, the test of the measure of damages is not what the plaintiffs have lost, but what benefit the defendant obtained by having the use of the berth; and he has been a trespasser, in my judgment, since Aug. 9, 1962. What benefit has the defendant obtained by having the use of it for this time? If he had moved it elsewhere, he would have had to pay, on the evidence, £ 37 10s. a week for a berth for a dock of this kind. But the damages are not put as high as that, and the damages are to be assessed in accordance with the law as I have stated it at the rate of £ 37 5s.

a week for a period commencing from Aug. 9,1962, which I would let run to Mar. 25,1963, because the dock has now been removed. I do not know what that sum will come to, but that can be a matter of calculation. I do not think that there is any call in the circumstances for a mandatory injunction or any other relief."

另在 Ministry of Defence v. Ashman 与 Ministry of Defence v. Thompson 两个先例，涉及军部因为军人离婚要把廉价的居所军人处收回，因为他不再符合居住廉价居所的条件，但军人妻子拒绝或延误迁出。在前一个先例，军部索赔廉价居所租金（95 英镑月租）与市场租金（500 英镑月租）的差价。上诉庭最后判只是与当地公务员居所的租金（145 英镑月租）差价，因为军部要把居所收回后的用途也不会去市场出租，而且该军人妻子根本也不会考虑去市场租房子。

在这些先例中，一直有争议到底这种赔偿是否属于返还性或是赔偿性。在 Ministry of Defence v. Ashman 先例，Hoffman 大法官认为是返还性，说："it has not been expressly stated that a claim for mesne profits for trespass can be a claim for restitution. Nowadays I do not see why we should not call a spade a spade. In this case the Ministry of Defence elected for the restitutionary remedy."

但在同一个上诉庭，Lloyd 大法官认为这只是作出损失赔偿，而返还性是法院无权作出。而另一位 Kennedy 大法官同意 Hoffman 大法官，但把它说成是"准合约返还"（quasi - contractual restitution）。

这些困难可节录《McGregor on Damages》（18th edn, 2009 年）一书 12 - 008 段如下："In the proprietary torts where restitutionary damages have flourished except in name, the courts have attempted to rationalize the damages awarded as compensatory on the basis of what is today generally referred to as the user principle, a phrase employed, and possibly initiated, by Nicholls LJ, as he then was, in Stoke City Council v. W & J Wass Ltd (1988) 1 WLR 1406 CA. The law has considered that a person should have a claim against one who has used his property without his consent, a claim to be measured by the amount which could reasonably be required to gain permission for the property's use, and has regarded the claimant as suffering loss or damage by virtue of not have received that amount. However, Lord Nicholls in Attorney General v. Blake recognises that, while the entitlement is established and uncontroversial, 'more difficult is the alignment of this measure of damages within the basic compensatory measure.' And he added: 'These awards cannot be regarded as conforming to the strictly compensatory measure of damage for the injured person's loss unless loss is given a strained and artificial meaning. The reality is that the injured person's rights were invaded but, in financial terms, he suffered no loss'."

7.3 合约的返还性损失赔偿

衡平法的"返还"（restitution）在合约关系中作出救济已经有很长历史。最为人所知的是如果没有合约规定报酬，或是合约终断，但一方当事人向对方提供服务并让对方得益,法院就会判对方要支付一笔由法院厘定的“按照得益的合理报酬”(*Quantum meruit* fee)。这方面的先例有:Planche v. Colburn(1831)8 Bing 14,131 ER 305;British Steel Corporation v. Cleveland Bridge & Engineering Co. Ltd(1984)1 All ER 504;Regalian Properties plc v. London Dockland Development Corporation(1995)1 WLR 212。对租约熟悉的人士也会知道在船舶不合理绕航而导致程租合约被自动中断,租约内约定的运费不再适用。但如果船东把船上的货物安全运到目的地,他还是可以要求货方支付一笔“*Quantum meruit* freight”。另一种衡平法会作出救济的是在货物买卖或者是提供服务的合约关系下,买方向卖方作出了支付,但卖方完全没有提供货物(或提供有缺陷的货物而被拒货)或服务。这一来,有说法是买方“完全得不到对价”(total failure of consideration),法院会因为这是一笔债务而要求卖方马上退还这一笔钱:Whincup v. Hughes(1871)LR 6 CP 78。

但本段所介绍的新发展的“返还性赔偿”(restitutionary damages)是针对不同的情况,就是在合约关系下违约要作出的额外赔偿,不再局限于侵权的行为。这种赔偿在Attorney General v. Blake(2001)1 AC 268 先例后也开始出现在特殊情况下适用在合约关系下的违约,虽然在合约赔偿损失的大原则,还是严格按照复原大原则作出金钱的赔偿。这已经较早时在谈到“加大损失”(aggravated damages)与“惩罚性损失”(exemplary damages)有提到过是不适用在违约。例如在 The “Siboen” and the “Sibotre”(1976)1 Lloyd's Rep 293 先例,涉及船东的被告在一个 3 年的期租合约下错误撤船。由于船东撤船后不久,油轮市场暴升,导致了船东通过违约赚了很多利润。这导致承租人的原告提出了交出利润的救济,也就是要求船东把撤船后赚的钱交出,不仅是局限在违约时的租船市场差价。但这一请求被 Kerr 大法官简短的拒绝,说是这种救济没有法律依据。这是显而易见的大道理,较早已节录了 Megarry V. C. 大法官在 Tito v. Waddell(No. 2)(1977)Ch. 106 所说的话。

另在 Surrey County Council v. Bredero Homes Ltd(1993)1 WLR 1361 先例,涉及卖方(Surrey 地区议会)出售一块土地给发展商。该买卖合约下是允许买方根据批准的图纸建造 72 栋房子,但成交后买方获得新的批准图纸加建了 5 栋房子。卖方向买方提出索赔,认为这一好处应该是给卖方。但这被上诉庭拒绝,认为买方的加建虽然是违约,但对卖方没有造成什么损失,所以只判给卖方一个 2 英镑名义上的损失赔偿,并被上诉庭所支持。其中上诉庭的 Steyn 大法官说是延伸违约下的损失赔偿大原则会带来问题,其中予没有真正损失的受害方一笔“利润”是否有必要? 这会否对商业活动不利? 而且,很多时候违约方会为他的责任投保,所以这一笔利润其实是由保险人掏出来,而保险人将来就会提高保费,对大众都没有好处。Steyn 大法官是这样说:“... The introduction of restitutionary remedies to deprive cynical contract breakers of the fruits of their breaches of contract will lead to greater uncertainty in the assessment of damages in commercial and consumer disputes. It is of paramount importance that the way in which disputes are likely to be resolved the courts must be readily predictable. Given the premise that the aggrieved party has suffered no loss, is such a dramatic extension of restitutionary remedies justified in order to confer a windfall in each case on the aggrieved party? I think not. In any event such a widespread availability of restitutionary remedies will have a tendency to discourage economic activity in relevant situations. In a range of cases such liability would fall on underwriters who have insured relevant liability risks. Inevitably underwriters would have to be compensated for the new species of potential claims. Insurance premiums would have to go up. That, too, is a consequence which militates against the proposed extension. The recognition of the proposed extension will in my view not serve the public interest. It is sound policy to guard against extending the protection of the law of obligations too widely. For these substantive and policy reasons I regard it as undesirable that the range of restitutionary remedies should be extended in the way in which we have been invited to do so."

但显然有人对 Surrey County Council v. Bredero Homes Ltd 的判决感觉到不公平，也就是让买方可在违约的情况下仍然获得了所有的好处。或可以说卖方可以在买卖合约中订约细一点，如说明如果加建房子要买方多支付多少钱。但问题是如果在订约时根本没有想到会有加建的问题，卖方是不会把所有无关有关的东西都写在买卖合约中，把它变为是一本厚厚的书。有不少人事后对这一先例感到不满意，认为是不公平。可以说这一个问题已经稍后在 Wrotham Park Estate Co v. Parkside Homes (1974) 1 WLR 798 先例中有了解决办法，法院可作出"交出部分利润"(account for profits)的判决，所以是这种赔偿也被称为"Wrotham Park 赔偿"。

但合约关系以前也不是没有过要求违约方交出部分利润（或节省了的费用）作为赔偿的先例，只是案例很少且没有重点或刻意针对这一点。这些先例有 Reid – Newfoundland Co v. Anglo – American Telegraph Co Ltd (1912) AC 555; British Motor Trade Association v. Gillbert (1951) 2 All ER 641; Strand Electric & Engineering Co Ltd v. Brisford Entertainments Ltd (1952) 2 QB 246; Lake v. Bayliss (1974) 1 WLR 1073 等。

这种受害方证明不了金钱损失去返还的问题很多出现在土地、财产的侵权，这导致违约方往往可以不必作出任何真正赔偿，也就大可以放心违约了。所以，针对这种金钱赔偿不足够作出救济的情况，英国法院往往是以另外一种救济的办法替代金钱赔偿损失，也就是作出"履约指令"(specific performance)或"禁令"(injunction)，只要是受害方会尽早与及时向法院作出申请。这方面可节录 Nicholls 勋爵在 Attorney General v. Blake 先例中有提到土地买卖在这方面的问题说："The classic example of this type of case, as every law student knows, is a contract for the sale of land. The buyer of a house may be attracted by features which have little or no impact on the value of the house. An award of damages, based on strictly financial criteria, would fail to recompense a disappointed buyer for this head of loss. The primary response of the law to this type of case is to ensure, if possible, that the contract is performed in accordance with its terms. The court may make orders compelling the party who has committed a breach of contract, or is threatening to do so, to carry out his contractual obligations. To this end the court has wide powers to grant injunctive relief. The court will, for instance, readily make orders for the specific performance of contracts for the sale of land, and sometimes it will do so in respect of contracts for the sale of goods. In Beswick v. Beswick(1968) AC 58 the court made an order for the specific performance of a contract to make payments of money to a third party. The law recognized that the innocent party to the breach of contract had a legitimate interest in having the contract performed even though he himself would suffer no financial loss from its breach. Likewise, the court will compel the observance of negative obligations by granting injunctions. This may include a mandatory order to undo an existing breach, as where the court orders the defendant to pull down building works carried out in breach of covenant."

7.3.1 先例之一:Wrotham Park Estate Co v. Parkside Homes

在合约关系下近期第一个作出返还性损失赔偿的重要先例是在 Wrotham Park Estate Co v. Parkside Homes(1974)1 WLR 798,案情涉及一块土地的买卖。卖方在买卖合约中限制了发展商的买方(或他的受让人)在该块土地上建造的房子必须按照卖方批准的图纸。但后来的受让人,也就是诉讼中的被告建造的房子是违反了上述的限制。这导致原告作为卖方保留了部分土地的承继人向英国法院申请一个禁制令要求把这些违约建造的房子全部清拆,但这被拒绝,原因是会造成不必要的资源浪费。这一来,剩下来的救济就只是金钱损失的赔偿。但被告的争议就是这些建造的房子并没有影响该块土地的价值,所以原告没有损失。英国法院认为这一抗辩看来并不公道,Brightman 大法官是这样说:"it was just that the plaintiffs should receive no compensation and that the defendants should be left in undisturbed possession of the fruits of their wrongdoing."结果是判被告要把他估计利润的 5% 作为赔偿,这赔偿是 Brightman 大法官认为如果原告被要求在买卖合约中放宽这一个限制,就会得到的一笔合理的金额(such a sum of money as might reasonably have been demanded... as a quid pro quo for relaxing the covenant)。相比较早前介绍的 Surrey County Council v. Bredero Homes Ltd(1993)1 WLR 1361 先例,这一个先例看来是公平得多,所以在 Attorney General v. Blake(2001)1 AC 268 先例中,贵族院有多位勋爵提到这一点。

7.3.2 先例之二:Attorney General v. Blake

而在合约关系中下一个要求违约方的被告"交出利润"(account for profits)的重要先例就是 Attorney General v. Blake(2001)1 AC 268,在该先例有说到是双方大律师没有找到任何的先例涉及原告向被告在合约关系中要求后者交出所有在违约下赚取的利润。有关的案情在本章第 1 段已经有介绍,这里只简单地重复一下,案情涉及英国特务 George Blake 实际上为前苏联提供情报,并成功潜伏在英国特务系统内很长一段时间,其间造成很大的破坏。他的身份是在前苏联解体之后被暴露出来,他也因

"叛国罪"被判终身监禁。之后,他决定把他的经历出版成书,并估计是由于他特殊的经历,这一本书是非常畅销。英国政府没有办法阻止他这样做,写书是他的人身自由,只能根据他为英国政府服务期间的雇佣合约,提出他是受到《公务人员机密法》(Official Secrets Act)的约束,合约内也有条文要求公务人员承诺保守机密,并说明是不能通过写书披露政府机密的资料,说:"I undertake not to divulge any official information gained by me as a result of my employment,either in the press or in book form. I also understand that those provisions apply not only during the period of service but also after employment has ceased."所以英国政府就以他违约为由提起诉讼,而至于损失的计算,英国政府根本没有办法证明出这本书与违反机密带来了什么真正的损失。这一来,英国政府所要求的救济只能是利润退还或者返还性损失,也就是把写书的所有版权费或稿费交给英国政府的原告。在贵族院,英国政府胜诉,判是违约下可以作出交出利润的救济办法,只要违约是在"特殊性案件"(exceptional case)。Nicholls 勋爵是这样说:"The present case is exceptional. The context is employment as a member of the security and intelligence services. Secret information is the lifeblood of these services... In considering what would be a just response to a breach of Blake's undertaking the court has to take these considerations into account. The undertaking,if not a fiduciary obligation,was closely akin to a fiduciary obligation,where an account of profits is a standard remedy in the event of breach. Had the information which Blake has now disclosed still been confidential, an account of profits would have been ordered, almost as a matter of course. In the special circumstances of the intelligence services,the same conclusion should follow even though the information is no longer confidential. That would be a just response to the breach ..."

Nicholls 勋爵也说:"Normally the remedies of damages,specific performance and injunction,coupled with the characterisation of some contractual obligations as fiduciary,will provide an adequate response to a breach of contract. It will be only in exceptional cases, where those remedies are inadequate,that any question of accounting for profits will arise. No fixed rules can be prescribed. The court will have regard to all the circumstances,including the subject matter of the contract,the purpose of the contractual provision which has been breached,the circumstances in which the breach occurred,the consequences of the breach and the circumstances in which relief is being sought. **A useful general guide,although not exhaustive,is whether the plaintiff had a legitimate interest in preventing the defendant's profit-making activity and,hence,in depriving him of his profit.**"(一般而言,金钱赔偿、履约指令、禁令与把部分合约承诺视为是诚信义务,[1]就已经

---

[1] 诚信义务下违约方可被视为是"推定的信托人"(constructive trustee),要把得到的利益交给委托人,请参考先例 The AG for Hong Kong v. Reid,Privy Council Appeal No. 44 of 1992。

足够对违约做出救济。只会是在特殊性的案件,这些救济办法才不足够而需要考虑要求违约方交出利润。但无法硬性规定什么才是特殊性案件,这要根据案件的不同情况,包括是什么性质的合约,被违反的承诺的本意是什么,违约的实际情况与后果,要求做出救济的情况。加黑部分是将原告是否有一个合法的利益阻止被告赚取利润,作为一个有用的指引判断被告是否必须要交出利润。这表示这一先例的判法主要还是基于公共政策/利益的考虑,就是英国政府不能允许前特务 George Blake 出卖国家机密而赚取利润。)

上述比较空泛的说法也带来了后来不肯定的案例,甚至带来疑问就是该先例贵族院并没有明确一般的合约关系下可以要求违约方的被告"交出利润",只有在特殊性案件(甚至是涉及公共利益)才可以作出交出利润的救济。但返还性损失赔偿没有这个要求,所以交出利润与返还性损失赔偿是不同的计算。这导致了后来的一些案例被视为是不足够"特殊"(exceptional)而被法院拒绝了交出利润的救济:Devenish Nutrition Ltd v. Sanofi – Aventis SA(2008)2 WLR 637;Experience Hendrix v. PPX Enterprises Inc(2003)1 All ER(Comm)830 CA 等。这也表示原告提出这方面的请求是需要清楚列明要求这两种替代的救济。这方面可节录《McGregor on Damages》(18th edn,2009 年)一书 12 – 006 段:"In many cases an account of profits would not be appropriate. This is so in the many cases where there is interference with the claimant's property rights,principally involving tort but occasionally branching out into contract,and would be impossible where the benefit arises from a saving of expense. And even where the court could contemplate the awarding of an account of profits Lord Nicholls makes clear in Blake that an award will be made only if the case is exceptional,as it was held to be in Blake itself. An exceptional quality is not needed for restitutionary damages so that in Experience Hendrix(2003)1 All ER(Comm)830 CA,as will be seen,where both an account of profits and restitutionary damages were claimed,restitutionary damages were awarded but an account was refused;a lesser award by way of resititutionary damage would suffice. Mance LJ was careful to point out in Experience Hendrix that,while Lord Nicholls had emphasized that an award of an account of profits was only appropriate in exceptional circumstances,'he did not... apply the same epithet or qualification' to an award of restitutionary damages. Indeed it is conceivable that cases could arise where it would be appropriate to award the claimant all the profits of the defendant as restitutionary damages even though there were not exceptional circumstances as would justify an account of profit."

7.3.3 先例之三:Experience Hendrix v. PPX Enterprises Inc

再接下去要介绍的是 Experience Hendrix v. PPX Enterprises Inc(2003)1 All ER(Comm)830 CA 先例,案情涉及在 1965 年,被告(PPX)与一位开始成名的吉他/歌手名为 Jimi Hendrix 签约。合约是一面倒对 PPX 有利,这包括歌手只能为 PPX 表演,而且所出的唱片只能获得很低的版权费。由于该歌手名气的增加,出现了很自然的发展，歌手要从原来对他不利的合约中脱身。PPX 就以歌手违约/毁约起诉，而歌手就以有关合约是"限制商贸/就业"（restraint of trade）作为抗辩。其间该歌手死亡，但诉讼以歌手遗属的名义继续下去。但开庭后不久，双方达成和解。和解协议中涉及了该歌手唱片的版权，这主要分为两个部分。第一部分涉及了 33 首歌的"母带"（masters）可以继续发行，但 PPX 需要大幅度提高（相比原来的合约）给歌手遗属的版权费。第二部分的 63 首歌的母带是约定不可以继续使用（不论是以唱片、录音带或任何其他方式），除非双方事前达成协议。但在接下去的 1995 年与 1999 年，PPX 违约并在没有达成协议下使用第二部分的 39 首歌曲，并赚取了庞大的利润。这导致了在 2001 年，原告（是歌手遗属成立的一家公司）向被告提出诉讼，向法院申请禁令、损失赔偿与要求交出利润。第一审的法院作出了禁令，阻止 PPX 继续违约，但拒绝了损失赔偿与交出利润的申请。在上诉庭，判是这一案例的案情并不属于太"特殊"（exceptional），不适合作出交出利润的救济。但可以命令被告作出赔偿，这赔偿就是一笔使用了歌曲母带的合理金钱。

7.3.4　先例之四：WWF World Life Fund for Nature v. World Wrestling Federation Entertainment Inc

在 WWF World Life Fund for Nature v. World Wrestling Federation Entertainment Inc (2008) 1 WLR 445 CA 的上诉庭先例，案情涉及原告的野生动物基金与世界摔角联会娱乐有限公司都有相同的"WWF"的简称，但前者是在国际上很有名气，并且比后者成立早得多。这导致了原告向被告提出诉讼，指后者侵犯了它的商标。这一个诉讼导致了双方达成和解协议，协议内容包括有条文禁止被告继续使用 WWF 的简称。但在接下去的时间，后者多次违反和解协议，继续使用 WWF 的简称，并因此带来经济上的好处。但这对前者的野生动物基金没有造成经济上的损失，前者也没有办法证明损失。这一来，就导致了前者在诉讼中提出以修改文书请求要求后者交出违约所带来的利润。这被法院拒绝，认为有关的案件并不是太特殊，可要求交出利润的救济。这一个先例在《McGregor on Damages》（18th edn，2009 年）一书 12－030 段被视为是一个在返还性损失赔偿发展上的倒退，因为上诉庭把"Wrotham Park 损失"与交出利润都视为是复原性或赔偿性的救济。

7.4　合约关系作出返还性救济的利弊

这里可总结一下在合约关系作出这种返还性损失赔偿救济的利与弊，其中的好处主要就是阻止违约方通过违约获得利益。它也可以保护一些很难证明违约带来什么经济损失的受害方，如名誉上的损失或是破坏机密的损失：AG v. Guardian Newspapers Ltd (No. 2) (1990) 1 AC 109。但它的坏处也不少，如与另一个大原则有冲突，就是"有效益违约"（efficient breach）的说法（本书第十二章 4.1 段有详细的介绍）。这就是说如果违约方能够履行他的"次要合约义务"（secondary obligations）对受害方做出金钱的赔偿（本书第十一章 1.1 段有详细的介绍），从而可以从原来的合约中脱身并追求更大的经济利益，而受害方也能够合理减少损失（本书第五章有详细的介绍),这是对整个社会或全世界的总体经济会发挥更大的效益。

另一个坏处是会带来违约(特别是商业合约)的计算损失不肯定、让受害方获利而不是赔偿损失这么简单等方面。例如,要求违约方交出利润的救济,就在很多情况下违约方所获得的利润是与违约关系不大,可以说是受害方自己没有办法赚取,因为可能是涉及违约方特殊的关系、技术与动力(甚至是他的好运气),这就会导致让违约方交出利润并不公平或很难计算。还有是怎样的违约才能适合作出交出利润的救济?什么才算是太"特殊的案件"(exceptional case)?即使是作出"返还性损失"(restitutionary damage),也是存在于一般性违约的救济只局限在复原并不明显。

7.4.1 可能作出返还性损失赔偿的三种违约的情况

在 Attorney General v. Blake(2001)1 AC 268 的上诉庭先例,Woolf 勋爵曾经建议三种情况的违约可以考虑作出交出利润或返还性损失的赔偿,这三种情况是:(1)被告以不履行合约而牟利(benefit by under - performance of the contract);(2)被告违反合约中明示的禁止性规定而牟利(benefit by breach of a negative stipulation in the contract);(3)被告违约是因为与第三人签订一个更赚钱的合约(benefit by making a more profitable contract with a third party)。但贵族院看来并没有支持这一观点。这方面可节录《McGregor on Damages》(18th edn,2009 年)一书 12 - 033 段:"The cases bringing in the new doctrine do not in themselves indicate how far it is going to extend and precisely where its limits lie. Indeed as Mance LJ said in Experience Hendrix (2003) 2 All ER (Comm) 830 CA, Blake leaves future courts with the task of 'hammering out on the anvil of decided cases' - the words he was applying were those of Lord Steyn in Blake - when and how far remedies such as the appellant... seeks should be available.' It is therefore thought useful to turn to Blake in the Court of Appeal where Lord Woolf MR, delivering the judgment of the court, not only dealt specifically with restitutionary damages rather than the account of profits favoured in the Lords but also helpfully made reference to specific type situations in which restitutionary damages could be considered. There were three such, in two of which the court thought that justice required restitutionary damages to be awarded while in the third it took the view that restitutionary damages would be inappropriate."

在第一种情况的不履行导致了返还性损失的赔偿,英国有这方面的案例,而贵族院的 Nicholls 勋爵也有说这种情况是不足作出交出利润的救济。在美国 Louisiana 上诉庭有一个类似的先例名为 City of New Orleans v. Firemen's Charitable Association 43 La. Ann. 447(1891),但索赔并不成功。该合约是涉及被告向原告的财产提供消防服务,并必须配备多少消防员、消防喉与马匹等。但被告为了省钱,消防员与设备等都不足数。但这并没有导致原告有什么损失,因为还是做到了灭火。

第二种情况比较多见,较早前介绍的先例有好几个都属于这种情况,看来是不足作出交出利润的救济,但可以作出返还性损失的赔偿。这方面可节录《McGregor on Damages》(18th edn,2009 年)一书 12 - 038 段:"All three of the key cases identified above which were prepared to award restitutionary damage fall squarely within this category. In Wrotham Park the developers had built houses which they had covenanted not to build; in Blake the spy had revealed information which he had covenanted not to reveal; in Experience Hendrix the producer had granted licences of master recordings that it had contracted not to grant. The way should therefore now be open to awarding restitutionary damages in contractual situations analogous to the admittedly diverse situations which have so far led to favourable outcomes for contractual claimants. It is true that in the House of Lords in Blake Lord Nicholls considered that this second categorization of Lord Woolf was defined too widely to assist but he said this in connection with the remedy of accounting for profits, and we are not concerned in this text with the remedy of account. One can see why Lord Nicholls would say that it did not suffice to bring the remedy of account into play because that remedy was to apply only in exceptional cases. But there is no such limitation for restitutionary damages."

第三种情况在后来有一个被报道的伦敦仲裁与一个案例有针对,但看来有不同结果。第一个伦敦仲裁是有报道,名为 The "Sine Nomine"(2001)1 Lloyd's Rep 805。案情是有关一个 4~6 个月的期租合约,但被二船东撤船。这撤船在仲裁中判是错误,并且在第二个中间裁决书判二船东必须赔偿违约/毁约时的市场差价给承租人。但由于二船东撤船的时间非常有利,估计赚了不少钱并导致承租人在第三个中间裁决书要求作出交出利润的裁决。但这一要求被仲裁庭拒绝,其中仲裁庭指出了这方面的困难,一个是原告往往不会知道被告在违约/毁约后的准确利润是多少。另是作出这样的裁决会是双重赔偿原告的损失,因为在第二个中间裁决书已经根据 The "Elena d'Amico"(1980)1 Lloyd's Rep 75 的大原则作出市场差价的"复原性"(compensatory)赔偿。仲裁庭说:

"It is by no means uncommon for commercial contracts to be broken deliberately because a more profitable opportunity has arisen. Or the contract - breaker takes an over - generous view of his rights, knowing that the law may ultimately be against him. In such a case he may have little or nothing to lose by taking the chance; the downside at worst is that he will have to pay the costs of both sides. International commerce on a large scale is red in tooth and claw. We do not say that the Respondents' action was either deliberate or cynical wrongdoing in this case; they had a respectable argument on liability, although a commercial judge refused their application for leave to appeal.

Our solution to the present problem is that there should not be an award of wrongful profits where both parties are dealing with a marketable commodity - the services of a ship in this case - for which a substitute can be found in the market place. In the ordinary way the damages which the claimant suffers by having to buy in at the market price will be equal to the profit which the wrongdoer makes by having his goods or his ships' services to sell at a higher price. It is in the nature of things unlikely that the wrongdoer will make a greater profit than that. And if he does, it is an adventitious benefit which he can keep. The commercial law of this country should not make moral judgments, or seek to punish contract - breakers."

但在同一周所作出的 Esso Petroleum Co Ltd v. Niad Ltd (2002) All ER (D) 324 判例看来是有不同结果。由于案件的报道十分简陋,所以不同之处没有办法说明。该先例是涉及原告的 Esso 石油公司向被告供应汽油,但要求以固定价格向市场出售。这固定价格显然是要顾及与 Esso 竞争的其他石油公司的价格。但被告不断违反协议,以更高的价格向市场出售。原告的 Esso 却没有办法证明它实际的损失,就是被告的违约影响了它的销量与利润到底是多少,甚至更可能是 Esso 没有损失。所以,Esso 向被告提出的是三种替代救济,这包括"复原性损失"(compensatory damage)、"交出利润"(account for profits)与"返还性损失"(restitutionary damage)。但在最后的判决由于报道简陋而看不出到底是哪一种救济被法院接受,但判决是判 Esso 有权向被告取回后者以较高价格出售汽油的额外利润,这看来是与"The Sine Nomine"的仲裁裁决不一致。

7.4.2　总结有关返还性损失与交出利润在合约关系下的不肯定

总结而言,这方面的发展还是未知数,照理由说 The "Sine Nomine" 与 Esso Petroleum Co Ltd v. Niad Ltd 都不是太特殊的案件。正如《McGregor on Damages》(18th edn, 2009 年)一书 12 - 044 段所讲:"In any event Niad can be reconciled with The Sine Nomine on the basis that in Niad the parties were not dealing with a marketable commodity for which a substitute could be found in the market, but the two decisions seem to reflect opposing attitudes to the issue of whether a profiteering defendant should be required to give up his gains to a claimant who has not lost out. Down which path courts and arbitrators will eventually go, and whether it will be the same path, remains to be seen."

这种利弊在 Attorney General v. Blake (2001) 1 AC 268 先例也有多处提到,如针对计算损失的不肯定与适用在哪一类违约的案件,Nicholls 勋爵认为问题并不严重,说:"The main argument against the availability of an account of profits as a remedy for breach of contract is that the circumstances where this remedy may be granted will be uncertain. This will have an unsettling effect on commercial contracts where certainty is important. I do not think these fears are well founded. I see no reason why, in practice, the availability of the remedy of an account of profits need disturb settled expectations in the commercial or consumer world. An account of profits will be appropriate only in exceptional circumstances. Normally the remedies of damages, specific performance and injunction, coupled with the characterization of some contractual obligations as fiduciary, will provide an adequate response to a breach of contract. It will be only in exceptional cases, where those remedies are inadequate, that any question of accounting for profits will arise. No fixed rules can be prescribed. The court will have regard to all the circumstances, including the subject matter of the contract, the purpose of the contractual provision which has been breached, the circumstances in which the breach occurred, the consequences of the breach and the circumstances in which relief is being sought. A useful general guide, although not exhaustive, is whether the plaintiff had a legitimate interest in preventing the defendant's profit - making activity and, hence, in depriving him of his profit."

但在贵族院唯一持不同意见的 Hobhouse 勋爵说："The principle of compensation is both intellectually sound as the remedy for breach and provides the just answer. The example discussed in my noble and learned friend's speech do not on the correct analysis disclose the supposed need to extend the boundaries of remedies for breach of contract... I must also sound a further note of warning that if some more extensive principle of awarding non - compensatory damages for breach of contract is to be introduced into our commercial law the consequences will be very far reaching and disruptive. I do not believe that such is the intention of your Lordships but if others are tempted to try to extend the decision of the present exceptional case to commercial situations so as to introduce restitutionary rights beyond those presently recognized by the law of restitution, such a step will require very careful consideration before it is acceded to ..."

所以在英国法律委员会 1997 年的报告《Report on Aggravated, Exemplary and Restitutionary Damages, Law Commission No. 247》有建议是针对可以作出履约指令的合约（这种合约会是金钱赔偿不足作出救济）与受信义务的合约是可作出返还性损失赔偿，但其他的合约（包括商业合约），就不应该理会违约方的被告从违约中获得的利益，不作出这种损失赔偿。这在 7.21 段有提到说："In the case of breach of contract we inclined to the view that the distinction that appears to be drawn between specifically enforceable contracts and contracts between fiduciaries where a restitutionary award may be made, and other contracts where the gain to a defendant from breach is irrelevant, reflects an appropriate balance of the respective interests of the parties."

在目前的法律地位，可以说是 Attorney General v. Blake 先例带来了很多疑问，需要进一步的案例解答与合理化。例如，该先例要求被告交出所有利润（所有版权费或稿费），并说是只在"特殊"（exceptional）案件这样做。但在 Wrotham Park Estate Co v. Parkside Homes（1974）1 WLR 798 先例，只要求被告交出部分利润（5%），而那一个案例应该谈不上特殊。这一来，这两个先例是否是根据同一个原则判？如果是，会否要求案件特殊性只是在要求交出所有利润的情况下？如果是，会否 Wrotham Park 的部分利润交出会是在将来的案件中大量出现，毕竟好像 Attorney General v. Blake 这种特殊的案件不会有太多。

另是交出部分利润的百分比是怎么样考虑，被告会否可抗辩指利润是通过他的特殊的关系、技术与动力（甚至是他的好运气）应减少交出利润等？

7.5 其他方面的考虑之一:被告是否故意与值得批评的违约

在上诉庭的 Experience Hendrix v. PPX Enterprises Inc(2003)1 All ER(Comm)830 CA 先例,有把被告的违约是否是刻意作为考虑之一。但在 Attorney General v. Blake (2001)1 AC 268 的上诉庭,Woolf 勋爵认为返还性损失的判决并“不光是根据被告的道德上错误”(not depend upon Defendant’s moral culpability alone)与被告“刻意与值得批评的违约并不是离开复原性赔偿的理由”(the fact that his breach of contract is deliberate and cynical is not by itself a good ground for departing from the normal basis on which damages are awarded)。

另是,在贵族院的 Nicholls 勋爵说“无意违约”(innocent breach)只能要求赔偿复原性损失,但“值得批评违约”(cynical breach)就可以要求返还性损失赔偿。这种说法也并不肯定,如这两种违约之间的分水线就并不明确,也很难证明:Surrey County Council v. Bredero Homes Ltd(1993)1 WLR 1361。只说,在 1977 年的《专利法》(Patents Act 1977)之 Section 62(1),是有说明被告如果是无辜或不知情的情况下破坏专利,就不作出交出利润的判决。

7.6 其他方面的考虑之二:有否及时向法院申请禁令

涉及返还性损失赔偿或交出利润的案件很多会是可以及时向法院申请禁令,毕竟这种案件根据违约赔偿的复原大原则是不足够救济,所以有必要做出禁令。但如果受害方的原告没有及时向法院或仲裁庭申请禁令,会否影响返还性损失赔偿或是赔偿的高低?这也是有许多不同的说法。例如在 Experience Hendrix v. PPX Enterprises Inc(2003)1 All ER(Comm)830 CA 先例上诉庭说不会影响,该先例本身是作出一个禁令并同时作出返还性损失赔偿。但《McGregor on Damages》(18th edn,2009 年)一书 12-049 段认为原告没有这样做会影响返还性损失赔偿的高低,说:“The fact that injunctive relief has not been claimed when it was available should not preclude a claim for restitutionary damages. Millett LJ’s attempt in Jaggard v. Sawyer(1995)1 WLR 269 CA to explain Surrey County Council v. Bredero(1993)1 WLR 1361 on the ground that damages were refused because the claimant had not sought an injunction when it could have had one is misconceived. Not only is there no sign of such reasoning in Bredero but the decision itself is now thought to be wrong, Millett LJ was no doubt trying to justify it but for the wrong reason. However, a failure on the part of the claimant to pursue the injunctive route when it was available to him might be considered relevant to the amount of damages to be awarded to the claimant; level of recovery is dealt with below. Thus it is there pointed out that Brightman J in Wrotham Park Estate Co v. Parkside Homes(1974)1 WLR 798 said that his award was conservative because of the claimant’s failure to warn the developer defendant in advance that no consent to the development would be forthcoming.”

7.7 其他方面的考虑之三:返还性损失的金额

这方面在违约还没有太多的指导性先例,但在侵权就已经有了不少。其中针对被告在没有原告的同意下使用后者的财产,许多先例是判有关财产在市场上可以收取的租金。这也可以以被告的违约替他省下了租用有关财产的费用,而需要把省下的钱作为返还性损失赔给原告。至于涉及土地侵入的先例,有关的金额高低没有一定的准则。但看来是很大程度针对被告侵权所得到的好处或利润是多少,然后作出一个百分比。这在《McGregor on Damages》(18th edn,2009 年)一书 12－053 段提到的有关先例对返还性损失金额的不肯定,如下:"Each case has to be taken separately and it appears impossible to lay down any general rules. Thus in Wrotham Park Estate Co v. Parkside Homes(1974)1 WLR 798 the award was of only 5 percent of the developer's anticipated profit of £ 50,000 whereas in Bracewell v. Appleby(1975)Ch. 408 as much as 40 percent was awarded, but since the profit was only £ 5,000 the total amount was less. These were both cases of the 1970s when the courts may have been feeling their way in this area, but 20 years later in Jaggard v. Sawyer(1995)1 WLR 269 CA the claimant received only £ 700 although this did represent a potential award of over £ 6,000 which would have been divisible between the 10 properties in the development other than the defendant's. By contrast, as an even later date in Amec Developments Ltd v. Jury's Hotel Management(UK) Ltd(2001)1 EGLR 81, where it was a hotel that was being built in breach of a restrictive covenant, the far larger award of £ 375,000 was reached, being based upon the gain the defendant would make by its breach and the discount which would be applied to that gain in negotiation. Later still in Tamares (Vincent Square) Ltd v. Fairpoint Properties (Vincent Square) Ltd(2007)1 WLR 2167, where a developer had infringed a right to light, somewhat under one third of the developer's profit, taken at £ 174,500, was awarded. Various factors other than profit and how the parties might have negotiated may influence the court in coming to a view as to the appropriate amount."

8. 非复原损失赔偿之三:名义损失赔偿

名义损失赔偿(nominal damages)是指原告在责任方面胜诉,但是没有办法证明他在有关的侵权或违约中蒙受什么损失,导致法院或仲裁庭只能作出一个名义损失的赔偿。名义损失最著名的定义是 Halsbury 勋爵在 The"Mediana"(1900)AC 113 中所说的:"'Nominal damages' is a technical phrase which means that you have negatived anything like real damage, but that you are affirming by your nominal damages that there is an infraction of a legal right which, though it gives you no right to any real damages at all, yet gives you a right to the verdict or judgment because your legal right has been infringed."

名义损失在很长的一段时间内有大量针对违约的案例判是 2 英镑:Child v. Stenning(1879)11 Ch D 82 CA;Columbus Co v. Clowes(1903)1 KB 244;Weld - Blundell v. Stephens(1920)AC 956;Groom v. Crocker(1939)1 KB 194 CA;Clark v. Kirby - Smith (1964)Ch 506;Aryeh v. Kostoris & Son(1967)1 Lloyd's Rep 63 CA;Francis Delzenne v. Klee(1968)112 SJ 583;Sykes v. Midland Bank Executor & Trustee Co(1971)1 QB 113 CA;The Kismet(1976)2 Lloyd's Rep 585;The Football League Ltd v. Edge Ellison (2007)PNLR 2 等先例。但也会有情况判是 1 英镑:James v. Hutton(1950)1 KB 9 CA;Armstrong v. Sheppard & Short(1959)2 QB 384 CA;Moore v. Buchanan(1966)197 EG 565;Boaks v. Associated Newspapers(1967)111 SJ 703;Grobbelaar v. News Group Newspapers Ltd(2002)1 WLR 3024 HL 等先例。也曾经有过一些先例判的金额是 5 英镑:Brandeis Goldschmidt & Co v. Western Transport(1981)QB 864 CA;Dean v. Ainley (1987)1 WLR 1729;Surrey County Council v. Bredero Homes Ltd(1993)1 WLR 1361; Berkowitz v. MW(St John's Wood)(1993)48 EG 133 等先例。

不论是 1 英镑或者 5 英镑,名义损失都是微不足道,所以很难想象有原告明知道他没有真正损失或证明不了损失还是会提出昂贵的诉讼,在索赔请求要求判他责任上胜诉与下令被告向他作出名义损失赔偿。在部分古老的案例如 Hanfstaengl v. WH Smith(1905)1 Ch 519,涉及版权的侵犯但受害方的原告证明不了他的损失而只能获得名义损失,Kekewich 大法官是这样说:"I adopt the plaintiff's argument that, if he desires to protect his copyright, he is bound to take actions even in a case which is, on the face of it, of a trumpery character, or run the risk of encouraging more serious infringements... I think the plaintiff is entitled to a verdict for nominal damages."但今天的原告不需要这样做,阻吓被告不得继续侵犯他的版权,原告大可以去法院申请一个禁令,阻吓力会是比名义损失赔偿大得多。

所以,在现实中名义损失通常只是原告同时提出的几项不同诉因所带来的损失其中的一项。反正原告免不了要提出诉讼,就索性把他没有办法证明真正损失的索赔也包括在内。这也会在被告提出反索赔的情况下出现,就是被告把他没有办法证明真正损失的反索赔包括在内,希望碰碰运气或增加和解谈判的筹码。而法院或者仲裁庭作出名义损失往往是在提出一方没有办法证明他蒙受真正损失,这可能是侵权或违约与损失扯不上因果关系。举例说,在上述提到的 The "Kismet"先例,涉及了一个海上救助合约。合约要求另一艘船舶名为 Statesman 轮供应 75 ~ 100 吨食水与在有必要时,把 Kismet 轮拖带去安全港口。在之后的诉讼,涉及 Statesman 轮的经营人(也就是海上救助合约的合约方)向 Kismet 轮船东索赔拖带费用。但 Kismet 轮反索赔指 Statesman 轮供应的食水不足够(只有 65 吨)与受到污染,导致 Kismet 轮没有足够的食水供应锅炉,不能以自己的动力开去安全港口。所以,要反索赔这部分的损失包括时间上的损失。但法院认定供应的食水其中 30 ~ 35 吨是由于 Kismet 轮自己不小心把开关开错了而流失,而剩下的食水即使是 Statesman 轮没有违约也不足够让 Kismet 轮以自己的动力开去安全港口,所以拖带是免不了。这一来,法院判 Statesman

轮违反救助合约,只有供水 65 吨而不是 75 ~ 100 吨的违约只能给予 2 英镑的名义损失。

真正会影响的是诉讼费用,这才是一笔比名义损失大得多的钱。在以前的先例,认为原告毕竟还是在责任胜诉,所以应该由被告承担有关的费用。但这种情况带来了疑虑,因为一个严重的后果就是会鼓励不必要的诉讼。这种要倚赖法院或仲裁庭“裁量权”(discretion)的不肯定的情况可节录 Devlin 大法官在 Anglo - Cyprian Agencies v. Paphos Industries(1951)1 All ER 873 先例中所说:“No doubt the ordinary rule is that, where a plaintiff has been successful, he ought not to be deprived of his costs, or at any rate, made to pay the costs of the other side, unless he has been guilty of some sort of misconduct. In applying that rule, however, it is necessary to decide whether the plaintiff really has been successful, and I do not think that a plaintiff who recovers nominal damages ought necessarily to be regarded in the ordinary sense of the word as a ‘successful’ plaintiff. In certain cases he may be, e. g. where part of the object of the action is to establish a legal right, wholly irrespective of whether any substantial remedy is obtained. To that extent a plaintiff who recovers nominal damages may properly be regarded as a successful plaintiff, but it is necessary to examine the facts of each particular case.”

但这种情况应该在减少,首先是在笔者的《仲裁法——从开庭审理到裁决书的作出与执行》(法律出版社 2009 年版)之 61 页提到了 Tramountana v. Atlantic(1978)1 Lloyd’s Rep 391 与 Alltrans Express Ltd v. CVA Holding Ltd(1984)1 WLR 394 等先例,判是胜诉的金额“极微小”(trifling)就不能向被告取回诉讼费用。显然,名义损失应该是属于极微小的胜诉金额。笔者也在同一页提到了被告可以尽早在法院诉讼或仲裁开始或之前支付或者作出一个足够金额的提议把钱存放到法院、或在仲裁作出一个秘密提议或 Calderbank 提议,就能够保护被告的诉讼费用。更重要的是已经有了先例说是原告如果只能成功取回名义损失,这算是败诉而不是胜诉。在 Hyde Park Residence Ltd v. Yelland(1999)RPC 655, Jacob 大法官说:“It seems to me that the whole question of nominal damage is at the end of this century far too legalistic. A plaintiff who recovers only nominal damages has effectively lost and in reality the defendant has established a complete defence.”

9. 违约与侵权的损失计算是否相同

在大原则下,违约与侵权的损失计算也是为了复原,对受害方做出赔偿。但经常会有一个有趣与常被提起的疑问,就是违约与侵权的损失计算是否相同?而简单的答案就是有时候侵权与违约的损失计算相同,但有时候并不同。这里首先可以看损失计算的目的是什么,首先在违约是为了把受害方回复到合约被履行的经济地位,也就是所谓的"复原"(*restitutio integrum*)。但侵权是为了把受害方回复到侵权并没有发生过的经济地位,也就是把受害方回复到 *status quo ante*。这在一定程度上也是复原,但由于侵权不涉及合约关系,而合约的经济地位会是千变万化与根据每一个合约不同的条文,所以在许多方面并不相同。

9.1 误述下违约与侵权诉因重叠的不同损失计算办法

这方面最好是以一个合约的"误述"(misrepresentation)作为例子。如果是由于误述而导致一个合约的产生,受到误述的受害方会有违约或是侵权的诉因。如果误述成为后来订立合约的条文,受害方显然是可以以违约向误述方索赔损失,而赔偿是把受害方回复到被误述的事实是真实的地位。举一个简单的例子,货方在租用一艘船舶时被船东误述说可以装运 500 吨货物,但实际上船舶只能装运 495 吨。受害的货方就可以索赔损失从经济上回复到该船舶的确能够装运 500 吨货物的经济地位,估计这种轻微的误述所带来的违约损失恐怕不会太大。但换一种情况是误述并没有成为后来订立合约的条文,这一来受害方就会根据侵权向误述方索赔损失。显然受害方在误述的诱导下导致了一个合约的产生,这合约是有严重缺陷。所以,英国法律一直以来是支持受害方可以终断合约。但这方面已经是有了立法的改变,也就是 1967 年《误述法》把疏忽与无辜的误述改为让法院或者仲裁庭有一个裁量权做出金钱赔偿作为终断合约的替代(因为终断合约毕竟是一种极端的做法,而且经常会在市场波动下被用来取巧),毕竟在现实中经常会有一些无关重要的误述会在双方的合约谈判中出现。这误述会是误述方不小心,做出陈述之前没有查清楚而构成疏忽,甚至是已经小心查清楚但得到的资料实际上是错误而构成无辜的误述。对这种无关重要的误述做出金钱赔偿也赔不了多少,重要的还是不能随意让受害方利用这一次机会在市场变为不利的时候终断合约。

但 1967 年《误述法》并不针对另一种会有严重后果的误述,就是"欺诈性误述"(fraudulent misrepresentation)。欺诈性误述会带来的后果还是按照英国普通法的地位针对,也就是受害方可以终断合约。但也会有情况是受害方不能或不想终断合约,这一来受害方主要的救济就是向误述方根据侵权索赔损失。这里可以先节录《Chitty on Contracts》(30th edn,2008 年)一书 6 - 107 段所介绍关于英国目前的法律地位如下:"**Present position**. The right to rescind for fraudulent misrepresentation is unimpaired by the Misrepresentation Act, but there is no longer any absolute right to rescind for negligent or innocent misrepresentation. Section 2(2) of the Act provides that the court now has a discretion to award damages in lieu of rescission wherever it is of the opinion that it would be equitable to do so, having regard to the nature of the misrepresentation and the loss that would be caused by it if the contract were upheld, as well as to the loss that rescission would cause the other party. It has already been observed that this is a wide discretion, and the court is not confined to a consideration of whether damages would be an adequate remedy to the representee."

针对欺诈性误述的损失计算可以是十分广泛,只要是欺诈性误述所导致的所有损失,都可以向误述方索赔,把受害方回复到一个没有发生过误述的经济地位。损失的计算与违约并不相同,正如贵族院先例的 Smith New Court Securities v. Scrimgeour Vickers(1997)AC 254 所说:"is to put the claimant in the position he would have been in, not if representation had been true, but if the representation had never been made. This is a more restrictive rule, as an action in tort does not take into account the loss of a bargain."以下可以节录《Chitty on Contracts》(30th edn, 2008 年)一书 6-049 段如下:"**Measure of damages for fraudulent misrepresentation.** The proper measure of damages for fraudulent misrepresentation was discussed by the Court of Appeal in Doyle v. Olby (Ironmongers) Ltd (1969) 2 QB 158. It was here held that damages for fraud were not the same as damages for breach of contract in that they were not designed to place the innocent party in the position he would have been if the representation had been true, but to put him in the position he would have been in if the representation had not been made. The presumption seems to be that if the misrepresentation had not been made, the claimant would not have entered into the contract. So the plaintiff ought to be awarded such damages as will put him back in the financial position he was in before the contract was made. This means that where a person is induced by fraud to buy some property, the proper measure of damages is *prima facie* the difference between the price paid and the fair value of the property."

欺诈性误述的损失计算也不考虑损失类别是否是误述方作为被告能够预见得到,所以不存在损失遥远性的说法。例如,受害方如果不是这一个欺诈性误述,就不会丧失了其他的机会可以赚取的利润,这可以作为损失的一部分。这方面可节录《Chitty on Contracts》(30th edn, 2008 年)一书 6-050 段如下:"**Unforeseeable losses.** In Doyle Olby (Ironmongers) Ltd, it was held that in cases of fraud the plaintiff was entitled to damages for any such loss which flowed from the defendants' fraud, even if the loss could not have been foreseen by the latter. Thus the claimant may recover not only the difference between the price paid and the value of what he received but also expenditure wasted in reliance on the contract and compensation for other opportunities passed over in reliance on it."

最后,也可以节录《Chitty on Contracts》(30th edn, 2008 年)一书 6-051 段有关欺诈性误述的损失计算大原则如下:"In Smith New Court Securities Ltd v. Scringeour Vickers (Asset Management) Ltd (1997) AC 254 Lord Browne-Wilkinson described Doyle v. Olby (Ironmongers) Ltd as re-stating the law correctly. He stated the principles applicable in assessing damages where a party has been induced by a fraudulent misrepresentation to buy property as follows: '(1) The defendant is bound to make reparation for all the damage directly flowing from the transaction; (2) although such damage need not have been foreseeable, it must have been directly caused by the transaction; (3) in assessing such damage, the plaintiff is entitled to recover by way of damages the full price paid by him, but he must give credit for any benefits which he has received as a result of the transaction; (4) as a general rule, the benefits received by him include the market value of the property acquired at the date of the transaction; but such general rule is not to be inflexibly applied where to do so would prevent him obtaining full compensation for the wrong suffered; (5) although the circumstances in which the general rule should not apply cannot be comprehensively stated, it will normally not apply where either (a) the misrepresentation has continued to operate after the date of the acquisition of the asset so as to induce the plaintiff to retain the asset or (b) the circumstances of the case are such that the plaintiff is, by reason of the fraud, locked into the property; (6) in addition, the plaintiff is entitled to recover consequential losses caused by the transaction; (7) the plaintiff must take all reasonable steps to mitigate his loss once he has discovered the fraud.'"

总结而言,从误述来看,违约与侵权的损失计算是很不一样。

9.2 违约与侵权损失分别之一:惩罚性赔偿/议定赔偿

有关惩罚性赔偿与议定赔偿的议题在本章第6段有详细的讨论,在这里只说,议定赔偿只存在于违约中,因为议定赔偿是合约双方在订立合约时就某一特定的违约/毁约约定违约方向受害方做出确定金额赔偿,但在侵权中就不会有这种议定赔偿。注意是议定赔偿也可以作为限制赔偿责任,这就是约定一个比真正损失估计是低的金额。这在合约关系完全可以这样做,但侵权就不会预先约定限制赔偿责任然后做出侵权行为。

至于议定赔偿可否约定一个比真正损失高的金额,答案就是不可以,因为这就会涉及合约关系是不允许惩罚性赔偿。这是目前英国的公共政策,就是在合约关系,能够做出惩罚性赔偿目前只限制在三种情况,这是规定在 Rookes v. Barnard (1964) AC 1129 先例中,在本章6.1段已经详细介绍过。

但惩罚性赔偿在侵权的范畴就经常会有。这种违约与侵权在惩罚性赔偿的差异也会收窄,如在加拿大已经有先例 Royal Bank of Canada v. Got 178 DLR (4th) 385 (2000) 判是违约也可以做出惩罚性赔偿。估计英国法院也将会面对能否允许违约像侵权一样做出惩罚性赔偿,而英国法院目前已经对这方面在放宽,特别是针对商业合约,这在本章6.5段已经介绍过。这方面可节录《McGregor on Damages》(18th edn, 2009年)之11-016段作为总结如下:"... Historically, the law has always set its face against awarding exemplary damages for breach of contract; outrageous conduct is the domain of tort rather than contract. Such a stance was famously taken by the House of Lords in Addis v. Gramophone Co. (1909) AC 488 in the context of wrongful dismissal of an employee by an employer and continued in the context of wrongful disturbance of a tenant by a landlord right to the verge of the decision in Rooks v. Barnard (1964) AC 1129. But may not the new limits on exemplary damages have permitted an enlargement of the situations in which awards may be made? Once the rationale has been changed so as to concentrate upon high – handed public conduct and profit – motivated private conduct, may not such conduct deserve the same sanction whatever the cause of action? Not many years ago exemplary damages were awarded by a Canadian court in Royal Bank of Canada v. Got 178 DLR(4th) 385(2000). Just as the English courts have now, since Attorney General v. Blake(2001)1 AC 268, countenanced restitutionary damages for breach of contract as well as for tort, so too, it has been rightly said, English courts will soon have to confront the issue of whether exemplary damages are allowable for breach of contract as well as for tort."

9.3 违约与侵权损失分别之二:减少损失、损失的证明、过去与将来的损失等

只是简单的说,在这些方面违约与侵权没有分别,这可以节录《McGregor on Damages》(18th edn, 2009 年)之 19 – 004 段如下:"No distinctions appear to exists in the rules as to mitigation of damage, or as to certainty of proof, or as to the extent to which recovery or past and prospective loss is allowed."

9.4 违约与侵权损失分别之三:分摊责任与损失

有关这一个方面,本书第八章有详细介绍,也就是受害方自己在事件中有部分疏忽,导致他向被告索赔损失会需要做出部分扣减,以反应原告自己要承担的责任。这是根据 1945 年《The Law Reform(Contributory Negligence)Act》在违约方/侵权方与受害方都有一定程度错误与疏忽的情况下分摊责任与损失。这一立法主要就是针对侵权的疏忽,如在涉及汽车撞伤行人的交通意外事故中,闯红灯的行人与醉酒驾驶的司机在侵权的诉讼中需要分摊事故的责任,受伤的行人(原告)只能向司机(被告)取回部分损失。

1945 年的立法能否适用在合约关系分摊赔偿责任是一个富有争议性的问题,导致了大量的先例,例如:De Meza v. Apple(1975)1 Lloyd's Rep 498;The "Shinjitsu Maru No 5"(1985)1 Lloyd's Rep 568;Vesta v. Butcher(1986)2 Lloyd's Rep 179;Barclays Bank plc v. Fairclough Building Ltd(1995)QB 214;The "Ardent"(1997)2 Lloyd's Rep 547;Raflatac v. Eade & others(1999)1 Lloyd's Rep 506 等。只简单说,在订约自由下合约条文会带来千变万化的合约责任。目前的英国普通法下,如果合约条文带来的合约责任与侵权的疏忽责任完全一致,就会允许把损失分摊。有关这方面的复杂问题,可参阅本书第八章。以下只节录《McGregor on Damages》(18th edn, 2009 年)之 19 – 004 段说明在这一方面违约与侵权有很大的差异,如下:"But with contributory negligence the position is different. While damages can be reduced by apportionment in the case of the claimant's contributory negligence when he is suing in tort, this is not possible in contract except where there is concurrent liability in contract and tort. This would appear to be settled law but its wisdom has been questioned."

9.5 违约与侵权损失分别之四:损失遥远性之一的因果关系

损失遥远性涉及两个方面,第一个方面就是因果关系。也就是最后造成的损失能否与违约或者侵权行为串起来,可以说是该违约或侵权造成了这一损失。在这一个方面违约与侵权没有差异,这方面可以节录《McGregor on Damages》(18th edn,2009年)之19-006段如下:"The principle of causation, however, cannot alter with the boundaries of contract and tort: in particular, what is a direct consequence for tort is a direct consequence for contract and causation remains immutable."

9.6 违约与侵权损失分别之五:损失遥远性之二的保护范围

"保护范围"(scope of protection)是指受害方的原告能够向被告成功索赔哪一些损失类别。也可以说是英国法律保护受害方可以成功索赔哪一些类别的损失,而不受保护的损失即使是存在也是受害方自己倒霉。众所周知,不论是违约或是侵权都有说法是太遥远的损失,如订约时无法合理预见的损失类别是不能够向被告取回。这方面的问题在本书第三章有详细的介绍。

在这一方面,违约与侵权有重大甚至是主要差异,并导致不少说法是违约与侵权在损失计算方面并不一样。

首先在损失遥远性的考验,已经提到过在合约关系下是要看双方订约时什么是他们能够合理预见的损失类别。这种能够合理预见的损失类别可以被称为"一般性损失"(normal or general damage),而他们不能合理预见的损失类别,就被视为是遥远。除非是违约方在订约前收到足够的通知,否则受害方是不能索赔这种遥远的损失,也被称为是"特别损失"(special damage)。这些就是著名的先例Hadley v. Baxendale(1854)9 Ex. 341中所规定的两种损失类别。

在侵权的损失遥远性的考验,就不存在订约时的预见,更加不会存在对特别损失预先做出通知的做法。只要是在做出侵权行为时可以预见得到会产生的后果或损失,都属于受到英国法律保护的范畴内。这方面最主要的先例是枢密院的The "Wagon Mound"(1961)1 Lloyd's Rep 1。由于这在本书第三章会有十分详尽的介绍,这里就不多谈了。

一般的说法就是侵权会是比违约在损失遥远性方面宽松,因为违约受到双方在订合约时能否预见或料想得到的限制。这方面在本书第三章有介绍,因为侵权下应否能够"合理预见"(reasonably foreseeable)的考验要比违约下双方在订立合约时能否"料想得到"(the contemplation of the parties)更为广泛。例如,针对非金钱的间接损失,这包括精神的创伤与压力、名誉损失等,在侵权通常会被接受,但在违约(特别是商业合约)就往往会被否定。正如A Burrows教授在他的《Remedies for Torts and Breach of Contract》(第三版,2004年)是这样说:"While a slight possibility of the loss occurring is required in tort, a serious possibility of the loss occurring is required in contract."

但从另一个角度来说,合约双方当事人在订立合约时,可能会通过预先的通知甚至约定赔偿的范围是包括某些特别损失，甚至会在特殊情况下是一些极其遥远的损失类别，那么受害方在这类损失产生时就可以依照合约条文向被告要求赔偿，因为这是在合约当事人料想之内的。但这类损失在侵权的诉因下可能就过于遥远而超出了被告的预见，受害方也就不能够取回。这可以节录《McGregor on Damages》（18th edn，2009 年）之 19 - 010 段如下："The contemplation of the parties may, however, work the other way and lead to the opposite and most frequently expressed view that the liability in contract is wider. This stems from the second rule in Hadley v. Baxendale that, where special circumstances are at the making of contract communicated to the party subsequently in breach, damages may be given in respect of these special circumstances since they were within the parties′ contemplation. There is no such communication beforehand to a tortfeasor, and therefore it is said that the liability in contract can be greater in this connection. . ."

可以总结而言，在损失遥远性之一的因果关系方面，侵权与违约的法律规定是一样，但是在损失遥远性之二的保护范围方面，有时侵权的保护会比违约广泛（这种情况较多），而有时违约的保护会比侵权广泛，这是取决于具体合约条文的约定。这可以节录《McGregor on Damages》（18th edn，2009 年）之 19 - 011 段总结如下："In summary, the law as to remoteness of damage appear to be the same in contract and in tort as far as the causation aspect of remoteness is concerned, but the scope of the protection afforded to the claimant is sometimes wider in tort and sometimes wider in contract, depending upon the voluntary factor in contract, varying from agreement to agreement, of the contemplation of the parties."

9.7 违约与侵权损失分别之六：纯经济损失

违约与侵权损失的另一个分别在于是否可以索赔纯经济损失。这个课题在本书第八章有详述，这里不重复。只是简单总结违约受害方索赔的往往都是纯经济损失，但英国法律下对侵权的受害方能否索赔"纯经济损失"（pure economic loss）就十分谨慎。有不少先例都判"疏忽"（negligence）造成的纯经济损失不能索赔，这方面主要的考虑是怕打开"大水门"（floodgate）导致没完没了的诉讼。但针对其他类别的侵权，如"滋扰"（nuisance），受害方是有可能索赔纯经济损失。这也在本书第八章的第 7 段针对海上油污损失赔偿有详细说明。

第二章　损失计算办法与损失的类别

1. 序言

本章第一部分就是接下去第一章所讲的损失赔偿大原则下,英国法院根据"复原大原则"(*restitutio in integrum*)对合约被违反时受害方的利益作出保障,强制要求违约方以金钱作出赔偿。这种受到保护的合约利益主要可以分三大类如下:

一是"返还性利益"(restitutionary interest),这在本书第一章之7.4段有介绍,其中包括了一些有关的重要先例,如Attorney General v. Blake(2001)1 AC 268等先例。这种利益是要强制违约方交出他在违约下所获得的好处,而不是追究受害方在违约中是否有蒙受损失。

二是"预期利益"(expectation interest),也称"履行利益"(performance interest)或"交易损失"(loss of bargain)等。这种法律强制保护的利益是复原大原则下最主要的一个"损失计算办法"(measure of damage),就是计算如果没有发生违约/毁约,合约得以顺利执行,受害方预计会有什么经济上的好处或利益。毕竟受害方投入金钱与精力订立一个商业合约,通常就是希望能够在顺利履行后获得经济利益。所以在理论与实际中,这也是最说得通的一种达致复原目的的损失计算办法。本书其他主要的章节如第十三与十四章的市场规则,都是针对预期利益的损失及计算办法。

三是"依赖利益"(reliance interest),这种法律强制保护的利益是受害方因为有这一合约的存在而投入的金钱。例如,购买设备、建设厂房、雇佣员工等,但被告违约/毁约导致这些费用都浪费了。本来如果合约获得顺利履行,受害方获得合约的预期利益,就不应该存在依赖利益,因为投入的金钱可以说是受害方的成本就是为了赚取合约获得履行下的预期利益。所以一贯的说法是受害方的原告只能选其中一种利益作出索赔,而不能同时索赔两种利益,因为可能会造成重复赔偿。显然在绝大部分的情况下,受害方会选择预期利益的损失计算办法,因为金额会高得多。但会有情况是受害方没有预期利益或是证明不了预期利益,变成只能证明他自己为了这一合约的存在花了多少钱,向违约方取回。

在本章第一部分会针对的是上述所讲的预期利益与依赖利益,以及他们之间的关系与近年来的有关先例。

而本章接下去的第二部分是针对违约下的损失赔偿的类别,这主要就是在保护受害方的预期利益下的不同损失类别。主要是分三大类，第一类别是“基本金钱损失”(basic pecuniary losses)，第二类别是“间接金钱损失”(consequential pecuniary losses)，第三类别是“非金钱损失”(non - pecuniary losses)。其中会谈到哪一些是在一般违约下法律不承认的损失类别，原因会是公共政策或其他的理由。

2. 预期利益与依赖利益的区别

在本章第1段已经有涉及，就是一直以来的说法是受害方因违约而会蒙受的一类主要损失是“预期利益”(expectation interest)，一般是指若没有违约受害方本可以在此合约下期望获取利益的丧失。这些是如“市场价格的分别”(difference in value)、“利润损失”(loss of profit)、“交易损失”(loss of bargain)，甚至是“补救费用”(cost of cure)。这在商业合约是最常见与普遍的损失索赔是完全可以理解，因为商业合约就是为了利润，双方在订立这种合约时绝少会是没有什么预期的利益。所以，如果对方违约不履行，通常都可以计算这预期利益是什么，而因为对方违约就变成是受害方的预期利益丧失。这种损失计算办法是最正宗，也能完全体现“复原”的基本精神，即在先例 Robinson v. Harman(1848) 1 Exch. 850, Baron Parke 勋爵所说如下：“The rule of the common law is, that where a party sustains a loss by reason of a breach of contract, he is, so far as money can do it, to be placed in the same situation, with respect to damages, as if the contract had been performed.”(金钱来令受害方回到一个合约被履行的经济地位)。说到底，如果合约被顺利履行，受害方就会达到其预期的目标，也就是赚取他估计从合约会赚到的利润。

另一类是“依赖利益”(reliance interest)，针对“浪费的费用”(waste of expenditure)，是受害方因为依赖有此合约而花费，但因为对方违约而浪费的费用。这些费用会包括受害方投入/投资的机器/设备或厂房，以及其他相关的各种费用。这在一定程度上不是用“金钱来令受害方回到一个合约被履行的经济地位”，而是“回到一个合约从未存在的经济地位”(put into the position he would have been in had the contract never been made)，因为受害方本来不必花这笔钱。看来，这是接近侵权的损失计算原则，就是把受害方复原到侵权行为没有发生的地位。

此外，在特殊情况下受害方也可在以上两类损失计算办法外多考虑追偿另一类不严格是“损失”的“返还”(restitution)。这是剥夺违约方已得的利益，如受害方给违约方预付了的金钱。一个简单例子是受害方的买方预付了一部分钱但违约方的卖方没有如期付运货物。

针对预期利益与依赖利益，可以节录《Chitty on Contracts》(30th edn, 2008 年)之 26 - 002 段：“**‘Expectation’ and ‘reliance’ interests.** A distinction has been drawn between the ‘expectation interest’ and the ‘reliance interest’ of the claimant: the former relates to the gains or benefits which he expected to receive from the completion of the promised performance of the other party's obligation but which were in the event prevented by the breach of contract committed by the latter; the reliance interest relates to the expense or loss which the claimant has himself incurred in reliance on the promised performance and which is wasted by the defendant's breach. Both interests are protected by the law on damages, but it is not yet clear whether English law permits the claimant to recover both his expected profit on the contract and the consequential expense he has incurred in reliance on the defendant's promise. In principle, he should be entitled to recover his expected net profit plus any of his incidental expenditure of a type reasonably contemplated by the parties at the time the contract was made, but not his gross profit(e. g. the full contract price) plus his disbursements which would have been incurred in earning that gross profit."。

从上面的节录可以看到英国法律对这一方面还没有明确,其中一个问题就是原告是否可以同时索赔预期利益与依赖利益。另没有提到的也是类似方面,就是预期利益或依赖利益被当做是完全不同的两种类别,可让原告作出选择,导致在一些比较罕见的情况下,原告作为受害方可以得利。这方面的近期先例 The "Mamola Challenger"(2011)1 Lloyd's Rep 47 有了进一步的发展。

以下会对以上利益种类加以分析来寻找真正的"复原"精神。

3. 预期利益

违约损失赔偿很大程度上可以说是对受害方"交易应得"的赔偿,毕竟双方订约都是为了牟利、为了从合约中得利。一方违约会给另一方带来的最直接、最常见的损失自然也就是受害方本可从合约获取的利益的损失,即预期利益的损失。可以说,绝大部分的违约损失索赔都是针对预期利益的。

比方说,A 与 B 签约从 B 处购买货物,货价是 500 元。到了交货日 B 拒绝交货,当时市场货价升到 600 元。不论 A 有否从市场另买进替代货物,他都可以向 B 索赔 100 元,因为这是他本可在 B 履约的情况下从合约中获取的利益。如果 B 履约,A 本可以在交货时拥有市值 600 元的货物,转售或是自用都可获取 100 元的利益。或者换一个角度看,现在他就要花多 100 元才能从市场上买到他原来所期望得到的相同的货物来替代。因此 B 赔偿 100 元给 A,这笔钱也是 A 的预期利益的损失,才能使 A 恢复至如同合约被履行的经济地位。

3.1 常见预期利益损失的例子与说法

预期利益的损失可以随便举出很多例子,例如:(1)买卖合约中一方违约/毁约造成另一方蒙受的针对买卖标的(货物、船舶、土地、房屋以及股票等)的市场价格与合约价格间的差价损失。(2)运输合约中承运方违约延迟交货造成货物在应交付日与实际交付日之间的跌价损失(The "Heron Ⅱ"[1967]2 Lloyd's Rep 457);又或者货物并无市场,只是用于自用,如某个生产设备、机器(承运人订约前清楚知道货主的经营业务、货物的生产),则延迟交货造成生产厂家(货方)丧失了在延迟期间若投入这台设备本可正常获取的合理生产利润(Hadley v. Baxendale[1854]9 Ex 341;Victoria Laundry v. Newman Industries(1949)2 K. B. 528)。(3)雇佣合约中雇员被非法解雇而带来的工资收入损失。(4)租船合约中承租人违约/毁约造成船东的运费或租金收入损失;船东违约/毁约不提供船舶而造成承租人另找高价替代船舶而蒙受的原租约与替代租约间的运费或租金差价等。(5)其他服务合约中被服务方违约/毁约造成服务方预期利润的丧失,如一方订约替另一方包办酒席,或者代销热门产品、代做广告等,如果对方违约/毁约,自然会造成该方预期利润的损失。(6)财产、房屋与租赁合约中一方违约/毁约造成另一方高价租赁替代标的差价损失等。

以上这些都可以统称为预期利益的损失。因此,预期利益是一个很广泛的概念,也充分体现了双方订约就是为了牟利的这一本质。而违约方没有实质履行合约的第一个责任,就需要履行合约的第二个责任,这就是以金钱赔偿让受害方回到合约被履行的地位。

预期利益通常是由原告也就是受害方作出证明,在程度上只要达到"平衡的可能性"(balance of probabilities)。也就是法院或者仲裁庭在平衡了所有的因素之后,认为有超过50%的可能性,即可以判原告胜诉。

针对预期利益,在澳洲最高院的先例 Commonwealth of Australia v. Amann Aviation (1991)66 ALJR 123,Mason 与 Dawson 大法官是说:

"The general rule at common law, as stated by Parke B. in Robinson v. Harman, is 'that where a party sustains a loss by reason of breach of contract, he is, so far as money can do it, to be placed in the same situation, with respect to damages, as if the contract had been performed'. This statement of principle has been accepted and applied in Australia.

The award of damages for breach of contract protects a plaintiff's expectation of receiving the defendant's performance. That expectation arises out of or is created by the contract. Hence, damages for breach of contract are often described as 'expectation damages'. The onus of proving damages sustained lies on a plaintiff and the amount of damages awarded will be commensurate with the plaintiff's expectation, objectively determined, rather than subjectively ascertained. That is to say, a plaintiff must prove, on the balance of probabilities, that his or her expectation of a certain outcome, as a result of performance of the contract, had a likelihood of attainment rather than being mere expectation.

In the ordinary course of commercial dealings, a party supplying goods or rendering services will enter into a contract with a view to securing a profit, that is to say, that party will expect a certain margin of gain to be achieved in addition to the recouping of any expenses reasonably incurred by it in the discharge of its contractual obligation. It is for this reason that expectation damages are often described as damages for loss of profits. Damages recoverable as lost profits are constituted by thecombination of expenses justifiably incurred by a plaintiff in the discharge of contractual obligations and any amount by which gross receipts would have exceeded those expenses. This second amount is the net profit."

3.2 必须避免受害方获得重复赔偿

如果允许受害方索赔依赖利益，再加上预期利益，经常会带来"重复赔偿"(double compensation)。毕竟，受害方为了赚取合约的利润，即使是一切顺利，他也要承担这些费用。所以他在预期利益中的利润损失索偿，只应是"净利润"(net profit)或"净价格"(net value)，而不是"毛利润"(gross profit)。但如果再包括依赖利益(浪费的费用)岂非又让受害方得回毛利润? 世界上哪有不付代价就获得利润的好事。因此，如果允许受害方同时获得两者的赔偿，等于是让受害方不付任何代价就赚取到合约预期利益，让他不当得利，这显然是行不通的。举一些简单的例子，如买卖合约下卖方违约不交货，当时市场货价涨了，买方当然可以索赔市价损失，这是一种预期利益的损失，是买方本可以在合约中获取的差价利润的丧失。但如果同时还要索赔开信用证，办货物进口手续所花的(也可以说是因为卖方违约浪费掉的)费用，那就显然讲不通了。因为这些费用是买方要获得合约差价利润本来就要花费的、他有权依约赚取的差价利润中已加入了这些支出，不可能重复索赔。又比如期租中租家毁约，船东不能既索赔租金差价损失，又索赔船员的工资、伙食支出以及船舶的正常维修保养费等，因为后者是船东为了赚取租金必须付出的花费，已包含在租金收入这项毛利润中。程租船也一样，船东把船开到装港，结果租家无货提供，那么船东也不能既索赔该航次总的运费收入损失(当然要扣减该航次不用履行省下的燃油费等)，又索赔船开往装港所花掉的燃油、港口费等，因为船东要赚取运费，后者的花费是免不了的。

这里也另可节录 Re Daniel(1917)2 Ch 405 先例，案情涉及了土地/房子买卖，但卖方不转让，判是买方可以索赔违约的损失，但不能包括他所花的调查土地/房子的物权调查费用。法院是这样说："即使是卖方没有违约把土地/房子转让，买方还是要花这笔钱"(if they had had the property conveyed to them, of course they would have had to incur all the expense of investigating the title)。

另在 The "Mamola Challenger"(2011)1 Lloyd's Rep 47 先例中，Teare 大法官也有说："In a typical claim for damages for breach of contract on the expectancy basis both expected profits and necessary expenses will be taken into account. The claimant will claim a sum equal to the benefit he expected to earn from performance of the contract less the costs he would have had to have incurred in order to earn that benefit, which costs would include not only any sum he would have had to pay to the party in breach but also any expenses he would have had to incur in preparation for performance of the contract. Damages calculated in that way would put the claimant in the position he would have been in had the contract been performed. The measure of loss thus compensates for the loss of bargain and in doing so takes account of the expenses the claimant would have incurred in reliance on the contract being performed. To ignore those expenses when assessing damages would put the claimant in a better position than he would have been in had the contract been performed. Equally, if those expenses had already been incurred at the date on which the contract was repudiated, **to award those expenses in addition to damages for loss of bargain would put the claimant in a better position than he would have been in had the contract been performed.**"

举一个简单的例子,A 是需要花一些订约前与订约后的"使费"(expenditures)或作出一些投资才能在一个供应或服务的合约中赚取 100 元的预期利益。这使费包括了 5 元给经纪人,另要花费 15 元的成本购买有关机器/设备才能做出相关供应或服务,另有关的设备需要在合约履行期间总共约 25 元的维修保养费用等,这些都需要扣减才能得出纯利润,并向违约的 B 提出索赔。

但现实中总会出现不容易计算损失的案件,如有关的机器/设备或厂房寿命是 5 年,但合约只有 2 年,所以违约也只能是有 2 年的预期利益。又或是投入的资金涉及部分使用在土地的购买,土地是有更长的使用寿命,甚至会增值。这一来如何扣减以计算出预期利益/利润的损失会富争议性。但大原则还是相对简单,就是必须避免在违约中让受害方获得重复的赔偿。

稍后在本章会有另段多举在这方面的有关先例。

3.3 投资仲裁的重复赔偿

"投资仲裁"(investment arbitration)在近年来是一个热门的仲裁类别,简单说,就是外国投资者向接受投资的主权国家直接提出索赔,原因是后者没有保障外国的投资者,甚至把有关的投资没收/充公/收归国有,关于这个话题可以详见杨良宜、莫世杰和杨大明合著的《仲裁法——从 1996 年英国仲裁法到国际商务仲裁》(法律出版社 2006 年版)一书的第一章第三节"外国投资协议仲裁"。这种投资很多是涉及长期投资,导致了损失的计算并不容易,往往要依赖专家证人以提高可信度以及把受害方的"争辩"(submissions)提升为"证据"(evidence)。外国投资者作为原告的损失通常是有两种:第一种就是依赖利益的损失,也就是他投放进去的投资;第二种就是预期利益的损失,也就是长期投资预期能够赚取的利润的损失。显然,长期投资预期的利润是完全靠推测或估计,一般使用的办法就是"贴现现金流"(Discount Cash Flow),把将来估计会遇到的通货膨胀与会减低预期利益的各种风险等扣减。这方面会在本书第十八章进一步讨论,只说由于这种计算办法涉及长时间与庞大的金额,所以扣减的数字(主要靠估计)只要有小小偏差,就已经会带来很大索赔金额的差异。但在本小段,主要探讨的是重复赔偿的问题。

在 Michael Pryles 教授的《Lost Profit and Capital Investment》一文,他提到在投资仲裁,有不少的索赔与争议是把原告所作出的投资金额加上预期的利润作为损失的索赔，但这就会带来重复赔偿的危险。有关文章的段节是："On the basis of such a statement one might presume that the correct method for determining damages is to:(a) calculate the amount spent by the claimant in performing the contract;(b) calculate any profit the claimant expected to receive;and(c) add the two together. Indeed it is not uncommon to find legal argument advocating such an approach. However, it is in fact the cause of one of the fundamental errors committed in damages calculations: double counting."

在同一文章内，提到了一个非常著名的投资仲裁名为 Karaha Bodas Co v. Perusahaan Pertambangan Minyak Das Gas Bumi Negara 364 F. 3d 274(5th Cir. 2004)。案情涉及在苏哈托总统时代所签下的一个合约，是印尼的 Pertamina(国家石油公司)与 P. T. PLN(Persero)(印尼国家电力公司)跟一家有美国背景的开曼群岛(Cayman Island)公司 Karaha Boda Company LLC(KBC)签了两个有关能源供应/供电(高达 400mw)的合约，时为 30 年之久，以美元支付。在 1997 年的亚洲金融危机后，印尼经济严重受创，电力需求大幅度减少并且币值下跌(相对美元就要支付更大的一笔钱)，而苏哈托总统也开始失势，儿子则被拘捕。两个合约再也无法履行，被印尼政府终断。而美国公司也就开始瑞士仲裁对付 PLN、Pertamina 与印尼政府，向其索赔约 30 年的损失。损失的总金额是 96,000,000 美元的"浪费的费用"(waste of expenditure)即依赖利益的损失，再加上 512,500,000 美元的利润损失即预期利益的损失。最后仲裁庭判是 KBC 可以成功索赔 111,100,000 美元加上 150,000,000 美元的预期利益。但这一裁决带来争议与批评，在文章中 Michael Pryles 教授认为是作出了重复赔偿，因为任何对一个计划的投资都是为了提供将来的利润。如果有关的计划顺利获得履行并取得预期的履约，通常是原来的投资也就类似于投进去的本钱而失去了。如果有关的投资如在本案件是能源供应/发电厂房与设备能够在 30 年后还有一些剩余价值，这往往也是微不足道，与本来的投资金额不能相比。而如果这剩余价值因为在 30 年后有一些特殊的情况变得十分值钱，这也通常是在双方订约时不会合理预见的。而在该案件的有关合约中，更加有条文说明是在 30 年后，有关的厂房与设备是归被告的印尼公司所拥有。这更加明确表示了 KBC 不应该索赔投资所花的费用作为依赖利益的损失，否则是重复赔偿。从另一个角度看，如果可以成功索赔投资的钱加上利润，原告在理论上可以把同一笔投资的钱在另外一个国家作出同样的投资并赚取利润，这表示原告只是通过花同一笔的钱或成本，可以获得两次的预期利益。这明显是不正确的损失计算。Michael Pryles 教授在该文章是这样说："The double counting problem arises from the tribunal's decision to award *damnum emergens*(这是费用损失或依赖利益的拉丁文) in addition to *lucrum cessans*(这是预期利益的拉丁文). This is problematic because, in projects such as this, from an economics perspective, the real value of an investment is usually its ability to generate a stream of profits over the lifetime of the project. Once the contract has lived its natural life, the expenses incurred in reliance on the contract are rarely recovered. Rather, they form part of an investment that is considered worthwhile in light of expected profits. If assets can be sold, they usually attract only a fraction of their initial value."

4. 依赖利益

已经说过,依赖利益的损失是指依赖有此合约而花费的金钱,因违约而浪费掉。举例是:(1)卖方毁约不交货,买方因此而浪费了的开信用证、办进口手续等费用。(2)FOB 买卖中,买方依约派船到了装港,结果卖方交不出货,买方派船来空跑一次的费用与损失(如作为承租人要对船东承担的毁约责任)。但由于违约时有关货物的市场价格下跌,买方很容易以更便宜的价格从市场买进替代货物,所以受害方的买方根本没有蒙受任何预期利益的损失,唯一的损失就是这一笔船舶空放的费用的依赖利益损失。(3)CIF 卖方租了船,把货运给了买方,但买方违约/毁约拒收。(4)在二手船买卖,卖方拒绝交船,或要非法敲一笔钱才肯交船,构成违约/毁约,买方所浪费的如派遣了全套船员到交船港(如中国的船员前往欧洲交接船港)、准备接船的费用,以及为买船而支出的其他合理费用如派人检查船舶才确认接受合约、代理费等。也会是受害的买方没有蒙受预期利益的损失,因为以同样价格在市场买进了另一艘姐妹船舶,导致买方唯一的损失就是上述所讲的依赖利益的损失。(5)程租下船舶到了装港,被承租人发觉违约(如不适航)导致过了销约期,承租人已花费了基于船舶应按期抵达去雇用的装货工人的费用、货物放在码头的仓租等。(6)船东在租约下空放去了装港,但承租人没有货装而违约/毁约,船东因此而花费的空放费用如燃油、代理费等。(7)在大型设备(如海上石油平台、导管等)的运输中,船东专门为其对船舶(如在甲板)进行了必要的改装,加强(如甲板下面加支撑)等,但结果承租人不履行运输合约。再次重复已经多番介绍过的假设情况,就是受害方的船东在承租人违约/毁约后,马上在市场上找到更高租金的替代运输合约。这导致了船东没有蒙受预期利益的损失,损失只是上述所讲的依赖利益损失。

这种浪费的费用,本来就是合约履行下必须要花费的,因为这些费用是要计算作为预期利益的纯利润本来就要扣减的。

一般应是合约订立前的费用不该包括在依赖利益,毕竟在如果合约谈不拢而未有订立时,这种费用亦应是花费掉而无法有补偿。但在特别情况(会是受害方合理估计有关合约肯定会订的下来,预先为合约的履行做准备),这种费用也可包括在依赖利益中,先例是在 Anglia TV Ltd. v. Reed(1972)1 QB 60。

该案原告(电视商)向被告演员索赔的花费费用,其实大部分在签约聘请被告出演主角前就产生了。签约前,原告就安排了拍片场地,聘请了导演、设计师以及舞台经理等。依约被告应于 9 月 9 日到 11 日出镜,但被告的经理人为他同时签订了两份时间有冲突的片约。结果 9 月 3 日被告正式通知原告将不参加拍片。9 月 11 日原告接受了被告的违约/毁约。同时努力寻找替代演员但未能如愿，最后只得放弃该片的拍摄。在法庭上，被告争辩，他只应对片约签订后原告花费的854英镑负责，其余款项是订约前产生的，原告不能追偿。上诉庭判定原告可获得全数2750英镑的赔偿，尽管大部分花费是在订约前发生的，法院指出，“订约前的花费”(pre-contract expenditure)虽然不是基于合约而产生，但原告无疑是依赖了会有此合约而放手花掉这些合约订立前的费用，原告也没有另找主角作后备直至时间太晚。

4.1 在什么情况下索赔依赖利益的损失

已经提到过常见的情况是违约索赔只针对预期利益的损失，而这些所谓的使费或成本，不论是已经花掉或者是预期履行合约需要合理花费的，都要扣减才能计算出纯利润。那么，什么情况下原告才会只索赔依赖利益的损失呢？这通常就是在一些原告作为受害方无法证明他有什么预期利益的情况。这可能是很难证明，因为利润损失太不肯定，或者合约本身是没有任何利润的。也会是违约后的市场变化导致了受害方没有蒙受损失，反而有了好处，正如在第4段介绍过的假设情况。这一来，如果索赔预期利益的损失，原告也只能取得“名义损失”(nominal damage)。如果原告是花了一笔使费准备履行该合约，但因为被告的违约/毁约而浪费掉，在这种情况下，原告就会有诱因索赔依赖利益的损失。

正如Denning勋爵在Anglia TV Ltd. v. Reed(1972)1 Q. B. 60所明确下来：“If he(原告)has not suffered any loss of profits or if he cannot prove what his loss of profit would have been he can claim in the alternative the expenditure which has been thrown away, that is wasted by reason of the breach.”

在《McGregor on Damages》(18th edn, 2009年)之2-021段也说：“The circumstances which compel a claimant to proceed for his out-of-pocket expenses instead of for his loss of bargain are the difficulty and uncertainty in proving the amount of the benefit that would have accrued to him from the bargain.”

4.2 原告很难证明预期利益或者有关合约是没有利润的情况

表面看来，这种情况不大会发生，因为商业合约是为了赚钱，不会有人订一个预期亏本的合约。但这种情况还是有的，只是不多。更有可能会发生的是会有预期利益，但很难证明。而法律是要求原告根据平衡的可能性证明他的损失。这表示在一些很难证明(如投机性或变数太多)的情况下，难以达到51%以上的平衡可能性要求证明会有这种损失。

这方面可举一些先例，如Sapwell v. Bass(1910)2 K. B. 486一案。在该先例，被告破坏一个涉及纯种马交配的合约，判是原告有关可能丧失的幼马利润的损失是太不肯定。

在McRae v. Commonwealth Disposals Commission(1951)84 C. L. R. 377先例，有关的合约涉及被告卖给了原告在澳洲海域搁浅的一艘油轮的残骸与该船上剩余的石油货物。这导致了原告花了3000英镑雇用一队人寻找该油轮，但没有找到并估计没有这一艘油轮的残骸存在。针对原告向被告索赔的预期利益的损失,法院判原告索赔300,000英镑的油轮残骸与石油价值“太可笑”(manifestly absurd)而被否定。判决被告只是赔偿给原告所花的费用3000英镑(依赖利益)加上之前付给被告的285镑(“返还利益”[restitutionary interest])。

较早提到的Anglia TV. Ltd. v. Reed(1972)1 Q. B. 60,亦是原告很难证明预期利益,因为原告根本无法说出或计算出预期利益,更不用说证明如果被告履约演出,该片拍成后会挣取多少利润。

确是有一些高风险、高投机的生意,无法事先估量,也没有同类市场或经历量度,就像一些近海石油勘探开采合约,石油公司与沿海国政府或属下主管公司签订该国领海或专属经济区内的石油开发合约,对石油公司来讲就是一项风险极高的投资。如可能勘探到有经济价值的油区,打井采油,与对方政府或其主管公司分成利润,但也很可能花了一大笔钱进行勘探,结果并未发现有油区或油区开采的经济价值很低,而被迫放弃继续投资,事实上等于在这项合约亏了本,并无得益(中国南海油田的开发初期就有不少这种外国石油公司最后找不到有价值油区而亏本的例子)。投资聘演员拍电影,请作者著书出版也是一样,电影卖不卖座,书畅不畅销,事先很难科学估算。如果这部电影或著作本来也不是作为盈利用途,则会是更加明显没有或证明不了预期利益。这类风险高的合约,对于风险投资的一方(如石油公司、电影商或出版商等)来说,他能否从合约获利是要等到合约履行到一定阶段甚至非要双方履行完毕之后一段时间才能明确的。所以如果对方(如沿海国政府、演员或作家等)事前或中途违约/毁约,受害方是很可能很难举证有什么利润损失要索赔的。这一来,受害方如果只能取回名义损失,可以说,根本就不值得打这一场官司。

但是,如果受害方确实基于这份合约而花费了合理与对方订约时可预见的准备或履行费用,他仍是可以通过索赔违约损失获得补偿的。这就是我们这里要讲的受害方索赔损失的另项选择——“依赖利益的损失赔偿”(a claim for reliance loss)。受害方可以以这种索赔取回他因为对方违约而浪费掉的基于合约而产生的费用。就像刚才所举的石油勘探例子,如果沿海国政府违约/毁约,合约下有责任,那石油公司最起码可以索赔回他白白花费掉的有关勘探设备投入等的费用,加上利息。

原告受害方可以把预期利益或利润损失作为首要的救济,同时把依赖利益或浪费费用作为“替代”(alternate)的救济,这就在不肯定的案件中比较万无一失。如果漏掉或太迟提出都会有危险,例如在North Sea Energy Holdings v. Petroleum Authority of Thailand(1997)2 Lloyd’s Rep. 418先例,就涉及受害方在开庭结束之后才在结案陈词中提出一个替代的损失计算办法。这被法院否定,因为除了提出的时间太晚外,替代的损失计算也没有证据,而因为开庭完毕后是不可能再来一次的处理证据。至于为什么这么晚提出替代损失计算或救济办法,一个可能是受害方开庭后感觉对自己不利才觉得有必要提出,也有可能是代表律师的疏忽,还会有其他的可能性,但不必理会了。Thomas大法官是这样说:“In their written closing submissions, MSH(受害方)first advanced a different alternative basis for their claim. They contended that if, contrary to their primary submission, they could not recover damages by reference to the Magoil offer(特别损失), they were nonetheless entitled to the loss of profits(普通损失)that would have normally arisen... However, it is not necessary for me to decide whether I would have shut out this alternative basis on the grounds that it was not raised until a very late stage of the trial. This is because there was no evidence before me on which I could possibly have made an assessment of a reasonable profit on this long term supply contract for Arabian crude."

5. 预期利益与依赖利益是两种完全不同选择的救济

针对这两种不同的损失计算办法,在一连串的先例中发展出一种说法是它们是完全不同的与相对独立的类别,而原告的受害方是有权选择其中一种作出索赔。其中一个重要的先例是 Cullinane v. British "Rema" Manufacturing Co(1954)1 QB 292 CA,上诉庭判原告可以提出索赔预期利益的损失或者依赖利益的损失(不论是订约前或订约后会花费的费用)其中一种,但不能两种同时索赔或混合在一起。Evershed 勋爵是这样说:"As a matter of principle also it seems to me that a person who has obtained a machine... which was unable to perform a particular function which it was warranted to perform may adopt one of two courses. He may... claim to recover the capital loss he has incurred... A claim of that kind puts the plaintiff in the same position as though he had never made the contract at all... But, alternatively... he may, in my judgement, make his claim on the basis of the profit which he has lost because the machine as delivered fell short in its performance of that which it was warranted to do..."

该先例把这两种损失计算办法区分为两个选择,在上述先例 Anglia TV Ltd. v. Reed(1972)1 Q. B. 60 中,Denning 勋爵也表示过这两种损失计算办法可以互相替代,并且由原告选择,更加显示了它们属于不同的救济。因为一涉及选择,就表示这两者是不可混合与不协调的。

另在《McGregor on Damages》(18th edn,2009 年)有多段曾说过这两种损失计算办法是基于两种"不同的基础"(different basis),其中在 2-018 段说:"It is important to notice in all the above cases that not only must the defendant be credited with the amount that the claimant has saved by no longer having to perform his side of the bargain, but the claimant cannot also recover, in addition to the basic loss which is intended to represent the loss of his bargain, any expenses he has incurred in preparation or in part performance. Such expenses represent part of the price that the claimant has to incur to secure his bargain. If he recovers for the loss of his bargain, it would be inconsistent that he should in addition recover for expenses which were necessarily laid out by him for his attainment."

另在 2 - 020 段说:"Sometimes, however, the claimant may be compelled by circumstances to frame his suit on a different basis as to damages, not on the basis of the loss of his bargain but on the basis of his out - of - pocket loss. In other words, he is claiming not to be put into the position he would have been in had the contract been performed, but to be put into the position he would have been in had it never been made, which is a normal measure of damages akin to that in tort. In such cases expenses incurred in preparation or in part performance will be properly recoverable and will not involve an inconsistency of compensation."

最后节录 2 - 032 段说:"Just as expenses rendered futile by the breach may generally be claimed as an alternative to the normal measure of damages, so they may also be claimed as an alternative to recovering for gains prevented by the breach. Again it is important to realise that such expenses form an alternative and not an additional head of damage, since they represent part of the price that the claimant was to incur in order to secure the gain. Sometimes this may have been lost sight of, and a double recovery involving an inconsistency of compensation allowed. This may have happened, for example, in Hydraulic Engineering Co v. McHaffie (1878) 4 QBD 670 CA where, on the defendant's failure to deliver on time a particular part of a machine that was designed to be used by the claimant in making the whole machine for a third party, the claimant recovered both the expense incurred in making the machine and the profits which he lost when the third party refused to take the machine because of its not being ready on time. Only if the profits claimed were net of the expense incurred would there be no double recovery, but whether the judgments are referring to gross or net profits cannot be culled from the report."

由原告选择的说法,在《McGregor on Damages》(18th edn, 2009 年)之 2 - 024 段说:"The situation, however, has since become much clearer. The Court of Appeal in Anglia Television v. Reed (1972) 1 QB 60 CA where the issue was whether the claimants could recover pre - contractual as well as post - contractual expenditure, accepted without argument that a claimant is entitled to claim for expenses rendered futile, and in CCC Films (London) v. Impact Quadrant Films (1985) QB 16, Hutchison J. held that a claim claiming damages for breach of contract had an unfettered choice to claim one measure or the other."

6. 依赖利益的索赔不能与预期利益同时提出以避免重复赔偿

6.1 这方面的权威案例与说法

本章较早前在 3. 2 与 3. 3 段已经提到了损失的计算一定要避免重复赔偿,这方面主要的先例是在 Cullinane v. British“Rema” Manufacturing Co(1954)1 QB 292 CA，案情涉及原告向被告购买一座粉碎粘土的机器，在合约中被告有保证粉碎的速度，但事实上被发现做不到，这等于是被告的卖方违约。原告向被告提出索赔，第一笔的依赖利益的损失是购买该机器的成本加上利息，但减掉折旧与尚未支付的部分货价。同时，原告索赔第二笔的预期利益的损失，也就是利润损失。但利润损失只局限在前三年，这三年是扣取成本的利息、3 年的折旧、维修保养费用等。但由于该机器的估计使用年龄高达 10 年，原告等于在后来的 7 年索赔的就是第一笔的依赖利益的损失。这样的混合索赔被上诉庭的多数意见所拒绝，Evershed MR 大法官是这样说："By stating that his claim for lost profit was limited to three years, he was not, in my judgment, then entitled to claim (as he, admittedly, could not claim if he had not placed the limitation on the profit) both for loss of capital and for loss of profit. Upon the question whether the plaintiff could have claimed for loss of profit up to the date of the hearing and have claimed an additional sum because he was at that date left with a machine which was less valuable than the machine as warranted, I say only that the plaintiff has not so claimed. If he had done so, the second part of the claim would appear to be no more than a method of computing profit for the possible profit – earning period after the date of the hearing."

这一个属于多数意见的上诉庭先例有争议之处，例如在《McGregor on Damages》(18th edn，2009 年)之 2 – 038 段是说："To the extent, therefore, that the claim in Cullinane was in respect of net profit together with capital outlay attributable to the first three years of user, it was not a claim split between the two available measures but a claim directed only at recovering for gains prevented by the breach of contract. It might then be argued that the claim in respect of the capital outlay for the remaining seven years of useful life should be acceptable because, although in one sense a claim based on the alternative measure, it could once again be regarded as a claim for potential loss of profit up to the limit of the claimant's capital expenditure. While this would appear to be acceptable to Morris LJ (这是上诉庭持不同意见的大法官) who dissented, the High Court of Australia may well be right in saying in TC Industrial Plant Pty v. Robert's Queensland Pty (1964) 37 A. L. J. R. 289 that: 'the justification for the refusal of the majority of the court in Cullinane's case to follow such a course lies, we venture to think, in the fact that since nothing was proved about the probable amount of the profits that would have been made in the final seven years of the machine's life, and therefore nothing about any probable excess of profits during the whole ten years of the machine's life over amounts of depreciation equalling the total capital cost, the plaintiff failed to show that the damages assessed on the loss – of – profits basis would be greater than damages assessed by reference to capital expenditure and interest.'"

但 Cullinane 先例的说法是需要看个别的案件，因为主要的精神是为了避免重复赔偿而不是说依赖利益损失的索赔绝对不能与预期利益损失同时提出。这里可以先节录《McGregor on Damages》(18th edn,2009 年)之 2 - 041 段如下:"That *Cullinane* must not be carried too far is well illustrated by two recent cases. The claimants in Browning v. Brachers(2005) EWCA Civ 753 ran a business of rearing goats on their farm. In their claim against the defendant for selling them a diseased goatherd, *Cullinane* was invoked to argue that they could not claim both for the resultant diminution in the value of the farm and for the resultant loss of profits. The argument was rejected both at trial and by the Court of Appeal. Such a claim could not involve double counting as the claimants had two distinct assets, the business and the farm, so that a combination of compensation for the revenue loss of profits and the capital loss in the value of the farm was appropriate. Somewhat similar is 4 Eng Ltd v. Harper(2009) Ch. 91 where the claimant, deceived into buying share capital in a worthless company, would but for the deceit have bought the share capital in a different company. It was held that there was no inconsistency in claiming for the loss of the income profits he would have made from the other company and the capital profit that would have been realised by its acquisition. Indeed in neither Browning nor 4 Eng was the claim being made for wasted expenditure and for the alternative measure; so Cullinane could have no application whatsoever. Counsel should not be bemused by Cullinane to thinking that claims for loss of income profits and loss of capital profits must be alternative and not cumulative."

上述节录部分提到的两个不同判法的先例会在接下去的段节中介绍。

6.2　不同判法先例之一:Browning v. Brachers

《McGregor on Damages》(18th edn,2009 年)提到了两个近期先例 Browning v. Brachers(2005)EWCA Civ 753 和 4 Eng Ltd v. Harper(2009)Ch. 91,可进一步解释有关案情。首先在 Browning v. Brachers 先例,案情涉及经常发生的律师疏忽处理案件被前客户索赔损失。被疏忽处理案件是前客户 Browning 夫妻在 1991 年 3 月向一位 Gilham 先生购买了一群山羊以及相关业务,以扩大原告在这方面的业务。但这一群山羊有一种名为"副结核性肠炎"(Johne's disease)的疾病,导致原告自己的山羊也被感染。这种疾病传染性十分厉害,对不超过 6 个月大的小山羊尤其致命。另是这一疾病的细菌有很长的潜伏期,可以长达 7 年,并可以在草原生存而感染给其他吃草的动物。遇上这种不幸的牧场能够解决的办法不多,一种是把所有的山羊全部一并处理并把受感染的牧场关闭两年以上,希望令细菌灭绝。另一种是为所有的山羊注射疫苗,但这种疫苗只有针对其他家畜有效的经验,没有针对山羊的记录,而且价钱不便宜。在该先例中,Browning 夫妻在疾病爆发后继续营运牧场,但在其间有大量的山羊死亡或被出售,而且生产的山羊奶产量也大幅度降低,导致了 Browning 夫妻需要向其他牧场购买山羊奶以供应他们的客户而蒙受损失。而在牧场的利润损失,证据是显示了:"In the following year, with emergence of the disease, profit before interest fell by £ 13,404 to a loss of £ 4,394 in 1991/2. Once Mr and Mrs Browning were able to effect steps to mitigate their losses caused by Johne's disease profitability improved and continues to do so."

在较早被疏忽处理的诉讼先是由 Gilham 先生向 Browning 夫妻索赔他被欠下的购买山羊的余下对价，而 Browning 夫妻在成功申请法律援助后委任 Brachers 为代表律师，提出了一笔更大的反索赔，但 Brachers 律师因为疏忽没有把 Browning 夫妻的反索赔有关证据及时提出，导致反索赔被法院撤销。这最终导致了在本先例，Browning 夫妻作为原告向被告的 Brachers 律师索赔这一笔损失。看来，被告的疏忽在责任方面没有争议，主要还是在赔偿方面。这里涉及两方面的考虑，第一步是考虑如果这一反索赔没有被撤销，到底会是多少金额？由于在较早的诉讼，法院根本没有做出审理与判决，所以在本先例法院只能是估计如果反索赔不被撤销并且能够成功，估计会是多少钱。第二步是明确了这笔反索赔的合理金额后，也就是 Browning 夫妻在本先例的损失索赔，才考虑反索赔成功的可能性，也就是计算原告的"机会损失"（loss of chance）。这一课题在本书第六章有详论，在这里不重复。只说 Browning 夫妻肯定会面对败诉或者反索赔金额只能部分取回的诉讼风险，毕竟再也不能知道 Gilham 先生会提出什么抗辩。而估计会提出副结核性肠炎的细菌来源是来自 Browning 夫妻从第三人牧场购买的山羊（因为 Browning 夫妻也有向另一家牧场购买山羊与业务），而不是来自 Gilham 先生的山羊也不能说是绝对没有成功的机会。再说是 Browning 夫妻在疾病爆发后有否合理减少损失也会有争议之处。所以，在该先例中法院判是有30% 机会损失，也就是 Browning 夫妻作为原告只能向 Brachers 律师索赔 70% 反索赔的合理金额。

什么是反索赔的合理金额在本先例中是更不容易认定，就要先提到 Browning 夫妻的五项索赔中包括其中的两项，一是"利润损失"（loss of profit），这根据专家证人的估计是从 1991/2 年到 2008/9 年，长达 18 年之久时间内整体牧场的利润损失是高达 1，308，215 英镑。二是"资本价值的减少"（diminution in capital value），也就是整个 Browning 夫妻的牧场、业务与客户关系因副结核性肠炎这一种疾病而导致贬值，金额估计为 261，180 英镑。而这两项索赔从表面看来会有重复赔偿的危险，因为对不少的业务如一个厂房或一台机器，赚取将来的利润，资本价值的减少是避免不了。同时索赔，就会有重复赔偿的危险。

在第一审与上诉庭，都不认为有重复赔偿的问题。因为在本先例中副结核性肠炎这一种疾病是分别带来了 Browning 夫妻在业务上的利润损失与牧场的资本价值的减少，不存在重叠的问题。其中上诉庭的 Jonathan Parker 大法官说："The judge（这是指第一审的大法官）would then have had to consider whether he should make a further award because the land, the herd and the goodwill of the business were reduced in value by reason of infection with Johne's disease. Citing Cullinane v. British Rema Manufacturing Co Ltd [1954] 1 Q. B. 292 Mr Croxford（被告代表大律师）submitted that Mr and Mrs Browning could not claim for loss in value and loss of profits. I accept that a claimant who buys a defective machine usually cannot claim both the drop in value of the machine by reason of the defect and the loss of the profits which he would have made if the machine had not been defective: for he would have had to purchase the machine to make the profits. I think that there is here an argument, with a fair chance of success, that the claim here is different. It is that the goats were infected, and this had two consequences: it lowered the earnings from the combined herd; it also reduced the value of the combined herd, the land and the goodwill of the business. In short, if a defendant gives the claimant's farm a disease which lowers his profits and reduces the value of his land etc, he has suffered loss under both heads and to include both is not double counting..."

但法院把 Browning 夫妻索赔的金额大幅度减少，如在利润损失，18 年的估计被大幅度减少到只有 6 年(从 1992 年到 1998 年)，而第一审是在 1996 年，换言之是多估计 2 年的利润损失。这可能是因为已经知道结果的 4 年中，牧场所受到的影响已经降低，做出长达 18 年的利润损失估计实在过度。另在资本价值的减少，法院也认为有关的业务与客户关系不是一个很重要的因素，而且名誉也很快在恢复，所以只是做出 15,000 英镑的牧场价值贬值赔偿。

6.3 不同判法先例之二:4 Eng Ltd v. Harper

在《McGregor on Damages》(18th edn, 2009 年)一书提到的另一个先例是 4 Eng Ltd v. Harper(2009) Ch. 91，案情涉及了"欺诈性误述"(fraudulent misrepresentation)，就是被告把一家名为 Excel 的工程业务公司出售给原告的 4 Eng Ltd，对价为£ 1,200,000。在谈判的过程与被告提供的文件中，显示了 Excel 的主要客户是一家名为 Mars 的英国公司。当原告把公司购买并接管过来后，才发觉被告以前在一段很长的时间中通过贿赂 Mars 的员工，以虚假或夸大的发票向 Mars 收取了高达£ 1,800,000 的钱，这笔钱估计在事发后是要退还给 Mars 的。这表示原告以为收购了一家价值£ 1,200,000 的公司，其实是一文不值的，而且原告也将会失去 Mars 这一重要的客户。换言之，被告先是欺骗了 Mars，后是欺骗了原告。

原告于是向被告提出索赔，而损失分为如下:(1)已经支付给了被告的部分对价£ 550,000。(2)收购所花的费用£ 72,370.50。(3)收购并接管 Excel 这一家公司后所要承担的责任，包括员工的工资、退休金与保费等，共计£ 384,651.08。(4)有关对 Mars 的欺诈长达 4 年的调查所花的费用£ 711,200。(5)丧失了收购另一家名为 Tarvail Ltd 的公司的机会导致估计利润与估计增值的损失。

以上的五项损失与本章有关系的只是第五项，Tarvail Ltd 是原告原先计划一并与 Excel 前后收购的两家公司，其中相隔是 3 个月。但由于先收购 Excel，并很快就出现问题(有关欺骗 Mars 的事实)，这使原告很快就陷入经济困境并且得不到银行的支持，最终导致了无法收购 Tarvail Ltd。而原告第五项的索赔就是他失去了如果成功收购 Tarvail Ltd 能够赚取的利润与 Tarvail Ltd 的增值。这一来，即使索赔能够成功，也存在能够赚取的利润作为预期利益与增值能否一并提出，有否重复赔偿的危险之争。David Richards 大法官认为不存在有重复赔偿，说:"The reasoning in Cullinane v.

British ‘Rema’ Manufacturing Co Ltd(1954)1 QB 292 is not applicable to the facts of this case. The claim for capital loss as it relates to Tarvail is not for a loss of capital in acquiring Tarvail. It is the reverse. It is for a loss of the opportunity to make a capital profit as a result of the acquisition of Tarvail which would be in addition to the income profits which 4 Eng would have derived from Tarvail during its period of ownership. The inability to acquire Tarvail which resulted from the defendants' deceit deprived 4 Eng of both those income profits and a capital profit realisable by it on a sale as at the date of trial. Unlike Cullinane's case they are cumulative, not alternative, losses. The fact that the capital value of Tarvail is estimated by reference to anticipated future earnings is irrelevant. It is not the capital value of past earnings; if it were, there would of course be double recovery. Past earnings are used by the valuer only for the purpose of establishing maintainable earnings for the future, thereby providing the figure to which the p/e ratio can be applied. The income profits assumed to have been extracted by 4 Eng during its period of ownership are not reflected at all in the capital value of Tarvail."

换言之,原告是可以向被告同时索赔 Tarvail Ltd 的估计增值与利润。这里也可以顺便一提的是英国法律对欺诈是十分敌视与严格,所以对欺诈所导致的损失是不必理会损失类别是否可以预见。故此,被告是不能抗辩说他在订约时无法预见原告的计划是同时收购 Tarvail Ltd。这方面 David Richards 大法官是这样说:"The foreseeability of a loss is irrelevant in the award for deceit, as the House of Lords established in Smith New Court Securities Ltd v. Scrimgeour Vickers (Asset Management) Ltd (1997) AC 254. A loss is too remote only if it is not in the eyes of the law directly caused by a defendant's deceit. Once it is accepted that the claimant would have purchased an alternative business, and is entitled to recover damages for the loss of profits which would have been earned during the period of ownership, why should the claimant not also recover for the loss of the capital profit in the rise of the value of the business? If the claimant had not been induced by the defendants' deceit to purchase their business, the claimant would have purchased an alternative business from which it would have benefited in two ways: first, it would have received profits from it while owning it and, secondly, it would have been able to sell the business at a profit over the price it had paid for it. Both are losses suffered by it was a direct result of the defendants' deceit."

7. 英国的近期先例明确依赖利益只是预期利益的分类

英国法律这方面有了一个很近期的先例 The "Mamola Challenger" (2011) 1 Lloyd's Rep 47。案情涉及该船舶被期租了 5 年,每天的租金是 13,700 美元。该租约条文要求船东在交船前对船舶作出一些改装，包括安装一个新的吊车。因此，船东在交船前就已经产生了不少费用。该租约是针对承租人再将船舶转租出去给一家尼日利亚公司，而转租是需要获得批准，但却没有及时获得。看来这就是一连串合约经常会出现的问题，就是没办法在同一时间把每一个合约敲定。这一来，夹在中间的当事人就会有风险，就是在第一个合约敲定后，但在下一个合约还需要批准或其他的先决条件没有满足时，没有办法同时敲定。但如果不把第一个合约敲定，又会存在一个问题，就是下一个合约敲定时就已经失去了第一个合约的机会。至于在第一个合约加上一个"后续条件"（condition subsequent）说明在下一个合约不成功时可以脱身，又可能会遇到对方的抗拒。

反正在该先例，船东就接受承租人的违约/毁约，把该5年的租约终断。估计船东这样做的原因之一是当时的租船市场比订约时更好，所以船东会掌握每一个机会终断合约，承租人的违约/毁约更是给船东提供了黄金机会。这就导致船东在接受违约/毁约后的替代营运，实际上比原来的5年期租赚得更多，每天租金高达21,347美元，显然船东是不会有预期利益的损失。但船东还是向承租人（也就是夹在当中的当事人）提出索赔，索赔的就是一些交船前改装的费用，金额高达675,000美元。由于承租人违约，这些费用变为是"浪费的费用"（wasted costs），因为这是依赖这一租约所花费的。承租人的抗辩自然是船东没有损失，因为终断租约后的替代租约赚的钱更多，足够抵销有余。但仲裁庭判是船东在替代租约下赚的钱不应该被考虑在内，根据先例是 C&P Haulage v. Middleton(1983)1 WLR 1461。有关裁决书部分是这样写的："[The expenses] were simply wasted as a result of the termination of the contract by the other party. The fact that the vessel might have been occupied in more gainful employment as a result of the termination of the Charterparty by the Charterers is not a matter to be brought into account on the authority of C&P Haulage v. Middleton (1983) 1 WLR 1461. The expenses, such as they were, were wasted in preparing for the Charterparty and were rendered irrecoverable not by any provision of the Charterparty but as a result of its termination. It seems to us that to take the Charterers' position and look at the net overall position is to mix this basis of claim with a claim based on the difference between contract and market rates inasmuch as the latter contains within it the concept of what the vessel should have earned overall from substitute employment as compared with what would have been earned under the Charterparty."

但这一裁决被批准上诉，并在高院被推翻。Teare大法官认为仲裁庭在法律方面犯了错，误以为预期利益与依赖利益是两类完全不同的损失计算办法，必须分开处理，即使是受害方可以恢复到比如果履行被终断合约更好的经济地位。这并不正确。Teare大法官在分析了一连串的先例（包括在美国、加拿大与澳洲的一些有关的先例）后，判基本上最重要的还是不能让受害方得到比他真正损失更大的赔付。他是这样说："I am not therefore persuaded that the right to choose or elect between claiming damages on an expectancy basis or on a reliance basis indicates that there are two different principles at work... This appears to be true and is the reason why both parties accepted that there was no binding authority as to the question which the Court has to decide. However, in circumstances where, for the reasons I have given, the weight of authority firmly suggests that an award of reliance damages is governed by the principle in Robinson v. Harman I consider that to award substantial damages, measured by wasted expenditure, where the Owners have, as a result of the Charterers' breach, been able to trade the vessel at the higher market rates and have 'more than recuperated' their loss, would be wrong in principle. Such an award would place the Owners in a better position than they would have been in had the contract been performed..."

该先例也有针对船东作为原告的争辩,如在一些根本没打算赚取利润的合约,这一来,就没理由不让受害方索赔浪费的费用。笔者想到的是一个慈善捐款合约(并假设这是一个有法律效力的合约),如果这个合约导致了接受捐赠的一方花钱做了一些准备,但承诺捐赠的一方违约/毁约。Teare 大法官说这种情况不会带来什么麻烦,因为被告如果抗拒这笔钱的索赔是不可能证明即使合约被履行,原告还是浪费这费用。他是这样说:"Mr. Brenton(船东的代表大律师)has a further criticism, namely, that there are many contracts where a party does not expect or aim to make a profit, such as where purchases are made for pleasure or for charitable purposes. He suggests that the expectancy basis would deny recovery of wasted expenditure in such cases. I disagree. In such cases the defendant will usually be unable to show that the expenses exceeded the benefit expected to be obtained from the contract and thus the expense will be recoverable as damages."

8. 依赖利益不能用来补救亏本生意

8.1 有关的英国先例

很明确的是,如果是"一盘亏本生意"(a bad bargain),即支出(履行的费用)大于收入(预期利润),受害方是不能说是无法证明而不索赔预期利益的损失,转而"选择"索赔依赖利益的损失。因为根据先例 The "Mamola Challenger"(2011)1 Lloyd's Rep 47,是不存在"选择"这一说法。举例说,较早所提的 McRae v. Commonwealth Disposals Commission(1951)84 C. L. R. 377 一案,如果油轮残骸与剩余的石油价值即使找到也不会超过2000 英镑,等于预期利益也只有 2000 英镑。这表示原告即使花了3000 英镑的费用也是自己做了亏本生意,而允许他索赔 3000 英镑的依赖利益损失等于帮他关了亏本的大门,把这亏本风险转嫁给了被告。这正是 Learned Hand 大法官所说的:"We cannot agree that the promisor's default in performance should under this guise make him an insurer of the promisee's venture..."

在上诉庭的 C. &P. Haulage v. Middleton(1983)1 WLR 1461 CA 先例,就涉及如果判受害方的原告能够从被告取回依赖利益,就会让原告恢复到比合约获得履行更好的经济地位。这不被上诉庭接受,Fox 大法官是这样说:"... it was equally likely to be wasted if there had been no breach, because the(licensors) wanted to get the(licensee) out and could terminate the licence at quite short notice. A high risk of waste was from the very first inherent in the nature of the contract itself, breach or no breach. The reality of the matter is that the waste resulted from what was, on the(licensee's) side, a very unsatisfactory and dangerous bargain."

所以,有了另一说法是即使能索赔依赖利益的损失,这金额也不能超出估计的预期利益,可以说这一方面已经是被 The "Mamola Challenger"(2011)1 Lloyd's Rep 47 先例所确定,因为在这种情况下,明显就是亏本生意。即使是没有违约/毁约的情况下,原告履行也难逃亏本。

这原则很公道,实源于损害赔偿的复原大精神,就是让受害方回复至合约未有被违反的经济地位,该盈则盈,该亏则亏,一切恢复至受害方原来应有的状态。

8.2 其他普通法国家法院的先例

其他普通法国家法院有说法是依赖利益只不过是预期利益的分类,不能完全视为是独立的。这里最主要的危险是预期利益非但没有,而且可以很肯定如果原告履行有关合约会亏本,不履行更好。这一来,如果允许原告索赔依赖利益的损失,而且同时不必履行一个会亏本的合约,就会带来原告通过索赔依赖利益的损失而得利的危险。针对这种说法,最著名的是一个美国案例 L. Albert & Son v. Armstrong Rubber Co(1948)178 Fed Rep 182,案情涉及一座机器的买卖,原告买方由于无法证明该机器将来会为他带来多少利润,所以他索赔为摆放该机器所建造地基而浪费的费用。而被告卖方也无法证明合约如果履行这笔费用就可以收回。反正在该案中,双方都无法证明如果该合约履行的话会带来什么经济后果。著名的 Learned Hand 大法官判买方应该可以索赔和取回浪费的费用,但这一笔费用应该减少,因为被告卖方是可以证明即使履行了合约,这笔费用也会被浪费掉,不会通过履行的利润而取回。Learned Hand 大法官是这样说的:"In cases where the venture would have proved profitable to the promisee(原告), there is no reason why he should not recover his expenses. On the other hand, on those occasions in which the performance would not have covered the promisee's outlay, such a result imposes the risk of the promisee's contract upon the promisor(被告). We cannot agree that the promisor's default in performance should under this guise make him an insurer of the promisee's venture; yet it does not follow that the breach should not throw upon him the duty of showing that the value of the performance would in fact have been less than the promisee's outlay. It is often very hard to learn what the value of the performance would have been; and it is a common expedient, and a just one, in such situations to put the peril of the answer upon that party who by his wrong has made the issue relevant to the rights of the other. On principle therefore the proper solution would seem to be that the promisee may recover his outlay in preparation for the performance, subject to the privilege of the promisor to reduce it by as much as he can show that the promisee would have lost, if the contract had been performed."

Learned Hand 大法官提到了索赔浪费的费用有几个限制，其中一个就是被告能够证明即使合约被履行，原告还是会有这方面的损失。他同意 Fuller 教授在 1936 年耶鲁大学法学院期刊的一篇文章《The Reliance Interest in Contract Damages, 46 Yale Law Journal》所说的："We will not in a suit for reimbursement for losses incurred in reliance on a contract knowingly put the plaintiff in a better position than he would have occupied had the contract been fully performed."

上述的美国案例被加拿大法院接受，在先例 Bowlay Logging Ltd v. Domtar Ltd (1978) 4 WWR 105，案情涉及了原告与被告的一个合约，约定由原告砍树而被告将砍下来的木材运走。但由于被告违约，没有提供足够的卡车，所以导致原告索赔浪费的费用。法院判由于被告能够证明即使合约被完全履行，原告仍会亏本，所以原告就不能够索赔浪费的费用，因为他并没有损失，只可以获得名义损失。Burger 大法官是这样说：

"The law of contract compensates a plaintiff for damages resulting from the defendant's breach; it does not compensate a plaintiff for damages resulting from his making a bad bargain. Where it can be seen that the plaintiff would have incurred a loss on the contract as a whole, the expenses he has incurred are losses flowing from entering into the contract, not losses flowing from the Defendant's breach. In these circumstances, the true consequence of the defendant's breach is that the plaintiff is released from his obligation to complete the contract – or, in other words, he is saved from incurring further losses.

If the law of contract were to move from compensating for the consequences of breach to compensating for the consequences of entering into contracts, the law would run contrary to the normal expectations of the world of commerce. The burden of risk would be shifted from the plaintiff to the defendant. The defendant would become the insurer of the plaintiff's enterprise."

另在澳洲最高院的先例 Commonwealth of Australia v. Amann Aviation (1991) 66 ALJR 123, Mason 与 Dawson 大法官是这样说："The amount of wasted expenditure will be the appropriate measure of damages in such a situation because, it having been established that the client would not have entered into the subsequent contract if proper advice had been given, it is not sensible to speak of loss of profits."

8.3 其他有关的例子

对以上原则可多举两三个例子如下：

(1)房东把房子出租给房客半年,但答应房客要先照他的品味来大装修。结果这装修的费用大大超出预算,比起将来半年的“净租金”收入会是更多的一笔钱。这明显是一宗亏本生意。如果房客后来违约/毁约,不承租已为他装修好的房子,房东只能索赔预期利益的损失,即半年的“净租金”(就算该经过古怪装修的房子再无法转租出去而空置,即并非没有试图减少损失)。房东不能够、也不应该索赔整笔庞大的装修费用(依赖利益)。

(2)买方买贵了货,该批货在市场上根本不值这个钱,对于买方来说是一宗亏本生意。但碰巧卖方交不出货而违约/毁约,买方本来就已经是捡了个大便宜,不必履行这个亏本的合约,所以不能索赔依赖利益的损失如白开了信用证费用等(假设这些费用有限,比不必履行这种亏本生意要节省得多)。

(3)船东把船舶空放去装港,花了10万美元(主要在燃油方面等)。但在装港没有货装,承租人违约/毁约。可是对于船东来说,实际上履行该程租也会是入不敷出,因为运费很低,只有20万美元,而使费要达30万美元。看来,这租约即使是履行也会为船东带来10万美元的亏蚀,所以不能只索赔依赖利益损失的10万美元。

又或是,该程租的使费非是30万美元,而只是15万美元,则表示“预期利益”(利润损失)只应是5万美元(因为运费收入为20万美元)。所以,船东不能够、也不应该索赔10万美元的空放费用(依赖利益),而应局限在5万美元的预期利益而已。

9. 以亏本生意对依赖利益作出否定或减少的举证责任在谁

至于证明预期利益会是入不敷出,务求否定或减少依赖利益的索赔,这应是被告的举证责任。对损失的举证责任本来是在原告,但针对这一方面,举证责任会转移到被告的头上,也可以说是对违约的被告一种惩罚。这一个问题在诉讼中是有实质的重要性,因为有举证责任的一方就会要面对更大的费用与工作,并且在不能满足举证责任的情况下会面对败诉的危险。而针对一个复杂的商业合约,要估计一个不被履行的合约会是有多少预期利益/利润损失不一定是容易。这方面可以节录 Learned Hand 大法官在先例 L. Albert & Son v. Amstrong Rubber Co(1948)178 Fed Rep 182 中针对谁有举证责任说:“Even without the assistance of such authorities, I should have held on principle that the onus was on the defendant. It seems to me that at least in these cases where the plaintiff's decision to base his claim on abortive expenditure was dictated by the practical impossibility of proving loss of profit rather than by unfettered choice, any other rule would largely, if not entirely, defeat the object of allowing this alternative method of formulating a claim. This is because, notwithstanding the distinction to which I have drawn attention between proving a loss of net profit and proving in general terms the probability of sufficient returns to cover expenditure, in the majority of contested cases impossibility of proof of the first would probably involve like impossibility in the case of the second. It appears to me to be eminently fair that in such cases where the plaintiff has by the defendant's breach been prevented from exploiting the chattel or the ring contracted for and, therefore, putting to the test the question of whether he would have recouped his expenditure, the general rule as to the onus of proof of damage should be modified in this manner."

在英国法律,这方面举证责任也是在被告,这可节录《McGregor on Damages》(18th edn,2009 年)之2–035 段如下:"This valuable decision brings to the forefront the question of the onus of proof, formerly dormant: does the claimant have to prove that the bargain was a good one or is it for the other side to show that it was a bad one? Since the question of whether the claimant's receipts would have exceeded his outlay, or whether he might even have gone on to make a net profit, is a question to which it may often be difficult, if not impossible, for either claimant or defendant to offer a resolution, the placing of the onus of proof becomes crucial. To the extent that the recovery of the pre–contractual expenditure in Anglia Television v. Reed(1972)1 QB 60 CA is explainable on the basis that it must have been assumed that the claimants would have recouped their total expenditure, that decision is consistent with a defendant's onus. However, the matter was fully aired in C. C. C. Films (London) v Impact Quadrant Films(1985) QB 16 where Hutchison J. arrived at the sensible conclusion that **the onus is indeed on the defendant**. A licence to exploit, distribute and exhibit in various countries three films was granted for a consideration of US $ 12,000 to the claimants by the defendants. The consideration was paid but the taped recordings of the films were, in breach of contract, sent uninsured and by ordinary post by the defendants and never arrived at their destination. Without these tapes the claimants were unable to make effective use of the licence. They claimed as damages for breach of the contract the US $ 12,000 expended by them in acquiring the licence but adduced no evidence that they would have recouped their expenditure; nor did the defendants adduce any evidence that without the breach the claimants would have failed to recoup their expenditure. Hutchison J held that, though a claim for wasted expenditure was likely to be motivated by an inability to prove loss of profits, a claimant was entitled to choose between loss of profits and wasted expenditure, and furthermore, though damages for wasted expenditure were unavailable if the expenditure would not have been recouped had the contract been properly performed, the burden was on the defendant to show this was so and thereby to displace the claimant's *prima facie* right to claim for his wasted expenditure. Accordingly, as the defendants has failed to discharge this burden the claimants were entitled to recover the US $ 12,000 by way of damages."(英国的 C. C. C. Films(London) v Impact Quadrant Films 先例是涉及原告向被告购买三部电影的许可,对价是 12,000 美元,原告也作出了支付。但被告在向原

告寄出这三部电影的胶片时疏忽,没有投保并且只是以一般的方式邮寄,结果中途丢失。但对被告的疏忽与违约,原告是没有办法证明他的利润损失,所以只是向被告索赔这一笔花费了的费用12,000美元。英国法院认为对亏本生意企图否定或减少原告索赔依赖利益的损失的举证责任是在被告,否则从表面看原告是有权索赔这笔费用。)

10. 对预期利益与依赖利益混乱的例子

最后介绍一个笔者曾经处理过的案子,用以说明预期利益及其赔偿计算办法在现实中对维护自己正当利益的重要性。

案件是有关一个买卖合约,国内一家外贸公司作为买方与美国一著名大公司订了一份购买4万吨食糖的CFR合约,分两次运输,中方开了信用证,也把进口许可证等有关文件全部办妥了,结果到装船期美方并未派船,同时因市场急升而宣称解约。当时中方公司与国内的其他公司签订了转售合约,这一下全泡汤了。中方于是致函美国公司提出索赔70万美元(开信用证等费用与象征式赔给国内其他公司的收货人5美元/吨的罚金,加上中方自己原来可赚取的5美元/吨差价),但美国公司不理会。拖了多月后,这家公司通过朋友找到笔者帮忙处理。在查看了当时的有关文件,再一比较对方违约/毁约当时市场报告所反映的货价,市场价比合约价高了1000万美元(总货价)以上,这无疑是违约/毁约造成中方的预期利益损失。按照损害赔偿的计算原则(毁约当时市场价与合约价之差),中方完全可以索赔此巨额差价。反而,正确的损失赔偿计算是不应理会分售给国内其他公司,因为转售合约没有在第一个合约中说明,他的赚或亏通常不被视为是双方订约时可以合理预见。这等于中方在这一次少赔给国内其他公司是不应该影响向美国公司索赔的损失计算,但如果是多赔给国内其他公司,如1500万美元,同样不应该影响向美国公司的索赔,而只是稳定地停留在1000万美元。这方面可节录《McGregor on Damages》(17th edn,2004年)之6-166段,所说如下:"... A profitable sub-sale which fails through the breach is often not allowed to augment the damages because it is not within the contemplation of the parties, while conversely an unprofitable sub-sale which is carried through despite the breach cannot, if outside the parties' contemplation, reduce the damages measured by a notional loss in market value..."

笔者向这家中方公司作了说明,并满怀高兴地说这个案子是难得一见的好案子,对方是一个很大的美国公司。而本案的责任非常明确,甚至已经被对方接受,在损失金额上也是再明确不过了。但可惜,后来该公司说:"我们中国公司做生意要诚实,这次对方违约/毁约,我们实际上只损失白开信用证、办货物进口手续、赔给收货人等方面所花的费用,要索赔也只能是这些。"笔者耐心解释道:"根据损害赔偿的有关原则,你的损失其实远不止是这些依赖利益。本案件并非是一种难以证明预期利益的情况,可以说,放弃了这一主要的计算损失办法,改为索赔依赖利益,根本就说不通。再说,对方如果履约,你本可拿到比合约价格高1000万美元的货物,现在对方违约/毁约剥夺了你这种利益,法律上你就有了预期利益的损失,完全有权全数追偿回来,这是非常明确的。至于中方公司与国内其他公司有一份转售合约,你有依约交货的责任,理论上讲你也要花多1000万美元从市场上买入替代货来履行转售合约的责任。至于中方公司如果只需要赔5元/吨就可以脱身,中方公司想赚钱的话大可以赔这笔钱,然后把美国公司所交的4万吨市场价格高涨的食糖在市场卖给其他买家,那么,就可以稳赚1000万了。现在食糖市场跟合约的差价明确,这是索赔中不可辨驳的最有力的证据,能依法向美国公司索赔回来,为什么要放弃呢?这不交货的预期利益的损失一般计算办法是清楚注明在英国法的《Sale of Goods Act 1979》Sction 51(3)为"*prima facie* the difference between the contract price and the market or current price of the goods at the time or times when they ought to have been delivered..."

但很可惜,笔者最后还是不能说服公司。仍坚持按70万美元的依赖利益的损失索赔,不想多赚也不想亏。笔者在无法改变现状的情况下只能照办,结果是在笔者的经验中最快速度把钱要了回来。做法上是给美国公司的法律部首次以笔者作为中方公司法律代理人的身份发了个电文,说:"我方早已向你公司索赔70万美元,至今拖了接近1年还没有任何答复,请不要逼迫我去约定的伦敦仲裁起诉。一旦我提出诉讼,你应该知道我主张的绝不止这个数,相信你也清楚这种损失是怎么样算法的。如果你不马上答复,我会马上开始仲裁。"这一来美国公司立即有了回电,要求开会谈判。会上我把有记录的食糖市场报告拿出来给对方看,并向对方的法律代表说:"我方现在索赔70万美元,你也清楚当时市价是多少,如果3天内我看不见你70万美元的付款支票,我就去仲裁告你违约/毁约,索赔1000万美元。"结果2天不到对方就赶忙把70万美元的支票送来了。从这个案子看出,如果能对损失赔偿计算办法的有关基本概念有一定认识,对于维护自己应有的权益是何等重要。否则,只能是白白放弃权利,承受损失(不论是看得见的或是潜在的)。

这个案例在本书第十六章第4段中也有介绍,但针对不同的重点。

11. 返还利益与预期利益的区别

在本章一开始也提到了"返还"(restitution)这说法,它会有关但也常会是无关。例如,买方付了一部分或全部货款,但没有为此得益,因为卖方无法交货。这一来买方可选择要求卖方根据返还的精神退还货款,或是他可索赔预期利益的损失(如跟市场比较的差价)。这两种做法肯定有重复之处。需要了解的是返还不是"损失",所以也没有复原的考虑或减少损失等义务。这一来,受害方在这方面如果面对一宗亏本生意可取巧。比如,市场下跌表示高价买进的货会亏本,受害方的买方可要求返还或退回已付的货款。但如果市场上涨,肯定是差价(市场与合约价)扩大,则应索赔预期利益的损失。

这些情况在近期的造船合约经常发生,外国船东在船价高涨时向中国船厂大量订造船舶,但现在市场下跌,外国船东希望能从合约脱身,或是以取消合约为借口压价。一个习以为常的手段就是外国船东以及他们的总管尽量找麻烦或不合作拖慢工程,导致船舶的建造过了销约期或死亡日期,就有了完全合法的借口终断合约。在这种情况下,外国船东要求把预付的船价加上利息退还,否则就要向作出"还款担保"(refund guarantee)的银行收取,这是根据造船合约有关条文行事。但会有情况是中国船厂违约/毁约,给了外国船东机会去终断合约,而依据的是法律默示地位,但造船合约中没有任何条文针对。这一来,外国船东拣了大便宜,这一合约不履行比履行好得多,根本不会有任何预期利益损失,所以谈不上有复原的问题。但外国船东还是可以根据返还的说法把已经预付给船厂的船价要回来,由于这不是造船合约内明示条文所针对,所以有可能利息部分(双方在造船合约会同意一些很高的利息,笔者近期就见到一个造船合约与还款担保的利息高达15%)就不存在返还了。其他包括在返还说法下的也有外国船东自己订购的并放在船上的那些昂贵的机器与设备。顺便在这里一提依赖利益,因为外国船东也有可能花了不少钱,如派遣总管长期在船厂监督造船。根据本来的说法,外国船东即使没有任何预期利益,甚至因不必履约而省了不少,是可以"选择"向船厂索赔浪费的费用。但看来在 The "Mamola Challenger"(2011)1 Lloyd's Rep 47 先例后,外国船东这种做法就不应该成功了,因为他避免了一个亏本的造船合约的履行,所得到的好处远远超过这笔浪费的费用。

12. 替代商品比原来合约的商品质量更高的情况

如果在原来的买卖合约违约/毁约下,导致买方取不到货而要去市场购买替代商品,经常会有情况是替代商品虽然是与原来的商品一样,但质量更高,而导致价格更高(即使撇开市场上的波动)。如果这两种商品之间的差价是作为预期利益的损失向违约方索赔,就会有让受害方得利的危险。所以在贵族院的先例 Westinghouse v. Undergrounds Railways(1912)AC 673,案情涉及一座有缺陷的涡轮机器,最后导致卖方购买另一座替代的涡轮机器减少损失。但由于替代的涡轮机器质量更高,操作起来会比原来合约的涡轮机器节省。针对这一方面带来的好处是否要一并计算在损失内,贵族院的答案是肯定的。

这也可以举一个简单的例子说明这方面的合理性:A 与车行 B 签订了一份买车合约,但 B 由于车价上涨而违约/毁约。A 如果去市场另买入替代商品,但买的不是原来 B 要提供的一辆比亚迪,而是买入一辆奔驰,然后向违约/毁约的 B 索赔差价,这显然是不公道的。这比较差价应该只是“苹果对苹果”(apple to apple)的比较。但有可能买入质量更高的替代商品是没有其他合理办法,如只有这一种替代商品可以在市场上买得到。加上无法证明或是看到受害方有什么真正的得益。以前,这种情况在船舶损坏经常会发生,可能是由于船舶碰撞或者是其他事故导致的。这种损坏经常要作出修理,而修理主要涉及换钢板。针对老船,就会是以新的与质量更好的钢板替换腐蚀的钢板。这就带来一个争议,就是在计算损失时应否折旧,类似以前木头船的年代要作出1/3的扣减。但相反的说法就是对整艘老船来说,只把损坏的部分换上了新的与质量更好的钢板到底带来了什么整体的好处?船舶年龄到了要拆废钢,也不会因某一部分换上了新的钢板而有什么改变,所以这一折旧的做法在现在已经被放弃了。

在笔者近期处理的一个伦敦仲裁中,涉及中国船厂违约/毁约,买方希腊船东转而与日本船厂签订替代的造船合约,并向中国船厂索赔两者之间的差价。包括笔者在内的仲裁庭也知道在日本与中国大陆建造同类船舶,不论是市场高低,两艘船舶的差价都可能大约有300万美元。但由于中国船厂不出庭抗辩,这令仲裁庭非常难做,因为不能自己提供争辩与相关的证据。但结果还是发出了一份电文给双方当事人,其中就问到这一方面。但这还是没有挑起中国船厂出来回应,结果只能是判希腊船东全部胜诉,可以把所有提出的预期利益损失(主要是与日本船厂订购替代船舶带来的差价损失)取回。

有关这个课题及有关的先例可参阅本书第九章之2.5段。

13. 基本或直接金钱损失

13.1 违约的基本金钱损失

合约都是双方当事人承诺向对方提供利益,如在买卖合约卖方承诺向买方提供财产/货物,而买方承诺向卖方支付货款。如果其中一方违约,另一方的受害方在法律上就有权提出索赔损失,而最基本的损失就是所谓的“交易损失”(loss of bargain),这也就是本章第一部分所讲的“预期利益”(expectation interest)的损失。计算这交易损失完全符合“复原”(*restitutio in integrum*)的损失大原则,就是让受害方回复到合约被履行的经济地位。这等于找出合约如果被履行会对受害方带来的实际经济利益,然后相比合约不被履行对受害方产生的实际经济后果,两者之间的差价就是受害方可以索赔的损失。对这一个简单与基本的道理,恐怕不会有太多异议。适用在一个简单的例子,在货物买卖中违约的卖方拒绝交出有关的财产/货物,受害的买方损失的就是该财产/货物在当时(也就是买卖合约中卖方最后必须交出该财产/货物的日期)的“价值”(value)。但这不是他的真正损失,因为如果没有发生违约,卖方在交出该财产/货物时,买方就需要支付该买卖合约约定的货价。由于卖方拒绝交出,买方也不会做出货价的支付。所以,买方的损失就是该财产/货物应该交付当天的价值,相比买卖合约的货价,两者之间的差价(在前者比后者金额高的情况)就是基本或直接损失。而如果前者比后者金额低的罕见情况下,就表示受害的买方没有实际损失,就算在责任方面胜诉也只会获得"名义损失"(nominal damage)。

针对上述所讲,可节录《McGregor on Damages》(18th edn,2009 年)之 2-002 段有关一般性损失计算的定义:"**Normal measure of damages**:Contracts are concerned with the mutual rendering of benefits. If one party makes default in performing his side of the contract,then the basic loss to the other party is the market value of the benefit of which he has been deprived through the breach. Put shortly,the claimant is entitled to compensation for the loss of his bargain. This is what may best be called the normal measure of damages in contract."

所以可总结说,违约所造成的"基本或直接金钱损失"(basic or direct pecuniary losses)也可被称为是"一般性损失"(normal damages)。

13.2 什么是财产/货物或服务的价值?

上述在《McGregor on Damages》(18th edn,2009 年)一书所提到的"价值"(value)或"市场价值"(market value)或是在投资仲裁中的"公平市场价值"(fair market value,简称 FMV)基本上是同一个意思。在《Black's Law Dictionary》的法律字典中,也有把 FMV 与国与国之间的"双边投资协议"(bilateral investment treaty,简称 BIT)经常会出现的不同写法如"actual value"、"fair value"、"full value"、"just value"与"true value"等同义。

不少情况下决定有关财产/货物在违约一天的价值会不一定容易,这在本书第十八章针对投资仲裁对一些财产如一家公司或一个合约权利的"估值"(valuation)可以充分地显示出其困难性。任何财产/货物甚至是一个合约承诺的价值总会需要依据一个真正或假设的交易,看交易的对方所愿意为该财产/货物支付的金额。英国有一句老话说:"一样东西的价值是它会带来别人愿意为它所支付的金额"(The worth of a thing is the price it will bring)。而拉丁语也对价值有一个同样的说法是:*tantum bona valent,quantum vendi possunt* (things are worth as much as they can be sold for)。针对价值,也可以节录一个加拿大先例 Irving Oil Co Ltd v. The King(1946)SCR 551 中的说法:"represent the sum which as a prudent man he would be prepared to pay rather than to fail to obtain or retain his property."

最后是美国估价师协会出版的《International glossary of Business Valuation Terms》,对公平市场价值(FMV)有一个定义,说:"the price,expressed in terms of cash equivalents,at which property would change hands between a hypothetical willing and able buyer and a hypothetical willing and able seller,acting at arm's length in an open and unrestricted market,when neither is under compulsion to buy or sell and when both have reasonable knowledge of the relevant facts."在这个定义下,价值或市场价值必须是一个金

钱上的价格。另是,这一个价格必须通过一个假设的交易确立。这假设的交易必须卖方与买方都愿意与能够(如有买方有这一个财力)进行,没有任何一方是在有压力下需要完成交易。再接下去是这一交易必须是一个"正常交易"(arm's length transaction),如买卖双方并不是兄弟的关系。另是,交易必须是在一个公开与没有受到任何限制的市场环境下进行。最后,要求买卖双方对这一交易的事实都有一个合理程度的了解,否则在无知的情况下,卖方或是买方都会做出一些不正常的反应,这不能为有关财产/货物确立一个尽量客观的价值。

在任何不同类别的诉讼中,受害方都会要证明有关财产/货物在违约一天的价值。在买卖合约,受害的买方就需要证明有关货物的价值。在侵权诉讼中,受害方也要证明被侵权方侵占或毁坏的财产在当时是什么价值,因为侵权的赔偿也是复原,把受害方回复到没有发生侵权的经济地位。这会是根据各种证明,如在侵占或毁坏,受害方会提供证明在早一天才购买该财产所付出的金钱。在买卖合约下交付了次货,受害的买方会提供把该批次货处理掉并出售给第三人的金额。正如在 Biggin v. Permanite(1951)1 KB 422 先例中,Devlin 大法官所说:"If the actual damaged goods are sold with all faults, good evidence can be obtained of the difference in value."

这些证明都可以说明有关财产/货物在违约当时的价值或市场价值。但这些个别交易的证明并非是结论性,因为往往有可争议与可怀疑之处。一种最常见的情况就是受害方掌握不好有关财产/货物买进卖出的价格,导致买了贵货或卖得太便宜。毕竟在现实中,卖低买高或卖高买低的情况在个别交易中经常发生。这会是由许多其他因素所导致,包括交易双方的谈判力量、水平、对前景不同的估计等。所以,如果有关财产/货物在违约一天有一个"可供买卖市场"(available market),涉及有大量同样财产/货物(如股票或商品市场)的交易与平均"市场价格"(market price),这就会比受害方提供的一个个别交易中的价格准确与客观得多。就算个别买卖或交易都免不了有买卖双方的主观因素与其他外来因素,但在一个可供买卖的市场中在同一时间或同一天内,有多个个别买卖或交易,就会相互抵销并可以达致一个相对肯定的客观"市场价值"(market value)。这也是英国法律下最喜欢采用的"市场规则"(Market Rule),也就是通过违约一天有关财产/货物的"市场价格"(market price)比较合约价格找出差价作为损失赔偿金额,英国早在 1894 年的《货物销售法》就把市场规则立法作为计算损失的表面规则。考虑到西方国家本来就是市场经济,绝大部分的商品或者服务都会有市场可找到同样的替代,所以以这种办法来计算损失是非常普遍的。而受害方的直接金钱损失也就是市场价格与合约价格之间的差价(如果有损失的话)。有关这一条重要的市场规则会在本书第十五与十六章详细讨论。在这里只提一个方面,就是应该针对同样的财产/货物比较找出差价作为损失金额。这一方面会在货物买卖更为严格,因为货物买卖对有关货物的描述本身会是明示或默示的条件条文,显示了对有关货物描述的重视。但在其他类别的违约或侵权案件,对同样的替代财产/货物就不会这么严格,即使是市场可找到的替代财产/货物不完全一样,只要实际的用途不受影响。例如，一艘替代船舶，就不可能吹毛求疵必须与毁坏的船舶一模一样，不论在船龄、设备、造船厂、维修保养等。

当然，一个可供买卖市场所报道的市场价格也不是结论性，所以市场规则也只能是作为一个"表面规则"(*prima facie* rule)，法院或仲裁庭可以在特殊的情况下认为这做不到令受害方复原，就可以摒弃适用这一条规则。这种特殊情况很早就有了 Peek v. Derry(1887)37 Ch. D 541 先例，案情涉及一家电车公司董事的责任，因为在招股书中做出错误陈述导致了受害的原告购买公司的股票，这一家公司最后倒闭。贵族院最后是判被告的董事没有责任，他们没有欺诈的意图，所以不存在损失的计算。但在上诉庭是做出不同的结论，判董事有责任，所以要进一步针对损失的计算。这涉及该批股票的价值，被告认为原告的损失就是合约价格与分配股票一天市场价格的差价，而这样比较就表示原告没有什么损失。但上诉庭不同意，认为该公司股票的市场价格只是被错误陈述而被提高，实际上该公司股票的价值远远低于市场价格。其中 Cotton 大法官说："Now, it must not be taken that the value of the shares must be what they would have sold for in the market, because that might not show the real value at all... the market might have been affected by the representations which were made by the Defendants, which induced the Plaintiff to act, and which might have induced others to act."

注意是在该先例，原告索赔的并非是有关的 400 份股票，而是他为该批股票所付出的 4000 英镑，所以法院要追究股票的真正价值。但如果是其他的争议，如被告的卖方没有转让股票，他在事后就不能说事后证明该股票的市场价格并不代表真正价值，所以他的违约所导致的损失只是零，因为买卖股票约定的价格远超于该事后倒闭公司的真正价值，而市场价格并不代表真正价值。

说到股票的价值，如果有关争议是涉及控制性数量的股票，价值就不光是个别股票的市场价格而会是更加高昂：Widrig v. Strazer(1964) SCR 376, 44 DLR(2d)1; Pelling v. Pelling(1982), 130 DLR(3d)761(BCSC)。

13.2.1 财产/货物有不同买进与卖出的价格，以哪一个金额为准？

市场规则下的市场价格还有一个问题是买进卖出的差价，这种情况在部分财产/货物的市场会出现，如黄金、外币等。这就涉及估计受害方的损失应该以哪一个价格为准。这会是要看受害方对有关财产/货物的意图，如涉及买卖而卖方不交出该财产(假设是外币)，受害的买方如果是为了自己使用，复原大原则下显然是应该以买进的价格为准，这才足够允许买方在市场买进替代金额的外币。但如果受害的买方是为了转售，这就看来以卖出的价格为准。

13.2.2 财产/货物涉及其他因素(如年龄、季节性)会影响价值

有关财产/货物的价值还会涉及其他许多的因素，如年龄。比方说，违约(如运输合约)或侵权把受害方的财产毁坏/损坏，如果该财产已经被使用了 10 年，做出的赔偿就不一定是市场价格。这是因为对同样财产的市场价格是针对新东西，与已经使用 10 年的毁坏财产比较并不合适。所以，就涉及需要折旧：African Steamship Co

v. Swanzy(1856)2 K & J 660,69 ER 947。但如果是部分损坏,就不一定需要折旧。例如一艘10年船龄的船舶被违约方或侵权方损坏,需要修理并更换新的钢板,就很难接受新钢板需要受害的船东在他的损失中折旧。原因是通常船东不会有选择,他不能要求修理厂找使用了10年的钢板作为更换。加上一艘旧船更换部分新钢板不会有实质好处,船舶也不会因此修理而变成一艘新船。这在 The "Gazelle"(1844)2 W. Rob. 279,166 ER 759(Adm)先例中 Dr. Lushington 是说:"... it does not affect the principle. In case of partial damage, the party claiming to be restored *in integrum* gains the advantage of having sound timber put into the vessel, instead of that which had been deteriorated by wear and tear. That arises from the necessity of the case. You could not select timber of the same kind as that which was in the vessel before the collision; you could not ascertain what degree of deterioration had taken place, nor could you put the vessel precisely in the situation in which she was before."关于折旧的问题还是有很多争议,这在本章第12段与本书第九章第2.5段有详论。

另一个有关找出财产/货物的价值的早期先例是 Piper v. Darling(1940)67 L1 LR 419(Adm. Div.)先例,案情涉及原告的一艘游艇被毁坏,当时是1938年。但由于是"二战"期间,根本没有买家对游艇感兴趣,这种情况维持到审判的一天,也就是1940年8月。这表示法院难以找出该游艇的价值,甚至可以被争辩为该游艇不值钱,因为没有买方出价,所以受害的原告没有损失。但在法院,最后是假设一个在和平时期的交易中该游艇值多少钱作为原告的损失。Langton 大法官是说:"A yacht is not like a work of art, a matter which is perhaps nothing to one person but is of almost incalculable value to another, but it is undoubtedly one in which the element of sentiment and predilection enters more fully, and, in considering the commercial value of a yacht, that is a matter that has to be borne in mind, more particularly when you may have to wait for your buyer."

另一个会影响财产/货物价值的因素会是季节。在 Fletcher v. Tayleur(1855)17 CB 21 先例中,案情涉及被告的船厂依照造船合约为原告制造客轮供他在澳大利亚营运,合约约定被告应该在8月交船,那个时候正是当地客运业季节性的高峰期,该客轮的价值也会相应高昂。但被告在第二年的3月才交船,当时客运已经到了低谷期。原告成功索赔了客轮在这两个不同时间的贬值,而贬值的推算就是根据被告按时交船的话原告本应获得的营运利润减去他实际在第一次营运所能获得的利润。本来,一艘船舶的价值就会与它能够赚取的利润有密切关系:The "Harmonides"(1903) p.1。在航运低潮时,一艘连带一个长期高租金的租约的船舶肯定在估价方面与吸引买方出价方面会比一艘没有租约在身的船舶更优越。Wright 勋爵在 Liesbosch v. Edison(1933)45 Ll. L. Rep. 123 先例中说:"In assessing that value(to the owner as a going concern) regard must naturally be had to her pending engagements, either profitable or the reverse. The rule, however, obviously requires some care in its application; the figure of damage is to represent the capitalized value of the vessel as a profit - earning machine, not in the abstract but in view of the actual circumstances. The value of prospective freights cannot simply be added to the market value but ought to be taken into account in order to ascertain the total value for purpose of assessing the damage, since if it is merely added to the market value of a free ship, the owner will be getting *pro tanto* his damages twice over. The vessel cannot be earning in the open market, while fulfilling the pending charter or charters."

法律的改变也会影响财产/货物的价值。在 Martin v. London County Council (1947) KB 628 先例,受害方所购买的珠宝因为加了购物税,所以受害方即使能够将来购买替代的珠宝,也因此要付出更高的代价。所以加的税赋也应该算在该珠宝的价值内。

13. 2. 3　财产/货物的价值是根据成本价或是售价或其他价格?

这也是经常会面对的一种情况,就是被毁坏的财产/货物,成本只需要 1 元,但售价是 10 元。这看来提价很多,但也不是不可能。例如,名贵的瓷器或其他的名牌商品,就会大幅度提价而导致了成本价与售价有很大区别。这一来,如果是因为侵权(如疏忽或侵权等行为)或违约(如运输不当)导致该财产/货物被损坏,他的价值应该是以 1 元或是 10 元计算?根据损失赔偿的大原则是去令受害方回复到没有遭受侵权或合约被履行的经济地位,这就表示有必要看有关财产/货物在侵权/违约时候对受害方的地位。比方说,一位游客在商店中把一个陈列的名贵瓷器不小心打碎,如果商店是根据售价的 10 万元索赔,就看来是过高。除非是该名贵瓷器很难再有供应,而市场是供不应求,甚至另有顾客等着购买或该名贵瓷器已经被预订了。这一来,商店所损失的实际上是一种"销售损失"(loss of sale),显然是应该以售价作为该名贵瓷器的价值。但换另一个极端,如果该名贵瓷器是供应商可以源源不绝的供应,而供应的价格也就是成本的 1 万元。这一来,如果疏忽顾客赔偿 10 万元,就可以让该商店向供应商买进 10 个名贵瓷器,这显然是"超额赔偿"(over compensation)。

看来在这种情况下,受害方如果想索赔售价作为财产/货物的价值,他需要证明在没有发生事故下,他应该可以根据售价出售该财产/货物给第三人。显然在某些情况下,明确是售价才是受害方的损失。例如在国际贸易,有关货物在海上运输被承运人毁坏,损失赔偿显然应是以买方在卸港的价值为准。在没有市场价格的情况下,就会要通过其他途径找出真正的价值,这包括买方转售的正常利润。违约的承运人不能以该货物的成本价作为损失的计算。

价值是根据成本价或其他价格的先例还可列举英国贵族院的 Banco de Portugal v. Waterlow & Sons (1932) AC 452,案情涉及被告为原告的葡萄牙银行印刷葡萄牙纸币,但由于被告的疏忽而导致了这批纸币被第三人偷去。在损失的计算,被告认为违约的价值只应该是重印该批纸币的成本,包括纸张、墨水与劳工,这显然是没有多少钱。但原告认为他的损失远远不止这笔钱,而是应该以该批纸币的面额为准。因为原告即使收回这一批纸币并重印,难保将来不会有无辜或表面无辜的持有人要求银行兑现或使用。原告作为一家银行,是不可能不承认自己发行的纸币。结果是原告与被告对损失的计算是天壤之别。这一个先例在贵族院带来了很不同的意见,最后还是以多数意见判损失是以该批纸币的面额为准。

Atkin 勋爵是这样说:"If (a man) manufactures for 1d. articles which can sell for 6d., the measure of damages against the wrongdoer is 6d., not 1d... So if he was by fraud induced to promise to deliver 500 of the 6d. articles so that the contract could be enforced by an innocent holder of the contract, it appears to me that on well established authority the damages would be 12l. 10s., not 2l. 1s. 8d."

但看来,这还是要看侵权或是违约的本质是什么。假设该批纸币是由于被告疏忽而在厂房被烧毁,这一来正确的损失计算应该只是冲印的成本,因为不会有危险让这批纸币在市场流通而造成将来会相等于纸币面额的损失。这方面可列举 Building & Civil Engineering Holidays Scheme Management v. Post Office (1966) 1 QB 247 先例,案件涉及原告发出的一些名为 Holiday Stamps 的奖券,它有相当大的流通性,不论是谁持有奖券原告也不得不承认。但这批有关的奖券在运输途中被偷去,被告需要负责。针对损失计算,Denning 勋爵把两种不同本质的毁坏做出区分。一种是火灾把奖券烧毁,损失只应该是重印的成本。另一种是运输中被偷去,该批奖券有很大机会被使用导致原告蒙受更大的损失。他是这样说:"(The defendant's) argument would be legitimate if the books of stamps had been destroyed by fire in transit: and could never be represented. But these books were not destroyed. They were stolen in transit. And... there was a good chance that they would be sold in the thieves' market and be presented for payment: and paid at face value. Every stolen stamp that was so presented and paid, meant a loss to the plaintiffs of the money paid."

13.2.4 财产/货物的价值不考虑受害方的感情

一个不会影响财产/货物价值的因素是受害方的感情,可称为是"感情价值"(sentimental value)。这方面的英国先例并不多,但还是可以列举枢密院的 Raja Vyricherla Narayana Gajapatiraju v. Revenue Divisional Officer, Vizagapatam (1939) AC 302 先例。在其他普通法的国家如加拿大,倒是有好几个被报道的先例。例如在 Clarke v. Fullerton (1871) 8 NSR 348 先例,涉及被告侵占了原告的一个望远镜,这望远镜是英国政府赠送给原告父亲的,有特殊的感情。但法院认为是不能加入这一个感情的因素而把望远镜的价值提升,因为这因素是太含糊与不肯定计算到底是值多少钱。Wilkins 大法官是这样说:"The mere *pretium affectionis*, or ideal estimate of the plaintiff or of her father, having relation to the circumstance which induced the gift of the instrument to the latter by the British Government, is too vague and uncertain to form our measure of value."

13.2.5 财产/货物的价值被侵权方/违约方的行为而提高

这种情况经常会在侵占的侵权行为中出现,如由于土地分界线不明确,导致侵权方有意或无意霸占了属于邻居的部分土地，并种植了果树。显然，如果邻居提出了侵权的指控并把有关土地取回（如设了围栏），侵权方也是无可奈何，也不可能向邻居索取种植果树的成本或收成。毕竟任何民事索赔必须是对方有侵权或违约的责任，但在这一个例子中，对方的邻居并没有侵权（侵占土地不是他）或违约，对方只是受害方。但如果邻居收回土地外同时向侵权方提出金钱上的索赔，这里就存在侵权方种植果树的成本或收成能否做出抵销，务求把索赔金额减少？

这方面可先简单介绍贵族院的 Livingstone v. Rawyards Coal Co.（1880）5 App Cas 25 先例，案情涉及原告拥有一块面积小的土地，本身是不值得开采煤炭。但该土地被旁边的邻居侵占，把这块土地与邻居的土地一并开采煤矿，这显然是侵占行为。在计算原告的损失，贵族院认定在井口的煤炭，减去开采的成本，是 500 英镑。但最终贵族院只判原告可以取回 171 英镑，认为在理论上，如果原告给被告这一个开采权就会是这一笔金额。但对这一个判决有一定的批评，说是没有解释清楚。如这 500 英镑是否包括了利润，而如果是，利润的好处应该是由受害的原告所得，而不是侵权的被告所得。

另可介绍一个较近期的澳大利亚先例名为 Bilambil - Terranora Pty Ltd v. Tweed Shire Council（1980）1 NSWLR 465，案情涉及被告在原告的土地上开采砾石长达 2 年之久。法院判原告可以取回该批砾石的价值，但减去开采的费用。针对被告的抗辩说原告本人没有也不会取得开采许可证，所以没有损失或该批砾石没有价值，Mahoney 大法官是这样说："... the fact that the owner of property does not desire to use it, or to use it to the best economy advantage, has not meant that its value is less than it would be in the hands of one who regarded it differently."而针对原告没有开采许可证，一起在上诉庭的 Reynolds 大法官说是即使开采是非法，原告本人本来是不能享有任何经济利益，也不代表侵权人可以不为他侵占的财产/货物支付它的价值给原告。而 Mahoney 大法官是说如果非法开采的好处是归侵权的被告而不是归受害的原告，这就会是太可笑的结论了。

13.2.6 有关先例介绍

计算与厘定有关财产/货物的价值在侵权与违约的诉讼中多不胜数，笔者只介绍很小部分的有关先例。

13.2.6.1 计算与厘定价值先例之一：O'Hanlan v. Great Western Ry. Co.

在 O'Hanlan v. Great Western Ry. Co.（1865）6 B&S 484 先例，案情涉及计算货物在一处地点的价值。在该地点没有可供买卖的市场，所以没有市场价格作为指引或比较。法院的计算是在另一处有可供买卖市场的市场价格，再加上把货物运输到该地点的费用（其中加上了合理承运人的利润），作为该票货物的价值。

13.2.6.2 计算与厘定价值先例之二：Borries v. Hutchinson

再介绍另一个类似的早期先例，是 Borries v. Hutchinson（1865）18 CB（NS）445，案情涉及买卖合约中约定卖方分别在 7 月、8 月和 9 月分三批付运给买方 75 吨苛性钠，这种苛性钠当时没有可供买卖的市场。卖方当时知道买方是要将这批苛性钠从 Hull 港运给其他的分买方。但是卖方直到 9 月才开始提供货物给买方,直到 10 月底才运输完第一批的 26 吨。而在延迟的这段期间,从 Hull 港向国外运输的运费和保险费上涨,导致买方在把这批 26 吨的苛性钠运给他的分买方时多付了 401. 17s。法院判是卖方需要赔偿受害的买方对剩余 59 吨没有交付的苛性钠所蒙受的利润损失,也就是买方与分买方转售合约中这 59 吨货物的价格比较买卖合约价格的差价,另加上在第一批延迟交货期间上涨的运费与保险费。针对这笔上涨的运费与保险费,法院认为是代表了这第一批货物在买卖合约约定交货当天与货物实际到达当天的价值差异,因为当运费和保险费上涨时,对买方来说,这批苛性钠的价值在延迟交付后实际是降低了。Wills 大法官是这样说:"We must, therefore, ascertain what was the value of the article contracted for at the time it ought to have been and at the time when it actually was delivered. Now, the value of such an article as this depends upon the existence of facilities for its transport to the place for which it is destined. If the caustic – soda had been forwarded to Hull at the times contracted for, it was capable of being sent to St. Petersburg(分买方所在地). When it was delivered, it was also capable of being sent to St. Petersburg, but only at a greater cost for freight and insurance than would have been incurred if it had been delivered in due course at Hull. It necessarily follows, therefore, that the soda was worth less when it was delivered, by the difference between the cost of forwarding it at that time to St. Petersburg and what the cost would have been if delivered at the times mentioned in the contract. The plaintiffs are clearly entitled to recover that as the direct and natural consequence of the defendant's breach of contract."

13. 2. 6. 3　计算与厘定价值先例之三:Clyde Navigation Trustees v. Bowring Steamship Co.

在 Clyde Navigation Trustees v. Bowring Steamship Co. (1929)34 Ll LR 319 先例,涉及被告的船舶超速导致碰撞,把原告的一艘"漏斗挖掘驳船"(hopper digger barge)碰沉。但由于当时这种驳船没有可供买卖市场与市场价格,所以认定侵权时的真正价值就必须通过其他途径。结果判的价值是以下三项的总和:(1)购买一艘二手的驳船;(2)估计把该驳船改装为可提供与沉没驳船具有同样特殊用途需要花的费用;(3)在其间长达两年的使用损失,因为直到有了替代驳船,原告才有驳船可以使用。

13. 2. 6. 4　计算与厘定价值先例之四:The "Liesbosch"

The "Liesbosch"(1933)45 Ll. L. Rep. 123 先例也是与先例之三类似的案例,就是涉及船舶碰撞。被告承认疏忽的责任,所以在这一个著名的先例只为了针对损失赔偿的金额。在船舶碰撞的受害方是一艘原告所拥有的疏浚船,当时它是在 Patras Harbour 进行挖泥,而挖泥的合约中针对工程延误是要面对高昂的议定赔偿。这导致受害方的原告赶紧以非常昂贵的租金租用另一艘疏浚船,以继续进行工程。这导致受害方向侵权方的索赔是大大超出了该沉没疏浚船的价值或潜在价值。但被告的抗辩是原告能够取回的损失只是局限在沉没疏浚船在碰撞地点与时间的真正价值。

这一个著名的先例最为人所知是原告由于穷困，所以不能以金额差别不大与很短时间内买进另一艘替代船舶的疏浚船，继续他的工程。在该先例，贵族院是判由于穷困所带来的额外损失，根据损失遥远性不能向被告取回。由于这方面的问题已经在本书第四章9.6.2.2段有详细介绍，所以不重复。在本段只会谈其他有关损失计算的方面。首先在贵族院，Wright勋爵重复了损失计算的基本大原则："What in such a case as the present is the true measure of damage? It is not questioned that when a vessel is lost by collision due to the sole negligence of the wrong – doing vessel the owners of the former vessel are entitled to what is called *restitution in integrum*, which means that they should recover such a sum as will replace them, so far as can be done by compensation in money, in the same position as if the loss had not been inflicted on them, subject to the rules of law as to remoteness of damage."

Wright勋爵提到了在船舶碰撞，毁坏船舶对受害方的价值就是当时作为牟利工具的实际价值，所以要把当时船舶的经营（不论是赚钱或亏损）一并考虑在内。他说："The true rule seems to be that the measure of damages in such cases is the value of the ship to her owner as a going concern at the time and place of the loss. In assessing that value, regard must naturally be had to her pending engagements, either profitable or the reverse. The rule, however, obviously requires some care in its application; the figure of damages is to represent the capitalized value of the vessel as a profit – earning machine not in the abstract but in view of the actual circumstances."

贵族院最后判沉没疏浚船在当时的真正价值是以下三项的总和：（1）一艘同类疏浚船在市场的价格；（2）把替代疏浚船改装、运输至 Patras Harbour 与投保的费用；（3）其间的使用损失。Wright勋爵是这样说："From these it follows that the value of the Liesbosch to the appellants, capitalized as at the date of the loss, must be assessed by taking into account (1) the market price of a comparable dredger in the substitution, (2) costs of adaptation, transport, insurance, &c., to Patras, (3) compensation for disturbance and loss in carrying out their contract over the period of delay between the loss of the Liesbosch and the time at which the substituted dredger could reasonably have been available for use in Patras, including in that loss such items as overhead charges, expenses of staff and equipment, and so forth thrown away, but neglecting any special loss due to the appellants' financial position. On the capitalized sum so assessed, interest will run from the date of the loss."

13.2.6.5　计算与厘定价值先例之五：Croudace Construction v. Cawoods Concrete Products

不同行业与不同的事实会影响有关财产/货物在违约的损失计算，例如在 Croudace Construction v. Cawoods Concrete Products (1978) 2 Lloyd's Rep 55 先例中，就是判

供应商延误交付使用在一个工程中的建筑材料给建筑商，这与一般的货物延误交付不同，是不理会有关材料在违约一天的价值。Parker 大法官是这样说："When selling building materials to a contractor for delivery on a building site, the difference in the value of the materials is, as a matter of common sense, wholly irrelevant. If between the date when the goods should have been delivered and the date when they were in fact delivered, there is a fall in the value, that is, as a matter of commercial reality, of supreme indifference to the contractor and in no real sense does he suffer any loss or damage as a result of the fall."

接下去 Parker 大法官也继续说这种延误的直接损失是闲置的设备与等待工人的费用，如果这延误供应是导致了停工的结果，"To take an example, suppose that a load of steel work is due on May 1, and the contractor has on site ready to install it a work force, scaffolding and lifting plant. The steel is however 14 days late. The most direct, immediate and natural damage caused by the delay is the expense of the work force, scaffolding and plant. If when the steel arrives 14 days later it is worth the same as, less than, or more than it was worth on May 1 makes not the slightest difference to the contractor."

在该上诉庭的先例，实际上更重要的是解释什么是"间接损失"(consequential losses)，因为在有关的供货合约内有一个明示条文豁免供应商对间接损失的责任。所以在建筑商所提出的损失，包括了"生产损失"(productivity loss)、"通货膨胀费用"(cost of inflation)与分承建商的索赔，要决定这些是否是间接损失。这方面稍后在本章第 14 段会探讨。

13.3 违约的类别/形式

在进一步探讨损失赔偿的类别前，先简单介绍合约利益与违约的种类。合约的利益可分为三大类：第一类是"财产"(property)、第二类是"金钱"(money)与第三类是"服务"(services)。而违反合约也同样可分为三大类或三大形式，第一类是"不履行"(non – performance)、第二类是"延误履行"(delayed performance)与第三类是"有缺陷履行"(defective performance)。简单以最常见的货物买卖为例，违约的卖方不履行就是拒绝交付货物给买方、延误履行就是不按照买卖合约的最后期限交付货物、至于有缺陷履行就是交付有瑕疵的次货。

13.4 不履行财产转让合约的基本利益损失与救济：与市场价格比较的差价

这是卖方不履行有关合约(不论卖的是什么财产如货物、土地/房子、股票等)最"基本的损失"(basic loss)，就是合约价格与"市场价格"(market price)(只要是有关财产有市场)比较所得出来的差价，这就是著名与重要的"市场规则"(Market Rule)。而与市场价格比较的一天，就是违约的一天，这就是另一个著名与重要的"违约一天损失规则"(Breach Date Rule)。如果没有可供买卖市场，有关的财产/货物就要找出在违约一天的真正"市场价值"(market value)。这可先简单节录《McGregor on Damages》(18th edn, 2009 年)之 2 – 004 段如下："**Non – performance**. Where the breach of contract consists in a failure to transfer property, the basic loss is the market value of the property, always deducting the contract price if it has not already been paid to the person in breach. The prime example of this is in sales of goods; it will also apply to hire of goods and hire - purchase of goods, to sales of stocks and shares, and today to all sales and leases of land."(如果违约涉及不把财产转移,基本损失就是该财产的市场价值减掉[1]有关合约价格。最显著的例子就是在货物买卖,但也适用在货物的租赁,股票买卖与土地买卖与租用。)

13.5 不履行服务性合约的基本利益损失与救济

接下去《McGregor on Damages》(18th edn, 2009 年)之 2-006 段针对不履行服务性合约如运输(包括海上运输)货物或乘客的合约、建造合约、雇佣合约等,"基本的损失"(basic loss)也是根据违约时对同样服务的市场价与合约的差价为准。这段是这样说:"Where the breach of contract consists in a failure to render services, the basic loss is the price the claimant would have to pay in the market in order to obtain such services, always deducting the contract price if that has not yet been paid. The best example is the contract of carriage, whether of goods or of persons. If the carrier fails to carry, the basic measure of damages is the market rate less the contract rate. Also, in building and construction contracts, the measure against the defaulting builder is what it will cost the claimant to have the work done less the contract price. Similarly, where an employer sues an employee for failure to carry out his contract of employment, the measure is the market price of similar services less the contract price."(如果违约涉及不提供服务,基本损失就是受害方的原告要在市场为同样的服务付出的代价减掉有关合约的代价。最好的例子是货物或乘客的运输合约,如果承运人不提供服务,基本损失就是市场价格或运费减掉有关合约价格或运费。在建造合约,承建商如果违约不提供服务,受害方的原告基本损失就是去市场另找人把相关工作完成的价格减掉有关合约的价格。在雇佣合约,如果雇主指雇员违约不提供服务,基本损失就是同样服务的市场价格或工资减掉有关合约的价格或工资。)

13.6 延误履行财产转让合约的基本利益损失与救济

至于卖方的延误履行的违约,《McGregor on Damages》(18th edn, 2009 年)之 2-008段是接下去说"基本的损失"(basic loss)计算是以准时交付财产一天的市场价值相比受到延误真正交付的一天的市场价值为准:"**Delayed performance**. Where the breach consists in a delayed transfer of property, the basic loss is the market value at the date of due delivery less the market value at the date of actual delivery. The prime example is once again the sale of goods, and again will apply to hire and hire - purchase of goods, to sale of stocks and shares, and today to all sales and leases of land."(如果违约是延误履行财产的转移,基本损失就是在应该准时交付一天的市场价值减掉真正交付但延误

〔1〕 减掉是因为有关合约价格肯定是比较低的金额,否则受害方就不会有损失可言。

了一天的市场价值。最显著的例子就是货物买卖,但也适用在货物的租赁,股票买卖与土地买卖与租用。)

13.7 延误履行服务性合约的基本利益损失与救济

针对延误履行服务性合约,有关以哪一天的市场价格做出比较以找出差价,《McGregor on Damages》(18th edn,2009 年)之 2 - 010 段是说:"Where the breach consists in a late rendering of services, the basic loss is the value to the claimant of the services if rendered at the due date less their value at the time actually rendered. In the case of a contract of carriage of goods, the basic loss is generally their market value at the date of due delivery less their market value at the date of actual delivery. Similar principles will apply in the case of building contracts and contracts of service; again there are no clear authorities."(如果违约是延误提供服务,基本损失就是在应该准时提供服务一天的价值减掉真正提供服务但延误了一天的价值。在货物运输,基本损失通常是准时交付一天的市场价值减掉真正但延误了交付的市场价值。同样的道理也适用在其他的建造合约或服务性合约,虽然没有明确的先例。)

13.8 缺陷履行的基本利益损失与救济

最后是针对有缺陷履行,《McGregor on Damages》(18th edn,2009 年)之 2 - 011 段是说:

"**Defective performance.** Where the breach is a transfer of property which is either defective or is not of the quality promised, the basic loss is the value of the property as represented less its market value in fact. This is well established for sales of goods, it will apply *mutatis mutandis* to hire and hire - purchase, and to sales of stocks and shares. It also applies to the sale and lease of land, but the cases on leases where the lessor is in breach of repair covenants indicate that the basic loss may be taken either as the diminution in the value of the claimant's interest in the property or the cost of repairs.(如果违约是交付了有瑕疵或者不符合质量要求的货物,"基本的损失"[basic loss]就是应当交付符合合约要求货物的市场价值减掉它有瑕疵的真正市场价值。最显著的例子就是货物买卖,但也适用在货物的租赁、股票买卖。这个道理也适用于土地买卖与出租,但在土地出租的情况下,如果出租人违反维修合约,基本损失可能是原告在有关土地利益的贬值或是维修费用。)

Where the breach of contract is in the rendering of defective services the positions are more diverse. If property is affected adversely, as where there isdefective performance of a building contract or where a carrier damages the goods in transit, the basic loss is the diminution in the value of the property. In the case of an ordinary service contract, however, there is no clear basic loss: perhaps most loss will be consequential. And in the case of a carrier who loses the goods, the basic loss is their value loss less the contract price of carriage if not yet paid.(如果违约是提供有瑕疵的服务,会出现很多种不同的情况,毕竟

瑕疵是千变万化。如果违约是有缺陷地履行建造合约或承运人损坏了在运输途中的货物,基本损失就是有关货物价格的贬值。然而,如果违约是发生在一个普通的服务性合约中,就没有明确的基本损失:可能大部分损失都是间接的。如果违约是承运人丢失了货物,基本损失就是损失的货物价格减去有关合约规定但尚没有支付的运费。)

Whether, in all these cases of defective performance affecting property, the claimant is entitled to measure his basic loss of thediminution in the property' s value only by the diminution in market price or may, alternatively, claim the cost of putting the property into proper condition, is a question to which no clear - cut answer is possible. Each case must be looked at separately to see what is reasonable. "(在所有关于财产/货物的缺陷履行案例中,受害方的原告的基本损失是有关财产/货物在市场价格的贬值,但作为替代的赔偿是把有瑕疵财产/货物恢复原状的费用[这通常就是修理费用]。由于这两种不同赔偿方式的金额通常不会一样,如很多情况下会是修理费用更加昂贵,这导致了什么情况适用哪一种赔偿方式经常有争议。这个问题没有明确的回答,每一个案例都必须要单独来看哪种赔偿方式是合理的。一般而言,如果估计修理费用[因为在审理期间还没有进行修理]是完全不合理,与财产/货物的贬值完全不成比例,就不会让受害方取回这一笔估计修理费用:Ruxley Electronics & Construction Ltd v. Forsyth [1995] All ER 1936)。

在现实中,由于财产/货物的缺陷会有不同的程度,所以有市场也不一定能够决定什么才是有瑕疵财产/货物的市场价值。如果能够把有关有瑕疵财产/货物转售给第三人,会可以假设这转售的价格就是市场价值。而针对一些没有市场或无法转售的财产/货物如机器,也就只能是以合理修理费用作为基本损失的赔偿。这方面可节录在 Biggin v. Permanite(1951)1 KB 422 先例中,Devlin 大法官说:"It seems to me that one can very rarely arrive at an accurate figure of unsound value. Where the breach is non-delivery, there is often a market price which can be quoted, or evidence can be given of the price at which at the relevant date similar goods were changing hands, but there is rarely any market price for damaged goods since their value depends on the extent of the damage. If the actual damaged goods are sold with all faults, good evidence can be obtained of the difference in value, but such a sale is not always possible, and a claim for substantial damages cannot be limited to goods which have been sold."

14. 基本损失外的间接金钱的损失

14.1 间接损失与特别损失是不同的损失类别

除了上述所介绍的基本损失(也就是合约获得履行的价值与不履行/有缺陷履

行的价值比较)外,受害方的原告会有可能加上他蒙受的“间接金钱损失”(consequential pecuniary losses),这种经常在违约索赔会见到的损失类别以下分段介绍。以货物买卖为例,如果违约/毁约是卖方拒绝提供货物或是延误交出货物,受害方的买方完全可以索赔真正蒙受的间接损失。可以说,如果有关货物是有“可供买卖的市场”(available market),导致了适用市场规则,合约价格与市场价格的差价就会是“直接金钱损失”(direct pecuniary loss),很少再会有间接损失。但如果有关货物没有可供买卖的市场,导致市场规则不适用,受害方的原告提出的索赔往往就会是间接损失,这包括了“营运利润损失”(loss of user profit)、“必要的使费”(expenses made necessary);“分销/转售的利润损失”(loss of profit on a resale);“对分买方的赔偿”(compensation paid to the sub - buyer);“针对分买方诉讼的辩护费用”(costs incurred in defending a sub - buyer's action);“名誉损失”(loss of goodwill)或“将来生意的损失”(loss of repeated orders)等。

而对每一项间接损失,买方都需要证明以及要满足“损失的遥远性”(remoteness of damages)(本书第三章与第四章),这包括了损失类别是在订约时可以“合理预见”(reasonably foreseeable, within reasonable contemplation)与满足“因果关系”(causation)。另外,买方也要证明与满足他有合理“减少损失”(mitigation),否则没有合理减少的损失部分就不能成功索赔(本书第五章)。

这表示间接损失与 Hadley v. Baxendale(1854)9 Ex. 341 先例的“特别损失”(special damages)并不是同一码事,因为有许多项间接损失是属于 Hadley v. Baxendale 的“一般性损失”(normal or general damages)。例如在上述所举的例子,“营运利润损失”就会是一般性损失,只因为没有可供买卖市场,受害方(原告)才需要索赔这一项间接损失。而如果这一项损失涉及了部分利润是不可预见与非正常的损失,就不能成功向被告索赔。这方面最明确的先例就是 Victoria Laundry v. Newman Industries (1949)2 K. B. 528。再多举一个例子,是有关名誉或将来生意的损失,这会是在个别业务中双方订约时可以合理预见的情况下,被判是可以向被告成功索赔的间接损失:GKN v. Matbro(1976)2 Lloyd's Rep 555。

可以总结说在英国法律默示的地位是特别损失在没有给违约方预先与足够的通知是不能成功索赔,但间接损失作为损失的类别之一是没有这个预先与足够通知的限制/要求,一直在英国法律下是可以成功向被告索赔。这可以节录 Mondel v. Steel (1841)8 M & W 858 先例中 Parke B 大法官所说(针对货物买卖或提供服务合约的违约)如下:“as well the difference between the price contracted for and the real value of the articles or of the work done, as any consequential damage, might have been recovered.”

另在 Davis & Co v. Afa - Minerva(1974)2 LLR 27 先例,案情涉及被告没有安装一个足够防止盗窃的警报系统,所需要面对的正常或一般性损失,是与安装一个足够并且妥善的警报系统之间的差价,而原告其他方面的损失如修理费用以及被盗窃财物的损失,就属于“间接损失并且是可以向被告索赔”(is consequential loss and claimable)。

14.1.1 间接损失的多个不同定义

首先对什么是间接损失进行探讨,这就回到在本章13.2.6.5段介绍过的Croudace Construction v. Cawoods Concrete Products(1978)2 Lloyd's Rep 55先例。在该先例之前,英国法律从来没有区分"直接损失"(direct losses)和"间接损失"(consequential losses),所以这样的分类有时会带来不稳定/不肯定。这种分类一定程度可能是受美国法律的影响,因为美国法院与法律书籍有尝试对这些种类作出区分。在另一个角度需要做出区分,就是经常会有合约条文豁免将来违约方赔偿间接损失。例如在Croudace Construction v. Cawoods Concrete Products先例,有关的免责条文可部分节录如下:"... We are not under any circumstances to be liable for any consequential loss or damage caused or arising by reason of late supply or any fault failure or defect in any material or goods supplied by us or by reason of the same not being of the quality or specification ordered or by any other matter whatsoever."

在Croudace Construction v. Cawoods Concrete Products先例,它有考虑以前有关的两个先例:Millars Machinery Co Ltd v. Way(1934)40 Com Cas 204和Saint Line Ltd v. Richardsons Westgarth & Co Ltd(1940)2 KB 99。其中在Saint Line Ltd v. Richardsons Westgarth & Co Ltd,Atkinson大法官提到了"间接"一词的不明确,说:"The word 'consequential' is not very illuminating, as all damage is in a sense consequential, but there is a definition in the Oxford English Dictionary to which both sides have appealed: 'Of the nature, of a consequence, merely; not direct or immediate; eventual.' It cites the definition of 'consequential damages' from Wharton as: 'Losses or injuries which follow an act, but are not direct or immediate upon it.'"

供应商的代表大律师提出了"间接损失"(consequential loss)可以有三种不同的解释。第一种就是它包括了"违约导致的所有损失"(all resulting damage),这等于是供应商在买卖合约豁免间接损失的条文上根本不必承担任何损失。但这看来不是一个合理的条文解释,原因之一就是不合理与不针对受益方严格解释(*contra proferentem*)。另一个原因就是如果这样解释,等于不给"间接"一词有任何意思,因为双方大可以约定豁免"所有损失",而不是"所有间接损失"。

第二种解释是除了"一般或通常损失"(normal or ordinary damage)外,其他所有的损失。而在货物买卖下的延误付运,市场价值的差价就是一般或通常损失。在该先例中,建筑商作为买方所提出的索赔项目包括"生产损失"(productivity loss)、"通货膨胀费用"(cost of inflation)与分承建商的索赔,这些正是间接损失,供应商根据上述条文被豁免赔偿的责任。

而第三种解释是作为违约第二阶段的损失,也就是并非违约在第一阶段马上会造成的损失。这方面可节录有关的段节如下:"consequences which did not follow as a first stage, or immediately, from the breach, but which were, nevertheless, damages which, in the absence of this clause, would have been recoverable on ordinary principles of the law as to damages."

上诉庭支持第一审 Parker 大法官对间接损失的解释,他是说:"It is in my judgment clear that the word 'consequential' is, in the present context, used to describe or indicate a type of loss or damage which is in some way less direct or more remote than that loss or damage which is to remain recoverable despite the exclusion. This appears to me to follow from the ordinary use of the words and from the fact that it would be commercial nonsense to give it any other meaning."

另在《McGregor on Damages》(18th edn, 2009 年)之 1-040 段也提到了正常或一般性损失与间接损失的区分可以是前者是由于违约所造成的"积极或肯定"(positive)的损失,会是某一类别的违约在正常情况下肯定会造成的损失。但间接损失是"消极或不一定"(negative)的损失,如受害方的利润损失或是一些违约所造成的特定费用,但不是订约双方不能预见或料想不到的。该权威书籍是说:"Consequential losses themselves also contain a useful and important division: this is the division into the negative loss of gains that the claimant would have made had the wrong not been committed and the positive expenses to which he is put by reason of the commission of the wrong. The former is best illustrated by the claimant's loss of profits ... being deprived of goods through their non-delivery in breach of contract... The latter finds a good example in the compensation a claimant buyer has to pay to his sub-buyer when the defendant seller fails to deliver the goods, delivers late or delivers them in a defective condition."

14.1.2 判间接损失与特别损失是同义的先例

Croudace Construction v. Cawoods Concrete Products (1978) 2 Lloyd's Rep 55 先例的判法,等于把间接损失视为是 Hadley v. Baxendale 先例中 Anderson B 大法官著名说法的两种损失中第二种的"特别损失"(special damages),受害方如果不在订约时通知违约方是不能成功向他索赔的。而第一种损失的"一般性损失"(general damages)才是受害方可以不需要在订约时做出特别通知下也可以向违约方取回的,因为双方可以合理预见到如果将来违约这一类损失就是很可能的后果。Anderson B 大法官针对第一种损失是说:"the damages which the other party ought to receive in respect of such breach of contract should be such as may fairly and reasonably be considered either arising naturally, i. e. according to the usual course of things, from such breach of contract itself, ***or*** such as may reasonably be supposed to have been in the contemplation of both parties, at the time they made the contract, as the probable result of the breach of it."

而在该先例中,由于供应商延误交付使用在一个工程中的建筑材料给建筑商被判是市场价值的差价是无关(在本章13.2.6.5 段介绍过),因为这不是货物买卖中的延误交付,所以在供应商违约的情况下造成工程延误,对建筑商所造成的三项损失(生产损失、通货膨胀费用与分承建商的索赔)就变成直接损失,是直接与自然的延误付运后果，不会是特别损失而需要订约前的通知，所以上述条文豁免间接损失是保护不了违约的供应商。但这样的解释说不通的地方是三项损失类别如果是属于"特别损失"，根据 Hadley v. Baxendale(1854)9 Ex. 341 先例，被告的供应商在订约时没有获得预先通知是不必承担后果。这是法律默示的地位，根本不必多加一条明示条文保护供应商不必赔偿间接损失。所以，"特别损失"不应该与"间接损失"有相同意思。

这种对间接损失的狭窄解释也在之后上诉庭或一审先例如 British Sugar v. NEI Power Products and Another(1998)14 Const. L. J. 365 先例中被确认，在这个先例中法院判是增加的生产成本和利润损失并不必然是间接损失。

间接损失的含义虽然在理论上很清晰，但适用在更加复杂的合约关系，特别是有一条豁免违约方损失赔偿责任条文的情况下，间接损失的含义还是很复杂。在 BHP Petroleum and Others v. British Steel Dalmine(2000)2 Lloyd's Rep. 277 先例中，法院认为在考虑是否间接损失会被合约针对间接损失免责条文豁免时，需要考虑被告在订约时是否预见到的因素。在这个先例中法院判是被告需要赔偿原告生产利润损失，因为这笔损失是由于被告提供的钢材不符合质量要求被原告要求替换，而导致原告工程的延误所造成的直接损失。

所以，在不少近期的先例，英国法院都把利润损失当作是直接损失，并且强调在订约时是否可以预见到。例如在 Deepak Fertilisers Ltd v. I. C. I. Chemicals Polymers Ltd(1999)1 Lloyd's Rep. 387，有关的合约中有一条免责条文明示排除利润损失责任与"非直接或间接损失"(indirect and consequential damage)。上诉庭说工厂损毁的直接损失是重建所需要的金钱和时间，加上期间的生产损失，但期间浪费的管理费用与利润损失同样是属于直接损失。虽然最后判是利润损失不能索赔成功，这是因为另有一条明示条文排除利润损失的索赔，不是因为其不是非直接或间接损失。上诉庭的 Stuart - Smith 大法官是这样说："The direct and natural result of the destruction of the plant was that Deepak was left without a methanol plant, the reconstruction of which would cost money and take time, losing for Deepak any methanol production in the meantime. Wasted overheads incurred during the reconstruction of the plant, as well as profits lost during that period, are no more remote as losses than the cost of reconstruction. Lost profits cannot be recovered because they are excluded in terms, not because they are too remote."

再接下去同一判法的上诉庭先例是 Hotel Services Ltd. v. Hilton International Hotels(UK)Ltd. (2000)BLR 235 CA，原告索赔拆除酒店房间有问题的迷你吧台的费用与利润损失，这损失可被视为是正常或一般性损失。而如果把它们视为是间接损失，也说到是先例不把它视为是免责条文所豁免的间接损失类别。也就是原告可以成功索赔。

再接下去的上诉庭先例是 Watford Electronics Ltd v. Sanderson CFL Ltd(2001) BLR 143 CA，其中 Chadwick 大法官把合约中所豁免的"间接损失"(indirect or consequential losses)视为 Hadley v. Baxendale 先例中的第二种损失类别。

最后可详细介绍 Addax Ltd v. Arcadia Petroleum Ltd(2000)1 Lloyd's Rep 493 一审先例,案情涉及一票高达 79 万桶的原油买卖 FOB 合约,约定买方(被告)必须在 1998 年 5 月 22 日至 23 日期间派船到装港装货,但买方指派的船舶直到 5 月 30 日才到达装港,卖方(原告)为了减少损失而去期货市场购买了对冲产品,以防止市场波动而蒙受进一步的损失(有关对冲产品这一方面的损失,请看本书第三章第 10.3 段)。由于买卖合约中有条文豁免买方对间接损失的责任,条文是说:"In no event shall seller or buyer be liable for indirect or consequential damages",所以有必要对间接损失的定义做出考虑,以决定这笔购买对冲产品费用的间接损失是否包括在免责条文之内。Morrison 大法官是这样说:

"... In principle, I accept that the normal measure of the claimants' loss is the difference between the price he received and the price he would have received had the contract been performed on time. That would be the true measure of damage, regardless of the profit or loss made by the claimants with their own suppliers. This was a commercial contract to be looked at on its own. In principle, therefore, had the claimants not limited their claim I would have held in principle that the damages were the figure of US $ 962,206.

If I were wrong about the measure of damages and the Court was required to take account of the claimants' position with their own suppliers, then I can think of no sensible or commercial reason why the Court should not take into account the cost of the hedging instruments. It seems to me that, if the direct loss to the claimant is that which represents their net position with the NPCC(分卖方/供应方), it is wrong in principle to ignore part of what actually happened by describing it as either too remote or as consequential loss. The costs of the hedging devices are an integral part of the calculation of the net position, and if the net position is a directly relevant loss, so must the hedging costs be so regarded. To extract the costs of the hedging devices is wrong in principle and has no commercial merit.

In any event, it seems to me that the sale and purchase of crude oil is part of a well-established trading pattern, where the slightest movement of price can make a significant difference to profitability of a deal. It must have been for this very reason that hedging contracts and contracts for differences were required and provided as an adjunct to trading in physical oil. It was, I think, wholly foreseeable that if the claimants took a position which was otherwise than back-to-back with their contract with the defendants, they would cover their position with one of a multitude of hedging transactions available. While the contract instrument used may well vary from trade to trade(or possibly trader to trader), the defendants must have foreseen the need for the claimants to get over. **The consequential damages provision was, I think, to cover those damages which would fall within the second limb of Hadley v. Baxendale(1854)9 Exch. 341.** The hedging costs were part and parcel of the claimants' position with their suppliers, NPCC."(黑体部分是笔者的强调)

换言之,Morrison 大法官把原告在期货市场对冲的做法与费用视为是订约双方可以预见,所以原告可以把所有的损失向被告成功索赔,而有关对间接损失的豁免也不能保护卖方对这一项的损失负责。这显然又是另一个例子把间接损失等同于 Hadley v. Baxendale 先例中的第二种损失类别,也就是特别损失。

14.1.3 对间接损失不令人满意的解释与怎样拟定一条保护性的免责条文针对间接损失赔偿

虽然有上述所介绍过多个一审与上诉庭先例,判是"间接损失"(consequential damage)等同于"特别损失"(special damage)。这是不令人满意的,与本章中将金钱损失区分为"直接损失"(direct damage)与"间接损失"的观点不一致,这方面可以参阅本章 14.1 段为什么间接损失与特别损失是不同的损失类别的解释。这些一审与上诉庭的判法,也并非完全肯定,因为贵族院或最高院还没有做出定论。在 Caledonian North Sea Ltd. v. British Telecommunications plc(2002)1 Lloyd's Rep 553 的贵族院先例,Hoffmann 勋爵更是说明会保留将来对这一方面做出判决以肯定上诉庭的多个判决是否正确,说"wish to reserve the question of whether, in the context of the contracts in the Hotel Services and similar cases, the construction adopted by the Court of Appeal was correct."

目前对这种看来有一定矛盾与不肯定的法律地位,最好的解释还是把间接损失定在一条免责条文,就会导致了针对受益方的严格解释(*contra preferentem*)。所以,近期的先例都给免责条文中所针对的间接损失一个非常狭窄的解释,并与 Hadley v. Baxendale 中的特别损失相提并论。这方面可以节录《McGregor on Damages》(18th edn, 2009 年)之 1-039 段至 1-040 段如下:"And even if the Court of Appeal's interpretation for exclusion clauses should prevail, the argument as to the term's proper meaning is still adhered to and retained generally in the text, providing, as it does, a useful and valuable analysis of the damages recoverable. What is proposed is that the term consequential loss should be construed narrowly where exclusion clauses are concerned by resort to *contra preferentem* rule and widely in all other cases..."

所以,结论就是要限制索赔损失的种类,最好就是在免责条文明确说明某类别的损失如利润损失或对第三人的责任不必赔偿。订约方应该避免使用一些概括性的措辞如"间接损失",因为利润损失或其他通常被视为是间接损失的类别在一条免责条文下会被视为不是间接损失。这里可节录 Gerard McMeel 教授的《The Construction of Contracts—Interpretation, Implication and Rectification》一书第 21.69 段如下:"It is submitted that the best approach to drafting such clauses is to use terminology which has a settled meaning in English law. For example, in *Deepak* the clause excluding 'lost profits' was efficacious, whereas the boilerplate phrase of 'indirect and consequential losses' was ineffective. If such phrases are to be used, further definition or guidance as to what is intended should be included in the clause."

举一个例子是在一个关于电脑软件安装工程合约的 Salvage Association v. CAP Financial Services(1995)FSR 654 先例,有关免责条文是:"CAP shall not be liable for any indirect or consequential losses, damage, injury, costs or expenses of any kind whatsoever including economic loss such as a loss of production, loss of profits or of contracts ..."

最后一提是这种免责条文经常在合约出现的背后原因是在不少的买卖合约或工程合约,卖方/供应商或承建商会担心在自己的履约中发生延误或缺陷而要面对索赔。但由于对对方的业务不充分了解,怕会面对庞大的利润或生产损失的索赔,所以需要加上。最安全的做法是说明要豁免的损失类别,而不是依赖概括性的措辞如间接损失。但把损失类别说得太清楚也会面对一定程度的困难,因为不了解对方的业务,并会带来对方的抗拒。

在上述对间接损失的定义做出解释后,以下段节把一般理解的间接损失细分为几个类别,进一步分别探讨。

14.2 间接金钱上的损失类别之一:使用/营运利润或额外支出的损失

有关营运利润损失(losses through loss of use/profit),在本书第十六章第 2.2.3 段所介绍的 The "Ile Aux Moines"(1974)2 Lloyd's Rep 502 先例可以显示,案情是有关二手船舶买卖。违约的卖方因为市场急升而拒绝交出船舶,受害的买方所提出的损失有两项。第一项就是在违约当天(1972 年 12 月 15 日)有关船舶的合约价格与市场价格差别的 26 万美元。第二项就是在违约日期直到在 1973 年 2 月 16 日买进替代船舶(姊妹船)并在 1973 年的 7 月才真正交船,这相隔好几个月的营运利润损失。

卖方的违约/毁约还可以带来买方其他方面的损失如额外支出,如在 Blackburn Bobbin Co v. Allen(1918)1 KB 540 与 Erie County Natural Gas Co v. Carroll(1911) AC 105 PC 先例。

而针对延误交出货物,这一个类别的损失也会是千变万化,可先简单节录《McGregor on Damages》(18th edn, 2009 年)之 20 - 046 段:"Apart from loss of user profits, expenses may be incurred as a result of the loss of use. Thus in Smeed v. Foord(1859) 1 E & E 602, where a threshing - machine was sold and delivered late, the buyer recovered the resultant expense in stacking his crops and also, the stacked crops having been damaged by rain, the expense of drying them. In Watson v. Gray (1900) 16 TLR 308, where steel plates were sold and their delivery delayed, the buyer recovered for the increased cost of building barges for which the plates had been intended. And in Henderson v. Meyer(1941) 46 Com. Cas 209 a crane manufacturer sold cranes to a timber importer for use in his timber yard and delivered them late so that the buyer suffered loss in loading by hand. The buyer recovered as damages the extra labour costs of handling his timber by hand instead of by cranes and also the extra cost of loading his lorries by hand. He failed, however, to recover damages in respect of additional demurrage on barges kept waiting to be unloaded and rent for storage of some timber awaiting unloading. Such items were held too remote: the seller as a crane manufacturer could not be expected to have contemplated such expenses as they depended on the length of the timber - importing season."(除了使用的损失外,还会涉及额外的费用。在 Smeed v. Foord 先例,涉及卖方延误交付脱粒机,导致受害的买方要把他的谷物堆放起来,这产生了费用。而堆放的谷物部分受到雨水淋湿,需要再花钱弄干。这些额外的费用都可以向违约的卖方取回。另在 Watson v. Gray 先例,涉及钢板延误交付,这导致需要这些钢板制造驳船的买方制造成本/费用增加,这也被判是可以向违约的卖方取回。另在 Henderson v. Meyer 先例,涉及卖方延误交付吊车,这导致买方需要以人力装货而产生了额外的劳工费用,这被判是可以向违约的卖方取回。但买方另外产生的额外费用,包括驳船需要等待而产生了滞期费与租用仓库把部分木材的货物堆放就因为满足不了损失遥远性的限制而索赔失败,因为违约的卖方作为吊车生产商是不能合理预见到有这笔涉及木材出口季节长短的费用)。

不把财产/货物转移(或交出)或延误转移或有瑕疵的转移经常会带来受害方使用的损失或/与营运利润的损失。这损失在延误转移所包括的期限应该明确,就是合约应该转移/交出的一天至真正延误转移/交出一天的损失。而完全不转移/交出,等于是违约的卖方不提供货物,损失的期限就是到受害的买方能够买进替代货物的一天为止。至于转移有瑕疵的财产/货物,损失的期限是到受害的买方能够修复或买进替代货物的一天为止。而在这一段期限内,受害方是有合理减少损失的义务。

这种先例有不少,如著名的 Victoria Laundry v. Newman Industries(1949)2 K. B. 528 先例,案情涉及原告洗衣馆订购的锅炉因为延迟交付导致正常利润的损失。另外也可以多举几个这方面的案例,如在 Elbinger Akitengesellschaft v. Armstrong(1874) LR 9 QB 473 先例,案情涉及卖方延误交货,而有关的货物是火车的车轴与车轮,这导致了不能制造"铁路货车"(wagon)以供使用。Blackburn 大法官判是这一笔不能使用铁路货车的真正损失可以向卖方索赔,说:"It is obvious that both parties contemplated that the wheels and axles were to be put into immediate use. Under such circumstances, the natural and almost inevitable consequence of a delay in delivering a set of wheels would be that the plaintiffs, if they meant the wagon for their own use, or their customers, if the wagon was bespoke, would be deprived of the use of a wagon for a period equal to that for which the set of wheels was delayed. At all events the plaintiffs were entitled to recover at a rate per day equal to whatever the jury should find to be reasonable compensation for the loss of the use of the wagons."

这方面的案例不能成功索赔的原因往往是受害方的使用/营运利润或额外支出的损失被视为是遥远或双方订约时不能合理预见,而不是因为这种损失类别在本质上不被法律所接受。

14.2.1 索赔使用/营运利润损失必须满足损失遥远性的限制

受害的买方向卖方索赔分销/转售的利润损失，曾被视为是遥远并且卖方在订约时不可以预见买方事先或稍后把货物转售给第三人与有关分合约的实际内容。这要求以前是很严格，但近期的先例比较放宽。这可节录《McGregor on Damages》(18th edn,2009 年)之 20－027 段："The earlier cases did not allow the buyer to recover the loss of profit on a resale, whether made before or after the purchase, where all the seller knew was that the buyer had bought with a general intention to resell, as in Thol v. Henderson (1882)8 QBD 457, or even where it was the practice, known to the seller, for buyers to resell before delivery, as in Williams v. Reynolds(1865)6 B&S 495. Later cases, however, have shown a more liberal tendency and allowed loss of such profit where the defendant knew the buyer would resell, or even where it was probable that the buyer would resell."

对卖方在订约时必须合理预见有关货物会分销/转售，要求会是严格。光是知道受害方的买方是一位贸易商，通常会把手中的商品/货物转售，是不足够证明卖方在订约时预知到有分销/转售，能够索赔转售合约的利润损失。所以，英国法律还很倾向比较市场价格（如果有可供买卖的市场）计算损失。而在有可供买卖的市场情况下，受害的买方在减少损失的责任下应该马上去市场买进替代货物交出给分买方，就可以不必蒙受分销/转售的利润损失。在 Kwei Tek Chao v. British Traders and Shippers Ltd(1954)2 Lloyd's Rep 114 先例，Devlin 大法官是这样说："It is perfectly true that the defendants knew that the plaintiffs were merchants who had bought for re－sale, but everyone who sells to a merchant knows that he bought for re－sale, and it does not, as I understand it, make any difference to the ordinary measure of damage where there is a market. What is contemplated is that the merchant buys for re－sale, but if the goods are not delivered to him he will go out into the market and buy similar goods and honour his contract in that way. If the market has fallen, he has suffered no damage; if the market has risen the measure of damage is the difference in the market price. There are, of course, cases where that *prima facie* measure of damage is not applicable because something different is contemplated. If, for example, a man sells goods of a special manufacture and it is known that they are to be re－sold, it must also be known that they cannot be bought in the market, being specially manufactured by the seller. In such a case the loss of profit becomes the appropriate measure of damage. Similarly, it may very well be that in the case of string contracts, if the seller knows that the merchant is not buying merely for re－sale generally, but upon a string contract where he will re－sell those specific goods and where he could only honour his contract by delivering those goods and no others, the measure of loss or profit on re－sale is the right measure."

但注意是在 Kwei Tek Chao v. British Traders and Shippers Ltd 先例，是有可供买卖市场，这表示一般情况下本来就难索赔这种间接损失。至于在没有可供买卖市场的情况下，受害的买方本来就可以索赔间接损失，能否索赔分合约的利润损失就会是根据可能性了。估计受害的买方是一个国际贸易商，会把有关商品/货物转售的可能性应该是比较大。这方面在比较后期的先例看来是宽松了，其中可介绍的是 Patrick v. Russo-British Grain Export Co(1927)2 KB 535 先例。在该先例，涉及的货物是小麦但被认定受害方的买方是没有可供买卖市场可买进替代货物。法院判是买方可以向卖方索赔分合约价格与原买卖合约价格之间的差价，也就是买方的利润损失。Salter 大法官认为买方能索赔分合约损失的利润是不需要卖方肯定知道买方转售，卖方只需要料想到买方有可能会转售就已经足够，说："that the seller should have known, when he sold, that the buyer was buying to implement a contract already made or that the buyer would certainly resell; it is enough if both parties contemplate that the buyer will probably resell and the seller is content to take the risk. I think, therefore, that the arbitrators' finding [that the probability of resale was contemplated] is sufficient to support a claim for loss of profit on a resale."

另在 Hall v. Pim(1928)33 Com. Cas. 324 HL 先例，有关货物是小麦。仲裁庭认定买方会把有关货物留给自己用或转售是一半一半的机会。但贵族院还是判买方可以索赔转售合约的利润损失，其中 Viscount Dunedin 大法官说："to make a thing probable, it is enough, in my view, that there is an even chance of its happening."另 Shaw 勋爵说："the chance of a not unlikely thing [i. e. a resale] happening... [was] of those chances which must be reckoned to have been within the contemplation of the parties when sub-contracts or transfers were the matter of express agreement between them."

从较近期的案例看来对待违约的卖方在订约时知不知道买方"很有可能"(probable)分销/转售而蒙受利润损失是比较宽松。

14.2.2　买卖合约与运输合约由于本质不相同对索赔使用/营运利润损失的不同对待

买卖合约与运输合约被视为是本质上不相同。这导致了受害的买方如果蒙受使用/营运利润或额外支出的损失，违约的卖方就会有更大的可能性要承担赔偿责任，因为卖方通过订约前的谈判或是有关业务上应该拥有的常识，预见到如果不提供有关的财产/货物会导致买方蒙受这种间接金钱上的损失。但如果是运输合约，如果违约的承运人没有或延误在目的地交出财产/货物，受害的收货人就往往不能成功索赔使用/营运利润或额外支出的损失，因为在订立运输合约时，承运人通常是不会拥有对运输的财产/货物这方面业务的常识，货方也通常不会特别告诉承运人。这方面最著名的先例就是 Hadley v. Baxendale(1854)9 Ex. 341，案情涉及违约的承运人延误把一根新的蒸汽机曲轴运到目的地，这延误导致了收货人的工厂停产。法院判收货人本可早复工而赚取到的生产利润的损失是承运人在订约时无法合理预见的，如没有办法预见收货人没有一根备用的蒸汽机曲轴，所以不必承担赔偿责任。

这方面可节录《McGregor on Damages》(18th edn, 2009 年)之 6-206 段：

"While claims against sellers for loss of profits on resale or in user have on the whole succeeded, similar claims against carriers who have failed to deliver goods, delayed their delivery, or delivered them in bad condition, have in the past practically always failed. These include the three important early cases of Hadley v. Baxendale (1854) 9 Ex. 341 itself and British Columbia Saw Mill Co v. Nettleship (1868) LR 3 CP 499 as to user profits, and Horne v. Midland Ry (1873) LR 8 CP 131 as to sale profits and also the later, equally unsuccessful claims for user profits in Heskell v. Continental Express (1950) 1 All ER 1033 and for sale profits in The Arpad (1934) P 189 CA. The reason for the more rigid application of the contemplation of the parties doctrine to carrier than to sellers follows as 'a natural result of the fact that a carrier is supposed to know less about the commodity he carries and to undertake less responsibility in connection with it'. So said Roche J in Montevideo Gas Co v. Clan Line (1921) 37 TLR 544, one of the successful claims made for loss of profits against carriers, where the carrier knew the coal carried was urgently required by the claimant to make gas and that another supply or an adequate substitute would not be quickly obtainable. This view was endorsed in two of the leading modern cases on remoteness of damage in contract. In Victoria Laundry v. Newman (1949) 2 KB 528 CA Asquith LJ, pointing to the fact that the courts had been slow to allow loss of profits against a carrier, said: 'This was not, it would seem, because a different principle applies in such cases, but because the application of the same principle leads to different results. A carrier knows less than a seller about the purposes for with the buyer or consignee needs the goods, or about other 'special circumstances' which may cause exceptional loss if due delivery is withheld.'(Asquith 大法官是说针对这一方面,适用的原则是一致的[即损失遥远性的可预见],只是同一个原则会得出不同的结果。相比卖方,承运人对有关货物的买方或收货人的实际要求或其他的环境通常知道得更少,所以不准时交货导致买方或收货人蒙受不正常的损失是不会预见到)

And in The "Heron II" (1969) 1 AC 350 Lord Upjohn said that, while each of the contracting parties 'must be taken to understand the ordinary practices and exigencies of the other's trade... it must be remembered when dealing with the case of a carrier of goods by land, sea or air, he is not carrying on the same trade as the consignor of the goods and his knowledge of the practices and exigencies of the other's trade may be limited and less than between buyer and seller of goods who probably know far more about one another's business.'(买卖双方应该被视为是知道对方一般性的做法与迫切需要……但对海陆空的承运人而言,他不是参与与收货人同一类的业务,所以通常被视为是对收货人是否迫切需要与怎样处理有关货物所知道的有限,比不上买卖双方对此的了解)

Yet, in The "Pegase" (1981) 1 Lloyd's Rep 175, Robert Goff J said that he could 'find in the cases no rule of policy either excluding, or imposing special criteria in respect of, the recovery of damages for loss of profits, whether the relevant contract be a contract of sale or a contract of carriage, whether the breach be non – delivery or delayed delivery, and whether the profits claimed to have been lost are resale profits or profits from loss of use.'（但 Goff 大法官是说，英国法律没有在政策上对买卖合约或运输合约针对利润损失的索赔有所不同，不论违约是不交货或延误交货，也不论索赔是分销利润的损失或是失去使用的损失。这表示针对违约的卖方与针对违约的承运人不同对待并非是法律的问题，而是事实的问题）

'In truth', as Roche J put it in Montevideo Gas Co v. Clan Line (1921) 37 TLR 544, where loss of user profits on a non – delivery was awarded, 'distinctions between the liability of a carrier and a seller depend on matters of fact and not of law'. Thus damages for loss of profits on a sale are found to have been allowed in The "Pegase" (1981) 1 Lloyd's Rep 175, where carriage of a cargo by sea was delayed, in the early Simpson v. LNW Ry (1876) 1 QBD 274 and Jameson v. Midland Ry Co (1884) 50 lt 426 where parcels carried by rail were delayed, and in Panalpina International Transport v. Densil Underwear (1981) 1 Lloyd's Rep 187, where there was a delayed consignment of goods by air.

在这里可简短介绍上述提到的两个比较近期的先例，第一个就是 The "Pegase" (1981) 1 Lloyd's Rep 175 先例。该先例涉及船东因为不合理绕航，产生了长达 65 天的延误才到意大利卸港。该船舶是涉及 FOB 买卖，有关的货物是铬铁矿砂。由于受害方的收货人不能在市场找到同样的货物，加上存货不足，所以蒙受了 65 天的分销利润损失。而船东的抗辩是他在订约时无法预见这类损失，也不会知道收货人的存货不足而对船上这票铬铁矿砂有迫切需要。仲裁庭是判船东胜诉，但在高院，Goff 大法官是这样说："On the findings of fact in the special case, it is plain that the receivers did in fact suffer a loss of resale profits by reason of the owners' breach of contract."接下去 Goff 大法官就提到在较早时节录的说法，就是英国法律没有在政策上对买卖合约或运输合约针对利润损失的索赔有所不同。而在本先例涉及十分严重的延误，Goff 大法官认为仲裁庭应该在两方面考虑收货人的利润损失做出决定。一是索赔的分销利润是否一般性而不是过高；二是船东即使是预见不了收货人对这票货物的迫切需要，因为他的存货不足，但由于延误严重，船东应该可以合理估计得到收货人即使有合理数量的存货，也不够维持，所以对合理存货可以维持的时间做出估计后，额外的延误还是需要做出赔偿。Goff 大法官是这样说："... on the facts found, that the owners should, on the knowledge available to them, have reasonably understood that they were assuming responsibility for such a loss in the event of a considerable delay appears to me to be unobjectionable in point of principle. But before assessing the damages on the basis of the resale profits actually lost by the receivers, the arbitrator ought, in my judgment, to have considered two questions in particular. First since the actual resale contracts were not known to the owners, he should have considered whether the actual profits lost by the receivers were out of the ordinary; clearly, they should not be entitled to recover profits for "extravagant or unusual bargains", but only at a reasonable level. Second, and more important, the arbitrator should have taken into account the fact that the owners had no knowledge of the limited storage space available to the receivers or of their having run down their stocks, and (as I understand the position) had no knowledge that the receivers had an immediate need of these goods for processing and resale. That being so, it was necessary for the arbitrator to make some allowance for a period during which stocks might have been used for the purpose of meeting commitments, in order to assess the loss of resale profits only by reference to the period during which, on the knowledge available to them, the owners (had they considered the position) ought reasonably to have contemplated that it was not unlikely that the receivers would lose resale profits for want of these goods. Such an exercise may well be a difficult one, and may call for a somewhat arbitrary conclusion; but it is an exercise which has, in my judgment, to be carried out if the principles of law are to be properly applied to the facts of the present case."

第二个就是 Panalpina International Transport v. Densil Underwear (1981) 1 Lloyd's Rep 187 先例。案情涉及空运的延误,这导致有关的货物(衬衣)延误运到尼日利亚。由于延误错过了圣诞节的销售旺季,收货人拒绝接收有关货物,最后被迫以低价在当地市场转售。由于在订立空运合约前,货方曾经告诉承运人有关货物需要在圣诞节之前运到尼日利亚以供应圣诞节市场,所以被法院判是承运人需要负责赔偿这一笔延误的损失,因为违约的承运人在订约前被通知有关的特殊情况,符合 Hadley v. Baxendale (1854) 9 Ex. 341 先例中的第二条规则。Fay 大法官是这样说:"Next arises the question as to remoteness of damage. The claim here is for a large sum of money reflecting a fall in the value of the goods because they missed the Christmas market. Under the second rule in Hadley v. Baxendale (1854) 9 Ex. 341 this is clearly an item of damage which is too remote in the ordinary course of events and can only be claimed if it was reasonably within the contemplation of the parties because the party to be charged had been given the information which enabled him to appreciate that this kind of damage would flow. I have already found that I accept Mr. Ram's(发货人) evidence to the effect that he informed Mr. Fagin (承运人) that the purchaser in Lagos wanted the goods before Christmas, for the Christmas market, and that he told Mr. Fagin that he accepted the Dec. 2 flight because the purchaser insisted he wanted them for Christmas. That seems to me, accepting it as I do, to bring the defendants' claim within the second rule in Hadley v. Baxendale. There was information given to the plaintiffs from which they could reasonably contemplate that the damages, if there were damages for delay, would be swelled by the loss of the Christmas market. Therefore, I hold that the defendants are over that hurdle, and I turn to look at the quantum of those damages."

14.2.3 过高的使用/营运利润损失被视为是遥远与不能合理预见

即使买卖合约下,使用/营运利润或额外支出的损失是可以被英国法律接受作为间接损失提出索赔,有关损失项目的本质与金额高低也要是违约方(不论是买方或是卖方)可以合理预见到。如果分销/转售的利润十分可观,不是一般性的买卖可以赚取,也会是卖方在订约时没有办法预料得到的损失而不能成功索赔。除非是违约的卖方在订约时被买方告知有关分销/转售合约的细节,主要是价格方面,才会要作出赔偿。这方面最著名的就是 Victoria Laundry v. Newman(1949)2 KB 528 CA 先例,上诉庭判受害的买方可以索赔延误交付订购的锅炉所带来的正常利润损失,但拒绝买方其余几项来自政府方面的可挣取极高额利润的合约损失。因为违约卖方在订约时没有特别被知会的情况下,不可能预见到买方会有这么值钱的几份合约在手。另在上一小段所介绍的 The "Pegase"(1981)1 Lloyd's Rep 175 先例,在节录的 Goff 大法官判词中也有明确说到这一方面,不重复。

总结,这方面可节录《McGregor on Damages》(18th edn,2009 年)之 20-029 段:"Where damages are allowed for loss of profit on a resale of which the seller knew the actuality or the probability, he will not be liable for an exceptional loss of profits unless he has been informed of the details of the sub-contracts and only then if he can be said to have taken the risk of such loss on his shoulders. This appears from the speeches in Hall v. Pim (1928)33 Com. Cas. 324 HL. Lord Dunedin said: 'The contracts... must be contracts in accordance with the market, not extravagant and unusual bargains.' And Lord Shaw said: 'It is not suggested that these prices were out of the ordinary course of business. Had this been so, different considerations might quite well have arisen.' Thus in Household Machines v. Cosmos Exporters(1947)1 KB 217, where the seller knew of the claimant's intention to resell but did not know the details of the sub-contract, Lewis J did not award the claimant the 12 per cent by which the sub-contract price was higher than the contract price, but gave only 10 per cent. Similarly, in Coastal International Trading v. Maroil(1988) 1 Lloyd's Rep 92 where the sub-contract, of which the defendants were fully aware, contained unusual terms rendering the claimants' profit under it unreasonable and such as would not have been within the contemplation of the parties, the profit awarded to the claimants was arrived at after eliminating the extravagant effect of the unusual terms"。

14.2.4 财产/货物涉及有可供买卖市场通常不能索赔使用/营运利润损失

已经提到过,买卖合约通常是可以成功让受害的买方在卖方违约(不论是不履行提供货物、延误履行或有缺陷履行)可以索赔使用/营运利润或额外支出的损失,但这里有一个重要的例外,就是有关的财产/货物有"可供买卖市场"(available market)可以马上买进替代。因为在这种情况下,在 Breach Date Rule 与 Market rule 下受害的买方就应该去市场马上买进替代货物。这一方面是买方必须合理减少损失的义务,另一方面是合约价格与更高的市场价格(通常卖方在市场上扬才会拒绝提供货物)之间的差价才是"基本的损失"(basic loss)或违约卖方在订约时可以合理预见的损失。所以,买方会蒙受的使用/营运利润或额外支出的损失,通常被视为是卖方在订约时没有办法合理预见或可以在买方合理减少损失的行动下避免。在"商品买卖"(commodity sales)就经常会是这种情况。但如果买卖的财产/货物是涉及一些没有市场或市场不容易找得到替代,就不一样了。例如是 Victoria Laundry v. Newman (1949)2 KB 528 CA 先例的锅炉,就明显不会有市场马上可买进替代,所以索赔一般性的利润损失就完全站得住脚。虽然大部分的商品如散粮、食糖、化肥等通常都有可供买卖市场,但也会有地区性的局限或/与少部分的商品(如一些石油产品)不是这种情况。如果法院或仲裁庭接受是没有可供买卖市场,受害的买方就可以向违约的卖方索赔使用/营运利润或额外支出的损失了。在上述所介绍的 The "Pegase" (1981)1 Lloyd's Rep 175 先例,就因为有关货物/商品的铬铁矿砂当时没有可供买卖市场让受害的收货人买进替代,所以涉及向船东索赔延误所带来的利润损失。

最后可以节录《Benjamin's Sale of Goods》(8th edn,2010 年)之 17－035 段作为总结:"If there was no market for the goods in question but the seller knew, or ought to have known, that the buyer bought the goods with a view to resale, the buyer is entitled to his loss of profit on the resale when the seller fails to deliver the goods. Thus, if the goods were to be specially manufactured for the buyer, and the seller knew that they were to be resold by him, the buyer's loss of profit is the measure of damages when the seller fails to deliver, the seller is taken to know that similar goods cannot be bought in the market. For the buyer to be entitled to claim his loss of profits under this principle, the sub－contract must be of a usual type, and the profit must be reasonable in amount."(如果有关货物没有可供买卖市场,但卖方知道或应该知道买方购买这票货物是为了转售,买方是有权向违约卖方索赔这一笔分销利润的损失。所以,如果是需要特别制造的货物,而卖方知道买方会转售,买方的利润损失就是卖方拒绝交出货物的一般性损失计算,因为卖方知道同样的货物是无法在市场上买得到替代。但买方要成功索赔利润损失,有关的分合约必须是一般性的类别与利润必须是合理)

14.3 间接金钱上的损失类别之二:名誉损失

名誉损失(loss of reputation)通常是视为"非金钱损失"(non－pecuniary loss),会在本章稍后详论。但在某一些类别如雇佣合约(在贵族院的 Mahmud v. Bank of Credit and Commerce International SA[1998]AC 20 先例)会被视为是属于金钱上的损失,因为可以把名誉损失量化。这可以节录《McGregor on Damages》(18th edn,2009 年)之 2－028 段如下:

"Loss of reputation generally makes for a non－pecuniary loss but it may also involve a pecuniary one for which damages may be awarded in contract. As Hallett J said in Foaminol Laboratories v. British Artid Plastics(1941)2 All ER 393:'A claim for mere loss of reputation is the proper subject of an action for defamation, and cannot ordinarily be sustained by means of any other form of action... [but] if pecuniary loss can be established, the mere fact that the pecuniary loss is brought about by the loss of reputation caused by a breach of contract is not sufficient to preclude the plaintiffs from recovering in respect of that pecuniary loss.'

It is thus established that a claimant can recover for such a pecuniary loss in three particular types of case: (1) where the wrongful dismissal of an actor causes him loss of publicity; (2) where there has been a failure or a mismanagement of the advertising of the claimant's business; and (3) where the defendant fails to honour the claimant's drafts thereby causing him loss of credit, or otherwise fails in breach of contract to sustain the claimant's financial credit.

This head of damage may be recoverable in other types of case; that these arelikely to be few is suggested by the fact that in the three established types of case the loss was particularly contemplated by the parties to the contract. There is, however, one important development. For long it was accepted - erroneously, it has always been submitted in this work - that the House of Lords in Addis v. Gramophone Co (1909) AC 488 had laid down that there could be no recovery for financial loss through loss of reputation arising from an employee's wrongful dismissal. Now in Mahmud v. Bank of Credit and Commerce International SA (1998) AC 20 the House has held that in principle damages may be awarded for such loss caused by breach of contract of employment where the breach is of the implied term of trust and confidence."

14.4 间接金钱上的损失类别之三:失去亲人提供服务的损失

这一个类别的损失很少会在商业合约出现,所以笔者不多讲,只节录《McGregor on Damages》(18th edn, 2009 年)之 2-029 段如下:"Very seldom will loss of the services of spouse, child or other relative ground recovery in contract, but that it is a possible head of damage is shown by the interesting case of Jackson v. Watson (1909) 2 KB 193 CA. The claimant bought tinned salmon which his wife ate. On her death through food poisoning, he successfully sued the seller for damages in respect of the pecuniary loss of his wife's services, being now required to employ extra servants in the house. In Farwell LJ's opinion the damages should be assessed 'on the basis of the probable duration of their joint lives and the loss to the husband during that period.'"

14.5 间接金钱上的损失类别之四:违约所带来的使费

14.5.1 违约所带来的使费只要满足损失遥远性就可以成功索赔

这一类别的损失会是千变万化,它也是英国法律所接受的损失类别,只要满足对损失限制的要求如损失遥远性,这包括订约时可以合理预见与满足因果关系。这方面可节录《McGregor on Damages》(18th edn, 2009 年)之 2-030 段如下:"Many types of expenses may be incurred by the claimant as a result of the breach which will constitute a recoverable loss. Reasonable expenditure by the claimant in inquiring and searching for goods, the delivery of which has been delayed by the defendant carrier, has been allowed (Heskell v. Continental Express[1950]1 All ER 1033); the same would apply in the case of goods lost by a carrier, or where their non – delivery or delayed delivery is under a contract of sale. And where goods sold are delivered late so as to dislocate the buyer's business arrangements and thus involve him in further expense, this expenditure is often recovered as damages. Examples in the cases are of extra freight and insurance incurred by the claimant in forwarding the goods to his sub – buyer at a costlier season of the year (Borries v. Hutchinson[1865]18 CB[NS]445); the increased cost of building barges through the delay in the arrival of steel plates (Watson v. Gray[1900]16 TLR 308); and the extra labour costs incurred in the claimant's timber – yard by reason of the late delivery of cranes (Henderson v. Meyer[1941]46 Com Cas 209). Similar principles will apply where the goods sold are never delivered, and where the contract is one of carriage with non – delivery or delayed delivery (SS Ardennes[Cargo Owners] v SS Ardennes[Owners][1951]1 KB 55). Conversely, where goods sold are not accepted, recovery has been allowed for storage charges until such time as another purchaser is found (Harlow & Jones v. Panex International [1967]2 Lloyd's Rep. 509). Again, where defective goods have been delivered to the claimant under a contract of sale he may recover various expenditures made necessary by the defect, such as the cost of pulling down and rebuilding a wall which he had constructed with defective mortar (Smith v. Johnson[1899]15 TLR 179), the cost of rebuilding a factory burnt down (Harbutt's 'Plasticine' v. Wayne Tank & Pump Co[1970]1 QB 447 CA), the cost of repairing a machine broken up in processing a defective supply of steel (Bacon v. Cooper[1982]1 All ER 397), management expenses and management time taken up (The Salvage Association v. CAP Financial Services Ltd[1995]22 FSR 654), or medical expenses which may result where the claimant is physically insured by the defect in the goods (Square v. Model Dairies[1939]2 KB 365 CA; Wilson v. Rickett Cockerell[1954]1 QB 598 CA). Indeed, physical injury to the claimant will in contract generally constitute a consequential loss, and expenses of cure therefore fall within this category. So too, where there is expense incurred, in acquiring a substitute for what the defendant has failed to provide, in excess of the cost of the substitute, recovery has been allowed for such outlay, as where an evicted lessee incurs expenses in moving to, and setting up in, new premises (Grosvenor Hotel v. Hamilton[1894]2 QB 836 CA); similarly, the cost of alternative accommodation may be recovered where a lessee is forced to move while his lessor's failure to repair is being remedied (Calabar Properties v. Stitcher[1984]2 QB 836 CA)."(受害的原告由于违约而产生的许多不同类别的使费/费用都可以向违约方取回。例如在 Heskell v. Continental Express 先例，被告的承运人延误付运而导致了原告花费合理费

用询问与寻找他的货物,被判是可以向被告取回。如果是承运人把货物丢失了或者是在买卖合约下卖方不做出付运或延误付运,受害的原告也是同样的地位。如果货物延误交出导致了受害的买方业务上脱节,因此产生了额外的使费,这笔费用是可以作为损失向卖方取回。这种例子有不少,例如在 Borries v. Hutchinson 先例中的额外运费与保险费把有关货物转运给分买方。在 Watson v. Gray 先例中钢板延误交付导致了买方制造成本/费用增加。在 Henderson v. Meyer 先例中延误交付吊车导致了买方需要以人力装货而产生了额外的劳工费用。反过来说是买方违约拒绝接受货物,在 Harlow & Jones v. Panex International 先例就允许受害的卖方向买方取回货物的储存费用直到找到另一位新买方。如果涉及有瑕疵的货物,受害的买方可以取回各种因为瑕疵所产生的费用。在 Smith v. Johnson 先例中,卖方供应有缺陷的砂浆导致了建好的墙壁需要推倒重建的费用。在 Harbutt's 'Plasticine' v. Wayne Tank & Pump Co 先例中,卖方在买方的工厂安装有瑕疵的设备,该设备在使用中着火导致工厂被烧毁而需要重建的费用。在 Bacon v. Cooper 先例中由于卖方供应有缺陷的金属切割机器,买方因为要购买替代的零部件而欠信贷公司的高额利息。在 The Salvage Association v. CAP Financial Services Ltd 先例中的管理费用与时间,或在 Square v. Model Dairies 等先例的有缺陷货物导致原告受伤。通常这种违约导致了人身伤亡的医疗费用都被接受为间接损失,可向违约方取回。其他的费用包括受害的原告找替代而产生的花费,如在 Grosvenor Hotel v. Hamilton 先例中被驱逐的租客因为寻找新住所的花费,或在 Calabar Properties v. Stitcher 先例中出租人违约不维修而导致租客另寻找新住所)

14.5.1.1　有关先例之一:延误带来增加进口税的损失

针对以上的先例,可挑部分做进一步解释。第一个先例是 SS Ardennes(Cargo Owners) v. SS Ardennes(Owners)(1951)1 KB 55,案情涉及原告的出口商通过被告的船东运输一批 3000 箱的橘子,因为船东代理口头承诺说船舶会直接开去伦敦,并会在 1947 年 11 月 20 日到达。但实际上,这艘船先开去了安特卫普,将原告的 374 箱橘子卸下留给其他的船舶运去伦敦。其中的 362 箱于 12 月 15 日运达伦敦(丢失 12 箱)。剩余的 2626 箱橘子在 12 月 5 日被这艘船舶在伦敦卸下。结果当这批货物到达伦敦时,伦敦当地的橘子进口税提升,而且其他出口商的橘子也运抵伦敦,橘子的市场价格下跌。法院判是被告的船东应赔付给原告的承运人相应的损失,这包括增加的进口税和市场价格的损失。

14.5.1.2　有关先例之二:因买方不接受货物而导致的货物储存使费

第二个要介绍的先例是 Harlow & Jones v. Panex International(1967)2 Lloyd's Rep. 509,案情涉及一票 1 万吨钢坯的 FOB 买卖合约,卖方是从俄罗斯供应商购入这一票钢坯,并转卖给买方,而买方也把该票钢坯再转售给了西班牙的分买方。卖方与供应商的合约中有关付运的条文是:"由供应商选择在 1966 年 8 月到 9 月之间付运"(Goods to be delivered during August/September in supplier's option)。在 7 月 14 日,卖方通知买方货物将于8月初在装港备妥,并要求FOB买方派船。但买方没有回应与采取行动。只在8月1日买方才通知卖方他要求分两船付运该票钢坯,其中第一船是5000吨,装船期在8月12日到22日之间。而第二船将会在8月底装余下的5000吨。在8月3日,买方告诉卖方由于卖方的延误确认导致了买方无法在8月派船。在8月11日,买方要求卖方保证在8月20日至27日有货可装,并要求其在24小时内回复。再到了8月22日,买方通知卖方说后者的上述不马上回应的行为构成违约/毁约,并被接受终断合约。而从买方的态度可以想象得到当时钢材的市场价格暴跌。事后卖方以FOB买方不接受货物的违约/毁约提出索赔,而在责任方面法院是判买方违约。由于有关货物的钢坯没有可供买卖的市场转售,卖方向买方提出的索赔包括了利润损失与卖方承诺补偿供应商的储存费用。其中有关这一笔金额颇大的储存费用,Roskill大法官认为是可以加在卖方总的损失向买方索赔,也不受到卖方与供应商之间的有条件协议的影响(条件是在成功向买方索赔才需要赔付给供应商),他说:"Next there are the storage charges. I do not propose to go through the correspondence on this detail. There are a number of letters and telexes. Mr. Dunn(买方代表大律师)correctly summarized the final position by saying that the bargain was that the Russian sellers would only claim against the plaintiffs if the plaintiffs could recover those charges from the defendants in this action. Mr. Dunn argued that an arrangement of that kind barred the plaintiffs recovering in this action. For my part I am unable to see why. The plaintiffs have - and this was not contested - apart from any agreement with the Russian sellers, a perfectly good claim for these storage charges. Why the plaintiffs should not make an arrangement with their own sellers, 'We will claim these and hand the proceeds over to you if we recover provided you let us off if we do not', I am unable to see. Nor do I see why the existence of such an arrangement should afford the defendants a defence which they would not otherwise possess. It seems to me an eminently sensible commercial arrangement. I think the storage charges are recoverable. The figure is £ 21,327 1s. 8d."

14.5.1.3 有关先例之三:设备有瑕疵导致火灾把工厂烧毁的工厂重建费用

在Harbutt's 'Plasticine' v. Wayne Tank & Pump Co[1970]1 QB 447 CA先例中,案情涉及原告的买方向被告购买并安装一批设备并导致火灾。原告是一家生产粘土的工厂,粘土的主要成分是一种称为硬脂的油蜡。之前原告一直是将液体的硬脂用油槽汽车运来,然后凝固成固体储存起来,需要使用时再拿出一小块加热融化成液体,再由人工运输给用来混合不同成分制造粘土的机器。但这种加热后的液体很容易燃烧。之后原告的员工提出,这些硬脂可以在整个过程中保持液体的状态。应该从油槽汽车运进工厂后,放进安装了加热系统的特殊储存容器中,然后通过加热的管道直接运进混合机器。可以在加热管道的尾部安装喷嘴来控制硬脂的流量。

被告的公司是制造传输管道的专家,他们对这个想法很有兴趣,并设计了图纸。

他们设计了两个新的储存箱，由软钢制成并加装了一根塑料来防止腐蚀。管道是用一种名为 dura – pipe 的塑料制成。外面包了一层加热器，用电线连在一起，使得电流得以通过以加热管道。上面还安装了一个恒温器来控制温度。

原告对这项设计非常满意并订购了这个设备，并由被告公司进行安装。在1963年2月5日，被告公司的两名测试员将设备安装好准备进行测试。硬脂被放在新的储存箱里等待流入管道。但是由于天气十分寒冷，硬脂还是固体的。到了很晚的时候还是不能开始测试。所以在当天下午四点时，一名测试员 Duncan 先生打开了加热器，认为如果加热器开整晚，就会令固体的硬脂变成液体然后流入管道，估计第二天早上就可以进行测试了。Duncan 先生在离开时，对原告公司的人员说，所有的设备都连接好了，如果明天早上通知我们温度足够高，就可以进行测试了。之后所有人在当天晚上离开原告的工厂，开着加热器，认为第二天早上硬脂就会融化，就可以进行测试了。然而第二天早上5点到6点之间，有浓烟从厂房冒出来，大火根本不能扑灭，造成了严重的损失。法院认定，造成火灾的原因是因为 dura – pipe 在高温下变形，而恒温器失效。之后 dura – pipe 出现裂缝导致硬脂流出而引起大火，火势蔓延得很快。法院认为是由于被告公司三个方面的错误导致火灾：(1)被告公司根本不应该使用 dura – pipe 这种塑料，而应该使用不锈钢。因为塑料传热很慢，而且在高温下容易变形。(2)被告公司不应该把电子加热器安装在塑料管道上。被告的公司一直是用金属的管道，从来没有用过塑料的，而恒温器在金属管道上可以正常工作，在塑料上会失效，加上塑料传热很慢，管道不同位置的温度很不一样。如果恒温器是安装在远离加热器的地方，显示的温度就很低，相反，如果恒温器安装在接近加热器的地方，温度高时就会发出危险信号。这个致命的疏忽导致恒温器根本没有发挥任何效用。(3)被告的员工不应该在2月5日晚上打开加热器，然后整晚都不管它，没有人监视。如果是在白天开启加热器并一直监视它，管道出现裂缝就会很明显，在着火之前应该就被发现。所以在没有人监视时，加热器应该被关闭。

责任明确了之后，针对有关的损失计算，其中主要的一项是关于赔偿原告厂房烧毁的损失。原告之前五层高的厂房在大火后根本不能再继续使用，不得不重新建造了一栋两层高的厂房。这是被高院支持，而上诉庭也在这方面持一致看法。Denning 勋爵是这样说："The destruction of a building is different from the destruction of a chattel. If a second – hand car is destroyed, the owner only gets its value; because he can go into the market and get another second – hand car to replace it. He cannot charge the other party with the cost of replacing it with a new car. But when this mill was destroyed, the plasticine company had no choice. They were bound to replace it as soon as they could, not only to keep their business going, but also to mitigate the loss of profit (for which they would be able to charge the defendants). They replaced it in the only possible way, without adding any extras. I think they should be allowed the cost of replacement. True it is that they got new for old; but I do not think the wrongdoer can diminish the claim on that account. If they had added extra accommodation or made extra improvements, they would have to give credit. But that is not this case. I think the judge was right on this point."（工厂的损毁与动产的损毁在损失计算方面不一样。如果一辆二手车被损毁，车主只能取回该二手车的价值，因为他可以去市场买进另一辆替代的二手车，他不能索赔一辆替代的新车。但在本案例工厂被损毁的情况，原告是没有其他索赔的选择。他只能尽快建立另一栋工厂作为替代，以保障他们的业务，进而减少利润损失［这利润损失本来是可以向被告取回］。原告建立的替代工厂没有增加什么额外的设备或建筑［如员工宿舍］，所以Denning勋爵认为原告可以把重新建造的费用从违约的被告取回。会是原告得到了一个新的工厂，索赔金额会需要折扣，但由于不明显原告在这方面有得益，所以在本案例的违约方不应该可以因此减少赔偿金额。如果原告在新的工厂加上或改良了设备或建筑，这好处是要扣去。但在本案例中没有这种情况，所以高院判原告成功索赔这一笔费用是正确的）

14.5.1.4　有关先例之四：房屋租赁因为违反维修义务导致租客另租用替代房屋的使费

在Calabar Properties v. Stitcher（1984）2 QB 836 CA先例中，案情涉及一个从1975年10月开始的一幢顶层房屋的租约。在这份租约下双方约定，被告的租客负责缴纳每年100英镑的地租，以及服务费、保险费和税费。而原告的房东负责外部维修。被告的租客夫妻取得房屋并重新装修之后，发现由于房屋外部的瑕疵，有水流进来导致潮湿和损坏。他们向原告投诉，而原告的房东坚持认为是因为水汽凝结导致潮湿和损坏，与房屋无关。1978年4月，原告的房东在地区法院起诉被告要求支付地租。之后案件被转去了高级法院。1978年6月被告提出反诉，要求原告赔偿因为他违反维修义务而对被告造成的损失。1981年1月，由于被告的丈夫在这幢潮湿的房屋中居住而生病，被告夫妻搬出了这幢房屋并找了另外一幢替代房屋居住。在责任方面，法院判是原告违反了维修的义务，应赔偿因此而造成的损失，这包括维修和重新装修房屋的费用（考虑到重新装修后使房屋比原来的更好，故在赔偿大原则下这总的花费应减去1/3），被告夫妻在这幢房屋居住期间因为失望、不舒服、失去快乐和生病所遭受的损失。但法院拒绝赔偿给被告因为房屋在不能居住期间所产生的税费、租金、运营费用（这包括服务费）以及间接使用的损失，因为这种费用本来也需要支付。但值得一提的是，Stephenson大法官和Griffiths大法官都指出，被告的租客没有提出该房屋在某个特定日期后不适合居住了，因此他们租了另一幢替代房屋。而如果被告夫妻提出了该项指控，关于租住替代房屋的使费是可以获得赔偿的。

14.5.2　在受害方索赔利润损失下避免对使费做出双重赔偿

卖方的违约还会带来买方表面看来是冤枉的花费，如在买卖合约中买方所花费的开出信用证的费用。这些间接损失也是可以索赔，但要小心是不要在买方索赔利润损失的情况下作出双重的赔偿。这是因为买方要赚取利润，即使没有违约，在履行下也逃不掉要支付这一笔费用。这方面可节录《McGregor on Damages》（18th edn,

2009 年)之 20 - 055 段:"Care, however, must be taken in allowing recovery of expenses rendered futile by the breach, for such recovery is alternative, and not additional, to a claim for loss of profits. Thus in Hydraulic Engineering Co v. McHaffie (1878) 4 QBD 670 CA, where the seller failed to deliver on time a part for a machine which the buyer was making for a third party, the court fell into error by allowing the buyer to recover both the expense incurred in making the machine and the profit which he lost when the third party refused to take the machine because it was not ready on time."

14.5.3　受害方赔付给第三人的赔偿与费用

而另一种常见的可以获得赔偿的使费损失是由于被告的违约而导致的原告支付给第三人(如分买方)的赔偿与费用(这包括诉讼费用)。这方面可以节录《McGregor on Damages》(18th edn, 2009 年)之 2 - 031 段如下:"One of the most interesting and probably one of the most frequent types of recoverable expenditure involves money paid by the claimant in proceedings with a third party which have been brought about by the defendant's breach of contract. Thus compensation paid to a third party, whether under a court judgment or by way of settlement, has been recovered as damages against the defendant, as where the third party is a sub - buyer of goods sold by the defendant to the claimant (Grebert - Borgnis v. Nugent [1885] 15 QBD 85 CA; Elbinger Aktiengesellschaft v. Armstrong [1874] LR 9 QB 475; Biggin v. Permanite [1951] 2 KB 314 CA; Hardwick Game Farm v. Suffolk Agricultural Poultry Producers Association [1969] 2 AC 31; Contigroup Companies Inc Glencore AG [2005] 1 Lloyd's Rep 241), a person physically injured by such goods (Mowbray v. Merryweather [1895] 2 QB 640 CA), or a buyer from the claimant of goods carried by the defendant for the claimant (The Ocean Dynamic [1982] 2 Lloyd's Rep 88). Similarly, fines paid by the claimant under a prosecution in respect of dangerous goods sold to him by the defendant have been held recoverable as damages (Crage v. Fry [1903] 67 JP 240; Cointat v. Myham [1913] 2 KB 220). And there are even more cases allowing the recovery as damages of legal costs incurred by the claimant in defending such actions and prosecution, sometimes successfully (Agius v. Great Western Colliery [1899] 1 QB 413) but usually unsuccessfully (Hammond v. Bussey [1888] 20 QBD 79 CA). Conversely, costs incurred by the claimant in bringing an action as a result of the defendant's breach have been recovered as damages, again whether the action has been brought successfully (Henderson v. Squire [1869] LR 4 QB 170) or unsuccessfully (Randell v. Trimen [1856] 18 CB 786).

14.5.3.1　有关先例之一:Contigroup Companies, Inc v. Glencore A. G.

也是介绍一些在上一段节录中所提到的先例,首先是在 Contigroup Companies, Inc v. Glencore A. G. (2005) 1 Lloyd's Rep 241 先例中,涉及的是丁烷(butane)与丙烷(propane)以 CFR 卖给中石油,卖方就是 Glencore,交货地点是中国温州,时间是 2002

年6月7日至12日。而Glencore就是在较早前向Contigroup买进一批丙烷并装在一只名为Sunway的船上。由于Sunway轮受到延误,所以根本赶不上交货日期。在5月31日,中石油才被告知交油的日期要比约定的日期晚3天(6月15日才会抵达温州),而当时中石油是急于要货的。再之后的6月5日,中石油终于被告知Sunway轮只有丁烷但没有丙烷。期间,Glencore想尽办法找其他的替代的丙烷,只要是能够在6月15日之前到达温州,但没有成功。由于Glencore在两方面违约:没有丙烷与延误交货,最后与中石油在6月10日达成和解协议,赔偿172,899.67美元给中石油或每吨减价8美元。而最终Sunway轮也在6月15日到达温州卸货。

Glencore后来向Contigroup索赔这笔钱的损失,因为Sunway轮的延误是来自Contigroup的。这里涉及两个争议,因为和解协议中的172,899.67美元肯定是和可供买卖的市场价格(如果有)不一样。由于在该先例没有可供买卖的市场,法院判是不适用Breach Date Rule与Market rule,所以Glencore可以向Contigroup成功索赔他真正的损失,也就是与中石油达成和解协议中所赔偿的172,899.67美元,这笔钱可以从Glencore欠下的货款中扣减(有关和解协议下做出的赔偿,在接下去14.5.4段会进一步详论)。

14.5.3.2 有关先例之二:The"Ocean Dynamic"

另一个先例The"Ocean Dynamic"(1982)2 Lloyd's Rep 88在本书第三章之"损失的遥远性之一:损失可否合理预见"会进一步介绍案情。只说在该先例,由于被告船东在运输途中让玻璃碎片混进一票樱桃的货物,在分买方用这批樱桃生产果酱时,玻璃碎片被发现,需要马上停止生产,并且把已经生产的果酱销毁,而没有用过的樱桃就被退货。之后分买方向原告的收货人提出索赔,最后达成大约24,000英镑的和解协议。收货人在做出赔付后向船东提出要求补偿这一笔损失。而船东抗拒,原因包括船东不了解分买方的义务,所以在订立运输合约时是无法料想到这笔损失。只说在该先例法院判是船东是要做出赔偿。

14.5.4 原告与第三人达成和解而赔付或需要赔付的金额是否可以作为间接损失向被告索赔

14.5.4.1 英国法律鼓励和解,避免劳民伤财把诉讼打到底

可以在这里顺便针对这一方面,因为在上文所介绍的两个先例都是原告与第三人达成和解并做出支付后才向被告提出索赔,看来没有任何问题。这也是可以想象得到,法律是不会要求受害方(原告)作为受害方与第三人之间必须要把诉讼打到底,有了判决或者裁决后才能向违约方(被告)成功索赔。毕竟,今天的诉讼费用昂贵,把诉讼打到底在大部分情况下都不是明智的做法。如果法律是这样重视把诉讼打到底,把每一个争议(特别是损失金额)都全面审理证据并全面考虑后做出判决才能作准,就不会把鼓励双方达成庭外和解作为公共政策推行,如在这些年来对"调解"(mediation)的鼓励。

这方面可以节录权威书籍《Benjamin's Sale of Goods》(8th edn,2010年)之17-

076 段与 17－078 段如下：

"**Compensation paid by the buyer to a sub－buyer.** This paragraph is concluded with the situation where the seller was in breach of his contractual undertaking as to the description or condition of the goods and it was within the reasonable contemplation of the parties, at the time of making the contract, that:(a) the buyer would, or probably would, resell the goods to a sub－buyer; and(b) that the contract of sub－sale would, or probably would, contain the same, or a similar, contractual undertaking as to the description or condition of the goods; and(c) that it was not unlikely that a breach of the seller's undertaking would cause the buyer to be in breach of his undertaking to the sub－buyer who would claim damages from the buyer for the loss or damage he suffered. If loss or injury occurs in these circumstances, as it may be inferred that the seller has assumed responsibility for such losses, the buyer who has paid damages and costs to his sub－buyer for breach of the undertaking in the sub－sale may recover this amount from the seller, together with his own costs in reasonably defending the sub－buyer's claim as damages for the seller's breach of the original contract....

Settlement out of court. The buyer need not defend the sub－buyer's claim to the point of a judgment against him. If he reasonably settled the sub－buyer's claim out of court, he may recover as damages from the seller a reasonable amount paid under such settlement: if litigation between the buyer and sub－buyer should have been in the contemplation of the parties, so should reasonable settlements. The fact that the settlement was made under legal advice is relevant to its reasonableness. The onus of proof is on the buyer to establish a *prima facie* case that the settlement was recoverable, but it is open to the seller to attempt to show that the buyer was not liable to pay anything to the sub－buyer or to produce new evidence or new factors to show that the sum paid was not reasonable. In addition to the damages paid under the settlement, the buyer will recover his reasonable costs."

但据知国内有部分律师的看法是和解赔付的金额不能作为损失的索赔，因为缺乏权威性与可信度。但这与国内大力鼓吹调解是有矛盾，因为商业上很多争议作出的和解赔付都会事后涉及向其他人（包括是保险人或上一手的违约方）要求补偿，而如果他们不肯补偿就会涉及诉讼。说实在，即使必须是法院判决或仲裁庭裁决的损失金额才能拥有权威性与可信性而向被告要求补偿，也不见得会在大部分情况下没有问题。例如，作为中国公司去看一个索马里或是乌干达法院或仲裁庭做出的判决/裁决，会否毫无疑问地认为是有权威性与可信性？如果中国公司有这样的倾向性，也可以换位思考的想想会否外国公司对待中国法院或仲裁庭所做出的判决/裁决也有同样的偏见或倾向。而即使是一个英国法院的判决，做出的赔偿金额是否一定具有权威性、可信性与合理性也是要考虑很多其他的因素，如由于原告的代表律师水平不足或疏忽而导致了在向第三人抗辩时损失计算被第三人严重夸大。说到底，作为夹在当中的受害方(原告),与第三人达成和解赔付或抗辩第三人的索赔损失,如果处理不当或在中间搞鬼,都会导致同样的结果。所以是否有一个法院判决或是仲裁裁决与私下进行的和解的结果在可信度上不应该有所区分。

14.5.4.2 与第三人达成和解而赔付的金额必须是合理与满足其他损失赔偿大原则

所以重复,英国法律是完全接受将通过和解而做出赔付的金钱作为间接损失。而其中一个关键就是根据所有的证据(特别是原告所披露的文件或/与在开庭审理中对原告做出和解的证人的盘问)看该和解是否合理。这方面也有不少先例,但由于合理与否是根据每一个不同案件的案情而定,所以笔者在现实中还是经常遇到这种仲裁案件,所针对的争议主要就是原告与第三人通过和解而赔付的金钱是否合理。这一个合理与否的标准,英国法院通常还会对受害的原告尽量宽松,毕竟是因为违约的被告所导致的尴尬环境。这方面可节录 Tomlinson 大法官在 Britvic Soft Drinks Ltd v. Messer UK Ltd(2002)1 Lloyd's Rep 20 先例中所说如下:"Britvic(受害的原告)must satisfy me that it was reasonable to conclude with Tesco(第三人之一)and Waitrose(第三人之二)the settlement which it did, the test of reasonableness being a generous one appropriate to a party placed in an awkward situation by another's breach, where the law recognizes that he is not expected to act in a manner which will imperil his existing business relationships. Against that background Britvic has satisfied me that the agreements to make these payments were reasonable."

14.5.4.3 有关先例之一:Biggin v. Permanite

这方面的一个重要先例是 Biggin v. Permanite(1951)2 KB 314 CA,案情涉及荷兰政府向原告购买一票 2500 吨的沥青黏合剂用来粘合屋顶的毛毡,原告将这个消息告诉给被告,被告因此向他的供应商订购了这批黏合剂来出售给原告。荷兰政府在收到货后把粘合剂卖给了不同的工程承包人,他们事后发现这批粘合剂质量不合格并向政府要求赔偿。荷兰政府转而向原告要求赔偿。在律师的法律意见之下,原告与荷兰政府在英国仲裁过程中达成了赔付 43,000 英镑的和解协议,并在本案中要求被告补偿这笔和解的费用以及原告与英国政府花费的仲裁费用。一审法院判是原告这笔和解的费用并不在当事人的预见之内,是原告自己主动承担的行为,所以不能作为原告向被告请求赔偿的依据。但这被上诉法院推翻,判是被告应该赔偿给原告这笔和解的费用。针对这个问题,上诉庭认为原告不仅需要证明和解协议是在当事人预见之内的,还要证明这笔和解费用的合理性。针对是否合理的问题,法院认为法律鼓励合理的和解,尤其是在举证会导致昂贵诉讼费用的情况下。和解协议是否在法律意见下做出是判断合理与否的相关因素。原告可以举证证明这笔和解的金额是否合理,被告也可以针对这些证据进行盘问。如果最后证明这笔和解金额是合理的,法院就应该按照这笔金额来判决应该赔偿的金额。这可以节录 Somervell 大法官的判词如下:"The question, in my opinion, is: what evidence is necessary to establish reasonableness? I think it relevant to prove that the settlement was made under advice legally taken. The client himself could do that, but I do not think that the advisers would normally be relevant or admissible witnesses. I say "normally". It may be that in special cases they might be. The plaintiff must, I think, lead evidence, which can be cross - examined to, as to facts which the witnesses themselves prove and as to what would probably be proved if, as here, the arbitration had proceeded, so that the court can come to a conclusion whether or not the sum paid was reasonable. The defendant may, by cross - examination, as was done here, seek to show-and perhaps successfully show - that it was not reasonable. He may do so, or call evidence which leads to the same conclusion. He might in some cases show that some vital matter had been overlooked. In the present case, of course, Sir Walter Monckton(原告的代表律师) relies, rightly, on the judge's finding with regard to the first head of damage, on the fact that the evidence showed that too much was bought, and so on; but if there is evidence at the end of the matter of the kind which I have indicated, on which the court can come to the conclusion that this was a reasonable settlement in the circumstances, then I think that it should be the measure."

14.5.4.4 有关先例之二:Britvic Soft Drinks Ltd v. Messer UK Ltd

在已经提到过的 Britvic Soft Drinks Ltd v. Messer UK Ltd(2002)1 Lloyd's Rep 20 先例,案情涉及被告向原告出售与供应的工业二氧化碳气体中有苯,导致原告所生产的饮料必须在市场中撤回,蒙受巨大损失。而损失的其中一项是与第三人的超级市场或最终买方达成的和解金额,因为超级市场由于这个事故而蒙受利润损失,这包括需要从货架中撤回与退还这些饮料,以及有一段时间没有这一种货品可供出售。其中针对这些和解金额的争议是卖方会否多赔付,毕竟任何货品的供应商必须重视他与超级市场的良好关系,以保证生产的货品有渠道出售。但这一来,就会导致被告关心或怀疑这一笔损失是否是他的违约所导致,因果关系是否被中断。在本先例中,针对原告通过和解赔付给一些英国著名的超级市场如 TESCO, Tomlinson 大法官是这样说:"Ultimately Britvic paid a total of £ 148,000 to Tesco, of which £ 21,673 is said to relate to the lost profit item. The evidence as to the negotiations which took place was exiguous. There can be no doubt whatever that the importance of maintaining a good trading relationship played some part in the level at which Britvic agreed to compromise-Mr. Ford volunteered the information that that was so. That is not in any way inappropriate-it is obvious that Britvic would quite properly wish to do everything which reasonably it could to maintain its good trading relationships and the law does not require it to do otherwise. So far as concerns Waitrose there is simply no evidence as to any discussion of its claim for loss of profit. Britvic's difficulty here is that the logic which informs these claims is that there must have been interruption in supply to these two retailers giving rise to unavailability of product on shelves whereas Britvic took the line at the time that there were no such difficulties, as perhaps one would inevitably expect that it would. Britvic has also confirmed in the context of the preparation of the expert evidence for this action that time off shelves was a minimal cause of lost profit. These are of course relatively small claims. The defendants contend that I should not assume that credit was properly given to Tesco and Waitrose in respect of this item. In my judgment there must be a limit to the extent to which Britvic could realistically be expected to go in challenging the assertion of customers such as Tesco and Waitrose that they had suffered loss of profit through unavailability of stock on shelves. It is obvious, with respect to the argument of the defendants to the contrary, that Britvic did have a legal liability to its customers in respect of their costs incurred and their loss of profits, if any, consequent upon the supply to them by Britvic of unsaleable product."

14.5.4.5 有关先例之三：General Feeds v. Slobodna Plovidba Yugoslavia

接下去介绍一个比较近期的有关先例，这是 General Feeds v. Slobodna Plovidba Yugoslavia (1999) 1 Lloyd's Rep. 688，案情涉及船东面对提单持有人或代位保险人的索赔做出和解赔付后，向承租人要求赔偿，因为是承租人的违约导致这笔和解赔付。Colman 大法官针对船东做出的和解赔付能否向承租人提出索赔是说：

"... assuming that loss attributable to a payment in settlement is not too remote, the plaintiff must prove that the fact and amount of the settlement were reasonable in all the circumstances. Unless he proves that, he fails to establish that the loss was caused by the relevant breach of contract by the defendant, for if and to the extent that an unreasonable settlement has been entered into, the loss has been caused not by the breach but by the plaintiff's voluntary assumption of liability under the settlement...

... when properly analysed, the overall exercise which the Court must do is to consider whether the specified eventuality (in the case of an indemnity) or the breach of contract (in a case such as the present) has caused the loss incurred in satisfying the settlement. Unless the claim is of sufficient strength reasonably to justify a settlement and the amount paid in settlement is reasonable having regard to the strength of the claim, it cannot be shown that the loss has been caused by the relevant eventuality or breach of contract. **That is not to say that unless it can be shown that the claim is likely to succeed it will be impossible to establish that it was reasonable to settle it. There may be many claims which appear to be intrinsically weak but which common prudence suggests should be settled in order to avoid the uncertainties and expenses of litigation. Even the successful defence of a claim in complex litigation is likely to involve substantial irrevocable costs.... Unless it appears on the evidence that the claim is so weak that no reasonable owner or club would take it sufficiently seriously to negotiate any settlement involving payment, it cannot be said that the loss attributable to a reasonable settlement was not caused by the breach by reason of which the goods are in a dam-**

aged condition."(加黑部分是笔者的强调,Colman 大法官在加黑部分的判词中说证明和解赔付的合理性并不需要证明第三人的索赔是否很可能会成功,因为有许多索赔表面看来是站不住脚,但一般的理性建议是最好尽早和解以避免诉讼的不肯定[特别是涉及法院的诉讼]与昂贵的费用。就算是能够成功抗辩一个复杂的诉讼,也会涉及庞大与不能取回的诉讼费用[如在中国大陆或在美国法院]。除非在表面看来有关索赔完全站得住脚,一个合理的船东或互保协会根本不会严肃对待并谈判和解做出赔付,否则是不能说合理和解的损失并非是由于承租人的违约所造成,在本案中就是装运发热的货物最后导致火灾)

14.5.4.6　有关先例之四:John F Hunt Demolition Ltd v. ASME Engineering Ltd

再接下去介绍的是更近期的先例 John F Hunt Demolition Ltd v. ASME Engineering Ltd(2008)1 All ER 180,Peter Coulson QC 大法官在总结了有关先例后是说:

" In addition,I consider that the judgment of Colman J in General Feeds provides a cogent explanation of the proper approach in cases of this sort,where A's liability to B may be difficult,if not impossible,to establish. The court must consider whether the breach of contract caused the loss incurred in satisfying the settlement. Unless the claim was(or was reasonably considered to be)of sufficient strength reasonably to justify a settlement,and the amount paid in settlement is reasonable having regard to the strength of the claim,it cannot be shown that the loss has been caused by the relevant breach of contract. On the other hand,the settlement of an intrinsically weak claim in order to avoid the uncertainties and expenses of litigation may well be reasonable;on Colman J's analysis(with which I respectfully agree)a claim will usually have to be so weak as to be obviously hopeless before it could be said that the settlement of the claim was unreasonable. In my view,in the passages of his judgment in the General Feeds case that I have cited above,Colman J provided an answer to preliminary issue 3("it is not necessary to prove that the claim settled... would probably have succeeded")and provided the clearest guidance as to the appropriate test to be applied("it is enough to establish that[the claim]had sufficient substance for the settlement of it to be regarded as reasonable")(Peter Coulson QC 大法官是针对并同意 Colman 大法官在较早所介绍的 General Feeds v. Slobodna Plovidba Yugoslavia 先例中所说,就是原告不必证明他与第三人和解并赔付是因为第三人的索赔很可能会胜诉,即使第三人的索赔本质上不是强而有力,但由于诉讼的风险与费用,原告达成和解并赔付还是会算合理。除非是第三人的索赔是本质上完全没有希望,原告达成和解并赔付才会被视为不合理。)

The authorities cited above do not demonstrate any rule or principle of law that A must prove that he was liable to B before recovering against C the sums which he paid to B by way of settlement. Of course,that is not to deny that,in the vast majority of cases,that liability will either be agreed by A and C or will,on investigation,be demonstrated. But there will be some cases, like the Comyn Ching & Co (London) Ltd v. Oriental Tube Co Ltd [1979] 17 BLR 56 and the General Feeds case where, even though investigation of the underlying facts demonstrated that there was in truth no liability at all, the settlement of the claim that had been made was found to be reasonable in all the circumstances. Furthermore, it seems to me that this is entirely in accordance with normal rules of foreseeability and remoteness of damage. It must be reasonably foreseeable, at the time that the contracts were made between A and C, that A might settle a claim brought by B arising out of the same subject matter, even if, on a detailed analysis, A's legal liability to B might actually be hard or even impossible to establish."(这是针对向第三人做出和解赔付后,如果在进一步的诉讼与调查中发现较早的赔付可能是多赔,这不影响较早和解赔付的合理性,因为确定合理与否的时间是在和解的一天。例如在 General Feeds v. Slobodna Plovidba Yugoslavia 先例,船东与提单持有人/代位求偿保险人达致和解赔付是因为被指控货物本身没有问题,发热/火灾是由于船舶错误堆载的问题。但事后船东向承租人索赔,被仲裁庭认定为火灾是由于货物本身的发热,与堆载无关。这一来,较早时赔付给提单持有人/代位求偿保险人的金额就是冤枉了,但和解还是合理。)

14.5.4.7 有关先例之五:Siemens v. Supershield

最后要介绍的是 Siemens v. Supershield(2009) EWHC 927 先例,Ramsay 大法官是这样总结说:

"In my judgment the following principles can, in summary, be derived from the authorities:(根据以往的先例,我的判决可以总结出以下的一些关于和解赔付的大原则)

(1) For C to be liable to A in respect of A's liability to B which was the subject of a settlement it is not necessary for A to prove on the balance of probabilities that A was or would have been liable to B or that A was or would have been liable for the amount of the settlement.(C 要对 A 向 B 作出和解赔付负最终责任,是不需要 A 根据平衡的可能性证明 A 是对 B 的确有责任或者会是要对和解赔付的金额负责任。这方面已经在较早的 General Feeds v. Slobodna Plovidba Yugoslavia 有介绍过。笔者还可以多举一个例子,如笔者在不久前的一个中国仲裁,外国船东与互保协会在仲裁庭调解中同意赔付索赔金额的50%而达成和解。但代表律师明确说明这一案件如果是在伦敦仲裁,他们是一毛钱也不肯赔付,因为他们有几乎肯定的胜诉把握。但在中国仲裁就基于不了解中国法律、诉讼的风险、中国称职律师的建议等因素做出了这一个和解赔付。显然,该外国船东之后向互保协会或是在另一个仲裁向承租人要求补偿,这一笔和解赔付的金额会被视为是合理,并且如果在责任方面成功就可以向对方取回)

(2) For C to be liable to A in respect of the settlement, A must show that the specified eventuality (in the case of an indemnity given by C to A) or the breach of contract (in the case of a breach of contract between C and A) has caused the loss incurred in satisfying the settlement in the manner set out in the indemnity or as required for causation of damages

and that the loss was within the loss covered by the indemnity or the damages were not too remote.（如果C需要对A与B的和解赔付负责，A必须证明A与B之间和解协议所涉及的损失是由C的特定事件或C违反与A之间合约的行为所造成，这是满足损失因果关系的要求，并且这笔和解赔付是在C需要给予A的赔偿范围内的损失，即这个损失并不是很遥远。例如，A与B的和解协议顺便把他们以前存在的一些争议一并扯进来，就会是满足不了这一个要求）

（3）Unless the claim is of sufficient strength reasonably to justify a settlement and the amount paid in settlement is reasonable having regard to the strength of the claim，it cannot be shown that the loss has been caused by the relevant eventuality or breach of contract. In assessing the strength of the claim，unless the claim is so weak that no reasonable party would take it sufficiently seriously to negotiate any settlement involving payment，it cannot be said that the loss attributable to a reasonable settlement was not caused by the eventuality or the breach.（考虑到B向A索赔的胜诉可能性，如果他们达成和解在有关诉讼中是合理的，并且和解赔付的金额也是合理的，那么这笔和解赔付就可以被视为是由相关事件或C的违约造成。在评估B胜诉的可能性时，如果胜诉的可能性极其微小，以至于合理的A根本就不会认真考虑做出赔偿的和解谈判，那么这笔和解赔付就不能视为是由相关事件或C的违约造成）

（4）In general if，when a party is in breach of contract，a claim by a third party is in the reasonable contemplation of the parties as a probable result of the breach，then it will generally also be in the reasonable contemplation of the parties that there might be a reasonable settlement of any such claim by the other party.（通常来说，如果C违约，B作为第三人的索赔是违约的可预见后果，也是在双方当事人[A与C]的预料范围内。所以在违约发生后，C也应该合理预料到，A会与第三人的B达成合理的和解）

（5）The test of whether the amount paid in settlement was reasonable is whether the settlement was，in all the circumstances，within the range of settlements which reasonable people in the position of the settling party might have made. Such circumstances will generally include：（和解赔付的金额是否合理要取决于，考虑到案件有关事实，有关和解是否在一个合理的人士处在和解双方的位置上会做出的和解范围内。这些合理要考虑的方面包括：）（a）The strength of the claim；（案件的强弱，这包括有关法律方面与证据方面）（b）Whether the settlement was the result of legal advice；（和解是否在称职律师[针对有关法律]的建议下做出）（c）The uncertainties and expenses of litigation；（诉讼的不确定性与花费）（d）The benefits of settling the case rather than disputing it.（当事人选择和解而不是继续诉讼的好处）

（6）The question of whether a settlement was reasonable is to be assessed at the date of the settlement when necessarily the issues between A and B remained unresolved."（决定和解是否合理的日期，应该是A与B达成和解的一天，当时双方的争议还没有解

决。这表示在和解赔付后如果有新的证据显示 A 向 B 赔付的和解金额应该大幅度减少,这不应该加以考虑,因为是事后诸葛亮。这方面请看上述介绍的 John F Hunt Demolition Ltd v. ASME Engineering Ltd 先例)

14.5.4.8 和解赔付金额能够成功向被告索赔的因素

最后总结原告通过和解赔付给第三人的金额(是否应该赔付与赔付金额的多少)能够成功向被告索赔的一些重要因素,因为这毕竟是经常会遇到的争议。其中最重要的因素就是在本章 14.5.4.2 段所讲到的"合理"(reasonableness),而且这一个合理的要求对受害的原告非常宽松。合理与否是没有一个标准或定义,每一个不同的案件都是看它不同的事实。很大程度也是要看双方争辩的水平,高水平的律师会在这种案件,也就是胜负取决于合理与否的情况下会为他的当事人的所作所为去尽量博得法院/仲裁庭的同情。

合理与否的例子不妨先提到在本书第五章的减少损失之 5.2.5 段,将会介绍的 Finlay v. Kwik Hoo Tong(1929)32 Lloyd's Rep 245 先例,案情涉及一个 CIF 孟买的食糖买卖合约。买卖合约涉及三票在 1920 年 7 月、8 月与 9 月的付运。到了 9 月这一票货物的付运受到延误,但被告(卖方)签发了一套倒签提单,这导致原告作为中间商也要对最后的买方为这一个延误负责。但由于在分销合约中有条文说明提单日期是作为付运日期的"决定性证据"(conclusive evidence),而倒签提单也与原告无关,他也是受害方。所以,在分销合约的条文下,原告实际上没有法律责任。但原告认为自己是有道义上的责任,所以还是向第三人做出了让步,不严格根据分销合约的条文迫使印度买方接受这一套倒签提单,而转去在市场把该票食糖的货物出售并蒙受损失。在向被告(倒签提单的卖方)提出索赔时,被告指原告没有减少损失,因为他完全可以合法要求分买方履行分销合约。但 Scrutton 大法官并不认同被告的抗辩,说:"Messrs. Finlay's answer to that is:'It is quite true that we had a contract under which the India buyer was bound to accept the date in the bill of lading as against the India buyer to recover the price of goods that we knew not to be in accordance with the contract, because of that term, would not be in the ordinary course of business and would ruin our credit in India, and as a matter of business, and of the standard of morality which should attach to an English firm of standing, we decline to bring an action against an India firm to compel them to take goods which we know are not in accordance with the contract. It would be different if we did not know and it was in doubt, and we could say:'Yes, we do not know which way it is, and you do not know, but here is a contract that the bill of lading date is to be taken'; that would be a different matter.' I personally cannot think that a man who has broken his contract can compel his buyer who has not broken his contract to take action to minimize the damages of a person who has broken his contract, by claiming money to which he knows he is not entitled, and to take action which will ruin his credit in the business world."

在 Finlay v. Kwik Hoo Tong 先例,倒签提单是严重的虚假行为,驱使原告不顾自己的商誉与道义,严格按照合约迫使分买方履行合约,并把损失(因为延误而市场价格大跌)转嫁给分买方有一点太过分。但即使是一般的违约行为,原告如果向第三人做出和解的赔付,即使是严格按照合约他不一定负责,在这一个先例的角度看来还是不一定代表原告不能向被告成功索赔。这看来还是主要根据合理与否,只能说是如果按照与第三人的合约条文没有任何责任,原告向第三人做出赔付就有一点令人怀疑与表面上感觉可能不合理,或是背后有其他原因。这会是需要原告提出其他的理由作为支持他的和解赔付是合情合理的并试图说服法院或仲裁庭。这些证据会是千变万化,如违约的性质的确是会影响原告的商誉与第三人的业务关系。或是由于第三人坚持把诉讼打到底(在海事诉讼甚至把原告的船舶扣押)或是仲裁庭的成员对有关争议的了解有怀疑,也会合理导致受害的原告向第三人做出一种"滋扰性金额和解"(nuisance value settlement)以利脱身。特别是受害的原告做出的和解赔付有称职律师的建议就会大幅度提升合理性。又或是受害的原告在做出和解协议之前曾经向被告做出通知,但被告没有回应,更加谈不上有提出任何质疑。

至于是受害的原告因为自己的原因尽快与第三人达成和解协议并做出赔付,如原告因为需要把公司上市或是有其他投资者进行收购,导致原告必须要早日了解与第三人的诉讼。这种和解赔付的金额会是在合理与否与因果关系方面有一定的争议,但是否合理还是会不肯定,原告还是有可能说服法院或仲裁庭。毕竟,原告是由于被告的违约导致需要和第三人达成和解协议并做出赔付,所以违约的被告最好还是做出同样的和解协议,做出部分赔偿/补偿。

也会是在披露出来的文件中或通过开庭中的证人盘问,受害的原告与第三人所达成的和解是说明属于"馈赠"(*ex gratia* payment),也就是法律上根本不需要负责的支付,如朋友或父子之间的馈赠。但一旦涉及商业关系,这种毫无法律责任或/与商业后果的馈赠也不大会有。所以即使是和解加上了馈赠这样的名称,但到底是否是没有任何对价的馈赠还是要看实质内容。毕竟在英国法律下一份文件的名称并不重要。如果它的确是一个馈赠,受害的原告向被告要求赔偿/补偿就会有一点问题。首先就是合理与否的方面,另是损失的遥远性(特别在有否合理减少损失),更加会涉及"因果关系"(causation)的争议,因为这一项所谓损失不像是由被告违约所直接导致。

最后介绍一个明显是不合理的和解,笔者在多年前曾经听闻在一单撞船事件中,两艘船舶分别是由中国船东与新加坡船东所有,由于该两家船公司的领导熟识,结果两家船公司出事后很快在未查明责任与没有任何称职律师参与的情况下,达成一人一半分摊损失的和解。该和解造成了事后向保险公司与互保协会要求赔付时的极大困难。

14.5.4.9　和解赔付是否要支付后才能成功取回

一般而言,如果在责任方面确定了被告违约,是要赔偿原告与第三人达成和解的损失金额，就会涉及原告到底有没有支付这笔钱与如果有支付，在哪一天。显然这针对利息的计算就已经是需要明确这一方面。问题是如果原告实际上还没有支付，所以没有办法在审理时提供给法院或仲裁庭支付的证明，原告是否不能成功向被告索赔，等于是在责任方面胜诉但损失方面只能取得一个名义损失的赔偿？这看来对原告并不合理，毕竟他即使还没有向第三人做出支付，也有一个支付的责任，第三人可能在不久后会追究。随便在一些权威的书就可以看到要明确支付给第三人的一笔钱，但还没有做出支付，原告还是可以向被告成功取回。例如《Benjamin's Sales of Goods》(8th edn，2010 年)之 17 - 077 段是说："**Costs paid or payable by the buyer**. If, in the circumstances set out in the first sentence of the preceding paragraph, the buyer has, as a result of the defect in the goods, reasonably incurred costs in defending a claim brought against him by a sub - buyer, he may recover from the seller both the reasonable costs paid or payable to the successful sub - buyer..."（上述的标题就已经显示了已经支付了[paid]或是还没有支付[payable]都会可以向违约的卖方成功取回。）

如果要举一个更明确的权威说法，可以是在本章之 14.5.1.2 有介绍的 Harlow & Jones v. Panex International(1967)2 Lloyd's Rep. 509 先例，Roskill 大法官允许卖方向违约的买方取回一笔十分庞大的储存费用，虽然卖方并没有支付给第三人的供应商，而只是达成了协议在成功向违约买方取回这笔钱之后才需要赔付给第三人。

另一个更近期的先例是 Total Liban v. Vitol(1999)2 Lloyd's Rep. 700，案情涉及一个 CIF 汽油的买卖，原告 Total 作为买方以货物质量有问题拒货，并之后向卖方 Mackay 索赔 500 万美元的损失。Mackay 只是中间商，他没有钱赔偿或打官司，于是他把对原卖方/供应方 Vitol 同样性质的索赔转让给 Total。这使得最后的仲裁是 Total 作为 Mackay 诉权的受让人与 Vitol 之间的诉讼。由于受让人的权利也就是 Mackay 的权利，所以 Vitol 作为被告的其中一个抗辩就是 Mackay 还没有作出支付给 Total。在伦敦仲裁，仲裁庭判 Vitol 胜诉，认为 Mackay 由于没有真正作出支付，只是对 Total 有一个责任赔付并不足够。这方面可节录仲裁庭裁决的总结："The arbitrator found in favour of Vitol and held that Total was not entitled to the relief claimed and liability without payment did not constitute a recoverable loss. The arbitrator noted that Mackay's claim for damage constituted solely of its liability to Total; there was no claim for any independent loss suffered by Mackay itself and concluded that the balance of authority favoured Vitol. Moreover Vitol's submission that liability without payment did not constitute a recoverable loss was supported by the fundamental principle that damages were intended to be compensatory."

这一个裁决书被上诉，在这一点是被英国高院推翻。Peter Gross 大法官在分析了所有有关的先例后判是在责任方面被确定胜诉后，受害方如果只有向第三人作出赔付的责任但实际上还没有支付，一样不影响向违约方索赔这一笔金钱的赔偿。这种情况经常会发生在穷困的受害方/原告在商业上有这种安排（如 Harlow & Jones v.

Panex International 先例中的做法),即是原告向违约方取回这笔钱才支付第三人。所以如果因为原告还没有真正支付给第三人就让违约方取巧并逃避作出赔偿的责任并不公平。Peter Gross 大法官的判决总结是:"(1)... if once there was a breach of contract and a proven liability satisfying the usual tests of causation and remoteness, then it was difficult to see why prior payment by Mackay to Total should be a requirement of law; and such rule of law was open to the objection on grounds of injustice, inconvenience and being at odds with everyday practice; (2)... liability without payment did found a claim for substantial damages..."

如果原告要支付给第三人的赔偿并不是明确的一笔议定金额或是债务,而是有争议性的"非议定赔偿"(unliquidated damage),原告向被告索赔向第三人的赔偿责任的损失就会有危险,即原告在最后与第三人达成和解的金额或是裁决下来的"裁决金额"(judgment debt)会是一个较低的金额。在这种情况下,仲裁庭可以采取的做法会是做出一个"宣告裁决"(declaratory award)说明被告要赔付给原告将来向第三人做出的支付,或只是对责任方面做出裁决,但保留权利稍后处理赔偿金额的计算。有关债务与损失的区别,请看本书第十一章。

这种问题笔者作为仲裁员经常遇到,如近期的一宗案件涉及中方的原告向被告索赔一笔已经支付了的岸上吊车费用,这笔费用是被告没有争议的。但争议是原告还没有支付这笔钱,而是由第三人做出支付。笔者的共同仲裁员(是一位香港大律师)认为原告没有办法提供支付证明,所以败诉。但笔者并不认同,因为对这笔钱的责任是明确在被告,也有证据显示第三人向原告要求支付。所以,原告没有办法提出支付证明并不代表他本来应该是胜诉但反而变得败诉。虽然不像 Harlow & Jones v. Panex International 的先例是原告与第三人达成了一个有条件的协议,而是笔者看来原告不想自己先掏腰包而希望从被告处成功取回后才支付给第三人,但在大道理笔者认为是同样的地位。或说,会否将来原告能够成功减少给第三人的支付,即使是一笔明确的金额?但法律上没有对原告有要求向第三人扯皮或尝试减少应该支付的这一笔岸上吊车费用,原告没有这种减少损失的责任。所以不存在要考虑这方面的问题。

14.5.5 受害方对抗第三人索赔的诉讼费用与其他

在 Grebert - Borgnis v. Nugent(1885)15 QBD 85 CA 先例,涉及违约的卖方接受要赔偿买方在分销/转售的利润损失,但不接受买方要面对分买方在法国法院面对的索赔与作出的赔偿。但卖方的抗拒并不成功,这方面可节录《McGregor on Damages》(18th edn,2009 年)之 20 - 030 段:"In an action for damages for non - delivery the seller again did not dispute liability for the loss of profit on the resale, but here the buyer successfully recovered the damages he had paid his sub - buyer in a suit in a French court. The Court of Appeal said that the damages given by the French court were not as a matter of law the exact amount the claimant was entitled to, but that this amount might be treated as a not unreasonable one at which the damages might be assessed. It is difficult to see how these two cases can be satisfactorily reconciled, and it is submitted that Grebert – Borgnis v. Nugent is to be preferred as a decision of the Court of Appeal and a decision showing the later more liberal tendency to allow recovery for loss on a resale. If the sub – sale is sufficiently within the parties' contemplation to allow loss of profits, it must surely also let in recovery in respect of compensation paid to the sub – buyer."

对受害的买方要花律师费用对抗分买方或第三人的索赔，例如在 Grebert – Borgnis v. Nugent 先例中在法国法院面对的诉讼，这一笔的费用支出看来是买方要满足它的合理性。如为了抗辩责任，就有可能被视为是不合理，因为买方没有向分买方提供货物(虽然是违约的原卖方所导致)是明确不过的违约/毁约。但如果是为了抗辩分买方或第三人提出看来是过高的损失金额，这就会是相对合理。这方面在《McGregor on Damages》(18th edn，2009 年)之 20 – 032 段提到说："If there is non – delivery to the buyer so that he cannot deliver to his sub – buyer he is so clearly in breach that he will seldom have any ground for defending an action brought against him by his sub – buyer. The costs of such a defence will therefore generally be on his own head since he cannot claim that they were incurred as the probable result of his seller's breach. The costs of a defence which succeeds in cutting down an exorbitant claim by the sub – buyer should, however, be recoverable."

最后一提是如果分销/转售合约有一些特殊的条文，如要求在没有提供货物的情况下支付给分买方一大笔惩罚性的议定赔偿(会有情况是分销/转售合约不适用英国法，所以不存在惩罚性条文无效的问题)，也需要违约的卖方在订约时被买方告知有关分销/转售合约的细节才会有责任赔偿或补偿这笔钱。

15. 非金钱损失类别

15.1 英国合约法下不承认非金钱损失类别

"非金钱的损失"(non – pecuniary losses)如"痛苦与受难"(pain and suffering)需要量化才能做出金钱上的赔偿是一直以来属于侵权的范畴，与合约下的违约没有什么关系。违约在一直以来的英国法律下只允许向违约方索赔经济损失，这也是唯一的一种被承认的损失类别。在 Sunley Ltd v. Cunard White Star Ltd(1939)2 KB 791 先例，Hallett 大法官说："in an action founded on breach of contract the only kind of loss... which is a subject for compensation is a financial loss."

所以违约的受害方索赔痛苦与受难的损失(如受害方因对方违约而晚上睡不着觉或是心脏病恶化)，就算是很有这种情况出现的可能，也不被视为是合法可以索赔的损失项目，在本章 13.2.4 段已经提到"感情价值"(sentimental value)太不肯定而不被接受。这方面可节录在 Hobbs v. London and South Western Railway Co(1875)LR 10 QB 111 先例,Mellor 大法官是这样说:"... for the mere inconvenience, such as annoyance and loss of temper, or vexation, or for being disappointed in a particular thing which you have set your mind upon, without real physical inconvenience resulting, you cannot recover damages. That is purely sentimental and not a case where the word inconveniences as I here use it would apply."

15.2　不承认非金钱损失类别的原因

英国法律在这一方面的地位估计是有以下的一些原因。

(1)非金钱损失类别很难准确与肯定地做出核算:Farley v. Skinner(2000)PLNR441(CA)。所以如果不严格控制或不予承认,这种损失会变得无所不在与太多,让诉讼索赔损失的大水门打开,是不符合公共利益的:A Burrows 教授在《Remedies for Torts and Breach of Contract》(3rd edn,2004 年)一书所说。另是上诉庭的 Staughton 大法官在 Hayes v. James & Charles Dodd(1990)2 All ER 815 先例中说:"I would not view with enthusiasm the prospect that every shipowner in the Commercial Court, having successfully claimed for unpaid freight or demurrage, would be able to add a claim for mental distress suffered while he was waiting for his money." 另 Bingham 大法官在 Watts v. Morrow(1991)1 WLR 1421 先例提到对一般商业合约的公共政策,主要就是避免在社会上太多的诉讼。这方面可节录 Steyn 勋爵在 Farley v. Skinner(2002)2 AC 732(HL)先例中说:"Like Bingham LJ in Watts v. Morrow(1991)1 WLR 1421, 1445H, I consider that awards in this area should be restrained and modest. It is important that logical and beneficial developments in this corner of the law should not contribute to the creation of a society bent on litigation(Steyn 勋爵认为对受压等这方面的赔偿应该受到约束与判赔的金额尽量少,否则会导致社会太多诉讼)。

(2)非金钱损失类别在合约关系(通常是商业关系)被视为是太普遍或太自然,不应该被视为是一种损失可以提出索赔。正如 Millett 勋爵在 Johnson v. Unisys Ltd (2003)1 AC 518 先例中所说的:"non - pecuniary loss is so commonly a consequence of a breach of contract that the parties must be regarded not only as having foressen it but as having agreed to take the risk of its occurrence."另 Cooke 勋爵在 Johnson v. Gore Wood (2002)2 AC 1 先例中说:"Contract - breaking is an incident of commercial life which players in the game are expected to meet with mental fortitude."(商业活动中违约是无可避免的事件,参与的人士都应该有足够的心理准备面对。)

(3)非金钱损失类别如受害方的"心理苦恼"(mental distress)或"不便"(inconvenience)在合约关系或商业关系会被视为是太遥远:Scott 勋爵在 Farley v. Skinner (2002)2 AC 732(HL)先例中之 75 段。

(4)非金钱损失也会被视为是等同惩罚性赔偿,而惩罚性赔偿是英国法律不予承认:E Peel 教授的《Treitel on the Law of Contract》(12th edn,2007 年[20 - 073]段);A

Burrows 教授的《Mental Distress Damages in Contract - A Decade of Change》(1984) LMCLQ 119 之 132 页;E Macdonald 教授的《Contractual Damages for Mental Distress》(1994)7 JCL 134 之 135 页;另可参阅 Perera v. Vandiyar(1953)1 WLR 672 先例与 Addis v. Gramophone(1909) AC 488 先例。

15.3 近年来对非金钱损失索赔的放宽

但这一个早期的说法在 1970 年后针对某些种类的合约有所放宽,其中在 Jarvis v. Swans Tours Ltd(1973) QB 233 先例中,Denning 勋爵说:"In a proper case damages for mental distress can be recovered in contract, just as damages for shock can be recovered in tort. One such case is a contract for a holiday or any other contract to provide entertainment and enjoyment"(在部分类别的合约,可以做出心理苦恼的损失,好像侵权一样。其中一种类别是有关娱乐和度假的合约)。

在接下去的 Jackson v. Horizon Holidays Ltd(1975)1 WLR 1468 先例,Denning 勋爵说:"In Jarvis... it was held by this Court that damages for the loss of a holiday may include not only the difference in value between what was promised and what was obtained but also damages for mental distress, inconvenience, upset, disappointment and frustration caused by the loss of the holiday... People look forward to a holiday. They expect the promises to be fulfilled. When it fails, they are greatly disappointed and upset. It is difficult to assess in terms of money; but it is the task of the judges to do the best they can. I see no reason to interfere with the total award of £ 1,100."

上诉庭的 Bingham 大法官在 Watts v. Morrow(1991)1 WLR 1421 先例总结了这方面的法律,说明一般的商业合约是不会有在这方面的损失赔偿,但除了一种是属于"例外合约"(exceptional contracts),说:"A contract - breaker is not in general liable for any distress, frustration, displeasure, vexation, tension or aggravation which his breach of contract may cause to the innocent party. This rule is not, I think, founded on the assumption that such reactions are not foreseeable, which they surely are or may be, but on considerations of policy. But the rule is not absolute. Where the very object of a contract is to provide pleasure, relaxation, peace of mind or freedom from molestation, damages will be awarded if the fruit of the contract is not provided or if the contrary result is procured instead"(违约方通常对苦恼、失望、不愉快、欺压、紧张或恼怒不必负责赔偿。这一个原则并非是因为这种损失无法在订约时预见得到或太遥远,而是因为公共政策的原因。但这一个原则并非是绝对。一种例外是如果合约涉及娱乐、休闲、安宁或免受骚扰[例如委任律师要求去法院申请禁令以阻止干预,但该律师违约]的目的,违约方就有可能在没有达到这一个目的的违约要对这方面损失作出赔偿)。

在近年来也有了一些先例针对 Bingham 大法官所讲的"例外合约"(exceptional contracts),毕竟涉及娱乐或休闲等方面的所谓"度假合约"(holiday contracts)就多了不少。但对一般的商业合约(如笔者涉及的国际货物买卖或租约/提单等方面),还是因为公共政策而不把这种非金钱上的损失视为是可以索赔的损失项目,除非合约的目的是为了娱乐或休闲。

总结而言,近年来放宽的先例涉及索赔非金钱损失类别最重要的就是合约有关娱乐、休闲、安宁或免受骚扰。其中涉及:(1)旅行社提供的住宿没有达到合约标准:Jarvis v. Swans Tours Ltd(1973)QB 233,Jackson v. Horizon Holidays Ltd(1975)1 WLR 1468,Milner v. Carnival plc(2010)1 Lloyd's Rep 374 等;(2)婚礼摄影师违约没有在婚礼上出现:Diesen v. Samson(1971)SLT 49;(3)坟场没有完成给予专属埋葬权的责任:Reed v. Madon(1989)Ch 408;(4)建造的游泳池太浅:Ruxley Eletronics and Construction Ltd v. Forsyth(1995)All ER 1936;(5)测量师的疏忽意见导致了客户购买的房子由于太接近机场而噪音太大:Farley v. Skinner(2002)2 AC 732(HL);(6)律师疏忽导致申请不到法院禁令令客户继续被骚扰,Heywood v. Wellers(1976)Q. B 446;等等。

另一种被放宽的索赔非金钱损失类别与上述所介绍的其实是差不多,涉及违约造成了身体上的不方便与不舒适:Watts v. Morrow(1991)1 WLR 1421 先例。这一个先例会在下一个小段详细介绍,这里不再重复。

至于索赔非金钱损失会否在其它类别的合约进一步放宽,就只能拭目以待了。

15.4 不同类别的非金钱损失赔偿

在接下去的段节,笔者会进一步细分不同类别的非金钱损失赔偿。

15.4.1 身体上的不方便和不舒适

如果违约导致受害方遭受巨大的身体上的不方便和不舒适(physical inconvenience and discomfort),他有权向违约方要求赔偿。例如在 Burton v. Pinkerton(1867) LR 2 Ex. 340 先例中,一名海员的雇主违反雇佣合约,把他放在一个国外的港口,导致了该位海员的不方便与不舒适,他因此而获得金钱上的赔偿。另在 Hobbs v. LSW Railway(1875)LR 10 QB 111 先例,被告铁路公司把原告和他的家人在深夜放在了一个错误的车站,迫使他们在雨中走了好几里路才到家,中途没有任何运输工具和旅店。受害方因此遭受身体上的不方便和不舒适,获得金钱上的赔偿。在这个先例中,Mellor 大法官十分谨慎地把"不方便"(inconvenience)限定为真正的身体上的不方便,而排除"因为生气或失望而导致的不方便"(the mere inconvenience of anger and disappointment)

现在的普通法依然遵循这两个先例的裁判。在 Bailey v. Bullock(1950)2 All ER 1167 先例,原告的受害方指示被告的律师尽快收回原告租给第三人的一幢房子。被告的律师所职员知道原告和他的妻子与孩子没有其他住所,但被告根本没有开始采取法律行动向第三人收回房子,还欺骗了原告长达两年,让原告误以为被告已经启动了收回房子的程序。当原告发现自己被骗后,他指示了其他的律师并收回了房子。但在这期间,原告不得不和他的妻子、孩子与他岳父母挤在一个小房子里,遭受了不方便和不舒适。他因此而获得针对这方面的金钱赔偿。

类似的不方便和不舒适还可能是因为旅行社为游客订了条件很差的旅店,而受害的游客直到抵达旅游目的地才发现,这已经是太迟而不能换房间,导致受害游客的整个假期泡汤:Stedman v. Swan's Tours(1951)95 SJ 727 CA。也有可能是因为受害原告房子里防水系统没有被恰当地安装,导致原告一直居住在有缺陷的房屋中而遭受不方便和不舒适:Rawlings v. Rentokil Laboratories(1972)EGD 744。在Watts v. Morrow(1991)1 WLR 1421 CA先例中,由于检验师的疏忽令受害原告的夫妻买了质量有问题的房子,导致他们的房屋一直在维修中,而他们实际上一直相当于住在建筑工地上。上诉庭支持一审法院的判决,认为原告应该因遭受不方便和不舒适而获得赔偿。Bingham大法官认为因为被告违反合约并使原告蒙受精神上的痛苦而导致原告身体上的不方便和不舒适,原告可以因此而获得赔偿:"recoverable for physical inconvenience and discomfort caused by the breach and mental suffering directly related to that inconvenience and discomfort."这种不方便与不舒适也有可能是因为受害的原告一直被过度的飞机噪音干扰而导致:Farley v. Skinner(2002)2 AC 732。

即使这种不方便并非来自于严格意义上身体的不适,也有可能是赔偿的考虑因素之一。在Piper v. Daybell Court - Cooper & Co(1969)EGD 535先例中,受害的原告打算买下一幢房子自己居住,而被告的律师疏忽没有告诉原告这个房子上存在一个通行权。结果原告买下该房子后,因为他的邻居在他窗前来回经过而对他造成不方便,法院判是被告的律师要因此而对原告进行赔偿。

15.4.2 痛苦、受难和舒适生活的损失

毫无疑问,因违约而导致的人身伤害赔偿中也会包括正常的非金钱损失,这包括了痛苦、受难和舒适生活的损失(pain and suffering and loss of amenities),这在之前被称为"对生命的期待"(expectation of life)。通常这种违约责任下还会有一个并存的侵权责任,最常见的例子就是铁路公司的疏忽导致了乘客的人身损害。但并非所有赔偿非金钱损失的违约责任下都需要有并存的侵权责任。例如在商品买卖中,卖方因违反买卖合约中的保证条款而导致买方在使用该商品时受伤。在Summers v. Salford Corp(1943)AC 283先例中,原告的租客在擦窗户时吊窗绳断裂,窗户掉落,而租客的双手也严重受伤。最终租客赢得了对房东的诉讼,因为房东在法律上有一项默示的提供适合居住的房屋的义务,而他违反了合约中的该项默示义务。而法院对损失的计算也是基于人身伤害的正常评估,并没有一个并存的侵权责任。同样在Cox v. Philips Industries(1976)1 WLR 638先例中,一位雇员起诉他的雇主,称其违反了雇佣合约,因为雇主把受害的雇员从一个适合的职位降级去了一个责任较少的职位,导致雇员生病。法院判是受害的雇员有权因此而获得赔偿。

除此之外,如果律师由于疏忽,延误了客户关于人身伤害的诉讼,从而导致客户在这段延误的日子里身体和精神状况恶化,法院也会倾向于要求律师给予赔偿。因为现代医学上承认,遭受人身伤害的人可能因为律师的拖延被一种名为"补偿性神经官能症"(compensation neurosis)进一步损害健康,直到他获得人身伤害诉讼的赔偿。在Wales v. Wales(1967)111 SJ 946和Malyon v. Lawrence Messer & Co(1968)112

SJ 623 两个先例中,法院都给予了这种赔偿。相反,在 Cook v. Swinfen(1967)1 WLR 457 CA 先例中,原告是之前一个离婚诉讼中的被告,而本案的被告是她的代表律师。由于律师在之前诉讼抗辩的疏忽,本案原告被判是败诉方,而没有为她自己和她的儿子争取到任何抚养费。但在本案中,她声称因为败诉而健康受到很大伤害,法院拒绝了她的赔偿要求。因为健康受损不是败诉的合理和可以预见的后果,因此这种损失过于遥远。

15.4.3　精神压力

对于违约而导致的合约当事人情感上的损害,法律是不会给予赔偿的。这种说法被许多先例支持:Hamlin v. GN Ry(1856)1 H&N 408;Hobbs v. LSW Railway(1875) LR 10 QB 111;Addis v. Gramophone Co(1909)AC 488;Groom v. Crocker(1939)1 KB 194 CA;Bailey v. Bullock(1950)2 All ER 1167。例如在 Addis v. Gramophone Co 先例中,案情涉及一名雇员被错误地解雇,贵族院判是该雇员获得的赔偿不应该包括对他情感上伤害的赔偿,就算他被解雇的方式是粗暴与侮辱性的。另在 15.4.1 段介绍过的 Bailey v. Bullock 先例中,原告称作为岳父的房客,而不是独立的户主,他遭受了"烦恼或精神压力"(the annoyance or mental distress),但法院判这种精神压力就不能获得赔偿。

但也应该有例外存在。在商业合约中,对于违约而造成的精神伤害通常被法律视为是不在合约当事人对交易风险的预料之内,因此通常的规则是违约而导致的精神伤害不应该给予赔偿。但涉及非商业的合约,这不但影响合约当事人的商业利益,还影响到他的个人、社会和家庭利益,法院如果认为在个别情况下精神伤害是在合约当事人订约时预料之内的,就应该判受害方得到赔偿。这方面可以节录《McGregor on Damages》(18th edn,2009 年)之 3 - 020 段如下:"The reason for the general rule is that contracts normally concern commercial matters and that mental suffering on breach is not in the contemplation of the parties as part of the business risk of the transaction. If, however, the contract is not primarily a commercial one, in the sense that it affects not the claimant's business interests but his personal, social and family interests, the door should not be closed to awarding damages for mental suffering if the court think that in the particular circumstances the parties to the contract had such damage in their contemplation."

对这种观点的支持在 1970 年后出现在大量的先例中。在一个苏格兰的先例 Diesen v. Samson(1971)SLT(Sh. Ct.)49 中,被告的摄影师违反合约没有出现在原告的婚礼上,导致原告的新娘失去了她婚礼的图片记录,法院判是原告有权获得因此遭受痛苦和失望的赔偿。这种观点也被上诉庭在不同的先例中肯定:Jarvis v. Swan's Tours(1973)QB 233 CA;Heywood v. Wellers(1976)QB 446 CA;Jackson v. Horizon Holidays(1975)1 WLR 1468 CA。在 Jarvis v. Swan's Tours 先例中,原告因为信赖被告旅行社"解释详细的宣传册和其中令人着迷的内容"(lavishly illustrated brochure with its ecstatic text),向被告预订了一个瑞士的冬季运动假期旅游。但原告最终发现被告的

"美好时光"(good time)的承诺没有兑现,许多因为被告承诺而原告期待的设施都没有。最终证明这个假期令原告很失望。上诉庭判是被告违约,要赔偿原告因此而遭受的失望、痛苦、烦恼和挫败感的损失。接下来在 Heywood v. Wellers 先例中,原告的受害方指令她的律师采取行动防止第三人骚扰她,但作为被告的律师把事情搞砸,导致第三人继续骚扰她。上诉庭判是律师应赔偿原告因此而造成的"精神压力和沮丧"(mental distress and upset)的损失。

在这些先例后的一段时间,上诉庭一直赞成在违约下针对精神压力给予赔偿,这方面的普通法也得到了进一步的发展。在 Perry v. Sidney Philips & Son(1982)1 WLR 1297 CA 先例,案情涉及房屋测量合约的违约,法院允许了针对精神压力的赔偿。在 Cox v. Philips Industries(1976)1 WLR 638 先例中,案情涉及一个雇佣合约(尽管案情有些特殊),原告(被告的雇员)并非声称自己被解雇,而是因为被降级到一个责任不大的职位,法院也判是原告应获得赔偿。在 McCall v. Abelesz(1976)QB 585 CA 先例,案情涉及土地出租的合约,房东对承租人进行骚扰和干涉的行为违反了租赁合约,侵犯了承租人在合约中享有的平静收益权。Denning 大法官认为承租人因此而遭受的精神压力应该获得赔偿。

但在 Bliss v. South East Thames Regional Health Authority(1987)ICR 700 CA 先例后,在违约下精神压力赔偿的地位开始下降。在该先例案情涉及原告的雇员声称雇主违反雇佣合约中默示的相互信任和信赖义务,但法院拒绝对雇员的精神压力给予赔偿,并推翻了之前的 Cox v. Philips Industries(1976)1 WLR 638 先例。Dillon 大法官在这个先例中重复他在 Heywood v. Wellers(1976)QB 446 CA 先例中的观点,认为只有在合约的主要目的是通过提供娱乐或排除痛苦来获得精神上的满足,才适合在违约时对精神上的伤害给予赔偿,但雇佣合约不属于这一类。接下来在一系列的先例中,上诉庭也因为这个原因拒绝给予赔偿。在 Hayes v. James & Charles Dodd(1990)2 All ER 815 CA 先例中,被告的律师在原告购买某处经营场所时提供了错误的信息,称该经营场所有必要的后门。但由于实际没有后门,原告之后不得不终止他的生意并处理了该处经营场所。对于原告因此而遭受的"痛苦和烦恼"(anguish and vexation),法院判是被告不应赔偿,因为这是一个商业合约。在本章 15.4.1 段介绍过的 Watts v. Morrow(1991)1 WLR 1421 CA 先例中,由于检验师的疏忽令受害原告的夫妻买了质量有问题的房子,导致他们的房屋一直在维修中,法院判是原告所遭受的精神上的痛苦不应该获得赔偿,因为被违反的是一个商业合约。

在 Johnson v. Gore Wood & Co 先例中,原告的房地产开发商请被告的律师为原告的土地收购提供建议,由于被告律师的马虎对待,原告和他的家庭陷入了漫长的诉讼过程和经济困窘,并导致了家庭关系的破裂。但由于当事人之间的合约是一个单纯的商业合约,贵族院判是被告不需要赔偿原告精神上的损失伤害。同样的,法院拒绝给予赔偿也出现在以下先例中:Channon v. Lindley Johnstone(2002)PNLR 41 CA 先例涉及律师在客户离婚诉讼中的马虎准备;Howell - Smith v. Official Solicitor(2006)PN-

LR 41 CA 先例涉及律师对诉讼的失误处理；Brighton v. Jones(2004)EMLR 26 先例涉及原告在一场成功演出后，没有被写在演出名单中而失去了曝光的机会；Wiseman v. Virgin Atlantic Airways plc(2006)EWHC 1566 QB 先例涉及航空公司职员错误对待原告，拒绝让他登机。

而在 Farley v. Skinner(2002)2 AC 732 先例中，涉及一个特殊的勘测合约，贵族院稍稍偏离了 Bingham 大法官建立的原则。原告雇佣了被告的勘测员勘测一幢房子，并强调要勘测是否有飞机噪音，因为原告特别希望避免飞机噪音干扰。但被告的勘测员由于疏忽没有发现这幢房子会被飞机噪音干扰。贵族院判被告要赔偿原告因为过度的飞机噪音而遭受的精神痛苦，因为他们之间的合约是属于 Bingham 大法官在 Watts v. Morrow 先例中提到的例外的合约类别。合约中关于保持平静、安宁和避免精神痛苦是合约订立的主要目的，所以原告有权因此而要求被告赔偿他的精神伤害损失。

而在 Ruxley Electronics v. Forsyth(1995)All ER 1936 先例中，案情涉及一个原告的屋主和被告的承建商订立合约要在他的花园里修一个游泳池，但由于承建商的违约，没有满足游泳池深度在合约中的要求。该深度的不足不会造成危险，也不会减少游泳池的价值或房子的价值。贵族院判是被告不用赔偿原告恢复原状的费用，因为重新修建泳池费用十分昂贵，为了一点点深度的差别是不合理的做法。但英国法院判是在该案例中的游泳池建造涉及“舒适生活的损失”(loss of amenity)，还是判原告可以获得这一方面的非金钱损失赔偿，金额是 2500 英镑。第一审的 Diamond 大法官说：“Mr Forsyth(原告)reminded me that ‘This is not a matter of commerce to be nicely measured in money. Swimming pools are not necessities, they are for fun. Due to(plaintiff's) default I have lost fun’. I think that where a contract is for the provision of a pleasurable amenity, such as a swimming pool, it is entirely proper to award a general sum for the loss of amenity. I accept that there has been a loss of amenity brought about by the shortfall in depth and I award damages for loss of that amenity in the sum of Pounds 2,500.”这等于是给了受害方的屋主一个安慰奖。

但是在这些发展中，都没有提到贵族院的 Addis v. Gramophone Co(1909)AC 488 先例，在这个先例中，贵族院建立了在合约关系下不能对精神损害给予赔偿的原则(所谓的“Addis 原则”)。贵族院在过去的一个世纪中都没有用到 Addis v. Gramophone Co 先例，除了在两个先例中提到了它：Johnson v. Gore Wood & Co(2002)2 AC 1；Johnson v. Unisys Ltd(2003)1 AC 518。尽管这两个先例都不是关于在雇佣合约中要求精神损失赔偿的(第一个先例是关于提供专业服务合约中的精神损失赔偿，第二个先例是关于雇佣合约中的金钱损失赔偿，而不涉及非金钱损失赔偿)，但在这两个先例中贵族院关于 Addis v. Gramophone Co 先例的阐述，表明 Addis 原则的地位十分危险。

在 Johnson v. Gore Wood & Co 先例中，Cooke 勋爵并不支持 Addis 原则。他认为，当时贵族院把雇主和雇员的关系仅仅看作一种简单的商业合约关系，因此对错误解雇的赔偿范围作了严格的限制,但现代观念已经大不同。在 Addis 原则下,在所有雇佣关系下都不会对精神损害作出赔偿,这个原则在加拿大和新西兰都不被采纳。因此 Cooke 勋爵怀疑 Addis 原则在英国法中是否也应该继续存在,他说:"I take leave to doubt the permanence of *Addis* in English Law"。

而在 Johnson v. Unisys Ltd 先例中情况更复杂。因为在之前的 Mahmud v. Bank of Credit and Commerce International SA(1998)AC 20 先例中,案情不仅涉及错误解雇的赔偿,还涉及对雇佣合约其他条文的违反,包括所谓的雇佣合约中默示的相互信任和信赖义务,贵族院已经判是在关于金钱损失方面不应适用 Addis 原则,但案情并不涉及非金钱损失赔偿。同样的在 Johnson v. Unisys Ltd 先例中,争议的只有金钱损失赔偿,但不涉及对相互信任和信赖义务条文或其他雇佣合约条文的违反。而针对不公平解雇有立法对雇员进行保护,因此法官们也不用考虑对错误解雇方面法律的扩张。依据相关立法,原告对于金钱损失的赔偿要求被法院拒绝,这样一来同样的非金钱损失赔偿也必然没有被法院支持。但是,如果在该案中有对雇佣合约其他条文的违反,有迹象表明法院可能会判给原告精神损害赔偿。Hoffman 勋爵提到在加拿大,如果雇主违反了他在雇佣合约中默示的诚实和禁止不公正行为的义务,而对雇员的名誉和声望造成伤害,法院会对雇员的精神损害做出赔偿的判决。他很支持这种观点,并说:"Such an approach would in this country have to circumvent or overcome the obstacle of *Addis*... Speaking for myself, I think that, if this task was one which I felt called upon to perform, I would be able to do so."这个观点 Millett 勋爵也表示赞同说:"the general rule[namely, of no recovery for non-pecuniary loss whether to feelings or to reputation] would seem to be a sound one, at least in relation to ordinary commercial contracts entered into by both parties with a view of profit... in *Addis's* case the House of Lords treated a contract of employment as an ordinary commercial contract terminable at will... contracts of employment are no longer regarded as purely commercial contracts entered into between free and equal agents."

以上先例中法官在附带意见里的观点表明,Addis 原则可能很快就会被废除。同时,我们也不应该太严格遵守相对有限的原则,仅仅看合约的主要目的是否是通过提供娱乐或排除痛苦来获得精神上的满足来决定是否给予精神损害赔偿,还应该考虑对某项损失的赔偿是否在合约当事方的预期之内。这可以节录 Millett 勋爵 Johnson v. Unisys Ltd 先例中所说的:"In such cases[namely, cases of ordinary commercial contracts], non-pecuniary loss such as mental suffering consequent on breach is not within the contemplation of the parties and is accordingly too remote."现在在英国普通法中,对于违反雇佣合约中默示的相互信任和信赖义务,法院不会给予精神损害赔偿:Bliss v. South East Thames Regional Health Authority(1987)ICR 700 CA;French v. Barclays Bank(1998)IRLR 646 CA;Gogay v. Hertfordshire County Council(2000)IRLR 703 CA。但笔者相信这种观点也不会维持太久了。

15.4.4 社会名誉的降低或名誉损失

名誉损害(loss of reputation)是属于“诽谤”(defamation)类别的侵权案件,通常是由陪审团来决定赔偿金额。对于名誉的损害在其他侵权类别与合约关系不能得到赔偿这种说法源自于对于“纯感情损害”(purely sentimental injury)不能得到赔偿的说法:Hobbs v. London and South Western Railway Co(1875)LR 10 QB 111。

在其他侵权类别不能索赔名誉损害可介绍英国上诉庭的 Dixon v. Calcraft(1892)1 QB 458 先例,案情涉及政府错误扣押一艘船舶,上诉庭判是因此而造成的名誉损害不能获得赔偿。Esher 勋爵说:“The damage alleged is that, by seizing the ship on a suspicion of being unsafe, an imputation was cast on the character of the plaintiffs as shipowners. No such claim for damages was ever yet sustained in an action for seizing a chattel. If compensation were given for such an injury, it would be a kind of compensation unknown to the English law. It seems to me clear that this damage could not be recovered in an action for such a detention of a chattel, if wrongful. It could not be given by way of aggravation of damages in respect of wounded feelings. Such a thing was never heard of. Nor could it be given for injury to character, because that would really be giving damages as for libel or slander, though the matter complained of is not anything written or spoken.”

至于在合约关系,特别是会涉及名誉损害的合约类别如雇佣合约,在著名的 Addis v. Gramophone Co(1909)AC 488 先例,案情涉及错误的解雇,贵族院判是雇员名誉降低所造成的非金钱损失不能获得赔偿。Atkinson 勋爵是这样说:“I can conceive nothing more objectionable and embarrassing in litigation than trying in effect an action of libel or slander as a matter of aggravation in an action for illegal dismissal, the defendant being permitted, as he must in justice be permitted, to traverse the defamatory sense, rely on privilege, or raise every point which he could raise in an independent action brought for the alleged libel or slander itself.”这种观点也被后来的先例采纳:Groom v. Crocker(1939)1 KB 194 CA 先例涉及社会声誉的降低,法院对于造成的非金钱损失拒绝给予赔偿;Bailey v. Bullock(1950)2 All ER 1167 先例涉及声望的降低,法院也拒绝给予赔偿。

但看来也并非是有一个基本抗拒在雇佣合约做出名誉损害的赔偿,说法是为了程序上的方便要把属于违约的错误解雇与属于侵权的诽谤诉讼分开。在一些加拿大的案例,就在错误解雇的诉讼一并考虑名誉损失的赔偿,或是把分开的诽谤诉讼合并在一起:Bilbrough v. Board of Education of Toranto(1934)OWN 44(HCJ);Cleary v. Cabletronics Inc.(1982)140 DLR(3d)110,39 OR(2d)456(HCJ);Johnston v. Muskoka Lakes Golf and Country Club Ltd(1983)40 OR(2d)762,33 CPC 239(HCJ);Foley v. Signtech Inc(1988)55 DLR(4th)152,66 OR(2d)79(HCJ);Ribeiro v. Canadian Imperial Bank of Commerce(1992)13 OR(3d)278,44 CCEL 165(CA)。

而在英国一个有关学徒雇佣合约的错误解雇先例名为 Dunk v. George Waller Ltd(1970)2 QB 163(CA),Denning 勋爵判是原告可以索赔他的名誉损害,影响他将来找工作的前景，说："We were also referred to Addis v. Gramophone Co(1909) AC 488, when it was said that an employee cannot get compensation 'for the loss he may sustain from the fact that his having been dismissed of itself makes it more difficult for him to obtain fresh employment'. I do not think that applies in the case of an apprenticeship. The very object of an apprenticeship agreement is to enable the apprentice to fit himself to get better employment."

正如在15.4.3段介绍过，在更近期的Johnson v. Gore Wood & Co(2002)2 AC 1和Johnson v. Unisys Ltd(2003)1 AC 518先例后，这方面的法律有了变化，法官在这两个先例中的观点表明，Addis原则可能很快就会被废除。但是这两个先例主要涉及精神损害所导致的金钱损失赔偿，这些讨论也推动了有关名誉与情感损失赔偿的法律。然而，在合约关系下精神损害赔偿的法律的宽松是否也会导致在合约下针对名誉损害的赔偿法律也变得宽松，这点还不能确定。也有可能这种新的思路以后只会适用在雇佣合约中，因为雇佣合约的违约(不合理解雇)最可能招致名誉损失。

在雇佣合约以外的合约类别，违约会带来名誉损害赔偿会是涉及歌手、演员。这在贵族院的Clayton & Waller Ltd v. Oliver(1930) AC 209(HL)先例，Buckmaster勋爵是这样说："Here both parties knew that as flowing from the contract the plaintiff would be billed and advertised as appearing at the Hippodrome, and in the theatrical profession this is a valuable right. In assessing the damages, therefore, it was competent for the jury to consider that the plaintiff was entitled to compensation because he did not appear at the Hippodrome, as by his contract he was entitled to do, and in assessing those damages they may consider the loss he suffered (1) because the Hippodrome is an important place of public entertainment and (2) that in the ordinary course he would have been "billed" and otherwise advertised as appearing at the Hippodrome. The learned judge put the matter as a loss of reputation, which I do not think is the exact expression, but he explained that as the equivalent of loss of publicity and that summarizes what I have stated as my view of the true situation."

其他合约类别会可以带来名誉损害赔偿会是有不少，如婚约的违约，银行错误把客户的支票退票，甚至是特殊情况下货物买卖不提供货物给买方等。在银行错误把客户支票退票的先例是Wilson v. United Counties Bank(1920) AC 102(HL), Atkinson勋爵是这样说："It would appear to me that injury to the credit and reputation of a trader is not only a natural and reasonable result of his being made a bankrupt, i. e., such a consequence was would, in the ordinary course of things, flow from it, but must, in the present case, have been in the contemplation of the parties when they entered into the contract as the result which would probably follow from the breach of it."

在货物买卖合约中，特殊的情况下卖方不提供货物或货物质量有缺陷的违约也会带来无辜买方的“名誉损失”(loss of reputation),如儿童的玩具含有毒物质,导致分售的百货公司在事情曝光后名誉扫地。该百货公司作为买方就有可能向玩具的卖方(他可能就是生产商)提出索赔,其中包括了名誉损失。根据合约的赔偿,大前提是名誉损失不能提出索赔,这只是属于诽谤的侵权范畴,这也会是太空泛与无法肯定合理赔偿的金额的原因:Addis v. Gramophone Co Ltd(1909)AC 488。但这里会有很多的例外,如雇佣合约、婚约、作家(如出版合约)、艺人(如表演合约)等。这方面在《Chitty on Contracts》(30th edn,2008 年)在 26 - 086 段与 26 - 087 段有提到,可部分节录如下:

“Damages for loss of reputation as such are not normally awarded for breach of contract, since protection of reputation is the role of the tort of defamation. However, where the breach of contract causes a loss of reputation which in turn causes foreseeable financial loss to the claimant, he may recover damages for that financial loss: in Malik's(Malik v. Bank of Credit and Commerce International SA[1998]AC 20)case, the House of Lords held that where, by conducting a dishonest and corrupt business, the employer had broken his obligation to his employee(under the implied 'trust and confidence' term)the employee could recover damages for the financial loss suffered by him where his future employment prospects were prejudiced by the stigma of his employment...

Another line of authority covers cases where the contract gave an opportunity to the claimant to enhance his reputation as an author(Tolnay v. Criterion Film Productions Ltd [1936]2 All ER 1625; Joseph v. National Magazine Co Ltd[1959]Ch 14)or an actor (Clayton & Jack Waller Ltd v. Oliver[1930]AC 209; Marbe v. George Edwardes Ltd [1928]1 KB 269): damages may beawarded for loss flowing from a failure to provide promised publicity, which loss may include loss to existing reputation. Subject to remoteness, damages are recoverable where the breach of contract causes loss commercial reputation involving loss of trade.”

估计一般货物的买卖合约应该是不属于这种例外情况。但上述的节录最后一句也有提到将来生意损失会是可以向违约方索赔,而其中提到几个先例 Cointat v. Myham & Son(1913)2 KB 220;GKN Centrax Gears Ltd v. Matbro Ltd(1976)2 Lloyd's Rep 555;Jackson v. Bank of Scotland(2005)1 WLR 377。

至于带来“将来生意损失”(loss of repeat orders),这看来也是与名誉损失有一点接近甚至是同一码事,有时候被称为是“loss of goodwill”,是有说法无辜买方只要举证成功(举证可以部分顾客作为证人说明如果不是货物的缺陷,他就会继续与无辜买方做生意)。大致是受害方的买方指卖方的违约导致他失去了其他的客户,并蒙受可以估计到的利润损失。这种损失类别通常不会成功,原因也是在遥远性,因为卖方不能合理在订约时预见到这种损失。但这也有例外,因为这项损失类别在本质上并非是不被法律所接受。这首先可节录《McGregor on Damages》(18th edn,2009 年)之

2 - 027 段:"On the other hand, recovery for loss of custom is generally refused both in sale and carriage, but again this is on the ground of remoteness and not because this is an impermissible head of damage; indeed recovery has been allowed in sale."

也可节录《Benjamin's Sale of Goods》(8th edn, 2010 年)之 17 - 069 段所说:"Where, at the time they made their contract, it was within the reasonable contemplation of the parties that defects in the goods supplied by the seller (in breach of his undertaking as to their quality) might lead to sub - buyers (customers of the buyer) withdrawing their custom from the buyer, damages may be awarded for loss of profits on 'repeat orders' from the sub - buyers. (A similar principle has been accepted by the House of Lords in the case [Jackson v. Royal Bank of Scotland [2005] 1 WLR 377] of breach of obligation to maintain confidence, which led to the claimant losing future profits from 'repeat orders' from his previous customers.) When some customers give evidence that they would have given repeat orders but for the breach of warranty, the damages are not limited in amount to the loss of custom from those customers: the court may draw inferences as to the probable total loss of business."

在一个关于卖方不提供货物的先例 Foaminol Laboratories Ltd v. British Artid Plastics, Ltd (1941) 2 All ER 393 (KB), 其中 Hallett 法官是这样说:"I think that, if pecuniary loss can be established, the mere fact that the pecuniary loss is brought about by the loss of reputation caused by a breach of contract is not sufficient to preclude the plaintiffs from recovering in respect of that pecuniary loss"。在这个先例中,案情涉及原告打算在市场上推出一种女士专用的夏日乳霜。这种乳霜是可以放在一种小而精致的容器中,便于她们随身携带。为了扩大宣传,原告和一些女士报刊专栏的美容编辑合作。这些编辑们不仅写文章对这款乳霜进行宣传,还接受顾客半价的预订。原告向被告订购了1万个这种特殊的容器,但被告除了提供了47个样品,剩余的容器都没有提供。原告起诉被告违反合约,并要求赔偿。法院判是原告可以获得三项赔偿:(1)利润损失;(2)在最初的促销中所支出的费用;(3)原告对那些预订了产品并支付费用的顾客的赔偿。但对于原告要求被告赔偿因此失去与美容编辑的合作而造成的名誉损失,法院拒绝赔偿。因为原告不能证明这项损失是在合约双方订约时可预料的,而且原告没有提出任何证据证明他遭受了具体的金钱损失。但法院认为,如果原告能够证明这两个方面,名誉损失是可以获得赔偿的。Hallett 大法官是这样说:"I think that, if pecuniary loss can be established, the mere fact that the pecuniary loss is brought about by the loss of reputation caused by a breach of contract is not sufficient to preclude the plaintiffs from recovering in respect of that pecuniary loss. Such a plaintiff has to overcome two difficulties. In the first place, he must prove with sufficient certainty the occurrence of the pecuniary loss, and, in the second place, he must prove that such pecuniary loss was within the contemplation of the defaulting party at the time when the contract was made. Otherwise it is not recoverable, having regard to the law respecting remoteness of damage. The plaintiff has failed to overcome these two difficulties."这看来在一般的货物买卖合约很难做得到,而涉及有"可供买卖市场"(available market)的货物是更加不会成功索赔名誉损失,因为受害的买方可以在市场买进替代货物就完全可以避免这一项的损失。(有关市场规则在本书第十五章与第十六章有详解)

这种说法在上诉庭的 GKN v. Matbro(1976)2 Lloyd's Rep 555 先例也有涉及,买方是叉车的建造商,而卖方是车轴的供应商让买方把车轴安装在叉车上。但由于车轴有缺陷,导致买方制造出来再分售给其他顾客使用后经常出现故障。这导致了诉讼,其中卖方向买方追讨3万英镑的欠下货款,但买方提出货物质量缺陷导致损失的索赔并要求抵销欠下的货款。而其中一项损失就是将来生意的损失,因为顾客再也不前来购买叉车,导致销售下降。Denning 勋爵同意这一种损失类别是可以成功索赔,说:

"I should have thought that loss of repeat orders was well within that principle. But Mr. Wilson(卖方代表大律师)submitted that a defendant ought not to be liable for such a loss unless he had expressly or impliedly undertaken to pay damages on that account. He relied on British Columbia Saw mill Co v. Nettleship(1868)LR 3 CP 499. but the observations in that case cannot survive the decision of the House of Lords in Czarnikov v. Koufos (1967)2 Lloyd's Rep 457. The principle was stated by Lord Upjohn at pp 484 and 421 and 422:... If parties enter into the contract with knowledge of some special circumstances, and it is reasonable to infer a particular loss as a result of those circumstances that is something which both must contemplate as a result of a breach...

That principle applies to loss of repeat orders as well as to other losses. Applying the principle here Centrax(卖方)knew as well as anybody the purpose for which these axles were required. It must have been within the contemplation of the parties that if these axles failed, it would cause much damage to the goodwill of Matbro(买方). Customers would be disappointed and would not order any more. It seems to me that the arbitrator was entirely correct. Loss of repeat orders from existing customers can be recovered where that is naturally within the contemplation of the parties as a consequence of the breach."

证明这种违约带来将来生意的损失会有一定难度,毕竟生意下跌会有其他各种原因,因果关系不容易成立。损失的举证责任虽然是在受害方,但在民事诉讼最后还是根据"平衡的可能性"(balance of probability)。所以有关的证人是否在证明有生意下跌的原因是来自货物的缺陷而且补救不了有说服力,就是至关重要。

至于这种损失类别因为遥远性不被法院支持的先例是 The "Pegase"(1981)1 Lloyd's Rep 175。该先例涉及在一个 FOB 买卖下的海上运输合约,而有关的货物是"铬铁矿砂"(chromite sand)。由于船舶不合理绕航导致了65天的延误,这导致了受害方的收货人索赔高价购买部分货物损失、转售利润损失与商誉损失。有关这个先例的其他方面在本章 14.2.2 段已经介绍过，在这里只针对商誉损失，英国高院的 Golf 大法官是这样说："Finally I must refer to the receivers' claim for damages for loss of goodwill. They claimed Italian lire 25,000,000 on the ground that, by reason of the incident, some of their customers failed to place repeat orders with them and transferred their custom to Laviosa; and the arbitrator found that the delay of 65 days did have the effect that a number of unspecified customers of the receives did transfer their custom to Laviosa and were permanently lost to the receivers, the resulting loss of profit to the receivers being assessed by him at the claimed figure of Italian lire 25,000,000. Even so, I do not see how, on the findings of fact in the award, this head of claim was recoverable by the receivers from the owners; because (quite apart from the fact that, on the findings of fact, it resulted from the whole delay of 65 days) there are no findings of fact in the award to found a conclusion that the owners ought reasonably to have contemplated any loss of goodwill as not unlikely to result from this breach contract. Indeed, without any knowledge of the receivers' business or of the circumstances in which they traded, any loss of goodwill must have been so speculative that it is difficult to see how it could be concluded that this head of claim was not too remote."

上述的两个先例可以看到除了合约本质不一样之外，货物的本质也不一样。在 GKN v. Matbro 先例，卖方在订约时是合理知道卖给买方的一批驱动轴是用来安装在买方生产与出售的叉车，可以预见到如果有缺陷会带来什么后果。但在 The "Pegase" 先例，承运人的船东除了不会合理预见收货人的转售合约（这与买卖合约不一样）或是没有可供买卖市场，更加不会预见到收货人没有这种商品的存货作为应急之用。

最后可节录 SM Waddams 著的《The Law of Damages》一书在 4.310 段的总结："It would seem from these cases that there is no cogent reason why damages should not be given for loss of reputation in a contract case, and it seems probable that the limitation expressed by Lord Atkinson in Addis v. Gramophone Co. Ltd (1909) AC 488 will continue to attract exceptions. The reason given by Lord Atkinson for excluding such damages was the possible procedural inconvenience of trying what would be in effect an action for defamation along with an action for breach of contract. There may in some cases be cogent procedural reasons for separating the actions, but it appears from the cases considered previously that these will not always be present, and that there is no inherent impossibility in combining the claims."

15.5 非金钱损失的计算

上述这种非金钱损失的赔偿还是需要量化为金钱做出赔偿，正如 Morris 勋爵在 Parry v. Cleaver (1970) AC 1 先例所讲的："But a money award is all that is possible. It is the best that can be done."

这就带来对这种非金钱损失的赔偿，量化是很不容易的问题。英国法律的大前提是受害方如果不能量化与证明他的损失，只能获得名义上的赔偿。这方面可节录

《McGregor on Damages》(18th edn,2009 年)之 8－001 段:“A claimant claiming damages must prove his case. To justify an award of substantial damages he must satisfy the court both as to the fact of damage and as to its amount. If he satisfies the court on neither, his action will fail, or at the most he will be awarded nominal damages where a right has been infringed. If the fact of damage is shown but no evidence is given as to its amount so that it is virtually impossible to assess damages, this will generally permit only an award of nominal damages; this situation is illustrated by the old cases of Dixon v. Deveridge(1825)2 C&P 109 and Twyman v. Knowles(1853)13 CB 222.”

但在英国法律承认的非金钱损失项目,如果有实质性的损失,即使量化有很大的困难也不是理由不这样做。这方面有许多的权威说法,如针对“机会损失”(loss of chance)(这课题在本书第六章之“损失的肯定性:将来的变数与机会损失”有介绍),著名的先例 Chaplin v. Hicks(1911)2 KB 786 CA 中 Vaughan Williams 大法官就说:“The fact that damages cannot be assessed with certainty does not relieve the wrongdoer of the necessity of paying damages.”他也另说:“No one has ever suggested that, because there is no market, there are no damages. In such a case the jury must do the best they can, and it may be that the amount of their verdict will really be a matter of guesswork.”另在 Biggin v. Permanite(1951)1 KB 422 先例中,Devlin 大法官也说:“Where precise evidence is obtainable, the court naturally expects to have it, [but] where it is not, the court must do the best it can.”另可节录在 Ratcliffe v. Evans(1892)2 QB 524 CA 先例中,Bowen 勋爵说:“In all actions accordingly on the case where the damage actually done is the gist of the action, the character of the acts themselves which produce the damage, and the circumstances under which these acts are done, must regulate the degree of certainty and particularity with which the damage done ought to be stated and proved. As much certainty and particularity must be insisted on, both in pleading and proof of damage, as is reasonable, having regard to the circumstances and to the nature of the acts themselves by which the damage is done. To insist upon less would be to relax old and intelligible principles. To insist upon more would be the vainest pedantry.”

但量化损失也不需要有绝对的肯定,通常的说法只是“合理的肯定”(reasonable certainty)。而对非金钱损失的举证责任通常只需要提供证明这方面的损失是可以“合理推断”(reasonably inferred)与提供“足够数据”(adequate data)可把损失的金额计算出来。在 Ashcroft v. Curtin(1971)1 WLR 1731 CA 先例,就是因为原告没有提供足够数据而导致索赔失败。

针对非金钱损失的赔偿,另有一些先例对这方面做出了一些指导思想。例如已经提到的 Farley v. Skinner(2002)2 AC 732(HL)先例,Steyn 大法官提到的赔偿应该受到约束与判赔金额尽量少。另也有说法是量化并不是容易的事,如针对“痛苦与受难”,Halsbury 勋爵在 The “Mediana”(1900)AC 113 先例中说到:“How is anybody to measure pain and suffering in moneys counted? Nobody can suggest that you can by arithmetical calculation establish what is the exact sum of money which would represent such a thing as the pain and suffering which a person has undergone by reason of an accident. But nevertheless the law recognizes that as a topic upon which damages may be given."而有关人身伤亡的侵权案件中针对这种非金钱损失的赔偿,在《McGregor on Damages》(18th edn,2009 年)之 35 -258 段至 35 -287 段有详细的介绍,不在本章重复。只说这方面的损失赔偿金额已经根据许多先例在 1992 年做出了一本名为《Guidelines for the Assessment of General Damages in Personal Injury Cases》的册子,到了 2008 年就已经是第九版。这本册子的目的是 Donaldson 勋爵在第一版的前言中所说提供这方面损失赔偿的一个指引或标准。而在第九版的前言,Waller 大法官是说:"The more established the work has become,the more its guidelines have been followed by the courts-and,anecdotal evidence suggests,in negotiated settlements."而在《McGregor on Damages》(18th edn,2009 年)之 35 -280 段,更是说明这一本册子对计算或量化非金钱损失赔偿在人身伤亡的案件是提供了重要的工具:"It is an essential tool in the assessment of damages for non - pecuniary loss in personal injury claims and relieves the author of a text on damages from further investigation of the detail of the level of awards."

违约的非金钱损失在本质上与人身伤亡的侵权案件中经常会涉及的"痛苦与受难"需要量化没有太大区别,而这是法院经常要做的事。这是 Singleton 大法官在 Stedman v. Swan's Tours(1951)95 SJ 727 先例所说:"Damages could be recovered for appreciable inconvenience and discomfort caused by a breach of contract. It might be difficult to assess the amount to be awarded, but it was no more difficult than to assess the amount to be given for pain and suffering in a case of personal injury."该先例是涉及一个"度假合约"(holiday contract),原告订的是一家一流酒店的超级海景房,但后来发觉提供的房间是低级与没有海景,原告也没有办法去其他酒店找到适合的房间而被迫接受,但假期的享受就受到破坏。另在一个类似的"滑雪度假合约"(skiing holiday contract),Denning 勋爵也有同样的说法(再重复):"In a proper case damages for mental distress can be recovered in contract, just as damages for shock can be recovered in tort. One such case is a contract for a holiday or any other contract to provide entertainment and enjoyment. If the contracting party breaks his contract, damages can be given for the disappointment, the distress, the upset and frustration caused by the breach. I know that it is difficult to assess in terms of money, but it is no more difficult than the assessment which the courts have to make every day in personal injury cases for loss of amenity."

也有说法是要尽量按照事实相同的判例,这显然是为了法律的肯定。Diplock 勋爵在 Wright v. British Railways Board(1983)2 AC 773 先例说:"Non - economic loss... is not susceptible of measurement in money. Any figure at which the assessor of damages arrives cannot be other than artificial and, if the aim is that justice meted out to all litigants should be even - handed instead of depending on idiosyncrasies of the assessor, whether jury or judge, the figure must be ‘a conventional figure derived from experience and from awards in comparable cases’.”

但度假合约的事实经常不会相同，这包括了假期的设施与要求、豪华程度、原告的目的等都不一样。这方面可节录 Cumming - Bruce 大法官在 Adcock v. Blue Sky Holidays Ltd (unreported decision of the Court of Appeal dated 13 May 1980) 先例中所讲的："Contracts for holidays vary on their facts very greatly. The facilities offered by the tour company vary enormously from case to case. It would be a grave mistake to look at the facts in, for example, the *Jackson v Horizon Holidays Ltd* (1975) 1 *WLR* 1468 case or the *Jarvis v Swan Tours Ltd* (1973) 1 *QB* 223 case and compare those facts with the facts in another case as a means of establishing the measure of damages."

但还是有一些方面的事实不同会导致量化的金额不同是已经有了共识。其中原告的目的会是一个重要的考虑因素，如为了度蜜月就会比一般的假期会获得更高的赔偿。或是度假合约是为了参加一种运动。在 Milner and Another v. Carnival (2010) 1 Lloyd's Rep 374 先例，就有提到这方面的统计。就是从有记录的度假合约，针对蜜月假期的赔偿金额是从 321 英镑到 1890 英镑，针对其他有特殊目的的假期赔偿金额是从 264 英镑到 1161 英镑，而一般的假期赔偿是从 83 英镑到 1876 英镑。但看来对有一些因素的考虑就有不同看法，如有钱人或是穷人。一个看法可以是穷人一生难得有一个假期，所以是如果度假合约发生违约导致他失去了应有的享受，就应该多赔偿一点。但有钱人就把一个假期看做是平常不过的事情，也很容易再安排另一个。对这种看法的先例有 Kepple - Palmer v. Exus Travel (2003) EWHC 3529 (QB), Gage 大法官是这样说："In my opinion she (原告) is entitled to a sum representing loss of enjoyment. In this respect, I take into account that this was designed to be a very luxurious holiday, coming after her, and her family's, difficult year. This is, however, not the case of a family unused to holidays. To be able to afford the cost of such a holiday indicates a degree of financial resources from which I infer that that the claimant and her family are used to some of the more expensive things in life, including regular holidays. For that reason, in my judgment, the sum for the loss of the enjoyment must be modest; I assess it in the sum of £3,000."

但在 Milner and Another v. Carnival 先例，Ward 大法官有不同的看法说："I am not sure that the loss of enjoyment must necessarily always be more modest for the wealthy than the poor; the level of distress is surely measured by the extent of the failure to meet reasonable expectations and a luxury holiday of a lifetime for the rich can be as spoilt for him as the more modest holiday of a lifetime for the poor, unless of course the poor man will never be able to afford another whilst the rich man can ameliorate his disappointment by immediately booking another jaunt to make up for his loss. It is a question of fact and degree in each case."

这方面的量化计算可以举一些先例作为介绍,其中有:Adcock v. Blue Sky Holidays Ltd(CA)13 May 1980, unreported;Farley v. Skinner(2002)2 AC 732(HL);Hobbs v. London and South Western Railway Co(1875)LR 10 QB 111;Jackson v. Horizon Holidays Ltd(CA)(1975)1 WLR 1468;Jarvis v. Swans Tours Ltd(CA)(1973)QB 233;Kepple – Palmer v. Exus Travel(2003)EWHC 3529(QB);Stedman v. Swan's Tours(CA)(1951)95 SJ 727 等。

在 Milner and Another v. Carnival(2010)1 Lloyd's Rep 374 先例,案情涉及 Milner 夫妻付出了约 6 万英镑的票价乘坐环游世界的游轮名为 Queen Victoria 轮,这是她的处女航并在 2008 年 1 月 6 日在英国南安普顿起航,途径纽约,然后通过巴拿马运河去洛杉矶,再去夏威夷,再去澳大利亚、香港、东南亚、印度,然后通过苏伊士运河去地中海,再回到南安普顿。整个环游世界的航次长达 106 天。当船舶离开南安普顿时,遇上了很坏的天气,原告夫妻的房间因船舱地板扭曲而产生噪音,影响了原告夫妻的睡眠。该游轮后来给原告夫妻提供了另外一间没有原来房间的良好设施的条件较差的房间。在抵达纽约前的 4 天原告夫妻都睡在该替代的房间里,只有在白天才回去原来的房间。从纽约去洛杉矶,航程是 17 天,该游轮提供给 Milner 夫妻一间非常高级的套房。虽然在起初只承诺给他们享用 2 ~ 3 天,但最终是让他们全程享用。游轮从洛杉矶起航后,Milner 夫妻被要求回去他们原来的房间。但不久后又遇上了坏天气,Milner 夫妻再度投诉因地板扭曲产生的噪音,并拒绝了游轮提供的另一个在船头的房间。Milner 夫妻表示他们不满意并准备在夏威夷离船,而事实上该游轮在 2 月 4 日抵达夏威夷后他们也的确离船。这表示在整个 106 天的航次,Milner 夫妻只完成了 28 天,剩下还有 78 天的环游世界航程没有完成。Milner 夫妻在夏威夷待了 6 个星期,是自己支付费用。最后他们乘坐了另一艘名为 Queen Elizabeth轮的游轮返回南安普顿,乘坐该游轮的费用是 13440 英镑。

在事后,Milner 夫妻向船公司提出的索赔是他们的游轮假期因为货不对版的贬值共 8500 英镑,"压力与失望"(distress and disappointment)共 50000 英镑,Milner 夫人浪费了的礼服费用(因为离船而没有机会去参加游轮的晚宴)共 4300 英镑与 Queen Elizabeth 轮的费用共 13440 英镑。在第一审,判是 Milner 夫妻总共可以获得赔偿 22000 英镑的损失。其中每人可获得 2500 英镑货不对版的贬值,每人 7500 英镑的压力与失望的赔偿,与 Milner 夫人浪费了的礼服费用 2000 英镑。

但一审法院的判决被上诉庭推翻。上诉庭认为损失赔偿应该从两个方面进行评估:(1)游轮假期的贬值;(2)Milner 夫妻的压力与失望。在第一个方面,游轮假期的贬值是游轮在合约中承诺提供的假期与实际提供假期的价值差异,不应考虑 Milner 夫妻个人对游轮假期贬值的看法。从事实来看,Milner 夫妻的游轮假期贬值了 1/3。根据船公司提供给 Milner 夫妻的游轮假期实际价格是 10812 英镑,Milner 夫妻应该因此而获得 3500 英镑的赔偿。在第二个方面,关于 Milner 夫妻所遭受的身体上的不方便、不舒适与精神压力,法院应该比较 Milner 夫妻的期待和现实情况。Milner 夫妻被船公司承诺了一个"终生难忘的经历"(experience of a lifetime),但实际上由于Milner夫妻在夏威夷主动放弃了旅程,大部分的游轮假期Milner夫妻都没有享受到。Milner夫妻的失望应该根据他们在船上的时间来评估。一审法院错误判决船公司应赔偿Milner夫人浪费了的礼服费用2000英镑,她没有机会参加游轮晚宴是因为他们在夏威夷主动放弃了旅程。被告的违约在因果关系上并没有导致这笔损失。Milner夫人由于没有机会穿礼服的失望应该作为在计算她的"压力"(distress)损失赔偿时一并考虑的因素。总之,一审法院判是被告应赔给Milner先生7500英镑,Milner夫人9500英镑以及每人2500英镑货不对版的贬值是太多和不成比例的。正确的应该是判给Milner先生4000英镑,Milner夫人4500英镑作为压力与失望的赔偿。两个方面的损失共计12000英镑。

在Kepple - Palmer v. Exus Travel(2003)EWHC 3529先例,第一被告的旅游代理为原告在第二被告拥有的位于巴巴多斯岛的豪华别墅内安排了一个价值88025英镑的假期。宣传册上承诺会提供给原告最佳品质的住宿和设施,还包括一名私人助理。原告自己安排了去巴巴多斯岛的交通,但被告仅安排了机场的接送。原告发现别墅根本达不到广告上的标准并向被告投诉了不达标的住宿状况,别墅内很多设施都没有,而私人助理提供了很差的服务。同时由于该别墅渗雨露风,使得原告居住在别墅里很不愉快。原告要求两被告赔偿她假期享受的损失和旅游假期的贬值。

法院判是被告违反合约并应提供给原告赔偿。原告的投诉已经超出了品质不同的范围,这些投诉清楚表明被告违反了与原告订立的合约。虽然被告不应该为恶劣天气负责,但不能提供充分遮蔽的房屋不可能被称为一流的或最佳品质的住宿。尽管原告的一些投诉是小事情,但并非这些小事情中的某一件,而是所有这些事情的积累导致了被告的违约。至于损失赔偿的量化,法院认为应该考虑两个方面的因素:(1)旅游假期的贬值;(2)原告在享受方面的损失或失望。在第一方面,原告要求赔偿假期价格的一半,而在第二方面,原告要求被告赔偿每天500英镑的损失,合计16500英镑。但法院考虑到,第二被告毫无疑问也提供了一些利益给原告。包括在千禧年的旺季提供给原告符合广告描述的房屋,有广阔的视野,还有一系列的利益包括高尔夫课程、私人沙滩和一个有大型游泳池的健身房。所以在第一方面的旅游假期的贬值赔偿,由于这是一个价格昂贵的旅游,原告有权期待一个很高标准的假期。而被告提供给她的是完全低于这个高标准。因此法官考虑到被告实际提供给原告的设施、地点和时间,在旅游假期的贬值方面的赔偿应该是合约价格的25%,也就是22000英镑。而针对原告在享受方面的损失或失望,法院认为原告有权获得赔偿。至于该项赔偿的量化,法院认为这是在她和她家人在度过困境后所计划的豪华假期。但这个假期对这个家庭来说是平常不过的。能够负担得起这样一个假期表明原告和她的家庭有经济能力并且很习惯于这种昂贵的生活,包括定期的旅游。因为这些原因,法院判是被告赔偿给原告在享受方面的损失或失望应该是最低的,也就是3000英镑。

第三章　损失的遥远性之一:损失可否合理预见

1. 为什么针对合约损失需要有遥远性的限制?

首先简单介绍什么是"损失的遥远性"(remoteness of damages)的限制,这来自两个方面。一是双方在订立合约时是否可以"合理预见"(reasonably foreseeable 或 within reasonable contemplation)违约很可能带来的损失类别(kind or type of loss not unlikely to result),如果不是,这部分的损失就不能向违约方取回。二是损失并非是真正因为违约方的过错而引起,这也就是"因果关系"(causation)方面的问题了。以下可节录《McGregor on Damages》(18th edn,2009 年)之 6 - 002 段:"A basic distinction, already referred to, is that the term 'remoteness' has more than one meaning, referring both to causation in the law and to scope of the protection afforded by the law."另在 19 - 006 段是说:"Damages may be too remote in one of the two ways: either because it is not caused by the defendant's act, or because, even if so caused, it is not within the scope of the protection afforded to the claimant."

可在无数先例有针对的挑一个近期的先例,The "Sylvia"(2010)2 Lloyd's Rep 81, Hamblen 大法官是这样说:"In the light of the authorities, the generally accepted test for remoteness has been whether the loss claimed was of a kind or type which it would have been within the reasonable contemplation of the parties at the time that the contract was made as being not unlikely to result."

在本章先探讨有关损失类别是否可以合理预见,这一个大原则适用在所有侵权与违约的损失,只会有很少的例外才会豁免,如"欺诈性误述"(fraudulent misrepresentation):Smith New Court Securities Ltd v. Scrimgeour Vickers (Asset Management) Ltd (1997) AC 254;4 Eng Ltd v. Harper (2009) Ch. 91。虽然在合约方面,有说法是 The "Achilleas"(2007)1 Lloyd's Rep. 19 带来了一些改变(这方面会稍后在第 8 段详细介绍),由"是否可以合理预见"变成是"客观看订约双方是否愿意承担赔偿的责任"(objective assessment in the voluntary assumption of responsibility),即双方所订的合约中有否明示或默示考虑到某一种类型的损失,并且违约方是否愿意承担后果。换言之,针对受害方可以在正常情况下向违约方索赔或取回的损失类别是有所收紧的。

区分损失的类别并且限制受害方取回全部损失的原因是如果要违约方承担不论

是否可以预见的所有损失被认为是太苛刻,甚至是不公平的。毕竟在双方谈判合约时,如果把这种无边无际的损失类别提出来要求对方如果违约就要承担,对方可能拒绝。这里可以举几个日常与假设的例子。第一个是一个乘客与一个出租车司机(或公司)约好第二天清早接他去机场。但第二天清早由于出租车司机睡过头爽约,原告因此误了班机,丧失了一宗大生意达1000万美元。那么司机是否要赔偿这1000万美元呢?旁观者马上会感到,要该司机赔这么大一笔钱有不妥、不公平之处。但能说得出什么法理上站的住脚的抗辩吗?第一个想得到的就是该乘客在过了约定时间之后没有看到出租车,为什么不另外找一辆出租车去机场?或是,早一班飞机赶不上就赶下一班飞机?这是涉及"合理减少损失"(reasonable mitigation)方面,本书第五章会详谈。但在这里就可以假设没有这一减损的合理机会,因为乘客住的地方很偏僻,清早根本无法找到其他的出租车。另外,飞机去的目的地是一个班机不多的地方,错过了清早这一班飞机就要等多几天才有班机,这一笔大生意就错过了。第二个想到的就是出租车司机不知道乘客原来有这么重要的事情要办,如果乘客早告诉他这一事实,他就会有不同做法。例如在早一天的晚上就在乘客的家门外等待,在出租车内睡觉,就万无一失不会爽约。甚至如果这是一个比较正规的租车合约,出租车司机会加上条文限制违约下的赔偿责任或是提高租车费。如果这样就会公道一点的话,就认为乘客在订车时应该在电话里提到接他去机场非常重要,因为他赶着签一个重要的合约,并承诺会给出租车司机多一点小费。这一来,假设乘客能够证明这些事实,是否足够与公平要出租车司机承担这1000万美元的损失呢?会否更公道的是要求该乘客清楚说明如果出租车司机违约/毁约的后果将会是面对1000万美元的索赔,并说明多一点小费是多少钱(如果没有说明小费多少或是只承诺给1美元区区小数,就会与承诺1万美元的小费显然是有所不同),然后让出租车司机自己考虑值不值得冒这个险来接这个生意?看来,法律这"一刀切"在什么地方并不是一件容易的事情。

香港高院Reyes大法官在2008年2月在香港大学的发言《Certainty in Contractual Damages Assessment - On Two Suggested Alternatives to the Rule in Hadley v. Baxendale》中也举到一个例子,可以在这里一提,这是从英国一首童谣引出来的:"For want of a nail the shoe was lost, for want of a shoe the horse was lost, for want of a horse the rider was lost, for want of a rider the battle was lost, for want of a battle the kingdom was lost, and all for the want of a horseshoe nail."

以上假设在国王和铁匠之间有一个以1英镑来提供马蹄钉的合约,在合约的谈判过程中,国王提到这个钉子是用在他的马匹上,而他即将骑这匹马去参加一场战役。国王声称这个钉子必须拥有最顶级的质量,否则他就会战败亡国。而铁匠以为国王只是说笑而没有提出任何条文免除或减轻提供有缺陷钉子的责任,也没有要求更高的报酬。结果铁匠提供的钉子质量上有缺陷,最终导致国王在战役中因为马失前蹄战败。在这种情况下,可不可以说铁匠要为国王战败与亡国的后果负责呢?换句话说,在与国王的谈判过程中,铁匠是不是要为了区区1英镑的收入承担国王战败与亡国的责任呢?

这个例子是极端的,但它引起了人的疑问:对损失类别的合理可预见性或者其他类似的标准可否作为限制合约赔偿的原则呢?这会否对订约双方更加公平?

2. Hadley v. Baxendale 先例的损失规定

显然,对于这种无法合理估计到的后果是应该有一个地方来一刀切断。这里就要介绍一个英国最著名的、在诉讼中被引用最多的先例 Hadley v. Baxendale(1854)9 Ex. 341,它就损失类别的合理预见性问题确立了一套基本的理论,称为其后这方面判例的一个总体指南。该案情是:原告的磨小麦、谷物的工厂(该工厂在当时是十分先进,该建筑物目前还是完整并已经被改为高级住宅)因蒸汽机曲轴断裂造成停产,原告急忙委托被告的承运人将断轴运送给英国某地的厂家供其依样再做一根新的。结果被告违约(运输合约)延迟了交付,造成新轴比原计划晚了好几天才交到原告厂里。为此,原告向被告索赔若没有这几天延迟工厂本可早点复工而挣取到的生产利润。法院判是延迟交送断轴给制造厂家造成原告工厂停产的损失是被告无法合理预见的,被告订约当时的全部认识只局限在为原告工厂运输这一条断轴,他并不知道原告没有任何备用轴可供应急,更不知道延误会带来停产。结果原告败诉。道理其实也很简单,虽然承运人确实是违约延迟了交货(这种运输中的延误在航运中经常发生,如船舶不合理绕航或不适航等),但所运的断轴仅仅是一个零件。以通常合理的眼光看,原告工厂晚了拿到新的零件损失了什么呢?被告的承运人并不知道原告没有备用的应急,以致弄到整个工厂停产这么严重。产值利润没了,工人没工开,收入没了,说不定家计都成了问题。这些都要承运人来赔,他肯定说:“你怎么不早讲这些后果啊!如果你订约当时就告诉我,这个断轴一定要某月某日前运抵,务必准时,否则整个工厂就开不了工,要倒闭,那我肯定不运了。即使运的话,我也会收很高的运费,因为责任太大了嘛!”这是一个很早的案件了,如果是现在的案件,承运人如船东可能还会说:“你要早讲明后果,运费多付一点我也会愿意运输,不过做法上就会不一样了。一旦半途船舶遇到什么麻烦,可能造成延迟的话,我就会马上设法把断轴转到岸上交飞机空运到目的地,以确保准时,高昂的飞机运输费用也只好支付了。”

这个案例判下来后,有关违约损害赔偿的判定就有了一个以违约方能否合理预见作为标准把损失分为两种类别的做法,或称为两条规则。一种是“一般损失”(ordinary damages,有时候被称为 general damage 或 incidental damage),或毁约会造成的自然与一般性后果,违约方要赔;另一种是“特别损失”(special damages,有时候被称为 consequential damage),或称非一般后果,违约方不用赔,除非订约当时或之前受害方已将会产生特别损失的后果告诉了违约方。其中,法院的判决如下:“We think the proper rule in such a case as the present is this:where two parties have made a contract which one of them has broken,the damages which the other party ought to receive in respect of such breach of contract should be such as may fairly and reasonably be considered either arising naturally,i. e. according to the usual course of things,from such breach of contract itself,or such as may reasonably be supposed to have been in the contemplation of both parties,at the time they made the contract,as the probable result of the breach of it. Now,if the special circumstances under which the contract was actually made were communicated by the plaintiffs to the defendants and thus known to both parties,the damages resulting from the breach of such a contract, which they would reasonably contemplate, would be the amount of injury which would ordinarily follow from a breach of contract under these special circumstances so known and communicated. But,on the other hand,if these special circumstances were wholly unknown to the party breaking the contract,he,at the most,would only be supposed to have had in his contemplation the amount of injury which would arise generally,and in the great multitude of cases not affected by any special circumstances,from such a breach of contract. For,had the special circumstances been known,the parties might have specially provided for the breach of contract by special terms as to the damages in that case;and of this advantage it would be very unjust to deprive them. Now the above principles are those by which we think the jury ought to be guided in estimating the damages arising out of any breach of contract."

有无数的案例探讨过对于这一个重要先例的理解,在这里只节录 Goff 大法官在 The "Pegase"(1981)1 Lloyd's Rep 175 先例的有关判词:"This statement of principle was at one time widely understood to embrace two 'rules',the first rule being concerned with the recovery of damages arising naturally,i. e.,according to the usual course of things, and the second rule being concerned with recovery of damages within the contemplation of the parties at the time when the contract was made. Furthermore,the application of the second rule was understood to be dependant upon knowledge of special circumstances which had not merely been communicated by the plaintiff to the defendant at or before the time when the contract was made(a requirement which is consistent with one reading of the succeeding passage in Baron Alderson's judgment),but had been so communicated that the defendant,by entering into the contract,assented expressly or impliedly to assuming the risk of loss flowing from such special circumstances."

接下去就有不少先例根据 Hadley v. Baxendale 的损失规定作出判决,看看损失类别到底是属于一般损失或特别损失。其中,被判是特别损失的类别,在订约时受害方没有预先作出通知,是不能索赔的,包括有:针对承运人,货方分销/转售合约的利润损失不能索赔的先例有:Wilson v. The Lancashire & Yorkshire Railway(1861)9 CB (NS)632;O' Hanlan v. The Great Western Railway(1865)12 LT 490;Great Western

Railway Co. v. Redmayne(1866) LR 1 CP 329; Horne v. Midland Railway(1873) LR 8 CP 131; The "Arpad" (1934) 49 Lloyd's Rep 313; Heskell v. Continental Express Ltd. (1950)83 Lloyd's Rep 438。针对货方在生产方面的损失或利润损失不能索赔的先例有: Hadley v. Baxendale; Gee v. Lancashire & Yorkshire Railway(1860) 6 H&N 211; British Columbia Saw Mill Co. v. Nettleship(1868) LR 3 CP 499。看来这些案件主要是针对货物买卖与货物运输,特别是海上运输,这也是早年最主要的商业活动。

但在 Hadley v. Baxendale 之后,普通法还是有进一步的发展。第一方面是通过 Victoria Laundry v. Newman Industries(1949) 2 K. B. 528 与 The "Heron Ⅱ"(1967) 2 Lloyd's Rep 457 这两个贵族院先例进一步给了判定损失类别的解读,并明确了一个判定标准,即双方在订立合约时,如果将来发生违约/毁约,哪些损失类别是属于违约方"推定知情"(imputed knowledge),哪些损失类别是"真正知情"(actual knowledge)。换言之,"一般损失"(ordinary damages)类别就是可推定违约方知情,但"特别损失"(special damages)就必须证明违约方真正知情才有的赔偿。

在 The "Heron Ⅱ",认为更好的测试办法是看将来发生违约/毁约,哪些损失是双方在订约时是"可以料想得到的"(within contemplation)而且"并非是不可能"(not unlikely)会产生,或者"很可能"(serious possibility)会产生,但不需要达到"极有可能"(probable)的程度。有说法是"possible"是有 50% 以下的可能性,而"probable"则有高达 90% 的可能性。这改变了每次考虑损失的遥远性,只需要根据这一条标准,而再也不需要 Hadley v. Baxendale 的两条损失类别规则。

在普通法下另一方面的发展,会是在扩大被视为是双方(特别是将来的违约方)应该是可以合理料想得到的损失类别。例如是在 Victoria Laundry,违约方是一家工程公司,也被视为是可以料想得到锅炉的延迟交付会导致洗衣馆的正常利润的损失。另在 The "Heron Ⅱ",违约方船东被视为是知道货物目的地港巴斯拉是有一个市场,船舶延误会带来市场下跌的可能性。可以说随着通讯发达与一般人知识面的不断扩大,所以估计认定在订约时双方应该可以合理料想得到的事情包括违约会造成什么损失也不断放宽。

在这里顺便一提的是 Hadley v. Baxendale 的损失规定是被全球所有普通法国家普遍接受,其中美国最高院早在 100 年前的一个先例就明确了这一方面。在 Globe Refining Company v. Landa Cotton Oil Company 190 US 540,543(1903)先例,涉及卖方没有向买方提供棉花籽油,买方向卖方索赔的损失包括了预订车皮的运费损失、顾客损失与名誉损失等方面,但被下级法院拒绝。最高院的 Holmes 大法官是这样说:"It is true that, as people when contracting contemplate performance, not breach, they commonly say little or nothing as to what shall happen in the latter event, and the common rules have been worked out by common sense, which has established what the parties probably would have said if they had spoken about the matter. But a man never can be absolutely certain of performing any contract when the time of performance arrives, and, in many cases, he obviously is taking the risk of an event which is wholly, or to an appreciable extent, beyond his control. The extent of liability in such cases is likely to be within his contemplation, and, whether it is or not, should be worked out on terms which it fairly may be presumed he would have assented to if they had been presented to his mind."

以下笔者将进一步地解释上述简单提到的案例。

3. Victoria Laundry 先例的进一步解读

这一个 Hadley v. Baxendale(1854)9 Ex. 341 先例的损失规定在 Victoria Laundry v. Newman Industries(1949)2 K. B. 528 的上诉庭先例有了进一步的解读。案情涉及原告洗衣馆向被告工程公司订购了一个锅炉，被告迟交货达 5 个月之久，原告诉称被告若按期交货，原告除了因使用锅炉可赚取正常利润之外(正常利润是每周 16 英镑)，还应可获得并完成几项来自政府方面的合约，可赚取极高额的利润(这极高利润是每周 262 英镑)。因此，被告要赔偿所有这些利润损失。法院判是被告在订约前已知晓原告是从事洗衣、印染行业，而且该锅炉是原告急待投入使用以扩大业务量的。因此对原告本可赚取的正常利润的损失，被告必须赔偿，因这是他在订约当时可以合理预见的一般损失。至于那几份获利奇高合约的利润损失，则被告无须负责。因为在原告没有特别知会的情况下，被告不可能预见到原告会有这么值钱的几份合约在手。这些合约本可带来的异常利润的损失客观上对被告来说，是遥不可及的特别损失。

相近的判决早在 Cory v. Thames Ironworks & Shipbuilding Co Ltd(1868)LR 3 QB 181 先例就已经出现。案情是涉及被告的船厂与原告的煤炭进口商约定被告向原告交付一个没有动力的船壳用于储存原告从大船卸下的煤炭，稍后再将煤炭转卸去驳船并运到岸上。这是双方订约时所知道的情况，但实际上原告后来发展出来一种更好的操作方法，就是为船壳加装吊车然后直接从大船卸下煤炭后马上转卸去驳船，根本不必先储存在船壳中(除非是在特别情况下)。这就大大加快了整个操作的流程与简化装卸而可以赚取更多的利润。事后被告违约，该船壳晚了六个月才能交付。但原告索赔的金额只是按照原来订约时知道的情况，而不是根据后来发展出来的操作方法而可以索赔更庞大的利润损失。原告接受在刚判了不久的 Hadley v. Baxendale 先例的大原则下，他是不能索赔后者的庞大利润损失。

从 Victoria Laundry v. Newman Industries 判例，读者可以再次看到，要判定某种损失类别可否合理预见与是否特别，受害方能否获赔，关键就是要看订约时违约方能否"合理预见到"(reasonably foreseeable)他一旦违约，就很有可能会导致某种类别的损失。如果推定能预见到，那么这种损失就是一般损失，违约方必须赔偿，反之则是不可合理预见的特别损失，违约方无须负责。

Victoria Laundry 先例实是对 Hadley v. Baxendale 先例的两条损失类别规定加以分析,然后列出著名的六项大原则,如下:

(1) It is well settled that the governing purpose of damages is to put the party whose rights have been violated in the same position, so far as money can do so, as if his rights had been observed: *Sally Wertheim v. Chicoutimi Pulp Co.* (1911) A. C. 301. This purpose, if relentlessly pursued, would provide him with a complete indemnity for all lose *de facto* resulting from a particular breach, however improbable, however unpredictable. This, in contract at least, is recognized as too harsh a rule. (这里指出受害方如果可以向违约方索赔全部损失,包括一些极不可能与估计不到的损失,会带来很苛刻的后果)

(2) In cases of breach of contract the aggrieved party is only entitled to recover such part of the loss actually resulting as was at the time of the contract reasonably foreseeable as liable to result from the breach. (如果违约,受害方只能索赔与取回在订约时可以合理预见的由于将会违约带来的损失)

(3) What was at that time reasonably so foreseeable depends on the knowledge then possessed by the parties or, at all events, by the party who later commits the breach. (什么是在订约时可以合理预见,是要根据双方订约当时应该知道的。这表示对合理预见性的测试,还要看违约方在订约时应该合理地对什么知情。例如在 Hadley v. Baxendale 先例,承运人不是搞工厂,所以通常不知道工厂是否有该断轴的备件,也不会知道工厂会因为缺少这个曲轴而导致停产。笔者可进一步举例,如果在该先例的违约方是做一个新的曲轴的工厂,如延误交货,他就会合理知道受害方不会有备件,因为全英国只有他能够制造。所以没有这一新的曲轴,原告很可能不能复工。这就表示他与承运人的合理知情程度是不一样,就会可能要对原告的利润损失负责。)

(4) For this purpose, knowledge "possessed" is of two kinds; one imputed, the other actual. Everyone, as a reasonable person, is taken to know the "ordinary course of things" and consequently what loss is liable to result from a breach of contract in that ordinary course. This is the subject matter of the "first rule" in Hadley v. Baxendale... But to this knowledge which a contract - breaker is assumed to possess whether possesses it or not, there may have to be added in a particular case knowledge which he actually possesses, of special circumstances outside the "ordinary course of things" of such a kind that a breach in those special circumstances would be liable to cause more loss. Such a case attracts the operation of the "second rule" so as to make additional loss also recoverable. (违约方在订约时应该知情的情况分为两种:第一种是推定知情,第二种是真正知情。第一种是假设一般人士或在该合约有关行业的人士都应该知道,这是轮不到违约方抗辩说他实际上是不知道,因为念书少或是愚蠢,但是无知不是抗辩理由。第二种真正知情是违约方真正知道的,这通常是由受害方通知。找出违约方是否真正知道是一个事实的认定。这真正知情与推定知情不一样的地方就是前者不是一般人士或在该合约有关

行业的人士应该知道的。这真正知情就会导致适用 Hadley v. Baxendale 的第二条规则，也就是让受害方可索赔特别损失的额外损失）

（5）In order to make the contract - breaker liable under either rule it is not necessary that he should actually have asked himself what loss is liable to result from a breach. As has often been pointed out, parties at the time of contracting contemplate not the breach of the contract, but its performance. It suffices that, if he had considered the question, he would as a reasonable man have concluded that the loss in question was liable to result...（找出违约方是否对一般损失或特别损失负责，是不必考虑他到底是否知道违约会带来什么损失。这是因为在订约时，双方只会考虑到如何履行与赚钱，不会想如果违约/毁约会带来的后果。所以只是假设在订约时，如果被问及，违约方作为一个合理的人士应该料想到某些损失会有可能或很可能产生就已经足够了）

（6）Nor, finally, to make a particular loss recoverable, need it be proved that upon a given state of knowledge the defendant could, as a reasonable man, foresee that a breach must necessarily result in that loss. It is enough if he could foresee it was likely so to result. It is indeed enough,... if the loss (or some factor without which it would not have occurred) is a "serious possibility" or a "real danger". For short, we have used the word "liable" to result. Possibly the colloquialism 'on the cards' indicates the shade of meaning with some approach to accuracy.（只要能够证明违约方在订约时能够预见到某种损失有可能或很有可能会发生，即要对损失负责，而不必要预见到这种损失一定会发生）

3.1　什么是推定知情

现在进一步解释什么是推定知情（imputed knowledge），在 Hadley v. Baxendale 先例中，违约方的推定知情是要对第一种的一般损失负责。认定违约方在订约时什么是应该知道或不知道是要根据每个案件的事实分析。但总的来说，是根据三个因素作出认定。第一个是订约双方（特别是原告受害方）的行业与专业。所以，有不少先例判是业务的损失或者转售利润的损失类别，针对有关货物的卖方与运载该货物的承运人是有不同的判法与松紧程度。显然，前者卖方是行业内的人士，他应该知道得更多。这在 The "Heron Ⅱ"（1967）2 Lloyd's Rep 457 先例中，Upjohn 勋爵也说："a carrier of goods... is not carrying on the same trade as the consignor of goods and his knowledge of the practices and exigencies of the other's trade may be limited and less than between buyer and seller of goods who probably know far more about one another's business."

另一个涉及土地/房子买卖的先例是 Diamond v. Compbell - Jones（1961）Ch 22，案情涉及买方向违约的卖方索赔损失，损失包括他预期可以赚取的利润，因为他向卖方买的位于伦敦的房子是计划把它们重新装修然后作为住宅与办公楼之用。Buckley 大法官只判违约方赔偿房子的市场价格减合约价格的差价，认为违约方通常不会知道受害方的业务与有什么打算，除非订约前已被通知。他是这样说："I cannot believe that Lord Wright, in... the Monarch Steamship Co v. A/B Karlshamns Oljefabriker (1940) 82 Lloyd's Rep. 137 meant that anyone entering into a contract must be treated as having constructive notice of the nature of the other party's business, or of its probable bearing on the loss which that other party might suffer in consequence of a breach of contract. In some cases the nature or the subject - matter of a contract or of its terms may be such as to make it clear that one of the parties is entering into the contract for the purpose of a particular business, and the circumstances may be such that the court will infer that the other party must have appreciated that this was so. It seems to me, however, that this can rarely be the case where the contract is for the sale of land. The vendor of a ship equipped for use as a butcher's shop would not, in my judgment, be justified by that circumstance alone in assuming, and ought not to be treated as knowing, that the purchaser would intend to use it for the business of a butcher rather than that of a baker or candlestick - maker, at any rate in the absence of covenants or other forms of restriction confining its use to butcher's business. Special circumstances are necessary to justify imputing to a vendor of land a knowledge that the purchaser intends to use it in any particular manner."

有说法是一个简单的行业可以推断违约方有更多的知情，而一个复杂的行业就会是违约方不会有太多的知情。这是 Juancey 勋爵在 The "Heron Ⅱ"先例说的："It must always be a question of circumstances what one contracting party is presumed to know about the business activities of the other. No doubt the simpler the activity of the one, the more readily can it be inferred that the other would have reasonable knowledge thereof. However, when the activity of A involves complicated construction or manufacturing techniques, I see no reason why B who supplies a commodity which A intends to use in the course of those technique should be assumed, merely because of the order for the commodity, to be aware of the details of all the techniques undertaken by A and the effect thereupon of any failure of or deficiency in that commodity. Even if the Lord Ordinary had made a positive finding that continuous pouring was a required part of industrial practice it would not follow that in the absence of any other evidence suppliers of electricity... should have been aware of that practice."

另有可能根据有关货物能推定违约方有更多或更少的知情，其中在涉及整批货物如一台完整的机器，相比只是一些零件，就可以作出不同程度的推定（如针对利润损失）。这是 Asquith 大法官在 Victoria Laundry 先例中所说："Significance in so far as it bears on the capacity of the supplier to foresee the consequence of non - delivery."

针对有"可供买卖市场"（available market）的价格涨跌会造成的损失，这通常被视为是双方在订约时可以推定知情。Parker 大法官在 Interoffice Telephones v. Freeman (1958) 1 QB 190 先例说："Whether it be a hiring agreement or a contract for the sale of goods, where the purchaser has failed to take delivery, the defaulting party must contemplate that damages will vary according to the state of the market, including questions of supply and demand."

3.2　什么是真正知情

3.2.1　订约后才就有关特别情况作出通知

如果要违约方承担某一种类别的特别损失,就必须认定他在订约的时候有真正知情(actual knowledge)。如果在订约后才有真正的知情,如受害方向违约方在违约之前作出通知,这是不管用的。虽然,曾经有一个古老的先例名为 Gee v. Lancashire & Yorkshire Railway(1860)6 H&N 211 说受害方可以对违约方在违约之前声明:"If you, after that notice, persist in breaking the contract, I shall claim the damages which will result from the breach.",就会导致违约方要承担特别损失。但这一说法是错误,这方面请看《McGregor on Damages》(18th edn, 2009 年)之 6 - 196 段。笔者看来,这显然是正确的,否则潜在的受害方可以留待合约一订立就马上通知对方有关一切违约会产生的特别损失,严重的程度是对方(潜在的违约方)从来没想过接受的。但由于合约已经订立,对方也没有退出或改变合约(如加上责任限制条文)的余地,这岂非是开玩笑。

3.2.2　订约前作出通知有关特别情况怎样才算是足够

更复杂的情况是如果受害方在订约时把有关的特别情况告诉违约方,怎么样才是足够保障将来对特别损失的索赔?例如买方告诉卖方他这票货已经转卖,这是否足够增加卖方的赔偿责任?看来这么简单的通知不像有什么作用。在国际买卖中,不少的商品或货物都会在海上运输期间转卖,不必通知也可以推定知情。这个问题在 Hadley v. Baxendale(1854)9 Ex. 341 先例之后的好几个先例都有涉及,第一个是 British Columbia Saw Mill Co v. Nettleship(1868)LR 3 CP 499, Willes 大法官说光是知道有关的特别情况并不足够,而是要受害方在订约时可以合理相信违约方是接受了这一特别情况下订约的。毕竟,知情可以是来自第三人的通知,但这并不足够。知情必须是受害方与违约方之间合约的一部分,明示或默示显示了违约方愿意接受这一赔偿责任。Willes 大法官是这样说:"The mere fact of knowledge cannot increase the liability. The knowledge must be brought home to the party sought to be charged, under such circumstances that he must know that the person he contracts with reasonably believes that he accepts the contract with the special condition attached to it... Knowledge on the part of the carrier is only important if it forms part of the contract. It may be that the knowledge is acquired casually from a stranger, the person to whom the goods belong not knowing or caring whether he had such knowledge or not..."

另在 Horne v. Midland Ry Co(1873)LR 8 CP 131 先例, Blackburn 大法官说:"that in order that the notice may have any effect, it must be given under such circumstances, as that an actual contract arises on the part of the defendant to bear the exceptional loss."

在近期的上诉庭先例 Mulvenna v. Royal Bank of Scotland Plc (2003) EWCA Civ

1112，Waller 大法官也说："simply drawing the attention of the payer of the money to special circumstances，does not necessarily impose a liability on the payer to be responsible for damages flowing from the special circumstances to which attention has been drawn."

但看来针对这一方面，大法官之间有不同的看法。在 The "Heron Ⅱ"(1967)2 Lloyd's Rep 457 先例，Upjohn 勋爵明确表示不同意，认为双方在知道一些特别情况下订立合约，就可以合理假设为双方有料想到违约/毁约会带来的后果，不需要再以合约条文明示或默示同意这种特别情况说明。Upjohn 勋爵说："If parties enter into the contract with knowledge of some special circumstances，and it is reasonable to infer a particular loss as a result of those circumstances that is something which both must contemplate as a result of a breach. It is quite unnecessary that it should be a term of the contract."

另在 Jackson v. Royal Bank of Scotland Plc(2005) UKHL 3 先例，Hope 勋爵说："Where knowledge of special circumstances is relied on，the assumption is that the defendant undertook to bear any special loss which was referable to those special circumstances."

Upjohn 勋爵在 The "Heron Ⅱ"的说法等于是对特别损失所需要的通知有所放宽，这可以节录 Goff 大法官在 The "Pegase"(1981)1 Lloyd's Rep 175 先例所讲的如下："The second development(这是指 Hadley v. Baxendale 先例之后针对这一方面的法律调整)has been a loosening of the rule，stated in earlier cases(of which British Columbia Saw Mill Co v. Nettleship is a typical example) that knowledge by the defendant of special circumstances is only relevant if so communicated to him(这是指违约方) that he，by entering into the contract，assented expressly or impliedly to assume the risk of loss flowing from such special circumstances. Indeed，in The 'Heron Ⅱ'，Lord Upjohn expressly dissented from the proposition that liability for damages resulting from special circumstances must be made a term of the contract. ... In the light of the decided cases，the test appears to be：have the facts in question come to the defendant's knowledge in such circumstances that a reasonable person in the shoes of the defendant would，if he had considered the matter at the time of making the contract，have contemplated that，in the event of a breach by him，such facts were to be taken into account when considering of his responsibility for loss suffered by the plaintiff as a result of such breach. The answer to that question may vary from case to case，taking into consideration matters as，for example，the nature of the facts in question and how far they are unusual，and the extent to which such facts are likely to make fulfilment of the contract by the due date more critical，or to render the plaintiff's loss heavier in the event of non – fulfilment."

对特别情况要给出通知的要求，合理之处就是被告违约方永远可以说是如果受害方在订约前告诉他的话，他根本不准备接受这种特别损失的赔偿风险。这种没有作出通知或足够通知导致被告成功抗拒赔偿特别损失的先例也不少。针对承运人，货方的分销/转售合约的利润损失与在生产方面的损失不能索赔的多个先例在上文第2段已有提及。

相反,如果是特别情况在订约前通知了被告违约方,而且是在一种情况下被告是接受,或者可以视为接受有关的风险,被告就通常要负责。而这种情况可以是被告漠不关心并订立合约,即使原告是给了足够与明确的通知。如果被告在通知后试图在合约增加一条责任限制条文,但最后不成功的情况下订立合约,被告接受有关风险就更明确了。这也是香港高院 Reyes 大法官的说法,他在2008年2月在香港大学的发言《Certainty in Contractual Damages Assessment - On Two Suggested Alternatives to the Rule in Hadley v. Baxendale》中说到:“In other words, the Court should conclude that a promisor undertook liability for an unusual loss **if and only** if the promisor expressly or impliedly agreed to do so. What has or has not been agreed depends as always on the peculiar facts of a case. But the Court should be able to apply the touchstone in a way that makes the Court's decisions reasonably foreseeable by all.”

这两个要求(通知与视为接受)两者都需要,这是 Diplock 大法官在 Robophone Facilities v. Blank(1966)1 WLR 1428 先例所说。例如在 Muhammad v. Ali(1947)AC 414, Trans Trust SPRL v. Danubian Trading Company(1952)2 QB 297, Wadsworth v. Lydall(1981)1 WLR 598,这些先例都让原告成功索赔因原告缺钱而导致的损失,因为在订合约的时候原告缺钱的情况是在双方料想之中。

3.3 笔者的一个近期仲裁案件

在笔者的仲裁中也经常会涉及这方面的争议,例如在近期的一个香港仲裁,涉及一票钢材从中国卖去南美洲,被买方指称货物质量有问题,这包括钢板的厚度、化学成分与机械性能等有所偏差。笔者作为仲裁庭也接受了货物质量是有一点偏差,主要在钢板的厚度。但除了责任以外,更重要的就是损失计算,因为南美买方索赔是高达200万美元以上的损失,因为这票钢材不能用来满足买方的用途,就是用作一个机械项目的材料。本来,按照专家意见,钢板的厚度与其他方面有一点偏差是不影响作为一般用途,如在建筑方面。所以,按照合约质量要求的钢板与有一点偏差的钢板估计在市场价格(如果是按照市场规则计算“一般损失”[general damage]的话,参见第十五章与第十六章)应该是相差不大。这表示最终来自南美买方的索赔是一种“特别损失”(special damage)。而买方支持这一种索赔是按照他所指称的在订约前一天曾经通过电话告诉了中国卖方有关这票钢材用作机械项目的材料。显然,中国卖方否认有这样的通话。但双方为了省钱,要求不开庭,令仲裁庭没有机会看到针对这一个重大的事实对证人进行的盘问。只是,双方证人各自提供了一份文书证人证言,对这方面有各自的说法。这使得包括笔者在内的仲裁庭最后根据举证责任判买方在这方面败诉,说:“This has caused the Tribunal to take a less desirable approach, namely, to see who bears the burden of proof. It is the Buyer's allegation that he has put the Seller on notice regarding the purpose of the Steel and therefore the Steel must be fit for the engineering purpose. In raising this allegation, the burden of proof is on the Buyer. Faced with a denial by the Seller, the Tribunal is left with a dilemma of no more than a 50 – 50 chance that the Buyer's allegation has to be correct. But this still does not discharge the Buyer's burden of proof which has to show a higher probability (even marginally higher)."

仲裁庭判买方在这方面败诉的另一个原因是买方指称在电话中简单说的一句话并非是一个足够的通知可以导致中国卖方要承担特别损失，裁决书在这方面是这样说："There is a further reason why the Buyer must fail in this allegation. That is, even if the Tribunal accepts that the alleged fact is correct, namely, the alleged notice of the Steel would be used by "a Brazilian buyer for an engineering project", the notice was still in all probability an inadequate notice. The Tribunal takes into considerations of: (ⅰ) Nothing was expressly stated in the Purchase Contract regarding the purpose of the Steel; (ⅱ) No documentary evidence to collaborate the oral conversation said to have taken place on 31 July 2008, such as, a subsequent brief fax or email; (ⅲ) Even if the notice was orally made, it must necessarily be brief and sketchy; An ordinary steel trader like the Seller would probably not be alerted in what specific requirement or care must go into the Steel if the ultimate purpose would be for a Brazilian sub – buyer (as against other sub – buyers) using the Steel for an engineering project (such as, what precisely was the engineering project?)."

3.4 真正知情可以带来更大或更小的损失

通常来说，违约方在订约时对特别情况知情就要负责赔偿特别损失，都会是指更高的损失。但也有情况会因知情而导致损失的减少，如在货物买卖中的分销或转售是双方都知情的，而且知道这是一个赚取很高差价的转售（估计这种情况不常见，因为买方不会希望卖方知道他的分销或转售是赚大钱的，所以不可能作出特别情况的通知）。这一来，说法是卖方违约/毁约拒绝供货的赔偿要依据这一转售，而不是市场价格的差价。当然在这种情况下，违约的卖方会可以争辩"市场规则"（market rule）还是适用，因为受害的买方可以去市场买进替代，然后供应以满足分销/转售合约，就不会失去赚取高差价的机会，但这是另一个问题，也就是合理减少损失。只针对遥远性，可节录在 Biggin v. Permanite (1951) 1 KB 422 先例，Devlin 大法官是这样说："If, however, a sub – sale is within the contemplation of the parties, I think that the damages must be assessed by reference to it, whether the plaintiff likes it or not... If it is the plaintiff's liability to the ultimate user that is contemplated as the measure of damages and it is in fact used without injurious results so that no such liability arises, the plaintiff could not claim the difference in market value, and say that the sub – sale must be disregarded."

但看来如果是一个双方在订约时都知情与作出过通知的分销或者转售，而且赚取的差价不高或甚至亏本，反正就是比违约/毁约时的市场价格低，看来也应该在计算损失时考虑在内，这会导致更低的赔偿金额。Pearce 勋爵在 The "Heron Ⅱ" (1967) 2 Lloyd's Rep 457 先例是这样说："Of course the extension of the horizon need not always increase the damage;it might introduce a knowledge of particular circumstances, e. g. a sub – contract,which show that the plaintiff would in fact suffer less damage than a more limited view of the circumstances might lead one to expect. ”

这种情况也在 Duncan Investment Ltd v. Underwood(1998)PNLR 754,CA 先例出现。案情涉及 15 栋房屋买卖,其中原告 Duncan 是地产商,而被告 Underwood 是估价师。原告想从接管人的米兰银行把 15 栋房屋(本来是 16 栋,但最终有 1 栋没有成交)以低价一并买下,然后分别出售赚钱。在行动之前,原告委任被告对这 15 栋房屋分别出售,估计在 6 个月内出售可以卖得的价钱。被告作出了估价,但事后才知道被告把价钱估高了。原告在这笔生意上亏了大本,所以向被告提出索赔,希望把自己的损失减低。针对损失的计算,原告认为是他从米兰银行对 15 栋房屋的支付价格减去把 15 栋房屋一并出售的差价,即 148253 英镑。但被告认为是原告的支付价格减去把 15 栋房屋分别出售的差价,即 41190 英镑。原因是一并出售与分别出售所得出的价格相差很远,是 25% 以上。毕竟,分别出售的话,麻烦会增加不少。原告认为是第一种计算办法比较正确,因为这是“苹果对苹果”(apple to apple,也就是对等)的比较。因为原告的支付价格是一并购买计算的,所以也应该以一并出售的价格来计算。上诉庭推翻高院的一审判决,判是应该赔 41190 英镑。这是因为被告在订约时并不知道原告从米兰银行购买的价格,他只知道原告将会把这 15 栋房屋分别出售。所以,损失计算应该是以违约方在订约时的知情与愿意承担的赔偿责任为准。上诉庭是这样说:“To put it another way,to measure Duncan's loss by reference to a basis of valuation which was not that on which Underwoods were asked to advise would impose on the valuer a liability greater than he could reasonably have thought he was undertaking. ”

看来这表示在一般情况下,在国际货物买卖或其他涉及市场的交易,买方在订约前通知卖方特别情况如分销或转售,不一定是明智之举。因为在毁约时,如果该货物或商品市场价格高涨(这也往往是导致卖方违约/毁约与拒绝供货的诱因),受害方买方根据“breach date rule”,也就是根据违约时市场价格与合约价格的差价提出索赔,会遇上违约方卖方抗拒说应该只能索赔分销合约与原合约价格的差价。这方面也可以节录 Thomas 大法官在 North Sea Energy Holdings v. Petroleum Authority of Thailand(1997)2 Lloyd's Rep. 418 先例中的有关判词:“If,in this case,MSH(受害方/卖方)could have claimed damages by reference to a market,then whether or not oil could have been delivered under the Magoil offer(供应方)would,in accordance with those authorities,be irrelevant. But,in this action,MSH base their claim to damages solely by reference to a specific offer which they say would have entitled them to very significant profits; it must follow that the party in repudiation,PTT(违约方/买方),can contend that those profits could never have been earned because that specific offer could never have been performed. The cases upon which MSH rely are not material to the factual issue in this case of the proof of damages by reference to the Magoil contract. ”

4. The "Heron Ⅱ"先例的解读

接下去是贵族院的重要先例 The "Heron Ⅱ"(1967)2 Lloyd's Rep 457。案情又涉及航运,该船舶从罗马尼亚装了 3000 吨食糖到伊拉克的巴斯拉港。本来这一个航次所需要的时间只是 20 天,但由于船舶在中途不合理绕航(去了另一个港口加装其他货物,但没有在租约内说明),导致了 10 天的延误。如果船舶准时抵达,该批食糖的应得价格是 97000 英镑左右。但因为延误,实得的价格只有 93000 英镑,两者相差 4000 英镑的市场损失。在仲裁中,被认定是船舶不合理绕航。剩下来的争议主要是在损失的计算,也就是违约方船东在订约时是否可以合理预见延误的结果有可能或很有可能造成食糖市场价格下跌所带来的损失。这也被法院认定是船东(即使不是一个食糖的贸易商)一般性应该知道,也就是属于"推定知情"(imputed knowledge)。其中,Morris 勋爵是这样说:"The carriage of sugar from the Black Sea to Iraqi ports (including Basrah) is a recognized trade. The appellant(船东) knew that there was a sugar market at Basrah. When he contracted with the respondents(货方) to carry their sugar to Basrah, though he did not know what were the actual plans of the respondents, he had all the information to enable him to appreciate that a delay in things result in their suffering some loss. He must have known that the price in a market may fluctuate. He must have known that if a price goes down someone whose goods are late in arrival may be caused loss... I think that it must follow that, where there is delay in arrival, in many cases the actual loss suffered (above the amount of which there ought not to be recovery) can be measured by comparing the market price of the goods at the date when they should have arrived and the market price when they did arrive. That *prima facie* is the measure of the damages."

在该先例贵族院对 Victoria Laundry 先例主要的一个批评就是在第二条损失规则的"合理预见"(reasonably foreseeable),Reid 勋爵认为这带来合约与侵权的混淆。因为在侵权下,被告作为一般人能够合理预见会发生的事十分广泛,包括一些最不寻常的损失类别,除非这种损失风险小到一种可以不去理会的情况:"The defendant will be liable for any type of damage which is reasonably foreseeable as liable to happen even in the most unusual case, unless the risk is so small that a reasonable man would in the whole circumstances feel justify in neglecting it."

Reid 勋爵认为在 Hadley v. Baxendale,可以作为正常损失向违约方索赔取回的损失不是合理预见的测试,而是看合约并找出双方订约时"可以料想得到"(in the parties' contemplation)有可能发生的损失类别。他是这样说有关 Hadley v. Baxendale:"... did not intend that every type of damage which was reasonably foreseeable by the parties when the contract was made should either be considered as arising naturally, i. e. in the usual course of things, or be supposed to have been in the contemplation of the parties. Indeed the decision makes it clear that a type of damage which was plainly foreseeable as a real possibility but which would only occur in a small minority of cases cannot be regarded as arising in the usual course of things or be supposed to have been in the contemplation of the parties: the parties are not supposed to contemplate as grounds for the recovery of damage any type of loss or damage which on the knowledge available to the defendant would appear to him as only likely to occur in a small minority of cases."

4.1 "合理预见"与"料想得到"的区别

可以说,在 The "Heron Ⅱ",贵族院是把 Victoria Laundry v. Newman Industries (1949) 2 K. B. 528 的"合理预见"(reasonably foreseeable)变成"料想得到"(within contemplation)。这两个标准中,前者是属于侵权范畴损失计算的测试,而后者属于违约范畴的,正如 Upjohn 勋爵在 The "Heron Ⅱ"所说:"it is better to use contemplate or contemplation in the case of contract, leaving foresee or foreseeability to the realm of torts." 表面看来,它们有一定的区别。例如,侵权的损失遥远性限制会比较宽(这方面稍后在12.1段会进一步介绍),也不会像合约的限制会有个别案件带来的多样变化,比如不同的行业就会带来不同的推定知情,双方也可以通过订约前的通知令对方能够对特别损失真正知情。但纯粹是从一般的违约方对某种损失能否合理预见或合理料想得到,这看来是没有什么差别。在 Parsons v. Uttley Ingham (1977) 2 Lloyd's Rep. 522 先例,Scarman 大法官是这样说:"it may be that the necessary reconciliation is to be found, notwithstanding the strictures of Lord Reid, in holding that the difference between 'reasonably foreseeable' (the test in tort) and 'reasonably contemplated' (the test in contract) is semantic, not substantial. Certainly, Asquith LJ in Victoria Laundry and Lord Pearce in The 'Heron Ⅱ' thought so, and I confess I think so too."

4.2 Hadley v. Baxendale 先例的两条规则实是一条规则的说法

普通法发展到 Victoria Laundry v. Newman Industries (1949) 2 K. B. 528 与 The "Heron Ⅱ" (1967) 2 Lloyd's Rep 457 的"可以合理料想到"(within reasonable contemplation)某种类的损失"不是不可能"(not unlikely)会因违约而产生,就可以区分某一种损失的类别是否可以或不可以向违约方索赔,开始有了说法是 Hadley v. Baxendale 的两条规则实质上是一条规则。这一条规则在 Victoria Laundry 先例的上诉庭有提出过是损失类别只要是"在订约时可以合理预见在将来如果违约的情况下会有可能产生"(loss actually resulting as was at the time of the contract reasonably foreseeable as liable to result from the breach),就可以向违约方成功索赔。

另可以节录 Goff 大法官在 The "Pegase" (1981) 1 Lloyd's Rep 175 先例是这样解释:"The general result of the two cases (Victoria Laundry v. Newman Industries 与 The Heron II) is that the principle in Hadley v. Baxendale is now no longer stated in terms of two rules, but rather in terms of a single principle - though it is recognized that the application of the principle may depend on the degree of relevant knowledge held by the defendant at the time of the contract in the particular case. This approach accords very much to what actually happens in practice; the Courts have not been over - ready to pigeon - hole the cases under one or other of the so - called rules in Hadley v. Baxendale, but rather to decide each case on the basis of the relevant knowledge of the defendant."

同一个说法在好几个重要先例都有涉及,例如在 Kpohraror v. Woolwich Building Society(1996)4 ALL ER 116 先例,案情涉及银行错误地不兑现客户的一张支票,法院判客户的信誉受到的损失可以根据 Hadley v. Baxendale 的第一条损失规则,也就是一般损失成功索赔。但客户生意上的损失就被视为是特别损失,这是不熟悉客户生意的被告银行在没有通知下料想不到的。上诉庭的 Evans 大法官是这样说:"The contentions for both parties were presented as if a straitjacket imposed by the strict application of the rule in Hadley v. Baxendale so as to require the separate consideration of each of the two limbs... I would prefer to hold that the starting point for any application of Hadley v. Baxendale is the extent of the shared knowledge of both parties when the contract was made... When that is established, it may often be the case that the first and second parts of the rule overlap, or at least that it is unnecessary to draw a clear line of demarcation between them."

笔者就可以接下去跳到一个最近期的先例,这是在 The "Achilleas"(2007)1 Lloyd's Rep. 19, Christopher Clark 大法官也有说 Hadley v. Baxendale 的两条规则在现代的做法是把它视为一条综合性损失规则(the modern approach is to treat the rule as a composite whole),而这个规则如下:"(a) The mere fact that a type of loss is foreseeable is not, of itself, sufficient to make it recoverable; some one may foresee a result that is very remote.(损失类别光是可以预见有可能产生并不足够,有一些人是可以预见很遥远的后果。)(b) A claimant is, however, entitled to recover damages in respect of a foreseeable result which either: -(原告受害方可以索赔损失是能够预见到,并且是)(i) will happen in the great majority of cases; or(在大部分的情况下会产生)(ii) in respect of which, on the facts known or available to the defendant, the chances of its happening are considerably less than evens but the occurrence of which would not be very unusual.(在被告违约方所知情或能够知情的事实情况下,会产生的机会是远低于50%,但如果产生的话并非不寻常)"

Christopher Clark 大法官看来还是用"合理预见"的测试,但把合约的合理预见加上了限制,变成与侵权有所区别。例如,在不知情的情况下,合理预见的损失类别必须是在大部分情况会发生或产生。

4.3 大部分情况下发生的程度是否包括产生损失的概率

能够料想到在大部分情况下会发生的损失是属于 Hadley v. Baxendale(1854)9

Ex. 341 先例中第一类的损失,就是在 The “Achilleas”(2007)1 Lloyd's Rep. 19 先例中被提到是大部分情况下会发生(will happen in the great majority of cases)。这让笔者注意到“概率”(odds)这个问题。表面看来,发生机率低的损失不应该是大部分会遇到的情况。但在一些著名的案例中并不是这样说,他们针对的并不是某一项损失的机率高低,而是看“损失的类别”(type of loss)是否在某一种违约/毁约情况下是大部分会遇到。这里第一个先例就是 The “Heron II”(1969)1 AC 350,Pearce 勋爵举了一个例子说明某种损失类别是属于某种违约很自然会导致的,但造成有关损失的机率不一定是高。他举的例子是针对高院的屋顶维修,但承建商没有把工程做好而构成违约。结果屋顶塌下来,把人压伤。作为损失的类别,可以说是最自然不过,因为屋顶维修有疏忽会塌下来并压伤人是小孩子都知道的。但如果把高院不上班的时候、周末与假期等都计算进去,就会发觉屋顶在塌下来的时候下面有人被压伤的概率只有 1/10。这就变成光看概率就不是属于多数遇到的情况。Pearce 勋爵是这样说:“I do not think that Alderson B. (in Hadley v. Baxendale) was directing his mind to whether something resulting in the natural course of events was an odds – on chance or not. A thing may be a natural (or even an obvious) result even though the odds are against it. Suppose a contractor was employed to repair the ceiling of one of the Law Courts and did it so negligently that it collapsed on the heads of those in court. I should be inclined to think that any tribunal (including the learned Baron [指判 Hadley v. Baxendale 的大法官] himself) would have found as a fact that the damage arose ‘naturally, i. e. according to the usual course of things.’ Yet if one takes into account the nights, weekends, and vacations, when the ceiling might have collapsed, the odds against it collapsing on top of anybody's head are nearly ten to one. I do not believe that this aspect of the matter was fully considered and worked out in the judgment. He was thinking of causation and type of consequence rather than of odds.”

另一个先例是 Parson (Livestock) v. Uttley Ingham & Co (1978) QB 791,上诉庭的 Scarman 大法官说:“It does not matter, in my judgment, if (the defendants) thought that the chance of physical injury... was slight, or that the odds were against it, provided they contemplated as a serious possibility the type of consequence, not necessarily the specific consequences, that ensued on breach. Making the assumption as to breach that the judge did, no more than common sense was needed for them to appreciate that food affected by bad storage conditions might well cause illness in the pigs fed upon it.”

5. 损失类别只要是在双方订约时料想到，损失程度的严重性会否有关？

上述所讲的实际会产生损失的概率不在考虑范围，也可以延伸考虑实际损失“程度”(extent)的严重性。有说法是只要损失类别是属于某一种违约的大部分情况下会产生，而且在订约时可以合理料想得到，这就已经足够。这方面的权威先例是 Parsons v. Uttley Ingham(1977)2 Lloyd's Rep. 522，案情涉及原告(养猪场场主)向被告(生产散装饲料储存漏斗的厂家)订造了一个漏斗以储存猪饲料。合约订明漏斗必须配有通风盖。漏斗造成后运到猪场安装时，被告忘了打开漏斗的通风盖。由于该漏斗高达 28 英尺，从地面根本无法看到通风盖是否开着，后来因为缺乏通风饲料逐渐霉变，而原告还懵然不知继续拿来喂猪，直到一些猪病了才发现问题。之后发生猪瘟共死了 254 头猪。该案主要是判被告要否赔偿原告猪死亡的重大损失。上诉庭判下来认为，被告只要有一般常识就应料想得到储存条件差会造成饲料变质，从而很可能引起吃这些饲料的猪发病。因此，猪发病死亡的损失类别是违约的被告可以在订约时合理料想得到的，他必须赔偿这一类损失。另外，Scarman 大法官特别指出，只要认定被告订约时应能合理料想得到某类违约会造成某类损失，就可以判令被告负责此类损失的赔偿，而不必再追究此类损失的具体程度如何、是否出于意料之外的严重。如该案中猪是病了还是死了、死了多少头等，这些都不必深究，反正要全赔。

该上诉庭判例的总结是说：“The defendant were liable for the illness and death of the pigs and that they ought reasonably to have foreseen that if the hopper, unventilated, was unfit for the storage of pignuts to be fed to the plaintiff's pigs, there was a serious possibility that the pigs might become ill... The fact that the pigs suffered from E Coli(大肠杆菌), a far worse illness than could then be foreseen did not lessen the liability since the type or kind of damage was foreseeable even if the extent of it was not.”

违约如果是如此，侵权行为更加明确是如此，只要造成的实际损失是可合理预见的类别，则后果严重程度将不加以理会，正如“egg - shell skull”与“shabby millionaire”都有这种精神在内(这将会在本章稍后 12.2.3 段会涉及)。有关违约与侵权的不同损失遥远性与 Parsons v. Uttley Ingham 先例的困难，本章第 7 段会进一步探讨。

但也有先例判是损失程度太严重会被视为是订约时不可以合理料想得到，变成属于“特别损失”(special damage)。涉及经济损失(如受害方的利润损失)，即使损失类别是在订约双方料想得到，也有不同的对待。例如在 Victoria Laundry v. Newman (1949)2 KB 528 先例，一般性的利润损失就可以成功索赔，但利润很高的就被视为是特别损失。显然，实际损失的程度严重与否是有区分的。所以在 Brown v. K. M. R. Services(1995)2 Lloyd's Rep 513 先例，上诉庭的 Stuart Smith 大法官是这样说：“I do not see any difficulty in holding that loss of ordinary business profits are different in kind from those flowing from a particular contract which gives rise to very high profits, the existence of which is unknown to the other party and who therefore does not accept the risk of such loss occurring."

在另一个先例 North Sea Energy Holdings v. Petroleum Authority of Thailand (1997) 2 Lloyd's Rep. 418,案情涉及石油的买卖,卖方有很大的利润损失,但是无法向违约的买方成功索赔。一个原因是因为买方在订约时根本不可能知道这票石油是卖方以低于合约价格非常多的价格从另外的供应商处买得,而这一买一卖的价格差本会为卖方带来极大的利润。

最后介绍一个有关人身伤亡的先例是 Smith v. Leech Brain (1962) 2 QB 405,案情涉及受害方在工作的时候被一块高温度的金属击中,嘴唇有了一小处烫伤,这本来是没有太大问题。但之后该烫伤引发了癌症,最终令受害方死亡。法院认定是该烫伤激发了癌症,而如果没有烫伤,癌症可能是不会出现。所以判被告要赔偿受害方妻子的原告所有的损失。其中 Parker 勋爵说:"The test is not whether these employers could reasonably have foreseen that a burn would cause cancer and that he would die. The question is whether these employers could reasonably foresee the type of injury he suffered, namely, the burn. What, in the particular case, is the amount of damage which he suffers as a result of that burn, depends upon the characteristics and constitution of the victim."

6. 双方在订约时料想到的一般损失可以多于一种

有些情况下,双方在订约时料想到的损失类别可能多于一种,在 The "Kriti Rex" (1996) 2 Lloyd's Rep 171 先例中,英国法院判船舶如果没有按约定准时到达装港装货,这种违约是可以产生两种损失的。第一种就是货方另去市场租用一艘替代船舶或以其他公司的船舶付运(如集装箱货物),多支付的运费就可以向违约的原船东索赔。第二种就是货方由于没有办法作出付运,损失就是在卸港这批货物的市场价格(要扣减付运的费用)。根据哪一种损失向违约船东索赔显然就要看货方在违约后是否能够找到替代船舶付运有关的货物。这有时候会做不到,而做不到的后果对货方的损失显然就是该批货物没有办法付运到卸港,所以真正的损失是这批货物在卸港的市场价格,也就是第二种损失。相反,如果货方在违约后是能够找到替代船舶,但不这样做,这就涉及货方没有合理"减少损失"(mitigate damage)的问题了。反正两种损失计算都会是"一般损失"(ordinary damages),是违约方在订约的时候可以料想得到的损失类别。Moore - Bick 大法官在 The "Kriti Rex" 先例是这样说:"In my judgment these decisions support Mr. Flaux's(货方大律师) submission that damages for failure to carry a cargo may be measured either by the difference between market and charter rates of freight or by reference to the value of the goods at the port of discharge(with appropriate deductions). Both measures of damage must be taken to have been within the contemplation of the parties because they are different ways of measuring the loss which the charterer suffers by not having his goods carried to the contractual destination. Which will be the appropriate measure in any given case will no doubt depend on the circumstances of the case, given that the plaintiff is under a duty to act reasonably to mitigate his loss. I do not consider that the passages in Scrutton and Voyage Charters to which I was referred are inconsistent with this view. They simply reflect the fact that in many cases alternative shipping space will be available, and if it is, it will probably be incumbent on the charterer to mitigate his loss by making use of it. I do not accept, therefore, that the charterer must be able to show that alternative space was not available before he can recover damages measured by reference to the value of the goods at the port of discharge, as Mr. Young(船方大律师) submitted. That does not, however, prevent the ship owner from seeking to establish that the charterer failed to act properly in mitigation, and I shall come to consider this aspect of the matter a little later."

顺便简单介绍一下这个案例的案情,涉及的是一艘冷藏船 Kriti Rex 轮被租用在南美洲的 Manzanillo、Santo Tomas 与 Big Creek 这几个港口装香蕉,目的地是英国的 Portsmouth 与比利时的 Zeebrugge。当船舶在 Manzanillo 装上 16530 箱香蕉并开向 Santo Tomas 时,中途发生机器故障,并且后来被法院认定是船舶不适航(因为主机的润滑油系统不清洁)。在 Santo Tomas 的香蕉已经被割下待装,但由于 Kriti Rex 轮无法准时到达,货方就想办法另找替代船舶,但找不到。最后的处置办法是通过与另一家美国的著名公司 Del Monte 达成的协议将该批香蕉卖到美国的 Galveston。至于在 Kriti Rex 轮上的 16530 箱香蕉,也因为船舶修理的延误而无法在腐烂前运至目的地,而在南美洲也无市场出售,结果货方把该批香蕉捐赠给洪都拉斯红十字会。事后货方向船方提出索赔,损失就是:(1)在 Santo Tomas 与 Big Creek 待装的香蕉在欧洲两个目的地的价值,减掉付运的费用与卖给 Del Monte 的那部分香蕉的价值;(2)在 Manzanillo 装上的 16530 箱香蕉的全损。货方与船方主要的争议之一是损失(1)应否替代船舶去欧洲的运费差价,这显然比货方要求的在欧洲两个目的地的价值要低得多。正如较早的解释,到底以哪一种损失类别为准,关键是看货方能否合理找到替代船舶将该批香蕉运至目的地。

7. 实质损失和经济损失的区别与困难

法律针对"实质的损失与伤亡"(physical injury and damage)与"经济损失"(economic loss)如利润损失,看来是有所区别,虽然这两类损失都是在订约时可以料想如果违约有可能会产生的“一般损失”(ordinary damages)。但困难是英国法下承认的“同步责任”(concurrent liability)可以同时提出侵权与违约的诉因。而侵权只是接受实质损失的赔偿，但不接受“纯经济损失”(pure economic loss)的赔偿(这在本章12.4段有详论)。疏忽的侵权只接受实际损失加上受害方的“间接经济损失”(consequential economic loss)而针对“损失遥远性”(remoteness)，侵权与违约的局限并不一致。这显然在同步责任的案件中会带来困难，在本章12.5段会进一步分析。在先例 Parsons v. Uttley Ingham(1977)2 Lloyd's Rep. 522 就涉及这一方面的困难，Denning 勋爵明确地作出了区分，认为针对前者的实质损失与伤亡，违约方在订约时只要料想得到有一个轻微的可能性就已经足够要他负责，而且后果严重与否不加以考虑。但针对后者的经济损失，就需要在订约时有一个重大的可能性才需要负责。他是这样说：“In the... loss of profit cases – the defaulting party is only liable for the consequences if they are such as, at the time of the contract he ought reasonably to have contemplated as a serious possibility or real danger... In the... physical injury or expense case – the defaulting party is liable for any damage which he ought reasonably to have foreseen at the time of the breach as a possible consequence, even if it was only a slight possibility ...”

Scarman 大法官也同意 Denning 勋爵的意见，并提出经济损失只涉及违约/毁约，而合约则有充分的订约自由，说：“I agree with Lord Denning, M. R., in thinking it absurd that the test for remoteness of damage should, in principle, differ according to the legal classification of the cause of action – though one must recognise that parties to a contract have the right to agree on a measure of damages which may be greater or less, than the law would offer in the absence of agreement ...”

针对实质的损失与伤亡，可节录《McGregor on Damages》(18th edn, 2009 年)一书之 6 – 157 段所说有关不理会实际损失的严重程度，如下：“It is submitted that, in contract as in tort, it should suffice that, if physical injury or damage is within the contemplation of the parties, recovery is not to be limited because the degree of physical injury or damage could not have been anticipated.”

结合本章第 7 段已经有提到，实质损失与经济损失在程度方面的对待看来有差异，前者比较宽松的一个原因是实质损失通常被视为违约/毁约所造成的“直接后果”(direct consequence)。另一个原因是 Denning 勋爵在 Parsons v. Uttley Ingham 先例所说的在该先例的同类情况下，受害方会有可能直接向供应商根据产品责任提出索赔，这就涉及侵权行为。所以，针对合理预见，合约与侵权针对这种实质损失就应该一致，比较宽松。这在实际伤亡也是一样，受害方可以直接根据侵权向责任方提出索赔，而不严格受制于合约关系。

针对经济损失(如利润损失)是比较严格对待，正如 Brown v. K. M. R. Services 先例所说，正常的业务所带来的利润与一些特殊合约带来的极高利润是被视为两种不同的损失类别。同样的说法也在近期的 Mayhaven Healthcare Ltd v. Bothma(2009)

EWHC 2634(TCC)先例出现。这等于是实际损失的程度严重与否是会带来区分。毕竟,违约方如果担心要负责极高利润的损失,由于有订约自由,他可以在订约时以合约条文(如免责条文或责任限制条文)减少损失赔偿。

8. The "Achilleas"先例对损失规定带来的不明朗

在这个重要的贵族院海事先例 The "Achilleas"(2009)1 AC 61(HL),涉及损失的遥远性问题,并且带来了不明朗与很大争议。即该先例是否对 Hadley v. Baxendale (1854)9 Ex. 341 有所改变,把本来是属于法律的问题变为一个事实问题(也就是看个别合约的双方当事人对风险分摊的订约意图)。详细讨论之前,不妨先介绍有关的案情。

8.1 案情介绍

这可节录杨大明律师所著的《期租合约》第125页,如下:

"首先笔者介绍该案例的有关事实。它是一个5~7个月的期租,并后来再续期5~7个月,租金是每天16750美元。反正,可计算出来的最后还船日期(terminal redelivery date)是2004年5月2日。在这一天之前之4月20日,承租人给了还船通知说是在4月30日至5月2日之间。这一来,船东就在市场订下下一个4~6个月的期租,租金是每天39500美元,而销约期是5月8日。可以说如果承租人能准时在5月2日还船,赶得及下一个租约的销约期。但最终船舶是在5月11日才在日本的大分港(Oita)卸清了煤炭并还船给船东。这一来超出或延迟的时间是9天,与市场租金的差价比较损失应是158301.17美元。但实际上船东的损失远不止此数,这是因为延迟至5月11日还船就错过了下一个租约的5月8日销约期,而当时市场租金急剧下挫,这导致船东最终被下一个租约承租人压价才保住这份租约。压的价是从原先订下的39500美元变为31500美元,等于每天损失8000美元。这乘以至少4个月的租约期,船东真正的损失就变成了1364584.37美元。

在伦敦仲裁,多数的两位仲裁员认为承租人应该赔偿船东真正的损失。但另一位不同意见的著名仲裁员认为针对这个问题的先例一直很稳定,只赔偿这9天船东租约租金与市场租金的差价,不应轻易改动而令人无所适从。他也在后来私下告知说他不相信该船东在下一个租约被压价是真实的,所以主要因为这个原因而持不同意见。这一个仲裁被败诉的承租人(香港的Transfield Shipping Inc)上诉去法院,但被驳回,Clarke大法官认为承租人在订约时应该可以合理预见这一个类别的损失并非是"不太可能"(not unlikely)会产生,即使这种情况会发生的概率是低于50%,这也是支持多数仲裁员所裁决的说法,就是这种损失可以在今天航运市场在订约时可以预见到。

这一来,何谓遥远的损失(remoteness)被扩大不少,特别是针对大家是在同一行业的合约双方,都被视为在订约时应该能够预见在该行业的一般做法与市场变化。看来仍会被视为是不可预见的遥远损失只会局限在只有索赔方自己才能知道的一些特殊、不平常与奇怪的方面所带来的损失,这种损失只能在订约时通知了对方才能成功索赔,但它不会是太多。反正是在著名的 Hadley v. Baxendale 先例中所作出的两个分支,即一般损失与特别损失,后者是要在订约前通知对方才能成功索赔,两者看来已经是没有什么区分了。"

杨大明律师的《期租合约》一书因出版时间较早,没有针对贵族院最后对 The "Achilleas"的判决。但可以说,多数仲裁员的裁决以及高院与上诉庭都认为船东这一种损失的类别是属于 Hadley v. Baxendale 中第一类别的"一般损失"(ordinary damages),所以是可以向违约(延误还船)的承租人索赔。至于实际损失是严重或是不严重,已经在先例 Parsons v. Uttley Ingham(1977)2 Lloyd's Rep. 522 介绍过这是不受影响的。但笔者是倾向同意这个少数仲裁员的不同意见,因为知道这样判法的危险性。原因是在期租合约,会导致延误还船的情况比比皆是。例如在卸港遇上坏天气就会拖延卸货时间几天,卸港拥挤又会延误靠泊几天,领港或拖轮罢工又会延误进港或开航几天,这种例子多不胜数,导致承租人在一个"航次期租"(time charter trip)或者一个期租最后的航次中根本没有办法掌握准确的还船时间。在航运市场上涨时,本来只支付延误还船那几天的差价是一直以来承租人可以接受的。但如果现在违约的承租人要面对船东可能因为延误还船而错过了下一个租约的销约期所带来的所有损失就很难接受了。而且笔者也担心一些精明的船东作假,就是把船舶的下一航次租给自己的联营公司(但表面看不出来,因为是一家巴拿马或利比里亚公司,要查他的底细也无从去查)。而租约是 10 年,租金订得很高,而销约期是只要原来的租约延误还船 1、2 天就会错过。这岂非是让船东在延误还船 1、2 天就可以向承租人索赔(或敲诈)一两千万美元金额的庞大损失?虽然精明的承租人可以通过订约自由在他的期租合约内规定如果发生延误还船只要赔偿超出时间的租金差价。但总有承租人会上当,所以法律的默示地位最好能够做到公平合理与配合实践。

8.2　贵族院的"客观看订约双方是否愿意承担赔偿的责任"测试的质疑

幸亏 The "Achilleas"的上诉庭判决在贵族院被改变过来,判承租人所需要赔偿的金额只是延迟的 9 天,乘以租约租金与市场租金的差价,也就是 158301.17 美元。但贵族院作出这个判决的原因却并不一致,其中 Hoffmann 勋爵与 Hope 勋爵是一致的看法。但 Rodger 勋爵和 Hale 女男爵的原因还是根据 Hadley v. Baxendale(1854)9 Ex. 341 先例以双方订约时无法料想到市场会有这么激烈的波动(这一个原因与其他的判例不一致,如在本章 8.3.2 段将要介绍的 Classic Maritime Inc v. Lion Diversified Holding Berhad[2010]1 Lloyd's Rep 59 先例。另可节录 Mustill 勋爵在 The "Gregos"[1995]1 Lloyd's Rep 1 先例说:"The fact is that in a volatile market, of which merchant shipping is by no means the only example, a contract breaker may find the consequences of a breach are multiplied to a surprising degree by adventitious factors.")而贵族院的第五

位成员 Walker 勋爵说他同意 Hoffman、Hope 与 Rodger 三位勋爵的理由，这表示 Walker 勋爵根本没有表态。

贵族院主要的判决原因是由 Hoffmann 勋爵作出，大致上是说，赔偿是要根据合约中双方所自愿承担的损失。而在该先例，客观看承租人在有关的租约下延误还船应该只愿意承担 9 天的差价，而不是下一个租约所有的损失。Hoffmann 勋爵是这样说：

"The findings of the majority arbitrators show that they considered their decision to be contrary to what would have been the expectations of the parties, but dictated by the rules in Hadley v. Baxendale as explained in The Heron II (1969) 1 AC 350. But in my opinion these rules are not so inflexible; they are intended to give effect to the presumed intentions of the parties and not to contradict them.

The owners submit that the question of whether the damage is too remote is a question of fact on which the arbitrators have found in their favour. It is true that the question of whether the damage was foreseeable is a question of fact: see Monarch Steamship Co Ltd v. Karlshamns Oljefabriker (A/B) (1949) AC 196. But the question of whether a given type of loss is one for which a party assumed contractual responsibility involves the interpretation, is a question of law. (船东说损失是否太遥远是一项事实的认定，而多数仲裁员已经判船东胜诉，这表示法院不应该再干预事实的认定。但 Hoffmann 勋爵说虽然损失在订约时可否预见或料想得到是事实问题，但某一类的损失是否是违约方愿意承担合约责任就涉及解释合约，这是法律问题。)

... In my opinion, the findings of the arbitrators and the commercial background to the agreement are sufficient to make it clear that the charterer cannot reasonably be regarded as having assumed the risk of the owner's loss of profit on the following charter. I would therefore allow the appeal. (在 Hoffmann 勋爵看来，仲裁庭的事实认定加上订约时的商业背景显示了承租人的被告不能被合理认为是愿意在租约中承担下一个租约中船东所损失的所有利润。)"

贵族院多数的上述意见是支持"客观看订约双方是否愿意承担赔偿的责任"(objective assessment in the voluntary assumption of responsibility)的测试，带来了不肯定与是否有改变了 Hadley v. Baxendale 与 Victoria Laundry 这两个一脉相承的重要先例确立的大原则的疑问，就是只区分一般损失与特别损失或是找出违约方在订约时是否可以合理料想得到有可能会产生损失的类别。这被视为是"法律默示的规则针对合约的遥远性"(a default rule of law governing remoteness of contract)。

但 Hoffman 勋爵在 The "Achilleas" 先例带来这一个新的说法也被称为"以合约为中心寻找遥远性"(an agreement - centred approach to remoteness)或"以双方订约意愿针对合约遥远性"(an intention - based view of contractual remoteness)，而不把损失遥远性当做是合约外的赔偿原则。这会带来要进一步考虑双方在合约中所愿意承担赔偿的责任就会带来额外争议，因为在每一个不同的合约针对双方愿意承担什么赔偿责任都会涉及谈判过程和合约的解释，这包括了更多“事实的认定”（finding of facts）与“法律的确定”（holding of law），这会令针对损失是否是遥远的诉讼变得是更昂贵与不肯定。由于许多的合约谈判都不会明示针对损失赔偿的遥远性问题（除了赔偿责任限制条文），所以很少比较可靠的证据。就表示法院往往在个别案子要找出双方的默示，如合约价格比市场价格更高或更低，是否代表了合约一方愿意或不愿意承担更大的赔偿责任。显然这些很不可靠与不肯定，所以有说法是以合约寻找遥远性是不可行的。例如，在《Lloyd's Maritime and Commercial Law Quarterly》季刊（2010年2月）中，在《Contractual interpretation and remoteness》一文中，有说：“A strong form of the agreement - centred approach to remoteness that seeks to resolve all questions of risk allocation solely on the basis of the parties' intentions and agreement as evidenced in the circumstances seems unworkable. Where an intention or agreement as to the allocation of a particular risk simply cannot be discerned, as seems not unlikely in the remoteness context, such an approach will not only be fictional, but will also involve the courts in rewriting the parties' bargain.”

这方面可以以一个上诉庭先例进一步解释，该案例名为 Brown v. KMR Service Ltd（1995）4 All ER 598。案情有关劳合社的一位成员向他的劳合社代理人以合约与侵权提出索赔，之后该代理人没有提出有关参与承保 Excess of Loss 再保险高风险的警告。在责任方面，代理人被判是要负责。但针对损失，就涉及在有关的延误中，所发生的前所未见的经济灾难所带来的损失程度是否太遥远。第一审与上诉庭都认为损失类别是属于可预料的范围，就不再理会程度方面的严重与否。换言之就是这前所未见的经济损失并非太遥远。但如果是同样该先例按以合约为中心寻找遥远性的原则，就应该对“前所未见的经济灾难”（unprecedented financial disasters）这种非常极端的情况，不可能在合约谈判时有明示或默示针对与得出一个结论是被告的劳合社代理人愿意承担赔付责任。首先，要一方同意承担过度庞大的责任并不是一个合理的情况，所以在明示条文欠缺下，做出默示就会需要得出一个结论是被告默示愿意承担所有的责任并作出赔偿，无论损失有多大。加上是面对原告是一个有经验的投资者以及与是有参与这种高风险的保险业务。所以，看来作出这样的默示结论是不容易的。这表示如果以合约为中心寻找遥远性的原则来判的话，显然这一案件就会有相反的判决结果了。

最后一提的是有说法 The “Achilleas”先例改变了一些已经明确下来从来也没有任何质疑的重要先例，例如在《Lloyd's Maritime and Commercial Law Quarterly》季刊（2012年2月）中刊登的《Contractual remoteness, “scope of duty” and intention》提到的 The “Heron II”（1967）2 Lloyd's Rep 457 先例如果是根据 The “Achilleas”的说法判就会有很不同的结果，说：“The claimants knew neither the date that they would arrive in Basra, nor whether the sugar market would be rising or falling at that point, and the only fact communicated to the defendants was that they were sugar merchants. What, then, would be the evidence from which the court could, on the intention - based rationale, infer that the risk of delay was allocated to the defendants rather than the claimants? Counterfactually, of course, the defendants 'must have realised that at least it was not unlikely' that the sugar was to be sold on arrival. But exactly the same is true of the possibility that the sugar was to be sold nine or ten days after arrival, in which case the defendants' deviation would have caused no loss. Further, even if the defendants had known of the intention of immediate sale, at least one background understanding prevailing at the time of contracting was that such a defendant could not be made the insurer of market loss. Accordingly, it is far more straightforward to explain - and to justify - decisions like The "Heron II" on the traditional approach to remoteness."

8.3 The "Achilleas"带来的新测试之后的先例

上一小段所说带来后来的一连串先例质疑 Hoffmann 勋爵的说法到底有没有改变 Hadley v. Baxendale 的损失规定，在以下段节会有介绍。

8.3.1 有关先例之一：The "Amer Energy"

第一个先例是 The "Amer Energy"(2009)1 Lloyd's Rep 293，它就是著名的有关首席仲裁员 Duncan Matthews QC 被法院在开庭时赶走的先例 ASM Shipping。但目前介绍的是该先例的续集，也就是针对实体的争议。案情是有关一个航次租约去科威特装一船汽油(gas oil)去地中海或红海港口。但由于船舶延误，导致承租人的联营公司(都属于 Sempra 石油集团的公司)失去了买卖合约，因为买方因延误而取消。所以，承租人向船东索赔的是利润损失，共达 75 万美元。结果是仲裁庭的 Bruce Harris、Tony Scott 与 Steven Berry QC(他替代了 Duncan Matthews QC 作为首席)判船东败诉，要赔付这笔钱。船东向英国法院申请批文，根据的就是 1996 年《英国仲裁法》之 Section 69。而有关的法律观点就是说，在 The "Achilleas"(2007)1 Lloyd's Rep. 19 后，针对损失遥远性的"新测试"(new test)就是这一种类的损失是否船东在订约时愿意承担责任(The damage of a type and kind for which the owners ought fairly to be taken to have assumed responsibility)，而船东认为裁决书是没有这方面的认定或确定，不能做出这样的结论。

胜诉承租人的一方代表大律师抗拒说，承租人在这一方面的利润损失是船东在订约时可以料想得到，不是"不可能"(not unlikely)会产生的损失类别。再说，即使是属于特别损失，承租人在谈判时也作出了通知，如下："the owners' agent Mr Moustakas had been told during the fixture negotiations that the proposed cargo of oil was being traded and that the charterers were part of a larger group. It would have been clear to him that, in the event the owners were in breach, charterers' affiliates and associates' would suffer losses. If contrary to the arbitrators´finding the matters which gave rise to the losses were not in the ordinary course of things but were special circumstances, the owners through Mr Moustakas had sufficient knowledge of those special circumstances. In other words, to the extent necessary, the charterers could satisfy the second limb of Hadley v. Baxendale."

最终是 Flaux 大法官拒绝作出上述的批文,并说明他不认为在 The "Achilleas",贵族院有任何意图作出任何新的测试改变有关 Hadley v. Baxendale 的损失计算规则,说:"To the extent that Lord Hoffmann was purporting to lay down some **new test** to recoverability of damages in contract, he was a minority. Although Lord Hope adopts a similar analysis at paras 30 and 36, he does so essentially by edges in paras 9 and 11 of his option that departure from the normal principles of foreseeability would be unusual. Although he refers to shipping as a market where limitations on the extent of liability arising out of general expectation in that market might be more common, I do not consider that he was intending to say that in all shipping cases (as opposed to the type of time charter case then under consideration) the rule in Hadley v. Baxendale as subsequently refined, will no longer apply. If he was saying that, it was not a view shared by the majority and it would be heterodox to say the least."

8.3.2 有关先例之二:Classic Maritime Inc v. Lion Diversified Holding Berhad

这是另一个有关的航运先例 Classic Maritime Inc v. Lion Diversified Holding Berhad(2010)1 Lloyd's Rep 59,案情涉及在 2008 年 8 月中订立的两个航次的"包运合约"(COA)准备运矿砂。众所周知,到了 2008 年 10 月左右,发生了全球的金融海啸,航运市场也受到很严重冲击,接下来下挫了高达 95% 以上。这导致承租人很大的压力,甚至也没有能力在卸港贮存与生产这些即将付运的矿砂。而承租人也在 2008 年 11 月取得了卖方的同意押后付运矿砂,导致再也不需要船东履行这一个包运合约。这无可避免地导致了承租人以"合约受阻"(frustration of contract)与不可以抗力为由拒绝履行合约,而船东也接受了毁约,并在英国法院申请了一个"简易判决"(summary judgment)。而承租人就要求英国法院"中止"(stay)审理,因为在包运合约中有一条仲裁条文。在船东的立场,一个包运合约在没有"法律上的障碍"(legal prohibition)或是实质性的无法履行(如唯一的装港/卸港发生灾难性的破坏),是很难因为市场改变导致受阻。其中一个重要的原因是包运合约不像一个航次租约,是为了将来的远期合约(forward contract)。这表示双方在很大程度就应该在这种合约里明示或默示分摊了将来有可能发生的变数所带来的后果或责任承担(如通过免责条文)。这方面的先例有贵族院的 Larrinaga & Co. v. Societe Franco Americaine des Phosphates (1923)14 Lloyd's Rep 457,说:"In effect, most forward contracts can be regarded as a form of commercial insurance in which every event is intended to be at the risk of one party or another. Each party is likely most to need the maintenance of such a contract exactly when the other would most wish to be rid of it. . . . All the uncertainties of a commercial contract can ultimately be expressed, though not very accurately, in terms of money, and rarely, if ever, is it a ground for inferring frustration of an adventure, that the contract has turned out to be a loss or even a commercial disaster for somebody. If a contract is really a speculative contract, as this plainly is, the doctrine of frustration can rarely, if ever, apply to it, for the basis of a speculative contract is to distribute all the risks on one side or on the other and to eliminate any chance of the contract falling to the ground, unless, indeed, the law has put an end to it. . . . No one can tell how long a spell of commercial depression may last; no suspense can be more harassing than the vagaries of foreign exchanges: but contracts are made for the purpose of fixing the incidence of such risks in advance, and their occurrence only makes it the more necessary to uphold a contract and not to make them the ground for discharging it."

笔者回到本章要针对的损失遥远性,针对这方面,船东索赔两个航次的金额高达1800万美元,而损失的计算是根据"breach date rule",也就是包运合约的运费与波罗的好望角型船舶指数(Baltic Capesize Index)的市场价格比较的差价作为基础。承租人认为索赔的金额过高,第一就是波罗的好望角型船舶指数不准确代表在某一天(也就是毁约的一天)的市场运费,这一方面承租人会将来在仲裁中提供专家意见作为证据。第二个承租人提出的抗辩是在The"Achilleas"先例,贵族院提出了一个新测试,就是这一种类的损失是否船东在订约时愿意承担责任(The damage of a type and kind for which the owners ought fairly to be taken to have assumed responsibility)。由于在2008年年底的历史性动荡,承租人是不应该在订约时愿意承担全部损失的,因为这是双方根本料想不到的。能够料想到的只能是一般运费市场的波动。这方面的争辩可节录如下:"An argument was raised with regard to The 'Achilleas'[2008]2 Lloyd's Rep. 275. Lion(承租人)submitted that the House of Lords had set out a new test for the recoverability of damages for breach of contract, namely whether the loss was a type of loss for which the party in breach could reasonably be regarded as having assumed responsibility. Because of the extreme volatility of the freight market in late 2008 it was submitted that Limbungan could not be liable for the full extent of the loss claimed by Classic(船东)which reflected the full 95% fall in freight rates, but only for the loss flowing from a fall in freight rates for vessels of the kind in question, of the magnitude which the parties would have contemplated, at the time of contracting, as being likely to occur in the ordinary course of things."

英国高院的Cooke大法官也是不认为The "Achilleas"针对损失遥远性的规定有作出任何改变,说:"I would be highly surprised, if this was the effect of their Lordships' decision. I note that Flaux J was wholly unpersuaded that the House of Lords had changed the law on remoteness – see The 'Amer Energy'(2009)1 Lloyd's Rep. 293."Cooke大法官认为市场的波动是双方在订合约时可以料想得到的损失类别,并且在分析了几个大法官在The "Achilleas"的判决后,认为只要损失的类别是料想得到,严重的程度是不在考虑之内的,说:"In my judgment, notwithstanding references to the unforeseen degree of fluctuation in the market, not one of their Lordships was saying that, if the type of loss was within the contemplation of the parties or that for which the party in breach must be assumed to have accepted responsibility, some of it might be irrecoverable because the extent of it was unexpected."

8.3.3 有关先例之三:GB Gas Holding Ltd v. Accenture

这一个 GB Gas Holding Ltd v. Accenture(UK) Ltd(2009) EWHC 2734(Comm)先例中涉及 The"Achilleas"(2008)2 Lloyd's Rep. 275 先例中所谓的新测试并不多,这不像其他几个在这里介绍的先例,但基本上还是依据了 Hadley v. Baxendale 的两种损失规则分析好几项不同的损失类别。

案情涉及向英国接近2000万顾客提供天然气与电力的原告英国天然气公司的大量的账目结算问题。所以在2002年初与被告 Accenture 达成协议,由后者设计、提供、安装与保养一套新的信息技术(IT)处理这些账单的问题。但到了2006年中,这方面出了大量的问题,最终导致原告指控被告违约并索赔损失。这些损失包括:原告需要雇用数以千计的额外雇员处理这些问题,包括对不满顾客的投诉做出解释;原告需要把数以百万英镑的没有的开出账单或者延误收费的坏账销账;原告需要做出大量的调查与针对大量问题做出解决等。

在有关的合约中,有一条明示条文豁免损失,豁免的损失包括了"直接或者间接的利润损失"、"直接或者间接的业务/收入损失"与"间接或惩罚性损失与费用"如下:

"16.2 Consequential Loss

Subject to Clause 16.7 or as otherwise expressly provided in this Agreement, in no event shall either Party be liable whether in contract, tort(including negligence) or otherwise in respect of any of the following losses or damages:

16.2.1 loss of profits or of contracts arising directly or indirectly;

16.2.2 loss of business or of revenues arising directly or indirectly;

16.2.3 any losses, damages, costs or expenses whatsoever to the extent that these are indirect or consequential or punitive;

save that this Clause 16.2 shall not apply in the event that either party terminates this Agreement other than in accordance with Clause 21."

双方同意在16条文的"直接"(directly)与"间接"(indirectly)就是指 Hadley v. Baxendale 的第一条损失规则与第二条损失规则。

针对各项不同类别的损失,第一项的 Gas Distribution Charges(高达1870万英镑),被告的抗辩是这属于收入损失或者利润损失,根据合约的第16条文是不必赔付的。原告的解释是他要向经销商批发买进天然气然后再供应给顾客,其间他需要把顾客消耗的天然气表所记录的数字转告给经销商,让经销商向原告收费。但由于被告对顾客账目的问题,导致无法提供15%顾客消耗的天然气数字给经销商,从而导致经销商作出偏高的估计向原告收费。针对这一项损失，Field 大法官判这不是一项收入或利润损失，而是 Hadley v. Baxendale 的第一条规则，是违约方在这一合约的本质下，在订约时就可以合理料想到会发生的一般损失。

第二项的名誉损失与赔偿给顾客的 800 万英镑，原告指这一问题导致了大量顾客的不满，在 2006 ~ 2007 年间，流失了 77 万以上的顾客。为了对这一名誉的损害作出补救，原告对一些顾客作出了赔偿，也就是这笔 800 万英镑。被告声称这笔支付并非是法律的责任需要支付，而是属于馈赠（*ex gratia* payment），并提到了 The "Achilleas" 先例。而英国法院的 Field 大法官只是简单针对被告的抗辩并判这笔损失也是在 Hadley v. Baxendale 的第一条损失规则内，说："Accenture（被告）contends that the sum paid out was paid *ex gratia* and is plainly an indirect or consequential loss. Mr Vos（被告的代表大律师）cited paragraphs 21 - 25 of Lord Hoffmann's judgement in The Achilleas[2009]1 AC 61. In my judgement this item of loss is neither indirect nor consequential but falls within the first limb of Hadley v. Baxendale. Having regard to the Amended JPA（有关合约）overall and to the relevant background, including Recital（A）I think it plain that one of the purposes of the new billing system was to improve customer relations and customer services. It is equally plain that in the context of the Amended JPA, Accenture assumed responsibility for losses in terms of compensation paid to customers if the billing system failed to perform as it was intended it should perform."

其他项目的损失类别包括了额外贷款费用的 200 万英镑、额外追偿顾客收费的约 39 万英镑与额外的通信与文书费用约 10 万英镑，Field 大法官都判是可以向违约的被告提出索赔。这些费用不属于间接损失，而是属于 Hadley v. Baxendale 的第一条损失规则，也没有被合约第 16 条文排除。但笔者不一一介绍了。

8.3.4　有关先例之四：Mayhaven Healthcare Ltd v. Bothma

在 Mayhaven Healthcare Ltd v. Bothma（2009）EWHC 2634（TCC）也显示了 Hadley v. Baxendale 的两种损失规则不是这么容易推翻。可简单介绍案情是有关"疗养院"（nursing home）的建筑工程延误所带来的预期利益损失/利润损失的计算。原告想将原来的收容老年残疾人士的计划改变为收容年轻（18 ~ 65 岁）残疾人士，因为这样可以大大增加利润。但仲裁庭判损失应该根据老年残疾人士的收入为准，认为原告计划收容年轻残疾人士属于特别损失，有必要在订合约之前通知被告。裁决书是这样写的："In this case, Mayhaven are developing a business plan, moving into the provision of care for YPD（这是指"年轻残疾人士"[young physical disable]）; in my opinion, this is not a special contract referred to in Victoria Laundry, nor are the circumstances similar to those in the Czarnikov case（这是指 The "Heron II" 先例）which related to a cargo of sugar. The circumstances relating to this case are a change in the provision of care to produce a significant increase in profit, to which Mayhaven（原告）were privy, and I find it is most unlikely that DAB（被告）could have discovered this possible change in Mayhaven's business plan."

原告不服上诉,认为其只需要证明疗养院是营利机构,所以利润损失是被告违约方应该知道在工程延误的情况下有可能会产生。而这只是 Hadley v. Baxendale 损失规则的第一条,被告根本不需要有真正知情。但在高院,Ramsey 大法官支持仲裁庭,认为年轻残疾人士的收容会带来高利润并非是一般损失,而是属于特别损失。Ramsey 大法官也提到利润损失不应该被视为只是一类的损失,一些特殊的、特别高的利润损失应该被视为属于第二条的损失规则,受害方若没有作出事前通知是不能索赔的。他是这样说:"In relation to question 2(b),'loss of profits' is not to be equated to 'loss of a kind' so as to make all profits recoverable. As Lord Hoffmann said in Transfield case(这是指 The "Achilleas"先例)at para 22,the loss of profits in the Victoria Laundry case are not a single type of case. Some may fall within the first limb(第一条损失规则)and some within the second limb(第二条损失规则). In this case the Arbitrator found that loss of profit for the use of the care home for the more lucrative YPD occupants was not recoverable for lack of actual knowledge under the second limb. I do not consider that there was any error on a question of law in that conclusion."

8.3.5 有关先例之五:Supershield Ltd v. Siemens Building Technologies FE Ltd

在另一个上诉庭的先例 Supershield Ltd v. Siemens Building Technologies FE Ltd (2010)EWCA Civ 7,案情是有关一栋大厦的消防灭火系统,由于一个螺丝钉与螺丝帽松脱,导致水箱的水满溢出来。本来该系统还有另外一个双重防御,就是有排水道将水引至污水渠。但在事发当时,不知什么原因导致排水道堵塞。当双重防御都失灵的情况下,地库的一整层楼都被水浸了。这导致住客庞大的损失,并向各有关方提出索赔。在诉讼过程中,Siemens 作为消防灭火系统的分承建商,作出了和解。而后 Siemens 向他的分分承建商 Supershield 要求补偿,而 Supershield 提出的其中一个争议是 Siemens 的水浸损失是太遥远,因为系统的双重防御同时失灵的概率非常低,可以说是"不可能"(unlikely)会发生。但在上诉庭,Toulson 大法官不接受,认为在复杂的机器或工程(不论是一架飞机、一辆车子、一条隧道或一栋大厦),通常是期待设计与安装的承建商会加入多重的防御措施,并希望这些措施不会同时失效,令出事故的概率是微乎其微。如果越小心与越多防御措施就反而令受害方在不幸遇上所有措施同时失效时的损失被视为是太遥远而无法索赔,显然,这样的逻辑不合理。这个期待承建商会加入多重的防御措施是依赖承建商做好他的工作,如果他没有这样做导致"不可能"的事故发生,承建商不需负责是没有理由的。而在该先例,Siemens 有一个合约责任做好他的工作防止水浸,即他作为订约方是愿意承担水浸损失的赔偿责任。这正是 Hoffmann 勋爵在 The "Achilleas"先例的新测试。

看来,Toulson 大法官是比较愿意接受对 Hadley v. Baxendale 的损失规则作出重新的解读,并认为损失的遥远性应该考虑订约方在合约中默示或明示愿意承担的赔偿责任。他是这样说:"The law on remoteness of damage in relation to claims for breach of contract is grounded on the policy that the loss recovered by the victim should be limited to loss from which the party in breach may reasonably be taken to have assumed a responsibility to protect the victim. It follows that the question of remoteness cannot be isolated from consideration of the purpose of the contract and the scope of the contractual obligation. The underlying policy is implicit in Lord Reid's speech in Czarnikow v. Koufos(这是指 The "Heron Ⅱ"先例),where he referred to what the parties may be supposed to have contemplated as grounds for the recovery of damages and linked this to the question whether the loss was sufficiently likely to result from the breach to make it proper to hold that loss of that kind should have been in the contract breaker's contemplation. It has been made more explicit in the decisions of the House of Lords in South Australia Asset Management Corp v. York Montague Ltd(1997) AC 191,212 and Transfield Shipping(这是指 The "Achilleas"先例)."

Toulson 大法官在考虑与解释 South Australia 和 The "Achilleas"这两个先例后,接下去说:"Hadley v. Baxendale remains a standard rule but it has been rationalised on the basis that it reflects the expectation to be imputed to the parties in the ordinary case,i. e. that a contract breaker should ordinarily be liable to the other party for damage resulting from his breach if,but only if,at the time of making the contract as reasonable person in his shoes would have had damage of that kind in mind as not unlikely to result from a breach. However,South Australia and Transfield Shipping(这就是 The "Achilleas"先例) are authority that there may be cases where the court,on examining the contract and the commercial background,decides that the standard approach would not reflect the expectation or intention reasonably to be imputed to the parties. In those two instances the effect was exclusionary;the contract breaker was held not to be liable for loss which result from its breach although some loss of the kind was not unlikely. But logically the same principle may have an inclusionary effect. If,on the proper analysis of the contract against its commercial background,the loss was within the scope of the duty,it cannot be regarded as too remote,even if it would not have occurred in ordinary circumstances."

事实上在 The "Achilleas"先例,贵族院大可以不必将 Hadley v. Baxendale 与 Victoria Laundry 这两个一脉相承的损失规则作出任何改变。在 The "Achilleas",延误 9 天的损失是 158301. 17 美元,这是违约方在订约时可以合理料想得到的,可以判是属于一般损失。但延误还船导致下一个租约中计算得出的 1364584. 37 美元的损失,是违约方在订约时没有料想到的,可以视为属于特别损失。

8.3.6 有关先例之六:The "Sylvia"

再接下去介绍 The "Sylvia"(2010)2 Lloyd's Rep 81 先例,案情涉及船东在一个期租合约的延误,导致承租人转租的一个程租合约错过了销约期而蒙受损失。由于船舶延误是船东违约所造成,所以承租人向船东索赔这一分租约中的损失。仲裁庭判船东没有恪尽职责令船舶适航与违反对船舶的维修保养的义务，需要对承租人这一笔损失负责，并认为是属于 Hadley v. Baxendale（1854）9 Ex. 341 先例中的“一般损失”（ordinary damages）。

但船东向高院提出上诉，认为根据 The “Achilleas”（2007）1 Lloyd's Rep. 19 的贵族院先例，承租人这种转租蒙受的损失是不能向船东提出索赔。船东认为他违约造成延误的损失只是在延误期间市场租金与租约租金的差价，这是非常有限的一笔赔偿。

在高院，Hamblen 大法官对 The “Achilleas”与之后有关的判决作出了总结并给予了一些十分有用的澄清。首先是 Hamblen 大法官不认为 Hadley v. Baxendale 先例的大原则有什么改变，而 The “Achilleas”先例所针对的案情是一种很特殊的情况，因为他会导致违约方（延误还船的承租人）面对可能是无法估计、无法预见、无法控制与不成比例的责任与损失。例如，延误还船一天可能会带来船东因此而错过的下一个长达 10 年利润奇高的租约，就会出现这样的情况。而且要承租人承担这些损失也不是市场上一贯的做法或认同，所以有这一个租约“客观看双方是否愿意承担赔偿的责任”（objective assessment in the voluntary assumption of responsibility）的测试，这在一般情况下并不适用。作为高院，Hamblen 大法官是不能不同意贵族院在 The “Achilleas”的多数判决，他只能在不同案件的事实作出“区分”（distinguish），这也是他所做的事。Hamblen 大法官是这样说：

“In my judgment, the decision in *The Achilleas* results in an amalgam of the orthodox and the broader approach. The orthodox approach remains the general test of remoteness applicable in the great majority of cases. However, there may be ‘unusual’ cases, such as *The Achilleas* itself, in which the context, surrounding circumstances or general understanding in the relevant market make it necessary specifically to consider whether there has been an assumption of responsibility. This is most likely to be in those relatively rare cases where the application of the general test leads or may lead to an unquantifiable, unpredictable, uncontrollable or disproportionate liability or where there is clear evidence that such a liability would be contrary to market understanding and expectations.

In the great majority of cases it will not be necessary specifically to address the issue of assumption of responsibility. Usually the fact that the type of loss arises in the ordinary course of things or out of special known circumstances will carry with it the necessary assumption of responsibility.”

但针对本先例，Hamblen 大法官认为市场与有关先例一贯是接受期租的承租人营运船舶就涉及转租，如果因为船东的违约导致了失去分租约的损失，这是可以向船东索赔：The “Derby”（1984）1 Lloyd's Rep 635。再加上，这种性质的索赔不会是“无法估计、无法预见、无法控制与不成比例”（unquantifiable, unpredictable, uncontrollable or disproportionate），如分租约的长短总不会比有关期租的租期更长。如果有关租约只剩下了2个月的租期,失去的分租约损失就不可能是一个10年的期租,这是与The "Achilleas"的延误交船不一样的。Hamblen大法官是这样说:"Trading will frequently involve subletting,and time charters will include an express liberty so to do. The trading of the vessel will often involve fixtures for the carriage of specific cargoes,usually by voyage charter but sometimes by a time charter trip. The lifting of such cargoes under the charter will almost invariably involve a laycan or a cancelling date. This is simply ordinary vessel trading. As such,one would expect it to be well within the reasonable contemplation of an owner that delay of significance in arriving or being ready to load at the designated load port may result in the loss of a fixture,as the tribunal found. If so,lost profit on such a fixture would equally be well within their reasonable contemplation."

Hamblen大法官最后是判仲裁庭的裁决没有对双方是否愿意承担责任加以考虑是法律正确,说:

"Finally,for completeness,I would add that,for reasons already stated,the features which made *The Achilleas* an 'unusual' case are not present here. As such,I do not consider that there was any requirement for the tribunal specifically to address the issue of assumption of responsibility. Such an assumption of responsibility followed from their conclusion that this was a foreseeable loss arising naturally and in accordance with the ordinary course of things.

For all these reasons I do not consider that the tribunal's conclusion on remoteness involves any error of law. They directed themselves correctly in law. In any event,their conclusion was not inconsistent with the application of the correct legal test,still less necessarily so."

8.3.7 总结The "Achilleas"先例后的判决

从以上的介绍,可以看到在The "Achilleas"(2007)1 Lloyd's Rep. 19先例后的多个判决都没有在"损失遥远性"(remoteness)的方面偏离Hadley v. Baxendale的测试。看来,The "Achilleas"先例并没有在这方面带来太大改变。但The "Achilleas"毕竟是一个贵族院先例,即使有争议与不被接受还是必须接受它对下一级法院与仲裁庭的约束性。有说法是The "Achilleas"先例只是在损失遥远性多加了一个注解,就是在一些案情特殊的案件,是可以考虑双方订约有否意图承担有关的责任。而这种特殊案情,在Supershield Ltd v. Siemens Building Technologies FE Ltd(2010)EWCA Civ 7先例,上诉庭给了一个例子,就是有关损失类别并不足够是在订约时可以合理预见,但在有关的合约条文下可以解释为违约方对这一类别的损失是愿意承担有关责任。

这表示合约的草拟还是必须小心,避免被解释为愿意承担一些会造成不能合理预见的损失类别,即使没有在订约前作出特别通知。这合约的草拟特别要小心一些条文会涉及双方在合约中愿意承担的风险,如不可抗力条文、议定赔偿条文、责任限制条文、免责条文、最高赔偿金额条文、排除损失类别条文(如排除间接损失的赔偿)、谁要负责投保的条文等。

9. North Sea Energy Holdings 先例的介绍

再介绍一个较早时提到过的先例 North Sea Energy Holdings v. Petroleum Authority of Thailand(1997)2 Lloyd's Rep. 418，该案涉及一个长达 5 年的供应沙特阿拉伯原油合约。第一年供应 1000 万桶，然后逐年递增，反正 5 年内供应共 7000 万桶。买方 PTT 是泰国的国营单位，主要买卖原油及石油产品。卖方 MSH 是一家为了与 PTT 做这笔生意而在 Netherlands Antilles 成立的公司（估计不会有太多的资产）。MSH 与另一家名为 Magoil 的摩洛哥公司稍后订立了一个同样的供应原油合约，且 Magoil 是与沙特阿拉伯皇室成员有关系。沙特阿拉伯原油的供应主要是控制在一家名为 Aramco 的公司，这是由 4 家最主要的美国石油公司共同组成的。Aramco 后来因沙特阿拉伯政府的参与而改名为 Saudi Aramco。成立该公司的主要原因说是沙特阿拉伯政府想针对原油出口的政策执行一连串的计划与控制，包括原油只卖给大的石油公司与最后的用家（这是指一些自己有炼油厂的用家）。反正，Saudi Aramco 不会向中间人和石油贸易商出售原油。对于卖给最后用家的原油，Saudi Aramco 也会规定价格，同样的原油会因目的地与国家的不同而以不同的价格出售。所以卖给这些用家通常有目的地的明示限制，即不允许他们转卖。在订约后，PTT 一直通过 MSH 要求沙特阿拉伯放宽目的地的限制，为了他的炼油厂在无法处理所有原油供应后将剩余的原油转售到其他东南亚的目的地。由于 PTT 曾经说话过了火，被 MSH 掌握机会接受毁约而终断合约。反正在责任方面，被英国法院的 Thomas 大法官判是 PTT 毁约。接下去就是处理 MSH 提出的 6650 万美元的索赔，索赔的计算是根据 Magoil 合约中供应原油的价格与 PTT 合约价格的差价。在该案中没有针对市场价格，因为无法算出原油市场价格在 5 年内的走势以及应该供应原油的时间点的市场价格。

PTT 作为被告提出的抗辩是 Magoil 不能够在这 5 年内去提供原油（如沙特阿拉伯不会承诺长过 1 年的石油供应），所以 MSH 实际上没有损失。但 MSH 的答辩是在违约/毁约并被受害方接受后而终断了合约，就应根据这一个时间点计算损失，不必再追究如果没有终断合约，受害方能否履行，这里有不少先例明确了这一方面。MSH 的答辩节录如下：

"MSH said that they did not have to show that oil could have been supplied under the Magoil offer because PTT repudiated the agreement before the time for performance of MSH's obligation to deliver oil had arisen.

It is not in issue that when a repudiatory breach has occurred, the innocent party is relieved from further performance of his obligations under the contract; the innocent party does not have to prove that he was ready, willing and able at the date of the repudiation to perform the contract in accordance with its terms. This is made clear in a number of cases, in particular D. H. Bain v. Field & Co. Fruit Merchants Ltd. ,(1920)5 Ll. L. Rep. 16 at P. 17, British and Benningtons LTd. v. North Western Cachar Tea Co. Ltd. ,(1922)13 L. 1. L. Pre. 67;(1923)A. C. 48 at pp. 63,66,and 72, Continental Contractors Ltd. v. Medway Oil and Storage Co. ,(1925)23 L. 1. L. Rep. 124 at pp. 132 – 133 and Bulk Oil(Zug)A. G. v. Sun International Ltd. ,(1984)1 Lloyd's Rep. 531 at p. 545. The innocent party is not required to prove, before being entitled to damages, either that he could perform at the time of termination, or that he could have performed in the future. Similarly, the party in repudiation cannot rely on arguments to the effect that the innocent party could not, or might not, have been able to perform the obligations which he had undertaken under the contract."

但 Thomas 大法官只同意如果 MSH 是根据毁约时市场损失提出索赔,以上的说法与先例便适用。但如果 MSH 是根据他与 Magoil 的合约计算损失(也就是实际损失),就有必要证明如果没有 PTT 的毁约,Magoil 是能够在这 5 年内履行合约。Thomas 大法官并提到其他有关的先例,如 British & Benningtons Ltd v. North Western Cachar Tea Co Ltd(1922)13 Lloyd's Rep 67;The "Mihalis Angelos"(1970)2 Lloyd's Rep 43; Berger & Co Inc v. Gill & Duffus SA(1984)1 Lloyd's Rep 27。他是这样说:"I therefore reject MSH's contention that the ability to obtain the oil under the arrangements with Magoil upon which they rely for their claim is immaterial as a matter of law: If under the Magoil offer no oil could ever have been delivered, MSH have lost nothing and are not entitled to US $ 66.5 m. which they claim by reference solely to the Magoil offer."

在开庭取证中,包括了在电话中答应 Magoil 供应原油的一位沙特阿拉伯王子,也通过视象会议接受盘问,Thomas 大法官最终根据平衡的可能性,认为是 MSH 没有办法供应这 5 年的大量原油,说:"On this evidence, I find, on the balance of probabilities, that the Saudi Prince would not have been able to make available this very large quantity of oil over a five year period. I make the finding because it is clear that it is only in very special circumstances that oil may be made available for the benefit of certain very senior members of the Saudi Arabian Royal Family, that there were no special circumstances that would explain the provision of oil to the Saudi Prince for sale to Magoil, that the general policy of Saudi Arabia is to make one year contracts and that it is therefore highly unlikely that oil sufficient to deliver under the agreement between MSH and PTT could in fact have been made available. This aspect of the action is dependent upon proof of a very special and highly profitable source of supply of oil. The fact that a decision was taken not to make available either Magoil's files or any direct evidence from the Saudi Prince or from Saudi Arabia may be explicable; it has had, together with the other factors to which I have referred, the consequence that I have concluded on the evidence on a balance of probabilities that oil could not have been made available to MSH through Magoil for delivery to PTT."

此外,由于 MSH 没在订约前把他与 Magoil 的供应原油合约通知 PTT(与 Magoil

的合约是在和 PTT 订约后才签订的),根据 Magoil 的合约价格索赔也属于特别损失而不是一般损失,更别说 MSH 根本无法证明有这一项的损失。Thomas 大法官说:"I therefore conclude that the offer made by Magoil is properly characterized as an extravagant and unusual bargain and even if oil could have been supplied through Magoil, damages could not be claimed by reference to the arrangements with Magoil."

10. 涉及 Hadley v. Baxendale 的损失规则的主要合约类别

损失遥远性的争议在各式各样的违约或侵权的案件中都会出现,而且非常频繁。这方面主要有两个种类的合约可以说是为这些年来发展这一条损失规则作出了很大的贡献与澄清,它们涉及无数的诉讼与先例。接下来将这两个种类的合约作出进一步的阐述并介绍有关重要的先例。

10.1 货物买卖合约的卖方违约

第一种是货物买卖,其中卖方由于市场价格上升或其它原因拒绝交货,或延误交货,或交的货物货不对版(主要是质量的争议)。这往往会导致买方面对分买方的困境,如要做出赔偿,利润的损失,或面对诉讼中对分买方提出索赔的抗辩。能不能索赔这些种类的损失在一定程度是要看违约方卖方在订约时是否知道有分买方的存在。

这里可以节录《McGregor on Damages》(18th edn,2009 年)之 6 - 204,205 段:

"Many cases have dealt with the situation of a seller of goods making default by non - delivery, delayed delivery, or breach of warranty, with the result that the buyer has been put in breach of a resale contract that he has made with a third party. The buyer has then claimed successfully or unsuccessfully loss of profit on the resale, sometimes in addition the compensation he had been obliged to pay his sub - buyer, and sometimes, even further, the costs he had incurred in the defense of an action brought against him for damages by the sub - buyer. Whether the claim has succeeded or not has turned upon whether the seller knew at the time of the contract that the buyer would resell. All of these cases are considered in detail when dealing with the contract of sale of goods; here it is only the general view that matters. It is significant that it is in the earlier cases that recovery is denied, and also that the second rule in Hadley v. Baxendale is squarely invoked to allow recovery less frequently as the cases progress in time. The high - water mark of recovery where there was a probability of resale without any definite knowledge on the part of the seller comes with the 1927 cases of Hall v. Pim in the House of Lords and of Patrick v. Russo - British Grain Export Co.

Fewer claims for loss of profits by user, as opposed to resale, appear in the books and those which do have generally been successful. The leading authority is Victoria Laundry v. Newman, which makes clear that such profits may be recovered under the first rule in Hadley v. Baxendale. Earlier successful claims were approved and applied."

货物买卖的损失计算经常会涉及是否有"可供买卖的市场"(available market),如果有的话,损失的表面计算办法就是根据合约价格与市场价格的差价。如果卖方违约,买方面对分买方蒙受更大的损失索赔或利润损失,是不能加在市场差价向卖方索赔。这是因为市场差价的损失计算办法已经是把损失遥远性与减少损失的考虑排除在外。但如果有关货物没有一个可供买卖的市场,不存在索赔市场差价,就要计算实际的损失。这一来针对受害买方的损失,能否加上分买方的损失索赔或利润损失(至少是合理的利润)这一项,就是要看双方订合约时能否料想到分销与转售。可以说在大部分的国际商品买卖,订约双方都应该想到有关货物会涉及分销与转售。这里可以节录 Goff 大法官在 The "Pegase" (1981) 1 Lloyd's Rep 175 先例中所说如下:"Thus, in a contract of sale, if at the time of making the contract it was sufficiently within the contemplation of the seller that the buyer would resell the goods and there was no available market to buy in substitute goods, or that the buyer would resell the goods on such terms as to exclude the possibility of buying in on the market, the damages may be assessed with reference to the resale price, provided of course that the resale price does not arise from "extravagant and unusual bargains" — See, e. g., *Patrick v. Russo - British Grain EXPORT Co.*, (1927) 18 Ll. L. Rep. 358; [1927] 2 K. B. 535, and in particular *R. and H. Hall Ltd. v. W. H. Pim (Junior) & Co. Ltd.*, (1928) 30 Ll. L. Rep. 159; (1928) 33 Com. Cas. 324 (especially at pp. 162 and 330, per Viscount Dunedin), a decision referred to with approval in the Heron II (see pp. 465 - 466 and 386 - 388, per Lord Reid)"

10.2 货物运输合约的承运人违约

第二种是货物运输合约,特别是涉及海上运输,而违约就涉及船东没有把货物运到目的地,或是延误运到目的地,或是运到的货物损坏。相比买卖合约中受害买方向卖方索赔分销或转售的合理利润通常会成功(在 Hall v. Pim [1928] 30 Lloyd's Rep 159 先例中判是只要订约时知道有可能转售就已经足够),受害方的买方向海上运输合约的承运人索赔同样的损失通常就不会成功。除了分销和转售的利润,收货人因为没有准时收到货物而带来的营运利润损失索赔也是不会成功的,这方面最主要的先例就是 Hadley v. Baxendale 与 British Columbia Saw Mill Co v. Nettleship (1868) LR 3 CP 499。虽然违约的本质看起来是一致(不交货、延误与货损),但买卖合约与运输合约有不同的对待是认为违约方的船东或承运人不比卖方,在订约时是不能够充分了解运输的有关货物的用途。所以,应该承担较低的赔偿责任。这是 Roche 大法官在 Montevideo Gas Co v. Clan Line (1921) 37 TLR 544 所说的:"a natural result of a fact that a carrier is supposed to know less about the commodity he carries and to undertake less responsibility in connection with it."

同样的说法也出现在另两个著名的先例 Victoria Laundry v. Newman Industries (1949)2 K. B. 528 与 The "Heron Ⅱ"(1967)2 Lloyd's Rep 457 中,在 Victoria Laundry 先例,Asquith 大法官是这样说:"This was not, it would seem, because a different principle applies in such cases, but because the application of the same principle leads to different results. A carrier knows less than a seller about the purposes for which the buyer or consignee needs the goods, or about other 'special circumstances' which may cause exceptional loss if due delivery is withheld."

另在 The "Heron Ⅱ"先例,Upjohn 勋爵是这样说:"... must be taken to understand the ordinary practices and exigencies of the other's trade... it must be remembered when dealing with the case of a carrier of goods by land, sea or air, he is not carrying on the same trade as the consignor of the goods and his knowledge of the practices and exigencies of the other's trade may be limited and less than between buyer and seller of goods who probably know far more about one another's business."

但 Goff 大法官在 The "Pegase"(1981)1 Lloyd's Rep 175 先例(有关这方面的案情稍后进一步介绍)中是说没有这方面的政策区分买卖合约与运输合约有关分售合约的利润损失,不同的判法纯粹是根据不同案件对不同事实的认定,说:"... find in the cases no rule of policy either excluding, or imposing special criteria in respect of, the recovery of damages for loss of profits, whether the relevant contract be a contract of sale or a contract of carriage, whether the breach be non - delivery or delayed delivery, and whether the profits claimed to have been lost are resale profits from loss of use."

10.3　对冲交易

"对冲"(hedging)是近年来商品贸易商经常会涉及的交易。在商品买卖,不论是石油、矿产、农产品等,甚至是相关的海上运输运费(这可看本书有关第十五章"市场规则之一"之 2.3.2 段所介绍的 Norden v. Andre(2003)1 Lloyd's Rep 287 先例)、外汇与利息都有活跃的期货市场可作为对冲之用。简单的说法是对冲可以让商人在一个波动十分大的市场中肯定将会进行实际买卖的预计利润。当然免不了有不少的商人或其他人士是利用这一对冲交易作为赌博或投机之用。

对冲交易也不是新鲜事物,数百年前在荷兰的郁金香交易与日本的大米交易就已经有对冲的做法。只是近年来,对冲交易变得是十分普遍。这就在损失遥远性方面带来一个疑问,就是对冲交易如果能够避免实际买卖所带来的损失,这对冲交易的好处可否被视为受害方合理减少损失所带来,需要在实际买卖的损失(按照市场规则)中减去?又或是,对冲交易如果加大了实际买卖的损失,这是否可以一并向违约方索赔?这到底是属于 Hadley v. Baxendale(1854)9 Ex. 341 的第一类或是第二类的损失类别?要知道,对冲交易即使是针对实际买卖,也不一定能够起到完全对冲的作用。一种风险是对冲交易的对象是否可靠,如在 2008 年底对上了雷曼兄弟的话就会要倒霉。另一种风险是对冲市场毕竟与实际市场还是有所不同,对冲市场只是反映了大部分在进行交易的人士对将来市场走势的预测或猜测。

对冲交易对实际损失的计算在近年来已经有不少先例与仲裁案件有针对,以下可做部分介绍,然后总结一下英国与其他普通法国家的法律目前在有关损失遥远性方面的地位。

10.3.1 案例之一:Trafigura Beheer BV and another v. Mediterranean Shipping Company SA

在 Trafigura Beheer BV and another v. Mediterranean Shipping Company SA(2007) EWCA Civ 794 先例,案情涉及 Trafigura 通过 MSC Amsterdam 轮把 18 个集装箱的“电解铜”(copper cathodes)从德班港运送至上海。这批货物在上海港口卸货后,由于假提单问题导致了真正的收货人 Trafigura 提取不到这批货物。之后 Trafigura 向船东提起“侵占”(conversion)的诉讼要求赔偿货物市场价值的损失,以及延迟交货所导致的对冲交易损失。法院认为船东需要负责,但对于损失赔偿的数额,法院判是以实际货物市场价值为准。但对于对冲的损失,法院认为商品交易商通常会进行对冲交易,但大多数承运人都不会太了解对冲损失。而且针对这种集装箱运输来说,承运人甚至都不关心集装箱内的货物种类,除非这种货物具有危险性,所以承运人不应该赔偿原告 Trafigura 对冲交易的损失。从以上的分析也可以看出,这个判法只能适用在集装箱运输中,而对于其他的运输可能就不会适用。

10.3.2 案例之二:Addax Ltd v. Arcadia Petroleum Ltd and Another

在 Addax Ltd v. Arcadia Petroleum Ltd and Another(2000)1 Lloyd's Rep 493 先例中,案情涉及一票高达 79 万桶的原油 FOB 买卖合约,约定买方(Arcadia)必须在 1998 年 5 月 22 ~ 23 日期间派船到装港装货,但买方违约,指派的船舶直到 5 月 30 日才到达装港。这里要一提的是卖方(Addax)的原油供应商是尼日利亚石油公司,他们之间的买卖合约价格是给了 Addax 一个选择,要么按照提单日期后的 5 天市场价格(根据实际市场 Brent crude oil ex Sullom Voe 的价格核算得出的数字),再加上 0.1 美元一桶的溢价。或是 Addax 可以选择推迟,以提单日期 14 天后的 5 天市场价格核算。而本案件 Addax 与 Arcadia 之间的买卖合约原油价格是按照前者的核算办法。这表示 Addax 在他与尼日利亚石油公司的买卖合约如果选择前者的核算办法,在货价方面就会是两份合约“背靠背”,Addax 不会蒙受损失。但 Addax 在与 Arcadia 签订了买卖合约后,他们预测市场价格会进一步下跌,所以原油价格越迟作出核算就对他们越有利。结果在签订合约后的一两个星期行使了选择权,以后一种核算办法与尼日利亚石油公司结算货价。这一来,对 Addax 而言,前后的两份买卖合约在原油价格方面再也不是“背靠背”。但这在一个激烈波动的市场是有危险,就是如果原油市场并非是进一步下跌而是猛烈上涨,Addax 就会蒙受损失,因为他要支付一笔更高的市场价格给尼日利亚石油公司。针对这一方面的风险,Addax 去市场购买了一种名为“contract for difference"(简称 CFD)的对冲产品。

由于 Arcadia 的违约,Addax 向 Arcadia 提出的索赔金额是 363,074.80 美元,这是如果 Arcadia 准时派船 Addax 可以赚取的利润。但由于这一个延误,Addax 针对实际延误日期要另购买 CFD 的对冲产品,这带来 453,476.05 美元的损失。这两笔金钱共计 816,550.85 美元。

Arcadia 拒绝赔偿对冲交易的损失,认为在法律上太遥远。这包括了因果关系方面,认为损失是来自 Addax 选择不以"背靠背"与尼日利亚石油公司结算原油价格。另是这种损失是属于 Hadley v. Baxendale(1854)9 Ex. 341 中的第二类损失,而他们之间的有关合约是有条文排除了间接损失的赔偿责任。但英国法院不同意,认为对于 Addax 与 Arcadia 这种有经验的石油贸易商,对冲交易十分正常并且是大家可以料想到的合理减少损失的做法。这种对冲交易是不需要在订约前向对方作出通知,所以 Addax 可以全数向 Arcadia 索赔。Morison 大法官是这样说:"The cost of hedging devices are an integral part of the calculation of the net position, and if the net position is a directly relevant loss, so must the hedging costs be so regarded. To extract the costs of the hedging devices is wrong in principle and has no commercial merit... It was I think wholly foreseeable that if the claimants took a position which was otherwise than back - to - back with their contract with the defendants, they could cover their position with one of a multitude of hedging transactions available. While the contract instrument used may well vary from trade to trade (or possibly trader to trader), the defendants must have foreseen the need for the claimants to get cover."

10.3.3 案例之三:Choil Trading v. Sahara Energy Resources Ltd

在 Choil Trading v. Sahara Energy Resources Ltd(2010)EWHC 374(Comm)先例,案情涉及 Choil(买方)以 FOB 价格向 Sahara(卖方)购买 30000 吨"挥发油"(naphtha),并约定在尼日利亚的哈克特港装货。但这批货物的质量出现严重问题,货物中掺杂了过量的 MTBE(Methyl Tertiair Buthyl Ether)人造杂质。Choil 本来将这批货物转售给葡萄牙分买方,但由于其中包含 MTBE 杂质而导致葡萄牙分买方拒绝接受。这迫使 Choil 另寻找替代分买方,并在两个月后因为挥发油的市场上涨,成功以更高的价格卖给了一家名为 Blue Ocean 的分买方。这一来,在实质的交易看来,Choil 并没有因为 Sahara 的违约(货物有杂质)而蒙受损失,但 Choil 蒙受了针这一个买卖而达成的对冲交易的损失,金额是 2,285,428.15 美元,并要求 Sahara 赔偿他这一笔损失。在该买卖合约中,有第 13 条文排除了对特别损失作为赔偿,说:"Neither party shall be liable for any consequential, indirect or special losses or special damages of any kind arising out of or in any way connected with the performance of or failure to perform the agreement."

这一来,要不要赔偿这一笔对冲交易的损失主要就是看它是否属于 Hadley v. Baxendale 的第二类损失。而法院认为是对冲交易的损失不属于间接或特别损失,所以不会被合约中的间接损失免责条款排除。换言之,法院判是对冲交易的损失是属于 Hadley v. Baxendale 的第一类损失。这可以节录 Christopher Clarke 大法官的判决如下：

"Trading companies such as Choil habitually hedge in order not to be caught with open positions in a volatile market. Choil was required to do so by its trade finance bank. When Petrogal(Choil 的葡萄牙分买方)rejected the naphtha as a result of MTBE contamination Choil was left with a long open position on naphtha. The evidence of Ms Driay(Sahara 的证人)Sahara was well aware of the likelihood of Choil hedging, and the reasonableness of its doing so. It would have done the same.

In my judgment Choil is*prima facie* entitled to recover \$ 2,285,428.15 as representing losses attributable to a reasonable attempt at mitigation. There is, in principle 'no sensible or commercial reason why the court should not take into account the cost of the hedging instruments' Addax Ltd v. Arcadia Petroleum(2000)1 Lloyd's Rep 496. In that case Morison J would, if he had been concerned with the claimant's position with their suppliers, have taken into account the hedging costs. In the present case the effect of Choil being left long in Naphtha was to expose it to the risk of severe losses if the market dropped. It was reasonable for it to protect itself against those losses if the market dropped. It was reasonable for it to protect itself against those losses by hedging in the way it did.

I do not regard the damages so far discussed as consequential, indirect or special. Such a limitation coversdamages within the second limb of Hadley v. Baxendale. The damages in issue constitute the difference between the sound arrived and damaged values of the goods as well as the estimated loss directly and naturally resulting, in the ordinary course of events, from the breach of warranty together with the reasonable cost of mitigation. In Addax Morrison J held that a limitation of consequential damages would not apply to hedging costs which were part and parcel of the claimant's positions with its suppliers(if that had been the relevant inquiry). It seems to me that a similar result should apply here where the hedging in question was part and parcel of the claimant's dealings in respect of the cargo unexpectedly left on its hands. Further in the trade in which both parties operated hedging was an every day occurrence. Anyone in Choil's position would have been expected to hedge, as Ms Driay made clear. (Her only criticism was that Choil had not hedged early enough). It did not require any special knowledge to realize that hedging was what Choil was likely to do. It was regarded as a normal and necessary part of the trade."

10.3.4 案例之四：Glencore Energy UK Ltd v. Transworld Oil Ltd

在 Glencore Energy UK Ltd v. Transworld Oil Ltd(2010)EWHC 141 先例，案情涉及一个 FOB 买卖，货物是尼日利亚原油，其中 Transworld 是卖方，Glencore 是买方。Glencore 在订约后开始出售这批原油并通过出售未来的原油来对冲他的投资。合约约定这批原油需要在一个中转油库装货，这个中转油库包含了浮动采油与储存设备，以及卸载设备。在 Glencore 派遣的油轮等待泊位装货时，本来打算帮助这艘油轮靠泊的拖船上一名船员被绑架，尽管这个绑架事件很快被解决，但拖船的船东基于安全的考虑，拒绝继续在这片海域为该油轮工作，导致油轮不能靠泊装货而最终离开。合约双方曾经尝试用其他方式来交付这批货物，但都不成功。最终法院判是 Transworld 没有交付货物的行为构成了违约，Glencore 有权获得按照“市场规则”(market rule)计算的损失赔偿共计 11,112,626 美元。但 Glencore 进行对冲交易来减少损失，并成功让 Glencore 的实际损失减少到了 8,665,496 美元。双方的争议就是哪一笔金额才是 Glencore 真正能够索赔的损失。Glencore 抗辩认为对冲交易是一笔单独的交易，发生在 Transworld 的违约之前，不属于合理减少损失的行为。Glencore 也曾经抗辩说对冲交易中所得到的好处类似保险赔偿，不应该让违约方从中得利。所以，Transworld 不能够因为 Glencore 在对冲交易中得到好处而获益。但法院认为 Glencore 的对冲交易是他与 Transworld 买卖合约交易的一部分，在计算损失时也应该被考虑在内。这可以节录 Blair 大法官的判决如下：“So far as the law is concerned, in the context of contracts for the sale of oil, it has been said that: ‘If a seller repudiates a contract before the time for performance arrives the buyer on existing authority is entitled to accept that anticipatory repudiation, treat the contract as at an end and claim damages. The basic measure of damages is such sum as will put the buyer in the same position as if the seller had duly performed the contract. The *prima facie* measure is, therefore, the difference between the contract price and the market price at the time of contractual performance. The seller is, however, only liable for such part of the buyer's loss as is properly to be regarded as caused by the seller's breach. If the buyer fails to take reasonable steps to mitigate his loss consequent on the seller's breach, he is debarred from claiming any part of the damage which is due to his neglect to take such steps. The seller's breach is not causative of that additional loss and therefore not recoverable.' Applying that approach, it is, in my view, plain on the evidence in this case that, having accepted Transworld's breach as bringing the contract to an end, Glencore not only did but was required to mitigate its loss by closing out its hedges. To have allowed them to run on would have been to speculate in the movement of the price of oil, which Glencore has asserted is no part of its business for present purposes. By doing so, in the words of its expert, it established its loss. I agree with Transworld that the position as regards the hedges is not *res inter alios acta*, nor is it equivalent to insurance. Hedging is on the evidence an integral part of the business by which Glencore entered into this contract for the purchase of oil, and since closing out on early termination established a lower loss than would otherwise have been incurred, that has to be taken into account when determining recoverable loss. To put it another way, if the seller had duly performed the contract Glencore would have closed out its hedges at the then current prices, and there is no reason to put it in a better position in the case of non-performance.”

10.3.5 案例之五:Prestige Marine Services Pte Ltd v. Marubeni International Petroleum(S)Pte Ltd

在 Prestige Marine Services Pte Ltd v. Marubeni International Petroleum(S)Pte Ltd (2011)SGHC 270 的新加坡先例,案情涉及 12 万吨的燃油买卖与运输合约,负责运输的买方没有运输这批货物而构成违约,新加坡高院判是买方需要赔偿卖方 1900 万美元的损失。其中的一个争议就是卖方因为进行对冲交易而获得的好处是否应该在损失赔偿中扣减。买方认为卖方进行对冲交易而获得的这一笔巨大好处应该在损失中扣减,但仲裁庭裁决认为这一笔对冲交易的利润与违约没有必然联系,而是卖方自己采取的投机性交易,所以不应该在损失中扣减,这也被新加坡高院支持,虽然这是与上述介绍的英国先例如 Glencore Energy UK Ltd v. Transworld Oil Ltd(2010)EWHC 141 不一样。这可以节录法院的判决如下:"A seller who wishes to speculate on the price of goods, as Marubeni(卖方)did in its paper transactions, is not in a position to foist his speculation losses onto the buyer. The arbitrator rightly noted that Marubeni alone bore the risk of the paper transactions. Had it made a huge loss ... it could not have held Prestige(买方)responsible for the loss. Similarly, Marubeni need not account to Prestige for any profit made in the paper transactions."

10.3.6 仲裁案件之一:Seaemblem Marine Ltd v. Jahre Services A/S v. Arochem International Inc., M/T Boni

在 Seaemblem Marine Ltd v. Jahre Services A/S v. Arochem International Inc., M/T Boni, SMA 3052(March 7,1994)的纽约仲裁案件中,涉及一个租约的争议。有关的船舶 Boni 轮在马来西亚与印尼装了两票原油去波多黎各卸货,但开航后不久,机房发生火灾。火灾最后被救援人员扑灭并被拖带去避难港口,但由于船舶严重损坏,再无法继续航行。这导致了船上的部分原油被卖给第三人,而其余的原油被另一艘船舶转运去目的地港波多黎各。

在该纽约仲裁,责任方面判是船东要对火灾负责,是船东自己的过错导致该船舶开航的时候就严重不适航。至于在损失计算方面,受害的承租人总共的索赔是 9133,192 美元,包括救助费用与对冲损失等。这对冲损失是包括了部分原油在新加坡被卖给第三人赚了一点,但其余的原油因为延误运去目的地港而蒙受巨大损失,而最后的净对冲损失是 2,315,418 美元。针对这一笔损失,仲裁庭是这样说:

"We now address Arochem's(承租人)claim. The general rule for an award of damages in a breach of contract action is to assess against the party in breach all damages resulting from the breach which could have reasonably been contemplated by the parties at the time the contract was executed. Hadley v. Baxendale, 9 Exch, 341, 156 Eng. Rep. 145 (1854) Damages should return the innocent party to the position it would have occupied had the contract not been breached, subject to the foreseeability standard referred to above. (这是提到损失赔偿的复原大原则,除非有关损失是不能预见)

It is generally recognized that the hedging of petroleum products and other commodities is a desirable and essential method of minimizing price fluctuations and exposure to loss. All of the experts before this panel testified on this point and there was no disagreement. Indeed, one may logically conclude that it is foolhardy and speculative not to do so. Seaemblem(船东) and Jahre knew Arochem operated a refinery in Puerto Rico and that it was also a sometime trader in the spot markets. Jahre's principal business is in the tanker lighterage trade and as such has close contract with a variety of petroleum operating companies. Seaemblem operates tankers and is presumed to have some understanding of the basic elements of the petroleum trade. After all, the very political and economic pressures impacting oil prices also affect tanker rates. We accept in this day and age that most companies are aware of the need and advantage of hedging products to assure price stability and a low risk profile.(所有专家证人都承认在石油产品以及其他商品买卖,以对冲交易减少价格的波动并且不会转盈为亏是十分重要与合理的做法,这是违约的船东应该知道)

The principal question we must now address is whether the transactions which form the basis of Arochem's equity loss claim are hedging losses on the Boni transaction or speculative position taking. Jahre's expert witness explained hedging in its simplest form:(在本案件主要要考虑的问题是承租人的对冲交易损失到底是否是来自 Boni 轮的买卖或是投机性的对冲) A hedge is placed by either party going long or short on the American Mercantile at a fixed month or fixed commodity at a fixed price by either buying in or selling out a relevant number of contracts to your open position in the wet oil, therefore performing the hedge. If you are long, for example, a cargo of 250,000 barrels of gasoline, then you go short, a relevant number of wet contracts per thousand barrel contracts on the New York Mercantile on the month you anticipated that cargo be delivered or the month you take a position so you lock in your prices.

We have carefully reviewed the alleged hedging transactions and conclude they are not in accord with Arochem's own stated procedure, nor are they placed in accordance with accepted industry standards. Hedges are never an absolute protection against the risks of market fluctuations, but if placed properly, and in a manner similar to the procedure which Arochem's witness described, they offer a large measure of price protection. They were not so placed here."(仲裁庭在考虑了有关这一个对冲交易的证据后,认为这一个对冲交易并非是按照承租人自己所说的做法或市场针对某一个特定买卖的做法,所以与 Boni 轮的买卖合约没有直接因果关系)

仲裁裁决的结果显然是承租人的对冲交易损失不被仲裁庭所接受,因为与船东的违约没有直接因果关系。

10.3.7　仲裁案件之二:Astra Energy Canada, Inc. v. Glencore Ltd.

在 Astra Energy Canada, Inc. v. Glencore Ltd, SMA 4109(December 2010)的纽约仲

裁案件中,案情涉及两票关于"普通出口质量"(normal export quality)的"埃德蒙顿混合低硫原油"(Edmonton mixed sweet crude oil 或简称 MSW)的 FOB 买卖。卖方为 Astra,买方为 Glencore,装运港是在加拿大的温哥华。Glencore 拒绝接受这批原油,声称原油被过量的"硫化氢"(hydrogen sulfide,简称 H_2S)污染。案件的争议是合约中要求的"普通出口质量"到底是什么标准,以及这批货物是否符合这个质量要求。

第一票原油被装上 Alpine Penelope 轮后由于硫化氢问题被 Glencore 拒绝接受,但该批原油在温哥华港口因为没有空的油柜而不能被卸下。所以 Glencore 被迫把船开往长岛,转载另一艘船后运往美湾,并最终以高出他的使费的价格出售,但这个价格低于他原本的转售价格。因此 Glencore 的索赔包括转售的利润损失、不同的花费以及一笔巨大的对冲交易损失。

第二票原油被 Glencore 拒绝接受后,Astra 将这批原油装上了 FR8 Pride 轮,然后转售给 ExxonMobil,转售的价格高于他出售给 Glencore 的价格。Astra 在对冲交易中的损失超过了400 万美元。在该买卖合约中,有第 17.2 条文排除了对间接损失的赔偿,说:"In no event shall either party be liable for loss of profits or special, indirect, exemplary or punitive, or consequential damages . . ."

Astra 认为 Glencore 在对冲交易中遭受的损失属于间接损失不应该获得赔偿,仲裁庭接受了这个观点。

但本案的有趣之处就是,Glencore 的对冲交易并非专门针对这笔买卖,而是针对公司的整体交易,他的证人证言也证实了这一点。在这一仲裁案件,由于在责任方面是判 Glencore 违反合约,所以不需要针对 Glencore 的损失问题。但看来,如果 Glencore 胜诉并可以索赔损失,他的对冲损失因为与违约没有直接的因果关系,估计也不会获得赔偿。但胜诉的 Astra 的对冲交易是专门针对这笔买卖,照理是可以获得赔偿。可是这被仲裁庭认为对冲损失只能是间接损失,所以可被合约中的 17.2 条文排除索赔。可以说,这一裁决是与一些较早所介绍的英国先例如 Addax Ltd v. Arcadia Petroleum Ltd and Another(2000)1 Lloyd's Rep 493; Glencore Energy UK Ltd v. Transworld Oil Ltd(2010) EWHC 141; Choil Trading v. Sahara Energy Resources Ltd(2010) EWHC 374(Comm)等案例的判法并不一致,在这些先例中,对冲交易损失被视为是双方订约时可以预见的 Hadley v. Baxendale(1854)9 Ex. 341 中的第一类损失,即属于一般损失。

10.3.8 对冲交易损失目前法律地位的结论

针对英国法律,可简单节录 Andrew Baker 御用大律师在《LMAA Law Review 2010 - 2012》中所说如下:"English law is still developing its thoughts on what to do with hedging transactions, actual or available, in damages assessments"(英国法关于在损失计算中如何对待对冲交易的法律地位还在发展)。估计这一个说法也包括了上述提到的先例都属于第一审的高等法院,还没有更高的法院对这方面作出一个定论。在同一文章中,Andrew Baker 御用大律师对目前的英国法律作出了以下结论说:"But then the effective availability,via hedging,of a fixed rate for the repudiated period,would seem to be relevant only if the owners actually hedge,as part of their mitigation effort,or there is a finding that no owner could reasonably fail to do so. "(对冲交易损失只会与损失计算有关,如果受害方的船东进行对冲作为他合理减少损失的行为,或者是在一种情况被仲裁庭认定每一个合理的船东作为受害方都会这样做)

针对美国法律(在商法方面,美国的最高院已经明确说明是完全依从英国商法,除非是涉及美国的公共政策。在较近期的 Senator Linie GMBH & Co KG v. Sunway Line,Inc. ,291 F 3d 145,170[2d Cir. 2002]先例说:"in matters of commercial law our decisions should conform to English decisions,in the absence of some rule of public policy which would forbid"),也可以节录 Jack Berg 先生作为著名的纽约海事仲裁员在 2012 年温哥华举行的国际海事仲裁员大会中所发表的说法,如下:

"Are hedging losses too remote? That depends in a large part on the nature and practice of the trade. The test is whether the loss being claimed is one that arises naturally and in the ordinary course of events and was within the reasonable contemplation of the parties when the contract was made. Commodity traders customarily hedge their physical commitments,therefore it would be difficult for others in the field or in related industries to argue that claims for hedge losses are too remote.(Jack Berg 先生认为对冲损失是否太遥远是看某一个行业的习惯做法,而测试的标准还是根据双方订约时能否合理预料到会有这种对冲的行为。商品贸易商习惯性会对他们的实质买卖做出对冲,则表示对一些抗辩指商品贸易商的对冲损失属于太遥远不容易被接受)

A court or arbitration panel,when considering a claim for hedging losses,will look to the nature of the trade and the parties experience in that trade,whether it is for hedges of petroleum products,metals,currency,freight,etc. A question that often arises is whether the alleged hedge is in reality a hedge or a speculative position in the market. A party seeking recovery for a hedge loss must establish that the hedge position in question is related to the specific cargo in question and not part of an overall hedging position.

There must be a causal link between a breach of the contract and a particular loss under the hedge. Proving the causal connection between a hedge loss and a breach related to the physical position will be difficult if the hedge cannot be clearly identified as relating to the physical contract.

Claims for hedging losses under sales contract will generally not failbecause they are too remote. Hedging losses being claimed against shipowners are not nearly as certain. Shipowners generally argue that hedging losses alleged by charterers are too remote and the objection that they raise is that they are not conversant with commodity trading and therefore do not possess the level of knowledge and experience to intelligently address the issue. The court in Addax Ltd v. Arcadia Petroleum Ltd and Another(2000)1 Lloyd's Rep 493 addressed this argument, nothing that although a shipowner may not know the different hedging instruments employed by the different trades, it should understand in a general sense that commodity traders utilize hedging transactions to protect themselves against market fluctuations."

在这里也可以简单谈谈在诉讼中会面对的问题，这就是索赔的原告如果在对冲交易中成功减少了部分损失，他很可能不会向被告披露这一个事实，而根据市场规则索赔"实际损失"(physical loss)，但隐瞒了"纸面利润"(paper gain)，而后者是可以减少原告的实际损失。例如在本章10.3.4段介绍的Glencore Energy UK Ltd v. Transworld Oil Ltd(2010)EWHC 141先例中，原告Glencore的对冲交易导致他的损失从11,112,626美元减少到了8,665,496美元，但估计Glencore不会主动向Transworld披露这一个事实，而是Transworld通过诉讼中的"文件披露"(discovery of documents)、"质询"(interlocutories)以及第三人的渠道(如对冲交易市场的了解)发掘出来。

在商业实践中，国际贸易商通常会对一个实际的商品交易作出对冲交易。如果在对冲交易中亏损，当事人就往往会在诉讼或仲裁中加入这笔损失的索赔，来把这笔损失转嫁到违约的被告身上。但如果对冲交易的好处可以成功隐瞒，就会对被告十分不公道。所以被告对这一方面的新发展千万不要掉以轻心，如果对方隐瞒了盈利的对冲交易，就可以请求法院或仲裁庭做出命令让对方当事人披露有关该笔对冲交易的文件(order discovery)。

11. 货损货差与其他方面的损失遥远性争议案例介绍

针对海上货物运输，如果运到的货物损坏，还会有其他各种各样的损失遥远性的争议。首先介绍一种情况是在Aikens大法官的《Bills of Lading》(2006年)一书之13.14段，这是有关货物损坏导致了货物价格的贬值。这表面看起来是违约的船东应该可以预见得到的损失，但特别是在某一些货物的运输，如化学品，很小的污染就会造成极大的损失或严重的价格贬值。也会是有关的货物对货方而言有特别的用途或价值，是承运人不知道的。这些情况都会导致损失遥远性的争议，虽然还没有见过有关的成功抗辩案例。以下可节录该段节："'Remoteness' arguments rarely avail a carrier in the context of claims concerning the diminution in the value of damaged cargo. However, in the chemical carriage trade in particular, very slight contamination of cargo (which may only be in the order of a few parts per million or less) caused by residues of previous cargo or from a tank coating, may contaminate the cargo in the sense of effecting a physical change which renders the cargo less valuable to the claimant. Sometimes the cargo is reduced in value because the claimant had intended a particular use for it, or because the contamination means that the cargo is in breach of a certain specification in a sale contract.

In either case it is reasonable for the carrier to be aware of the position. In such circumstances the carrier ought in principle to be able to argue that it could not be contemplated or foreseen that the presence of minute quantities of ‘contaminant’ would result in the loss alleged by the claimant. There are, however, no reported cases in which this argument has succeeded, no doubt because in general terms a carrier is to be taken to have the requisite knowledge of the cargo being carried and because seaworthiness and cargo care obligations are assessed by reference to the cargo in question and not in the abstract.”

11.1　轻微货损导致在卸港延误的 The “Forum Craftsman”

现在还经常会有另一种情况，就是在部分港口卸货，即使是发生很小的货损，都会导致非常严重的延误，这特别是在一些中东国家。例如在 The “Forum Craftsman”(1991)1 Lloyd's Rep 81 先例，船舶去伊朗的 Bandar Abbas 港卸糖。开始卸的时候发觉有几袋食糖受潮，但应该不会影响货物本身。可是不久后船卸货被港口当局终止并命令转移去锚地等候。反正最后导致了船舶在 Bandar Abbas 延误长达 79 天。在伦敦仲裁庭认为船东在订约时应该可以合理预见或料想到发生这种货损的违约(因为是不适航所导致的)，就会导致延误卸货大概一个星期，但不会是这么久。所以在船东向承租人索赔滞期费时扣减了大约一个星期的时间，但其余的滞期费就要支付。在高院，针对这方面的争议主要就是损失(延误)的遥远性问题。Hobhouse 支持仲裁庭的决定，说：

“The arbitrators in the present matter were clearly of the opinion on the evidence before them that the extreme delay which occurred arose from matters which were outside the contemplation of the contracting parties as possible consequence of a breach of contract on the part of owners such as owners' breach of cl. 42(不适航导致货损) in this case.

In arriving at the conclusion that, at the most, charterers could recover about a week of delay as a result of the breach by the owners of their obligation to make the ship seaworthy at the commencement of the voyage and in particular not to cause damage to the cargo through leaking hatch covers, the arbitrators have not made any error of law and this ground of criticism of the arbitrators' award and reasons fails.”

这种案件还真不少，近期报道的有另一个伦敦仲裁案件(2010) LMLN 809，案情涉及少量的散粮受到水损，但在卸货港导致严重的延误。仲裁庭说：“As to remoteness, Toulson LJ had recently reviewed the leading cases in Supershield v. Siemens(2010) 1 Lloyd's Rep 349. In the present case the purpose of the charter in so far as it concerned the relevant voyage was to load, transport and discharge the grain in question. No reasonable businessman could have contemplated that there was a serious possibility or a real danger that the ingress of so small an amount of seawater resulting in 0.1% damage to the cargo (and largely concentrated in one out of seven holds) would be likely to result in the extreme reaction of the authorities prohibiting discharge of the entire cargo, as opposed to the usual segregation procedure. The charterers would not have had the delay in contemplation as the sort of loss ' arising in the usual course of things'. Accordingly, the loss claimed was too remote."

11.2　船舶延误但收货人紧急需要有关货物的 The "Pegase"

再介绍一些有关先例,首先就是已经多次提到(如在本书第二章之 14.2.2 段)的 The "Pegase"(1981)1 Lloyd's Rep 175。案情是涉及 3100 吨的"铬砂"(chromite sand)从非洲运去意大利,原告是该批货物的 FOB 买方,并且在付运前几个月就已经把有关的货物分售给了意大利的几个不同分买方。虽然这是 FOB 买卖,但卖方同意代买方租船。在租船期间,卖方告诉了船东谁是收货人,但除了名字外没有提供给船东进一步的资料以及他的业务。但在货物付运的航次中,船舶不合理绕航导致了长达 65 天的延误。这显然是违约,责任方方面应该明确,但在损失计算方面就有了很大的争议。对受害方的收货人,由于货物的延误他提出的索赔包括三项损失:(1)在整段延误期间分售利润的损失;(2)由于货物立刻要提供给分买方,导致了收货人需要向竞争对手以高价买入 206 吨替代货物的损失;(3)商业信誉的损失。船东作为被告所提出的抗辩就是在订约时他是不会料想到延误会导致分售利润的损失以及收货人没有足够的存货在货物会发生延误时有供应给分买方。显然,这就导致了损失遥远性的争议。在高院,曾经提到过另一个先例 Gee v. The Lancashire and Yorkshire Railway Co.,(1860)6 H & N 211,涉及承运人的火车公司不知道货物(棉花)是原告紧急需要(原告的厂房是一个新的工厂,没有任何棉花的存货),所以承运人违约延误了 4 天,但不必对原告的利润损失与额外费用负责赔偿。而针对本先例,Goff 大法官根据仲裁员所认定的事实就是收货人没有足够存货是船东订约时没有料想到的,不知道收货人紧急要这票货满足分买方,认为船东不应该对收货人的利润损失负责。但 Goff 大法官也认为船舶不合理绕航导致 65 天延误,这么长的时间是应该可以料想到受害方的收货人会有一些合理利润损失。至于是什么利润损失就要仲裁庭进一步认定一些事实,特别要考虑到两个方面。第一个方面就是这利润损失不能够是过于庞大与不正常的损失。第二个方面是在正常情况下,收货人应该有正常的存货提供给分买方,并且维持一段时间,但之后还是会有一些合理利润的损失。Goff 大法官是这样说:"there is no finding that the owners had any knowledge of the extent of the receiver's storage space, or of the extent of their stocks. On these findings, it is difficult to see how a Court or an arbitrator could conclude that it was sufficiently within the contemplation of the owners that the receivers would have an immediate need of these particular goods for resale, to justify a conclusion that the owners were responsible for loss of profits which might have been earned on sales of goods covering the whole period of delay. No doubt the owners could, on their knowledge at the time of making the contract, reasonably have contemplated as not unlikely that (in the event of there being no available market for buying in substitute goods except after a considerable delay) the receivers would, after a delay so great as in the present case, lose some resale profits ...

But before assessing the damages onthe basis of the resale profits actually lost by the receivers, the arbitrator ought, in my judgment, to have considered two questions in particular. First, since the actual resale contracts were not known to the owners, he should have considered whether the actual profits lost by the receivers were out of the ordinary; clearly, they should not be entitled to recover profits for 'extravagant or unusual bargains', but only at a reasonable level.

Second, and more important, the arbitrator should have taken into account the fact that the owners had no knowledge of the limited storage space available to the receivers or of their having run down their stocks, and had no knowledge that the receivers had an immediately need of these goods for processing and resale. That being so, it was necessary for the arbitrator to make some allowance for a period during which stocks might have been used for the purpose of meeting commitments, in order to assess the loss of resale profits only by reference to the periodduring which, on the knowledge available to them, the owners ought reasonably to have contemplated that it was not unlikely that the receivers would lose resale profit for want of these goods. Such an exercise may well be a difficult one, and may call for a somewhat arbitrary conclusion ..."

至于第三项的损失,也就是商业信誉的损失,也是因为损失的遥远性,是船东订立租约的时候没有料想得到,而被 Goff 大法官所拒绝,说"Indeed, without any knowledge of the receivers' business or of the circumstances in which they traded, any loss of goodwill must have been so speculative that it is difficult to see how it could be concluded that this head of claim was not too remote."

11.3 货损造成分买方损失的 The "Ocean Dynamic"

在 The "Ocean Dynamic" (1982) 2 Lloyd's Rep 88,案情涉及原告收货人向一家美国公司买了 50 吨的樱桃,并且转手把该批货物转售给了一家英国公司名为 Samor。Samor 是一家专门生产果酱的公司,而这批樱桃就是为了这个用途。该批樱桃通过海上与公路的付运,最后抵达了 Samor 的工厂,并很快开始生产果酱。但在生产的过程中,被发现了有玻璃碎片,其中还有碎片显示是一种著名的威士忌(Johnnie Walker)的酒瓶碎片。这导致了大灾难,需要马上停止生产,并且把已经生产的果酱销毁,而没有用过的樱桃就被退货。之后,Samor 提出向原告的诉讼,索赔有关的损失,而原告最后是与 Samor 达成庭外和解。原告在做出的是什么原因造成这些玻璃碎片混杂在樱桃中的调查,认定最大可能是发生在船舶上,其中是该班轮在同一航次同一船舱中装了这种威士忌酒。估计会是装卸工人在装货的时候偷酒喝并把空酒瓶乱摔导致玻璃碎片进入到樱桃中。反正这也是最后被高院同意的可能性与认同的事实,所以船东根据《海牙规则》是需要负责的。但在损失方面,其中针对原告收货人与 Samor 达成和解并且赔付了一笔共达大约 24,000 英镑的金额,船东就提出了异议,说是船东在订合约时不能料想到有这种属于分买方的损失，也不会知道 Samor 生产的过程会造成这种损失。但这被 Goff 大法官拒绝，认为作为船东或承运人，虽然比不上买卖合约中卖方对有关货物以及它的用途的了解，但还是可以料想到冷藏樱桃是有可能会在目的地被原告收货人转售给分买方用做生产。如果这些樱桃是有玻璃碎片，在生产时被发觉就有可能会产生这种类别的损失。所以，船东是要负责赔付。Goff 大法官是这样说，"I am unable to accept this submission. Of course, I accept that in any particular case a carrier may be fixed with less knowledge of relevant facts than a seller of goods; see *The Pegase* at pp. 184 – 85, and the cases there cited. But even making every allowance for this, it must have been within the general knowledge of any reasonable person involved in the business of carriage of goods by sea that cartons of block frozen cherries were not unlikely to be the subject of processing after arrival at their destination, and that the importer was not unlikely to sell them on to a manufacturer for that purpose. These were not, after all, dessert cherries, but block frozen cherries. Common sense would have told any reasonable shipowner, had he considered the matter, that these would in all probability be used in the manufacture of some edible foodstuff, whether jam or cherry pies, or anything else within that category. That being so, any reasonable shipowner should likewise have appreciated that if fragments of broken glass were, by reason of his breach of contact, included in some of the cartons, it was not unlikely that they would be discovered in the course of the proceeding, with consequent waste of part of the consignment, of other materials used in the processing, and of labor costs. This was the type of loss claimed by Samor from the plaintiffs which the plaintiffs are now seeking to pass on the first defendants. The precise form of processing involved appears to me to be of no moment, provided that it had no unusual features. Their loss therefore falls within the type of loss which should, in my judgment, reasonably have been contemplated by the first defendants, if they had considered the matter, as not unlikely to occur as a result of the relevant breach. In fact, it makes no difference whether the processing was done by the importer himself or by a third party to whom he had sold on the goods, as in the present case. I therefore hold that the sum of 23,925 pounds is recoverable by the plaintiffs."

11.4 船舶不适航去不了装港导致割下待装香蕉损失的 The "Kriti Rex"

在 The "Kriti Rex"(1966)2 Lloyd's Rep 171 先例中（具体的案情介绍请见本章第6段），有关受害方承租人（原告）的另一项损失类别就是在第二个装港 Santo Tomas已经被割下待装的香蕉，但由于 Kriti Rex 轮无法准时到达，而承租人找不到替代船舶，最后的处置办法是通过与另一家美国的著名公司 Del Monte 的协议将该批香蕉卖到美国的 Galveston。承租人向船东索赔的损失包括他赔付的分承租人（也是货方）因此而蒙受的损失。船东的抗辩就是他不知道有关的做法，也没有料想到承租人会要对分承租人承担这一种损失的类别。

在高院，Moore - bick 大法官首先是认为损失来自分承租人是船东可以料想到，因为期租合约通常约定承租人可以分租或转租，说："When a vessel is time chartered for a period of three years for worldwide trading the owners will almost inevitably contemplate that it may be sub - chartered for some if not all of the period of the charter. Many charter forms make specific provision for sub - letting as the charter in this case does therefore, clearly within the owners' contemplation, as is the likelihood that a breach of charter on their party which renders the vessel unseaworthy will cause the charterers in turn to incur liability to the owners of cargo."

而针对在 Santo Tomas 被割下待装的香蕉最后处理掉所蒙受的损失，Moore - bick 大法官也不认为是太遥远，说："What is said to render the loss in the present case too remote is the peculiar nature of vessel's arrival and is unable to withstand prolonged delay waiting for alternative transport . . . I do not accept, therefore, simply as a matter of fact that the owners in this case were unaware of the particular nature of this trade of the consequences that might follow if the vessel were unable to load a cargo as a result of a breakdown of the kind which occurred. Moreover, if a loss measured by the replacement cost of the cargo at the destination is to be regarded as within the contemplation of a carrier by sea regardless of precisely how it comes about (as was held to be the case in Nissho v. Livanos (1941) 69 Lloyd's Rep. 125), it is difficult to see that a loss of that kind sustained by the charterer under his sub - charter can be outside the owner's contemplation."

11.5　银行泄露客户资料违反机密的 Jackson v. Royal Bank of Scotland

这 Jackson v. Royal Bank of Scotland (2005) UKHL 3 先例涉及苏格兰国家银行为客户处理一个可转让的信用证过程中把客户向泰国购买的狗粮由泰国出口商做出的发票错误交出给英国的分买方，这令分买方知道了该客户所赚取的庞大差价并在接下去的生意中撇开该客户，直接向泰国出口商购买。这是银行明显的违约，所以责任方面没有什么好争议，最后上诉到贵族院的也只是有关损失的计算。这损失计算的困难是在该客户到底损失（失去业务可赚取的利润）是多少，这在第一审判是估计 4 年业务的利润损失，但在上诉庭被减为 1 年的利润损失，最后在贵族院被重新改为是 4 年的利润损失。显然多少年业务会因为银行的违约而蒙受损失是很难准确做出估计，但这种业务关系显然是不会太长久，因为英国的分买方知道泰国的供应商，也迟早会通过其他渠道知道该客户所赚取的利润而把他撇开，也会因为市场的改变或其他的原因向该客户压价，反正是可以预料到该客户所赚取高额差价的好日子是不会太长。但怎样做出一个合理估计是涉及因果关系、订约方合理预见等多方面。针对合理预见的遥远性方面，贵族院判是这种损失是违约的银行可以合理预见，其中 Walker 勋爵说："It points on agency and breach of fiduciary duty. It was only in the penultimate paragraph of the reply that Samson（原告的客户）pleaded that the Bank knew or should have known: (a) Economy Bag（英国分买方）did not know of the plaintiffs' profit margin;(b)that upon the information being disclosed to Economy Bag the trade between the plaintiffs and Economy Bag would be liable to cease;(c)accordingly it was or ought to have been within the reasonable contemplation of the defendant(被告的银行)that by reason of the wrongful communication of the information to Economy Bag the plaintiffs would suffer the loss complained of."

贵族院推翻上诉庭的损失计算一个主要原因是不同意上诉庭以违约一天为准来决定违约的银行对损失可否合理预见,改判是以订约一天为准。Hope 勋爵是这样说:"In my opinion there are two errors in this approach to the assessment of damages. This first may appear to be the somewhat technical point, that it is the date of the making of the contract, not the date of the breach, that was identified as the relevant date in Hadley v. Baxendale. I say that it may appear to be somewhat technical because in this case the date of the making of the contract and the date of the breach were only about two months apart. There is no evidence that the facts that were relevant to what the Bank had in reasonable contemplation changed to any significant extent between Jan. 22, 1993 when the letter of credit was issued and Mar. 15, 1993 when the Bank sent Pet Products' invoice to Economy Bag. But the error was an error of principle. The choice of dates is more important than the differences, if any, in those facts. The parties have the opportunity to limit their liability in damages when they are making their contract. They have the opportunity at that stage to draw attention to any special circumstances outside the ordinary course of things which they ought to have in contemplation when entering into the contract. If no cut-off point is provided by the contract, there is no arbitrary limit that can be set to the amount of the damages once the test of remoteness according to one or other of the rules in Hadley v. Baxendale has been satisfied ..."

11.6 货损索赔代理收取固定报酬的 The "Eurasian Dream"

在 The "Eurasian Dream"(2002)2 Lloyd's Rep 692 先例,案情涉及船上的火灾损坏了汽车货物,最终导致了该船全损。保险公司后来委托了 WK Websters 作为索赔代理向船东提出索赔。该索赔代理是收取索赔金额的5%作为报酬。这笔钱后来有了争议,就是违约的船东是否要负责这一项的损失。Cresswell 大法官判这笔损失是订约时船东料想不到的损失类别,但会可以视为是诉讼费用向船东索赔。

11.7 支付给西班牙政府的税项的 Sandeman Coprimar SA v. Transitos y Transportes Integrales SL

最后要介绍的是 Sandeman Coprimar SA v. Transitos y Transportes Integrales SL (2003)QB 1270 CA,案情涉及被告(承运人)将一批原告(货方)的威士忌酒从西班牙通过公路运输至苏格兰,而原告已经向西班牙税务当局取得了"完税封"(tax seal)。货物在运输途中发生全损,但还是导致原告要向西班牙税务局支付一定金额的税项。原告向被告承运人提出索赔,这一笔钱又涉及遥远性的争议。但法院认定承运人在订约时是知道这一完税封与事后支付税项的情况,所以判承运人要负责。

12. 侵权损失遥远性的限制

12.1 侵权与违约的损失遥远性限制松紧之别

针对侵权所造成的损失,一贯以来最重视的就是侵权行为与损失之间的"因果关系"(causation),而不是损失类别是否在侵权时"合理预见"(reasonably foreseeable)。但侵权还是有合理预见的要求,只是它与违约的限制并不一样。这也可以理解,因为合约要求在订约时违约方对可以"合理料想得到"(reasonable contemplation)或"推定知情"(imputed knowledge)在将来违约的情况下会带来的"一般损失"(ordinary damage)需要负责,但对不能合理料想得到的"特别损失"(special damage)就不必负责,这是完全讲得通,因为违约方可以拒绝订约或者坚持有关合约加上限制责任或免责的条文等。但侵权就不存在有同样的情况,总不能说侵权方要承担高昂的"特别损失"类别就不侵权,并怪责受害方为什么在他没有侵权前作出特别通知。另在较早的时候也提到了是不同的行业就会带来在不同的合约有不同的推定知情,这也会带来对损失遥远性的不同限制。但侵权也是不会有这一方面的考虑,不论是侵权方或者是受害方都不会考虑他们的行业,侵权往往只是针对整体的社会保护受到侵权伤害的受害方。所以,侵权的合理预见的限制一向被视为是比违约的订约时合理料想得到的限制宽松,如在贵族院的 Henderson v. Merrett Syndicates(1995)2 AC 145;(1994)2 WLR 761 先例就有说到"the rules as to remoteness of damage... are less restricted in tort than they are in contract"。这种法律地位在许多侵权的案例中都可以显示出来,如涉及人身伤亡的所谓"egg - shell skull"或"shabby millionaire"案例。

12.2 侵权与违约在可索赔损失类别的不同之一:遥远性/预见性方面

有关违约造成损失的预见性方面在本章之前的段节已经介绍过,最重要的先例就是 Hadley v. Baxendale(1854)9 Ex. 341,不重复。但在侵权造成损失的预见性方面显然是不同,最主要的先例是 The "Wagon Mound"(1961)1 Lloyd's Rep 1,所以这就会带来到底应该采用"Hadley v. Baxendale 限制"或是"The Wagon Mound 限制"来确定损失的范围。

可以先简单节录一些有关侵权与违约在损失遥远性的区别,首先是 Michael Furmston 教授所著的《The Law of Contract》(第四版,2010 年)之 1810 页所说:"However the significant difference between the two tests is only apparent when it is asked 'How likely must the loss be to be recoverable?'. The tortuous test may permit recovery in respect of an item of loss which was foreseen (or contemplated) as a mere possibility, whereas to satisfy the contractual test the preferred formulation is that the loss must be a 'not unlikely' one. The latter statement of Scarman LJ should be interpreted as referring to this distinction."

(这里提到的 Scarman 大法官的说法是在 Parsons v. Uttley Ingham(1977)2 Lloyd's Rep. 522 先例,在本章第 7 段已经有介绍)

12.2.1 侵权造成损失的遥远性先例之一:Re Polemis

最早涉及这一方面的一个著名侵权先例 Re Polemis(1921)8 Lloyd's Rep 351,上诉庭判是"只要损失是直接来自疏忽行为,就算是不能合理预见的损失类别侵权方也必须要负责"(a defendant could be liable in negligence for unforeseeable damage so long as the damage is in fact directly traceable to the negligent act)。该先例的案情是这样:船舱内的货物包括有桶装的汽油,漏出易燃气体。承租人的工人在船舱上搬动舱盖板时不小心掉了一块进舱内,产生火花引致爆炸,最后全船毁灭。船东与承租人在仲裁中同意以侵权基础而非是以租约来决定责任,仲裁庭判是船舶的毁灭不是错误一方(疏忽的工人)可在侵权时"合理预见"(not reasonably foreseeable)的损失。一般是,掉了一块舱盖板下去只会穿个洞,这又不是油轮,不会想到内有不应存在的易燃气体并引起爆炸。但即使如此,上诉庭仍判承租人要负责所有后果,因为工人的疏忽与全船爆炸是一气呵成,没有新介入因素。而不论可否合理预见,只要是"直接后果"(direct consequence),错误方即要承担负责。

12.2.2 侵权造成损失的遥远性先例之二:The "Wagon Mound"

但 Re Polemis 被枢密院的著名先例 The "Wagon Mound"(1961)1 Lloyd's Rep 1 否定。该先例的案情涉及该船舶在澳大利亚悉尼停留时漏出大量"燃油"(fuel oil)。这是疏忽引起的侵权行为,造成的自然后果显然可见是污染。但说是燃油在海上会引起大火,这是一般人不会相信的。因为燃油即使在船上的油柜,没有漂散,用在主机也非要加热至高温约 130 度,否则根本烧不起来。燃点一只火柴抛进未加热的燃油,后果与抛进海水一样,火柴会马上熄灭。但"Wagon Mound"漏出的燃油很巧,它漂去一个船厂的码头下面,而且没有漂散。在码头上正在进行修理的一艘小船烧焊的火花掉落至水面,碰巧有一块碎布也同时掉下并被火花点燃,这燃烧的碎布把附近漂浮的燃油加热并引起大火,居然把船厂码头与码头上待修的一条小船烧毁。这应是万中无一的巧事,但根据 Re Polemis,恐怕船东难逃责任,这损失明显是漏油的直接后果。但枢密院判是错误方只要对可以合理预见的损失负责,而在该先例这种损失类别是侵权方在侵权时不能合理预见的。

这一个判法的背后大原则是 Viscount Simonds 大法官所说:"It does not seem consonant with current ideas of justice or morality that for an act of negligence, however slight or venial ... the actor should be liable for all consequences, however unforeseeable and however grave, so long as they can be said to be 'direct.' It is a principle of civil liability, subject to qualifications which have no present relevance, that a man must be considered to be responsible for the probable consequences of his act. To demand more of him is too harsh a rule, to demand less is to ignore that civilised order requires the observance of a minimum standard of behaviour."

12.2.3 侵权造成损失的遥远性在人身伤亡的先例:Bourhill v. Young

在侵权行为中不好解释的一种预见性是人身伤亡的损失赔偿。如果受害方身体特别脆弱,头盖骨像蛋壳一样一敲就碎,所谓"egg - shell skull"的情况,常会有侵权方争辩说谁会知道受害方年纪轻轻的,居然是弱不禁风,一碰就出大事情?这是不可合理预见的。再进一步说,该受害方不是受伤,而是被打了一拳后死亡,会否受伤与死亡是不同类别的后果,不光是程度上不同,而死亡是不可合理预见?

在这方面,大原则大精神是受害方身体特别脆弱,又带来意想不到的严重伤亡后果,亦算是可合理预见,侵权方需要负责。如 Wright 勋爵在 Bourhill v. Young(1943) A. C. 92 的名言:"侵权方碰到了怎么样的受害方就要承担相应后果"(If the wrong is established the wrongdoer must take the victim as he finds him)。除受害方身体脆弱外,还会有另一情况是受害方可能蒙受意想不到的重大经济损失。例如,碰死碰伤美国总统或是香港首富,侵权方会面对天文数字的索赔。或会是该首富一点不起眼,衣衫褴褛,所谓"shabby millionaire",错误方又怎能会合理预见呢?但同样,法律不接受这个抗辩,Scrutton 大法官在 The "Arpad"(1934) P. 189 有以下的话:"You negligently run down a shabby - looking man in the street, and he turns out to be a millionaire engaged in a very profitable business which the accident disables him from carrying on; or you negligently and ignorantly injure the favourite for the Derby whereby he cannot run. You have to pay damages resulting from the circumstances of which you have no notice. You have to pay the actual loss to the man or his goods at the time of the tort."

这种案件还有不少,可以介绍的就是 Smith v. Leech Brain & Co(1962)2 QB 405,案情涉及原告的丈夫在被告的公司工作,他在工作中被融化了的金属烧伤,这激发了他本身潜在的癌症,他在 3 年后死亡。这种情况在医学上是非常罕见的,但法院还是判被告要对原告负责,虽然这种后果是不可以合理预见的。另在先例 Robinson v. Post Office(1974)1 WLR 1176,案情涉及一个邮政局雇员从楼梯摔下时擦伤了腿,可是他对破伤风血清过敏,最后导致他大脑受损。法院判雇主对该员工的脑炎和腿伤都要负责。

12.2.4 侵权造成损失的遥远性在财产损坏的先例:The "Fedra"

先例 Bourhill v. Young(1943) A. C. 92 与后来的先例都涉及人身伤亡,法院可能会对受害方有一定程度上的同情。如果是涉及财产损失的侵权案件,可能判罚会不一样。但这也说不定,在近期的 The "Fedra"(2002)1 Lloyd's Rep 453,案情涉及船舶碰撞。当时船龄达 20 年以上的 Fedra 轮满载了一船的散装水泥,她与另一艘 Seafarer 1 轮碰撞,是 Fedra 轮的船头碰到 Seafarer 1 轮的右舷。这造成了 Fedra 轮的船头舱进水,但船头的"防撞舱壁"(collision bulkhead)并没有损坏,显然,后面的船舱看来也没有任何损坏或进水。但碰撞后 9 天,船舶的第三与第四舱开始进水,这发展到后来船舶被推定全损。照理由说,该进水的地点是与碰撞受到损坏的船首离得很远,超过 80 米。进水的原因是由于第四舱的一个排水箱破裂所导致,该排水箱被严重腐蚀,估计它与碰撞的关系是碰撞带来的强烈震动把已经严重腐蚀的箱子给震破了。结果在两艘船之间的诉讼,Fedra 轮的船东索赔全损,但最终没有成功。原因是高院的Aikens大法官认为 Fedra 轮的船东没有成功举证证明第四舱进水在碰撞前没有发生,而只是在碰撞后才发生(这才表示与碰撞有关系)。但虽然是没有太针对"egg - shell skull"的说法到底是否适用在这种财产损失的争议,双方也不像要提出上诉介绍的先例,但在相对简单的判决中,看来 Aikens 大法官是接受这一个说法的适用,就是表示在船舶碰撞这种经常会发生的侵权,如果一艘船舶被对方船舶轻轻地一碰就沉没或是发生严重后果,对方船舶还是要负责所有的后果。正如 Seafarer 1 轮会要负责赔偿 Fedra 轮的船头直接碰撞造成的损坏外,还有第四舱漏水(即使这是因为该船舶的老龄与情况欠佳)而造成的船舶全损。

在该先例,有关"egg - shell skull"说法的争议,Fedra 轮的船东代表律师是这样说:"The defendants riposted to this in two ways. First, by asserting that if the ingress was made the more likely as a result of the pre - existing poor state of the bottom plate, that did not prevent the ingress being caused by the negligence that led to the collision. That is because a tortfeasor must take his victim as he finds him, including pre - existing conditions such as the wasted bottom plate. The issue remains whether, assuming that state of affairs, in 'common sense' the collision caused the ingress to the No. 4 hold. Secondly, the defendants said that if the collision (as opposed to the pre - existing condition of the bottom plate) did cause the ingress, then the resulting damage must be foreseeable. That is because this type of physical damage to goods is bound to be foreseeable if caused by a collision resulting from negligent navigation."

Seafarer 1 轮的代表律师争论道:"... the so - called 'egg - shell skull' principle does not apply to property damage, but only to personal injuries. Therefore it could not be relied on by the defendants in this case."(争辩是说'egg - shell skull'的原则不适用在财产损失,只能适用在人身伤亡。)

最后 Aikens 大法官的判词是:"... I think that two conclusions necessarily follow. First no issue on 'foreseeability' can arise. Physical damage caused by the acts or omissions that resulted in the collision and ingress of water into the No. 4 hold must be foreseeable. But in law it does not matter if the precise extent of that physical damage is not foreseeable. Secondly, there would be no need to explore the interesting question of the scope of the 'egg - shell skull' principle. So I will not even attempt to grapple with that issue here."(判词是说可以有两个结论。第一个是损失的预见性,船舶碰撞之后导致第四船舱受损并进水肯定是可以预见到的。在侵权的法律也不需要深究是否预见得到损失的程度。第二个结论是因为有了第一个结论,法院再也不需要探讨有关有趣的'egg - shell skull'原则。)

所以可以总结说,"egg - shell skull"这一原则是否可以适用于财产损失,到现在还没有定论。

12.3 侵权与违约在可索赔损失类别的不同之二:非金钱间接损失

侵权与违约在损失的遥远性不同之处,其中一个重要的方面是在一些"非金钱的间接损失"(non - pecuniary consequential damages),如精神的创伤与压力、名誉损失等。这种类别的损失在侵权就通常会被接受,但违约(特别是商业合约)就往往被否定。而通常的理由就是这种损失类别并非是双方在订约时能够合理预见。有关这一方面在本书第二章之第15段有详解,就不重复。只节录《McGregor on Damages》(18th edn,2009年)之19-008段如下:"... And it is the consideration that contracting parties may contemplate liability on a narrower range than what is reasonably foreseeable that largely explains the disallowance of recovery for non - pecuniary loss in contract, contract being concerned primarily with commercial matters.... but damages for mental distress are now not available in commercial contracts as opposed to consumer contracts, and there are still denied to a claimant complaining of breach of contract damages for non - pecuniary injury to reputation. The only satisfactory rationale of the exclusion of these heads of damage, which are frequent in tort, is that they are not within the contemplation of the parties to a contract, and this rationale is now supported by the fact that the breakthrough in allowing damages for mental distress has occurred in contracts where the parties may be taken to have contemplated such damage, as the contracts have not primarily been commercial ones but ones affecting also the claimant's personal and social interest.. . All these cases illustrate where the liability in tort is wider because of the limiting doctrine in contract of the contemplation of the parties."(法律认为在合约关系[特别是商业合约]中,非金钱损失是双方订约时不能料想到的,所以不允许提出这种损失的索赔。但这种类别的损失索赔在侵权诉讼中就经常会成功。看来合约就在这一方面是比较局限,因为受到了订约双方是否能够料想得到的限制。但是现在法律开始允许一些在涉及个人与社交的合约中受害方得以成功索赔非金钱损失,理由就是这种类别的损失是在订约时双方料想得到的。)

但违约比侵权在非金钱损失赔偿方面更加局限也说不定,原因是在合约关系,受害方可以通过在订约前给违约方足够通知,令其能够在订约时就可以合理预计到如果违约要承担"特别损失"(special damage)的更严重后果。这是在侵权无法做到,因为受害方不可能有机会在侵权行为发生之前对侵权方做出足够的通知。

这方面可以节录《McGregor on Damages》(18th edn,2009年)之19-010段如下:"The contemplation of the parties may, however, work the other way and lead to the opposite and most frequently expressed view that the liability in contract is wider. This stems from the second rule in Hadley v. Baxendale(1854)9 Ex. 341 that, where special circumstances are at the making of contract communicated to the party subsequently in breach, damages may be given in respect of these special circumstances since they were within the parties' contemplation. There is no such communication beforehand to a tortfeasor, and therefore it is said that the liability in contract can be greater in this connection. . ."

12.4 侵权与违约在可索赔损失类别的不同之三:纯经济损失

首先可以解释在"疏忽的侵权"(tort of negligence),也是经常见的一种侵权,对不论是人身或是财产的"实体损失"(physical loss)同时带来的经济损失,是与另一种不涉及实际损失的"纯经济损失"(pure economic loss)有不同对待:Cattle v. Stockton Waterworks Co(1875)L. R. 10 Q. B. 453;SCM(United Kingdom)Ltd v. W. J. Whittal & Son Ltd(1970)3 All ER 245;Spartan Steel and Alloys v. Martin & Co Ltd(1973)QB 27;The "Mineral Transporter"(1985)2 Lloyd's Rep 303 等。美国也有类似的先例,Robins Dry Dock & Repair Co v. Flint(1927)275 U. S. 303。换言之,纯经济损失是不能向疏忽的侵权方索赔,或不被法律所承认,这背后原因主要是怕"大水闸"(floodgate)打开会有太多诉讼。

所以,侵权的法律只想保护主要或直接的受害方,而不是次要的受害方。否则在一个简单的车祸中,除了无可争议可以提出索赔的车祸受害方(他会同时蒙受了实体损失与经济损失),会同时跟进了一大批的次要受害方提出纯经济损失(如车祸受害方的家人、亲戚、朋友、雇主等)。有关这一个重要的课题,会在本书第八章第5段详细介绍。

但在违约的损失索赔,可以说是绝大部分都是纯经济损失,不存在有这一方面的限制,也没有怕大水闸打开的考虑与需要防止滥诉的公共政策。

12.5 侵权与违约重叠的选择

这种受害方与"错误方"(wrong - doer)同时拥有侵权与违约诉因的"同步或替代责任"(concurrent or alternative liability)的案件会有不少,主要是合约在双方约定的责任与侵权的责任(一般是不能疏忽)是一致的,如约定必须尽谨慎的义务或是履行责任不能疏忽,就会出现了重叠的问题。这种合约关系大量出现在某些类别的协议如雇用专业人士类似律师:Groom v. Crocker(1939)1 KB 194;雇用设计师:Bagot v. Stevens Scanlan & Co. Ltd.(1966)1 Q. B. 197;银行:Hedley Byrne & Co. Ltd. v. Heller & Partners Ltd. [1964] A. C. 465 等。这些专业人士一旦在履行合约时疏忽,就同时构成了违约与侵权。

英国法律在近几十年来的先例是明确承认这一个同步或替代责任的说法。其中一些著名先例中的说法可节录,首先是在 Midland Bank Trust Co. Ltd. v. Hett, Stubbs & Kemp(1979)Ch. 384 先例中,Oliver 大法官说:"There is not and never has been any rule of law that a person having alternative claims must frame his action in one or the other. If I have a contract with my dentist to extract a tooth, I am not thereby precluded from suing him in tort if he negligently shatters my jaw:Edwards v. Mallan(1908)]1 K. B. 1002 . . ."

另一个重要的近期先例 Henderson v. Merrett Syndicates(1995)2 AC 145,贵族院也有针对侵权与违约之间的重叠与不同对待的问题,Goff 勋爵同意 Oliver 大法官的观点,认为服务合约中通常存在同步或替代责任,原告有权选择对他最有利的救济,除非根据所适用的合约,当事人同意限制或排除侵权救济。这可以节录如下:"It is however my understanding that by the law in this country contracts for services do contain an implied promise to exercise reasonable care(and skill)in the performance of the relevant services;... My own belief is that,in the present context,the common law is not antipathetic to concurrent liability,and that there is no sound basis for a rule which automatically restricts the claimant to either a tortious or a contractual remedy. The result may be untidy; but,given that the tortious duty is imposed by the general law,and the contractual duty is attributable to the will of the parties,I do not find it objectionable that the claimant may be entitled to take advantage of the remedy which is most advantageous to him,subject only to ascertaining whether the tortious duty is so inconsistent with the applicable contract that,in accordance with ordinary principle,the parties must be taken to have agreed that the tortious remedy is to be limited or excluded.... an assumption of responsibility coupled with the concomitant reliance may give rise to a tortious duty of care irrespective of whether there is a contractual relationship between the parties,and in consequence,unless his contract precludes him from doing so,the plaintiff,who has available to him concurrent remedies in contract and tort,may choose that remedy which appears to him to be the most advantageous."

12.5.1 侵权与违约重叠带来的利弊

涉及这种重叠的同步责任案件,由于侵权与违约在许多方面有不同的法律地位,所以会带来很不一样的实际结果,如"诉讼时效"(time bar)的方面。虽然侵权与违约的法定时效都是6年,但由于起算的日期不一样,所以会是根据合约关系时效已经错过,但侵权方面还是有效。如果在同步责任下的侵权责任不被承认,原告可能会在毫不知情的情况下发现他的诉讼请求已经过了诉讼时效。这种可能性在针对专业人士的诉讼中尤其大,如律师或者设计师,因为他们的疏忽造成的后果很有可能在违约发生之日起6年或更短的合约诉讼时效过去后才被发现。但侵权的时效,通常是由造成损失的一天才开始起算这6年的时间,变成往往是比违约更晚的时间。另外,根据《Latent Damage Act 1986》,诉讼时效开始计算的日期可能会被推迟至原告知道疏忽所造成的后果的一天,但这只适用于侵权疏忽的案件(这在本书第十七章有详论)。其他的实际问题可能包括:(1)针对受害方也有部分疏忽的情况,违约方往往在合约关系下是不能要求双方分摊责任与损失,但在侵权关系中就可以要求(这在本书第八章有详述);(2)在本章12.3段所针对的损失遥远性问题,因为违约一般而言比侵权更局限。

但如果随便让受害方的原告可以自由选择损失遥远性较宽松的诉因提出索赔,也会带来问题。如果以侵权作为诉因,会是与双方的合约有冲突,如合约有限制责任、赔偿金额的条文或是时效条文。允许原告任意取巧显然也是有不妥之处与违反支持双方订约自由下所达成的合约尊严。针对这一方面,看来目前还没有直接的先例针对。比方说,违约时没有办法索赔某一个类别的损失(如因为属于非金钱赔偿的类别或是订约时不可预见),但原告改为是根据侵权作为诉因提出索赔。《McGregor on Damages》(18th edn,2009 年)一书在 19 - 008 段之注脚 57 是认为不应该允许原告这样做,因为原告与被告有合约的关系,损失的程度也应该受到双方能否预见/料想所约束,说:"Now that the tort of negligence has been expanded to allow recovery for pure economic loss so that in cases of professional negligence there is concurrent liability in contract and in tort, the question arises whether, where it could make a difference, the victim of the negligence may rely on the wider tortious test of reasonable foreseeability and ignore the stricter and more limiting contractual test of contemplation of the parties. It is thought that there is much to be said for not allowing him to do so. Where the claim in tort is in the context of a contractual relationship, the parties are not strangers, as most tortfeasors and tort victims are, and they should be bound by what they have brought to their contractual relationship in term of what risks have been communicated the one to the other. This question has not yet been faced by the courts but one day it will have to be."

但应该是明确是已经有先例说明了受害方不能以侵权逃避合约的明示条文作出的限制(如果有的话)。由于订约自由,所以会有各种限制例如是更短的诉讼时效或是损失赔偿不超过某一个金额。这一来,受害方是不能通过以侵权的诉因绕过这些合约的限制。这方面的英国先例有 Midland Bank Trust Co. Ltd. v. Hett, Stubbs & Kemp (1979) Ch. 384。另在之后的 Central Trust Co. v. Rafuse (1986) 31 D. L. R. (4th) 481 先例,针对律师由于疏忽对客户承担合约与侵权责任的问题,加拿大最高法院的 Le Dain 大法官对英国和加拿大相关案例进行了详尽调研,并得出了与 Midland Bank Trust Co. Ltd. v. Hett, Stubbs & Kemp 先例中 Oliver 大法官一致的结论,如下:"A concurrent or alternative liability in tort will not be admitted if its effect would be to permit the plaintiff to circumvent or escape a contractual exclusion or limitation of liability for the act or omission that would constitute the tort. Subject to this qualification, where concurrent liability in tort and contract exists the plaintiff has the right to assert the cause of action that appears to be the most advantageous to him in respect of any particular legal consequence."

但合约条文很少会针对损失的遥远性问题,所以这方面还是有它的困扰。其中 Parsons v. Uttley Ingham 先例就是一个明显的例子, Denning 勋爵把实体损失(猪的死亡)与经济损失(可以在一个案件中同时出现)以较宽松的"The Wagon Mound 限制"考虑,而不是以较紧的"Hadley v. Baxendale 限制"或"The Heron Ⅱ限制"考虑。但这带来有很多说不通的地方,在以下段节会更加详细介绍这一个困难的先例。

12.5.2 侵权与违约重叠带来困扰的先例:Parsons v. Uttley Ingham

在以上所介绍侵权与违约的不同,特别是在损失遥远性的一宽一紧,就会带来困难。这是因为受害方会同时拥有侵权与违约的诉因提出索赔,这就会导致在同一案情下，因为一宽一紧的损失遥远性而带来不同的索赔结果。这显然是不理想，正如 Scarman 大法官在 Parsons v. Uttley Ingham（1977）2 Lloyd's Rep. 522 先例所说："I agree with Lord Denning, MR, in thinking it absurd that the test for remoteness of damage should, in principle, differ according to the legal classification of the cause of action-though one must recognise that parties to a contract have the right to agree on a measure of damage which may be greater or less, than the law would offer in the absence of agreement... the law must be such that, in a factual situation where all have the same actual or imputed knowledge and the contract contains no term limiting the damages recoverable for breach, the amount of damages recoverable does not depend upon whether, as a matter of legal classification, the plaintiffs' cause of action is breach of contract or tort."

受害方可以同时拥有侵权与违约的诉因提出索赔会有许多不同情况。一种情况是"同步责任"（concurrent liability），就是在同一份合约中的错误做法涉及违约与侵权的重叠。另一种情况是如在 Parsons v. Uttley Ingham 先例中，涉及购买与安装的漏斗疏忽没有打开通风盖，受害的买方就可以选择以侵权的产品责任向生产商提出索赔，这就会导致损失遥远性以较宽的所谓"The Wagon Mound 限制"考虑。但买方也可以以违约向中间商（他从生产商订购）提出索赔，但这会导致以较紧的"Hadley v. Baxendale 限制"或"The Heron Ⅱ限制"考虑。这也是在 Parsons v. Uttley Ingham 先例中面对的棘手问题，而 Denning 勋爵是选择针对因猪瘟而死的 254 头猪的实体损失是以"The Wagon Mound 限制"考虑。Denning 勋爵是这样说："We were told that in some cases the makers of these hoppers supply them direct to the pig farmer under contract with him; but in other cases they supply them through an intermediate dealer-who buys from the manufacturer and resells to the pig farmer on the self - same terms-in which the manufacturer delivers direct to the pig farmer. In the one case the pig farmer can sue the manufacturer in contract. In the other in tort. The test of remoteness should be the same. It should be the test in tort."（Denning 勋爵是考虑到漏斗可以由生产商出售给受害的买方，双方有直接合约关系。但也有很大的可能是生产商通过中间商把漏斗出售给受害的买方，双方没有直接合约关系。受害买方在前者的情况下以违约提出索赔，但在后者的情况向生产商提出的索赔则是以侵权为基础。所以如果损失计算办法不一样，就会是很不理想。所以，针对遥远性的标准测试应该是一致。）

但 Parsons v. Uttley Ingham 先例是一个买卖合约的索赔，只不过索赔的损失碰巧是实体损失（猪的死亡）。如果是纯经济损失，就会是与侵权沾不上边了。Denning 勋爵在该先例的判决理由与上诉庭其余两位大法官也并不相同，这可以节录 Michael Furmston 教授所著的《The Law of Contract》（第四版，2010 年）之 1808 页所说："According to Lord Denning the former test was applicable where physical damage was concerned and the latter where economic loss was suffered. In Parsons the loss was physical and so Lord Denning permitted recovery under the Wagon Mound Test."

但这样的判决理由还是有很多不如意的地方,如实体损失与经济损失有时候会分不清。例如如果在该先例猪并没有因为猪瘟而死亡,只是严重消瘦导致买方的猪农在出售这批猪的时候收入大减。这一来,这一个索赔到底算是实体损失还是经济损失?又或是在侵权的经济损失也要区分纯经济损失或是人身、财产的实体损失同时带来的经济损失,在后者的情况下是侵权可以同时索赔的损失类别。这一来会否是只要这批猪有一只死亡,买方就可以同时成功索赔所有经济损失?

至于在该先例的其他两位上诉庭大法官,他们的判决理由是猪的死亡是属于订约时可以料想得到的损失类别,这一来就不理会最后造成损失的程度是否严重,都可以一概索赔成功。这方面可节录 Michael Furmston 教授所著的《The Law of Contract》(第四版,2010 年)之 1809 页的总结如下:"The majority of the Court of Appeal permitted recovery on the more conservative basis that it is the type of loss but not its extent that must be reasonably contemplated. The defendants were in breach of contract by supplying a hopper unfit for the purpose of storing animal food and it was within the reasonable contemplation of the parties that such a breach would result in illness for the pigs. That the illness was more serious(extensive) than would have been reasonably contemplated did not matter as the loss that did occur(the death of the pigs) was of the same type as the loss which was reasonably contemplated(illness to the pigs)."

但这多数意见的分析也是有它说不通的地方,就是程度太严重或者范围太广泛在违约的损失遥远性会被视为是订约时不可以合理料想得到,变成属于"特别损失"(special damage)。损失程度的严重与否没有这方面考虑的只是在侵权。这在本章第 5 段已经有针对,并提到了有关的以下先例如 Victoria Laundry v. Newman(1949)2 KB 528;Brown v. K. M. R. Services(1995)2 Lloyd's Rep 513 与 North Sea Energy Holdings v. Petroleum Authority of Thailand(1997)2 Lloyd's Rep. 418 等,不重复。

看来在 Parsons v. Uttley Ingham 先例后,还没有在这方面有一个比较明确的说法。所以,在 Michael Furmston 教授所著的《The Law of Contract》(第四版,2010 年)之 1808 页,还是指 Parsons v. Uttley Ingham 先例是一个"麻烦"(troublesome)的先例。

第四章　损失的遥远性之二:因果关系

1. 序言

因果关系(causation)是“损失遥远性”(remoteness of damages)对受害方能否向“侵权”(tort)或“违约”(breach of contract)的被告取回他的损失的限制中的一种。可以说凡事(不论是追究责任方面或是国家大事)都要考虑因果关系,这在计算损失赔偿方面更是重要。受害方因侵权或违约方面提出损失赔偿时,首先要证明的就是被告的侵权或违约为“前因”与受害方原告蒙受的损失为“后果”。正如在《Chitty on Contracts》(30th edn, 2008 年)之 26 - 032 段所说如下:“**Requirement of a causal connection**. The important issue in remoteness of damage in the law of contract is whether a particular loss was within the reasonable contemplation of the parties, but causation must first be proved: there must be a causal connection between the defendant's breach of contract and the claimant's loss. The claimant may recover damages for a loss only where the breach of contract was the 'effective' or 'dominant' cause of that loss. The courts have avoided laying down any formal tests for causation: they have relied on common sense to guide decisions as to whether a breach of contract is a sufficiently substantial cause of the claimant's loss. The answer to whether the breach was the cause of the loss or merely the occasion for the loss must 'in the end' depend on 'the court's common sense' in interpreting the facts.”(在合约法,损失的遥远性是十分重要,这是看某一项的损失是否是在双方当事人的合理预见/料想内。但因果关系必须先证明,就是证明被告的违约与原告的损失有一定的关系。原告能够向被告取回他的损失,但只是在被告的违约就是损失的有效或主要原因。法院避免说死因果关系的正规测试是什么。法院是依赖它的一般的常识来决定到底违约是否足够重要导致了原告的损失。在不同的案件,法院都要依赖它的常识决定到底有关的违约是造成损失的原因或仅是提供了机会。)

不论是侵权或者是违约,受害方的原告都需要满足“要不是”(but for)的测试,也就是说明与证明这一个因果关系的事实:“要不是”被告的侵权或是违约,他就不会蒙受这一个损失。这看来是简单合理的道理,在大部分涉及单一的侵权或违约行为的案件中都是很容易作出判断。例如,疏忽的驾驶员把一个行人碰伤,后者的损失

（包括他的医疗费用、经济损失与身体受到伤害的赔偿等）显然与驾驶员的侵权行为有直接关系，可以说是明确不过。如果涉及违约，如卖方拒绝交付货物或是交付了有缺陷的货物，导致买方市场价格的损失，也是因果关系明确不过。只要受害方的买方证明卖方的违约（会有情况在明确与证据确凿的违约下，卖方干脆就承认责任）与损失金额，因果关系很可能都不会提到。

但如果不是涉及单一的侵权或违约行为，而是同时有两个或多个侵权或违约造成了同一个损失，这就会增加了考虑因果关系的困难。这种情况在航运的案件中经常会遇到，如承租人的违约如指定不安全港口或装运危险品，但同时由于船舶不适航或船员疏忽与处理不当，造成了损失。这就经常会带来到底哪一个原因才是主要或有效的原因造成了损失的困难，因为结果会完全不同：主要原因如果是不安全港口或危险品，承租人要负责赔偿损失；但主要原因如果是不适航或船员疏忽，船东要负责赔偿损失。虽然，同时有多个近因造成同一个损失的情况不会是太多，往往在时间上有先后，但还是会有。在保险的范畴就在20世纪70年代开始发展起来这一个“同时有多个近因”的说法，并发展出三种情况分别规定保险人是否赔付。第一种就是同时多个近因都属于承保的风险，保险人显然必须赔付。第二种是其中一个属于承保的风险，但其他的近因既没有说承保，但也没有说是排除，保险人依然必须赔付。最复杂的是第三种情况，就是一个近因属于承保的风险，但另一个是属于排除的风险。这些问题在笔者所著的《海上货物保险》一书第六章4.5段有详论，内容很多，不重复。

另一种主要情况会带来考虑因果关系的困难是在一项侵权或违约行为产生后，往往会引发一连串的后果（损失），因果之间实际是一个连续的、不可逆转的过程，每一项后果都是之后一项后果的前因。有人把这称之为“因果链”（chain of causation）。如果在这个过程中间插进了“新介入事件”（new intervening event 或是拉丁文的 *novus actus interveniens*），中断了因果链，那么之后的后果（全部或部分损失）与原先的违约就不存在因果关系了，这等于是以新介入事件为起点造成了之后的后果。在许多的先例中，可节录 Sumner 勋爵在 Latham v. Johnson ［1913］ K. B. 398 先例所说：“... No doubt each intervener is a *causa sine qua non*, but unless the intervention is a fresh, independent cause, the person guilty of the original negligence will still be the effective cause, if he ought reasonably to have anticipated such interventions and to have foreseen that if they occurred the result would be that his negligence would lead to mischief.”（每一个第三人介入的行为都会有可能中断因果链，但这介入的行为必须是一个全新与独立的事件才有这一个后果。否则原来疏忽的被告还是造成最后损失的有效原因，如果他能够合理预见到会有这种不足以中断因果链的第三人行为并与它造成的后果。）

另 Wright 勋爵在 The “Oropesa” （1943） 1 All ER. 211 先例也有有关新介入事件的说法：“To break the chain of causation it must be shown that there is something which I will call ultraneous, something unwarrantable, a new cause which disturbs the sequence of events, something which can be described, as either unreasonable or extraneous or extrinsic. ”(中断因果关系必须说明有一些不应该发生的,是全新的,可以说是不合理与外来的事件。这与上一段 Sumner 勋爵所说没有矛盾, 因为这种事件是被告不能合理预见到的事件,而该事件所造成的损失或额外损失也是被告不能预见的。)

至于为什么法律要对受害方的损失有这一个限制,是因为侵权或违约会引发的一连串后果可以是没完没了。侵权或违约后经常会涉及第三人的行为或其他独立因素的介入。这方面的政策可以节录 The “Liesbosch” (1933) 45 Ll L Rep 123 先例中,Wright 勋爵所说:“The law cannot take account of everything that follows a wrongful act: it regards some subsequent matters as outside the scope of its selection, because ‘it were infinite for the law to judge the cause of causes’, or consequences of consequences.”

这可以用一个简单的例子说明,受害方的船舶被侵权(这种情况会是被另一艘船舶碰撞)或违约(这种情况会是承租人的小工疏忽所导致)所损坏,虽然损坏并不严重,但因为影响适航而被安排去中国修船。如果在航行去中国的途中,该船舶发生了另一次独立的碰撞或极大风浪,导致了更严重的损坏。或在中国修船时,又不幸遇上了重大灾难如大地震或大海啸,最终导致船舶全损。在整件事来看,的确是如果没有最早的侵权或违约,该船舶根本不必去中国修船。所以,最早的侵权或违约是引发了后来一连串后果。但如果要该侵权方或违约方承担所有的损失,包括船舶的全损,看来是过分。这就是有必要通过因果关系与因果链看后来的损失哪一些是最早的侵权或违约应该负责,而哪一些就不必负责。而不必负责的损失也就是一般被律师称为是中断了因果链。

大部分重要的因果关系先例都涉及侵权(特别近期是人身伤亡与医疗,但早期则是涉及船舶碰撞与救助方面的海事事故),这估计是因为大部分的侵权案件不像违约,相对不会有太多方面的争议。例如在侵权经常会涉及的一般性疏忽,会是不难成立被告的疏忽(不论是严重还是轻微),这导致被告在剩下不多的重要争议往往会是因果关系,即是否由于他的疏忽而造成了这一个后果或是索赔的损失(全部或部分)。这也是所谓的“要不是”(but for)的测试,就是受害方的原告要证明“要不是被告这一个疏忽,就不会导致这一个损失”。而被告的抗辩就是他的疏忽并没有或一定会导致这一个损失或全部的损失,或是这一个损失本来就逃不了,或是被告即使没有疏忽也不会有改变,或是有后续的其他人士包括原告自己的疏忽才是真正造成这一个损失的有效原因。先举一个简单的例子说明这种争议,就是被告的车主因为驾驶疏忽碰撞了原告的行人,而原告被送去医院,在医院内受到严重的感染或医疗疏忽而带来严重后果。在无可否认的疏忽下,被告的抗辩会是:我的侵权并不会导致你这个严重后果/损失。而原告的请求会是:“要不是”你的侵权,我根本不必进医院,而进医院就有可能会受到感染或医疗疏忽,这都是你的疏忽所引起的后果。这样看来,“要不是”测试也不应是唯一的测试看被告是否要对受害方原告负责。

但在合约的范畴,也不表示这一个因果关系的问题没有重要的关系与复杂性,违约与损失也是需要满足同样的"要不是"测试,这将会在本章探讨。

因果关系会有不同的解说,如在 The City of Lincoln (1980) P 15 是说被告要赔偿的损失是"在一般情况下来自他的错误行为"(in the ordinary cause of things would flow from his wrongful act)。其他说法包括是损失是否是侵权或者违约所带来的"自然后果"(natural consequence),或是"直接后果"(direct consequence),或是"一般性后果"(ordinary consequence),或是"很可能的后果"(probable consequence),或是"可预见的后果"(foreseeable consequence)。而针对某一项的侵权或违约,也会被说是造成损失的"最重要原因"(predominant cause)/"主要原因"(main cause),或是"近因"(proximate cause),或是"有效的原因"(effective cause),或是"真正原因"(real cause),或是"引发的原因"(operative cause)等。反正是通过一个"要不是"测试找出如果不是某一个特定的原因,是不会造成后来的损失。

2. 因果关系是根据一般人常识的判断

由于因果关系被说是根据一般人的"常识"(common sense),而不是根据"哲理"(philosophical)或"科学"(science)吹毛求疵。这说法可以说在几乎每一个涉及因果关系的先例中法院都会强调。可以在许多先例中随手挑一些说法,首先是在 Canada Rice Mills Ltd. v. Union Marine & General Insurance Co. Ltd. (1940) 67 Lloyd's Rep. 549 先例中,Wright 勋爵是这样说:"Causation is to be understood as the man in the street, and not as either the scientist or the metaphysician, would understand it. Cause here means what a business or seafaring man would taken to be the cause without too microscopic analysis but on a broad view."

下一个是 Royal Greek Government v. Minister of Transport (1950) 83 Lloyd's Rep 228 先例,案情涉及船舶装了挥发易燃的煤炭而导致爆炸,仲裁庭认为事故是由五个可能的原因所造成,并认定了哪一个才是主要原因。上诉去了高院,Devlin 大法官针对有关常识判断因果关系是这样说:"The arbitrator is the person whom the parties have chosen, as they are entitled to do, to apply finally the standard of common sense; and common sense is, I believe, the only test that can be applied to the choice between several causes, all of which are sufficient in law. In my judgment, an arbitrator's finding on causation, unless he can be shown to have misdirected himself on some principle of law or on some point of construction, or to have acted on insufficient evidence, is conclusive."(仲裁员是当事人选择使用他的常识作出判断,从几个不同造成事故的原因中选择一个有效原因。仲裁员认定的因果关系,除非能够证明仲裁员对有关法律或法律的解释被错误适用,他的认定就是最终的)

接下去介绍 The “Wagon Mound” (1961) 1 Lloyd’s Rep 1 先例,Viscount Simonds 大法官说:“... since he is judged by what the reasonable man ought to foresee, corresponds with the common conscience of mankind, and a test (the ‘direct’ consequence) be substituted which leads to nowhere but the never ending and insoluble problems of causation. ‘The lawyer,’ said Sir Frederick Pollock, ‘cannot afford to adventure himself with philosophers in the logical and metaphysical controversies that beset the idea of cause.’”

另在 The “Sivand” (1998) 2 Lloyd’s Rep 97 先例,上诉庭的 Evans 大法官说:“Causation is a matter of common sense. No sensible person could doubt but that the whole of the cost they incurred was the measure of the loss caused to them by the negligent handling of ship.”

同样说法也在 BCCI v. Ali (No 2) (2002) EWCA Civ. 82 先例中被提到,Robert Walker 大法官说:“In deciding [causation] the trial judge may draw inferences in a commonsense way. The fact that the loss cannot be quantified precisely need not be a barrier to a finding that it was caused by the breach or to an assessment of the loss in a commonsense way.”

在一个古老的船舶碰撞先例 The “San Onofre” (1922) P 243 CA,有说法是因果关系与损失遥远性的判断往往就是法院的第一印象,这也是类似一般常识的说法。Scrutton 大法官是这样说:“The question whether damage is sufficiently direct consequence of negligence to be recoverable, or is too remote, is rather a question of first impression. I am clear that if a negligent driver on the road injures himself in a collision with another vehicle, whose driver and a stranger thereupon take the injured man to hospital and meet with an accident in so doing, neither of them can recover damages for the accident from the negligent driver as consequences of his original negligence. The present case seems to me exactly similar.”

所以有说法是这一个问题其实并不困难,一般有常识的人士也可以作出判断(虽然有更多的说法是因果关系的判断会是十分困难、不可捉摸与不肯定)。但这也不好说,经常见到部分人士对因果关系的判断是笔者接受不了如目前发生的不幸或幸运事件是上天的意志。

笔者也有感觉部分人的“常识”(common sense)就经常会在因果关系方面十分混乱。这种态度并不是好事,因为出了严重后果如果不找出真正的前因,而是随便找一个原因推搪过去,就永远不能解决问题,也学不到教训。而在法律的层面,如果追究责任或索赔损失不理会因果之间的“一定关系”(casual relationship),岂非会怪责侵权方或违约方甚至是谋杀犯的母亲生了他,这才是无辜受害方蒙受损失的主要或有效原因,而该母亲才应该受到惩罚或/与作出赔偿?

这看来可笑,因为两者之间的因果关系可以说是实在太遥远与间接。但同样道理,有时候会不明显,所以在日常生活中也经常会见到这方面的争议,难以作出定论。

例如,在同样的情况改为是母亲没有教育好她的孩子,甚至教唆他犯罪,在一定程度上可以合理预见在这种家庭环境长大的孩子迟早会出大事,只是无法预见会出什么大事。这一来母亲与她孩子的犯罪因果关系就会相对接近甚至有一定的关系。更进一步说如果母亲教唆她的孩子犯某一项特定的罪,如盗窃或杀人,而她的孩子是没有自己的独立思维(年纪太小或有智障),这与母亲的教唆会是有非常密切关系,甚至是直接的因果关系,盗窃或教唆盗窃或杀人的罪名会是落在母亲而不一定是孩子的头上。可以说,每一个不同的案件中的因果关系都会受有关案件的不同事实所影响,这就是所谓的"事实敏感"(fact - sensitive),并以一般常识对这些事实作出因果关系的判断。

再多举一个日常生活会遇到的例子,就是A与B是好朋友,一天晚上A打电话约B出来,说是有要事商量。B本是不想出来,他的夫人也阻止说是太晚了。但A还是坚持,B最后只好答应。结果,B在半途被车撞了,这会是他自己不小心,晚上也是视力差,又或是第三人的驾驶员疏忽。也会是B半途被抢劫而受伤,因为当地的治安并不是太好。但B的夫人仍是埋怨A,因为要不是他这么晚约B出门,根本不会有这种不幸的事。不少人都会有这种心态,但真正分析起来往往是没有道理的,因为A约B的行为与B的受伤之间无因果关系,毕竟B是有他自由选择的权利,而且晚上出去并不会"无可避免的遇上车祸或抢劫"。只要举个反例好了:如果B的不幸可怪A,那么如果B遇到幸运的事会否应由A来独享,如B在半途捡到一块黄金?

笔者介绍一个仲裁案件,因为该案件中因果关系是裁决结果的主要甚至是唯一的原因。这是一个金额不大的案件,案情涉及一艘船舶抵达菲律宾的一个卸港时,船舶吊车的缆索太长(比规格长了2.5米),无法把抓斗吊高至岸上的漏斗上。由于没有其他卸货的办法,结果大家同意的解决办法是把船舶中间的第三吊车缆索切掉12米。再把船上煤炭用第三吊车卸下一部分,船舶吃水升高后最终能够允许其他吊车也可同时卸货。但双方存在的争议就是谁要承担这些延误与替代缆索的费用。承租人指称船东的缆索太长是违约,但笔者作为独任仲裁员觉得因果关系有问题。因为第三吊车的缆索如果是切掉2.5米或以内的长度,可以说损失是因为该船舶的缆索比规格长而导致了这一个事故。但问题是切掉12米才能解决问题,这也导致了切断的缆索不能再使用,因为它的长度到不了舱底抓货,在下一个航次就会有问题,所以要另在第三舱更换替代缆索。所以笔者不接受承租人认为原来的缆索长了2.5米是损失的主要或有效原因的说法,并判事故的原因与码头结构包括漏斗的高度相关。

最后可以把因果关系适用在一连串事件的责任方面,如在国际贸易中就经常会有争议是FOB买方派船到装港,但由于不可抗力甚至是受阻的原因,卖方没有办法提供货物。争议会是卖方是否可以依赖不可抗力的合约条文或是法律的默示地位逃避赔偿损失,甚至谈不上有违约责任。这往往先要卖方证明他准备装在该船的一票货物遇上了不可抗力或受阻事件而导致无法履行合约。例如这票货物已经是明确等待装船,甚至已经安放在码头仓库,但不幸在装船前遇上了台风或火灾,被严重摧毁,这一来卖方就有机会成功依赖不可抗力或受阻,因为他证明了遇上不可抗力或受阻事件的货物就是合约有关要提供给 FOB 买方装船的货物。如果卖方本身没有特定的一票货物备妥,而是要不时向其他的分卖方收购,并稍后“划归”(appropriate)在这一个 FOB 买卖合约下,但在划归前该货物已经因不可抗力或受阻事件而损毁,卖方就会很难抗拒 FOB 买方的索赔。原因是卖方很难证明损毁的货物就是他要划归给 FOB 买方的货物,它们之间的因果关系建立不起来。这些案例有不少,如 European Grain & Shipping Ltd v. J. H. Rayner & Co. Ltd (1970) 2 Lloyd's Rep. 239; Avimex v. Dewulf (1979) 2 Lloyd's Rep 57 等。在 Avimex v. Dewulf 先例,Goff 大法官针对这一点是这样说:

“I turn then to the first issue on liability, which is whether a *force majeure* event occasioned delay in the shipment of the goods, as required by cl. 22 (这是买卖合约中的不可抗力条文). It is not in dispute that there was a *force majeure* event (该先例是明确发生了不可抗力事件)...

Mr. Russell, for the sellers,(卖方的代表大律师)submitted that it did. He invited me to infer from the telex quoted in par. 8 of the award that American shippers, Admisa, (分卖方与供应货物装船的付运人)were shippers of goods which the sellers intended to appropriate to the contract, and to conclude that the *force majeure* event occasioned delay in shipment of those goods. Now I am satisfied that, to invoke cl. 22, the sellers have to show that the *force majeure* event occasioned delay in the shipment of goods which they intended to appropriate to the contract. These sellers were not shippers; so, in order to discharge this burden, they have to trace a string, i. e. a chain of contracts, back from themselves to an affected shippers... par. 4 of the award, in which the Board of Appeal(GAFTA 上诉仲裁庭)found that – ‘The sellers did not intend to ship the Contract goods themselves, but intended to fulfil the Contract by appropriating to it goods bought in from other sources but they produced no evidence that they had entered into a contract for the purchase of any such goods ... ’

This is a most striking finding: obviously, if the sellers had themselves entered into a contract for the purchase of such goods, they would have been able to prove it, and they have failed to do so. So they are unable to establish the first link in the chain which they have to prove.”

3. 因果关系是一个事实与法律混合的问题

因果关系可分为“事实上的原因”(cause in fact)与“法律上的原因”(cause in law)。针对事实上的原因,普遍被接受的就是以“要不是”测试,这稍后会进一步解释。但这一测试并不代表法律上的原因,因为原因或始因即使与损失有一定关系,法律上也会有其他考虑,不接受两者之间有法律上的因果关系。在《McGregor on Damages》(18th edn, 2009 年)一书 6-008 段就有提到是否可以通过"要不是"测试把一宗谋杀案件中的杀人犯与他母亲对他的生养建立因果关系,但法律是不会接受两者之间有因果关系,如不会允许受害方的家属向他母亲提出民事诉讼,要求赔偿。该6-008段是这样说:"Causation in law takes us into an entirely different field. It is never enough simply to satisfy the 'but for' test in order to establish legal cause. To take an extreme example. A mother gives birth to a son who, when he grows up, commits a murder. Yet 'but for' the mother's decision to have a child the murder would never have happened; on the 'but for' test she is a cause in fact of the murder. In simple, if mundane, terms this shows what lies behind the grander, frequently cited maxim of Bacon that 'it were infinite for the law to judge the causes of causes and their impression one of another'. While, of course, it is true that the mother will bear no responsibility for the murder on account of lack of negligent or other tortuous activity on her part, it is the law that removes her from being a cause of the murder through the mechanism of legal cause."

所以有说法是因果关系是一个事实与法律混合的问题。这一个方面重要之处是在英国仲裁,仲裁庭认定的事实是终局。但他所作出的法律判决是有机会上诉去法院(这是根据 1996 年《仲裁法》之 Section 69)。同样情况也是在英国法院,在第一审所认定的事实是终局,但涉及法律问题是可以上诉至上诉庭。这一来,涉及因果关系的争议显然主要是对事实的认定,毕竟有说法是一般人的常识也可以作出准确的判断。但在英国法律,因果关系一直被视为是一个事实与法律混合的问题,就表示有上诉的机会。这方面首先可介绍 The "Coxwold" (1941) 70 Ll L Rep 160 先例,Caldecote 勋爵说:"Some questions arose as to whether that ought to be treated as a finding of fact which could not be disturbed unless there was no evidence to support it, but if one looks at the familiar cases on questions of this sort one sees that a finding to this effect has always been treated as a question of law which is open to review."

Devlin 大法官在 Royal Greek Government v. Minister of Transport (1950) 83 Lloyd's Rep 228 先例说到:"Questions of causation can give rise to problem both of law and of fact; once the problem has been formulated, it will be seen whether its solution requires the application of some point of construction, or is to be obtained by resolving a matter of fact or inference from fact."

4. 事实的因果关系:"要不是"测试

特别在侵权,有说法第一步成立被告的错误或疏忽与原告的损失有不可切断的因果关系,就是通过“要不是”测试(“but for” test)排除一些无关或没有造成损失的错误或疏忽行为。在往往是同时或前后多过一个错误或疏忽(如来自第三人或原告自己)的情况下,法院是想找出最主要或有效造成损失的原因,然后把赔偿所有损失的责任加在该原因上。“要不是”测试就是问一个问题:“要不是被告的错误或疏忽,原告会否有这一个损失?”(would the damage of which the claimant complains have occurred “but for” the negligence [or other wrongdoing] of the defendant?)

4.1　举证责任

当然,对这一个“要不是”测试的举证责任是在原告。但这一举证责任只需要达到超过50%的可能性,就可以满足对民事诉讼的要求。关键是举证要成功说服法院肯推断被告的错误/疏忽是与原告的损失有一定的关系。法院对“因果关系的法律推断”(legal inference of causation)会根据提供的证据作出,这可以是“几乎肯定”(almost certain)的程度或只能是“合理可能”(reasonable probable)的程度下作出对原告有利的推断。但如果提供的证据不能满足这一个对原告有利的推断,就会判原告在因果关系的举证责任败诉:The “Popi M” (1985) 2 Lloyd's Rep 1; Davis and Docherty v. Balfour Kilpatrick Ltd (2002) EWCA Civ. 736。

这里不妨先介绍The “Popi M” (1985) 2 Lloyd's Rep 1重要先例的案情:有关这艘船舶在风平浪静的海面上航行时沉没,而且沉没地点水深至无法派潜水员下去调查真正沉没原因。在这种情况下沉没,保险人总免不了怀疑可能的真相是船东故意“凿沉”(scuttle)骗保险费;或是船舶因“损耗/磨损”(wear and tear)导致破裂进水。而两种情况下保险都不赔付。但问题是这纯属臆猜,难以找证据支持。

由于保险人拒赔,船东被迫起诉。但船东也面临问题,而且比保险人先一步头疼。因为船舶保险是采用“列名风险”(named perils)的做法,船东有责任先举证船舶是由于其中一项的列名风险所引起损失的。而船东从生还船员所知道的有限事实是:一声巨响,船舶震动,船尾机房船底出现一大洞,海水迅速涌入,根本无法挽救,船舶迅速沉没。船东根本无法从这事实去试图说服法院作出对他有利的推断。说是火灾或碰船等常见的列名风险当然不可以,因为与所知事实一点也没有关系。其中没有证人看到一点火光或其他船舶的踪影,怎能赖火灾或碰船呢?

结果,船东依赖于“海难”(peril of the sea)为列名风险,而根据有限的事实,指真相可能是:(1)船舶碰上了浮木等东西;(2)被苏联潜水艇浮上水面时碰上了。而保险人则以“消耗/磨损”(wear and tear)为由而抗辩。双方差一点没有指是遇上水怪,因为是更加不可信与没有任何证据,船东也可以肯定英国法院不会作出这样的推断。

但技术上去考验,以上的“指控”(allegations)都不可能或不大可能成立。首先是水上浮木等东西,因为船舶在前进,造成的水流会把浮木往外推而不是往里吸,所以技术上不可能发生浮木碰上船舶的后部分。再是船舶磨损,这一般不会造成如此巨大/突然的破裂,故此这指控也过不了技术考验的一关。这只留下了苏联潜水艇的一项指控了。船东还煞有介事的写信给前苏联的海军司令部问当时当地(地中海在亚尔及西亚对开海面)是否有潜水艇在活动?有否与不明物体碰撞等?但苏联海军部不予理睬,这也可以想得到。

这可能性有吗?听说几年前美国潜水艇在夏威夷附近因为急速升上水面而碰沉了一艘日本渔船,可知道这种意外并不是不可能。但可能性大吗?又不见得。Popi M轮上船员没有人在事故前后曾看见有潜水艇浮起。该潜水艇也应在碰撞中受了重创,怎会仍不浮出水面?可总结说:Popi M轮沉没的真实原因会是被苏联潜水艇在浮出水面时碰上的可能性的百分比之低是绝不应达致民事诉讼的51%的多数可能性要求。

在高院与上诉庭,他们把"不可能"(impossible)的指控排除在外,在不情愿下接受了"不大可能"(improbable)的"潜水艇理论"(submarine theory)。在高院,说是Bingham大法官受了福尔摩斯小说的影响。福尔摩斯先生教导华生医生有关调查真相是把不可能的原因一项项排除,最后留下来的不大可能的原因也就是真相。这在(1985) 2 Lloyds' Rep之6页说:"... the late Sir Arthur Conan Doyle in his book 'The Sign of Four', describes his hero, Mr Sherlock Holmes, as saying to the latter's friend Dr Watson: 'how often have I said to you that, when you have eliminated the impossible, whatever remains, however improbable, must be the truth?' It is, no doubt, on the basis of this well-known but unjudicial dictum that Mr Justice Bingham decided to accept the shipowners' submarine theory..."

但这被贵族院推翻,认为他们(高院与上诉庭)"捉错路"(misdirect)。Brandon勋爵判说:"In my opinion Mr Justice Bingham adopted an erroneous approach to this case by regarding himself as compelled to choose between two theories, both of which he regarded as extremely improbable, or one of which he regarded as extremely improbable and the other of which he regarded as virtually impossible. He should have borne in mind, and considered carefully in his judgment, the third alternative which was open to him, namely, that the evidence left him in doubt as to the cause of the aperture in the ship's hull, and that, in these circumstances, the shipowner had failed to discharge the burden of proof which was on them."

看来,高院根据福尔摩斯小说所作出的被视为是较准确"猜测"(conjecture)并没有法律举证的价值。但根据提供的证据所作出来的"推断"(inference)就不一样。虽然它们之间的区别并不容易区分,连Bingham大法官这种极高水平的人士也会"错判"。这一点可节录Macmillan勋爵在Jones v. Great Western Ry Co (1930) 47 TLR 39先例所说:"The dividing line between conjecture and inference is often a very difficult one to draw. A conjecture may be plausible, but it is of no legal value, for its essence is that it is a mere guess. An inference in the legal sense, on the other hand, is a deduction from the evidence, and of it is a reasonable deduction it may have the validity of legal proof."

在接下去的Davis and Docherty v. Balfour Kilpatrick Ltd(2002) EWCA Civ. 736近

期先例也是根据 The “Popi M”先例作出同样的判法。但这种案例还是很少会出现,这是要原告提出的有关因果关系证据都是“不大可能”(improbable),没有一项是可能。这种情况在现实中很少见,正如上诉庭的 Thomas 大法官在 Ide v. ATB Sales Ltd; Lexus Financial Services (t/a Toyota Financial Services (UK) Plc) v. Russell (2008) EWCA Civ. 424 先例说到:“In the vast majority of cases where the judge has before him the issue of causation of a particular event, the parties will put before the judges two or more competing explanations as to how the event occurred, which though they may be uncommon, are not improbable. In such cases, it is... a permissible and logical train of reasoning for a judge, having eliminated all of the causes of the loss but one, to ask himself whether, on the balance of probabilities, that one cause was the cause of the event. What is impermissible is for a judge to conclude in the case of a series of improbable causes that the least improbable or least unlikely is nonetheless the cause of the event.”

会有特殊的情况是原告举证不了,而原因是被告的行为所导致,法院会认为更公道是由被告承担举证的责任:Cook v. Lewis (1951) SCR 830。这一先例会在本章 4.3.4 段介绍。

4.2　满足不了“要不是”测试的先例

“要不是”测试在侵权与违约都会是必要,这才能把被告错误或疏忽的行为与原告蒙受的损失串联起来。以下举一些案例说明这一点。

4.2.1　先例之一:Barnett v. Chelsea and Kensington Hospital Management Committee

已经提到过,如果根据所提供证据作出的推断是“这一个损失本来就逃避不了”,不受到被告侵权或违约的影响,就属于其中一种的不能满足“要不是”测试。这一点不妨以一个先例说明,就是 Barnett v. Chelsea and Kensington Hospital Management Committee (1969) 1 QB 428。该先例的案情涉及原告的丈夫由于严重的肚子痛被送到医院的急救室,但他在当天稍后时间死亡,并被证明是砒霜中毒。医院虽然在较早时接收了这一个病人,但没有派出人手马上或尽快处理。事后原告作为受害方的遗孀向医院提出起诉并索赔损失,医院承认疏忽,没有尽快处理与尝试治疗她的丈夫。但医院提供证据证明这一疏忽与她丈夫的死亡是没有直接因果关系,因为即使是马上或尽快处理,该病人也肯定会死亡,因为是中了砒霜的毒。这被法院接受而导致原告败诉。

4.2.2　先例之二:McWilliams v. Sir Williams Arrol & Co

也提到过,如果法院作出的推断是“被告即使没有疏忽也不会令最后的损失有改变”,也属于一种不能满足“要不是”测试的情况,这与上述介绍的“这一个损失本来就逃不了”说法本质上非常接近。这方面可举 McWilliams v. Sir Williams Arrol & Co (1962) 1 WLR 295 HL 先例作为介绍,案情涉及一个钢铁工人从 70 尺的高空跌下地面死亡,雇主的被告被认定违反法律的责任不提供安全设施给该工人,也就是防止高空跌落的保护带。但被告提出证明是即使提供了,他也不会使用。这导致了原告(死者家属)的索赔败诉,因为满足不了"要不是"测试的要求。在贵族院,Reid 勋爵强调是不应该太轻率作出受害方被提供了保护带也不会使用的推断,因为人类的行为是会随时改变,即使他以前有经常罔顾安全的做法不代表这一次他不会突然改变主意。但 Reid 勋爵认为这一个案件的证据证明这一个钢铁工人不会使用保护带实在是"压倒性的"(overwhelming)。

4.2.3 先例之三:Kay's Tutor v. Ayrshire and Arran Health Board

另一个满足不了"要不是"测试的先例也是涉及人身伤亡,这先例也充分显示了医学的不肯定导致了这一个测试的困难。在 Kay's Tutor v. Ayrshire and Arran Health Board (1987) 2 All ER 417 HL 先例,涉及一个小孩患了脑膜炎。他在医院时被过度注射了盘尼西林,几乎死亡,但最终还是恢复。虽然是如此,他被发现失去听觉。耳聋会是脑膜炎的并发症,但是从来没有数据或前例是与过度注射盘尼西林有关。医院承认过度注射盘尼西林的疏忽,但指出这一个疏忽是与耳聋没有关系。虽然受害方的原告提供不了证据把医院的疏忽与他的耳聋扯上一定的关系,第一审的法官还是判原告胜诉,推断是过度注射盘尼西林很可能令受害方身体更加虚弱而导致了出现脑膜炎的并发症。但这个判决在贵族院被推翻,认为是满足不了"要不是"的测试。

4.3 "要不是"测试不适用或放宽的例外情况

任何法律的原则都会有例外情况,所以非要有例外情况放宽或不要求这一个"要不是"测试。反正是不同的案件都会有不同程度的要求,最终还是取决于法院认为侵权方或违约方应该对有关的损失有什么责任。但正如 Hoffman 勋爵在 Kuwait Airways Corp v. Iraq Airways Co (2002) UKHL 19 先例所说,不论是怎样的程度,总会需要侵权行为与最后的损失有"一定程度的因果关系"(some causal connection),否则就不是理性的侵权法律制度。Hoffman 勋爵是这样说:"... no uniform causal requirement for liability in tort. Instead, there are varying causal requirements, depending upon the basis and purpose of liability. One cannot separate questions of liability from questions of causation. They are inextricably connected. One is never simply liable; one is always liable for something and the rules which determine what one is liable for are as much part of the substantive law as the rules which determine which acts give rise to liability."

以下是分段针对这种"要不是"测试的例外情况。

4.3.1 例外情况之一:侵占的严格责任

如果涉及"侵占"(conversion)的严格侵权责任,就不需要满足"要不是"测试。

这可以举 Kuwait Airways Corp v. Iraq Airways Co (2002) UKHL 19 先例作为例子。案情涉及 1990 年伊拉克侵略科威特的海湾战争。伊拉克的一个重要侵略目标是科威特机场,而起初的侵略可谓十分成功与快速,半天不到的时间就已经控制了科威特机场。当时有 15 架属于"科威特航空公司"(Kuwait Airways Corporation)的民航飞机停泊在科威特机场,全部落入伊拉克军的手中。在 9 月 17 日萨达姆政权的伊拉克通过命令把科威特航空公司解散并把它的资产全部转交给伊拉克航空公司。伊拉克航空公司受命将其中10架飞机(8架是空中巴士,2架是波音767)从科威特开去伊拉克并把飞机占用。在1991年1月17日,联军的军事行动开始。其中4架飞机在摩苏尔(伊拉克北部城市)被摧毁,其余的6架从巴格达飞去伊朗逃避战火。科威特航空公司在英国开始诉讼,索赔它的10架飞机被侵占的损失高达约8亿美元,而第一个被告就是伊拉克航空公司,第二个被告就是伊拉克政府。伊拉克航空公司提出了一个初步争议,就是他能否在整个事件中享有外交豁免。这在贵族院最初是判伊拉克航空公司受命把飞机从科威特转移的行动是可以享有外交豁免,但之后的继续占用是不能享有外交豁免。反正这方面带来大量的争议与问题是与本段想针对的问题没有直接关系,有兴趣的读者可看 KAC v. IAC (2003) 1 Lloyd's Rep 448 的报道。

在本段所要针对的是有关伊拉克航空公司作为被告争辩说他的侵占责任与科威特航空公司索赔的损失必须能够满足"要不是"测试,但这显然是做不到。因为科威特航空公司的10架飞机的损失已经是定论,伊拉克航空公司后来的侵占与否都是改变不了这个事实。萨达姆政权的伊拉克怎样都会占用这10架飞机,不拨给伊拉克航空公司也会拨给其他的国家机构或国家公司。贵族院同意"要不是"测试满足不了,而需要根据整体的价值观看被告是否需要负责作为判决。其中 Nicholls 勋爵是这样说:"the court may treat wrongful conduct as having sufficient causal connection with the loss for the purpose of attracting responsibility even though the simple 'but for' test is not satisfied. In so deciding the court is primarily making a value judgment on responsibility. In making this judgment the court will have regard to the purpose sought to be achieved by the relevant tort, as applied to the particular circumstances."

Hoffman 勋爵说:"The liability is strict. Thus the causal questions are answered by reference to the nature of the liability."

所以,虽然伊拉克航空公司最初不是自己侵占这10架飞机,而是伊拉克军队的作为,而且伊拉克航空公司即使不侵占,还是难逃被第三人(伊拉克萨达姆政权)侵占,所以不能满足"要不是"测试。但这些争议还是不能让伊拉克航空公司作为被告逃避责任。这方面也可节录 Nicholls 勋爵说:"Each person in a series of conversions wrongfully excludes the owner from the possession of the goods. This is the basis on which each is liable to the owner. This is the nature of the tort of conversion. The wrongful acts of a previous possessor do not therefore diminish the plaintiff's claim in respect of the wrongful acts of a later possessor. Nor ... is it anything to the point that, absent the defendant's conversion, someone else would wrongfully have converted the goods. The likelihood that, had the defendant not wronged the plaintiff, somebody would have done so is no reason for diminishing the defendant's liability and responsibility for the loss he brought upon the plaintiff."

4.3.2 例外情况之二:欺诈或故意损害受害方

欺诈是不需要满足"要不是"测试,这在一定程度是政策上的考虑以严厉对待不诚实的言行。早在 Quinn v. Leathem (1901) AC 495 先例,Lindley 勋爵说:"The intention to injure the plaintiff ... disposes of any question of remoteness of damage."他是说故意损害受害方的原告排除了损失遥远性的要求,而"遥远性"(remoteness)包括了因果关系的说法。

例如被告疏忽的误述导致依赖误述的原告订立合约而蒙受损失,原告需要说明误述与他订立合约的因果关系,这是"要不是"测试,这误述只需要是原告后来订约的一个重要原因,不必是决定性原因。这可节录 Stephenson 大法官在 JEB Fasteners Ltd v. Marks Bloom & Co (1983) 1 All ER 583 先例所说:"as long as a misrepresentation plays a real and substantial part, though not by itself a decisive part, in inducing the claimant to act."但如果是欺诈性误述,就不必满足"要不是"测试了。在 Downs v. Chappell (1997) 1 WLR 426 先例,上诉庭说到:"The judge was wrong to ask how the claimants would have acted if they had been told the truth. They were never told the truth. They were told lies in order to induce them to enter into the contract. The lies were material and successful."

另举一个例子说明欺诈不适用"要不是"测试,如果 A 对 B 作出了一个虚假陈述,B 也就相信了,但这是疏忽,因为在正常情况下 B 应该自己查核就可以理解真相,不应该贸然轻信 A 或 A 的雇员。这一来,A 是不能向 B 争辩说"你不该相信我(或我的雇员),这是你的疏忽所造成的损失",这种情况在《Clerk & Lindsell on Torts》(20th edn, 2010 年)一书之 2-20 段说到"The rule that the 'but for' test does not apply in actions for deceit is based on the paradigm fact - situation where A makes a fraudulent statement to B, who believes the statement, even though he should not have done so if he had made proper enquiry. B was negligent, but A cannot say 'you should not have believed me', nor can A's employer say 'you should not believe him'."

但这也有不同判法的先例,就是 Barings Plc (In Liquidation) v. Coopers & Lybrand (A Firm) (2003) EWHC 1319 (Ch)先例。案情涉及 1995 年惊动世界的百年老店霸菱银行的倒闭。该倒闭起因于年仅 28 岁的新加坡霸菱期货公司总裁兼首席交易员尼克李森(Nick Leeson),因错误对赌了经济萧条已久的日本股市将自谷底复苏,自 1994 年起便陆续持有高达 4 万个"新加坡国际金融交易所"(SIMEX)及"大阪证券交易所"(OSE)的日经指数期货契约的多头部位以及"日本长期公债"(JGB)与欧洲日圆期货契约。但日本经济却因遭逢阪神大地震及金融机构超贷倒闭事件而继续疲弱不振,在一年内爆跌近 4000 点。具有 232 年历史、素以经营保守而著称的霸菱银行,最后落得以 1 英镑象征性的价格,被荷兰国际银行(ING)收购。

在这个事件后引发了一连串诉讼,其中 Barings Plc (In Liquidation) v. Coopers & Lybrand (A Firm)先例就是在清盘中的霸菱银行向他的核数师提出索赔,指后者在没有疏忽的情况下应该可以及时发觉尼克李森的不法行为。而被告核数师的其中一项抗辩是尼克李森不法的掩盖损失,对被告造成欺诈性误导/误述而导致被告签字确认审计报告。而尼克李森是属于霸菱银行的雇员,后者必须为前者的错误言行负责。但这又带来争议是被告不应该贸然轻信,应该自己独立调查,否则就是疏忽。英国法院是判霸菱银行作为雇主应该是要为尼克李森的错误言行负责,但面对被告是不需要负这个责任。原因是被告作为核数师对霸菱银行是有一个基本责任,就是通过审计查出这种掩盖损失的不法行为。如果核数师疏忽,但反过来抗辩说是委任他作为核数师的公司的雇员的欺诈行为,公司要负责,所以核数师不必负责或损失可以获得补偿。这一来就变成专门被委任核数师的工作即使做不好也不需要负责。

4.3.3　例外情况之三:公共政策

在这方面放宽或不必满足"要不是"测试,有许多例子是在工业意外与人身伤亡的案件。只举一个例子说明这公共政策的例外情况,这就是英国每年都有上千人患上"间皮瘤"(mesothelioma),这是一种非常致命的癌症,潜伏期长达40年,但通常在发现后的两年会死亡。这种癌症的病原还没有科学上的定论,但绝大部分的例子显示了是由于病人曾经接触"石棉"(asbestos)。在英国所作的统计是每年的患者中,只有50~60人没有接触过石棉,但多达1500人是有接触过石棉的历史。此外,这一种癌症不像另一种涉及石棉的"肺尘症"(pneumoconiosis)是一种累积性的疾病。所以,没有办法科学地说明患者是哪一次接触石棉才引发了间皮瘤。这就表示患者如果曾经两次为不同的雇主服务的时候接触过石棉,就没有办法较科学的证明哪一位雇主应该为他的患病或死亡负责。换言之,患者作为原告是满足不了"要不是"测试。这一方面可节录Bingham大法官在Fairchild v. Glenhaven Funeral Services (2003) AC 32先例所说如下:"So if C is employed successively by A and B and is exposed to asbestos dust and fibres during each employment and develops a mesothelioma, the very strong probability is that this will have been caused by inhalation of asbestos dust containing fibres. But C could have inhaled a single fibre giving rise to his condition during employment by A, in which case his exposure by B will have had no effect on his condition; or he could have inhaled fibres during his employment by B, in which case his exposure by A will have had no effect on his condition; or he could have inhaled fibres during his employment by A and B which together give rise to his condition; but medical science cannot support the suggestion that any of these possibilities is to be regarded as more probable than any other. There is no way of identifying, even on a balance of probabilities, the source of the fibre or fibres which initiated the genetic process which culminated in the malignant tumour."

在Fairchild v. Glenhaven Funeral Services (2003) AC 32先例,上诉庭判是患者(原告)没有办法证明因果关系,因为涉及一位以上的雇主,原告是没有任何办法或证据说明是他在为哪一位雇主服务时导致他致命的癌症。但去了贵族院判决被改变过来，Bingham 勋爵认为在其他许多国家都会通过要求被告有举证责任或根据其他的说法给原告一个救济，认为从公共政策考虑也必须这样做，说："... there is a strong policy argument in favour of compensating those who have suffered grave harm, at the expense of their employers who owed them a duty to protect them against that very harm and failed to do so, when the harm can only have been caused by breach of that duty and when science does not permit the victim accurately to attribute, as between several employers, the precise responsibility for the harm he has suffered. I am of opinion that such injustice as may be involved in imposing liability on a duty - breaking employer in these circumstances is heavily outweighed by the injustice of denying redress to a victim."

可以说贵族院在 Fairchild v. Glenhaven Funeral Services (2003) AC 32 先例是判只要被告的侵权行为增加了原告患癌的风险，就已经是与原告最后患上间皮瘤之间成立了因果关系。此外，也引进了"连带责任"(joint and several liability)的说法，就是每一个雇主都要对原告负全责。这一个先例在《McGregor on Damages》(18th edn, 2009 年)一书 6 - 021 段说："*Fairchild* marks the high point in English law of the departure from the requirement that cause in fact must be shown before damages can be awarded."

但接下去，另一个贵族院的先例 Barker v. Corus (UK) Plc (2006) 2 AC 572 认为原告可以向任何一个雇主索赔全部的损失也有不公平之处，判是应该只分摊。Hoffman 勋爵是这样说："In my opinion, the attribution of liability according to the relative degree of contribution to the chance of the disease being contracted would smooth the roughness of the justice which a rule of joint and several liability creates. The defendant was a wrong doer, it is true, and should not be allowed to escape liability altogether, but he should not be liable for more than the damage which he caused and, since this is a case in which science can deal only in probabilities, the law should accept that position and attribute liability according to probabilities."可值得一提的是，在该先例其中一位原告曾经三次接触过石棉，两次是不同的雇主，但另一次是原告自雇，并且在期间没有小心与妥善地为自己作出保护以免暴露在石棉中。所以要求其中一位雇主负全责，就会变为是原告自雇期间的疏忽也要这个雇主负责。

在 Barker v. Corus (UK) Plc 先例后，很快带来 2006 年《The Compensation Act》立法的修改。这是在 Section 3，说明有责任的被告导致或者允许原告暴露在石棉，而原告事后间皮瘤发作，但没有办法确定是否是由于被告导致的暴露或是其他的暴露引致发病，被告还是要负责任并需要负责原告所有的损失，责任是连带性。这连带性责任是不管有否其他侵权责任的第三人(other than by the defendant, whether or not on circumstances in which another person has a liability in tort)或是被告本人有情况是没有侵权的责任(by the defendant in circumstances in which he has no liability in tort)。在前一种情况，没有侵权责任的第三人显然可以是包括原告本人，他在自雇的时候没有采取保护措施而暴露在石棉下,但自己不会对自己有侵权责任。而在后一种情况,会是包括如在被告雇用的时间,其中一段是有作出充分的保护措施,所以不存在有侵权的责任。但被告还是会对其余有侵权或违反法律的一段时间需要负全责。可见,立法已经恢复到 Fairchild v. Glenhaven Funeral Services (2003) AC 32 先例之后与 Barker v. Corus (UK) Plc (2006) 2 AC 572 先例之前的普通法地位,充分保障受害方与明确不适用"要不是"的测试。

值得一提的是《The Compensation Act》立法的修改只是针对间皮瘤病,对其他的涉及工业的病症,Fairchild v. Glenhaven Funeral Services (2003) AC 32 先例与 Barker v. Corus (UK) Plc (2006) 2 AC 572 先例的普通法地位还是适用。

4.3.4 例外情况之四:同时发生的侵权造成同一损失

如果同时发生两个独立的侵权行为,任何一个就足以造成有关的损失。这一来,又是一种情况不要求"要不是"测试。举一个例子,两个着火点同时来自 A 与 B,但两个着火点之间没有相互关系,这两个着火点同时蔓延损坏了 C 的房子。如果 C 向 A 提出索赔,但没有或不能把 B 也拖进来一并审理,A 就可以根据"要不是"测试说,即使不是我的疏忽,你的房子也会被火烧毁。但 C 如果向 B 提出索赔,也会面对同样的争辩。显然这是说不通,唯一合理的做法是判 A 或 B 都要个别承担 C 的损失。但这一来,判决是主要考虑谁应该负责的问题而并非侵权与损失之间的因果关系问题。这方面可节录 Nicolls 勋爵在 Kuwait Airways Corp v. Iraq Airways Co (2002) UKHL 19 先例所说:"In this type of case, involving multiple wrongdoers, the court may treat wrongful conduct as having sufficient causal connection with the loss for the purpose of attracting responsibility even though the simple 'but for' test is not satisfied. In so deciding the court is primarily making a value judgment on responsibility."

有类似的判法是加拿大最高院的 Cook v. Lewis (1951) SCR 830,案情涉及 A 与 B 到树林里去打猎,并同时以为看到猎物向同一个方向开枪,但结果伤害了 C。C 的伤害是来自一颗子弹,但没办法证明是来自 A 的枪还是 B 的枪,所以满足不了"要不是"测试的举证责任。加拿大最高院判是 A 与 B 的侵权行为导致了 C 无法举证,所以举证责任改为是在 A 与 B。如果他们满足不了(这是极可能的事),就判 A 或 B 都要个别及连带承担 C 的损失。

4.3.5 例外情况之五:"要不是"测试不足够认定主要原因

有说法是"要不是"测试有必要确立最早的侵权与违约行为与最后造成损失之间有一定的关系,但不足以这一个测试认定造成最后损失的主要或有效原因。毕竟,法律的因果关系受到其他政策上的影响(特别是侵权)与/或根据"价值观"(value judgement)考虑是谁最应该负责最后的损失。这方面可节录 Aikens 大法官的《Bill of Lading》(2006 年)一书之 10.129 段所说:"The 'but for' cause is usually a necessary but rarely sufficient criterion for legal causation. It is necessary because damage is rarely caused by an event if it would have happened anyway, and not sufficient because for obvious policy reasons not all the ‘but for’ causes of an event are legally causative. The ‘but for’ test is rarely relevant, except where specific words, such as ‘directly or indirectly arising’ in Article Iv. rule 6(这是指1924年《海牙规则》的条文), make it applicable.”

这方面可介绍The “Kamilla” (2006) 2 Lloyd’s Rep 238先例,案情涉及船舶不适航(第二舱盖没有密封关上)而导致了在航次中海水渗入并损坏了约30吨的扁豆,但这只是整票货物的1%。在阿尔及利亚的卸港,当局却拒绝整票货物,这导致收货人在卸港扣船并最终逼迫船东作出赔偿约38万美元的损失。而如果损失只局限在30吨的扁豆,只有大概9300美元的区区小数。这事后带来船东与承租人之间的争议,就是根据“互保协会内部协议”(Inter - Club Agreement)[1]怎么样分摊,因为如果整票货物的损失原因是不适航则要船东自己承担,不存在分摊。但如果货物大部分的损失主要原因是阿尔及利亚当局的过激反应(这种情况在中东国家并非是罕见),就存在不同的分摊损失了。在仲裁裁决书,判是损失主要原因来自不适航,这导致败诉船东上诉至英国法院。船东上诉的理由是仲裁庭只简单的考虑“要不是”测试,认为没有不适航导致这30吨扁豆的损坏就不会带来后来发生的重大损失。但完全没有考虑船东的争辩绝大部分的损失的近因或有效原因并非是不适航,而且阿尔及利亚当局的过激反应拒货是完全不能合理预见到的损失。以下可节录船东在这方面的争辩:“Mr Berry QC for the owners(船东代表大律师), who was not instructed to appear before the arbitrators, submitted that the assumed facts, in paras 1 - 3 of the agreed document, gave the owners a strong case for saying that unseaworthiness was not a proximate cause of the claim. He drew attention especially to the assumed facts that only about 1 per cent of the cargo was wetted; that the damaged cargo was separated out by the crew; that the receiver’s request for inspection by the DCP (阿尔及利亚当局) was unusual and was not within the reasonable contemplation of the parties; and that the decision of the DCP was irrational, unjustified and unreasonable and not within the reasonable contemplation of the parties. The arbitrators decided that the only fact that needed to be proved or assumed was that stated in para 1. 1. In other words, they ignored the other facts. They did so because they were misled by the charterers’ arguments into thinking that they had to apply what for shorthand could be called the ‘but for’ test of causation. This is reflected in para 31 of the decision where they say that the cargo would not have been rejected ‘but for the unseaworthiness of the vessel.’ He argued that when the arbitrators used the word ‘triggered’ in para 34 that was, again, a sign that they had applied a ‘but for’ test. He made the same point in relation to the words ‘not mere coincidence’ in para 36. Thus in excluding the alleged facts and by applying the simple ‘but for’ causation test, and in excluding remoteness, the arbitrators erred in law. As a matter of law, the courts look to proximate

---

[1] 有关协议可看杨大明所著的《期租合约》一书第25.3段。

cause and not to the infinity of causes and their impulsion in one another. . . It must be erroneous to exclude evidence of all the facts which would enable common sense to be exercised."

在高院，Morison 大法官同意“要不是”测试并不足够找出最后损失的有效原因或近因，但也不同意船东的争辩说损失必须是违约方能够合理预见到。Morison 大法官是同意与支持仲裁庭对因果关系的判决，认为不适航是造成船东所有损失的有效原因，虽然部分损失与严重性是船东预见以外，但这种过激反应的拒货在中东港口并非是罕见，正如仲裁裁决书所说：“by no means unprecedented in our experience”（para 31）。Morison 大法官是这样说：“The test for causation is whether the act or default complained of is a ‘proximate cause’ of the alleged damage. The ‘but for’ test is appropriate to establish whether there is a causal link between the act or default and the alleged damage. It is a necessary but not sufficient test. But for the choice of this vessel the incident would not have occurred but no – one could suggest that the choice of vessel was a proximate cause of the damage. It was unfortunate that the charterers appeared to espouse a ‘but for’ test. I suspect that they were provoked into doing so by the equally erroneous approach of the owners in argument before the arbitrators that the damage which was not reasonably foreseeable could not have been caused by the wetting that occurred due to unseaworthiness. Yet foreseeability ‘is not the criterion for deciding whether a person caused something or not. People often cause things which they could not have foreseen’: per Lord Hoffmann in Environmental Agency (Formerly National Rivers Authority) v. Empress Car Co (Abertillery) Ltd (1999) 2 AC 22 at page 34. However the argument arose and were initially presented, I agree with the charterers that the correct test for causation was applied by the arbitrators when they found that ‘provided the unseaworthiness of the vessel could be said in a practical sense to be a [and I stress the use of the indefinite article] cause of the loss, it was not appropriate to embark upon a further inquiry as to whether it was the [and I stress the use of the indefinite article] effective cause of the loss. . . ’ In my judgment the arbitrators dealt with causation in precisely the way required in law and they were not distracted from their task by some of the submissions which counsel made to them."

5. 不涉及新介入事件或行为的侵权或违约与最后损失有直接/自然的关系并可以预见

首先针对不涉及新介入事件或行为的情况，也就是不会涉及中断因果关系或因果链。这种情况通常是侵权或违约事件或行为直截了当造成最后的损失，它们之间没有发生过任何新介入事件或行为。例如在 Re Polemis (1921) 8 Lloyd's Rep. 351

的卸货工人疏忽把船舶的舱盖板掉下船舱并造成船舶损坏或是 The “Wagon Mound”(1961) 1 Lloyd’s Rep 1 的船舶漏油造成火灾,这都是不涉及其他新介入事件或行为。

侵权或违约行为造成最后损失是否是有“直接与自然原因”(direct and natural cause)关系是因果关系的测试,它们之间会是没有新介入事件或行为,例如是 Re Polemis。而在违约时或订约时对损失类别的合理预见/预料是针对第三章的损失遥远性的另一个测试。它们会在许多情况能够满足这两个要求,但还是有情况这两个要求并不能走在一起。

曾经有说法是侵权或违约与最后损失有直接与自然关系,没有新介入事件或行为,就已经足够要求错误方的被告作出全数赔偿:Re Polemis (1921) 8 Lloyd’s Rep. 351; Thurogood v. Van Den Berghs (1951) 2 KB 537 CA。在后一个先例,上诉庭的 Asquith 大法官说:“Directness of causation is the sole criterion of recoverability. The actual damage may be wholly different in character, magnitude or in the detailed manner of its incidence, from anything which could reasonably have been anticipated.”(直接的因果关系是赔偿成功与否的唯一的考虑。至于真正造成的损失会是完全不能合理预见,不论是在损失的性质上、严重程度或是其他细节,不是考虑的因素。)

但上述的先例,特别是 Re Polemis,已经被后来枢密院的先例 The “Wagon Mound” (No. 1) (1961) 1 Lloyd’s Rep 1 推翻,认为直接与自然的因果关系造成最后的损失并非是唯一的考虑,而是要看最后的损失是否是侵权方可以预见到会发生。有关这方面,在本书第三章之 12.2.2 段已经有详细介绍,不再重复。只节录 Viscount Simonds 大法官在 The “Wagon Mound”先例中所说:“The ‘sovereign principle’ is that liability does not depend solely on the damage being the ‘direct’ or ‘natural’ consequence of the precedent act... thus foreseeability becomes the effective test’.”(最重要的大原则是损失赔偿责任并不应该只考虑是否是侵权行为‘直接’或‘自然’的后果,所以可否预见才是最有效的测试。)

这一说法是针对最早的侵权或违约与最后造成的损失并没有新介入事件或行为的情况,这一来就是以损失是否可以合理预见/料想得到为准。而侵权与违约的合理预见/料想得到在时间上与程度上并不相同,这也在本书第三章之 12.1 段有详细介绍,也不再重复。

最后一提的是可合理预见的损失作为是最重要的测试只是针对疏忽的侵权,但在其他类别如涉及严格责任的侵权,因果关系会应是重要的测试。这可节录《McGregor on Damages》(18th edn, 2009 年)一书 6-012 段如下:“But causation cannot be so easily superseded. This becomes particularly clear when one looks beyond the tort of negligence itself. For in many torts where liability is strict and independent of negligence, foreseeability cannot *ex hypothesi* be the test of the extent of liability. Thus causation must remain the test of the extent to which a defendant is liable under the rule in

Rylands v. Fletcher (1868) LR 3 HL 330: indeed, some of the so - called 'defences' to that particular tort, such as that based upon the act of a stranger, may perhaps be said to stem from the fact that the damage is causally too remote. Cattle trespass is another tort in point. If the defendant's trespassing animals should infect the claimant's animals with disease, it is submitted that the defendant should be liable for this damage although he could not reasonably have foreseen that his animals were suffering from infectious disease at the time of the trespass. And it is also significant that in *The Wagon Mound*, where the claimants had claimed both in negligence and in nuisance, the Judicial Committee remitted the case on the issue of nuisance. Furthermore, in the tort of negligence itself, as indeed in all other torts, it must be shown that the defendant's breach of duty of care has, as a matter of fact, caused the damage to the claimant, and in certain cases the defendant will not be liable for foreseeable damage because he cannot be shown to have caused it in fact."

6. 新介入事件或行为会否中断因果链

在侵权或违约行为(作为前因)与损失(作为后果)之间,往往会出现"新介入事件或行为"(intervening act or event),导致了最后的损失或额外损失。这种新介入事件或行为好像是一波接着一波,它们之间都应有"一定的关系"(casual relationship)。可以说,如果侵权或违约与最后损失之间有一个"直接与自然"(direct and natural)的关系,就表示没有新介入事件或行为。但如果说两者之间只是有"间接关系"(indirect relationship),就已经显示了有了新介入事件或行为。现实中有不少这种实例,因果关系更会是一波未平,一波又起的情况。常要看这新的一波或新介入事件或行为是否是足够分量中断因果链。

新介入事件或行为会是千变万化,可大可小,包括外来事件(如在船舶碰撞的侵权后,受损船舶在开去避难港口途中遇上了风暴或另一个碰撞)、第三人行为(如在船舶碰撞后受损船舶在维修港口遇上领航员或修理厂工人罢工而导致了额外损失)或受害方自己的行为。而如果是受害方的行为,也通常会是他减少损失的行为,但这一个行为事后看会是做得不好,甚至是疏忽了。这就给了侵权方或违约方的抗辩机会说是最后造成的损失或额外损失主要与有效原因是来自新介入事件或行为。

如果违约方或侵权方的争辩能够成立,就可以说是新介入事件或行为中断了原来侵权或违约行为与最后损失的因果关系或"因果链"(chain of causation)。

新介入事件或行为会是可以合理预见到会可能发生,也不是受害方自己的疏忽或错误(如侵权的受害方在医院治疗就会容易受到其他的感染;违约受害方的船东去安排船舶在船厂进行修理时遇上罢工:The "Mineral Transporter" (1985) 2 Lloyd's

Rep 303 等)。但也会有新介入事件或行为是不能合理可以预见(如受害方在医院治疗时发生火灾或房子倒塌;船舶在船厂进行修理时遇上地震或船厂倒闭),或这些行为/事件涉及受害方或第三人的严重疏忽或错误。反正是这些不同性质的新介入事件或行为会在中断因果关系方面有完全不同的后果。

针对以上的简单介绍,可以在无数先例中的权威说法挑 Vinmar v. Theresa Nav. (2001) 2 Lloyd's Rep 1 先例中 Tomlinson 大法官所说如下:"Questions of causation arise in many contexts and they are often elusive. They fall to be decided as matters of fact and common sense. Where there is an act of decision of a party independent of the contract or duty breaker which is said to sever the chain of causation between breach and loss, the quality of that act or decision must be examined in its context in order to determine whether it should be regarded as having that effect. In principle that enquiry is no different whether the independent party is a stranger to the transaction or is the claimant himself or someone for whose acts the claimant is responsible. However in practice it is perhaps inevitable that it is in general easier to establish a *novus actus interveniens* where the act relied on is that of the claimant or someone for whom the claimant is responsible. Furthermore, an act or decision is the more likely to be regarded as breaking the chain of causation if it can be characterized as involving a want of appropriate care by a person under a duty to take such care."(因果关系的问题经常出现而且是难以捉摸。这问题是根据不同案件的事实与一般的常识作出判断。如果是有一位与违约方或侵权方无关的独立人士所作出的行为,这会否中断原来违约或侵权与损失之间的因果链就要根据该行为或决定的分量而判断到底会否能够中断。原则上这一个独立人士是完全无关的第三人或是受害方原告本人或是原告的代理人,都不会有区别。但在实际中,受害方原告或他的代理人所作出的行为是更容易中断因果链。另是该独立人士的行为或决定是涉及疏忽,而他本来是有责任小心,就会更加容易中断因果链。)

以上的结论简单提到不是所有的新介入事件或行为都可以中断因果链,而是要看是什么事件或行为。其中,它提到了受害方自己或他的代理人疏忽的行为是更容易中断因果链。以下的段节可以分段详细分析一些重要说法有关什么样的新介入事件或行为会或不会有这个后果。

6.1 说法之一:新介入事件或行为能合理预见才不会中断因果链

在中国人所讲的"一波未平,一波又起"的新介入事件或行为,就会有争议最后的损失到底是上一波还是下一波所导致,或是第二波是否中断了第一波的前因与最后损失的因果关系或因果链。一个关键的测试是上一波能否"合理预见"(reasonably foresee)有这下一波。而如果第二波是不可合理预见,也往往表示第二波带来的损失是与上一波的侵权或违约事件或行为没有直接关系,侵权方或违约方也是不必负责最后的或第二波造成的额外损失。但如果第二波是第一波引发后可以合理预见,就表示要对第一波负责的侵权方或违约方还是要赔偿最后造成的所有损失。

所以，船舶因航次中不合理绕航或不适航导致延误开航会为该航次带来延误，这是违约并且船东要对延误的损失负责。但如果延误开航导致在航次中遇到“雷击”（thunderbolt）而船货被毁，就不应怪船东为什么不准时开航，否则可以避过该雷击。原因是两者（船东违约与新介入事件的雷击）没有一定的直接与自然关系，也不能合理预见。虽然的确是因为船舶的延误开航，否则不会遇上这一下的雷击，但人类不应能合理预见得到延误会增加或减少遭受雷击的风险（这是 Normand 勋爵在 The “British Monarch” (1947) 80 Lloyd's Rep. 151 先例的讲话：it might be said that if the ship had not been delayed she would not have been at the place where the thunderbolt struck her, but no human being could have foretold that delay would in any degree increase the risk of destruction by a thunderbolt）。

但同样的船东违约，船舶延误开航或不合理绕航带来航次无法准时完成，因为第二次世界大战爆发，这导致了船舶去不了卸港，货方蒙受损失，船东就会要负责赔偿。这是因为在订约时船东可以“合理预见”战争的危险，当时欧洲已是战云密布，在这种情况下，显然是尽早完成航次就会减少风险。所以，新介入的事件或行为，也就是第二次世界大战，并不能中断船东违约造成延误与最后损失的因果链。在 The “British Monarch” (1947) 80 Lloyd's Rep. 151 先例，Normand 勋爵说：“In the present case, the outbreak of war in September, 1939, was not, of course, predictable in the same way as the closing of a port by ice is predictable, but on the statement of Mr. Sherriff, one of the witness for the appellants, the risk of war was in April, 1939, causing the appellants grave concern, and it was for that reason that the war deviation clause was specially inserted in the contract. The outbreak of war, therefore, and the almost inevitable consequence that British ships would then be diverted from Karlshamn（卸港）, though not certain, were within reasonable human foresight and were in fact foreseen by the appellants, as the contract itself shows. And, further, the shipowners must have known that the undue prolongation of the voyage was more likely to bring it within the operation of a wartime embargo than if the voyage were prosecuted without delays and with ordinary speed. There is accordingly a connection between the unseaworthiness of the ship and the operation of the embargo and the consequent non-fulfilment of the voyage, and it is a connection which is real and not fortuitous.”

也有不少先例对第二波能否合理预见采取比较宽松的态度，毕竟有很多情况是能够预见会有困难或麻烦，但不能预见到底会是什么困难或麻烦与程度上会否严重。而如果太轻易让第二波中断因果链，也会对受害方不公平。所以，不少先例判是只要不是“不自然与不正常”（unnatural & extra-ordinary）与完全独立的新介入事件，一般不会判是中断了因果链。

例如是在 The “Sivand” (1998) 2 Lloyd's Rep 97 先例，案情涉及一个简单的侵权，就是被告的船舶 Sivand 轮在挂靠时把受害方原告的油码头碰坏。之后，受害方雇佣了承建商对油码头进行修理，双方签署了承建合约，是根据著名标准格式合约的

ICE。它其中有一条第12条文约定在工程途中遇上了一些有经验承建商也无法合理预见的障碍,额外的费用与时间是要雇主承担。在工程进行的途中,涉及一艘工作驳船是以支架伸去海床作为支撑。由于海床的泥土不能支撑而导致了支架倒塌并导致工作驳船的全损,这是有经验的承建商也无法合理预见的事件。根据ICE第12条文,承建商成功在伦敦仲裁向雇主(也就是受害方)取回这笔损失。接下去是受害方向被告(Sivand轮船东)要求赔偿损失,其中也包括了这一项赔给承建商的损失。被告的抗辩是这发生在工程进行中的第二波所造成的额外损失是不可预见,这显然是有经验承建商也无法预见。但上诉庭是判船东的被告败诉,认为被告可以合理预见原告需要修理被损坏的油码头,也可以合理预见修理工程以经常被使用的ICE标准格式合约,其中包括了第12条文。再进一步,被告可以合理预见修理工程中会发生事故(特别是考虑到海床工程难以预测与科技上的局限)导致被告需要根据ICE标准格式合约第12条文赔偿承建商的损失。上诉庭的Pill大法官是说:

"I do not accept as a general principle that the extent of a wrongdoer's liability to his victim can be determined by the terms of the victim's contract with a third party. I am not however surprised at the defendants' concession in this case that it was reasonable for the plaintiffs to contract with the repairers on ICE terms including cl. 12. They are in common use for such contracts and the possibility that they would be used could have been foreseen by all parties. Having made the concession, the defendants cannot escape liability on the basis they claim. It was, as Lord Justice Hobhouse puts it by reference to Counsel's submission, 'the end of the matter'.

However I also consider that the same result would follow even if there had been no such concession. In the present contract, the victim's right to contract on cl. 12 terms no more than reflects the extent of the tortfeasor's potential liability to him. Given the vagaries of the seabed and the limitations of technology, it was foreseeable that ground conditions might be encountered which competent contractors could not be expected to foresee. It was the defendants' misfortune that the damage their vessel caused was caused to a structure located at a point above the seabed where a combination of difficult ground conditions was liable to and did occur. The liability of the defendants is founded on one aspect of the principle that a tortfeasor takes his victim as he finds him. The conditions encountered cannot in my judgment be equated with an earthquake or freak storm."

The"Sivand"先例与较早前一个涉及航运的"共同海损"(general average)先例判法也是一致。众所周知,共同海损是针对在船舶与货物面临海上风险时候为了共同的利益船长"刻意"(intentional)作出的牺牲或费用,在航次安全完成后要求受惠的船舶与货物需要分摊损失。这是英国的普通法地位,也是通常作为共同海损计算的《约克-安特卫普规则》(York - Antwerp Rules)中的规定。但共同海损可以是与侵权或者违约走在一起,就是遇上风险需要作出牺牲或费用的起因是由侵权方或违约方所造成。例如,有一票货物隐瞒了危险性,结果在航次中爆炸,导致船舶与船上其他货物的风险需要做出共同海损的牺牲或费用。或是船东违约的船舶不适航,导致在航次中发生风险并带来同样的后果。这一来,整个共同海损最终还是要侵权方或违约方承担责任。由于共同海损是延续一段时间的行为,所以经常会有因果关系的争议,就是最后造成的牺牲或费用与原来的侵权或违约或共同海损行为是否中断因果链。其中有不少先例是针对能否合理预见最后严重的后果。与 The "Sivand"先例判法一致的是 Coastal Shipping v. Green (1971) 1 QB 456,案情涉及遇事的船舶需要拖带去安全港口,船东也作出了安排,这拖带的费用显然是共同海损。但在拖带过程中,拖缆断了,并且部分缆绳卷到拖轮车叶导致拖轮失去动力并最后全损。船东与拖轮公司的协议是根据著名的标准格式合约 United Kingdom Standard Towage Conditions,约定拖轮在拖带过程中发生任何损坏(包括对拖轮造成的损坏),即使是拖轮的疏忽,也是一面倒要求船东承担责任与作出赔付。这是一面倒的合约,但拖轮公司所持的理由就是这种拖带作业涉及很大的危险,所以他们没有办法承担责任,而是要由雇主承担责任。这一先例的争议就是该拖轮的全损,也就是船东要赔付给拖轮公司的钱,能否作为共同海损。在上诉庭,判是可以。而针对可否合理预见后来发生的新介入事件或行为(就是指拖轮在拖带时的疏忽造成额外损失),所需要的只是有一点点会预见发生的可能性就业已足够,不会中断因果关系/因果链。Denning 勋爵是这样说:"If the master, when he does 'the general average act', ought reasonably to have foreseen that a subsequent accident of the kind might occur - or even that there was a distinct possibility of it - then the subsequent accident does not break the chain of causation... If, however, there is a subsequent incident which was only a remote possibility, it would be different."

多介绍一个共同海损有关的先例是 Anglo - Grecian v. Benyon (1926) 24 Ll L Rep 122,案情涉及有关的船舶由于事故导致船壳进水,有沉没的危险,船长在领航员的协助下决定把船舶冲上浅滩搁浅。但由于计算错误,船舶漂流去礁石搁浅而造成船舶严重的损坏。法院判是这一个额外的损坏也算作是共同海损的牺牲,需要船货分摊,因为后来的新介入行为(船长计算错误)并没有中断因果关系/因果链。Roche 大法官是这样说:"... although the grounding on the rocks was not at any rate foreseen as either a necessary or even a probable consequence by the pilot, yet it was not a subsequent accident unconnected with the grounding. It was at all times a possibility and it was a possibility which did not render the action of beaching illegitimate, or render the subsequent materialisation of the possibility into an actuality so disconnected with the beaching which brought it about as to break the chain of causation and prevent the plaintiffs from recovering in respect of the damage done by the rocks."

6.2 说法之二:新介入事件或行为必须是受害方的合理行为才不会中断因果链

这种一波未平一波又起的情况很多时候是涉及受害方"减少损失"(mitigation of

damage)，如船舶碰撞后受害方安排救助，或是承租人在一个长期租约中违约/毁约后船东另找替代租约让有关船舶可以赚一点租金与减少损失，或是雇员被非法解雇后另找替代工作而不是待在家中等待索赔所有失去的工资等。而在这些减损的过程中，受害方不幸地遇上了第二波的事件或行为。例如，船舶被救助的时候发生另一宗海难，如碰撞或者搁浅。或是雇员在寻找替代工作时被新雇主欺骗而蒙受更大的损失。所以因果关系很多时候与减少损失难以区分，新介入事件或行为也就与后来的减损行为是否"合理"(reasonable)分不开。正如 Templeman 大法官在 The "Liesbosch" (1933) 45 Ll L Rep 123 先例所说："Whatever principle is invoked – whether it be the principle of causation or mitigation – the acid test in the present circumstances must have been reasonableness; and, if the interest charges were reasonable, they were not damages for which the managers were liable. I agree with Mr. Johnson that in some circumstances different principles may require different tests and produce different results, but in the present case, if these interest charges were unreasonable – they were too remote; they were not caused by the breach; they were not part of a reasonable form of mitigation – all these matters hang together."

另可引述 Lindley 大法官在 The "City of Lincoln" (1890) 15 P 15 的一句话说："I take it that reasonable human conduct is part of the ordinary course of things. So far as I can see my way to any definite proposition I should say that the ordinary course of things does not exclude all human conduct, but includes at least the reasonable conduct of those who have sustained the damage, and who are seeking to save further loss."(这句话大致上是指合理的人类行为是自然与一般性会发生的，也是可以合理预见到的，所以不会中断因果链。)

其他权威说法也可节录 The "Metagama" (1927) 29 Ll L Rep 253 先例，Viscount Dunedin 大法官是这样说："But it is always the duty of the person who is damaged to do his best to minimise his loss. This is really the same thing as to say that, if he might reasonably have avoided any part of the damage he has suffered, to that extent the damage is not such as arises directly from the act complained of. In many cases the question is stated as to whether, after the original fault which started matters, there has been a *novus actus interveniens* which was the direct cause of the final damage. *Novus actus interveniens* may be the act of a third party, so that in this case I think the best way of stating the question is, was the pursuer guilty of such negligence after the collision as to make that negligence the direct cause of the final damage?"

另在 Canadian Pacific Ry v. Kelvin Shipping Co (1927) 138 LT 369 HL 先例，Haldane 勋爵说："Where those in charge of the injured ship do to save it may be mistaken, but if they do whatever they do reasonably, although unsuccessfully, their mistaken judgment may be a natural consequence for which the offending ship is responsible, just as much as is any physical occurrence. Reasonable human conduct is part of the ordinary course of things, which extends to the reasonable conduct of those who have sustained the damage and who are seeking to save further loss."

较近期的说法有 The "Sivand" (1998) 2 Lloyd's Rep 97 先例,上诉庭的 Evans 大法官总结有关先例,说:"The language was that of causation (*novus actus interveniens*) and the judgments are authority for the propositions (1) that reasonable human conduct is part of the ordinary course of things, for the purposes of the underlying common law rule (cf. The 'City of Lincoln'), and (2) that the defendant is not liable for damage, or increased damage, caused by negligence of the claimant or those for whom the claimant is responsible. The second proposition is substantially equivalent to the rule that the plaintiff is in breach of duty if he and those for whom he is responsible fail to take reasonable steps to mitigate the loss he has suffered by reason of the defendant's wrongdoing."[说法是因果关系的中断而权威的判决是说:(1)合理的人类行为是自然与一般性会发生的;(2)被告不需要负责因为是原告或原告需要负责人士的疏忽所造成的损失或增加了的损失。以上第二个说法也等同是说面对被告的错误行为,但原告没有合理减少损失。]

6.3　说法之三:新介入事件或行为改变不了原来侵权或违约的后果

即使是严重分量与性质的新介入事件或行为(如受害方严重疏忽),足可以中断因果关系,但由于改变不了原先侵权或违约所带来的后果,还是不会中断因果关系。笔者在 4.2.1 段介绍的 Barnett v. Chelsea and Kensington Hospital Management Committee (1969) 1 QB 428 先例就是对这一重要说法的很好例子,这也等于新介入的医院疏忽行为不能满足"要不是"(but for) 测试,满足这一测试还是原来的砒霜中毒导致了无可避免的后果,就是死亡。可另举一个船舶碰撞的先例,在 The "Bharatkhand" (1952) 1 Lloyd's Rep. 470,是两船相撞,受害方的船舶事后沉没。但有责任的侵权方指沉没船舶的船长应做一些事情防止沉没,但法院根据专家意见认定是即使做了,也不会令船舶浮太久,可以等到救援船(拖轮)抵达并拖去安全港口,所以改变不了沉没的命运。Willmer 大法官并认为侵权方指船长应该做的事情太具有投机性,毕竟受害方的减损责任只需要是合理,而举证责任是在他。如果侵权方是指船舶碰撞的"前因"与船舶沉没的"后果"之间有一个新介入事件或行为,他必须说明这是什么。在这一先例中不存在有第三人的行为或疏忽作为新介入事件,而剩下来的新介入行为只有是指称沉没船舶的船员有疏忽,没有合理减损,这也是会中断因果链的新介入行为。但侵权方必须证明受害方船员疏忽外,还要进一步证明如果没有这一疏忽,船舶沉没的命运就可以改变了。Willmer 大法官是这样说:"It appears to me that in those circumstances the onus is upon those who allege that there was a *novus actus interveniens* to prove that there was. There is here no question of any act on the part of a third party – which, of course, in some cases is the *novus actus* relied upon. Here the only *novus actus* which has been, or could be, suggested is fault on the part of the plaintiffs' servants themselves. On the facts of this case, therefore, it seems to me that, in order to displace the plaintiffs' *prima facie* case, the defendants have to prove, first, that the plaintiffs' servants failed in their duty to minimize the damage by omitting to take some precaution which good seamanship required; and, **secondly**, having done that, **they must go on to prove that if that precaution had been taken the loss complained of would probably have been averted.**"(黑字是笔者的强调)

6.4 说法之四:新介入事件或行为必须是造成损失或额外损失的主要或有效原因

新介入事件或行为能够中断因果链,必须是令原来的侵权或违约行为再也不是损失或额外损失的有效原因,变为"历史事实"(historical fact)的部分,而新介入事件或行为才是主要或有效甚至是唯一的原因。这往往也表示新介入事件或行为不能是太轻微或无关重要。这方面可节录 Vinmar v. Theresa Nav.(2001)2 Lloyd's Rep 1, Tomlinson 大法官所说如下:"The conduct of those for whom the claimants are responsible cannot be regarded as breaking the chain of causation between the admitted breach of contract and the loss unless that conduct can be regarded as the sole cause of the loss to the exclusion of any efficacy of the breach - see per Mr. Justice Devlin in Heskell v. Continental Express Ltd.,(1950) 83 LL. L. Rep. 438 at p. 457, col. 2. 'The contract breaker is liable so long as his breach was 'an' effective cause of the loss; the Court need not choose which cause was the most effective' - Chitty on Contracts, 28th ed., par. 27-033."

6.5 说法之五:侵权或违约前已经存在的历史事实不属于新介入行为或事实

在理念上,在侵权或违约前已经存在的"历史事实"(historical fact)很难被接受为新介入事件或行为并中断因果链,成为最后损失的有效原因。这在时间上与逻辑上都说不通。

6.5.1 "脆弱头壳"案例受害方的身体弱不禁风被视为是历史事实

在侵权的案例,有一个说法是已经存在的因素是不能中断侵权与损失之间的因果关系或因果链。其中最为人所知的一些名为"脆弱头壳"或"鸡蛋壳头壳"(thin - skull 或 egg - shell skull)的说法,这是指一些受害方在侵权之前可能有一段长时间就已经是弱不禁风,碰一碰他就会一倒不起。这导致侵权方的被告会抗辩说他的侵权行为(如疏忽驾驶或是不小心在露台掉了一些东西而导致受害方受伤)对正常人而言是造成微不足道的伤害,但由于受害方的原告身体状况,造成了严重事故甚至死亡,所以这才是死亡的主要原因。但一连串的先例,其中包括 Dulieu v. White(1901)2 KB 669、Bourhill v. Young(1943)AC 92 与 Smith v. Leech Brain & Co Ltd(1962)2 QB 405 先例,已经明确了侵权方碰到了怎样的受害方就要承担这些后果,也就是"the defendant takes the plaintiff (victim) as he finds him"的说法。在 Dulieu v. White 先例,Kennedy 大法官说:"If a man is negligently run over or otherwise negligently injured in his body it is no answer to the sufferer's claim for damages that he would have suffered less injury, or no injury at all, if he had not had an unusually thin skull or an unusually weak heart."

同样的说法是"衣衫褴褛的百万富翁"(shabby millionaire),这在 The "Arpad" (1934)49 Llyod's Rep 313 先例, Scrutton 大法官说:"You negligently run down a shabby - looking man in the street, and he turns out to be a millionaire engaged in a very profitable business which the accident disables him from carrying on; or you negligently and ignorantly injure the favourite for the Derby (英国的大赛马会,1780 年德贝伯爵所创立) whereby he cannot run. You have to pay damages resulting from the circumstances of which you have no notice. You have to pay the actual loss to the man or his goods at the time of the tort."

这一个判法,被视为在考虑被告侵权所带来的后果,是不考虑已经存在的因素,如受害人的身体弱不禁风。这可节录上诉庭 Evans 大法官在 The "Sivand" (1998) 2 Lloyd's Rep 97 先例中所说:"A feature of 'thin - skull' cases is that the plaintiff's physical characteristics, which have the effect of increasing the scale or extent of physical damage caused to him by the defendant's negligence, are already in existence when the negligence occurs. It has therefore been suggested that there is a rule of law to the effect that pre - existing factors of this sort have to be disregarded when determining what are the consequences of the defendant's act: see for example McGregor on Damages (16th edn) pars 200 et seq."

6.5.2 不被视为历史事实的 The "Eurus"先例

但涉及违约,看来这一个说法很有疑问。在 The "Eurus" (1998) 1 Lloyd's Rep 351 先例,案情涉及一个租约的纠纷。有关船舶被航次租用去尼日利亚装 12.2 万吨原油,在该买卖合约,该批原油价格是按照提单日期为准(这是石油买卖惯常的结算办法)。在船舶抵达装港前的 1 月 23 日,承租人(也是 FOB 买方)就知道 2 月的原油价格会比 1 月低,很希望取得 2 月日期的提单。所以承租人命令船长不要在 1 月 31 日的 11:00 时之前递交"准备就绪通知书"(Notice of Readiness) 并且不要进港靠泊,这就有保证船舶会在 2 月才装完货。而有关的程租合约中,是有一条第 36 条文要求船东按照承租人的航次指示,否则要赔偿承租人所有的损失。但船长在 1 月 31 日的 00:30 时就进港靠泊,而在 11:00 时递交通知书时,船舶实际上已经在装货的中途。当承租人知道后,马上想办法让装货放慢。事实上,船舶是在 2 月 1 日的 01:30 时装完货物。但在尼日利亚装港有一个已经有 18 年历史的习惯做法是只要在第二天 08:00 时之前才装完的货物,都属于早一天的提单日期。但这一习惯做法是船东与承租人都不知道的,所以承租人并没有通知船长要想办法拖延至 2 月 1 日 08:00 时之后才装完货物。反正是承租人作为 FOB 买方最后要多支付了约 70 万美元的额外货价给尼日利亚的卖方,并向船东提出索赔损失,要求赔偿。这里所涉及造成损失的主要原因有两个,一是船长没有按照承租人的航次指示不要在 1 月 31 日的 11:00

时之前递交通知书，而不递交也表示不应靠泊。二是尼日利亚装港特殊的“08:00 时规定”(8 a. m. rule)。

如果是按照一般人的常识看承租人的损失是什么主要或有效的原因所造成，而估计很多人会毫不犹豫说是“08:00 时规定”所造成。但由于这是已经在违约前存在的事实，所以“08:00 时规定”能否被视为是新介入事件中断因果链是有疑问。仲裁庭看来不接受并在裁决书说：“It seemed to us that there were very real conceptual difficulties in Total(船东)argument that the 8 a. m. rule, which had existed for some 18 years at least before the conclusion of the charterparty contract, constituted an effective or intervening cause of Arcadia's(承租人)loss. The 8 a. m. rule was certainly part of the causal link between the failure to obey Arcadia's instructions and the loss suffered by them, but as an already extant factor at the time of the conclusion of the charterparty, it could not be considered as an effective or intervening cause of the loss...”

船东上诉去了法院，第一审的 Rix 大法官不同意仲裁庭的说法，认为法律并没有禁止认定违约前已经存在的事实才是造成损失的主要或有效原因，并举了 The “Almak” (1985) 1 Lloyd's Rep 557 先例。Rix 大法官是这样说：“As for the 8 o'clock rule itself as a candidate for the proximate cause, the arbitrators excluded it on the ground that it preceded Total's(船东)failure to comply. It will be recalled that in par. 58 of their award the arbitrators had spoken of the ‘very real conceptual difficulties’ in Total's argument that a rule which had preceded the charter for some 18 years constituted an ‘effective or intervening cause’. I agree that such a rule could not be properly considered an ‘intervening’ cause, even though its manifestation followed Total's failure, but for reasons which I have sought to explain above I do not see why it could not be an or indeed the effective cause... In my judgment it was a possible cause, and indeed once admitted as a candidate, became a strong contender in the light of the parties' ignorance of the rule and its unforeseeability from their point of view.”

之后上诉庭的 Staughton 大法官也不认同这一个说法，说：“It is common to refer to a chain of causation between the wrongful act and the plaintiff's loss, and to an intervening act which may or may not break the chain. If that is always the appropriate metaphor, of course it must follow that an event occurring before the wrongful act cannot break the chain. It is as simple as that. But I for my part do not accept that the chain metaphor is an appropriate one for causation in contract. Instead one has to ask whether in common sense the wrongful act was a cause of the plaintiff's loss, or whether something else was.”(一般的说法是错误行为与原告蒙受的损失之间有一个因果链，而如果发生新介入事件或行为，这会否中断因果链。如果这是一个恰当的比喻，显然，在错误行为发生之前已经存在的事实是不能中断因果链。但对我来说，我不认为这一个因果链的比喻适用在合约中的因果关系。而是应该依赖一般的常识查问什么造成了原告的损失——是

错误行为还是其他原因?)

至于比较一些“脆弱头壳”的案例,Staughton 大法官是这样说:“Hart & Honore (指这两位教授所著的《Causation in the Law》一书) cite the eggshell skull cases, the rule that a wrongdoer takes his victim as he finds him, as an example of the general principle; and they suggest that there is a similar rule for inanimate objects. I am not persuaded that there is such a general principle. It seems to me at least as likely that the eggshell skull cases are a separate category where the law allows compensation as a matter of policy, and not an example of a general principle.”(Staughton 大法官不认为“脆弱头壳”案件确立了一个通用的大原则,他认为这种案件是一个不同的类别,而法律允许索赔损失是基于公共政策,不是一个普遍性原则。)

但还有一个考虑是根据 The “Wagon Mound” (1961) 1 Lloyd's Rep 1 先例,只要是不大可能、不正常与不能合理预见的损失是不能向被告取回,即使损失是由于被告的侵权或违约所引起。这一来即使可以考虑“08:00 时规定”是主要或有效原因,看来这一个“08:00 时规定”所造成的损失应该是属于不大可能、不正常与不能合理预见的损失。这一点在《McGregor on Damages》(18th edn, 2009 年)之 6-032 段有提到说:“The important point, which Staughton L. J. would appear not to have appreciated, is that policy would have seen to it that liability would not have followed upon the elimination of the 8 o'clock rule as a relevant cause. For it is stated in the above text after the general rule for causation that whether the defendant will escape liability where the third factor is improbable, abnormal and unforeseeable turns on policy since *The Wagon Mound*, as we shall see, has favoured no liability in respect of the improbable, abnormal and unforeseeable. The 8 o'clock rule would have satisfied all three eptithets.”

6.6　说法之六:侵权或违约行为只是提供了机会但不是造成损失的有效原因

有部分的案例是判较早的侵权或违约行为只是为后来的事件或行为提供了机会并造成了最后的损失。这方面可先介绍 Galoo Ltd v. Bright Grahame Murray (1994) 1 WLR 1360 先例,案情涉及核数师的被告在审计原告公司账目的时候犯了错误,导致没有显示该公司实际上已经是无力偿付债务。原告向被告提出的损失是如果审计正确,让原告知道了公司无力偿付债务,他就不会继续营运并产生额外的损失。上诉庭判这一核数师的错误或疏忽只是提供了机会,但并非是导致后来的营运损失的主要或有效原因。而提供损失的机会与因果关系是有很大区别。营运损失的有效原因毕竟可以有很多,如原告自己经营不善或运气不好,毕竟正常的情况下营运是可以赚钱而不是蒙受损失。这一个案件也可以从其他角度来看,如违约的核数师没有办法合理预见他的疏忽会造成这一类别的损失,这一点可看《McGregor on Damages》(18th edn, 2009 年)一书 6-049 段的注脚 192。在这里也可节录该段节的内容如下:“Finally, it should be noted that there may be occasions when the defendant will be held not to have caused the loss but only to have provided the occasion for the loss by making the intervening act possible. This was the position in Saddington v. Colleys Professional Services (1999) 1 Lloyd's Rep PN 140 CA and again in Moore v. Zerfah (1999) 1 Lloyd's Rep PN 144 CA. Loans on mortgage were made to wives and their husbands, and the money lent was lost by the husband or by the husband's company. Actions were brought by the wives against valuers and brokers respectively on the basis that the wives would not have agreed to the loans but for negligence on the part of the defendant professionals. Both claims failed. The defendants' breach of duty did not cause the loss of the money but merely gave the opportunity for the loss to occur through the intervening act of the husband or the husband's company."

7. 新介入事件或行为之第一类:外来事件

这与第三人或受害方行为的不同之处是新事件的介入,不严格是追究第三人或受害方行为上错误或疏忽,或是他们合理或不合理的行为。

在这问题上,大原则与上述6.1段及接下去的段节所讲的道理一样。因为是外来事件,如遇上坏天气,所以也往往不关系到人为错误的问题。能否成为新介入事件中断因果链,主要是看可否合理预见下一波的发生。可以说与人类(不论是受害方或第三人)无关的天灾或自然现象也会有情况可中断因果链,但这种情况不多。毕竟太轻易中断因果关系对受害方并不公平,只是善待了侵权方或违约方。法院对侵权方或违约方有敌意的说法有许多例子,可节录Harlow & Jones, Ltd v. Panex (International), Ltd (1967) 2 Lloyd's Rep 509先例,Roskill大法官所说:"The defendants broke this contract. It is they who put the plaintiffs in this difficulty. Of course, a plaintiff has always to act reasonably, and of course he has to do what is reasonable to mitigate his damages. But he is not bound to nurse the interests of the contract breaker, and so long as he acts reasonably at the time it ill lies in the mouth of the contract breaker to turn round afterwards and complain, in order to reduce his own liability to a plaintiff, that the plaintiff failed to do that which perhaps with hindsight he might have been wiser to do."

例如在6.1段提到的The "British Monarch" (1947) 80 Lloyd's Rep. 151先例的雷击就被视为是不可合理预见的,可中断船东延误开航的违约与造成最后损失的因果关系。但反过来,受害方船舶在碰撞后进行修理,期间发生下雨或是暴热影响工程进度并带来额外损失,在很大程度上这种自然现象是可以合理预计到,所以不应该中断因果链。即使进行修理的船厂遇上了比较异常的下雨或是暴热,也不应该轻易让它中断因果关系,善待侵权方。但又反过来,如果是一场大地震/大海啸,如日本2011年3月11日发生的大地震,对进行修理中的船舶造成严重的损坏或全损,这种独立事件就会不一样。说是不能中断因果关系,要求原来侵权或违约而造成了船舶轻微的损坏是要这一次修理,赔偿大地震/大海啸造成的全损,可以说是有说不通之处。毕竟这种百年难得一见的大地震/大海啸会是属于 The "Wagon Mound" (1961) 1 Lloyd's Rep 1 先例所讲的"不大可能、不正常与不能合理预见"的损失,没有新介入事件也不需要侵权方或违约方赔偿。这种新介入事件也是6.1段所讲的上一波不能合理预见有这下一波。

针对以上所讲,可多举一个有关坏天气的新介入事件的 The "Carslogie" (1951) 2 Lloyd's Rep 441 先例。案情也是涉及船舶碰撞后,受害方被碰坏的船舶去纽约进行永久修理。但在开往纽约的中途,遇上的大风浪给船舶造成额外损坏。结果在纽约,总共花了30天的时间修理大风浪的损坏,但其中10天是同时修理碰撞的损坏。原告向碰撞的侵权方索赔这10天的时间损失,并被上诉庭所接受。但贵族院推翻上诉庭判决,认为碰撞虽然是引发了去纽约修理,但航程中遇到大风浪的外来事件造成船舶进一步的损坏中断了因果链。因为这一独立的新介入事件无可避免地令船舶需要30天的修理时间,加上修理是一并进行的,所以原来的碰撞所需要的10天的修理时间是可以包含在这30天之内的,碰撞的侵权方就不需要对10天延误损失负责。

除了坏天气,其他方面的新介入外来事件能否中断因果链的案例也有很多,可介绍少数的例子。

第一个案例要介绍的是 The "Malcolm Baxter, Jr" (1928) 31 Lloyd's Rep. 200 先例,船舶在美国的新奥尔良装货去法国的波尔多。船舶因不适航导致需要绕航去古巴的哈瓦那修理,但这延误带来航次无法完成,因为在其间美国下令禁运,不准船舶开往法国的波尔多。货方因此向船东索赔庞大损失,包括转运费用等。但美国最高法院判船东只是负责不适航带来延误所导致的货物差价损失,而对新介入事件的美国禁运,船东不必负责,因为这不可以合理预见。

第二个案件是在 LMLN No. 351 报道了1993年一个伦敦仲裁,该案中船东将船舶程租给承租人运货,租约规定船舶一到卸港承租人必须马上提供"抵港可达"的泊位(berth reachable on arrival)。船舶抵达卸港当天因天气恶劣未能立即开往泊位(根据上述条文承租人等于违约:The "Laura Prima" (1982) 1 Lloyd's Rep. 1;The "Sea Queen" (1988) 1 Lloyd's Rep. 588)。于是就在锚地抛锚,同时递交了"卸货准备就绪通知书"(notice of readiness to discharge),当时船舶已进入"滞期"(demurrage)。第二天天气转好,船舶在起锚准备开往泊位时却发现起锚机因"潜在缺陷"(latent defect)而发生故障(注意:这故障并非船舶的错误与疏忽),不能起锚。结果因为需要重装一台新的锚机方能起锚,一直拖了7天后船舶才靠了泊。仲裁中船东提出滞期费(这是属于违约的议定赔偿)要从递交通知书后起一直计算,承租人抗辩船舶递交的通知书无效,因为锚机有问题。而且即使通知书有效,承租人也只须负责整段滞期时间中的第一天滞期。因为本来船舶抵港后第二天即可靠泊,只是因为船舶的锚机发生故障,起不了锚才引起之后的滞期。所以承租人原先的违约(就是没有在船舶抵达卸港马上提供"抵港可达"的泊位)的因果链已被锚机故障这一个新介入事件中断。仲裁庭裁决认为:(1)船东递交的通知书有效。之后船舶的不妥是因承租人违约引发的,因为船舶抵港时完全适合卸货,如能直达泊位(因为承租人在租约承诺提供“抵港可达”的泊位)就根本不需要在锚地抛锚等候,就不会有锚机故障而带来额外的滞期;(2)承租人完全可以预见到如果没有依约马上提供抵港可达的泊位,很可能会因稍后介入的其他事项而引起进一步的滞期。比如泊位又被其他船舶占用了,或者装卸工人、引水员或拖轮人员罢工等,这些都是承租人可以预见到的违约之后的新介入事件,并不能中断承租人违约与最后损失之间的因果链。因此,这类事件引发的滞期均属承租人违约的直接后果,本案的锚机故障引起进一步滞期亦在此例。结果承租人仍是要赔偿所有滞期费。不过仲裁庭在案中也提到如果承租人违约之后的进一步延误是由船舶本身的错误或疏忽引起的,如锚机故障是因为缺乏维修保养,则这部分损失承租人不需要负责。毕竟是船东(受害方)本身的错误或疏忽,中断了因果链所要求的程度会是低多了,这稍后会进一步详论。

在以上判决或裁决,可见到一般法院或仲裁庭在一方当事人违约下,都不会太容易允许后来的外来事件中断因果链,令无辜受害方无法获得部分损失的赔偿,而要自己承担。

8. 新介入事件或行为之第二类:第三人的行为

新介入事件或行为比较多会产生争议的是第三人的行为或受害方自己的行为,考虑这种新介入行为到底有否中断因果链也是相对复杂。这方面可先简单节录《Chitty on Contracts》(30th edn, 2008 年)之26-033 段所说如下:“The problem of causation most likely to arise concern intervening acts of either a third party or of the claimant: but an issue of causation may also arise when the alleged loss is claimed on the basis of a hypothesis as to what the claimant or a third person would have done had the defendant not broken the contract.”

本段先探讨有关第三人的行为会否中断因果链,但显然是可以发生。这在上述6.2 段所介绍的 The “Metagama” (1927) 29 Ll L Rep 253 先例,Viscount Dunedin 大法官有讲到:“*Novus actus interveniens* may be the act of a third party,”表示第三人的行为也可以中断因果链。这方面也可节录 The “Sivand” (1998) 2 Lloyd's Rep 97 先例中的说法,大致上是说第三人即使没有错误或疏忽,也可以中断因果关系,因为这是一个独立的事件或因素。但可以说,第三人如果有错误或疏忽,而且严重,就更有可能中断因果关系,毕竟这造成的损失或额外损失也属于不能合理预见。这方面可节录 Evans 大法官在 The “Sivand” (1998) 2 Lloyd's Rep 97 先例中所说:“Viscount Dunedin referred to the act of a third party as another possible type of *novus actus interveniens*. It is not necessary, in my judgment, that the third party's act must have been negligent for it to have this effect, although if it is negligent then it may be more likely to do so. I would hold that when the independent act of a third party is properly regarded as the effective cause of damage, to the exclusion of the negligence for which the defendant is responsible, then that is because the intervening act was independent, not because it was or may have been negligent. This therefore is a question of fact, to be answered on a common sense basis for the reasons suggested above, although considerations both of negligence and reasonable foreseeability may be relevant to it."(这是说第三人的行为不必要是疏忽才能中断因果关系,虽然涉及疏忽就更容易中断。Evans 大法官认为最主要还是认定第三人行为是否是一个独立的行为,并且是造成损失或额外损失的有效原因。虽然在这方面会涉及疏忽与合理预见的考虑。)

综合以上所说,第三人的行为能否中断因果链涉及四个重要的考虑:(1)新介入事件是否导致了原来的侵权或违约变为历史事件的一部分。(2)第三人行为的新介入事件是否是选择性或故意,也不合理。(3)新介入事件是否可以合理预见。(4)第三人行为是否完全独立,与被告没有关系。

显然,这是要看每一个案件不同的事实才能下判断,正如在 Hogan v. Bentinck West Hartley Collieries (Owners) Ltd (1949) 1 All ER 588 先例所说:"... can only be answered on a consideration of all the circumstances and, in particular, the quality of that later act or event."(必须全面考虑所有的情况后,特别是该行为的质量。)

以下进一步探讨并把这第三人行为分类为第三人有无责任,或是有无选择的行为与第三人独立的恶意或疏忽行为。

8.1　第三人无侵权责任也没有真正选择的行为

举例说是涉及无知小孩的行为作为新介入的事件,如车主不小心安放车子而后来被无知小孩开动闯祸。又例如,第三人受惊作出反应,或想作出自卫行为的新介入事件。以上这些例子一般都不会中断因果链,后果仍是由原来错误或疏忽一方负责,被视为可以合理预见。如 Hamilton 大法官在 Latham v. Johnson (1913) 1 KB 398 先例所讲:"Children acting in the wantonness of infancy and adults acting on the impulse of personal peril may be and often are links in a chain of causation extending from such initial negligence to the subsequent injury... unless the intervention is a fresh, independent cause, the person guilty of the original negligence will still be the effective cause, if he ought reasonably to have anticipated such interventions and to have foreseen that if they occurred the result would be that his negligence would lead to mischief."

在同样的道理下,动物(如家畜)的行为作为新介入的事件也通常不会中断因果链:Cox v. Burbidge (1863) 13 CB NS 430; Manton v. Brocklebank (1923) 2 KB 212 CA; Buckle v. Holmes (1926) 2 KB 125 CA; Arneil v. Paterson (1931) AC 560; Wormald v. Cole (1954) 1 QB 614 CA。另在 Aldham v. United Dairies (1940) 1 KB 507 先例,Greene 勋爵说:"If a man negligently relaxes his hold on an animal it does not necessarily follow that he is liable for the damage caused by the animal in its state of freedom, for that damage may be due to a spontaneous act of the animal for which the want of care gives the opportunity, but of which it is not the cause." Parcq 大法官也说:"... even if a defendant's omission to control or secure his horse is negligent, an act on the part of the horse which is contrary to its ordinary nature cannot be regarded, in the absence of special circumstances, as being directly caused by such negligence."(这是说被告如果不小心控制或捆绑他的马匹,导致马匹因失控而伤害被告,除非有特别的情况,原来疏忽的马主还是要对被告的损失负责。)

作为对违约被告的错误行为,第三人如果合理为了保护他或其他人的利益而作出了对原告造成损失,被告也要负责。针对第三人为了保护他自己的利益,可节录《McGregor on Damages》(18th edn, 2009 年)一书 6-039 段所说:"Where a wrongful act of the defendant interferes with the rights of a third party who, in the exercise or defence of his own rights, acts in such a way that the claimant suffers injury, the defendant will be liable for his injury"。针对第三人为了保护其他人的利益,可节录《McGregor on Damages》(18th edn, 2009 年)一书 6-041 段:"It is established that where a claimant intervenes to rescue the person or property of a third party from the results of the defendant's tort and is himself injured, his act of rescue is not a new cause which will prevent him from recovering damages from the defendant. Analogously, if the claimant is injured in the decourse of a third party's attempt to rescue him or another in such circumstances, the defendant ought to be liable for that injury."这种情况可以诽谤的侵权为例,在 Speight v. Gosnay (1890) 60 LJQB 231 CA 先例,判是作出对原告诽谤的被告,是要对第三人重复被告的诽谤负责,只要该第三人是有一个道德上的责任去重复。换言之,第三人重复诽谤的后果并不会因此被视为中断因果链。这在 Derry v. Handley (1867) 16 LT 263 先例,案情涉及 A(被告)向 B(第三人)对 C(原告)作出了诽谤,B 把这一诽谤重复告诉了他的妻子,因为他的妻子就是 C 的雇主。这一来,后果就是 C 被解雇并蒙受损失。C 成功向 A 索赔损失,因为 B 是有道德上的责任向他的妻子重复 A 的诽谤,没有中断因果链。

8.2 第三人无侵权责任但有真正选择的行为

不像没有选择的上一小段,第三人一有"选择"(free chooser),即表示这损失(或额外损失)不必要发生。所以,这行为作为新介入行为会中断因果链的机会大增。但要是第三人无责任,也就是没有错误或疏忽,这会好多了。不像是第三人既是错误,也是自由选择行为,后者往往会中断因果链。这方面可节录《McGregor on Damages》(18th edn, 2009 年)一书 6-043 段:"Where there is full and free choice in the intervening act, the defendant is much less likely to be held liable. The basic reason for this is that where a completely free intervening act is a lawful one damage does not generally result, and where it is a wrongful one it will be held to form a new cause. This is, however, only the general position: there are exceptional cases and there are difficult cases. ”

例如,受害方的船舶被损坏后在修理期间遇上合法罢工,这带来额外延误损失。看来,原来的侵权方或违约方要对此负责:H. M. S. London (1914) P. 72,这罢工既是合法,即是无责任,但工人或工会也是自由选择罢工。在该案法院说:“in the ordinary course of business industrial disputes may and do occur, and strikes ensue. ”在 The “Mineral Transporter” (1985) 2 Lloyd's Rep 303 先例也有同样的判法。从另外一个角度看,遇上罢工也是可以合理预见。即使遇上非法罢工也在很多情况下是合理预见,也不应该中断因果链。

罢工是如此,其他新介入行为也是如此。所以,如果违约方(如承租人)要对船舶修理负责,他就不能推卸部分赔偿责任,例如,救助船或拖带船的疏忽,导航员的罢工或延误上船去领航进修理港,修理工人懈怠令 3 天工作变了 4 天等。

再一例是承租人或发货人的危险品泄漏易燃气体,没有人觉察,有吸烟的船员经过而发生爆炸。应该是承租人或发货人的责任不能推给吸烟的船员,争辩说毕竟他不吸烟就不会导致船舶爆炸并全损,所以本身是一个新介入事件。但这种争辩不应该会成功,因果链不应被中断,即使是吸烟的船员是身在禁止吸烟区,应该说是严重错误,但他不知有这易燃气漏出,仍是不应中断因果链。如在 Philco Radio v. Spurling (1949) 2 All E. R. 882 先例的上诉庭所讲,如果这“吸烟”人士是故意引起火灾,则情况不一样了,因果链应可中断了。

以上介绍的简单先例在很大的程度上是第三人的行为(如罢工、懈怠、抽烟等)是可以合理预见到会发生,而可以合理预见到的行为,通常是不容易中断因果链。

8.3　第三人行为既是错误,也是自由选择

在这种情况下,如上小段所讲,经常会中断因果链。经常引用的一句名言是在 Wild – Blundell v. Stephens (1920) A. C. 956 先例由 Sumner 勋爵所讲:“... in general... even though A is in fault, he is not responsible for injury to C which B, a stranger to him, deliberately chooses to do. Though A may have given the occasion for B's mischievous activity, B then becomes a new and independent cause. ”(就算 A 是对 C 犯错,他不必对第三人 B 对 C 所造成的损失负责,即使是 A 的错误提供了机会给 B 做这种错误的行为。B 的错误变为一个新的与独立的原因。)

这在《McGregor on Damages》(18th edn, 2009 年)一书 6 – 050 段这样说:“Nor can any hard and fast rule be laid down as to wrongful intervening acts. The tendency has been to hold the defendant not liable for the further damage. ”(很难对错误介入的行为作出一些硬性的规定,趋势是认为被告不需要对这种行为所造成的额外损失负责。)

特别是第三人的错误或疏忽是允许受害方可以另向第三人起诉要求赔偿损失,则原来的侵权方或违约方应有更大可能可当作已有一个独立的新介入行为中断了因果链,造成了损失或额外损失他是不必负责的。

以下介绍一些第三人严重错误或疏忽可中断因果链的先例。

8.3.1　先例之一:Ruoff v. Long

这一先例涉及被告把他的卡车停在公路边,在没有人看管下,有两个军人潜上卡车乱开,把受害方原告的商店撞毁。法院判是被告胜诉,因为在该先例的事实中,他把卡车停在公路边并没有疏忽。但法院也提到即使是被告有疏忽,他也不会对原告负责赔偿损失,因为两个军人作为第三人的错误与自由选择行为已经中断了因果链。

8.3.2　先例之二:The "Paludina"

两船碰撞后,在第一次碰撞中无辜的受害方船舶(原告)又与另一艘船舶(第三人)发生第二次碰撞并且导致另一艘船舶沉没,但法院根据提供的证据认为另一艘船舶应有足够的时间(有 20 分钟时间)避开但没有这样做,所以难逃责任。加上法院认定另一艘船舶作为第三人在第二次碰撞时并非是在本章 9.1.3 段所讲的"in the grip of the casualty"或"agony of the moment"下作出的反应或行为,而且另一艘船舶可以自由选择躲避,这一切的事实认定导致了中断因果链,也就是对第一次碰撞的侵权方船舶不必对第二次碰撞带来的损失负责。需指出的是,在该贵族院先例,是以 3:2 的多数认定另一艘船舶(第三人)有错误或疏忽,所以中断因果链,不必要原来负责的被告的 Paludina 轮负责。而在贵族院之前的第一审,是判第二次碰撞的第二波是由第一波直接导致,所以 Paludina 轮要负责两次碰撞所有的损失,包括另一艘船舶的沉没。但去了上诉庭,这个判决又被推翻。可见在同样的证据下,得出的有关受害方或第三人的错误与疏忽会否中断因果链的结论很不一样。毕竟,谁对谁错在很多情况下并不是黑白分明,特别是在提供的证据并不完善的情况下。

8.3.3　先例之三:Hogan v. Bentinck Collieries

在侵权或违约的受害方受伤时,如果治疗时医生疏忽带来更大伤害、毛病、甚至死亡,原来的侵权或违约方是否可以不必负责,指医生疏忽是新介入的事件或行为把因果链中断?毕竟是受害方可以独立控告医生。这个说法以前站得住脚,在贵族院的 Hogan v. Bentinck Collieries (1949) 1 All E. R. 588 先例,Normand 勋爵说:"... if a surgeon, by lack of skill or failure in reasonable care, causes additional injury or aggravates an existing injury and so renders himself liable in damages, the reasonable conclusion must be that his intervention is a new cause, and that the additional injury or the aggravation of the existing injury should be attributed to it and not to the original accident. On the other hand, an operation prudently advised and carefully carried out should not be treated as a new cause, whatever its consequences may be."

但这种先例毕竟涉及人权,而且涉及受伤与医疗就会一定有不同程度的风险,可以合理预见到。所以在该 Hogan v. Bentinck Collieries 先例,另一位贵族院大法官 Reid 勋爵是在不情愿下接受这方面先例的约束,但表达了很强的意见认为医疗的疏忽必须是"非常严重"(grave lack of skill and care),并且是明确证明如果有恰当的医疗就可以把受害方医好,才能中断因果链。其中也有 MacDermott 勋爵的不同意见说:"When, in order to rid himself of his incapacity for work, a workman reasonably submits himself to surgical treatment at the hands of a qualified practitioner, why should the risk of some error of judgment or some lack of efficiency on the part of the latter in the course of the treatment fall on the workman so as to rob him of his right to compensation?"

8.3.4 先例之四:The "Ness"

另一个可介绍的较早的 The "Ness" (1952) 2 Lloyd's Rep. 294 先例。被告的 Ness 轮是一条驳船,它没有人看管,这被判是错误或疏忽的行为,被告显然是要对这一个行为的后果负责。之后不知名第三人恶意解掉该驳船靠挂在码头的缆绳,引起 Ness 轮在港内漂流而碰上另一条靠在码头的 Ellen 轮。原告的 Ellen 轮提出损失索赔,结果败诉。这是因为不知名第三人的恶意行为已经中断了被告没有派人看管 Ness 轮的错误或疏忽的因果链。而这第三人的恶意行为不是"自然与正常"的,不像是 Ness 轮妨碍了第三人船舶的出口航道,而由于 Ness 轮又没有人看管与让路,导致第三人非要这样做,这至少在一定程度上说的过去或属于合理,就不至于会中断因果链。Willmer 大法官有以下讲话:"It does not necessarily follow, therefore, that because human conduct intervenes between an act of negligence and ultimate damage, the chain of causation is broken. But it must, in my judgment, be reasonable human conduct. It is urged that the act of the unknown person in this case, the trespasser who cast the barge adrift, was really nothing else, if he found the barge was obstructing his passage, than an ordinary and natural thing for him to do. No doubt the temptation to cast off the 'Ness' existed, but I am quite unable to regard it as a natural and ordinary thing to do, because quite clearly, it was a wrongful thing to do... The lighterman in charge of the "Ness" may have created the occasion for the unknown person's mischievous activity during the night, but that unknown person then became, in my judgment, a new and independent cause. "(简单说,Willmer 大法官判是驳船的错误或疏忽只是给一位不知名的第三人提供了机会,他的恶意行为才是造成损失的一个新的与独立的原因。)

8.3.5 先例之五:Rahman v. Arearose Ltd

这是上述 8.3.3 段介绍过的 Hogan v. Bentinck Collieries (1949) 1 All E. R. 588 先例在普通法的进一步发展,开始普遍接受医疗的疏忽不会中断因果链。例如在 Rahman v. Arearose Ltd (2001) QB 351 先例,受害方的原告受到攻击,并把右眼弄伤。但在后来的医疗疏忽,导致了受害方右眼瞎了,并带来严重的心理压抑。在上诉庭,判新介入事件或行为(医疗疏忽)并不一定会中断因果链,其中 Laws 大法官是这样说:"... it does not seem to me to be established as a rule of law that later negligence always extinguishes the causative potency of an earlier tort. Nor should it be. The law is that every tortfeasor should compensate the injured claimant in respect of that loss and damage for which he should justly be held responsible. To make that principle good, it is important that the elusive conception of causation should not be frozen into constricting rules. It is true that the idea of supervening cause – *noves actus interveniens* – is generally deployed in cases where it is suggested that the first tortfeasor should bear responsibility for the effects of the second tort, and this is not such a case: [counsel for the hospital] accepts that the second defendants are solely responsible for the loss of the eye. However the spirit of *noves actus* rattles its chains at the suggestion that the first defendants should bear some responsibility, given that this is not a case of concurrent torts, for the continuing effects of the claimant's psychological damages after the loss vision in the right eye."

8.3.6 先例之六:Wiseman v. Virgin Atlantic Airways plc

相比侵权,违约涉及第三人中断因果关系的案例并不多,其中一个近期的案例是 Wiseman v. Virgin Atlantic Airways plc。案情涉及维珍航空公司违约,一个乘客被滞留在一个地方,并不幸被抢劫。该乘客向维珍航空公司提出索赔损失,这被判是太遥远。看来,在这一个先例中不幸被第三人(盗贼)抢劫是新介入行为,这显然是错误与自由选择的行为,中断了因果链,而且这也不是可以合理预见的损失。

8.4 严重第三人错误与自由选择行为不能中断因果链的例外情况

涉及第三人错误与自由选择的行为不能中断因果链的例外情况,最重要是在最早的侵权或违约方本来就有责任防止第三人造成损失,而他偏偏因犯错或疏忽给了第三人这样的机会,这就不能说该第三人就是一个新介入的行为而中断因果链。另一角度看,这最早的错误或疏忽与后来第三人所造成的损失实是完全可以合理预见,这可节录 Reid 勋爵在 Dorset Yacht Co v. Home Office (1970) AC 1004 先例中所说:"Unfortunately, tortuous or criminal action by a third party is often the 'very kind of thing' which is likely to happen as a result of the wrongful or careless act of the defendant. ... I think that the taking of a boat by the escaping trainees and their unskilled navigation leading to damage to another vessel was the very kind of thing that these Borstal officers ought to have seen to be likely."

例如,受害方找了一家警卫公司看门,但他偏偏犯错或疏忽,没有锁好大门,让盗贼进来。这警卫公司不可以指盗贼这第三人严重新介入行为带来损失,可中断因果链。这种后果完全可以合理预见到。这方面相近的案例有 Potrovitch v. Callinghams (1962) 2 Lloyd's Rep. 386。这方面可比较在较早前介绍过的 Wiseman v. Virgin Atlantic Airways plc (2006) EWHC 1566 QB 先例。

另一著名先例是 London Joint Stock Bank v. Macmillan (1918) A. C. 777。该案被告(储户)给他的职员开了一张 2 英镑的支票,由于金额书写得很随便,那个职员后来轻易地将支票改成为 120 英镑,到银行提取了钱后逃掉。结果判下来被告的储户要承担银行付出的 120 英镑损失,作为第三人的职员的错误行为没有中断因果链。因为储户对银行有义务防止这种事情发生,而疏忽令这事情发生也完全可以预见,也是一个"自然的后果"(natural consequence of the carelessness)。

针对同一课题,比较近期的有 Barings Plc (In Liquidation) v. Coopers & Lybrand (A Firm) (2003) EWHC 1319 (Ch)先例,案情已经在本章第4.3.2段介绍过。

9. 新介入事件或行为之第三类:原告受害方的行为

不论是侵权或者是违约,涉及受害方的行为导致会否中断因果关系的争议是最多会发生的。在发生侵权或违约后直到最后的损失之间(如船舶发生碰撞后直到最后把损失修妥,这会有可能是拖上半年一年,其中包括了救助、暂时修理、永久修理等),来自受害方的行为也远比其他第三人的行为多,这些行为经常会涉及减少损失。一旦涉及受害方的错误或疏忽的行为,没有合理减少损失,或是涉及受害方"自由选择"(free choser)采取某一种行为,结果导致了损失或额外损失,都会带来被告指称原告的受害方没有合理减少合理损失或原告的行为中断了因果链,不能要求被告赔付。

一般而言,受害方原告自己的行为作为新介入行为,会涉及其他损失赔偿的大原则,如由于涉及双方的错误或疏忽会需要分摊责任与损失、合理减少损失与本章所讲的损失遥远性的因果关系。有时候区分与适用哪一条大原则会有一定的困难。这可节录《McGregor on Damages》(18th edn, 2009年)一书6-061段:"Where the intervening act is that of the claimant himself, the problem may find solution by way of the doctrines of contributory negligence or of mitigation of damage which here compete with that of remoteness. The difficulties in separating these three doctrines when it comes to a particular set of facts have already been considered."

9.1 受害方有否错误或疏忽的合理或不合理行为

首先针对这一个方面,就是原告受害方没有错误或疏忽的行为,完全是合理减少损失,这通常被视为是完全可以合理预见的反应,不应该中断原来侵权或违约所带来的因果关系。这方面可重复本章6.2段所介绍的 The "Metagama" (1927) 29 Ll L Rep 253 与 Canadian Pacific Ry v. Kelvin Shipping Co (1927) 138 LT 369 HL 等先例,不重复。

这方面可以船舶碰撞后受害的船舶(通过船长或是船东)作出的减损行为中的一些有关先例作以介绍。

9.1.1 受害方在减少损失中合理行为的船舶碰撞案例

这种一波未平一波又起,但不涉及受害方有错误或疏忽都是合理的行为,在笔者熟悉的如船舶碰撞的海事侵权行为方面有非常多先例,这些案例都判是不会中断因果链,令最后的损失都要原来的侵权方负责赔偿。简单举几个先例:

(1)受害方船舶在被碰撞之后,船长希望把船舶开去最近的安全港口,但在途中搁浅而导致船舶全损,判是搁浅的损失是原来碰撞一部分,造成碰撞的对方船舶要负全责，船长在没有疏忽的情况下发生搁浅并没有中断因果链：The "City of Lincoln" (1890) P 15；The "Waalstroom" (1923) 17 Lloyd's Rep. 53。

(2)也是在船舶碰撞后，其中一艘损坏严重的船舶放下了救生艇开去另一艘船舶准备与对方船长商讨如何协助本船的对策（估计当时还没有无线电可以方便通讯）。但由于海浪大，救生艇翻船而导致了部分船员死亡。死亡船员家属事后向另一艘对碰撞负责的船舶提出索赔，该船东抗辩说对方船长决定放下救生艇的行为是新介入行为，中断了因果关系。但上诉庭并不接受，认为该船长的行为合理，不能中断因果链：The "Oropesa" (1943) 74 Ll L Rep 86。

(3)疏忽导致走锚的船舶在发生第一次碰撞后随即再第二次发生碰撞，判是第二次碰撞没有中断因果链。除了整件事是一气呵成外，第二次碰撞的受害方船舶没有错误或疏忽，不存在有新介入行为可中断因果链：The "Epiros" (1946) 79 Lloyd's Rep. 498。

(4)在船舶碰撞后，其中一艘严重损坏的船舶拒绝了另一艘与之碰撞的船舶愿意拖带去安全港口的承诺，决定等待船东已经安排了的拖轮。但在 5 个小时拖轮抵达后并拖带了 7 个小时后，该严重损坏船舶沉没。另一艘船舶对全损的索赔提出抗辩指该船长拒绝拖带的协助是属于新介入行为，中断了因果关系。而如果接受承诺，另一艘船舶提供的拖带会有机会在船舶沉没前抵达安全港口，或至少可以省时间在半途把严重损坏船舶转交给拖轮。所以，船舶沉没的主要或有效原因是船长拒绝拖带的协助。但法院认为在视野不清与当时困难的环境下，依赖两艘大船进行拖带是危险与困难的做法，这包括连接上拖缆、双方通讯与大船难以灵活操作等。所以，只会在根本没有其他拖带办法的情况下，沉没船舶的船长拒绝另一艘船舶的拖带承诺才有可能是不合理与会中断因果链。但在这一个案件中，该船长完全合理，而合理的行为是不会中断因果链：The "Guildford" (1956) 2 Lloyd's Rep 74。

9.1.2 受害方在减少损失中不合理行为的船舶碰撞案例

新介入行为如果是"不自然与不正常"(unnatural & extra - ordinary)通常会中断因果链，如受害方在事后减少损失中有相对独立、严重与不能预见的错误或疏忽。这与"合理预见"的要求实际上相同，因为不自然与不正常的行为与损失，是不能合理预见的。而其中受害方在事后的行为有错误或疏忽就会被视为是这种不能合理预见的情况。比如，继续列举早期船舶碰撞的受害方船舶因为在减少损失中有错误或疏忽行为而导致了中断因果链的案例：(1)在碰撞之后，受害方船舶的船长不必要的、疏忽的弃船，法院判是有责任的侵权方只要赔受害方估计修理碰撞损坏所产生的费用：The "Thuringia" (1872) 1 Asp. M. C. 283。(2)在碰撞之后，受害方船舶的船长与领航员不明智的、错误的决定开进 Blyth 港口，而不等待拖轮的协助，结果在半途搁浅并造成另外损失。法院判是船长与领航员的疏忽中断因果链：The "Glendinning" (1943) 76 Lloyd's Rep 86。

9.1.3 受害方的行为合理与否应尽量宽松看待

顺便一提是认定受害方是否有错误或疏忽必须是合理与现实,毕竟受害方的困境是由于侵权方或违约方所造成。在船舶碰撞这类侵权案件(或相关的事故)必须考虑在出了第一波事故,船舶身处危险,或失去动力,或操纵困难,通常船长在当时有高度压力,都会造成了船长在危急时候作出的决定事后看并非是最好的反应或行为。所以要现实的考虑这种因素,所谓的"in the grip of the casualty"或"agony of the moment"下作出的反应或行为,就不要"事后诸葛亮"作出批评。只要船长当时的决定谈不上不合理,仍然可说是这第二波的船长行为是第一波持续的直接与自然的后果,也可以合理预见到。所以,不应把第二波的行为轻易当作为新介入行为,令因果链中断。换言之,第二波行为产生的损失应与第一波的损失加在一起。

在违约的受害方,也有同样的说法。Macmillan 勋爵在 Banco de Portugal v. Waterlow (1932) AC 452 先例中说:"Where the sufferer from a breach of contract finds himself in consequence of that breach placed in a position of embarrassment the measures which he may be driven to adopt in order to extricate himself ought not to be weighed in nice scales at the instance of the party whose breach of contract has occasioned the difficulty. It is often easy after an emergency passed to criticise the steps which have been taken to meet it, but such criticism does not come well from those who have themselves created the emergency. The law is satisfied if the party placed in a difficult situation by reason of the breach of a duty owed to him has acted reasonably in the adoption of remedial measures and he will not be held disentitled to recover the cost of such measures merely because the party in breach can suggest that other measures less burdensome to him might have been taken."

9.1.4 受害方有错误或疏忽的程度到哪里才能够中断因果链

受害方在侵权或者违约后自己有错误或疏忽会中断因果关系应该是明确,但问题是这一个错误或疏忽到底到什么程度才足够达到中断因果关系。从先例或者一些说法中看到还是不肯定,有宽有紧,毕竟疏忽会是十分轻微或是严重。例如像著名的"市场规则"(market rule),背后的说法是受害方如果有可供买卖的市场就必须在违约一天采取行动,否则就被视为是中断因果关系。但受害方会有许多十分合理的原因不能这样做,根本扯不上任何错误或疏忽,但在市场规则下都被漠视。在上一小段所介绍的几个有关海事的案例如 The "Stork" (1955) 1 Lloyd's Rep. 349;The "Houston City" (1954) 2 Lloyd's Rep 148;The "Dagmar" (1968) 2 Lloyd's Rep. 563;The "Polyglory" (1977) 2 Lloyd's Rep. 353;The "Mary Lou" (1981) 2 Lloyd's Rep. 272 等,接受事故后船长的航行疏忽是属于一时冲动的所谓"agony of the moment"。这就带来一个疑问就是在一般的案件,会是以什么程度的错误或疏忽才会中断因果关系?这在一个近期的先例 Borealis v. Geogas Trading (2011) 1 Lloyd's 482 (CA)有针对。案情涉及 5200 吨的"丁烷"(butane)买卖,该批丁烷是作为原料生产乙烯和丙烯作为塑料。但丁烷受到了氟化物的污染,这导致了在正常的生产过程中产生了"氢氟酸"(hydrofluoric acid),对买方的设备与机器造成严重损坏与生产停顿,导致了利润损失。

在双方的争议中,卖方承认提供了货不对版的丁烷的责任,但在损失赔偿这一方面卖方作为被告提出了各方面的抗辩,包括了因果关系、损失遥远性与合理减少损失。其中针对因果关系是否被中断,卖方提出了几个方面如买方应该在收到丁烷的时候就对该批货物进行包括对氟化物的测试,但最重要的还是在9月12日,在卸下丁烷其间,PH值测试系统曾经发出警报,显示了PH值过低,但买方没有采取行动。

上诉庭的Gross大法官针对受害方错误或疏忽的程度列为五个方面作出考虑,如下:

(1) Although an evidential burden rested on the defendant insofar as it contended that there was a break in the chain of causation, the legal burden of proof rested throughout on the claimant to prove that the defendant's breach of contract caused its loss.(虽然对中断因果关系的指控,举证责任是在被告,但原告还是有全程的举证责任说明损失是被告违约所导致。)

(2) In order to break the chain of causation, the conduct of the claimant had to constitute an event of such impact that it "obliterated" the wrongdoing of the defendant. The true cause of the loss had to be the conduct of the claimant rather than the breach of contract by the defendant and the claimant's subsequent conduct were concurrent causes, it was unlikely that the chain of causation would be broken. In circumstances where the defendant's breach of contract remained an effective cause of the loss, at least ordinarily, the chain of causation would not be broken.(要成功中断因果关系,受害方原告的行为必须达到"擦去"被告的错误。真正的损失变为原告的行为多于被告的违约所导致。如果原告后来的行为只能是一个共同的原因导致损失,就不大可能会中断因果关系。在一些情况是被告的违约仍然属于导致损失的有效原因,因果关系不会被中断。)

(3) Anything less than unreasonable conduct on the part of the claimant was unlikely to be capable of breaking the chain of causation. However, mere unreasonable conduct on a claimant's part would not necessarily do so, eg where the defendant's breach remained an effective cause of the loss, albeit in combination with the claimant's failure to take reasonable precautions in its own interest. Reckless conduct by the claimant would ordinarily break the chain of causation.(任何谈不上是原告不合理的行为是不大会中断因果关系。但仅是不合理行为并不一定会有这个效果,如被告的违约仍然属于导致损失的有效原因,虽然这也同时发生了原告没有采取合理行动保障他自己的利益。但原告轻率、鲁莽与不顾危险的行为通常是会中断因果关系。)

(4) The claimant's state of knowledge at the time of and following the defendant's

breach of contract was likely to be a factor of very great significance. For the chain of causation to be broken, the claimant need not have knowledge of the legal niceties of the breach of contract; nor would the chain of causation only be broken if the claimant had actual knowledge that a breach of contract had occurred – otherwise there would be a premium on ignorance. However, the more the claimant had actual knowledge of the breach, of the dangerousness of the situation which had thus arisen and of the need to take appropriate remedial measure, the greater the likelihood that the chain of causation would be broken. Conversely, the less the claimant knew the more likely it was that only recklessness would suffice to break the chain of causation.（原告对被告违约的知识与了解程度会是一个非常重要的考虑因素。原告并不需要知道是否在有关的合约下有违约[因为违约后受害方才有合理减轻损失的责任],否则会让一个无知的原告得益,说是他不知道违约所以不合理减损。但在原告对违约事实知道得越多的情况下,就会带来一个危险的情况就是原告越应该知道需要采取补救行动与采取什么行动。相反是原告合理看是应该知道较少,不充分理解有关的危险,就会只在他轻率、鲁莽与不顾危险的情况下才会中断因果关系。）

（5）Ultimately, the question of whether there had been a break in the chain of causation was fact sensitive, involving a practical inquiry into the circumstances of the defendant's breach of contract and the claimant's subsequent conduct. It was always a question of degree at what point the damage claimed for ceased to flow naturally and directly from the breach.（最后是中断因果关系是以个别案件的不同事实为准,法院或仲裁庭需要调查被告违约与原告事后行为的情况。通常是看程度的问题,就是从哪一点开始有关的损失再也不是由起初违约所导致的有效原因。）

接下去 Gross 大法官把以上五个方面的大原则适用在 Borealis v. Geogas Trading 先例,特别是有关 PH 值测试系统曾经发出警报,显示了 PH 值过低的事实与买方没有采取行动会否打断因果关系。Gross 大法官首先是不认为买方的反应是不合理、其中很大的原因是买方不会有卖方违约与带来危险这方面的知识与了解,说:"In my judgment, it is essential to keep uppermost in mind my earlier conclusion: namely, that Borealis（买方）did not know and could not reasonably have expected to know of the kind of acid introduced into the system by the Geogas（卖方）breach of contract and the nature of the threat it posed. Again, as already concluded, the pH system was not designed or intended to deal with acids of such a nature. It is correct that the sudden and considerable drop in pH and the triggering of the pH alarm indicated an acid of the kind typically encountered by the plant, nothing untoward would have resulted from the operators waiting until the routine samples were taken on the Monday (15 September). In the light of the experience of those at the plant, this would not have been a problem. That the operators could have done better, as indeed they did when pH dropped significantly after discharge of the Stanlow cargo (a cargo mentioned above), is one thing – and as already underlined amply justifies the conclusions in the Report. But, against this background, to characterise as unreasonable the operators' failure to achieve best practice, seems to me a step too far. It should also be noted that operators and supervisors (including Mr Andersson) on the shift/s subsequent to that when the pH levels first fell, reacted in the same manner as those on the initial shift. It might be said that the focus must then move (away from the initial operators and supervisors) to the training given to operators and others in the production department in the plant. If so, however, the same conclusion is reached: until the occurrence of this incident and in the light of experience hitherto, Borealis had no reason to anticipate that low pH would or could have consequences of this nature."

接下去 Gross 大法官说即使买方没有采取行动是不合理、错误或疏忽,也不会中断因果关系。第一个原因是卖方并没有指称买方的不合理程度上是轻率、鲁莽与不顾危险。第二个原因是在本案例的事实中,比起有关的先例,是可以值得原谅。在 9 月 12 日的 PH 值系统警报,买方是完全有权站在一个起点是他买了一票高质量与没有污染的丁烷,而这票丁烷受到污染的事实是买方根本不知道。第三个原因是 Gross 大法官认为买方的不行动根本没有擦去卖方的违约才是设备损坏最有效与一般性的原因(Approached as a question of fact and degree, I cannot begin to say that any failure/s on the part of Borealis, "obliterated" or destroyed the "causative potency" of the anterior Geogas breach of contract. It seems plain to me that the Geogas breach of contract remained, at the least, an effective cause of the Borealis loss and damage, regardless of any failure/s on the part of Borealis. Though Borealis knew or ought to have known of the presence of an acid in the system, it remained in the grip of an unknown breach giving rise to an unknown danger)。

9.2 受害方没有错误或疏忽但属于自由选择的行为

与 9.1 段不同的是另一种情况,就是受害方没有错误或疏忽,甚至在受害方(或第三人)的角度看来是合理的行为,但只要是涉及受害方自由选择,还是会有很大可能会中断因果链。这一个问题可以在以下段节去分几个不同的情况作出分析。

9.2.1 货物买卖的市场规则下假设受害方做出的选择

在国际货物/商品买卖,经常出现的争议就是在市场价格暴升暴跌时,受严重影响或亏损的卖方或者买方就会扯皮,如卖方拒绝交付有关的货物,或是买方拒绝接收有关的货物。这一来,受害方在接受违约中断买卖合约后,就有了减少损失的责任。最正常的做法就是转售有关货物(受害方如果是卖方)或是买进替代货物(受害方如果是买方)。但现实中受害方即使这样做,也会在每一个不同的案件中有不同的做法。其中在时间方面,如受害方的买方会在卖方违约后第二天就去市场买进替代货物,但也会是等两个星期后,甚至是一个月或三个月后不等的时间。而背后的原因会是有很多,其中经常包括买方自己预测市场的走势后决定尽快或稍后买进替代货物,这就涉及受害方自己的选择。如果买方预测的对,在等待三个月后买进替代货物,价格上更加便宜,变为卖方的运气,因为买方成功减少损失的好处是要给卖方。但如果买方预测不对,买进了更昂贵的替代货物,违约的卖方就可以抗辩说这额外的损失是由于新介入行为,也就是买方选择等待,事后证明这样做是并不明智,所以中断了因果链。这种先例很多,随便介绍是 Kaines(UK) Ltd. v. Osterreichische Warenhandelsgesellshaft Austrowaren Gessellschaft mbH (1993) 2 Lloyd's Rep. 1 先例。案情涉及受害的买方不及时买进替代货物,而在原油市场赌博,希望货价会下跌,但"投机"失败,这额外损失被判是不能向违约/毁约的卖方索赔,因为受害的买方自由选择"博市"的行为已是一个新介入的行为,中断因果链。

由于这种因果关系与减少损失的争议太多与太麻烦,所以英国法律有了一套相对简单与快捷的办法计算损失,这个办法就是"市场规则"(market rule),它在 1979 年《货物销售法》的 Section 50 (3)和 Section 51 (3) 有所规定。以市场规则计算损失在英国法律下也是适用在其他的商业活动,反正只要是有市场,如租船合约或是股票转让合约都可以适用。但只有货物买卖才是立了法,并说明这是计算损失的"表面规则"(*prima facie* rule)。

市场规则相对简单的主要原因是它不追究无辜受害方因为违约而蒙受的"真正损失"(actual loss),而是针对一个"客观损失"(objective loss)或"推断损失"(notional loss)。这就是推断或假设违约卖方(作为例子)如果拒绝交付货物,无辜买方就马上去市场买进替代货物,而将来向卖方索赔的就是违约一天的买卖合约价格与当天市场价格的差价。反过来,买方如果拒绝收货,无辜的受害卖方就马上去市场转售有关货物。至于其他方面的违约,如卖方交付是次货,只要次货也是有市场价格,损失也可以同样作出比较与计算。这就是所谓的市场规则,它的好处就是不必再理会真正损失所带来的局限大原则的争议与举证,如因果关系与合理减少损失等。一个简单的计算也可以看得出它的公平之处,就是 A 卖价值 100 元的货物给 B,B 再把同样的货物以 120 元转卖给了 C。但由于市场价格上涨或其他原因,A 拒绝提供货物,而当时的市场价格是 140 元。这表示 B 去市场马上买进替代货物,以履行他与 C 的买卖合约,就表示 B 损失了 40 元的差价,这是可以向 A 提出索赔。或是 B 不去市场买进替代货物,就会面对 C 向他的索赔,在该合约下市场与合约价格的差价是 20 元,B 要赔偿给 C。但 B 可以同时向 A 提出索赔,这差价就扩大至 40 元,其中 20 元赔了给 C,剩下的 20 元也就是如果合约被履行 B 应该能够赚取的利润。

这方面可节录 Shearson Lehman Hutton Inc. v. Maclaine Watson & Company Ltd (No. 2) (1990) 1 Lloyd's Rep 441 先例中所说:"... the object of the provision is to avoid uncertainty of damages, of a presumption that if there is an available market the plaintiff seller can obtain the market or current price of the goods on the date of the breach, that his damages are to be measured by reference to that price whether or not it would have been reasonable or sensible for him to have waited before going into the market and selling the goods, and that neither is to be adversely affected by price fluctuations either before or after the date of the breach. For these reasons the requirements of reasonable mitigation, which would ordinarily apply to a claim for damages, do not apply when the measure of damages is governed by s. 50 (3)."

市场规则是完全不理会受害的买方(为例)去市场买进替代货物并非是马上进行,甚至在违约后根本不买进。反正就是推断损失是以违约当天的市场价格为准,就表示在现实中这得出来的推断损失与真正损失总免不了有差别,导致无辜方会赚会亏。比如受害买方在卖方违约后的一个月(这延误可以是买方自己下不了决心,想投机,公司官僚主义,进口手续,期间长假,涉及货物数量庞大可以分批购买等原因)才去市场购买替代货物,由于市场一直在上涨,他的实际损失就显然会比推断损失更大。也会是受害买方在卖方违约后根本没有去市场买进替代货物,因为暂时不需要这票货,甚至是有第三人送了一票同类货物给买方,表面看来买方没有真正损失,但他还是可以向卖方索赔根据市场规则所得出来的推断损失。

虽然市场规则也免不了有争议,如有关的商品是否有市场。因为针对不同的商品在全球不同的违约地点与时间,不一定都有进行买卖的市场。至于要求无辜方马上在市场购买替代货物,立法条文是说明在违约的"时候"(at the time or times)。但现实中这是不大可能的事,尤其是有关货物/商品数量庞大,可以说无辜方转售或买进都需要时间。但如果考虑太多什么才是对无辜方合理的时间,就会令市场规则所针对的推断损失靠近无辜方真正损失,最终会令1979年《货物销售法》中 Section 50 (3)和 Section 51 (3)所追求的肯定性与客观性计算损失会被冲淡甚至否定。

市场规则虽然解决了大部分的商品买卖损失计算,因为商品通常都有市场并且有很完整的市场报告可以作为市场价格的证据,但还是避免不了即使是国际货物买卖,有小部分商品以及其他的货物(如机械设备等)没有市场。这一来,就只能回去索赔真正损失,并受到计算损失各种限制大原则(如第三章的损失在订约时可否预见/料想得到、本章的因果关系与第五章的减少损失)的约束。有关市场规则的损失计算,也会在本书第十五章与第十六章会详论。

9.2.2 受害方穷困的原因做出的选择

受害方的穷困经常会导致他在没有办法的情况下选择一些不是最好的办法减少损失,导致最后损失会因此加大。对侵权或违约方而言,就经常会抗辩受害方的穷困导致因果链的中断。虽然穷困谈不上是受害方的错误或疏忽,但通常会涉及他的选择作出一些谈不上合理减少损失的行为。

这方面最重要与最早是在 The "Liesbosch" (1933) LL. L. Rep. 123 的先例。案情涉及船舶碰撞,由于受害船东自己财力不足,不能另购买一艘替代疏浚船履行疏浚合约,改为以高租金租入一艘船舶履行。但这增加了损失的金额,向侵权方索赔损失的时候遇到抗拒。虽然受害船东在做法上没有不合理,但被贵族院判是他的穷困中断了因果链,导致额外的损失不能向对方船舶取回。Wright 勋爵也判是这额外的损失太遥远,有关说法在较早的1段与6.2段已经节录,不重复。Wright勋爵这样说:"The respondents' tortuous act involved the physical loss of the dredger(该先例涉及一艘疏浚船在碰撞后沉没); that loss must somehow be reduced to terms of money. But the appellants'(受害方) actual loss in so far as it was due to their impecuniosity(该先例中受害方船东因为贫穷而不能买另一艘替代疏浚船继续工作)... arose from that impecuniosity as a separate and concurrent cause, extraneous to and distinct in character from the tort; the impecuniosity was not traceable to the respondents' acts, and in my opinion was outside the legal purview of the consequences of these acts. The law cannot take account of everything that follows a wrongful act; it regards some subsequent matters as outside the scope of its selection, because 'it was infinite for the law to judge the cause of causes', or the consequences of consequences. Thus the loss of a ship by collision due to the other vessel's sole fault, may force the shipowner into bankruptcy and that again may involve his family in suffering, loss of education or opportunities in life, but no such loss could be recovered from the wrongdoer. In the varied web of affairs, the law must abstract some consequences as relevant, not perhaps on grounds of pure logic but simply for practical reasons. In the present case if the appellants' financial embarrassment is to be regarded as a consequence of the respondents' tort, I think it is too remote, but I prefer to regard it as an independent cause, though its operative effect was conditioned by the loss of the dredger."(在船舶碰撞后,受害方如果被迫倒闭或导致他的家庭经济陷入困境,如孩子没有钱受教育或错失了人生的好机会,这种损失都不能向侵权的被告取回,否则是没完没了。在这一个先例,受害方的贫穷所带来的结果如果也算在被告侵权的头上,Wright勋爵认为是太遥远,宁愿把它视为一个独立的原因中断因果链。)

在近期的违约先例还是有涉及这一穷困会中断因果链的问题或被视为是没有合理减少损失,在Geofizika v. MMB International & Greenfields (2010) 1 Lloyd's Rep 458先例,案情涉及原告Geofizika作为买方向被告MMB购买3辆救护车,买卖是以CIP(Carriage & Insurance Paid to利比亚的特里波利)方式,价格是74,952英镑。在买卖合约负责运输的MMB委托货代Greenfields安排运输与保险。但在海上运输,该3辆救护车被错误安放在船舶的甲板,结果在经过比斯开湾(Bay of Biscay)的时候遇上风浪,导致其中2辆被冲下大海。根据买卖合约的条文,说明运输必须是以"正常条件"(usual terms),这被法院认定是该3辆救护车应该被装在船舱内,这表示MMB违反了买卖合约。MMB也违反了另一方面,就是提单说明是允许船东可以有选择权把货物装在甲板上(的确也是这样做了),但保单说明是必须装在船舱内。这表示两份付运文件不一致,甚至是提供了一份无效的保单,Geofizika作为受害方是没有办法向保险人要求赔付。所以,Geofizika只能向MMB提出索赔,而且责任是相对明确,有争议的还是在损失的计算。Geofizika索赔的金额有两个部分:第一个部分没有争议,就是被冲下大海两辆救护车的价格共57,890英镑,加上替代救护车的付运的运费及保险费共3200英镑,这也代表了有关货物的真正价值。第二部分就有很大争议,这涉及Geofizika长期(从2006年12月下旬到2007年11月9日)以高昂的代价租用其他车辆用来替代冲下海的两辆救护车,共达90,000英镑。Geofizika指称他不能马上买入替代的救护车是由于他没有这笔钱或外汇,而如果他能够有资金买入替代的救护车,这也需要一段合理时间安排,包括订立另一个买卖合约与付运。这估计Geofizika还是需要租用其他车辆一直到2007年3月31日,换言之从2006年12月下旬货物应该交付直到这一天所花的高昂租金,作为合理解决办法所花的费用,还是可以向MMB索赔。至于2007年3月31日到2007年11月9日这一段时间所花的高昂租金,就涉及无辜方的穷困所导致的额外损失可否向违约方索赔,英国高院认为没有证据显示MMB在订约时可以合理预见Geofizika的穷困。Mackie大法官是这样说:"There is no evidence that MMB knew of these genuine difficulties and, as I see it, it could not reasonably have foreseen that such expenses would be not unlikely to result from any breach." 结果是判对于这部分的损失,也就是租用其他替代车辆的额外租金,是不能向违约卖方索赔。

但The "Liesbosch"先例中受害方的贫穷可以中断因果链的说法特别涉及"侵权"(tort)的案例经常被质疑,毕竟是涉及其他有关人身伤亡的侵权案件,当时已经有针对"脆弱头壳"或"鸡蛋壳头壳"(thin - skull 或 eggshell - skull)的先例说是侵权方碰到了怎么样的受害方(身体状况本来就差),就要承担这些后果,也就是"the defendant takes the plaintiff (victim) as he finds him"的说法。当时也接受了受害方如果赚钱能力很高,被告伤害了他就会要比伤害一个乞丐要支付更高赔偿的"shabby millionaire"的说法。但在The "Liesbosch"先例,贵族院解释受害方贫穷导致没有办法合理减少损失是一个"外来因素"(extrinsic),这区分看来并不是很有说服力,照说这也应该是属于"the defendant takes the plaintiff (victim) as he finds him",就是侵权方碰到了一个穷困的受害方,这与碰到了身体差的受害方本质上是一样。受害方的贫穷或受害方的体质都可以被视为侵权之前就已经存在历史事实。反正在近期的Lagden v. O'Connor (2003) UKHL 64贵族院先例,已经认为The "Liesbosch"先例不再代表英国目前的法律,Hope勋爵是这样说:"The wrongdoer must take his victim as he finds him... This rule applies to the economic state of the victim in the same way as it applies to his physical and mental vulnerability. It requires the wrongdoer to bear the consequences if it was reasonably foreseeable that the injured party would have to borrow money or incur some other kind of expenditure to mitigate his damage."

9.2.3 受害方行使合约中的选择权

受害方"行使选择权"(exercise an option)的情况下,也会是新介入事件,中断因果链。一个典型例子会是船东因承租人晚了支付租金而乘机撤船,众所周知,纽约土产期租格式有条文是给予船东在承租人没有准时支付足够租金时一个撤船的选择权。在普通法下,如果承租人晚付了租金,或是少付了金额,即使是违约也只是违反

"保证条文"(warranty),不足以可撤船来中止租约。所以,撤船的发生应是来自船东行使租约赋予的选择权而非是承租人在延误支付租金的轻微违约。这一来,船东会面对的其中一项主要损失,就是来自在装了货签发了运费已预付提单后才撤船,就根据提单合约必须完成航次,否则会面对提单持有人的违约/毁约的索赔,会要自己承担。这些损失包括完成航次所花的时间、燃油费用与港口费用等。在船东的角度来看,这些损失是来自承租人在"雇佣条文"(employment clause)下要求船长签发运费已预付提单所带来的后果与损失,所以承租人应该作出补偿。但法律对"补偿条文"(indemnity clause)的要求是严格的因果关系,这方面在本章第10.4段会进一步解释。这一来承租人就会抗辩他的命令与指示与船东的损失没有直接因果关系,因为如果船东不行使选择权撤船,承租人肯定要继续支付租金直到航次的完成,并要支付燃油与港口费用等。所以船东蒙受的损失完全是来自他自己选择撤船,这就中断了因果链。这方面的讨论可看The "Tropwind" (No. 2) (1981) 1 Lloyd's Rep. 45先例。而最近也另有The "Kos" (2010) 1 Lloyd's Rep 87先例,Andrew Smith大法官同意的说:"I cannot accept that the owners' claim is recoverable as damages for the failure to pay hire. I agree with the charterers' submission that, once the breach is not said to be repudiatory, it is an answer to the claim that the loss was not effectively caused by their failure to pay hire on time because the owners' decision to withdraw the vessel breaks the chain of causation. This is, I think, why Lord Denning MR said in Tropwood AG of Zug v. Jade Enterprises Ltd (The Tropwind) (No 2) [1982] 1 Lloyd's Rep 232 at page 237 (in a passage to which I refer further below): 'The damages for such a breach would be trifling'."

这种合约的选择权也出现在其他合约,如近年来发生大量争议的造船合约的条文中,其中涉及分期支付船价的标准造船格式。如果买方不准时作出支付,造船合约会明确规定船厂有的救济办法,其中包括在一段时间后中断造船合约。例如在日本造船格式之Article XI 3(b):

"If any default by the BUYER continues for a period of fifteen (15) days, the BUILDER may, at its option, rescind this Contract by giving notice of such effect to the BUYER by cable confirmed in writing. Upon receipt by the BUYER of such notice of rescission, this Contract shall forthwith become null and void and any of the BUYER's Supplies shall become the sole property of the BUILDER.

In the event of such rescission of the Contract, the BUILDER shall be entitled to retain any Instalment or Instalments therefore paid by the BUYER to the BUILDER on account of this Contract. . . ."

在今天航运低迷,买方普遍想逃避高价的造船合约,船厂经常会遇到买方到期时不支付船价。船厂有各种合约的救济,如通过仲裁向买方施压。但如果船厂选择根据上述的条文行使合约选择权中断造船合约,就要明白这不一定是足够让船厂索赔损失。这一损失在今天的航运市场会是非常庞大,可能是涉及上千万甚至是数以千万美元的金额。如果买方没有支付船价只涉及违约/毁约,如向船厂明确说明他没有经济能力支付,并被船厂接受中断造船合约。这一来,就不会影响船厂索赔损失的权利,这权利是来自普通法的地位。但如果船厂是根据合约选择权中断造船合约,这船厂只能是根据合约中明示的救济,但很可能就不能索赔船厂所有的损失了。这种区别到底是否有实际的意义当然还需要看其他方面,如买方是否是一家大的船公司,或是一家皮包的方便旗公司?而如果是后者,船厂是否有背后财雄势大母公司的履约担保等。

9.2.4 受害方选择不接受治疗

这种争议在侵权也有不少,只简单介绍,因为侵权并不是本书的重点。这方面相比违约的争议往往会多了公共政策的考虑,如在本章8.3.3段与8.3.5段已经提到的有关医疗疏忽的第三人行为的新介入因素有关先例 Hogan v. Bentinck Collieries (1949) 1 All E. R. 588 与 Rahman v. Arearose Ltd (2001) QB 351。在本段,是针对受害方自己的行为而不是第三人如医院或医生的疏忽行为,比方说是受害方的原告在侵权后因为宗教的原因或其他的原因拒绝接受治疗,这种选择可被视为是完全不合理与没有减少损失。但这在一个"刑事"(criminal)的案例,已经被判是不影响因果关系。在 R v. Blaue (1975) 1 WLR 1411 先例,上诉庭的 Lawton 大法官说:"It does not lie in the mouth of the assailant to say that his victim's religious beliefs which inhibited him from accepting certain kinds of treatment were unreasonable. The question for decision is what caused her death. The answer is the stab wound. The fact that the victim refused to stop this end coming about did not break the causal connection between the act and the death."但 Lawton 大法官在该先例也提到如果受害方向被告提起民事诉讼,就有可能受害方拒绝接收输血与治疗会被视为是中断因果关系。

这种问题在很大程度是看拒绝治疗是否合理(这方面请看本章之6.2段),如有关治疗涉及一定程度的风险或后果不明确。这可以节录《McGregor on Damages》(18th edn, 2009年)一书6-076段所说如下:"In a number of modern cases it has been held that whether a claimant's refusal to undergo an operation after being physically injured by the defendant debars him from recovery for damage that would not otherwise have been suffered, turns on the reasonableness or the unreasonableness of the refusal. In two workmen's compensation claims, the House of Lords held in Steele v. Robert George (1942) AC 497 and Richardson v. Redpath (1944) AC 62 that on the facts of both the refusal was reasonable and did not prevent the claimant from recovering for his full loss; the conclusion of the Judicial Committee of the Privy Council has been the same in two damages claims, Selvanayagam v. University of the West Indies (1983) 1 WLR 585 PC and Geest plc v. Lansiquot (2002) 1 WLR 3111 PC. A contrary result was reached by the Court of Appeal in Marcroft v. Scruttons (1954) 1 Lloyd's Rep. 395 CA on the ground that the claimant's refusal was unreasonable. It is submitted elsewhere, however, that these cases are more properly based upon the mitigation doctrine than upon that of remoteness."

另可介绍的例子是涉及不成功绝育手术导致受害方的原告再度怀孕,并向进行绝育手术的医生提出索赔损失,而损失就是抚养孩子成人的一大笔费用。被告提出的抗辩就是原告应该接受堕胎就可以把损失减到最少,而原告不这样做才是导致生育与抚养孩子的主要或有效原因。在 Emeh v. Kensington, Chelsea and Westminster AHA (1985) QB 1012 CA 先例,第一审是判受害方的原告败诉。但去了上诉庭被推翻,判是受害方在怀孕 18 周之后决定堕胎是有一定风险。也认为是除了很特殊与极端的情况下,一般受害方选择不接受堕胎都不能被视为不合理与没有减少损失。之后在贵族院的 McFarlane v. Tayside Health Board (2000) 2 AC 59 先例,已经明确受害方选择不接受堕胎或是拒绝把孩子交给其他家庭抚养都不被视为不合理的行为,也不会中断因果链。

另在 Parkinson v. St James and Seacroft University Hospital NHS Trust (2001) EWCA Civ. 530 的同一类有关不成功绝育手术的先例,涉及孩子生育时有残疾,导致抚养费用的大幅度增加。法院判是生育时的残疾并不会中断因果链,被告还是要负责赔偿。但上诉庭强调如果残疾是在怀孕至生育这一段时间"由于外来的因素"(by some ultraneous cause)所引致,被告就不必负责由于残疾所带来的额外费用。

9.3　受害方有错误或疏忽的自由选择行为

受害方的自由选择如果涉及有错误或疏忽的行为,就有很大的可能会中断因果链。从合理的角度看,受害方的错误或疏忽越是严重,就表示这行为越不合理与无法合理预见,也就越有可能中断因果链。这在较早时本章第 6 段在节录 Vinmar v. Theresa Nav. (2001) 2 Lloyd's Rep 1 的先例中 Tomlinson 大法官的讲话就有涉及。至于错误或疏忽的程度到哪里才会中断因果关系或因果链,这在 9.1.4 段的 Borealis v. Geogas Trading (2011) 1 Lloyd's 482 (CA)先例已做了详细介绍。

首先看一些有关的著名先例:

(1)在货物买卖,违约方的卖方在提供次货或在拒绝交付货物时,受害方自己明知的情况下使用次货或不良替代品而带来损失或受伤,受害方这自己选择的错误行为会中断因果链。在 Quinn v. Burch Bros. (Builders) (1966) 2 Q. B. 370 先例可看到这精神,该案的被告(违约方)没有依约向受害方提供一把梯子,结果受害方的原告自己"胆大"径自使用一个不大稳固的支架作为替代时摔伤。法院判是受害方自己的错误或疏忽中断了因果链,不能从被告处取得赔偿。

(2)当然,如果受害方使用次货是因为看不出,不知道不妥或要检查,加上有其他的枝节如被告的违约方曾出保证没有这方面不妥,则受害方继续使用次货直至出事与蒙受损失,就谈不上有受害方自己选择的错误或疏忽行为了。例如,汽车中的主要零件有问题,继续使用后出事,这方面的讨论可看贵族院 Lexmead v. Lewis and others (1981) 2 Lloyd's Rep. 17 先例。

(3) Quinn v. Burch Bros. (Builders)先例实质是采纳了另一宗海事判决的精神，这另一案例是著名的 The "Stork" (1955) 1 Lloyd's Rep. 349 先例。它是关于承租人违约，提供了不安全港口/码头，在出了事之后，承租人怪责船长疏忽或有错的行为是新介入事件，中断了因果链。但法院不接受船长行为有不合理之处，上诉庭的 Hodson 大法官说："The question is one of causation. If the master, by acting as he did, either caused the damage by acting unreasonably in the circumstances in which he was placed, or failed to mitigate the damage, the charterers would be relieved, accordingly, from the liability which would otherwise have fallen upon them."

(4) 同样的争议也发生在 The "Houston City" (1954) 2 Lloyd's Rep 148 先例，Dixon 大法官说："The chain of causation was broken, it was suggested, because the decision of the master to rely upon the fine weather and not to put out a stream anchor intervened. The master knew the berth to be unsafe, so it was said, or liable to become unsafe on a change of weather. His action in going to the berth with that knowledge, it was said, was the true cause of the damage ..."

(5) 另外有的同类案例有 The "Dagmar" (1968) 2 Lloyd's Rep. 563; The "Polyglory" (1977) 2 Lloyd's Rep. 353, The "Mary Lou" (1981) 2 Lloyd's Rep. 272 等。看来，船长行为即使是错误或疏忽，或事后看来应有更好做法，但应考虑他当时的矛盾，特别是船舶在危急时，常有一时冲动的所谓"agony of the moment"。通常受惊情况下作出错误反应是不应被视为有选择的行为。故此，只要船长行为不是客观看来不合理，即使有改进的余地，也一般不会中断因果链。这方面在本章 9.1.3 段有这方面的讨论。

(6) 在 Schering Agrochemicals Ltd v. Resibel Nv. SA (CA) 26 November 1992 (unreported)先例，被告受聘为原告厂房安装火灾的安全设备，但该设备的设计有缺陷，没有做出火灾的防护。这导致在 1987 年 9 月 30 日原告工厂发生了严重火灾并造成重大损失，原告向被告提出索赔。但在该天火灾前大概三个星期，也就是在 9 月 8 日，就已经发生了一个非常轻微的火灾但足够程度让原告知道该套安全设备有缺陷。应该在那个时候就带来一个危险信号，原告应该终止生产并去做出进一步的检查，但他没有采取行动。在该先例，高院与上诉庭都判原告的索赔不成功，原因是因果关系的中断与没有合理减少损失。其中上诉庭的 Hobhouse 大法官认为原告没有采取合理的行动是"破坏了原来违约带来损失的效力"(destroyed the further causative potency of the pre - existing breach of contract)。

(7) 在 Beoco Ltd v. Alfa Laval Co. Ltd (1995) QB 137 先例，涉及违约方提供了一个有缺陷的机器，但受害方在不足够的修理后也没有经过测试就重新使用，这导致机器爆炸，造成机器的全损与生产中断的损失。上诉庭判受害方可以索赔机器原来有缺陷的损失，但后来的机器爆炸造成了的损坏与损失就是受害方自己所造成，不能要违约方赔偿。

(8)在本章第6段有提及的 Vinmar v. Theresa Nav. (2001) 2 Lloyd's Rep 1 的先例,涉及一个货损的案件。有关货物是高纯度的乙烯,而买卖合约是 CFR,而租用的船舶名为 Atrice 轮。在装港,船舶装了大约一尺高的乙烯后,取了样品化验并发觉有严重的污染。造成污染的是由于船舶上一航次的货物没有清洗,导致船舱与管道把乙烯污染,这也表示船舶不适货,船东也承认责任。所以,双方争议的只局限在损失的计算。这争议主要是来自发觉污染后,承租人与发货人决定继续装货,而船长并没有阻止。这导致把所有的货物装上船之后,都受到严重污染,最后这票货被作为是"跳楼货"(distress cargo)贱价出售。船东对损失计算的抗辩就是只接受原来约一尺高乙烯受到污染的损失,认为后来继续装船导致整船的货物受到污染而蒙受重大损失是承租人与发货人自己的错误或疏忽所导致,而这一决定是完全不负责任的决定,船长并不知道。

但 Tomlinson 大法官判是承租人与发货人作为受害方的决定并非是主要或唯一的原因造成这一个扩大的污染损失,并提到了受害方的困境与矛盾,这方面可看本章9.1.3段。Tomlinson 大法官也认为对扩大污染的损失主要或有效原因还是来自船舶的不适货,加上船长不采取行动阻止继续装货。所以,承租人与发货人的新介入行为并没有中断因果链。

(9)在 The "Aconcagua" (2011) 1 Lloyd's Rep 683 先例,涉及发货人中化集团把一个装载了次氯酸钙的集装箱交给 Aconcagua 轮付运。作为一般性的介绍,次氯酸钙是一种中国出口非常多的货物,但极度危险,非常容易引起爆炸与火灾,已经出过许多大事故,如 The "Kapitan Sakharov" (2000) 2 Lloyd's Rep 255 先例。在1998至1999年间,更有多达4宗重大事故。这导致国际互保协会组织成立了专门小组进行研究与作出有关建议。这种货物经常是装在集装箱,如果一个集装箱装满了这种货物的桶,它在摄氏30度时就已经很危险了。这根本就是一般的气温,其危险性可想而知。看来,这种货物要安全运输,是需要冷藏的集装箱能够保持温度在摄氏10度以下。再看这一先例,Aconcagua 轮在航次的半途中,次氯酸钙发生自燃与爆炸,这导致了严重损失。船东向期租的承租人 CSAV 提出2775万美元的索赔,而 CSAV 再向中化集团作为发货人提出补偿的要求。中化集团所做出的抗辩就是这种货物是在联合国的规定(IMDG Code)是要求在船舶上堆放的地方必须远离任何会发热的源头,但该集装箱偏偏就装在第三货仓的燃油柜附近,而在航次半途中燃油柜曾经为燃油加热,这种受害方自己疏忽的选择行为导致了因果关系的中断。但这被第一审的高院所拒绝,中化集团上诉去上诉庭并提出了有可能是其他不知道的原因造成这一爆炸。但这也被上诉庭拒绝,Longmore 大法官的判决可以总结如下:"Only two possible causes of the explosion had been canvassed at the trial; either the cargo blew up without any external trigger other than ordinary ambient temperature conditions during the carriage, or it blew up because the heating to which the cargo was subjected by reason of its stowage position and the heating of the bunker tanks was a contributory trigger. Sinochem now accepted that the ambient carriage temperatures were "ordinary", and that bunker heating did not play any causative role. The judge did not merely reject Sinochem's case that the explosion was caused by exposure to excessive heating. He relied on expert evidence to form a conclusion that the explosion must have been caused by the rogue nature of the cargo. The judge's findings in relation to that expert evidence could not be challenged."大致上是说第一审的高院通过专家意见证据认定爆炸是出自该票次氯酸钙有不正常的本质,有过低的"临界环境温度"(Critical Ambient Temperature [CAT]),会导致在正常温度下也会发生爆炸,邻近燃油的加热不会造成因果链中断的效果。而在装货的时候,船东或 CSAV 是不知道这票次氯酸钙是有这一个"不正常本质"(rogue nature)。

(10)笔者多年前曾经处理一个案件,是涉及国内卖方在 FOB 买卖下装了货后去银行议付信用证,但付运文件上(货物检查证书,其中一项质量要求中与买卖合约有偏差)有问题而结不到汇。外国买方乘机想敲一笔钱。首先,他吓卖方有关的船舶因为没有提单提货而在卸港会延误,将来会向卖方索赔高昂的滞期费,要求卖方把付运文件在不要求同时支付货款下先交出给买方提货。国内卖方起初不肯,结果双方僵持了不少时间,终于卖方在大幅减价下把文件交出给买方。但船舶已产生了近 2 个月的卸港滞期费,船东先是向承租人(外国买方)索赔,这是一笔大钱,也逃避不了。外国买方在赔付给了船东后转而向中国卖方要求赔付,原因是中国卖方最初的违约所导致。这宗案件是在一个场合中提出来向 7、8 个中方专家咨询的,笔者记得竟然是有不少专家认为卖方有责任,要承担这笔高昂的滞期费。原因是如果一开始卖方不在付运文件上有问题,是不会出这件事情与这笔损失。但笔者的看法完全相反,而且认为非常明确,是:

(a)即使是货物质量有问题(因为货物检查证书有偏差),买方的救济会是可以拒绝这一套单证并让卖方自己另外对这票浮动货物作出处理,如转售给在同一卸港的其他买方。或是买方可以接受货物,但索赔质量方面的损失。后者的损失计算方法有规定在 1979 年《货物销售法》之 53(3)段节,即是以质量良好商品与次货的市场价格比较,差价就是损失金额。但在该案件,外国买方两样合法的做法都没有作出(拒单或拒货)很想要这票商品(估计因为市场价格上涨了),所以不拒货。但也没有放弃向中国卖方借这一问题"敲竹杠",而"敲竹杠"的办法就是不接受付运单证,也因此不能向船舶提货,而以船舶在卸港的延误威胁卖方,希望逼迫卖方让步。结果完全成功,而且提前占了大便宜,因为成功把货价减了几乎一半来换取付运文件。这是小小的质量问题,根本按照市场价格的差价不会有这么大的赔偿金额。

(b)换言之,在买方逼迫卖方减价的延误所导致的船舶的滞期费是买方自己不合理与不合法做法所引起的后果。这额外的滞期费损失是受害方(买方)自己选择敲卖方一笔钱所引起的,这选择也是有错与不安好心。所以,这已中断因果链,这滞期费的产生与卖方在质量上有小偏差根本是扯不上关系了。质量偏差合理预见到的直接与自然后果只能是被买方拒单/拒货或接收付运单证与货物但事后索赔市场差价(如果有市场的话),根本不会是受害的买方两样都不做,造成了不卸货所带来滞期费的额外损失。大家只要想想,如果这艘船舶不是只延误2个月,而是2年,因为外国买方一直坚持决不付钱要这一套付运文件,但又不拒单,引致双方僵局打不破呢?

以上分析看来,卖方连最初的货价也不必大幅减价,甚至不必减价。他根本可马上向买方指出:(i)交出付运文件与支付货款在FOB或CIF买卖下是同步行为,买方如果想要这一套文件,但不肯付钱(因信用证已失效)是买方违约。(ii)质量即使有不妥与(i)的双方责任扯不上关系。买方大可以提出质量问题的损失索赔。(iii)质量问题可在事后依照《货物销售法》处理,或仲裁,或和解,不是事前买方可向卖方敲一笔的借口。买方有减少损失的责任,其中根据市场规则在违约时的计算就已经是把这一个因素考虑在内。(iv)船舶是买方自己租的,船东也明知提单在卖方手中,不肯无单放货,所以买方因不肯付钱取不到付运文件要自己承担所有船舶延误后果,肯定压力在买方,不是卖方。(v)而令笔者感到难以接受的是有好几个中国专家认为外国买方有道理,可以成功索赔这一大笔高昂的滞期费,因为有效的原因是来自货物质量问题与付运单证中的货物检查证书不符。但笔者没有办法接受,并认为外国买方自由选择向中国卖方压价导致船舶在卸港延误,不论成功与否(在这一个案件是完全成功),都打断了因果关系。从另一个角度看,中国卖方的违约是无法合理预见到会带来这种损失,也就是卸港一大笔的滞期费。

9.4　侵权下受害方错误或疏忽中断因果链与分摊责任/损失的区别

侵权也是与违约一样,如果受害方由于自己的错误或疏忽而造成更严重的损失,往往就会中断因果链。而中断因果链之后,这造成额外损失的主要或唯一原因就是新介入行为,变为受害方额外损失全部要自己承担。但在本书第八章有提到过1945年《The Law Reform (Contributory Negligence) Act》的立法,这表示受害方即使是有错误也会根据该立法分摊责任/损失,不至于一毛钱的损失都不能向侵权方取回。可以说在大部分案件涉及新介入事件或行为中断了因果链是不会涉及分摊责任,对额外损失作出了非黑即白的决定也是正确。但会有少数的案件额外损失是由于原来的被告疏忽与新介入行为的原告疏忽共同造成,这就表示更好与更公平的做法是按照1945年立法分摊责任/损失。但这里的分水线不容易界定,而且太轻易或动辄分摊责任/损失会带来对被告一个新的赔偿责任,原来并不存在。这在《McGregor on Damages》(18th edn, 2009年)一书4-018段有提到说:"The danger of too easy an adoption of the solution chartered by the *The Calliope*(1970) P 172 is that it could lead to imposing new liabilities on defendants which were not there before. Thus it is generally accepted that if the claimant, on his way to hospital from a street accident in which the defendant has tortiously injured him, is injured further by a falling tree or by a motorist, whether negligently or not, the defendant is not liable for the further injury. It therefore should not be in any way arguable that the defendant could become subject to a partial liability for such further injury if the claimant himself, by proceeding negligently to the hospital, has contributed to its occurrence. Or, to take the illustration from what is generally regarded as the mitigation sphere, it has never been suggested, where a claimant, run down by a negligent defendant, has unreasonably failed or refused to enter hospital for treatment, that the court should make an apportionment as between claimant and defendant in respect of the loss which the claimant, acting reasonably, could have avoided."(太容易引进分摊责任会导致强加新的赔偿责任在被告。毕竟是一贯接受如果原告因被告的侵权而受伤并入院,途中因倒塌的树木或遭遇交通意外[不论有否涉及疏忽]而蒙受额外的人身伤害,原来的被告是不必为这些新介入事件而负责。不应该说被告也需要对新介入事件负责,并需要与自己也后来有疏忽的原告分摊责任。或者在另一种情况,原告被疏忽的被告撞倒,原告拒绝接受治疗,这应该是有否合理减少损失方面的问题,但法院分摊责任,根据被告最早的疏忽与原告后来拒绝治疗的疏忽分摊,这是从未有过的说法。)

总体针对这一个问题,也另可节录《McGregor on Damages》(18th edn, 2009 年)一书 6-074 段所说如下:"Where the claimant is a free chooser the defendant is much more likely to be relieved of liability for increased damage resulting from the claimant's act. It is at this point that the distinction between contributory negligence, remoteness and mitigation becomes most acute. Since it is here that it becomes most likely that the claimant may fail in his action in respect of the increased damage, it is of great practical importance whether the axe falls by way of contributory negligence, where the claimant can at least recover an apportioned part of his increased damage; by way of remoteness, where the onus is on the claimant to prove the defendant liable for the increased damage; or by way of mitigation, where the onus is on the defendant to show himself not liable for the increased damage. The difficulties of these distinctions need not be analysed again, but it is important to keep them in mind when considering the following cases; the decision in The Calliope (1970) P 172, applying the contributory negligence doctrine in preference to the remoteness doctrine so as to allow a limited recovery in a ship collision case, is of particular significance."(如果受害原告的行为是自由选择,这就造成最大的可能是被告不需要对原告的行为造成额外损失负责。在这个时候,会是分摊责任、损失遥远性与减少损失的区分最为尖锐。由于原告对额外损失会不能向被告索赔成功,所以如果判是可以分摊责任,就会让原告至少可以向被告取回部分的额外损失。如果是根据损失遥远性的因果关系,则举证责任是在原告证明被告要对额外损失负责。而如果是根据减少损失,则举证责任在被告证明他不需要对额外损失负责。这些区分的困难不必再进一步分析,其中在 The Calliope 先例是适用了分摊责任而不选择适用损失遥远性,这导致原告在该撞船的先例能取回部分损失,这先例会稍后进一步介绍。)

这方面可先介绍一个著名的先例McKew v. Holland and Hannen and Cubitts (Scotland) Ltd (1969) 3 All ER 1621,涉及被告的侵权行为导致受害方的原告大腿受伤,但原告在事故几天后作出危险的行动,涉及抱一个孩子爬一个很陡的楼梯而进一步摔伤。在贵族院,他被认定是由于他自己的愚蠢与完全不合理的行为而造成后来的伤害。Reid勋爵是这样说:"If the injured man acts unreasonably he cannot hold the defender liable for injury caused by his own unreasonable conduct. His unreasonable conduct is *novus actus interveniens*. The chain of causation has been broken and what follows must be regarded as caused by his own conduct and not by the defender's fault of the disability caused by it."

但在McKew v. Holland and Hannen and Cubitts (Scotland) Ltd先例,受害方没有请求根据1945年《The Law Reform (Contributory Negligence) Act》要求分摊责任与损失,而法院也没有主动这样做或不认为适用,所以在判决中也没有作出任何分摊。这表示在受害方的原告自己也有疏忽或判断错误的情况下,根据1945年立法要求分摊责任与损失会比因果关系的测试更加公平。

而这方面重要的先例(也在上述节录的《McGregor on Damages》一书中有提到)是The "Calliope" (1970) 1 Lloyd's Rep 84,也是涉及船舶碰撞。Calliope轮在发生碰撞后在事后的操作因为疏忽而蒙受了额外的损坏。Brandon大法官认为他不需要判Calliope轮的船东对额外损坏全部能够取回或全部要自己承担,而可以判额外损坏是部分由于原来的碰撞与部分由于操作的疏忽,并可分摊这额外损坏。结果是在原来船舶碰撞的责任分摊,Calliope轮是要承担55%。但针对后来的额外损坏,Calliope轮就要承担50%。Brandon大法官也说明Calliope轮即使在原来的船舶碰撞没有责任,对额外损坏也可作出分摊。Brandon大法官这样说:"Looking at the question from the point of view of principle, I cannot see any logical reason for denying to the court the right to apportion, or subapportion, liability in the circumstances contemplated. Where all relevant negligence on both sides precedes the original casualty, the fact that A's negligence occurs later than B's negligence, and possibly also in a different place, does not prevent an apportionment of liability for such casualty. The view that it did so was enshrined in the so-called last opportunity rule, which is, to this extent, dead and buried. I find it difficult to see why, as a matter of principle, it should make any difference that, in relation to a particular part of the damage arising, or alleged to arise, from the casualty, the later negligence of B should follow rather than precede the casualty itself. Why should later negligence of B before the casualty be held not necessarily to break the chain of causation, but later negligence of his after the casualty be held necessarily to do so?"

Brandon估计也了解到他这个判法与一般的判法是不一致所以也提到要进一步分摊责任的案件会是很少,说:"... cases where it would be right to find that such damage was caused both by such intervening negligence and by the original negligence which resulted in the casualty may well be comparatively rare."

接下去在 March v. E & MH Stramare Pty Ltd (1991) 99 ALR 423 先例,涉及侵权方的被告把卡车停泊在一条六车道的马路中间,导致其他车道的部分视线被遮挡。原告是另一辆车的司机,他事发时喝了酒,反正就碰撞了这一辆停驶的卡车而受伤。在澳大利亚法院第一审,判是原告与被告都有错误或疏忽,原告是醉酒驾驶,被告是把卡车停在马路中央,但判是受害方原告的错误或疏忽才是最主要与有效的原因导致这一事故。在上诉庭,是把判决改变过来,认为被告对所有其他公路使用者有一个小心的责任,这包括对一些不小心与受到酒精影响的第三人,所以改判原告自己要承担与分摊到70%的责任与损失,这表示被告只分摊到赔付30%的损失。而如果改以损失遥远性的因果关系对待而不是分摊责任,原告就会是要承担全部的责任与损失,是一个非黑即白的结果。

再一个要介绍的是在本章 4.3.2 段已经介绍的 Barings Plc (In Liquidation) v. Coopers & Lybrand (A Firm) (2003) EWHC 1319 (Ch)先例,在该先例法院是分段处理。在前阶段是分摊责任/损失,从 50% 开始到 80%。在后阶段就判是中断了因果链,是一个非黑即白的结果。

这方面在《McGregor on Damages》(18th edn, 2009 年)一书 4 - 019 段有说到:"Barings Plc (In Liquidation) v. Coopers & Lybrand an extremely lengthy litigation arising out of the disastrous Barings collapse, provides an interesting and unusual application, to events following upon the wrong, of contributory negligence and remoteness in combination. The defendant auditors had negligently failed to uncover unauthorised trading by an employee which had resulted over time in huge losses to the claimant employer companies, but mismanagement of the companies was such that for long the unauthorised trading, and hence the losses, went undetected by them. The trial judge after a very lengthy and thorough analysis concluded that there had been increasing contributory negligence, starting at 50 and finishing at 80 percent, until eventually the chain of causation had been broken. Thus for a time only contributory negligence was in issue; then remoteness took over."(霸菱银行对永道国际会计所的诉讼是一个十分漫长与昂贵的案件,案情涉及霸菱银行的倒闭。在该案例中,分摊责任与损失遥远性的因果关系两个大原则混合适用。被告的永道国际会计所因疏忽而没有在查账时发现霸菱银行的一个雇员的非法交易并造成大量损失。但原告的霸菱银行也涉及疏忽管理,竟然没有在较长时间内发觉这些非法交易,也不知道自己蒙受庞大的损失。法院最后的判决是起初的阶段分摊责任,原告与被告一人一半,并在后来把原告的责任增加至80%。而随着时间的过去,也就是疏忽管理更加严重,中断了被告疏忽与损失的因果链。这一来,之后的损失就是有了一个黑白分明的结果,原告因为中断了因果链而要自己承担损失。)

该先例的 Evans - Lombe 大法官针对责任分摊与因果链的中断是这样说:"In the

light of this fault I have concluded that the damages to which BFS(原告) is entitled from November 1992 to April 1994 should be reduced by a proportion which rises over time from 50% to 80%. From the end of April 1994 onwards (that is, for the period during which by far the largest part of BFS´loss was suffered), BFS´fault was so great as to be the only cause of the losses suffered, and D&T (被告)have no further liability from that date. The detailed calculation of BFS' damages is to be agreed between the parties (or, if necessary, decided at a further hearing) in the light of the conclusions I have set out above and two further points of principle upon which I have ruled."

10. 合约下的因果关系

以上针对新介入事件或行为能否中断因果关系或因果链,主要介绍的先例都是与侵权有关,虽然也有少部分是合约关系。以下段节分别简单针对笔者熟悉的合约类别(租船合约、海上货物运输合约、海上保险合约、补偿条文)中会发生的新介入事件或行为(不论是外来事件、第三人行为或受害方行为)会否中断因果链。

10.1 有关租船合约的新介入事件或行为的案例与例子

租船合约经常会有新介入事件或行为的争议,说是原先的违约与最后的损失再也没有直接关系。在较早的时候已经介绍过不少这种案件,都涉及租约关系。如在本章之9.3段已提及的先例 The "Stork" (1955) 1 Lloyd's Rep. 349;The "Houston City" (1954) 2 Lloyd's Rep 148;The "Dagmar" (1968) 2 Lloyd's Rep. 563;The "Polyglory" (1977) 2 Lloyd's Rep. 353;The "Mary Lou" (1981) 2 Lloyd's Rep. 272等,这些案例都涉及承租人对租约中安全港口的违约,但这与最后造成的损失涉及新介入的行为,就是船长的疏忽或不合理行为到底能否中断因果链的争议。这种争议也涉及期租合约通常会有的一条"雇佣与补偿条文"(employment and indemnity clause),有关补偿条文是否会因船长的疏忽或不合理行为而中断了因果链,会在本章之10.4段详论。另在9.2.3段也提到了 The "Tropwind" (No. 2) (1981) 1 Lloyd's Rep. 45与The "Kos" (2010) 1 Lloyd's Rep 87先例,涉及承租人的违约(没有准时支付租金),之后因船东行使撤船选择权并导致最后的损失。

笔者在这里多举一个有关租船合约的例子:假设在一个航次租约,涉及船舶抵达欧洲装港但被承租人违约/毁约说是没有货物可装,船东被迫找替代租约以减少损失。能够找到的一个租约是要在美湾交船,这表示船舶要从欧洲空放去美湾。但在这替代租约的履行过程中,另有不幸的第二波(第一波是承租人违约),如:(1)美湾装港是不安全港,带来船舶损坏。(2)空放途中与另一船舶相撞,除损坏外,也赶不上替代租约的销约期而被取消,加大了总的损失金额。(3)替代租约的承租人签发了运费已付的提单后,发生经济困难倒闭,带来船东严重损失来完成提单航次。

(4)在空放途中的大西洋上遇上坏天气,赶不上替代租约本来已是很短的销约期,也无法延长,加大了总的损失金额。

在以上四个例子,都是没有原先的违约就不会有替代租约,在一定程度上也能满足"要不是"测试(but for test)。所以表面看来承租人要负责全部的损失,即使是损失严重程度有所扩大。但以笔者看来,只有(4)是合理可预见的第二波,是受害方的船东在没有办法的情况下冒一定的险,明知冬天横渡大西洋会遇上坏天气,会造成航次的延误,但仍希望赶上替代租约的销约日,因为没有其他更好的选择。所以,预见与冒的险不幸成真,加大损失应是原来违约/毁约的"直接与自然后果"(direct and natural consequences),也可以合理预见到。但其他三例,都会是新介入事件,中断了因果链。

10.2 有关海上货物运输合约新介入事件或行为的案例

海上货物运输合约在这方面的著名先例也不少,其中就是在6.1段所介绍过的The "British Monarch" (1947) 80 Lloyd's Rep. 151先例。重复与补充下,案情是涉及船东在中国的伪满洲装货(大豆)去瑞典,但在开航时由于不适航而造成航次的延误与减速,令本来只需要60天航程拖延至5个月后才能抵达欧洲。延误期间发生"二战",英国海军命令该船舶要改港去英国格拉斯哥港卸货,这导致货方严重的损失。双方的争议是这一个改港带来的损失是主要由什么原因造成,到底是船东违约也就是船舶不适航导致延误,或是英国海军的命令?或即使最早的原因是船舶不适航,但会否英国海军的命令属于新介入事件或行为,中断了因果关系?贵族院是判在签发提单时,船东就应该可以"合理预料"(reasonable contemplation)到战事的爆发,因为当时欧洲局势已经十分紧张,航次延误时间越长战争风险就越大,所以船东作为违约方要对所有的损失负责。贵族院的Porter勋爵是这样说:"... delay, at a time when war is likely to occur, gives more opportunity for its incidence than a speedy and proper dispatch would give. Where, however, the basis of liability is delay, it is, as I think, the reasonable anticipation which matters."

在上述先例,有提到较早的另一个先例The "Wilhelm" (1866) 14 LT 636,案情涉及船长延误开航导致了船舶由于寒冬而被冰封在港要滞留至第二年的春天才能开航。船东被判要承担所有的延误损失,因为这一个结果是完全可以合理预见到。

但在Associated Portland Cement v. Houlder (1917) 86 LJKB 1495先例,涉及被告的船舶延误一天抵达装港,这事后导致了船舶遇上德国潜水艇被击沉。这被判是船东的违约只需要承担一天的延误,因为德国潜水艇的新介入事件是不可以合理预见。这与之前6.1段提及的The "British Monarch"先例中,船舶延误开航导致被雷击(thunderbolt)的道理是一样的。

10.3 有关海上保险合约新介入事件或行为的案例

海上保险合约在这方面的重要先例也有不少,这是因为在1906年的《英国海上保险法》之 Section 55 规定了保险人是要赔付承保风险作为“近因”(proximate cause)所造成的损失,该条文规定:“55. **Included and excluded losses** (1) Subject to the provisions of this Act, and unless the policy otherwise provides, the insurer is liable for any loss proximately caused by a peril insured against, but, subject as aforesaid, he is not liable for any loss which is not proximately caused by a peril insured against.”

这就表示在任何事故,如果起因与最后造成的损失相隔时间很短,就通常不会有“近因”(proximate cause)的争议。如一个风暴或一个水雷马上把船舶摧毁沉没,前者的近因显然是风暴,承保水险的保险人要赔付。而后者的近因是水雷,变为战争保险人要赔付了。但如果这一起因与最后造成的损失相隔时间很长,当中就会发生许多新介入事件或行为(包括是受保人的行为、第三人的行为、保单除外的风险等),这就会带来最后损失到底是由什么近因造成。所以在这种近因的争议,也就是因果关系有否中断的争议。

这方面介绍一个重要的贵族院先例,这是在 Leyland Shipping v. Norwich Union (1918) AC 350 (HL),该先例明确了保险立法的近因也就是“有效原因”(effective cause) 的同义。之前,近因是被视为在一连串事件或行为中与最后损失在时间上最接近的原因。例如,船舶碰撞后需要修理,延误导致了船上香蕉腐烂,近因被视为是香蕉的内在本质(这不在承保的范围内)而不是看来更有效造成延误的船舶碰撞(这是承保的海上风险):Taylor v. Dunbar (1869) LR 4 CP 206; Pink v. Fleming (1895) 25 QBD 396。但在 Leyland Shipping v. Norwich Union 先例,贵族院作出重大改变,认为保险立法的近因主要是找出在一连串事件或行为中最主要与最有效的原因,而不是看时间上与最后损失的远近。这一来,保险近因的争议也变为与本章所针对的新介入事件或行为是否是主要与有效原因是一致的,这方面请看本章 6.4 段。

Leyland Shipping v. Norwich Union 先例的案情涉及承保的船舶 Ikaria 轮在第一次世界大战期间,1915 年的 1 月 30 日,在离目的港法国勒阿弗尔港(Le Havre)还有 25 海里处,被德国潜艇发射的鱼雷击中,并造成严重损坏,第一货舱全部进水,海水也同时进入第二货舱。通过拖船的救助,总算把船舶拖进勒阿弗尔港并挂靠泊位。如果船舶能够在泊位停留并进行修理,船舶可以说是安全。但在第二天,即 1 月 31 日,勒阿弗尔港受到飓风的袭击,导致船舶不断与泊位碰撞。港口当局担心该船舶在泊位处沉没,而该泊位有重要的军事用途,所以命令船舶必须离开去外锚地搁浅或在防波堤抛锚。这最终导致船舶在 2 月 1 日折断,变成全损。这就涉及最后的损失到底是归咎原来的起因,也就是被德国潜艇的鱼雷击中或是新介入事件的飓风袭击?毕竟,前者是由战争险承保,后者是由不同保险人的水险承保。船东以“海上灾难”(peril of sea)提出索赔,但贵族院判是战争险而不是水险的保险人来负责赔偿,因为船舶被鱼雷击中后从来没有脱离严重的风险,所以战争才是近因或有效原因。贵族院也提到了发生时间上的远近(飓风在近,鱼雷在远)并非是决定性的,根据常识得出真正造成最后损失的有效与最重要的原因才算是近因。Shaw 勋爵这样说：

"I will venture to remark that one must be careful not to lay the accent upon the word 'proximate' in such a sense as to lose sight of or destroy altogether the idea of cause itself. The true and the overruling principle is to look at a contract as a whole and to ascertain what the parties to it really meant. What was it which brought about the loss, the event, the calamity, the accident? . . .

To treat*proxima causa* as the cause which is nearest in time is out of the question. Causes are spoken of as if they were as distinct from one another as beads in a row or links in a chain, but—if this metaphysical topic has to be referred to - it is not wholly so. The chain of causation is a handy expression, but the figure is inadequate. Causation is not a chain, but a net. At each point influences, forces, events, precedent and simultaneously meet; and the radiation from each point extends indefinitely. At the point where these various influences meet it is for the judgment as upon a matter of fact to declare which of the causes thus joined at the point of effect was the proximate and which was the remote cause.

What does 'proximate' here mean? To treat proximate cause as if it was the cause which is proximate in time is, as I have said, out of the question. The cause which is truly proximate is that which is proximate in efficiency. That efficiency may have been preserved although other causes may meantime have sprung up which have not yet destroyed it, or truly impaired it, and it may culminate in a result of which it still remains the real efficient cause to which the event can be ascribed."

Shaw 勋爵接下去也解释了为什么船舶被鱼雷击中才是有效的近因："In my opinion the real efficient cause of the sinking of this vessel was that she was torpedoed. Where an injury is received by a vessel, it may be fatal or it may be cured: it has to be dealt with. In so dealing with it there may, it is true, be attendant circumstances which may aggravate or possibly precipitate the result, but which are incidents flowing from the injury, or receive from it an operative and disastrous power. The vessel, in short, is all the time in the grip of the casualty. The true and efficient cause never loses its hold. The result is produced, a result attributable in common language to the casualty as a cause, and this result, proximate as well as continuous in its efficiency, properly meets, whether under contract or under the statue, the language of the expression 'proximately caused'."

10.4 有关补偿条文新介入事件或行为的案例

"补偿合约/条文"(indemnity contract/clause)出现在不同类别合约中,其中期租合约就经常有一条"雇佣与补偿条文"(employment and indemnity clause)。这种条文与因果关系有密切关系,而补偿条文就是指一些合约条文说明一方当事人如果按照该条文的要求做,带来的后果就会有另一方作出补偿。一般经常会遇到的担保或保函也是属于这种合约或条文。有时候,什么是补偿条文与"免责条文"(exception clause)或其他类型的条文也不容易区分,因为在订约自由下经常会用词不当。例如在本章10.4.6段提及的 The "Eurus" (1998) 1 Lloyd's Rep 351 先例,就有争议有关的条文是否属于免责条文,仲裁庭认为是,但法院不同意。但还是有一些很明确是属于补偿条文,如著名的纽约土产标准期租合约中的第8条文(名为"雇佣条文"[employment clause])要求船长按照承租人的命令与指示让承租人营运船舶。即使没有明示条文说明承租人必须补偿船东因为他所作出的命令与指示所带来的后果与损失,已经有很多的先例判是有这一个默示的补偿责任:The "Ann Stathatos" (1949) 83 Ll L Rep 228。至于另一份名为 BALTIME 的标准期租合约,雇佣条文更加是明示说明承租人要作出补偿,如下:"The captain (although appointed by the owners) shall be under the orders and direction of the charterers as regards employment, agency or other arrangements; and the charterers hereby agree to indemnity the owners from all consequences or liabilities that may arise from the captain signing bills of lading by the orders of the charterers or of their agents, or in otherwise complying with the same..."

补偿条文与违约的损失赔偿并不相同,前者是没有后者的各种限制,如"损失遥远性"(remoteness)或是"合理减少损失"(reasonable mitigation)。但它们之间有一个共同的限制,这就是"因果关系"(causation)。补偿条文也通常不涉及违约不违约,因为在期租合约下,承租人的合法命令与指示导致船东损失经常并不涉及任何违约、错误与不合理之处:The "Athanasia Comninos" (1990) 1 Lloyd's Rep 277。补偿条文是严格要求寻求补偿的原告(船东)证明造成他的损失的"近因"(proximate cause)或"有效原因"(effective cause)就是被告(承租人)的在期租合约下作出的命令与指示,也没有任何新介入事件或行为中断因果链。正如 Donaldson 大法官在 The "White Rose" (1969) 2 Lloyd's Rep 52 先例所讲如下:"A loss may well arise in the course of compliance with the time charterers' orders, but this fact does not, without more, establish that it was caused by and is in law consequence of such compliance and, in the absence of proof of such causation, there is no right to indemnity."这种先例在期租合约很多,包括 Strathlorne Steamship v. Andrew Weir (1934) 50 Ll L Rep 185; The "Ann Stathatos" (1949) 83 Ll L Rep 228; The "White Rose" (1969) 2 Lloyd's Rep 52; The "Aquacharm" (1982) 1 Lloyd's Rep 7; The "Sagona" (1984) 1 Lloyd's Rep 194; The "Erechthion" (1987) 2 Lloyd's Rep 180; The "Nogar Marin" (1988) 1 Lloyd's Rep. 412; The "Berge Sund" (1992) 1 Lloyd's Rep 460; The "Island Archon" (1993) 2 Lloyd's Rep 388; The "Greek Fighter" (2006) 1 Lloyd's Rep 99。

在这种案例,承租人拒绝作出补偿所提出的中断因果链的新介入行为是船长不应该依从他所作出的命令与指示(特别是一些表面就看得出是不合理或有疑问的命令与指示),这等于是说船长自己愚蠢或是疏忽导致最后的损失。也会经常提出的新介入行为是承租人的命令与指示作出后船长在执行时有错误或疏忽,这中断了因果链。以下对部分的先例做简单介绍。

10.4.1 案例之一：The "White Rose"

有关船舶被期租承租人命令与指示去美国 Duluth 港装粮，期间有一个小工从二层舱摔下舱底而受伤，并在美国法院向船东提出索赔，最后双方以约 3000 美元的赔偿达成和解。之后，船东向承租人提出要求补偿，因为是他的命令去 Duluth 港装货。仲裁庭认定了几个可以造成这一个事故与损失的原因，包括是承租人的命令去该美国港口；装货工人包括受伤小工没有经验；没有足够的安全指引给受伤小工；船舶没有按照船籍国芬兰的规定要求二层舱安装围栏；受伤小工自己不小心等。在高院，Donaldson 大法官认为船东没有满足举证责任证明这个损失的近因就是承租人的命令。而根据仲裁庭认定的事实，会是有其他新介入事件或行为造成这一个损失。在这个先例中，依据一般常识就可以很容易感觉到承租人去某一个港口装货的命令怎会与装货小工摔下舱底的损失串在一起？Donaldson 大法官是这样说："The shipowners in the present case have undoubtedly established that their 'potential liability' to Mr. De Chambeau（受伤工人）and their actual loss of £ 2935 5s. 5d. were incidents of and occurred in the course of complying with the charterers' orders to load grain at Duluth. But were they caused by such compliance? The judge of fact, the learned umpire, has found that the accident itself was caused partly by the absence of fencing, but it is clear from his conclusion that the time charterers themselves were at no time guilty of any improper or negligent act and that they were not responsible for the lack of fencing. He has found that the shipowners were in breach of Finnish law, but I do not think that that is material. What connected the accident with, and gave rise to, a potential liability and an actual loss were the provisions of Minnesota law. Unless it can be said that this law was so unusual as to constitute Duluth a legally unsafe port to which the vessel should not have been ordered – and no such contention was advanced – or that the time charterers engaged stevedores who were incompetent by local standards, which is negatived by the findings of fact, I do not consider that it can be said that there is the necessary causal connection between the order to load and the loss."（Donaldson 大法官认为只在很特殊的情况下把受伤小工的意外与承租人的命令去 Duluth 港装货之间才有可能有因果关系。例如，强加在船东的责任与赔偿金额的明尼苏达州法律［Duluth 港口在该州］是十分不寻常，这导致了 Duluth港变成了是一个法律上不安全的港口。比方说，法律是规定即使小工自己疏忽甚至自杀，船东也需要赔偿整艘船舶的价值给该受伤小工。但在本案例，明尼苏达州法律并非是这种不寻常的法律。另一种情况会是承租人在 Duluth 港雇佣的小工是相完全完全低于当地标准的，如没有受过任何装货安全培训，这导致他们在船上作业即使不摔下船舱也会掉入大海或遭遇其他在船舶上的意外。）

10.4.2 案例之二：The "Sagona"

有关船舶装运了约 3 万吨的汽油（gasoil）去德国 Nordenham，船东在较早时收到承租人命令把货物卸下给收货人名为 Mabanaft，船长也就这样做了。对油轮而言，无单交货是经常有的做法。但这一次就出了问题,由于发货人因付运文件的不符点导致了无法在信用证取得货款,所以把船舶扣押并索赔无单放货所造成的损失。这一个问题事后获得解决,但船东还是蒙受损失,主要是扣船所造成的时间损失与有关费用。船东于是向承租人提出要求补偿,因为是他作出的命令与指示而无单放货。但承租人提出的抗辩是他无权作出无单放货的命令与指示,这是侵占第三人货物的做法,所以船长根本不应该依从。而如果依从,就构成了严重的疏忽而中断因果链。在高院,Staughton 大法官认为船长依照一般的油轮做法无单放货,当时也没有值得船长怀疑之处,所以不构成疏忽,更不是可中断因果链的严重疏忽。他是这样说:

"This point is, in my judgment, one of causation. (这是因果关系的问题) The doctrine is well - established in the case of an order by a time charterer to proceed to a port which is, in fact, unsafe. See Scrutton on Charterparties (18th ed.) p. 124:

Where a ship is ordered to an unsafe port and the master acts negligently in entering or remaining in the port, the charterer will be free from liability if, but only if, the negligence is sufficiently serious to sever the causal connection between the order and the damage to the vessel. (同样的道理在期租承租人命令船舶去一个不安全港口的案例中经常涉及,就是一艘船舶被命令去一个不安全港口,但船长发现不安全因素后还是错误或疏忽进港或在没有做出预防措施的情况下停留在该港口并造成损失,如果船长的疏忽是足够严重中断承租人命令与船舶损坏之间的因果链,承租人就可以免去补偿责任。)

So here, when the charterers ordered the owners to deliver the cargo to Mabanaft, the question is whether that order caused the owner's loss, or whether the conduct of the master in obeying it without further enquiry was a *novus actus interveniens*. Seeing that the master followed his normal practice and that of other master, and there being no circumstances to arose, his suspicion, I consider that the charterers' order caused the owners' loss. They are entitled to be indemnified in the sums that have mentioned." (所以在本案件,到底是承租人无单放货的命令或是船长听令这样做才是有效原因,中断因果关系?考虑到油船经常是无单放货,船长只是依从一贯的做法,也没有情况值得他怀疑,所以主要或有效的原因还是承租人命令无单放货。)(笔者一提的是油轮经常有无单放货的做法,但在干散货船就不是同一回事。所以本案例如果涉及散货船,判法应该是不同。)

10.4.3　案例之三:The "Erechthion"

有关船舶被承租人命令去尼日利亚的 Port Harcourt,并稍后通过 Port Harcourt 港务局命令船舶去一处锚地(名为 Dawes Island)抛锚。但在航行途中该船舶搁浅受损,并导致船舶救助与最后进行修理。船东事后向承租人提出补偿要求,并在仲裁胜诉。但上诉去了法院被认为裁决书所认定的事实并不明确船舶搁浅的有效原因是由于承租人的命令或是领航员的航行命令,而船东是自己要对航行的风险负责,领航员的命

令也不等同是承租人的命令。所以,法院把该裁决书发还给仲裁庭明确这一点。Staughton 大法官是这样说:

"However, when one looks at the tribunal's findings, it is apparent that this award, which is otherwise admirably lucid, contains some error or confusion, for two reasons. First, the arbitrators say in the passage to have numbered (4) that the vessel was ordered by the charterers to lighten at anchor between buoys 11 and 12. but the instruction of the harbour authority was only proceed to the Dawes Island anchorage; it was the advice of the pilot, not given on behalf of the charterers, which pointed to a place between buoys 11 and 12. Secondly, in the passage numbered (3) it is said that there was no other way of proceeding to the anchorage indicated by the harbour authority than that adopted by the vessel. From other findings in the award that is manifestly incorrect. If the pilot has advised or the master had decided that the vessel should anchor in some other part of the anchorage, for example between buoys 12 and 13 where a number of other vessels were anchored, there would have been no need for the vessel to pass through the waters where the casualty occurred.

Those points convince me either that the arbitrators were treating the pilot's advices as part of the charterers' orders, or at least that there is a real risk that they may have done so. In the circumstances I do not think it right to infer a finding on the part of the arbitrators that the damage to the vessel was proximately caused by the charterers' orders to proceed to Dawes Island anchorage. I shall remit the award to the arbitrators and ask them to state whether they do in fact reach that conclusion."

10.4.4 案例之四:The "Nogar Marin"

在这一个先例,是关于船长疏忽依从承租人(估计也是 CIF/CFR 卖方)的命令与指示签发了清洁提单,而事实上货物装船时不妥(钢条有生锈)。船东对收货人作出赔偿,但事后向承租人要求补偿时被拒,承租人指是船长错误不在提单上批注已中断因果链。仲裁员同意承租人这一个的抗辩说:"... intervening negligence of the master broke the chain of causation between the charterer's act of presenting inaccurate shipping documents and the subsequent claim by cargo – interests."

在上诉庭,Mustill 大法官强调了船长有自由选择去批注提单,所以船长错误选择不这样做就足以中断因果链。他说:"Furthermore, on the facts of the present case (and we would suspect on the facts of most cases) the argument must found on causation. The charterers tender the document. The master has a free choice whether or not to clause it. He chooses not to do so. Later, those acting for the owners (这是指船东代理人) have the opportunity to clause the bill of lading, so as to protect the owners. Again they let the opportunity pass."

10.4.5 案例之五:The "Berge Sund"

这一个先例涉及一个长达 20 年的期租合约,船舶一直被用来装运丁烷和丙烷,也不涉及清洁船舱。但在过了 10 个月的营运后,该船舶(在沙特阿拉伯港口的 Ras Tanura 等待装货前)发觉在第 2 与第 3 舱有污染,不能通过一个名为"copper strip corrosion test"的检验。不能通过检验的原因被仲裁庭认定为有三个,这包括:前一票去日本的货物有过量硫磺或承租人检验师以没有代表性的样品作出检验。反正仲裁庭最后是认定这一次问题是船东与承租人都没有过错与责任,检验不通过后,承租人要求清洁船舱,而船舶也用"苛性钠液体"(caustic soda solution)清洁妥,但这带来了 20 天的延误。争议就是这 20 天应否是停租或是承租人应该补偿船东这些损失,因为是依照承租人的命令与指示装运这票去日本不合规格的货物。

Steyn 大法官说:"The difficulty is, however, that the indemnity only extends to direct consequence of complying with the relevant orders. The burden rested on the owners to establish a direct cause or link between the orders and/or loading and the loss of time. There is no express finding that the loss of time resulted directly from compliance with the charterers' order. (困难的地方是必须有关命令所带来的直接后果才有补偿,而举证责任是在船东。在这个裁决书没有认定这 20 天的延误是承租人命令直接带来的后果。)

The only question is whether from the primary facts set out in the award there is only one answer, namely that it was a direct consequence... The arbitrators said that the loss of time was not the natural result of the loading of the cargo. It must follow that the arbitrators did not regard the loss of time as directly resulting from the orders to load. At the very least it is uncertain what their conclusion would have been if they had grappled with the issue which is probably one of mixed fact and law. It is also important to note that in par. 62 the three causes which I have mentioned are cited as examples of one of a number of reasons why the vessel failed the test. In any event, it is not clear whether the arbitrators might have regarded testing and sampling at Ras Tanura by charterers' surveyors as a cause interrupting the chain of causation. (仲裁庭认定时间的损失并非是装载有关货物所带来的自然后果。另外,仲裁庭认定了有三个原因造成了这一污染。也不清楚仲裁庭是否认定承租人检验师的疏忽中断了承租人的命令与最后损失的因果关系。)

It is simply not possible on the facts set out in the award to infer that the problem at Ras Tanura was the direct consequence of the charterers' orders or the loading of the cargo."

10.4.6　案例之六:The "Eurus"

这个先例在本章之 6.5.2 段已经介绍过,不重复,只说承租人向船东索赔多支付了约 70 万美元的额外货价给尼日利亚的卖方,原因就是船长没有按照承租人的航次指示不要在 1 月 31 日的 11:00 时之前递交通知书,而不递交也表示不应靠泊。事实上,船舶是在 2 月 1 日的 01:30 时装完货物。这严格看来,船长的违约并没有造成后果或损失,因为承租人应该还是可以取得 2 月份的提单。但尼日利亚装港特殊的

“08:00 时规定”(8 a. m. rule)才是真正原因导致了承租人只能取得1月份的提单。在仲裁庭,判船长是违约,但这个“08:00 时规定”的损失是不能合理预见与太遥远,这只是尼日利亚的特殊规定/做法。而根据另一个诉因,也就是租约的一条特殊条文要求船长必须依照承租人的航次指示,否则要赔偿所有的损失,如果视为是一条“补偿条文”(indemnity clause),就只需要关心因果关系,而不必理会损失太遥远的问题。由于“08:00 时规定”已经在订立租约前存在18年之久,所以不能在因果关系加以考虑,这变成只能考虑船长的违约,这与最后造成的损失是没有任何新介入事件或行为,所以仲裁庭判是船东需要对承租人作出补偿。但已经介绍过,这个案件上诉去了法院,被高院与上诉庭推翻认为最重要的还是找出造成损失的最主要与有效原因,这极可能就是“08:00 时规定”,而法律也没有禁止考虑违约前已经存在的因素。

10.4.7 案例之七:The “Greek Fighter”

有关船舶是一艘油轮,期租给承租人并在阿拉伯联合酋长国的 Khorfakkan 港口外抛锚,作为浮动油库。按照承租人的命令与指示,船舶从另一艘名为 Gulf Prince 轮接受过来一票原油,但船长不知道这票原油是来自伊拉克。当时是有联合国对伊拉克作出禁运(起因来自伊拉克侵略科威特),而阿联酋是支持与执行的,并且有法律规定任何违反禁运的船舶将会被没收,而船东知道与否是不能作为抗辩。反正是最后该船舶被阿联酋没收与公开拍卖,蒙受损失的船东根据雇佣条文向承租人要求补偿,因为是依从他的命令与指示接受这批来自伊拉克的原油。在高院,Colman 大法官判承租人败诉,因为承租人违反租约装运违禁品。Colman 大法官也针对另一个假设情况,就是如果货物并非是违禁品,但船舶还是被阿联酋政府没收,承租人是否还是需要根据雇佣条文对船东作出补偿。Colman 大法官是认为在这种情况下,承租人就应该胜诉,因为即使是承租人的命令与指示装货所引起,但阿联酋政府根据不合理的怀疑没收船舶就变为非法与不合理,这一行为就中断了补偿条文下的因果链。

11. 订约自由下合约条文带来的变化

合约与侵权不一样的地方就是前者有订约自由,这包括了对因果关系的要求。合约会有条文严格要求因果关系,或是排除要求因果关系,这些都是完全有效的合约条文,但也会无可避免带来对因果关系作出不同的判决。一个针对性说法是 Rix 大法官在 The “Eurus” (1996) 2 Lloyd's Rep 408 的一审中所说:“Contracts create their own private worlds (within the world at large). Their terms define the parties' mutual obligations and duties. Moreover the parties' knowledge or reasonable contemplation of each other's business may itself be a private matter (within the more general expectations of their industry) and will most probably be affected in some degree by the terms of their own private bargain. So it is that even though issues of causation and of reasonable contemplation may be formally separate, they are both affected by the parties' contract, its matrix and their expectations."

11.1　合约条文不同的解释会带来对因果关系不同的理解

解释合约条文会带来对因果关系有不同的理解。这方面可节录 Devlin 大法官在 The "Ann Stathatos" (1950) 83 Ll L Rep 228 先例所说："When questions of causation arises in contracts, points of construction are often involved. The contract defines the event which sets in motion the train of consequences. If in this respect the contract is misconstrued and the angle of view is, as it were, incorrectly plotted, the view will be wrong. Thus, in the war risk insurance cases, when the event was 'warlike operations,' error at one time arose because the adjective rather than the noun was thought to point to the direction which the inquiry should take, and it was supposed that the consequences must always be attributable to the warlike character of the operation... The terms of the contract may restrict or expand the field of causation which has to be examined. There is no rigid rule that a cause to be operative must be the proximate cause. The rule is based on the intention of the parties."

上述节录的第一段是指船舶战争保险在 1983 年前的 200 年都是以劳合社的 SG 保单进行投保所有船舶在海上会遇到的风险，只是以一条名为"捕获和扣押不保条文"(Free of Capture and Seizure Clause)把 SG 保单中的战争风险排除在外，该条文其中排除的一种风险是"敌对或类似战争行为的后果"(consequence of hostilities or war－like operations)。但在著名的贵族院先例 The "Coxwold" (1942) 73 Ll L Rep 1，判是按照护航军舰官员确定航向的航行船舶发生搁浅是类似战争行为的后果，所以是战争保险人要去赔付。但问题是在"二战"期间，所有的英国船舶都是要参加护航与按照军舰官员的命令行事。如果事后发生搁浅碰撞等原属于水险的新介入事件也被视为是战争险，就会导致在"二战"期间船舶根本不需要投保水险，劳合社也就没有生意可做(因为只有水险是商业市场承保，战争险是主要由政府承保)。所以许多人认为这一案例破坏了水险保险人和战争险保险人之间的市场平衡。本来船舶的事故与损失主要或有效原因是战争险或是水险造成在"二战"期间也是不容易掌握，因为战争险往往导致水险的风险大大增加，如避开德国潜水艇而采取危险的航线带来搁浅或关灯航行带来船舶碰撞。但 The "Coxwold"被认为是错判应该是共识，这也带来了后来对"捕获和扣押不保条文"的修改恢复市场平衡。而根据上述 Devlin 大法官的说法，就是贵族院错误解释有关条文的"战争行为"一词，把重心放在形容词的"战争"，导致了对什么是主要或有效原因的错判。

11.2　合约以明示条文收紧或是扩大因果关系的做法

合约方面的规定影响因果关系的问题在保险合约就经常会有，可节录笔者所著的《海上货物保险》一书第六章。

"近因原则的默示法律地位在上述已经介绍过，但在现实中保险人会希望在承保不同的风险时想将该近因原则进行扩大或限制，这就只能通过明示条文超越默示地位。举例说，在协会货物保险条文之4.7条，条文是排除核武器的风险。由于保险人惧怕核武器/装置的杀伤力太大与影响深远，所以不希望只是依赖近因原则的默示法律地位，而是说明损失只要是直接或间接由于核武器/装置引起就被排除在外。例如在引爆核武器之后，广泛受影响的地区肯定是会变得无法无天，纵火抢劫会大量发生并造成进一步损失，就会有争议纵火抢劫的错误与自由选择的第三人行为会否中断因果链。而'直接或间接导致'一词可以说是在海上保险中含义最广泛的用词，该条文为：'In no case shall this insurance cover—4.7 loss damage or expense **directly or indirectly caused by or arising from** the use of any weapon or device employing atomic or nuclear fission and/or fusion or other like reaction or radioactive force or matter.'

另一个极端是以明示条文限制'近因原则'(proximate cause)的适用，即规定只有承保的风险是损失发生的'唯一'(solely)、'绝对'(exclusively)与'直接'(directly)原因的情况下，受保人才可以得到赔偿。这里可以介绍香港的先例 Vastgrand Industrial Ltd. v. Hong Kong and Shanghai Insurance Co. Ltd. (2002) HKEC 494，案情涉及原告投保的保险合约规定是只承保台风与风暴造成的损失。后来有了很大的风暴(这可算是起因)，这风暴导致珠江水位大涨(这可算是新介入事件)，原告的工厂也因此而被淹没。作为被告的保险人否认自己有责任，并争辩说在洪水前几天，风暴已经减弱。法院的观点是该损失是在承保的范围内，并说直接原因不必是最重要的原因，只要是重大的原因造成损失就已经足够。这样看来，这种方法大致是与近因原则是相同的。

在货物保险的条文中还会有其他明示条文试图改变近因原则，但许多在效力上有疑问。这里还存在一个问题就是如果放宽，是要放宽到什么程度？而正如前面介绍过的，一个人的出生也可以说是他死亡的一个间接原因(因为没有出生的起因，就不会有死亡的后果)，但这间接是要到什么程度才算是合理？不妨先介绍明示条文中应该可以说是最广泛的'直接或间接导致'(directly or indirectly caused by or arising from)一词。这里首先介绍案件：Coxe v. Employers Liability Assurance (1916.) 2 KB 629，案情涉及一个军官在检阅士兵的时候被火车撞死，因为当时是在'一战'期间，灯火管制导致路轨周围昏暗。有关的保险合约说明是不赔偿军官直接或间接由战争引起或导致的死亡(This policy does not insure against death... directly or indirectly caused by, arising from, or traceable to ... war...)。在第一审，判近因是战争。在上诉庭，Scrutton 大法官认为有'间接'(indirectly)这一词，所以不能干预仲裁庭的裁决。他也认为无法理解什么才是'间接的近因'(indirect proximate cause)，但可以清楚看到是双方想排除近因原则，说：'... the words which I find it impossible to escape from are 'directly or indirectly.' There does not appear to be any authority in which those words have been considered, and I find it impossible to reconcile them with the maxim *causa proxima non remota spectatur*. If it were contended that the result of the words is that the proximate cause, whether direct or indirect, is to be looked at, I should reply that that result does not appear to me to be consistent or intelligible. I am unable to understand what is an indirect proximate cause, and in my judgment the only possible effect which can be given to those words is that the maxim *causa proxima non remota spectatur* is excluded and that a more remote link in the chain of causation is contemplated than the proximate and immediate cause.'

但 Scrutton 大法官也感觉到'间接'这一词很难给它一个合理的限制,他提到该军官的出生也可以认为是他死亡的一个间接原因。但他也给了一些指引说:'a more remote link in the chain of causation is contemplated.'。而在 Spinney's v. Royal Insurance (1980) 1 Lloyd's Rep. 406 先例,Mustill 大法官认为将'间接'应该限制在与损失有'关系'(connection)的范围,而不是到一个地步使该原因再也不是造成损失的原因而变了是历史的一部分(an event ceases to be a cause of the loss, and becomes merely an item of history)。Mustill 大法官比较详细的判词是如下:'I now turn to the question whether there was a sufficient causal connection between the operation of the excepted perils and the losses which I have described. The type of connection required is defined by the causation clause, and the mode of proof by the reverse burden clause. The meaning of the former was the subject of citation and argument at the trial. I do not find it necessary to discuss the reported decisions on the meaning of various individual words of the clause, for whatever they may mean on their own, **it is quite clear that the draftsman has gone to great lengths to ensure that the doctrine of proximate cause does not apply. Plainly, there must be some limit on the application of the clause, for the chain of causation recedes infinitely into the past. The draftsman must have intended to stop somewhere: and that place must be the point at which an event ceases to be a cause of the loss, and becomes merely an item of history. The draftsman has not explained how that point is to be identified, nor indeed do I believe that words can be found to do so. It is, eventually, a matter of instinct——but an instinct guided by the fact that this is a policy which (unlike others in which similar clauses can be found) expressly insures against violent acts**. In essence, the task is to assess whether the particular act of violence simply takes place against the background of a 'warlike' state of affairs, or whether it has itself (even if in a rather remote way) a warlike aspect of its own.'(加黑部分是笔者的强调)

另在先例 Oei v. Foster and Eagle Star Insurance Co. Ltd. (1982) 2 Lloyd's Rep. 170,也是类似的判法。最后一提的是《O'May on Marine Insurance》一书中,O'May 律师建议最好避免使用'indirect'一词,因为给间接的因果关系一个合理的限制会是很困难(in view of the difficulty in setting any reasonable limits to indirect causation)。

另一个用词也会是改变与扩大近因原则是‘可归因于’(attributable to)或‘可合理归因于’(reasonably attributable to),在海上保险也是保险人用在比较严重的风险,所以要更广泛的把它排除在外,这就是受保人的‘恶意行为’(wilful misconduct)。这种恶意行为在海上保险最典型的就是船东恶意凿沉船舶,在岸上保险最典型就是纵火。把近因原则扩大就可以在受保人做这种事情的时候,如果有其他原因共同导致或者扩大损失,保险人也有保障可拒赔。这可以节录2009年协会货物条文之4.1是规定:‘In no case shall this insurance cover loss damage or expense **attributable to** wilful misconduct of the Assured.’,这与1906年《英国海上保险法》之 Section 55(1)(a):‘The insurer is not liable for any loss **attributable to** the wilful misconduct of the assured...’对比之下就可以看到两者都采用了相同的措辞‘可归因于’。

《Arnould's Law of Marine Insurance and Average》第16版对‘attributable’一词的解释如下:‘It seems, however, to be clear in principle that wilful misconduct of the assured is a defence not only when it is the proximate cause of loss but also when it is only one of the effective causes of, or factors contributing to a loss. A similar rule appears also to obtain in cases, of the type provided for in section 39(5) of the Marine Insurance Act 1906, where the ship is sent to sea in an unseaworthy state, with the privity of the assured.’

从这个意义上说,‘可归因于’的意思不必局限在近因,而只要是受保人的恶意行为是导致损失的其中一个有效原因就已经是足够。

另是在这一个用词,不论有没有在前面加上‘合理地’(reasonably)应该都是同一个意思。《Arnould's Law of Marine Insurance and Average》关于该词到底有怎样的作用论述如下:‘The test for causation under the words ‘reasonably attributable to’ may be less stringent than the proximate cause test. In principle, it appears that reasonable evidence of a causal link between the specified peril and the loss claimed is sufficient under this part of the clause.’

但在 The ‘Salem’ (1982) 1 Lloyd's Rep. 369(CA)先例,上诉庭 Kerr 大法官有不同的看法认为‘可归因于’是不能改变近因原则。他是这样说:‘But I think that these words ‘may have been attributable to’ are neutral words which cannot be read as intended to alter the well-established principles of causation in this field.’这在 John Dunt 2009年所著的《Marine Cargo Insurance》第130页分析该案例,认为是该案件的情况特殊,并且 Kerr 大法官只是‘随口讲讲’(*obiter*)。John Dunt 的结论还是:“‘Attributable to’ is wider than proximately caused by and covers the case where the risk is ‘a’ cause of the loss even where it is only one of the effective causes or factors contributing to the loss.”

毕竟,如果是用明示的合约条文改变默示的法律地位就必须说得十分清楚。其实现在什么样的用词可以将近因原则有效的排除还不是很明朗,像‘caused by’、 'resulting from'、'due to'、'arising from'、'consequences of'这些用词都不足够改变近因的原则。

首先介绍'caused by'，Scrutton 大法官在 Coxe v. Employers Liability Assurance (1916) 2 KB 629 先例中是说：'They are words which always have been construed as relating to the proximate cause.'

接下去介绍'resulting from'，上诉庭的 Potter 大法官在先例 Lloyds TSB General Insurance Holdings Ltd. v. Lloyds Bank Group Insurance Co. Ltd. (2002) Lloyd's Rep. IR 113 中是说：'In my view the expression 'result from' undoubtedly imparts the notion of causation which, in turn, in all branches of insurance law, involves application of the notion of proximate cause, applied with good sense, so as to give effect to and not to defeat the intention of the parties.'

关于'due to'与'arising from'，《Arnould's Law of Marine Insurance and Average》，第 16 版在第 938 页是这样说："Words such as 'due to' 'resulting from' 'arising from' in an exceptions clause in a policy have been construed as excluding only those losses proximately caused by the events mentioned."

这种以明示条文针对因果关系的要求也不仅是在保险合约，在租约也一样会有。例如在 Reardon Smith Line Ltd v. Ministry of Agriculture, Fisheries and Food (1961) 1 Lloyd's Rep 385 先例，其中一个争议涉及装港罢工的时间是否有对船舶造成延误，而有关条文是说明罢工所造成的延误船舶装卸不算装卸货时间。这就涉及罢工与船舶延误的因果关系，在上诉庭 Sellers 大法官说：'I would agree with Mr. Justice McNair that the decision established and applies the principle that the mere existence of strike is not sufficient; it must have some causative effect upon the operations of the particular ship concerned.'这表示罢工必须与有关船舶的延误有一定程度的因果关系，而不是太间接的关系。例如在船舶抵达装港之前就已经发生罢工，造成了货物与船舶的积压，令有关船舶无法马上靠泊装货。"

12. 同步原因

对于同步原因(concurrent cause)或先后有多个近因造成一个损失的情况，要在这些同步原因或多个近因之间找出哪一个才是造成损失最重要与最有效的原因。这种争议往往是与因果关系是否中断的争议十分接近，最后得出的答案也往往一致，在本章 6.4 段有提到损失的起因或新介入事件或行为也存在要找出哪一个才是最重要与有效的原因。虽然被称为是同步原因，但仍是在时间上会有先后，只是可能会十分接近与有时候不容易肯定，毕竟两个或以上的原因发生在同一时刻的情况会是绝少。在笔者所著的《海上货物保险》一书第六章 4.5 段就介绍了在保险范畴如何处理有多个近因的情况,因为这几个近因会包括在承保的风险,也会有排除在承保外的列名风险。这方面在本章不重复,只除了重复在该书提到的一个重要先例,就是 Wayne Tank & Pump v. Employers' Liability (1973) 2 Lloyd's Rep 237,这个有关火灾的先例是工厂里面安置了一个有缺陷与危险的设备,起火是因为在没有人监管的情况下将该设备开动,这涉及雇员的疏忽。这就带来到底是危险设备还是雇员疏忽才是近因的问题,前者是雇员责任保险合约的除外风险,后者是在保险合约承保的范围内。Denning 勋爵在上诉庭认为根据正常思维或是"常识"(common sense)应该是危险设备,说:

"So I would approach this case by asking which of the two causes was the effective or dominant cause? I should have thought that it was the first cause, the dangerous nature of the installation, and thus within the exception. So that the Employers' Liability were not liable under this policy. (Denning 勋爵是找出有危险设备与雇员疏忽这两个原因到底哪一个是有效或主要造成火灾的原因,他认为是前者,所以雇员责任保险不必赔付。)

The Judge was much inclined to hold that it was the dangerous installation which was the dominant cause. But he was dissuaded from that view by Mr. Le Quesne (原告代表大律师), who argued, with his usual persuasiveness, that the act of the man (in switching on the heating tape) was a *novus actus interveniens* which was predominant in effectiveness. It was the cause of the fire. It did not come within the exceptions. So the Employers' Liability were liable. (但在第一审的法院,大法官被原告代表大律师说服,该雇员的疏忽中断了因果关系,导致了这一个新介入行为才是火灾最重要的有效原因。这一来,雇员责任保险就需要赔付所有的损失。)

I must say that I do not care for this emphasis on *novus actus interveniens*. It seems to me to be going back to the old and forsaken test of the latest in time. I would reject *novus actus*. I would ask, as a matter of common sense, what was the effective or dominant cause of the fire? To that question I would answer that it was the dangerous installation of a pipe which was likely to melt under heat. It seems to me that the conduct of the man in switching on the heating tape was just the trigger – the precipitating event – which brought about the disaster. There would have been no trouble whatever if the system had been properly designed and installed. (Denning 勋爵拒绝接受新介入事件或行为中断因果链的说法。他认为这有危险再回到根据行为与事件发生时间距最后损失产生远近作为找出近因的唯一标准的过时说法[这可看本章 10.3 段有关 Leyland Shipping v. Norwich Union (1918) AC 350 (HL)先例的介绍]。Denning 勋爵说是根据常识作出判断什么才是火灾的有效或主要原因,他认为是有危险的设备,而雇员的行为只是引发了这一灾难。如果设备是没有问题,根本不会发生这样的结果)(注:在本章 8.2 段有介绍 Philco Radio v. Spurling (1949) 2 All E. R. 882 先例,提到船员在禁止吸烟区疏忽吸

烟而导致船舶爆炸,因为他不知道承租人违约把危险品装在船上并漏出易燃气体,仍是不应中断承租人违约与最后损失的因果链,可以说是与本先例的道理是一致的。)

Seeing that the dangerous installation was the dominant cause, it comes within the exception and the Employers' Liability company are not liable on this policy."(所以,在本案例雇员责任保险公司不需要赔付损失。)

接下去笔者介绍一些与保险无关的先例,在做法上也是在涉及同步原因或多个先后的原因造成同一个损失中找出哪一个是最重要与有效的原因。在 The "Kapitan Sakharov" (2000) 2 Lloyd's Rep 255 先例,涉及受害方的船东向两位提供有关货物的发货人(DSR 与 CYL)提出索赔损失。案情是一艘俄罗斯集装箱船 Kapitan Sakharov 轮在波斯湾港口航行,出事的时候,船舶所装运的货物大部分是属于两位被告提供的货物。而事故就是"堆装"(stow)在甲板的一个集装箱先发生爆炸与引起大火,火灾蔓延到船舱,最后导致船舶沉没。这一个集装箱后来被认定是装了一种名为"次氯酸钙"(calcium hypochlorite)的危险品,很容易引起爆炸与火灾,在本章 9.3 段所介绍的 The "Aconcagua" (2011) 1 Lloyd's Rep 683 先例也涉及同样的货物。在这一个案例中,DSR 作为次氯酸钙的发货人没有向船东宣告这一个集装箱内是装有次氯酸钙的危险品,这是违反 1924 年《海牙规则》与英国法律的默示责任。所以后来是判 DSR 对集装箱爆炸与发生大火所造成的损失负责。但问题是该船舶出事后,爆炸与大火如果只局限在船舶的甲板上是不至于令船舶沉没。而船舶沉没的原因是大火蔓延去船舱,而船舱内堆装了几个属于第二被告 CYL 提供给船东的装有另一种名为"异戊烷"(isopentane)的危险品的集装箱。它的危险来自易燃,程度上比汽油更厉害,它的燃点是摄氏 0 度,而沸点是摄氏 28 度。所以在波斯湾的正常气温,就已经比沸点更高,会造成异戊烷的挥发。本来这种货物是应该堆装在甲板上,而即使是堆装在船舱内,该船舱也必须有良好的通风以防止挥发了的易燃气体累积而产生危险。偏偏 Kapitan Sakharov 轮没有良好的通风设备,但船东还是把装有异戊烷的集装箱放置在第三舱内。这被法院认定为船舶因为装货不恰当而导致船舶不适航并且船东没有"恪尽职责"(due diligence),这才是最后导致船舱发生大火并激发了船底仓柴油柜的爆炸并最终导致船舶沉没的"有效原因"(effective cause)。在第一审,Clarke 大法官是这样说:"... the position at common law is as follows, assuming for present purposes that the shippers were in breach of a common law duty not to ship dangerous cargo. If (as here) there were two effective causes of the relevant loss, which in this context was the sinking, one of which was the plaintiffs' breach of Article III rule 1 and the other of which was a breach of duty at common law on the part of the shippers, the plaintiffs' claim fails. It fails because, just as the plaintiffs can say that they are entitled to recover damages for the shippers' breach of their duty at common law, so the shippers can say that they are entitled to recover by reason of the breach of Article III rule 1. Both claims would fail, as it were, for circuity of action. I would add in passing that I do not think that this is a situation in which the plaintiffs' claim can properly be said to have failed by reason of a break in the chain of causation, although the result is the same."[假设在本案例是有两个有效原因造成最后损失，也就是船舶的沉没，第一个有效原因就是船东违反了《海牙规则》之 Article III (1)有关船舶适航的责任，而第二个有效原因就是被告 DSR 违反了普通法要求对危险品作出宣告的责任。这一来，原告与被告之间的索赔与反索赔都不会成功，原因这是迂回反复诉讼。]

在上诉庭，双方也有争议是如果两个违约原因(DSR 没有宣告危险品与船东把异戊烷堆装在没有良好通风设备的船舱内导致船舶不适航)，不是同时发生，而是先后发生，船舶的不适航是否被 DSR 违反普通法作为一个新介入事件或行为中断了因果链。代表 DSR 的大律师是这样争辩："... any explosion or fire on deck for which DSR might be responsible did not of themselves cause the vessel to sink. The true and intervening cause of that was the plaintiffs' stowage of isopentane below deck in hold 3 in breach of its duty under art. III, r. 1 of the Hague Rules to exercise due diligence to make the vessel seaworthy. He argues that the significance to causation of such breach is that it is a finding of a wrongful act vis - à - vis DSR, including an awareness or imputed awareness of its breach of MOPOG (这是船旗国俄罗斯版本的《国际海上危险品法规》) and duty of due diligence, and also of a reasonable foreseeability that it would exacerbate any fire and/or make its consequences more serious. Such intervening conduct, especially by reason of its element of breach of duty, should, he submitted, relieve DSR from liability for the damage and losses caused by the isopentane fire. He relied upon The 'Sivand' (1998) 2 Lloyd's Rep 97, in which this court held that the defence is available where the intervening act is the effective - in effect the exclusive - cause of damage."(即使 DSR 违反普通法地位不作出"次氯酸钙"危险品的宣告，这也只会导致堆装在甲板的集装箱发生爆炸与火灾，造成较局限的损坏，但不会导致船舶沉没。真正与有效的原因是装在第三舱的"异戊烷"危险品，也就是根本不应该这样堆装，导致船舶不适航。所以不论船舶不适航是起因或是新介入事件，它才是船舶沉没的主要与有效的原因。)

而最后上诉庭判决是认为因果链有没有中断并不重要，重要的是认定船舶不适航才是船舶沉没的主要或有效原因，也就是船东没有恪尽职责令船舶适航。所以，针对各项索赔与反索赔，判是：(1)船东向 DSR 索赔最初在甲板爆炸与火灾的损失成功。(2)船东向 DSR 索赔船舶沉没的损失与船舶沉没造成对第三人的责任(如船员死亡与造成污染)不成功，因为 DSR 违反普通法的不宣告集装箱内的次氯酸钙危险品并非是造成船舶沉没的有效原因。(3)船东向 CYL 提出的索赔不成功，因为 CYL 不存在违约，而是船东自己把装满异戊烷的集装箱错误堆装在第三舱，并且没有良好通风。(4)DSR 向船东反索赔次氯酸钙与集装箱的损失不成功，因为这是他自己违法所导致。(5)CYL 向船东反索赔由于 DSR 的集装箱在甲板上发生爆炸与火灾造成的部分异戊烷与集装箱的损坏不成功,因为即使装载了 DSR 的危险品,但由于 DSR 没有作出宣告,船东无法知道,不存在违反《海牙规则》,只要求恪尽职责令船舶适航。(6)CYL 向船东反索赔装载在第三舱的异戊烷与集装箱因后来在第三舱内与船底柴油柜的火灾与船舶发生沉没所造成的进一步损失成功,因为是船东违约把有关货物堆装在第三舱内,造成了船舶不适航。这违反了《海牙规则》中的船东应该恪尽职责令船舶适航与小心/谨慎堆装货物的责任。

第五章　减少损失

1. 序言

受害方向违约方或侵权方索赔损失时，被告常常会争辩道，“即使我违约（或侵权），可是我违约本来也不会造成这么大后果啊！是你没有采取合理措施减少损失，才会有这么多的损失，我只能赔你这部分，其他一概不赔！”的确，除了“损失的遥远性”（remoteness）的“可预见”（foreseeable）与“因果关系”（causation）的局限外，还有受害方合理减少损失的责任，而且这三个局限赔偿的大原则都是相互有密切关系的。在减少损失的大原则下，每个受害方都应该合理地减少自己的损失，如果没有合理减少损失，他就不能把自己应能减少而没有减少的那部分损失向违约方索赔回来。这一大原则是有几个方面的大道理支持，如下：(1)与因果关系有一定的关系，就是违约方/侵权方虽然有赔偿责任，但受害方没有合理减少损失而造成的部分额外损失与原来的违约或侵权没有直接的因果关系。(2)与损失的可预见也有一定关系，就是违约方/侵权方没有料想或预见到受害方是不合理减少损失，导致小事变大事，所以额外的损失在本质上太遥远。(3)要求受害方合理减少损失是为了避免整体的经济损失与浪费。(4)这涉及公平对待双方当事人，就是受害方如果想多花钱如买进被损坏产品的替代品（如买进一架最新型号的劳斯莱斯汽车以替代被被告损坏的夏利汽车），他可以自己掏腰包，没有理由要违约方/侵权方承担他的奢侈行为。这方面可节录 Pearson 大法官在 Darbishire v. Warran(1963)1 WLR 1067 所说如下：“... he is fully entitled to be as extravagant as he please but not at the expense of the defendant.”

针对减少损失的大原则，最权威的说法是在先例中，贵族院的 Viscount Haldane 说：

“The fundamental basis (of damage assessment) is thus compensation for pecuniary loss naturally flowing from the breach; but this first principle is qualified by a second, which imposes on a plaintiff the duty of taking all reasonable steps to mitigate the loss of consequent on the breach, and debars him from claiming any part of damage which is due to his neglect to take such steps.”（在计算损失，最基本的道理是以金钱赔偿来自违约的损失，但这是第一个大道理，要受到第二个大道理的约束，就是有一个强加在原告作为受害方的“责任”要采取所有的合理行动减少因为违约所带来的合理损失，并禁

止他索赔任何由于其疏忽没有采取这些行动而造成的损失部分。)

要求受害方合理减少损失的道理也很简单,可以一个简单例子说明。如买方因为市场价格下跌或己方原因拒绝收货,卖方应当合理尽快地在市场上把货物转售出去以取回一定货价。而不应任由该票货物闲置而导致最后霉坏不值一文,甚至还有一大笔的仓储费用与弃置处理费用,而这种情况在现实中会出现,特别是在受害方意气用事,明显不可行但仍坚持买方让步的情况下。这很容易客观看到如果要求买方(即使违约/毁约的责任是完全明确)赔偿全部货价并加上各种费用,是非常不公平的。这里当然会涉及每一个案件不同的事实,如同样造成这一个严重结果的原因是由于卖方没有办法合理找到替代的买家,如该票货物比较特殊,根本没有其他人要,或当时遇上金融海啸根本没有市场或替代买方。这一来,要求买方承担所有的损失客观看就是理所当然了,因为卖方有设法合理减少损失,只是没有成果罢了。又例如该票货物(如一台特殊制造的机器)根本没有市场或找不到替代买方,也不代表卖方没有办法减少损失。例如尽快安排把货物转运回自己的工厂,在改装后转售给第三人。或是以废铁价格尽快处理掉以减少仓库费用。或是以大幅度减价出售给原来的买方,但不放弃卖方将来索赔的权利:Payzu Ltd v. Saunders (1919) 2 KB 581; A. B. D. [Metals & Waste] Ltd v. Anglo Chemical & Ore Company Ltd (1955)2 Lloyd's Rep 456 等。反正就是能够合理减少损失,即使成效不会太大,受害方还是应该这样做。在 1979 年《英国货物销售法》之 Section 50(3)针对买方对卖方的违约/毁约,也就是本段所介绍的情况,就说明表面的损失计算就是根据合约价格与市场价格的差价,只要是在违约当时有一个可供买卖的市场,如在买方拒绝接受货物的情况下:"50(3) Where there is an available market for the goods in question the measure of damage is *prima facie* to be ascertained by the difference between the contract price and the market or current price at the time or times when the goods ought to have been accepted or (if no time was fixed for acceptance) at the time of the refusal to accept. (如果有关货物是有一个可供买卖的市场,表面的损失计算是根据合约价格与买方拒绝接受货物当天的市场价格的差价。)

背后的大道理就是要求受害的卖方应该尽快合理减少损失,而只要有一个可供买卖的市场,在该市场把货物处理掉是最合理的做法。同时,通过这样的处理,也可以找出受害方实际的损失,也就是找出违约/毁约的买方应该负责赔偿的金额,因为通过市场出售给替代买方而取得的价格是体现违约一天该货物的真正价值,然后比较合约价格得出的差价就是受害方的损失。正如 The "Clyde" (1856) Swab 23 先例中,Dr. Lushington 大法官是这样说:"It is the market price which the Court looks to, and nothing else, as the value of the property. It is an old saying, 'The worth of a thing is the price it will bring'."

在进一步探讨减少损失的大原则之前,不妨先简单介绍一下 British Westinghouse Electric & Manufacturing Co Ltd v. Underground Electric Rys. Co of London Ltd

(1912) AC 673 与 Darbishire v. Warran(1963)1 WLR 1067 的案情。在 British Westinghouse 先例,涉及一座蒸汽机的出售,用在火车的车头。由于该蒸汽机不符合买卖合约的要求,操作上有缺陷,导致了在后来的诉讼中,受害方作为原告索赔替代蒸汽机的价格以及其他有关的损失,但并不成功,因为判是替代蒸汽机所带来的更高利润是足够抵销买方的损失的。也就是说,受害方通过合理减少损失购买另一台更大动力的蒸汽机作为替代,完全成功避免被告较早的违约所带来的损失。

在 Darbishire v. Warran 先例中,涉及被告将原告的车子损坏,原告安排修理,但修理是不符合经济的做法的。上诉庭判是被告只需要负责赔偿损坏车子所导致的"市场价格的减损"(diminution in market value),而不是高昂的修理费用。

2. 减少损失的三条规则

损害赔偿中,受害方减少损失的"责任"实际上包括三条规则:(1)如果受害方可以采取合理行动减少损失而没有采取,则对其所受损害的赔偿只限于若他采取了合理行动仍然会承受的那部分的损失。(2)一方违约/毁约后,如果受害方采取的行动事实上避免或减少了一部分损失,那么损失赔偿亦要相应免除或扣减这部分减少的损失。即使受害方所作所为已超出了合理减少损失所要求的范围,他也不应借助违约或侵权向被告多赚一笔。(3)受害方为减少损失采取合理行动而作出的花费,不论成功与否都可以得到赔偿。

这方面可以节录《Chitty on Contracts》(30th edn, 2008 年)之 26 - 101 段:"**Mitigation**. There are three rules often referred to under the comprehensive heading of 'mitigation': they will be considered in turn. First, the claimant cannot recover damages for any part of his loss consequent upon the defendant's breach of contract which the claimant could have avoided by taking reasonable steps. Secondly, if the claimant in fact avoids or mitigates his loss consequent upon the defendant's breach, he cannot recover for such avoided loss, even though the steps he took were more than could be reasonably required of him under the first rule. Thirdly, where the claimant incurs loss or expense in the course of taking reasonable steps to mitigate the loss resulting from the defendant's breach, the claimant may recover this further loss or expense from the defendant."

这三条规则在著名先例 British Westinghouse Electric & Manufacturing Co Ltd v. Underground Electric Rys. Co of London Ltd (1912) AC 673 中有针对,第一条规则是这样说:"... imposes on a plaintiff the duty of taking all reasonable steps to mitigate the loss consequent on the breach, and debars him from claiming any party of the damage which is due to his neglect to take such steps."而第二条规则是这样说:"When in the course of his business [the claimant] has taken action arising out of the transaction, which action has diminished his loss, the effect in actual diminution of the loss he has suffered may be taken into account even though there was no duty on him to act."至于第三条规则,基本上就是第一条规则的衍生。

3. 减少损失是否为受害方承担的责任?

Viscount Haldane 在著名先例 British Westinghouse Electric & Manufacturing Co Ltd v. Underground Electric Rys. Co of London Ltd (1912) AC 673 中,把减少损失称为是受害方的一种"责任"(duty of taking all reasonable steps to mitigate the loss of consequent on the breach),这一说法就带来了一些争议。这是因为受害方如果有这一默示责任,就表示一旦他没有合理减少损失,就变成是违约并导致违约方/侵权方可以倒过来向他索赔。但实际上没有减少损失的后果只是不让受害方索赔由于他没有合理减损而造成的这部分额外的损失。所以后来有不少先例对这一"责任"是有所澄清,说明并不是这样一回事。首先,可节录 Pearson 大法官在 Darbishire v. Warran(1963)1 WLR 1067 中所说:"For the purposes of the present case it is important to appreciate the true nature of the so - called 'duty to mitigate the loss' or 'duty to minimise the damage'. The plaintiff is not under any actual obligation to adopt the cheaper method: if he wishes to adopt the more expensive against the defendant or anyone else. The true meaning is that the plaintiff is not entitled to charge the defendant by way of damages with any greater sum than that which he reasonably needs to expend for the purpose of making good the loss."

另在 The"Solholt"(1983)1 Lloyd's Rep. 605 先例的一审中,Staughton 大法官是这样说:"In this context it is perhaps worth repeating that the duty to mitigate is not in any sense an obligation, contractual or otherwise. It is a condition attached to the right to claim damages: see Mr Justice Robert Goff in Koch Marine Inc. v. D'Amico Societa Di Navigazione ARL (1980) 1 Lloyd's Rep. 75."这一个先例去了上诉庭,Donaldson 大法官也有同样的说法:"A plaintiff is under no duty to mitigate his loss, despite the habitual use by the lawyers of the phrase 'duty to mitigate'. He is completely free to act as he judges to be in his best interests. On the other hand, a defendant is not liable for all loss suffered by the plaintiff in consequence of his so acting. A defendant is only liable for such part of the plaintiff's loss as is properly caused by the defendant's breach of duty."

4. 减少损失大原则与其他计算损失大原则之间的关系

较早时候已经提过,减少损失大原则与其他计算损失的大原则,包括损失的遥远性的可预见与因果关系，甚至是整体减少浪费，都有一点关系。但它们实际上还是不同的大原则或者说法，虽然它们经常会混淆在一起，如在针对受害方穷困而无法减少损失的情况下，就往往与损失的遥远性分不开，这稍后在第9段会解释。针对损失的遥远性，是不理会受害方到底合理或者不合理，只要损失类别是订约时双方料想不到的，就会属于遥远的损失类别。但减少损失就非常讲究受害方的合理性。它们之间的不同可以举两个先例作为介绍，第一个是 The "Borag"（1981）1 WLR 274 先例。案情涉及被告错误扣押原告的船舶，迫使原告提供银行担保去放船。但由于原告的资信很差，导致他要支付给银行全部担保金额的高额利息。Denning 勋爵说从来没有听说过银行有这么严格的做法，由此被告提出受害方有否减少损失的争议。在上诉庭判是这一损失属于太遥远的损失类别，与受害方是否减少损失无关。Denning 勋爵说："It seems to me, as a matter of common sense and common law, that expenditure made to obtain the release of a vessel from arrest should be regarded as an item of damages, and not as mitigation. It is the natural way of dealing with it. They are entitled to all the reasonable expenditure which they incurred as a result of the wrongful arrest and getting the ship released: but not 'unheard - of' overdraft interest of this kind."

另一个是 Simpson v. Grove Tomkins & Co（1982）Sol J 347 先例，案情涉及被告律师的疏忽（没有与对方律师及时交换合约），导致他原来的客户也就是本案的原告失去了一个购买房屋的合约，并最终导致了该土地被转售给第三人而原告再以非常高昂的价格向第三人购买。第一审法院认定原告这样做是合理的，并判被告要根据原告向第三人购买的价格做出赔偿，金额是38,285英镑。但去了上诉庭，判决被改变，认为损失赔偿只应该局限在该土地原来在合约中约定的价格与当时的市场价格之间的差价，金额是20,542英镑。至于向第三人以高昂价格购买，被认为是不可预见的损失。上诉庭这样说："The question was whether the purchase of the identical property by the plaintiff, if the original agreement to purchase fell through, ought reasonably to have been foreseen by the defendant. The answer is no, even if it was reasonable for the plaintiff to pay the price that he did."这等于判原告没有不减少损失，因为在做法上合理。但原告还是不能把向第三人购买的高昂价格向被告取回，这是因为损失遥远性的不可预见的局限。

减少损失大原则与整体社会减少浪费也不一定有关系，如在涉及受害方要去市场买进或者卖出的最常见案件，就通常不会涉及整体社会的资源浪费，只会在受害的卖方放任货物闲置一隅进而最后霉坏不值一文才会涉及整体社会的经济浪费。

有看法是减少损失的大原则主要还是与因果关系大原则的关系最密切。这里可节录上诉庭 Potter 大法官在 Standard Chartered Bank v. Pakistan National Shipping Corp（No. 4）(2000) 2 Lloyd's Rep 511 先例中所说："The orthodox view is that the rule as to avoidable loss is merely an aspect of the fundamental principle of causation that a plaintiff can recover only in respect of damage caused by the defendant's wrong. The rule is...

that the plaintiff... cannot recover for a loss avoidable by reasonable action on his own part, because, if he could reasonably have avoided it, it would not be regarded as caused by the wrongdoer."

但在 Uzinterimpex JSC v. Standard Bank (2008) 2 Lloyd's Rep 456,上诉庭的 Moore－Bick 大法官就减少损失与因果关系大原则之间的关系是这样说:"There was a certain amount of debate in the course of argument about whether mitigation should be understood in terms of causation. For my own part I accept that it can be viewed in that way, but I am not sure that to do so adds greatly to one's understanding of the principles. If one analyses a failure to mitigate in terms of a new event which breaks the chain of causation between the wrongful act and the subsequent loss, it is necessary to recognize that the way in which the test of a new supervening cause has traditionally been formulated must be adapted or applied so as to take into account the relatively undemanding level of the duty to mitigate which the law imposes on the victim of a wrongful act. It may be that in this case it sharpens one's appreciation of the issues to view mitigation through the prism of causation..."

另是《McGregor on Damages》(18th edn, 2009 年)之 7－018 段的最后一句有提到许多有关减少损失的先例,并没有提到因果关系大原则。(it is significant that the cases on the avoidable loss aspect of mitigation are not full of references to causation.)

最后一提的是减少损失的案例虽然大部分都涉及违约,但同样的道理也适用在侵权,正如在涉及侵权的船舶碰撞先例 The "Liverpool" (No. 2) (1963) P 64 CA 中, Merriman 勋爵说:"The classic statement [namely of Lord Haldane], although made in an action arising out of a breach of contract, applies equally, *mutatis mutandis*, to tort."

5. 受害方怎样才算是合理减少损失

总的来说,受害方合理与否,是要根据每个案件不同的事实看。但由于受害方是受害方,而且面临违约/毁约时经常是处于困难的境地。所以,针对受害方所作出的补救行为,法院或仲裁庭通常会是以非常宽松的态度对待。有一个说法是受害方无需做任何特别的事情减少损失,除非这是他平时也会做的。如 Viscount Haldance 在 British Westinghouse Co. v. Undergound (1912) A. C. 637 先例之 689 页所说:"the plaintiff is not under any obligation to do anything other than in the ordinary course of business."

另在 Harlow & Jones, Ltd v. Panex (International), Ltd (1967) 2 Lloyd's Rep 509 先例,Roskill 大法官说:"The defendants broke this contract. It is they who put the plaintiffs in this difficulty. Of course, a plaintiff has always to act reasonably, and of course he has to do what is reasonable to mitigate his damages. **But he is not bound to nurse the interests of the contract breaker**, and so long as he acts reasonably at the time it ill lies in the mouth of the contract breaker to turn round afterwards and complain, in order to reduce his own liability to a plaintiff, that the plaintiff failed to do what which perhaps with hindsight he might have been wiser to do."(加黑部分显示了受害方不必考虑违约方的利益。)

但也有另一个说法是强调这合理与否是从受害方的角度看,而不是从违约方,就已经可以被接受。但也有明确的说法是受害方除了考虑自己的利益,也需要想到违约方的利益:Smailes v. Hans Dessen (1906) 94 LT 492。比较近期在这方面的先例有 Darbishire v. Warran (1963) 1 WLR 1067,上诉庭说:"The true question was whether the plaintiff acted reasonably as between himself and defendant and in view of his duty to mitigate the damages."另在贵族院的 Dimond v. Lovell (2002) 1 AC 384 先例,判是受害方高价租用替代车辆的行为虽然对他是合理,但这笔费用不能从侵权方取回。

在现实中,受害方只要对他的减少损失行为有一个合理的解释,加上保留一些证据(通常是文件证据)作为支持,就已经足够。宽松对待受害方,而不动不动就质疑受害方到底有否合理减少损失,也符合常理。原因是一般的受害方都知道无论违约/毁约的责任如何的明确,将来的索赔损失也不会是一帆风顺。撇开谁对谁错或其他的如诉讼风险等问题,仅是一些客观环境就表示了受害方能够最后完全取回所有损失的机会是不高的。这些客观环境包括像实质得到的金钱补偿肯定会有时间上的延误,期间被告会发生经济问题甚至倒闭,也有可能发生受害方自己因为资金流动的问题而被迫接受被告提出的很不足够的和解要约等。但如果能够合理减少损失,受害方就在发生违约/毁约时马上可以得益,通常就是可以少亏一点钱,而且这是不影响将来向违约方的索赔。而索赔的金额能够减少,也表示受害方(原告)向违约方(被告)的诉讼行动会相对容易与快捷。

这表示在现实中没有合理减少损失的案件,导致受害方的部分损失无法向违约/毁约方取回,往往是因为受害方明确误解了法律的地位,加上一定程度的意气用事或不现实面对问题,致使损失的扩大。举例说,在货价上涨时,卖方根据买方的违约(如没有准时开出符合买卖合约要求的信用证或指定卸港)终断买卖合约,然后马上向买方作出另一个"新的要约"(re - offer),但要求在原来的货价基础上增加 20%。如果该货物是有市场,当时市场的价格还要高,如比原来的货价高 40%。如果买方是意气用事或不现实面对问题,坚持卖方要以原来的货价交货,导致最终一拍两散,买方会有可能是成为最终的输家。在后来的诉讼,如果在责任方面判是终断买卖合约的卖方胜诉,就不存在买方可以向卖方索赔损失的问题。但买方还是损失了一个可以比市场价格便宜 20%(40% ~20%)根据一个新的买卖合约向卖方买回同一票货物的机会。但如果诉讼结果是反过来,责任方面判是终断合约的卖方败诉(如判信用证并非是不符合买卖合约的要求),就会接下去计算受害买方向卖方能够索赔的损失。表面看来,如果根据"市场规则"(market rule),就很容易算出违约的损失,即该票货合约价格与市场价格的差价,上涨的40%。但由于违约的卖方曾经作出新的要约,如果买方接受,就可以减少一半的差价损失即原货价的20%。这就有危险是法院或仲裁庭会判这一半的损失是由于买方没有合理减少损失所导致,应该扣减。当然,如果买方对没有接受卖方的新要约有一个说得过去的理由,这就有机会被视为是合理。例如,买方指出卖方的新要约是有其他不合理的条件,如要求买方必须放弃将来对他的指控或索赔;或是规定了一个很短的回复时限及无条件接受,令买方这类型的公司(如国营公司)无法在这么短时间内做出决定;又或是买方在卖方违约后的很短时间就已经与"分买方"(sub - buyer)达成和解协议,给分买方一笔钱作为不交货的赔偿,这令稍后卖方提供这票货物的新要约变得毫无意义;亦或是买方有一点理由怀疑卖方这一票货物有问题,如质量上的问题等。这种能够说的过去的理由是千变万化,反正重复的是要求受害方合理减少损失的责任并不严格。怕就怕买方根本给不出任何不接受卖方新要约的理由,甚至有当场的文件证明买方是意气用事或蛮不讲理,这就对买方有危险了。例如对卖方说:"我以后再也不跟你这种人做生意了!"如果有关的合约是一个长期的合作协议,买方倒还可能有一个说得过去的理由支持他的做法是合理,即缺乏长期与卖方合作的信心,因为卖方动不动终断合约。但如果在这里介绍的是一票货物买卖,买方也明知道有一票质量没有问题甚至已装船的货物,买或者不买,就不存在需要考虑跟什么人做生意了。这一来,同样的一句话"我以后再也不跟你这种人做生意了!"就可能不足以证明受害方的合理,甚至会被视为是意气用事。这方面可节录 Devlin 大法官在 Heaven & Kesterton Ltd v. Establishment Francois Albiac & Cie (1956) 2 Lloyd's Rep 316 (QB)先例所说如下:"If goods are rejected in a c. i. f. contract for some reason that has nothing to do with quality - the shipment date was wrong, or documents were not in order, or something of that sort, so that the goods are properly rejected - and then the buyer goes out into the market to buy goods of the contract quality, it is open to the seller to go to him and say: 'Well, then, I tender you these goods. These goods are of the contract quality. You are looking for goods of the contract quality. You rightly rejected them upon a basis that had nothing to do with their quality. If you are looking, therefore, for goods to make good your loss, here they are, and I can supply cheaper than you would be able to buy them at the market rate outside.' If the seller does that, that is a matter which must be taken into consideration in answering the question of whether or not the buyer has acted reasonably, as it is his duty to do, in mitigating damage."

以下内容会对这一问题作进一步的详细讨论。

5.1　合理与否是根据事实的认定

在每一个案件,由于事实不会完全相同,所以合理与否是要根据双方当事人提供的证据作出事实的认定。在 McAuley v. London Transport Executive (1957) 2 Lloyd's

Rep 500 先例中,上诉庭的 Jenkins 大法官是这样说:“The question must be one of fact, as I see it, in each particular case: Was the advice, and were the prospects of success of the proposed operation or treatment, clearly put to the plaintiff so that he, as a reasonable man, would appreciate that he was being advised that this treatment or operation would put him right. If the evidence shows that, then it seems to me that the plaintiff, as a reasonable person, ought either to accept that advice, or else go to his own doctor and say: ‘Doctor, this is what I have been advised by Mr So - and So, the surgeon at Such - and - Such a hospital; what do you think about it?’ Of course, the plaintiff here never did any such thing as that.”

在该先例,案情涉及被告在雇用原告期间,原告因公而导致手腕割伤,并同时切断了神经。原告曾经被外科医生诊断过,认为他如果动手术,就会有机会在3~6个月之内大程度的康复,并且有90%的机会可以令手指进行大动作的活动或35%的机会令手指进行比较细致的活动。否则,这样下去就会导致肌肉萎缩与严重程度的变形。但原告不听从医生的建议,并被法院看来是想打完官司才处理。Jenkins 大法官是这样说:“It seems that the plaintiff was averse to having the left wrist dealt with until his legal claim in regard to the injury to the right wrist had been attended to.”这导致了上诉庭判原告没有合理减少损失,而损失的计算只能是假设原告如果动手术并康复的情况下所蒙受的损失。这方面 Jenkins 大法官是这样说:“In that state of affairs, what is the effect, if any, on the quantum of damages of the plaintiff's conduct in relation to the advice he received from these two medical men? It is not in dispute that, inasmuch as in a case of this sort it is the duty of the injured party to mitigate damages, it is his duty to act on any medical advice he receives to the effect that this or that treatment will give this or that prospect of success. If he receives medical advice to the effect that an operation will have a 90% chance of success, and is strongly recommended to undergo the operation and does not do so, then the result must be, I think, that he has acted unreasonably, and that the damages ought to be assessed as they would properly have been assessable if he had, in fact, undergone the operation and secured the degree of recovery to be expected from it.”

另在 The “Solholt” (1983) 1 Lloyd's Rep 605 先例中,Donaldson 大法官也说:“whether the loss is avoidable by reasonable action on the part of the plaintiff is a question of fact not law”,并说这一点已经在上诉庭的先例 Payzu v. Saunders (1919) 2 KB 581 有了定论。

这带来的结果就是如果在第一审(不论是高院还是仲裁庭)认定了原告有或者没有合理减少损失,原告就没有机会能够上诉来对这一事实的认定作出改变。

但减少损失的大原则也会涉及法律的问题,这主要在受害方是否有“责任”要减少损失方面。例如在对方有一个“预期违约”(anticipatory breach),而受害方拒绝接受违约的情况下,受害方是否需要减少损失,毕竟双方还是有一个合约关系的存在。

又或是受害方并非索赔损失，而是有索赔“债务”(debt)的选择下，受害方是否需要减少损失。这些问题会在本书关于第十一章“债务与损失的分别”一章详细介绍，只在这里简单说受害方没有“责任”。

5.2　对受害方合理的要求程度不高与认定并不肯定

已经在第4段提到过，英国法律对这种合理的要求并不会太高，毕竟始作俑者是违约方/侵权方，他的违约/侵权已经使受害方处于不同程度的困难境地。因此只要受害方采取了一些看来适当与解释得过去的补救行动，他就可以获得全部赔偿。重复这方面只是为了节录有关的权威说法，就是在 Banco de Portugal v. Waterlow & Sons, Ltd (1932) AC 452 中 Macmillan 勋爵所说：“Where the sufferer from a breach of contract finds himself in consequence of that breach placed in a position of embarrassment the measures which he may be driven to adopt in order to extricate himself ought not to be weighed in nice scales at the instance of the party whose breach of contract has occasioned the difficulty. It is often easy after an emergency has passed to criticize the steps which have been taken to meet it, but such criticism does not come well from those who have themselves created the emergency. The law is satisfied if the party placed in a difficult situation by reason of the breach of a duty owed to him have acted reasonably in the adoption of remedial measures, and he will not be held disentitled to recover the cost of such measures merely because the party in breach can suggest that other measures less burdensome to him might have been taken.”

另在本章第5段提到的 Harlow & Jones, Ltd v. Panex (International), Ltd (1967) 2 Lloyd's Rep 509 先例也有类似的权威说法。

虽然对受害方合理程度的要求不高，但这只是一个说法或原则。适用在个别的案件，还是会有很多变数，只能说合理与否本身就是一个非常不肯定的看法。由于每一个人(包括法官与仲裁员)对合理的看法都有一定差异，加上每个案件的事实不同，所以在这一方面的先例也往往对之后的案件起不到太大的指导作用。针对这一方面的不肯定，笔者可节录 Rajah 大法官在 The “Asia Star” (2010) 2 Lloyd's Rep 12 的新加坡上诉庭先例作为介绍如下：“The many sub - rules, qualifications and nuances that have built up around the reasonableness inquiry may not infrequently appear to be confusing and unwieldy. Nevertheless, when one takes a step back to look at the object of this inquiry as a whole, it becomes clear that the inquiry amounts to nothing more than the common law's attempt to reflect commercial and fact - sensitive fairness at the remedial stage of a legal inquiry into the extent of liability on the defaulting party's part. The concept of reasonableness in the context of mitigation is a flexible one. In essence, it bars an aggrieved party from profiting or behaving unreasonably at the expense of the defaulting party, and encapsulates notions of fairness, the principle of mitigation confers on the courts considerable discretion in evaluating the facts of the case at hand in order to arrive at a commercially just determination. The principle embodies a fact - centric flexibility which, whilst remaining in harmony with sound business practice, stands in vivid contract to the strictness with which rules in other areas of contract law are applied."

接下去就分段介绍在各种不同情况下被视为是合理与否减少损失的先例,可以进一步理解笔者上述所讲。

5.2.1 受害方对减少损失的选择并非是最有效或最省钱的情况

经常见到违约方会辩称:受害方本来还有其他更有效更省钱的措施可选择,可以更大程度减少损失,甚至令他不需要赔偿,但这种说法通常不会被法院或仲裁庭接受。比如在租船业务中,经常是违反租约的船东辩称承租人后来找的替代船太贵,据他所知当时还有另外几艘更便宜的船舶可以租进,承租人没有租进更便宜的船舶就是没有减少损失。但这是不能被接受的说法,因为这种指责往往只是事后诸葛亮。在现实中,在发生违约时受害方往往是无法看到全局的市场情况的,所以受害方不会被视为是没有合理减少损失,因为事后看,受害方是有可能找到比较便宜的替代船舶,但并非表示受害方不合理。这方面有许多权威的说法,首先重复节录 Banco de Portugal v. Waterlow(1932)A. C. 452 先例中,贵族院的 Macmillan 勋爵说:"... it is often easy after an emergency has passed to criticize the steps which have been taken to meet it, but such criticism does not come well from those who have themselves created the emergency."

另在 Emeh v. Kensington Area Health Authority (1985) QB 1012 CA, Purchas 大法官说:"It would be intolerable if a defendant... having ... placed the plaintiff in the position in which a choice or decision had to be made, was able closely to analyse that decision so as to show that it might not have been the right choice and thereby escape his liability."

最后详尽介绍一个有关先例 Gebruder Metelmann GmbH v. NBR(London)Ltd. (1984)1 Lloyd's Rep 614,它涉及受害方去期货市场作出对冲,但反而令损失扩大。这带来的问题是该对冲是否属于受害方减少损失行为的一部分,如果是,这扩大的损失才可以一并向违约方取回。案情是原告卖方 Metalmann 出售 2000 吨食糖给被告 NBR,FOB 欧洲的价格是 803 美元/吨,付运期是 1981 年 1 月。但 NBR 违约/毁约,拒绝接受该批货物。该违约/毁约令 Metalmann 手中多出 2000 吨货物,而当时食糖市场价格也在不断下跌。为了在一个不断下跌的市场中令自己的损失减少或者得到对冲,Metalmann 在巴黎的食糖期货市场沽空 5 月付运的 2500 吨食糖,价格是 673 美元/吨(这种在期货市场对冲实际买卖中价格风险的做法是食糖贸易中的常见做法)。这价格比违约/毁约当时的实际食糖价格市场略低,该价格是 680 美元/吨。这里要稍微解释一下食糖有两个价格,一个是"实物市场价格"(physical market price),这是针对实际货物的买卖,的确是存在付运与交货。另一个是"期货市场价格"(terminal market price),这些食糖并不进行真正的买卖,而是一些机构如巴黎或伦敦的食糖交易所让大家对赌。换言之,贸易商进行买卖的对象是市场,而不是另一位贸易商。实物市场与期货市场的价格走势大致是一致的,但并不完全一样,而且每天的波动非常厉害。在该先例的第一审,Mustill 大法官认为 Metalmann 没有必要在期货市场沽空,所以这一做法与减少损失无关,赔偿只能根据实物市场价格的 680 美元/吨,说:"A sale in the futures market is, for the reasons already stated, an effective measure of protection where a seller finds that he has unexpectedly been left long in goods for physical delivery on a falling market, and where it is plain that some time will elapse before the goods can be resold.(当卖方在一个价格下跌的市场中因为出乎意料的原因而多持有了一票货物[形成多头仓位],并且转卖该票货物很明显需要一定的时间,那么他去期货市场上进行沽空来对冲自己在实物买卖市场上的进一步损失是一个有效的减少损失的方法)The potential loss resulting from the fact that the market will have fallen by the time the resale is made, is matched by the opportunity to make a profit on the margin, by repurchasing the terminal contract.(转卖该票货物时由于市场下跌而造成的潜在进一步损失可以通过在期货市场通过回购期货合约赚取的利润来弥补)In other words, the seller protects himself in respect of the market risk during the interval before he is able to make a substitute contract.(换句话说就是卖方在找到替代合约把手中的一票货物转售之前,用此种办法来降低自己会承担的市场风险)The theory of this device will, however, only produce a practical result if (a) the seller is left long in physical goods; (b) he does resell them for physical delivery (c) the goods are actually delivered; and (d) the futures transaction is closed out as soon as the new physical sale is made, at which time the falling market has ceased to be a source of loss. As I see it, none of these conditions existed here. [这种策略只有在以下四个条件被满足时才能够起作用:(a)卖方在实物买卖市场上形成多头仓位;(b)卖方将会转卖该票多出来的货物;(c)货物被实际交付;(d)期货交易在实物转卖作出之时结算,下跌的市场也就不会造成进一步的损失。但是据我(Mustill 大法官)所见,所有的条件在这个案件均不存在] Thus - (a) Metelmann never came into possession of 'the' 2,000 tonnes of physical goods (b) Metelmann did not resell 'the' 2,000 goods were for physical delivery hence (c) 'the' goods were not actually delivered and hence also (d) the closing - out of the terminal transaction (whenever it happened) was not related to any resale of physical goods. [因此:(a) Metelmann 从来都没有真正在实体上拥有过该票货物;(b) Metelmann 也没有通过实体的交付而转卖过该票货物;(c) 所以该票货物实际上没有被交付;(d)而且期货合约的出售与转卖该票货物没有关系。]In these circumstances, I consider that the futures transaction did not serve to mitigate any real loss by Metelmann. This does not mean that I disbelieve the evidence of Mr. Robertson to the effect that the future sale was intended as a stop - loss measure to protect Metelmann and hence NBR from further loss on a falling market.(在这种情况下,我认为 Metelmann 在期货市场上的交易并不是用来减少他在实物买卖市场上的真正损失,但是这并不意味着我不相信 Mr. Robertson 提供的

证据证明该期货交易的意图是在一个不断下跌的市场保护 Metelmann,进而也让 NBR 可以减少将来赔偿损失的金额。)I do accept this evidence, and I also accept that if the transactions had afterwards been carried out differently, the futures sale might properly have been brought into account.(我接受这个证据,并且也接受如果这个交易后来改变,后来期货沽空的交易可能可以考虑。)In the events which actually happened, however, the sale in the Paris market did not go to mitigate Metelmann's loss. It was entirely independent of the loss, which must be computed as if the forward sale had not been made."(真实的情况是,在巴黎期货市场上的沽空交易并不是为了减少 Metelmann 的损失,而是完全独立于该实物交易市场的损失。所以计算 Metelmann 的损失时不应该考虑该沽空交易。)

但这一判法在上诉庭被推翻,Donaldson 大法官说是:"As a result of the default of NBR, Metelmann was left long or longer to the extent of 2,000 tonnes of sugar on a falling market. Whether they were in possession of that sugar or had merely entered into a contract to purchase it is immaterial. The reasonably anticipated consequence was that their losses would increase day by day, subject to minor unpredictable and short-lived upward movements in the price. Their duty was to take all reasonable measures to prevent this increase in loss. In a less sophisticated market, the only available measure would have been to conclude another contract for the sale of 2,000 tonnes of sugar as soon as possible and at the best price obtainable. However, in the sugar market they had the alternative of selling 2000 tonnes on the terminal market. Furthermore, on the evidence, this is what any reasonable trader would have done, since it involved no delay."(NBR 的违约令 Metelmann 在一个不断下跌的市场形成了 2000 吨的多头仓位。Metelmann 是否实际拥有该票食糖的货物或者只是与第三人签订了一个购买食糖的合约并不重要。能够合理预想到的后果就是 NBR 的违约令 Metelmann 的损失在一个货物价格不断下跌的市场上是一天一天不断增加,除了在少数不可预测的短期价格上涨的情况。Metelmann 应该采取所有合理的措施阻止损失的增加。在一个相对简单的市场,唯一可以采取的措施应该是尽快以当时市场上能够找到的最好的价格订立另一个卖出 2000 吨食糖的买卖合约。但是在食糖交易市场,有另一个可供选择的办法就是在期货市场上出售这2000吨食糖。进一步说,根据证据,这是任何一个合理的贸易商应该做的事情,因为这样做是最快能令损失减少的。)

这一个案例也是配合在本书第三章之 10.3"对冲交易"一段。简单来说,在商业实践中,国际贸易商通常会对一个实际的商品交易作出对冲交易以减少损失 。因此,不论在对冲的实际成效中,损失是增加还是减少,对冲交易都应予以考虑。这方面可参考 10.3 段已经提及的一些先例:Trafigura Beheer Bv. and another v. Mediterranean Shipping Company SA (2007) EWCA Civ. 794;Addax Ltd v. Arcadia Petroleum Ltd and Another (2000) 1 Lloyd's Rep 493;Choil Trading v. Sahara Energy Resources Ltd (2010) EWHC

374 (Comm);Glencore Energy UK Ltd v. Transworld Oil Ltd (2010) EWHC 141;Prestige Marine Services Pte Ltd v. Marubeni International Petroleum (S) Pte Ltd (2011) SGHC 270。

5.2.2 受害方对减少损失的选择并不要求向第三人提出诉讼

这方面的先例是在 Pilkington v. Wood (1953) Ch 770,Harman 大法官是说:"the so - called duty to mitigate does not go so far as to oblige the injured party, even under an indemnity, to embark on a complicated and difficult piece of litigation against a third party."该先例的案情涉及受害的原告原来的律师疏忽,没有把原告购买的土地产权查清楚。事实上,原告所购买的土地产权有问题,因为卖方只是该土地的信托人。在原告向原来的律师(被告)提出索赔损失时,被告的抗辩是他已经向原告提供诉讼费用的担保,要求原告向产权有问题土地的卖方提出索赔损失,作为原告减少损失的"责任"。不过这一抗辩被法院拒绝,因为虽然在卖方经济与诉讼费用保障上看来原告值得向卖方索赔,但这一个法律行动从表面看来还是不清楚是否有明确胜诉的把握,所以原告没有必要这样做来减少损失。这种同类的近期案例有不少如 Horsfall v. Haywards (1999) Lloyd's Rep PN 332 CA;Pozzolanic Lytag v. Bryan Hobson Associates (1999) 63 Con LR 81;Center Optical (HK) Ltd v. Jardine Transport Services (China) Ltd (2001) 2 Lloyd's Rep 678(香港案例);Williams v. Glyn Owen & Co (2004) PNLR 20 CA 等。另是即使向第三人提出起诉并达成和解,法院也不接受被告的争辩指该和解的金额太低,应该争取更好的和解:British Racing Drivers' Club v. Hextall Erskine & Co (1996) PNLR 523。

上述不少案例是针对专业人士作为被告,如原告指律师的疏忽而导致损失。而针对这种案件,近期的法律有一点改变,如果受害方向第三人提出索赔并不是很困难也不需要花费庞大的费用,但受害方并不这样做而只向专业人士索赔,这就会被视为受害方没有合理减少损失。这方面可以节录《McGregor on Damages》(18th edn, 2009年)之7-083段所说如下:"However there is now a preparedness, appearing in professional negligence cases, for the courts to see a failure to claim against a third party before suing the professional himself as a failure to mitigate: the classic Pilkington v. Wood is becoming interpreted as being concerned with the need to embark only on complex, difficult and uncertain litigation. Illustrations are Western Trust & Saving Ltd v. Travers & Co (1997) PNLR 295 CA and Walker v. Medlicott & Son (1999) 1 WLR 727 CA."看来,如果有这一个倾向,会是针对当今受害方大量向专业人士(尤其是律师)作为首要(而非次要)的索赔对象的做法,有一定的保留。以下可进一步介绍一些这方面的先例。

在 Western Trust & Saving Ltd v. Travers & Co 先例中,法院判有抵押权的贷款人应该先采取行动把抵押的财产占有,而不是向被告的律师提出全数索赔,否则就是没有合理减少损失。把抵押的财产占有并非是一个执行担保的不正常或者困难的办法。

在同样的道理下，如果有多于一位对受害方需要负责（特别是在侵权）的所谓的“共同侵权方”（joint tortfeasors），被告不能要求受害方原告向其他共同侵权方提出索赔，要求他们负责至少是他们应该承担责任的部分损失。在 The “Liverpool”（No. 2）（1963） P 64 CA 先例，即使第三方就他所应负责的部分承诺赔付并提供了一笔保证金，受害方原告也没有必要接受这一笔金钱来减少被告需要赔付的损失。Harman 大法官说：“It has never been the law that a creditor having a security against a third party for his debt must give credit for that when proving in the bankruptcy.”在该先例，涉及船舶在碰撞之后沉船，港口当局（英国 Mersey 港）需要把残骸清除。碰撞的责任是 100% 在 Liverpool 轮的头上，但另一艘无辜的船舶 Ousel 轮反而是沉没的船舶。根据当地的立法规定，沉船船东即使是无辜也必须承担清除残骸的责任与费用。港口当局（原告）向 Liverpool 轮的船东（被告）索赔有关的费用与损失，法院判是港口当局没有必要向 Ousel 轮的船东（第三方）要同样的一笔钱来作为减少损失的“责任”。而且也不需要在对 Liverpool 轮的船东索赔损失时扣减将来可能会从 Ousel 轮的船东取得的一笔钱。

针对 The “Liverpool”先例，在《McGregor on Damages》（18th edn，2009 年）之 7-085 段，有解释如下：“A claimant need not take steps to recover compensation for his loss from parties who, in addition to the defendant, are liable to him. This is an undoubted principle. Indeed, as Harman LJ said in The ‘Liverpool’, ‘it is a principle which, strictly speaking, stands on its own feet independently of mitigation, a principle without which it would have been unnecessary for the legislature to make provision for contribution and indemnity between joint and several tortfeasors’. And the ‘Liverpool’ shows that, even if the third party offers payment of the amount for which he is liable, the claimant is not required to accept it in mitigation. In that case the defendants' ship through negligence came into collision in port with another ship which sank. The claimant harbour board sued the defendants, whose liability was limited, for expense incurred and damages sustained in clearing the port of the wreck. However, the claimants had also taken steps to enforce their statutory right against the owners of the wreck to recover from them any expenses outstanding after raising and selling the wreck, and not only had this amount been established but the money had been tendered, refused by the claimants, and then put on deposit by the owners of the wreck. In such circumstances the Court of Appeal held that the claimants were under no duty to satisfy part of their damages by accepting the money already on deposit. Harman LJ, delivering the court's judgment, pointed to the analogy that ‘it has never been the law that a creditor having a security against a third party for his debt must give credit for that when proving in the bankruptcy’.”

有同样的说法就是原告可以选择任何一个被告索赔，在 The International Factors Ltd v. Rodriguez（1979）1 QB 351 先例，David Cairns 大法官是这样说：“A plaintiff who has two causes of action cannot be met when he makes a claim against one defendant by the answer: 'Oh, no; you've suffered nothing by my tort because you have a cause of action against somebody else.' That clearly cannot be right."另在近期 Peters v. East Midland Strategic Health Authority (2009) 3 WLR 737 的上诉庭先例与 Haugesund Kommune v. Depfa (2010) 2 Lloyd's Rep 323 先例,也有同样说法。

这种情况经常会发生,就是受害方有多过一个途径索赔损失。这就可以联想到受害方通过一个途径取回他全部的损失,但稍后在其他途径索赔同一样的损失,受害方就会从中获利,这是完全违反损失赔偿只应该是复原的大原则。有关这方面的预防,将会在本书第九章第3段会详论。在这里只一提,在部分侵权的案件还比较容易处理,因为法院是容许把第三人加进来一并审理的。这表示在"共同侵权方"(joint tortfeasors)的情况下,其中一位侵权方被受害方选中作为被告,他可以向法院申请把其他共同侵权方一并列为共同被告,然后让法院审理他们之间的责任与赔偿分摊。至于在合约方面,问题就比较复杂了。简单的一个事故,如船舶受到危险品货物的损坏是货方或者承租人的责任,甚至是两方都有责任。船东就可以选择向货方索赔,或是向承租人索赔。由于今天在不少这种合约内都有仲裁条文,更加不存在合并审理的做法。另是,船东会有可能选择只向保险公司要求赔付,这是另一个取回损失的途径。笔者见过船东向保险公司获得赔付后,再向承租人索赔同样的损失,并在成功后不退还或告诉保险公司。这种行为对代位求偿权警觉性不高的保险公司危险尤其之大。针对这一个问题,在本章第11段会进一步探讨,在这里只是为了说明受害方并没有"责任"要向第三人提出索赔作为合理减少损失的行为。

5.2.3　受害方对减少损失的选择并不要求对第三人放弃权利

在先例 Elliott Steam Tug Co. v. Shipping Controller (1922) 1 KB 127,案情涉及原告租进了一条拖轮,租约容许原告无限期使用,直到他提前14天发出通知终断租约。在使用期间,拖轮被英国海军征用。但有立法对受害方作出赔偿,所以原告承租人就向英国政府提出赔偿要求,损失是有两项:第一项是在征用期间要付给拖轮船东的租金,因为租约并没有规定在船舶被征用的情况下可以不付租金;第二项是原告如果能够使用该拖轮所带来的利润。一审法院判原告可以胜诉并获得赔偿,但赔偿只是局限在30天的租金与利润,理由是认为原告有减少损失的"责任",就是向拖轮船东作出14天的通知终断租约,就可以避免多支付租金。该先例最后没有针对第一项的损失上诉(看来是一个错误的决定),但上诉庭的 Scrutton 大法官看来是不同意一审法院的决定,说:"the owner of a ship while under a duty to act reasonably to reduce damages is under no obligation to destroy his own property to reduce the damage payable by the wrongdoer. The leasehold tenant of a house would not be bound to stop paying rent to his superior landlord during the period during which a wrongdoer prevented him using the house, because by so doing he would reduce the damages the wrongdoer had to pay if by so doing he lost the tenancy of the house after the wrong of the tortfeasor was repaired, or finished in its effects.”(作为受害方的船东或二船东,虽然有一个合理减少损失的“责任”,但并不要求他为了减少对被告的损失而毁灭他的财产[原告向拖轮船东终断租约就有这一种的味道]。一个房子的长期租客如果他的居所因为被告的原因而没有办法使用,是没有必要为了减轻被告的赔偿责任而对房东终止租约以减少租金的支付的。这一来,被告会可以少赔一点,但原告就可能失去了一个长期的租约。)

但情况稍有改变就会得出不同结果,在先例 Weir v. Dobell (1916) 1 KB 722 中,原告是二船东,他把有关的船舶分租给被告。但分租约比第一份租约的运费费率低,这表示如果租约获得履行,原告会要赔钱,因为被告作为分承租人所支付给原告的运费不足以支付他向原船东支付的运费。这种情况也经常会有,夹在当中的合约方不一定能够赚取差价,根据租入(或买入)的市场高低比较租出(或转售)的市场高低,会有机会赚取或亏蚀的差价。在本先例,被告在履行的时候拒绝装货,这构成了违约/毁约。对原告而言,第一份租约容许他有裁量权终断合约。结果在双方的诉讼中,判是原告应该行使他的合约权利终断第一份租约以减少损失。这被视为是合理的做法,而该先例中事实与 Elliott Steam Tug Co. v. Shipping Controller 先例有所不同。第一个方面是第一份租约与分租约是针对一模一样的航次,第二是该航次结束之后第一份租约也没有剩下来的租期需要保留。这估计是造成了原告二船东根本无法合理地解释为什么不行使裁量权终断第一份租约。不这样做的真正原因有可能是:(1)二船东没有这方面的法律知识,不知道裁量权是何物;(2)二船东疏忽,要么是没有留心第一份租约的条文,或是延误导致了想行使裁量权时已经过了规定或合理的时间。反正什么是真正的原因,都会离不开二船东没有合理减少损失。

5.2.4 受害方对减少损失的选择并不需要花费太多的时间与精力

这里有涉及合理与否的情况,要求受害方做太多或太困难的事情减少损失就看来没有这个必要了。在 Lesters Leather & Skin Co. Ltd v. Home & Overseas Buyers Brokers, Ltd (1948) 64 TLR 569 先例,案情涉及原告作为买方向被告购买一批蛇皮,在英国港口交货。但货物运到的时候,被原告因为质量问题拒货,上诉庭判原告胜诉并可取回他的利润损失,并否定了被告所作出的原告应该在印度购买蛇皮以减少损失的抗辩。这一判决的原因包括受害方不需要冒太多险与花费太多精力减少损失。其中,Goddard 大法官说:“I cannot say that the buyers are bound to go hunting the globe to find out where they can get skins.”(我不能要求买方必须全世界寻找蛇皮。)另 Singleton 大法官重复了第一审 Sellers 大法官所说:“It is one thing to enter into a contract. It would be another thing to get the goods.”

类似的说法在 Harlow & Jones, Ltd v. Panex (International) Ltd (1967) 2 Lloyd's Rep 509 先例也有提到,Roskill 大法官说:“he has to do what is reasonable to mitigate his damages. But he is not bound to nurse the interests of the contract breaker...”

这里也可以举一个比较近期的加拿大先例,Costello v. City of Calgary (1995) 163 AR 241。案情涉及原告受害方准备在一块他所拥有的土地上建造一个 40 个房间的酒店,但该土地被当局(也就是被告)错误没收,加拿大最高院作出决定认为这是属于非法没收。这导致原告后来向被告提出索赔损失,而在责任方面是十分明确,就是被告侵占了原告的土地。被告面对损失赔偿的其中一个抗辩,就是原告应该减少损失,就是应该购买附近另一块土地并建造一座同样的酒店,而原告的财力完全是能够做得到的。但法院不同意,认为这是一笔很大的钱,没有理由要求受害方这样做。加拿大 Alberta 法院是这样判:"... the evidence also established that the [plaintiffs] had sufficient credit capacity to make such a purchase [i. e., to purchase another plot of land as a replacement for Ranch Site] had they so wished. However, the point is that the argument of the [defendant] must be rejected because it has failed to establish that other comparable property was available at [the] equivalent compensation [which] the [defendant] was offering, and the law is clear that the plaintiffs need not incur unreasonable expenses to mitigate a loss caused by the defendant. ."

5.2.5 受害方对减少损失的选择并不需要损害他的名誉或影响商业关系

在 Finlay v. Kwik Hoo Tong (1929) 32 Lloyd's Rep 245 先例,案情涉及一个 CIF 孟买的食糖买卖合约。买卖合约涉及三票在 1920 年 7 月、8 月与 9 月的付运。到了 9 月这一票货物的付运,时间上发生了延误,食糖是在 10 月 2 日才装上船舶。这表示货不对版,因为付运日期一直被视为是合约的"条件条文"(essence of contract),买方有权可以不要这一票货物。但卖方交出了一份提单,日期是在 9 月 30 日。这就涉及做外贸与航运的人士最熟悉的不良做法,就是倒签提单。至于导致延误付运的原因会有许多,如 CIF 卖方自己晚了租船或者把货物备妥,或者是在装船前的运输(该票食糖是要通过驳船运输)发生延误,又或者遇上坏天气拖慢了运输或装货,反正原因是千奇百怪。任何一个原因就已经足够延误一两天而导致了 9 月付运的食糖变为 10 月。这些原因可能涉及 CIF 卖方本人的过错或疏忽,但也可能是他完全无辜或控制不了。但这都不会影响 CIF 卖方的违约,因为他在买卖合约承诺了出售 9 月付运的食糖,而合约的承诺是严格责任。

再回到本先例,原告 Finlay 接受了这份倒签提单,并交给了一个印度的分买方(这票食糖较早前就已经转售给了分买方)。而分买方估计到食糖的延误付运,加上当时的食糖市场价格下跌,继而拒绝接受提单。这导致了原告 Finlay 被迫以拍卖的形式低价出售该票食糖,造成了很大损失。

在本先例,Finlay 作为受害方到底有没有合理减少损失的争议涉及在分销合约中有一条条文说明提单注明的日期就是"决定性证据"(conclusive evidence)。这表示根据买卖合约的明示条文,Finlay 可以坚持要分买方接受该票货物或向分买方索赔他不按合约拒货的损失,因为提单本身是注明 9 月付运。由于倒签提单并不涉及 Finlay 的不诚实行为,所以不影响分销合约中这一条文的有效性。但 Finlay 解释他不这样做的理由是为了保障他在印度食糖市场的名誉,不想强制印度分买方接受一套倒签提单。上诉庭判 Finlay 并没有不合理减少损失,其中 Scrutton 大法官是这样说："Messrs. Finlay's answer to that is：'It is quite true that we had a contract under which the India buyer was bound to accept the date in the bill of lading as against the India buyer to recover the price of goods that we knew not to be in accordance with the contract, because of that term, would not be in the ordinary course of business and would ruin our credit in India, and as a matter of business, and of the standard of morality which should attach to an English firm of standing, we decline to bring an action against an India firm to compel them to take goods which we know are not in accordance with the contract. It would be different if we did not know and it was in doubt, and we could say：'Yes, we do not know which way it is, and you do not know, but here is a contract that the bill of lading date is to be taken'; that would be a different matter.' I personally cannot think that a man who has broken his contract can compel his buyer who has not broken his contract to take action to minimize the damages of a person who has broken his contract, by claiming money to which he knows he is not entitled, and to take action which will ruin his credit in the business world."

说实在，好像这种案件的事实真相（特别是全面的真相）没人能说清楚，如会否是 Finlay 向印度分买方在事前或事后根据合约的条文加压，指出分买方无权拒绝接受提单与货物，结果是印度分买方答应给 Finlay 一些"好处"作为交换 Finlay 不向他索赔损失。把这些"好处"量化为金钱，应该也在损失中作出扣减，只要这是在判决前能够曝光。但现实中如果有这种情况，Finlay 也不会把这笔"台底交易"的好处自动说出来，而这种交易也不是被告 Kwik Hoo Tong 所能自己查出来或通过文件披露而知道。所以，是否懂得法律并能够从中钻空子会是有天壤之别，短期还看不出分别（因为受到短暂运气好坏的影响比较大，如一路没有发生意外），但中长期就会有极大的差别，懂法律的一方很可能从中赚取很大的利益。

另一个有关的先例 The "Lily Prima" (1976) 2 Lloyd's Rep 487，案情涉及一个长期的程租租约，总共要履行 24 个连续的航次。租约也涉及分租约，也就是"Lily Prima"轮在第一个租约被船东（被告）租给了本先例的原告承租人 Yamashita Shinnihon，而原告再分租给分承租人 Nichimen。在分租约内有一条免责条文，说明在这 24 个连续航次的履行，如果发生了 Yamashita Shinnihon 作为二船东无法控制的原因造成了延误，承租人就可以免责。

履行了 8 个航次之后，Lily Prima 轮在第 9 个航次发生了延误。在 1973 年 8 月 8 日到 8 月 30 日，原告 Yamashita Shinnihon 一直催促被告船东通知有关第 9 航次的履行日期。但船东一直给不出日期，到了 8 月 31 日才说是估计要到 12 月 25 日才能履行。而事实上船舶是到了 1974 年 1 月 12 日才能够交船履行。在这段期间，原告为了履行他的分租约，在 9 月初的时候，以高价在市场租入一艘替代船舶履行第 9 个航次，并在事后向被告索赔高达 1,759,826 美元的运费差价。而被告船东提出的其中一个抗辩就是原告可以拒绝履行分租约的第 9 航次，依据的就是分租约中的免责条文。但这不被英国法院接受,认为原告受害方没有必要行使他在分租约中的所有法律权利,他只需要合理。估计原告只需要作出合理的解释,如他必须对分承租人Nichimen履行,不管合约中有怎样的条文,因为大家都是日本公司,法院极可能会接受。其中,第一审的Kerr大法官是这样说:"The other point on which the owners relied, though Mr. Saville(船东的代表大律师)did not press it strongly, is that the charterers should have relied against Nichimen on cl. 17 of the sub - charter and claimed that the voyage in question was delayed by causes beyond their control, because the Lily Prima was unavailable to them at the material time and there was no right of substitution. However, if a party to a contract is put in a dilemma or difficulty in relation to his commitments by the other party's breach he is not bound to exercise all his legal rights in order to extricate himself; he is only bound to act reasonably in all the circumstances: see the authorities summarized in McGregor on Damages, (13th ed.) par. 233. Since it is found that the charterers acted reasonably, and indeed chartered the substitute tonnage after being advised to do so by the owners' brokers, there is nothing in this point."

5.2.6　受害方对减少损失的选择是否需要预先通知违约/侵权方?

笔者一直是觉得受害方在减少损失时,合理与否是要看很多的因素的。如果时间上容许,向违约/侵权方预先通知有关受害方将会采取减损的行动并非是"坏事",但这充其量只是看整个行动是否合理的其中一个因素,而且不一定是重要因素。做出预先通知的好处就是如果违约/侵权方不马上做出反对或异议,将来就很难抗辩说受害方的行动不合理。例如,受害方船东在修理之前告诉可能要承担损坏责任的承租人,船舶将会在美国的下一个港口装货前进行修理。如果承租人默不作声,或只是说"我不予评论,因为我没有责任",这都会在将来令承租人被指称这种做法不合理,因为在美国修理太昂贵。但笔者认为这并非是决定性的,最后还是要看整体的合理与否,而这方面的因素就会是很多了。比如,船舶是否可以等待下一个航次回到亚洲才进行修理?船舶是否会在下一个航次回去亚洲?这种修理在亚洲是否的确会比美国便宜很多?船东有否其他有说服力的原因必须要在美国修好?承租人如果做出评论或反对,会否改变船东在美国修理的事实或决定等。

但不论笔者怎么样想,最近就有一个新加坡的上诉庭先例,认为受害方如果在减少损失时不预先通知违约/侵权方,就会是一种不合理的做法,这就是The "Asia Star"(2010)2 Lloyd's Rep 12先例。案情涉及该船舶被租用一个航次,去印尼与马来西亚的装港装运21,500吨的棕榈油去中东、土耳其与黑海港口。但船舶有延误,而且在装港被检查的时候(2004年1月19日),船舱被发觉不够清洁来装运棕榈油。最终,这一艘船舶没有跑这一个航次并在1月21日离开了印尼装港,这导致了承租人(也是CIF卖方)的损失。因为他这票棕榈油的供应是来自三位分卖方,其中一位由于付运的延误而取消了供应,结果只有两票货物能够用其他船付运,这就导致了承租人的利润损失高达698,889美元。承租人也蒙受了其他的损失,如因为付运的延误要赔给买方 823,800 美元与棕榈油的额外仓库费等。反正整个索赔高达 200 万美元。

但在船东违约后(船舱发觉不清洁被拒绝装货)的 1~2 天,曾经在市场上有另一艘 Puma 轮可以作为替代的船舶,而当时承租人也在市场寻找替代船舶,发觉只有这一艘船舶,虽然比 Asia Star 轮大(Puma 轮是 40,000 吨载重量),但还是可以作为替代。反正是双方在 1 月 20 日的谈判,作出了很快的"发盘与还盘"(offer and counter-offer)。最后大家只差 2 美元的运费,但 Puma 轮的船东就不再理会,显然是有其他更好的租约了。在金钱方面,就算是根据 Puma 轮最后要求的运费,与 Asia Star 轮的租约运费相差也只是 399,500 美元。这就带来了承租人有没有合理减少损失的争议。如果有,就可以成功索赔约 2,000,000 美元。如果没有,承租人只能向船东索赔 399,500 美元。

在新加坡法院的第一审,"助理司法常务主任"(Assistant Registrar)在核算损失的时候,认为承租人没有合理减少损失,只能获赔 399,500 美元,所持的理由就是承租人明知棕榈油市场在上涨,面临被供应商因为延误付运而取消的很严重危险,没有理由不尽一切努力租下 Puma 轮作出替代船舶。毕竟要多支付的运费差价与整个航次买卖可以赚取的利润(高达 1,500,000 美元)完全是不成比例的。但这一判决上诉去了高院,Judith Prakash 大法官有不同的决定,认为承租人没有不合理,也不应该事后作出批评。她是这样说:"The Assistant Registrar had erred on the issue of mitigation. Acting reasonably in mitigation did not mean that the charterers had to accept the terms offered by Puma's owners without negotiation. Mitigation principles did not require the injured party to incur extraordinary expenditure or act otherwise than in the ordinary course of business. In the ordinary course of business, a charterer of a ship would negotiate with the shipowner to get the best possible terms in the prevailing market. The defendant had called no evidence as to what the prevailing freight rates and demurrage rates were on 20 January 2004, or as to whether the charterer were acting unreasonably in relation to the terms of their offer to the owners of Puma. The fact that events showed that the charterers would have lost less had they chartered Puma did not mean that the charterers acted unreasonably in relation to their negotiations with Puma's owners."

但这去了新加坡上诉庭又被推翻,并挑出一项被视为是承租人不合理的做法,就是没有把可能租用 Puma 轮作为替代船的事实告诉违约方船东。这可节录 Rajah 大法官所说:"In our view, one important issue which the judge should have considered was whether, in the circumstances, the respondent(受害方承租人)should have notified the appellant(违约方船东)of the option of chartering Puma at the freight rate offered by her owners. This would have given the appellant the opportunity to object to this option if it did not deem it reasonable. The essence of the respondent's submissions on this point was this: where additional expense had to be incurred in mitigating loss, it was reasonable for an aggrieved party which was experienced in the ways of business to simply unilaterally evaluate whether the additional sum was an amount which it was willing to pay, and then decide whether or not to proceed with the mitigation measure in question. There is, according to the respondent, no obligation whatsoever on the aggrieved party's part to notify or consult the defaulting party *vis - a - vis* the available options for mitigating losses."

新加坡上诉庭并依赖了一个古老的先例名为 Mitchell v. Kahl (1862) 175 ER 1250 的说法:"If you think either that the plaintiffs might have got a smaller vessel, or that the improperly neglected to give the defendants notice of the substitute charter, so as to give them the option of using the surplus space, you may find for the defendants; otherwise, for the plaintiffs, for the sum claimed."

对这一个先例,笔者由于没有看证据,所以很难作出有价值的评论。只是观察到掌握"合理或不合理"的确是非常不肯定,大家都会有不同的看法或侧重点。虽然在这一个先例是不存在这个问题,但在国际仲裁经常会涉及不同文化背景的仲裁员,他们之间看待合理或不合理更有时会是有天壤之别,这不能简单说偏袒或不公正就解释得过去的。另一个笔者的观察涉及受害方在采取减少损失行动前向违约方作出预先通知,这方面的复杂问题已经在本小段开头有涉及。而针对租船业务,笔者也有一定的经验,就是发盘与还盘来的很快,经常会有短至 10 分钟或 5 分钟的时限要求对方马上作出回应。这种情况也发生在 The "Asia Star"先例。看市场对谁有利,会有一方,如船东同时与几个不同的潜在承租人同时谈判,经常会有一位承租人决定无条件接受了船东在 10 分钟前的还盘,但船东回应说:"你刚过了 1 分钟(甚至没有超过时限,但由于时限并非是一个有约因的承诺,船东不遵守也没有责任),我把船舶已经租给另一位承租人了。"所以无论如何,怎样有诚意谈判,也不能保证一定谈得拢。想有一定的把握能够谈得拢,就是不要作出任何的反盘,也就是不要谈判,船东只要肯给出一个发盘就马上全面接受。在这种情况下,向违约方作出预先通知是否现实与希望取得什么实际的效果,笔者是有疑问的。至于新加坡上诉庭指称在该案例中如果做出预先通知,会有可能违约方愿意承担或承担一半租入 Puma 轮的运费差价,笔者觉得是更加不现实。

5.3 合理减少损失要求较严格的说法

以上 5.2.1 至 5.2.6 段都是一些经常会有争议的情况,说明法律对受害方在合理减少损失方面的要求是尽量宽松与善待,只要受害方能够说得出一些道理支持他的选择就会被接受。但这方面也并非是没有不同的说法,虽然不多见。这不是法律,但说法是在减少损失的行为方面应对受害方有较紧的要求,因为这对大家都好。往往有情况是受害方需要冒一定程度的风险或多花费一些钱才会带来更好更大的"净现值"(net present value,简称 NPV)或经济效益,可减少损失。但目前在普通法下,是不要求受害方冒风险或多花费,认为合理减少损失并不要求这样做。但这就不一定带来最好的经济效益,如在本章第 1 段所介绍的 British Westinghouse Electric & Manufacturing Co Ltd v. Underground Electric Rys. Co of London Ltd (1912) AC 673 先例,就涉及受害方的买方以更高价格购买另一台更大动力的蒸汽机作为替代,结果带来的高利润成功把违约方(供应一台有缺陷的蒸汽机的卖方)本来要赔偿的损失全部抵销掉。在多伦多大学一个报告〔by MacIntozh and Frydenhnd (1987) 37 University of Toronto LJ 113〕,有结论是(在147与157页):

"... damage should be assessed as the difference between the NPV. of the contract and the NPV. of mitigation strategy, both measured as of the date of breach, and without regard to the actual results of the mitigation or of the notional contract performance... (This approach would involve) a reversal of the common law policy that the non - breacher need not take any considerable degree of risk in mitigating damages: the 'duty' to mitigate should extend to a risky strategy where it has the highest NPV. of all available mitigation strategies... Equally, it will reverse the common law rule that the plaintiff need not invest any non - trivial sum of money in the effort to mitigate: the duty to mitigate should extend to non - trivial investment where justified by the NPV. of the mitigation strategy.

By comparison, the economic approach suggests that the rules should be structured so as to encourage the plaintiff to adopt his best mitigation strategy, whether or not this involves investment beyond that contemplated in the original contract (albeit, where an ex post rule is used, without taking inordinate risk.) If purchasing the new machines was clearly the soundest decision that the plaintiff could have made (and this appears to have been the case) then this investment decision should be encompassed within the duty to mitigate. "

6. 受害方对违约/毁约方提出新要约的情况

众所周知,在合约一方声称对方违约/毁约(不论是否最后能够成立)并且接受违约/毁约的情况下,就表示原来的合约已经终断。将来即使是判另一方并没有违约/毁约,也不会带来原合约的重生,只会是声称对方违约/毁约并接受的一方自己变为是违约方。反正在发生了这样的事情后,通常双方会进行谈判,试图继续履行有关的合约。往往会有两种做法:第一种就是"恢复原合约"(reinstate original contract),但会对该原合约的条文做出一些修改,如抬高或减低原来的价格。第二种做法就是签订一份新的合约作为替代,其中有新的合约条文,但这是与原合约分开,也不影响原合约的争议与索赔权利。这表示在新合约下,价格比原合约会是有所抬高或减低。这显然会导致合约一方的损失,他可以提起诉讼,指称他没有在原合约违约/毁约,而是对方违约/毁约,而带来的损失就是原合约与新合约之间的差价。

要有一个新的合约,就涉及新的"要约"(offer)与"接受"(acceptance),反正是与产生一个有效合约的要求是完全一致。通常会是违约/毁约方或担心自己会成为违约方向受害方提出新的要约,这里的其中一个目的是为了迫使受害方减少损失。的确也有情况是客观来看这种新的要约是不失为减少损失的有效方法。那么,受害方不合理的拒绝违约方的新要约会构成没有合理减少损失的行为,其日后的损失赔偿请求也会被相应限制。

6.1 在个人服务合约或商业合约中受害方应否接受新要约的不同对待

受害方是否要接受违约/毁约方的新要约?这要从两个方面考虑:第一个就是商业合约,一般来说,这种情况下应尽量接受该新要约以减少损失;第二个方面是个人服务合约,由于涉及感情上的因素,所以受害方接受新要约与否的合理性会有更大程度的宽松。这方面可先节录在 Payzu v. Saunders(1919)2 K. B. 581,McCardie 大法官所说:"I felt no inclination to allow in a mercantile dispute an unhappy indulgence in far - fetched resentment or an undue sensitiveness to slights or unfortunately worded letters. Business often gives rise to certain asperities. "另在上诉庭,Scrutton 大法官也说了同样的话:"In certain cases of personal service it may be unreasonable to expect a plaintiff to consider an offer from the other party who has grossly injured him;In commercial contracts, it is generally reasonable to accept an offer from the party in default. However, it is always a question of fact. "

另节录 Bankes 大法官针对个人服务合约的新要约,他在 Payzu v. Saunders 有以下的话:"There may be cases where as matter of fact it would be unreasonable to expect a plaintiff to consider any offer made in view of the treatment he has received from the defendant. If he had been rendering personal services and had been dismissed after being accused in presence of others of being a thief, and if after that his employer had offered to take him back into his service, most persons would think he was justified in refusing the offer, and that it would be unreasonable to ask him in this way to mitigate the damages in an action for wrongful dismissal. "

6.2 个人服务合约

个人服务合约由于涉及个人的尊严与感受,所以受害方应否接受违约/毁约方新要约的合理性就要考虑这些因素,即使这些因素有时候是很主观的。这与基本上只是为了金钱的商业合约有所不同。但大原则上,个人服务合约还是要看受害方有否合理减少损失,顶多是对合理程度的要求比较低。这种案例大量存在于雇佣合约,毕竟劳资纠纷是经常会有的。以下介绍的案例是涉及雇主无理或错误解雇雇员,但事后作出新要约表示愿意重新雇用。

首先简单介绍有关受害方雇员没有合理减少损失的先例。在 Brace v. Calder (1895)2 Q. B. 253 先例,案情涉及 4 位被告合伙经营一间公司,他们与原告签约 2 年让他负责公司的业务管理。2 年雇佣期届满前,其中 2 位合伙人退出并且令公司解散,但另 2 位合伙人又重组了公司继续经营业务。结果原告声称由于原公司解散造成其雇佣合约的终断,他要求索赔他在余下雇佣期本可挣取的工资收入。实际上当时余下的2位合伙人曾向原告提出依照原合约、原条件继续聘用他，但被原告拒绝。上诉庭判定雇佣合约的确是被告不当终断，但责任虽然明确，在损失方面原告仅可获得象征性赔偿。因为他本应合理接受余下的合伙人提出的继续聘用邀请，可把损失减少至零。

但有更多的先例是尊重与考虑受害方雇员的尊严与感受。比如雇员是在一种屈辱的情况下被解雇的，那么考虑到他先前所遭受到的待遇，再要求他接受雇主的重新聘用是不合理的。如果一个雇员被雇主当众斥责为“内鬼”、“窃贼”后遭到不当解雇，之后雇主又提出聘回他，那么该雇员拒绝受聘也是完全合理的。因为若要求他以这种方式减少因非法解雇而蒙受的损失，显然并不合理。这方面的先例在英国、美国、加拿大等普通法国家都有不少：Yetton v. Eastwoods Froy (1967) 1 WLR 104 (QB)；Robertson v. Wing (1978) 95 DLR (3d) 424 (BCSC)；Allison v. Amoco Production Co (1975) 58 DLR (3d) 233 (Alta SCTD)；O' Grady v. Ins Corp of British Columbia (1975) 63 DLR (3d) 370 (BCSC)；Thiessen v. Leduc (1975) 4 WWR 387 (Alta SC)；Washer v. British Columbia Toll Highways & Bridges Authority (1965) 53 DLR (2d) 620 (BCCA)；Herrschaft v. Vancouver Community College (1978) 91 Dlr (3d) 328 (BCSC)。

如果新要约涉及要求受害方雇员与他以前吵过架的同事一起工作，也会被视为是可以不接受：Shindler v. Northern Raincoat Co (1960) 1 WLR 1038。

另是，如果要求受害方雇员在重新接受聘用时，放弃向违约/毁约的雇主针对较前的不合理解雇追索的权利，这种新要约也是可以不接受：Shindler v. Northern Raincoat Co (1960) 1 WLR 1038；Washer v. British Columbia Toll Highways & Bridges Authority (1965) 53 DLR (2d) 620 (BCCA)；Campbell v. MacMillan Bloedel Ltd (1978) 2 WWR 686 (BCSC)。

在以上谈的是雇佣合约，但估计把受害方的感受加入作为合理与否的考虑，也会出现在其他类别的案件，即使这些案件不严格属于个人服务。例如，在一个长期的商业合约被违约/毁约而终断后，受害方对违约方的新要约不予接受，就可能涉及个人的感受，如是否对违约方继续履行合约有信心。如果受害方说得出一个有板有眼的理由，这会是可以作为针对有否合理减少损失质疑的反驳。但也会有不太令人信服的理由，例如，受害方指称违约方是一家经济实力不强的公司，甚至是一家巴拿马公司，所以没有信心。但这个情况是在受害方与违约方订立原合约时就存在。所以，受害方的这个借口看来并不太合理。说到底，合理与否都是在法院与仲裁庭的一念之间。

笔者估计，另一种有可能在一定程度涉及受害方感受的就是在 Udale v. Bloomsbury Area Health Authority (1983) 1 WLR 1098 和 Emeh v. Kensington & Chelsea & Westminster Area Health Authority (1985) QB 1012 之后带来的一连串同类先例。这种本质上是属于侵权的先例涉及医生进行绝育手术，但手术失败，导致病人受孕所带来的损失计算。例如在 Udale v. Bloomsbury Area Health Authority，涉及一位已经有3个小孩的母亲进行绝育手术后再度怀孕。这种案例涉及的损失是将来把该不想要的孩子养大与提供教育的所有费用,直到他能够自立为止。正如在 Allen v. Bloomsbury Area Health Authority (1993) 1 All ER 651,Brooke 大法官所说:"... in this type of case defendants are liable to pay for all such expenses as may be reasonably incurred for the education and upkeep for the unplanned child, to his condition in life and his reasonable requirements at the time the expenditure is incurred."

显然,这样计算出的损失是一笔很大的钱。所以,当地医管局作为被告通常会试图减少金钱赔偿而提出抗辩就是受害方应该接受堕胎,否则是没有合理减少损失。这一来,被告即使是要承担疏忽的责任,也只是要赔偿有限的堕胎费用。但有关的先例是一直否定受害方拒绝堕胎有任何不合理,这里涉及堕胎毕竟还有一定程度的风险并会给受害方带来痛楚与不适。但估计也是照顾了受害方不愿意接受堕胎的个人感受。在 Allen v. Bloomsbury Area Health Authority 先例中是说:"the defendant... did not try to contend that (the plaintiff) had acted unreasonably in deciding not to have a termination."(被告没有试图争辩原告拒绝接受堕胎是不合理的。)

还有其他估计涉及受害方感受的案件,可以举一个先例 R v. Blaue (1975) 1 WLR 1411 (CA)为例。案情涉及受害方因宗教的原因拒绝输血而濒临死亡,被侵权方指称没有合理减少损失,但这不被法院接受。

6.3 商业合约

在大原则上,商业合约一般是要求受害方更谨慎考虑违约/毁约方的新要约,特别这是能够解决当时的困难或减少损失。已经是提到过,商业合约不应该涉及感情因素,或是个人尊严。如果受害方没有一个说得过去的理由就拒绝违约方的新要约,就会有危险。这尤其是在一次过的买卖合约。比如违约/毁约的卖方拒绝以原合约条件或价格交货,或违约/毁约的买方拒绝接受交货,但同时又提出以其他条件或价格交货或收货。若根据客观情况判断,受害方当时拒绝这项新要约是不合理的,那他日后的索赔金额就会打折扣了。已多次提及的重要先例 Payzu v. Saunders (1919) 2 K. B. 581 就是这样一种情况,被告卖方与原告买方签订有关的买卖合约,分 9 个月交货。付款为赊购方式,原告可以每期交货后一个月内支付货款。第一期付款由于原告晚了开支票支付,被告以此为由终断了合约,但法院认为是被告违约/毁约。被告曾经在同时提出订立新合约继续向原告供货,建议的新合约除了付款改为交货即付(原告作为买方在收货时立即支付货款)之外,其余条文并无改变。但原告拒绝接受,等于是拒绝了被告的新要约。当时市场价格一路上涨,原告向被告索赔市场价格与原合约价格的差价。法院判定原告本应接受被告签订新合约的建议,并认定新要约是"善意"(*bona fide*),虽然是付款方式改为交货即付,但原合约价格毕竟维持不变,这样原告本可以避免支付市场的差价,从而减少损失。因此,原告只能索赔他如果可以每期赊付但变为是交货即付所带来的利息损失,也就是他若接受被告合理作出新要约仍会蒙受的有限损失。

已经提过,法院在判决时提出,在商业合约方面,要求受害方接受违约方的新要约通常并没有什么不合理。对此我们要引起重视,因为实务中不时会遇到这种情况。比如航次租约中承租人因为备货、买卖合约等出问题,造成原来约定的租约船舶无货可装,变为非要违约/毁约不可。而他或他的联营公司在装港或附近港口有另一批货物可付运,那么他就会一方面告诉船东原租约运输的货物已落空(通常船东就会被迫接受承租人违约/毁约),另一方面向船东提出新要约就是另一个替代的航次并显然需要把原来租约的一些条文作出改变,包括运费。这时船东都应以平和的心态加以合理考虑,最好不要断然拒绝。如果船东当时还有其他市场上的替代租约可供选择,利润与好处(这会包括很多方面,如卸货地点)不少于承租人的替代航次,船东还可以硬气得起来。但若是不幸揽不到其他生意,船东断然拒绝承租人的新要约就有危险了,可能日后会被认定没有合理接受承租人的新要约以减少损失,令损失赔偿受到限制。

6.3.1 新要约的条件必须合理

在著名 Payzu v. Saunders(1919)2 K. B. 581 先例的一审,McCardie 大法官说:"I feel no inclination to allow in a mercantile dispute an unhappy indulgence in farfetched resentment or an undue sensitiveness to slights or unfortunately worded letters. Business often gives rise to certain asperities. But I agree that the plaintiffs in deciding whether to accept the defendant's offer were fully entitled to consider the terms in which the offer was made, its *bona fides* or otherwise, its relation to their own business methods and financial position, and all the circumstances of the case; and it must be remembered that an acceptance of the offer would not preclude an action for damages for the actual loss sustained."(以上的第二句话就说到原告决定是否接受被告的新要约时,完全有权考虑新要约的条件、是否有诚意或其他方面,特别是关系到原告自己的生意模式与经济状况[例如,在该先例把支付条件改为交货即付会否导致原告资金流通的困难]。同时,必须要记得新要约不能要求受害方放弃对已造成的实际损失的索赔。)

根据这一说法,就可以举一个例子是被告同意以 10 美元/吨的价格卖给原告一批货,但在市场上涨到 12 美元/吨时,被告拒绝交货并构成违约/毁约。但被告随即作出新要约以 11 美元/吨的价格卖给原告,并说明这是原合约的"全面与最后的和解"(full and final settlement)。在这种情况下,原告拒绝该新要约并非是不合理减少损失。但如果被告作出新要约是同样以 11 美元/吨的价格卖给原告,但说明这是不损害原告索赔他的损失(也就是比原来合约价格多付了 1 美元)。原告还是拒绝接受,并没有其他合理的原因解释此行为,就有危险被视为没有合理减少损失。

这方面还可以举另一个先例 Heaven & Kesterton Ltd v. Establishment Francois Albias & Cie (1956) 2 Lloyd's Rep 316 (QB)。该先例涉及买方对一批货物(木材)因货不对版而拒货,卖方同意减价要求买方收货,但买方仍然拒绝。在后来的仲裁,仲裁庭判买方拒绝卖方的新要约是没有合理减少损失。但这上诉去了法院后被推翻,认为拒绝新要约是合理,并说买方如果必须接受减价的新要约,就等于剥夺买方因货不对版可以拒货的权利。Devlin 大法官是这样说:“What, in effect, the arbitrator is saying is: ‘From a business point of view’ – if I may put it that way – ‘you could very well have taken up these goods and suffered no business disadvantage, providing you were given an allowance of £ 1 per standard for the defects in quality. ’ Of course, that is tantamount to depriving a buyer of his right to reject altogether, and saying that, notwithstanding that he is properly rejecting, he is to be put in precisely the same position as if he had taken up the goods, and as if his only remedy was to be compensated for the damage on the basis of defective quality.”

但看来如果不涉及货物质量的问题,而是当事人以其他理由终断买卖合约,如是在一个 CIF 买卖,卖方迟延付运货物或者是交出的付运文件有不符点(这是会导致信用证无法结汇),情况就有不同。如果买方是因为货物质量问题要求受害方接受减价作为和解,就是要求受害方放弃他的权利。但如果是涉及非货物质量而导致买卖合约终断的情况,就没有要求受害方放弃他任何的权利。正如 Devlin 大法官所说(这段话在本章第 5 段已节录过):“If goods are rejected in a c. i. f. contract for some reason that has nothing to do with quality – the shipment date was wrong, or documents were not in order, or something of that sort, so that the goods are properly rejected – and then the buyer goes out into the market to buy goods of the contract quality, it is open to the seller to go to him and say: ‘Well, then, I tender you these goods. These goods are of the contract quality. You are looking for goods of the contract quality. You rightly rejected them upon a basis that had nothing to do with their quality. If you are looking, therefore, for goods to make good your loss, here they are, and I can supply cheaper than you would be able to buy them at the market rate outside. ’ If the seller does that, that is a matter which must be taken into consideration in answering the question of whether or not the buyer has acted reasonably, as it is his duty to do, in mitigating damage.”

在另一个先例 Strutt v. Whitnell (1975) 1 WLR 870 (CA)中,案情涉及被告向原告(房子的开发商)购买了一栋房子,事后出现缺陷。但由于没有合约关系,所以被告不能向需要负责的承建商提出索赔。结果是原告建议把该房子从被告手中购买回来,然后由原告开发商根据他与承建商的合约向其索赔。双方的确也这样做了,并且完成了回购的交易。在回购合约中,被告承诺当时的租客会搬走。但原告买回房子之后发生变化,租客不肯走,也无法将其赶走。这导致原告只能向被告提出索赔,因为空置的房子价值应该比有租客的房子高。但在知悉将会被起诉时,被告对原告说,“不要这样做,我可以把房子买回来”(Don't do that, we will buy it back),但这被原告拒绝。在诉讼中,被告有责任是没有争议的,但被告辩称原告没有接受新要约去合理减少损失。在英国上诉庭,判是原告拒绝新要约是合理的。其中,Cairns 大法官认为被告所作出的新要约太简单,原告不考虑没有不合理之处。MacKenna 大法官把本案例与 Payzu v. Saunders(1919)2 K. B. 581 先例作出区分。因为在本案例,涉及被告要求原告受害方放弃属于他自己的货物(房子),否则,就会失去索赔金钱损失的权利,这是不合理的。MacKenna 大法官是这样说:"the seller cannot compel him to forgo his right to substantial damages as the price of retaining what has become his own property."

另一个先例是 Ideal Phonograph Co v. Shapiro (1920) 48 OLR 618,案情涉及一个房屋的租赁,租赁合约中要求承租人安装电梯,否则出租人可以自己安装然后向承租人收取不超过 350 加元的费用。但承租人没有安装,这是违约,而事实上出租人安装电梯的费用是超过了 350 加元。法院判出租人有权在合约下作出安装,但这是他的裁量权。也不存在出租人有一个减少损失的"责任",就是作出安装电梯后再向承租人取回 350 加元,因为这导致他无法把安装费用全部取回,也等于解除了承租人部分的安装责任。反正是法院认为这对受害方出租人不合理。

最后可介绍 The"Solholt"(1983)1 Lloyd' s Rep. 605 先例,案情涉及二手船的买卖。由于卖方在最后一个航次的延误,没有办法在合约规定的最后交船日期赶到交船港口 Southampton,结果被买方取消二手船买卖合约。而根据该合约的文字,船舶延误赶不上最后交船日期是构成违约,所以案例主要针对的是损失的计算,特别是有否合理减少损失。该案例涉及一种比较奇怪的现象,就是在买方合法终断合约时,该船舶的市场价格比买卖合约价格还要高,前者是 550 万美元,后者是 500 万美元。按照常理,能够占到便宜买方不会贸然终断合约,即使在合约下他是有权利终断。毕竟,将来索赔损失也是劳民伤财与有不肯定之处。但该案例的买方就是这样做,终断合约后再向卖方索赔 50 万美元。买方这种做法虽然奇怪,但背后会有各种千奇百怪的商业原因。例如,买方怀疑该船舶有问题,但又证明不了,就乐得以这一合法理由终断合约。或是买方突然对航运市场中长期变得很悲观或买方突然决定不搞航运。当然,在这种情况下,如果有便宜货,还是可以接受船舶然后转售以牟利,但会是有一些船型不容易转售出去。只多举一个有可能理由,就是买方打算终断合约后,再向卖方压价。在本先例,的确也有报道说买方在终断合约后曾向卖方作出新要约,欲以 475 万美元购买该船舶,后被卖方拒绝。表面看来,买方会是异想天开,因为当时的市场价格是 550 万美元。但实际上笔者也不是没有见过这种情况,就是一些厉害的买方会以将来索赔市场损失来威胁卖方,加上卖方怕麻烦,结果作出一些让步。但显然,在 The "Solholt"先例中的这一做法是不成功的。最后,卖方以 580 万美元把该船舶转售给其他人。

在买方向卖方提出索赔 50 万美元的损失,一个主要争议就是买方有否合理减少损失。卖方的一个争议就是买方根本不应该终断合约,不这样做就不会导致这一笔损失。但这一争议站不住脚,因为合理减少损失的"责任"是在违约/毁约后才出现。卖方的另一个更重要的争议就是如果买方提出一个新要约,以原来的合约价格 500 万美元购买该船舶,并且是不损害买方索赔 3 天延误交船的损失(这估计是很少钱),卖方肯定会答应。但买方没有这样做,反而压低价格,这不是合理减少损失。

双方当事人针对这方面提交给法院的证据如下：盘问买方 Economakis 先生："After the vessel was cancelled, you caused an offer to be made at ＄4,750,000... "Economakis 先生回答："... There are always brokers. I got bombarded by them. A broker suggested a reduction in price and I said to try it. "盘问买方 Economakis 先生有关他是否在当时知道 Solholt 轮仍然在寻找买方，回答是："The sellers had the ship in Southampton. It is natural to assume that the vessel was still available for sale. "另在卖方 Holter－Sorensen 先生被问及："If after the cancellation, you had been asked whether you would sell to Mr. Economakis for ＄5,000,000, what would have been the answer?"卖方 Holter－Sorensen 先生回答："I would have done so. It would have needed at least two directors to approve the decision. "此外，Holter－Sorensen 先生也表明了船舶因没有买方而滞留在 Southampton 港，他不知道应该怎么办，并感到担心。因为再寻找其他买方涉及新的谈判、新的合约、买方需要检查船级记录与船舶的表面状况，甚至再要进干坞检查船底，以及会要面对 Economakis 的诉讼。结果这些证据说服法院只要买方作出按照原合约的船价的新要约，卖方几乎肯定是会接受。这导致了买方 50 万美元的市场差价索赔败诉。

在这一个先例，比较特殊的地方至少有两个方面。一是违约方指受害方没有作出新要约，而不是一般情况下的由违约方向受害方作出新要约，这估计是因为受害方的确有作出一个看起来不合理的新要约。可以看得出，合理与否是从整体的事实看，而且每个案件的事实都不一样。二是该案例看来奇怪的结果，就是受害方索赔不成功，但违约方反而可以把市场上涨的高达 80 万美元的差价全部据为己有。针对这一点，一审的 Staughton 大法官有针对，并对没有市场转售的货物与很容易转售的商品作出比较，认为在这方面有不同之处。针对后者，Staughton 大法官以 100 吨小麦为例，卖方同意出售并在 8 月份付运，但发生违约。到了 9 月 2 日，当时的小麦市场上涨，卖方作出新要约同意以原来合约价格供应该 100 吨小麦，但买方不合理拒绝。法律地位应该是买方虽然蒙受损失，但索赔不成功。相反，卖方就可以把该 100 吨小麦高价转售所得的利润据为己有。Staughton 大法官说："In any event I would have some doubt whether a ship is a readily marketable commodity in the same sense as 100 tons of wheat, although on the facts of this case the sellers did obtain the benefit of the increased value of the ship when they later resold. And it does not greatly disturb me that these sellers have made an adventitious profit merely because the buyers failed to adopt the course which would have secured that profit to themselves by accepting the vessel even after the contract was cancelled. The claim for damages fails. "

6.3.2　对待新要约合理与否的不肯定裁决

虽然，有了不少有关的先例关于新要约合理与否，但在笔者处理的仲裁案件中，还是经常有不肯定，毕竟合理与否的掌握难以拿捏，也经常会因人而异。在 The"Xi Hai"（伦敦仲裁，1991 年）案件，船舶被程租从马来西亚装运木薯片（tapioca）去欧洲。

但去了装港没有货物提供，承租人另要求船舶开去泰国改为装运 palm kernel expeller 去欧洲，船东反对而引致后来是否合理拒绝新要约之争，因为关系损失计算。船东反对理由有二：(i)木薯片不是危险品，但 palm kernel expeller 是易燃品，加上该船舶没有二氧化碳灭火装置。(ii)船东(原告)不是原船东，只是二船东，要取得原船东同意装危险品非是易事。

但仲裁庭判是船东没有合理接受新要约来减少损失，因为仅是新要约涉及危险品并无大碍，而船东也没有积极向原船东争取同意装危险品的证据。

看来这个先例对受害方"合理"的尺度要求相对严格。但这不必太关注，同样的事实在另一个不同人士组成的仲裁庭会有完全相反的裁决。甚至即使是同一个仲裁庭的成员，也会在另一场合改变以前的看法，这确是在 The"Xi Hai" 案件发展下发生的现象，但不再详谈以免扯得太远。

另一案件名为 The"HBS"(伦敦仲裁，1995)是以挪威买卖格式合约的二手船买卖。在船价订约后下跌的情况下，希腊买方在上船检查时指船东没有给他充分机会检查，所以要求第二个检查。但这一拖时间，中国卖方有极大困难，因他不能在该二手船买卖合约受到约束下转卖或出租，而航运市场在开始下跌。而且会有希腊买方要求了第二个再会有第三个检查的危险等，无限期地拖下去，因为该买卖合约并没有说是只能有一个检查。根据挪威买卖格式合约下的规定，买方在检查后如果不满意，在一段约定的时限(如 72 小时)内有一个选择权终断买卖合约，即不确认接受。

在拒绝给予第二个检查并提醒买方在时限内作出选择后不久，中国卖方在 72 小时时限届满后终断合约，因为买方不曾确认接受。

但为了小心起见，卖方之后马上几次以诚恳的文字向买方提出新要约，说明对方如果还要这艘船舶，可马上交接，以原条件、原价格，只要不再在重新检查方面纠缠下去拖时间。毕竟买方已检查了该船舶两次，对船舶的情况有了解。当时市场下跌，可想象到是买方没有理睬中国卖方的新要约。之后卖方以更低价格把该船转售给第三人。

但希腊买方并不满足于只是省去买进一艘高价(比起当时市场)的船舶，而更进一步向卖方索偿买船不成的营运利润(当时只是靠估计)的损失：The "Ile Anx Moines"(1974)2 Lloyd's Rep. 502。这就关系到其中一项争议是买方应否合理接受卖方在终断合约后几次提出的新要约？而如果接受了，则不会有这估计的损失了。

买方争辩说他不必接受这新要约的唯一理由是他失去了仔细检查的权利但要马上接受该船舶，这不合理。而卖方则争辩买方已有分别两次长达一天的检查，即使时间仍不足够，买方认为没有充分机会看清楚某些地方，也应是可以对该船舶的状况有一个合理的印象足够决定接受与否。而且 Paysu v. Saunders(1919)2 K. B. 581 先例也是违约方把赊购改为交货即付，即表示买方接受新要约还是会有一点吃亏，但并不表示可以拒绝。

但仲裁庭判是希腊买方不接受这新要约完全合理，不存在没有减少损失。笔者的感觉就是仲裁庭成员如果改变,就有可能从有关的事实看透了希腊买方是在市场下跌但走势还不明确的情况下,希望以重复检查的借口拖延时间。所以失去了仔细检查的权利(这毕竟是一个很空泛与主观的说法),只是一个借口,不应该被接受为合理拒绝新要约的借口。把本案件与The"Solholt"(1983)1 Lloyd's Rep. 605的判决相比,就可以看出两者有着显著区别。

较早时提及的两个伦敦仲裁庭中,有一位共同仲裁员。笔者对案情细节有所了解,笔者认为合理与否,或宽或紧,均有理由。而且仲裁庭对此事实的认定是完全终局。

撇开这种个别案件裁决的不肯定性,大原则仍是明确的,在Payzu v. Saunders (1919)2 K. B. 581的先例,商业合约相比个人服务合约对这方面的合理程度应要提高,要较严格要求受害方接受违约方的"新要约"(re-offer)来减少损失。

7. 举证责任

对于原告受害方没有合理减少损失的指控,应该是被告违约方必须负举证责任,这早在Roper v. Johnson (1873) LR 8 CP 167先例,并在贵族院的Garnac Grain Co v. Faure & Fairclough, Ltd (1967) 1 Lloyd's Rep 495先例获得确认。但也曾经有过不同的说法,如在Selvanayagam v. University of the West Indies (1983) 1 WLR 585先例,涉及人身伤亡,英国枢密院判是原告要为他拒绝治疗来减轻伤害举证,说明这样做是合理的。也有可能是枢密院在该先例把减少损失与"损失遥远性"(remoteness)混为一谈。但看来,主流的说法应该是被告对原告没有合理减少损失负举证责任的。在上诉庭的London and South of England Building Society v. Stone (1983) 1 WLR 1242先例,Stephenson大法官说:"the question [is] whether the [plaintiff] lenders acted reasonably... or rather whether the [defendant] valuer has proved that the lenders had acted unreasonably."另在Gebruder Metelmann GmbH v. NBR(London)Ltd. (1984) 1 Lloyd's Rep. 614先例,上诉庭的Donaldson大法官说:"it is no doubt true that the burden of proof lies upon the defendant."

举证责任在被告会有实质的重要性,这在Saunders v. Williams (2003) BLR 125 CA先例中可以看到。案情涉及被告把原告的财产损坏,但原告部分是因为穷困的原因,反正是过了三年后才进行修理。但在第一审,法院并没有针对原告押后进行修理是否合理的事实做出认定。加上上诉庭也看不到有任何资料针对这方面的合理性。所以案件中上诉庭就面对要么就把案件返还给高院作出这一方面的审理,要么就核算损失。最后上诉庭决定核算损失并判被告没有证明原告有任何不合理减少损失,而这方面的举证责任是在被告,所以判原告索赔的损失可以全数取回。

考虑到将来举证责任,中方当事人就要很小心保留证据,特别是文书证据。例如中方当事人如果将来有可能成为违约方,向对方做出新要约,就要留下文书证据。而如果中方当事人是受害方,对方做出新要约,要拒绝接受,也必须合情合理,并把这种情况留下文书证据。另是受害方如果做出减少损失的行为(特别是估计这一做法将来会有争议),时间上来得及的情况下,应该尽量给违约/侵权方一个预先的通知,看看他是否反对或者有什么话要讲:The "Asia Star"(2010) 2 Lloyd's Rep 12。

8. 减少损失的费用与后果不理想

受害方在减少损失时,通常会产生费用。这种费用的例子有很多,比如:(1)买卖合约中买方违约拒绝收货,而交货当地并无市场可转售。卖方只好把货物转运到最近有市场的地方卖掉。那么这笔运输费就是减少损失所作出的合理费用,买方自然要负责。(2)房屋租赁合约中房客违约退房,房东按照通常的做法在报纸的分类广告栏重新招租,这笔广告费房客要赔偿,即使是广告并没有吸引替代的租客。(3)或者货物运输中的货损,收货人重新包装散包货物(如散包水泥重新灌包)、分开清洁货与霉变货等,这笔费用应该可以向对货损负责任的承运人索赔。

有某些种类的费用会有争议,如受害方为了减少损失所花的时间可否收费(the value of plaintiff's own personal time and services expended in an effort to reduce the loss resulting from the defendant's wrongdoing)。这在美国是有一些不一致的判例,在《Handbook on the Law of Damages》(St. Paul, Minn., West Publishing Co., 1935)有提到,其中支持受害方可以把这笔费用向被告取回的是 St. Louis & San Fransisco Railway Co v. Sharp, 27 Kan. 134 (SC 1882),但不支持的有 Spencer v. Murphy, 6 Colo A 453, 41 P 841 (CA 1895)。

总结一下,受害方这些实际支付出去的费用只要合理,就都可以向侵权方/违约方索赔。很多时候这些费用甚至是与受害方其他的损失混合在一起,如在人身伤害的案件中,受害方的医疗费用就往往与他的其他损失(如收入的损失)算在一起。已经提到过,这是本章第2段所讲的有关减少损失大原则的第三条规则,它是根据第一条规则的衍生而来。通常这些减少损失的花费也不会受到质疑,特别有关行为的确是能够成功减少损失。但更重要的就是作出了这种花费,结果是不能成功减少损失,甚至加大了损失,这会有什么结果?看来现在已经有不少先例清楚说明是只要受害方的行为与费用是合理,还是不影响他的索赔。

在 Wilson v. United Counties Bank (1920) AC 102 先例中,Atkinson 勋爵说:"If one man inflicts an injury upon another the resort by the sufferer to reasonable expedients for the *bona fide* purpose of counteracting, curing or lessening the evil effects of the injury done to him, does not necessarily absolve the wrongdoer, even though the sufferer's efforts should, in the result, undesignedly aggravate the result of the injury. ”(最后的部分是说明即使受害方在减少损失的行为中无意中扩大了损害,还是不会让犯错的一方逃避赔偿责任。)

在 The“World Beauty”(1969) 1 Lloyd’s Rep 350 有关船舶碰撞的计算损失先例中,上诉庭的 Winn 大法官说:“but it is implicit in the principle, that if mitigating steps are reasonably taken and additional loss or damage results notwithstanding the reasonable decision to take those steps, then that will be in addition to the recoverable damage and not a set – off against the amount of it. ”(如果减少损失的行为是合理的,但发生了额外的损失,那么这些损失仍然是可以索赔的。)

另在本章 5.2.1 段已经介绍过的 Gebruder Metelmann GmbH v. NBR (London) Ltd. (1984)1 Lloyd’s Rep. 614 先例中,Browne – Wilkinson 大法官说:“In addition to the basic damages... Metalmann is entitled to be compensated for the additional damage flowing from the attempt to mitigate.... If there are two methods of mitigating damage, both of which are practicable and reasonable in the circumstances known to the innocent party at the time the mitigating action is required, it is not possible to say that the innocent party acted unreasonably in selecting one of these methods just because, in the light of later events, it turns out that the loss would have been less had the other method been adopted. ”有关这一个案例,可重复一提就是上诉庭判是受害方 Metelmann 去巴黎期货市场沽空 2500 吨食糖是属于合理减少损失的行为,即使沽空后果不理想,带来额外损失,这部分也可以向违约的 NBR 取回。

这方面还有其他的著名先例可简单介绍,如在 Lloyds and Scottish Finance v. Modern Cars and Caravans (Kingston) (1966) 1 QB 764 先例,涉及被告出售给原告一辆货车,但实际上被告是没有该货车的所有权的。而这种情况在美国经常发生,就是车子被盗窃,然后去其他地区出售,车子可能还会继续被转售。但无论善意转售多少次,卖方不拥有该货车所有权的事实还是改变不了,卖方也无法有效转让所有权给买方。再回到这一先例中,该货车后来被警察扣押,这导致一个受害方原告在被告的建议下向法院作出“互争权利诉讼”(interpleader action),等于让法院在听过各方争辩之后来决定货车的所有权究竟属于谁。但在诉讼途中,受害方的律师建议受害方撤销诉讼,因为不会成功。这一来,就涉及在整个减少损失的行为中产生了额外的律师/诉讼费用。之后受害方向被告提出索赔,因为被告出售的货车没有所有权,索赔的损失除了货车的价格外,也包括了这笔额外的费用。Edmund Davies 大法官认为受害方原告合理减少损失,特别是该浪费的诉讼是在被告的建议下作出的。所以,可以把额外的费用一并索偿成功。Edmund Davies 大法官是这样说:“mitigation were taken at the instigation of the defendants, I do not think it is open to them to assert that such steps were not reasonable. ”

另一个是 Esso Petroleum Co v. Mardon (1976) 2 Lloyd’s Rep 305 先例,案情涉及

原告 Esso（大石油公司）想在 Southport 建一个加油站，他们先作了一个调查。根据估计的车流量得出的调查结果表明每年应可售出汽油 20 万加仑之多。但在事后向当局申请执照时，加油站不被批准在面对大路的地方修建。这一来，肯定车辆的流量会减少。事实在营运的第一年（从 1963 年到 1964 年 4 月），只出售了约58370加仑的汽油。但 Esso 并没有减低每年出售 20 万加仑的估计，并在租约谈判的时候以此数字告知 Mardon 先生，这导致 Mardon 先生以高价向 Esso 租了这个加油站 3 年来营运。无可避免是 Mardon 先生亏了大本。到了 1964 年 8 月份，Esso 知道 Mardon 先生经济情况严峻，他所有投入加油站的资金已经赔光，所以作出一个新要约大幅度减低租金。Mardon 先生也接受了这一新要约，并在 1964 年 9 月 1 日与 Esso 订立了一个新合约。但可惜还是不能扭转亏损的厄运，最后以倒闭收场。Esso 后来向 Mardon 先生提起诉讼，追索欠下的油钱，而 Mardon 先生向 Esso 反索赔这疏忽"误述"（misrepresentation）所带来的严重损失。这著名的先例主要是针对误述，但在本章所要针对的问题是损失的计算。主要与本段有关的内容是针对在 1964 年 9 月 1 日后的新合约下的损失。第一审法院认为新合约下的损失与原来租约的误述无关，因为双方已经知道原来的误述，不会再诱使 Mardon 先生订立新合约，所以 Esso 不必赔付这部分的损失。这样的判法看来是根据损失赔偿中的"因果关系"（causation）大原则。但去了上诉庭，法院把新要约（这方面在本章第 6 段有详论）与新合约视为是合理减少损失的行为，新合约并不代表是一个新开始。而受害方 Mardon 先生在新合约中的损失也可以被视为是没有完全成功的减少损失行为，所以这额外的损失可以被视为是原来向违约方索赔的损失的一部分。Denning 勋爵是这样说："The Judge（第一审的 Lawson 大法官）limited the loss to the period from April, 1963, to September, 1964, when the new agreement was made. He said that from Sept. 1, 1964, Mr. Mardon was carrying on the business 'on an entirely fresh basis, of which the negligent mis – statement formed no part.' I am afraid I take a different view. It seems to me that from Sep 1 1964, Mr. Mardon acted most reasonably. He was doing what he could to retrieve the position, not only in his own interest but also in the interest of Esso. It was Esso who were anxious for him to stay on. They had no other suitable tenant to replace him. They needed him to keep the station as a going concern and sell their petrol. It is true that by this time the truth was known — that the throughput was very far short of 200,000 gallons — but nevertheless, the effect of the original mis – statement was still there. It laid a heavy hand on all that followed. The new agreement was an attempt to mitigate the effect. It was not a fresh cause which eliminated the past. It seems to me that the losses after Sep 1 1964, can be attributed to the original mis – statement, just as those before."

这方面近期还有几个相关的海事案例，都明确了合理减少损失的行为但后果不理想而导致了更大损失都可以向违约/侵权方取回，这些案例包括 The "Windfall"（1998）2 Lloyd's Rep 664；The "Sivand"（1998）2 Lloyd's Rep 97 与 Vinmar International Ltd v. Theresa Navigation SA (2001) 2 Lloyd's Rep 1。比较简短地介绍这些先例就可以直接节录《Mcgregor on Damages》(18th edn,2009 年)之 7 - 096 段:"It is thought that the principle is now fully accepted. Evidence of this is to be found in a series of modern shipping cases. In The 'Windfall' it was held that the claim for the loss of the sale of a vessel wrongfully arrested would still succeed even if the loss of the sale turned out to be because of the claimant's chartering and reflagging of the vessel, a reasonable act of mitigation made in an effort to obtain the vessel's release; here the attempt at mitigation would have caused the whole loss claimed. In The 'Sivand', where the claimant's harbour installations had been damaged by the defendant's vessel and the act of mitigation was the common one of repairing the damage done, it was held to be no good reason for not allowing the full outlay that the repair had cost much more than had been foreseen. In Vinmar International Ltd v. Theresa Navigation SA where the claimant cargo owner's decision to continue loading cargo although there was a serious risk of its being contaminated by the cargo already loaded was seen by the court as a reasonable but unsuccessful attempt at mitigation."

9. 受害方因为穷困带来额外损失或无法减少损失

9.1 有关的先例

受害方如果是因为穷困或其他如财政困难而没有办法或没有采取合理行动来减少损失,针对这个问题有一些不肯定的判例,而且会与本书第三与第四章所介绍的损失遥远性(remoteness of damage)大原则混在一起,其中因果关系大原则是在第四章 9.2.2 段有针对。这方面首先介绍的是一个重要的贵族院先例,它是判受害方自己穷困的原因所带来的额外损失是不能向对方责任方索赔:The "Liesbosch" (1933) 45 Ll. L. Rep. 123。案情是因 Edison 轮的过错把 Liesbosch Dredger 在港内工作的一艘疏浚船弄沉,但 Liesbosch Dredger 自己财力不够,无法很快买入另一艘疏浚船来代替。但港口当局逼迫它尽快进行工作,否则会采取行动如没收履行保证金等。Liesbosch Dredger 被迫租进另一艘疏浚船继续工作,这是更昂贵的做法并带来额外损失。贵族院判是受害方只能索赔一艘同类疏浚船的市场价格,加上直至在合理时间内买入另一艘替代疏浚船能去替代沉没的一艘期间内其他没法履行疏浚合约的损失。但一切因受害方经济差所带来的额外损失(主要是更长的延误与高价租入替代疏浚船的费用),所以不必赔偿。其中,Wright 勋爵是主要根据因果关系判受害方不能成功索赔这笔额外损失,说:"The appellants' actual loss in so far as it was due to their own impecuniosity arose from that impecuniosity as a separate and concurrent cause, extraneous to and distinct in character from the tort; the impecuniosity was not traceable to the respondents' acts, and in my opinion was outside the legal purview of the consequences of these acts."

但这一先例看来把穷困带来的额外损失视为与被告的侵权行为没有直接关系,不像是指受害方没有合理减少损失。而且这一先例与贵族院较早的另一个以减少损失的大原则看待的先例也不一致,这是 Collins 勋爵在 Clippens Oil Co. v. Edinburgh and District Water Trustees(1907)A. C. 291 先例说:"... if the position of the latter is aggravated because he is without the means of mitigating it, so much the worse for the wrongdoer, who has to be answerable for the consequences flowing from his tortious act."

在 The"Liesbosch"先例,贵族院也没有否定 Clippens Oil 案例,Wright 勋爵只是说:"(前一先例)dealing not with the measure of damage, but with victim's duty to mitigate damage, which is quite a different matter."(Clippens Oil 先例是针对合理减少损失,这是另一码事。)

但这两个先例就带来了混乱,就是不确定穷困应该是遥远性的问题还是合理减少损失的问题。如果两个大原则都有关,就拿不准在哪一点就可以不必理会遥远性的问题而让减少损失大原则接手。总之它们之间的界限很难分清,但两个不同大原则会带来截然不同的结果。

The"Liesbosch"先例与 Clippens Oil 先例之后有不少案例可以部分介绍,如下:

(1)Trans Trust SPRL v. Danubian Trading Company Ltd (1952)2QB 297:案情是有关一个 1000 吨钢材的 FOB 买卖,以信用证付款,该案例的原告与被告都是中间商,但在他们之间的合约中,原告是卖方。作为中间商的卖方能够向上一个卖方开出信用证往往是需要买方的信用证作为担保,这才可以让卖方的银行视为有足够担保可以替他开出信用证(所谓的"背靠背信用证")或作出融资。正如 Denning 勋爵所解释:"He may, for instance, be himself a merchant, who is buying the goods from the growers or the manufacturers, and has to pay for them before he can get delivery; and his own bank will only grant him facilities for the purpose if he has the backing of a letter of credit."但在本案例,原告与被告的协议更加干脆,就是要求最后的美国买方开出信用证给最后的卖方,也就是原告的卖方,作为受益人。结果美国买方没有开出信用证,这导致被告对原告违约/毁约,而原告也对最后的卖方(也就是钢材的生产商)违约/毁约。没有开出信用证是一个明确的违约/毁约,责任无需质疑,争议还是在损失的计算。被告的争辩是原告可以向最后卖方履行开出信用证或作出支付,就不会对最后买方有责任或造成如此大的利润损失。显然这就涉及原告到底有没有财力或能力这样做以减少损失的问题。上诉庭认为原告由于穷困或无法支付最后卖方的损失是在双方订买卖合约时可以料想到的,Denning 勋爵是这样说:"It was... said that the damages were the result of the impecuniosity of the sellers and that it was a rule of law that such damages are too remote. I do not think there is any such rule. In the case of breach of contract, it depends on whether the damages were reasonably foreseeable or not. In the present case they clearly were."(被告作为买方说是原告作为卖方的贫穷所带来的损失涉及损失遥远性的大原则,Denning 勋爵说没有这一个规定,针对违约的损失,只是看有关损失是否能够合理预见,而在本案例是清楚可以预见。)但接下去 Denning 勋爵也有针对合理减少损失,说:"There is one way, however, in which the buyer might be able to rely on the rise in price. It might be a ground for mitigation of damages. I can well understand that the buyer might in some cases be able to say that the seller ought to have offered the goods elsewhere and got someone else to provide a letter of credit. But no such case can be made here. The seller acted very reasonably throughout. He kept the matter open for the buyer in the hope and expectation that the credit would be provided, and eventually lost his own option because the credit was not provided. He has, therefore, lost his profit without any fault on his part and is entitled to recover it from the buyer as damages."(这大致上是说原告作为卖方并没有不合理减少损失)看来在本先例,Denning 勋爵是把原告的穷困视为合理减少损失的问题,与损失遥远性的合理预见没有关系,也没有针对因果关系的大原则。

(2)Robbins of Putney v. Meek (1971) R. T. R. 345:受害方因穷困而过早把被拒的货物处理掉,但法院判这不影响受害方的索赔。

(3)Martindale v. Duncan (1973) 1 W. L. R. 574 (C. A.)与 Bunclark v. Hertfordshire C. C. (1977) 243 E. G. 381 and 455:受害方的穷困带来修理的延误,但法院判这不影响受害方的索赔。

(4)在 Wroth v. Tyler (1974) Ch 30 先例,涉及房屋买卖,双方在订合约时料想到了房价上升。被告是知道原告受害方的穷困的,法院认为这是一个针对原告能否减少损失的有关考虑,并判是:"... had no financial resources beyond [the price] that they could have put together for the purchase of [the seller's house]... [The purchasers] were therefore to the [seller's] knowledge unable at the time of breach to raise a further 1,500 pounds to purchase an equivalent house forthwith, and so... mitigate their loss."

(5)但在 Dodd Properties v. Canterbury City Council (1979) 2 All E. R. 118,涉及原告的房屋被被告的地基作业损坏,但拖了 10 年也不修理。法院判是不能索赔 10 年后高昂的修理费用,只应是赔偿造成损坏当时的市场价格。在这一先例,上诉庭是以受害方有否合理减少损失作为考虑,Megaw 大法官是这样说:"Once it is accepted that the plaintiff was not in any breach of any duty owed by him to the defendant in failing to carry out repairs earlier than the time when it was reasonably for the repairs to be put in hand, this becomes, for all practical purposes, if not in theory, equated with a plaintiff's ordinary duty to mitigate his damages."

(6)在 Wadsworth v. Lydall (1981) 1 WLR 598 先例,被告没有在最后限期支付 1 万英镑给原告,而且明知原告是需要这笔钱去买一个农场的。上诉庭判被告需要赔付原告因这一违约而要承担的额外利息与法律费用,并视为是一种"特别损失"(special damage)。

(7)在 Bacon v. Cooper (1982) 1 All ER 397 先例,案情涉及被告给原告出售一票不妥的钢料,把原告的碎裂机打烂。这导致原告把钢料碎裂的业务停顿,直到原告以"融资租赁"(hire purchase)的方式买进一个新的转轮(rotor)以替代损坏了的老转轮。以融资租赁的方式是由于原告的财力不足以买入一个新的转轮,但也多花了融资的钱。这被判是可以向被告索赔。

(8) 在一个近期有关侵权的贵族院先例,Lagden v. O Connor (2004) 1 AC 1067,案情涉及原告的车子由于被告的疏忽而损坏,但原告由于没办法支付定金,不能向一般的租车公司租入一个替代的车辆,而要以更高昂的办法"accident hire"(这一办法不需要支付定金)租入。贵族院的多数判是原告可以向被告索赔这一笔更高的损失,Hope 勋爵说:"... requires the wrongdoer to bear the consequences if it was reasonably foreseeable that the injured party would have to borrow money or incur some other kind of expenditure to mitigate his damages."可以说针对侵权案件,这一先例已经明确了原告的穷困不影响他索赔所有的损失。

(9) 回去违约/毁约涉及穷困的问题,在本书第四章之 9. 2. 2 段介绍过的 Geofizika v. MMB International & Greenfields (2010) 1 Lloyd's Rep 458 先例,不重复案情,只说原告 Geofizika 作为买方因为被告 MMB 的违约而蒙受损失,但由于原告的穷困,导致了额外的损失。英国高院认定没有证据显示 MMB 在订约时是知道 Geofizika 的穷困, Mackie 大法官是这样说:"There is no evidence that MMB knew of these genuine difficulties and, as I see it, it could not reasonably have foreseen that such expenses would be not unlikely to result from any breach."(这是判 MMB 无法合理预见到有这种困难与这种花费。)

(10) 在 The "Asia Star" (2010) 2 Lloyd's Rep 12,有关的案情在本章第 5. 2. 6 段已有详述。只说在该先例的上诉,受害方多提出了一个他为什么没有租入替代船舶 Puma 轮的解释,就是多支付 399,500 美元的运费差价对公司是一个沉重的经济负担。Rajah 大法官简单针对穷困导致损失扩大或不能合理减少损失,说:"The respondent's impecuniosity argument is based on the principle set out in para 7 - 088 of《McGregor on Damages》that "[an aggrieved party] will not be prejudiced by [its] financial inability to take steps in mitigation" [emphasis in original]. This principle appears to be a corollary of the eggshell - skull rule that the defaulting party must take the aggrieved party as it finds the latter. If the position of the aggrieved party is aggravated because it lacks the mean to mitigate the loss suffered, the defaulting party nevertheless remains answerable for the consequences flowing from its wrongful act (see Clippens Oil Co Ltd v. Edinburgh and District Water Trustees [1907] AC 291 at page 303). Applied in the context of a claim for damages for breach of contract, this rule entails that, so long as the aggrieved party acts reasonably to mitigate its loss, it will not be the disbarred from pursu-

ing its claim for the actual loss suffered simply because it was unable to take certain mitigation measures which it could otherwise have taken had it had the requisite financial resources."（穷困与"鸡蛋壳头壳"是同一个必然的推论，即违约/侵权方碰到了怎样的受害方，就要承担这些后果。只要受害方合理减少损失，他就不会因为他没有财力采取某一些减少损失的行为而无法取回损失。）

9.2 侵权与违约如何针对穷困带来额外损失或无法减少损失

总结以上介绍的部分先例，其中有侵权也有违约，这就涉及如何看待受害方穷困所带来的损失。在大原则，侵权与违约在这方面都是应该一致，正如 Wright 勋爵在 Monarch SS Co v. Karlshamns Oljefabriker（1949）AC 196 先例所说："the difference in the result did not depend on the difference（if any）between contract and tort in this connection."

但这个观点在侵权方面前受到质疑，因为这方面早就有一个著名的说法，也多次在本书提及，就是 Wright 勋爵在 Bourhill v. Young（1943）A. C. 92 的名言："If the wrong is established the wrongdoer must take the victim as he finds him."如侵权造成了极大与不成比例的严重后果，如轻轻地碰受害方一下，就导致对方严重的伤害，原因可以是受害方身体衰弱或年老。还会有另一种情况是受害方可能因为侵权行为而遭受"意想不到严重"的经济损失。如果碰伤美国总统、香港首富，会面对天文数字索赔。或会是该首富一点不起眼，衣衫褴褛，所谓"shabby millionaire"，错误一方又会说谁能合理预见呢？但同样，法律是不接受这个抗辩，Scrutton 大法官在 The "Arpad"（1934）49 Lloyd's Rep 313 有以下的话："You negligently run down a shabby - looking man in the street, and he turns to be a millionaire engaged in a very profitable business which the accident disables him from carrying on; or you negligently and ignorantly injure the favourite for the Derby whereby he cannot run. You have to pay damages resulting from the circumstances of which you have no notice. You have to pay the actual loss to the man or his goods at the time of the tort."

这样的判法估计很大程度上是因为公共政策，因为不少侵权的案件涉及人身伤亡。但无法协调的就是为什么受害方的穷困会有不同对待，正如 Donaldson 大法官在 Dodd Properties v. Canterbury City Council（1979）2 All E. R. 118 先例中所说："it is not at once apparent why a tortfeasor must take his victim as he finds him in terms of exceptionally high or low profit - earning capacity, but not in terms of pecuniosity or impecuniosity which may be their manifestation."看来，侵权案件已经普遍把受害方的穷困导致损失扩大视为是侵权方可以预见的损失，而在因果关系也把受害方的贫穷与"鸡蛋壳头壳"的身体虚弱视为是已经存在的历史事实（这在第四章 9.2.2 段有介绍），这表示 The "Liesbosch"（1933）45 Ll. L. Rep. 123 先例的说法已经不被重视。事实上，这一方面针对侵权案件而言，已经是被 Lagden v. O Connor（2004）1 AC 1067 的贵族院先例所替代。这方面可节录《Mcgregor on Damages》（18th edn，2009 年）之 7 - 090

段:"Fortunately, this problem has now evaporated since at last the House of Lords in Lagden v. O'Connor has departed from Lord Wright's long controversial ruling in The Liesbosch. From now on therefore it matters not by which route the impecunious claimant is protected, the cross - over point need no longer be investigated and our rule based on Lord Collins's dictum need no longer be concerned that it may be displaced by arguments on remoteness."

而针对违约,受害方因穷困所带来的损失,看来是属于 Hadley v. Baxendale (1854) 9 Ex. 341 先例的第二条损失规则中的"特别损失"(special damages),这要看双方订合约时是否可以合理预见或料想得到。这方面可节录《Chitty on Contracts》(30th edn, 2008 年)之 26 - 106 段所说如下:"The claimant's impecuniosity will be relevant in contract if the second rule in Hadley v. Baxendale is satisfied viz if, at the time of contracting, the contract - breaker had actual knowledge of special circumstances under which a breach was likely to cause the claimant greater or different loss from that to be normally expected under normal circumstances. The claimant's impecuniostiy could be a 'special circumstance' under this rule if, with his knowledge of it, the defendant could foresee that the claimant could mitigate his loss caused by the breach only by incurring greater expense than would be incurred by a financially secure person. The claimant must act 'reasonably' in his mitigating actions but what is reasonable for a claimant known to be impecunious may be different from the case of a person with financial resources."

10. 预期违约

10.1 有关预期违约所带来的困难

在"违约"(breach)、"毁约"(repudiation)后,受害方应当在可能的范围内采取合理的行动减轻违约/毁约引发的损失,否则他不能对采取合理行动本可避免的损失获得赔偿,这是"减少损失"(mitigation)的最基本精神或是本章第 2 段所介绍的第一条规则。也会有情况是违约的后果暂时看不出来,如一栋房子的缺陷。这一来,就有说法是在缺陷暴露出来或受害方应该知道这一缺陷时就有了减少损失的"责任":Youell v. Bland Welch & Co Ltd (1990) 2 Lloyd's Rep 431;Toepfer v. Warinco (1978) 2 Lloyd's Rep 569。

但还有一种违约称为"预期违约"(anticipatory breach 或 renunciation)的合理减少损失"责任"就比较复杂了。这里首先是要解释什么是预期违约,就是在履行的时间尚未到或尚未完成,履行方已明确以行动或者文字表示他不会履约,或表示他只会以非合约规定的方式来履行(如必须加价或减价),这就构成了预期违约。这种情况经常发生,就是预期违约方会把话说过头。例如船东威胁承租人说如果不给船员支付奖金,就命令船员以后不为你干活。或是租客对房东说房价市场下跌,你如果不同意减租,我就会延迟支付下一期的租金。反正这种威胁性的过火语言经常会发生,这种违反后来的合约履行的言论,都会是预期违约。英国普通法很早就已经有先例说预期违约虽然是针对后来的合约履行,但本身就是一个"现有的违约"(present breach),可以让受害方"接受"(accept)终断合约并马上提出损失的索赔:Hochster v. De La Tour (1853) 2 El & Bl 678。在这方面 Esher 勋爵在 Johnston v. Milling (1886) 16 QBD 460 先例有权威的说法如下:"A renunciation of a contract, or, in other words, a total refusal to perform it by one party before the time for performance arrives, does not, by itself, amount to a breach of contract but may be so acted upon and adopted by the other party as a rescission of the contract as to give an immediate right of action. Where one party assumes to renounce the contract, that is, by anticipation refuses to perform it, he thereby, so far as he is concerned, declares his intention then and there to rescind the contract... The other party may adopt such renunciation of the contract by so acting upon it as in effect to declare that he too treats the contract as at an end, except for the purpose of bringing an action upon it for the damages sustained by him in consequence of such renunciation."

针对减少损失的大原则而言,在这种情况下受害方的"责任"应该没有问题,就是在接受预期违约终断合约后就马上有了这一减少损失的"责任"。但困难是在另一种情况,也就是受害方在对方预期违约下另有一个被称为是"不受节制的选择"(unfettered discretion),就是拒绝接受该违约并坚持对方履行合约。这第二个选择也在 Johnston v. Milling 先例中有提到,Cotton 大法官是这样说:"The promisee, if he pleases, may treat the notice of intention as inoperative, and await the time when the contract is to be executed, and then hold the other party responsible for all the consequences of non - performance; but in that case he keeps the contract alive for the benefit of the other party as well as his own; he remains subject to all the obligations and liabilities under it, and enables the other party not only to complete the contract, if so advised, notwithstanding his previous repudiation of it, but also to take advantage of any supervening circumstances which would justify him in declining to complete it."

这种情况在现实中也经常出现,如在航运市场下跌时,承租人向船东说,你不必把船舶开来交船地点,因为我不会接船,也不会履行我们较早时候订立的三年期租合约。但船东拒绝接受这一预期违约并坚持承租人必须履行有关的期租合约,并对承租人作出威胁,如表示会扣押承租人的船舶或冻结他的资产。这最后导致承租人回心转意,到要履行的时候乖乖地接船。这一来,正如 Asquith 大法官在 Howard v. Pickford Tool Co Ltd (1951) 1 KB 417 先例中所说,较早前没有被船东接受的预期违约就好像"没有发生过的镜花水月"(a thing writ in water)。

当然在责任方面,预期违约的课题还有许多其他困难的地方,但这不是本书所针对的重点,只简单一提。例如,有说法是接受预期违约终断合约的受害方是否能够证明他自己是否是“备妥与愿意”(ready and willing)履行有关的合约。因为如果受害方自己也是不能履行,就没有理由向对方索赔损失。正如在 D. T. R. Nominess Pty. Ltd v. Mona Homes Pty. Ltd (1978) 138 CLR 423 先例中所讲:“A party in order to be entitled to rescind for anticipatory breach must at the time of recission himself be willing to perform the contract on its proper interpretation. Otherwise he is not an innocent party, the common description of a party entitled to rescind for anticipatory breach...”但在较近期的一个澳大利亚高院的判决看来,这受害方的备妥与愿意的举证责任十分轻微,很多情况下更可以被假设:Foran v. Wight (1989) 168 CLR 385。

另一个在责任方面经常带来困扰的是受害方如果拒绝接受预期违约,就表示有关的合约仍是有效。这表示受害方也必须继续履行他的合约责任,除非他的履行是直接受到对方预期违约的影响。这一来,其他的一些合约法理论就可能会适用,包括“禁止反供”(estoppel)、“阻止原则”(prevention principle)、法律不要求受害方做无谓的事情等。在这些合约法理论下,就不能让违约/毁约方事后指受害方既没有接受预期违约终断合约,但他自己也没有履行合约。这方面有不少先例,如近期香港终审法院的一个十分详尽针对的先例 Kensland Realty Ltd v. Whale View Investment Ltd & Anor (2001) 4 HKCFAR 381。笔者希望能通过假设一个简单的例子说得更清楚,就是一个 CIF 卖方在付运前收到买方因为市场下跌而拒绝接受货物的通知,但卖方拒绝接受这一个预期违约并坚持买方收货。但由于买方持续拒货而导致了卖方没有准时从装港付运这批货物去卸港,这导致买方在诉讼的抗辩中指卖方自己也违反了有关合约的条件条文,也就是准时付运。这种情况看来是卖方作为受害方值得同情,毕竟买方的预期违约是与卖方的不履行有直接关系,卖方付出昂贵的费用把货物运到卸港而不被买方接受会导致更严重的损失与更被动的情况。但如果这批货物不是运给订立合约并拒绝将来支付货价的买方而是运给第三人,并且第三人也从来没有表示拒绝接受这批货物。在这种情况下,卖方没有准时付运就可能会有问题,因为买方的预期违约或拒绝履行与卖方的不履行看来没有直接的因果关系,阻止原则看来也不完全适用。

笔者回归探讨损失方面,就是给予受害方在对方预期违约下这一个不受节制的选择是否终断合约的法律地位也带来了两个方面的困难,一是与受害方需要合理减少损失的“责任”有冲突,二是与“有效益违约”(efficient breach)的说法有冲突。以下进一步分析。

10.2 受害方不接受预期违约终断合约是没有减少损失的“责任”

根据较早前的假设,预期违约不被接受就表示合约一直有效存在,直到需要履行合约的时候如果违约方仍然拒绝履行,如在较早介绍的例子中,承租人拒绝受害方船东的交船,这构成了实际的“违约/毁约”(repudiation),船东作为受害方才有了减少损失的“责任”。在这以前,如果受害方船东选择不接受承租人的预期违约,则法律上认为该三年的租约一切如常，所以不存在要受害方船东减少损失的问题：Shindler v. Northern Rainco at Co. Ltd. （1960）2 All ER 239。事实上，在这期间如果船东有其他很好的机会，如另一个租金相比市场很不错的租约，船东也不敢或不应该试图订立。因为船东这样做很危险，他会被夹在两个租约之间，因为原来的三年租约仍然有效。船东也千万别考虑减少损失，因为合约依然有效，双方唯一的责任就是严格履行合约。至于稍后在交船时发生了实际的违约/毁约，承租人作为违约方是不能指称船东为什么没有在较早前有机会出租但不加以理会去减少损失的，因为船东是没有这一"责任"的。

这种情况在 White and Carter(Councils) Ltd. v. McGregor （1962） A. C. 413 的先例中出现。该案例的原告为当地议会长期提供垃圾箱，他与被告签约在垃圾箱上为被告的修车场业务做广告，为期 3 年。被告于签约当日后即反悔并且说明他的预期违约。大概是被告的想法有了改变，在垃圾箱上做自己的业务广告，人家会想"我的车拿到你那里修理恐怕真的要变成垃圾啦"，谁还敢找你！或是认为这样做广告功效不显著，有其他更好的办法。反正是被告在合约墨迹未干时就要反悔。可原告并不接受被告的预期违约，继续按照合约为被告做广告（也真够损的），整整 3 年！最后原告索赔依据合约履行他应得的收费（广告费）。上诉庭以多数意见判定原告可全数索回其履约应得的收费，原告可以选择接受被告的预期违约去终断合约并索赔违约/毁约的损失。而一天没终断合约，就不存在有减少损失"责任"的说法。结果原告胜诉并把所有的合约收费成功取回。但该先例中也有少数法官认为，原告本应终断合约以减少损失，因为他本可接受对方预期违约而从那时起索赔有关损失，如将来估计的利润等，但原告却选择了花费更多的钱去执行一个对方不再需要的合约。这虽然没有违反合理减少损失的大原则，但整体说是一种无谓的浪费，这正是违反了有效益违约的说法。这听来也不无道理，但毕竟这个判例更倾向于支持另一种大原则，即受害方有权选择是否接受预期违约。

另一提的就是 White and Carter(Councils) Ltd. v. McGregor 先例也有对受害方自由选择是否接受预期违约终断合约加了两个限制。第一个限制就是受害方如果再也没有"重大与合法利益"（substantial and legitimate interest），就不能再坚持不接受预期违约，这方面会在本章 10.4 段进一步详论。第二个限制就是受害方的原告可以单方面履行合约，不需要违约方的合作，才可以坚持履行，并且把预期违约本来应该带来的损失计算变为在履行后"债务"（debt）的索赔，进而避开了减少损失的"责任"。但这种做法在很多需要双方合作才能履行的合约中是不可行的。如在买卖合约中，如果买方作出预期违约，说明不要这批货。就很难想象卖方怎么能坚持把这批货硬交出给买方，并进一步索赔货价的债务。另一种合约也必须是双方合作才能履行的就是雇佣合约，否则雇员硬要上班，雇主还是可以把他拒之门外。所以好像雇佣合约，就不存在受害方雇员可以不接受预期违约，坚持要履行合约的情况。

10.3 不接受预期违约会与有效益违约的说法有冲突

从合理减少损失的实际效用,亦即受害方如采取合理行动本不应该产生的损失不能获得赔偿这一角度来看,这一大原则也可以被视为一种防止整体经济上资源浪费的有效手段。在这个意义上看,减少损失甚至可以说是对"有效益违约"(efficient breach)的鼓励,是符合发挥社会或全世界总体经济效益的需要。实际上,如果违约方在依法按照合约赔偿受害方损失后,尚能从另一项生意中获取比原合约"更大的收益"(a greater benefit),或是可避免比赔偿受害方损失更大的损失,那么在整体的经济活动等于是发挥了更好的效益。毕竟,在无损对方的前提下(指受害方可通过损失赔偿的救济恢复到合约被履行一样的经济地位),违约方为追求更大的利益而抛弃原合约也没什么大不了的。正是由于有受害方应当合理减少损失这一个对损失赔偿的限制,让商业社会的实务中不必太墨守合约严格不可破坏的信条。为获得更大利益,在可行的情况下违约/毁约也无妨。由于损失赔偿是补偿性的,受害方如果没有实际损失,责任方面胜诉也只能取得"象征性赔偿"(nominal damage)。同时,法律上对受害方也有合理减少损失的要求,因此,在适当的情况下违约/毁约对某一方来说并不失为一种好的选择。以下不妨在"有效益违约"这一方面举一些笔者熟悉的租船业务的先例。

10.3.1 "有效益违约"例子之一

船东与一家巴拿马公司的承租人刚订立了一份2年的期租合约,随后有一家信誉很好的大公司要来租这条船,一租5年,租金等各方面的条件都很优厚。这时如果船东考虑过取消已订2年租约将要承担的赔偿责任后,仍然认为将船舶期租5年更有利,那么船东大可以与后一家大公司签约并对原来2年的承租人作出预期违约,并愿意赔偿损失。另说明第一份租约的承租人是一家巴拿马公司,这表示2年租约的承租人信誉与财力也有问题,更加表示船东预期违约可能是一个非常明智的做法。如果在预期违约时的航运市场同类船舶多的是,而且租金下跌,那么该巴拿马承租人根本不会有什么损失,因他可以找到更便宜的船舶替代,要索赔也只能拿象征性赔偿。即使市场租金涨了,比租约价格高,要赔偿巴拿马承租人的差价损失也已是船东另订5年租约前已考虑进去的。更可以放心的是法律要求巴拿马承租人有合理减少损失的义务,他不能听任航运市场租金一路上涨而不尽快租回替代船舶,否则租金再上涨的额外损失船东也不用赔偿。

10.3.2 "有效益违约"例子之二

例如期租中最后航次的卸港距离租约规定的还船地点很远,如卸港是在波斯湾,但租约的还船地订在日本,而且船舶在卸港附近也不难找到下一个航次的租约(只是前往日本方向的不一定有)。显然,明智的承租人会有很大的诱因不理租约,卸完货物就坚持在波斯湾卸港还船,等于故意作出预期违约的通知,因为按照合约他应该继续履行把船舶开去日本才能还船。如果船东接受承租人的预期违约,就要合理减少损失,如在波斯湾附近找其他租约,船东也不受制于下一个航次的目的地,因为再也不存在要在日本还船的问题了。这样一来,船东如果有损失,即使是计算会比较复杂,但肯定是会比承租人如果循规蹈矩地履行租约,将船舶空放回日本交船地点的航次费用(燃油、港口费等)与继续支付给船东的租金为低。

10.3.3 "有效益违约"例子之三

再举一个期租的例子。租约规定租期是1年,租金2万美元/天,结果离租期届满前10天,承租人已完成了计划中的最后航次。当时租金市场跌得很厉害,这类船租金只有1万美元/天,这样承租人就很为难了。一方面船东当然坚持要承租人至少在租期届满时才还船,能拖长一点更好,毕竟租约租金比市场租金高很多。而另一方面,承租人不可能这么巧找到刚好在短短10天就能够完成的航次,能找到的最短航次至少也要30天,而且实际往往会比估计更长。这等于"超出"(overlap)至少的一年租期20天,租金仍按合约的2万美元/天计算(不论是否超过约定的最长 maximum 租期),这20天的租金等于每天比当时市场租金要多1万美元,总数即多付20万美元,但如果让船闲置10天专门等租期届满就还船,也是要白白支付10天租金的20万美元。这时承租人最现实的办法就是预期违约,跟船东说:"我现在正式还船给你,终断租约。"甚至这话早讲以免浪费船东要减少损失到市场找下一个租约的时间。船东会要接受承租人的预期违约,因为不接受的话会在将来面对承租人的指控,就是没有"重大与合法利益"(substantial and legitimate interest)的情况下坚持租约必须维持,直到10天后租期届满。与其让船干等10天,还不如尽快找其他生意,否则就有可能因为没有合理减少损失,日后连损失都索赔不回来,更何况打官司本身已是劳民伤财,也不肯定。这样一来,船东就会尽快把船再租出去,除非他这10天内一直不能把船舶租出去,而且没有不合理的成份,承租人要赔偿的只是10天租金扣减船东这10天找到的替代租约的收入(替代租约的收入就会是减少损失的成果)。而且对于船东来讲,这10天内他找下一个租约在灵活性与伸缩性比承租人多,他可以找任何或长或短的期租、程租又或是"航次期租"(Time Charter Trip),也不必受制于任何不同的卸港或营运地点。这些选择都是考虑船东有否合理减少损失的因素,船东如果说他只会寻找与原租约一样的1年租约与交船地点就不合理,因为不必局限自己。

10.3.4 "有效益违约"例子之四

期租承租人常常会遇到要将船舶在还船前修妥的问题。一个租期届满,有时候船舶难免会有一些小损坏(如在最后一个航次中有承租人雇佣的小工造成或是不安全泊位造成)。但根据一般的期租租约,还船的状况要如同当初交船时一样良好(正常损耗除外)。因此是按照期租合约,承租人必须把船舶修好后再还船。但这一来,无疑承租人要多付修理期间的租金,而且如果还船地点是美国、欧洲等地,会是不易安排与修理费用昂贵,令承租人即使想履行合约也非常头痛。更会有情况是在还船地点根本无法修理,或是修理需要的零件要等几个月才会有。但其间,该船舶可以继续营运,船级社也批准,就可以在营运中等待零件。这一来,承租人可以利用预期违约这一招告知船东不会进行修理就还船。如果船东说："不行，根据租约，你必须把船修理好再还"。承租人会回应说："修是肯定不修的了，船东如果在没有重大与合法利益去拒绝接船，加上这些损坏并不严重，根本不影响船舶的适航性，船东完全可以日后等待到更廉宜的地方修理或者等船舶进干坞年检才一并修理。现在船东坚持不接船明显是不合理，因此一切后果你自己承担。"

这方面是有一个著名的先例，The "Puerto Buitrago"（1976）1 Lloyd's Rep. 250，涉及一艘光船租约的还船，当时船舶有严重的损坏被拖去德国的 Kiel（这是一个修理费用昂贵的港口），而承租人也对部分的损坏承认需要修理的责任。船东拒绝承租人的还船，要求他履行光租合约修好船舶后才能还船。在第一审，Mocatta 大法官也是认为在预期违约的情况下，受害方船东有一个无限制的选择权不去接受，判承租人一定要把船舶修妥后才能还船，而其间必须继续支付租金。但去了上诉庭，该判决被推翻，上诉庭认为船东必须接受预期违约，并减少损失。Denning 勋爵是这样说："Either the charterers pay the charter hire for years to come, whilst the vessel lies idle and useless for want of repairs. Or the charterers must do repairs which cost twice as much as the ship would be worth when repaired."

10.3.5 "有效益违约"例子之五

同样理论也用在还船时不够期租租约规定的燃油数量，笔者记得看见过一个案件是希腊船东在还船时成功逼迫国内承租人先去另一港口（不是在最后的卸港，也就是承租人预计的还船港口）多添加 20 吨柴油才能还船。这多花了不少钱，而且延误好几天（当时市场下跌，这也是希腊船东能拖就拖的理由，可赚取租约高昂的租金）。这里涉及风险问题，如果船舶在另外的加油港遇上领航员或拖轮罢工等意外事件无法开去原来的港口还船，承租人一直支付昂贵租金可能要面对破产。显然，即使是燃油数量不足够，承租人还是希望坚持还船，这才是明智的做法。

总结，10.3.1 至 10.3.5 段举了不少有关租船下的承租人需要预期违约的例子，这才是比较明智与符合整体经济利益的做法。但要小心是最近有了 The "Aquafaith"（2012）EWHC1077（Comm）的先例，对受害方的船东是否需要接受预期违约终断租约有很大程度的放宽，这是会影响上述所举的例子，该先例会在本章 10.5 段介绍。

10.4 重大与合法利益理论的出现

在 White and Carter（Councils）Ltd. v. McGregor（1962）A. C. 413 先例，贵族院的多数大法官也看到了容许受害方无限制的选择是否接受预期违约会带来上述的一些问题，结果 Reid 勋爵在该先例中提出了一个说法或是限制，就是如果受害方没有一个"重大与合法利益"（substantial and legitimate interest）继续维持合约的存在，他就必须接受预期违约。Reid 勋爵是这样说："If I may revert to the example which I gave of a company engaging an expert to prepare an elaborate report and then repudiating before anything was done, it might be that the company could show that the expert had no substantial or legitimate interest in carrying out the work rather than accepting damages: I would think that the *de minimis* principle would apply in determining whether his interest was substantial, and that he might have a legitimate interest other than an immediate financial interest. But if the expert had no such interest then that might be regarded as a proper case for the exercise of the general equitable jurisdiction of the court. But that is not this case. Here the respondent did not set out to prove that the appellants had not legitimate interest in completing the contract and claiming the contract price rather than claiming damages; there is nothing in the findings of fact to support such a case, and it seems improbable that any such case could have been proved."

但这一重大与合法利益的说法并不容易适用，Reid 勋爵也没有说清楚这一分水线究竟如何划分。在上述节录的判词中，Reid 勋爵所举的例子是一家公司雇佣一位专家要求做出一份详细的报告，但在还未开始做报告之前公司就已经预期违约，告诉专家不再需要这份报告。这一来，Reid 勋爵认为该专家是没有重大与合法利益继续做报告，然后再向公司收取庞大的费用。专家必须接受预期违约并索赔损失，这损失就是专家失去这份工作所损失的利润，但专家必须减少损失寻找替代的工作，这会在很大程度上减少公司的赔偿。但问题是与 White and Carter (Councils) Ltd. v. McGregor 先例的分水线究竟在哪里，毕竟该先例中在垃圾箱刊登广告的原告与 Reid 勋爵举例中的专家有什么不同是很难区分的。有说法是把受害方对违约/毁约方的"不合理做法"（这是在他有权选择时可以做的）与"完全不合理做法"作出区分，显然是十分困难。在 The "Dynamic" (2003) 2 Lloyd's Rep 693 先例，Simon 大法官是认为"完全"并没有特别的意思，反正就是要极端的情况才会要求受害方必须接受违约方的预期违约，说："Although, the use of the qualifying word wholly in the expression wholly unreasonable in the Odenfeld property emphasizes that the rule is general and the exception only applies in extreme cases, it adds nothing to the text."

所以，在 The "Puerto Buitrago" (1976) 1 Lloyd's Rep. 250 先例，Denning 勋爵判是船东必须接受承租人的预期违约，并针对 White and Carter (Councils) Ltd. v. McGregor 先例是这样说："The decision has been criticized in a leading textbook... it is said to give a 'grotesque' result. Even though it was a Scots case, it would appear that the House of Lords, as at present constituted, would expect us to follow it in any case that is precisely on all fours with it. But I would not follow it otherwise. It has no application whatever in a case where the plaintiff ought, in all reason, to accept the repudiation and sue for damages — provided that damages would provide an adequate remedy for any loss suffered by him."

Denning 勋爵这段话的意思是说他不会依照 White and Carter (Councils) Ltd. v. McGregor 的苏格兰先例（虽然上诉去了枢密院，审理的大法官与贵族院一样），认为只要在合情合理的情况下，受害方必须接受预期违约，并索赔损失，只要损失赔偿是足够的救济。也可以说是在这种情况下受害方再也没有一个重大与合法利益不接受预期违约。但上诉庭其余的两位 Orr 大法官与 Browne 大法官虽然是与 Denning 勋爵得出同一个结果,但主要是与 White and Carter(Councils) Ltd. v. McGregor 先例的事实作出区分。

同样的说法在 The "Odenfeld"(1978)2 Lloyd's Rep. 357 先例,看来是重大与合法利益就是看损失赔偿是否足够的救济与受害方不接受预期违约是否完全不合理。Kerr 大法官是说:"... in extreme cases, viz, where damages would be an adequate remedy and where an election to keep the contract alive would be wholly unreasonable."(极端的例子,就是损失赔偿是足够的救济,而且选择让合约继续有效是完全不合理的。)

另也可以介绍一个加拿大最高院的判例,名为 Asamera Oil Corp Ltd v. Sea Oil & General Corp (1979) 1 SCR 633,案情涉及被告违约没有退还股票给原告。该股票在违约时价值是每股 0.29 加元,但后来在市场上涨到超过 45 加元,到了开庭审理的一天,价值变为 21 加元。这表示选择哪一天的股票价值计算损失会带来重大区别,差别会高达数以百万加元。最高院判是原告在违约后的一段合理时间内应该在股票市场购买替代股票以减少损失,这带来了一个争议是原告申请的履约指令(本书第十二章)是否解除了原告减少损失的"责任"。Estey 大法官是这样说:"It is, of course, an eminently reasonable position to take if, as Lord Reid suggests in White and Carter (Councils) Ltd. v. McGregor, in the case of anticipatory breach, there is substantial and legitimate interest in looking to performance of a contractual obligation. So a plaintiff who has agreed to purchase a particular piece of real estate, or a block of shares which represent control of a company, or has entered into performance of his own obligation and where to discontinue performance might aggravate his losses, might well have sustained the position that the issuance of a writ for specific performance would hold in abeyance the obligation to avoid or reduce losses by acquisition of replacement property. Yet, even in these cases, the action for performance must be instituted and carried on with due diligence. This is but another application of the ordinary rule of mitigation which insists that the injured party act reasonably in all of the circumstances. Where those circumstances reveal a substantial and legitimate interest in seeking performance as opposed to damages, then a plaintiff will be able to justify his inaction and on failing in his plea for specific performance might then recover losses which in other circumstances might be classified as avoidable and thus unrecoverable; but such is not the case there."(这一段话的意思就是如果受害方对该合约的履行是有一个重大与合法的利益,他就可以不接受预期违约,也没有责任减少损失。例如,受害方认为如果终断履行会导致他的损失加大,他会考虑向法院申请履约指令,强制对方履行合约。这一来,他就可以延后作出任何减少损失的行动,如买入替代的股票。但即使申请履约指令,法律是要求受害方尽快作出申请。这等同于是从另一个方面减少损失,要求受害方要合情合理。在这种情况下,就显示了受害方对

合约的履行是有一个重大与合法利益的,他就有权不行动。)

最后一提的是稍后在 10.5 段将会介绍的 The "Aquafaith" (2012) EWHC1077 (Comm)先例也有全面针对什么是重大与合法利益。

接下去的段节会先介绍在 White and Carter(Councils) Ltd. v. McGregor 先例后的一些著名先例。

10.4.1 有关案例之一:The "Odenfeld"

在 The "Odenfeld" (1978) 2 Lloyd's Rep. 357 先例,涉及一个长达 10 年的期租租约,在履行了大约 2 年后的 1975 年,运费市场暴跌。承租人在 1976 年 1 月发出通知拒绝继续支付租金,这显然是一个预期违约。但船东肯定是不接受,双方僵持到 1976 年 9 月,承租人向法院申请要一个宣告判决,说明租约在 1976 年 1 月就已经终断。在高院,Kerr 大法官考虑了 White and Carter(Councils) Ltd. v. McGregor(1962) A.C. 413 与 The "Puerto Buitrago" (1976) 1 Lloyd's Rep. 250 两个主要先例,认为它们是有约束力并且局限了受害方有一个几乎是没有限制的权利拒绝接受预期违约,说:"... a presently binding authority on this Court in limiting or qualifying the generality of the principle of a virtually unfettered right of election in favour of the innocent party."

但 Kerr 大法官认为直到 1976 年 9 月,受害方船东还是有权选择不接受承租人的预期违约,这也是他所需要做出判决计算损失的一段时间。但针对在余下的时间内(这是一个 10 年长的租约)船东什么时候必须接受违约,他看来就有一点犹豫不决,说:"However, in saying this I must not be thought to be implying that Occidental (船东) and the plaintiffs(原告是租金的受让人) could necessarily have maintained the same position for a further six years. As was pointed out by the Court of Appeal in the Decro - Wall case (Decro - Wall International SA v. Practitioners in Marketing Ltd [CA] [1971] 1 WLR 361), the reality is that deadlocked situations of this kind are usually resolved by the practicalities. Moreover, the passage of time might in itself alter the legal position of the parties, because an insistence to treat the contract as still in being might in time become quite unrealistic, unreasonable and untenable. I am only saying that in my view on the facts of the present case this had not happened by September, 1976."

10.4.2 有关案例之二:The "Alaskan Trader"

在 The "Alaskan Trader" (No. 2) (1983) 2 Lloyd's Rep. 645 先例也涉及同样的问题。案情是有关一个 2 年的期租租约,履行了 11 个月后,船舶主机出了严重故障,结果一修就是半年(这期间自然算停租)。期间租约市场也在下跌。所以承租人拒绝在修理完毕后接受该船舶,可以说是单方面终断了租约。实际上这构成了预期违约,因为就算船舶有严重问题,不适航要修理,承租人也只能停租,而不能取消合约,这方面是有著名的先例 The "Hongkong Fir" (1961) 2 Lloyd's Rep 478。但船东并不接受承租人的预期违约(因为还没有到租期届满),导致船舶在修妥后的 8 个月(直到 2 年租期的期租租约届满的一天)一直处于待命听候承租人调度状态,船东也不理会承租人要求他另找替代租约以减少损失的要求,反而配备全套船员。船东是有该租约租金的担保,因为承租人开出了一份备用信用证作为履约的保证,这令船东根本不必担心收不到钱,反正到时候就向银行结汇。所以,这一个诉讼反而是承租人向船东要求退还多支付的租金,约200万美元,这是假设船东应该在承租人作出预期违约的时候接受。在伦敦仲裁,独任仲裁员判是船东没有一个重大与合法利益继续这个租约,所以必须归还多收取的200万美元租金。裁决书是这样说:

"The Charterers refused to accept the vessel and made it clear they never would. At that stage, there was nothing contingent or anticipatory about the Charterers' action. It was clear that the charter was dead. The Owners, however, did not accept that the moribund condition of the charter was equivalent to termination in the legal sense. They contended that all was required of the vessel under the charter was that she should be at Charterers' disposal; the hire there by fell due and it would be unjust to permit the Charterers to avoid a debt by requiring the Owners to accept repudiation and claim damages.

There is a superficial logic in this argument but it is apt to lead to absurd situation. In this case, the Owners contend that they kept the vessel with a full crew and engine ready for over seven months, waiting for orders which they well knew would never come. I am satisfied that this commercial absurdity is not justified by a proper interpretation of the decided cases."

结果上诉去了高院,Lloyd大法官拒绝干预该裁决书,说:"... the Court would in the exercise of its general equitable jurisdiction, decline to grant the owners the remedy to which they would otherwise have been entitled, since they had no legitimate interest, financial or otherwise, in performing the contract rather than claiming damages, and that there was no error of law in the arbitrator's approach..."

10.4.3 有关案例之三:The"Dynamic"

在The"Dynamic"(2003) 2 Lloyd's Rep 693先例,是另一个同样问题。船舶以航次期租从中国大连装一船散装水泥去美湾的Myrtle Grove港,是说明在该港"领航员离船"(drop off pilot)的时候还船。船舶在Myrtle Grove港卸完水泥前的一天,承租人把船舶扣押,要求取得诉前担保以保障对船东的索赔。这导致船舶在8月3日卸完货,直到8月17日一直没有办法开航。承租人坚持在8月3日卸完货就已经是还船。而即使这说法不正确(因为还船根据合约是要开航与领航员离开船舶),还船是要在8月17日后,承租人辩称船东在承租人8月3日坚持还船并扣押船舶时就应该接受预期违约。如果船东真的接受预期违约而终断该航次期租租约,就表示接下去船舶被承租人扣押后直到8月17日,船东都会自己承担这一段时间的损失。正常想来,笔者认为承租人指称船东必须要接受承租人的预期违约是有点牵强的。在该判决,高院把裁决书退还给仲裁员,要求其重新作出考虑,在这里笔者想说的只是Simon大法官在考虑了所有的有关先例后,总结有关受害方到底在怎样的情况下才是必须接受违约方的预期违约,说:"These cases establish the following exception to the general rule that the innocent party has an option whether or not to accept a repudiation: (i) The burden is on the contract – breaker to show that the innocent party has no legitimate interest in performing the contract rather than claiming damages. (ii) This burden is not discharged merely by showing that the benefit to the other party is small in comparison to the loss to the contract breaker. (iii) The exception to the general rule applies only in extreme cases: where an election to keep the contract alive would be unreasonable."

10.4.4 有关案例之四:Reichman v. Beveridge

在这一方面还可以列举一个非海事的上诉庭先例,名为 Reichman v. Beveridge (2007) 1 P & CR 20 CA。案情有关一个长达5年的房屋租赁合约,被告是一家律师事务所。但三年之后,该律师事务所停止营业并终止支付租金。原告在一年后向被告成功索赔没有支付的一年租金,其间原告既没有终断租约,也没有试图终断租约再转租给第三人以减少损失。

10.4.5 重大与合法利益的不肯定

从上述有限的这方面先例看来,什么是受害方重大与合法利益的分水线并不明确。虽然案例发展下去也开始有了一些比较完整的说法,如在 The "Dynamic" (2003) 2 Lloyd's Rep 693 先例,Simon 大法官就已经比较有针对性地说,光是违约方的损失会比受害方的损失严重并不是一个足够的原因指称受害方就应该接受预期违约以终断合约。笔者早期在处理好几个伦敦仲裁案件时也感觉分水线并不明确。比如在一个程租租约中,如果在离开租约受载期还早的时候,承租人对船东说:"你的船不要来了,现在出口地政府禁止此类货物出口,我生意做不成了,要取消合约。"这等于是承租人的预期违约,因为依约为船舶提供指定货物的责任尚未到期,他就明确宣称不干了。但船东回应说:"我不接受你的预期违约,船舶还是一样会开航去装港。"之后船东真的让船舶空放10多天到装港,又等了一段时间后才肯面对现实终断程租租约。其间,承租人曾再三向船东强调因为出口禁令确实无法提供货物了。在这种情况下,笔者觉得船东不接受承租人预期违约而坚持派船空放到装港,扩大了损失,应该说是不能满足有"重大与合法利益"。这批货物因为出口禁令无法付运已是很明确,船东也知道承租人没有办法,加上装港附近也不容易找到合适的替代租约。这种情况下还是硬派船去装港只会增加费用与时间损失,船东自己也没有好处。否则如果船东一早在承租人预期违约的时候就接受,并寻找替代租约,损失会大幅度减少。这样看来,船东的行为实属完全不合理,他索赔损失也应该只能按若合理接受了承租人预期违约的情况来估计。但真正去了诉讼,也难保船东不会提出一些理由支持他这样做的合理性。例如,根据船东自己调查得知装港政府禁止有关货物出口的决定随时会有改变;或是程租租约是针对了几种替代货物,承租人是有责任提供其他不受禁令影响的货物,所以希望去装港迫使承租人履约等。

这方面的不肯定性可以一个笔者涉及的早期伦敦仲裁为例,在 The "Nyon" 一案，该船舶在1992年以航次期租被租来跑一个20天的航次，从印度Mangalore港装矿砂至印尼。承租人在确定租约的第二天，马上从发货人处知悉装港Mangalore刚发生大水灾，全港封闭，无限期的拒绝船舶去装矿砂。事后证实这封港延续一个月之久。反正在当时，承租人在7月25号发电文给船东告知此事，并紧急要求对方同意把早一天所订的航次期租租约终断。但船东回电说不答应，并坚持要求承租人履行租约。承租人只好请求船东"修改"(vary)租约，延长20天的租期并且交还船地点从Mangalore港改为去Madras港等，因为承租人可以有另一个航次自Madras港装货去日本。但船东要求是大幅度提高每天的租金，以致这修改租约提议也告吹。这迫使承租人在7月28号发出电传给船东说明："... Force Majeure has cancelled original cargo"。这电传看似不太明确是预期违约，但从船东的马上回电可见到这仍是被这样理解的。该回电是说："We must point out that it is not up to charterers to decide whether they 'agree to carry on the charter' or whether they should 'drop ship' which would be a repudiation of the charter."

此时，船舶一直从新加坡空放去装港Mangalore交船。之后承租人再有电文请船东不要继续去Mangalore港，免得浪费金钱，而替代生意在Mangalore港附近难找，反而在新加坡附近机会更好，但船东并不理会。直至船舶快到Mangalore港，承租人再度表明不会接船，船东才接受预期违约让租约终断，把船舶开回头，当时已是8月3号。可笑的是，该船舶找到的替代生意是在新加坡交船。

船东在伦敦仲裁提出索赔损失，是去Mangalore港兜了一圈的所有费用(包括昂贵的燃油)，金额不少。承租人认为船东完全不合理，该航次期租租约是明确了这个航次，不能另去他港装货(所以需要修改承租人才能去Madras港)，而他完全知道Mangalore港的封港，是公开消息。而且当时情况混乱，有不少消息是说会延长多个月而不是事后的一个月。所以在这种情况下，船东没有理由仍让船舶空跑一趟。

但裁决书作出后，判是该租约没有"受阻"(frustrated)，因为Mangalore港大水灾不影响船在港口外"交船"(delivery)等。这也不奇怪，因为受阻很难成立。但裁决书判船东可全数取回损失，说："... the charterers argued that the owners could have had no legitimate interest in continuing the voyage towards Margalore after they had been told on 25th July of the position. Such an argument could only avail the charterers if there had been a repudiatory breach after which the owners had sought to treat the contract as subsisting. But here there was no repudiatory breach until 3rd August, and at that time the owners accepted the charterers' breach."

裁决书接下去很正确的说船东在8月3号前没有减少损失的"责任"，所以不能怪责他继续派船舶往Mangalore港开，或不肯答应改去Madras港交船装货，因为该租约仍然存在。

但可以留意到仲裁庭忘了针对7月28号的相对明确预期违约(明确是在船东的回电中被理解为预期违约)，而承租人针对这方面的书面抗辩是说："The charter was terminated on 25/7/92. Alternatively, it was not later than 28/7/92 when it was repudiated. But the owners continued to press on with the vessel sailing towards Mangalore. By then, they have no legitimate interest to do so. "

所以,第三人是看不出裁决书有错,表面上是有理有据,但当事方是知道仲裁庭遗漏了主要之处,也有完整的文件证据证明,连船东也没有对这方面作出否认。问题是裁决书即使有错,也不一定有救济(remedy),特别是在对事实的认定方面。

10.5　这方面不肯定的可能解决办法

涉及预期违约没有被接受,合约仍然存在与有效的情况下不存在减少损失的"责任",看来英国法律应该参考美国法律。美国法律虽然也是有预期违约需要合理减少损失的说法,但就不区分到底受害方有没有接受预期违约,反正之前与之后都应该合理减少损失。

这在《McGregor on damages》(18th edn, 2009 年)之 7－030 段的最后一句所说如下:"It is salutary to look at the long held position in the United States where, as Lloyd J said, in The 'Alaskan Trader', 'the courts take the uncomplicated view that whether the repudiation is accepted or not, the innocent party is always obliged to mitigate his damages'"。该美国的先例是 Clark v. Marsiglia, 1 Denio 317 (NY 1845)。

但这在一个近期涉及租约的名为 The "Aquafaith" (2012) EWHC1077 (Comm) 的先例,看来还是重视受害方是否接受违约方作出预期违约的自由选择,而不是减少损失。该先例的案情涉及中国江苏沙钢集团下的沙钢船务有限公司(Shagang Shipping Co Ltd)在航运好景时长期期租(长达 5 年)了该艘船舶,但到了 2011 年 7 月 6 日,沙钢船务作为承租人决定提早还船,并通知船东在船舶完成航次并在中国卸货后,马上把船交还。但船东拒绝接受这一预期违约并开始了伦敦仲裁,其间船舶停在卸港等待进一步消息。伦敦仲裁的仲裁庭判是船东需要接受承租人提早还船的预期违约,并在终断租约后在航运市场营运以减少损失,最后向承租人索赔有关的损失。但船东不服,上诉去法院,这一个裁决被英国高院推翻。Cooke 大法官分析了所有有关的先例,从 White and Carter (Councils) Ltd. v. McGregor (1962) A. C. 413 的先例开始与接下去的 The "Puerto Buitrago" (1976) 1 Lloyd's Rep 250; The "Odenfeld" (1978) 2 Lloyd's Rep 357; The "Alaskan Trader" (No. 2) (1983) 2 Lloyd's Rep. 645; The "Dynamic" (2003) 2 Lloyd's Rep 693; Stocznia Gdanska SA v. Latvian Shipping Co (1996) 2 Lloyd's Rep 132 与 Reichman v. Beveridge (2007) Bus LR 412 先例。Cooke 大法官判仲裁庭错误裁决 White and Carter (Councils) Ltd. v. McGregor 先例不适用,认为期租合约是与该先例的合约本质一样,可以单方面履行合约,也就是船东不需要承租人的合作把租约履行完毕。他是这样说:"The question, to my mind, is very simple. Could the owners claim hire from the charterers under this time charter without the need for the charterers to do anything under the charter? The answer is yes. If the charterers failed to give any orders, the vessel would simply stay where it was, awaiting order but earning hire. Although the master is under the orders of the charterer, the master and crew are the servants of the owners and the ship is available to the charterers for any order they wish to give. Hire continues to be earned. Although the charterers are obliged under the terms of the charter to provide and pay for fuel, should the bunkers run out whilst awaiting orders, it is open to the owners to stem the vessel and to charge that to the charterers' account. In order to complete their side of the bargain, the owners do not need the charterers to do anything in order for them to earn the hire in question. The earning of hire after purported redelivery was not dependent on any performance by the charterers of their obligations."

这一来,本先例是与 White and Carter 先例一样,可以单方面履行合约的受害方船东可以自由选择接受或不接受预期违约去终断合约,除非受害方再也没有"重大与合法利益"(substantial and legitimate interest)。Cooke 大法官判是如果说受害方再也没有重大与合法利益,就必须是:(1)违约方必须证明受害方将来索赔损失是一个完全足够的救济;(2)违约方必须证明受害方的行为是完全不合理或荒谬/反常的。Cooke 大法官是这样说:"He (指仲裁员)understood the nature of the test when eliminating from his consideration anything other than that part of the speech of Lord Reid (这是指 White and Carter 先例中的 Reid 勋爵) which referred to 'no legitimate interest'. He ignored what was said by Lord Reid about the irrelevance of reasonableness in itself, and he ignored all the subsequent explanations of the meaning of 'legitimate interest', by reference to the need for the contract breaker to show that damages were an entirely adequate remedy and that the conduct on the part of the innocent party was beyond all reason, wholly unreasonable or, to use my expression perverse."

Cooke 大法官针对了本先例,第一个测试是对受害方的船东而言,将来的损失赔偿是否是一个足够的救济?他的答案是否定的,并说:"It is plain from the arbitrator's recitation of the submissions made by the parties that the owners had submitted that damages were an inadequate remedy because the charterers were in financial difficulty. The owners were therefore at risk of the charterers directing their limited funds to meet obligations to other parties, whilst delaying payment of any sums owing to the owners until the end of the charterparty and the assessment of what was due in damages. Instead of paying hire up front, semi-monthly in advance, with all the cashflow implications of that, the charterers wished to compel the owners to trade the vessel in mitigation of loss and leave themselves liberty to argue about the quantum of damages at the end of the relevant period and pay whatever they could at that stage...."

至于第二个测试是受害方的船东的行为(也就是拒绝接受承租人的预期违约)是否是完全不合理或荒谬/反常?Cooke 大法官也不认为是,其中涉及船舶去航运市场营运以减少损失。这显然不是太容易的事情,因为市场实在是太差。但 Cooke 大法官认为船东在终断合约后自己去市场营运相比租约仍然存在,让承租人自己转租

(期租合约都有条文允许这样做),结果没有什么不一样。所以没有必要强加在船东身上一个在市场营运减少损失的“责任”,而船东拒绝这样做也谈不上是完全不合理或荒谬/反常的。

总结,Cooke 大法官认为船东完全有重大与合法利益坚持承租人履行合约。从这个先例可以看出,承租人想甩掉一个亏大本的长期租约不是这么容易的,而且较早的部分先例如 The “Alaskan Trader” (1983) 2 Lloyd's Rep. 645 也会有疑问。不论承租人怎么样坚持提早还船,恐怕船东还是可以不理睬,反正就是不接受预期违约去终断租约。船东只需要等到支付租金的日期届满(期租通常是 15 天,预付一期租金),承租人如果不支付,船东就可以去仲裁庭要求作出一个中间裁决针对这一笔债务的支付。如果承租人想终断长期租约,看来需要满足上述提到的两个测试才能成功指称受害方的船东没有合法利益可拒绝接受预期违约。例如在第一个测试,会是在作出预期违约时提供给受害方一流银行担保可以足够赔付将来证明的损失。至于第二个测试,满足更加困难。这会是一些个别的情况,如受害方的船东有一个肯定机会把有关船舶(特别是一艘特殊用处的船舶)高价出售,如果这样做就可以大幅度减少甚至抵销了承租人单方面提早还船的预期违约。但承租人对有关船舶不拥有所有权,无法做同样的事情减少损失。另在较早的 10. 3. 1 至 10. 3. 5 段举了不少有关租船下的承租人需要预期违约的例子,才是比较明智与符合整体经济利益的做法,也在 The “Aquafaith”先例下需要十分小心。

11. 对受害方的好处需要或不必做出扣减的情况

如果侵权或违约发生后受害方采取的某种行为(即使是法律上并不要求的),事实上减免了损失或得到一些“好处”(benefits),那么他就不能再就这些已减免的损失获赔。但到底哪一些好处是需要作出扣减,英国法律并不完全明确分水线如何划分。总的说,一个“遥远”(remote)、“间接”(indirect)、“独立”(independent)与“完全是附属的好处”(complete collateral benefit 或拉丁文中的 *res inter alios acta* [意思是说法律上无关的行为或英文:legally irrelevant acts])是不能用来扣减损失。Reid 勋爵在 Gourley's Case (1956) AC at p. 214 是这样说:“I do not think that it is possible to formulate any principle by which it can determined what is and what is not too remote. 《Mayne on Damages》, 11th ed., p. 151, refers to ‘matter completely collateral,’ and for a general description of what is too remote I cannot find better words, but I do think that every case can be solved merely by applying those words to it.”

另是 Denning 勋爵在 Liffen v. Watson (1940) 1 KB 556 先例说:“I can find no sound principle for saying what matters should or should not be taken into account in reduction of damages. As each new point comes up, it is decided by the courts according to what is best policy to adopt: and thenceforward it governs subsequent cases."（Denning 勋爵在分析了有关先例后说是找不出有什么大原则针对哪一些好处可以或不可以对损失作出扣减。每一次出了新的争议，法院就要个别考虑什么是最好的政策，而判了之后希望对以后同样的案件有了指引。）

但如果受害方在违约后所采取的行为是违约所带来的结果，这带来的一些"好处"(benefits)就需要作出扣减了，这一个大原则应该是明确。这方面的权威性说法就是 Viscount Haldane 在 British Westinghouse v. Underground(1912)A. C. 673 先例中所强调的，说："the subsequent transaction, if to be taken into account, must be one arising out of the consequences of the breach and in the ordinary course of event."针对这一个权威性说法，《McGregor on Damages》(18th edn, 2009 年)之 7－098 段说："Where steps are taken by the claimant after the wrong which cut down his loss, the important practical question is therefore to ascertain which, if any, of the steps taken come within and satisfy Viscount Haldane's formulation, what subsequent transactions of the claimant are to be regarded as arising out of the consequences of the wrong and also, in the case of contract, as arising in the ordinary course of business. This question will be considered in due course; it represents the core of the problem of mitigation by way of avoided loss."

可以说有些好处需要从损失中扣减是属于简单明了。例如针对有多位"共同侵权方"(joint tortfeasors)的情况，如果受害方已经向其中一位成功取回了部分损失，这些好处是必须在事后向另一位共同侵权方索赔时作出扣减的：Burn v. Morris（1834）2 Cr & M 579。针对违约也是同样的道理，这方面的近期先例有 Geofizika DD v. MMB International Ltd Greenshields Cowie & Co Ltd（2010）1 Lloyd's Rep 45 和 Haugesund Kommune and Another v. Depfa ACS Bank Wikborg Rein & Co（2010）2 Lloyd's Rep 323。另针对受害方的货物被侵占，但货物事后物归原主，受害方就不能向侵占方索赔货物的损失：Moon v. Raphael（1835）2 Bing NC 310。

可以说基本大原则就是在减少损失的行动中获得的好处通常需要作出扣减，这可节录《Mcgregor on Damages》(18th edn,2009 年)之 7－109 段："In any event, it is suggested that the basic rule is that the benefit to the claimant, if it is to be taken into account in mitigation of damage, must arise out of the act of mitigation itself; this approach has been adopted by the courts in quite a number of cases. It may be regarded as simply another way of expressing Viscount Hadane's requirement that the transaction giving rise to the benefit 'must be one arising out of the consequences of the breach'."

针对这方面的大原则也就是本章第 2 段所讲的第二条规则(为了方便阅读，第二条规则是说："一方违约/毁约后，如果受害方采取的行动事实上避免或减少了一部分损失，那么损失赔偿亦要相应免除或扣减这部分减少的损失。即使受害方所作所为已超出了合理减少损失所要求的范围，他也不应借助违约或侵权向被告多赚一笔")。这条规则可以区分为三个部分，在接下去的段节做进一步的介绍。

11.1 受害方在侵权或违约前采取的行动带来的好处不需要扣减

另考虑到底哪一些好处是需要作出扣减时,很重要的就是受害方采取的行动在时间上要划分。如果受害方在侵权或违约前就已经采取了行动,对后来的损失作出保障,这是不存在扣减。因为在时间上受害方还没有减少损失的"责任",这些行为谈不上是减少损失。

11.1.1 受害方事前的投保

这种情况最常见的就是受害方在侵权或违约前已经做出了投保,这方面已经有明确的先例说明保险的好处是不必在向被告索赔损失的时候被扣减:Bradburn v. G. W. R. (1874) L. R. 10 Ex. 1。在该先例,Bramwell B 大法官是说:"In Dalby v. India & London Life Assurance Co (1854) 15 CB 365, it was decided that one who pays premiums for the purpose of insuring himself, pays on the footing that his right to be compensated when the event insured against happens is an equivalent for the premiums he has paid; it is a *quid pro quo*, larger if he gets it, on the chance that he will never get it at all. That decision is an authority bearing on the present case, for the principle laid down in it applies, and shows that the plaintiff is entitled to retain the benefit which he has paid for in addition to the damages which he recovers on account of the defendant's negligence."

另 Pigott B 大法官也是有同样的说法:"The plaintiff is entitled to recover the damages caused to him by the negligence of the defendant, and there is no reason or justice in setting of what the plaintiff has entitled himself to under a contract with third persons, by which he has bargained for the payment of a sum of money in the event of an accident happening to him. He does not receive that sum of money because of the accident, but because he has made a contract providing for the contingency; an accident must occur to entitle to him to it, but it is not the accident, but his contract, which is the cause of his receiving it."

这种涉及受害方事先购买的保险好处不能用来作为扣减的先例有:Bristol and West Building Society v. Bevan May May & Merrimans (1998) 1 WLR 336; Portman Building Society v. Bevan Ashford (2000) PNLR 336; Banque Bruxelles Lambert v. Eagle Star Insurance Co Ltd (1995) 2 All ER 769; Brown v. KMR Services Ltd (1994) 4 All ER 385; Arab Bank plc v. John D Wood Commercial Ltd (2000) 1 WLR 857 CA; FNCB Ltd v. Barnet Devanney (Harrow) Ltd (2000) PNLR 248 CA; Parry v. Cleaver (1970) AC/(HL)等。

11.1.2 受害方事前与第三人订立的合约

这种情况比较复杂,可介绍有关房屋租赁的两个先例:Joyner v. Weeks (1891) 2 QB 31 CA 与 Haviland v. Long (1952) 2 QB 80 CA。案情大致上都是涉及前租客在租约届满时退还的房屋需要修理,但在这之前房东已经为房屋找到新租客,并且是由新租客对房屋作出装修(包括修理)。表面看来,房东没有损失,不应该向前租客索赔修理的费用。但已经有明确的先例说明新租客租约的"好处"是不能用来扣减向前租客索赔的损失。在 Joyner v. Weeks, Wright 大法官是这样说:"Many cases may be put in which it is plainly immaterial that at the commencement of an action for a breach of contract the plaintiff is in fact no worse off than he would have been if the contract had been performed... The person whose breach of contract has caused the damage is not the less liable because the damage has been made good, or its effect compensated by an extraneous event of such a kind that if it had operated the other way it would not have increased his legal liability. Nor does it seem to us that the relation between the plaintiff and the defendant is directly, if at all, affected by the terms of an agreement made by the plaintiff with a third person before the expiration of the defendant's term. That agreement might be rescinded, or might never be performed. When it was made the parties to it could not foresee, and did not contract on the basis, that there would at the end of the defendant's term be any breach of the contract to deliver up in repair. It must be not the making but the performance of the new agreement to which the supposed effect would be attributable. But if so, then at the moment of the termination of the defendant's tenancy and before the new agreement was performed, a cause of action vested in the plaintiff against the defendant, and this could not be taken away or affected by the subsequent *res inter alios acta.*"

在 Haviland v. Long 先例,上诉庭的 Denning 勋爵说得更加清楚,是:"The fact that the landlord has an undertaking from a new tenant to do the repairs does not go in diminution of damages. It is *res inter alios acta.*"

上述所讲的情况也适用在货物买卖,就是卖方供应了有缺陷或延误付运的货物,但买方只是中间商,他早就已经把货物转售给分买方,而且分买方接受了这批有缺陷或延误付运的货物而没有异议,并支付了全数的货价。至于分买方为什么这样做,可以有各种理由,如货物缺陷或延误并不严重。如果分买方接受货物,买方表面看来就是没有损失。但已经有明确先例判是这不影响买方可以/应该根据市场规则索赔(交货时质量良好货物的市场价格与有缺陷货物的市场价格之间的差价):Rodocamachi v. Milburn (1886) 18 QBD 67; Williams v. Agius (1914) AC 510; Slater v. Hoyle Smith (1920) KB 11 (CA)。在这些先例,有两个是涉及原告作为中间商,在发生违约前已经把货物转卖,转卖的价格高于原合约的价格但低于违约时候的市场价格,所以以市场价格来计算损失,对原告更有利,而且看来不是原告的真正损失。举例说,如原合约的价格是 10 元,转卖的价格是 12 元,而当时的市场价格是 15 元,如果原合约的卖方违约不提供货物,中间商的买方以市场价格索赔是 5 元的差价,但以转卖的价格计算只有 2 元的差价。但法院还是判原告以市场价格为准获得赔偿。简单介绍一下前两个先例,可以节录《McGregor on Damages》(18th edn, 2009 年)之 7 - 156 段:"With breach by non - delivery the leading case is Williams v. Agius decided in 1914. Having bought a cargo of coal from Agius, Williams resold before the time fixed for delivery a cargo of similar amount and description to one Ghiron at a price higher than the contract price but lower than what turned out to be the market price at the time when Agius failed in breach of contract to deliver. The House of Lords held that the normal measure of damages applied and that the sub – sale price to Ghiron was irrelevant to reduce Williams's damages. In so doing their Lordships strongly approved the Court of Appeal's decision in Rodocamachi v. Milburn where the contract that was breached was not one of sale but of carriage of goods, the non – delivery resulting from the goods being lost at sea in the course of carriage. The price at which the charterer had sold the goods in advance of the breach of contract, a price lower than that at the time of due delivery, was not allowed to reduce the damages."

至于在 Slater v. Hoyle Smith 先例,案情涉及棉布的买卖,被告卖方所交的货质量有缺陷,但该批货原告(中间商)已经转售给了第三人,并且原告收到全额的货价,没有受到货物质量缺陷的影响。之后原告向被告提出索赔,损失的金额就是买卖合约所规定的良好状况的棉布的市场价格与该批有质量缺陷的棉布的市场价格之间的差价。但由于原告是收到全额的货价,这比这批质量有缺陷的棉布的市场价格为高,所以带来被告指称原告没有真正损失的争议。被告的抗辩被上诉庭所拒绝,Scrutton 大法官是这样说:"if the buyer is lucky enough, for reasons with which the seller has nothing to do, to get his goods through on the sub – contract without a claim against him, this on principle cannot affect his claim against the seller."

同样的判法也出现在 The "Sanix Ace"(1987) 1 Lloyd's Rep 465,案情涉及 7558 吨货物(DIR pellets)的 FOB 买卖。承租人也就是货物的买方已经在事前把该批货物转售给了 11 个最终分买方,但发生事故的时候货物的所有权还没有转让给分买方(也就是把提单转让)。但货物的风险在装船后就已经转移给了分买方。反正是最后承租人从分买方取得了全额的货款,这导致被告船东(因为他在租约中对该批货物的损坏要负责)抗辩说承租人没有真正的损失。但 Hobhouse 大法官拒绝船东的抗辩说:"the owner of goods is entitled to sue and recover damages in respect of loss or damage to those goods... In contract, although nominal damages can be awarded, the right to recover substantial damages can be proved by proving possession or ownership of the relevant goods. The carriers' argument before me that the claimants had suffered no damage because they had subsequently been paid by the end users is misconceived. As soon as the goods are damaged the owner of the goods of full value and subsequently he is the owner of goods with only a reduced value. He has suffered a loss. Whether or not he is able to recover his loss from others is a separate question."

11.2 受害方在侵权或违约后来自第三人的帮助与其他情况不需要扣减

这方面的问题最明确的就是受害方在发生侵权或者违约的损失后,从第三人得到一些的礼物或者帮助。例如,受害方由于被告的侵权或违约而导致房屋被烧毁,他的父母或者孩子会掏钱出来帮助他。问题是这笔钱是否应该用来扣减被告对损失的赔偿？如果不能扣减损失，岂不是会让受害方从这一个不幸事故中获利，毕竟大原则是损失只为了复原？但也会有其他说法（如在贵族院先例的 Hunt v. Severs [1994] AC350 的"reimbursement route"说法）是受害方在成功取回损失后，可以把馈赠的金钱或好处归还给父母、孩子或朋友。再说被告的过错没有理由要无辜的第三人资助他赔偿损失。总之，这方面的答案应该是明确，礼物是不能用作扣减损失赔偿，如在先例 Parry v. Cleaver (1970) AC 1 (HL)，Reid 勋爵说："It would be revolting to the ordinary man's sense of justice, and therefore contrary to public policy, that the sufferer should have his damages reduced so that he would gain nothing from the benevolence of his friends or relations or of the public at large, and that the only gainer would be the wrongdoer. We do not have to decide in this case whether these considerations also apply to public benevolence in the shape of various uncovenanted benefits from the welfare state, but it may be thought that Parliament did not intend them to be for the benefit of the wrongdoer."

在 Cunningham v. Harrison (1973) QB 942 (CA) 先例，涉及一个有同情心的雇主给了受害方一笔补助，Denning 勋爵认为在这种情况下受害方即使是收到比复原还要多的金钱，这多出来的钱可视为作出馈赠的雇主给受害方的信托。

但什么是礼物也不容易说清楚，这方面尤其有很多涉及人身伤亡的先例。Parry v. Cleaver 先例针对的是受害方的雇主给他的一笔"残疾退休金"（disable pension）是否算是礼物。这在较早前的一个上诉庭先例 Browning v. War Office (1963) 1 QB 750，判是雇主给的好处包括退休金应该从损失中扣减。在 Parry v. Cleaver 先例，贵族院有了不同的判法，认为残疾退休金（不论该笔退休金受害方是否根据雇用合约是应该赚取的）以及其他的退休金都不应该从受害方可以向被告索赔的损失中扣减。贵族院认为唯一的例外是受害方如果继续赚取工资（如在治疗期间），就不能向被告索赔工资的损失。

较早前提到的 Parry v. Cleaver 先例，Reid 勋爵的判词对以前在这方面的判例会有冲击，如受害方的"失业救济金"（unemployment benefit）。在较早的先例 Parsons v. BNM Laboratories Ltd (1964) 1 QB 95 判是这笔钱需要在受害方索赔损失中扣减，上诉庭的 Pearson 大法官是这样解释："In the end one comes back to the question: Is the plaintiff's receipt of unemployment benefit a matter too remote to be taken wrongful dismissal? The common - sense answer is that of course it is not too remote. It is not 'completely collateral.' The dismissal caused the plaintiff to become unemployed, and therefore entitled, as a matter of general right under the system of state insurance and not by virtue of any private insurance policy of his own, to receive unemployment benefit. The effect of the dismissal was not to deprive him of all income but to reduce his income by substituting unemployment benefit for his salary. It would be unrealistic to disregard the unemployment benefit, because to do so would confer on the plaintiff, to the extent of 59 2s. 6d., a fortuitous windfall in addition to compensation. Sir Andrew Clark（被告代表大律师）also put his argument in this way：the plaintiff has a duty to mitigate the damage, resulting from the wrongful dismissal, by seeking other employment and drawing unemployment benefit in the meantime. I think that is correct, although the word ' duty ' is used in a special sense, meaning only that the plaintiff cannot charge the defendant with any part of the loss which the plaintiff could have avoided by taking reasonable steps."

至于受害方从父母处取得帮助是不必在向被告索赔的损失中扣减，有关的先例是 Liffen v. Watson（1940）1 KB 556，受害方获得的好处是在意外发生后父母提供的免费住宿与膳食。在上诉庭，Slesser 大法官说："... there is no reason why in the assessment of damages, the loss of board and lodging should not stand on the same footing as the loss in cash of the wages. If, since the plaintiff's discharge from hospital, her father has provided her with board and lodging in his home, there is no reason why she should not be heard to say that her loss of the board and lodging previously provided by her employer was as much a loss to her as if she has loss the actual sum in money. It has been said that there is no authority on this matter. None is needed, it is a matter of general principle ... that a wrongdoer must recompense a plaintiff for all the damages which naturally flow from the wrongdoing."

这方面的先例也不只是局限在人身伤亡的案件，例如在 Garner v. Marsh & Parsons（1997）1 WLR 489 先例，涉及被告的测量师没有发觉房屋有严重的结构缺陷，这导致原告买方（购买的房屋是租借业权，不是永久业权）向该测量师索赔损失，并被判损失是根据购买当天该幢有缺陷房屋的价值来计算。上诉庭不理会在购买该房屋后的 5 年，房东愿意把房屋修妥的事实，上诉庭认为房东作为第三方的行为只能算是附属的好处或拉丁文中的 *res inter alios acta*。

在一个比较近期的先例 Hamilton - Jones v. David & Dnape（2004）1 WLR 924，案情涉及原告向她之前委任的律师提出索赔，因为该律师疏忽而导致她的子女被她的前夫带去 Tunisia 而离开她。原告的索赔包括了一笔原告需要多次坐飞机去 Tunisia 探望她的子女的费用，但实际上原告的母亲已经对这笔很大的费用作出了支付。Neuberger 大法官认为应该适用与人身伤亡索赔同样的大原则，说："... see no reason, in logic or policy, as to why the principal should be limited... the principal can be said to be based on the proposition that the gratuitous payment of money by third parties to the claimant is *res inter alios acta*, as between the claimants and the defendants." Neuberger 大法官另说："There is no reason why payment made to the claimant by third parties, particularly when those payments are made out of natural love and affection for the claimant, should be credited to the benefit of the person whose negligence has harmed the claimant, and to the disadvantage of the claimant. Indeed, it would seem almost absurd if that were the law."（没有理由让第三人出于自然的亲情帮助受害方的原告，这好处要给了疏

忽的被告,是被告造成了对原告的伤害,导致原告站在一个不利的地位。如果这是法律地位,这就太可笑了。)

在其他一些特殊的情况下来自第三人的好处要在损失中扣减,如被告侵占了原告的财产,但有关的财产减轻了原告向第三人的债务,这就可以在原告索赔的损失中作出扣减。这方面的先例有上诉庭的 Underwood v. Bank of Liverpool (1924) 1 KB 775 CA,案情涉及被告银行错误把属于原告公司的支票兑现给了该公司唯一的董事,这也属于是被告侵占了原告公司作为法人的财产。获得好处的董事(第三人)把部分金钱清偿原告公司的债务,看来上诉庭的 Scrutton 大法官认为原告以侵占向被告索赔损失,这笔来自第三人的利益不可以被扣减。可以节录《Mcgregor on damages》(18th edn,2009 年)之 7 - 140 段:"the defendant bank had converted cheques of the claimant company by crediting them to the company's sole director. Although the question of damages was not up for decision, Scrutton LJ took the view, with which Atkin LJ agreed, that the fact that the sole director had used some of the proceeds of the cheques in discharging the claimant company's liabilities might go in mitigation of damages, and an inquiry as to the exact facts in this regard was directed. He referred to the dictum of Byles J in Edmondson v. Nuttall that '*you could not mitigate damages for conversion of a bag of money by showing that the defendant had out of the bag of money converted paid the debt of the claimant*', and added that he was: 'not sure that the learned judge had in his mind the equitable doctrines under which a person who had in fact paid the debts of another without authority was allowed the advantage of his payments'."

11.3 受害方在侵权或违约后采取的行动好处需要扣减

在侵权或违约后,受害方所采取的相关行动主要就是为了减少损失(不论是否合理),这如果带来利益或好处,是要在索赔的损失中扣减。

基本的精神就是,如果有关的行为是在侵权或违约后所采取的减少损失行为的一部分,所获得的好处就要在索赔损失中作出扣减。毕竟,合理减少损失不仅是为了保护受害方自己,也在一定程度上是为了保护侵权方或违约方的利益。

在本章第 1 段提过的 British Westinghouse v. Underground(1912)A. C. 673 先例中,涉及出售的火车蒸汽机不符合买卖合约的要求,受害方买方购买另一台更大动力的蒸汽机作为替代,从而获得了更高的利润。在后来的诉讼中,判是替代蒸汽机带来的好处要在受害方的损失中扣减,由于这些好处所带来的更高利润比买方索赔的损失还要高,所以受害方只能取得象征性赔偿。

在一个来自加拿大的枢密院先例 Erie County Natural Gas & Fuel Co v. Carroll (1911) AC 105 (PC)中,涉及受害方原告把煤气租用给被告,只保留了部分煤气来供应自己的业务所需要的机器。但事后被告切断煤气的供应,导致原告需要从其他途径租用煤气并同时自己生产煤气来供应自己的业务。后来原告高价出售他的生产设施,完全可以抵消利用其他途径租用煤气以及自己生产煤气的损失。英国枢密院判是这高价出售业务的好处必须用来扣减损失，否则“受害方会因为被告的违约而获利”（a profit by the defendant's breach of their obligation of about $128,965.22, a somewhat grotesque result.）。结果是判原告只能取得象征性损失。Atkinson 勋爵是这样说：“It would have been competent for the plaintiffs to have abstained from procuring gas in substitution for that which the defendants should have supplied to them, and have sued the defendants for damages for breach of their contract. They did not take that course. They chose to perform on behalf of the defendants, in a reasonable way, that contract for them and to obtain from an independent source a sufficient quantity of gas similar as near as might be in character and quality to that which they were entitled to receive. In such cases it is well established that the measure of damages is the cost of procuring the substituted article when procured could have been sold by the person who has procured it.”

下一个介绍的先例是 Lavarack v. Colchester (1967) 1 QB 278 CA，涉及雇员被雇主无理解雇。在解雇后，该雇员找到了另一份工作，工资不高，并买了一些该公司的股票。但该股票后来大幅增值，导致该雇员赚了一笔钱。上诉庭判是该笔赚的钱也应该在向原来的雇主索赔的损失中扣减。值得注意的是该雇员同时间也买了一些其他公司的股票并赚了钱，但法院判这些利润就不能用来扣减了。这里的区别是雇员在雇主违约后找到了另一份工作，这是受害方减少损失行为的一部分，得到的好处包括工资，是应该用来扣减的。至于购买该公司的股票并赚钱，这虽然不是受害方需要采取的行动，不做也没有人说是不合理。但既然是做了，这好处就应该在损失中扣减。估计没有这解雇，受害方不去另一家公司，是不会买它的股票的。但受害方同时间购买了其他公司股票赚钱，这是与原雇主的违约没有直接关系的，也与减少损失的行为扯不上关系，所以不能作出扣减。

11.3.1 “lost volume”如果能够证明，就不需要扣减

在这里还有一个变数，就是假设买方违约拒绝接受货物，这导致受害方卖方把货物转售给另一位替代买方，价格与合约价格是一样的。表面看来，受害方没有任何损失。但会有情况是受害方是有多余的货物作出供应，所以买方如果不拒货，受害方在找到替代买方时可以给他供应多余的货物，就可以赚取两份利润。这种所谓的“lost volume”的争议可以举一个加拿大先例说明：APECO of Canada, Ltd v. Windmill Place (1978) 2 SCR 385。案情涉及一位租客违约/毁约，租期还未届满就搬走，但房东很快找到了另一位替代租客。加拿大的最高院判替代租客的租金是不需要用来扣减的，说：“an independent transaction which in no way arose out of the consequences of the breach by the appellant.”估计这样判最重要的原因是这间房屋只有半满，表示如果原租客没有违约/毁约，房东找到了替代租客后也有其他房间可以供应给他。

11.3.2 市场规则下的好处是否需要扣减

在本书第十五与十六章会更详尽的针对以“市场规则”（market rule）计算损失，就是假设了受害方合理减少损失就应该可供买卖的市场马上或尽快买入或出售。在

本段只是针对受害方索赔损失是否要作出扣减的问题。简单说，只有在可供买卖市场马上或尽快买入或出售的行为中得到的好处，法律才要求在损失中作出扣减。如果受害方是事后才真正买入或出售并且从中得到好处，但这是与市场规则没有关系，法律是不要求在损失中作出扣减。

简单地说，例如受害方卖方供应的货物被买方拒绝接受，受害方应该马上或尽快在市场出售，如果当时市场价格比合约价格更高，这一个好处必须在损失中扣减，也表示受害方向买方索赔只能取得象征性损失赔偿。同样的道理也适用在受害方买方被卖方拒绝供货，受害方就应该马上或尽快在市场买入替代货物。如果当时市场价格比合约价格还要低，表示受害方如果买入就更省钱，他就只能向卖方索赔象征性损失。当然在现实中，大部分卖方拒绝供货都是因为市场上涨，表示在当时的市场买入替代货物需要支付的价格都会比合约的价格高。所以，这两者的差价就是受害方的损失，通常不会是象征性损失的情况。重要的是，这市场规则只是一个假设，也是一条表面计算损失的规则（*prima facie* rule）。一根据这样的办法计算，就不再理会受害方到底有没有在市场买入或出售。这表示，受害方如果后来（谈不上是马上或尽快）才买入替代货物或出售有关货物，这就已经不算是合理减少损失行为的一部分。这表示受害方买方在卖方拒绝供货后的 3 个月（为例），才去市场买入货物，如果当时的市场价格是比卖方违约/毁约当天的市场价格低，表示受害方买了更便宜的货物，这里的差价好处是属于受害方，不需要从向卖方索赔的损失中扣减。原因是受害方在卖方拒绝供货时就应该马上合理减少损失，在市场买入。但是受害方在 3 个月后才去市场买入，这已经是脱离了市场规则，就再也不能算是减少损失行为的一部分。

同样道理也适用在卖方供应有缺陷的货物，而受害方买方的索赔是根据市场规则，也就是按照合约应该提供的良好货物与缺陷货物的市场价格的差价。至于受害方如果稍后将该票货物转售，即使是没有损失（如市场价格上涨导致有缺陷的货物也可以卖一个好价钱），也被认为是无关。这里的原因主要是损失已经根据市场价格来计算，所以后来转售的好处不存在扣减：Jones v. Just（1868）LR 3 QB 197。

这方面的大原则主要是来自一个古老的有关股票买卖的枢密院先例，在 Jamal v. Moolla Dawood（1916）1 AC 175，买方拒绝接受一批股票，但后来市场上涨，卖方得以高价出售。枢密院判是卖方的这一个好处是不能用来扣减他对买方造成的有关损失，枢密院是这样说："The question therefore is the general question and may be stated thus: In a contract for sale of negotiable securities, is the measure of damages for breach the difference between the contract price and the market price at the date of the breach – with an obligation on the part of the seller to mitigate the damages by getting the best price he can at the date of the breach – or is the seller bound to reduce the damages, if he can, by subsequent sales at better prices? If he is, and if the purchaser is entitled to the benefit of subsequent sales, it must also be true that he must bear the burden of subsequent losses. The latter proposition is in their Lordships' opinion impossible, and the former is equally unsound. If the seller retains the shares after the breach, the speculation as to the way the market will subsequently go is the speculation of the seller, not of the buyer; the seller cannot recover from the buyer the loss below the market price at the date of the breach if the market falls, nor is he liable to the purchaser for the profit if the market rises."

在 Campbell Mostyn v. Barner (1954) 1 Lloyd's Rep 65 CA 先例,案情涉及从南非出口的500箱火腿罐头,买方在接受了150箱货物后,拒绝接受余下的350箱。在1951年10月24日,双方同意这就是违约/毁约的一天,因为卖方以一封信函接受了买方的违约/毁约,说:"With reference to the past correspondence we have to inform you that having duly tendered the above contracts and you having refused to accept these tenders we must inform you that we reserve our full rights to sell these goods against you and debit you with any difference should a loss be incurred."但当时的市场是十分困难与萧条,火腿罐头价格下跌。但在违约/毁约后大概两个星期,英国政府刚刚换届并作出了控制有关货物进口的命令,再加上圣诞节即将到来,这导致火腿罐头在市场上的价格上升。结果是在11月7日,受害方卖方将该批火腿罐头成功出售,价格是远超过10月24日违约/毁约一天的市场价格。这样看来,违约的买方应该可以松一口气,因为卖方没有任何损失。但第一审的审判官(Master)根据 Jamal v. Moolla Dawood 先例定下来的大原则判买方要赔偿损失,依据的就是在违约一天的市场价格与合约价格的差价。至于卖方在后来高价出售,算是他自己的决定、运气或远见所赚取的利润,不能用来扣减向买方索赔的损失。第一审判决被上诉庭支持,而在上诉庭买方的主要争辩是两点。一是当时没有可供买卖的市场,因为当时市场十分萧条。二是由于没有办法或很难在市场出售,卖方延后出售实际上是减少损失行为的一部分,所以利润应该扣减损失。但这些争议都被上诉庭拒绝,因为第一审已经认定了违约/毁约时有一个可供买卖的市场。

除了货物买卖,其他有可供买卖市场的损失计算也是适用同样的原则。例如租船市场,就通常有可供船舶租出(如果船东是受害方)或是租入替代船舶(如果承租人是受害方)的市场。这方面可节录 Goff 大法官在 The "Elena d'Amico" (1980) 1 Lloyd's Rep 75 先例中所说:"In my judgment the same principles are applicable in the assessment of the damages to be awarded where there has been a repudiation by a shipowner of a time charter. If, at the date of breach, there is an available market, the normal measure of damages will be difference between the contract rate and the market rate for chartering a substitute ship for the balance of the charter period. **If however the time charterer decides not to take advantage of that market then, generally speaking, that will be his own business decision independent of the wrong; and the consequences of that decision are his. If he judges the market correctly, he reaps the benefit; if he judges it**

incorrectly, then the extra cost falls upon him."（黑体是说受害的承租人如果不在可供买卖市场租进替代船舶，而是事后才租进，这是他自己的商业决定，与船东的违约无关，所以后果也是他自己承担。如果他准确预测了市场走势，这好处是属于他自己的。如果他预测错误，额外损失也是属于他自己的。）

11.3.3 市场规则适用但双方订立新合约的好处需要扣减

即使有"市场规则"(market rule)相对简单地计算损失，但还是会有千奇百怪的案件导致不同的结果，在这里可以介绍 Pagnan & Fratelli v. Corbisa Industrial Agropacuaria (1970) 1 WLR 1306 CA 先例。案情涉及的货物是一票巴西玉米，该 CIF 买卖合约为1965年5月20日，合约价格为每吨64美元。卖方无法按照合约规定的时间交货，买方同意卖方延迟交货，但是在延期的过程中与卖方达成口头协议就是如果将来货物运到之后质量无法令买方满意，他就有权拒绝货物。在经历了严重的延误后部分货物在卸港被发现损坏，买方于是拒绝了整批货物。在拒绝货物后，买方在卸港所在地的法院申请了对于该票货物的扣押令，用来作为卖方归还他已经提前支付给卖方的运费、保险费等费用的担保。卖方在归还了买方一部分款项之后，被扣押的货物也被部分释放出来。在此过程中，买方与卖方针对该票货物在1965年11月13日又重新订立了一份买卖合约，合约的价格为每吨51.40美元。但由于新合约中没有说清楚这是包括了对原来买卖合约最终与全面的和解，导致买方后来取巧进一步向卖方索赔原来买卖合约下他的违约（货物质量不妥而被拒货）损失，而计算损失是根据市场规则，也就是合约价格与拒货一天（10月19日）的市场价格的64.5美元至65美元。这市场价格是比后来双方达成新合约的每吨51.40美元还要高的多，显然卖方是为了息事宁人或者没有办法处理该批货物才不得不同意以如此低价再次卖给买方。在该先例，针对与本段有关的损失计算争议就是买方在新合约以低价买入该批玉米而获得的这一好处是否要在根据市场规则计算的损失中扣减。如果不是原来双方有新合约而是把该批玉米高价或者低价出售给第三人，根据 Jamal v. Moolla Dawood 先例的大原则，分售都可以不予理会，只要玉米在违约/毁约时有可供买卖的市场就有了损失计算的基础。上诉庭显然认为是不能让买方取巧，因为第二个合约是第一个合约中交易的延续，两个合约根本上应该被视为同一单交易。那么在第一个合约中按照违约一天市场价格与合约价格差别计算出来的损失可以与第二个合约中买方以低于市场价格购买货物的获利相抵销。Salmon 大法官是这样说：

"I come now to the main point taken on behalf of the buyers. Mr. Goff(买方代表大律师) argues that when considering the buyers' claim for damages in respect of the sellers' failure to deliver goods in accordance with the May contract, the purchase of November 13 must, in law, be treated as irrelevant and that accordingly any profit which the buyers may have made from it must be ignored. Since the November purchase was not a transaction independent of or disconnected with the May contract but formed part of a continuous dealing between the same parties in respect of the same goods resulting, on balance, in a profit to the buyers, Mr. Goff's argument (however attractively he puts it), on analysis, comes to this — that the buyers, who in reality have made a handsome profit, are, in law, entitled to recover damages for a fictitious loss. I should be reluctant to come to such an absurd and unjust conclusion unless compelled to do so by the clearest authority. Mr. Goff contends that such authority is to be found in Jamal v. Moolla Dawood, Sons & Co. [1916] 1 A. C. 175 and Campbell Mostyn (Provisions) Ltd. v. Barnett Trading Co. [1954] 1 Lloyd's Rep. 65. I am afraid that I cannot agree with this contention. The principle of law is that where a buyer wrongfully neglects or refuses to accept and pay for the goods or a seller wrongfully neglects or refuses to deliver the goods to the buyer, the innocent buyer or seller as the case may be may maintain an action for damages for breach of contract. The measure of damage in each case is the estimated loss directly and naturally resulting in the normal course of events from the breach of contract. Where there is an available market for the goods, the measure of damage is *prima facie* to be ascertained by the difference between the contract price and the market price at the date of the breach: see sections 50 and 51 of the Sale of Goods Act, 1893. The two authorities relied on by Mr. Goff do no more than illustrate instances in which the *prima facie* rule relating to the measure of damages applies. In such cases the innocent party is not bound to go on the market and buy or sell at the date of the breach. Nor is he bound to gamble on the market changing in his favour. He may wait, if he chooses; and if the market turns against him this cannot increase the liability of the party in default; similarly if the market turns in his favour, the liability of the party in default is not diminished. Normally if the innocent party goes on to the market and buys or sells after the date of the breach, this is *res inter alios acta* so far as the party in default is concerned.

The present case, however, is quite different. The purchase of November 13, 1965, was certainly not inter *alios acta*; it was between the self-same buyers and sellers who were parties to the contract of May 20, 1965, and it related to the self-same goods that were the subject-matter of that contract. Moreover, as already stated, the tribunal found that it was not an independent or disconnected transaction but formed part of a continuous dealing between the parties; and these findings of fact cannot be challenged in this court. Accordingly the *prima facie* rule for ascertaining the measure of damages cannot apply because the buyers suffered no loss or damage but instead made a handsome profit in spite of the sellers' breach. ..."(Salmon 大法官在这两段大致上是说买方的原告已经通过第二个新合约把这票货很便宜地买回来,如果再让他根据市场规则向可怜的卖方多索赔一笔假设的损失,买方就可以发大财。这会令法律变得不公平与可笑。1893 年《英国货物销售法》的市场规则只是一条表面规则,不是强制性适用。而第二个新合

约虽然与市场规则无关,但已经被认定是买方拒货后双方持续交易的过程,针对的是同一票货,不能被视为是一个独立或无关的事后买卖。所以没有理由新合约的好处不作出扣减。)

上诉庭的另一位 Megaw 大法官基本上是与 Salmon 所说的一样:

"For my part, I think the argument fails. The rule in section 51 (3) of the Sale of Goods Act, 1893, does not purport to be more than a*prima facie* rule. There is nothing in the cases cited, or in any other case which was brought to our attention, to elevate its status above that which is involved in "*prima facie.*" In particular, the cases cited were not concerned with a situation, as here, in which, after a breach of contract by non - delivery, or rejected delivery of defective goods, the self - same goods became the subject - matter of a contract of purchase and sale between the self - same parties at a price which differed from the then - prevailing market price.

Despite the attractive argument of counsel for the buyers, I am not persuaded that the ordinary principle of mitigation of damages, as laid down in the British Westinghouse case (1912) A. C. 673 should not be allowed to have effect in such a case, where the tribunal of fact concludes that the ultimate sale is a part of a continuous dealing."

11.3.4 部分其他侵权案例有关好处是否需要扣减的介绍

在这方面,可以先以一个船舶碰撞的上诉庭先例作为例子:The "World Beauty" (1969) 1 Lloyd's Rep 350。该先例涉及两艘油轮在苏伊士湾发生碰撞,其中一艘 Andros Springs 轮被严重损坏,需要在当地作出暂时修理,并要减速去法国勒阿弗尔港完成航次并继续去荷兰鹿特丹进行全面修理。从碰撞的一天(1958 年 4 月 21 日)直到修理完毕(6 月 7 日),总共的延误是 37 天。在碰撞当时该油轮是以多航次的程租合约出租给一家 CFR 公司的承租人,租金为 3659.48 美元/天,该租约估计要履行到 9 月 15 日才终止。但船东在 1957 年 9 月 8 日就把该油轮期租给了美孚石油,期限为 7 年,Laycan 是 1958 年 8 月 1 日到 10 月 31 日,这表示该油轮若在这段时间中交船就可以开始赚取该期租合约的租金。反正船东在出租给 CFR 和美孚石油时市场都非常好,但到了 7 个月后,在发生碰撞时,运费市场暴跌,市场租金只降到了原来运费或租金的 1/10。

Andros Springs 轮船东(算是受害方)为了减少损失,租进了一艘替代船舶 Andros Thunder 轮。由于当时的运费市场很低,所以租入的费用不高,船东以该艘船舶履行 CFR 的多航次程租合约。但 Andros Thunder 轮比较旧,船速也慢,所以只履行了 3 个航次,而不是 Andros Springs 轮本来可以履行的 4 个航次,所以运费也相应赚少了。至于空出来的 Andros Springs 轮在 6 月 7 日修妥后,本来还要大约 3 个月时间(根据本来在 CFR 的程租合约是要履行到 9 月 15 日)才能交船给美孚石油并赚取高租金。但船东成功取得美孚石油的同意把交船日期提早了 3 个月,这导致了 Andros Springs 轮提前 100 天赚取美孚石油的高昂租金。双方的争议就是如何计算减少损失所带来好处的扣减。

受害方提出的损失是假设 Andros Springs 轮如果没有这一碰撞事故,就可以赚取以下的 4 个航次的利润,共计 542,068.55 美元。但这需要扣减减少损失的好处,而好处是分两个部分。第一部分就是 Andros Thunder 轮在 3 个航次中赚取的利润,共计 369,169.08 美元。以上两个金额双方没有争议,有争议的是第二部分减少损失的好处,也就是 Andros Springs 轮可以提早 100 天赚取美孚石油的高租金应该如何计算。侵权方 World Beauty 轮的代表大律师认为这 100 天让受害方赚取了总共 350,705美元,这与第一部分的好处加起来就表示受害方根本没有损失。但 Denning 勋爵不同意,并接受了第一审 Willmer 大法官的看法,就是美孚石油的租约早在侵权前已经订立,不应该算是减少损失行为所带来的好处(这方面请看本章之 11.1 段),说:"The earning of these profits [that is, the $350,708 in three months] flowed not from measures taken in consequence of the collision, but from the fact of the charter having been the fact of the charter having been negotiated months previously. Collision or no collision, these profits would have been earned in any event..."

加上碰撞为受害方带来的唯一好处就是把美孚石油租约提前了 100 天,整个租期还是 7 年。问题就是这一提前好处应该如何计算。Willmer 大法官的计算就是把 350,708 美元的利润或租金的赚取乘以 5% 的复息,再乘以 7 年。这样得出的受害方真正损失是 71,934.47 美元。但上诉庭的 Winn 勋爵不同意,他认为应该把提前收到的 350,708 美元的折现值算出,这得出的受害方真正损失是 113,003 美元。但 Denning 勋爵的上诉庭多数意见不同意两种算法,认为准确的算法是假设 Andros Springs 轮在 6 月 7 日修妥后,直到交船给美孚石油,会在当时的市场赚多少钱。根据专家证据,当时的市场租金是 392 美元/天,可以在市场赚的钱就是 52,528 美元。这一来得出的受害方真正损失是 162,178.47 美元,也就是 World Beauty 轮船东作为被告所需赔付的金额。这里也涉及举证责任的问题,这是在侵权方,也就是 World Beauty 轮船东。上诉庭的 Fenton Atkinson 大法官同意 Denning 勋爵判决的原因就是他认为侵权方没有办法明确证明受害方在美孚石油租约提前了 100 天到底得到什么好处,所以只能以 Denning 勋爵的算法并得出了最大金额的真正损失。

之后的另一个先例是 Bellingham v. Dhillon (1973) QB 304,案情涉及交通事故造成原告受伤。原告本人经营一个汽车驾驶学校,因为这一意外事故导致他失去了一个购买驾驶模拟器的机会,并且因此造成了 3 年半的利润损失。但在 3 年半后,他在一次清盘的过程中有机会以很低的价格买进了一台驾驶模拟器,而这里节省的钱是完全可以抵销这 3 年半的利润损失的。法院判这一好处必须在损失中做出扣减,导致原告受害方根本没有办法证明有可索赔的损失。

但在 Hussey v. Eels (1990) 2 QB 227 CA,这一案例中的好处被判是不必扣减。案情涉及被告的一个有关卖给原告的房屋不会下沉的误述(这是可以构成侵权)。事后因为修理十分昂贵,原告决定把该房子拆除并申请在该地点新建两栋房子的批文。最后原告把该土地与批文出售给了一位地产商,价格高达78,500英镑,这比原来向被告购买的53,200英镑高得多。之后原告向被告提出索赔,损失的计算就是在买卖一天该房屋的合约价格减去该存在问题的房屋应该值的价格。但被告指称原告没有损失,因为他以高价把房屋出售给了地产商。法院判是后来的出售并非是原来违约的延续性交易的一部分,事实上原告买了该房屋之后曾经在里面住过一段时间,在后来发觉该房屋的发展价值或潜力,原告纯粹是为他自己的利益着想出售给地产商,与减少损失无关。

第六章　损失的肯定性:将来的变数与机会损失

1. 序言

重复一次耳熟能详与不能偏离的损失赔偿最基本的大原则,这就是在 Robinson v. Harman (1848) 1 Exch 850 先例中, Parke B 大法官所说的:"The rule of the common law is that where a party sustains a loss by reason of a breach of contract he is so far as money can do it *to be placed in the same situation as if the contract had been performed.*"(普通法的规定就是一方当事人如果因为对方违约而蒙受损失,计算的办法就是用金钱来令他作为受害方回到一个合约被履行的经济地位。)

受害方有证明损失的责任,这包括证明有关损失的事实与金额。如果他没有办法证明或是实质上没有真正的损失,就算在责任方面原告的受害方胜诉,法院或仲裁庭也不会给予金钱赔偿的救济或顶多是给予"名义损失"(nominal damage)。

但如果是有真正损失,只是损失计算起来十分困难,这不是法院或仲裁庭不找出答案的理由。正如 Vaughan Williams 大法官在著名的 Chaplin v. Hicks (1911) 2 KB 768 先例所说:"The fact that damages cannot be assessed with certainty does not relieve the wrongdoer of the necessity of paying damages."

但法律并不要求"绝对肯定"(absolute certainty),因为要求原告对他每一项的损失都达到一个绝对肯定的证明程度就会导致原告在绝大部分的案件中都无法获赔。

1.1　过去的损失

原告的受害方能够肯定证明的损失类别会很有限,这就是原告能够在审理的时候提供无可质疑或明确的文件或口头证据证明"过去的损失"(past losses),因为这已经成为了"事实"(fact)。例如,受害方已经真正损失了的"收益"(loss of earnings)与他支付了的"真正使费"(actual expenses)。在本书第二章谈到的"依赖利益"(reliance interest)主要是针对依赖有关合约而花费的费用,显然就是针对过去的事实,原告应该可以提供完整的证据。此外在财产/货物损失/损坏,针对基本损失(如损失/损坏货物在违约一天的价值或损坏货物的真正修理费用)与间接损失(如营运利润的损失与有关的支出),也通常在审理时是属于过去的事实并可以提供证据。

但许多"过去的损失"类别有证据还会有一定程度的不肯定,如根据"违约一天损失规则"(breach date rule)计算出来的合约价格与市场价格的差价,虽然是在审理一天已经属于过去,但由于市场规则只是假设的损失计算,所以通常不会是受害方肯定的损失。总的来说,针对已经发生的过去损失的事实,在大部分的情况之下法院或仲裁庭还是需要根据双方的争议与所提供的证据,根据"平衡的可能性"(balance of probability)作出"事实"的认定。最后对赔偿的决定就只有两种可能:"完全获偿或毫无赔偿"(all or nothing),也就是非黑即白。如果被认定某个事实发生的可能性比没有发生的可能性大,这认定的事实也就在法律上变为肯定的事实。这是不存在法院或仲裁庭在考虑了证据后,认为有60%会发生过这一事实,在赔偿金额上也作出40%的折扣。这是Reid勋爵在Davies v. Taylor (1974) AC 207先例中说:"When the question is whether a certain thing is or not true—whether a certain event did or did not happen—then the court must decide one way or the other. There is no question of chance or probability. Either it did not happen. But the standard of civil proof is a balance of probabilities. If the evidence shows a balance in favour of it having happened then it is proved that it did in fact happen."

1.2 将来的损失

以上是针对过去的损失,但损失类别针对"将来事实"(future fact or event)与"将来的损失"(future loss)也有不少,如"预期违约"(anticipatory breach)或拒绝履行合约的"违约/毁约"(repudiation)并且被受害方接受而令合约根本没有被履行或只是被部分履行就是典型的例子。这一来要估计的就是该违约/毁约的有关合约没有履行部分如果被履行会是怎样的结果,如会赚取多少利润。另也在经常会发生的人身伤害案件中受害方将来所需要的医疗、照顾费用与收入的损失。这些都是需要对将来"事实"作出估计,而且要达到合理的肯定性。对将来"事实"如果涉及会有什么损失产生,这还是相对容易。而如果将来"事实"是涉及有没有机会合理减少损失,会是更加困难与不肯定。但往往可以肯定的是这种估计出来的损失要么是高估,要么是低估。

"将来损失"因为是还没有发生的事情(会否真正变为事实是天知道),由于合约根本还没有被履行,做出估计就会是很困难。这方面有两个特定的困难可以介绍:(1)订约自由会带来千变万化的合约规定,每一个合约都会有它特殊的明示条文。这表示要估计如果合约被履行会是怎样的结果,就必须先对有关合约做出解释:Duffen v. Frabo (2000) 1 Lloyd's Rep 180。这需要对合约条文有正确、合理与整体性的解释,而合约解释本身是一个大学问,可参阅笔者所著的《合约的解释》(法律出版社2007年版)。(2)估计完全是假设性的情况,因为这是从来没有发生过的"事实",根本不存在有太肯定的证据。但法律是要求对这一个将来的"事实"证明必须是根据一些可信的证据(通常是专家意见证据)得出的有一定合理肯定程度的估计,而不能是毫无根据的"凭空臆猜"(pure guesswork)。例如,根据一些数据做出"估计的损失"(estimated loss)与引入专家意见证据支持。这一个困难在本书第十八章第六段有关投资仲裁以"贴现现金流"(discount cash flow)来计算出预计的利润损失就可以看出。

但正如 Vaughan Williams 大法官在 Chaplin v. Hicks (1911) 2 KB 768 先例中所讲,尽管将来的损失不能够完全确定,但仍然要对损失的金额做出判断,不能在明知道有损失的情况下让违约方可以轻易脱身。针对将来的"事实",法院或仲裁庭能够做的只能是根据"可能性"(probability)或"机会"(chance)做出估计或给其一个价值。这可以节录 Reid 勋爵在 Davies v. Taylor 所说的名言:"You can prove that a past event happened, but you cannot prove that a future event will happen and I do not think that the law is so foolish as to suppose that you can. All you can do is evaluate the chance."

另也可以节录在澳大利亚高院的先例, Wardley Australia Ltd v. Western Australia (1992) 175 CLR 514 中所说:

"The answer to the question when a cause of action for negligence causing economic loss accrues may require consideration of the precise interest infringed by the negligent act or omission... With economic loss, as with other forms of damage, there has to be some actual damage. Prospective loss is not enough.

When a plaintiff is induced by a misrepresentation to enter into an agreement which is, or proves to be, to his or her disadvantage, the plaintiff sustains a detriment in a general sense on entry into the agreement. That is because the agreement subjects the plaintiff to obligations and liability which exceed the value or worth of the rights and benefits which it confers upon the plaintiff.

But, as will appear shortly, detriment in this general sense has not universally been equated with the legal concept of 'loss or damage'. And that is just as well. In many instances the disadvantageous character or effect of the agreement cannot be ascertained until some future date when its impact upon events as they unfold becomes known or apparent and, by then, the relevant limitation period may have expired. To compel a plaintiff to institute proceedings before the existence of his or her loss is ascertained or ascertainable would be unjust. Moreover, it would increase the possibility that the courts would be forced to estimate damages on the basis of likelihood or probability instead of assessing damages by reference to established events. In such a situation, there would be an ever-present risk of under compensation, the risk of the former being the greater."(以上所讲是指预期会发生的损失并不足够。受害方在误述的诱导下订立了一个对他不利的合约,导致他承担了比他合约价值或权利更大的合约责任,这种不利之处并不是法律承认的"损失"。这不利之处只在将来才会暴露出来并才会知道造成怎样的经济损失,但如果等到那个时候受害方才提起索赔的诉讼,有可能是法定或合约的时效已经届满。但如果要求受害方在损失还没有出现的时候就提起诉讼[这种诉讼会只是针对责任,如误述的责任,而金钱损失的计算留待将来核算],这对受害方不公平,因为要求他花费律师费用而将来不利之处会否造成损失还是天知道。这种诉讼也会是要迫使法

院根据会出现的可能性或机会对将来的损失作出估计。这就会带来无可避免多赔或少赔给受害方的风险。)

1.3 过去事实与将来“事实”的不同举证责任

在这里可以介绍普通法对“已经发生事实”与将来“事实”是有不同的举证责任,后者的要求更高。这可先节录 Michael Furmston 教授所著的《The Law of Contract》(4th edn, 2010)之 1703 – 1704 页所说如下:“In order to succeed in an action for breach of contract a claimant must establish liability upon the normal civil burden of proof i. e. the balance of probabilities. By extension it might be thought that the claimant's right to recover substantial damages (where loss must be shown) is dependent upon proof of loss to the same standard. However as Lord Nicholls observes in Gregg v. Scott (2005) UKHL 2 '... the common law has drawn a distinction between proof of past facts and proof of future prospects'. A past event either occurred or did not and falls to be established in civil proceedings upon the balance of probabilities. Claims for wasted expenditure will fall within this category. However, where the loss being claimed requires an investigation of future events, a different approach is taken; 'proof of future possibilities is approached differently'. Then damages are only recoverable if the item of loss claimed for can be proven with reasonable certainty. The policy behind the application of different burdens of proof in respect of past facts and future events is unclear. It is possible that the risk of exaggeration and falsification in relation to the latter is thought to justify the imposition of a higher standard of proof.”

这是说针对“过去事实”(包括违约所带来的损失),受害方举证的责任是“平衡的可能性”(balance of probabilities),也就是法院或仲裁庭认为证据只要能满足超过50%的可能性就可以认定为事实。但针对将来“事实”,受害方的举证责任是要提高至“合理肯定”(reasonable certainty)。这里的原因可能是对将来“事实”的估计会有夸大或虚假的危险。

要说明的是合理肯定的举证责任关键词是“合理”,这就表示不能一概而论的说对将来“事实”的证明就必须要比对“过去事实”的证明提供更多与更可信的证据,因为不同性质的案件会在举证方面有不同困难,甚至会有情况是不可能有证据,如果法院或仲裁庭接受受害方有蒙受损失,就需要根据十分有限的证据对损失做出最接近事实的估计。

这方面最清楚的说明是在 Ratcliffe v. Evans(1892)2 QB 524 先例,上诉庭的 Bowen 大法官说:“In all actions accordingly on the case where the damage actually done is the gist of the action, the character of the acts themselves which produce the damage, and the circumstances under which these acts are done, must regulate the degree of certainty and particularity with which the damage done ought to be stated and proved. As much certainty and particularity must be insisted on, both in pleading and proof of damage, as is reasonable, having regard to the circumstances and to the nature of the acts themselves by which the damage is done. To insist upon less would be to relax old and intelligible principles. To insist upon more would be the vainest pedantry."

针对这一方面,Diplock 勋爵在一个人身伤亡意外的案例 Mallett v. McMonagle (1970) AC 166 (HL)中也有类似的说法:"The role of the court in making an assessment of damages which depends upon its view as to what will be and what would have been is to be contrasted with its ordinary function in civil actions of determining what was. In determining what did happen in the past a court decides on the balance of probabilities. Anything that is more probable than not it treats as certain. But in assessing damages which depend upon its view as to what will happen in the future or would have happened in the future if something had not happened in the past, the court must make an estimate as to what are the chances that a particular thing will or would have happened and reflect those chances, whether they are more or less than even, in the amount of damages which it awards."(Diplock 勋爵认为过去的事实是根据平衡的可能性,一旦被认定有更大的可能会发生过就变为肯定的事实。但在核算损失时针对将来的事实法院就只能估计其会发生的机会,看看机会是高是低,然后做出赔偿金额的判决。)

另在几年后的 Davies v. Taylor (1974) AC 207 先例,Reid 勋爵是与 Diplock 勋爵说同样的话:"When the question is whether a certain thing is or is not true - whether a certain event did or did not happen - then the court must decide one way or the other. There is no question of chance or probability. Either it did or it did not happen. But the standard of civil proof is a balance of probabilities. If the evidence shows a balance in a favour of it having happened, then it is proved that it did in fact happen... You can prove that a past event happened, but you cannot prove that a future event will happen and I do not think that the law is so foolish as to suppose that you can. All that you can do is to evaluate the chance. Sometimes it is virtually 100 percent: sometimes virtually nil. But often it is somewhere in between. And if it somewhere in between I do not see much difference between a probability of 51 percent and a probability of 49 percent."(Reid 勋爵说针对过去的事实只有发生过与没有发生过两种可能性,只能从证据中根据平衡的可能性找出非黑即白的答案。这样一来,虽然能够证明过去的事实确实发生过,但是仍然无法证明将来的"事实"一定会发生,而且法律也不会愚蠢地认为将来"事实"能够被证明一定会发生。能够做的就只是估计某一"事实"将会发生的机会有多大。它有可能是接近100%,有可能是接近0,但通常是会介乎于这两个数字之间。如果机会是介于这两个数字之间,我认为49%与51%是没有太大区别的,所以不适合用平衡的可能性。)

对将来"事实"估计的困难并不表示可以不努力这样做,因为在不少的损失类别是非要估计损失不可。例如,涉及"机会损失"(loss of chance)的著名选美先例 Chaplin v. Hicks (1911) 2 KB 786 (CA),就涉及受害方的少女因为选美当局的违约而失去了进入选美决赛赢取奖金的机会,法院需要估计这机会损失到底是赔偿多少才恰当,Davies 大法官是这样说:"It was clearly impossible under the facts of that case to estimate with anything approaching to mathematical accuracy the damage sustained by the plaintiffs, but it seems to me to be clearly laid down there by the learned Judges that such an impossibility cannot 'relieve the wrongdoer of the necessity of paying damages for his breach of contract' and that on the other hand the tribunal to estimate that whether jury or Judge must under such circumstances do 'the best it can' and its conclusion will not be set aside even if 'the amount of the verdict is a matter of guess work."(很明显要精确计算出原告的损失是不可能的。但是不能因为这种不可能而让违约的被告能够什么都不赔。陪审团与法官还是要在这种情况下尽力做出决定,即使该决定只是通过猜测做出,但仍然是有效。)

会有先例是因为证明不了甚至猜测不出将来会是什么预期利润的损失,导致在少数著名的先例中受害方只能索赔在本书第二章已经提到的"依赖利益"(reliance interest)。例如在 McRae v. Commonwealth Disposals Commission (1951) 84 CLR 377 先例中针对搜索与救助一艘不存在船舶残骸的费用(abortive salvage of a non – existent ship); Anglia Television v. Reed (1972) 1 QB 60 (CA)先例针对一部没有拍摄的电视剧(the production of a TV play); CCC v. Impact Quadrant Films (1985) QB 16 先例针对三部恐怖录像片的发行(distribution of three 'video nasties')等。

针对损失的不肯定性,主要有以下三种将来的"变数"(contingency):(1)变数来自原告受害方自己;(2)变数来自被告违约方;(3)变数全部或部分来自第三人。这将会在接下去的段节分别介绍。

2. 变数来自原告的受害方

这种变数在航运或外贸最常见的例子就是合约给了原告受害方一个百分比的选择权。例如是买卖合约,如果涉及卖方拒绝供应货物(通常是有关的商品市场价格上涨,但也可以是其他的原因),无辜的买方接受违约/毁约后就免不了会有一个诉讼去向卖方索赔损失。在该有关的合约中,货量是30,000吨,有加减 10% 的伸缩性,由买方选择(英文会是"30,000 tons,10% more or less at buyer's option")。这样的约定通常会是在 FOB 买卖,原因是由买方派船装货,但最后能实际装上的货物是要根据装货时船上的燃油以及其他会有变数的实际数量,这是事前吃不准的。如果装货的船舶当时因为船上燃油数量比较多(原因可以是耗油比估计的低,或是在装港有价钱便宜的燃油供应,这都会导致该船舶燃油数量比事先的估计为多),就会导致装货的载重量相应减低。这一来,船舶的宣载可能只是在 29,000 吨,而不是 30,000

吨,更加不会是 31,000 吨。有关的程租合约与买卖合约有了这 10% 的伸缩性,就不至于造成船东因为少装货对承租人买方违约,而买方也不至于对卖方违约。如果情况相反,船东宣载 31,000 吨,因为船上燃油或吃水实际数量比事先的估计低,所以船东也希望能装多少就尽量装,以多赚取运费。而只要船东是在 10% 伸缩性的范围内,承租人必须提供货物,否则要承担亏舱费的赔偿。在以上解释了为什么船东与派船的 FOB 买方希望在合约中争取 10% 的装货量伸缩性。接下来就继续讨论在卖方拒绝供应货物的违约/毁约情况下,怎样计算损失的问题。这是因为有 10% 伸缩性的变数,而由于船舶从来没有装货与宣载,这 10% 伸缩性到底会否需要行使,而如果行使,到底是多装还是少装,就很不肯定。这会严重影响最后的损失金额,因为受害方买方会根据市场规则要求以货物的合约价格与违约/毁约当天市场价格的差价作为计算损失的基础,假设差价是 20 美元/吨,乘以29,000吨,30,000 吨和 31,000 吨都会有不同的损失金额。对原告受害方而言,他显然会说是以 31,000 吨为准,因为是由他行使选择权的,而对被告的违约方而言,他会说违约后将来没有发生的事情不应该加以考虑,所以损失要么是按照 30,000 吨计算,要么就是按照29,000吨。

在这种情况下,针对将来原告会否行使选择权应该根据"平衡的可能性"(balance of possibility)来决定。这里可节录 Toprak v. Finagrain (1979) 2 Lloyd's Rep. 98 的先例。在该案例,合约中对于货物数量的规定是 350,000 吨,有加减 10% 的伸缩性,由卖方行使这选择权。但卖方是受害方,该案是买方为违约方,拒绝收货。如果这选择权在违约的买方,计算损失应以对他最有利的选择为准,即只是算315,000吨的损失,这方面稍后在第 3 段有详论。

但问题是该案例的选择权是在受害方。这变得损失应是依照 315,000 吨?或是 350,000 吨?或是 385,000 吨?当然是 385,000 吨的损失金额会大得多。Goff 大法官判是以 385,000 吨作准,他说:"... the buyers submitted, damages should be assessed on the basis most favourable to them. Again, I cannot accept this submission: indeed, if it was right, the buyers would only be liable in damages in respect of 350,000 tonnes less 10 per cent., i. e. on 315,000 tonnes. No doubt, where under a contract an option was to be exercised by the party in default, damages may have to be assessed on the basis that option would have been exercised in the manner most favourable to the party in default, because the innocent party cannot prove that any greater damages have been suffered: See Re Thornett and Fehr and Yuills Ltd (1921) 1 KB 219. But I can see no reason why, where the option fell to be exercised by the innocent party, he should not, for the purposes of assessing damages, call evidence to establish how, on the balance of probabilities, he would have exercised the option. Indeed, evidence of this kind is frequently called by claimants in legal proceedings, both in Court and in arbitration. Only by assessing damages on such a basis can the fundamental principle of assessment of damages, viz. *restitutio in integrum*, be complied with... Mr. Lloyd(被告大律师) sought to avoid the consequences of this conclusion by saying that, in any event, it could only be relied upon by the sellers if they could show that they had in fact exercised their option. In my judgment, however, that is not correct in law. The sellers have only to show that, on the balance of probabilities, they would have exercised their option..."(Goff 大法官大致是说损失计算是不能以对违约方/买方最有利的货量为基础，例如是以 315,000 吨为准。如果合约的选择权是在违约方,损失计算就会以对违约方最有利的数目计算,因为受害方是没有办法提供证据说明违约方会怎样行使选择权。但在本先例,合约的选择权是在受害方,这一来就没有理由不容许受害方提供证据说明他很有可能会行使这一个选择权供应给违约方 385,000 吨[这种证据会是口头证据佐以文件证据,如受害方有大量货物可以供应,合约价格偏高,受害方在近期的其他合约中都是供应有关合约允许最大的货量等],然后让法院或仲裁庭根据平衡的可能性作出决定。)

看来原则虽是清楚,实际"适用"(application)仍非容易。笔者多举三个例子：

(1)期租合约的租期为 1 年再加 1 年(延长与否由承租人在期租履行 9 个月内行使选择权),而船东一开始违约/毁约引致租约终断。问题是损失应是按照 1 年期限或是 2 年？要是以 2 年为准,这损失会大得多,甚至是加倍。大家也可以想象得到,承租人会否选择延长 1 年应是顶多一半一半的机会而满足不了平衡的可能性,这往往是根据交船后 9 个月的市场情况与对接下去 1 年市场走势的预测来决定。即使违约一天的航运市场非常低落,也不表示承租人不选择延长租期的可能性会高。或是把诉讼日期拖至违约/毁约后 1 年才开始,届时已知悉航运市场上升或低落,承租人会或不会在 9 个月内的最后几天行使选择权,倒是相对容易判断,因为已成了事实,不必再估计航运市场的高低。但如果换了是一个 5 年或 10 年的期租合约,总不能去拖太久作出判决或裁决吧。

(2)更复杂的情况,2 年期租加上了承租人有权以 500 万美元买这艘船,这种选择权可称为是"购买选择权"(option to purchase)。这一来,船东如果拒绝交船,这违约/毁约后的变数应如何处理？船价会急升急跌,受害方的承租人可以是"事后诸葛亮"的态度找出 2 年期间船舶价值最高的几天,说届时他会选择以 500 万美元买进这条船再转卖图利,这与市场的船价之间的差价会是一笔巨大的损失。但在把这一个合约权利量化为金钱的问题上就会涉及许多变数或"假设"(assumptions)。例如,会有可能租约在船东没有责任下发生受阻,如船舶沉没或战争,令这个"购买选择权"也同时失去。或是承租人自己不小心违约,如迟付租金,导致船东合法撤船。或是根本等不到船舶价值高的几天,在第一年航运市场低落时,承租人已经找到机会终断租约,如根据一条停租 14 天可终断租约的条文。以上许多凭空想象出来与千变万化的假设也不应考虑,这种"购买选择权"争议可见 The "Griparion" (1994) 1 Lloyd's Rep. 533 先例,而且法院并没有原则性否定这种类别的索赔。

(3)买卖合约也经常会有这种变数,如受害的买方在合约已同意的货量上有权往后追加要求违约的卖方提供额外的货量。

在以上的例子,要是根据 Toprak v. Finagrain (1979) 2 Lloyd's Rep. 98 先例的说法,受害方只要举证他更有可能行使这权利即可,举证的尺度只是可能多于不可能,所谓"平衡的可能性"(balance of probability)。通常违约/毁约的发生越接近履行的时间,原告作为受害方就越容易有证据证明他会行使这一选择权。例如,原告作为 FOB 买方在市场上租了一艘载重量比较大的船舶,可以轻松的把选择的 10% 的增加货量也一并装运。又或者原告已经达成协议把该批货物转售,而货量也是包括选择的 10% 的增加量。也有可能当时市场正在上涨,市场价格比合约价格为高。这些证据都显示受害方为了他自己的利益是有更大的可能行使选择权的,这就把一个不肯定的情况变成一个可预测或推断的情况了。反过来说,如果违约/毁约的时间距离履行时间仍然很长,仲裁庭认为受害方是否会行使选择权几乎完全是要看将来的市场涨跌,但没有谁会知道,也没有办法推断。这一来,就有可能原告受害方没有办法满足平衡的可能性了。

可举另一个先例 Sudan Import Co. Ltd. v. Societa Generale de Compensation (1958) 1 Lloyd's Rep. 310 来说明根据双方提供的证据让法院以平衡的可能性做出决定到底受害方会怎样行使属于他的裁量权。该先例案情涉及一个 2000 吨苏丹花生的 FOB 买卖合约。合约中也同时规定了卖方在提供的货物数量方面有加减 10% 的伸缩性。订约后不久,买方通知卖方他开不出信用证并需要取消买卖合约,最后买卖合约也就被终断。这种司空见惯的案件在责任方面可以说没有什么可争议的,所以双方主要的争议还是在损失方面,即应该是以 2000 吨还是 2200 吨或者其他的中间数字为基础计算损失。受害的卖方显然是力争以 2200 吨为准,因为越大的数字,乘以合约价格与市场价格的差价,得出的损失金额就会越大。毕竟有关买卖合约中给予受害方的伸缩性是没有限制的。但从双方披露出来的证据来看,法院注意到卖方曾经在双方的通信往来中说明货物已经准备好,而且在之后的一份给买方的发票中,货物数量注明是 2000 吨。这些证据显示如果买卖合约被履行,卖方会提供装船的货物只是发票中注明的 2000 吨而不是 2200 吨,所以损失计算的基础是以 2000 吨为准。上诉庭的 Evershed 勋爵是这样说:"The contract provided that the option was the sellers' option and that they were entitled to perform the contract by delivering not necessarily 2,000 tons, the exact figure stated in the contract, but a sum either 10 per cent in excess of 2,000 or 10 per cent less than 2,000, or (I assume) any intermediate figure. It was, therefore, submitted, and has been submitted in this Court by Mr. MacCrindle, that, in assessing the damages, you must, against a wrongdoer, give the benefit to the seller of assuming that, when the time came for performance, the seller would have delivered, or offered to deliver, the maximum which the contract allowed him under the option, namely, 2,200 tons. It appears, however, that, in this case, there are some additional facts which, in my judgment, have a conclusive bearing upon the question. In the first place, as I have already indicated, by the cable of Aug. 22, the sellers have intimated that they had already allocated an amount of seeds to the contract, for they had said 'entire quantity now ready'. That, standing alone, might be ambiguous; but, over a month later, and after acceptance of repudiation – a debit note was apparently transmitted by the sellers to the buyers which showed that the figure for which the buyers were debited was a figure arrived at by calculating the contract price in respect of 2,000 tons, the exact figure in the contract, and not any figure 10 per cent in excess or any intermediate figure."

有关以平衡的可能性认定受害方会怎样行使选择权或怎样做,可以再介绍其他领域的案例,就是 McWilliams v. Sir William Arrol & Co. Ltd (1962) 1 WLR 295 先例,案情涉及一个雇主违反了《Factories Act 1937》立法强制的责任,没有提供安全带给高空作业的雇员,导致了他跌落死亡。但他的遗孀向雇主提出索赔并不成功,因为雇主能够提供十分可信的证据证明即使提供给受害方安全带,他也不会或不选择在作业时系上。这是一个特殊的案件,也估计在今天的公共政策下会有不同判法。在这里只是说明针对受害方选择的估计,会是根据平衡的可能性看提供的证据。

3. 变数来自被告的违约方

3.1 与损失以违约方最低合约责任为准计算一并考虑

如果将来的变数是来自违约方,问题就会比本章第 2 段介绍的变数来自受害方复杂得多。原因是如果合约给予违约方一个选择权或者允许违约方有一个弹性的做法,这就需要与另一个以违约方最低合约责任为准计算损失的大原则一并考虑,这一个大原则会在本书第十章介绍,所以会尽量减少在本章重复。只说起点是根据一个很简单的道理:就是违约方行使他的选择权或履行合约,在任何时间都会以对他最有利的经济后果做。这表示违约方如果要做出赔偿,也会以一个合约允许下需要赔偿的最低金额赔付给受害方。

这一个大原则在多个历史悠久以及近期先例有提到,例如 Thomas v. Clarke (1818) 2 Stark 450; Cockburn v. Alexander (1848) 6 C. B. 791; Robinson v. Robinson (1851) 1 De G. M. &G. 247; Deverill v. Burnell (1873) L. R. 8 C. P. 475; Re Thornett & Fehr (1921) K. B. 219; Abrahams v. Herbert Reiach Ltd (1922) 1 KB 477; Kaye Steam Navigating Co v. Barnett (1932) 48 TLR 440; Withers v. General Theatre Corp. (1933) 2 KB 536 (CA); Lavarack v. Woods of Colchester Ltd (1967) 1 QB 278; The "Mihalis Angelos" (1970) 2 Lloyd's Rep. 43; The "Rijn" (1981) 2 Lloyd's Rep. 267; Paula Lee v. Robert Zehil & Co. (1983) 2 All E. R. 390; Spiliada Maritime Co v. Louis Dreyfus Co (1983) Com L R 268; Johnson Matthey Banking v. The State Trading Corporation of India (1984) 1 Lloyd's Rep. 427; TCN Channel 9 Pty Ltd v. Hayden Enterprises Pty Ltd (1989) 16 NSWLR 130; The "World Navigator" (1991) 2 Lloyd's Rep

23;The "Seaflower" (2000) 2 Lloyd's Rep 37; And So To Bed v. Dixon (2001) FSR 935; The "Golden Victory" (2007) 2 Lloyd's Rep 164; Durham Tees Valley Airport Ltd v. BMI Baby Ltd. (2011) 1 Lloyd's Rep 68 等。这些先例大部分会在本书第十章做出详细介绍。在这里只抽样节录与简单介绍这个以违约方最低合约责任为准计算损失大原则的少数先例。

这一个原则在 19 世纪就已经出现。这可节录 Cockburn v. Alexander (1848) 6 CB 791 先例中 Maule 大法官说:"Where there are several ways in which the contract might be performed, that mode is adopted which is the least profitable to the plaintiff and the least burdensome to the defendant."(如果合约可以有几种不同的履行方法,就要以一种对原告产生最低利润与对被告带来最轻责任的方法计算损失。)

之后可节录 Diplock 大法官在 Lavarack v. Woods of Colchester Ltd 先例所说:"The general rule as stated by Scrutton L. J. in Abrahams v. Reiach (1922) 1 KB 477 that in an action for breach of contract a defendant is not liable for not doing that which he is not bound to do, has been generally accepted as correct ..."(在违约的诉讼中一般的规定是被告不需要对合约中他没有必要履行的部分造成的损失去负责,这说法被认为是正确的。)

另在 The "Mihalis Angelos" 中,上诉庭的 Denning 勋爵也明确说出了这一假设或原则:"that if the defendant has under the contract an option which would reduce or extinguish the loss it will be assumed he will exercise it."(如果被告在合约中有一个选择权可以减少或免除损失赔偿,应该假设他会行使这一个权利。)

3.2　部分有关先例的介绍

在这里在以下段节挑几个较早期的先例作简单介绍,让读者可以看到在涉及违约方的裁量权或是弹性做法履行合约的话,损失会怎样计算。

3.2.1　先例之一:Kaye Steam Navigating Co v. Barnett

在 Kaye Steam Navigating Co v. Barnett (1932) 48 TLR 440 先例,案情涉及货方没有给船舶提供货物而构成违约/毁约,但损失的计算是假设违约/毁约的货方会选择一个在真正履约时船东花费最大的卸港(租约中允许货方在一个地理范围内的多个港口中选择一个作为卸港,但航次没有履行,所以货方没有做出选择,只是计算损失时作出假设),进而减少船东索赔的预期损失/利润损失。Branson 大法官是这样说:"But once you have the principle that in assessing damages to be paid by a person who has broken his contract you must see that you do not impose on him more than he has contracted to give to the plaintiff, one cannot avoid the conclusion that in calculating the loss of profit which a charterer who has broken his charter-party must pay to the ship, any option which the charterer is given under the charter-party, the exercise of which would reduce the profit which the shipowner could have earned, must be taken into account in assessing damages."

3.2.2 先例之二:The“Mihalis Angelos”

第二个先例是 The“Mihalis Angelos”(1970) 2 Lloyd's Rep. 43,案情涉及一个程租合约,装港是当时北越的海防。租约中有一个销约期,是1965年7月20日。但实际上 Mihalis Angelos 轮在上一个航次发生了严重的延误,在香港卸货也要到7月23日才能完毕,然后还需要时间开去海防,所以显然赶不上销约期。但承租人也遇上了困难,因为车皮的问题而无法把货物拉去装港。可以说在这种情况下,双方都无法履行合约。希腊船东肯定船舶无法在销约期前抵达海防港装货了,就跟承租人说:“船可能赶不及了,你现在就告诉我是延长销约期还是取消租约吧。”注意船东这一个电文仅是询问,未表明他拒绝把船舶开去装港。但承租人也憨得可爱,电文回应说:“没关系啦,反正我也没货,你不要来了。”这一来希腊船东马上就不安好心了,一个电传打给对方说:“你声称没货可装,构成‘预期违约’(anticipatory breach),我要索赔。”承租人在有很多不同的说法回应甚至可以不理睬船东的情况下,却做出了一个最笨的回应。这可以采用的很多不同的回应包括承租人可以回应说:“如果船舶晚到了,我到时肯定会解约”,这没有问题因为这只是告知船东将来的意图,而且这是一个合法的意图。承租人更加可以进一步“敲竹杠”说:“如果船舶晚到了,我到时肯定会解约,如果船东不想白跑一趟,你就要赔给我2万美元,这只是你可以省下的燃油费用,我可以提早让你脱身并寻找替代租约。”至于承租人自己的货物没有准备好也就不必这么坦白告诉希腊船东了,反正船舶赶不及在销约期之前抵达装港肯定会被取消,货物有没有备妥再也没有关系。

后来船东真开始伦敦仲裁向承租人索赔,并证明到他有损失,因为他找到的另外一个替代航次利润并没有原本这个航次高,等于是利润上损失了一些。第一审判下来,承租人提出的当时是依合约销约期终断合约的抗辩并不成立。法院认为,程租合约清楚订明,船舶错过销约期,承租人取消租约的权利是要在销约期已届满并且船舶抵达装港并递交了“装货准备就绪通知书”(notice of readiness)后才能行使的。英国高院最后判定承租人要赔船东损失。于是承租人上诉。在上诉庭(Court of Appeal),Denning 勋爵等大法官判定承租人只需赔偿象征性的损失。因为损害赔偿的大原则是要使受害方恢复至合约未被违反的经济地位,损失衡量应该是看合约如果被履行与实际没有履约的区别。本案中船舶就是到了装港海防也会过了销约期,在当时情况下承租人肯定会行使销约权取消合约,这是承租人估计履行的做法,等于租约违约/毁约后被取消的情况是“注定会发生”(predestined to happen)。这一来,即使是继续履约,船东仍是不能保住租约,经济地位与承租人提前的违约/毁约无区别,因此船东实际上没有蒙受损失,结果高院判决被上诉庭推翻。这样的判法在很大的程度上与以违约方最低合约责任是一并考虑,就是他如果将来根据合约有一个可以合法终断的机会,就会假设他会把握。

3.2.3 先例之三:Spiliada Maritime Co v. Louis Dreyfus Co

第三个先例是 Spiliada Maritime Co v. Louis Dreyfus Co (1983) Com L R 268,案情

涉及承租合约中,承租人没有给船舶提供货物而构成合约的违约/毁约,但损失的计算是假设承租人如果履行,就会用尽所有租约下约定的免费装卸时间,进而把航次履行的时间延长,减少船东计算的预期损失/利润损失。这是因为能够赚取的运费是一笔固定的金额,但这并非是船东作为受害方的损失,因为租约如果履行是需要成本的。显然如果履行的时间越长,成本就越高,而船东的预期损失也就越少。会是租约约定的免费装卸时间(如总共 15 天)比现实中偏高,而船东可以提供证明如果履行的话,正常装卸顶多只需要 10 天。但由于违约方的承租人可以免费享有 15 天,就是假设他会用完这 15 天以减少对船东的损失赔偿。这方面读者再看接下去第五个先例就会更加明白。

3.2.4　先例之四:Johnson Matthey Banking v. The State Trading Corporation of India

第四个先例是 Johnson Matthey Banking v. The State Trading Corporation of India (1984) 1 Lloyd's Rep. 427,涉及白银的买卖,但由于印度政府下禁令阻止白银的出口而导致了卖方(也就是被判是违约方的被告)无法履行,买方接受了违约/毁约并提出索赔损失。简单说就是英国法院判买方胜诉,但所能成功索赔的损失是根据合约价格与市场价格在违约一天的差价,但要减掉卖方有 1.5% 货量的伸缩性。Staughton 大法官是这样说:"No silver was delivered. On Mar. 31, 1980, the buyers treated the sellers as in default. In my judgement the buyers are entitled to damages from the sellers under the Sale of Goods Act. It is not suggested that Indian law provided any different measure of damages from English law. They are entitled to the difference between the contract prices and the market price on Mar. 31, 1980. That produces a figure of 1,175,675.75 pounds. From it must be deducted a tolerance of 1.5%. (see the buyers' letter of Aug. 15, 1977) Since the sellers might lawfully have made use of that tolerance in performing their contracts. That leaves 1,158,040.50 pounds."(其中提到的1977 年8 月15 日的信中就涉及卖方有 1.5% 的伸缩性。)

3.2.5　先例之五:The "World Navigator"

第五个先例是 The "World Navigator" (1991) 2 Lloyd's Rep 23,案情涉及以 FOB 出售的30,000 吨玉米,分三批付运。在 FOB 买方派船到南美的装港时,由于卖方还没准备好文件,导致船舶延期靠泊装货,延误是从 1985 年6 月13 日至7 月11 日。买方于是索赔这段延误期间的损失,而在责任方面英国法院判是卖方违反了一条默示条文,即卖方需要合作让买方派遣的船舶尽快靠泊装货。但在损失计算方面就有更大争议。卖方认为,在买卖合约中有条文针对在靠泊后装货率是 500 吨一个"好天气工作天"(weather working day),这一来,针对该批 12,000 吨玉米的装货就需要 24 天。所以,即使没有违反默示条文,船舶在靠泊后卖方也可以慢慢装货用尽这 24 天,而不是以实际快速得多的装货率去装货(由于有实际履行,所以是知道船舶在 7 月 18 日至 22 日的 4 天内装完)。从而令停留在装港总的时间是差不多,所以买方没有损失。这一个先例很有争议性,因为案情不涉及违约的卖方有一个选择权,所以以违约方最低合约责任为准计算损失的大原则是否适用有争议。其中第一审的 Phillips 大法官判违约的卖方败诉,但去了上诉庭该判决被推翻,其中上诉庭的 David Croom - Johnson 大法官说:“最低合约责任大原则的适用并不局限在违约方有一个选择权”(The application of the general rule is not dependent on there being an option)。

这一个先例会在本书第十章会有更详细的介绍。

3.3 对损失以违约方最低合约责任为准计算持不同意见的先例

在3.1段中所提到的大量先例中有少数不同的同时期判法,就是不让违约方在没有限制的情况下假设他会行使选择权或选择有利的弹性做法减少损失赔偿金额,而是另以一个估计是合理与实际会发生的做法(如果合约被履行)为准限制违约方。这方面在接下去的段节简单介绍以上提到的两个比较早期的先例。

3.3.1 先例之一:Abrahams v. Herbert Reiach

这里第一个先例(并会在第十章6.2段详述)是 Abrahams v. Herbert Reiach Ltd (1922) 1 KB 477,案情涉及被告印刷商承诺了原告出版原告的文章/书籍,并同意按照出版的数量支付原告稿费。但被告后来拒绝出版,这构成了违约/毁约。在计算损失方面,被告声称他可以决定出版的格式、定价、出版日期与复印的本数,并以这种方式(主要是复印的本数)把原告的损失也就是稿费压到最低。这里不涉及违约方一个明示的选择权,但他如果履行合约允许弹性的做法,只是实际中他不会这样做。上诉庭判损失计算不能照违约方的争辩,其中 Scrutton 大法官是说被告必须“按照一个不低于正常履行合约的情况下会复印的本数”(will bound to make such a publication as could be considered reasonable in the circumstances)作为赔偿的标准。在这一先例可以看到,除非合约中有明确规定违约方的选择权,否则在只有一个弹性的做法时,还是需要考虑如果履约怎样才是合理的做法。

3.3.2 先例之二:Paula Lee v. Robert Zehil & Co

另一个先例是在本书第十章6.7段有详述的 Paula Lee v. Robert Zehil & Co. (1983) 2 All E. R. 390,案情涉及原告制衣商与被告分销商订立买卖合约,被告承诺每一个季度向原告购买1.6万件衣服,可以选择不同的式样、种类和价格的衣服。被告违约/毁约后在计算要支付的损失赔偿时指出应以1.6万套最便宜的衣服为准,这也会把原告的索赔金额压到最低。但法院判在该合约条文下,被告不能也不会如此履行,合约要求是对不同种类衣服有一个合理选购,但在计算上仍是以这“合理选购”下被告会支付的最低价格为准(in terms of that reasonable selection which would yield the lowest price)。Mustill 大法官是这样说:“Accordingly I consider that the agreement must be construed as subject to an implied reasonable manner. Since selection would be a matter of judgment, this leaved open the very strong possibility that there would not be a unique reasonable selection, but a range of such selections, some yielding a greater total price than others for the 16,000 chosen garments. On this basis, the damages should, as I have already suggested, be assessed in terms of that reasonable selection which would yield the lowest price."

3.4　对损失以违约方最低合约责任为准计算太偏袒违约方的批评

在近年来对以违约方最低合约责任为准计算损失的大原则有了不少批评,并令这方面的法律地位目前并不明确,这方面会在本书第十章有详论。在这里只是说这一个问题已经变得越来越复杂,而在 3.1 段中所列举的大量先例还没有哪一个直接到贵族院或最高院并对这方面给出权威的说法。

赔偿损失的起点就是复原,也就是让受害方恢复到合约被履行的地位。至于怎么样才算是被履行,也要解释有关的合约条文。目前的法律是发展到将来的履行如果涉及违约方的变数,就要把这个变数区分为:(1)是否给违约方一个"绝对或没有任何限制的选择权"(absolute or unrestricted option);(2)是否给违约方一个选择权,但明示或默示有限制;(3)违约方"单一的履行责任"(single obligation),但这一个责任有一定的弹性。看来,只有在(1)违约方才是可以以他最低合约责任为准计算损失。但在(2)与(3),法院看来是更愿意默示违约方如果行使选择权或选择有利的弹性做法中有各种的限制,包括合理、实际、真诚与善意。

4. 变数全部或部分来自第三人

这是在违约/毁约与合约被终断后的损失计算中,对将来变数的三种中最难掌握的一种情况。而且法律也发展出来另一种计算损失的办法,即不再看这一变数是否能够满足平衡的可能性,而是根据一种名为"机会损失"(loss of chance)的办法。这种计算办法除了适用在合约外,也适用在侵权的经济损失计算。

这在 Allied Maples Group Ltd v. Simmons & Simmons (a firm) (1995) 1 WLR 1602 先例中,Stuart – Smith 大法官所说:

"what has to be proved to establish a causal link between the negligence of the defendants and the loss sustained by the plaintiffs depends in the first instance on whether the negligence consists of some positive act or misfeasance, or an omission or non – feasance. In the former case, the question of causation is one of historical fact. The court has to determine on the balance of probability whether the defendant's act, for example the careless driving, caused the plaintiffs loss consisting of his broken leg. Once established on balance of probability, that fact is taken as true and the plaintiff recovers his damage in full. There is no discount because the judge considers that the balance is only just tipped in favour of the plaintiff; and the plaintiff gets nothing if he fails to establish that it is more likely than not that the accident resulted in the injury. (一般而言,疏忽与损失之间的因果关系是根据平衡的可能性,如果法院认定疏忽[这是已经发生了的事实]的可能性比没有疏

忽的可能性更大,即使是大一点点,也会是认定疏忽的事实是正确的,并让原告可向被告取回全部的损失。这可能性是不存在对损失的金额有任何扣减,判决的结果是全部取回损失或没有任何赔偿。)

Questions of quantification of the plaintiff's loss, however, may depend upon future uncertain events. For example... whether he will continue to earn at the same rate until retirement, whether, but for the accident, he might have been promoted. It is trite law that these questions are not decided on a balance of probability, but rather on the court's assessment, often expressed in percentage terms, of the risk eventuating or the prospect of promotion, which it should be noted depends in part at least on the hypothetical acts of a third party, namely the plaintiff's employer."(对于原告将来的损失,如原告将来会否升职或只会赚取同样的工资直到退休,就涉及第三人[也就是他的雇主]的裁量权与变数。法律已经明确下来对这方面的认定不是根据平衡的可能性,而是由法院作出核算,通常是一个百分比。)

4.1 "机会损失"的大原则

在机会损失(loss of chance)的大原则下,也有不少近期的重要先例与发展,但仍存在很多不明确问题。例如在 Allied Maples Group Ltd v. Simmons & Simmons (a firm) (1995) 1 WLR 1602 先例(针对律师的专业疏忽),这是有关"机会损失"(loss of chance)的最重要先例,它解读了多年前的 Chaplin v. Hicks (1911) 2 KB 786 先例,并明确了是有这一种损失类别。这一种损失类别与传统的"平衡的可能性"(balance of probability)很不一样,所根据的只是"possibilities"找出一个损失赔偿的百分比。众所周知,"possible"是指 50% 以下的可能性,而"probable"则是指可以高达 90% 的可能性。在之后的法律也明确了原告受害方是不能在同一个案件中同时以传统的平衡的可能性与机会损失来提出救济,因为他们是相互排斥的,而是要根据不同案件的本质决定损失赔偿应该是根据哪一种的准则来提出救济(案件本质是涉及完全或部分的第三人变数才能适用机会损失的救济)。在 Gregg v. Scott (2005) UKHL 2(针对医疗疏忽),Baroness Hale 大法官解释了原因,就是允许这种做法会令损失的计算变得复杂与不肯定。而且太善待原告,Baroness Hale 大法官说:"heads you lose everything, tails I win something"(这是指投掷硬币,如果是正面,也表示根据平衡的可能性胜诉,原告可以成功索赔全部的损失。如果是背面,根据机会损失,原告也可以成功索赔一部分的损失)。Baroness Hale 大法官也讲到这对被告很不公平,因为他没有同样的这两个机会。

另也在 Stovold v. Barlows (1996) PNLR 91 先例中上诉庭明确说明如果损失只是根据第三人的变数,原告与被告都可以坚持以机会损失来核算赔偿金额。

机会损失的救济可以适用在哪一类的案件已经比较明确了,如大量的专业人士(主要是律师)因为专业疏忽被索赔损失就已经很明确是根据机会损失来计算/核算的。但还是有不明确的地方,这方面在本章第 5.5 段的商业案件与第 7 段的海事案件会介绍。其中在有关医疗疏忽的先例 Hotson v. East Berkshire Area Health Authority (1987) AC 750 中,涉及被告对原告的延误诊断,就把机会损失的救济从合约与经济损失扩张到侵权与人身伤亡的范畴。但之后在 Gregg v. Scott (2005) UKHL 2 先例中,贵族院拒绝在医疗疏忽的案件中依赖机会损失的救济。

这些方面以及其他方面会在接下去的段节进一步探讨。

4.1.1 第三人的变数经常不会有证据作出平衡的可能性判断,只能推断与估计机会损失

这里的困难就是如果将来的变数是来自第三人,不一定会有第三人(第三人可以是数目庞大的人士)举证他会怎样做。正如 Allied Maples Group Ltd v. Simmons & Simmons (a firm) (1995) 1 WLR 1602 先例中所说:"the third parties' attitude must be a matter of inference. In many cases direct evidence from the third party will not be available, as in the cases of the deceased husbands in Hall v. Meyrick (1957) 2 QB 455 and Davies v. Taylor (1974) AC 207."笔者也想到在国际层面,第三人如果不愿意举证,也很难强制把他传召到法院来举证。

而即使第三人肯举证,他的说法也不一定在某一些案件会被视为是有用的证据,正如 Allied Maples Group Ltd v. Simmons & Simmons (a firm)先例中所说:"It will not avail the plaintiffs (原告) if Gillow (第三人) say: 'We might have yielded; we might not. It is really not possible to say.' That does not lead to the conclusion that there was a 50% chance, or any substantial chance: it is still all speculation. Nor will it avail the plaintiffs to obtain apparent admissions from Gillow that: 'Of course we might have yielded; so there was a chance,' and then to drive the witness into hazarding a percentage by asking: 'A 50% chance? 40%? 30%?' until he reluctantly accepts a figure. That would not be inviting the witness to give evidence, but to speculate."

这不像上述介绍的变数是来自原告或者被告,他们是可以举证(虽然是可以估计到他们提供的证据都会是"自我保护"[self - serving]),并可根据平衡的可能性作出判断。所以在很多这种涉及第三人的变数,要根据平衡的可能性证明有 50% 以上的发生可能性是很难做得到的。会有许多情况是明显原告受害方因为被告的违约/毁约或疏忽而遭受了预期经济损失或机会,只是这损失会有太多变数,导致完全获偿或毫无赔偿的结果都是不公平。Reid 勋爵在 Davies v. Taylor (1974) AC 207 先例说得很明白,节录如下:"I do not think that the law is so foolish as to suppose that you can. All that you can do is to evaluate the chance. Sometimes it is virtually 100 per cent.: sometimes virtually nil. But often it is somewhere in between. And if it is somewhere in between I do not see much difference between a probability of 51 per cent and a probability of 49 per cent... If the balance of probability were the proper test what is to happen in the two cases which I have supposed of a 60 per cent and a 40 per cent probability? The 40 per cent case will get nothing but what about the 60 per cent case? Is it to get a full award on the basis that it has been proved that the wife would have returned to her husband? That would be the logical result. I can see no ground at all for saying that the 40 per cent case fails altogether but the 60 per cent case gets 100 per cent. But it would be almost absurd to say that the 40 per cent case gets nothing while the 60 per cent case award is scaled down to that proportion of what the award would have been if the spouses had been living together. That would be applying two different rules to the two cases. So I reject the balance of probability in this case."

另也可节录Parker大法官在先例Kitchen v. Royal Air Force Association（1958）1 WLR 563所说："If the plaintiff can satisfy the court that she would have had some prospect of success, then it would be for the court to evaluate those prospects, taking into consideration the difficulties that remained to be surmounted."

4.1.2 机会损失会带来的问题：大量诉讼与社会的沉重负担

这马上想得到允许机会损失作为救济所带来的问题，就是本来受害方对于索赔机会不高的案件会放弃诉讼，也就是受害方没办法满足"平衡的可能性"（balance of probability）测试，但现在有了机会损失的救济，受害方就会蠢蠢欲动。这种案件即使是只有10%或20%的可能性，原告也值得向被告提出索赔。甚至在做法上提出的救济是主要以平衡的可能性，希望如果举证成功就可以索赔全部损失。但为了避免不成功就什么赔偿也得不到或只有名义赔偿，并因此要承担诉讼费用，原告就以"替代案件"（alternative case）要求"机会损失"（loss of chance）的救济，希望拿到10%或20%的赔偿也是聊胜于无。

毕竟，诉讼没有一定会胜诉或败诉的案件，总会有机会成为例外。例如，一个现在是穷光蛋的美国小青年能否在20年后变为美国首富，比David Rockefeller先生（美国Exxon石油公司的创办人）或Bill Gates先生更富有，就难以说是他完全不可能，1%的机会总会有。而如果在涉及该小青年伤亡的侵权案件中，他或他的家人索赔的金额庞大，判他可以获得David Rockefeller先生或Bill Gates先生财富的1%作为他将来的损失也会是非常庞大的金额。

所以就要严格控制包括要求原告先要超越哪一些障碍才能以机会损失计算损失。这方面的障碍在本章4.1.4段有针对，就是这一个损失的机会必须是真正与实质的。毕竟，机会损失只为了针对第三人的变数，而不是其他变数。而来自其他的变数，还是要根据平衡的可能性作出判断。例如，以上述所讲的一个穷青年20年后变为比David Rockefeller或Bill Gates更富有，就会涉及千千万万的变数。这包括他的教育、才智、判断能力、勤奋、雄心或野心、家庭背景、社会环境、个人机遇与运气等，这些因素都不涉及第三人的变数，要作出判断是需要满足平衡的可能性，之后才能考虑机会损失。

另一方面需要严格控制是区分究竟哪一类案件可以得到机会损失的救济，哪一些就必须满足"平衡的可能性"。另外也需要严格控制某些类别的案件，因为一开放可以以机会损失提出救济，就会带来大量的诉讼，给整个社会带来不安宁与沉重的负担。这是政策的问题，所以在 Gregg v. Scott（2005）UKHL 2 先例，贵族院判医疗疏忽是不可以根据机会损失提出救济的。这导致了医生与律师两个专业在这方面有完全不同的对待，前者没有机会损失的救济，但后者就有这个救济。这个决定显然只是考虑公共政策，与公平合理或逻辑性没有关系。这些方面都会在稍后作出进一步的介绍。

4.1.3　机会损失的推断与估计不能针对责任

针对机会损失的推断与估计，一个困难是上诉庭在 Allied Maples Group Ltd v. Simmons & Simmons（a firm）（1995）1 WLR 1602 先例所说的不容易掌握因果关系的中断与计算损失的开始（where causation ends and quantification of damage begins）。这是因为被告的疏忽所导致的损失，包括两者之间的"因果关系"（causation），是责任的一部分。在判了被告有责任后，才针对损失的计算。而针对责任的判决，通常是要根据平衡的可能性。但在 Allied Maples Group Ltd v. Simmons & Simmons（a firm）先例中已经明确下来，针对涉及机会损失的案件（主要因为涉及第三人的变数），在因果关系上可以有一个比平衡的可能性测试更低的举证标准，就是只需要证明违约/毁约或疏忽导致一个"真正"（real）与"实质"（substantial）的损失，而不是太具"臆猜性"（speculative）。"太具臆猜性"在 Mount v. Barker Austin（a firm）（1998）PNLR 493 先例中被 Simon Brown 大法官认为应该更恰当的被称为"成功机会微小"（negligible prospect of success），下一小段会进一步解释这一问题。在这里只是说不少案例中把确立责任的部分（因果关系）与核算损失的部分（机会损失）混为一谈。比方说，在处理实际案件中经常会遇到一种错误的做法，就是把因果关系确定为40%（本来根据平衡的可能性，应该没有责任），并在接下去核算损失时也同样把机会损失确定为40%。这一问题在 Jill Poole 教授的《Loss of chance and the evaluation of hypotheticals in contractual claims》一文中有提到，说："For the courts have not always maintained a clear distinction between causation and quantum when approaching the determination of loss of chance claims. **As a result, they have fallen into the trap of identifying liability by reference to matters which should figure only in the assessment of quantum once that liability has been established.** The danger is that the precise mathematical evaluation of the chance of the hypothetical occurring becomes the calculation which determines liability and whether the loss of chance is, in principle, established; rather, the test for causation, and hence liability, is whether the loss is 'real' or 'substantial', which has no precise mathematical equivalent."

该文章接下去在结论部分这样说："Of course, this begs the question: how are the courts to determine whether the lost chance is substantial or speculative? It has been argued here that the great danger in using quantitative terminology is that it suggests the necessity to prove a substantial loss of chance as a percentage chance when a more instinctive, less mathematical, response is called for. **The liability exercise involves a discretion, not statistics. The statistics should relate only to the fixing of the quantum for the lost chance, ie. its actual measurement. To this end it is vital that the courts avoid a temptation to dismiss loss of chance claims where something of value.** It may therefore be preferable to amend the terminology accordingly. It would also be preferable to restore a chronological structure to the identification and quantification of lost chance claims. **Quantum should not be used to determine liability**—or, for that matter, to determine whether the loss turns on a past fact or hypothetical."(加黑部分是笔者的强调)

总结上述 Jill Poole 教授所说的主要意思就是机会损失是不应该适用在责任方面,而只能适用在涉及来自第三人变数的损失计算。针对责任方面还是要看因果关系,而因果关系是根据"平衡的可能性"(balance of probability),法院或仲裁庭根据提供的证据以常识作出一个"直觉上"(instinctive 或 gut feeling)的判断,要么就是有责任,要么就是没有责任。责任的确定方面是不涉及对一些假设情况的发生几率做出精确的数学计算,这种计算只能适用在确定损失的金额。但 Jill Poole 教授说是很多法院的先例也把责任与损失的确定混为一谈,都适用机会损失的判定标准。比如是认为有 20% 的几率也适用在责任的确定,但是根据平衡的可能性,20% 是肯定不足够确定被告有责任,而没有责任就根本不会需要确定损失金额。

4.1.4 机会必须是真正与实质的,不能太具臆猜性

机会必须是真正与实质的说法也在 Davies v. Taylor (1974) AC 207 先例与 Allied Maples Group Ltd v. Simmons & Simmons (a firm) (1995) 1 WLR 1602 先例中有提及。这两个案例的案情在稍后有详述,不重复。只说看是否是一个真正和实质的机会是在因果关系的阶段就要针对。照理说如果太具臆猜性,也应该过不了平衡的可能性测试。但看来,针对机会损失的救济,在因果关系方面的要求是比平衡的可能性为低的。在 Allied Maples Group Ltd v. Simmons & Simmons (a firm)先例中,上诉庭的 Stuart - Smith 大法官是这样说:"But, in my judgment, the plaintiff must prove as a matter of causation that he has a real or substantial chance as opposed to a speculative one. If he succeeds in doing so, the evaluation of the chance is part of the assessment of the quantum of damage, the range lying somewhere between something that just qualifies as real and substantial on the one hand and near certainty on the other. I do not think that it is helpful to seek to lay down in percentage terms what the lower and upper ends of the bracket should be."

上述的说法显然不是针对平衡的可能性,虽然 Stuart - Smith 大法官拒绝给出一个明确的百分比上下限,但说明是不需要超过 50%,这是不足够满足平衡的可能性的要求。另外,Millett 大法官说得更加清楚:"The prospects of the ultimate success (or, in the case of litigation, of receiving an offer of settlement) may be less than 50%, but they are nevertheless capable of objective evaluation."

这方面也可以看 Sellars v. Adelaide Pertroleum NL (1994) 179 CLR 332 先例与 Blue Circle Industries Plc v. Ministry of Defense (1999) Ch 289 先例。另在 Spring v. Guardian Assurance Plc. (1995) 2 A. C. 296 先例中(稍后会介绍),也提到了只需要证明“失去了被雇佣的合理机会”(lost a reasonable chance of employment)就已经足够进一步核算机会损失了。

在因果关系方面不需要达到 51% 以上的平衡的可能性就已经足够证明有一个真正与实质的损失,这在 Allied Maples Group Ltd v. Simmons & Simmons (a firm) 等接下去的很多先例有显示,如在涉及律师疏忽的 Normans Bay Ltd v. Coudert Bros (2004) EWCA Civ 215 先例,因果关系被认定只有 40%(照理由考虑责任方面是不应该作出这种百分比),但这已经是足够进一步核算机会损失了。另在 Dixon v. Clement Jones (a firm) (2004) EWCA Civ 1005; (2005) PNLR 6; (2004) TLR 396,案情涉及原告因他的会计师漏给了一个专业意见而导致损失,于是原告聘用律师起诉该会计师,然而该律师没有把索赔请求送达,导致索赔被法院撤销,原告转而向该律师提出索赔。法院判该原告在被撤销的案件中只有 30% 的胜诉机会,因为从表面证据看来,会计师即使给了专业意见,也不会影响原告的商业决定,这表示该案件并非是一个强有力的案件。被告的律师提出上诉指第一审的大法官既然认定会计师即使给了意见也不影响原告的决定,就表示律师的专业疏忽与原告声称的损失之间的因果关系很难成立。而即使能够成立,顶多也只有 5% ~ 10%,这是典型的臆猜性的损失。但上诉庭不接受这一争议,认为法院在因果关系上只需要做出一个“对索赔结果的合理核算”(reasonable assessment of outcome of the claim),其中 Rix 大法官说:“provided the underlying claim is of some real value, then the separate causation issue which arises in the instant claim out of the loss of underlying litigation answers itself.”

在商业方面(而不是主要适用机会损失的专业疏忽)被视为太具臆猜性的先例可看在本书第十章之 6. 12 段介绍的 Automotive Latch Systems Ltd v. Honeywell International Inc (2008) EWHC 2171 (Comm)先例,被法院拒绝适用机会损失。在本章 5. 5 段会介绍一个笔者的仲裁案件中,被告的中国医学仪器生产公司的代表大律师曾经提供了一份计算损失的流程以协助仲裁庭决定有关机会损失的适用。该流程的第一步是要先根据"平衡的可能性"(balance of probability)决定原告的欧洲公司违约/毁约或是被告违约/毁约,这是因为在案件中双方指责对方违约与无法履行合约责任。这方面涉及责任,决定要适用平衡的可能性在本章之 4. 1. 3 段有介绍。流程的第二步是假设被告违约/毁约,就要根据平衡的可能性决定原告是否能够满足所有的要求或条件把从被告购买的医学仪器推向国际市场与向国际卫生组织投标。这包括生产过程中原告能否按照合约严格提供的设备与技术援助、能否向国际组织与有关国家的主管单位取得有关医学仪器的批文或许可证等。流程的第三步是根据平衡的可能性整体看这种医学仪器是否在国际市场中有卖点,可以在已饱和的市场中占一席之地。这才来到流程的第四步,也就是机会损失。到了这一步,不再是根据平衡的可能性而只是根据该医学仪器在国际市场被第三人接受的机会。换言之,这一步的考虑纯粹是估计市场中第三人(包括国际卫生组织)的变数。这一个变数会根据该医学仪器对使用者的吸引力、出售的价格、其他竞争者同类产品的比较、会出现突破性技术新产品的可能性等,最后决定一个百分比作为机会损失。这可以低至10%或高至80%~90%不等,而如果低至10%也不代表原告的索赔太具臆猜性。

4.2 最早期的涉及第三人变数的先例

这方面的先例最早出现在Richardson v. Mellish (1824) 2 Bing 229,案情涉及一个船长为被告所雇用在船上航行两个航次,但雇佣合约中规定第二个航次是否允许该船长航行取决于东印度公司(第三人)的决定。虽然一贯的做法是东印度公司会允许船长继续服务。之后被告违约/毁约,导致船长作为原告提出索赔。其中一个重要的争议就是第二个航次的船长报酬是否应该计算在内,因为有一个第三人决定的变数。英国法院是支持原告应该取得赔偿,其中Best大法官说:"Common sense says you are not to be paid for consequences which might not turn to in your favour; but the plaintiff is entitled to have a compensation for being deprived of that which almost certainly happens in these cases."看来这一个古老的先例针对将来第三人的变数是根据平衡的可能性而不是本章所讲的机会损失。

另一个先例The"Empress of Britain" (1913) 29 TLR 423,案情涉及原告的一艘船舶因为被告的侵权行为而沉没。该船舶有一个7年的租约,沉没的时候只是第二年,但在租约剩下的5年,合约说明每一年都给承租人(第三人)取消合约的选择权。英国法院判在计算预期损失时,整个租约以及所有的变数都应该考虑在内。

4.3 "机会损失"的先例Chaplin v. Hicks

但真正被视为是带来"机会损失"(loss of chance)计算办法的先例就是一个出名的选美先例Chaplin v. Hicks (1911) 2 KB 786。有关的案情涉及选美,本来是有12个奖,就是3年的剧院雇佣合约,其中头4个奖是每周5英镑的工资,接下去4个奖为每周4英镑,最后4个是每周3英镑。本来的计划是将24个进入决赛的美女照片刊登在报纸上由读者投票确定中奖的人选,但由于反应出乎意料的热烈(大概有6000人)导致选美组织改变了规则。变为在英国的10个地区各选出5个美女,这等于总共有50个参赛者。但最后的12个胜利美女则是由被告Hicks先生挑选,他本人是一个演员的经理人。Hicks先生的挑选是在伦敦的Aldwych剧院进行,基本上是一个面试,估计除了看她们的样貌外,另外也包括了考察她们的演技与记台词的能力。原告Chaplin小姐是伦敦地区排名最高的参选人,她很晚才收到选美组织的通知要求她与Hicks先生面试,但她当时在英国另一个城市Dundee演出(她本来已经是一名演员),根本赶不回伦敦,因此被淘汰。这导致原告(Chaplin小姐)向被告(Hicks先生)提出索赔,认为被告违反合约作出了不合理的通知,这也被英国法院所接受,但问题主要出在如何计算原告的损失。显然,原告是不能根据这12个奖索赔损失,因为平均的几率是每一个由地区选出的美女只有1/4的机会得奖。除此之外还有其他的变数,如由 Hicks 先生决定谁得奖以及原告自己在面试的表现等,反正被告的抗辩是认为原告根本没有办法来准确算出她的经济损失。但英国上诉庭不同意,认为被告的违约即使是令损失很难计算,因为有太多变数,但也不是不尽量根据几率作出计算的理由。Vaughan Williams 大法官说:"It was said that the plaintiff's chance of winning a prize turned on such a number of contingencies that it was impossible for anyone, even after arriving at the conclusion that the plaintiff had lost her opportunity by the breach, to say that there was any assessable value of that loss. It is said that in a case which involves so many contingencies it is impossible to say what was the plaintiff's pecuniary loss. I am unable to agree with that contention. I agree that the presence of all the contingencies upon which the gaining of the prize might depend makes the calculation not only difficult but incapable of being carried out with certainty or precision. The proposition is that, whenever the contingencies on which the result depends are numerous and difficult to deal with, it is impossible to recover any damages for the loss of the chance or opportunity of winning the prize... I agree... that damages might be so unassessable that the doctrine of averages would be inapplicable because the necessary figures for working upon would not be forthcoming... I only wish to deny with emphasis that, because precision cannot be arrived at, the jury has no function in the assessment of damages."

上诉庭认为原告显然损失了一个好机会,是一个"有价值的机会"(something of value),不应该不做出计算。上诉庭这样说:"The existence of contingency, which is dependent on the volition of a third person, is not enough to justify us in saying that the damages are incapable of assessment... where by contract a man has a right to belong to a limited class of competitors, he is possessed of something of value"

结果陪审团(当时英国法院的民事案件也是由陪审团认定事实)判原告可以成功向被告索赔 100 英镑,这比 1/4 的得奖机会还要偏高,估计是考虑到原告是伦敦地区 5 名获选美女中排名最高的,另加上她本身已经是演员,所以如果能够继续参选,获奖的机会应该比平均要高。

已经提到过,这一个"选美先例"一直被视为带来"机会损失"(loss of chance)的计算办法。但实际上这是有疑问的,因为最后决定哪一个美女得奖不是第三人,如一个选举团(这是今天选美活动中普遍的做法)做出决定,而是由被告 Hicks 先生来做出决定。这表示针对将来的变数如果要被告做出选择或者裁量,就应该根据平衡的可能性。而带来的结果也就是"全部获偿或者毫无赔偿"(all or nothing),这也无法避免多赔或少赔的不良后果。也就是如果原告 Chaplin 小姐能够满足平衡的可能性,她得到的赔偿就以得奖计算。而如果不能满足,她就无法取得任何金钱赔偿了。显然,如果由地区选出的美女只有 1/4 的机会得奖,是无法满足平衡的可能性的。但由于有了"机会损失"的计算办法,这导致 Chaplin 小姐成功索赔 100 英镑,这在 100 年前不是一笔小数目。针对这一疑问,Jill Poole 教授的《Loss of chance and the evaluation of hypotheticals in contractual claims》一文中的注脚 21 有提到说:"The assumption is that this case involved the hypothetical action of the interviewing panel, a third party, whereas the evidence was that, as the defendant had determined to make the decision alone, the hypothetical rested on the action of the defendant. It might follow that this should not be treated as a case to which 'loss of chance' principles applied, despite the fact that it is regarded as a seminal authority on the point."

4.4 对"机会损失"全面探讨的先例 Allied Maples Group Ltd v. Simmons & Simmons

适用机会损失大原则的律师专业疏忽先例有不少,受害方客户的损失显然不会是全部的索赔金额(不论是原告的索赔金额还是被告所面对的索赔金额),因为谁都知道诉讼是一件复杂的事情,会有许多变数(包括无法控制的第三人,主要是法院和仲裁庭的决定)会影响到最终的诉讼成败。而且即使是胜诉,能够变为金钱还是有另外的变数,主要是在执行判决或裁决方面。换言之,即使是严重与明确的专业疏忽,如律师错过了索赔的时效,也不代表律师要赔偿给客户他在有关案件中索赔的一笔钱。这里就显然涉及机会损失的大原则了。其中重要的是对损失机会的价值尽量准确地作出评估,一个重点是有关案件的强弱与相应的胜诉机会,虽然这是没有办法太准确。但明确的是原告证明他案件的强弱与胜诉机会,是不需要达到 51% 或以上的平衡的可能性测试。在机会损失的测试,即使只能证明胜诉的机会只有 15%,也可以向被告进行索赔有关案件全部索赔金额的 15%,而不是由于无法满足平衡的可能性而导致毫无赔偿或只有象征性损失赔偿。这可节录 Stuart - Smith 大法官在 Allied Maples Group Ltd v. Simmons &Simmons (1995) 1 WLR 1602 先例所说如下:"Secondly, Mr. Jackson submitted that the plaintiffs can only succeed if in fact the chance of success can be rated at over 50%. It so happened that in Kitchen v. Royal Air Force Association (1958) 1 WLR 563, Otter v. Church, Adams, Tatham & Co. (1953) Chi. 280 and Hall v. Meyrick (1957) 2 QB 455, to which I shall shortly refer, the plaintiff did recover more than 50% of the full value of the loss. But this is fortuitous and there is no reason in principle why it should be so. In Yardley v. Coombes (1963) 107 SJ 575 Edmund Davies J. awarded one - third of the full liability value of the plaintiff's claim against the negligent defendant solicitors."

律师专业疏忽的先例多不胜数,可以感觉到律师这一行业的危险性,难怪收费要这么高才付得起专业疏忽保险的高昂保费。听说一些国际律师所在他们的支出中除了工资,专业疏忽的保费就要排第二了。除了上述提到的先例,其他先例还有 Kitchen v. Royal Air Force Association, Otter v. Church, Adams, Tatham & Co. (1953) Ch 280 和 Hall v. Meyrick (1957) 2 QB 455 还有本章在其他地方会提到的 Normans Bay Ltd v. Coudert Bros (2004) EWCA Civ 215, Dixon v. Clement Jones (a firm) (2004) EWCA Civ 1005; Hanif v. Middleweeks (a firm) (2000) Lloyd's Rep. PN 920, Pearson

v. Sanders Witherspoon & Another (2000) P. N. L. R. 110; Mount v. Barker Austin (a firm) (1998) PNLR 493; Inter – Leisure Ltd v. Lambert (1997) MPC49 等。只介绍其中一个典型的先例 Kitchen v. Royal Air Force Association,就是涉及律师最要小心的不错过索赔时效,否则原告的索赔根本起不了步,而律师错过索赔时效的专业疏忽也就是明确不过的。英国上诉庭同意法院对损失的核算,就是该索赔金额的2/3,也就是2000英镑。上诉庭拒绝了被告的抗辩说要求原告必须满足平衡的可能性去证明她的索赔应该会成功。上诉庭认为只要原告能够证明她有一定程度的成功机会,法院就可以作出核算。Parker 大法官是这样说:"If the plaintiff can satisfy the court that she would have had some prospect of success, then it would be for the court to evaluate those prospects, taking into consideration the difficulties that remained to be surmounted."

再重新回到 Allied Maples Group Ltd v. Simmons &Simmons 的重要先例,上诉庭有机会把有关机会损失方面的法律全面考虑,并作出了总结。案情涉及被告律师所作为原告的代表律师在一个合并收购的交易中漏给了原告一个重要的法律意见,导致原告蒙受了损失。律师漏了给一个法律意见的案件不多,也不像其他的专业疏忽(如错过了时效或是提供了错误的法律意见)有明显的疏忽与后果。除了这一个先例,其他类似的先例还有 Otter v. Church, Adams, Tatham & Co 与 Hall v. Meyrick。

这个遗漏的法律意见是收购的财产/公司如果是有"或有负债"(contingent claims),会计的做法是不会反映在公司的"资产负债表"(balance sheet)。结果是原告在交易完成后面对"或有负债"的损失,向被告提出索赔。原告声称,如果被告有给这一个法律意见,原告就会坚持在谈判中向卖方(也就是收购公司的母公司)要求作出保障,而且估计卖方会同意。在这里就可以看到有两个变数。第一个变数就是原告的确会坚持向卖方提出要求保障,这一个变数是本章1段所针对的情况。第二个变数就是本段所针对的情况,就是涉及第三人(也就是卖方)的变数。案例还涉及了其他重要的方面,以下分段针对。

4.4.1　责任方面

这在英国法院是一个"先决争议"(preliminary issue),就是被告是否有专业疏忽的责任。被告的抗辩包括原告的公司负责人本人是专业会计师,应该知道所谓遗漏的法律意见。但笔者不多讲,因为责任问题不是本书要针对的。只简单说,英国高院判被告的确是犯了专业疏忽。

4.4.2　因果关系

在本先例中所针对的被告漏了提供法律意见,但要确定是否有违约的责任,还要看这违约是否导致最后的损失,也就是因果关系的测试。这因果关系测试的考虑包括了原告即使得到了这一个法律意见,他会否向第三人的卖方坚持要求保障,而卖方在对自己会是很不利的情况下会否答应或只会提供部分保障等。这些都是变数,包括来自第三人卖方的变数。

针对原告自己,法院根据"平衡的可能性"(balance of probability)接受原告如果得到这一个法律意见,是会向卖方要求保障的。这毕竟是对原告有利,这一情况发生的机会是很大的。比较困难的就是第三人的卖方会否答应或部分答应提供保障。这一变数涉及谈判,关系到谈判双方的议价能力、谈判技巧与水平、主观愿望、其他客观环境与时机等。反正没有人能够知道一个复杂的谈判会带来的结果,也没有办法"假设"(infer)。另外也往往没有客观的准则考验,如在某一些简单与常见的交易,只要一方提出建议,另一方几乎肯定会接受。这可节录在上诉庭,Millett 大法官所说如下:

"The chance of which the plaintiffs complain they have been deprived is the chance of persuading Gillow(第三人卖方)to act against their own interests by reinstating a warranty which their own solicitors had already struck out or to give some other protection against a risk for which their own solicitors had not thought fit to provide. Gillow might have yielded to the plaintiffs' demand, of course, particularly if they believed (wrongly) that they might lose the deal if they did not. But there are no objective criteria by which the chance can be evaluated. Gillow would no doubt have consulted their solicitors. If so, they would if correctly advised have learnt that it was not standard conveyancing practice for vendors to give the protection which the plaintiffs were seeking: vendors sometimes gave it but often did not; and the decision whether to accommodate the plaintiffs was a commercial one for Gillow to make. The outcome would then have depended on Gillow's perception of the relative strength of the parties' bargaining positions, the extent of the risk which they were being asked to assume and the effect on the deal if they refused. These are all subjective matters; none of them is known and none can be inferred.

... The 'chance' of which the plaintiffs claim to have been deprived is the chance that they might have negotiated better terms from their vendors. In the absence of evidence from Gillow, what would have been the outcome of such negotiations is a matter of pure speculation. No case has gone so far as to allow damages in such a situation, and in my view it would be wrong to do so. The nearest is Davies v. Taylor (1974) AC 207, where the outcome depended on whether a married couple who had separated would have had a reconciliation; it was held that this was too speculative to sound in damages. I call to mind the words of Vaughan Williams L. J. in Chaplin v. Hicks (1911) 2 KB 786, 792 - 793: (这一段 Millett 大法官认为原告所损失的只是一个可与第三人卖方谈判获得一个更有利的条文的机会。在没有第三人提供证据,这一个谈判最后的结果会是怎样只是一个纯粹的臆猜。从来没有先例给一个臆猜作出损失赔偿,我也觉得这样做是不对的。最近的先例是 Davies v. Taylor,结果是根据分居的夫妻有否机会复合,这被判是太具臆猜性,没有办法作出金钱上的损失赔偿。接下去 Millett 大法官是引述"选美"先例中的话)'There are cases, no doubt, where the loss is so dependent on the mere unrestricted volition of another that it is impossible to say that there is any assessable loss resulting from the breach. 'In my judgment this is just such a case."

这一问题在本章第4.1.4小段有详述,在这里进一步探讨。Millett大法官认为原告的机会损失太具“臆猜性”(speculative),谈不上是一个“真正”(real)与“实质”(substantial)的损失,不应该给予任何赔偿的救济。上述的节录也引用了Chaplin v. Hicks先例中的说法,就是如果一个变数完全是依赖第三人的“没有限制的意愿”(unrestricted volition),就会根本没办法核算到底损失了什么机会。笔者估计还会有其他的微妙考虑,就是在本案例中第三人卖方如果答应给原告提供保障会对自己不利,就可以推断第三人会抗拒。相反,如果谈判是对双方都有利的,就比较容易推断这一谈判令合约得到进一步改善的机会是比较真正与实质的机会了。换言之这一变数就从“不肯定”(uncertain)变为“可预测”(predictable)了。

但由于该先例是针对一个先决争议,判决本身并非是终局的,所以上诉庭允许原告让第三人卖方出庭举证,然后认定会否有真正与实质的机会损失,以及机会的百分比。Millett大法官也提到了第三人在这种谈判的情况下的举证也未必有用,这在本章第4.1.1小段已经有提及。

4.4.3 推断与核算第三人变数的种类

较早提到第三人的变数是最难掌握的,因为没有办法提供证据或者有用的证据找出机会损失。但如果责任能够成立,这在因果关系方面包括证明违约的确会导致一个真正与实质的损失,就一定要想办法推断/核算第三人的变数与找出机会损失的百分比来厘定损失金额。在已经判过的Allied Maples Group Ltd v. Simmons & Simmons (a firm) (1995) 1 WLR 1602先例中,法院认为可把第三人的变数分为三或四类,这可以在以下进一步分析。

4.4.3.1 第一类的第三人变数:有限制的意愿

在这一类别,由于第三人不是没有限制地喜欢怎样决定就怎样决定,所以是可以对第三人会怎样决定有一个客观的标准,进而找出机会损失。这种案件包括了Chaplin v. Hicks (1911) 2 KB 768先例,就是原告失去了选美比赛中得奖的机会。假设这是由陪审团决定,原告会失去机会的百分比应该可以核算出来。另一个案例是Kitchen v. Royal Air Force Association (1958) 1 WLR 563,这是律师疏忽错过时效的案例。原告因此失去了起诉的机会。在这些案例里,原告明显失去了一些有价值的东西。所以应该可以计算/核算中奖或可以起诉的机会的损失。即使成功机会低过50%,但还是可以客观计算它的百分比的。这里可以节录Allied Maples Group Ltd v. Simmons & Simmons (a firm)先例中Millett大法官针对这一类别,说:“There are first those cases where the outcome is not dependent on the unrestricted volition of a third party, since his decision must be justifiable by objective criteria. Into this category fall the cases of the loss of the right to be a finalist in a competition (Chaplin v. Hicks [1911] 2 K. B. 786) or to bring legal proceedings (Kitchen v. Royal Air Force Association [1958] 1 W. L. R. 563). In these cases the plaintiff has clearly lost something of value and its value must be assessed however difficult the task may be. The prospects of ultimate success (or, in the case of litigation, of receiving an offer of settlement) may be less than 50 per cent. but they are nevertheless capable of objective evaluation."

4.4.3.2 第二类的第三人变数:做法上符合第三人利益

在这一类别,由于第三人的变数是合乎他自己的利益,所以可以推断这一变数的结果会朝哪一个方向发展。如果这一变数有很大可能会发生并且如果发生的话对原告有利,就可以判原告能够成功索赔所有的损失,只对一些比较不重要的变数作出扣减。这里可以节录 Allied Maples Group Ltd v. Simmons & Simmons (a firm) 先例中 Millett 大法官针对这一类别,说:"Secondly, there are those cases where the outcome depends upon whether a third party who had been properly advised would have acted in accordance with his own best interests. Kitchen v. Royal Air Force Association [1958] 1 W. L. R. 563 and Otter v. Church, Adams, Tatham & Co. [1953] Ch. 280 must be classified in this category, though it was probably wrong to treat it as a case of a loss of a chance at all. In these cases there is obviously a very strong probability that the third party would have acted in his own interests, and accordingly the plaintiff is likely to be awarded the full amount of his damages less a discount to allow for the possibility that something might have occurred to prevent his doing so."

这里可以顺便介绍一下上述的 Otter v. Church, Adams, Tatham & Co. 先例,这也是一个律师漏了给客户法律意见的案例,导致客户没有在死亡之前采取一些行动保护他的财产而失去了这些财产。客户的"遗产执行人"(adminstratrix)向被告的律师提出索赔,Upjohn 大法官判被告要赔偿所有的损失,但因存在一定的变数扣减了10%,因为即使是提供了法律意见,该客户也不一定会采取行动(即使这是符合客户的利益的)。这里有说法是这一案件其实不涉及第三人,应该根据"平衡的可能性"(balance of probability)判,不应该再扣减10%,因为这是"完全获偿或毫无赔偿"(all or nothing)的做法。这种错判的说法在 Sykes v. Midland Bank Executor and Trustee Co. Ltd (1971) 1 QB 113 和 Allied Maples Group Ltd v. Simmons & Simmons (a firm) (1995) 1 WLR 1602 先例都有提到。但如果把客户与遗产执行人视为不同的当事人,而客户作为第三人,不会也不能提供证据,这一来当作是机会损失而扣减10%也就无可厚非了。

4.4.3.3 第三类的第三人变数:没有限制的意愿但可以根据客观因素推测

在这一类别,由于第三人的变数没有限制意愿,变得很难对变数的结果作出客观的核算。但由于有其他客观的因素,可以对第三人会怎样做作出一个预计。在一定程度上,第三类与第二类的分别并不是太大。这里可以节录 Allied Maples Group Ltd v. Simmons & Simmons (a firm) 先例中 Millett 大法官针对这一类别,说:"Thirdly, there are cases where the outcome appears to depend on the unrestricted volition of a third party but there are objective considerations which make it possible to predicate how he would have acted. Into this category fall Hall v. Meyrick [1957] 2 Q. B. 455 (where the outcome depended on whether a man who had already made a will in favour of his fiancee would have made a fresh will in her favour after his marriage to her if advised that this had had the effect of revoking it — clearly a strong likelihood and such as to make the case virtually indistinguishable from the second category); Dunbar v. A. & B. Painters Ltd. (1986) 2 Lloyd's Rep. 38 (where the outcome depended on whether an insurance company would act against its commercial interests; again unlikely and virtually indistinguishable from the second category); and Richardson v. Mellish (1824) 2 Bing. 229 (where evidence of the third party's customary practice was available). Spring v. Guardian Assurance Plc. (1995) 2 A. C. 296 probably falls into this category."

以下也可以对上述节录提到的部分先例加以介绍。第一个是 Hall v. Meyrick 先例,案情涉及被告的律师漏了给原告一个法律意见,这就是原告与一位 H 先生委托被告为他们议定遗嘱,相互把关于自己死亡的利益赠予对方。当时他们还没有结婚,只是准备结婚。这一事实被告的律师也知道,但漏了告诉他们在法律上,如果结婚的话,就会导致原来的遗嘱无效,除非特别明示针对。结果在 H 先生死后,由于原告没有取得 H 先生的遗产,所以向被告提出索赔。但这里有几个相对来讲不是太重要的变数,就是 H 先生会否同意与会否事后作出改变。但总的来说,高院是认为这些变数会对原告有利是有一个合理的机会,所以判原告可以索赔全部的损失,但针对这种变数作出了约 35% 的扣减。高院的判决被上诉庭根据其他原因推翻。

下一个要介绍的是 Dunbar v. A. & B. Painters Ltd. 先例,案情涉及原告工人在屋顶工作时从一个 40 层以上高度的"脚手架"(scaffold)摔下来严重受伤,被告雇主是要对原告的受伤负责并根据强制性投保的立法《Employers' Liability (Compulsory Insurance) Act 1969》向他的保险人要求补偿。但在该保单中有一条明示豁免条文说明如果工作是在 40 层以上的高度,保险人是可以拒赔所造成的事故损失的。由于保险人是第三人,而变数就是他会否依赖保单中的豁免条文拒赔,这里就涉及到机会的损失,上诉庭的 May 大法官是这样说:

"Thus I think it is clear, on the law applicable, that the proper approach for the learned judge to have adopted in the present case was to have assessed the chances that the insurers would have taken the height point and, having so assessed the chances, tailored his award of damages accordingly.

With respect to the learned Judge, I think that the phraseology which he used in his judgment and which I have quoted, is susceptible to the construction that he was adopting the wrong approach and deciding the question at issue on the balance of probabilities. Nevertheless, it would be surprising if in truth he had done so, because the relevant passage in the judgment follows immediately after his reference to Fraser's case and it is common ground before us that Counsel, in their final speeches below, did address the learned Judge on the basis that the question for his decision on this point should be answered on a consideration of the balance of probabilities. In any event the learned Judge made a specific finding (which I have quoted) that insurers would not have relied on the height point, and for my part I do not think that his reference to ' unlikely ', in the same breath as his reference to ' unthinkable ' a little later, in the context used detracts from that which I think he was saying, namely that, on all the evidence he had heard, he concluded that insurers would not have taken the point; in other words that the chances of their doing so were nil."

换言之,法院认为保险人由于商业或声誉的原因,拒绝赔偿的机会是零。以上上诉庭的判词中,说明正确的损失计算应该以"机会损失"(loss of chance)而不是"平衡的可能性"(balance of probability),并批评高院判决中的措辞会被人误解为他采用了错误的损失计算办法,也就是根据平衡的可能性。

最后介绍的就是 Spring v. Guardian Assurance Plc. 先例。案情涉及原告向他的前雇主(被告)提出索赔,因为他在推荐信里提供了许多对原告不利的不准确内容,导致原告没有被第三人雇用。在责任方面判是被告对原告有一个小心谨慎的义务,被告违反这个义务就构成疏忽。被告的抗辩是第三人无论如何都不会雇用原告。贵族院判被告要赔偿原告的损失,原告并不需要证明在平衡的可能性之下,如果不是这一不利的推荐信,第三人是会雇用他的。原告只需要证明因为被告的错误,导致原告损失了一个合理的机会,Lowry 勋爵是这样说:"Once the duty of care is held to exist and the defendants' negligence is proved, the plaintiff only has to show that by reason of that negligence he has lost a reasonable chance of employment (which would have to be evaluated) and has thereby sustained loss: McGregor on Damages, 14th ed. (1980), pp. 198 – 202, paras. 276 – 278 and Chaplin v. Hicks (1911) 2 KB 786. He does not have to prove that, but for the negligent reference, Scottish Amicable (第三人) would have employed him."(只要被告的疏忽被证明,原告只需要证明由于这一个疏忽导致他损失了合理被雇佣的机会。原告不需要证明要不是疏忽的推荐,第三人就会雇用他。后一个因果关系的证明是根据平衡的可能性,这是在证明机会损失中不要求的。)

4.4.3.4 第四类的第三人变数:没有限制的意愿

在这一类别是 Millett 大法官在 Allied Maples Group Ltd v. Simmons & Simmons (a firm) (1995) 1 WLR 1602 先例中没有提到的,就是第三人的变数没有限制他的意愿,而且也没有其他因素来对变数的结果作出客观的核算。在这种情况下,应是在因果关系的一关就已经过不了,因为这一第三人变数就变得"太具臆猜性"(too speculative),根本就谈不上是损失了一个"真正"(real)和"实质"(substantial)的机会。这样看来这第四类就不能算是机会损失核算方面的一个类别了。

这方面的先例另有 Davies v. Taylor (1974) AC 207 可以稍作介绍。该先例涉及在原告的丈夫(本先例中的第三人)因为交通意外死亡前不久,他们夫妻之间有严重的争执,并且原告离开了她的丈夫,而丈夫也知道她的婚外情。原告的丈夫曾经要求她回到他的身边，但被原告拒绝后，丈夫就委任律师开始了离婚程序，也取得了原告男朋友承认的证据。另要一提的是他们并没有孩子。在这种情况下，原告自己离开丈夫就等于不要求赡养费了。在原告丈夫死亡后，原告向应该对他丈夫的死亡负责的被告（疏忽驾驶的司机）提出索赔，根据的是1846－1959年《Fatal Accidents Acts》的立法。在这个立法下，原告是需要证明他有合理机会可以从死亡的丈夫获得金钱上的利益。贵族院判是原告只有一个臆猜性的机会会回到她丈夫的身边，而并非是实质性机会能够由她丈夫继续维持她的生活或提供金钱上的利益。贵族院是这样判："the test of a claim by a dependant under the Fatal Accidents Acts 1846 – 1959 was whether there was a reasonable expectation of pecuniary benefit from the deceased, which meant in the case of a deserting widow who had forfeited any right to maintenance that she had to show that there was some significant prospect, as opposed to a mere speculative possibility, of a reconciliation with her husband had he lived; and that in the present case, since the plaintiff had failed to establish such a prospect of reconciliation, her claim failed."

4.5　机会损失核算的方法与不肯定性

机会损失的核算是完全依靠法院或者仲裁庭的裁量权，所以有很大的不肯定性。而且双方当事人可以不凭证据任意发挥的讲"故事"，把将来会发生的来自第三人的变数会尽量说成对己方有利，反正没有人能说的准。难怪有说法是在这一类的案件中（也就是涉及第三人的变数），针对损失赔偿争议最好的解决办法就是双方"调解"（mediation）。

法院也尝试尽量把核算的办法科学化，如原告将来会得到的好处或者会避免的损失是根据：(1)"一连串情况的发展"（chain of events）；(2)"替代情况"（alternative events）的出现。

在(1)，可举 Pearson v. Sanders Witherspoon & Another (2000) P. N. L. R. 110 的先例，在该先例中，被告律师延误了原告的索赔，导致索赔人不能及时执行对第三人公司的判决，因为第三人公司在稍后已经破产。而被告在第三人公司破产前就一直知道该公司的财务状况前景不妙。在核算机会损失的恰当扣减时，上诉庭考虑到：(a)索赔及时提出，律师没有延误的情况下获得胜诉的几率为75%，(b)根据第三人公司的财务状况，对第三人公司的胜诉判决在及时执行的情况下可以成功的几率为50%。将这两个几率相乘，得到的最终结果37.5%就是法院最终确定的机会损失的百分比。

Hanif v. Middleweeks (a firm) (2000) Lloyd's Rep. PN 920 也可以算是属于第(1)种情况的另一个先例，案情涉及被告律师的延误最终导致原告的索赔被法院撤销。而被撤销案件中的被告是保险人（第三人），他提出了一些抗辩，是显然会影响原告在该案件中的胜诉机会的。这些抗辩包括了：(a)原告作为受保人违反了保险合约；(b)误述；(c)火灾造成的损失是原告自己纵火。法院估计原告针对这些保险人的这三项抗辩的成功几率分别为80%、60%与25%，并核算机会损失为25%。结果去了上诉庭，认为保险人提出的三项抗辩是连贯的，表示只要有一项原告不成功，整个被撤销的案件就会败诉。所以，不应该分别看这三项的成功几率，而是应该整体对待，这表示机会损失应该降低到12%。但这三项抗辩也有关联之处，就是法院会否接受原告作为受保人的答辩很大程度上是根据"可信性"(creditability)。这表示如果原告针对保险人的起诉没有被撤销，如果原告的举证在抗辩(a)被法院接受，就有较大的可能性抗辩(b)与抗辩(c)也被接受。这表示机会损失应该提升，上诉庭最后判是20%。

针对第(2)种替代情况，可以 Inter - Leisure Ltd v. Lambert (1997) MPC49 先例为例，在该先例中，被告律师在为原告草拟房屋租约时有疏忽，加入了一条重新调整租金条文，除了允许租金上调以外还允许租金下调。由于这一条文，导致后来租金向下进行了调整。法院判决是被告的疏忽剥夺了原告的两种不同的收益机会：(a)有25%的机会租客(第三人)同意租金只可上调条文，并且在原告提出增加租金时租客没有终止租约，在这种情况下原告可以通过租金增加获得383,000英镑的收益；(b)有66%的机会租客同意租金只可上调条文，并且在原告提出增加租金之初租客终止租约，在这种情况下，原告的空置房屋可以增值40,000英镑。法院判决383,000英镑的25%加上40,000英镑的66%就应该为该案件中原告的机会损失。

4.6 第三人能够出庭举证的情况

已经提到过，机会损失是针对第三人的变数，因为这是难以掌握的并且没有办法提供证据。但如果在少数的案件是第三人可以出庭举证，这就带来了是适用"机会损失"(loss of chance)计算损失还是回到以"平衡的可能性"(balance of probability)计算的争议。毕竟，针对第三人提供的证据，法院或仲裁庭接受与否，这是根据平衡的可能性。这方面在 Stone Heritage Developments Ltd v. Davis Blank Furniss (unreported) 31 May 2006 先例与 4 Eng Ltd v. Harper (2009) Ch. 91 先例有涉及，在后一个先例(案情稍后在5.3段详细介绍)的答案看来是如果所有涉及的第三人都可以出庭举证，就应以平衡的可能性为准。但如果还有部分甚至是次要的第三人不提供证据，还是可以适用机会损失。这方面可以节录后一个先例的 David Richards 大法官判词：

"Mr. Leech (被告代表大律师) submitted that the position was different where the claimant called, or was able to call, the third party. In such a case, the court could assess the likelihood that the third party would have acted as the claimant contends, just as well as in the case of the claimant himself. As 4 Eng had called Mr. Tapp (这是有关的第三人，可决定是否出售 Tarvail Ltd 给原告), the court should decide whether Tarvail would have been sold to 4 Eng, or at least whether Mr. Tapp would have agreed to sell his shares in Tarvail, on the balance of probabilities. Mr. Leech relied on the decision of Judge Hodge QC in Stone Heritage Developments Ltd v Davis Blank Furniss (unreported) 31 May 2006, in which it was held that where all of the available evidence was before the court, the court should apply the balance of probabilities. The decision in the case was partly reversed on appeal [2007] EWCA Civ 765, but this issue was not considered by the Court of Appeal.

The state of evidence in this case is such that the court must in any event, in my judgment, apply the approach established in the Allied Maples case. Although Mr Tapp gave evidence, and it is reasonable to assume that Mr Rogers(他也是另一位第三人但没有出庭举证,但估计是否出售 Tarvail Ltd 给原告的决定与 Tapp 先生一致)would have taken the same decisions and adopted the same approach as Mr. Tapp, there are other witnesses who did not give evidence nor would appear to have been available to do so. The ultimate decision of Mr. Tapp and Mr. Rogers would have been affected in very important respects by the advice of their solicitors and accountants and by the attitude of Mr Dalton and Mr Ede, directors who worked full time in the business. **Without evidence from these people, there is no basis for applying the balance of probabilities.** I prefer to express no view on whether, if all the evidence relevant to the conduct of Mr Tapp and Mr Rogers had been available, the balance of probabilities would have been the right test to apply to the issue as to whether Mr Tapp and Mr Rogers would have sold Tarvail to 4 Eng."

5. 其他适用机会损失的案件类别

5.1 律师以外专业人士的疏忽

机会损失的案件还可以包括其他不同类别的案件,从上述介绍的有关律师"专业疏忽"(professional negligence)的大量案件就可以引申到其他专业人士也会有这样的危险,如会计师、经纪人、测量师等。举一个常见的例子,如果被告经纪人(假设是保险经纪人)错误或漏了告诉原告他投保的 A 保险公司并不适合(如在信誉方面),这就会带来好几个变数了。第一个就是如果没有漏了告知,原告受害方会否向 B 或其他保险公司投保。这是受害方自己的选择,要根据平衡的可能性来决定,在本章的第 1 段有详述。但第二个变数就会涉及第三人的变数,就是 B 或其他保险公司会否以同样的保费承保这一个风险,以及是否能够提供给原告保障。这就涉及了机会损失的核算。

5.2 银行的疏忽

也会有案件是双方当事人对适用机会损失来核算赔偿金额没有争议,这看来是应该以这一办法核算。在贵族院的先例 Jackson v. Royal Bank of Scotland (2005) UKHL 3,涉及中间商(原告)由于其银行(被告)疏忽把可转让信用证的资料泄露给买方,导致他作为中间商所赚取的差价(高达 19%)被买方知道后在以后的交易中就跳过了原告直接向泰国的供应商订购货物(狗粮)。高院判被告有疏忽责任,因为他违反了保护客户机密的义务。但在损失这方面的计算就很麻烦,第一审的高院判是原告可向被告索赔4年的预期利润的损失(也就是在这4年中可以赚取的差价,而估计的货量就是根据以往的货量)。但去了上诉庭,被认为4年的预期利润太多,判只有1年的预期利润是肯定的,接下去年份的预计损失被认为是太遥远与太不肯定。上诉庭的Potter大法官是这样说:"On the assumption that the evidence (as I read it) showed that, but for the Bank's error, Samson (原告) was virtually certain to have retained Economy Bag's (买方) business in dog chews for the year 1993/94, the loss of profit on the figures adopted by the Judge would have been $38,831, to which should be added 5% commission, less overheads, giving a total of $47,278.15. I would round down that figure to $45,000 to reflect the small degree of uncertainty inherent in even the closest of trading relationships and would award that sum together with interest by way of general damages for loss of profit."

但接下去原告就向贵族院提出上诉,认为只要被告在订约时是可以"预料得到"的(within contemplation)并且"并非是不可能"(not unlikely)会产生的损失类别,就不必再理会损失的严重性:Hadley v. Baxendale (1854) 9 Ex. 341;Parsons v. Uttley Ingham (1977) 2 Lloyd's Rep. 522。这表示被告要赔原告作所有预期利润的损失,不受年份的限制。而被告的抗辩是说原告可以继续赚取19%的差价是具臆猜性的与机会太微小的,因为买方会不断压低原告作为中间商的利润,即使没有被告的违约,也不会让原告持续赚取如此高的差价。

这先例并不明显是针对机会损失,但贵族院Hope勋爵有提到Allied Maples Group Ltd v. Simmons & Simmons (a firm) (1995) 1 WLR 1602的先例,并认为要把案件发还给一审法院认定事实,也就是仔细的核算4年的预期利润的损失,因为涉及了许多变数,包括随着时间过去,买方会不断压价(这是来自第三人的变数)。Walker勋爵也认为一审大法官很可能高估了利润,说:"The Judge's quantification of the loss was open to criticism on some points, as my noble and learned friend Lord Hope has explained, I think that the Judge probably overestimated, and certainly did not underestimate, Samson's (原告) recoverable loss. But the Court of Appeal erred in principle in reaching its decision, and after all the time that has elapsed it would not be acceptable to remit the matter for a fresh assessment of damages, especially as it would on any view involve so many imponderables. The least unsatisfactory course is to make the order which Lord Hope proposes."

看来,贵族院也认为在该先例中,机会损失是一个比较恰当的核算损失的方法,而不是"损失遥远性"(remoteness of damages)的可预见或可预料得到的问题。

5.3 欺诈性误述

4 Eng Ltd v. Harper (2009) Ch. 91是第一个针对"欺诈性误述"(fraudulent misrepresentation)的侵权或违约是否能够适用机会损失的先例。David Richards大法官认为是看不到什么原则性的理由不能适用,说:"It does not seem to me to be an objec-

tion that the loss is assessed as a loss of chance, not as a loss established on the balance of probabilities. It is true that it does not previously appear to have been decided that damages for loss of a chance are recoverable for deceit, but there is in my judgment no objection in principle. If damages for loss of a chance are recoverable in negligence, why should they not also be recoverable in deceit?"

在该先例,涉及被告的欺诈性误述导致原告失去了购买一家名为 Tarvail Ltd 的公司的机会,带来了估计的利润损失与增值损失。而有关的机会损失是假设不存在欺诈性误述,原告能否成功购买这一家公司。这显然涉及许多的变数,包括原告自己的变数与来自第三人(主要涉及 Tarvail Ltd 的有关人士)的变数。针对原告的变数(如能否成功融资方面),这是以"平衡性的可能"(balance of probability)为准考虑原告提供的证据(主要是口头证据)。但针对来自第三人(Tarvail Ltd 的有关人士)的变数,这就以机会损失来考虑。Tarvail Ltd 的主要大股东 Tapp 先生有出庭作证并确认愿意把他的股份出售给原告,而另一位主要大股东 Rogers 先生没有出庭,但估计他与 Tapp 先生的想法一致。可是还有其他第三人如在 Tarvail Ltd 工作的 Dalton 先生与 Ede 先生,他们也是 Tarvail Ltd 的股东并持有没有投票权的普通股。他们的服务对 Tarvail Ltd 的继续成功营运十分重要,如果他们辞职会对原告是否购买这一家公司有影响,而他们没有出庭举证。这也是该先例中 David Richards 大法官认为针对这第三人的变数,还是要根据机会损失而不是根据平衡性的可能考虑证据。最后,判是有 80% 的机会 Tarvail Ltd 会被出售给原告。

5.4 笔者仲裁案件之一:租约纠纷

机会损失的救济也开始出现在笔者的仲裁案件中,其中一个近期的租约仲裁中,被告就提出了机会损失作为减少索赔金额的理由。有关的案情是司空见惯的,租约是一个航次从黑海装运了 6 万吨铁矿石去中国。但估计是航运市场上涨或其他原因,原船东在船舶开去装港前撤船,而根据市场报道是以更高的运费另转租给了其他承租人到美湾装货。但笔者作为独任仲裁员涉及的是航次承租人与二船东之间的租约,所以对二船东与南韩原船东之间的租约发生了什么事情导致原船东撤船并不了解。反正在笔者涉及的租约下,二船东不能履行显然是一个明确不过的违约/毁约。责任没有好争的情况下,主要的争议还是在损失赔偿金额。受害方的承租人后来是很快去市场另租了替代船舶履行了这一个航次,但需要付出高昂的运费,这导致了承租人蒙受近 100 万美元的损失并向二船东提出索赔。其中的一个争议是二船东指称承租人太快去市场另租替代船舶,导致他们失去了一个说服原船东不要撤船与履行这一个航次的机会。二船东唯一能够提供的证据就是他们曾经接触原船东提出这一个要求,但根本没有其他证据显示原船东有否回应与有什么回应,也没有证据显示二船东曾经向承租人要求给他一点时间说服原船东履约。除了没有证据外,笔者对这种情况也经历很多,就是夹在中间的二船东希望说服原船东不要撤船,但估计成功的机会不高,毕竟笔者是看不到证据或有说服力的解释。要知道当时航运市场高涨,不论原船东的撤船是否站得住脚(笔者对这方面是不知道),恐怕原船东都不愿意回来原租约赚取更低的租金。或者是原船东会在二船东愿意把原租金提高的情况下才不撤船,但这又涉及二船东愿不愿意这样做。再加上这种谈判会要花时间,但承租人由于销约期的关系根本没有办法等待。更不用说有可能在当时高涨的市场下,原船东很快就已经把该船舶出租给了其他承租人。所以,笔者认为这是一个很明确不能考虑机会损失救济的案件,因为二船东的说法是太具臆猜性。笔者的裁决书有简单针对这一方面,说:

"One final point being, the Owners' Counsel, during the first hearing, raised an issue of 'a loss of chance'. I have asked for a percentage of the loss, if any. This was never put forward to me. But in the Closing Submissions, this issue was maintained in paragraphs 59 – 62, which I can cite in part as follows: '... Charterers' unlawful conduct deprived Owners of the chance to persuade the Head Owners to deliver the Vessel. Damages can be assessed to take into account the value of the loss of a chance: Allied Maples Group v Simmons & Simmons (1995) 1 WLR 1602 and Equitable Life Assurance Society v Ernst & Young (2003) EWCA Civ 1114.'

My decision is simple in that the Owners' argument must fail by reason of the chance, if any, to persuade the Head Owners to perform was too speculative and of no real value. I have said it in Paragraph 31 above. The reasons which I have concluded earlier can be repeated, are for instance: the '有关船舶' was chartered/fixed to another charterers; a rising market which must have induced the Head Owners to walk away from the head – C/P in the first place, etc. I also find a complete lack of evidence to show the existence of such a chance. As was said in Allied Maples Group Ltd v Simmons & Simmons by Mr. Justice Stuart – Smith: 'But, in my judgment, the plaintiff must prove as a matter of causation that he has a real or substantial chance as opposed to a speculative one. If he succeeds in doing so, the evaluation of the chance is part of the assessment of the quantum of damage, the range lying somewhere between something that just qualifies as real and substantial on the one hand and near certainty on the other. I do not think that it is helpful to seek to lay down in percentage terms what the lower and upper ends of the bracket should be.'

In another word, until and unless the Owners can prove that the chance being lost is not speculative and of some real value, the evaluation of the loss of chance does not even begin."

5.5 笔者仲裁案件之二:医学仪器生产合约

这是笔者另一个近期涉及机会损失的仲裁案件,案情涉及一家欧洲公司与中国公司订立一个生产医学仪器的合约,有关合约规定的交货日期非常短。中国公司的延误令其根本无法按照该日期交货,所以看来违约的责任是明确。因为在英国法律中作出合约承诺是严格责任,不存在有中方当事人经常会拿来抗辩的合理不合理或者不可抗力问题。剩下来只是损失如何计算的问题,在这方面欧洲公司就提出了一个非常庞大的索赔金额。交货日期很重要是因为欧洲公司计划用这些产品在国际卫生组织投标,以取得一个利润非常高的长期供应合约。但由于中国公司的延误令这个机会落空。所以,欧洲公司是索赔机会损失,这机会就是成功取得国际卫生组织这一个供应合约的百分比,如70%。而损失也就是成功取得该供应合约后总利润的70%。固然这种争议还会涉及损失遥远性的问题,就是中国公司在订约时是否知道欧洲公司这一个意图。而就算欧洲公司给了通知,这通知是否足够让中国公司知道这是一个长期的供应合约以及利润很高。但在本段不是谈损失遥远性的问题,而是探讨机会损失。在该案件的中间程序中一个非常有争议的地方是欧洲公司大力抗拒专家证人,坚持这是一个浪费。但中国公司的代表律师看来在这方面也是很熟悉与精明,他们坚持要仲裁庭批准有3位专家。其中一位专家证人是会计师,他会对国际卫生组织的长期供应合约带来的总利润进行核算,而其余的两位专家,一位是针对国际卫生组织的招投标做法与竞标成功的机会有多少提供专家意见,另一位是针对医学仪器市场包括世界上有多少公司涉及这方面的业务与其他竞争者给出意见,这也是针对机会损失。

显然欧洲公司要索赔机会损失还是要为他们的机会是多少提供证据,这证据是欧洲公司的两位高级雇员所做出的证人证言。中国公司也有他们的雇员作为证人,但显然中国公司不会像欧洲公司那么了解国际卫生组织招投标的做法、有多少竞争者、竞争者的背景与机会等。

这里也可以顺便一提就是在诉讼或仲裁程序中,仲裁庭是管不了当事人认为需要出庭的事实证人,也不应该管。但针对专家证人,由于在道理上是为了协助仲裁庭了解技术性的证据,所以有说法是专家证人是为了帮助法院或仲裁庭。但这一来,专家证人是否可以委任就必须先取得法院或仲裁庭的批准,因为法官或仲裁员总可以说是我不需要这方面的协助。

笔者是由中方公司指定的仲裁员,而首席是一位退休的大法官。他十分不喜欢专家证人,认为这种证据都是偏袒委任方并且浪费大量的金钱。但笔者就考虑到专家证人的偏袒程度总不会比当事人自己的事实证人更严重。再加上仲裁庭在程序上是必须要平等对待双方。这一来,就要考虑到对于国际卫生组织招投标以及国际上有关竞争的做法,中国公司的事实证人肯定是不会熟悉,特别是在盘问的过程中,相比欧洲公司的事实证人就会明显吃亏。这一来,为了让双方能够享有平等的陈述案件的机会,就有必要允许中国公司委任懂行的专家证人。而中方公司的代表律师是一家很出名的国际律师所,所以寻找这些专家证人也不困难。笔者纯粹是为了平等对待双方,说服了首席仲裁员,而最后也成功。

笔者继续本章所针对的机会损失,也就是成功取得国际卫生组织这一供应合约的百分比,表面看来是适合机会损失的计算办法,因为国际卫生组织是第三人。当然作为原告的欧洲公司还是需要满足平衡的可能性和本章4.1.4段的要求,即机会要是真正与实质，不能太具臆猜性。但笔者主要想介绍的是代表中国公司的大律师提出一个有趣的争议，就是机会损失不适用在这一类的案件。这是因为传统的机会损失案件所针对的情况都是原告的受害方只会有赚而不会有亏，问题只是赚多少，这包括像涉及选美的 Chaplin v. Hicks (1911) 2 KB 786 (CA)先例或专业人士疏忽的 Allied Maples Group Ltd v. Simmons & Simmons (1995) 1 WLR 1602 先例。但在本仲裁案件，原告并不是这样的情况，因为如果无法获得国际卫生组织的这一供应合约，他还是需要向中国公司接收与支付一个最低数量的医学仪器（这是合约规定）。如果不能全数在市场出售，原告会面临严重亏损。而如果假设获得国际卫生组织的供应合约机会是 20%，就会有 80% 会是严重亏损，这一个因素表示原告不能在损失计算时只考虑获得国际卫生组织供应合约利润的 20% 机会，而漠视 80% 严重亏损的机会。据悉，这方面还没有有关先例，而在本仲裁案件中也不需要作出考虑。只说这方面的争辩对笔者而言是很有说服力，但分水线划在什么地方还是个问题。因为是涉及选美的 Chaplin v. Hicks 先例也不能说是原告的美女不会有任何损失，落选后只是哭一场。她至少会要花费交通费用参加选美，在落选后这些钱就等于泡了汤。而在 Allied Maples Group Ltd v. Simmons & Simmons 类似的律师疏忽的先例（这种案件最普遍适用机会损失估计诉讼风险），也在原告如果在被告律师疏忽涉及的官司中败诉，会面对法院判他要承担的第三人的诉讼费用。所以，也不能说死是机会损失只能局限在会有赚而不会有任何亏损的案件。当然，这种例子比起笔者仲裁案件中原告的欧洲公司所会面对的亏损金额已然很小。所以还要看将来英国法院会否发展出来对亏损的程度有一条分水线作为适不适用机会损失的准则，或是把原告成功的机会损失加上另一条公式计算亏损的机会，才乘以原告的利润损失索赔金额。

5.6　笔者知悉仲裁案件：运输服务的分配利润协议

这一个仲裁案件的案情是一个有关中国在一个非洲国家的庞大工程需要大量的货物运输，而涉及的不同货物数量高达 250～270 吨。其中有两家中资背景的公司（可称为 A 与 B）达成协议由 B 出面取得这一个运输合约，并约定在 B 获得货物的分配后由 A 完成运输，而受到的运费在扣除成本后剩下的利润就由 A 与 B 平均分摊。但由 B 出面订立的运输合约中，包括了另一家物流公司（可称为 C），等于在该合约中有两位承运人的 B 与 C。运输合约中规定实际交付运输的货物类别与数量给哪一位承运人是完全由运输合约中的货方（可称为 D）全权决定。有关运输合约的条文是这样约定："在本协议履行过程，D 有权指定 B 或 C 中的任何一承运人承担单船货物的海运服务……"，另有条文约定"……货物数量由 D 决定……"。

该仲裁案件涉及在履行了两次运输后，A 与 B 之间的合作与分配利润协议被 B 单方面终断。这导致了 A 向 B 提起北京仲裁并索赔该协议的"预期利益损失"（expectation interest loss）或"利润损失"（loss of profit）。有关案件对责任方面应是十分简单，因为 B 单方面粗暴地终断协议，可以说违约/毁约是明确不过。问题还是计算损失，这方面被认为在 B 作为其中一位承运人的运输合约中，D 拥有绝对决定性对货物的分配权（分配给 B 或 C），所以 B 会获得的承运货物有极大不确定性。而如果 D 不分配货物给 B，也就不存在 A 可以完成运输再与 B 分摊获得的利润。而 A 所说的"B 与 C 会是交替完成货物的运输"纯粹是一厢情愿的臆猜。所以，A 向 B 索赔的利润损失不能够成立。

笔者不了解中国法律（适用在该仲裁的有关利润分配协议），但觉得在 B 明确的违约/毁约下，竟然不必对受害方的 A 做出实质的赔偿是在公平的角度说不过去的。但怎么样才能比较科学地计算实质的赔偿？看来这一个所谓的不确定性主要还是因为有第三人的变数，也就是 D 在运输合约下拥有一个绝对对需要运输货物做出分配的权利。但显然 D 作为第三人是不会不想顺利完成履行这一个非洲庞大工程的运输，也没有理由或证据显示会在两个承运人之间偏袒其中一个，如把所有的货物都交给 C 运输，而对 B 却置之不理。所以笔者认为北京仲裁的仲裁庭应该是采取英国法律下的"机会损失"（loss of chance）处理第三人 D 的变数。特别是有关的运输合约已经是小部分履行，从中也可以找得出一些数据估计到 D 会是怎么样在 B 与 C 之间分配运输货物以及支付有关的运费。

6. 其他不适用机会损失的案件：医疗疏忽

这方面重要的发展是在医疗疏忽领域的侵权案件，其中要介绍的就是贵族院的 Gregg v. Scott（2005）UKHL 2 先例。案情涉及原告 Gregg 先生在 1994 年 11 月（当时 43 岁）看门诊医生（被告），咨询有关他腋下的肿块。被告告诉他没有关系，也没有推荐他去医院做进一步的检查。9 个月之后，原告因为搬家而找了另一位门诊医生并且被推荐去医院做进一步检查，发现得了癌症。这后来带来了一连串的化疗与其他痛苦的治疗，但总算生存下来。原告在 2001 年向被告起诉，而被告也承认了疏忽与误诊。而损失就是这 9 个月的误诊带来的寿命减少以及疾病的困扰。根据专家证据与后来双方同意的事实，原告如果正确与及时的就医检查，在今后的 10 年会有 42% 的机会健康生存下去，但误诊 9 个月就把这一几率降低为 25%。

从数字上可以看到，根据平衡的可能性，原告是无法成功索赔损失的，因为无法证明被告的误诊导致原告损失的可能性是超过 50%。但根据机会损失就不一样了。反正这一案件在不同法院的大法官面前也有很大的争议。在第一审，高院认为原告没有能够证明有任何真正与实质的损失。到了上诉庭，也是判原告败诉，但以 2∶1 的多数作出判决。到了贵族院，最后还是判原告败诉，但也是以 3∶2 的多数作出最后的判决。而且 5 个勋爵分别以不同的理由写出了他们的决定，导致了整个判决长达 227 个段节。

贵族院少数的意见认为被告应该作出机会损失的赔偿，其中 Nicholls 勋爵是这样说："This surely cannot be the state of the law today. It would be irrational and indefensible. The loss of a 45% prospect of recovery is just as much a real loss for a patient as the loss of a 55% prospect of recovery. In both cases the doctor was in breach of his duty to his patient. In both cases the patient was worse off. He lost something of importance and value. But, it is said, in one case the patient has a remedy, and in the other he does not. This would make no sort of sense. It would mean that in the 45% case the doctor's duty would be hollow. The duty would be empty of content."

贵族院多数(包括 Hoffmann 勋爵、Phillips 勋爵和 Baroness Hale 大法官)的判决是机会损失不适用在医疗疏忽特别是误诊的案件,所以原告败诉。但多数判决中每一位大法官的侧重点也不完全一样。其中一点是国家政策的原因,因为把水闸打开容许机会损失的索赔,就会令英国的"国家医疗服务"(National Health Service)与保险公司面临大量的索赔从而在财政上无法负担。其他的原因大致上有:

(1)如果延误诊断,可以说一般的尝试肯定会带来一些不好的后果,但经常是没有办法准确认定到底造成了什么伤害或后果;如果不理会后果而核算机会,Baroness Hale 大法官认为两者是不可在人身伤亡的法律并存的,说:"that personal injury law should transform itself. It should never be about outcomes but only about chances. It seems to me that this is the real problem in this case. How can the two live together?"

(2)医疗疏忽与合约的经济损失在本质上是不一样的,Hoffmann 勋爵在 Gregg v. Scott 先例中也同意机会损失更适用在经济损失。在医疗疏忽,往往涉及其他更重要的原因导致了受害方的伤害或损失。这一重要原因就是原告本身就已经有疾病(特别是致命的病),这是已经"发生了的事实"(past fact)。后来的医疗疏忽或误诊充其量只是增加了伤害或者减少了生存几率,这往往是不足以打断因果关系的。这一来如果根据平衡的可能性,导致原告最后结果主要的原因往往仍然是他本身就有的疾病。原告不应该在不能成立平衡的可能性情况下,改为适用机会损失作为救济。以 Hotson v. East Berkshire Area Health Authority (1987) AC 750 先例为例,误诊导致原告因"骨疽"(necrosis)而瘫痪的机会是25%。这就表示即使是没有误诊,也有75%的几率会导致同样的结果。在 Gregg v. Scott 一案中,认定误诊对导致最后的结果只占42%机会,也表示即使没有误诊,Gregg 先生有58%的机会是无法避免这一最后结果的。这里可节录 Jill Poole 教授的《Loss of chance and the evaluation of hypotheticals in contractual claims》一文中所说:"In medical negligence claims, unlike contractual claims for loss of chance, there is an underlying medical condition which pre-dates the alleged wrong or the context for that wrong. It also follows that, unlike contractual claims, there are other forces at work, apart from the human intervention of the defendant, which give rise to the context for the claim. In Hotson, for example, Lord Mackay of Clashfern stated that, before the moment when the plaintiff in that case had arrived at hospital, there had been no chance to lose because, based on the objective prognosis fixed at the particular point in time, the permanent disability would have followed in any event. The cause of the loss (permanent injury) was therefore classified as a question of past fact to which the probability text applied. On the balance of probabilities, it was the accident that had caused the injury rather than the failure to diagnose in good time. That conclusion could not be altered by formulating the claim as one for loss of chance. Similarly, in Gregg v. Scott the breach of duty involved a delay in the diagnosis and treatment of cancer due to the defendant's negligence in failing to refer the claimant to a specialist. The trial judge had found that on the initial visit to the defendant the claimant had had (past fact) a 42% chance of surviving cancer and that the delay in referral to the specialist had resulted in this chance failing to 25%. The House of Lords, by a 3:2 majority, rejected the claim for damages for loss the opportunity to improve the claimant's chance of survival. Thus, rather than formulating the question in terms of what the claimant had lost as a result of the defendant's actions (ie, the chance of a better survival rate), the question is formulated in terms of whether it can be established, as a probability, that he would otherwise have survived."

(3)医学本身是一个很困难与不肯定的科学,例如在 Gregg v. Scott 先例中,原告可以生存这样久的时间并不符合统计数字。而法院处理这方面的专家意见也被批评为不准确与不称职,例如在 Hotson v. East Berkshire Area Health Authority 先例中,原告的25%机会是在第一审法院对双方当事人的专家意见证据都感到不满意后取的平均数。估计这也是被视为无法接受机会损失救济的原因之一。

(4)还有是在医疗疏忽之类的案件,通常并没有涉及第三人的变数,这就不应该适用机会损失的救济。

7. 其他不适用机会损失的案件:船舶碰撞

机会损失的救济也首次出现在船舶碰撞的侵权案件,有关的案例是 The "Vicky 1" (2008) 2 Lloyd's Rep. 45。该船舶与原告的一艘名为 Front Ace 的超级油轮在印尼水域于2002年12月12日发生碰撞,并对 Front Ace 轮造成了严重的损坏。在责任方面,Vicky 1 轮的船东作为被告是承认了碰撞责任,所以双方的争议停留在损失的核算上。Front Ace 轮的船东作为原告证明在碰撞前一天,他已经与 Chevron 油公司订立了一个利润非常高的程租合约,租约横跨的时间为2002年12月20日到2003年1月20日,每天的利润高达62,000美元。但油轮市场在该租约订立后急剧下跌,该碰撞导致了 Front Ace 轮错过销约期,并被 Chevron 借这个黄金机会解约。最终 Front Ace 轮在12月底修妥之后只能找到一个西非的航次租约,承租人是 Vitol,履行的时间一直维持到2003年4月18日,每天的利润只有35,000美元。双方的争议涉及如何计算 Front Ace 轮的利润损失,原告指应该以"time equalisation method",就是把 Chevron 租约应该赚取的利润加上从2003年1月20日到2003年4月18日这一段时间内在当时油轮市场可以赚取的利润,反正就不理会 Vitol 的租约的实际利润。这样计算损失高达 2,360,000 美元。但被告认为应该以"ballast - laden method"方法计算,就是把 Chevron 租约应该赚取的每天利润,减去 Vitol 租约的每天实际利润,然后乘以受影响的期间,也就是只算到 2003 年 1 月 20 日。这样计算出的损失只有 850,000 美元。在第一审,法院认为原告的计算办法才是正确,但由于是有变数(包括第三人的承租人变数),所以原告的 2,360,000 美元的损失要减掉 20%。到了上诉庭,这一机会损失的说法被推翻,Clarke 大法官是这样说:

"I would accept those submissions. I am not persuaded that this is a case for the application of the loss of a chance approach discussed in Allied Maples among many other cases. This is not as I see it a case in which, as Stuart - Smith LJ put it . . . the plaintiff's loss depends on the hypothetical action of a third party, either in addition to action by the plaintiff, as in this case, or independently of it.

It is not a case where the claimants' loss depends upon a chance of making a particular contract. The exercise upon which the experts were engaged was to find the appropriate market rate for the use of the vessel in the relevant 57 days in circumstances in which it was established that she would have been profitably employed during that period. The experts agreed the appropriate figure. So indeed did the parties, at any rate assuming that it was appropriate to adopt the time equalisation approach, which in my opinion it was.

There are many cases in which courts or arbitrators have to determine what rate or profit would have been earned but for a tort or breach of contract. As I see it, in a case of this kind, where the court has held that the vessels would have been profitably engaged during the relevant period, **where there is a relevant market and where the court can and does make a finding as to the profit that would probably have been made (and has been lost), there is no place for a discount from that figure to reflect the chance than the vessel would not have been employed.** (加黑部分是笔者的强调)

It has not in my experience been suggested in the past that any such discount should be made. This situation is to be contrasted with a case in which it is not shown that the vessel would have been profitably employed but she might have been. It may be that in those circumstances it would be possible to approach the problem as a loss of a chance. However, I would not wish to express a firm view on that question in this case, where it does not arise on the facts. Here, given the exercise carried out by the experts and given the figure agreed by them, there is in my opinion no warrant for a reduction of 20%, either to reflect a risk that the vessel would not have been employed or for contingencies to reflect that the figure agreed might not be accurate."

从上述 Clarke 大法官的判词中,是可以感受到"机会损失"(loss of chance)并没有远离船舶碰撞或者任何其他针对将来利润损失的案件(如租约或者买卖合约的违约/毁约)，只要能够扯上第三人的变数。在 The“Vicky 1”先例中，机会损失的计算办法被上诉庭拒绝，因为原告提出并被法院接受的“time equalisation method”实际上是不涉及第三人(如 Vitol)的变数的。原告主要是根据市场的租金/运费。这一来，根据专家意见证据所估计的市场租金/运费应该已经考虑了原告的船舶 Front Ace 轮能不能找到生意或找到租金更高的生意。所以，没有理由再做出 20% 的扣减。但如果不是根据市场的租金/运费，而是根据某一个特定的租约索赔利润损失，就会涉及第三人(如特定租约的承租人)的变数，这在本章 4.1 段提到 Stovold v. Barlows (1996) PNLR 91 的先例有介绍过，就是原告与被告都可以坚持以机会损失核算金额。

总结而言，这种以“possibility”替代“probability”的损失计算办法还是有许多的疑问尚待解决，包括在笔者熟悉的商事案件(这在本章之 5.5 段有提到的仲裁案件)与海事案件中，估计在接下去的案例会在这一方面有不断的发展。

第七章　第三人损失与第三人规则

1. 英国法律下的第三人规则

1.1　第三人规则的原因与来由

简单说,一旦在一个合约中发生违约的情况,除了合约的受害方以外,第三人也会蒙受损失,而且经常会有这种情况。但英国法律下,根据损失赔偿的"复原大原则"(*restitutio in integrum*),只是把合约受害方回复到合约被履行的经济地位,没有把第三人的损失包括在内。这一个问题也带出了另一个更严重与更广泛的问题,并且上百年来都对英国法律造成了困扰。这问题就是"第三人规则"(Third Party Rule)。它的广泛性不止包括合约受害方不能向违约方索赔第三人蒙受的损失,也包括合约受害方不能根据合约向第三人索赔或第三人不能向合约方主张合约利益。换言之是第三人即使是与有关合约有密切的关系,英国法下合约只是严格属于订约双方,不论是责任或是权利,只有订约双方才需要履行或能够享有。第三人规则是在英国法律下严格的"合约相互性"(privity of contract)与"约因/对价"(consideration)大原则下衍生出来的。在合约相互性下,只有合约的双方才谈得上能够依赖并主张他们之间的权利与义务。另外,一份有效合约必须要存在约因/对价的原则下也要求合约双方都必须相互做出承诺或提供好处。这令第三人不可能为有关的合约做出任何约因/对价,因为他从来没有机会也从来不会想这样做。这一来,第三人如果向合约的承诺方主张合约的权利(如要求支付一笔钱或是依赖合约免责条文),马上面对的困难是他没有作为被承诺方向承诺方提供的约因/对价,这也是英国一句著名的"Consideration must move from the promise"。

换言之,英国法律是不承认 *jus quaesitum tertio*(这拉丁语的英文翻译可以是"an acquired right of third party to recover from one who is under an obligation"): Tweddle v. Atkinson (1861) 1 B. & S. 393. 这方面可以节录很早的一个先例 Dunlop Pneumatic Tyre Co Ltd v. Selfridge & Co Ltd (1915) AC 847 中 Viscount Haldane 说:"Our law knows nothing of a *jus quaesitum tertio* by way of contract."英国这一个法律地位可以说是自从 Tweddle v. Atkinson 先例后才明确起来,以前是没有这一个说法,正如在 Drive Yourself Hire Co (London) Ltd v. Strutt (1954) 1 QB 250 先例,Denning 大法官说:"It is often said to be a fundamental principle of our law that only a person who is a party to a contract can sue on it. I wish to assert, as distinctly as I can, that the common law in its original setting knew no such principle. Indeed, it said quite the contrary. For the 200 years before 1861 it was settled law that, if a promise in a simple contract was made expressly for the benefit of a third person in such circumstances that it was intended to be enforceable by him, then the common law would enforce the promise at his instance, although he was not a party to the contract."

1.2　合约变更才能让第三人承担合约履行责任

针对合约的责任不能让第三人参与是完全可以理解,否则会是与订约自由的大原则起冲突。毕竟一方当事人如果愿意与另一方订立合约,在合约下是有许多明示约定的责任需要对方履行,就会涉及对对方的信心无论是对财政或是技术等各种考虑因素。如果让不知底细的第三人参与合约责任的履行,并替代原来订约方把合约责任接过来,可以说被履行的当事人不会愿意,也不是订约的意图。所以合约责任不存在第三人的参与也不能单方面通过"转让"(assignment)合法转移让第三人履行,并让原来的履约方脱身。唯一能够让第三人参与责任的履行,就是通过合约"更替"(novation)。这就需要每一位涉及更替的当事人同意,这包括原来订约的双方同意终止原合约,而准备接管该合约的第三人也在同时接过来并与原合约的一方继续履行,而原合约的另一方也就退出了该合约,甚至可以说原合约已经被"杀死"了,取而代之的是更替合约。有关合约更替的法律,可节录Steel大法官在The "Tychy" (No. 2) (2001) 1 Lloyd's Rep 10说:"(a) Novation involves the creation of a new contract where an existing party is replaced by a new party. (b) Thus, novation requires the consent of all parties, including in particular the party which is thereby accepting a new person as his debtor or as his counterpart under an executory contract. (c) The consent may be apparent from express words or inferred from conduct. (d) The consent must be clearly established on the evidence as being only consistent with the intent of achieving a novation."

1.3　转让才能让第三人取得合约的权利或利益

上述只是针对合约责任(虽然合约更替也同时把有关合约权利让第三人接管过来变为是新的合约方),但如果是涉及合约的权利或利益,在现实中不存在上述的考虑与法律要求,英国法律除了在为数不多的限制下,是完全允许合约权利的"被承诺方"(promisee)让第三人参与,也就是把合约权利转让给第三人。对合约权利下的"承诺方"(promisor)而言,特别是涉及一些谁来主张合约权利都没有区别的情况。例如支付一笔租金或其他债务给合约的被承诺方,或是在被承诺方要求下支付给第三人,对承诺方而言都没有任何关系,只要在支付之后就履行了他在合约下作出的承诺即可。现实的商业社会经常需要把这种合约利益交出给第三人,如被承诺方向银行贷款,就会需要在贷款协议中把合约的租金(如果该合约的收益是作为担保)交出给银行。银行是不会放心合约承诺方先把合约租金支付给被承诺方,然后依赖后者的信用按照贷款协议把这笔钱转给银行。但在英国普通法下,这"第三人规则"

(Third Party Rule)是禁止这样做,这导致在早期的英国衡平法法院对普通法僵化的立场作出救济,名为"衡平法转让"(equitable assignment):Crouch v. Martin (1707) 2 Vern. 595; Row v. Dowson (1749) 1 Vern Sen. 331; Ryall v. Rowles (1750) 1 Ves. Sen. 348; Wright v. Wright (1750) Ves. Sen. 409。而到了1925年的《财产法》之Section 136(1)也有了"立法转让"(statutory/legal assignment)。

1.4 对第三人规则的批评

第三人规则是十分严重的问题,因为在日常的生活中与商业活动中经常出现。简单地举个例子说明这一个英国法律地位就是作为合约受害方的原告因为被告的违约而损失了100万美元,原告可以成功向被告取回这笔钱。但如果这100万的损失并非是在原告,而是第三人(即使该第三人与原告有密切的关系,如是联营公司),而且原告对第三人也没有责任,原告就不能向被告索赔。即使是在责任方面明确了被告的违约,原告能够取回的只会是"名义损失"(nominal damage),这其实是败诉,原告恐怕还要承担所有的诉讼费用。至于蒙受真正损失的第三人,能否直接向违约方索赔这笔100万美元的损失就要看个别案件了,如他们之间是否拥有直接的合约关系(但即使有也根据不同的合约条文会有局限与困难,如错过了更短暂的索赔时限),或是能否以侵权起诉(但要考虑到侵权通常是不能索赔纯经济损失)等。

这一法律地位带来很多麻烦,可以说是非常令人不满意。早在1937年,"法律改革委员会"(Law Revision Committee)就已经作出建议(Cmnd. 5449之44段)认为应该让第三人能够执行一个与他利益相关的合约下的承诺。该委员会的主席Wright勋爵的建议是:"Where a contract by its express terms purports to confer a benefit directly on a third party, the third party shall be entitled to enforce the provision in his own name, provided that the promisor shall be entitled to raise as against the third party any defence that would have been valid against the promisee. The rights of the third party shall be subject to cancellation of the contract by the mutual consent of the contracting parties at any time before the third party has adopted it either expressly or by conduct."

但由于其他的原因,如法律改革委员会曾经一度转移注意力想先改革约因/对价的问题,所以一直没有进一步的改革。这带来在Woodar Investment Development Ltd v. Wimpey Construction UK Ltd (1980) 1 WLR 277先例,贵族院的大法官都对这一个英国法律地位作出了批评,并要求尽早改革。其中Salmon勋爵是说,"I would add that, in my opinion, the law as it stands at present in relation to damages of this kind is most unsatisfactory; and I can only hope that your Lordships' House will soon have an opportunity of reconsidering it unless in the meantime it is altered by statute."

Keith勋爵也说,"I would also associate myself with the observations of my noble and learned friend, Lord Scarman, as to the desirability of this House having an opportunity of reviewing, in some appropriate future case, the general attitude of English law towards the topic of *jus quaesitum tertio*."

最后节录 Scarman 勋爵说,“ First, the ‘*jus quaestitum tertio.* ’ I respectfully agree with Lord Reid that the denial by English law of a ‘*jus quaestitum tertio*’ calls for reconsideration. In Beswick v. Beswick (1968) A. C. 58, 72 Lord Reid, after referring to the Law Revision Committee’s recommendation in 1937 (Cmnd. 5449) P. 31 that the third party should be able to enforce a contractual promise taken by another for his benefit, observed: ‘And, if one had to contemplate a further long period of Parliamentary procrastination, this House might find it necessary to deal with this matter. ’ The committee reported in 1937: Beswick v. Beswick was decided in 1967. It is now 1979: but nothing has been done. If the opportunity arisen, I hope the House will reconsider Tweddle v. Atkinson and the other cases which stand guard over this unjust rule. ”

而要求英国国会议院作出这方面的法律改革在 1995 年还在 Darling Borough Council v. Wiltshier Northern Ltd(1995)1 WLR 68 先例中出现,上诉庭的 Steyn 大法官说:“The case for recognising a contract for the benefit of a third party is simple and straightforward. Thee autonomy of the will of the parties should be respected. The law of contract should give effect to the reasonable expectations of contracting parties. Principle certainly requires that a burden should not be imposed on a third party without consent. But there is no doctrinal, logical, or policy reason why the law should deny effectiveness to a contract for the benefit of a third party where that is the expressed intention of the parties. Moreover, often the parties, and particularly third parties, organise their affairs on the faith of the contract. They rely on the contract. It is therefore unjust to deny effectiveness to such a contract. I will not struggle with the point further since nobody seriously asserts the contrary. ”

1.5　第三人规则带来问题的简要介绍

第三人规则带来很多严重的麻烦与不公平,在进一步探讨之前,可先简单说明以下问题:(1)违约导致第三人蒙受损失,如果他无法取得任何救济会是不公平。(2)经常会出现的情况是合约的受害方能够向违约方起诉,但真正的损失或大部分的损失并不严格是在他本人,而是在第三人(重复这第三人可以是与受害方关系十分密切,如配偶或联营公司),但蒙受损失的第三人却不能起诉违约方。正如 Beswick v. Beswick (1968) AC 58 先例中,贵族院表示:“The person who has suffered the loss cannot sue, while the person who has suffered no loss can sue. ”(3)即使合约的受害方或“被承诺方”(promisee)可以替第三人取得损失赔偿,被承诺方也可能不能(如死亡[自然人]或者倒闭[公司法人])或不愿意(原因很多,如与违约方关系好,但与第三人却不是关系密切;不愿意打官司与花律师费,而即使费用有第三人补偿下也怕麻烦等)起诉违约方。英国法律是无法帮助第三人强制合约的被承诺方代他向违约方索赔损失。(4)为了解决这个严重的问题,英国已经是发展出许多第三人规则的例外情况,这种情况会稍后介绍。但问题是这些例外情况导致英国法律在这方面是十分复杂、不肯定与牵强。(5)英国已经与其他英联邦与普通法国家的法律脱节,如美国、澳大利亚(部分州)与新西兰都已经通过立法排除第三人规则。(6)英国虽然已经是欧共体国家的成员之一,但在第三人规则方面与其他欧洲国家不一致。其他的国家法律都已经解决了这个问题,如法国(《民法典》之 Article 1121 与 1165)、德国(《Burgerliches Gesetzbuch》之 Article 328)、意大利(《民法典》之 Article 1411)、澳大利亚(《民法典》之 Article 881)、西班牙(《民法典》之 Article 1257 第二段)、葡萄牙(《民法典》之 Article 443)、荷兰(《民法典》Book 6 Article 253)、比利时(基本遵循《法国民法典》)、卢森堡公国(模仿《法国民法典》)、希腊(《民法典》之 Article 411)。

2. 第三人规则问题的例子

这不满意的法律地位的例子数不胜数,举一些很简单的日常例子可以显示其不实际与不公平,如下:

(1)例如,一位父亲或是一位母亲代表家庭成员与旅行社订了一个旅游合约,但事后货不对版(如约定的著名五星级酒店爆满,该家庭成员被迫住在一个三星级酒店),导致该父亲(或母亲)作为签约方向旅行社索赔损失。毫无疑问,如果责任方面能够成立,该父亲或母亲可以索赔他/她本人的损失,但他/她不能索赔作为第三人的损失,也就是他/她家人的损失,因为家人是属于第三人。这种问题也不能以其他说法解决,如说该父亲或母亲是他/她家人的代理人。这个说法会太虚假或牵强,如家人包括了一个婴儿,很难说得通该婴儿授权他父亲或母亲订立有关旅游合约。另一个说法就是信托关系,这也是很难说得通。因为整个行动与信托扯不上关系,也不涉及信托资金或信托财产。

(2)再举一个日常例子就是一位男士或女士邀请多位朋友参加晚餐,唯一与餐厅订合约的就是这位男士或女士,他/她的朋友就是第三人。这一来如果出了什么问题,能够索赔的损失只能局限在该男士或女士,而第三人的损失就束之门外。如果是涉及餐厅提供不卫生的食物导致多人拉肚子,这倒还可以让第三人向餐厅以侵权起诉。但如果是涉及合约方面的权利,如提供食物货不对版等,又带来了问题就是第三人不能向该餐厅提出索赔或通过邀请的男士或女士代他向餐厅索赔。

(3)另一个日常例子是一个乐队的代表或是一个会议的代表安排交通负责接送,与当地的旅游巴士管理公司订了合约。但如果该公司违约,在子夜的时候没有安排巴士来接送,最后导致乐队的成员或会议代表各自要以昂贵的费用乘坐的士或要住酒店,也会导致他们作为第三人的损失无法向巴士管理公司提出索赔。

(4)A 向 B 承诺他会支付给 B 妻子每年 5000 美元生活费直到她死亡,作为交换是 B 把他的一盘生意或他昂贵的房子转交给 A。在这个协议后不久,B 因病去世,而 A 也在不久后停止支付给 B 妻子的生活费。这一来,B 的去世已经不可能起诉 A 的违约。但 B 妻子也不能向 A 提出索赔,因为她不是合约方,只是第三人。(这案情与著名的 Beswick v. Beswick [1968] AC 58 先例类似。)

(5) A 是一位十分富有的老人,他准备在死后把所有的家产捐出给一个 C 的慈善机构。所以,A 就委托了 B 的律师所为他拟定一份遗嘱,但由于 B 的疏忽与延误,A 突然得病很快就死亡了,而遗嘱还没有拟定。C 知道消息后感觉到十分气愤因为它失去了这一笔捐赠,并向 B 提出诉讼,毕竟 B 是有投保专业疏忽的保险,赔得起。但 C 是第三人,不能根据合约向 B 提出索赔。(这案情与著名的 White v. Jones [1995] 2 AC 207 先例类似。)

(6) 一家公司为它的雇员购买意外保险,订约方是公司与保险人,雇员是第三人。这表示将来出了意外第三人是不能直接向保险人索赔损失而是会要通过有关的公司。但如果该公司倒闭或是停止业务,雇员的索赔就会有问题。(这种案件很多,如 Green v. Rusell [1959] 2 QB 226)

(7) 第三人规则特别困扰保险,多举一个例子是 B 向 A 投保一个工程的责任保险,其中受保人包括了 B 集团的分公司、承建商、分承建商等有关人士。C 是一位分承建商,在工程进行中被指疏忽而导致了一位工人受伤,C 希望通过 B 与 A 的保险合约获得补偿,但 C 与 A 是没有合约关系。而即使是通过 B 向 A 要求补偿,也存在争议就是损失是在第三人 C。

(8) 至于外贸,这种情况无时无刻不会出现。早期中国的外贸进口(如机械)必须依赖外贸代理商与外商之间签订的合约,然后由外贸代理商把有关机械转交给中国的最终使用者,甚至是通过他自己向船舶提货。如果该机械有问题,就会带来最终使用者的损失,甚至是严重损失。根据外贸代理商与外商的合约,外商有明确的责任。但问题是损失并不在外贸代理商,而且外贸代理商会是大国企,不存在对最后使用者有任何责任或有法律依据(如他们之间的合约)可让最后使用者向外贸代理商提出同样的索赔。如果任由最后使用者直接向外商索赔,他们之间并没有合约关系,甚至也不能以侵权提出。这一来,就表示外商可以在违约后"逍遥法外",而中国的最终使用者就要承担这一笔可能是庞大的损失,可以说是陷进了英国法下的"法律黑洞"(legal black hole),[1] 也就是臭名远播的第三人规则。

(9) 上一个例子是涉及中国外贸,但几百年来英国法下国际贸易也面临相同的严重困难。国际贸易离不开航运,一直以来与承运人或船东订立的海上运输合约

[1] 法律黑洞的说法在苏格兰先例之 GUS Property Management Ltd v. Littlewoods Mail Order Stores Ltd (1982) SLT 533 中,由 Keith 勋爵首先提到。接下去在 Linden Gardens v. Lenesta Sludge Disposals Ltd. and others (1993) 3 All ER 417 先例,Browne – Wilkinson 勋爵说:"Therefore, it is said, neither of the plaintiffs has any right to substantial damages: [the building owner] has incurred damage (being the cost rectifying the faulty work) but has no cause of action; [the building employer] has a cause of action but has suffered no loss. If this is right, in the words of my noble and learned friend, Lord Keith of Kinkel... 'the claim to damages would disappear... into some legal black hole, so that the wrongdoer escaped scot – free.'

(这包括提单),通常是卖方或发货人。这包括是绝大部分的班轮运输,或是散货的CIF或CFR买卖,甚至在部分的FOB买卖(买方委托卖方作出付运)。但如果货物在航程中发生损坏,而且涉及船舶的违约(如不适航),损失通常是在买方或收货人。而且在卖方与买方之间的买卖合约,通常的做法是运输的风险是在买方,这表示卖方对货物在航程中发生损坏是没有责任。这导致了船东索赔损失,会带来尴尬的局面就是与船东有合约关系的卖方有权索赔,但他没有损失(包括没有对第三人有任何责任)。而与船东没有合约关系的买方或收货人作为第三人是蒙受损失,但他没有合约关系可以索赔。这种情况在Lickbarrow v. Mason (1794) 5 Term Rep. 683先例,确认通过提单的转让,可以把有关货物转让并可以根据正本提单向船舶提货的做法。这也是提单作为"物权凭证"(document of title)说法的来由。但在这个说法下还是没有办法解决买方或收货人蒙受损失不能根据提单的运输合约向承运人索赔,因为Lickbarrow v. Mason先例只是根据贸易习惯确认交出提单相等于转让货物所有权,但没有说法是交出提单也可以同时把提单合约关系从发货人与承运人之间变为收货人与承运人之间,如果想这样做还是需要通过合约"更替"(novation)的做法,这通常不会发生。这方面的问题直到1855年英国《提单法》的生效才有了解决,立法是强加一个提单合约的"更替"(novation),就是卖方把提单通过背书转让给买方的同时,除了把有关货物转让外,也同时把提单所代表的运输合约转让。这等于是把买方或收货人与承运人或船东通过立法扯上合约关系,虽然他们之间从来没有普通法要求一个有效合约必须要有的条件,如"要约"(offer)、"接受"(acceptance)、"约因"(consideration)等。1855年英国《提单法》已经被1992年《海上货物运输法》替代,但其中的大道理还是一样的,就是通过立法允许买方根据提单合约(通常1924年《海牙规则》强制适用)向承运人或船东索赔他所蒙受的货损货差损失。但在1855年的立法之前,普通法已经发展出一些"例外"(exceptions)情况提供一些救济,让有合约关系的卖方代买方向船东索赔货损货差的损失。这种例外情况包括"托管"(bailment)、"代理"(agency)、"订约意图"(contractual intention)等。这些例外情况稍后会分段介绍。这种例外即使是有了1855年或1992年的立法还是有必要,如The "Albazero" (1976) 2 Lloyd's Rep 467先例,就涉及买方因为错过了1924年《海牙规则》的1年时效,所以需要通过卖方作为承租人与船东订立的期租合约索赔货损货差的损失,而该期租合约是有6年时效。另是特别在1855年立法下,由于适用的情况比较局限,所以在立法不适用的案件下,作为第三人的买方通过订约方的卖方向承运人索赔损失还是要依赖普通法下的例外情况。有关这方面的详细介绍,可参阅笔者所著的《提单及其他付运单证》一书。

(10)另举的例子是涉及房屋建造与买卖,这也是另一个严重受到第三人规则困扰的商业活动。通常开发商与承建商的合约中会对房屋的质量要求、建造标准等作以约定,并明确要求承建商应对因建造与合约不符而造成的损失对开发商负责任。但涉及房屋买卖时,合约则发生在开发商与作为小业主的购房者之间。如果房屋出现了任何与建造有关的质量问题,小业主不能直接向承建商索赔,因为他们之间没有任何合约关系,也不能以侵权索赔(如质量问题不一定涉及承建商的疏忽或过错,也很难证明,但合约往往涉及严格责任),除非有当地法律对此作出特别规定,以保护小业主的权利。这一来,小业主就要自行承担这一笔损失,这看起来是有失公平的。同样的情况也会出现在造船合约,这种合约通常会有条文针对船厂向买方做出各种承诺,如在交船后的1年或更长的时间内,船舶如果发生故障,船厂保证会免费做出修理。但如果在交船后,买方很快把有关船舶出售给另一位新船东,这就带来问题如果在这一个保证的期限内发生故障,该新船东作为第三人是没有办法直接要求船厂作出修理或赔偿损失。会是在船舶出售给新船东时,买方可以把造船合约内的权利或利益同时"转让"(assign)给新船东。但造船合约通常会有一条"禁止转让条文"(prohibition of assignment clause),导致买方没有办法这样做。这种情况也通常出现在较早介绍的房屋建造,承建商与开发商之间的合约中也往往有一条禁止转让条文,导致开发商出售房子给小业主,也往往没有办法把承建商作出的承诺利益转让给小业主:Linden Gardens v. Lenesta Sludge Disposals Ltd. and others (1993) 3 All ER 417先例。

3. 第三人规则的例外情况

上述所讲的来自"合约相互性"(privity of contract)与"约因/对价"(consideration)导致的"第三人规则"(*jus quaestitum tertio*)所带出来的困境以及英国法在针对不同领域/行业在这些年来发展出来许多的例外情况,可节录Miller勋爵在McAlpine Construction Ltd v. Panatown Ltd (2001) 1 AC 518先例的说法:"There are several apparent but well-established exceptions to the general rule of English law that in an action for breach of contract a plaintiff can only recover substantial damages for the loss which he has himself sustained. I say 'apparent' exceptions for I regard most of them as explicable in a manner consistent with the rule."

同样的说法也可把权威书籍的《Chitty on Contracts》(30th edn, 2008年)之18-052段节录如下:"**Damages in respect of third party's loss: exceptions in general.** Judicial awareness of the unsatisfactory results which can flow from the general rule ... has led the courts to create a number of exceptions to that rule. For example substantial damages for breach of contract can be recovered by a trustee even though the loss is suffered by his *cestui que trust*; by an agent even though the loss is suffered by its undisclosed principal; by a local authority even though the loss is suffered by its inhabitants; and by a shipper of goods for breach of his contract of carriage with the shipowner in respect of the loss of the goods, even though that loss is suffered by a person to whom the shipper has sold the goods and to whom the risk and property in them has passed but who has not himself acquired any rights under the contract of carriage against the shipowner; it will be convenient to refer to this last rule as 'the *Albazero* exception' after the leading modern case in which it is recognised. In all these exceptional cases, a person recovers substantial damages for breach of contract, even thought the breach caused no loss to him, but only to a third party. ."(法院明白第三人规则作为一个普遍适用的一般性规则带来的不令人满意的结果,所以针对这条规则发展出了许多例外情况。例如,合约的受害方可以向违约方取得第三人的实质损失赔偿,依据是他与第三人有一个信托关系,这第三人变为受益人。合约的受害方也可以以他是一位代理人索赔"没有披露委托人"所蒙受的实质损失。当地政府往往可以作为合约方对居民的第三人蒙受的实际损失要求违约方做出赔偿。船东违反与卖方或发货人订立的货物运输合约造成了货物损失/损坏,卖方或发货人可以要求船东赔偿,即使货物的所有权和风险已经在装船后转移给了买方或收货人。也就是说实质损失是在买方或收货人,但买方或收货人对船东没有运输合约的关系。所以对第三人[也就是买方或收货人]的损失,能够向违约的船东索赔也就必须发展一个例外,这也就是著名的"The 'Albazero' 例外"。在上面的所有例外中,合约的受害方可以取得违约所带来的实质损失赔偿,即使违约没有对他本人造成损失,而是对一些相关的第三人造成了损失。)

由于这个第三人规则带来很多让人不满意的情况,所以这些年来普通法与衡平法下与立法发展出来许多的例外情况,以下可以做出进一步的介绍。

3.1 第三人规则例外之一:托管关系

这是在早期的国际贸易案件中让有运输合约关系的卖方代买方向船东索赔货损货差的损失的一种主要例外情况,这到 1855 年英国《提单法》的生效后才告一段落。这个例外就是根据"托管"(bailment)与"禁止反供"(estoppel)的说法,大致上是指"寄托人"(bailor)交出货物给"托管人"(bailee),如果货物在托管期间因后者的疏忽而损坏,后者是"禁止反供"(estopped)质疑寄托人对有关货物的所有权。换言之,前者的寄托人可以向后者索赔所有的损失,即使真正的损失是在第三人(货物所有权人)。这一个说法是为了"商业方便"(commercial convenience)。这可节录 Martin B 大法官在 Cheeseman v. Exall (1851) 6 Exch 341 先例中所说:"There are numerous cases in connection with wharfs and docks, in which, if the party entrusted with the possession of property were not estopped from denying the title of the person from whom he received it, it would be difficult to transact commercial business."

换言之,在托管的关系下,寄托人是可以向受托人索赔第三人的损失。由于海上运输真正涉及了托管的关系,所以有不少的早期先例是根据这一种例外情况由卖方(作为寄托人)向承运人或船东(作为托管人)索赔航程中的货损货差,虽然这一方面的损失会是落在买方或收货人(作为第三人)。这可节录 The "Albazero" (1976) 2 Lloyd's Rep 467 先例中 Diplock 勋爵所说:"The reason why in the early cases right of suit and the right to recover substantial damages for loss of the goods were treated as always vested in the same person may have been because the contract for the carriage of goods involves a bailment. The person on whose behalf the goods are delivered to the carrier is the bailor and the carrier is the bailee. If sued before the Common Law Procedure Act, 1852, whether in case upon the common custom of the realm or in assumpist, the carrier was estopped from denying his bailor's title to the goods at the time when possession was delivered to him."

这种例外情况最大的困难是"禁止反供"(estoppel)并没有太多的先例支持,也往往经不起考验。例如在一个少见的有关先例 Sheridan v. New Quay Company (1858) 4 CB NS 618,判是托管人并没有禁止争辩寄托人对有关货物的所有权,因为托管人曾经获得真正货物所有权人的指示。

3.2 索赔第三人损失例外之二:代理关系

也是在早期的国际贸易案件中,如果明确知道委托人(也是发货人)与收货人是不同人士,这一来可以根据另一种例外情况让委托人向承运人或船东索赔航次中的货损货差,即使损失是在买方或收货人,这就是根据代理关系(Agency)。在这一个关系下,就是假设委托人把货物交出给承运人或船东做出托运(托管与运输),他是以买方或收货人的代理人身份这样做。毕竟在早期的国际贸易中,也没有合法的途径在航次半途中通过提单背书与交出转让货物的所有权,这是直到 Lickbarrow v. Mason (1794) 5 Term Rep. 683 先例后才有的说法。这方面也可以节录 The "Albazero" (1976) 2 Lloyd's Rep 467 先例中 Diplock 勋爵所说:"The question who stood in relation of bailor to carrier and so was entitled to sue him for the full value of the goods lost or the full amount of the damage could only arise where the consignor and consignee were different persons. In such a case the presumption was that the bailor was the person named as consignee and that in delivering possession of the goods to the carrier the consignor was acting and purporting to act as agent only for a designated principal—the consignee. The possibility that the property in the goods might be transferred from consignor to consignee while they were in the possession of the carrier did not arise in practice until the close of the 18th century when the bill of lading was recognized in Lickbarrow v. Mason (1794) 5 Term Rep. 683, as a document of title capable of transferring the property in the goods to which it related by endorsement and delivery."

但这一个代理关系的说法在许多国际货物买卖十分牵强,因为双方明显是有一个买卖合约的关系。而且在常见的 CIF 买卖,合约是规定了卖方负责运输。这一来卖方租用船舶,与船东或班轮公司订下了运输合约,在发生货损货差后为了向船东提出索赔,把买卖双方的关系扭曲成为是代理关系,订立运输合约是因为买方或收货人的委托是说不通的。

简单地说,代理关系分两种。第一种涉及"披露委托人"(disclosed principal)。

代理人是以他的委托人的名义订立一个合约,所以不存在代理人可以起诉或被诉,他根本不是合约的一方。也没有必要让这种代理人向另一合约方索赔属于他的委托人的损失,委托人自己可以索赔。英国法律针对代理人是只要他在授权的范围内订立一份合约,在合约订立后,代理人就会"消失"(drops out of the picture),代理人既不能起诉也不能被诉:Wakefield v. Duckworth (1915) 1 KB 218。即使代理人订立一份合约是在他授权范围外(如授权书只允许代理人以不能低于某一个价格出售一批货物,但代理人还是没有依照做了),也有"表面授权"(apparent/ostensible authority)的说法,披露委托人还是要对越权代理人订立的合约负责,必须向不知内情的另外一方做出履行。

第二种涉及"没有披露委托人"(undisclosed principal),这种说法是普通法的一种特色。可以说是在这种关系下,直到代理人披露谁是背后的委托人,另外的合约方根本不知道有这位背后的委托人,他会以为代理人就是合约的另外一方。没有披露委托人的说法会导致合约方直到背后委托人出现,才知道原来他与一位根本不愿意打交道的一方有了合约关系。所以这一种合约关系难以说是有合约的相互性和订约意图。难怪 Reynolds 教授在权威书籍《Bowstead and Reynolds on Agency》(18th edn, 2006 年)中指出:"It is difficult to deny that the undisclosed principle is really a third party intervening on a contract which he did not make."

但普通法有这一个说法是为了配合商业上的方便,如拍卖古董或名画就经常会出现没有披露的卖方或买方。正如 Lloyd 勋爵在 Siu v. Eastern Insurance Co. Ltd (1994) 2 AC 199 先例说:"It seems to be generally accepted that, while the development of this branch of the law may have been anomalous, since it runs counter to fundamental principles of privity of contract, it is justified on grounds of commercial convenience."但这一个特色的说法也会对不懂的商业人士带来危险。

这种没有披露委托人的代理关系在 Siu v. Eastern Insurance Co. Ltd (1994) 2 AC 199 先例,Lloyd 勋爵总结说:"(1) An undisclosed principal may sue and be sued on a contract made by his agent on his behalf, acting within the scope of his actual authority. (2) In entering into the contract, the agent must intend to act on the principal's behalf. (3) The agent of an undisclosed principal may also sue and be sued on the contract. (4) Any defence which the third party may have against the agent is available against his principal. (5) The terms of the contract may, expressly or by implication, exclude the principal's right to sue, and his liability to be sued."

另在 The "World Era" (1992) 1 Lloyd's Rep 45 先例,Hobhouse 大法官说:"... it is recognised in English law that a party who has entered into a contract as the undisclosed agent for his principal may sue on that contract and recover substantial damages even though the financial interest in the contract may be entirely that of his principal. ... The performance of a contract has value and the mere fact that the agent has to account for that value to this principal is irrelevant to his right to recover that value from the contract breaker. . . ”

最近期的有关“没有披露委托人”(undisclosed principal)的权威说法是 Novasen SA v. Alimenta SA (2011) EWHC 49 (Comm)先例,Mackie 大法官是这样总结:“(1) an undisclosed principal may sue and be sued on a contract made by an agent on his behalf, acting within the scope of his actual authority(没有披露委托人可以在一个通过实际授权代理人所订立的合约下提起诉讼或被起诉);(2) in entering into the contract, the agent must intend to act on the principal's behalf(在订立合约的时候,代理人必须是意图代他的委托人订约);(3) the agent of an undisclosed principal may also sue and be sued on the contract(没有披露委托人的代理人也可以在有关合约下提起诉讼或被起诉);(4) any defence which the third party may have against the agent is available against his principal(第三人可以有同样的抗辩针对代理人或是他的委托人); and(5) the terms of the contract may, expressly or by implication, exclude the principal's right to sue, and his liability to be sued. The contract itself, or the circumstance surrounding the contract, may show that the agent is the true and only principal. ”(合约条文可以明示或默示排除没有披露委托人提起诉讼的权利与被诉的责任。合约本身或其他相关情况也可显示代理人是否是真正与唯一的委托人:The “Virgo”[1976] 2 Lloyd's Rep 135; The “Scaplake” [1978] 2 Lloyd's Rep 380;The “Sun Happiness” [1984] 1 Lloyd's Rep 381)

这方面的先例也有不少,如在一个名为 James Laidlaw & Sons Ltd v. Griffin (1968) SLT 278 的苏格兰先例,案情涉及原告向被告索赔供应两个在船舶上使用的锅炉的货价余额,而被告反索赔由于锅炉缺陷带来的损失。但在诉讼的披露过程中,才发觉与原告一直打交道的被告只是代理人,他只是该船舶的“管理人”(managing agent),而不是真正的船东。这一来,原告对反索赔的抗辩是真正蒙受损失是第三人的船东,不是被告。在第一审的法院也是判原告在反索赔的抗辩胜诉,但在上诉后被推翻。上诉庭的依据就是英国的“没有披露委托人”(undisclosed principal)说法,Ormidale 勋爵认为原告不能要求被告自付货款,把被告的代理人作为是合约的一方,但同时抗辩反索赔,指被告不是合约的一方,说“... ignoring it to the effect of forcing the price of the boilers from the agent, as the parties liable therefore under the contract, but calling it in aid to disentitle the agents from stating any counter - claim otherwise competent to them under the identical contract. ”

另多举一个英国的先例 Corfield v. David Grant (1992) 29 Con LR 58,案情涉及一对夫妻与一位建筑师的建造合约,把位于牛津的一幢房子改装成为一个酒店。改装后,该酒店是由一家有限公司营运,该对夫妻只是背后拥有。事后双方有了争议,该建筑师作为原告向被告的夫妻索赔还没有支付的费用,而被告反索赔改装不妥善所带来的损失。但这又带来了问题,就是原告抗辩蒙受损失的是营运的有限公司,不是被告的夫妻。在第一审，法院判是被告的夫妻可以以"没有披露代理人"的身份向原告反索赔这笔损失。Bowsher 大法官说："Any damages awarded to the defendant(该对夫妻)are to be treated as awarded to him as trustee for the company(营运酒店的有限公司法人), and any action by the company in respect of the same subject matter hereafter would no doubt be stayed as an abuse of the process of the court."

总结，"没有披露委托人"(undisclosed principal)的说法被视为第三人规则的一种例外是因为表面看来是一位完全与合约没有关系的第三人冒出来说他蒙受损失，要求向违约方索赔，但根据的理由是他实际上是背后的委托人，也就是合约的真正受害方。

3.3 索赔第三人损失例外之三：对合约承诺的信托

在很早的一个先例 Tomlinson v. Gill (1756) Amb 330，案情涉及被告向死者的妻子承诺如果她同意被告和她共同管理遗产，当资不抵债时，被告将会偿还死者余下的债务。之后，死者的债权人要求被告偿还死者欠下的债务并履行他的承诺。Hardwicke 勋爵判："The plaintiff is proper for relief here for two reasons: Firstly, he could not maintain an action at law, for the promise was made to the widow; but he is proper here, for the promise was for the benefit of the creditors, and the widow is a trustee for them."(原告[死者的债权人]有权向被告索赔。虽然在法律上严格说来，原告并无索赔的权利，因为被告的承诺是向死者的妻子作出的；但是在该案例中，他却有权利这样做，因为被告的承诺是为了债权人的利益，而该死者的妻子是债权人的受托人。)

这种合约承诺的信托(trust of promise)的说法适用在航运最为人所知的就是在合约(租约或船舶买卖合约)中有条款作出承诺支付给经纪人一笔佣金，作为他把双方合约方介绍在一起订约的报酬。例如在 Les Affreteurs Reunies SA v. Leopold Walford Ltd (1919) AC 801 先例中，案情涉及一个船舶的租约，其中有条文规定了船东需要支付经纪人的佣金，说："A commission of three percent on the estimated gross amount of hire is due to the broker on signing the charter."由于船东没有支付，原告的承租人委托的经纪人向船东提出索赔，但原告显然不是合约方。在该先例，原告把承租人也加进来同一个诉讼作为"共同原告"(co - plaintiffs)，因为承租人在该租约下是经纪人的受托人，这被英国法院支持说经纪人可以这样做。而如果承租人拒绝对经纪人作出协助，经纪人作为信托的受益人是可以把船东与承租人一并列为是共同被告。

在这个先例后，很快在早期的商业活动中，只要是合约承诺支付一笔钱给第三人，都被广泛解释为这种信托关系，而第三人就变为信托下的受益人。正如在《Privity of Contract: Contracts for the Benefit of Third Parties》Law Com No. 242 之 2.8 段所说："The court were once prepared to infer this from the simple intention to benefit a third party, an approach which reached its high water mark in Les Affreteurs Reunies SA v. Leopold Walford Ltd (1919) AC 801."

但这种合约承诺的信托的例外情况后来有了很大局限,第一个局限是在后来的先例显示了此例外只适用在合约的承诺必须是支付一笔金钱或者是转移财产,但其他形式的合约承诺就不适用:Southern Water Authority v. Carey (1985) 2 All ER 1077 与 Norwich City Council v. Harvey (1989) 1 WLR 828。

第二个更大的局限是信托的协议必须是有此"信托意图"(intention to create trust)。这包括提供"利益"(benefit)给第三人,但不能强加责任与义务。这利益又不能纯是捐赠,变得必须是受托人对受益的第三人是有合约或受信关系(fiduciary)下要照顾。信托的协议成立后,也"不可撤回"(irrevocable)。更重要的是,订约方不能再双方同意中止或改变这有信托的协议,因而损害受益的第三人。比方是租船人与船东可同意改变租约每一条文,但不能改变给经纪人的佣金,如免除支付或减一半。这些方面可部分节录《Chitty on Contracts》(30th edn, 2008 年)之 18 – 079 段:"A promise will not be regarded as a trustee for the third party unless he has the intention to create a trust. Such an intention can be made clear by using the word 'trust' or 'trustee', though even where this is done the further question may arise whether the trust, which no doubt exists, is one in favour of the particular third party who seeks to enforce the promise which is the subject – matter of that trust. A trust may, moreover, be created without using any particular form of words; and where the word 'trust' or 'trustee' has not been used, the question whether there is an intention to create a trust gives rise to very great difficulty. . . . "

这一个要求信托的订约意图是在上诉庭的 Re Schebsman (1944) Ch 83 先例中明确下来。案情涉及一位 John Schebsman 先生为一家公司服务并在 1940 年雇佣合约终结时与公司达成另一个协议,就是公司 6 次支付给他 5500 英镑。协议也约定如果 John Schebsman 死亡,这 6 次分期付款的没有支付部分就支付给他的妻子或女儿。后来在 1942 年 3 月 5 日 John Schebsman 被法院宣布破产,而 John Schebsman 稍后在 5 月 12 日死亡。这导致这个法院委派的破产执行人向法院申请命令公司应该把 6 次支付 5500 英镑的钱不是给 John Schebsman 的妻子或女儿而是交给破产执行人,让他之后平均分配给债权人。但 John Schebsman 的妻子作为被告抗辩说 John Schebsman 和公司的协议为她和女儿"成立信托"(create a trust)。上诉庭最后判这一个协议并没有一个信托的存在,因为根本看不出有这个订约的意图。Greene 勋爵是这样说:"The first question which arises is whether or not the debtor (John Schebsman 先生) was a trustee for his wife and daughter of the benefit of the undertaking given by the English company in their favour. An examination of the decided cases does, it is true, show that the courts have on occasions adopted that may be called a liberal view on questions of this character, but in the present case I cannot find in the contract anything to justify the conclusion that a trust was intended. It is not legitimate to import into the contract the idea of a trust when the parties have given no indication that such was their intention. To interpret this contract as creating a trust would, in my judgment, be to disregard the dividing line between the case of a trust and the simple case of a contract made between two persons for the benefit of a third. That dividing line exists, although it may not always be easy to determine where it is to be drawn. In the present case I find no difficulty."

总结而言,信托作为一种例外十分局限。在绝大部分的情况下,一个合约的订立即使涉及给第三人一些利益,也只是一个简单的合约而不会是订约双方有为第三人成立一个信托的意图。毕竟双方也不会想放弃他们之间的订约自由,如将来通过协商对合约做出改变,包括给第三人的利益部分。这是因为已经谈到过,一旦成立了一个信托的协议就是不可撤回。

3.4 索赔第三人损失例外之四:转让

在本章1.3段有简单介绍过通过转让(Assignment),可以把合约的权利与利益单方面转交给第三人。也有提到普通法在严格的第三人规则下,是不允许把合约的权利与利益转让给第三人,也就是不承认这一个转让的权利。但在早期与普通法院分开的衡平法院,就承认这一个做法,可称为是"衡平法转让"(equitable assignment),这显然是对第三人规则做出了另一种例外情况。

接下去有许多个别的立法针对与允许有关合约权利与利益的转让。例如,针对海上运输中的提单,就有了1992年的《海上货物运输法》。针对海上保险的保单,就是1906年的《海上保险法》之s. 50(2)。另外针对公司股份就有2006年的《公司法》之s. 544,针对流通票据就有《Bill of Exchange Act 1882》,针对专利有《Patents Act 1977》ss. 30, 32,针对版权就有《Copyright Design and Patents Act 1988》ss. 90, 94。而其中面最广也是最重要的就是《Law of Property Act 1925》之s. 136承认"立法转让"(statutory assignment),说:"(1) Any absolute assignment by writing under the hand of the assignor (not purporting to be by way of charge only) of any debt or other legal thing in action, of which express notice in writing has been given to the debtor, trustee or other person from whom the assignor would have been entitled to claim such debt or thing in action, is effectual in law (**subject to equities** having priority over the right of the assignee) to pass and transfer from the date of such notice..."(黑字是笔者的强调,中文可以翻译为"要基于总的公平",稍后会进一步解释)

衡平法转让或立法转让可以适用在任何的合约权利或利益,除了少数例外,如合约说明不准或限制转让,"个人合约"(personal contract)不能转让,纯是一个"诉讼权益"(mere rights of action)不能转让,"公共政策"(public policy)不允许转让等。以下十分简单地解释这些例外。

第一种对转让的限制也是尊重订约自由,双方可以在他们的合约中加上一条"禁止转让条文"(Prohibition of Assignment Clause),这完全有效。这种做法也非常普遍,特别涉及一些合约的其中一方或双方不喜欢将来与不知名的第三人打交道,即使只是局限在合约承诺的利益。例如,在造船合约或岸上的建筑合约都普遍加上这一条文,这可以看 Linden Gardens v. Lenesta Sludge Disposals Ltd. and others and St Martins Property Corporation Ltd v. Sir Robert McAlpine Ltd (1994) 1 AC 85 (HL)先例。

第二种对转让的限制是因为个人合约的双方涉及自然人,他们之间往往不会喜欢第三人插进来。例如,出版商不能转让一位作家与他订约写书的利益给第三人,因为其中会涉及该名作家只信任这家出版商而不是其他任何出版商的因素:Stevens v. Benning (1854) 1 K, & J. 168。又例如,雇主不能转让雇员会提供服务合约的利益给第三人,因为雇员一般不会想为任何人都做出服务。

第三种对转让的限制是说一个"纯诉讼权"(如侵权)不能转让。例如,A 被 B 袭击或诽谤,A 不能把索赔损失的诉权转让给 C。更加要小心不能转让的是一个诉讼的权利(不论是合约或侵权)并且不涉及任何商业因素,例如,把诉权"出售"给律师所或追债公司。这会构成"揽讼或助讼"(maintenance or champerty),曾经在《Criminal Law Act 1967》出现前长期被视为是犯法与侵权。

最后一种对转让的限制与商业运作没有太大关系,如英国曾经不准公职人员把他们在雇佣合约中会赚取的工资转让给第三人(如银行、贷款公司或高利贷),以防止他们无法维持自己的生活,并保持尊严与减少贪污等。

针对上述《Law of Property Act 1925》之 s. 136 提到的"要基于总的公平"(subject to equities)的进一步说明可节录《Chitty on Contracts》(30th edn, 2008 年)第 19-074 段:"Assignee cannot recover more than assignor. A further aspect of the idea that an assignee takes an assignment 'subject to equities' is the principle that an assignee cannot recover more from the debtor than the assignor could have done had there been no assignment. . . "(这是说"受让人"[assignee]不能向"债务人"[debtor]主张比"转让人"[assignor]更多的权利。换言之如果在没有转让的情况下,转让人能够合法向债务人索赔的金额,也是受让人在发生转让的情况下可向债权人索赔的局限。)

这表示在"subject to equities"的说法下,立法转让还是不能解决*jus quaestitum tertio* 原则所带来的问题,也就是损失如果是在第三人身上而不是在合约的受害方,该合约受害方把合约权利转让给受让人,受让人还是不能索赔第三人的损失,就算是该第三人也就是受让人本人。这是在《Chitty on Contracts》(30th edn, 2008 年)第 19-075 与 19-076 段所说(虽然它也提到了好像 Offer-Hoar v. Larkstore Ltd. 的近期先例已经另有说法与涉及建筑合约有例外情况,则会后详):

"The application of this principle has given rise to particular difficulty in relation to building contracts or tort claims for damage to buildings. Say, for example, a building is sold at full value along with an assignment to the purchaser of claims in contract or tort in relation to the building. The building turns out to need repairs as a result of a breach of the builder's contract with the assignor (whether that breach is prior, or subsequent, to the sale to the assignee) or of a tort (damaging the building prior to the sale). The assignee pays for the repairs. It might be argued that the assignor in that situation has suffered no loss so that, applying the governing principle that the assignee cannot recover more than the assignor, the assignee has no substantial claim. If correct, 'the claim to damages would disappear ... into some legal black hole, so that the wrongdoer escaped scot – free'. Acceptance of the argument would also nullify the purpose of the governing principle which is to avoid prejudice to the debtor and not to allow the debtor to escape liability. Perhaps not surprisingly, therefore, that the argument was rejected in Offer – Hoar v. Larkstore Ltd. (2006) EWCA Civ. 1079. The Court of Appeal said that, in applying the principle that the assignee cannot recover more than the assignor, one should be asking what damages the assignor could itself have recovered had there been no assignment and *had there been no transfer of the land* to the assignee. Substantial damages were, therefore, recoverable where the assignor had sold its land to an assignee along with, or prior to, the assignment of the relevant cause of action relating to the land.（这是举例说把房子按照市价卖给新买方，并转让给他一个合约或侵权的索赔权利。事后房子被发觉有缺陷导致需要进一步修理，而缺陷是由于承建商的违约或侵权行为。这就会带来争议转让人没有蒙受损失[因为房子再也不是属于转让人，修理费用也不是他付出]，所以新买方作为受让人也不能索赔比转让人能够索赔的更大的损失。这一来，就会导致受让人实质支付了的修理费用掉进了法律的黑洞。而且这样的说法也违反了基本的公平原则，就是既不让承建商作为债务人或违约方受到损害，向受让人做出要赔付比转让人更大的损失，但同时也不要让承建商不必做出任何赔偿。所以毫不奇怪，这种说法被上诉庭在 Offer – Hoar v. Larkstore Ltd. 先例中拒绝，认为适用受让人不能向债务人或违约方主张比转让人更多的权利，也就是"要基于总的公平"[subject to equities]原则时，要问的问题是如果没有这个房子与权利的转让，转让人会有什么损失，所以受让人是可以向承建商取回实质损失。）

The problem has, in any event, normally been circumvented because of the courts' recognition that, where a third party is, or will become, owner of the defective or damaged property, there is an exception to the general rule that a contracting party can recover damages only for its own loss and not the loss of the third party. Where the exception applies, the contracting party (the assignor) is entitled to substantial damages for the loss suffered by the third party (the assignee): by the same token, there is no question of an award of substantial damages to the assignee infringing the principle that the assignee cannot recover more than the assignor."（这一个问题通过另一个途径也可以解决，就是法院认定如果一个第三人也就是新买方拥有这个有缺陷的房子，那么就有一个第三人规则的例外情况适用了。当这种例外情况适用时，转让人就有权向违约方索赔是属于受让人蒙受的损失。）

3.5 第三人规则例外之五：侵权

蒙受损失的第三人可以通过"侵权"(tort)向违约方或侵权方索赔是早在 Donoghue v. Stevenson (1932) AC 562 先例就被确认下来。该先例涉及啤酒生产商 A 将啤酒卖给 B,B 再将啤酒卖给消费者 C,而 C 把买来的啤酒给了 D (Donoghue 夫人)。D 在喝啤酒时发现啤酒瓶底有一只腐烂的蜗牛后觉得身体不适。C 与 D 是朋友,所以 D 不想向 C 索赔损失,加上 C 甚至 B 在事件中都没有任何过错或疏忽,想索赔也无从说起。所以 D 直接向 A 提起侵权诉讼。A 只跟 B 有合约关系,也就是说 D 是第三人。A 抗辩说他对第三人没有责任。贵族院判 A 对 D 有一个"小心谨慎的责任"(duty of care),这也是侵权成立的一个基本要求。

但侵权还是有其他局限,如长期以来不允许索赔"纯经济损失"(pure economic loss),以防止把侵权门开得太大。因为就算一个简单的车祸,受害方由于身体蒙受损伤肯定是索赔他的损失,也包括了他的经济损失。但如果纯经济损失的话,加进来的受害方就可能没完没了,如车祸受害方的雇主、配偶、其他家庭成员、朋友或有关人士(如车祸受害方订了餐馆吃饭但因为车祸而去不了,有关的餐馆就少了一票生意)。这些人士都是因为疏忽造成车祸的侵权人而蒙受了纯经济损失。有关这一个课题会在本书第八章第 5 段有进一步详论。

但纯经济损失索赔也在侵权的个别类别有所放宽,例如在 Hedley Byrne and Co Ltd v. Heller and Partners Ltd (1964) AC 465 先例。案情涉及 Hedley Byrne 要与 Easipower 公司做生意,于是 Hedley Byrne 从 Easipower 公司的银行 Heller 处取得了认定 Easipower 公司资信良好的报告。但事实上 Easipower 公司的经济状况并不好,银行在有疏忽的情况下做出的这份资信报告并不正确,令 Hedley Byrne 依赖该资信报告在后来与 Easipower 公司做生意时蒙受了经济损失。贵族院认为,如果一方有"特别的技能"(special skill)与知识,用来协助另一方给予"意见"(advice)或"信息"(information),他就有了一个"小心谨慎的义务"(duty of care)。如果有疏忽,破坏了这义务,他(如银行、律师、会计师)应该有侵权责任。而在这种情况下,被侵权方索赔的一般也都是纯经济损失。

在作了以上的介绍之后,就可以介绍有关第三人规则例外的主要先例。

第一个案例是贵族院的 Junior Books Ltd v. Veitchi Co Ltd (1983) 1 AC 520 先例。原告的业主与总承建商订立了建筑合约建造一家工厂,总承建商雇佣了被告的分承建商进行地板的工程。原告声称地板有缺陷并以分承建商有疏忽构成侵权而直接向他索赔,贵族院判该索赔成功。一般来说这种情况应该以合约关系提起诉讼:原告向总承建商索赔,总承建商再向分承建商要求"补偿"(indemnity),这样责任就沿着"合约关系链"(chain of contracts)一级级传下来。Junior Books 先例让原告跳过了合约关系链直接向分承建商提起诉讼。在航运方面也有类似先例,如 The "Antonis P. Lemos" (1985) 1 Lloyd's Rep 283。这个先例严格来说并不涉及第三人规则,因为总承建商对原告有合约责任,原告可以通过合约关系向总承建商索赔损失,然后总承建商向被告的分承建商要求补偿。换言之,总承建商并非是在没有对原告有任何责任下向分承建商索赔原告作为第三人所蒙受的损失。

第二个与第三人规则有直接关系的先例是在本章第2段提到过的 White v. Jones (1995) 2 AC 207 先例。White 先生指示他的律师 Jones 先生为他拟定一份新遗嘱,但是由于 Jones 的疏忽,直到 White 先生死亡新遗嘱都没有拟定。White 先生的两个女儿作为新遗嘱的受益人向 Jones 索赔因为 Jones 的疏忽造成的损失。贵族院以3比2的多数判 White 先生的两个女儿有权以侵权向 Jones 索赔损失。贵族院作出这个判决的一个重要原因是 White 先生的两个女儿作为受害方蒙受了损失,如果她们不能向疏忽的一方提起诉讼,这将会掉进法律的黑洞。这是第三人以侵权诉讼的方式使合约履行的最好例子。原告的受害方和被告的侵权方之间没有任何合约关系也不能用合约关系链串起来。被告的侵权方作为律师对受害方有一个小心谨慎的义务,被告的疏忽破坏了这个义务,就有侵权责任。但要说明贵族院这个先例是3比2的多数作出可见第三人规则是很富争议性的。例如 Mustill 勋爵就持少数意见,认为受益人明显是依赖有关的合约向 Jones 索赔,但受益人并非是合约方。Mustill 勋爵是这样说:"... the intended beneficiaries did not engage the solicitor, undertake to pay his fees or tell him what to do. Having promised them nothing he has broken no promise. They nevertheless fasten upon the circumstance that the solicitor broke his promise to someone else..."

但总结这一个第三人规则的例外情况还是有很大局限,就是它必须涉及被告的疏忽,才存在第三人可以以侵权向被告起诉。但如果涉及合约关系,许多做出的合约承诺会是严格责任,这一来承诺方一旦没有履行就会构成违约,不论是什么理由造成的不履行合约承诺,完全不限制在疏忽与否。另一个局限就是在第三人向被告起诉并索赔损失,必须先证明被告的疏忽以及对第三人有一个小心谨慎的义务,而有这种对第三人的义务会是局限,如被告的承诺方拥有特别的技能(会计、律师、银行等)。

3.6 第三人规则例外之六:运输合约的"喜马拉雅条文"

在著名的 Midland Silicones v. Scruttons (1961) 2 Lloyd's Rep 365 先例,贵族院认定作为第三人的小工,是不能依赖船东与货方之间的提单合约,来要求享受《1924年海牙规则》下给予船东的保障,如100英镑一件货物的限额赔偿、1年索赔时效等。在另一著名先例 Adler v. Dickson (1955) 1 QB 158, Adler 在一艘名为"喜马拉雅"的客轮上受伤,但发觉客票(这是船公司与旅客的合约)上的条文规定船东可对此疏忽免责。于是她转而以侵权告船长疏忽,法院判是船长是客票这一份合约以外的第三人,他不能依赖客票的免责条文作为抗辩。

当然,船长因为在工作中的疏忽而要对第三人负责,往往船东还是难免要在背后拿钱出来。从以上两个先例可以看出,这种起诉船长或小工疏忽的做法实际上等于绕过了有关合约给予船东的保障,因为船长与小工是合约的第三人,他们无法依赖有关的责任限制与免责条文。这导致船东自己想办法对第三人规则作出例外,就是在所有的海上运输合约(提单或客票)加上一条"喜马拉雅条文"(Himalaya Clause)。这种条文是有不同版本或措辞,内容大致上是说船东作为代理人或受托人身份把本是第三人的小工、船员等人也拖进来作为合约一方。这一个课题在笔者的《国际商务游戏规则——英国合约法》一书中第四章有详论,不在本章多讲。在这里多一提的是这种条文也不光是海上运输合约适用,同样的理念下是可以适用在任何其他业务的合约,只要是其中一位合约方想让替他履行的仆人或独立分包人也能享有合约的权利。

只说这种条文的有效性已经被英国贵族院或"枢密院"(Privy Council)确认是有效,这是在 The "Eurymedon" (1974) 1 Lloyd's Rep. 534 (PC)先例,Wilberforce 勋爵说:"... brought into existence a bargain initially unilateral but capable of becoming mutual, between the shipper and the [stevedores], made through the carrier as agent. This became a full contract when the [stevedores] performed services for the benefit of the shipper was the consideration for the agreement by the shipper that the [stevedores] should have the benefit of the exemptions and limitations contained in the bill of lading."(这就是解释这种条文怎么样可以配合合约法的要求。大致上是说船东作为代理与货方或发货人订约的时候,针对小工而言由于他还没有出现,只能算是一个单方面的合约。但后来小工真正出现并为货方履行装卸货物,单方面的合约变为双方同意下的完整合约,而小工做出的服务也就是提供了约因/对价,而取得的权利就是在提单中的免责条文或责任限制条文)

简单总结这"喜马拉雅条文"的牵强解释,可节录 Goff 勋爵在 The "Mahkutai" (1996) 3 WLR 1 先例中所说如下:"There can be no doubt of the commercial need of some such principle as this, and not only in cases concerned with stevedores; and the bold step taken by the Privy Council in The "Eurymedon" (1974) 1 Lloyd's Rep. 534 (PC), and later developed in The "New York Star" (1980) 2 Lloyd's Rep. 317 (PC), has been widely welcomed. But it is legitimate to wonder whether that development is yet complete. Here their Lordships have in mind not only Lord Wilberforce's discouragement of fine distinctions, but also the fact that the law is now approaching the position where, provided that the bill of lading contract clearly provides that (for example) independent contractors such as stevedores are to have the benefit of exceptions and limitations contained in that contract, they will be able to enjoy the protection of those terms as against the cargo owners. This is because (1) the problem of consideration in these cases is regarded as having been solved on the basis that a bilateral agreement between the stevedores and the cargo owners, entered into through the agency of the shipowners may, though itself unsupported by consideration, be rendered enforceable by consideration subsequently furnished by the stevedores in the form of performance of their duties as stevedores for the shipowners; (2) the problem of authority from the stevedores to the shipowners to contract on their behalf can, in the majority of cases, be solved by recourse to the principle of ratification; and (3) consignees of the cargo may be held to be bound on the principle in Brandt

v. Liverpool Brazil and River Plate Steam Navigation Co. Ltd. (1924) 17 Lloyd's Rep. 142. Though these solutions are now perceived to be generally effective for their purpose, their technical nature is all too apparent; and the time may well come when, in an appropriate case, it will fall to be considered whether the courts should take what may legitimately be perceived to be the final, and perhaps inevitable, step in this development, and recognise in these cases a fully – fledged exception to the doctrine of privity of contract, thus escaping from all the technicalities with which courts are now faced in English law. It is not far from their Lordships' minds that, if the English courts were minded to take that step, they would be following in the footsteps of the Supreme Court of Canada (see London drugs Ltd v. Kuehne & Nagel International Ltd. [1992] 97 DLR [4th] 261) and in a different context, the High Court of Australia (see Trident General Insurance Co. Ltd. v. McNiece Bros Pty Ltd. [1988] 165 CLR 107). Their Lordships have given consideration to the question whether they should face up to this question in the present appeal. However, they have come to the conclusion that it would not be appropriate for them to do so, first, because they have not heard argument specifically directed towards this fundamental question, and second because, as well become clear in due course, they are satisfied that the appeal must in any event be dismissed."

简单解释,Goff 勋爵是说毫无疑问这个"喜马拉雅条文"是有商业上的需要,持续发展并广受欢迎。在这种条文下小工等独立分包人也可以享有合约中的限制责任和免除责任条文。但这种条文还是在解释起来面对很多技术性的争议:(1)有关约因/对价的问题;(2)小工有否授权船东作为代理人订约的问题,因为船东在装港签发提单时,往往还没有指定在卸港的小工。虽然在大部分情况下授权的问题还可以以"追认"(ratification)解释,但还是会有问题。例如,有卸港的小工是由港口当局指定,船东与小工根本从来没有接触过;(3)收货人作为与小工的另一方的合约方,可以根据"默示合约"(implied contract)作出解释,也就是根据 Brandt v. Liverpool Brazil and River Plate Steam Navigation Co. Ltd 先例,收货人以行动接受小工的服务,在卸港接收货物。Goff 勋爵呼吁承认这种条文作为"合约相对性"(privity of contract)的全面例外情况,并摒弃在每一个案件中"挑骨头"并允许太多技术性的争议。这也是对第三人规则做出例外情况的说法。

有关喜马拉雅条文更详尽的介绍与许多有关的先例可参阅笔者的《国际商务游戏规则——英国合约法》一书的第四章之第 5 段,在这里就不再多谈。

3.7 第三人规则例外之七:保险合约关系

保险合约(Insurance Contract)是受到第三人规则严重影响的商业活动,举一个简单的例子,就是在保险合约下保险人在赔付给受保人之后,经常会以自己名义(这是美国法或中国法)或以受保人的名义(这是英国法)向侵权方或违约方提出索赔,希望把赔付给受保人的钱能全部或部分取回,这就是著名的"代位求偿"(subrogation)

原则或说法。显然，在英国法律下，作为受害方的受保人向侵权方或违约方提出的索赔，损失是在他的保险人。但这一地位是没有人会质疑，因为1906年《英国海上保险法》之Section 79明确了代位求偿的说法，说："Where the insurer pays for a total loss, either of the whole, or in the case of goods of any apportionable part, of the subject - matter insured, he thereupon becomes entitled to take over the interest of the assured in whatever may remain the subject - matter so paid for, and he is thereby subrogated to all the rights and remedies of the assured in and in respect of that subject - matter as from the time of the casualty causing the loss."

但保险合约在许多其他方面都受到影响，所以有许多的立法针对不同的情况。立法针对第三人规则的例外情况有：

(1)人寿保险，可节录《Married Women's Property Act 1882》之Section 11如下："A married woman may ... effect a policy upon her own life or the life of her husband for her [own benefit]; and the same and all benefit thereof shall enure accordingly.

A policy of assurance effected by any man on his own life, and expressed to be for the benefit of his wife, or of his children, or of his wife and children, or any of them, or by any woman on her own life, and expressed to be for the benefit of her husband, or of her children, or of her husband and children, or any of them, shall create a trust in favour of the objects therein named, and the moneys payable under any such policy shall not, so long as any object of the trust remains unperformed, form part of the estate of the insured, or be subject to his or her debts: Provided, that if it shall be proved that the policy was effected and the premiums paid with intent to defraud the creditors of the insured, they shall be entitled to receive, out of the moneys payable under the policy, a sum equal to the premiums so paid. The insured may by the policy, or by any memorandum under his or her hand, appoint a trustee or trustees of the moneys payable under the policy, and from time to time appoint a new trustee or new trustees thereof, and may make provision for the appointment of a new trustee or new trustees thereof, and for the investment of the moneys payable under any such policy. In default of any such appointment of a trustee, such policy, immediately on its being effected, shall vest in the insured and his or her legal personal representatives, in trust for the purposes aforesaid ... The receipt of a trustee or trustees duly appointed, or in default of any such appointment, or in default of notice to the insurance office, the receipt of the legal personal representatives of the insured shall be a discharge to the office for the sum secured by the policy, or for the value thereof, in whole or in part."

也就是说，如果一个人给自己买了人寿保险，合约明示受益人是他/她的配偶或子女，根据这条法律是为他们建立了一个信托关系，保险人直接赔付给受益人。

(2)火灾保险，《Fire Prevention (Metropolis) Act 1774》之Section 83说："And in order to deter and hinder ill - minded persons from wilfully setting their house or houses or other buildings on fire with a view of gaining to themselves the insurance money, whereby the lives and fortunes of many families may be lost or endangered: it shall and may be lawful to and for the respective governors or directors of the several insurance offices for insuring houses or other buildings against loss by fire, and they are hereby authorised and required, upon the request of any person or persons interested in or entitled unto any house or houses or other buildings which may hereafter be burnt down, demolished or damaged by fire, or upon any grounds of suspicion that the owner or owners, occupier or occupiers, or other person or persons who shall have insured such house or houses or other buildings have been guilty of fraud, or of wilfully setting their house or houses or other buildings on fire, to cause the insurance money to be laid out and expended, as far as the same will go, towards rebuilding, reinstating or repairing such house or houses or other buildings so burnt down, demolished or damaged by fire, unless the party or parties claiming such insurance money shall, within sixty days next after his, her or their claim is adjusted, give a sufficient security to the governors or directors of the insurance office where such house or houses or other buildings are insured, that the same insurance money shall be laid out and expended as aforesaid, or unless the said insurance money shall be in that time settled and disposed of to and amongst all the contending parties, to the satisfaction and approbation of such governors or directors of such insurance office respectively."

根据这条法律,当被保的房屋或建筑被火烧毁,保险人可以根据任何有相关利益的人士要求支付赔偿金修缮房屋或建筑。也就是说,一个租客(第三人)可以在他的房东的保险下要求赔付,或者一个房东(第三人)可以在他的租客的保险下要求赔付。

(3)车辆保险,《Road Traffic Act 1988》之 Section 148(7)节录如下:"(7) Notwithstanding anything in any enactment, a person issuing a policy of insurance under section 145 of this Act shall be liable to indemnify the persons or classes of persons specified in the policy in respect of any liability which the policy purports to cover in the case of those persons or classes of persons."

也就是说,在该立法之 Section 145 条下订立的保险合约的保险人,应该负责赔偿在保险合约包括的第三人的责任,如驾驶公司车辆的职员或驾驶家庭车辆的其他家庭成员或朋友在驾驶时所造成的事故与责任。

(4)针对蒙受损失的第三人可以直接向保险公司索赔损失,在《Third Parties (Rights Against Insurers) Act 1930》之 Section 1 说:

"Rights of third parties against insurers on bankruptcy &c. of the insured

(1) Where under any contract of insurance a person (hereinafter referred to as the insured) is insured against liabilities to third parties which he may incur, then— (a) in the event of the insured becoming bankrupt or making a composition or arrangement with his

creditors; or (b) in the case of the insured being a company, in the event of a winding – up order being made, or a resolution for a voluntary winding – up being passed, with respect to the company, or of a receiver or manager of the company's business or undertaking being duly appointed, or of possession being taken, by or on behalf of the holders of any debentures secured by a floating charge, of any property comprised in or subject to the charge; if, either before or after that event, any such liability as aforesaid is incurred by the insured, his rights against the insurer under the contract in respect of the liability shall, notwithstanding anything in any Act or rule of law to the contrary, he transferred to and vest in the third party to whom the liability was so incurred.

(2) Where an order is made under section one hundred and thirty of the Bankruptcy Act, 1914, for the administration of the estate of a deceased debtor according to the law of bankruptcy, then, if any debt provable in bankruptcy is owing by the deceased in respect of a liability against which he was insured under a contract of insurance as being a liability to a third party, the deceased debtor's rights against the insurer under the contract in respect of that liability shall, notwithstanding anything in the said Act, be transferred to and vest in the person to whom the debt is owing."

这一个 1930 年的立法可以与上一个车辆保险的立法《Road Traffic Act 1988》串起来,较早车辆保险是说公司车辆在职员驾驶时发生事故,保险公司会负责赔偿。在这里是说,如果发生车祸的受害方向公司要求赔偿,公司却已经破产或清盘。清盘人即使是获得保险公司的赔付后,这笔钱要按照顺序或平均分给所有债权人,受害方可能得不到全额赔偿。在这个立法下,受害方可以跳过清盘人直接向保险人提起诉讼并取得全额赔偿。

3.8 第三人规则例外之八:其他针对性的立法

其他方面的立法可部分介绍如下:

(1)在《Solicitor Act 1974》中允许律师协会替它的会员订立合约,让第三人获益。例如,律师协会可以替会员购买专业疏忽保险。Diplock 勋爵在 Swain v. Law Society (1983) 1 AC 598 先例中解释说:"The policy of insurance which the Society is empowered to take out and maintain by Section 37(2)(b) is a contract which creates a *jus quaesitum tertio*. It does so by virtue of public law not the ordinary English private law of contract. This makes it unnecessary in the instant case to have recourse to any of those juristic subterfuges to which courts have, from time to time, felt driven to resort in cases in which English private law is applicable, to mitigate the effect of the lacuna resulting from the non – recognition of a *jus quaesitum tertio* – an anachronistic shortcoming that has for many years been regarded as a reproach to English private law..."

(2)在《Law of Property Act 1925》之 Section56(1)是说:"A person may take an immediate or other interest in land or other property, or the benefit of any condition, right of entry, covenant or agreement over or respecting land or other property, although he may not be named as a party to the conveyance or other instrument."

针对这个法律条文 Denning 大法官在 Drive Yourself Hire Co (London) Ltd v. Strutt (1954) 1 QB 250 先例认为这废除了 Tweddle v. Atkinson 先例确立的原则,也就是"第三人规则"。Beswick v. Beswick 先例认为这个法律条文对 A 仅仅向 B 承诺给 C 钱的情况不适用。这个法律条文针对第三人利益的范围看来用字很广,但是实际的适用范围还不明朗。

(3)《Companies Act 1985》之 Section 14 说明注册的公司章程大纲约束公司的法人以及公司的成员,并每一位都被视为是签署了这份文件。

(4)《Package Travel, Package Holidays and Package Tours Regulations 1992》之 Section 15(1) 绕过了第三人规则,让旅游合约的受益人可以直接向订立合约的旅行社要求赔偿。

(5)《Carriage of Goods by Sea 1992》之 Section 2(1) 有关提单合约的转让是说:"2 Rights under shipping documents. (1) Subject to the following provisions of this section, aperson who becomes— (a) the lawful holder of a bill of lading; (b) the person who (without being an original party to the contract of carriage) is the person to whom delivery of the goods to which a sea waybill relates is to be made by the carrier in accordance with that contract; or (c) the person to whom delivery of the goods to which a ship's delivery order relates is to be made in accordance with the undertaking contained in the order, shall (by virtue of becoming the holder of the bill or, as the case may be, the person to whom delivery is to be made) have transferred to and vested in him all rights of suit under the contract of carriage as if he had been a party to that contract."

还有其他的立法对第三人规则做出例外情况,如《Bill of Exchange Act 1882》等,就不逐一介绍。

4. 其他普通法国家对第三人规则的法律改革

普通法国家因为"合约相互性"(privity of contract)与"约因/对价"(consideration)的理念也不约而同的受到第三人规则的困扰,这是大陆法国家不存在的。在这里可以介绍这些国家怎样针对第三人规则做出的改革。

首先是在美国上诉庭的 Lawrence v. Fox 20 NY 268 (1859) 先例基本上接受了第三人可以直接执行一个对他做出利益承诺的合约。但由于依赖判例,一直没有办法对哪一类的第三人可以执行做出全面或满意的规定。所以在 1932 年的《first Restatement of Contracts》在 Section 133 把第三人受益人分类为"馈赠受益人"(donee beneficiaries)、"债务受益人"(creditor beneficiaries)、"偶然受益人"(incidental beneficiaries)。大致上前两类的第三人因为合约的履行能够满足对他的一个实际承诺,所以可以执行一个合约对他们做出的利益承诺。但最后一类的偶然受益人就不能直接执行一个合约对他偶然会带来的利益,因为这把范围拓得太宽了。在 1981 年有《second Restatement of Contract》,基本上把第三人受益人分为两种,分别是"意图受益人"(intended beneficiaries)与偶然受益人,其中第一类受益人可以直接执行一个对他做出利益承诺的合约,但后者就不行。在 Section 302,该立法针对这两类受益人是这样说:"(1) Unless otherwise agreed between promisor and promisee, a beneficiary of a promise is an intended beneficiary if recognition of a right to performance in the beneficiary is appropriate to effectuate the intention of the parties and either (a) the performance of the promise will satisfy an obligation of the promise to pay money to the beneficiary; or (b) the circumstances indicate that the promise intends to give the beneficiary the benefit of the promised performance. (2) An incidental beneficiary is a beneficiary who is not an intended beneficiary."

接下去要介绍的国家是澳大利亚,分别在不同的州都有个别的立法针对第三人规则。首先是在西澳大利亚的《Western Australian Property Law Act 1969》中,针对第三人规则是说:"... where a contract expressly in its terms purports to confer a benefit directly on a person who is not named as a party to the contract, the contract is... enforceable by that person in his own name..."另在昆士兰州《Queensland Property Law Act 1974》之 Section 55 说:"A promisor who, for a valuable consideration moving from the promise, promises to do or to refrain from doing an act or acts for the benefit of a beneficiary shall, upon acceptance by the beneficiary, be subject to a duty enforceable by the beneficiary to perform that promise."

再接下去介绍新西兰的立法《New Zealand Contracts (Privity) Act 1982》,其中在 Section 4 规定:"Where a promise contained in a deed or contract confers, or purports to confer, a benefit on a person, designated by name, description or reference to a class, who is not a party to the deed or contract... the promisor shall be under an obligation, enforceable at the suit of that person, to perform that promise."

另一个亚洲的普通法国家新加坡在较近期有《Contracts (Rights of Third Parties) Act 2002》的立法,内容主要是根据英国 1999 年的《Contract (Right of Third Parties) Act》立法(在稍后的本章第 6 段将有详述)并已经发展出一些重要的先例,如 CLAAS Medical Centre Pte Ltd v. Ng Boon Ching (2010) 2 SLR 386。

至于在香港特区,据悉正在考虑这方面的立法。2007 年法律改革委员会提出关于合约相互性的报告,建议内容主要是根据英国的《Contract (Right of Third Parties) Act 1999》的立法,现在还处于咨询阶段,具体内容可查询香港法律改革委员会官方网站,http://www.hkreform.gov.hk。

5. 普通法对第三人规则的例外情况：订约时双方知道有涉及第三人的利益

5.1 国际贸易与海上货物运输带来的 Dunlop v. Lambert 说法与 The Albazero 原则

在早期的国际贸易案件中，上述所介绍的例外情况都有其局限，不论是托管关系、代理关系还是信托关系都不能适用在卖方与买方之间的买卖合约关系。所以在1855 年英国《提单法》生效前，普通法在著名的 Dunlop v. Lambert (1839) 6 CI & F 600 先例中发展出了一个新的说法。在该先例的说法是发货人或卖方与船东在订立海上运输合约时都知道/默认合约是为了以后这票货物的买方利益所订立的，因为国际外贸几乎一定是这种情况，提单与货物在航次中转让/转售给买方，所以卖方作为订约方，虽然在发生货损货差事故时，卖方已经失去了货物所有权，本身没有任何损失，可以代买方（合约利益方，在订立海上运输合约时双方已知道）索赔全部在航程中发生货损货差与其他（如不合理绕航或航次延误等）的损失：“... is entitled to recover by way of damages for breach of contract the actual loss sustained by those for whose benefit the contract is entered into.”

这著名说法是根据双方“订约意图”（contractual intention），也就是发货人或卖方与承运人或船东订约时（不论是租约或是订舱单），双方就知道在货物装船后会要签发提单，而这份提单就会通过背书与交出把这票货物转售给买方或分买方。这导致最后以正本提单来提货的收货人才是真正因为航程中发生货损货差而蒙受损失的受害方。但他不是合约方（因为当时还没有 1855 年的英国《提单法》），所以他的损失必须是通过发货人才能向船东提出索赔，这是双方订约时知道或应该知道，就是发货人是“以第三人的利益去订立合约”（contract for the benefit of third party）。

在接下去的有关海上运输的先例，也不断有先例引用这一个说法，其中最著名的是在 The “Albazero” (1976) 2 Lloyd's Rep 467 先例，Diplock 勋爵是这样说：“The only way in which I find it possible to rationalize the rule in Dunlop v. Lambert so that it may fit into the pattern of the English law is to treat it as an application of the principle, accepted also in relation to policies of insurance upon goods, that in a commercial contract concerning goods where it is in the contemplation of the parties that the proprietary interests in the goods may be transferred from one owner to another after the contract has been entered into and before the breach which causes loss or damage to the goods, an original party to the contract, if such be the intention of them both, is to be treated in law as having entered into the contract for the benefit of all persons who have or may acquire an interest in the goods before they are lost or damaged, and is entitled to recover by way of damages for breach of contract the actual loss sustained by those for whose benefit the contract is entered into. ”

这一个在海上货物运输著名的“The Albazero 原则”是说:“发货人有权向船东索赔并取回所有的损失,只要他们之间有合约关系,即使是发货人再也不拥有这票运输的货物,也不必承担货物的风险。而发货人如果成功向船东索赔后,这笔取回来的钱是要向真正货方,也就是受害方的买方,负责交出。”(that the consignor may recover substantial damages against the shipowner if there is privity of contract between him and the carrier for the carriage of goods; although if the goods are not his property or at his risk, he will be accountable to the true owner for the proceeds of his judgment.)

这一个普通法的地位也不能满意解决国际货物买卖与海上运输在这方面的问题,因为还是需要与船东订约的卖方或发货人提出索赔,这在货物如果涉及多次转卖(这经常在海上运输发生,以提单作为中心的 CIF 单证买卖),最后蒙受货损货差损失的买方或收货人根本找不到谁是最初的发货人,也不会认识他。所以最理想的还是由真正蒙受损失的收货人可以直接根据提单合约向船东提出索赔,但他们之间实际是没有合约关系,所以在普通法是没有办法解决的问题,最终还是需要依赖立法,也就是 1855 年的《提单法》。这 1855 年的立法也在 1992 年有了更新的版本,名为《海上货物运输法》。这方面的问题与演变可节录 Goff 勋爵在 Alfred McAlpine Construction Ltd *v.* Panatown Ltd (2001) 1 AC 518 所讲如下:“... let us look first of all at the rule in Dunlop v. Lambert 6 CI &c F 600. As Lord Diplock himself explained, this rule should be seen in context of commercial contracts concerning goods, and in particular of contracts for the carriage of goods by sea. It is a commonplace of such contracts that the goods may be shipped pursuant to a contract of sale, under which the property in the goods may pass to the consignee while the goods are in transit. However, the rule of privity of contract requires that, if the contract of carriage is (as it usually is) made between the consignor and the carrier, it can be enforced only by the consignor and not by the consignee. This creates manifest problems where the goods are lost or damaged in transit after the property in them has passed to the consignee. The rule in Dunlop v. Lambert provided a practical solution to these problems by giving the consignor the right to recover damages for such loss or damage for the benefit of the consignee, to whom he was accountable. The shortcoming of this rule must, I imagine, have been that it left the initiative with the seller, rather than with the consignee who was the person who had suffered the loss of or damage to the goods. It is not surprising, therefore, that Parliament intervened only 15 years later, in 1855, to pass the Bills of Lading Act that year, under section 1 of which a person to whom the property in the goods had passed upon or by reason of the consignment to him of the goods or the indorsement to him of the bill of lading acquired a direct right of action against the shipowner on the terms of the bill of lading. (The 1855 Act has recently been repealed and replaced by the Carriage of Goods by Sea Act 1992.) The more effective remedy given by statute must have meant that the useful life of the rule in Dunlop v. Lambert was relatively short. ”

5.2 适用 Dunlop v. Lambert 说法与 The Albazero 原则的建筑合约 Linden Gardens v. Lenesta Sludge Disposals Ltd. and others 与 St Martins Property Corporation Ltd v. Sir Robert McAlpine Ltd 先例

这一个来自海上货物运输的“The Albazero 原则”在有了 1855 年的英国《提单法》后已经不大适用,后来却被其他商业活动借用,主要就是在建筑行业。至于在建筑行业以外的合约将来会否适用“The Albazero 原则”作为 *jus quaesitum tertio* 原则的例外情况也不好说,因为允许太多例外就会导致原来的大原则失去意义。

在著名的 Linden Gardens v. Lenesta Sludge Disposals Ltd. and others 与 St Martins Property Corporation Ltd v. Sir Robert McAlpine Ltd (1994) 1 AC 85 (HL)先例中(这两个建筑案例同时被贵族院一并审理,因为针对的争议是一致)。该 Linden Gardens 先例的案情涉及原告与被告订约,合约要求后者的承建商把一个老房子的有毒石棉清除。但承建商违约,没有把这一个工程按照合约完成。但在承建商的违约后不久,原告作为原来的房东就把房子卖给了第三人。但原告受到合约中一条禁止转让条文的限制,无法把这一个工程合约的利益同时转让给房子的新买方。最后由于承建商的违约没有把有毒石棉清除干净,迫使房子的新买方(工程合约的第三人)另花钱聘用其他承建商完成清除。这导致原告(原来的房东)与第三人(房子的新买方)同时作为共同原告向被告的承建商提出起诉,要求赔偿损失。

在第二个一并审理的 St. Martins 先例,案情涉及在发生违约之前就已经把有关的房产转移。St. Martin Corporation 作为雇主与被告 McAlpine 的承建商订立了建筑合约发展一个伦敦的地产项目。订约后不久 St. Martin Corporation 把建筑合约的利益转让给了一个附属公司的 St. Martin Investments。St. Martin Corporation 和 St. Martin Investments 都是科威特基金控制的 St. Martin Holdings 下的子公司。这样转让与公司内部结构是为了合法逃避英国的税务。但工程完毕后发现这个建筑有缺陷,不得不再与另一个建筑商签订一个工程合约做出补救。这笔额外费用先由 St. Martin Corporation 支付,之后由 St. Martin Investments 转账给 St. Martin Corporation。这样看来,St. Martin Corporation 没有实际损失,损失是在第三人的 St. Martin Investments。而且由于建筑合约是有条文“禁止权利的转让”(prohibition of assignment clause),所以整个内部的转让也是在有关合约下无效。但 St. Martin Corporation(转让人)和 St. Martin Investments(受让人)作为共同原告向 McAlpine 要求赔偿损失。

贵族院判原合约方(St Martin Corporation)可以获得额外费用等的损失赔偿。贵族院中大多数认为可以把“The Albazero 原则”应用到建筑合约中,Browne - Wilkinson 勋爵是这样说:“The contract was for a large development of property which, to the knowledge of both Corporation and McAlpine, was going to be occupied, and possibly purchased, by third parties and by Corporation itself. Therefore, it could be foreseen that damages caused by a breach would cause loss to a later owner and not merely to the original contracting party, Corporation ... McAlpine had specifically contracted that the rights under the building contract *could* not without McAlpine's consent be transferred to third parties who became owners or occupiers and might suffer loss. In such a case, it seems to me proper as in the case of the carriage of goods, to treat the parties as having entered into the contract on the footing that Corporation would be entitled to enforce contractual rights for the benefit of those who suffered from defective performance but who, under the terms of the contract, could not acquire any right to hold McAlpine liable for the breach."（有关合约是涉及一个庞大的地产发展项目,双方在订立建筑合约时完全知道房子将来会出售给第三人。所以双方能够预见违约的损失将来是会由第三人的新买方承担,而不是原来的订约方或雇主。有关的建筑合约还有一条"禁止转让合约利益"条文,显示雇主如果没有承建商的同意是不能把合约利益转让给第三人,包括将来的新买方。这些都显示了双方的意图是允许原合约方的雇主可以为第三人向承建商索赔损失）

这一个先例还是不能解决许多疑问,这也是根据双方"订约意图"(contractual intention)作为依据的缺点,因为要在每一个案件的不同事实下看双方到底有什么订约意图,这会带来不肯定与昂贵的诉讼。例如,在一个有可能是自住的小型地产发展项目,双方在订立建筑合约时就不会知道房子将来会否出售给第三人？更好的说法会是在部分类别的合约,只要受害方没有获得违约方承诺的履行,就被视为蒙受损失,而不必理会损失是否在受害方或有关的第三人。后者的说法就等于把问题视为"法律问题"(issue of law),再也不必理会每一个不同案件的"事实问题"(issue of fact)。这后者的说法也是在本先例中 Griffiths 勋爵所倡议的"广泛地位"(broader ground),但他在本先例只是少数意见,其他贵族院的勋爵多数意见还是以所谓的"狭窄地位"(narrow ground)做出同样结果的判决,也就是适用"The Albazero 原则"作为第三人规则的例外。在这个方面英国法律还是有持续的发展,稍后会进一步介绍。

另在上述先例,Browne - Wilkinson 勋爵以建筑合约的"禁止转让合约利益"条文支持他的看法,就是双方意图让原合约的一方可以代第三人向违约方索赔损失,不需要第三人通过转让介入,会有一定程度的牵强。这种常见的条文应该更恰当地被视为是双方订约方不希望有第三人通过转让获得该合约的利益或关系。

这"以第三人的利益订立合约"(contract for the benefit of third party)的说法被视为是一个法律观点(不是一个事实问题而需要每一个案件看双方有什么订约意图)可能会带来更大的肯定。

最后可总结在权威书籍《Chitty on Contracts》(30th edn, 2008 年)之 18 - 055 段提到贵族院在该先例多数的意见时这样说:"This treats the loss as having been suffered by the third party rather than by the employer, but concludes that the employer could nevertheless recover substantial damages as the case fell within the rationale of *Albazero* exception to the general rule that a party can recover damages only in respect of his own loss. The rationale of this exception was that, in the carriage of goods cases to which it applies, the shipper and carrier must have contemplated that property in the goods might be transferred to third party after the contract had been made, and that the shipper must therefore be treated in law as having made the contract of carriage for the benefit of all personal who might after the time of contracting acquire interest in the goods. This rationale applied equally to the facts of the *Linden Gardens* case since the contractor could foresee that parts of the new development were going to be ' occupied and possibly purchased by third party' so that ' it could be foreseen that damage caused by a breach would cause loss to a later owner. ' The contractor could also foresee that a later owner would not have acquired rights under the building contract against contractor since that contract expressly prohibited assignment by the employer without the contractor' s written consent, which had not been sought. The effect of *Linden Gardens* case was thus to extend the scope of the *Albazero* exception from contracts for the carriage of goods by sea to contracts generally, but it was consistent with two factors which had restricted the scope of that exception: namely that (a) the loss or damage was caused to property which had been transferred by one of the contracting parties to the third party; and (b) the third party had not acquired any rights under the building contract and it was foreseeable (by reason of the prohibition against assignment) that he would not do so."(最后的一句是说"The Albazero 原则"的适用要满足两个要求:[a]被损坏的财产是从其中一位原订约方转让给了第三人;[b]第三人在原来的合约没有任何权利,也预见不会有,如有条文禁止转让。)

5.3 建筑合约的 Darlington BC v. Wiltshier Northern Ltd. 先例

在接下去的 Darlington BC v. Wiltshier Northern Ltd. (1995) 1 WLR 68 先例,对"The Albazero 原则"的适用进行了扩展。建筑公司 Wiltshier 作为承建商和财务公司 Morgan Grenfell 订立建筑合约为 Darlington 地方议会建娱乐中心。土地与将来造好的娱乐中心都属于 Darlington 地方议会所有,Morgan Grenfell 由头到尾都没有任何财产权。这一个涉及 Morgan Grenfell 作为中介人士的安排,原因是根据当地法律 Darlington 地方议会借款建造娱乐中心有限制,除非由部长批准才行,这显然会很麻烦。所以 Darlington 与 Morgan Grenfell 达成协议由后者订立建筑合约,Darlington 将来归还这笔费用,而在建造合约订立后 Morgan Grenfell 将合约所有权益转让给 Darlington。

娱乐中心建成后 Darlington 发现建筑有非常严重的缺陷,于是作为受让人向 Wiltshier 要求赔偿。一审法院认为 Darlington 作为受让人能够取回的只是"名义损失"(nominal damage),原因是在本章 3.4 段提到的"subject to equities"的说法下,受让人通过转让取得的权利只能是转让人(Morgan Grenfell)在合约下的权利。由于 Morgan Grenfell 从来不拥有土地与娱乐中心,所以没有任何损失,也表示能够转让给 Darlington 的利益只能是名义损失。

请注意在本案例,“The Albazero 原则”如果适用,就有了扩展。原因是在 The “Albazero”与 Linden Gardens v. Lenesta Sludge Disposals Ltd. and others 先例,都涉及订约方原来拥有有关的货物或财产,而在订约期间,双方都可以合理知道将来拥有者会把该货物或财产转让给第三人。所以如果另外一方作为承运人或承建商如果违反合约导致该货物或财产蒙受损失,双方知道真正蒙受损失的不是订约方而是第三人。但在本案例,Morgan Grenfell 从来不拥有有关的货物或财产(土地),也不存在转让给 Darlington。

接下去该先例在上诉庭被推翻,允许原告的 Darlington 作为受让人获得实质赔偿。上诉庭认为 Morgan Grenfell 从来不拥有有关财产并不重要,“The Albazero 原则”还是可以适用。其中 Dillon 大法官是这样说:“Mr. Blackburn(被告 Wiltshier 的大律师)also sought to distinguish the decision in the McAlpine case on the ground that in the present case Morgan Grenfell never acquired or transmitted to the council any proprietary interest in the Dolphin Centre(娱乐中心). I do not see that that matters as the council had the ownership of the site of the Dolphin Centre all along. It was plainly obvious to Wiltshier throughout that the Dolphin Centre was being constructed for the benefit of the council on the council's land. Accordingly, I would allow this appeal by direct application of the rule in Dunlop v. Lambert as recognised in a building contract context in Lord Browne - Wilkinson's speech in the McAlpine case.”

Steyn 勋爵也说:“... I would rule that the present case is within the rationale of Lord Browne - Wilkinson's speech. I do not say that the relevant passages in his speech precisely fit the material facts of the present case. But it involves only a very conservative and limited extension to apply it by analogy to the present case. For these reasons I would hold that the present case is covered by an exception to the general rule that a plaintiff can only recover damages for his own loss.”

5.4　建筑合约的 L/M International Construction Inc (now Bovis International Inc) v. The Circle Ltd Partnership 先例

在 L/M International Construction Inc (now Bovis International Inc) v. The Circle Ltd Partnership (1995)49 Con LR 12 的上诉庭先例,判决的结果也与上述的先例一致,就是被告(承建商)以雇主在被告违约时对有关财产没有财产权所以没有蒙受损失的抗辩不被法院所接受。在这里只简单介绍有关当事人,可以显示在建筑行业中,这种复杂的合约安排并非罕见。该先例涉及伦敦塔桥附近的一个庞大的住宅建造工程,其中拥有土地的所有权人雇用了一个发展商发展这一个工程,而所有权人与发展商实际上是联营公司。发展商另与一家管理公司订立一个合约,让后者监督工程的进行。发展商也同时向一个财团取得贷款,并把发展商的财产权益抵押给该财团的代表人 Shire(这是一家财务公司),而将来的还款将会是来自出售住宅所得的金钱。

由于工程进度慢,导致发展商要向承建商索赔延误的损失。这也带来承建商的抗辩就是发展商没有损失,因为在违约是发生在发展商把有关的土地与建筑抵押给了 Shire 之时,发展商当时是没有财产权。

5.5 建筑合约的 Alfred McAlpine Construction Ltd v. Panatown Ltd 先例

在 Alfred McAlpine Construction Ltd v. Panatown Ltd (2001) 1 AC 518 的贵族院先例,再度显示了"The Albazero 原则"或"以第三人的利益订立合约"(contract for the benefit of third party)作为"事实问题"(issue of fact)在每一个不同案件中做出认定的局限。本先例的合约安排其实相对简单,就是 Alfred McAlpine 作为承建商与 Panatown 订立一个办公楼工程的设计与建筑合约。但实际上有关的一块土地是由一家名为 UILP 所拥有,但 UILP 与 Panatown 是同一个集团下的联营公司,而这样的合约安排也是为了避免"增值税"(VAT)。这一个案件唯一的不同是在订约时,Alfred McAlpine 同时签了一份名为"小心谨慎契约"(duty of care deed ,简称 DCD)给 UILP,这表示本来是属于第三人的 UILP 与 Alfred McAlpine 有了直接的合约关系。虽然是 DCD 这一份文件的条文与建筑合约的条文并不一致,如 DCD 并没有一条仲裁条文;DCD 只要求 Alfred McAlpine 合理谨慎,但建筑合约对 Alfred McAlpine 的要求是严格责任等。只说在这一个事实下,贵族院判是作为订约方的 Panatown 是不能向 Alfred McAlpine 索赔第三人(UILP)的损失,也就是说"The Albazero 原则"不适用。

这方面的顾虑也可以说得通,就是会对 Alfred McAlpine 造成"双重赔偿"(double compensation)的危险。也就是 Alfred McAlpine 在建筑合约下赔偿了给 Panatown 后,在 DCD 下再度被 UILP 追偿同一笔损失。毕竟每一个合约是独立看待。UILP 与 Panatown 是同一个集团的联营公司也不保证不会出问题,如其中一家公司因为清盘而被清盘人接管等。而更大的危险是 UILP 把这一份 DCD 转让给其他人,如新的买方。这一来如果办公楼的设计与建筑有缺陷,DCD 的受让人会向 Alfred McAlpine 索赔,但 Alfred McAlpine 已经赔了一次给 Panatown。这一个危险 Browne - Wilkinson 勋爵有提到说:"The theoretical objection to giving the contracting party A substantial damages for breach of the contract by B for failing to provide C with a benefit which C itself can enforce against B is further demonstrated by great practical difficulties which such a view would entail. Let me illustrate this by postulating a case where, before the breach occurred, UPIL had with consent assigned the benefit of the DCD to a purchaser of the site, X. What if Panatown itself was entitled to, and did, sue for and recover damages from McAlpine? Presumably McAlpine could not in addition be liable to X for breach of the DCD: yet Panatown would not be liable to account to X for the damages it had recovered from McAlpine. The result would therefore be another piece of legal nonsense: the party who had suffered real, tangible damage, X, could recover nothing but Panatown which had suffered no real loss could recover damages. Again suppose that X agrees with McAlpine certain variations of McAlpine's liability under the building contract. What rights would Panatown then have against McAlpine?"

贵族院的判决可节录 Clyde 勋爵所说:"I have no difficulty in holding in the present case that the exception cannot apply. As part of the contractual arrangements entered into between Panatown and McAlpine there was a clear contemplation that separate contracts would be entered into by McAlpine, the contracts of the deed of duty of care and the collateral warranties. The duty of care deed and the collateral warranties were of course not in themselves building contracts. But they did form an integral part of the package of arrangements which the employer and the contractor agree upon and in that respect should be viewed as reflecting the intentions of all the parties engaged in the arrangements that the third party should have a direct cause of action to the exclusion of any substantial claim by the employer, and accordingly that the exception should not apply. There was some dispute upon the difference in substance between the remedies available under the contract and those available under the duty of care deed. Even if it is accepted that in the circumstances of the present case where the eventual issue may relate particularly to matters of reasonable skill and care, the remedies do not absolutely coincide, the express provision of the direct remedy for the third party is fatal to the application of The Albazero exception. On a more general approach the difference between a strict contractual basis of claim and a basis of reasonable care makes the express remedy more contractual basis of claim and a basis of reasonable care makes the express remedy more clearly a substitution for the operation of the exception. Panatown cannot then in the light of these deeds be treated as having contracted with McAlpine for the benefit of the owner or later owners of the land and the exception is plainly excluded."

再重复从这个先例就可以看出"The Albazero 原则"的局限,如果案情的事实有改变,如在本先例中 DCD 的存在,就会造成最后的判决结果不同。所以在这一个先例中在"广泛地位"(broader ground)和"狭窄地位"(narrow ground)贵族院再度有分歧,其中少数意见的 Goff 勋爵和 Millett 勋爵支持广泛地位。在广泛地位适用的情况下,就不必理会 Panatown 本身是否蒙受实际损失,它也可以向 Alfred McAlpine 索赔与取回实际损失。其中 Millett 勋爵批评狭窄地位说这是会计师只会看资产负债表内有关违约所带来的损失数字(the product of the narrow accountants' balance sheet quantification of loss which measures the loss suffered by the promise by the diminution in his overall financial position resulting from the breach)。Millett 勋爵也支持 Griffiths 勋爵对广泛地位的说法,说:"[Lord Griffiths] was insisting that, in certain kinds of contract at least, the right of performance has a value which is capable of being measured by the cost of obtaining it from a third party... There has for some time been a growing consensus among academic writers that English law adopts an unduly narrow approach to the concept of loss, and that it ought to recognise that the performance of a contractual obligation may have an economic value of its own which is capable of sounding in damages. Such damages may be measured by the cost of obtaining alternative performance, but they may also take account of loss from delay and other consequential loss."

5.6 普通法下广泛地位与狭窄地位的总结

从上述的建筑行业有关先例就已经可以看到这个普通法下"The Albazero 原则"或以第三人的利益订立合约(contract for the benefit of third party)说法的缺点,也就是根据每一个案件的不同事实会带来完全相反的结果,这带来不肯定与昂贵的诉讼。所以在 Alfred McAlpine Construction Ltd v. Panatown Ltd (2001) 1 AC 518 先例后还是不断有案例对广泛地位与狭窄地位持不同看法。如支持广泛地位的先例有:Earl's Terrace Properties Ltd v. Nilsson Design Ltd and Charter Construction plc (2004) EWHC 136 与 Mirant Asia - Pacific Construction (Hong Kong) Ltd v. Ove Arup & Partners International Ltd (2007) EWHC 918。对广泛地位持异议的先例就有 Rolls - Royce Power Engineering plc v. Ricardo Consulting Engineers Ltd (2003) EWHC 2871。可以说英国法律到目前对是否采纳广泛地位作为第三人规则的例外还是没有定论,也没有直接针对的先例。

当然,广泛地位如果被接受,本身也会带来很多的问题,这包括有:

(1)适用在什么类别的合约或商业活动?而 Griffiths 勋爵在倡议广泛地位是主要考虑建筑合约,但他没有考虑与也没有理由局限广泛地位适用在更多不同类别的合约关系,可参阅:J Cattwright 教授的《Compensatory Damages: Central Issues of Assessment》,收录在 A Burrows 教授与 E Peel 教授主编的《Commercial Remedies: Current Issues and Problems》(2003 年)中与 E Peel 教授的《Treitel on the Law of Contract》(12th edn,2007 年)之 14 - 033 段。

(2)就是会导致英国法律针对受害方的复原与"赔偿原则"(compensation principle)、受害方对他的经济损失"举证责任"(burden of proof)、合理"减少损失"(mitigation)、损失类别是否在订约时可以合理预见或料想到(remoteness)等方面的根本性改变,也带来"双重赔偿"(double jeopardy)的危险与诉讼程序的不配合等。例如在诉讼程序的文件披露,被告能否成功要求原告披露有关第三人实际损失的文件,毕竟这些文件不一定是原告能够有权利取得,即使第三人是它的联营公司:Lonrho Plc v. Al Fayed (1994) QB 775 (HL)。

部分的问题是 Seymour 大法官在 Rolls - Royce Power Engineering plc v. Ricardo Consulting Engineers Ltd 先例所说如下:"Lord Griffiths´ approach has not so far been adopted as a matter of decision in any case in England and Wales which Counsel had been able to discover. It seems on its face to divorce the assessment of damages for breach of contract in a case in which it is adopted from proof of any particular loss sustained by the claimant, substituting some more or less notional quantification of damages for loss of bargain. As it is a notional loss of the actual claimant, if the person who has actually sustained the loss has some independent ground of claim, for example in tort, it would seem that the wrongdoer could find himself having to pay compensation for one wrong twice over. Settlement of the claim of the other contracting party would not obviously be a defence to the claim of the person who in fact sustained loss. Again, leaving aside that difficulty, it does not seem at all easy just as a practical matter to apply Lord Griffiths´approach in any case other than one in which the alleged damage is damage to, or failure to repair, property and there is no suggestion of any consequential loss. It may be that the cost of repairing damage to a house or a car or some other type of corporeal property is likely to be similar no matter who sustains it. It may be that the diminution in the value of an item of corporeal property is likely to be similar no matter who owns it. However, the nature and extent of any consequential loss — for example, loss of income from inability for a period to turn property to account — may well depend critically upon the particular circumstances of the owner and what he or she does with the property. A simple example is that an owner of a flat may live in it as his main residence, or he may keep it empty for occasional use by himself, or he may let it and derive an income from it. Inability to use the flat because it has been damaged in some way may cause no loss beyond the cost of repair in the second case — the owner can live in his main residence — and the measure of the loss in the other two cases may well be different, either the cost of renting alternative accommodation or loss of rental income. In a case such as the present, in which there has been no damage to corporeal property as a result of the defendant's alleged breach of contract, it is impossible to see how any assessment of damages could be made other than by reference to what actually happened to the other contracting party. "(上述 Seymour 大法官首先提到了双重赔偿的危险,就是蒙受损失的第三人可以根据侵权向违约方索赔,但违约方已经在较早时赔付给了合约下的受害方[根据广泛地位索赔第三人蒙受的损失],违约方不能在一个后来的侵权诉讼中以这个理由作为抗辩,就很容易会产生双重赔偿的危险。接下去 Seymour 大法官也提到在这种建筑合约,缺陷建造主要的损失赔偿是修理[或估计修理]费用或有关建筑/房子的贬值,这一方面的损失是不受广泛地位的影响,因为合约受害方[或房产所有人]或真正蒙受损失的第三人提出索赔的修理费用或贬值都是针对有关或特定的建筑/房子,损失计算不会有变化。但如果涉及间接损失,就会很受受害方的影响。例如在合约下,受害方是计划把有关的房子作为度假屋,他就不会因为违约方造成的缺陷需要修理而蒙受损失。而如果受害方是计划把有关的房子作为居所,他就可能因为房子需要修理而蒙受间接损失,如需要另租房子暂时居住甚至住在酒店。但第三人的间接损失就会因人而异,变为完全不是这么回事。)

(3)即使采取了广泛地位,也不能解决第三人规则在本章 5.1 段简单提到过的海上货物运输和国际贸易方面的问题,也就是蒙受损失的第三人不一定能够取得合约方替他向违约方索赔实际损失。在上述介绍的著名建筑合约中的先例,没有涉及这方面的问题,往往合约方与第三人是联营公司。但这种情况是说不定,很有可能会出现第三人与合约下的受害方是没有任何关系，甚至互不认识或有敌意。

5.7 转移损失的说法

最后一提是在普通法下也曾经出现过“转移损失”(transferred loss)的说法，这个说法据说是来自德国的“Drittschadenliquidation”原则或说法。但这个说法的寿命远比 Dunlop v. Lambert 说法要短，它在 The “Aliakmon”（1986）2 Lloyd’s Rep 1 的上诉庭先例中被 Goff 大法官提出说：“There is a recognisable principle underlying the imposition of liability, which can be called the principle of transferred loss. Furthermore, that principle can be formulated... Where A owes a duty of care in tort not to cause physical damage to B’s property, and commits a breach of that duty in circumstances in which the loss of or physical damage to the property will ordinarily fall on B but (as is reasonably foreseeable by A) such loss or damage, by reason of a contractual relationship between B and C, falls upon C, then C will be entitled, subject to the terms of any contract restricting A’s liability to B, to bring an action in tort against A in respect of such loss or damage to the extent that it falls on him, C.”(Goff 大法官的说法下给的例子是 A 对 B 的财产有一个小心谨慎的侵权责任[在 The “Aliakmon”先例，由于无法成立海上运输合约的关系，所以受损货物的买方以侵权向承运人提出索赔]，A 在正常情况下是可以预见到他如果疏忽造成对 B 财产的损坏，是要向 B 做出赔偿。但由于 B 与另一位 C 订立了一个合约关系[如本案例的货物买卖合约]，导致原来在 B 身上的损失通过该合约转移到了 C。这一来，法律应该允许 C 向 A 索赔这一笔原来是要赔偿给 B 的损失)

但这一个转移损失的说法在上诉后很快被贵族院否定，其中 Brandon 勋爵是这样说(其他贵族院大法官也同意)：“With the greatest possible respect to Lord Goff the principle of transferred loss which he there enunciated, however useful in dealing with special factual situation it may be in theory, is not only not supported by authority, but is on the contrary inconsistent with it. Even if it were necessary to introduce such a principle in order to fill a genuine lacuna in the law, I should myself, perhaps because I am more faint-hearted than Lord Goff, be reluctant to do so. As I have tried to show earlier, however, there is in truth no such lacuna in the law which requires to be filled. Neither Sir John Donaldson, M. R. nor Lord Justice Oliver (now Lord Oliver of Aylmerton) was prepared to accept the introduction of such a principle and I find myself entirely in agreement with their unwillingness to do so.”

最后一提的是在 Alfred McAlpine Construction Ltd v. Panatown Ltd (2001) 1 AC 先例，Clyde 勋爵也有提到这一个转移损失的说法，但看来 Clyde 勋爵举的例子是第三人把损失转移给合约下的受害方，让受害方代他向违约方索赔实际损失。看来，由于转移损失的说法没有进一步的发展，所以实际损失是谁转移给谁还没有定论。Clyde 勋爵是这样说：“If by a special contract the goods were the property or at the risk of the consignor then the loss would be his. That indeed was recognised in Dunlop v. Lambert.

The second part of the passage which I have quoted however advances beyond such a position. What is there propounded is, as was noticed by my noble and learned friend, Lord Goff of Chieveley, in White v. Jones (1995) 2 AC 207, 267, a case of transferred loss. This is not a situation where the loss is that of the promisee(合约的被承诺方). It is a loss suffered by the third party but transferred to the promisee who is then accountable to the third party. Thus the loss becomes that of the employer instead of and in place of the third party, a point emphasised by Hannes Unberath in his recent article 'Third Party Losses and Black Holes: Another View' (1999) 115 LQR 535. (上一句指 Hannes Unberath 先生的德国律师所发表的文章把德国的'Drittschadenliquidation'与转移损失串了起来) The promisee is deemed to have suffered the loss so that it is he and not the third party who is able to pursue the remedy in damages...

It seems to me that a more realistic and practical solution is to permit the contracting party to recover damages for the loss which he and a third party has suffered, being duly accountable to them in respect of their actual loss, than to construct a theoretical loss in law on the part of the contracting party, for which he may be under no duty to account to anyone since it is to be seen as his own loss..."(笔者的理解是 Clyde 勋爵也不认同转移损失的说法,因为这不像是上述 3.2 段所讲的代理关系或是 3.3 段提到的信托关系,合约受害方在获得实质损失赔偿后在法律上有责任把这笔钱交还给真正蒙受损失的第三人。如果采取这一个转移损失的说法,在法律下视为是合约受害方自己的损失,那么就很难限制原告把取回的金钱赔偿怎样处理,如要交出给第三人。英国法律通常是不理会原告怎样处理他取回的金钱赔偿,如意外伤害的原告从侵权方取得估计医疗赔偿金完全可以用作支付他孩子的学费,而自己的医疗能省就省。)

6.《Contract (Right of Third Parties) Act 1999》的立法

看来通过法院建立起来的普通法没有办法完善解决的法律问题,还是需要通过一个普遍性的立法对第三人规则做出改变。虽然有一贯的说法是不同案件会有千变万化的情况,往往是立法没有或不能想得到。所以法律的改革最好还是通过大量的案例先让法院针对不同案情慢慢组织出一套体系与说法。但问题是后者的做法在时间上需要太长与很难有这么多的机会让法院(特别是贵族院或最高院)通过大量的同类案件建立一套体系或说法。正如 Steyn 大法官在 Darlington BC v. Wiltshier Northern Ltd. (1995) 1 WLR 68 先例所说,"But that requires the door to be opened by the House of Lords reviewing the major cases which are thought to have entrenched the rule of privity of contract. Unfortunately, there will be few opportunities for the House of Lords to do so."

显然是立法如果订的好与全面,就会有希望很快能够解决大部分的问题。针对非合约方的第三人损失或利益,在英国的重要立法就是《Contract(Right of Third Parties) Act 1999》,它是根据法律委员会1996年242号报告中建议取消"第三人规则"(Third Party Rule)做出回应。这一个立法在笔者的《国际商务游戏规则——英国合约法》之82~98页有详论,不在本书重复。本章只针对该立法的两方面重点(Section 1与Section 2),并介绍一些近期的先例。

6.1 Section 1:有关第三人可直接强制执行合约

这就是立法Section 1的第三人可直接强制执行合约条文到底是哪些人,这一个英文可称为是"Test of enforceability"也是整个立法的中心问题,可以说是十分重要,也在目前看来涉及最多的先例。

6.1.1 可直接执行的第三人范围不能太宽或太窄

这里的轻重是很不容易掌握,因为太宽或太窄都会带来严重后果。如果太宽,就是任何在一个合约的执行都会合理得利的第三人都可以执行,就会对合约违约方带来很严重后果。举例说,一个演唱会的协议,其中会合理得利的第三人可以说很多,包括可能是数以千计的听众、安排转播的电视台等。如果演唱的歌手违约,他要对主办演唱会的合约受害方负责并赔偿损失是理所当然的。但如果有数以千计的听众或电视台或其他受影响的第三人都可以向违约的歌手提出索赔,这就会对违约方带来不可预计的赔偿责任与麻烦。

再多举一个例子,就是当地政府宣布把某一块地发展成为一个公园或是建造一条主要的公路,并与承建商订立合约。这一个消息把附近的房价抬高并持续上涨。如果承建商顺利与准时完成建造,这应该是皆大欢喜。但如果承建商违约,如工程拖慢了3年才完成甚至是完成不了,面对与它订约的当地政府提起的索赔固然是无话可说。但如果根据消息抢了买房子的第三人,也因为这一个违约而蒙受损失,如房价下跌或是提早搬了进去但由于公路还没建好而带来交通的不便与昂贵,也可以向违约的承建商提出索赔,带来了严重的不可预计赔偿责任,甚至承建商是购买了责任保险也不足赔偿的。所以保障第三人这一份合约的利益与不能让他蒙受损失不能放得太宽。

但立法如果把第三人的范围订得太窄,就会失去了立法的意义,而且不能较大面积保护第三人的利益或损失。这里可以举一个例子就是澳大利亚的《Western Australian Property Law Act 1969》的Section 11说,"... where a contract expressly in its terms purports to confer a benefit directly on a person who is not named as a party to the contract, the contract is... enforceable by that person in his own name..."这就被批评是订得太窄,其中在新西兰的商业法律改革委员会1981年《Privity of Contract》的报告中,就有说:"(i) it does not appear to permit enforcement by third parties who are not in existence or ascertained at the time of formation of the contract;(法律条文不像让在订约时还没有存在或无法确定是谁的第三人强制执行合约权益)(ii) it seems to require express naming of the third party;(法律条文看来是要求在合约中明确说明谁是第三人,这在现实中是很少会发生)(iii) it seems to exclude implied terms in favour of third parties;(法律条文看来是排除任何默示的第三人,只允许明示第三人)(iv) it requires the joinder of each person named as a party to the contract in any proceedings commenced by the third party;(法律条文要求第三人开始诉讼时必须把合约的所有当事人加进来)(v) it does not clearly express the necessity for the promisor and promisee to have intended to confer a legal right on the third party."(它没有明确要求订约双方有意图提供给第三人一个合法利益)

6.1.2 英国1999年立法对可直接执行的第三人的范围

英国的立法在这方面的轻重掌握,为了方便参阅可先把《Contract (Right of Third Parties) Act 1999》之 Section 1 节录如下:

"1. Right of third party to enforce contractual term

(1) Subject to the provisions of this Act, a person who is not a party to a contract (a 'third party') may in his own right enforce a term of the contract if— (a) the contract expressly provides that he may, **or** (b) subject to subsection (2), the term purports to confer a benefit on him.

(2) Subsection (1)(b) does not apply if on a proper construction of the contract it appears that the parties did not intend the term to be enforceable by the third party.

(3) The third party must be expressly identified in the contract by name, as a member of a class or as answering a particular description but need not be in existence when the contract is entered into.

(4) This section does not confer a right on a third party to enforce a term of a contract otherwise than subject to and in accordance with any other relevant terms of the contract.

(5) For the purpose of exercising his right to enforce a term of the contract, there shall be available to the third party any remedy that would have been available to him in an action for breach of contract if he had been a party to the contract (and the rules relating to damages, injunctions, specific performance and other relief shall apply accordingly).

(6) Where a term of a contract excludes or limits liability in relation to any matter references in this Act to the third party enforcing the term shall be construed as references to his availing himself of the exclusion or limitation.

(7) In this Act, in relation to a term of a contract which is enforceable by a third party—'the promisor' means the party to the contract against whom the term is enforceable by the third party, and 'the promisee' means the party to the contract by whom the term is enforceable against the promisor."

英国立法是把这可直接执行的第三人分两类或两部分。

6.1.2.1 可直接执行的第三人的第一部分

第一部分(也就是在 Section 1[1][a]与 Section 1[3]所针对)是合约明确说明第三人有权执行有关合约,或有关合约的某一部分。该第三人必须是明示规定,但该立法的 Section 1(3)也说明第三人不需要在合约中明示他的名字,可以只是明示哪一个类别的人士(如经纪人、装卸小工、房子的买方、北京长安街 10 号的居民、将来住客等)。另外,这第三人甚至不需要在订立合约时就已经存在,如在保险合约中把合约利益提供给还没有出生的婴儿,或是提供给一个还没有注册的有限公司。

但这一部分的第三人并没有要求订约双方把合约利益提供给他,这是因为在现实中会有情况合约约定某位第三人有权执行该合约,而命名的第三人并没有任何合约利益。这在法律委员会 1996 年 242 号报告之 7.13 段的提到两个例子会出现这样的情况,可节录如下:"... Two main examples were given of where the parties might seek to contract to create obligations which would benefit a range of persons not party to the contract but in the interests of simplicity and certainty might wish to confine the ability to enforce the rights arising to a third party who was not a beneficiary. First, A contracts with B to transfer Pds. 10,000 to C, which C is hold on trust for the benefit of D; and C is expressly given the right to enforce A's obligation to B. It was argued that, in that situation, C should have the right to enforce the contract even though the performance of A's obligation would be for the benefit of D and C could perhaps be said not to "benefit" from the performance by being made a trustee of the benefit. Secondly, A (a developer) and B (the client) might wish to designate C (a management company) as having the right to sue to enforce warranties in the construction contract for D-Z (the tenants)...."(第一个例子是 A 与 B 订立合约约定 A 支付给 C 一笔 1 万英镑的金钱,但实际上 C 只是 D 的受托人,C 收到这笔钱后要交出给受益人的 D[甚至有好几个受益人],严格说 C 并没有这一个合约的利益,但合约明示规定了他可以执行。第二个例子是 A 作为发展商与 B 的客户约定指定一家管理公司的 C,规定了 C 可以为租客 D-Z 执行建造合约中的一些保证。)

在立法后的先例看来,对这第一部分所识别的第三人解释起来是相当严格。在 Avraamides v. Colwill (2006) EWCA Civ. 1533 先例,法院判是不能通过对整个合约的解释或默示确定第三人,因为立法规定是有关合约必须"明示"(express)。

6.1.2.2 可直接执行的第三人的第二部分

可直接执行的第三人的第二部分是在立法的 Section 1(1)(b),1(2)与 1(3)就比较复杂,有说法是这部分只针对合约"默示"(implied)给第三人一个合约的利益,这与第一部分所针对的"明示"(express)并不一样。第二部分会是合约根据 Section 1(1)(b)有条文"提供合约利益"(confer a benefit)给第三人,而且谁是第三人根据 Section 1(3)要在合约中明示,这看来就与第一部分的情况相同。

6.1.2.2.1 什么是提供合约利益?

提供合约利益看来还是解释得比较宽松,但还是会有复杂的问题,如订约双方有订约意图提供合约利益给第三人(an intentional to confer a benefit)就与第三人通过合约的履行也会碰巧获得利益(a third party incidentally gain some benefit from the performance of certain terms in a contract)就会有微妙的区别。这在 Dolphin Maritime v. Sceriges Angfartygs Assurans (2009) 2 Lloyd's Rep. 123 先例有针对。首先简单介绍该先例的案情,它涉及一船的废钢从美国装运去土耳其。船舶名为 New Flame 轮,在直布罗陀附近的海域发生碰撞与搁浅,导致严重货损。货物保险人在赔付后取得代位求偿权,开始在美国提出"海事诉讼"(action in rem)向两艘船舶索赔,简单一提在美国提起这种诉讼索赔是对货方非常有利的,在笔者的《海事法》第七章 10.3 段有详论。同时货物保险人也指定了索赔代理人 Dolphin Maritime 代他追偿,双方也订了一个协议就是如果成功追偿,这笔取回来的钱有一个百分比是给索赔代理人。这种所谓"不成功,不付费"(no cure, no pay)的安排在海事索赔代理人的行业中非常普遍。这一个协议中也有条文规定了保险人不得直接与对方(也就是指被告的船东或他的互保协会)谈判与讨论有关本案件,同时保证追偿回来的金钱必须先支付给索赔代理人。这些也是行业中非常普遍的条文,为了保障索赔代理人做了很多工作之后,委托他的保险人直接与被告的船东或互保协会私下达成协议。进一步更会是被告把赔付的钱直接支付给保险人,绕过索赔代理人并导致他失去了先收取赔偿,可以扣起了百分比费用后才把余下金额支付给保险人的机会。

在美国的这个诉讼也导致了 New Flame 轮的互保协会 Sceriges Angfartygs Assurans 提供了一个金额高达 1750 万美元的保函,作为货方或代位的保险人不扣船的对价。但之后,有了一个私下的会议,双方谈判的就是船东互保协会与保险人,但 Dolphin Maritime 完全不知道,这就是绕过了他并达成了船东赔付 850 万美元的和解协议。在大约 2 个月后 Dolphin Maritime 知道了这种情况后曾经电邮给船东互保协会投诉他不应该绕过他直接与保险人接触,并需要根据他所提供的保函把 850 万美元的和解金额直接给他而不是保险人。但最终船东互保协会并没有理会,并把这笔钱直接支付给了保险人。这导致了 Dolphin Maritime 在本先例向船东的互保协会索赔他应该有的费用,而诉因是根据侵权的"诱导他人违约"(induce breach of contract),也就是诱导了保险人破坏与 Dolphin Maritime 的"不成功,不付费"协议。另外,Dolphin Maritime 认为它可以根据 1999 的《Contract (Right of Third Parties) Act》立法向船东互保协会强制执行在保函中提供给他的合约利益。

对于 1999 立法的关系是互保协会提供的 1750 万美元的保函订约双方是船东互保协会与货方或代位的保险人,索赔代理人只是第三人。但在保函中有明示条文说明船东互保协会在做出赔付是通过索赔代理人支付给保险人。英文是:"In consideration of the cargo interests consenting to the release from arrest and/or refraining from arresting New Flame for the purposes of obtaining security in respect of claims against the vessel or her owners in respect of the cargo now in question the Club undertook: **to pay to [Dolphin] on your behalf or to any solicitors you may appoint** such sums as may be due pursuant to a final and unappealable judgement issued by a US court or as may be agreed to be recoverable from the owner of the ... ship in respect of claims in respect of the cargo up to a total of US $ 17.5 million."(加黑的一句是支付给 Dolphin Maritime 或是保险人会委任的代表律师)

这就带来了第一个争议,也就是有关合约(保函)这样的写法是否提供了合约利益给 Dolphin Maritime 作为第三人。Dolphin Maritime 的代表大律师举了三个例子说明不同的写法与有否算是提供合约利益,如下:

(1) A 向 B 承诺支付给 C 850 万美元(在这种情况明显双方有订约意图把合约利益提供给第三人的 C,如果 A 不支付的情况下 C 是可以根据立法向 A 直接提出索赔)。

(2) A 向 B 承诺支付给 B 850 万美元,这笔钱是通过 C 银行的账号或是代表 B 的 D 律师所的客户账号支付给 B (在一定的程度上,如果 A 履行合约做出支付,第三人的 C 银行或是 D 律师所也是会获得利益,如可以把这笔钱抵销 B 作为客户所欠下的钱或费用。但这种合约利益只是"碰巧"[incidental],一般人士都会把这种安排视为是这笔钱的受益人只是 B,而双方的订约意图也只是想提供合约利益给他,而不是其他第三人。所以如果 A 不做出支付,是不会除了 B 以外要面对合约提到的第三人如银行、律师所或是代理人根据 1999 年立法向 A 提出索赔。)

(3)这一个例子就是本案例的情况,有关保函的合约,A (货方或代位保险人)与 B (New Flame 轮的互保协会)达成协议,把赔偿金额支付给 C 的索赔代理人(Dolphin Maritime),这看来与第二个例子的情况差不多。但解释合约是要考虑订约时的背景,这包括:B 是与 C 谈判并取得这一份保函;C 是保函的抬头上所注明的人士;保函规定了支付赔偿金额是给 C 代 A 收取,有一些证据显示了 B 是应该知道这是索赔代理人惯常的做法。所以,作为 C 的 Dolphin Maritime 争辩说他有权根据 1999 年的立法以第三人的身份向 B 执行保函的合约,并索赔损失。

在英国高院,Christopher Clarke 大法官不同意 Dolphin 代表大律师的争辩,认为第三个例子其实也是第二个例子,充其量 Dolphin Maritime 只是合约如果履行会有一个碰巧的合约利益,说:

"A contract does not purport to confer a benefit on a third party simply because the position of that third party will be improved if the contract is performed. The reference in the section to the term purporting to "confer" a benefit seems to me to connote that the language used by the parties show that one of the purposes of their bargain (rather than one of its incidental effects if performed) was to benefit the third party.

In my judgment the term in question does not purport to confer a benefit on Dolphin... The provision of in the LOU(保函) that payment should be made to Dolphin or underwriters solicitors are an agreement as to the means by which the Club's obligation (船东互保协会的承诺) to underwriters was to be discharged. It was not an indication that the agent payee was an intended beneficiary of the promise. The intended beneficiaries were the underwriters on whose behalf the payment was to be reserved. ... The provision in the LOU that payment should be made to Dolphin or underwriters' solicitors was an agreement as to the means by which the Club's obligation to underwriters was to be discharged. It was not an indication that the agent payee was an intended beneficiary of the promise. The intended beneficiaries were the underwriters on whose behalf the payment was to be received."(有关保函支付说明赔偿金额是支付给 Dolphin Maritime 或是保险人的代表律师,要加上代表律师是因为 Dolphin Maritime 只是索赔代理人,而不是合资格的律师。所以 Dolphin Maritime 可以处理这一个案件,包括谈判,但去法院[美国法院或英国法院]就必须通过合资格律师作为代表。在海事索赔代理人的行业,索赔代理人通常都有熟悉或有联系的律师所。这一来如果委任了代表律师,通常在双方达成和解或是法院诉讼后做出的支付会是给律师所的客户账户。这也表示了为什么保函说明赔偿金额会是支付 Dolphin Maritime 或是代表律师,但无论他们有什么背后的安排,针对船东互保协会或是保函而言,他们都只是货方或代位保险人的代理人。)

6.1.2.2.2　复杂与富争议的订约双方有否让第三人获得合约利益的订约意图

但在 Section 1(2),比较复杂的是通过解释有关的合约并认定另有明示或默示条文否定,显示了双方订约方并没有订约意图让第三人获得合约利益并让他直接执行,这是受到承认。换言之,订约自由还是完全受到尊重。这种否定的条文可以十分直接如说明"C 作为第三人不能执行这一份合约",或是一条禁止转让条文(prohibition of assignment clause),或是干脆否定适用这一个立法说"A person who is not a party to this contract shall have no rights under the Contracts (Right of Third Party) Act 1999 to enforce any of its terms"。但问题以上述条文清楚订明合约双方没有意图让第三人获得合约利益并让他直接执行的情况是非常少见的,大多数案件会涉及对合约条文的解释支持或否定有否这一个订约意图。解释合约是一个非常复杂的问题,近 30 年来在英国法院对传统解释合约的做法有了很大改变,并涉及大量重要的先例,其中不少是贵族院或是最高院的先例,如 Charter Reinsurance Co. Ltd v. Fagan (1997) AC 313; Mannai Investment Co. Ltd v. Eagle Star Life Assurance Co. Ltd (1997) AC 749; Investors Compensation Scheme v. West Bromwich Building Society (1998) 1 WLR 896; BCCI v. Ali (2002) 1 AC 251; The "Starsin" (2003) 1 Lloyd's Rep 571; Chartbrook v. Persimmon Homes (2009) UKHL 38; Re Sigma Finance Corp (2009) UKSC 2; Rainy Sky SA v. Kookmin Bank (2011) UKSC 50 等。简单说,传统的合约解释是比较重视双方所用的文字/措辞,但近期的合约解释可称为是"目的解释"(purposive construction),也有称为"本质解释"(contextual construction),或"商业解释"(commercial construction),或"自由解释"(liberal construction)。对这一重要的法律问题,请参阅笔者的《合约的解释》一书。只总结一下这也是为什么 Section 1(2)的情况会这么复杂的原因,并会在下述的先例介绍。

在立法后的先例有不少,看来对第二个部分的第三人可否享有合约利益是比第一个部分宽松,特别是前两个先例包括了 Nisshin Shipping Co Ltd v. Cleave & Co Ltd (2004) 1 Lloyd's Rep 38 与 The "Laemthong Glory" (No. 2) (2005) 1 Lloyd's Rep 688。但第三个与第四个先例有不同的判法 Prudential Assurance Co Ltd v. Ayres (2007) EWHC 775 与 Dolphin Maritime v. Sceriges Angfartygs Assurans (2009) 2 Lloyd's Rep. 123。第五个先例是新加坡的 CLAAS Medical Centre Pte Ltd v. Ng Boon Ching (2010) 2 SLR 386。以下会个别介绍。

6.1.2.2.3 有关案例之一:Nisshin Shipping Co Ltd v. Cleave & Co Ltd

第一个 Nisshin Shipping Co Ltd v. Cleave & Co Ltd (2004) 1 Lloyd's Rep 38 先例涉及 9 个期租合约,租约中都有一条涉及佣金的条文说明船东要支付给 Cleave & Co 作为其中一位的船舶经纪人。由于船东没有支付,经纪人直接根据这一立法向船东提出索赔。在本章 3.3 段提到这类案件经纪人也可以通过承租人作为受托人向船东索赔,并把取得的钱退还给经纪人。另经纪人也可以以信托的受益人向船东索赔。但估计会麻烦一点,不如直接根据这个立法向船东索赔,如果经纪人可以这样做。这在该先例被 Colman 大法官接受,认为租约的佣金条文明显是提供给第三人 Cleave & Co 一个合约利益。

首先是根据 1999 年的《Contract (Right of Third Parties) Act》立法的 Section 1(3),必须明示谁是第三人。这在这个先例中没有什么可以争议,合约中清楚写明了经纪人的名字 Cleave & Co。富争议的还是 Section 1(2)针对的,合约方是有或是没有意图给经济人一个合约利益让他可以有权利直接执行合约。被告的船东显然抗辩是说没有,第一个理由是有关的 9 份租约没有任何有关这方面的条文或显示,说:"It is argued by Mr. Ashcroft (船东代表大律师) on behalf of Nisshin (船东) that there is no positive indication in the charter - parties that the parties did intend the brokers to have enforceable rights. There is no suggestion in those contracts that the owners and charterers were mutually in agreement that the brokers should be entitled to claim against the owners as if they were parties to the contract."

针对这方面 Colman 大法官判是有关合约即使是中立(就是也没有明确显示有或是没有这一个订约意图),但由于 Section 1(2)条文的举证责任是在被告,所以被告的船东只根据有关合约只是"中立"(neutral)或"沉默"(silence)并不足够。

另一个抗辩理由是指经纪人既然有通过承租人作为受托人向船东索赔的权利,就根本没有必要再让经纪人有直接向船东索赔的权利。但这也被 Colman 大法官拒绝,说:"This proposition is, in my judgment, entirely unsustainable. The fact that prior to the 1999 Act it would be the mutual intention that the only available facility for enforcement would be deployed by the broker does not lead to the conclusion that, once an additional statutory facility for enforcement had been introduced, the broker would not be entitled to use it, but would instead be confined to the use of the pro - existing procedure. Indeed, quite apart from the complete lack of any logical basis for such an inference, the very cumbersome and inconvenient nature of the procedure based on the trustee relationship (described by Lord Wright as a 'cumbrous fiction') would point naturally to the preferred use by the broker of the right to sue directly provided by the 1999 Act. Not only would that original procedure be inconvenient, but it might involve risk that the broker would be prevented from recovering his commission, for example, in a case where the charterer had been dissolved in its place of incorporation or where, in the absence of co - operation by the charterer, proceedings had to be served on it outside the jurisdiction and service could not be effected. There are therefore very strong grounds pointing against any mutual intention to confine the brokers to the old procedure and to deny them the right to rely on the 1999 Act."

6.1.2.2.4 有关案例之二:The "Laemthong Glory"(No.2)

第二个先例 The "Laemthong Glory"(No.2)(2005)1 Lloyd's Rep 688 涉及一批 14,000 吨食糖在亚丁卸港的无单放货。这是很危险的行为,船东这样做很容易构成对货物的"侵占"(conversion),这是严格责任。反正在该先例,这种危险的做法也按照了惯常的做法,就是收货人提供了一份保函给二船东,而二船东作为承租人也给了原船东一份背靠背的保函。结果出事,该船舶被持有正本提单的银行(因为收货人没有去赎单)扣押,看来原船东要赔付这笔高达 300 多万美元货价的责任是难逃了。原船东于是向承租人(也就是二船东)与收货人提起诉讼并索赔这笔钱与有关的损失(如扣押期间的船期损失)。原船东向承租人的索赔应该是没有任何问题,撇开租约关系,根据保函就已经有十分广泛的条文承诺对船东因为无单放货造成的损失做出全面保障与赔偿。但原船东向收货人主张同样的权利就有问题,因为收货人提供给二船东的保函,原船东只是第三人。这里会涉及很多千变万化的现实问题,如承租人/二船东是一家大公司,相反收货人是一家小公司,原船东根本不用动脑筋,只要盯了承租人要求他根据保函履行他承诺对无单放货的保护与赔偿,不必理会收货人。但反过来如果承租人是一家皮包公司但收货人是一家资金雄厚的大公司,原船东就会希望能够盯了收货人做出的保函所承诺的保障与赔偿。在该先例,原船东的争辩简单介绍是:(1)发货人的保函有提供合约利益给原船东,因为无单放货只有原船东才能这样做,而且事后的严重后果也是原船东要承担。所以收货人做出的保函,收货人与二船东在订约时肯定会想到提供的利益实际上是给原船东。(2)发货人的保函也有明示针对了原船东这一种类别的第三人,因为保函的措辞是说明补偿"你,你的仆人与代理人"(to indemnify you, your servants and agents and to hold all of you harmless in respect of any liability, loss, damages or expense of whatsoever nature which you may sustain by reason of delivering the cargo in accordance with our request.)。这是无单放货保函的一些标准措辞,而原船东指"代理人"(agents)针对了他这一个类别的第三人。

这些原船东的争辩被上诉庭接受,同意收货人的保函的确是提供了合约利益给原船东。但看来主要又是出在双方订约方(收货人与二船东)到底有否订约意图提供这一利益。这带来了一个争议就是在法律委员会 1996 年 242 号报告中的 7.18 段曾经提到在建筑行业中经常有一连串合约的关系,如发展商与承建商有一个合约,接下去承建商与分承建商又会是另一个合约,分承建商会与分分承建商或物料供应商又有另一个合约。在这种一连串合约关系下,报告认为是建筑行业的惯例,只向合约的一方索赔损失而不会绕过合约在另一个其他合约中采取行动即使是后者的合约会提供给他一些合约利益。这 7.18 段是这样写的:"We should clarify that... we do not see our second limb as cutting across the chain of sub – contracts that have traditionally been a feature of [the construction] industry. For example, we do not think that in normal circumstances an owner would be able to sue a sub – contractor for breach of the latter's contract with the head – contractor. This is because, even if the sub – contractor has promised to confer a benefit on the expressly designated owner, the parties have deliberately set up a chain of contracts which are well understood in the construction industry as ensuring that a party's remedies lie against the other contracting party only."

这带来收货人的争辩说,在本案例所提供的无单放货保函,正是一连串的合约关系,所以应该有同样的考虑就是不应该绕过合约关系,即使其他的合约有提供利益给第三人。但这也被高院与上诉庭所否定,认为法律委员会的说法顶多只是局限在他们所理解的建筑行业,这不代表只要是有一连串合约的关系,就会是否定了 1999 年的《Contract (Right of Third Parties) Act》的适用。其中上诉庭的 Clarke 大法官是这样说:

"Mr. Berry(收货人代表大律师) submitted that similar considerations apply to the chain of LOIs(无单放货保函) here. He recognized that this was not a chain of quite the kind which commonly exists in the construction industry but he drew attention to the fact that the report referred to chains of sale contracts and submitted that chains of charter – parties are common in the maritime industry, as for example a time charter, a sub – time charter, a voyage charter and a sub – voyage charter, and that similar considerations should apply both to them and to these two LOIs. His essential point was that, as in the case of other chain contracts, the parties had expressly set up the contractual arrangements as described above, namely between the owners and the charterers and between the charterers and the receivers.

The Judge(指一审高院的大法官) did not accept those submissions when they were made to him. In par. 45 of his judgment he referred to the two examples of chains in the Law Commission Report, said that the contents of the Report did not assist the receivers any more under his head than they had done under s. 1 (1) (a) of the 1999 Act, and added:

Those situations are well – known and provide a commercial background of practice to contracts which are unlikely to cut across the legal framework customarily employed. Here there is no such background. Letters of indemnity take a number of different forms and have given rise to a wealth of arguments between parties as to their terms. Each has to be construed according to its own terms.

We agree with the Judge. We say nothing about the position on the case of a chain of charter – parties but we agree that there is no tradition of chain LOIs similar to the examples given in the report. All depends upon the construction of the receivers' LOI. The reasons we have given in reaching our conclusion under the first issue also point to the correct resolution of this issue. If we are right in agreeing with the Judge that both cll. 1 and 3 of the LOI were intended to be for the benefit of the owners, it makes no sense to hold that it was nevertheless intended that receivers' liability should not be directly to the owners. For example, as pointed out earlier, it was the owners who needed the benefit of cl. 3 in order to secure the release of the vessel from arrest. They needed the bail or other security, not the charterers. We see nothing in the LOI to lead to the conclusion that the parties did not intend cll. 1 and 3 to be enforceable by the owners. The whole purpose of the receivers' LOI was on the one hand to ensure that the receivers received the cargo from the ship without production of the original bill of lading and on the other hand to ensure that the owners were fully protected from the consequences of arrest or other action which might be taken by the holders of the original bills of lading. In short, in our judgment, the Judge was correct on this second issue as well as the first. ”

6.1.2.2.5 有关案例之三：Prudential Assurance Co Ltd v. Ayres

第三个是上诉庭的 Prudential Assurance Co Ltd v. Ayres (2007) EWHC 775 先例，是有关办公楼的租约由英国著名的保险公司 Prudential Assurance 作为二房东(它实际上也是租客,但获得房东的许可转租)把部分的办公楼出租给一家美国律师所的 Ayres 律师与另一位合伙人。事后 Ayres 在获得房东与二房东的许可下再把部分办公楼转租给了另一家美国律师事务所 Altheimer & Gray,并在 2001 年 6 月 8 日四方(房东、二房东、Ayres 与 Altheimer & Gray)签了一份合约,而其中一条有关的重要条文是第 6 条,其中 6.3 条文要求 Altheimer & Gray 必须准时支付租金。另在 6.4 条文说明 Altheimer & Gray 如果违约不支付租金,Ayres 就要支付租金给 Prudential Assurance。可以说这 6.4 条文等于是一条“补偿条文”(Indemnity Clause)或 Ayres 是作为 Altheimer & Gray 会准时支付租金的担保人。

稍后在 2001 年 6 月 21 日,Prudential Assurance 与 Altheimer & Gray 再签订了一份“附加契约”(Supplemental Deed),其中有 2.1 条文说明 Altheimer & Gray 如果付不起租金,Prudential Assurance 索赔的损失只能局限在律师所的资产,不能索赔合伙人

个人的资产。另外2.2条文说明 Altheimer & Gray 如果清盘而且清盘人有权向合伙人提出额外的索赔,Prudential Assurance 也不能参与。Prudential Assurance 如果向清盘人证明 Altheimer & Gray 欠它的债务,也必须披露这份契约的存在。其中重要的一句英文可节录,因为它根据 Section 1(3)有提到第三人:"... Consequently any recovery by the Landlord (指 Prudential Assurance), against the Tenant (Altheimer & Gray) **or previous tenant** (指以前的租客,这也是第三人的描述) under the Lease for any such default shall be limited to the assets of the Partnership and shall not extent to the personal assets of any individual partner therein other than the capital and current accounts of such partners in the Partnership."

显然在附加契约,Altheimer & Gray 的目的就是减少合伙人律师的个人责任,希望把租约的责任只局限在律师所的资产(而一家律师所的资产恐怕是很少,因为律师所赚钱的本事就是靠个别律师的头脑)。但这一个契约,Ayres 并没有参与。另一提的是 Prudential Assurance 与 Altheimer & Gray 契约的条件实际上在2001年的3月份就已经谈妥,这是在四方合约签订之前的事情。接下去是这家 Altheimer & Gray 由于业务不好在2003年11月21日清盘。期间,也欠下了大约150万英镑的租金。而 Prudential Assurance 也就开始向 Ayres 索赔这笔钱。这就涉及一个很重要的抗辩并涉及1999年的《Contract (Right of Third Parties) Act》,就是 Ayres 指称附加契约提供了一个合约利益给第三人,也就是限制赔偿责任,而 Ayres 正是符合附加契约中对第三人的描述,也就是"以前的租客"(previous tenant)。

在第一审是判 Ayres 胜诉,但这个判决之后被上诉庭推翻,可见对 Section 1(1)(b)与 Section 1(2)所针对的情况的争议性和不肯定。上诉庭不认为 Prudential Assurance 与 Altheimer & Gray 在订立附加契约的时候有订约意图让 Ayres 获得合约利益,Moore - Bick 大法官的判决内容只小部分节录如下:"One can therefore fairly summarise the position as known to both parties immediately prior to the execution of the Supplemental Deed as follows: (a) the Prudential had agreed to an assignment of the lease to Altheimer & Gray on terms that the respondents (指 Ayres) guaranteed payment of the rent and the performance of all its other terms, notwithstanding any arrangements that it might itself make with Altheimer & Gray; (b) the respondents had agreed to assign the lease to Altheimer & Gray on terms that Altheimer & Gray undertook to perform its terms and to indemnify them against any failure to do so; (c) the Prudential had agreed to limit its right of recourse in the event of any default by Altheimer & Gray in the performance of the lease to partnership assets; (d) the respondents were aware of that; (e) the scope of the respondents' liability to the Prudential had not arisen for consideration; (f) the scope of Altheimer & Gray's liability to the respondents had not arisen for consideration."[这里是简单总结了双方签订附加契约时的背景:(a)Prudential Assurance 同意 Ayres 把租约转让给 Altheimer & Gray,但要求 Ayres 保证租金准时支付和其他条款的履行,不管 Prudential Assurance 自己和 Altheimer & Gray 之间的安排。(b)Ayres 同意把租约转让给 Altheimer & Gray,只要 Altheimer & Gray 履行条款,如果没有履行要对他进行赔偿。(c)Prudential Assurance 同意把 Altheimer & Gray 赔偿责任限制在律师所的资产。(d)Ayres 知道这个情况。[e]Ayres 对 Prudential 的责任范围没有考虑。(f)Altheimer & Gray 对 Ayres 的责任范围也没有考虑。]

从上诉庭对订立附加契约时的背景做出总结,可以看到现在英国法院对合约的解释更注重合约方的真正订约意图,而不是只关注合约的用字/措辞。这就表示订约时的背景十分重要,这会显示了他们到底在合约的用字或措辞代表了什么意图。接下去 Moore - Bick 大法官提到了附加契约如果提供合约利益给 Ayres 会带来十分不肯定与困难的情况,说:"If the clause is to be construed as limiting the Prudential's rights against the respondents(指 Ayres), it is necessary to read it as if it provided that the amount that could be recovered from the respondents should not exceed the value of the assets of the partnership or, perhaps, the amount that could be recovered from the partnership in a liquidation. Such a construction gives rise to great uncertainty, however, because in the event of a failure to pay rent the Prudential might wish for purely practical reasons to pursue the respondents rather than Altheimer & Gray. If it were to do so, there would be considerable uncertainty about how much it was entitled to recover and the date at which that was to be determined. Both the background to the transaction and the absence of any provision addressing questions of that kind suggest that it was not what the parties had in mind."(其中一个困难是如果 Altheimer & Gray 没有支付租金, Prudential Assurance 很可能直接起诉 Ayres 而不是参与 Altheimer & Gray 的清盘作为其中一个债权人。如果发生这种情况就会对 Ayres 需要赔偿的金额造成极大的不肯定,因为无法确定 Altheimer & Gray 有多少资产与清盘后会分摊给 Prudential Assurance 的债务多少钱。)

Moore - Bick 大法官继续从附加契约与四方合约约定与签订的日期(这也是背景的部分)与大家的做法做出考虑,发觉很难接受 Prudential Assurance 与 Altheimer & Gray 有这种提供利益给 Ayres 的订约意图说:"Given the background to the Supplemental Deed I find it very difficult to accept that the parties to it intended to limit the scope of the respondents' liability to the Prudential or the Prudential's right to enforce that liability in the ordinary way. Had that been their intention, they would surely have made the respondents a party to the Supplemental Deed and would have included a provision which clearly limited the scope of their liability to the Prudential. Equally, it is highly unlikely that, having settled the terms of the Supplemental Deed some months earlier, they would have entered into a Licence(指四方合约) containing unqualified covenants on the part of the respondents in relation to the performance of the obligations under the lease. I think there is much force in Mr. Trace's (Prudential Assurance 代表大律师) submission that the respondents' construction substantially deprives the Prudential of the benefit of those covenants in the very circumstances in which they were most needed..."(在这个附加契约的背景下,Moore - Bick 大法官认为很难接受 Prudential Assurance 和 Altheimer & Gray 有意图限制第三人 Ayres 对 Prudential Assurance 在四方合约的补偿或担保责任。如果他们有这样的意图,就很容易可以在契约中把 Ayres 拉进来让他变成其中的一方或有明确条文写明限制 Ayres 的补偿或担保责任。同样的,也不大可能在附加契约已经谈妥的3个月后的四方合约中也不限制 Ayres 的补偿或担保责任。Moore - Bick 大法官也接受 Prudential Assurance 的代表大律师所说是如果 Ayres 可以限制补偿或担保责任,Prudential Assurance 就在它最需要保障的情况下失去了绝大部分利益。毕竟是如果赔偿只局限在 Altheimer & Gray 清盘的资产,Prudential Assurance 大可以参与清盘而不再需要 Ayres 提供担保了。)

再接下去是 Moore - Bick 大法官接受他这样判法是与附加契约的2.1条文的文字/措辞有冲突,但这是较早前贵族院在被视为合约的传统解释方法和现在的解释方法的分水岭先例的 Investors Compensation Scheme v. West Bromwich Building Society (1998) 1 WLR 896 有同样的做法,就是找出双方订约时的意图作为合约的解释,即使是与合约文字/措辞有矛盾。Moore - Bick 大法官说:

"The judge felt unable to accept the Prudential's argument in this case because it involved an ungrammatical reading of the second sentence of clause 2.1 which he regarded as part of a conscious design to exclude recourse by the Prudential to the partners' personal assets through the medium of the respondents. I can quite see that from the partners' perspective that would be a desirable course, but it is one that has significant implications for the Prudential and for the respondents themselves. Taking an objective view of the language used by the parties in the Supplemental Deed set against the background to which I have referred, I think it is clear that the purpose of the Supplemental Deed was to limit the scope of the assets to which a claimant should be entitled to have recourse to enforce claims under the lease. I find it impossible to accept that the parties intended to alter in a significant way the nature of the relationship between the Prudential and the respondents that had been established under the Licence.

I recognise that to construe the Supplemental Deed in this a way may be said to do violence to its language, but I am fortified by the approach taken to the not dissimilar problem in Investors Compensation Scheme v. West Bromwich Building Society. There too the judge felt that the construction he favoured as reflecting the parties' intention might be open to the criticism that it did violence to the language of the document, but his approach was upheld by a majority of their Lordships, who clearly did not draw the line at correcting errors of syntax in the course of interpreting the document in the manner that reflected the intention of the parties."

6.1.2.2.6 有关案例之四:Dolphin Maritime v. Sceriges Angfartygs Assurans

在6.1.2.2.1段提到的Dolphin Maritime v. Sceriges Angfartygs Assurans (2009) 2 Lloyd's Rep. 123先例,主要讨论的是船东互保协会的保函有没有根据1999年的立法Section 1(1)(b)提供给Dolphin Maritime合约利益。这里主要讨论即使保函提供给Dolphin Maritime合约利益,双方是否根据Section 1(2)有订约意图让Dolphin Maritime的第三人有合约利益让他可以直接执行合约。

这里再节录一次保函的相关部分:"The LOU was to:'The Owners and/or Underwriters of the cargo detailed below ("the Cargo Interests") c/o Dolphin Maritime & Aviation Services Ltd. ... The Club undertook to pay to Dolphin on your behalf or to any solicitors you may appoint such sums as may be due pursuant to a final and unappealable judgement issued by a US Court or as may be agreed to be recoverable from the owners of the (Vessel) in respect of claims in respect of the cargo up to a total of US $17.5 million...'."

上诉庭的Christopher Clarke大法官是这样说:

"It seems to me unreasonable to suppose that the parties to the LOU intended the provision for payment to Dolphin or some solicitor of the underwriters to preclude payment to the underwriters direct. If, however, the contract must be construed as having that effect, the next question is whether the parties would vary that agreement by agreeing to make and receive payment direct. Dolphin must necessarily contend that section 2 of the Act prevents such a variation since, if the parties were entitled to vary the agreement, they must be taken to have done so by asking for and making payment to the underwriters. (Christopher Clarke大法官说他看来保函不像有这样的订约意图提供利益与必须支付赔偿金额给Dolphin Maritime或者保险人将来会指定的律师所,而不能直接支付给保险人。如果保函能够这样解释,下一个问题就是1999年立法之Section 2会否限制互保协会与保险人事后改变这个合约的订约自由,就是改为把钱直接支付给保险人。)

It appears to me unrealistic to suppose that, by agreement that the Club would pay Dolphin or any solicitors appointed by the underwriters, the Club and the underwriters intended that Dolphin should, were no solicitors had been appointed by the underwriters, have an enforceable right to require payment of the settlement monies to it, with the result that, although the underwriters could, consistently with the LOU, appoint solicitors and ask the Club to pay them, they could not without breaching Dolphin's rights under the LOU legitimately agree with the Club that it should be paid direct. (这里说不通的地方如果货方或代位保险人没有指定代表律师,保函可以被解释为Dolphin Maritime根据立法有一个权利作为第三人向船东互保协会强制执行,迫使后者支付这笔850万美元。但如果保险人指定代表律师[虽然这一个指定是通过Dolphin Maritime,但在名义上该律师还是货方或代位保险人的代理人,不可能是Dolphin Maritime的代理人,因为它根本不是当事人],显然根据保函规定就会是船东互保协会把赔偿金额支付给该代表律师而不是给Dolphin Maritime。这一来,岂非船东互保协会还是会破坏了Dolphin Maritime 在1999年立法下的权利,可以向船东互保协会提出索赔?)

If such a right was intended to exist it is unclear what the position would be if a solicitor or solicitors were in fact appointed by the underwriters. It would be surprising if Dolphin, assuming it had a right beforehand, would now have no right at all. . . . "(如果 Dolphin Maritime 有这一个立法的权利,但这个立法权利因为货方或代位保险人事后指定了代表律师而失去,就有一点讲不通到底怎样造成这个结果,从有权变为无权。)

6.1.2.2.7 有关案例之五:CLAAS Medical Centre Pte Ltd v. Ng Boon Ching

第五个先例是新加坡的 CLAAS Medical Centre Pte Ltd v. Ng Boon Ching (2010) 2 SLR 386,Dr. Ng 和5位医生作为股东成立了 CLAAS。Dr. Ng 在之前就拥有一家名为 BCNG Holding 的公司。在2005年4月,Dr. Ng 以192万新加坡币的价格将 BCNG 的60%的股份出售给 CLAAS,并在买卖合约中给 CLAAS 一个选择可以在2年内以128万新加坡币的价格购买剩下的40%。在2005年11月,所有股东签订了另一个合约,其中包括一条"禁止竞争条文"(non-competition clause),约定股东在出售股票3年内不得从事与 CLAAS 有竞争的业务,如果违反 Dr. Ng 要支付100万新加坡币的罚款,其余的5位看来名气没有这么大的医生如果违反则支付70万新加坡币的罚款。2007年4月,Dr. Ng 开了一家开展与 CLAAS 类似业务的医疗中心。之后Dr. Ng 起诉 CLAAS 要求支付购买 BCNG Holding 的余款。CLAAS 反诉 Dr. Ng 违反了禁止竞争条文,要求赔偿100万新加坡币。

这个先例首先要解决的问题是 CLAAS 能否根据新加坡立法的《Contracts (Rights of Third Parties) Act 2002》之 Section 2(1)(b)(内容与英国1999年的《Contract [Right of Third Parties] Act》之 Section 1[1][b]相同),作为第三人要求执行这一个禁止竞争条文。在一审中,新加坡高院认为合约写明了如果有股东违反了这个禁止竞争条文,是要赔偿 CLAAS 并规定了具体金额,所以该条文毫无疑问是提供给了 CLAAS 一个合约利益。但最富争议的是,合约方(就是所有的6位医生)是否有订约意图让 CLAAS 有权利执行这个条文。11月的合约的第12.1(ii)条文表示如果所有合约方书面同意,他们可以终止这个合约,并没有提到需要 CLAAS 的同意。这与合约方有订约意图提供给 CLAAS 一个合约利益有不符,因为合约方随意可终止或改变合约就可以随意剥夺提供了给第三人的利益。另合约的第14.5条文是"禁止转让条文"(Prohibition of Assignment Clause),除非有其他合约方的书面同意。法院认为根据这两条条文可以看出合约方的订约意图是为了保护合约方(6位医生)的利益,而并没有意图让 CLAAS 作为第三人获得合约利益并有权执行这一个禁止竞争条文。

这个判决在上诉庭被推翻,上诉庭对两个条文的解释都有不同意见。简单的合约方保留终止或修改合约的权利或者禁止转让条文,并不能说明合约方没有订约意图让第三人获得合约利益并有权执行合约条文。上诉庭的大法官是这样说:

"These provisions(指11月的合约的条文),by spelling out the circumstances which would restrict the liberty of the contracting parties to rescind or vary their contract, would suggest that the mere fact that a term in the contract permits the parties to terminate it does not *ipso facto* mean that benefits conferred therein on a third party is not intended to be enforced by the third party. Of particular significance is s 3(3)(指新加坡的《Contracts (Rights of Third Parties) Act 2002》之 Section 3[3],内容与英国 1999 年的《Contract (Right of Third Parties) Act》的 Section 2[3]相同) which provides that for the parties to override the rights acquired by the third party pursuant to the latter's assent or reliance, the contract must expressly provide that the parties may rescind or vary the contract without the consent of the third party. If the mere presence of a reservation of a right to the contracting parties to terminate or vary the contract would amount to there being no intention to confer on a named third party a right to sue for the benefits conferred thereunder, then there would not have been any need to have those elaborate provisions in s 3. Chitty on Contracts vol 1 (Thomson Reuters (Legal) Limited, 30th Ed, 2008) at para 18 – 091, states the following: Nor is the presumption rebutted merely because in the contract, A and B had reserved the right to rescind or vary the contract: this follows from the provisions with regard to such rescission or variation made in s 2 of the [UK Act]...

Turning to cl 14.5, which prohibited the assignment of rights and benefits under the Agreement without the prior consent in writing of the other parties, and which provision the Judge took to be a factor in determining that it was not the intention of the parties to confer a right on the Appellant(指 CLAAS) to sue for the benefits prescribed in its favour under cl 11, we think, with respect, that this view involves the conflation of two different concepts. There is nothing inconsistent or incompatible between the express conferment of a benefit on a named third party and the restriction on the right of assignment of a contracting party without the consent of the other contracting parties. When the parties by express terms confer a benefit upon a third party, that is not an assignment and has nothing to do with assignment..."(最后一段与在本章 5.2 段介绍的建筑合约的 St Martins Property Corporation Ltd v. Sir Robert McAlpine Ltd (1994) 1 AC 85 (HL)先例的说法类似。一种看法是禁止转让条文说明合约双方不想让第三人参与这一个合约并享有权利,可以解释是没有订约意图让第三人有权执行这个合约。另一种看法[也是新加坡上诉庭的看法]是说,禁止转让条文与给第三人一个合约利益并让他有权执行合约是两回事情。毕竟有权执行合约的第三人必须在合约中明示,而转让可以把合约利益转让给任何人。这两者之间并没有什么不一致与有矛盾的地方。)

6.1.2.2.8　Beswick v. Beswick 先例是否能明确订约双方有否订约意图的探讨

本章较早前已经有多处提到这个重要的贵族院先例 Beswick v. Beswick (1968) AC 538,可以说这 1999 年《Contract (Right of Third Parties) Act》立法的重要动力之一就是这个先例所带来的一些严重问题。在本小段探讨的就是在目前的立法下,Beswick v. Beswick 先例能否明确订约双方是有订约意图提供给第三人(Beswick 夫人)一个合约利益。

这里首先简单介绍该先例的案情,涉及一个名为 Peter Beswick 的老先生把生意交给了他名为 John Beswick 的侄子。作为交换的是侄子承诺会在伯伯死后照顾他的妻子(侄子的伯母或 Beswick 夫人,名为 Ruth),每周给她 5 英镑的生活费用。但在该老先生死后,他的侄子不履行承诺,Beswick 夫人不能以自己的名义起诉,因为她只是有关合约的第三人。该先例总算是通过另一个途径申张了正义,就是 Beswick 夫人以她丈夫遗产执行人的名义向贵族院取得一个"履约指令"(specific performance),强制侄子履行合约。但如果 Beswick 夫人没有这个身份,就根本没有人或什么名义可向法院申请救济了。

法律委员会 1996 年 242 号报告之 7.46 段认为立法就可以解决这一个先例的问题,让 Beswick 夫人可以以自己的名义起诉(通过申请履约指令或索赔损失)他的侄子,说:"the provision of old Mr Beswick's contract with his nephew providing for payment of an annuity to Mrs Beswick would give Mrs Beswick a presumed right of enforceability under our second limb. The nephew promised to confer the benefit (the annuity payments) on Mrs Beswick, who was expressly named. The presumption could only be rebutted if the nephew could demonstrate that, on the proper construction of the contract, he and old Mr Beswick had no intention at the time of contracting that Mrs Beswick should have the right to enforce the provision. In our view, the nephew would not be able to satisfy the onus of proof so that Mrs Beswick would have the right of enforcement."

上述是指该侄子有举证责任,但不容易成功证明他与 Beswick 老先生订约的时候没有意图给 Beswick 夫人一个合约利益,所以 1999 年立法应该就可以解决这类案件。但这被著名的 Treitel 教授在《Some Landmarks of Twentieth Century Contract Law》(Oxford University Press,2002 年)一文中质疑,就是有关的合约是 Beswick 老先生与他的侄子交给律师拟定,如果他们有这一个订约意图,可以很容易告诉律师在合约中说明 Beswick 夫人有这个权利或甚至把她加进来作为合约的一方。这一来,为什么该律师没有这样明确写明,这又可以有几种不同的可能性,如律师疏忽或是双方没有这一个订约意图。而没有这一个订约意图的原因又可能是当律师告诉了 Beswick 老先生与他的侄子如果他们提供给第三人这一个合约利益,他们将来对有关合约条文做出改变的权利就会失去,这导致了他们两位不愿意失去这一灵活性。

当然上述所讲纯粹是猜测,但可见这一个方面是非常复杂和不肯定。

6.2 Section 2:原订约双方能终止或改变合约权利的凝结点

Section 2 的措辞/用字部分如下:

"Variation and rescission of contract.

(1) Subject to the provisions of this section, where a third party has a right under section 1 to enforce a term of the contract, the parties to the contract may not, by agreement, rescind the contract, or vary it in such a way as to extinguish or alter his entitlement

under that right, without his consent if—(a) the third party has communicated his assent to the term to the promisor, (b) the promisor is aware that the third party has relied on the term, or (c) the promisor can reasonably be expected to have foreseen that the third party would rely on the term and the third party has in fact relied on it.

(2) The assent referred to in subsection (1)(a)—(a) may be by words or conduct, and (b) if sent to the promisor by post or other means, shall not be regarded as communicated to the promisor until received by him. . . ."

这一个问题的重要性是在订约自由的大原则下,原来的订约双方可以有完全的自由订立双方愿意接受的条文。订约自由也包括在合约还没有履行或履行完毕之前,双方同意解除合约。订约自由更加是包括了双方只要愿意,可以在任何合约有效与在履行期间对部分条文做出修改。但有了1999的《Contract (Right of Third Parties) Act》的立法后,这一个订约自由的权利就需要受到局限,否则会严重影响第三人。例如在一个简单与明确的案件,A承诺B支付1万美元给C,但A没有履行,这导致C根据1999年立法向A强制执行。但如果A与B之间还是有订约自由,A可以找B说我们的关系这么好,但你与C的关系只是泛泛之交,C只是你的经纪人或是代理人,根本不必理会他的利益。这一来A与B同意解除或改变他们之间原来的合约,如把支付1万美元给C的条文删除或改为10美元。在订约自由下,A与B完全能够这样做。但如果他们这样做的时间是在C已经委任了律师向A采取诉讼行动,甚至快要开庭,但因为A与B之间同意解除或改变合约条文,C就会突然从有权变为无权推进这个诉讼,而必须撤回向A的诉讼,并可能要赔付A的律师费用。这样再加上C的律师费用与花费的大量工作会令C损失惨重。

从上述例子看来,只要涉及第三人的利益,就不能让A与B的订约双方太晚对合约做出解除或修改。但如果太早就禁止订约双方的A与B不准对有关合约做出解除或修改,也是个问题。例如,A承诺B在一个月后支付1万美元给C,但在订约后的第二天,A发觉计算错误如漏了做出一些扣减,应该只支付8000美元。在通知了B之后,B也同意这一个计算并愿意做出修改。而当时C甚至还不知道有这样的安排,B也没有通知C。难道因为合约中存在有关条文提供利益给C,所以合约一经生效A与B就再也不能做出任何改动?这显然也不是好的法律,因为过分干预A与B的订约自由。

所以,必须找出一个公平合理的"凝结点"(crystallization)。在这个凝结点之前订约双方有完全的订约自由,但之后订约双方就再也没有权利解除或修改有关的条文影响获得合约利益的第三人。

要在两个极端(一个是订约方可在合约有效的任何时间内随意解除或修改合约,另一个是订约方一在合约提供利益给第三人,马上就失去解除或修改合约有关条文的权利)当中找一个中间点,又能是合理、实际与明确,并不容易。而在1999年立法,它找的一个"凝结点"是在:

(i) Section 2(1)(a)中规定的第三人告知合约的承诺方他同意提供利益给他的条文。至于告知的方法在 Subsection (2)(a)与(b)中有说明,是十分宽松,以口头与行动就可以足够成立。相比"立法转让"(statutory assignment),它是立法规定需要"转让人"(assignor)书面通知债务方把有关的金钱或财产转让给"受让人"(assignee)。所以为了尽快把凝结点确认下来,第三人应该尽快向合约的承诺方做出通知,好像 Dolphin Maritime v. Sceriges Angfartygs Assurans (2009) 2 Lloyd's Rep. 123 先例中 Dolphin Maritime 所做的那样。

(ii)合约承诺方知道有第三人依赖有关条文。估计这种情况会是像一个雇主为公司员工投保医疗保险,保险人知道有员工(第三人)依赖,故不能在没有员工的同意下"私下"与原订约方的雇主解除或修改保险合约,除非这样做不会影响员工的"利益"(benefit)。这估计也是香港法例为什么强制规定公司要将为雇员投保的保险合约展示在雇员都可以看到的地方的背后的原因。

(iii)合约承诺方可以"合理预计"(reasonably expect)会有第三人依赖有关条文,而第三人确也是依赖。这情况应该是与(ii)差不多,但合约内容给予第三人的利益可能比较隐蔽,需要作出合理预计。

而如果订约方"私下"解除或修改合约而妄顾了第三人的利益,后果会是第三人(C)直接起诉合约承诺方(A)时后者不得以此作为抗辩理由。或是第三人可向合约非承诺方(B)索赔损失,诉因可以是后者"诱导他人(合约承诺方)违约"(induce breach of contract),这可参阅本章 6.1.2.2.1 段和 6.1.2.2.6 段介绍的 Dolphin Maritime v. Sceriges Angfartygs Assurans 先例。

但最早订立的合约是用如何的措辞/用字仍是有至高无上的地位,即订约自由仍受到尊重。所以,Subsection 2(3)说:"2(3) Subsection (1) is subject to any express term of the contract under which— (a) the parties to the contract may by agreement rescind or vary the contract without the consent of the third party, or (b) the consent of the third party is required in circumstances specified in the contract instead of those set out in subsection (1)(a) to (c)"

从条文措辞/用字可见,订约方大可以一开始在订立合约时就明示规定可事后任何时间私下解除或修改合约,即使这样做会直接或间接影响第三人。这一开始已在合约中订明的规定是有效,但给予第三人一个利益而第三人同意或依赖了有关条文,双方再想规定同样的内容则是无效。

6.3 有关《Contract (Right of Third Parties) Act 1999》立法的总结

在部分介绍了这一个立法后,笔者可以说这个曾经被不少人认为是非常重要的可以让第三人很简单的主张他在一份非定约方合约权利的立法,,但看来也不是这么简单,而且也不可能包罗万有。例如 Treitel 教授在他的《The Law of Contract》(12th edn,2007 年)一书说,在本章第 2 段中提到的旅游合约的问题[类似 Jackson v. Horizon Holidays Ltd (1975) WLR 1468 先例],在这个 1999 年的立法下基本已经解决。但是如果案情涉及一位先生或女士只是以自己名义租用了一间度假屋,并没有明示有哪些第三人会一起使用这间度假屋(如配偶、子女等),那么1999年的立法就不适用。

另外事实上,有许多国际上通用的标准格式,已经普遍加上了一条标准条文(boiler - plate clause)针对这一个1999年立法的适用。例如在BIMCO拟定的名为NEWBUILDCON的标准造船合约格式的48条就说"Unless expressly identified in this Contract, no third parties shall have the right to enforce any terms of this Contract."至于背后的考虑是什么,笔者作为BIMCO文件委员会的副主席也说不清楚,反正就是害怕不知名的第三人前来主张他认为合约提供给他的利益,加上这也会影响订约双方在事后修改甚至解除合约的权利的灵活性。

如果这是一个商业社会的普遍与持久的做法,带来的结果就是令1999年立法所花的心血与时间白费了,这也表示不令人满意的第三人规则还是得不到解决。看来普通法还是需要在这方面想办法基本上解决这一个困境,如进一步放宽"例外情况"(exceptions),除了上述已经在3.1小段介绍的托管关系,3.2小段介绍的代理关系,3.3小段介绍的信托,3.4小段介绍的转让,3.7小段介绍的保险以及5段介绍的货物买卖和建筑合约等。另外在本章5.2、5.5与5.6小段提到的"广泛地位"(broader ground)也会是一个重要的发展。

第八章　同步/竞合责任、纯经济损失与合约纠纷中分摊责任与损失

1. 合约与侵权的同步责任

大部分的国家法律都承认合约与侵权的民事责任,在一般情况下它们是独立存在的。但也有不少情况下它们同步发生,也就是某一行为在违反合约的同时也构成侵权。举例说,违反“小心谨慎责任”(duty of care)的侵权责任很早就已经加在一些公共承运人(船舶)、托管人与雇主的身上,这在 Bagot v. Stevens Scanlan & Co Ltd (1966) 1 QB 197 先例中,Diplock 大法官说到:“... where the law in the old days recognised either something in the nature of a status like a public calling (such as common carrier, common innkeeper, or a bailor and bailee) or the status of a master and servant.”

针对实质货损货差的侵权责任,早在 Hayn v. Culliford (1879) 4 CPD 182 先例就已经判是船东有一个小心谨慎的责任。在该先例,案情涉及船东错误把食糖装在氧化锌下面。船东作为托管人也对货负有小心谨慎的责任:The “Kapetan Marcos” (1987) 2 Lloyd's Rep 321 先例。但许多情况下船东与货方也会有合约关系,这合约关系通常就是一份提单,而提单是强制适用 1924 年的《海牙规则》,其中 Article 3(2) 是要求船东作为承运人必须要妥善而小心谨慎地装卸与照管货物(the carrier shall properly and carefully load, handle, stow, carry, keep, care for, and discharge the goods carried)。这就是一个违约与托管/侵权同步发生的典型例子。

这一来,会带来怎样处理的问题,因为违约与侵权会带来很多不同的后果,这是由于侵权是属于“一般性法律”(general law),它的地位不会在个别不同的案件中有所变化。但在订约自由下,违约会导致要承担(或不承担)千变万化的不同的责任与损失赔偿。

2. 侵权与违约的不同后果

这些不同的后果在接下去的段节会介绍。

2.1　侵权可以规避合约中的管辖条文

在 The "Sindh" (1975) 1 Lloyd's Rep 372 先例，争议涉及提单下的侵占货物。受害方可以违约或侵权向船东起诉，而如果根据违约就受到提单中一条法国马赛的排外管辖条文约束，必须去该法院起诉。但如果根据侵权就不受到提单条文的约束，可以在英国法院以侵权作出起诉。

2.2　计算损失遥远性违约会是比侵权严格

这方面可举一个简单的例子，在《Clerk & Lindsell on Torts》(20th edn, 2010 年)一书之 1－03 段就提到惩罚性赔偿与返还性赔偿在侵权案件中经常会做出，但在违约案件中就不大会出现(for example, punitive and restitutionary damages may be awarded for torts where liability is imposed, but not for contract where the obligation was voluntarily undertaken and should give rise to remedies which compensate rather than punish)。

2.3　1945 年《The Law Reform (Contributory Negligence) Act》立法的适用

这是一个十分重要的不同后果，也是本章要针对之处。这就是双方都有错误与疏忽的情况下，在侵权案件中就可以根据 1945 年《The Law Reform (Contributory Negligence) Act》分摊责任与损失。在做法上基本与熟悉航运人士所知道的船舶碰撞责任与损失的分摊一致，这是依据早期的国际公约，也就是 1910 年的《碰撞公约》(Collision Convention)。但在违约案件中，就不适用该 1945 年的立法，也不是该立法所针对的。这表示在合约双方(或在 1945 年立法前的侵权双方)都有部分错误与疏忽的情况下(经常会有，双方互相指责与举证是对方的错误与疏忽导致损失)，法院或仲裁庭只能根据证据认定谁的错误与疏忽。而错得多的一方，即使只是 51/49 的比例，就要承担所有的损失。至于胜诉方后来的错误与疏忽，只要不能中断因果链，就不予考虑。而如果他的错误与疏忽的严重程度足够中断因果链，后果就是他要承担所有的损失，导致他从胜诉方变了败诉方。换言之，判决或裁决只能是一面倒，非黑即白。但是在侵权的情况下如果可以根据 1945 年立法分摊责任与损失，原告与被告之间的错误与疏忽被认定为 49/51，原告就只能向被告取回 51% 的损失，而不是全部了。这方面可先节录《Clerk & Lindsell on Torts》(20th edn, 2010 年)一书之 3－63 段所说："At common law the defence of contributory negligence was not available in contract, and nothing in the 1945 Act expressly extends contributory negligence to actions for breach of contract. Difficulty arises, however, when there is concurrent liability in contract and tort." 上述的节录提到了"同步/竞合责任"(concurrent liability)，也就是原告的诉因可以违约与侵权提出，就会带来 1945 年立法是否能够适用的困难。这也是本章要分析的重点。

2.3.1　1945 年立法的有关条文

在这里可先简单介绍 1945 年的立法，就是在侵权的诉讼中，如果受害方自己有部分过错，就不能成功向侵权方提出这部分损失的索赔，这是为了改变或补救普通法的严格性。在 1945 年立法下，如果受害方自己有部分过错，法院只是会减少他所索赔的损失赔偿,或受害方需要与侵权方分摊责任。在 Section 1(1)是说:"where any person suffers damages as a result partly of his own fault and partly of the fault of any other person or persons, a claim in respect of that damage shall not be defeated by reason of the fault of the person suffering the damage, but damages recoverable in respect thereof shall be reduced to such extend as the court thinks just and equitable having regard to the claimant's share in the responsibility for the damage."

至于对"fault"(错误)的定义,实是指错误与疏忽,并且会带来侵权的后果。这是在立法的 Section 4 所说:"'Fault' means negligence, breach of statutory duty or other act or omission which gives rise to a liability in tort or would, apart from this Act, give rise to the defence of contributory negligence."

2.3.2 分摊责任与损失比重的考虑

而如何在这规定下分摊损失,百分比如何,Denning 大法官在 Davies v. Swan Motor Co (1949) 2 KB 291 先例中说是不完全考虑"因果关系"(causation),而应是以"公道"来看这件不幸事件中双方应被怪责的比重:"Whilst causation is the decisive factor in determining whether there should be a reduced amount payable to the plaintiff, nevertheless, the amount of the reduction does not depend solely on the degree of the causation. The amount of the reduction of such an amount as may be found by the court to be 'just and equitable', having regard to the claimant's share in the responsibility for the damage. This involves a consideration, not only of the causative potency of a particular factor, but also of its blameworthiness."

2.3.3 1945 年立法适用的范围

这立法当时是明显要针对"侵权的疏忽行为"(tort of negligence),所以像车祸这种不幸的人身伤亡事件肯定是受其管制。但它不包括被告刻意对受害方的原告造成损失的欺诈性行为,这表示原告的损失索赔不会因为他有一定程度的错误与疏忽而被减少:Corporacion Nacional del Cobre del Chile v. Sogemin Metals (1997) 1 WLR 1396; Nationwide Building Society v. Thimbleby (1999) PNLR 733; Standard Chartered Bank v. Pakistan National Shipping Corp (No. 2)(2003) 1 AC 959。其他对是否适用这 1945 年立法有争议的近期侵权先例包括:Corr v. IBC Vehicles Ltd (2008) AC 884; Gary v. Thames Trains Ltd (2009) 2 WLR 351 CA。

本章主要探讨该立法能否适用在合约,如在违约时分摊损失?毕竟,1945 年立法没有排除合约,虽然它在措辞上是明确针对侵权。

2.3.4 针对合约争议能否适用的混乱判例

这方面有不少先例可介绍,首先可介绍 Quinn v. Burch Bros (Builders) (1966) 2 QB 370 先例。该先例中受害方的分承建商自己使用一个不稳固的支架,引致受伤,法院判是这新介入因素中断了因果链。但受害方提出他应该可以依据 1945 年的立法索赔一部分损失,即使不是全部,因为被告的承建商毕竟是有错误与疏忽,是他没有先提供一架稳固的梯子而带来整件不幸事件。

Paull 大法官觉得“发明”一新名词叫“疏忽违约”(negligent breach of contract)有点别扭,因为多数违约与疏忽没有关系。例如,承租人对安全港口、泊位的严格责任;船东的严格适航责任或“恪尽职责”(due diligence)适航责任,即使是委任了有水平的劳合社验船师,如果他犯了错船东还是需要承担责任:The “Muncaster Castle” (1961) 1 Lloyd's Rep 57 先例等,这都会是在违约方自己或他的雇员没有疏忽的情况下违约。但 Paull 大法官认为 1945 年的立法应该可适用在某些合约的争议,只要合约引进了疏忽的责任。只是在 Quinn v. Burch Bros (Builders)的先例中,受害方原告的损失被视为是太遥远。这一个先例的一审与上诉庭的判决在《McGregor on Damages》(18th edn,2009 年)一书有说:“... Applying these principles to the case before him, in which the defendant building contractors had in breach of contract failed to supply a step-ladder to the plaintiff sub-contractor who had then injured himself by using unsuitable equipment, Mr. Justice Paull held that this breach of contract did not constitute negligence for the purposes of the Act. Accordingly, the plaintiff could not invoke the apportionment provisions to support a limited recovery and his claim failed *in limine* because the damage was too remote. This decision was subsequently affirmed but without touching upon the contributory negligence issue; the Court of Appeal was content to hold for the defendants on the ground that their breach of contract did not cause the plaintiff's injury ...”

同样的判决还有 De Meza & Stuart v. Apple Van Straten Shena & Stone (1975) 1 Lloyd's Rep 498 (CA)先例,这在第一审被判是 1945 年立法适用,责任与损失分摊是被告要承担 70%,原告要承担 30%。但在上诉庭,双方都不愿意在这一方面争议,所以上诉庭没有机会作出任何判决。

但接下去有关 1945 年立法是否适用的先例持相反看法,这包括 Basildon District Council v. J E Lesser (Properties) (1985) QB 839 与 The “Shinjitsu Maru No 5” (1985) 1 Lloyd's Rep 568。

可以说这些不同判法直到 Vesta v. Butcher (1989) 1 Lloyd's Rep 331 先例才有了肯定性的说法。这些案例稍后会在本章第 11 段分段介绍。

2.4　不同索赔时效起算

另一个至关重要的不同后果就是在索赔时效的不同。虽然合约与侵权根据 1980 年的《Limitation Act》都有 6 年的时效,但由于起算的时间不同,导致侵权的时效一般比违约更为宽松。针对违约,时效的起算通常是针对被告违约的时间。但很多的违约通常不会马上造成损失与后果,原告也不会警觉。这特别是一些专业人士的错误与疏忽,如律师、工程师、建筑师或者医生作出了错误的专业意见,又或是建筑师的错误导致了新造的房屋有内在缺陷,多年后才会暴露出来。侵权时效的起算通常是针对损失的出现,所谓“有诉因的侵权”(actionable tort)是需要证明侵权方带来什么损失,这方面甚至会有立法针对如 1986 年的《潜在损失法》(Latent Damage Act),

显然对原告是好得多。现实中许多原告提出同步责任，把侵权也拖进合约的关系来，往往就是为了这一方面的优势。对航运熟悉的人士会知道在1924年《海牙规则》下，向承运人提出货损货差的索赔是受到在卸货港交货后的1年时效限制。这一年是很短的时间，不少收货人或他的代位保险人都会错过。这导致不少案件试图通过以侵权或同步责任，从而适用侵权的6年时效以得利。这导致了在1968年的《海牙—维斯比规则》中Article Ⅲ加上了一条条文加以约束说："The defences and limits of liability provided for in this Convention shall apply in any action against the carrier in respect of loss or damage to goods covered by a contract of carriage whether the action be founded in contract or in tort."

有关上述所讲，也可节录《Clerk & Lindsell on Torts》(20th edn，2010年)一书之32-17段所说："A breach of contract is actionable per se, and so a cause of action for breach of contract accrues, and the limitation period starts from, when the contract is broken rather than from when the damage flows from the breach. As this contrasts with the accrual of a cause of action in the tort of negligence which does require damage. Accordingly, in a case of concurrent liability in contract and tort, (which arises in many professional-client relationships) where damages occurs at a later point in time than the breach of duty it will be to the claimant's advantage for limitation purposes to sue for the tort of negligence rather than for breach of contract."

另也可以节录Goff勋爵在The Lloyd's Litigation (1994) 2 Lloyd's Rep 468先例中所说："I think it is desirable to stress at this stage that the question of concurrent liability is by no means only of academic significance. Practical issues, which can be of great importance to the parties, are at stake. Foremost among these is perhaps the question of limitation of actions. If concurrent liability in tort is not recognized, a claimant may find his claim barred at a time when he is unaware of its existence. This must moreover be a real possibility in the case of claims against professional men, such as solicitors or architects, since the consequences of their negligence may well not come to light until long after the lapse of six years from the date when the relevant breach of contract occurred. Moreover the benefits of the Latent Damage Act, 1986, under which the time of the accrual of the cause of action may be postponed until after the plaintiff has the relevant knowledge, are limited to actions in tortuous negligence. This lead to the startling possibility that a client who has had the benefit of gratuitous advice from his solicitor may in this respect be better off than a client who has paid a fee. Other practical problems arise, for example, from the absence of a right to contribution between negligent contract-breakers."

Goff勋爵上诉所讲的倒数第二句是举了一个有关律师提供错误的法律意见的例子，这会带来违约或侵权的诉因。如果客户支付了费用，这表示律师与客户之间有合约关系，时效是从提供错误法律意见的时间起算。但如果客户没有支付费用，律师纯粹是提供免费法律意见，这表示他们之间没有合约关系，因为没有对价或约因。但这一来，客户反而能够享有更长的时效。例如在多年后出事才发觉律师提供的法律意见是错误的，会是侵权的时效只是刚开始，但违约的时效已经届满。这显然是不令人感到满意的结果，怎会客户支付费用给律师反而是站在更不利的地位？

3. 处理违约与侵权同步责任的两种不同办法

基本上，能够处理的办法不外是两种。第一种办法就是强制原告必须按照合约起诉对方违约，不得以侵权起诉。法国法律就是这一个说法：The "Sindh" (1975) 1 Lloyd's Rep 372。但也并不是欧洲大陆所有的国家都接受同样的处理办法，如德国。而在英国，在早期的时候也一度是与法国一样，原告必须只按照合约起诉：Bean v. Wade (1885) 2 TLR 157 先例与 Groom v. Crocker (1939) 1 KB 194 先例。在后一个先例，涉及律师的错误与疏忽，就是判受害方必须根据合约关系起诉。英国是在相对近期才发展起来这一种所谓同步责任的法理。

第二种办法是允许受害方的原告自由选择根据违约或是侵权起诉，而如果原告以侵权起诉，法院或仲裁庭就必须看双方有关的合约中是否约定有与以侵权为诉因时法律地位不同的条文（如有更短的时效或赔偿金额限制）。如果有，就以双方约定的条文为准。可以说同步责任是英国目前的法律地位，这可节录《Clerk & Lindsell on Torts》(20th edn，2010 年）一书之 1－05 段所说："**Principles of tort and contract interact in two situations.** The first is where there is a contractual relationship between claimant and defendant but the claimant wishes to sue in tort in order to escape the narrower limitation principles in contract or to be able to make a claim going beyond what was agreed in the contract. In this situation, the courts will allow concurrent liability provided there is nothing in the contract which expressly or impliedly excludes liability in tort ..."

这里不妨随便拣一个笔者熟悉的海上运输中货损货差的案例来简单说明这一点，这是 The "Dong Do", Hong Kong High Court (Admiralty Jurisdiction Folio No 95 of 1988）先例。案情涉及一票电子产品从日本神户运来香港，但持有正本提单的收货人发觉货物损坏，于是在香港扣船并向船东提出索赔。但由于提出索赔的时候是已经过了 1924 年《海牙规则》或相关强制性法律（不论是日本或是香港都有相关立法）的 1 年时效，所以收货人是不能以违反提单合约向船东提出索赔，而需要改为以"托管或/与侵权"（bailment and/or tort）提出索赔，这是可以有长达 6 年的时效。这就带来了一个有关的争议，就是船东与收货人之间是否有合约关系。如果有，即使收货人有权以托管/侵权向船东提出索赔，香港法院也会倒过来看合约是否有不同约定的条文，并以该条文为准，也就是 1 年的时效还是避不开的。但如果船东与收货人之间没有合约关系，收货人以侵权提出起诉就完全不会受到任何的约束。这种情况也的确会出现，其中一个经常会出现的争议就是提单到底是“船东提单”（owner's bill）或是“承租人提单”（charterer's bill），因为船舶涉及租约，由承租人营运，就会任由承租人签发船东或他自己作为承运人的提单合约。这毕竟是订约自由，1924年《海牙规则》也没有干预。这方面的问题可看笔者《提单及其他付运单证》的第三章。再回来去看The“Dong Do”先例，如果提单是承租人提单，这表示收货人与船东之间并没有合约关系。由于货物是在船舶运输过程中由于船东/船员没有尽到小心谨慎的义务而导致了货损货差，收货人的托管/侵权诉讼就应该不成问题。但最后在该先例香港法院判是有关的提单属于船东提单，这表示双方有合约关系，收货人不能以同步责任的侵权诉讼回避合约中的1年时效，所以收货人败诉。Sears大法官的结论是：“The result is that I find this is a shipowner's bill and the plaintiffs' claim is defeated by virtue of the time-bar.”

4. 什么是疏忽的侵权？

侵权可以说是一种“民事过错”（civil wrongs），即如果被告违反了一个法律强加在他头上的责任，而这一个违反影响了一位无辜方或原告的利益，法律就会允许原告以个人的名义向被告提出赔偿的请求（breach of a legal duty which affects the interests of an individual to a degree which the law regards as sufficient to allow the individual to complain on his or her own account rather than as a representative of society as a whole）。

侵权有很多不同种类，本章无意涉及，如一些涉及严格责任的侵权，它们通常是通过立法把严格责任强加在个别人士，如针对危险动物的1971年《Animal Act》，针对产品责任与消费者保护的1987年《Consumer Protection Act》，海事业务人士熟悉的美国1990年《油污法》（Oil Pollution Act）等。

虽然普通法也有在少数的情况下强加严格责任的侵权，特别是针对土地权利的保护。例如，“侵入他人的土地”（trespass）或“滋扰”（nuisance）：Rylands v. Fletcher (1868) LR 3 HL 330。但在大部分的情况下是本章要涉及的侵权，就是被告的“错误与疏忽的侵权”（tort of negligence）。造成这种侵权需要四个要求，如下：（1）the existence in law of a duty of care situation, i. e. one in which the law attaches liability to carelessness. There has to be recognition by law that the careless infliction of the kind of damage in suit on the class of person to which the claimant belongs by the class of person to which the defendant belongs is actionable（法律要求一类人士对另一类人士负有一个“小心谨慎的责任”[duty of care]，如果因为错误与疏忽前者没有尽到小心谨慎的责任并导致后者的损失，后者就会变为原告，而前者变为被告）。（2）breach of the duty of care by the defendant, i. e. that it failed to measure up to the standard set by law（这基本与上述一致，就是被告违反了一个小心谨慎的责任，而是否小心谨慎是根据法律在不

同情况下认定的标准)。(3) a causal connection between the defendant's careless conduct and the damage(被告的错误与疏忽与原告的损失有直接因果关系)。(4) that the particular kind of damage to the particular claimant is not so unforeseeable as to be too remote(原告的损失并非是不能预见的,不会是太遥远)。

在这里主要先进一步解释法律怎样会强加一个"小心谨慎的责任"(duty of care),这在著名的先例 Caparo Plc v. Dickman (1990) AC 605,贵族院的 Bridge 勋爵提了三个要求:(1) foreseeability of damage arising from the negligent performance of the relevant operation(错误与疏忽的言行对所造成损失的可预见性)。(2) the existence of a sufficient relationship of proximity between the parties and(原告与被告之间的邻近关系)。(3) whether or not as a matter of legal policy it is "fair just and reasonable" that a duty of care should exist, the direct infliction of foreseeable physical damage is an established category of case where a duty exist(强加这一个小心谨慎的责任在被告是否公平与合理,这涉及公共政策的考虑)。

这三个要求带来了许多先例,笔者不妨先节录《Clerk & Lindsell on Torts》(20th edn,2010 年)一书有关这三个要求的进一步权威说法。首先是节录 8-16 段有关第一与第二的要求,如下:

"**Foreseeable and proximity** The criterion of reasonable foreseeability focuses on the knowledge that someone in the defendant's position would be expected to possess. The greater the awareness of the potential for harm, the more likely it is that this criterion will be satisfied. If the risk of harm is farfetched, a duty will not arise. Proximity focuses on the broader relationship between the parties. In a much cited passage of his judgment in Sutherland Shire Council v. Heyman (1985) 60 ALR 1, Deane J. described the requirement as follows: 'It involves the notion of nearness or closeness and embraces physical proximity (in sense of space and time) between the person or property of the plaintiff and the person or property of the defendant, circumstantial proximity such as an overriding relationship... of professional man and client and what might (perhaps loosely) be referred to as causal proximity in the sense of the closeness or directness of the causal connection or relationship between the particular course of conduct and the loss or injury sustained. It may reflect as assumption by one party of a responsibility to take care to avoid or prevent injury, loss or damage to the person or property of another or reliance by one party upon such care being taken where the other party ought to have known of such reliance. Both the identity and relative importance of the factors which are determinative of an issue of proximity are likely to varyin different categories of case.'

Thus proximity may consist of various forms of closeness - physical, circumstantial, causal or assumed. It involves considering the relationship from the perspective of both the defendant and the claimant. At root, it will reflect 'a balancing of the plaintiff's moral claim to compensation for avoidable harm and the defendant's moral claim to be protected from an undue burden of legal responsibility'. As such it will inevitably overlap with considerations of justice between the parties."

这第一个要求的可预见性与第二个要求的邻近关系,看来是十分接近或是同一回事,所以可一并解释。笔者只进一步说这些要求存在的原因是如果不加以限制会带来危险的后果与太多的侵权,这并非是好事。简单的例子是律师或是会计师提供给他的客户一个错误或疏忽的意见或报告,他们只要针对因该过错而导致的损失(不论是否有合约关系或有否收费)对客户负责。这是因为除了可预见的损失外,双方的关系也是邻近。但如果其他第三人看到了这一个文书的意见与报告,并依赖它而蒙受损失,第三人要求该律师或会计师承担侵权的责任就会是太危险了。毕竟,假设该错误的法律意见或财务报告被公开而导致有许多人参阅与依赖,这受害方会有上千上万的人。

接下去节录8-17段的有关第三个要求,如下:"**Fairness, justice and reasonableness** Justice and reasonableness is a test of 'ordinary reason and common sense'. It has been said that, in itself, 'the expression means little more than that the court should only impose a duty of care if it considers it right to do so'. It has been also referred to as an 'exercise of judicial pragmatism, which is the same as judicial policy'. As such it encompasses a wide range of considerations. At its narrowest, it focuses on justice and fairness as between the parties. At a broader level, it will consider the reasonableness of a duty from the perspective of legal policy, focusing on the operation of the legal system and its principles. At a still wider but more controversial level, it may take account of the social and public policy implications of imposing a duty."

已经在较早时提到过,这一个考虑往往涉及公共政策。例如涉及航运业务人士就知道"船级社"(classification society)在检查与确认船舶适航的时候犯错与疏忽,在英国法律下不必对船上货物因此蒙受损失负侵权责任,这是在贵族院的先例 The "Nicholas H"(1992) 2 Lloyd's Rep 481 确定。贵族院认为船东才是需要对船舶的适航负最主要的责任,船级社的检查作用只是从属性。而货方与船级社之间不存在任何合约的关系,也没有任何接触,货方只是依赖船东恪尽职责令船舶适航。换言之,货方与船级社之间没有一个太邻近的关系。但这样的判法也涉及公共政策的考虑,贵族院认为船级社是一个"为整体航运利益"服务的机构,履行了应由船籍国完成对船舶安全监督的功能,如果令船级社承担责任就会使船级社面临大量的索赔。

再多举一个英国普通法不对消防员强加一个小心谨慎责任的例子:Digital Equipment Co Ltd v. Hampshire CC (1997) 2 Lloyd's Rep 161。毕竟在一个紧急的情况下,消防员会犯错与疏忽是经常会有。例如在救火的过程中把灭火系统过早关闭,或者摸错地点导致晚到火场。

5. 侵权造成实质损失与纯经济损失的不同对待

疏忽的侵权造成“实质损失”(physical loss),包括人身伤亡或是财产损失,是一直不存在问题,只要该损失不会是太遥远。而如果有了实质损失,受害方的原告也可以同时索赔他的“间接经济损失”(consequential economic loss)。例如无辜的行人可向错误与疏忽的车主索赔他的实质损失,这主要包括了他的伤亡,也同时可包括经济损失如误工损失与医疗费用等。但英国法律对另一种名为“纯经济损失”(pure economic loss)就十分谨慎,这些损失很多是来自被告的侵权而导致第三人由于与受害方原告之间的关系而蒙受损失。例如,原告与第三人订下的合约因为侵权而无法履行。但第三人完全不存在他自己有人身伤亡或是财产损失,所以被称为纯经济损失。这种先例有很多,如:Cattle v. Stockton Waterworks Co (1875) L. R. 10 Q. B. 453;SCM (United Kingdom) Ltd v. W. J. Whittal & Son Ltd (1970) 3 All ER 245;Spartan Steel and Alloys v. Martin & Co Ltd (1973) QB 27;The “Mineral Transporter” (1985) 2 Lloyd's Rep 303 等,美国也有类似的先例,Robins Dry Dock & Repair Co v. Flint (1927) 275 U. S. 303。

5.1 疏忽的侵权不允许受害方索赔纯经济损失的权威说法

早在 Allan v. Barclay (1864) 2 M. 873 先例,Kinloch 大法官就说:“The grand rule on the subject of damages is, none can be claimed except as naturally and directly arise out of the wrong done; and such, therefore, as may reasonably be supposed to have been in the view of the wrongdoer. Tried by this test, the present claim appears to fail. The personal injuries of the individual himself will be properly held to have been in the contemplation of the wrongdoer but he cannot be held bound to have surmised the secondary injuries done to all holding relations with the individual, whether that of a master, or any other.”

另在贵族院的 The “Aliakmon” (1986) 1 Lloyd's Rep 1 先例,Brandon 勋爵说:“My Lords, there is a long line of authority for a principle of law that, in order to enable a person to claim in negligence for loss caused to him by reason of loss of or damage to property, he must have had either the legal ownership of or a possessory title to the property concerned at the time when the loss or damage occurred, and it is not enough for him to have only had contractual rights in relation to such property which have been adversely affected by the loss of or damage to it.”

5.2 谨慎的原因与政策

英国法律针对这方面谨慎的原因是怕允许索赔纯经济损失会引起“打开大水门”(floodgate effect)的效应而导致没完没了的诉讼。例如在一个简单的车祸导致一个无辜行人受伤,会有许多与上述无辜行人有关系的人士蒙受纯经济损失。他的哥哥/弟弟会放下工作去医院探望他、他的公司很需要他及时完成工作否则就会有损失，但他就是上不了班、等待他完成工作的一些公司客户也因为这一宗交通事故而蒙受延误等，这都会导致他们的纯经济损失。

这方面的谨慎已经被视为是英国法律的一个政策上的考虑，这在不少先例谈到，例如 Candlewood Navigation Corporation Ltd v. Mitsui Ltd（1985）2 Lloyd's Rep. 303 先例，Fraser 勋爵说："... the justification for denying a right of action to a person who has suffered economic damage through injury to the property of another is that for reasons of practical policy it is considered to be inexpedient to admit his claim."

这也在 The "Aliakmon" 先例中，Brandon 勋爵有提到说："Mr. Clarke（被告代表大律师）said, rightly in my view, that the policy reason for excluding a duty of care in cases like The Mineral Transporter and what I earlier called the other non-recovery cases was to avoid the opening of the floodgates so as to expose a person guilty of want of care to unlimited liability to an indefinite number of other persons whose contractual rights have been adversely affected by such want of care."

最后可节录《Clerk & Lindsell on Torts》(20th edn, 2010 年）一书，提到纯经济损失要严格控制是有三个理由，其中第一个就是"大水门"的考虑。8－91 段是这样说："One person's negligent conduct may cause financial loss to another unrelated to any physical damage where that other is dependent upon that person's services for his financial well being or relies on that person's statements when making for his financial decisions. Such a loss is referred to as a 'pure' financial or economic loss as it is not the consequence of physical damage to the person's body or property. Three features distinguish such loss from loss resulting from physical damage. *First*, whilst the links between negligence and physical damage depend largely on the laws of nature and necessarily limit the type of relationship giving rise to a claim, those between negligence and pure financial loss are primarily human in creation and can form a complex web through which financial losses can ripple out from the one negligent act. *Secondly*, because the economic relationships are frequently created rather than imposed, the participants in the web have a greater opportunity to use contracts to determine the level of risk to be taken and the degree of protection from loss required. Furthermore, in some situations legislation provides a framework for relationships in which risk, protection and responsibility are already balanced. *Thirdly*, as Hobhouse LJ has observed, 'in a competitive economic society the conduct of one person is always liable to have economic consequences for another and, in principle, economic activity does not have to have regard to the interests of others and is justifiable by the actor having regard to his own interests alone'. Furthermore, as McHugh J, has noted, 'pure economic losses frequently result in mere transfers of wealth. The claimant's loss is the defendant's or a third party's gain [whereas] harm to a person or property ordinarily involves a new loss to social wealth'. These features have led the courts to take a more restrictive approach to the imposition of a duty of care in relation to pure financial loss than in relation to physical damage. A special relationship between the parties is required to justify a duty. The starting point for any analysis of the required relationship is the decision of the House of Lords in Hedley Bryne & Co Ltd v. Heller & Partners Ltd (1964) AC 465."

5.3 有关先例之一:The "Mineral Transporter"

这方面可以介绍其中一个重要的先例,把这一个问题说得更明白,这是英国枢密院的 The "Mineral Transporter" (1985) 2 Lloyd's Rep 303 先例。案情是有关船舶在澳大利亚 Port Kembla 发生碰撞,抛锚的 Ibaraki Maru 轮受损并需要在澳大利亚进行暂时修理与在日本进行最后修理。法院判决碰撞的另一船舶 Mineral Transporter 轮承担100%的责任。蒙受损失的 Ibaraki Maru 轮不是真正船东,而是光租承租人,他需要承担所有的修理费用与租金损失,他请求的损失赔偿是没有问题,因为在英国法律下蒙受财产损失的"真正所有权人"(legal ownership)或"托管权人"(possessory title)是可以向侵权方索赔损失:The "Aliakmon" (1986) 2 Lloyd's Rep 1。但光租承租人在当时把船舶期租给了另一家公司,他也蒙受损失,因为在修理的期间无法营运该船舶赚取更高的运费或租金。换言之,期租承租人所索赔的是纯经济损失。这在澳大利亚法院被判是可以成功,但最后上诉去了英国枢密院被改变过来,判期租承租人败诉。Fraser 勋爵是这样说:"... the argument, if accepted, would have far-reaching consequences, which would run counter to the accepted policy of the law. If this exception to the rule against allowing recovery by persons who are in merely contractual relationship with the injured party were admitted, these appears to be no reason why contracts under time charters should be treated differently in this regard from other contracts between the owner or disponent owner of a ship and other parties. On the not uncommon case where the damaged vessel is the subject of a chain of sub-charters and sub-sub-charters, made at different dates, some of the charters may be profitable to the charterer though the respective rates of profit may be different, and some charters may result in a loss to the charterer. Is a sub-charterer who is wholly or partly released from a loss-making charter to be expected to contribute to the damages fund(这是指船舶最高赔偿责任基金), in order to relieve the wrongdoer pro tanto? That would be surprising, yet it seems to be the logical consequence of treating the damages as a fund which is divisible among those who have suffered loss in proportion to their loss. And if claims for economic loss by sub-charterers are to be admitted, why not also claims by any person with a contractual interest in any goods being carried in the damaged vessel, and by any passenger in her, who suffers economic loss by reason of the delay attributable to the collision? An exceedingly wide new range of liability would be opened up. Their Lordships accordingly reject this submission."(Fraser 勋爵大致上说如果接受与受害方只有合约关系的当事人[如期租承租人]在碰撞蒙受损失时也可以

提出索赔纯经济损失,就没有理由只局限租约,这就会带来大量与受害方有合约关系的第三人前来索赔纯经济损失,如本来安排在新加坡添加燃油或新加坡修理但由于船舶碰撞改了不再去新加坡,这导致燃油商或新加坡修理厂也蒙受纯经济损失可以提出索赔。而光是租约,经常会有一连串的租约,变了“分分租家”也可以前来分一杯羹。在碰撞也不是只有船东或光租承租人是受害方,船上的货物或乘客如果蒙受损坏或伤亡也是受害方,可以向对方负责的船舶提出索赔。但如果与他们有合约关系的第三人也受到该碰撞的影响前来索赔纯经济损失,就真的是没完没了。涉及船舶碰撞或其他海事事故,还会有另一个方面的重大影响,就是有过错或疏忽的船舶很早以来就可以限制赔偿责任,让所有在该事故的受害方按比例分摊这一笔总的金额。这方面目前已经有国际公约作出规定,就是 1976 年的《Convention on Limitation of Liability for Maritime Claims》。这一来,允许太多与太间接的纯经济损失前来分摊这一笔固定的总金额,如只有 500 万美元,就会导致了传统与更加值得赔偿的直接受害方的分摊相应薄了或少了。)

在该先例中 Fraser 勋爵也提到英国普通法一直以来就不允许受害方索赔纯经济损失,除非与实质损失走在一起,虽然这在 Hedley Bryne & Co Ltd v. Heller & Partners Ltd (1963) 1 Lloyd's Rep 485 先例中有不同的判法,说:“It started by accepting that historically the policy of the common law in the Untied Kingdom and the Untied States of America, and also in the Australian States, has been to impose strict rules limiting the right to recover compensation from a wrongdoer for loss caused by his fault. In particular liability was limited by the rule that a plaintiff was not entitled to recover for economic or financial loss which was not consequential upon damage to his person or property. That limit was breached by the decision of the House of Lords in Hedley Byrne v. Heller.”

最后贵族院还是认为需要严格控制纯经济损失的索赔,虽然是会有例外情况。Fraser 勋爵是这样说:“Their Lordships consider that some limit or control mechanism has to be imposed upon the liability of a wrongdoer towards those who have suffered economic damage in consequence of his negligence.”

5.4 有关先例之二:Murphy v. Brentwood

本先例涉及一种常见的情况,这种情况就是有关货物买卖的质量问题导致用家或消费者损失。损失如果是涉及人身伤亡或财产损失,这种实质损失可向疏忽的制造商索赔是没有问题。但如果是纯经济损失,如用家或消费者提早发现产品有缺陷,在没有造成进一步的人身伤亡或财产损失前把它修妥的费用,就不一定能够以侵权向制造商提出索赔这一笔纯经济损失,除非他们之间有非常密切的关系(如制造商向消费者提供说明产品是不会有缺陷),甚至有合约关系(这要看合约怎么样约定,如发现产品有缺陷的时候仍在保用期间或是卖方对货物质量有保证)。这可先节录在贵族院的 Murphy v. Brentwood DC (1991) 1 AC 398 先例,Bridge 勋爵是这样说:“If a manufacturer negligently puts into circulation a chattel containing a latent defect which renders it dangerous to persons or property, the manufacturer, on the well known principles established by a case Donoghue v. Stevenson (1932) AC 562, will be liable in tort for injury to persons or damage to property which the chattel causes. But if a manufacturer produces and sells a chattel which is merely defective in quality, even to the extent that it is valueless for the purposes for which it is intended, the manufacturer' s liability at common law arises only under and, by reference to the terms of any contract to which he is a party in tort to persons to whom he owes no duty in contract but who, having acquired the chattel, suffer economic loss because the chattel is defective in quality. If a dangerous defect in a chattel is discovered before it cause any personal injury or damage to property, because the danger is now known and the chattel cannot safely be used unless the defect is repaired, the defect becomes merely a defect in quality. The chattel is either capable of repair at economic cost, or it is worthless and must be scrapped. In either case, the loss sustained by the owner or hirer of the chattel is purely economic. It is recoverable against any party who owes the loser a relevant contractual duty. But, it is not recoverable in tort in the absence of a special relationship of proximity imposing on the tortfeasor a duty of care to safeguard the plaintiff from economic loss. There is no such special relationship between the manufacturer of a chattel and a remote owner or hirer."

5.5　有关先例之三:The "Rebecca Elaine"

另可介绍同样道理的先例,就是 The "Rebecca Elaine" (1999) 2 Lloyd' s Rep 1。案情是有关船舶(是一艘渔船)的建造,由于船东对一种名为 Gradner 的主机有信心,所以决定将该主机装配在新船上。主机建造商并不直接把主机卖给船东,而是卖给船厂。之后在交船后,该主机建造商通过船厂给了船东一份说明书,其中说明活塞可使用 2 万小时以上不需要拆除与更换(pistons would run for 20,000 hours or more without dismantling and before replacement is necessary)。在交船的 2 年后,主机建造商开始不断收到其他船舶的报告说主机的活塞破裂。事实上那些活塞只过了 1/3 的使用时间就已经出问题了。但主机建造商知道了这个消息并没有警告其他装配了该主机的客户,或是发出任何其他形式的警告。回去说 Rebecca Elaine 轮,当它在海上航行的途中,主机的活塞出问题令主机动不了,最终船舶是被拖带去港口,并需要修理船舶。此外,该渔船船东也有利润损失。

但由于交船后 2 年已经过了担保期,所以船东不能根据造船合约向船厂提出索赔。因此船东只能向没有合约关系的主机建造商(但当时已经被船厂收购)根据侵权(疏忽)提出索赔,而疏忽就是没有预先警告船东有关主机活塞的问题。在一审,判是主机建造商只对人身与财产的实际损失有责任,但对经济损失没有责任。在上诉庭,也是同样的判决。而针对作出警告的责任,Tuckey 大法官是这样说:"Under English law I do not think that there is any basis for putting failure to warn of a known danger into a category of its own... My review of the authorities shows that the general rule is that a manufacturer in the position of the respondent owes no duty of care to avoid the economic loss. Exceptionally, he may be under such a duty if he assumes responsibility to his consumers in a situation, which is akin to contract. The duty may include a duty to warn, but it would be much more difficult to infer in the case of mere silence than in the case of misrepresentation. Reliance by the consumer is relevant whether there has been an assumption of responsibility and the essential has to causation."

5.6 其他普通法国家的弹性处理

英国法律严格控制纯经济损失的索赔也导致了不令人满意的情况，其中包括好像油污等重大事故，因为有许多受害方都会蒙受纯经济损失，如渔民无法捕鱼或海边的酒店或餐馆失去大量顾客（这方面稍后在本章第7段会进一步探讨）。这导致了部分普通法国家弹性处理，如澳大利亚的高院在 Caltex Oil (Australia) Pty Ltd v. Dredge "Willemstad" (1976) H. C. A. 65 先例，涉及一条疏浚船因为航行疏忽把一条海底油管毁坏了，而这个油管是连接炼油厂和码头的。油管属于炼油厂，所以炼油厂可以向疏浚船公司索赔实质损失和经济损失。但码头是属于另一家石油公司名为 Caltex，该事故中并没有对码头造成任何实际损失，但 Caltex 公司需要在海底油管修理期间花费额外的运输费用把石油产品从炼油厂拉过来另一个码头以避免分销中断。之后，Caltex 公司向疏浚船公司索赔这一笔纯经济损失。澳大利亚的高院明确允许 Caltex 公司取回这一笔损失，尽管它自身的财产并没有蒙受损失。

另一个例子是加拿大最高院的 Canadian National Railway Co. v. Norsk Pacific Steamship Co (1992) 1 S. C. R. 1021 先例。案情涉及被告的一艘驳船与一座铁路桥发生了碰撞，桥被撞坏了，该桥梁是属于政府所拥有。但事故显然是影响了使用该桥梁的火车公司 Canadian National Railway，虽然并没有火车因事故而受到损坏，但蒙受庞大的纯经济损失。加拿大法院判火车公司胜诉，其中 McLachlin 大法官说：

"The fundamental illogicality of any line drawn between physical damage and economic loss as a way to prevent indeterminate liability has led in recent decades to the abandonment of any such inflexible exclusionary rule. Its abandonment, however, has provoked a measure of uncertainty and inconsistency in the case law. The need for some check upon potentially unlimited liability for economic loss is plain, and the limit should ideally be a relatively clear one, so as to facilitate the identification of legal risk, especially in commercial contexts. The issue is one of policy, and its resolution is unlikely to be attained by reference to any single, simple criterion. （实质损失和纯经济损失的区分因为过于不灵活而在近年来被部分的法院废弃。但这种废弃也造成了案例法下的不肯定与不统一[各有各的判法]。对纯经济损失责任需要做出限制的必要很明显，并且这种限制应该相对明确与肯定，以便让大家能够确定法律风险。这是一个政策问题，但看起来很难设定一个单一、简单的标准来解决。）

... In this case, the evidence supported a finding of proximity necessary to establish liability. The property of CN had itself been at risk; it could not fully be enjoyed without the use of the bridge; CN was engaged in the management and repair of the bridge and was its most frequent user; the contractual nexus between CN and the bridge owner was very close, tantamount indeed to a "joint venture" situation. The plaintiff's position, as against the tortfeasor, was scarcely distinguishable from that of an owner. The danger of indeterminate liability did not arise, since casual bridge users, or persons incidentally affected by the damage, were excluded from the category. (在本先例中,法院认为证据显示原告火车公司的损失在邻近性方面足够让被告负责。原告自己的财产[火车]也面对风险,虽然最终没有在事故中受到损坏。事故后,原告的财产在不能使用桥梁的情况下无法完全起作用。原告本人对桥梁进行管理与维修,并且是桥梁最频繁的使用者。可以说原告和桥梁的所有权人之间的合约关系十分密切,几乎相当于联营的情况。对于侵权方来说,原告的火车公司与桥梁的所有权人之间几乎分不出来。这样判并不会造成允许索赔纯经济损失会带来没完没了的责任所带来的不明确。但如果原告只是属于桥梁偶尔的使用者或者因为桥梁损坏而意外受到不利影响的人士,并不包括在这个类别之内,不能要求赔偿纯经济损失。[也就是说,如原告的乘客因为桥梁损坏造成的延误与火车要暂停服务,导致不便或要改坐其他交通工具如飞机而多花了的费用,不能向被告要求赔偿,因为这种关系是太遥远。])"

6. 法律承认纯经济损失赔偿的侵权

侵权现在也有了许多例外情况允许赔偿纯经济损失,这是因为这种侵权很少会造成实质损失,但又非得承认不可。这种例子有:(i) 噪音: Shelfer v. City of London Electric Lighting Co (1895) 1 Ch 287; Kennaway v. Thompson (1981) QB 88 等先例。(ii)"滋扰"(nuisance): Imperial Gas Light & Coke Co v. Broadbent (1859) 7 HL Cas 600 等先例。(iii) 污染水源的滋扰: Pride of Derby and Derbyshire Angling Association Ltd v. British Celanese Ltd (1953) Ch 149 等先例。(iv)"侵入"(trespass): Behrens v. Richards (1905) 2 Ch 614; Armstrong v. Sheppard & Short Ltd (1958) 2 QB 384; Woollerton & Wilson Ltd v. Richard Costain Ltd (1970) 1 WLR 411; Leagie Against Cruel Sports Ltd v. Scott (1985) 2 All ER 489 等先例。(v)"引诱破坏合约"(induce breach of contract): Emerall Construction Co Ltd v. Lowthian (1966) 1 All ER 1013 等先例。(vi)"诽谤"(defamation): Saxby v. Easterbrood (1878) 3 CPD 339; Bonnard v. Perryman (1891) 2 Ch 269 等先例。(vii)"侵犯版权": Performing Right Society Ltd v. Mitchell & Booker Ltd (1924) 1 KB 762 等先例。

这里可节录《Clerk & Lindsell on Torts》(20th edn, 2010 年)一书 1-42 段,如下:"**Pure economic loss** As Hobhouse L. J. has observed, 'in a competitive economic society the conduct of one person is always liable to have economic consequences for another and, in principle, economic activity does not have to have regard to the interests of others and is justifiable by the actor having regard to his own interests alone'. Hence, economic interests received limited protection. Pure economic loss will normally take two forms; wasted expenditure or loss of a gain, profits or profitability. The tort of deceit and the expanded tort of passing-off protect economic interests of both kinds where loss results from deliberate or reckless statements or conduct designed to induce the claimant to act against his interests, or to damage those interests with third parties. Hedley Byrne v. Heller (1963) 1 Lloyd's Rep 485 allowed recovery of economic loss in negligence within the boundaries of a 'special relationship' of a kind rendering it appropriate to require the defendant to safeguard the economic interests of the claimant. The outer limits of such 'special relationship', which will generally relate to wasted expenditure, are now set largely by the judgments in Caparo Industries plc v. Dickman (1990) 2 AC 287. loss of profits, loss of a potential damage, normally though not inevitably fall outside the ambit of torts."

可以说,随着商业活动的大量增加,纯经济损失的侵权也会增加而且越来越复杂。本章也不会进一步针对这一复杂的课题,除了上述节录中所讲的有关"特殊关系"(special relationship),因为它与本章所要探讨的同步责任有密切关系,稍后在本章第8段会进一步介绍。

7. 油污责任与索赔纯经济损失的问题

海上油污(不论是油污来自船舶或是钻油平台)所造成的重大影响众所周知,有许多案件属于世界性的大新闻。如 Torrey Canyon 轮(英法附近海域,1967 年)、Exxon Valdez 轮(阿拉斯加,1989 年)、Sea Empress 轮(英国威尔士,1996 年)、Erika 轮(法国,1999 年)、Prestige 轮(西班牙,2002 年)、Hebei Spirit 轮(韩国,2007 年)等。至于钻油平台造成的油污有著名的 Montara Wellhead (澳大利亚北部,2009 年)、更著名的 Deepwater Horizon(墨西哥湾,2010 年)、蓬莱 19 - 3 油田 B、C 平台漏油(中国渤海,2011 年)、Gannet Alpha(苏格兰,2011 年)等。其中钻油平台所造成的油污更加会是影响深远,因为在理论上在任何一个事故会漏出的石油会是无止尽,这不像一艘超级油轮,每一滴油都漏到大海里面充其量也就是它所装载的 20 万吨或 30 万吨。随着钻油平台必须更深的海域钻探石油,这方面的问题会更加严峻。据闻,如果钻探的水深超过 1000 米,最乐观的时间把漏油的钻井封死也需要 140 天之久。这一来,看是什么海域发生这种事故以及当时的天气与水流,运气不好的时候会把整个国家海域的海水由清澈全部变黑。所以,这些问题近几十年来一直都是一个国际上十分关注的问题,而对中国而言由于大量进口石油与海上钻油活动也导致问题变得越来越严峻。

油污问题虽然是会造成人命或财产损失，如在 Deepwater Horizon 事件中就有 11 个钻油平台上的工人死亡以及钻油平台的沉没，这些就是明显的实质损失。其他受到油污影响的岸上设施也会有实质的损失，如设施或者建筑物需要清除油污才能重新使用。但肯定的是绝大部分受害方都是属于纯经济损失，如渔民失去了生计，但在海上还没有捕获的鱼或受影响的水域明显不属于这些渔民。所以在没有任何人命或财产的损失的情况下，渔民以及大量其他受影响的人士（如酒店、餐馆等）所损失的都是纯经济损失。而本段只是针对这一方面探讨这一个问题，而不会深入研究关于整个油污事件的复杂问题，但为了方便了解以下也会简单谈谈关于船舶或海上钻油平台造成油污的赔偿问题。

7.1　油轮造成的油污

首先针对油轮的油污，已经有了《Civil Liability Convention 1992》（CLC 1992）的国际公约针对（CLC 1992 取代了 CLC 1969）。CLC 强加一个“谁漏油、谁负责”的严格责任（不再是一般法律的过错或疏忽责任）在船东，除非是 4 项主要免责的其中一项。也就是说，油污责任与船东是否疏忽无关。CLC 强制了船东投保足够的油污责任险（通常是向船东互保协会投保），这好像岸上汽车的强制性投保第三人保险一样。CLC 也允许受到油污损失的受害方直接向有关的责任保险人（也就是船东互保协会）直接要求赔偿。对赔偿的最高金额 CLC 也有了限制，作为对船东的保障，也允许船东为他的油污责任可以进行投保。但同时也通过保险作出了一笔独立与相对庞大的赔偿基金，作为对油污受害方的保障。CLC 也允许油污受害方将索赔“导向”（channel）船东，将船东作为索赔对象，而船东的背后就是船东互保协会，这可以保证肯定有这笔基金赔付。至于其他人士如船东的雇员或代理人、船员、领航员、承租人（包括光租承租人）、船舶经理人或营运人、救助人或其他有关人士去采取保障行为等都在 CLC 之 Article Ⅲ(4) 被排除作为索赔对象。

对于庞大的油污损害索赔会是仅靠 CLC 的赔偿最高金额是不足够，加上造成油污的货方也应该对赔偿作出贡献不应该仅由船东支付。所以，有另一个名为《Fund Convention 1992》（FC 1992）的国际公约（FC 1992 取代了 FC 1971），加上另进一步提高赔偿金额的《2003 Supplementary Fund》。在这个国际公约下，是成立一笔国际油污赔偿基金叫 International Oil Pollution Compensation Fund（the IOPC Fund），在 CLC 的最高赔偿金额不足时，由 IOPC Fund 加上 FC 1992 的最高金额 2.03 亿“特别提款权”（SDR，约等于 3.15 亿美元）。而针对承认《2003 Supplementary Fund》的国家，更加可以把最高赔偿金额提高至 7.5 亿特别提款权（约等于 11.6 亿美元）。这笔油污赔偿基金的财政来源是通过缔约国的石油进口数量去征收。总的来说，CLC 1992 加上了 FC 1992 为油轮与石油行业造成的油污赔偿建立了一个相对令人满意的体系。这可以从承认 CLC 与 FC 的国家数量看出来，截至 2012 年 3 月 31 日，有 127 个国家承认 CLC 1992，109 个国家承认 FC，28 个国家承认《2003 Supplementary Fund》。

CLC 之 Article I(6)对于"油污损害"(Pollution Damages)定义的措辞/用字如下："(a) loss or damage caused outside the ship by contamination resulting from the escape or discharge of oil from the ship, wherever such escape or discharge may occur, provided that compensation for impairment of the environment other than loss of profit from such impairment shall be limited to costs of reasonable measures of reinstatement actually undertaken or to be undertaken. (b) the costs of preventive measures and further loss or damage caused by preventive measures. "在 Article I(7)是说："'Preventive measures' means any reasonable measures taken by any person after an incident has occurred to prevent or minimize pollution damage. "(针对 preventive measures 的定义是说任何人在事故发生后采取合理的措施避免或减少油污损失)

7.2 船舶燃油造成的油污

但 CLC 1992 加上 FC 1992 只是解决了海上污染包括石油污染的一部分问题,如并非是油轮的干货船或集装箱船等也可以造成严重的油污,这就是来自它们的燃油。这些船舶很容易有数千吨的燃油,而这些燃油造成的污染,虽然数量上相对较少,但严重性可能会比油轮所运输的原油或石油产品造成的污染更甚。这是因为燃油相对较厚不易蒸发,造成的污染影响比较持久,且干货轮的路线多变化,造成的燃油污染一般比较近海岸影响比较严重。在统计上看,燃油的漏油事故也比较多,在国际船东互保协会提供给国际海事组织(IMO)的数字,在 2000 年至 2009 年 8 月期间,有统计的事故有 595 件之多。这导致另一个公约在 2001 年出台,名为《International Convention on Civil Liability for Bunker Oil Pollution Damage》,或简称 Bunkers Convention。这一个公约在 2008 年 11 月已经有足够国家承认并生效,目前已经有高达 60 个承认的国家并且估计会不断增加。

Bunkers Convention 对目前的法律制度改变不多,它主要的要求是油轮以外的船舶,船东需要为燃油造成的油污承担严格责任并作出保险与提供证明等。Bunkers Convention 不像 CLC/FC 1992 建立一笔独立的赔偿基金,除非个别国家根据自己的立法这样做(如加拿大的 Ship-source Oil Pollution Fund)。

7.3 海上钻油平台造成的油污

而另一个海上石油污染目前还没有国际公约针对的是钻油平台所造成的油污。从 Deepwater Horizon 事故中可以看出,如果不是英国石油公司及时把海底油井封死,钻油平台造成的石油污染连英国石油公司这种巨无霸公司都可能会被拖垮。但即使如此,根据 2012 年 11 月的报道,英国石油公司要面对高达 210 亿美元的民事索赔与支付给美国政府 45 亿美元的罚款。

以国际公约建立一套好像 CLC/FC 1992 的体系,早在 1977 年国际海事委员会(CMI)就草拟一份文件给国际海事组织(IMO),名为《Draft International Convention on Offshore Mobile Craft》,也被称为是 Rio draft。这份文件建议把 CLC/FC 的体系延伸至海上钻油平台造成的油污赔偿。Rio draft 在国际海事委员会的 2004 年会议作出了一些修改,名为 Sydney draft,但本质上还是一样的理念。

但这一个理念实际操作起来会很困难,因为海上钻油平台与油轮的行业是很不一样的。除了已经提到油污的严重程度不一样之外,还有其他很多重要的方面。第一个方面就是油污责任保险,到目前为止,CLC 能够有很好的操作,是因为油轮基本都参加了船东互保协会,而国际船东互保协会通过已经多年来所成立的互保以及再保的安排才能为庞大的油污责任提供保险。但海上钻油平台还是依赖一般商业市场上的保险,船东互保协会一般不承保这种风险。如果海上钻油平台的油污责任也加进 CLC,很怀疑传统的船东互保协会会否愿意为这种新的险种提供油污责任保险。这一来,海上钻油平台要建立好像油轮目前的保险体系会很困难,因为这是要依赖市场上一些商业保险人。另一个困难是 FC,这不像目前的 FC 是从进口的石油每吨征收税款,这可以说是简单得多,但海上钻油平台要建立这种赔偿基金就会很困难,因为涉及许多不同的利益方与沿岸国家。可以说怎么样征收这笔庞大的基金会有很严重与政治化的争议。另一个令人担心的问题是 CLC/FC 1992 如果延伸去海上钻油平台会否减低它的吸引力,因为有不少国家并没有在蓬勃的海上钻油活动中分到一杯羹。所以,2012 年 10 月,国际海事委员会在北京召开的第 40 届大会上,提出为海上钻油平台草拟一份独立的国际公约,交给国际海事组织,希望能够成为另一个针对海上油污的国际公约。

至于在目前针对海上钻油平台造成油污的责任赔偿的机制,纯粹是在 1975 年来自石油公司"自发"(voluntary)与通过合约建立起来的一个赔偿制度名为"Offshore Pollution Liability Agreement"(简称 OPOL)针对欧洲的海上钻油平台。OPOL 的最高赔偿金额是 2.5 亿美元。OPOL 在做法上好像在 1967 年的 Torrey Canyon 轮油污事件后,在 1969 年油轮船东与互保协会很快地建立了一种自发的油污赔偿制度名为"'Tanker Owners' Voluntary Agreement concerning Liability for Oil Pollution "(简称 TOVALOP)与 1971 年石油公司自发的"Contract Regarding an Interim Supplement to Tanker Liability for Oil Pollution"(简称 CRISTAL)。这种民间或业界自发的赔偿制度显然是因为国际公约的拟定需要时间太长,而业界也希望立法不要对他们太苛刻,并同时希望显示给民众他们是有责任心的生意人。而到了国际公约的 CLC 1969/FC 1971 出台后,TOVALOP 与 CRISTAL 完成历史任务而自动消失。

OPOL 对油污损失的定义是:"direct loss or damage by contamination which results from a discharge of oil."

7.4 危险品与有毒物品的污染

早在 1984 年,国际海事组织(IMO)法律委员会在外交会议上提交了一份有关除石油外危险品与有毒物品造成污染的相关责任及损害赔偿的国际公约草案。但这份草案并没有被通过成为国际公约。之后国际海事组织法律委员会着手修改草案,在 1996 年的外交会议上提交了做了重大修改的内容,并顺利通过了这份名为《与危险品及有毒物品海上运输相关的责任及损害赔偿》的国际公约("International Convention on Liability and Compensation for Damage in Connection with the Carriage of Hazardous and Noxious Substances by Sea 1996",或简称 HNS 公约)。

HNS 公约沿用了 1992 年 CLC/FC 双层赔偿体系。第一层赔偿来自船东(与船东互保协会),最高赔偿金额为 2.5 亿"特别提款权"(SDR,约 3.85 亿美元)。对第一层赔偿没有覆盖的事故或最高赔偿金额不够赔的情况,赔偿将由第二层——HNS Fund 支付。HNS Fund 的财政来源是向缔约国的港口与码头运输危险品的收货人征收。

HNS 公约在很多方面都比 CLC/FC 1992 复杂:(1)它只是一个公约,而不像 CLC/FC 是两个公约。(2)它覆盖了上千种货物,包括如散装固体材料如化肥、硝酸钠与硝酸钾、硫磺和一些鱼粉;散装液体如甲醇、二甲苯与苯乙烯、硫酸、磷酸、苛性钠、动植物油脂;液态气体如氨气、乙烯、丁二烯、乙烷、丙烯等。(3) HNS 公约对于损失的定义要比 CLC/FC 1992 针对油污损失广泛得多。HNS 公约包括了人身伤亡,船舶外的财产损失,采取预防措施的使费;为恢复环境采取的合理措施的使费与"环境污染造成的经济损失,如渔业、海洋生物养殖业、旅游业"(economic losses resulting from contamination of the environment, e. g. fisheries, mariculture and tourism sectors)。

HNS 公约没有明确说明"经济损失"(economic losses)只包括"间接经济损失"(consequential economic loss)(如渔民在清洗捕鱼用具期间不能捕鱼)或"纯经济损失"(pure economic loss)。但是它应该是与 CLC/FC 1992 下的 IOPC Fund 的立场一致,即只有能够证明与污染有足够邻近的因果关系的纯经济损失才能获得赔偿。也就是说,"次要"(secondary)的纯经济损失不能获得赔偿:Landcatch Ltd v. IOPCF (1998) 2 Lloyd's Rep 552 先例与 The "Sea Empress" (2003) 1 Lloyd's Rep 327 先例。这可节录前 IOPC Fund 负责人 Mans Jacobsson 先生在《Pollution at Sea Law and Liability》(2012 年)一书中的说法:"The HNS Convention does not explicitly indicate whether a pure economic loss qualifies for compensation under the convention. The corresponding provisions in the Civil Liability and Fund Convention ('loss or damage caused outside the ship by contamination') have been consistently interpreted by the governing bodies of the IOPC Fund to cover in principle pure economic losses, and these bodies have developed certain criteria for the admissibility of claims for such losses, in particular that there must be a sufficiently close link of causation between the contamination and the loss. It is submitted that the concept of damage in the HNS Convention should be interpreted in the same way."

要使最初版本的 HNS 公约有足够国家承认并生效可谓是困难重重。其中一个困难就是危险品行业与有关国家怎样建立实际的海上运输"包装危险货物"(packaged hazardous cargoes)数据收集与报告系统,并向收货人征收。所以在 2010 年的外交大会上,包装货物从"摊款货物"(contributing cargo)中删除,往往只剩下了是大宗货的散装货物。

截至2012年3月31日,还没有国家承认2010年议定书。

7.5 普通法在海上污染中的地位

虽然油轮造成的油污责任有了国际公约的约束与代取(如变为严格责任),但普通法或者其他国家的"一般法律"(general law),针对海上污染还会有一个重要的地位,原因有以下方面:第一,并不是所有有关人士都受到如好像CLC 1992的保护,在他们面对油污受害方索赔损失的时候就要依赖普通法。第二,海上污染在许多方面还没有国际公约的约束,亦没有较完善的本国法律(如美国的《Oil Pollution Act 1980》)针对,如海上钻油平台造成的油污或危险品造成的污染。而涉及普通法或许多国家的一般法律,根据过失责任针对,又会涉及纯经济损失能否索赔的问题。

7.5.1 CLC受保护的人士

上面已经提到,CLC 1992的目的之一是希望把大量油污的受害方通过索赔船东获得赔偿,因为船东的背后是提供油污责任保险的互保协会,虽然有金额上的限制但肯定赔得起,并同时Article Ⅲ(4)规定不能向其他与船东有关人士(如船员、领航员、承租人等较早已经提到过的有关人士)索赔。但还是会有情况油污的受害方不能或不想根据CLC 1992向船东提起索赔,而需要依赖普通法赋予的权利。例如,CLC 1992只是要求运载多过2000吨的油轮进行强制保险或取得财物担保,这就会造成运载2000吨以下的油轮由于没有保险而赔不起。另一个情况是CLC充其量只是赔偿比较有限的纯经济损失,如在受油污影响海域作业的渔民(Landcatch Ltd v. IOPCF [1998] 2 Lloyd's Rep 552先例与The "Sea Empress" [2003] 1 Lloyd's Rep 327先例),受到其他纯经济损失的受害方会希望求助普通法可能会给他更广泛的救济。也会有情况是赔偿基金设立的管辖地法院可能不吸引在其它国家的油污受害方去该法院索赔。这些不能或不想根据CLC 1992向船东提起索赔的受害方,会选择在普通法下的侵权向CLC 1992不保护的有关人士索赔,只要是能够找到他们的过错或疏忽。这些人士包括如货方、船级社、船厂等。当然找这些CLC 1992以外的人士索赔显然要考虑被告的经济状况,要他们赔得起才行,在实际情况中,他们往往也会赔得起。这种索赔就不会是根据CLC 1992或有关国家的立法,而是要根据普通法或一般法律。

货方会是赔得起的对象,这特别是指发货人。他们的过错或疏忽比较少会出现在原油的运输,但涉及危险品就大有可能。这些过错包括没有把货物的危险特征向船长宣告(如有关货物不能装在甲板上或是接近发热源附近)、包装不足、集装箱内的堆货不妥等。这种情况会造成在航次中的严重事故,并造成对第三人的损失,包括污染。这种先例有The "Orjula" (1995) 2 Lloyd's Rep 395,案情涉及集装箱内的桶装盐酸(hydrochloric acid)因为装得不好导致盐酸倾倒泄漏并对船舶造成污染,船东(实际上是光租承租人)要花费额外的清洗费用。于是船东向发货人的第一被告和装集装箱的第二被告(这种被告就要关心他的经济状况)索赔这笔费用。

下一个会赔得起的对象是港口当局,港口当局可以对污染的事件有过错或疏忽,如对航道或港口设备的维修保养不妥善或对一艘危险的沉船没有及时设下标记与警告，导致港口变得不安全而造成事故，而事故的发生导致污染（不论是油污或是危险品的污染）。这种先例有美国的 US v. Bear Marine Services 696 F. 2d 1117 (1983) 与英国的 Michell v. Milford Haven Port Authority (2003) EWHC 1246 (Admiralty); The "Charlotte C" (2005) 2 Lloyd's Rep 626。

再下一个会是赔得起的对象是船级社，向船级社提出索赔的案件已经是不少，毕竟船舶如果发生事故很容易就会责怪有关的船级社没有对船舶安全与适航把好关。但能否成功向船级社索赔目前在世界各地的法院还是不肯定，这是因为船级社特殊的地位与作用。这方面可以在英国的贵族院先例 The "Nicholas H" (1995) 2 Lloyd's Rep 299 中看到。简单的案情涉及 Nicholas H 轮在装满了铅铝精矿（lead and zinc concentrates）后，发觉船壳板出现裂缝。日本船级社于是被船东邀请前来检验，而第一次是要求船东作出永久修理，即要完全修妥才开。但这一来会对船东非常不利而且昂贵，如当地附近没有适当或廉价的修船设备；船舶已装满货物，要卸下来一部分才能修等。于是船东派代表飞来装港与日本船级社检验师交涉。最后估计在压力下，日本船级社把永久修理的要求改为暂时修理后即可开航。在途中，裂缝扩大导致船舶沉没。看来，日本船级社这暂时修理的决定是错误的、有疏忽的。货方在起诉船东并获得互保协会赔偿的 50 万美元后（这金额是《海牙规则》下的限额），对余下赔不到的 550 万美元向日本船级社追偿。

英国贵族院最后是判日本船级社不需要负责。原因如下：(1) 主要在公共利益大前提下不应强加船级社一个对货方"小心谨慎的责任"（duty of care），这是疏忽的侵权必须要达到的要求。如果船级社有了这个责任，不知会扩散到什么地步，如对其他的受害方如船员、乘客、承租人、二手船买卖或建造新船的船东等。而船级社以后处处防范，不敢下决定，整体对全球航运不是好事。所以，在政策上并非是公正（just）、公平（fair）与合理（reasonable）强加在船级社身上一个小心谨慎的责任，要求船级社作为船舶安全的最终负责人。(2) 负责船舶安全适航的主要是船东，不是船级社。(3) 船东如果违约造成货损货差，已有各种国际公约针对，如《海牙规则》，船舶可以吨位限制责任的 1976 年《伦敦公约》等。如果允许船级社被货方起诉，将来船级社又会对在替船东检验时（双方有合约关系）要求给予"补偿"（indemnity）等，即会搅垮整个国际公约所建立起来的风险分摊制度。

美国也有类似的判决，这是 Reino de Espana v. American Bureau of Shipping, Inc 729 F. Supp. 2d 2010 A. M. C 1877 (2010) 先例。案情涉及 Prestige 轮 1992 年在西班牙造成的严重油污事件，原告的西班牙政府在美国法院向美国船级社索赔。美国上诉庭（Second Circuit）判是要求船级社作为海上不受到污染的最终负责人并不恰当。但在该先例中并没有在法律上作出定论是船级社不必负责任，而最后美国船级社的胜诉还是以证据不足为由，所以船级社在美国法律下仍然是不能安心。上诉庭的 Livingston 大法官是这样说："We conclude that we need not resolve the question whether a classification society may be held liable in tort to a third party such as Spain for reckless conduct in connection with the classification of vessels. Rather, we assume arguendo for purposed of this appeal that defendants did owe the claimed duty to Spain. In our view, Spain has nonetheless failed to adduce sufficient evidence to create a genuine dispute of material fact as to whether defendants recklessly breached that duty such that their actions constituted a proximate cause of the wreck of the 'Prestige'."

对于船级社要不要负责还不肯定,也可看另一宗著名油污事件的 Erika 轮。她在英法边界的比斯开湾造成的严重油污事故中,受害方要求的赔偿超出了 CLC/FC 1992 设定的最高赔偿金额约 2 亿欧元。于是拿不到足够赔偿的受害方(法国政府)向 15 名被告提起了刑事疏忽的诉讼。最终有 4 名被告被判刑事疏忽,即船东 Savarese 先生,船舶管理人 Pollara 先生,货方 Total SA 与意大利船级社 RINA SpA,指他们不受 CLC 1992 之 Article Ⅲ(4)保护,而法国上诉庭也同意。但这个判决很受争议,因为船东 Savarese 先生与船舶管理人 Pollara 先生明显是在 CLC 1992 规定的范围内。但获悉最后是大家达成了和解,具体的和解方案是没有公开但是可以估计船级社也是出了钱。

最后要一提的不受 CLC 保护的人士会是修理厂、生产商或船厂,他们会负责任是因为修理或建造有疏忽导致事后船舶发生事故与漏油事件。至于生产商,会有产品的严格责任,而涉及的事件会是他供应的主机或其他机件或零件有潜在的故障导致船舶发生事故与漏油,有关的先例有 The "Esso Bernicia" (1989) A. C. 643。至于这些人士赔不赔得起可能是庞大的油污赔偿就要看个别公司的经济状况了。

7.5.2　油污/污染造成的实质损失与纯经济损失

油污或者危险品会造成的污染会是影响广泛与深远,其中部分受害方会是有实质损失,如他的财产受到油污而需要清洁,甚至油污造成火灾把他的财产烧毁: The "Wagon Mound" (1961) 1 Lloyd's Rep 1 先例。这种实质损失的受害方也可以在同一个诉讼中索赔他们的"间接经济损失"(consequential economic loss)。但这种事故会有可能大部分的受害方只是蒙受"纯经济损失"(pure economic loss),就是他们的财产并没有受到油污或污染的直接影响,但实际上还是蒙受了经济损失。这种经济损失主要是估计的利润/业务损失,但还可以是包括许多其他方面。这种受害方会是:

(1)油污的污染几乎肯定会带来庞大的清洁与预防措施费用。如果这个费用是涉及清洁原告的受害方所拥有的土地,这并不属于纯经济损失。但更大的可能会是有关当局由于社会压力或者当地的法律进行油污或污染的清洁与预防措施费用。针对这方面英国以前有成功的先例向疏忽的侵权方索赔清洁费用,如 The "Ella" (1915) P 111 先例与 Dee Conservancy Board v. McConnell (1928) 2 KB 159 先例,但这些早期的判决被视为是根据"公共滋扰"(public nuisance)的诉因而不是"疏忽"(negligence)的诉因:Tettenborn 教授的《Pollution at Sea Law and Liability》(2012 年)一书之212页。

但美国法律在 Matter of Oil Spill By Amoco Cadiz,954 F.2d 1279 先例,美国法院提到是在美法两国都有"公共服务免费"(free public service doctrine)的说法,不允许政府部门就提供公共服务的费用向疏忽的侵权方索赔,如警察提供保护的费用或者消防员救火的费用:Chausson v. Prefect of Valice (Cour de Cassation Jan. 9,1866);X v. Bouches-du-Rhone Firefighting Service,No. 87 - 10.359 (Cour de Cassation Jan. 10,1990);District of Columbia v. Air Florida,Inc.,750 F.2d 1077,1079 - 80 (D. C. Cir. 1984);Flagstaff v. Atchison,Topeka & Santa Fe Ry.,719 F.2d 322 (9th Cir. 1983)等先例。

针对清洁费用,已经在许多的国际公约特别是已经生效的 CLC/FC 1992 与 Bunkers Convention 都有所规定。CLC 1992 之 Article Ⅰ(6)、Article Ⅱ规定,预防措施在任何地方采取均可视为赔偿的损害,即使为减少在领海或专属经济区内的污染而在公海上采取也不例外。虽然什么算是"合理"(reasonable)的清洁费用还是经常会有争议,因为是否合理还是要根据每个案件的具体情况进行判断,没有办法说死。但至少在原则上说,已经明确了清洁费用作为纯经济损失,可以获得赔偿。

(2)环境/自然资源损失以及恢复环境的合理措施费用。这也是很富争议性的损失类别,但本段并非针对油污问题,不会进一步探讨。只说,CLC 1992 之 Article Ⅰ(6)已是明示针对,但该损失应发生在缔约国的领土,包括领海及专属经济区内。

(3)这一类的受害方会是渔民以及海产养殖厂或是其他依赖受油污/危险品污染海域的经营的生意。这一类的受害方会有"实质损失"(physical loss),如海产养殖厂受到污染导致鱼类或贝壳类的死亡。这种损失也包括了因污染导致的财产清洁、修理、重置费用。受害方根据普通法或者一般法律的过错责任通常是可以同时索赔"间接经济损失"(consequential economic loss),这是因为财产被污染而遭受的收入损失。

(4)但会有更多的受害方是"纯经济损失"(pure economic loss),如没有蒙受实质损失的渔民就谈不上拥有受到污染海域的财产权,也谈不上拥有还没有捕获的海产或鱼类,变成索赔就只能是纯经济损失。这种受害方也包括其他靠海吃饭的人士,如受污染海域是海滨浴场或是渡假胜地,由于污染而导致游客大减,这无疑会影响附近的酒店、餐厅、游乐场,甚至提供运输的渡轮、巴士、出租车等的生意。如果把这种受害方的供应链或合约链进一步扩大,蒙受这种纯经济损失的受害方会在一个大的油污/污染的事故中无限度地扩大。如酒店/餐厅受到影响,为它提供食物的供应商或是为它提供洗涤服务的干洗店等显然也会蒙受纯经济损失。又如受到港口封闭而延误的船舶会到不了十分遥远的目的地港而导致港口的工人、码头、领航员、驳船等都丧失了这票业务带来纯经济损失。

针对过错或疏忽原则的普通法或是许多国家的一般法律,这种纯经济损失(不论是与油污/污染的事故有否密切关系)都不被接受可以向侵权方提出索赔,这方面在本章 5.1 段有详论。

7.6 CLC/FC 1992 与 IOPC Fund 对纯经济损失的立场

纯经济损失在针对油轮造成油污的 CLC 1992 与针对船舶燃油造成油污的 Bunkers Convention 2001 并没有明示针对。CLC 1992 对污染损失的定义可以重复节录说:"loss or damage caused outside the ship by contamination resulting from the escape or discharge of oil from the ship..."

但在 IOPC 的《索赔手册》(IOPC Fund Claims Manual, December 2008 Edition),[1] 明确了可赔偿的损失类型并且详细解释了各种类型损害的可赔偿范围,其中包括纯经济损失,即财产未受污染的人确因油污而引起的收入损失及为减少该经济损失而采取的合理措施费用,但强调必须与油污有密切关联的因果关系。

而针对因果密切关联性是否存在,应考虑以下因素:索赔人商业活动与污染区域的地理相近性、索赔人的业务在经济上对受事故影响资源的依赖程度、索赔人获得替代供应资源或商业机会的可能程度、索赔人的业务在构成受事故影响区域中部分经济活动的程度(如索赔人的业务是否位于受影响的区域,是否为生活在该区域的人提供就业)。

所以在伦敦的 IOPC Fund 一贯的立场[2]是包括直接受到污染影响的纯经济损失,但抗拒赔偿一些所谓的"次要"(secondary)纯经济损失,如相隔受污染海域很远的受害方或是中间隔了一个受害方。IOPC Fund 的立场可以节录苏格兰的 Landcatch Ltd v. IOPCF (1998) 2 Lloyd's Rep 552 先例如下:"... the Fund did not dispute that 'loss' for the purpose of s. 1 was apt to include pure economic loss, but this was so long as it could be seen to be a direct result of contamination as opposed to the merely secondary or relational. 'Damage' and 'loss' could not be used interchangeably in practice. Economic loss was more likely to be relational in nature. It was accepted on behalf of the Fund that Shetland fishermen who were prevented from fishing in the sea within the exclusion zone would have suffered an economic loss which was admissible. They would not have suffered the loss of anything owned by them, since they owned neither the sea nor the fish in it. Their economic loss would have been a direct result of the contamination, without any party or relationship interposed. The same would not have applied, or at least would not necessarily have applied, in the case of a fisherman whose home port was further afield. This was because statute indicated that it was imposing liability for damage, including loss, which was

---

[1] 该版本由全体成员国大会于 2004 年 10 月通过,2007 年 6 月修订。全体成员国大会是 IOPC Fund 的最高权力机构,有权批准向该基金提出的索赔。

[2] 虽然索赔对各成员国并无法定约束力,只是基金本身认定索赔的依据,但自 1978 年基金公约生效以来,绝大多数事故中索赔人均可以与基金达成一致而无须诉诸法院解决。但亦有三个先例会作出介绍,说明哪一些是 IOPC Fund 拒绝赔偿的次要纯经济损失索赔。即 Landcatch Ltd v. IOPCF 与 P & O Scottish Ferries Ltd v. The Braer Corporation 以及 The "Sea Empress"先例。

localized. The central idea was physical contamination. This pointed to a place or thing which was contaminated, and hence to a geographical location. The terms in which ss. 1 and 13 were expressed envisaged that the contamination and the damage or loss would be in the same area. While every claim of economic loss would require to be considered on its own merits, the further away that a claimant's economic activities were from the scene of the contamination the more difficult it was to fit his claim within the scope of the Act."（IOPC Fund 对于立法 s. 1 中对于损失的定义是接受纯经济损失，但坚持这个纯经济损失必须是污染的直接后果而不是次要或仅仅扯得上关系。纯经济损失通常在本质上涉及关系的远近。IOPC Fund 接受 Shetland 的渔民不能在专属区域捕鱼而蒙受的纯经济损失，因为他们没有蒙受任何属于他们的财产的损失，他们既不拥有海洋也不拥有还没有捕获的鱼类。但他们的纯经济损失是污染的直接后果，中间没有插进任何第三人或别的关系。而对于那些基地在很遥远的地方的渔民，IOPC Fund 认为立法就不适用，至少是不一定适用。这也是因为立法的措辞显示船东只需要对当地的损失负责。尽管所有的纯经济损失都需要个别考虑有关的事实，但受害方的经济活动和发生污染的地点离得越远，他的纯经济损失越难被 IOPC Fund 接受属于立法包括的范围。）

IOPC Fund 对于纯经济损失的立场，也就是针对个别不同案件的有关事实考虑是否是油污直接造成并决定是否赔付，是受到了英国法院的支持。英国法院也认为很难硬性规定一条因果关系的分水线，现实的做法还是任由 IOPC Fund 做出决定。这是在 The "Sea Empress"（2003）1 Lloyd's Rep 327 先例中上诉庭的 Chadwick 大法官所说："It is necessary, also, to avoid the temptation to offer guidelines as to the causative test to be applied by the Fund when making decisions in the future. The Fund has not suggested that it needs assistance in this respect. It recognizes the need, on pragmatic grounds to draw a line so as to include some claims and exclude others. It would, no doubt, assert that, with the benefit of its accumulated experience in the administration of claims over the past thirty years, it is likely to be in a much better position than the Court to decide where the line should be drawn in particular cases; and that its decisions have generally commanded confidence. At the least, it can say that it has not yet been held to be wrong. That is not, of course, to suggest the Fund is not subject to the control of the Court; nor that the Court should not correct a decision which does not accord with the Fund's obligations under statute. It is only to recognize that the precise extent of those obligations is best left for determination on a case by case basis."

7.6.1 先例之一：Landcatch Ltd v. IOPCF

在这里不妨进一步介绍 Landcatch Ltd v. IOPCF（1998）2 Lloyd's Rep 552 先例的案情。案情涉及 Braer 轮 1993 年在苏格兰的 Shetland（这是大不列颠岛以北的群岛，主要经济来源是渔业和北海海底的石油）附近搁浅并导致了 85,000 吨的原油与 16,000 吨的燃油泄漏，当局作出了禁令警告民众不要食用附近海域的三文鱼。原告的 Landcatch Ltd 的三文鱼养殖场向 IOPC Fund 索赔它在业务上蒙受的损失包括生意减少，在 1993 与 1994 年需要大幅度降价与增加使费特别处理在养殖的三文鱼。但 Landcatch Ltd 并不成功，苏格兰法院认为普通法从来不接受这种属于"次要"(secondary)的纯经济损失，因为开了门就会带来漫无止境的索赔。苏格兰法院也不认为 CLC/FC 在英国的立法《Merchant Shipping (Oil Pollution) Act 1971》有做出这方面的改变。因为如果立法是有这个意图，就可以用很简单的文字表达清楚。估计也不会有这种意图，其中一个原因是允许太多的次要纯经济损失加进来向同一笔赔偿基金索赔，就会分薄了其他严重受到油污影响的首要损失赔偿，如实质损失并加上了间接经济损失，以及立法规定的减少油污损失的合理措施。例如 McCluskey 勋爵说："... the issue is whether or not the words used in the sections governing damage are apt to extend the liability of the responsible shipowner much wider, so as to make him potentially liable to compensate an indeterminate number of claimants who would not, under the common law, have had a claim, because their claims would have been regarded as too remote. I cannot see that the legislature would have left such a result to inference."

7.6.2　先例之二：P & O Scottish Ferries Ltd v. The Braer Corporation

第二个有关的先例是 P & O Scottish Ferries Ltd v. The Braer Corporation (1999) 2 Lloyd's Rep 535，这也是与 Braer 轮搁浅漏油事故有关。原告 P & O 是一个渡轮公司，提供往返 Shetland 与英国或苏格兰本土的渡轮服务。P & O 提出的索赔是由于油污事件，去 Shetland 的游客大大减少，导致渡轮生意受到很大影响。这包括了旅客与运货的拖车运输都比起过去几年大幅度减少，这些损失项目都琐碎(除了旅客的客票外还包括他们在船上买东西、免税烟酒、赌博等收益)，但都算得出来，而加起来就变成很大的一笔数目。但 P & O 也好像 Landcatch Ltd 一样索赔并不成功，理由是与 Landcatch Ltd 先例基本一样。P &O 的损失明显是插进了第三人，如旅客的减少。Gill 勋爵认为有关 CLC/FC 1992 的立法并没有清楚改变普通法的政策，就是侵权方的过错需要承担的责任不能是无止境的，而必须要有一个合理与现实的限制。而在本先例，Gill 勋爵认为 P & O 的索赔是非常间接，说："... these losses were not the direct consequence of the escape of oil. They were no more than an indirect consequence of adverse publicity affecting the image of Shetland as a source of fish and fish products and as a holiday destination. The adverse publicity was in turn a consequence of the contamination of other parties' property. It is obvious that many of those who failed to enter into contracts with the pursuers, for example ferry passengers, had themselves suffered no damage from contamination by oil."

7.6.3　先例之三：The "Sea Empress"

最后介绍英国上诉庭的 The "Sea Empress" (2003) 1 Lloyd's Rep 327 先例。这一个油污事件是 1996 年 Sea Empress 轮在 Milford Haven 海域附近搁浅而泄漏 72,000 吨原油，造成严重油污。这导致当局禁止食用在威尔士海域的海产品长达 6 个多月。

这影响了一家在Devon(离开Milford Haven大概4个小时车程)处理海产品的公司。该公司作为原告向IOPC Fund提出索赔643,557英镑。原告的诉讼理由可以简单概括为:(1)从立法措辞上看油污"损害"(damage)包括了"损失"(loss);(2)因此理论上说,原油泄漏造成的污染引起的纯经济损失应该可以获得赔偿;(3)原告的纯经济损失是油污引起的,因为如果没有原油泄漏事件当局就不会禁止捕鱼,满足因果关系;(4)原油泄漏导致了"利润损失"(loss of profit);(5)这项损失是可预见的,不是太遥远。

而被告IOPC Fund的抗辩是:(1)原告(1)~(4)的主张是正确的,换言之是接受原告的损失满足因果关系与可预见;(2)尽管损失是可预见的,但是并不足够使纯经济损失获得赔偿;(3)原告的损失是源自与油污首要受害方(也就是渔民)的商业关系,等于插进了第三人;(4)根据Landcatch Ltd先例这种"次要"(secondary)损失不能获得赔偿。

IOPC Fund认为必须要对纯经济损失有一定的控制,否则会有很多原告前来索赔,包括受影响的当地政府、渔民、酒店(包括它的食物或其它物料的供应商)、餐厅(包括它的供应商)、商店等。反正从供应链算下去,许多人都是或多或少会受到影响,他们都前来索赔的话会变得无止境。而索赔项目也会是千变万化,如生意额度下跌、业务损失、税收减少(受影响的当地政府)、商誉损失等。这些损失通常都可以满足与油污的因果关系以及可以预见。

已经较早提到过IOPC Fund接受直接受到影响的经济损失,如当地的渔民,虽然油污所影响的海域与鱼类并非是属于受影响渔民的财产,但IOPC Fund认为本先例属于次要损失就不应该赔。在本先例的第一审法院与上诉庭都判原告的纯经济损失属于次要的纯经济损失,不能获得赔偿。上诉庭的Mance大法官是这样说:"Despite the difficulty of drawing the line in any case such as the present, I consider, at the end of all the arguments, that the appellant falls on the wrong side of it. It was not engaged in any local activity in the physical area of the contamination. Its interest was in landed whelks(海螺), not in the whelks in their natural habitat. The contamination has prevented local fishermen, whose physical activities are closely affected by the contamination of the waters and of whelks, from supplying the appellant with the landed whelks for which it had contracted. The appellant's resulting loss arises from its inability to carry out processing and packing and deliveries of processed and packed whelks at points far away from the contaminated areas. I consider that this is a form of secondary economic loss, which is outside the intended scope of a statute which is closely focused on physical contamination and its consequences."

7.7 公共滋扰

7.7.1 公共滋扰与私人滋扰的区别

滋扰分为私人滋扰与公共滋扰。私人滋扰很早就有这一方面的法律,这主要是对土地或者财产的拥有人如果因第三人的行为而导致他无法享用,在很多方面已经受到法律的保障。例如,第三人的行为导致他的土地或者财产的损坏,这通常可以根据侵权的疏忽索赔损失。如果土地或者财产的拥有人受到第三人的侵入,也有侵入的法律作出保障。但问题是如果不涉及这两种情况,而是第三人的行为影响他享用他的土地或财产,如在一个河流上游的邻居建造一个水坝或湖泊而导致了受害方无法享用充足的供水或容易造成大水,这就会是第三人对受害方作出滋扰。由于这个滋扰只是影响个别人士,这会是"私人滋扰"(private nuisance)。但如果第三人的行为是更大程度会影响河流下游的公众,这就会是"公共滋扰"(public nuisance)了。

虽然私人滋扰与公共滋扰都名为滋扰,但实际上它们十分不同。这两种滋扰的区别可节录 Colour Quest Ltd v. Total Downstream UK (2009) 2 Lloyd's Rep 1 先例中 Steel 大法官说:"(a) Private nuisance involves interference with someone's private right to enjoy his own land. Public nuisance involves the endangering of the health, comfort or property of the public. (b) It follows that a collection of private nuisances can constitute a public nuisance: but it does not follow either that in consequence the claim in private nuisance is sub-sumed or that a public nuisance involving interference with health or comfort cannot be freestanding."(私人滋扰涉及第三人干预土地拥有人享用的权利。公共滋扰涉及危害公众的健康、舒适或者财产,这些被危害的人士并无需拥有土地。)

上述的简单定义可以看到两种滋扰的不同,首先私人滋扰是要与土地的享用扯在一起,但公共滋扰的面就会广得多。这方面的区别也在更近期的 Jan De Nul (UK) Ltd v. NV Royal Belge (2000) 2 Lloyd's Rep 700 先例有涉及,Moore-Bick 大法官是这样说:"Liability in public nuisance, however, raises more difficult questions. Although it does sometimes arise for consideration in the context of an interference with the plaintiffs use and enjoyment of land similar to that which would support a claim in private nuisance (see, for example, Attorney General v. PYA Quarries Ltd [1957] 2 QB 169), that is not its essential nature. Perhaps it is most commonly encountered in the context of obstruction of the highway or of a navigable waterway interfering with the public right of passage, but, as the editors of Clerk & Lindsell point out in para 18 – 05, the scope of public nuisance is wide and the acts and omissions to which it applies are all unlawful. Private nuisance, on the other hand, is only concerned with interference with the use and enjoyment of land and may be committed by doing acts which are not necessarily unlawful in themselves."

以上的说法可以总结私人滋扰与公共滋扰的区别有以下:(1)私人滋扰只是侵权行为,公共滋扰长期以来视为是刑事犯罪,但蒙受特殊伤害或者损失的个别人士也可以民事诉讼向造成公共滋扰的被告提出索赔,这方面会后详。(2)私人滋扰能索赔的损失主要是他的土地或者货物的损失,但公共滋扰能索赔的损失可以包括人身伤亡与纯经济损失。(3)在私人滋扰,是否要涉及滋扰方的疏忽或过错,看来是不肯定。Wilberforce 勋爵在 Goldman v. Hargrave (1967) 1 AC 645 先例中提到:"the tort of nuisance, uncertain in his boundary, may comprise a wide variety of situations, in some of which negligence plays no part, in others of which it is decisive."这个说法看来是说有些私人滋扰是严格责任,而另一些要看被告是否有过错或疏忽。在公共滋扰,这方面也是不太肯定,估计还是要滋扰方的行为涉及疏忽或是过错。但不像侵权的疏忽需要原告证明,公共滋扰通常可以假设被告有过错,没有过错的举证责任是在被告。

由于本段是探讨油污或污染造成的庞大经济损失索赔,这与私人滋扰关系不大,所以接下去主要针对公共滋扰。

7.7.2 公共滋扰是属于刑事范畴,不存在民事诉讼的索赔

在权威书籍《Archbold's Criminal Pleading, Evidence and Practice》(58th edn, 2010年)对公共滋扰的定义如下:"Every person is guilty of an offence at common law, known as public nuisance, who does an act not warranted by law, or omits to discharge a legal duty, if the effect of the act or omission is to endanger life, health, property, morals, or comfort of the public, or to obstruct the public in the exercise or employment of rights common to all Her Majesty's subjects."(任何人的行为如果没有被法律允许或者没有尽法律规定的责任,而这种行为或不作为对公众的生命、健康、财产、道德或舒适造成了威胁,或者阻碍了公众行使他们的权利,那么他就会被判犯了普通法下的公众滋扰罪。)这一个定义也可参阅 R v. Shorrock (1994) QB 279 先例与 Wandsworth London Borough Council v. Railtrack plc (2001) EWCA civ. 1236 先例。

这是一个非常广泛的定义,可以说是包括了刑法、侵权或者立法的救济,所以被认为是一个十分危险的普通法理念。

早期的公共滋扰被视为是犯罪行为,采取诉讼行动的是政府而不是个人,这与私人滋扰并不一样。在 1768 年 William Blackstone 之《Commentaries on Laws of England》一书,是这样说:"... common nuisances are such inconvenient or troublesome offences, as annoy the whole community in general, and not merely some particular person; and therefore are **indictable only, and not actionable**; as it would be unreasonable to multiply suits, by giving every man a separate right of action, for what damnifies him in common only with the rest of his fellow subjects."(加黑部分是笔者的强调)

比较近期有 Denning 大法官在 Attorney General v. PYA Quarries Ltd (1957) 2 QB 169 先例之 191 页解释说:"a public nuisance is a nuisance which is so widespread in its range or so indiscrimination in its effect that it would not be reasonable to expect one person to take proceedings on his own responsibility to put a stop to it, but that it should be taken on the responsibility of the community at large."(公共滋扰面实在是太广,所以不能让个别人士采取法律行动如禁制令阻止这种行为。)

涉及公共滋扰的案例或者案件是非常多,这是因为它的面开得很广。比方说,虚报炸弹并且影响大众(如要疏散人群或飞机乘客)显然就是一种公共滋扰。当然如果真的放了炸弹,这进一步变为一种恐怖主义行为。也有不少案件涉及公路的阻碍,

例如 A-G v. Castonia Coaches Ltd (1977) RTR 219 先例就涉及十六架大巴堵塞了交通。在 Lyons, Sons & Co v. Gulliver (1914) 1 Ch 631 先例就涉及被告的剧院每天下午两点半到六点半都会排起长队造成原告的店铺被人群阻挡。法院认为这也构成了公共滋扰,并出了禁令。在比较近期的先例 Re Rimmington (2006) AC 459 是涉及被告开玩笑给他朋友寄了些食盐,没想到在邮局被工作人员发现以为是炭疽而紧急疏散了人群。被告也被以公共滋扰起诉,虽然最后贵族院判他是无罪。另外近年来由于对于环境的关注也导致了越来越多的公共滋扰案件,如涉及危险的废料:Gertsen v. Municipality of Metropolitan Toronto (1943) 41 DLR (3d) 646 先例与 Anthony v. Coal Authority (2005) EWHC 1654 QB 先例;工业臭气:Halsey v. Esso Petroleum Co Ltd (1961) 1 WLR 683 先例与 Shoreham-by-sea UDC v. Dolphin Canadian Proteins Ltd (1973) 71 LGR 261 先例;严重的噪音:Halsey v. Esso Petroleum Co Ltd (1961) 1 WLR 683 先例与 R v. Shorrock (1994) QB 279 先例。

7.7.3　受害方蒙受特殊伤害或特殊损失可以侵权提出索赔

已经在较早时提到过公共滋扰早期是属于刑事的范畴,不存在个别人士可以通过民事诉讼向滋扰方的被告索赔他的损失。但这在 Sowthall v. Dagger (1535) YB 27 Hen. 8 先例,对个别受害方开了门,认为他们只要蒙受了"特殊伤害"(special hurt)就可以索赔损失。该先例说:"I agree well that each nuisance done in the King's highway is punishable in the Leet and not by action, unless it be where one man has suffered greater hurt or inconvenience than the generality have; but he who has suffered such greater displeasure or hurt can have an action to recover the damage which he has by reason of this special hurt. So if one makes a ditch across the highway, and I come riding along the way in the night and I and my horse are thrown into the ditch so that I have great damage and displeasure thereby, I shall have an action here against him who make his ditch across the highway, because I have suffered more damage than any other person."(这大致上是说受到公共滋扰的受害方如果蒙受了一些损失,是其他同样受到滋扰的公众人士通常不会蒙受,该受害方就可以根据民事诉讼索赔这一些特殊伤害或损失。)

这看来也有必要,否则公共滋扰的广泛性,再加上受到一般影响的人会是很多,没有这个特别伤害或特别损失把关就会带来数不清的诉讼。就是一个简单的车祸也会带来许多受到短暂交通阻塞造成的不便的其他车辆的人士可以对造成车祸的驾驶人士提出索赔。

7.7.4　公共滋扰下受害方能否索赔纯经济损失?

与侵权的疏忽不一样,公共滋扰一直以来的先例都可以索赔纯经济损失。这方面可以举一些近期的先例:

(1) Blundy Clark & Co Ltd v. London and North Eastern Railway Co (1931) 2 KB 334 (CA)先例,案情涉及出售砂石的原告因为被告堵塞运河而导致砂石运不出去,蒙受了利润损失的纯经济损失。上诉庭判原告可以成功索赔这笔钱,其中 Greer 大法官说:“If the diminution in value of business premises due to an unauthorised obstruction gives the owner a good cause of action, it seems to me that the interference with his business which gave rise to the loss of business earnings ought a fortiori to be regarded as particular damage giving him a cause of action.”

这种同类的先例在岸上是非常多,就是被告不合理堵塞了马路导致受影响的商店的原告蒙受利润损失并成功索赔。正如 Steel 大法官在近期的先例 Colour Quest Ltd v. Total Downstream UK (2009) 2 Lloyd's Rep 1 说:“... there is long standing and consistent authority in support of the proposition that a claimant can recover damages in public nuisance where access to or from his premises is obstructed so as to occasion a loss of trade attributable to obstruction of his customers' use of the highway and liberty of access.”

(2) Gravesham Borough Council v. British Railways Board (1978) Ch. 379 先例,案情涉及英国铁路公司因为亏损而准备减少渡轮的班次,这导致当地区议会以及伦敦港务局的不满,认为影响乘客。他们向英国法院申请禁令阻止英国铁路公司,但最终败诉,因为英国法院认定受影响的乘客并不多。该先例中涉及公共滋扰的问题,以及能否索赔纯经济损失。Slade 大法官认为业务的损失在公共滋扰一直以来都可以获得赔偿,说:“In all the circumstances there is, in my judgment, sufficient authority for the statement of the law by Greer L. J. in the Blundy Clark case, where he said at p 365: ‘In my judgment it is the law that where a plaintiff has property near a highway which he uses for the purpose of his business, and the highway, whether a canal or a roadway, is unlawfully obstructed, and he is thereby put to greater expense in the conduct of his business, or suffers loss by the diminution of his business, he is entitled to recover damages as a person who has suffered special or peculiar damage beyond that which has been suffered by other members of the public wanting to use the highway or waterway.’ ... I respectfully agree with both the statement of law and the reasoning of Greer L. J. in that case.”

7.7.5 受害方能否索赔次要纯经济损失?

这方面可以先介绍 Colour Quest Ltd v. Total Downstream UK (2009) 2 Lloyd's Rep 1先例。案情涉及2005 年一个位于英国名为 Buncefield Oil Storage Depot 的油库的爆炸,这造成了严重的损害并带来大量受害方的损失索赔。这也是一个公共滋扰的案例,而被告的 Total 石油公司(他是该油库的大股东)不抗拒在这个诉因下是可以向他索赔纯经济损失。在该先例的受害方的原告分两大类,第一类是属于“范围内”(inside the fence)的受害方,他们是在油库内有经营的场所,Total 不抗辩他们对纯经济损失的索赔。但问题是该爆炸影响了很大的范围与许多在“范围外”(outside the fence)的建筑,包括在这些建筑中的600 个工厂雇用的16,500 个员工,其中有一小部分还受到了实质破坏。爆炸也造成很深远的影响包括在受影响地区范围内有多条公路被封闭。这些在范围外的受害方,Total 做出抗拒,认为他只需要负责赔偿受害方的财产是在造成公共滋扰的地区。这方面可以部分节录 Salmon Rainey QC 在 2012 年发表的《To the Great Damage and Common Nuisance of All Liege Subjects of Our Lady the Queen"：Oil Pollution Claims and Public Nuisance》一文如下："Total nevertheless sought to argue, in the context of public nuisance claims brought by 'outside the fence' claimants and which were founded solely upon the widespread closure of roads around the affected site, that the entitlement to damages extended only to a claim where the damage that is alleged to be particular, substantial and direct was caused by injury to proprietary rights of the claimant in, as it was expressed, 'hereditaments in proximity to the public nuisance'. Total argued that the economic loss had to be tied in this context to the existence on the part of the claimant of proprietary rights in the immediate vicinity of the public nuisance. **This was rejected by the Court on the basis that the only restriction on the entitlement to recover was that of the sufficiency of the causative link.** While it might follow as a matter of fact that a person who suffered economic loss and whose property was far away from the affected rights of way might not be entitled to claim damages on the basis that his loss was not sufficiently directly caused by the nuisance, there was no legal principle that only those who adjoined the right of way could claim."（加黑部分是笔者的强调，意思是说法院拒绝了 Total 的抗辩说是范围内才可以获得赔偿，只说唯一的局限是损失必须与事故有足够的因果关系。）

在该先例，Steel 大法官是这样判："It was common ground that it was no bar to recovery of damages in public nuisance that the loss was economic loss and that an individual claimant had to establish a loss which was particular, substantial and direct, over and above that suffered by the public at large... A claimant was entitled to recover damages in public nuisance where not only was his access to his premises obstructed but loss of trade was caused by reason of his customers' right of free passage to the premises being likewise obstructed... There was no requirement for proximity in proprietary terms, so that it was not only those with proprietary rights that could claim..."

这样看来针对次要纯经济损失的立场还是会跟本章 7.6 段提到的 IOPC Fund 的立场差不多。毕竟，普通法的政策就是侵权方的过错需要承担的责任不能是无止境的，而必须要有一个合理与现实的限制。只是到底英国法院和 IOPC Fund 对于个别案件的因果关系要求的宽紧是否一样还是不肯定，毕竟公共滋扰的起点是属于刑事范畴。

7.7.6　公共滋扰与油污/污染的索赔

从上述的介绍可以看到涉及海上油污/污染如果没有国际公约的约束下，受害方还是要依赖普通法或者一般法律索赔损失，特别是纯经济损失（不论是首要还是次要），在英国法律下是完全不能依赖疏忽的侵权，而需要依赖公共滋扰。但据悉还没有这方面的直接案例，虽然有一些比较相关的先例如 The "Wagon Mound"（No. 2）

(1976) 1 AC 617, Environment Agency v. Milford Haven Port Authority (1999) 1 Lloyd's Rep 673, Esso Petroleum Co. Ltd v. Southport Corporation (1956) AC 218。

8. 疏忽的侵权在有特殊关系下可以索赔纯经济损失

本章第6段已经介绍过在英国十分重要的 Hedley Byrne & Co Ltd v. Heller & Partners Ltd (1963) 1 Lloyd's Rep 485 先例,发展起来有"特殊关系"(special relationship)的侵权是可以作为索赔纯经济损失的例外。特殊关系的定义可节录上诉庭的 Ormrod 大法官在 Esso v. Mardon (1976) 2 Lloyd's Rep 305 先例中有说:"There is no magic in the phrase 'special relationship'; it means no more than a relationship the nature of which is that one party, for a variety of possible reasons, will be regarded by the law as under a duty of care to the other."(特殊关系一词没有什么巧妙,它是指双方的关系在本质上是其中一方由于各种原因,法律视为是他对另外一方有一个小心谨慎的责任。)

这特殊关系也在 Hedley Byrne & Co Ltd 先例中有详细针对,如 Reid 勋爵解释是一方当事人向对方寻求消息并会相信与依赖这一个消息,而另一方当事人也知道对方会合理依赖他提供的消息,双方就有了特殊关系,说:"the party seeking the information and advice was trusting the other to exercise such a degree of case as the circumstances required, where it was reasonable for him to do that and where the other gave the information or advice when he knew or ought to have known that the inquirer was relying on him."

另是 Devlin 勋爵也解释说特殊关系是"雷同合约"(equivalent to contract)的关系,只是双方不严格拥有法律要求的有效合约必须拥有的条件,如欠缺对价(或其他方面)。他是这样说:"... the categories of special relationships, which may give rise to a duty to take care... are not limited to contractual relationships or to relationships of fiduciary duty, but also include relationships which... are 'equivalent to contract' that is, where there is an assumption of responsibility in circumstances in which, but for the absence of consideration, there would be a contract."

特殊关系是有两大类,第一类是侵权方对无辜方有一个"受信的关系"(fiduciary relationship),第二类是侵权方对无辜方提供特殊技能的意见/消息或服务,并且可以合理估计到后者会依赖这些言行并蒙受纯经济损失。这方面可节录 Browne-Wilkinson 勋爵在 White v. Jones (HL) (1995) 2 AC 207 先例的说法:"Though the categories of cases in which such special relationship can be held to exist are not closed, as yet only two categories have been identified, viz. 1. where there is a fiduciary relationship and 2. where the defendant has voluntarily answered a question or tendered skilled advice or services in circumstances where he knows or ought to know that an identified plaintiff will rely on his answers or advice. In both these categories this special relationship is created by the defendant voluntarily assuming to act in the matter by involving himself in the plaintiff's affairs or by choosing to speak. If he does so assume to act or speak he is liable to have assumed responsibility for carrying through the matter he has entered upon."

8.1　侵权方是否愿意承担责任的考验

看来,特殊关系的重要之处是看侵权方是否有在他的言行中"愿意承担责任"(undertake to assume responsibility)。例如在本章一开始有谈到有关实质的货损货差,船东作为货物的托运人是有侵权的责任。但货方如果向船东索赔纯经济损失,就需要额外的要求,也就是这一个愿意承担责任的要求。这可节录 Aikens 大法官《Bills of Lading》(2006 年)一书之 182 页,注脚 9 提到说:"In the context of a claim for damages for economic loss, as opposed to a claim for damages for physical loss or damage, the key test is whether the defendant has assumed responsibility."

在 The Lloyd's Litigation (1994) 2 Lloyd's Rep 468 先例中,Goff 勋爵提到了 Hedley Byrne & Co Ltd v. Heller & Partners Ltd (1963) 1 Lloyd's Rep 485 先例所确立的大原则就是在这一方面,说:"we can derive some understanding of the breadth of the principle underlying the case. We can see that it rests upon a relationship between the parties, which may be general or specific to the particular transaction, and which may or may not be contractual in nature. All of their Lordships spoke in terms of one party having assumed or undertaken a responsibility towards the other. On this point, Lord Devlin spoke in particularly clear terms... Further, Lord Morris spoke of that party being possessed of a special skill which he undertakes to apply for the assistance of another who relies upon such skill."

在这一个考验下,表示受害方与被指控的侵权方关系隔得越远,就越是谈不上有一个愿意承担责任的因素。例如,律师与他的长期客户是有特殊关系,该客户向律师咨询法律意见,律师在没有收费或正式接受委任的情况下提供了意见,事后被证明是错误与疏忽,并导致了客户的损失。显然在目前的英国法律,律师是被视为是要对客户的损失负责,因为他提供法律意见的时候就可以被视为是愿意承担责任。但如果关系隔了一层,该客户把同样的错误法律意见给了他的亲友,是该律师根本不认识或知道的人士,就很难说是律师愿意对客户的亲友承担责任。

8.2　这是一个客观而不是主观的考验

看违约方是否愿意承担责任,是不理会他的主观想法,毕竟这也无法证明违约方到底是怎么想的。考验是法院或仲裁庭客观看违约方是否愿意对受害方承担责任。例如,在 Hedley Byrne & Co Ltd v. Heller & Partners Ltd (1963) 1 Lloyd's Rep 485 先例,违约方的被告在提供的错误的资信报告中就加上了一句"不负任何责任"(without responsibility),这就是明确的证据说明被告不愿意承担责任,贵族院也是因为这个原因判是被告不必对受害方的原告负责。针对这一个客观的考验,可节录 Williams v. Natural Life Health Foods Ltd (1998) 1 WLR 830 先例中,Steyn 勋爵所说如下:"The touchstone of liability is not the state of mind of the defendant. An objective test means that the primary focus must be on things said or done by the defendant or on his behalf in his dealings with the claimant. Obviously, the impact of what the defendant says or does must be judged in the light of the relevant contextual scene. Subject to this qualification, the primary focus must be on exchanges... which cross the line between the defendant and the [claimant]."

8.3 不存在向受害方承担责任的先例

这可介绍贵族院的 Commissioners of Customs and Excise v. Barclays Bank Plc (2007) 1 AC 181 先例,案情涉及英国法院作出冻结令,把原告债务人的存款冻结,而存款是在被告的银行。但由于被告的疏忽,让这笔存款流走。这里会涉及藐视法院的课题,但这也补救不了原告的损失。所以原告以民事诉讼向被告银行提出这一笔纯经济损失的索赔,指被告对原告有一个小心谨慎的责任。在贵族院,这一个说法被否定,认为被告从来没有向原告表示过愿意承担责任,而对于法院作出的冻结令,被告银行唯一需要承担的是面向法院的责任。Mance 勋爵是这样说:"it was 'difficult in any meaningful sense to speak of the bank(被告) as having voluntarily assumed responsibility even for the task in relation to which it was allegedly negligent, let alone responsibility towards the Commissioners(原告) for the task. In a very general sense any bank, indeed any one carrying on any activity during the course of which they might have cause to hold the monies or possessions of another, might be said to accept the risk that a third party might obtain a freezing order in respect of such monies or possessions. But that is to assign to the concept of voluntary assumption of responsibility so wide a meaning as to deprive it of effective utility.'"

8.4 考虑被告是否愿意承担责任的因素

考虑被告是否愿意承担责任是要根据每一个不同案件的事实客观考虑各种因素。在 James McNaughton Paper Group Ltd v. Hicks Anderson & Co (1991) 2 QB 113 先例中,上诉庭的 Neill 大法官举了六个要考虑的因素:(1) the purpose for which the statement was made(作出有关意见的目的);(2) the purpose for which the statement was communicated(提供意见给受害方的目的);(3) the relationship between the adviser, the advisee and any relevant third party(提供意见与接受意见及其他相关第三人之间的关系);(4) the size of any class to which the advisee belongs(接受意见方的人数有多少);(5) the state of knowledge of the adviser(提供意见方的知识程度);(6) reliance by the advisee(接受意见方依赖的程度)。

另在 Reeman v. Department of Transport (1997) PNLR 618 贵族院先例,Bingham 勋爵是这样说:"[claimant]-specific; that is it must be given to the actual [claimant] or a member of an [identifiable] group to which the [claimant] belongs. Secondly, the statement must be purpose-specific: the statement must be made for the very purpose for which the actual [claimant] has used it. Thirdly, the statement must be transaction-specific: the statement must be made with reference to the very transaction into which the [claimant] has entered in reliance upon it."

以下简单介绍这上述应考虑的一些因素。

8.4.1 考虑因素之一:有关的意见(或服务)是什么目的与作用

这是在要求的意见中,需要让对方明确了解是为了什么目的,这可让提供意见的被告衡量有关的风险,决定是否收取费用与什么费用,甚至拒绝提供意见。这可介绍 Reeman v. Department of Transport (1997) PNLR 618 先例,受害方的原告根据被告所做出的一份船舶适航证书购买了一艘渔船。但由于被告的船舶检查有错误与疏忽,导致了该证书不正确,并事后被撤回。这令原告不能使用该渔船而蒙受纯经济损失。但法院认为该证书只是为了证实船舶安全而作出的意见,不是为了让原告依赖作为投资。

除了意见外,提供服务也是有同样的考虑因素。在 West Bromwich Albion FC Ltd v. El-Safty (2006) EWCA Civ. 1299 先例,案情涉及原告的球会推荐了一位医生给他的受伤球星进行治疗。但由于该医生的错误与疏忽,导致了该球星必须结束足球生涯。球会在该球星的合约中损失高达 300 万英镑,并向该医生提出这一笔纯经济损失。但在上诉庭,判是该医生并没有意愿对球会承担责任,因为医疗服务只是为了把该球星医好,从来没有考虑到球会的经济损失,与后者没有一个邻近的关系。Rix 大法官是这样说:"there was no proximity as the dominant relationship is that of the doctor and his patient, and the dominant context is that of the [patient's] health, not his employer's financial security."

Rix 大法官也提到要求医生承担这种纯经济损失并不公平的原因:"if WBA(球会)had wanted [the defendant's] advice for the purpose of its own interests, it could have made that plain to him. He would then have been in a position where he could choose to charge for that advice and the risks involved in giving it and/or disclaiming liability."

8.4.2 考虑因素之二:提供意见与接受意见人士之间的关系与类别

这一个主要是"大水门"的考虑,所以必须严格控制提供与接受意见方的关系是否紧密,被告在提供错误与疏忽意见的时候是否可以理解到会有这一个后果。在 Preston v. Torfaen BC (1993) 36 Con LR 48 先例,涉及一个工程师在检查地基时有错误与疏忽,导致了建造的房屋有问题。但法院判是该工程师对该房屋的后来买方没有一个特殊关系可让后来买方向工程师索赔纯经济损失。毕竟在工程师犯错的时候,受害买方是谁也不会知道,工程师不会愿意对他承担责任。

上诉庭的 Henry 大法官在 Omega Trust Co Ltd v. Wright Son & Pepper (1997) PNLR 424 先例也是这样说:"It seems to me that this professional valuer, valuing expensive properties in a commercial context, was entitled to know who his client was and to whom his duty was owed. He was entitled... to refuse to assume liability to any unknown lender, indeed, I would go further and say that he is entitled to refuse to assume liability to any unknown lender to whom he had not agreed. He was entitled to increase fee... as a term of permitting the second lender to rely on the valuation because... potentially it can be more expensive to be sued by two lenders rather than one."

8.4.3 考虑因素之三:合理的依赖与信任

这一个考虑因素是因为在一些案例中,原告并没有事实依赖被告所提供的意见或服务作出决定,并蒙受纯经济损失。在 Spring v. Guardian Assurance Plc (1995) 2 AC 296 先例中,案情涉及原告因为其前雇主的被告疏忽错误准备了一份推荐信给他的新雇主而导致原告丢了工作,法院判是雇佣关系证明原告可以合理依赖被告所提供的服务。Goff 勋爵是这样说:"The provision of such references is a service regularly provided by employers to their employees;... Furthermore, when, such a reference is provided by an employer, it is plain that the employee relies on him to exercise due skill and care in the preparation of the reference before making it available to the third party."

原被告之间的关系是否是依赖与信任,主要就是看原告依赖被告的小心谨慎责任是否合理。比如说被告是否有技能提供意见或服务,如在 Mutual Life & Citizens' Assurance Co Ltd v. Evatt (1971) AC 793 颇有争议的贵族院先例中,被告保险人提供有关投资的意见。另在 Stevens v. Bermondsey and Southwark Group Hospital Management Committee (1963) 107 SJ 478 先例中,判是医院的医疗人员错误提供有关法律责任的意见而导致原告蒙受纯经济损失是没有 Hedley Byrne & Co Ltd v. Heller & Partners Ltd (1963) 1 Lloyd's Rep 485 先例的责任,他们的责任只是能够针对医疗意见或服务。反过来,如果原告依赖被告的错误与疏忽根本不合理,也是有同样的结果,在 Williams v. Natural Life Health Foods Ltd (1998) 1 WLR 830 先例,贵族院判是原告作为一家公司的客户,是不合理地依赖公司董事(被告)会尽小心谨慎责任。在 McNaughton Paper Group Ltd v. Hicks Anderson & Co (A Firm) (1991) 2 QB 113 先例中,判是原告作为一家有经验的公司进行收购是不会只依赖被告所草拟的账目。上诉庭的 Neill 大法官说:"in business transactions conducted at arms' length it may sometimes be difficult for an advisee to prove that he was entitled to act on a statement without taking any independent advice."

此外,被告在一些很随意与非正式的场合下提供专业意见,也会被判是不足够可让受害方的原告依赖:Tidman v. Reading BC (1994) 3 PLR 72, Electra KPMG Peat Marwick (1998) PNLR 135; Fashion Brokers Ltd v. Clarke Hayes (A Firm) (2000) PNLR 473 等先例。

9. 法律强加小心谨慎的责任给提供特殊技能的人士与专业人士

这里首先要介绍的是重要贵族院先例 Hedley Byrne & Co Ltd v. Heller & Partners Ltd (1963) 1 Lloyd's Rep 485。该先例涉及被告的银行给原告提供了其客户的错误的资信报告,结果该客户清盘而导致原告蒙受损失,原告向被告提出索赔损失,指他作出的资信报告没有尽合理小心谨慎的责任。在该先例,被告提供的资信报告是没有收取任何报酬,所以双方也谈不上有合约关系,因为欠缺了有效合约必须拥有的"对价"(consideration)。这表示被告必须要有一个侵权的责任填补这一个漏洞,而且要对原告的纯经济损失负责,才会有胜诉的机会。贵族院判是如果双方有特殊关系(主要是指一方提供给另外一方一些特殊技能的服务或者特殊消息,并估计后者会依赖),那么就存在一个合理小心并提供准确消息的特殊责任(不论双方是否有合约的存在),说:"There could be a special relationship between parties which imposed a duty to give careful advice and accurate information; but responsibility could attach only to the single act (the giving of the reference), and only if the doing of the act implied a voluntary undertaking to assume responsibility."

Hedley Byrne & Co Ltd v. Heller & Partners Ltd 先例带来后来许多其他先例的延伸,也涉及许多属于纯经济损失的同步责任。一个主要原因就是特殊技能所带来的特殊关系有很宽松的解释,正如 Goff 勋爵在 Spring v. Guardian Assurance (1995) 2 AC 296 先例所说的:"to be understood in a broad sense, certainly broad enough to embrace special knowledge and that this could include situations where the defendant has access to information and fails to exercise due care... in drawing on that source of information."这就带来了一个经常会出现的问题,特别是涉及一些有特殊技能的专业人士。他们提供的意见或消息通常都会有合约关系,但也不排除有情况是涉及没有收取报酬。反正是只要这一个意见或消息是错误与疏忽,应该说是根据合约或者根据侵权(因为不涉及报酬),都应该带来同样的后果,就是要对受害方的实质损失或纯经济损失负责。

许多类别的专业人士都负有这种小心谨慎的责任,如:针对律师:White v. Jones (HL) (1995) 2 AC 207; Midland Bank Trust Co Ltd v. Hett, Stubbs & Kemp (1979) Ch 384 等先例。针对测量师与估价师:Smith v. Eric S Bush (1990) 1 AC 831 等先例。针对会计师:Caparo Industries plc v. Dickman (1990) 2 AC 605 等先例。保险经纪人:Youell v. Bland Welch & Co Ltd (The Superhulls Cover Case No. 2) (1990) 2 Lloyd's Rep 431; Punjab National Bank v. De Boinville (1992) 1 Lloyd's Rep 7; Vesta v. Butcher (1986) 2 Lloyd's Rep 179 等先例。劳合社经纪人:The Lloyd's Litigation (1994) 2

Lloyd's Rep 468;Aiken v. Stewart Wrightson Members Agency Ltd (1995) 2 Lloyd's Rep 618 等先例。向购买船舶基金提供商业资信与技术援助的公司:The "Ardent" (1997) 2 Lloyd's Rep 547 等先例。

9.1 非专业人士愿意承担责任也会有同样结果

上一小段所针对的专业人士是可被假设有特殊技能并且受害方会依赖,但普通法非常灵活,在其他的情况下可假设一位非专业人士"愿意承担责任"(undertake to assume responsibility),而受害方也合理依赖而蒙受损失,法律也会增加一个侵权的小心谨慎责任。例如在 The Lloyd's Litigation (1994) 2 Lloyd's Rep 468 先例中,Goff 勋爵就提到了 Hedley Byrne & Co Ltd v. Heller & Partners Ltd (1963) 1 Lloyd's Rep 485 先例中 Devlin 勋爵的一段话,是指在每一个不同的案件最主要看侵权方是否愿意承担责任。例如一位被告对受害方的原告说"你可以省下找专业人士的钱,我会替你办妥,你大可以放心"。这被告就不会因为他并非是专业人士,没有特殊技能而没有责任。Devlin 勋爵是这样说:"Since the essence of the matter in the present case and in others of the same type is the acceptance of responsibility, I should like to guard against the imposition of restrictive terms notwithstanding that the essential condition is fulfilled. If a defendant says to a plaintiff: 'Let me do this for you: do not waste your money in employing a professional, I will do it for nothing and you can rely on me.' I do not think he could escape liability simply because he belongs to no profession or calling, had no qualifications or special skill and did not hold himself out as having any."

9.2 非专业人士拥有受害方会依赖的资料也有同样结果

已经提到过特殊关系并不严格局限在专业人士,显然"特殊技能"是有一个宽松的解释,包括侵权方有受害方会依赖的一些资料。这可介绍 Esso v. Mardon (1976) 2 Lloyd's Rep 305 先例,案情涉及 Esso(美国与全球最大的石油公司)想在 Southport 建立一个加油站,并进行一个可行性调查。该调查结果显示了根据车流量,该加油站每年应可出售汽油达 20 万加仑之多。但事后情况发生了变化,就是 Esso 申请执照时,加油站不被批准面对大马路修建。这一来,经过加油站的车流量会减少。但 Esso 并没有降低他在较早调查中所作出的估计,并以此告知受害方的 Mardon 先生,导致 Mardon 先生以高租金向 Esso 租用了这一个加油站 3 年的营运许可权。但事实上该加油站每年只能出售 8 万加仑的汽油,因此 Mardon 先生亏大本,并提起这一个诉讼。

先要说明该案例发生在 1961 年,当时的 1967 年《误述法》(Misrepresentation Act)还不存在,所以 Mardon 先生如果指称 Esso 对事实有误述就必须证明是"欺诈性"(fraudulent)才能索赔损失。而另一个困难是误述方对将来所作出的估计并不属于一个误述,误述只能是针对已经存在的事实:Bisset v. Wilkinson (1927) AC 177。在第一审也被判是不存在一个"附带保证"(collateral warranty),因为 Esso 并没有向 Mardon 先生保证每年可出售 20 万加仑汽油。所以 Mardon 先生必须要依赖 Hedley Byrne & Co Ltd v. Heller & Partners Ltd (1963) 1 Lloyd's Rep 485 先例确立下来的"特殊关系”(special relationship),就是 Esso 是否明知道 Mardon 先生会依赖,而有一个对车流量估计的错误与疏忽陈述的侵权责任。而 Mardon 先生在第一审与在上诉庭都在这方面胜诉。

Denning 勋爵是这样说:

“A professional man may give advice under a contract for reward; or without a contract, in pursuance of a voluntary assumption of responsibility, gratuitously without reward. In either case he is under one and the same duty to the use of reasonable care: see Cassidy v. Ministry of Health (1951) 2 KB 343 at pp. 359 – 360. In the one case it is by reason of a term implied by law. In the other, it is by reason of duty imposed by law. For a breach of that duty, he is liable in damages; and those damages should be, and are, the same, whether he is sued in contract or in tort. . .

It seems to me that Hedley Byrne, properly understood, covers this particular proposition: If a man, who has or professes to have specialknowledge or skill, makes a representation by virtue thereof to another - be it advice, information or opinion - with the intention of inducing him to enter into a contract with him, he is under a duty to use reasonable care to see that the representation is correct, and that the advice, information or opinion is reliable. If he negligently gives unsound advice or misleading information or expresses an erroneous opinion, and thereby induces the other side into a contract with him, he is liable in damages. . . .

Applying this principle, it is a plain that Esso professed to have – and did in fact have – special knowledge or skill in estimating the throughput of a filling station. They made the representation – they forecast a throughput of 200,000 gallons – intending to induce Mr. Mardon to enter into a tenancy on the faith of it. They made it negligently. It was a ‘fatal error’. And thereby induced Mr. Mardon to enter into a contract of tenancy that was disastrous to him. For this misrepresentation they are liable in damages. ”

10. 特殊关系下合约关系所带来的同步责任

较早时候已经提到过,受害方与专业人士之间通常都会有合约关系的存在,英国法律是承认违约与侵权的同步责任。也就是受害方的原告可以选择以违约(一般与专业人士的合约即使没有明示条文,也会有默示要求他们提供专业与小心的服务)或者以侵权向被告提出起诉,索赔损失。

在本章第 3 段已经提到过,目前英国的法律在涉及违约与侵权的情况下,做法上会是先考虑有关侵权的责任,然后看有关的合约是否有条文豁免或者减轻有关侵权的责任,正如 Goff 勋爵在 The Lloyd ' s Litigation (1994) 2 Lloyd ' s Rep 468 先例中所说："Approached as a matter of principle, therefore, it is right to attribute to that assumption of responsibility, together with its concomitant reliance, a tortious liability, and then to enquire whether or not that liability is excluded by the contract because the latter is inconsistent with it."

在该贵族院重要先例，Goff 勋爵在分析了有关这一个同步责任的问题后，也同意加拿大最高院的 Le Dain 大法官在 Central Trust Co v. Rafuse (1986) 31 DLR 4th 481 先例所说的有关违约与侵权同步责任的处理："A concurrent or alternative liability in tort will not be admitted if its effect would be to permit the plaintiff to circumvent or escape a contractual exclusion or limitation of liability for the act or omission that would constitute the tort. Subject to this qualification, where concurrent liability in tort and contract exists the plaintiff has the right to assert the cause of action that appears to be the most advantageous to him in respect of any particular legal consequence."

Goff 勋爵也表示同意另一个新西兰的先例 Rowlands v. Collow (1992) 1 NZLR 178，案情是针对特殊技能人士（一位工程师）错误或疏忽提供意见或消息的责任，新西兰的 Thomas 大法官是这样说："The issue is now virtually incontestable; a person who has performed professional services may be held liable concurrently in contract and in negligence, unless the terms of the contract preclude the tortuous liability."

11. 受害方本人有部分过错的分摊

说到分摊责任与损失，本段所针对的是侵权方有错误与疏忽外，受害方也或多或少有一部分错误与疏忽，这种情况在现实中是大部分。本段不针对的是侵权方的被告有错误与疏忽外，还有其他第三人也有一定的责任，这种情况可称为是"多位侵权方"（multiple tortfeasor）。这种情况对无辜与本人没有过错的受害方而言，是不存在分摊。被告不能说如果分摊我只能是50%的责任，只赔50%的损失，其余你向第三人索赔。这是因为侵权方对受害方的损失是要承担"共同与连带责任"（jointly and severally liable）。所以一位侵权方被受害方起诉，但他认为有其他侵权方也会需要负责，在法院他就应该申请把这些第三人也拉进来作为第二或第三被告，一并作为共同被告，然后让法院在判决责任的时候同时作出分摊。另外的做法是侵权方的被告可事后向其他第三人要求分摊他的赔偿责任，这是根据 1978 年的《Civil Liability (Contribution) Act》。有关这一个课题将会在本书第九章之第 3 段有详述，在这里不重复。

接下去是探讨侵权与违约的一个重要不同后果，就是可否根据 1945 年《The Law Reform (Contributory Negligence) Act》在违约方/侵权方与受害方都有一定程度错误与疏忽的情况下分摊责任与损失。如果受害方本人有过错或疏忽，但不足以中断因果链的情况下，在合约方面怎么样处理损失赔偿是并不容易。在这方面针对侵权，已经提到过早在1945年就有了立法。这立法是《The Law Reform（Contributory Negligence）Act》，但它并不是针对合约下的违约。这就带来违约下的损失计算的困难，特别是受害方自己有部分过错的情况经常发生。例如，受害方通过保险经纪人投保，但由于他的过错与疏忽，导致投保金额不足，或是漏了披露以致白白投保，或是没有排除一些受害方履行不了的承诺性保证等。这些显然都是主要的前因，导致了受害方后来要求保险人赔付的时候赔不足或拒赔的后果。但保险经纪人经常可以指称受害方自己也有过错与疏忽，即使轻微至10%或20%，如没有跟进或紧密跟进，受害方后来有许多的机会知道这种缺陷但没有作出补救。在接受受害方自己也是有错的情况下，问题就是这错误能否中断因果链而导致保险经纪人完全可以免责？看个别案件的事实而定，可以说是大部分情况下受害方的错误是相对轻微，不足中断因果链。受害方的原告会为了避免根据1945年立法的分摊，而只是向被告提出合约的索赔。如果受害方也要为他的轻微错误与疏忽付出部分代价，在合约的关系下看来只能是适用1945年立法（如果可以的话）才有可能。以下介绍在这一方面的其他案例。

11.1 De Meza 先例

在De Meza v. Apple（1975）1 Lloyd's Rep 498先例，案情是关于被告的核算师疏忽在保单内填了一个错误而且较低的金额，带来"投保不足"（under-insured），在事后原告（律师事务所）的办公楼因为火灾而蒙受损失（这正是受保的事项），令受害方赔不足。但受害方与他的律师也有错，如果可以发觉保单的这个错误，就可及时纠正。在高院一审，Brabin大法官认为1945年立法适用，以70/30分摊损失。但到了上诉庭，上诉庭却不肯对这1945年立法是否适用作出任何决定。但这一来，De Meza的先例就被之后许多合约关系下的仲裁案件依赖以支持他们分摊损失的做法。

在该先例中法院是判受害方自己要承担30%的损失，只能向被告成功索赔70%的损失。Brabin大法官是这样说：

"If the claim is one in contract only, I find that the omissions by Mr. de Meza do not amount to a*novus actus interveniens* following upon the breach of contract by the defendants. There were two effective and continuing causes which resulted in the damages suffered by the plaintiffs, namely, the fault of the defendants and the conduct of Mr. de Meza who did not in his own interest exercise reasonable care for the plaintiffs and thereby contributed to the damage. It follows that the damage to which the plaintiffs are entitled in this action must, by virtue of the Act（这是指1945年的立法）which I consider applies to this case, be apportioned according to the causative potency of the acts and also the blameworthiness of the parties.

Looking at this matter broadly and bearing in mind that the plaintiffs are the persons they are, acting in the circumstances in which they find themselves, I apportion liability and damage as to70 per cent. in the defendants and 30 per cent. in the plaintiffs."

11.2 The "Shinjitsu Maru No. 5"先例

这个情况维持到 The "Shinjitsu Maru No. 5" (1985) 1 Lloyd's Rep 568 先例,这方面的问题才再度被英国法院重新考虑。该案例涉及装运的货物在海上移动,船舶被迫回航"重新堆装"(restow),这自然带来时间损失与额外费用,争议是承租人或船东谁要承担这笔损失。

仲裁庭判是:(i)承租人在该租约条文下对船东有一个"小心谨慎的责任"(duty of care),是要他的发货人小工与验货师小心工作。(ii)发货人不许用叉车是不合理。(iii)船员的木匠没有处理好"垫货料"(timber dunnage),这是船东的责任。(iv)承租人的验货师疏忽的对船长保证货物堆装满意,可以开航。(v)船长疏忽,没有妥善的监督与控制"装货与堆装"(loading and stowing)。

根据以上裁定的事实,仲裁庭裁定船长的责任是有60%,承租人则有40%,损失亦是如此分摊。如果不是适用这1945年立法的分摊,就有可能根据因果关系判主要原因是船长的过错与疏忽,船长要承担所有的损失了。

但上诉去了高院,Neill 大法官判是1945年的立法并不适用在合约,他说:"... the words in Section (1) of the 1945 Act were directed towards tortious liabilities alone and were not apt to cover breaches of contractual duties of care or breaches of statutory duty which gave rise liabilities other than tortious liabilities; the 1945 Act had no application to a claim in contract and the charterers were entitled to succeed in full in their claim against the owners."

11.3 Vesta v. Butcher 先例

接着是 Vesta v. Butcher (1986) 2 Lloyd's Rep 179 的重要先例,Hobhouse 大法官在该案例中不同意 Neill 大法官在 The "Shinjitsu Maru No 5"的判决,认为1945年的立法并没有排除适用在合约的关系,说:"I do accept that the Act was not concerned with displacing contractual rights as is demonstrated by provisos (a) and (b) in s. 1(1), but these very provisos contemplate that the Act is capable of application where there is a contractual relationship between the parties and thus cast doubt on the approach adopted by Lord Justice Neill."

可以先简单介绍 Vesta v. Butcher 先例的案情是关于一个在挪威养鱼场的保险,其中一项投保是"任何原因导致养鱼的损失"(loss of living fish from any cause whatsoever)。在12个月的保单中,有一个"承诺性保证"(promissory warranty)养鱼场要每天24小时有人当值。保险中的"承诺性保证"非同小可,它必须被严格执行,否则保险合约马上自动终止。

事后,受保人(养鱼场主人)发觉这"保证"执行不了,向保险公司 Vesta 提出修改保单免去了这承诺性保证。Vesta 另叫他的保险经纪人 Butcher 向伦敦再保人提出同样修改要求,但不知为何,保险经纪人忘了此事,而且大家都忘了跟进直至6个月后出事。不幸之事是一场暴风雨令养鱼场损坏,所养的鱼全部流失。再保人拒赔,是指承诺性保证未被严格执行。这拒赔理由是完全能成立,但这一来,Vesta 夹在当中可就惨了。于是他向保险经纪人提出索赔,指他疏忽,没有尽到“合理小心谨慎”(reasonable care)的责任。

经纪人抗辩说他即使有错,Vesta 也有错,他自已也忘了跟进,所以在之后 6 个月未出事前 Vesta 明知这 24 小时承诺性保证仍未被修改,也是不跟进。法院判是双方都有过错,但 Vesta 的过错程度更高。Hobhouse 大法官判是要保险经纪人承担 1/4 的责任,但 Vesta 承担 3/4 的责任。

接下去的就要考虑在损失方面能否以 1945 年立法 1/4 ~ 3/4 分摊,因为如果不能,则 Vesta 要全部承担损失了,因为他的过错,他应受的“怪责”(blame),才是出事的“主因”。

Hobhouse 大法官认为合约责任有三大类:

(1)合约条文有严格责任(或只是极轻微责任,又或是另一个极端的索性免责,反正这都是订约自由,只要订约双方你情我愿),与被告是否有疏忽没有关系(Where the defendant's liability arises from some contractual provision which does not depend on negligence on the part of the defendant)。这合约责任是与侵权责任无关系的,明显是 1945 年立法不适用。

(2)有关的合约条文也有约定合理小心谨慎的责任,但不存在有独立的侵权责任。换言之,一旦脱离了合约的关系,原告就不能以侵权向被告提出侵权的索赔(Where the defendant's liability arises from a contractual obligation which is expressed on terms of taking care [or its equivalent] but does not correspond to a common law duty to take care which would exist in the given case independently of contract)。这方面是有一定的争议与不明朗,照说是在这一类的责任,一脱离了合约,这就不能成功以侵权行为起诉,则 1945 年立法也不适用。但已经介绍过曾有个别案件如 De Meza v. Apple (1975) 1 Lloyd's Rep 498 先例,属于第二类的责任,在一审时被判是 1945 年立法适用,但上诉去了上诉庭,拒绝在这方面作出任何决定。

(3)合约条文带来的责任与侵权行为责任完全一致,两种责任也同时存在。这一来,由于英国法律承认“同步责任”(concurrent liability),受害方可以选择对他最为有利的办法提起诉讼,则 1945 年立法也应该适用(Where the defendant's liability in contract is the same as his liability in the tort of negligence independently of the existence of any contract)。Hobhouse 大法官认为这第三类的合约关系或责任适用 1945 年立法分摊责任与损失十分明显,并说:“It is commonplace that actions are brought by persons who have suffered personal injuries as the result of the negligence of the person sued and that there is a contractual as well as tortious relationship. In such cases apportionment of blame is invariably adopted by the Court notwithstanding that the plaintiff could sue in contract as well as in tort. The example normally cited in the present context is the decision of the Court of Appeal in Sayers v. Harlow UDC (1958) 1 WLR 623, which concerned a contractual visitor to premises (a lady who had paid to use a public lavatory). The Court of Appeal said it did not matter whether the cause of action was put in tort or in contract and proceeded to apportion blame awarding her three-quarters of her damages. This was a decision on a category (3) case."

在该 Vesta v. Butcher 先例,Hobhouse 大法官判是属于第三类的合约责任,所以 1945 年立法适用。Hobhouse 大法官是这样说:"I consider that, in the present case and in any similar category (3) case where there is no express contractual provision which defines the parties' rights and liabilities in a different way, apportionment of blame and liability is open to the tribunal. My reasons are twofold. First, I am bound by the Court of Appeal so to decide in a category (3) case. Secondly, the correct analysis is that independently of contract there is a statutory or common law relationship which exists between the parties and which can then give rise to tortious liabilities which fall to be adjusted in accordance with the 1945 Act and the relevant question in any given case is whether the parties have by their contract varied that position. Here they patently have not."

该先例上诉到贵族院,但维持原判:(1989) 1 Lloyd's Rep 331。

上述三类不同的合约责任是一个十分复杂的问题,稍后会另段详解,特别是它涉及合约与侵权的"同步责任"(concurrent liability)问题。

11.4 Barclays Bank plc v. Fairclough Building Ltd 先例

在 Barclays Bank plc v. Fairclough Building Ltd (1995) QB 214 先例,案情涉及承建商的被告为原告的大楼进行装修工程时,错误与疏忽以不当的办法,用高压水冲洗含有石棉的屋顶而造成了"石棉尘"(asbestos dust),并大面积的造成污染而给原告带来严重的损失。但被告以原告没有劝止与监督作为理由,要求根据 1945 年立法承担部分责任与损失。本来根据装修工程合约,被告是在这方面有严格责任。在第一审,判是被告的疏忽是造成损失的主要原因,但原告也是有部分过错,所以原告自己要承担 40% 的损失。注意这是涉及双方的合约关系中有一个严格的责任,也就是在 11.1 段提到的在 De Meza v. Apple (1975) 1 Lloyd's Rep 498 先例后,即使是合约的关系下也被法院与许多仲裁案件依赖以支持分摊损失的做法。

但一审的判决被上诉庭推翻,认为 1945 年立法根本不适用于严格责任。合约一方愿意承担严格责任,也代表了否定受害方要分摊责任与损失。

11.5 Raflatac v. Eade & others 先例

Raflatac v. Eade & others (1999) 1 Lloyd's Rep 506 先例的案情涉及原告的受害方与第一被告订下合约对他的办公室进行装修,其中包括更换灭火洒水器装置。针对灭火洒水器的工程,被告另承包给另一家公司,该公司也是先例中的第二被告。在第二被告开始进行工程的第一天,工人错误地在没有把水源切断前就把洒水头拆下,这导致大量的水涌进把办公室淹没,并造成很大损失。受害方事后向两位被告提出起诉,针对第一被告是违约,而针对第二被告是侵权(因为与第二被告并没有合约关系)。第二被告的抗辩只能是受害方自己也有过错,需要承担部分损失,这些过错包括受害方没有事先告诉第二被告有关灭火洒水装置设备的结构,受害方不应该把受损的东西(主要是文件)放在地上而不放在书架上,与受害方不应疏忽让排水口堵塞,导致淹没变得严重。最后受害方与第二被告是达成庭外和解。但针对第一被告,由于双方是合约的关系,就涉及1945年有关分摊责任是否适用的争议,而这针对第二被告的侵权是毫无疑问可以分摊责任的。

这里就涉及第一被告对受害方是否有一个类似侵权的责任,也就是"小心谨慎的责任"(duty of care)。有许多合约的关系,如买卖合约或者租约,法律是不另强加这种责任,变成双方之间完全就是看合约的约定。但在本案件中这种关系,法律会强加一个小心谨慎的责任在第一被告(可以说是承包了这一个装修工程)的身上。这方面的法律可节录Colman大法官在Raflatac v. Eade先例中所说如下:

"On the authority of D & F Estates Ltd v. Church Commissioners for England (1989) AC 177 and Aiken v. Stewart Wrightson Agency (1995) 2 Lloyd's Rep 618, where an employer contracts with a main contractor that a sub-contractor will carry out certain work with reasonable skill and care, the main contractor will not normally owe to the employer a co-extensive and concurrent duty of care in tort to carry out such work with reasonable skill and care.

The only exceptions to the absence of an independent duty of care in such cases are those cases where the courts have held the main contractor's duty to be non-delegable, as where he is under a statutory duty for the safety of the plaintiff, for example as an employee, or because the main contractor is carrying out some kind of hazardous operation which, if done negligently, could, because of the high risk of physical damage or personal injury, cause serious losses."

上述是说英国侵权法律下如果一位人士(假设是承包商)是有权委任或分包部分工作给其他的独立承包商,只要他是恰当的委任一位表面看来是称职的分承包商,他是不必为该分承包商在工作期间的错误与疏忽负责,也就是除了合约外没有一个侵权的责任。唯一的例外是一种属于"不可下放"(non-delegable)的责任,如独立承包商必须提供一个安全工作地点的法定责任。或是涉及一些危险的工作,容易引起人身伤亡或其他损害,这时雇主作为受害方可以依赖他的承包商会尽小心谨慎的责任,不论有否委任或分包给其他人。这种不可下放的责任对航运人士并不陌生,1924年的《海牙规则》针对船东令船舶在开航前适航的恪尽职责就是一种不可下放的责任,船东不能通过委任第三人下放适航的责任:The "Muncaster Castle" (1961) 1 Lloyd's Rep 57。这也表示在前者的情况,承包商与受害方之间只是有合约关系,但在后者的情况就除了合约关系外有了一个类似侵权的同步责任,会涉及1945年立法的适用。

再回到Raflatac v. Eade先例,Colman大法官认为根据受害方与第一被告之间的合约关系是要求第一被告必须尽合理小心谨慎的责任。但第一被告对灭火洒水器装置并没有特别的技能，而需要委任或分包给第二被告，这是双方的合约允许，而第二被告是有这一方面的特别技能。这一来，Colman 大法官认为要求第一被告在对第二被告的错误与疏忽也需要承担类似侵权的责任并不现实与合理。他是这样说："In the present case there is no doubt whatever that the first defendants were under a contractual obligation to exercise reasonable skill and care in the conduct of their work on the plaintiffs' premises. But what was the actual relationship between them and the plaintiffs in respect of the carrying out of the work? It was quite simply that it was agreed that the first defendants would enter into a sub-contract with the second defendant in order to provide the plaintiffs with the benefit of his knowledge and experience in relation to the plaintiffs' sprinkler system. Thus, if one assumes no more than a voluntary undertaking in respect of the work in question, all that the first defendants volunteered was at the highest to exercise reasonable care to procure the second defendant to carry out the works in question. In particular, it would be quite unrealistic to conclude that they undertook any responsibility for the skill and care with which, when he had been appointed, the second defendant undertook the works. Indeed, the whole purpose of his appointment was to make available to the plaintiffs the benefit of the knowledge and experience which he had and the first defendants did not have."

所以，由于受害方与第一被告之间除了合约责任外不存在有一个类似侵权的责任，导致受害方如果撇开合约关系是不能独立以侵权向第一被告起诉。所以即使是有关的合约是要求第一被告必须尽合理小心谨慎的责任，也只能是属于 Vesta v. Butcher (1986) 2 Lloyd's Rep 179 先例的第二类合约责任，不适用1945 年立法。Colman 大法官是这样说："I therefore conclude that there is no arguable basis on which it can be said that the first defendant owed to the plaintiffs a parallel duty of care in tort in respect of the conduct of the contract works. It follows that this is not a case to which the principles of contributory negligence apply. It is a class (2) case, as defined in Vesta v. Butcher, sup, -'where the defendant's liability arises from some contractual obligation which is expressed in terms of taking care (or its equivalent) but does not correspond to a common law duty to take care which would exist in the given case independently of contract'. Accordingly, the 1945 Act does not apply.

上述介绍是有关雇主与承包商之间的合约与侵权关系，这也可以适用在许多其他的情况，如在 1990 年中期，英国法院就涉及大量的有关劳合社的重要先例。因为在 20 世纪 80 年代，来自美国因为石棉污染的再保赔付导致了英国劳合社的保险人严重亏损，几乎没有能力赔付以至于要破产。在短短的 3 年期间，劳合社保险人亏损了 60 亿英镑（当时是天文数字），其中在 1990 年，亏损是 29 亿英镑，这是劳合社从来没有过的亏损。由于英国 1720 年的《Bubble Act》只允许个人的保险人经营业务，这正是劳合社的做法,就是以个人名义参与名为“syndicate”的各种保险集团。所以这天文数字的亏损需要分摊到每一个保险人,就是平均每个人在该年度要承担10万英镑。这些保险人都是自然人,不像有限公司可以法人局限损失,他们也纯是投资者,希望有一个可观的回报,而本人并不一定懂得保险,只是交给“劳合社代理人”(Lloyd's agent)的“受保代理”(underwriting agent)或“管理代理”(managing agent)接受投保,并依赖他们的专业技能与小心。反正当年的亏损导致好几个保险人自杀或/与倒闭,因为大家都是以个人的名义承保而需要承担无限责任。这种恶劣情况到1993年劳合社委任了新的主席与首席执行官并做出了一些基本性的改革,成功吸收了有限公司的“大量资本”(corporate capital)后才慢慢恢复。

这里也可以一提的是每一位投资人的自然人加入一个syndicate的保险集团,他是需要通过劳合社代理人,他的工作会是只局限于替该投资人介绍与安排加入某一个保险集团(不同集团会针对不同的险种,也有不同的业绩),但事后并不一定参与受保或管理的工作。这一来该劳合社代理人只能是属于一位劳合社“成员代理”(member agent)。而该投资人作为劳合社的一个“名字”(name),他与受保代理的关系隔了一层,双方没有直接的合约关系。有直接合约关系的只是成员代理。

出了劳合社严重亏损的事情,显然有不少的劳合社保险人或名字希望转嫁损失,其中一个主要的诉讼对象就是劳合社代理人,特别是负责接受投保的受保代理,因为如果有过错或疏忽就应该是受保代理或管理代理。这种案例有不少,如贵族院的The Lloyd's Litigation (1994) 2 Lloyd's Rep 468;Aiken v. Stewart Wrightson (1995) 2 Lloyd's Rep 618与Brown v. KMR Services Ltd (1995) 2 Lloyd's Rep 513。

在The Lloyd's Litigation先例,贵族院明确了受保代理或管理代理对有关的投资人有一个侵权下的“小心谨慎责任”(duty of care)。而该受保代理也会有可能与投资人之间有合约关系(根据劳合社当时的规定),合约中也有同样的小心谨慎责任。这变为一种同步责任,投资人可以自己选择以合约或侵权向受保代理提出索赔。Goff勋爵针对这方面的总结是这样说:“*prima facie* a duty of care was owed in tort by the managing agents both to direct and indirect Names; so far as the direct Names were concerned, there was plainly a contract between them and the managing agents in the terms of the pre-1985 byelaw form of agency agreements in which a term fell to be implied that the agents would exercise due care and skill in the exercise of their functions as managing agents under the agreement; that duty was no different from the duty of care owed to them by the relevant Names in tort and the contract did not operate to exclude the tortuous duty, leaving it open to the Names, to pursue either remedy against the agents.”

在这种情况下,如果投资人或名字也涉及有部分的过错与疏忽,就会涉及1945年立法的分摊责任了,但通常并没有这种情况的存在,因为投资人一般不涉及保险业务。

但如果所涉及的成员代理并没有事后涉及接受投保与管理保险业务,这关系就变为类似承包商与分承包商一样。在 Aiken v. Stewart Wrightson 先例,就涉及成员代理(类似承包商)除了对投资人或名字有一个合约的责任外,是否还有一个侵权的责任?毕竟,这不涉及"不可下放"(non-delegable)的责任或一些危险的工作,所以成员代理唯一的责任就是恰当的替投资人委任一位表面看来是称职的受保代理或管理代理,他是不必为该代理在接受投保期间的错误与疏忽负责。在该先例,Potter 大法官有提到成员代理在这方面的抗辩,说:"It is submitted for the members' agents that such authorities have no application or bearing in a case such as the present in which (i) the work is not of an inherently hazardous kind and/or of a type likely to cause physical injury or otherwise requiring protection for a plaintiff as a matter of policy, (ii) the risk of injury to the plaintiff is not physical but purely economic, (iii) the practice of Lloyd's, known to all the syndicate Names, involves the performance of the actual underwriting function by an independent contractor working in the course of his own business and not that of the members' agents, and (iv) there is an express contractual right (which the parties expect to be exercised) to delegate the entire underwriting function to such agents."

Potter 大法官判成员代理没有在这方面的侵权责任,总结说:"the common law duty of care was no more than a duty to exercise care at the level and in the respects ordinarily to be expected and required of a competent members' agent; and therefore in respect of the detailed conduct of the underwriting function and the day to day management of the syndicates' affairs in connection with it, the common law duty to be imposed was no more than one of reasonable care in the selection of and liaison with the managing agents coupled with general oversight of the members' interests; it was no part of the members' agents' function (unless put on inquiry as to competence of the managing agent) to supervise or interfere in managing agents who were employed for that purpose pursuant to the practice and requirements of the Lloyd's market; the syndicate was in a position where the common law duty of care on which it relied was one which fell short of the specific obligation or duty imposed by the express term of contract, unless that common law duty of care could be shown to be non-delegable in character for the purposes of law of tort; however there were no policy provisions which dictated a finding of non-delegable duty for the purposes of the law of tort; thus the members' agents owed a duty in contract (but not in tort) to the syndicate to act with reasonable care and skill ..."

Potter 大法官上述的话可简单总结说,普通法不外是追求公平合理。在成员代理不能参与并监督有关的保险业务,就没有必要增加它在合约以外的侵权责任。这与 Raflatac v. Eade & others (1999) 1 Lloyd's Rep 506 先例的承包商一样,如果合约责任可以下放,他对分承包商(相等于劳合社的受保代理或管理代理)的过错与疏忽,没有一个侵权的责任。如果成员代理与投资人或名字之间的合约关系也是有一个小心谨慎的责任,则充其量只属于 Vesta v. Butcher (1986) 2 Lloyd's Rep 179 先例中的第二类合约责任。

希望通过上述的解释,读者能够更加明确区分 Vesta v. Butcher 先例中第二类与第三类合约责任的区别。

11.6 The "Ardent"先例

The"Ardent" (1997) 2 Lloyd's Rep 547 先例是涉及一个名为"红海"(Red Sea)的开曼群岛公司,他实际上是一个准备购买船舶的基金,而该基金主要的金钱是来自"沙特阿拉伯国家商业银行"(NCB)。NCB 主要是认为二手油轮值得投资,可以赚大钱而进行这一个业务。NCB 通过纽约大通银行的介绍认识了 Basil Papachristidis 先生并最后接受他旗下两家英国顾问公司的服务,其中 NCB 与一家名为 Papachristidis Ltd (PL)的公司签下了一份商业顾问合约,并与另一家名为 Papachristidis Ship Management Services Ltd (PSMSL)签下一份提供技术顾问合约。

但这一个投机性很大的商业活动最终是以该红海基金严重亏损惨淡收场。亏损的严重程度可从四艘船舶购进的价格与最后出售的价格之间的差别感受到。第一艘名为 Armour 轮的船舶在 1989 年 5 月 16 日以 11,680,000 美元买进,但只能在 1992 年 1 月 8 日以 7,321,627 美元卖出,但这是亏蚀最少的一艘船舶。第二艘名为 Archer 轮的船舶在 1989 年 7 月 26 日以 20,000,000 美元买进,结果在 1993 年 6 月 14 日以 3,835,868 美元卖出。第三艘名为 Arrow 轮的船舶在 1989 年 8 月 16 日以 15,500,000 美元买进,在 1993 年 2 月 22 日以 2,228,609 美元卖出。第四艘名为 Ardent 轮的船舶在 1989 年 8 月 30 日以 12,018,200 美元买进,最后在 1993 年 4 月 22 日以 2,621,414美元卖出。

这一来,NCB 背后的红海基金公司就想寻找转嫁损失的对象,并向 Basil Papachristidis 先生,PL,PSMSL,Anderson 先生(他是一位 PSMSL 雇用的验船师)与 Dunn 先生(他是 PL/PSMSL 两家公司的总经理)提出违约与侵权的索赔。显然红海基金公司只是与 PL,PSMSL 两家公司有合约关系,要把其他三位自然人拖进来只能是根据侵权。

红海基金公司指控的侵权就是他们身为被告所提供的就是特殊技能,所以双方有一个特殊关系,而这五位被告是违反了小心谨慎的责任。至于其中被指控的错误与疏忽是涉及 Ardent 轮在决定购买之前没有好好检查,其中船舶的"压水舱"(permanent ballast tanks)严重腐蚀,导致交船后产生庞大的修理费用,远超出 200 万美元的预算修理费。在 Anderson 先生上船检查时,由于压水舱满载海水,所以没有办法作出检查。如果能够检查并发觉严重腐蚀的情况,PL 与 PSMSL 就不应该让红海基金公司购买这一艘船舶。这被英国法院的 Mance 大法官接受是疏忽,认为被告应该坚持进行另一次上船的检查以明确了解压水舱的腐蚀情况。Mance 大法官不接受当时市场上涨就没有其他状况更佳的油轮可供选择的说法,他是这样说:"All this occurred against the background of a rising market and his own imminent departure on holiday, and betrays an over-optimism about the market and a feeling that it was important to get into the market as soon as possible, which can be seen in retrospect to have been only too obviously misplaced, but which appear to have been generally shared in the market at the time. Mr. Anderson's negligence occurred in or involved the misguided and over-hasty pursuit of his duties."笔者的上述案情介绍主要是为了说明违反小心谨慎的责任是非常容易的事,因为只要是疏忽,就不再追究疏忽是大是小,反正是要承担赔偿损失的后果。

Mance 大法官最后是判 PL 与 PSMSL 对红海基金公司有这一个侵权的责任,再加上他们之间是有合约关系,正是一个同步责任的典型。而对于其他三位自然人的被告,Mance 大法官判是没有这一个侵权的责任。原因应该是这三位被告通过 PL 与 PSMSL 两家公司与原告隔得很远,并作为这两家公司的雇员,对红海基金公司的关系就不是这么邻近。

至于与 PL/PSMSL 的同步责任也带来了 1945 年《The Law Reform (Contributory Negligence) Act》立法的分摊责任与损失。PL 与 PSMSL 作为被告是指称红海基金公司的原告自己也有错误与疏忽,因为 NCB 委派了他的三位雇员加入红海基金公司的董事局,他们作为公司董事有机会与责任警觉购买 Ardent 轮之前的验船是不足够,并可作出纠正。所以根据 1945 年立法是需要分摊 50% 的损失,也就是说即使是成功索赔,PL 与 PSMSL 也只需要赔偿红海基金公司 50% 的损失。但 Mance 大法官不接受两位被告的说法,认为 NCB 或红海基金公司自己不了解航运,所以依赖被告。他是这样说:"These allegations in my view lack substance. PL and PSMSL were engaged because Red Sea could not itself command the necessary commercial and technical expertise. Their role together was to identify and recommend suitable tankers for the fund's purpose, and to take all steps appropriate to that end. As Mr. Anderson acknowledged in evidence, the other Red Sea directors had 'absolutely no reason' to think that PL and PSMSL might go ahead with a vessel such as Ardent without the benefit of a thorough inspection. No-one expected or would have expected Messrs. Bouckley, Baarma and Henderson (这就是红海基金公司自己委任的董事) to involve themselves in this process or to seek to formalize themselves with its execution or with individual vessels identified by PL and PSMSL in any way which could have led to their discovering the failings in the process of inspection and recommendation which occurred in respect of Ardent."

12. 违约依照双方错误与疏忽的不同程度分摊损失的总结

12.1　总结三类合约条文与责任可否分摊损失

看了以上的先例,可见这问题非常复杂。在大部分违约下,看来 1945 年立法并不适用。这是因为合约的承诺与责任是以严格责任作为起点。在英国的法律委员会所出的第一个名为《Contributory Negligence as a Defence in Contract》(No. 114,1990)的报告中,曾经建议双方有错误与疏忽分摊损失也适用在所有的合约责任。但这会带来严重的后果,就是会减轻或混淆合约的严格责任。此外,也会带来昂贵的诉讼费用,因为涉及严格责任,通常作出判决或裁决是相对简单,往往只涉及解释有关的合约条文。但如果把双方错误责任扯进来,就会涉及许多的争辩与证据,必须要涉及“事实的调查与取证”(factual investigation),可以说是费时失事,导致严格责任也会变为昂贵的诉讼。所以在法律委员会接下去与最终的一个报告也就是《Contributory Negligence as a Defence in Contract》(No 219,1993)中放弃了这一个建议。

相反,这个问题对于第二类合约责任则不大明显。由于这类合约中有约定合理小心谨慎责任的条文,而在判决或裁决时亦需要衡量被告与原告有没有错误与疏忽。反正在考虑损失计算的其他方面大原则如因果关系、近因与合理减少损失也需要这一方面的争议与证据。这是与考虑分摊损失的原理相似,所以即使考虑分摊损失亦不会为这一场诉讼带来太多额外的负担。加上由于在这类合约中双方的错误与疏忽的责任均为“未能达到合约条文中的合理小心谨慎程度”,而且受到相同的合约条文所约束,故在比较双方的小心程度和损失的分摊时亦来得容易。其次,在这类合约中被告只承诺了一个合约中的小心谨慎责任,而没有承诺一个确保合约特定结果的严格责任。在原告有一定的责任下仍要被告完全承担所有损失实在有欠公平(即使只是51/49的比例,就要承担所有的损失),故应有分摊损失的机制。

第三类的合约条文,由于其带来的责任与侵权行为责任完全一致,加上受害方可以选择对他最为有利的诉因提起诉讼,所以处理此类合约条文亦理应和对待侵权行为责任的方法相同——允许损失的分摊。在这里英国法律委员会的看法和Hobhouse大法官在Vesta v. Butcher (1986) 2 Lloyd's Rep 179 先例中认为第三类的合约关系或责任适用1945年立法分摊责任与损失的看法颇为相近。

可以说目前在英国还没有相关立法的情况下(或把1945年立法作出修改,把违约也加进去),普通法针对合约责任的地位是1945年立法对第一类合约责任肯定不适用。第二类合约责任可能适用但可能性不大(判是适用的有De Meza v. Apple [1975] 1 Lloyd's Rep 498 先例,但判是不适用的有Raflatac v. Eade [1999] 1 Lloyd's Rep 506 先例)。而第三类合约责任明显就是适用,而在The Lloyd's Litigation (1994) 2 Lloyd's Rep 468 先例后,的确是多了很多同步责任的案件。

12.2　能够按照1945年立法分摊责任与损失的吸引

这一来,在涉及双方都有一定程度的错误或疏忽的违约,而且适用侵权责任时,仍会是看谁的过错是主要或有效引致损失的原因,有主要过错的一方就要负责全部损失,是“非黑即白”的判决。假设受害方不减少损失,只是把这部分多出来的损失“非黑即白”否定掉,也不是双方分摊总的损失。如果双方的过错或疏忽涉及时间上的前后,也是看后来的过错会否中断因果链,如果不足够中断因果链,也表示后来的过错根本不考虑。

这样看来,1945 年立法下按照原告与被告之间所认定的错误与疏忽作出分摊责任与损失看来是有吸引,有一点像是调解的结果。但在目前英国的普通法下还是不容易适应在合约的关系。这一来为了肯定,可以利用订约自由明示加入条文说明在该合约中的争议可适用这 1945 年立法的分摊。如果合约是有严格责任,或者要顾虑如果按照 1945 年立法分摊责任与损失会导致该诉讼的复杂性与费用大幅度增加,就在合约中写明不适用 1945 年立法的分摊。但至少在第二类的合约条文,只要求合理小心谨慎的责任,但又不涉及属于同步责任,就更加应该明示约定在有关的争议中是否适用 1945 年立法的分摊。

12.3　原告提出违约的请求被告可否以同步责任要求分摊损失的探讨

另在争议中,也会有个别的诉讼技巧需要注意。例如原告如果认为对他造成损失的对方被告的错误与疏忽十分明显,但难保被告会提出原告也应该承担部分的责任,如自己应该小心或应该向被告提出警告等表面看来是无关紧要的理由,会造成 1945 年立法的责任与损失分摊。即使原告只需要分摊很小的部分,但原告能避免还是最好。所以安全的做法就是原告不要提出同步责任,而只是以合约关系索赔,就可以避免。这方面的做法有美国的 Pepsi Cola Bottling Co. of Anchorage v. Superior Burner Service Co. 427 P. 2d 833 (1967) (Supreme Court of Alaska) 先例与澳大利亚的 Astley v. Austrust Ltd (1999) 161 ALR 155 (HCA)先例。在后一个先例,涉及一位律师给了客户疏忽的法律意见,这是典型的同步责任,律师在合约与侵权下都是有责任。该律师作为被告在他的抗辩中指出他的客户也有疏忽,需要分摊责任与损失。但法院的多数拒绝作出分摊,判是有关的立法不适用在一个合约的关系。法院也提到了原告可以自由以违约提出起诉,避开立法对责任与损失的分摊。这一个问题在 Vesta v. Butcher (1986) 2 Lloyd's Rep 179 的上诉庭判决也有针对并看来是不支持原告取巧,其中 O'Connor 大法官是这样说:"There are two further possible arguments for saying that there is a power to apportion in a category (3) case even though the claim is made in contract. I will state them but do not find it necessary to analyse or reach a conclusion upon them:(i) That contributory negligence was a defence in category (3) cases pleaded in contract before 1945. The argument is supported by railway cases and banking cases. (ii) That just as it has been held that a plaintiff cannot escape the Limitation Act by pleading a negligence case as trespass to the person so here the Court should hold that a plaintiff cannot escape apportionment by pleading the case in contract. See Letang v. Cooper (1964) 2 Lloyd's Rep 339."

但在另一个情况是原告不肯定自己一定能够胜诉,判被告的错误与疏忽所造成的损失不会被原告后来的错误与疏忽中断因果关系,更安全与更好的做法,就是适用 1945 年立法的分摊,希望把损失按照各自承担的责任部分取回来。正如《Clerk & Lindsell on Torts》(20th edn,2010 年)一书之 2 - 121 段所说:"On this basis,it is suggested that where a defendant has been negligent and the claimant has also been negligent (or has made a 'misjudgement') the power to apportion damages for contributory negligence provides a better solution in reaching a 'fair' outcome than finding that the claimant's mistake breaks the chain of causation."反正是如果原告有这个希望,就必须提出这一个请求,要求在他属于的侵权或同步责任案件中适用1945年立法的分摊。例如在贵族院的McKew v. Holland and Cubitts (Scotland) Ltd (1969) 3 All ER 1621 HL先例,案情涉及被告疏忽导致原告的腿伤。但在不久后受害方的原告在自己腿部受伤的情况下做一些危险的事情(从一些没有扶手与很陡的阶梯走下来而摔伤,造成更严重的腿伤),贵族院是判原告自己愚蠢的行为中断了因果关系,所以这严重的腿伤被告不需要负责。但在该先例后的Spencer v. Wincanton Holdings Ltd (2009) EWCA Civ. 1404先例,在判决的22段有提到McKew先例是没有"替代请求"(alternative plead)要求分摊责任与损失,估计原告如果这样做就可能拿回一部分损失。

另在March v. E & MH Stramare Pty Ltd (1991) 99 ALR 423先例,涉及侵权方的被告把一辆卡车停在马路中央,导致其他车道的部分视线被遮挡。原告是另一辆车子的司机,他事发时喝了酒,就撞上了这一辆停在路中央的卡车而受伤。在澳大利亚第一审法院,判是原告与被告都有错误与疏忽,原告是醉酒驾驶,被告是把卡车停在马路中央,但判是原告的错误与责任才是导致这一事故的最主要原因。但上诉庭把判决改变过来,认为被告对所有其他公路使用者是有一个小心谨慎的责任,这包括一些不小心与受到酒精影响的第三人,所以改判原告自己要承担并分摊70%的责任与损失,这表示被告只需要赔付30%的损失。而如果改以因果关系对待而不是分摊责任,原告就要承担全部的责任与损失,是一个非黑即白的结果。

12.4 同步责任下分摊损失与百分比的近期先例

近年来,由于金融市场的波动,带来了大量涉及这方面的先例,主要是作为受害方的原告向一些专业人士的被告提起诉讼,而这些被告(如律师、估价师、测量师等)通常是涉及同步责任。这些先例会涉及不同的分摊,如在First National Commercial Bank v. Andrew S Taylor Commercial Ltd (1997) PNLR 37先例,原告损失扣减75%。在Birmingham Midshires Mortgage Services v. Phillips (1998) PNLR 468先例,原告损失扣减60%。在Omega Trust Co Ltd v. Wright Son & Pepper (No 2) (1998) PNLR 337先例,原告损失扣减70%。在Nationwide Building Society v. Littlestone & Cowan (1999) Lloyd's Rep PN 625先例,原告的损失扣减66%。在Nationwide Building Society v. Archdeacons (1999) Lloyd's Rep PN 549先例,原告的损失扣减90%。在Nationwide Building Society v. Balmer Radmore (1999) Lloyd's Rep PN 558先例,原告的损失扣减75%。但也有扣减不多的先例,如The Mortgage Corp v. Halifax (SW) Ltd (1999) Lloyd's Rep PN 159先例中扣减了20%。

12.5 1967年《误述法》下的分摊责任与损失

在这方面可简单节录《McGregor on Damages》(18th edn,2009年)一书5-017段

所说如下："That the 1945 Act applies to claims for damages under section 2(1) of the Misrepresentation Act 1967 follows from the existence of the concurrent tortuous liability at common law for negligent misrepresentation. Sir Donald Nicholls VC so decided in Gran Gelato v. Richcliff (Group) (1992) Ch 560 following the Court of Appeal's reasoning in Vesta v. Butcher (1986) 2 Lloyd's Rep 179; (1989) 1 Lloyd's Rep 331. By contrast, the 1945 Act should not apply to a claim under section 2(2), which deals with innocent misrepresentation, as there will not be a concurrent liability in tort for misrepresentation that is not negligent."

12.6 分摊责任与损失遥远性及合理减少损失之间的关系

这一个复杂与不稳定的问题在本书第四章9.4段已经有很详细的针对，就是在1945年《The Law Reform (Contributory Negligence) Act》立法下的分摊责任与损失遥远性之因果关系与受害方需要合理减少损失之间的关系。其中也详细介绍了The "Calliope" (1970) 1 Lloyd's Rep 84 等的先例，所以不重复。

13. 对中国内地有关合约分摊损失个别做法的想法

最后，笔者可以一提在与部分中国内地的法官或仲裁员在贸仲仲裁或其他仲裁（包括香港仲裁）的共事经验中，他们有倾向或喜欢在合约争议中根据双方可能会存在的错误与疏忽分摊责任与损失。这分摊通常也是一个十分粗略的比例，如三七分或一人一半。但经常他们说不出中国法律对这方面的立场与理由。一个说法是中国法律下合约关系与侵权是完全分开的诉因，不像英国法律的同步责任要把他们一并考虑（但也有部分学者认为，即使受害方以侵权为诉因索赔损失，仍然需要考虑合约的具体条文，但这两种观点都没有法律条文支持）。另在中国《合同法》针对同步/竞合责任，第122条是说："因当事人一方的违约行为，侵害对方人身、财产权益的，受损害方有权选择依照本法要求其承担违约责任或者依照其他法律要求其承担侵权责任。"但看起来这个条文并没有针对本章主要涉及的纯经济损失的问题，也没有提供任何关于合约争议下（合约损失主要是纯经济损失）分摊责任与损失的依据。

笔者对此还是充满了疑虑。因为从本章较早的介绍可以看到，合约关系与侵权是完全来自不同的基础。合约关系千变万化，通常都是艰辛谈判相互妥协的结果。但侵权只是违反法律所强加的小心谨慎责任，不存在当事人可以作出改变。这一来，如果在一些涉及同步责任的合约关系（如有特殊关系的专业人士提供服务），假设有一位专业人士在一个复杂、危险性高与责任重大的委任中，坚持要在合约中局限责任或赔偿金额才肯接受委任，并且为雇主接受。但如果最后出了事，就很难接受在中国法律下，雇主可以完全撇开合约关系和有关条文，选择以侵权作为诉因并可以轻易回避他较早前在合约中所作出的让步。

这显然不是英国法律的地位，它是把合约关系与侵权一并考虑。正如在本章第3段与第10段所讲的，合约条文下的责任如果比侵权责任要轻，那么仍以合约条文下的责任为准。但如果合约条文下的责任比侵权要重，如违约方要承担严格责任，就如本章11.3段的 Vesta v. Butcher (1986) 2 Lloyd's Rep 179 先例，分摊责任与损失不适用，剩下来适用的就是真正的同步责任，也就是 Vesta v. Butcher 先例中所讲的第三类的情况。这个复杂与细微的法律地位是为了保障受害方的侵权权利，但充分尊重合约条文的规定。毕竟合约条文及其会带来的后果是双方当事人在经过可能是漫长与昂贵的谈判后心甘情愿接受的。

这也不是英国法律要面对的问题，其他法治国家也面对同样的问题，这许多其他的国家（包括部分大陆法国家）都有在英国法律委员会的报告《Contributory Negligence as a Defence in Contract》（No 219，1993）中被提到。

简单想想，合约条文是通过双方深思熟虑后达成的约定。其中针对责任方面会有千变万化的约定，包括有一方订约方接受绝对或严格责任，但另一方完全豁免责任；或一方即使有责任也不需赔偿任何损失等。不论是怎么写法，或者对谁有利或不利，至少在理论上他们是通过谈判尽量保护自己，而且完全理解有关后果，心甘情愿接受的最后协议。上一句提到"理论上"是因为在现实中有大量不懂得谈判，没有水平理解一些条文对自己的影响的人士，在中国大陆会经常见到。但任何国家的法律特别是针对国际性的商业协议是不会接受以无知作为抗辩或加以考虑。

以海上运输合约的船舶适航责任为例，根据合约条文的写法与约定就会带来许多不同层次的责任。例如，合约条文如果写作"tight，staunch and strong and in every way fitted for the voyage"是被解释为船东接受绝对或严格适航责任，即使涉及船舶的潜在缺陷也不能豁免责任。但另一个极端是船东完全不接受适航责任的许多不同写法如：(1) Weiner & Co v. Wilsons & Furness-Leyland Line (1910) 15 Com Cas 294 先例中条文写作："（船东不负责）unseaworthiness or unfitness of the vessel at commencement of or before or at any time during the voyage"；(2) Elderslie SS Co v. Borthwick (1905) AC 93 先例中条文写作："Neither the steamer, nor her owners, nor her charterers, shall be accountable for the condition of goods shipped under this bill of lading, nor for any loss or damage thereto, whether arising from failure or breakdown of machinery, insulation, or other appliances, refrigerating or otherwise, or from any other cause whatsoever, whether arising from a defect existing at the commencement of the voyage or at the time of shipment of the goods or not."；(3) Ingram & Royle v. Services Maritimes (1914) 1 KB 541 先例中条文写作："It is agreed that the maintenance by the shipowners of the vessel's class... shall be considered a fulfilment of every duty, warranty or obligation and whether before or after the commencement of the voyage."

在约定绝对或严格适航责任与完全豁免适航责任的两个极端之间也会有千变万化的不同责任层次。例如在1924年《海牙规则》或类似合约条文的"恪尽职责"（due diligence)令船舶适航,这是接近严格责任但至少豁免了一些船东避免不了的不适航,如船舶的潜在缺陷。另一个著名的不同层次就是金康租约的"船东与船舶管理人个人(令船舶适航)的恪尽职责"(personal want of due diligence on the part of the owners of their manager to make the vessel in all respects seaworthy and to secure that she is properly manned, equipped and supplied, or by the personal act or default of the owners or their manager.),这被解释为接近豁免船东适航责任。还有其他不同层次的适航责任,如只针对某些设备(如冷藏设备)有严格的适航责任但其他方面就宽松。

这一来如果出现了不适航的事故,仅是凭案情的事实认定双方对事故的错误与疏忽而粗略地把责任与损失在船东与货方身上作三七分或一人一半,所带来的结果就会是:(1)完全罔顾了双方在有关海上运输合约中所约定与接受的不同层次适航责任;(2)法官或仲裁员改写双方定下的合约条文,而他们并不是订约方;(3)即使是凭空泛的公道而言,这三七分或一人一半同样适用在船东接受严格适航与/或完全豁免适航责任的两个极端的合约关系,不作出区分或调整分摊的幅度,这是否算是公道也有问题。

在笔者不久前涉及的中国内地的一个仲裁案件中,案情涉及货物买卖,卖方看来是提供了有缺陷并且不符合合约描述的货物。但卖方怪责买方没有在卸港尽早检查货物并及时找到问题,而买方的反驳是这检查并不容易进行。还有是笔者也看不出提早发现问题到底能够带来什么补救,估计顶多就是最后的损失可以稍微减轻。但这就导致了笔者的共同仲裁员认为买方也应该负一部分责任,要把损失分摊一人一半。笔者觉得很难接受,毕竟该合约下卖方提供清洁与符合合约描述的货物是一个严格责任。

话说回来,看来中国法律在这方面的理念与 UNIDROIT Principles of International Commercial Contracts 接近,后者的 7.4.7 条文是节录如下:"**ARTICLE 7.4.7** (*Harm due in part to aggrieved party*) Where the harm is due in part to an act or omission of the aggrieved party or to another event for which that party bears the risk, the amount of damages shall be reduced to the extent that these factors have contributed to the harm, having regard to the conduct of each of the parties."

上述条文看来并没有像英国法律一样区分三大类的合约条文与责任,而是适用在所有的合约关系。但笔者涉及适用 UNIDROIT Principles of International Commercial Contracts 的争议并不多,也没有做这方面的研究,只是表达这方面的疑虑,只能略过不谈。

第九章　避免超额赔偿之一:净损失规则

1. 损失计算必须避免重复赔偿

首先重申,损失赔偿的"复原"大原则就是要让受害方回到假设合约被履行的经济地位。在计算损失时,就要与合约获得履行的经济地位相比较,损失赔偿金额不可以赔偿不足(除了一些法律的限制,如损失遥远性与合理减少损失等),也不可以令受害方获得超额赔偿。

针对不可以超额赔偿,有好几个需要注意的方面或损失计算的规则,如"净损失规则"(Net Loss Rule)、"不得重复规则"(No Duplication Rule)与"最低合约责任原则"(Minimum Performance Principle)等。这些方面会在本章与本书另章探讨。但首先可随手节录有关损失计算不能赔偿不足也不能超额赔偿的权威说法,在近期的贵族院先例 The "Golden Victory" (2007) 2 Lloyd's Rep 164,Scott 勋爵说:"The lodestar is that the damages should represent the value of the contractual benefits of which the claimant had been deprived by the breach of the contract, *no less but also no more*."

净损失规则与不得重复赔偿规则经常在一起,这个问题在本书多处有提到,如第二章的3.2段与第十章等。就是受害方能成功索赔的损失并不是他的依赖利益与预期利益的损失的总和,因为这会带来"重复赔偿"(duplicated or double compensation),而是他在预期利益损失中的"净利润损失"。因为通常受害方在赚取合约利润时要支出一些使费,这些费用是需要受害方自己承担的。如在程租合约中,如果承租人在船东把船舶开往装货港之前违约/毁约,声称没有货物装船,船东也不需要派船了。船东可以向承租人成功索赔的损失就应该是如果合约被履行,他在这一次航程中能赚取的净利润如10万美元,而不能索赔该航次总的运费收入损失如100万美元。因为要赚取这100万美元的运费,船东必须花费燃油费(包括空放去装港的航次加与装货的航次)、港口费等各项使费共计90万美元。所以能够成功索赔的净利润或"预期利益"(expectation interest),只是10万美元。这是一个很简单的例子,甚至没有把船东为该船舶找到替代航次进一步减少损失所赚取的净运费或租金一并考虑,但在现实中笔者作为仲裁员还是经常见到有这种粗糙与明显的错误损失计算。

2. 损失计算必须扣减由侵权或违约直接或自然带来的好处

这方面针对净损失规则计算损失是适用在许多其他不同的情况,以下可先介绍少部分案例。

(1)在 Charter v. Sullivan (1957) 2 QB 117 先例,如果卖方的货物供不应求,完全可以转售给第三人,就不能向原来违约/毁约的买方索赔损失,因为并没有造成无辜卖方的任何损失,不论是利润损失或是"交易损失"(loss of sale)。

(2)在 Nadreph v. Willmett & Co (1978) 1 All ER 766 先例,案情涉及原告的律师(被告)疏忽提供给原告法律意见与建议中断了原告与租客之间的租约,这导致该租客搬出了这处房子并向原告索赔一笔 145,000 英镑的违约赔偿。原告向疏忽的律师要求补偿这笔损失。法院判是在计算被告应该承担的损失时,原告因为提早获得房子腾空的好处(如以更高租金转租,这也是原告要尽的合理减损义务)也应该被考虑在内,这好处是要从原告所要求补偿的 145,000 英镑中"抵销"(set off)。

(3)在 Platt v. London Underground Ltd (2001) 2 EGLR 121 先例,案情涉及原告(租客)租下了伦敦某个地铁站临近出口与入口的两个商铺,这个地铁站只有这两个出入口。伦敦地铁公司(被告)在租约订立后改变地铁站出口的关闭时间,这导致每天有 3/4 的时间出口都是关闭的,而原告临近出口商店的客流量也大大减少。所以原告以"租约权利减损"(derogation of grant)的名义起诉被告并要求被告补偿生意减少的损失。法院判是被告确实违反了租约,但在计算损失赔偿时,应该将原告位于入口的第二个商铺增加的收益考虑在内并从原告要求的赔偿中抵消,因为关闭地铁站出口的直接后果就是乘客会从地铁站唯一的入口离开,从而增加了第二个商铺的客流量,弥补了原告在第一个商铺的生意损失。考虑其他好处是否能抵消损失主要是看"遥远性"(remoteness),特别是已经提到的"因果关系"(causation)。如果伦敦地铁公司的违约并不自然会带来乘客要从另一个入口离开的直接后果,判法就会不一样。例如在 Jebsen v. East & West India Dock Co (1875) LR 10 CP 300 先例,涉及船舶的延误导致乘客取消并需要退票,其中有不少的乘客另订了同一家船公司的其他船舶的船票,这方面的好处不被法院接受可令减少损失。

(4)在 Hamilton v. Osborne (2009) 83 OLR (3d) 157 先例,案情涉及原告通过被告(经纪人)的介绍雇佣了一名建筑工人来为她建造房屋,但事后发现这名建筑工人缺乏水平并且不能完成原告指定的工作,原告以"误述"(misrepresentation)为理由要被告承担责任与赔偿因此造成的损失。法院判是除了原告在 1998 年 6 月之前交给建筑工人的押金,所有损失被告都不需要赔偿,因为"因果关系"(causation)不能成立。而针对这 15,000 美元的押金损失,法院判是原告没有尽到减少损失的义务而不能成功索赔,因为原告本可以从 ONHWP(the Ontario New Home Warranty Program)基金项目中要求退还这笔押金,从而避免损失。这是法律授予她的权利,因此原告不能向被告索赔这笔押金而获得重复赔偿。

(5)在 Ng v. Ashley King (Developments) Ltd (2010) EWHC 456 (Ch)先例,案情涉及原告 A 向被告 B 购买了一幢房子,但是后来发现这幢房子根本不适合居住。事后通过 A 与 B 的调解,B 同意以 38 万英镑回购这幢房子(但最后实际没有做到),而同时 A 再以同样的价格购买第三人的一幢房子作为替代。两个买卖合约中都约定没有押金,但是有特殊条文规定卖方给予买方"完成通知"(notice of completion)后,买方需要支付一笔房价 10% 的押金,如果买方违约/毁约没有购买这幢房子,卖方就有权没收这笔押金。最后 B 支付了押金但由于没有完成回购这幢房子,A 也没收了这笔房价 10% 的押金。但这违约/毁约也同时导致 A 对第三人的违约/毁约,因为 A 再没有余钱购买第三人的房子。A 起诉要求 B 赔偿他对第三人违约而白白支付了的房价 10% 的押金。一审法院判是 A 有权获得 B 应支付给他的房价 10% 的押金,但是无权获得他白白支付给第三人的押金。上诉庭判是 A 应该从 B 处有权获得他支付给第三人的押金,而 B 依照合约支付给 A 的违约金应该从赔偿中抵消,因为损失赔偿的原则是让受害方得到赔偿而不是惩罚违约方,一旦 A 没收了 B 的押金,这笔赔偿就应该从 B 应该承担的损失中扣减,而两笔钱是一样的数目。

2.1　什么是直接或自然带来的好处?

如果侵权或是违约带来的好处并非是直接或自然会产生的,就会有另外一个说法是这一个好处属于"遥远"(remote),可以不必在损失计算扣减。在本书其他章节(特别是第三与第四章)已经介绍过,遥远主要是指两个方面:一个是"因果关系"(causation),另一个是"可否预见"(foreseeability)。所以简单的解释是对受害方带来的好处并非是与原来侵权或违约行为有直接因果关系,也不是在侵权或违约时可以合理预见会导致有这样的结果,就可以说是这一个好处属于遥远,可让受害方享有而不必在损失计算中扣减。也有另一个常见的说法是这一个好处"完全是附带的好处"(complete collateral benefit 或拉丁文的 *res inter alios acta*),也就是说好处不来自原来的交易,也是不必在损失计算中扣减。这些方面都在本书有关"减少损失"(mitigation)的第五章有详论,课题本身也是与减少损失密切相关,所以尽量不重复。

与受害方减少损失行动无关所带来的好处也会被视为是"独立"(independent)与"附带"(collateral),不被接受可在损失计算扣减。但这些千奇百怪的案情与不同的好处什么可以扣减与什么不可以扣减法院也不容易掌握,导致这方面的先例还是不少。但有一些类别减少受害方的损失的好处是应该很明确不会被视为是可扣减。这种类别的好处在本书第五章有详细介绍,在这里只简单一提。这就是第三人在损失发生后为了各种私人的原因馈赠或资助受害方,这好处已经被视为是公共政策不得在损失计算中扣减。这里重复 Reid 勋爵在 Parry v. Cleaver (1970) AC 1 (HL)先例中所说:"It would be revolting to the ordinary man's sense of justice, and therefore contrary to public policy, that the sufferer should have his damages reduced so that he would gain nothing from the benevolence of his friends or relations or of the public at large, and that the only gainer would be the wrongdoer. We do not have to decide in this case whether these considerations also apply to public benevolence in the shape of various uncovenanted benefits from the welfare state, but it may be thought that Parliament did not intend them to be for the benefit of the wrongdoer."(公共政策不会接受受害方的亲友提供的利益或是公共援助实际上是不能令受害方得益,反而是让错误方得益,因为要把这些利益或援助作为减少损失并让错误方少赔一点。在本案不需要考虑公共援助是否需要在损失计算中扣减,但可以估计立法的议院不会有考虑把立法提供的好处让错误方得益。)

有许多被视为独立与附带的好处是出现在人身伤亡的侵权或违约案件,这包括是受害方的"保险好处"(insurance benefits)、"雇佣好处"(employment benefits)、"福利好处"(welfare benefits)、"失业救济"(unemployment benefits)、"劳工赔偿"(workers'compensation)与"医疗保险"(health insurance)等。这背后的原因可能是公共政策、人权保障、生命无价,或是立法的结合。

在笔者涉及的国际商品买卖与航运,也有一种好处是不可以在计算损失扣减,这就是在"市场规则"(market rule)适用的情况下。如果适用,就会以违约一天的市场价格作为计算损失的标准,而受害方如买方如果在更后的时间买进更便宜的替代商品(或船舶),这一个好处也被视为是独立与附带的好处,在计算损失中不予理会。所以在笔者作为仲裁员的案件中,如果违约的卖方要求受害的买方披露他事后买进替代商品的有关文件,笔者在损失计算是以市场规则为准的情况下,通常是会拒绝这种披露的申请,因为这些文件无关。这方面可节录重要的航运先例 The "Elena d'Amico" (1980) 1 Lloyd's Rep 75, Goff 大法官说:"In considering the submission that these lost profits are recoverable from the owners as damages, in my judgment guidance is provided ... by cases concerned with the sale of goods. Taking ... the case of non-delivery, where goods are not delivered on the due date, or the contract is repudiated, the buyer is placed in a situation where he has to decide whether or not to buy in and, if he is going to buy in, whether he should buy in immediately or wait for a time and buy in later. The position in law appears to be that, generally speaking, if there is an available market for the goods in question at the time when they ought to have been delivered, then if the buyer decides not to buy in on that date, which he is fully entitled to do, he cannot visit the consequences of that decision upon the seller. If he buys in later he may, of course, either buy in ... at a higher price or at a lower price than the available market price at the date when they ought to have been delivered. But if he has to buy at the higher price he cannot, generally speaking, claim the extra cost from the seller; and **if he makes a saving then that saving is not, generally speaking, to be brought into account to reduce the damages which are**

recoverable from the seller."(加黑部分是笔者的强调)

大道理是这样，但适用在每一个案件还是不容易。案件的事实稍微不同，就可能会对损失计算产生很大影响。例如，较早第2段介绍的 Platt v. London Underground Ltd (2001) 2 EGLR 121 先例与不同判法的 Jebsen v. East & West India Dock Co (1875) LR 10 CP 300 先例。

2.2 直接或自然带来的好处之一：成功合理减少损失

关于是否遥远或附带的好处可介绍其中一个权威的说法，是上诉庭的 Peter Gibson 大法官在 Gardner v. Marsh & Parsons (1997) 1 WLR 489 先例中说："unless such conduct flows inexorably from the original transaction, and can properly be seen as part of a continuous course of dealing with the situation in which the plaintiff originally found himself"(如果受害方的行为是毫无疑问由原来的交易导致，可以被恰当地视为是由于违约所带给受害方的困境后一个持续的处理)。在这一个说法下，表示在本书第五章所提到的"减少损失"(mitigation)是要求受害方在违约后采取合理行动与持续处理，希望减少损失，就表示合理减少损失的行动如果成功，给受害方带来的好处就不会是遥远，并且必须在计算损失的时候加以扣减。

在本书第五章提到很多有关的先例，在这里只简单介绍两个著名的先例，就是 British Westinghouse Electric Co Ltd v. Underground Electric Railways of London Ltd (1912) AC 673 与 Laverack v. Woods of Colchester Ltd (1967) 1 QB 278。

在 British Westinghouse Electric Co Ltd 著名先例，涉及出售的火车涡轮机不符合买卖合约的要求，卖方在买卖合约下显然是违约。受害的买方作出决定另购买一台替代涡轮机，但是属于一个新的型号，有更大的动力。这一个合理的商业决定导致了在后来的操作上带来比原来一台涡轮机(即使没有缺陷)更大的效益与利润。在后来的诉讼中，判是替代涡轮机带来的好处要在受害方的损失中扣减，由于这些好处所带来更高的利润比买方索赔的利润损失还要高，这导致受害方胜诉也只能取得"名义赔偿"(nominal damage)。这个先例可以看到受害方采取合理减损的行动，如果成功，这好处是要在损失计算中作出扣减。

但在 Laverack v. Woods of Colchester Ltd 先例，涉及一名高管雇员被雇主无理解雇。在被解雇后，该雇员找到了另一份工作，工资虽然不高(这表示无理解雇对该雇员造成工资的损失)，但他同时买了新就职公司50%的股份并参与该公司的管理。该股份后来大幅增值，导致该雇员赚了一笔钱。上诉庭判是该笔赚的钱也应该在向原雇主索赔的损失中扣减，毕竟该雇员如果不换工作就不会买该公司的股份并参与管理令股份增值。Denning 勋爵是这样说："... His salary of £1500 was very low for a man of his ability: and it looks as if he was getting, in addition, a concealed remuneration by a profit on his shares in the company."

值得注意的是，该雇员同时间也买了一些其他公司的股票并赚了钱，其中一家公司还是原雇主的竞争对手，这是该雇员如果没有离开原雇主的公司是不能购买的。

这部分赚的钱法院判就不能用来扣减了,因为属于遥远与附带好处。其中 Denning 勋爵说:"He might have invested his money in any other company and made similar profits. It is sheer speculation whether he would do better in Ventilation (原雇主的竞争对手) than in others. I realise that the plaintiff was only at liberty to invest in Ventilation because his employment was terminated. But nevertheless the benefit from that investment was not a direct result of his dismissal. It was an entirely collateral benefit, for which he need not account to his employers."

这里的区别是雇员在原雇主违约后找到了另一份工作,这是受害方减少损失行动的一部分,得到的直接或自然的好处包括工资、佣金、其它的福利、养老金等应该用来扣减向原雇主索赔的损失。至于同时购买该新就职公司或其他公司的股票并赚了钱,一般而言与原雇主违约即使有一点关系,但这关系也很小,并与减少损失的行动扯不上关系,完全是附带的好处,所以不能在损失计算中作出扣减。但在本先例中,原告的雇员与新就职公司的股票增值关系密切,可以算是一种很罕见的例外。

2.3 直接或自然带来的好处之二:不涉及受害方自己的决定或抉择

涉及是否"遥远"(remote)或"附带"(collateral)的好处也会考虑这侵权或违约后带来的好处是否主要来自受害方自己作出的独立决定或抉择,而不是较早时的侵权或违约直接或自然所带来。这可介绍贵族院的 Jamal v. Moolla Dawood, Sons & Co (1916) 1 AC 175 先例,案情涉及股票买卖,约定在 1911 年 12 月 30 日交付,当天股票价格碰巧暴跌,所以买方拒绝接受股票。受害的卖方没有把有关的股票在市场转售减少损失,而继续持有这些股票并在后来的月份(直到 1912 年 8 月)分批在市场上出售。这些出售的金额加起来令卖方的损失大幅度减少,但问题是这个股票在后来增值的好处是否要在计算损失时加以考虑? Wrenbury 勋爵是说:"If the seller retains the shares after the breach, the speculation as to the way the market will subsequently go is the speculation of the seller, not of the buyer; the seller cannot recover from the buyer the loss below the market price at the date of the breach if the market falls, nor is he liable to the purchaser for the profit if the market rises."这等于是说受害的卖方没有在违约一天或尽快在市场转售减少损失,而决定或选择保留有关的股票。这是属于卖方自己的眼光准确(如果股票增值)或是自己投机失败要承担的风险(如果股票价格持续下跌),不应在损失计算中予以考虑。这一个判法是与较早时在 2.1 段所提到的 The "Elena d' Amico" (1980) 1 Lloyd's Rep 75 先例是一致。

同样的考虑也出现在其他的先例,如在新西兰的先例 Turner v. Superannuation & Mutual Savings Ltd (1987) 1 NZLR 218。案情涉及一栋在奥克兰商业大厦的买卖,价格是 110 万新西兰元。但在这一个买卖中买方是做了冤大头,因为合约价格比市场价格超出了 40 万新西兰元。但毕竟是订下了买卖合约,也不存在卖方有误述或其他非法的行为导致这一个合约的产生,所以买方还是需要履行。但买方拒绝履行,这导致卖方最终把该房子留给自己使用,并向违约的买方索赔这 40 万新西兰元的差价。

买方的一个抗辩是卖方没有损失,因为在诉讼时该房子已经升值到 700 万新西兰元。但问题是把该房子留下而不去市场另找替代买方作出转售,是卖方自己做的决定与选择,所以该商业大厦后来的升值好处也只是属于卖方自己的。新西兰法院判是卖方可以成功索赔这 40 万新西兰元。

同样的考虑也出现在英国上诉庭的 Hussey v. Eels (1990) 2 QB 227 先例,案情涉及受害的买方因为卖方误述而买进一幢严重有缺陷的"单层小屋"(bungalow)。但买方在违约后决定采取一些行动,就是把整幢房子拆除并重建。这重建与事后出售的行动给买方带来了很大利润,违约的卖方显然争辩说受害方没有蒙受损失。但这不被上诉庭接受,判是这一个重建的利润并非是原来的买卖在违约后的(卖方的误述导致合约的订立)持续性行动所带来。Mustill 大法官在分析了有关的先例后说:"Ultimately, as with so many disputes about damages, the issue is primarily one of fact. Did the negligence which caused the damage also cause the profit—if profit there was? I do not think so. It is true that in one sense there was a causal link between the inducement of the purchase by misrepresentation and the sale 2.5 years later, for the sale represented a choice of one of the options with which the plaintiffs had been presented by the defendants' wrongful act. But only in that sense. To my mind the reality of the situation is that the plaintiffs bought the house to live in, and did live in it for a substantial period. It was only after two years that the possibility of selling the land and moving elsewhere was explored, and six months later still that this possibility came to fruition. It seems to me that when the plaintiffs unlocked the development value of their land they did so for their own benefit, and not as part of a continuous transaction of which the purchase of land and bungalow was the inception."

2.4　直接或自然带来的好处之三:不涉及受害方与第三人之间的独立与附带合约

这方面权威说法可先节录《Chitty on Contracts》(30th edn. 2008 年)之 26－117 段所说如下:"**Benefits independent of mitigation**. . . .　On a similar principle, advantages gained by the claimant from wholly independent transactions, especially those entered into before the defendant's breach of contract, as for example, a sum due under an insurance policy, cannot be relied on in mitigation of loss arising from the defendant's breach. So where the claimant, by another contract with a third party entered into before the defendant's breach of his contract with the claimant, has made an arrangement which should or does in fact prevent loss to the claimant from the defendant's breach, the defendant cannot rely on that other contract to reduce his damages; it is *res inter alios acta*, or an extraneous circumstance. Even where a benefit to the claimant arises in the course of his mitigating action, there may not be a sufficient causal connection between the defendant's breach and that benefit to justify taking it into account in assessing the claimant's damages."

如果受害方与第三人之间的合约为受害方的损失作出部分或全部的补偿,这也不是侵权人或违约方可以在损失计算中扣取的好处。特别是在侵权或违约前就已经订立的合约,更加是与减损没有任何关系。这种情况最明显的是保险合约,但还是经常有侵权人或违约方对受害方争辩说:“你的损失可以向保险人取回,为什么还要向我索赔?”这种说法明显站不住脚,特别是在保险的范畴,因为在 1906 年的英国《海上保险法》(Marine Insurance Act 1906)之 Section 79,明确规定了保险人在赔付了受保人后,可以代位向侵权人或违约方索赔有关的损失。这种“代位求偿权”(subrogation right)也在许多其他国家包括中国的保险法内有规定。英国《海上保险法》也不仅是针对海上保险,该立法的原则包括代位求偿也完全适用在其他范畴的保险。所以这一个被视为是受害方(受保人)与第三人(保险人)之间的补偿合约,所带来的好处不会被视为侵权或违约直接或自然带来,可在损失计算中做出扣减。这些非海事保险的有关先例有:Naumann v. Ford (1985) Times, March 13; Brown v. KMR Services Ltd (1994) 4 All ER 385; Bristol & West Building Society v. May, May & Merrimans (No. 2) (1998) 1 WLR 336; Portman Building Society v. Bevan Ashford (2000) PNLR 336。

特别在违约的情况,这说法更加讲得通。毕竟受害方与第三人的合约关系通常是完全独立,不能与受害方同违约方之间的合约串联在一起。所以撇开保险合约,如果受害方与第三人(如银行或是母公司)之间有一份“补偿合约”(indemnity contract),在出现违约时受害方得到部分或全部的损失补偿,违约方还是不能把该不同合约的好处扯进来计算损失。这里虽然不涉及代位求偿,但受害方完全是可以把他向违约方索赔损失的权利“转让”(assign)给第三人,让第三人以自己的名义提出索赔,或是第三人以受害方的名义继续向违约方索赔,反正就是违约方不能从中得益。

同样清楚不过的是货物买卖合约,特别是有关货物有“可供买卖的市场”(available market)。在这种情况下,英国法律已经是明确不过规定如果卖方违约不提供/付运有关货物,损失计算是不会理会分销合约的损失(这可能比市场的差价更大或更小,甚至分销是为了慈善或援助用途),因为分销合约与第一份合约是两份独立的合约,不必也不能混在一起。即使违约的卖方在订立第一份合约时是明确知道或应该知道有分销合约,在有市场价格可以比较的情况下,损失计算还是不理会。所以在权威的《Benjamin's Sale of Goods》(8th edn,2010 年)之 17 - 028 段是这样说:“Where a market price at the date of the seller's breach is ascertainable, a higher or lower price at which the buyer has resold the goods to a sub-buyer is generally irrelevant to the assessment of damages for the seller's failure to deliver: the damages are to be calculated on the basis of the market price of similar goods at the date (and place) of the failure to deliver.”这一个问题在杨大明律师所著的《国际货物买卖》之 543 至 548 页有详论,不去重复。同样,在较早时的 2.1 段提到的 The “Elenad'Amico” (1980) 1 Lloyd's Rep 75 先例也有针对。

这种情况也出现在其他千奇百怪的案例有:Legal & General Mortgage Services Ltd

v. Underwoods (1997) PNLR 567;Interallianz Finanz AG v. Independent Insurance Co Ltd (1997) NPC 89;Banque Bruxelles Lambert SA v. Eagle Star (1995) All ER 769;Mobil North Sea Ltd v. PJ Pipe & Valve Co Ltd (2001) EWCA Civ. 741 等。

只介绍 Mobil North Sea Ltd v. PJ Pipe & Valve Co Ltd 先例,案情涉及北海天然气平台的工程,有关当事人包括美孚北海(该平台的运营商)雇佣 Fluor 做总承包商,而 PJ Pipe 是与 Fluor 订约的分包商,PJ Pipe 的任务是供应活塞气门。在施工过程中,PJ Pipe 供应的活塞气门出现了质量问题。为了赶在工期之内完成,这部分活塞气门全部被美孚北海替换,损失高达 130 万英镑。这导致了美孚北海与 Fluor 分别根据违约向 PJ Pipe 提出这一笔损失的索赔。Fluor 与 PJ Pipe 之间的合约应该是明确存在,而且责任也是明确。而美孚北海与 PJ Pipe 之间应该是没有直接合约关系,但从案例报道中对这方面的简单介绍来看,美孚北海主张 Fluor 与 PJ Pipe 之间的合约合并了美孚北海与 Fluor 之间的工程合约中有关条文,所以 PJ Pipe 对美孚北海有一个对活塞气门的"附带保证"(collateral warranty)。PJ Pipe 同时面对美孚北海与 Fluor 两方的索赔,估计是不想打一场有关活塞气门技术问题的昂贵诉讼或财力不足,所以在本先例他采取了一个战略上的做法,就是根据《民事诉讼规则》之 Part 24. 1 先向法院申请撤销 Fluor 的索赔,而如果这第一步能够成功,就可以第二步争辩美孚北海与 PJ Pipe 本身是没有直接合约关系。而走第一步,照说是已经提到的合约责任明确,所以希望能够成功撤销索赔就需要在其他方面说得通。针对这一方面,PJ Pipe 找到的理由就是指 Fluor 实际上没有蒙受损失。这种做法跟本书第七章 5.2 段提到的 Linden Gardens v. Lenesta Sludge Disposals Ltd. and others (1994) 1 AC 85 (HL)等先例大同小异。

按照 PJ Pipe 的说法,Fluor 有没有蒙受损失是先要看 Fluor 与美孚北海之间的工程合约条文,另看 Fluor 与美孚北海事后为这件事达成的和解协议。有关的工程合约第 10 条文内容与解释可节录 Rix 大法官所说如下:"... it rendered Fluor liable to Mobil for defective valves;that Fluor was obliged to obtain a proper sub-contract under which the sub-contractor would be liable in turn for providing defective valves; that Fluor was obliged to take proceedings to enforce that sub-contract in the event of something going wrong;that if, as a result of those proceedings, Fluor was unable to obtain any recovery against the sub-contractor, then Fluor had no liability itself (save in circumstances where Fluor was responsible for some personal failing), and that such provisions against it was to be **regarded simply as a mere conduit for the supply of defective valves coming from a sub-contractor**... Provided the finance with which Fluor could carry out such replacement or repair as defective supply might make necessary. Mobil also agreed under Article 10 to bear the costs of Fluor's litigation. Any recovery from that litigation from the sub-contractor would go to Mobil in extinction of the finance provided and Mobil's liability in general." 换言之,在加黑部分是说工程合约把 Fluor 视为是一个没有任何经济责任的

“中转人”(conduit),替美孚北海寻找活塞汽门的供应商。即使 Fluor 针对 PJ Pipe 的违约要对美孚北海负责,也只限于根据分承包合约向 PJ Pipe 追讨赔偿(而且有关的诉讼费用也是由美孚北海承担),而赔偿给美孚北海的钱也只限于能够成功向 PJ Pipe 取回来的钱。

至于美孚北海与 Fluor 达成的和解协议,有关内容与解释也是可以节录 Rix 大法官所说如下:I turn now to the settlement agreement, where Mobil again represented all its consortium partners. This provides, in essence, as follows. First of all it is stated that, subject only to some detailed provisions which would come into play if the claim against PJ Pipe were compromised in circumstances where one out of Mobil and Fluor wished to settle but the other did not, Fluor was guaranteed what is called a guaranteed minimum payment of £ 250,000, plus interest from the beginning of 1999. It is then provided that any monies recovered from PJ Pipe in a sum greater than twice that guaranteed minimum payment should be split 50/50 between Fluor and Mobil. Mobil would continue to pay all the costs of litigation, at any rate so far as external lawyers are concerned. Each side would bear its own internal legal costs. There were detailed provisions to deal with various possibilities as to settlements at various levels and the willingness of one party to proceed in circumstances where the other party wished to withdraw. I need not go into all those details.”

该和解协议还有一条文说明和解是双方对有缺陷活塞气门问题的全面与最终的和解,说:“The agreement set out in this letter is in full and final settlement of any claim that Mobil, SAGE (这是指北海天然气平台背后投资的财团) or Fluor may have against each other in connection with the defective materials supplied by PJ Valves”。

PJ Pipe 就是根据以上的条文作为理由声称 Fluor 没有实际损失,但这在第一审判是 Fluor 与美孚北海之间的和解协议是一个“独立”(independent)与“附带”(collateral)的合约,不存在可以作为 Fluor 向 PJ Pipe 索赔损失的扣减。PJ Pipe 请求撤销 Fluor 索赔的申请被高院驳回后,它又向上诉庭提出。

上诉庭同样也驳回了他的抗辩,理由是有三个。第一个理由是 Fluor 向 PJ Pipe 的索赔纯粹是他们之间合约下的违约所带来的损失,并非是一个要求 PJ Pipe“补偿”(indemnify) Fluor 要赔偿给美孚北海的损失,这从文书请求中就看得到。如果是一个补偿,才会是由于 Fluor 不需要赔偿美孚北海,就不存在需要补偿了。第二个理由是 Fluor 与美孚北海之间的和解协议所用的措辞与文字,明确说明是要继续向 PJ Pipe 提出索赔。与本章关系最大的就是第三个理由,就是分析美孚北海与 Fluor 之间的和解协议是否是完全独立与附带的交易,也就是拉丁文的“*res inter alios acta*”。而如果是,显然 Fluor 所取得的好处就不存在可扣减他向 PJ Pipe 索赔的损失。上诉庭认为答案是明确,Fluor 与美孚北海之间的所谓和解协议与 Fluor 的合理减少损失义务毫无关系,也没有减损的意图。和解协议只是 Fluor 与美孚北海之间为了向 PJ Pipe 索赔损失的一个关系重组与确定(如针对谁应该做什么),正如 Rix 大法官所说:“...

as being simply a reorganization of the terms upon which those two parties were (or were not) going to conduct litigation against PJ Pipe"。另 May 大法官说:"Further, the loss arising from the need to replace the defective pipes was not avoided by the settlement agreement. On the contrary, it remained but became subsumed in modified accounting arrangements between Fluor and Mobil which took account of other matters as well."

2.5 直接或自然带来的好处之四:不是强加在受害方的好处(更好的替代)

这种情况可举的例子是受害方的财产/货物如果被侵权人或违约方损坏需要做出修理,在工程中受害方被迫使用一些更好或更新的材料,这种可能会带来的好处是不被视为可扣减损失的计算:Bacon v. Cooper (Metals) Ltd (1982) 1 All ER 397。同样的道理也可以适用在提供的电脑有缺陷而需要以更好的机型做出替换,这好处也不被视为可扣减损失的计算:Pegler Ltd v. Wang (UK) Ltd (1999) 70 Const LR 68。这些先例接下去介绍。

2.5.1 先例之一:Harbutt's 'Plasticine' Ltd v. Wayne Tank & Pump Co Ltd

这种情况的一个主要先例是英国上诉庭的 Harbutt's 'Plasticine' Ltd v. Wayne Tank & Pump Co Ltd (1970) 1 QB 447,清楚说明对于违约后的好处是强加在受害方是有不同对待。这个先例的案情在本书第二章之14.5.1.3段有详细介绍,在这里只做简单讲解。案情涉及原告(买方)向被告购买一批生产粘土的设备并由被告进行安装。但由于被告提供的产品有瑕疵以及被告雇员在安装过程中的疏忽,这批设备引起了大火并烧毁了原告的工厂。

针对有关的损失计算,其中主要的一项是关于赔偿原告工厂烧毁的损失。原告之前五层高的工厂在大火后根本不能再继续使用,不得不重新建造了一个两层高的新工厂。被告的抗辩是原告有了一幢新工厂,这一个好处需要扣减。但高院支持原告的索赔判是这笔重新建造工厂的费用可以全数取回,而上诉庭在这方面也持一致看法。Denning 勋爵是这样说:"The destruction of a building is different from the destruction of a chattel. If a second-hand car is destroyed, the owner only gets its value; because he can go into the market and get another second-hand car to replace it. He cannot charge the other party with the cost of replacing it with a new car. But when this mill was destroyed, the plasticine company had no choice. They were bound to replace it as soon as they could, not only to keep their business going, but also to mitigate the loss of profit (for which they would be able to charge the defendants). They replaced it in the only possible way, without adding any extras. I think they should be allowed the cost of replacement. True it is that they got new for old; but I do not think the wrongdoer can diminish the claim on that account. If they had added extra accommodation or made extra improvements, they would have to give credit. But that is not this case. I think the judge was right on this point."(工厂的毁坏与动产的毁坏在损失计算方面不一样。如果一辆二手车被毁坏,车主只能取回该二手车的价值,因为他可以去市场买进另一辆替代的二手车,他

不能索赔一辆替代的新车。但在本案例的工厂被毁坏,原告没有其他选择。他只能尽快建造另一幢工厂作为替代,以保障他们的业务,进而减少利润损失[这利润损失本来是可以向被告取回,所以尽快建造新工厂是一个合理减损行动]。原告建造的替代工厂没有增加什么额外的设备或建筑[如员工宿舍],所以 Denning 勋爵认为原告可以把重新建造的费用从违约的被告处取回。原告得到了一个新的工厂,表面看来索赔金额会需要折旧,但由于原告在这方面没有明显得益,所以在本案例的违约方不应该可以因此扣减赔偿金额。如果原告在新的工厂加入或改良了设备或建筑,这好处是要扣减。但在本案例中没有这种情况,所以高院判原告能够成功索赔这一笔费用是正确的)

2.5.2 先例之二:Bacon v. Cooper (Metals) Ltd

在 Bacon v. Cooper (Metals) Ltd (1982) 1 All ER 397 先例,案情涉及原告(废金属交易商)与一家信贷公司签订融资租赁合约购买金属切割机器。这种机器的零部件包含一个“旋转器”(rotor),通常寿命为 7 年,但如果损坏就需要更换一个全新的旋转器。后来被告放在原告那里寄卖的钢材在切割时损坏了这台机器,导致其中的旋转器完全不能修理好并使原告的业务暂停。这被损坏的旋转器本应该还有 3.75 年的寿命,等于已经使用了一半的寿命。为了继续他的业务,原告不得不以高昂的利息与信贷公司签署了另一份融资租赁合约,以 41,500 英镑的价格购买了一个新的旋转器。毫无疑问被告违反合约应该承担责任。但针对损失赔偿,原告声称被告应该赔偿他重新购买旋转器的所有费用,以及他多支付的信贷费用。被告抗辩说,旧的旋转器还有 3.75 年的剩余寿命,应该计算出剩余寿命与旋转器总寿命的比例,他们只应该赔偿新旋转器价格中这个比例的金额,这大约只是赔一半。而针对原告多支付的信贷费用,被告认为新的融资租赁合约下高昂的利息是由原告的经济状况造成的,不应该由被告承担。法院最后判是原告胜诉,被告应该承担购买新旋转器的费用以及原告多支出的信贷费用。因为如果没有被告的违约,原告在剩余的几年中本来不需要购买新旋转器。而现在原告被迫购买这个新的零件。原告通过融资租赁合约购买新旋转器是合理的行为,甚至也是被迫要做的事,而蒙受高昂的利息也是不能避免的。

看来这也是善待受害方,让他以一个有 7 年寿命的新旋转器替代违约损坏的 3.75年寿命的旧旋转器,而这个好处不必在损失计算中扣减。但这种判法在事实稍有不同的案件中就可能会有不同,如旧旋转器只剩下了 1 年不到的寿命,或是替代的新旋转器有更长的寿命,或有可能找到只有短暂使用寿命的替代旋转器等。

2.5.3 先例之三:Pegler Ltd v. Wang (UK) Ltd

在 Pegler Ltd v. Wang (UK) Ltd (1999) 70 Const LR 68 先例,案情涉及原告与被告签订合约购买一套一体化的计算机系统。原告是一个生产机械、管道铜制品的公司,它的产品包括室内用龙头、搅拌器、散热器阀门与管道设施等 4000 多种不同产品。它在 1990 年拥有 3600 个顾客,1500 名原材料供应商,并在业界因为产品质量优良具有很高的声誉。而被告是总部设在美国的一家计算机硬件、软件和相应服务的生产与供应商，创办人是当时中国人很熟悉的王安先生。原告为了提高公司的服务与管理（特别涉及购买原料、生产与分销它的产品），打算向被告购买一套全新的一体化计算机系统来代替旧的电脑。之后在1991年12月，原告与被告签订了一份长达3年的计算机系统买卖合约，规定由被告向原告提供价值1,198,130英镑的计算机硬件、软件与订制系统，以及每年价值235,000英镑长达3年的维护和业务进程管理服务。但之后被告不断违约（一些违约是技术性），其中一项违约是他在合约中承诺向原告提供业务进程管理服务，但在1994年2月，被告在只完成了一部分合约责任后，关闭了提供服务的伦敦分公司，并停止向原告履行任何合约责任。原告在2月底向被告发出违约通知并要求他进行补救，但被告没有任何补救并放弃了这个合约。在1997年4月1日原告接受了被告的毁约并要求行使合约权利终止合约。1997年5月，原告任命KPMG（毕马威）来评估原告的计算机需求并对安装一体化计算机系统提供建议与补救被告违约所带来的问题。所以直到当时，原告才开始采取减少损失的行动。

在1996年2月，原告在英国法院出了告票，向被告索赔的金额是2300万英镑。但真正推进诉讼的程序是在1997年5月底才开始。这2300万英镑的损失是12项不同类别损失之和，包括：（1）Lost home Sales 12,530,000英镑（业务损失）；（2）Lost opportunity to increase margins（included in A）（提高边际效益的机会损失）；（3）Lost opportunity to make staff cost savings 2,124,642英镑（失去节省雇员花费的机会损失）；（4）Amounts paid to third parties 150,217英镑（对第三人的损失赔偿）；（5）Ongoing expenditure（up to 31 July,1999）47,334英镑（直到1999年7月1日的正在进行中的花费）；（6）Further expenditure to be incurred 1,744,206英镑（未来会发生的花费，主要包括聘请KPMG的费用与更换新的一体化计算机系统的费用）；（7）Contract sales discounts 205,279英镑（合约交易的折扣）；（8）Planned maintenance 2,637,217英镑（计划的维护费用）；（9）Reduction in home trade debtors 107,920英镑；（10）Reduction in inventory 774,400英镑（存货减少的费用）；（11）Wasted management time 1,114,056英镑（浪费的管理时间成本折算的费用）；（12）Purchasing. 1,463,200英镑（购买的费用）。

本章节所要讲的课题，就是针对索赔中F项下的更换新的一体化计算机系统，这套新的替代系统是KPMG所建议的TROPOS。TROPOS比被告没有提供与部分提供但有缺陷的计算机系统FACT的性能更好与型号更新，这方面的好处是否要做出扣减涉及许多的争议，包括计算机系统本来是否需要一套更新更昂贵的替代系统，但这里只节录法院有关的判决如下。

法院是判针对这种争议，举证责任是在被告的违约方，Bowsher大法官说："245... The evidential burden of establishing betterment is on the defendant: Oswald v. Countrywide Surveyors Ltd. (1996) 50 Con L. R. 1 at 6, Skandia Property (UK) Ltd. v.

Thames Water Utilities (1997) 57 Con. L. R. 65 at p. 80. Wang(王安公司的被告)have not satisfied that burden and accordingly I make no allowance for betterment."

而针对双方的证据,法院首先认为是电脑的发展一日千里,所以原告不可能要求找一套完全相同的替代电脑系统。Bowsher 大法官说:"242.... it would have been impossible as well as commercially nonsensical for Pegler(原告) to buy a system which had not been advanced technically beyond the system sold to them some years earlier by Wang. The pace of computer development has been so fast that one simply cannot buy new computers built to old specifications. Moreover, it would have been an act of madness for Pegler to buy a second hand computer and no one has suggested that they could or should have done so. When buying a replacement computer, Pegler was inevitably going to get something better than the 1994 FACT(王安公司提供的计算机系统). Sometimes, replacement of defective goods involves paying a higher price, but a refreshing feature of the remarkable advances in development of computers is that they have been accompanied be equally remarkable reductions in price: hence TROPOS(替代计算机系统) cost less than FACT."

另是针对新的系统性能更好与拥有更多的功能,Bowsher 大法官认为原告购买 TROPOS 并没有选择,不能减少新功能换取费用的降低,说:"244. It follows from Dr. Worden's(被告的专家证人)evidence that Pegler could not have bought TROPOS more cheaply by omitting those features which he says are betterment because 'they are usually not separable from the cost of the main TROPOS product'. If Pegler could have bought a package omitting the alleged 'betterment' features, it would have been possible [if the case on betterment were accepted] to compare the price of TROPOS as bought with the price of TROPOS without the alleged betterment features and deduct the difference from the damages. An alternative approach might have been to compare TROPOS with other systems on the market without the alleged betterment features. Neither Dr. Worden nor any other witness sought to identify another cheaper product which did not contain those features. If he had done so, it would have both been possible to put a precise figure on the sum which, according to Wang, ought to have been saved and to investigate whether Pegler ought reasonably to have bought that other system. There is no evidence that SSI were able to raise the price of TROPOS above the cost of competing products because of the alleged betterment features other than Dr. Worden's bland assertion. Before Pegler contracted with SSI, they went out to tender. There was no attempt to suggest to Pegler that they ought to have accepted a tender given at a lower price. I do not even know whether other tenders were at higher or lower prices than the price tendered by SSI. Pegler had the advice of KPMG when they contracted with SSI and the contract was made to satisfy what was in the new ITT, not to obtain those additional features. It is not suggested that the new ITT required features which constituted betterment."

最后总结这一问题，Bowsher 大法官是说："如果替代品比侵权或违约损坏的产品有更长的使用年限，或是更新的型号，或是有额外的性能等，这一般不接受可做出扣减，除非当时有二手市场可找到与原来产品相同的替代品"(248. The mere fact that a party purchasing a substitute product acquires something with a longer life span, or which is more modern, or has additional features than the original would have had does not require an allowance for betterment, still less recovery limited to the financing cost of acquiring the replacement early: Harbutt's Plasticine v. Wayne Tank; Bacon v. Cooper Metals [1982] 1 All ER 397; Dominion Mosaics v. Trafalgar Trucking [1990] 2 All ER 246. In particular, where there is no ready second hand market for goods, or where there might be uncertainty as to the reliability of such goods, no credit need be given for the fact that a new and up-to-date replacement has been purchased: Moore v. DER Ltd. [1971] 1 WLR 1476.)

以上介绍的先例与在 2.2 段提到的 British Westinghouse Electric Co Ltd v. Underground Electric Railways of London Ltd (1912) AC 673 先例不同之处应该是后者涉及原告做出一个商业上更明智的决定购买一台新型号的涡轮机带来了更好的效益，这好处并非是强加在原告。

3. 同一个诉因有多位共同侵权人或违约方

"共同侵权人"(joint tortfeasors)是指受害方对他们的诉因是完全一样，证明他们的侵权责任也是根据同样的证据。"多位侵权人"(several tortfeasors)是指他们对同一个受害方造成不同程度的损害，而受害方向他们个别起诉的诉因并不一致，受害方可以向他们取得他们分别造成的损害赔偿。在没有证据可以区分受害方的损害，赔偿就会要所有不同的侵权人按比例分摊。它们在普通法下的分别是共同侵权人只能在一个诉讼中作出处理，只要有一个共同侵权人被原告选为被告，并被判要赔偿受害方所有的损失，其他没有作为共同被告的侵权人不能再被起诉，即使有关的判决并没有获得支付(如被告倒闭)。但涉及多位侵权人，受害方可以分别起诉每一个侵权人，直到取回所有的损失。

但这些区别已经不再重要，因为共同侵权人与多位侵权人的分别已经通过立法取消，该立法就是《Law Reform (Married Women and Tortfeasors) Act 1935》之 Section 6。但该立法没有针对违约，也已经被《Civil Liability (Contribution) Act 1978》废除。《Civil Liability (Contribution) Act 1978》之 Sections 1,3 和 6，是针对侵权人或违约方之间对赔偿给受害方损失的分摊。Section 6(1)要求分摊的损失是可以针对任何"法律基础"(legal basis)的责任，这包括侵权、违约、信托的违反或任何其他形式的过错。

3.1 受害方可以自由选择向任何一位侵权人或违约方索赔所有损失

这一种情况是经常会出现,特别是在一个侵权。也就是在同一个诉因下,涉及多位侵权人或违约方。在这种情况下,法律已经是非常明确规定受害方可以选择任何一位侵权人或违约方向他索赔所有的损失。被选中的被告,可以说是"共同与连带"(jointly and severally)要负责这一个损失赔偿。也不必考虑他的选择是否合理,所以是不存在被受害方选中的被告抗辩说:"你为什么不向另一位侵权人或违约方索赔?向他索赔会是更加合理或有把握。"这方面可节录 Sir David Cairns 大法官在 International Factors Ltd v. Rodriguez (1979) 1 QB 351 先例中所说:"A plaintiff who has two causes of action cannot be met when he makes a claim against one defendant by the answer: 'Oh, no; you've suffered nothing by my tort because you have a cause of action against somebody else.' That clearly cannot be right."

这方面最早与最重要的先例是 The "Liverpool" (No. 2) (1963) P 64 CA,案情涉及在 Mersey 河道上船舶碰撞,碰撞责任全是 Liverpool 轮的过错。碰撞后另一艘船舶 Ousel 轮在河道沉没,需要移走沉船。Ousel 轮虽然是无辜,但该英国港口有强制性法律要求船东承担责任移走沉船,但有一个金额限制是 10,835 英镑。由于这一个立法责任明确不过,所以 Ousel 轮船东主动提出支付与存放这一笔钱给 Mersey 河道当局,但被拒绝。而当局向 Liverpool 轮提出的侵权索赔,由于不受限制,所以包括移走沉船的所有费用或损失,高达 128,382 英镑。Liverpool 轮的船东抗辩说当局应该减少损失,向 Ousel 轮船东要求赔偿并减少损失的金额。但上诉庭判是当局作为原告并没有这方面的减损责任,他有权向任何一个有责任做出赔偿的被告起诉。换言之,受害方有权选择任何一位侵权人或违约方的权利并不属于"合理减少损失"(reasonable mitigation)义务的范畴,这在《McGregor on Damages》(18th edn, 2009 年)之 7-085 段说:"**A claimant need not take steps to recover compensation for his loss from parties who, in addition to the defendant, are liable to him**. This is an undoubted principle. Indeed, as Harman L. J said in *The Liverpool* (*no.* 2). It is a principle which, strictly speaking, stands on its own feet independently of mitigation, a principle without which it would have been unnecessary for the legislature to make provision for contribution and indemnity between joint and several tortfeasors. And *The Liverpool* (*No.* 2) shows that, even if the third party offers payment of the amount for which he is liable, the claimant is not required to accept it in mitigation."

这一方面的法律地位应该是明确不过,在 The "Liverpool" (No. 2)先例后,有不少的先例都明确了这一方面的说法,这包括 International Factors Ltd v. Rodriguez [1979] QB 351; London and South of England Building Society v. Stone (1983) 1 WLR 1242; Cottingham v. Attey Bower & Jones (2000) Lloyd's Rep PN 591; Standard Chartered Bank v. Pakistan National Shipping Corporation (2001) CLC 825; Peters v. East Midlands Strategic Health Authority (2009) 3 WLR 737; Haugesund Kommune v. Depfa (2010) 2

Lloyd's Rep 323 等先例。

其中在上述的 Peters v. East Midlands Strategic Health Authority 先例,涉及医疗疏忽的索赔,被告争辩说原告有一个法律规定的权利可向当地政府取得医疗与住院的福利,所以不能够向被告索赔这些损失。但上诉庭不同意,认为这一个案例在本质上是与 The "Liverpool"(No. 2)先例一致,其中 Dyson 大法官是这样说:

"Having reviewed these authorities, we can now express our conclusion on this issue. We can see no reason in policy or principle which requires us to hold that a claimant who wishes to opt for self-funding and damages in preference to reliance on the statutory obligations of a public authority should not be entitled to do so as a matter of right. The Claimant has suffered loss which has been caused by the wrongdoing of the Defendants. She is entitled to have that loss made good, so far as this is possible, by the provision of accommodation and care. There is no dispute as to what that should be and the council currently arranges for its provision at The Spinnies. The only issue is whether the Defendant wrongdoers or the council and the PCT should pay for it in the future.

It is difficult to see on what basis the present case can in principle be distinguished from the case where a claimant has a right of action against more than one wrongdoer or a case such as *The Liverpool* (*No.* 2) where a claimant has a right of action against a wrongdoer and an innocent party. In *The Liverpool* (*No.* 2), those two cases were treated alike. In our judgment, the present case should be treated in the same way. It is true that in the present case, the Claimant's right against the council is the statutory right to receive accommodation and care. But the fact that there is a statutory right in the claimant to have his or her loss made good in kind, rather than by payment of compensation, is not a sufficient reason for treating the cases differently."

另在 Haugesund Kommune v. Depfa 先例,案情涉及挪威一家著名的律师所 Wikborg Rein 在 Depfa 银行提供一笔庞大的贷款给当地政府的事件中疏忽提供法律意见。但这一个贷款的合约在挪威法律下是无效,导致 Depfa 银行实际上没有办法根据违约向当地政府取回该笔贷款,唯一可以通过"复原"(restitution)的诉因向当地政府取回,但这在挪威法律是一个不肯定的救济,估计是这个原因 Depfa 在英国法院向 Wikborg Rein 索赔这一笔庞大的损失。在本先例,被告的 Wikborg Rein 律师所抗辩说他要负责的损失必须扣减 Depfa 银行向当地政府能够取回的金额。

但 Tomlinson 大法官判是说:"英国法律允许受害方向任何一位被告索赔所有的损失,不管将来是否有可能向其他被告取得赔偿"(The law permitted recovery in full of the outstanding loss, that loss being assessed independently of the possibility of further recoveries)。此外,"受害的原告是不需要向其他有责任赔偿的当事人提出索赔"(A claimant was not required to take steps to recover compensation for his loss from persons who were, in addition to the defendant, liable to him)。

3.2 受害方向侵权人/违约方索赔损失必须扣减他已经从其他侵权人/违约方处取得的部分赔偿

这种情况会出现在受害方向他选择的第一位侵权人或违约方提出索赔,但由于各种原因(不论是受到法律或合约的责任限制或是庭外和解)导致受害方并不能把所有的损失取回来,所以他要找第二位“共同侵权人”(joint tortfeasor)或违约方索赔他余下的损失。这一来,向第二位被告索赔的损失,就必须扣减从第一位被告已经取得的部分赔偿,这就是净损失原则下的大道理。如果受害方已经从第一位被告取得所有的损失,也就表示他向第二位被告的索赔只会是局限在“名义损失”(nominal loss)。这方面的英国法律地位可节录《Halsbury's Laws of England》(4th Edition),Volume 12(1)之825段:“Where, however, a claimant who has concurrent claims against two obligors in respect of the same matter recovers the whole or part of his loss from one of those obligors, the amount which the claimant thus recovers is applied in diminution of the damages which are awarded to him against the other obligor. A claimant cannot recover more than the total sum due in respect of his loss, merely by reason of the fact that his claim may lie against more than one person. The rule reflects a general judicial dislike of overcompensation.”

这方面可先介绍一个违约的先例名为 Townsend v. Stone Toms & Partners (1981) 1 WLR 1153,案情涉及受害的发展商向承建商提出有关工程缺陷的索赔与向测量师索赔他疏忽没有监督有关工程的损失。在诉讼期间,承建商把3万英镑存放进法院(这种做法在笔者所著《仲裁法—从开庭审理到裁决书的作出与执行》一书第一章5.3.3.3.6.1段有详论)。这实际上是向受害方提出和解,并把这一笔钱做为是和解的底线并期望在金额上能够保护将来如果要继续的诉讼费用。这笔存放进法院的钱说明是“in satisfaction of all the causes of action in respect of which the plaintiffs claim”,并且被受害方接受了。这导致了第二被告(测量师)要求中止向他提出的诉讼,不应该允许继续下去。但这被拒绝,其中上诉庭的 Eveleigh 大法官是这样说“如果有两个不同的诉讼行动,满足了一个并不会阻止另一个行动的推进”(where there are two separate causes of action, satisfaction of the one should not be a bar to proceedings on the other)。

但该先例在最后的审理 Townsend v. Stone Toms & Partners (No. 2) (1984) 27 BLR 26,法院认定3万英镑是完全足够赔偿受害方的所有损失,所以把他向测量师的索赔请求撤销,原因是受害方再也没有任何损失。也有说法是如果受害方向其中一位侵权人或违约方取回所有的损失,受害方再也没有诉因去针对其他的侵权人或违约方。这是 Atkin 勋爵在 Clark v. Urquhart (1930) AC 28 先例中所说的:“... damage is an essential part of the cause of action and if already satisfied by one of the alleged tortfeasors the cause of action is destroyed.”

另也可节录 Tang Man Sit v. Capacious Investments Ltd (1996) AC 514 先例中 Nicholls 勋爵所说如下:“A third limitation is that a plaintiff cannot recover in the aggregate from one or more defendants an amount in excess of his loss. Part satisfaction of a judgment against one person does not operate as a bar to the plaintiff thereafter bringing an action against another who is also liable, but it does operate to reduce the amount recoverable in the second action. However, once a plaintiff has fully recouped his loss, of necessity he cannot thereafter pursue any other remedy he might have and which he might have pursued earlier. Having recouped the whole of his loss, any further proceedings would lack a subject matter. The principle of full satisfaction prevents double recovery.”

但这样的法律地位显然在细节上有很多问题要解决,例如:(1)第一位被告岂不是站在非常不利与不公平的地位?因为他要承担所有的损失,反而在他赔付了所有损失后,其他的侵权人或违约方就可以脱身。受害方能够向第一位被告取回所有损失的可能性也比较大,因为选择索赔对象时,其中一个主要考虑是被告能否有财力做出赔付。(2)什么情况会被视为是受害方能够向第一位被告取回所有的损失?(3)作为第二位甚至是第三位的被告,如何能够知悉受害方已经从较早的被告处取回部分或是全部的损失?这些问题会在接下去的段节做进一步的探讨。

3.2.1 共同侵权人或违约方之间对受害方损失赔偿的分摊

多位共同侵权人或违约方之间,如果其中一个被受害方选中为被告并且对所有的损失作出赔偿,在普通法下是不能要求其他共同侵权人或违约方对这笔损失赔偿做出分摊:Merryweather v. Nixon (1799) 8 TR 186 先例。法院在该先例认为原告不允许以他自己也有过错的事件作为诉因向其他共同侵权人或违约方强制要求分摊损失。这一个不令人满意的地位已经被立法改变。这一个立法是《Civil Liability (Contribution) Act 1978》,以下可简单节录 Section 1 的部分条文,主要是针对在本章所说的问题:“**1 Entitlement to contribution**. (1) Subject to the following provisions of this section, any person liable in respect of any damage suffered by another person may recover contribution from any other person liable in respect of the same damage (whether jointly with him or otherwise).... (4) A person who has made or agreed to make any payment in bona fide settlement or compromise of any claim made against him in respect of any damage (including a payment into court which has been accepted) shall be entitled to recover contribution in accordance with this section without regard to whether or not he himself is or ever was liable in respect of the damage, provided, however, that he would have been liable assuming that the factual basis of the claim against him could be established. (5) A judgment given in any action brought in any part of the United Kingdom by or on behalf of the person who suffered the damage in question against any person from whom contribution is sought under this section shall be conclusive in the proceedings for contribution as to any issue determined by that judgment in favour of the person from whom the contribution is sought.”

关于这个立法的解释,可以节录 Michael Furmston 教授所著的《The Law of Contract》(4th edn,2010 年)之 6.344 段如下:

"In principle, if a joint or joint and several debtor has paid the whole debt, he can recover contribution from the other debtors.

Obviously, this rule can be varied by agreement between the debtors. As between principal and surety, the assumption would be that the debt should fall wholly on the principal. Between other co-debtors the assumption would be that each would pay the amount of the debt divided by the number of solvent debtors at the time when the right to contribution arose.

Contribution between those liable in respect of the same damage (as opposed to the same debt) is now governed by the Civil Liability (Contribution) Act 1978. The same damage may be caused by two tortfeasors or by two defendants, one of whom is a tortfeasor and the other of whom is a contract breaker or by two contract breakers who are breaking different contracts but are causing the same damage. The Act does not apply however where two economically connected contracts are broken but the effect is to cause different damage. This was the point of the important decision of the House of Lords in Royal Brompton Hospital NHS Trust v. Hammond (No. 3) (2002) UKHL 14, in which there were possible claims by an employer under a building contract against the main contractor and against the architect. It was held that even if the claims were established they would not be in respect of the same damage. The breach of contract alleged against the contractor was based on delay in performing the contract, which would lead to late delivery of the building. The claim againstthe architect was that it had incorrectly evaluated the contractor's claim for an extension of time. This if correct would have led to different damage."

在多位共同侵权人之间分摊损失,该立法之 Section 2(1)是这样规定:"Subject to subsection (3) below, in any proceedings for contribution under section above the amount of the contribution recoverable from any person shall be such as may be found by the court to be just and equitable having regard to the extent of that person's responsibility for the damage in question."另一提的是在该立法中,Section 1 是规定了 2 年的时效,起算是在有权要求分摊的一天为准。

显然多位共同侵权人或违约方事后要求分摊是出现在其中一位侵权人或违约方被受害方作为被告并通过判决或是和解赔偿全部损失的情况下,如果受害方在同一个诉讼中把所有有责任的侵权人或违约方都加在一起作为共同被告,就可以避免事后需要通过另一个法律行动分摊。即使是作为原告的受害方不把所有的有关人士都加进来作为共同被告,被告的侵权人或违约方也可以向法院申请加入其他共同侵权人或违约方作为共同被告。这也是在侵权很普遍的做法,也是一个较好的做法。有关的《民事诉讼法》(Civil Procedural Rules)之 r. 19.1(2)说:"The court may order a person to be added as a new party if it is desirable to add the new party so that the court can resolve all the matters in dispute in the proceedings, or there is an issue involving the new party and an existing party which is connected to the matters in dispute."

但如果有所遗漏或被索赔的侵权人或违约方不知道其他被告的存在，导致了多位共同侵权人或违约方被分别先后索赔损失，这就涉及受害方不能向不同的侵权人或违约方取回多过他实际蒙受的损失，所以必须扣减他已经从其他侵权人/违约方取得的部分或全部赔偿。这种情况也会涉及多位共同侵权人或违约方需要事后分摊损失。

针对违约的情况，由于今天绝大部分跨国性的商业合约中是有一条仲裁条文，而由于仲裁的机密性以及仲裁是基于双方约定才会赋予仲裁庭管辖权，更加是谈不上可以合并审理。所以如果涉及有多位共同侵权人与违约方，受害方难免要分别向不同的被告提出索赔，事后再让他们分摊所赔付的这一笔损失。

针对本段与上一段所讲的，可节录 Bingham 勋爵在 Heaton v. Axa Equity and Law Life Assurance Society plc (2002) UKHL 15 先例中以简单的例子所介绍的相互关系，说：

"A（受害方）brings an action against B（侵权人）claiming damages for negligence in tort. The claim goes to trial, and judgment is given for A for £ x. There is no appeal and the judgment sum is paid by B to A. £ x will thereafter be taken, in the ordinary way, to represent the full value of A's claim against B. A cannot thereafter maintain an action for damages for negligence in tort against C as a concurrent tortfeasor liable in respect of the same damage for two reasons: first, such a claim will amount to a collateral attack on the judgment already given; and secondly, A will be unable to allege or prove any damage, and damage is a necessary ingredient for a cause of action based on tortious negligence. A cannot maintain an action against C in contract either, in respect of the same damage, for the first reason which bars his tortious claim. There is however no reason of principle, in either case, on the assumptions made in this example, why B should not recover a contribution from C under the Civil Liability (Contribution) Act 1978 as a party liable with him for the same damage suffered by A.

In a second example the facts are varied. A brings an action against B claiming damages for negligence in tort. The action does not proceed to judgment because B compromises A's claim by an agreement providing that he will pay A damages of £ x, which he duly does. If £ x is agreed or taken to represent the full value of A's claim against B, A cannot thereafter maintain an action against C in tort in respect of the same damage for the second reason given in the last paragraph, and although he is not precluded from pursuing a claim against C in contract in respect of the same damage he cannot claim or recover more than nominal damages. There is again, in the ordinary way, no reason of principle in either case, on the assumptions made in this example, why B should not recover a contribution from C under the 1978 Act as a party liable with him for the damage suffered by A."

3.2.2 什么情况会被视为是受害方能够向第一位被告取回所有的损失

受害方的损失,一般不是"议定赔偿"(liquidated damage)。换言之是需要经过审理并且可能是复杂的事实认定与法律争辩才能最后确定损失的金额。所以"非议定赔偿"(unliquidated damage)的金额就是"称职的法院"(competent court)所判决的金额。如果这一笔钱已经从第一位被告取回,就代表受害方再也没有损失可向其他共同侵权人或违约方索赔。如果受害方不服原来法院的判决,认为胜诉的金额太少,或是审理后情况的改变导致损失加大,也不能改变这一个事实,因为同一个诉因不能再重新审理,即"一事不再审"(*res judicata*)原则。

现实中,不少诉讼的双方当事人会达成和解,这和解会是针对责任方面或是赔偿金额方面,也有可能是针对两方面。这一来,这个和解的金额是否代表受害方所有的损失就会要看和解协议的措辞与文字,因为不通过审理是永远不会明确肯定。显然通过和解达成的赔偿金额是可以让法院做出一个"同意判决"(consent judgment),而判决是被视为等同于一般法院审理后的判决:Knight v. Rochdale Healthcare NHS Trust (2004) EWHC 1831。但和解的金额通常会比受害方蒙受的全部损失为低,受害方如果不让步也达不成和解。这表示如果受害方知道他还可以向其他的共同侵权人或违约方追讨还没有全部取回的损失,曾经有说法是他在与第一位被告的和解协议中的措辞与文字需要十分小心,不要表达他已经取回所有的损失。例如在 Dillon v. Napier Shanks & Bell (1893) 30 SLR 685 先例中,案情涉及人身伤害的索赔,受害方在与其中一位侵权人的和解协议中明确约定保留向其他侵权人索赔的权利,而且写明这位侵权人的赔偿并不是用来弥补受害方所有的损失。法院判是在这种情况下,受害方有权向其他侵权人追讨金额不足的部分。同样的先例还有 Crawford v. Springfield Steel Co Ltd, July 18, unreported, Carrigan v. Duncan (1971) SLT (Sh. Ct.) 33 与澳大利亚的 Ruffino v. Grace Brothers Pty. Ltd (1980) 1 NWSLR 732 与 Boyle v. State Rail Authority, (NSW), (1997) 14 NSWCCR 374。

但如果较早的和解协议可以被解释为全部损失已经取回,曾经有说法是这会有令稍后针对其他共同侵权人或违约方的索赔变为"无效"(incompetent)的危险。这种案件出现在两个不同判法的贵族院先例 Jameson v. CEGB (1999) 1 Lloyd's Rep 573 与 Heaton v. Axa Equity and Law Life Assurance Society plc (2002) UKHL 15。

在 Jameson v. CEGB 先例,案情涉及 Jameson 先生曾经分别为两个不同的发电厂雇主工作并接触石棉的毒害而感染了"间皮瘤"(mesothelioma),这种情况在本书第四章4.3.3段有详细介绍。并值得一提的是,在2006年《The Compensation Act》有立法的修改,其中 Section 3 规定,如果有责任的被告导致或允许原告接触石棉,而原告事后发作间皮瘤病,但没有办法确定是否由于被告导致或是其他的接触引致发病,被告还是要负责任并需要负责原告所有的损失,责任是连带性,不管有没有其他共同侵权人存在或被告本人可能没有侵权责任。在该先例,Jameson 先生作为原告先向第一位被告名为 Babcock 的雇主提出索赔。在该诉讼中,Babcock 在 1988 年 3 月 30 日存进法院一笔 75,000 英镑的金额,而 Jameson 先生的代表律师在 4 月 19 日与 Babcock 的律师同意庭外和解,金额是 80,000 英镑。这笔钱也在 4 月 29 日支付了,并说明这笔钱是"in full and final settlement and satisfaction of all the causes of action in respect of which the claims"。而碰巧是 Jameson 先生在 4 月 29 日的 5 天前因为间皮瘤而死亡。在大约一年后,Jameson 先生的遗产执行人根据当时的立法《Fatal Accidents Acts 1976》之 Section 1(这在之后被《Administration of Justice Act 1982》之 Section 3[1]替代)向 CEGB(第二位雇主)起诉要求赔偿 Jameson 先生的遗孀抚养费和丧失生活依赖的损失,这一笔损失的金额是 142,000 英镑,而且根据立法的规定,是不需要扣减已经向 Babcock 取回的 80,000 英镑的部分损失,这笔钱已经是属于 Jameson 先生的遗产。看来,对 Babcock 与对 CEGB 的诉因并不相同,但索赔的损失基本上是一致与重复。从整体来看,每一方的说法都有合理与不合理之处。Jameson 先生的遗孀显然还是有大部分的损失没有取回,而且情况也有了改变。对 Babcock 而言更加是不合理,他以为达成和解的 80,000 英镑已经把整件事情了结,但如果第二被告(CEGB)真的赔付 142,000 英镑,CEGB 会向作为共同侵权人或违约方的 Babcock 根据《Civil Liability (Contribution) Act 1978》要求分摊。第一审和上诉庭都是判根据《Fatal Accidents Acts 1976》,CEGB 需要向原告赔偿损失,之后 CEGB 有权根据《Civil Liability (Contribution) Act 1978》向 Babcock 要求分摊损失。但到了贵族院,这被多数意见的判决推翻。多数判决是由 Hope 勋爵的判词代表,他认为法院看较早的和解金额是否能够代表受害方所有的损失只应局限在和解的措辞与文字,而在这一个先例,Jameson 先生与 Babcock 的和解协议显然是明确了所有的损失都已经取回,Hope 勋爵是这样说:"The question therefore is, as Mr. McLaren, QC (CEGB 的代表大律师) put it, not whether the plaintiff has received the full value of his claim but whether the sum which he has received in settlement of it was intended to be in full satisfaction of the tort. In this case the words used cannot be construed as meaning that the sum which the deceased agreed to accept was in partial satisfaction only of his claim of damages. It was expressly accepted in full and final settlement and satisfaction of all of his causes of action in the statement of claim. I would hold that the terms of his settlement with Babcock extinguished his claim of damages against the other tortfeasors."

但持不同意见的 Lloyd 勋爵主要认为庭外和解通常是不会满足所有的损失,而《Fatal Accidents Act 1976》规定了在计算 Jameson 先生死亡的损失赔偿时,是不必考虑他的遗产中会给遗孀的好处,也就是不必考虑 Babcock 的 80,000 英镑赔偿。Lloyd 勋爵认为在《Fatal Accidents Act 1976》的立法,没有考虑双重赔偿的问题。他是这样说:

"In the ordinary case, where the deceased has died without having first brought an action of damages, the application of this provision will produce a fair result and ought not to give rise to any difficulty. But the question whether the plaintiffs can satisfy its requirements has an additional significance in this case. This is because s. 4 of the 1976 Act, as substituted by s. 3(1) of the Administration of Justice Act, 1982, provides that in assessing damages in respect of a person's death in an action under that Act the benefits which have accrued to any person from his estate or otherwise as a result of his death shall be disregarded. The first named plaintiff has inherited the whole of the sum of 80,000 which was received from Babcock under the settlement of the deceased's claim together with the remainder of the deceased's estate. As this is a benefit which accrued to her as a result of the death it must be disregarded. So the CEGB cannot take into credit, by way of set-off against any liability to the plaintiffs in this action, the amount which was paid to the deceased in order to settle his claim against Babcock. . . .

The trial Judge said that he had reached this result with regret because it might work an injustice on Babcock. I agree. It seems unjust that Babcock should be exposed to the risk of having to pay damages twice for the same harm and that the plaintiffs should be able to obtain for the first named plaintiff what, in the circumstances, would amount to double recovery in respect of the same loss. It seems unlikely that, when the substituted s. 4 of the Fatal Accidents Act, 1976 was enacted, Parliament contemplated that a person could become entitled to a double recovery in these circumstances."

这一个贵族院先例并不受欢迎,如新西兰上诉法院的 Allison v. KPMG Peat Marwick (2000) I NZLR 560 先例就不接受,Jameson v. CEGB 先例被视为只要受害方与其中一位共同侵权人或违约方达成了一个"全面与最终的和解"(full and final settlement),就再也不能向其他侵权人或违约方索赔他可能还没有满足的损失。

英国贵族院在不久后作出了不同的判决。这是在 Heaton v. Axa Equity and Law Life Assurance Society plc 先例,它也没有去推翻 Jameson v. CEGB (1999) 1 Lloyd's Rep 573 先例,只是在对这两个案件的案情作出区分之后,作出相反的判决。该先例案情涉及两个投资产品的经纪合约,是两个委托人 A 与 B(本案被告)分别与同一个经纪人(本案原告)签订。A 与 B 都是做金融投资产品的生意,在公司结构和业务上有关联,会共享一些信息。合约履行过程中,A 声称经纪人有"财务违规行为"(financial misconduct),取消了他与经纪人的合约。B 相信了这一"丑闻",也取消了他与经纪人的合约。这不仅给经纪人的生意带来困难,也对他的名誉造成影响。

经纪人先向 A 起诉违约及侵权。A 承认他宣称经纪人财务违规是错误的,并收回这个说法。经纪人于是修改了具体诉因。后来经纪人与 A 达成和解,A 向经纪人做出损失的赔偿。和解协议的关键措辞是"所有当事人(指经纪人与 A)就已经或可能产生的所有索赔和潜在的索赔相互达成全面和最终的和解"(in full and final settlement of all claims and potential claims which the parties had or might have against each other)。经纪人转而向 B 索赔。与 A 的看法不同,B 坚持认为经纪人是有财务违规行为。这就导致经纪人对 B 的诉因与对 A 的诉因有一些不同了。

第一审的高院认为经纪人向 A 索赔的损失与向 B 索赔的损失完全重复,既然他与 A 已经达成全面最终的和解,他就等于放了 B 一马,不应再向 B 索赔,也不应再将诉讼进行下去。但上诉庭与贵族院均不同意第一审判决,认为通过解释经纪人与 A 的和解协议的措辞,可以得出结论是这份和解协议并没有一次性解决各方之间所有的争议。经纪人起诉 A 与 B 虽然是针对同一损失,但贵族院 Mackay 勋爵认为经纪人对 A 的诉因不同于对 B 的诉因。另外,B 不是和解协议中的当事方,和解协议也没有排除经纪人向 B 索赔的权利,所以经纪人仍然有权向 B 索赔损失。

这一个先例对 Jameson 先例的改变主要体现在对第一个和解协议的解释,这也是针对合约的解释,这在笔者所著的《合约的解释》(法律出版社 2007 年版)一书中有介绍。在这个先例,贵族院接受和解协议是与法院判决不同,经常涉及受害方的让步,导致和解金额不代表受害方所有的损失。这一来,如果不允许受害方向其他的侵权人或违约方索赔其余的损失,就会造成不公平。Bingham 勋爵是这样说:"There is, however, an obvious difference between the action which culminates in judgment and the action which culminates in compromise: that whereas, save in an exceptional case (such as Crawford v. Springfield Steel Co Ltd [unreported] 18 July 1958, Lord Cameron), a judgment will conclusively decide the full measure of damage for which B is liable to A, a sum agreed to be paid under a compromise may or may not represent the full measure of B's liability to A. Where a sum is agreed which makes a discount for the risk of failure or for a possible finding of contributory negligence or for any other hazard of litigation, the compromise sum may nevertheless be regarded as the full measure of B's liability. But A may agree to settle with B for £ x not because either party regards that sum as the full measure of A's loss but for many other reasons: it may be known that B is uninsured and £ x represents the limit of his ability to pay; or A may wish to pocket a small sum in order to finance litigation against other parties; or it may be that A is old and ill and prefers to accept a small sum now rather than a larger sum years later; or it may be that there is a contractual or other limitation on B's liability to A. While it is just that A should be precluded from recovering substantial damages against C in a case where he has accepted a sum representing the full measure of his estimated loss, it is unjust that A should be so precluded where he has not."

任何的和解协议都会有可能是约定了受害方所蒙受的所有损失,这就涉及有关和解协议的解释。而 Bingham 勋爵认为 Jameson v. CEGB 先例中多数意见对和解协议的解释是"有一点太绝对"(a little too absolute),就是只要说明"全面与最终"就代表所有损失被双方约定。

针对合约的解释,其中必须考虑的是达成和解的"事实背景"(factual matrix),也就是不再严格看一个合约的措辞/文字并给它一个字面的解释，而是从谈判的事实背景找出订约双方真正的意图。一考虑双方和解谈判时的事实背景与订约双方的意图，就马上想到 A 与 C 达成和解协议的时候根本不可能想到 B 的好处，并让他可以在违约中脱身。至于和解协议所用的措辞/文字不论是紧是松，都不应该有这一个后果。A 与 C 达成和解协议时，也通常不会把 B 拖进来，如说明是他保留将来向 B 起诉权利，因为一般情况下这根本不关 C 的事。所以 Jameson v. CEGB 先例要求在和解协议不要约定全面与最终和解并要保留向其他共同侵权人或违约方索赔的权利并不现实。而对达成和解协议的侵权人或者违约方而言，如 C，如果这一个和解金额赔得越少，他为了将来的好处就更加要争取和解协议是用紧密的措辞/文字说明和解是全面与最终的，以保证这同一个索赔不会让 A 将来钻空子。所以仅考虑和解协议中措辞/文字的紧松，与双方订约的意图不一致。至于说是否会导致 B 在事后赔付后，再根据《Civil Liability（Contribution）Act 1978》向 C 要求分摊，导致了 C 与 A 较早的和解协议只是一场空。Bingham 勋爵是说这些问题很容易解决，完全可以在与 A 的和解协议中多加一条条文就是将来如果 C 被其他途径追讨同样的损失或被要求分摊，A 必须补偿 C 在这方面的损失。这种条文在航运中的无单放货保函经常会见到。总结以上所讲，可简单节录 Bingham 勋爵所说如下：

"In considering whether a sum accepted under a compromise agreement should be taken to fix the full measure of A's loss, so as to preclude action against C in tort in respect of the same damage, and so as to restrict any action against C in contract in respect of the same damage to a claim for nominal damages, the terms of the settlement agreement between A and B must be the primary focus of attention, and the agreement must be construed in its appropriate factual context. In construing it various significant points must in my opinion be borne clearly in mind:

(1) The release of one concurrent tortfeasor does not have the effect in law of releasing another concurrent tortfeasor and the release of one contract-breaker does not have the effect in law of releasing a successive contract-breaker.

(2) An agreement made between A and B will not affect A's rights against C unless either (a) A agrees to forgo or waive rights which he would otherwise enjoy against C, in which case his agreement is enforceable by B, or (b) the agreement falls within that limited class of contracts which either at common law or by virtue of the Contracts (Rights of Third Parties) Act 1999 is enforceable by C as a third party.

(3) The use of clear and comprehensive language to preclude the pursuit of claims and cross-claims as between A and B has little bearing on the question whether the agreement represents the full measure of A's loss. The more inadequate the compensation agreed to be paid by B, the greater the need for B to protect himself against any possibility of further action by A to obtain a full measure of redress.

(4) While an express reservation by A of his right to sue C will fortify the inference that A is not treating the sum recovered from B as representing the full measure of his loss, the absence of such a reservation is of lesser and perhaps of no significance, since there is no need for A to reserve a right to do that which A is in the ordinary way fully entitled to do without any such reservation.

(5) If B, on compromising A' s claim, wishes to protect himself against any claim against him by C claiming contribution, he may achieve that end either (a) by obtaining an enforceable undertaking by A not to pursue any claim against C relating to the subject matter of the compromise, or (b) by obtaining an indemnity from A against any liability to which B may become subject relating to the subject matter of the compromise."

3.2.3　第二位被告如何能够知悉受害方已经从较早的被告取回部分或是全部的损失?

如果所有共同侵权人或违约方都参与在一个诉讼中作为共同被告,这方面不会是个问题。但如果受害方是先后分别向不同侵权人或违约方提出索赔,被告就需要警觉会有危险是原告的受害方有可能从不同侵权人或违约方取回比他真正损失更大的一笔赔偿,被告是需要知道后才可以把原告的索赔金额减少(扣减原告已经取回的部分损失),甚至是撤销索赔因为再也没有诉因。也有可能在赔付后,需要向其他共同侵权人或违约方根据《Civil Liability (Contribution) Act 1978》要求分摊。要全面知道就需要通过各方面的行动,如独立的调查,向其他潜在的共同侵权人或违约方的查询,在诉讼中向原告要求"文件披露"(discovery/disclosure of documents),甚至向原告作出"质询"(interrogatories)等。

3.2.4　共同侵权人或违约方对受害方所有的损失要负上共同与连带责任的问题

本小段还可以谈谈这个"共同与连带"(jointly and severally)责任的问题,这问题在近年来针对一些专业人士如会计师、工程师、建筑师、测量师、律师等尤其重要。这些专业人士在80年代以来所出的商业大事件中,如公司的倒闭或遇上困难,经常会被列为是共同被告。而他们会被视为有部分的过错或疏忽通常是因为在他们的工作中,没有通过他们的专业知识把有关的问题暴露出来。例如,如果一个建筑有缺陷,承建商显然要在有关的合约下负责。但有可能负责设计与监督的建筑师也要负上部分责任,因为他监督不力,否则这缺陷本来是可以及时发现。在20世纪90年代,国际上有好几个大型企业与跨国公司突然之间垮台,这导致为这些企业或公司做出年度审计的会计师也事后被债权人起诉。这类事件中最著名的就是安达信会计师事务所(Arthur Andersen)因美国安然公司(Enron)假账问题而解体。2001年10月,安然公司造假账等多项罪行被揭发,而作为其审计师的安达信不仅没有审查及披露这些问题,反而在不到一个月时间内销毁了安然公司数千页文件。随后安达信被美国司法部以妨害司法罪名起诉并被判有罪,导致吊销会计师执照、被迫解体的严重后果。

作为这种事故的受害方,他们免不了要找恰当的被告,也就是有能力与财力赔偿他们损失的被告。往往剩下值得通过诉讼索赔损失的共同被告就是专业人士。他们就算本身不是很有钱,但通常会对他们的"专业疏忽"(professional negligence)的责任有投保,而保险的范围与程度也会是非常完善。换言之,这些专业人士是一般受害方眼中的"提款机"(deep pocket)被告。而在整件事故,这些专业人士即使是有错,一般也不会是主要过错。但在共同与连带的侵权与合约责任下,他们如果被受害方选中为被告还是要对所有的损失作出赔偿。理论上,他们可以在事后根据《Civil Liability (Contribution) Act 1978》要求其他的共同侵权人或违约方分摊这一笔损失,但现实是做不到,因为其他共同侵权人或违约方已经倒闭或濒临倒闭。

这带来的后果是近年一些承保专业人士疏忽责任的保险公司倒闭、部分保险公司完全撤出了"专业人士责任保险"(professional indemnity insurance)与剩下的保险公司大幅度提高保费。会有情况是保费高昂不说,根本没办法有保险公司承保这方面的责任。这导致专业人士要求对这一个共同与连带责任进行法律改革,并在英国有好几个由政府或专业人士成立小组对这方面作出研究,并提交了有关的报告,如法律改革委员会的《Feasibility Investigation of Joint and Several Liability》(London:HMSO,1996),英国贸易与工业部的《Professional Liability:Report of the Study Teams》(London:HMSO,1989)(可称为 Likieraman 报告),政府和各行业的《Constructing the Team》(London:HMSO,1994)(可称为 Latham 报告),以及专业人士团体的《Professional Liability》(1989)、《Professional Indemnity Insurance and Joint and Several Liability in the Construction Industry—The Case for Reform》(2004)。在 Likieraman 报告中建议解决的办法是把共同与连带责任改变为"按比例责任"(proportionate liability),也就是在共同侵权人或违约方之间,他们对受害方的赔偿(除了人身伤亡)再也不是所有的损失,而是按照他们的过错占整个事故中的百分比作出相应的赔偿。这表示如果建筑师或会计师在事故中只占了 5% 的责任,他们的赔偿也只需要局限在受害方 5% 的损失。

但看来法律改革委员会报告并不认同这一个建议办法。主要是认为这把共同与连带责任对共同侵权人或违约方的不公平,转变为对受害方不公平,这可以说在公共政策上更加不可以接受。在按比例责任下,估计受害方能够取回全部损失的赔偿机会不高。而且受害方选择被告(不论是单独一个或多个被告)会有很大的矛盾,跟以前的做法不同。如果选了一个提款机被告,但估计他在整个事故中的过错不会超出 5%,就不一定是恰当的对象。对部分共同侵权人或违约方死亡或倒闭的风险,也从原来的由被原告起诉的第一被告承担转变为由受害的原告自己承担。

估计按比例责任也违反了一般英国法律的传统就是对被告错误的程度与损失赔偿高低的分别对待。这就是被告如果犯了很轻微的错误/疏忽,但碰巧有关的案件中所造成的损失十分高昂,从来没有说法是被告可以赔少一点。这种案件经常出现,如一些"蛋壳脑袋"(egg-shell skull)与"衣衫褴褛的超级富豪"(shabby millionaire)就是这种案件的典型。所以,专业人士说他在事故中只有犯5%的错误/疏忽所以不应该承担全部责任对不少人来说就不是很有说服力。

法律改革委员会还是倾向于考虑其他解决办法,虽然办法也不多。其中一个如立法针对专业人士的赔偿封顶,另一个是建议专业人士在他们为客户服务的合约中加上按比例责任的条文。这种条文在英国皇家建筑师标准合约格式中已经有加上,说:“The Architect's liability for loss or damage shall be limited to such sum as the Architect ought reasonably to pay having regard to his responsibility for the same on the basis that all other consultants, specialists, and the contractor, shall where appointed be deemed to have provided to the Client contractual undertakings in respect of their services and shall be deemed to have paid to the Client such contribution as may be appropriate having regard to the extent of their responsibility for such loss or damage.”当然,以合约解决这个问题也会带来许多其他的问题,如不像法律一样可以统一做法,变为会有合约加上类似的条文,但也会有其他合约欠缺(不论是因为当事人不懂而没有加上,或是专业人士的谈判力量不够争取)。也会是加上类似条文但措辞不一致或有争议,反而导致许多昂贵的诉讼。还有是1977年的英国《公平合约法》(Unfair Contract Terms 1977)会对这种条文有所控制,要求符合公平合理。

最后一提的是,澳大利亚已经在2003年前后对这方面有了改革,引进了按比例责任替代共同与连带责任。而在不同州份的相关立法有:《Civil Liability Act 2002》(NSW) Pt,4;《Wrongs Act 1958》(Vic),Pt IVAA;《Civil Liability Act 2002》(WA) Pt 1F;《Civil Liability Act 2003》(Qld),Ch 2,Pt2;《Civil Law (Wrongs) Act 2002》(ACT),Ch 7A;《Proportionate Liability Act 2005》(NT);《Civil Liability Act 2002》(Tas),Pt 9A;《Law Reform (Contributory Negligence and Apportionment of Liability) Act 2001》(SA),Pt 3。据说在不同州份的做法中也面临许多困难,包括带来不肯定。例如针对不出庭的被告,部分州(New South Wales,Queensland,the Northern Territory 和 the Commonwealth)是可让法院对不出庭与出庭的共同侵权人或违约方会要承担的责任百分比一并加以考虑。但部分州(Victoria)只对出庭的被告要承担的责任百分比加以考虑,并严格禁止考虑不出庭的共同侵权人或违约方(除非对方已经是死亡或倒闭)。两种做法都会有问题,前者会对不出庭的共同侵权人或违约方认定的责任百分比有偏差,因为他们根本没有出庭抗辩与提供证据。后者还是会保留以前的做法就是受害的原告选择恰当的共同侵权人或违约方作为被告,而其他不恰当的对象就有可能是不会出庭。另一个困难是有关的立法有可能干预订约自由,这可以举建造合约经常会有的合约安排为例。在这种合约中,业主经常会与一位总承包商订约,业主也会关心并满意总承包商的财政状况后才会订约,保证如果将来出了事故能够根据合约向总承包商取得所有的赔偿。而总承包商会在事后把不同的工程分包给分包商。这表示根据合约的关系,工程如果出了事故就会是业主向总承包商索赔损失,而总承包商向分包商要求补偿。如果分包商倒闭,这是总承包商的风险,与业主无关。但有了这方面的立法之后,法院按照共同侵权人或违约方的错误程度判他们按比例承担责任,就会有可能干预他们之间的合约关系。在建筑合约的履行方面,工程会是总承包商监督,但主要是由分包商施工。所以一旦有问题,他们都会是共同侵权人或违约方,而且分包商会要承担大部分的责任。这表示受害的业主作为原告提出索赔,他变为只能向他的违约方(总承包商)按他责任的比例取回部分损失。大部分的损失会是要向分包商按照侵权的疏忽(因为他们之间没有直接的合约关系)索赔。这表示业主在订约时也要关心分包商的财政状况以及他是否有能力赔偿损失,甚至要限制总承包商能够聘用的分包商。由于本章不是主要针对这一方面,所以不进一步探讨这一个十分重要与复杂的课题。

4. 税务的问题

4.1 税务问题曾经被视为是太遥远,计算损失时不必加以考虑

针对税务的问题英国法院看来是在1933年之前都不加以理会,这方面的原因会是税务问题被视为是“太遥远”(*res inter alios acta*),被认为是涉及受害方与第三人(税务局)的个人问题。加上在那个年代税务的问题也不大,因为税率不高。从1933年直到British Transport Commission v. Gourley (1956) AC185先例,有一些英国的一审判决与上诉庭判决都认为侵权或违约的损失计算,可以不必理会税务的问题,也就是损失金额不必因税务作出扣减。但在贵族院的British Transport Commission v. Gourley先例,案情涉及铁路公司的疏忽导致了乘客Gourley先生的人身伤害,并提出向铁路公司索赔。Gourley先生当时是一位非常成功的工程师,所以他的索赔金额相对庞大,而主要就是他的收益损失。显然如果他没有受到伤害并能够继续工作,他的收入也需要缴纳入息税。但如果是损失赔偿,就不必缴纳税费。这导致了贵族院判他的损失赔偿需要扣减估计的税费。

在British Transport Commission v. Gourley先例贵族院的大部分意见是认为税务问题并非是太遥远,其中Goddard勋爵说:“The mere fact that the item arises as between the claimant and a third party would not seem to be the test”,他也有说漠视税务是不现实。另Earl Jowitt大法官列举了一个苏格兰的先例McDaid v. Clyde Navigation Trustees 1946 SC 462来支持他的观点说:“When you get a liability to which all earnings are subject and which depends not upon any circumstances peculiar to the individual but upon a general law of the land universal in its application, it would be wrong to ignore the existence of the liability.”

上述所讲显然是考虑到受害方与第三人(税务局)之间税务的问题并非是个人的问题,如受害方为损失买了保险或与个别第三人有合约导致他真正损失金额的增加与减少是可以不必理会,但税收的问题是一般性法律,涉及每一个人。

4.2 British Transport Commission v. Gourley 先例的两个先决条件

税务的问题在 British Transport Commission v. Gourley 先例订下了两个考虑因素或先决条件,必须都满足才会在损失计算中扣去税费。这就是:(1)如果没有侵权或违约造成损失,受害方蒙受的这笔损失(不论是可以赚取的利润或是工资)本来需要缴纳税费;(2)受害方获得的这笔损失赔偿本身是不需要缴纳税费的。

这两个先决条件满足的情况简单说就是受害方的收益或利润在没有发生侵权或违约时是需要纳税,但变为以损失赔偿的方式,受害方就不需要纳税。这显然是为了避免被告多赔或少赔受害方,因为如果条件一是满足而条件二是否定,也就是受害方在稍后的时间把损失取回来还是要支付税费给税务局,在损失赔偿扣减任何税费的情况下造成了重复的扣减。这不是善待侵权人或违约方让他少赔,而是在净损失的原则下,计算受害方真正蒙受的损失。正如在 British Transport Commission v. Gourley 先例中,Earl Jowitt 大法官是这样说:"My Lords, it is, I think if I may say so with the utmost respect, fallacious to consider the problem as though a benefit were being conferred upon a wrongdoer by allowing him to abate the damages for which he would otherwise be liable. The problem is rather for what damages is he liable? And if we apply the dominant rule, we should answer: 'He is liable for such damages as, by reason of his wrongdoing, the plaintiff has sustained....' I see no reason why in this case we should depart from the dominant rule or why the respondent should not have his damages assessed upon the basis of what he has really lost, and I consider that in determining what he really lost the judge ought to have considered the tax liability of the respondent."

这种情况可以一个经常会发生的人身伤害案件为例,如果涉及收益损失,也就是工资的损失,条件一肯定可以满足。但针对条件二,英国已经有立法规定了受害方的损失赔偿是可以免税。这可以节录《McGregor on Damages》(18th edn, 2009 年)之 572 页,注脚 95 所说:"Mirroring the earlier legislation from 1960 onwards, s. 406(b) of the Income Tax (Earnings and Pensions) Act 2003 exempts from the charge to tax on termination of employment a payment provided 'on account of injury to, or disability of, an employee'. And following upon legislation from 1971, s. 751 of the Income Tax (Trading and Other Income) Act 2005 exempts from tax the interest given on personal injury damages, whether by court order or by settlement. This latter exemption does not justify awarding a lower rate of interest: Mason v. Harman (1972) RTR 1."

所以,条件一与条件二都可以满足,在 British Transport Commission v. Gourley 先例下,损失计算就需要扣减税费。这两个条件要同时满足的要求也适用在以后所有的案例,但这个问题也就变得越来越复杂。

税务问题的复杂性是在好几个方面,一是税制越来越复杂与经常有改变。不同的司法区域都会有不同的税制,而任何税制都是一个极其复杂的系统。举例来说,中国的就有流转税、所得税、资源税、增值税、财产税、行为税等多种体系。而每一体系下也有不同的税种。再加上不同的司法区域又有不同的税务概念,如地域/全球性来源征税原则,资本性/一般性收入/支出,集团亏损税项关联等。因此,如果把税务问题考虑进损失计算会是一个复杂的问题,正是“牵一发而动全身”。而从以下的举例(4.4.1段)也可看到,法院/仲裁庭在做出判决或裁决时也只能就单一项的税种/税率的影响做出调整。而且法院/仲裁庭如果没有专家证人(一般是会计师)的协助,一般是十分困难甚至无法做出一个正确的计算。

涉及人身伤害的工资损失,估计如果没有意外能够顺利赚取的工资会缴纳多少税费就已经要考虑许多变数。如有关税法的税率、法定免税额或减税、其他的税务优惠如子女的抚养和父母的赡养、配偶是否有收入、受害方有无其他的收入等。如果针对公司法人的利润损失,可能更加复杂并且涉及更多方面的考虑(如是否集团公司、在有关的年度会否亏损或少赚、会否有计划做出资本投资等)。如果涉及外国业务或是跨国公司,通常会有复杂的避税或减税做法,导致不少有跨国业务的公司如船公司或是贸易商根本是在一个不抽税的环境下强大起来。但如果要对税务问题加以考虑,往往会要考虑外国的税务问题:Julien Praet et Cie., S/A v. H. G. Poland, Ltd (1962) 1 Lloyd's Rep 566。把税务问题一并考虑在内才能判定损失赔偿的金额,就经常会需要会计师与税务专家等专家意见证据,这表示整个诉讼会变得更加昂贵与延误。这一个考虑在很多先例中都提到,包括在 British Transport Commission v. Gourley 先例。Earl Jowitt 大法官说:“It would, I think, be unfortunate if, as the result of our decision, the fixation of damages in a running-down case were to involve an elaborate assessment of tax liability. It will no doubt become necessary for the tribunal assessing damages to form an estimate of what the tax would have been if the money had been earned, but such an estimate will be none the worse if it is formed on broad lines, even though it may be described as rough and ready. It is impossible to assess with mathematical accuracy what reduction should be made by reason of the tax position, just as it is impossible to assess with mathematical accuracy the amount of damages which should be awarded for the injury itself and for the pain and suffering endured.”

在同一先例,Reid 勋爵是这样说:“Another element to be considered is whether bringing in the matter of liability to tax would seriously increase the duration and expense of trials; for practical as well as theoretical considerations weigh in determining what is too remote. But I do not think that there would be serious practical effects.”

但如果涉及税务,对损失计算影响会很大,原因是今天许多国家征收税款的税率十分高。所以,如果受害方的损失赔偿可以免税,就会涉及侵权人或违约方多赔付了受害方真正的损失,虽然公道地说这一个好处也不应该是他可占有,而是应该由第三人的税务局与它代表的民众享有。

4.3 税务问题太复杂与避免考虑的说法

这方面的复杂性导致不少先例对税务的问题采取一个比较粗略的对待,如在

Deeny v. Gooda Walker (1995) STC 439 先例,涉及劳合社保险代理人疏忽承保导致有关“保险小组”(syndicate)的劳合社会员蒙受损失。由于涉及的劳合社会员受害方有3000 人左右,所以 Potter 大法官拒绝考虑损失是否需要考虑税务的问题,即使考虑税务会对个别人士有好处,因为这会大大增加诉讼的时间与费用。

第二方面是不同的损失类别会受到不同的税制影响,如针对财产/货物的损坏、侵占或摧毁的损失计算,如果有关的财产/货物是属于“资本资产”(capital assets)或受害方的生产工具,这一般是免税,所以满足不了条件一,也就根本不必考虑条件二。这可以列举 Clyde 勋爵在 Burmah SS Co v. IRC (1931) 16 TC 67 先例中所举的有关受害方的船舶被侵权人的船舶撞沉的例子,这船舶只是受害方的生产工具,不存在有税务的问题。他说:“Suppose ... that one of the appellant's vessels was negligently run down and sunk by a vessel belonging to some other ship-owner, and the appellant recovered as damages the value of the sunken vessel, I imagine that there could be no doubt that the damages so recovered could not enter the appellant's profit and loss account because the destruction of the vessel would be an injury inflicted, not on the appellant's trading, but on the capital assets of the appellant's trade, making (so to speak) a hole in them, and the damages could therefore ... only be used to fill that hole.”

但如果有关的财产/货物是属于“营业库存”(trading stock),就会涉及买卖与贸易中的利润。所以,就会存在条件一满足但条件二否定的情况,因为受害方会需要把取回的损失赔偿当做公司的利润并交纳税费。但这种情况会是千变万化,需要考虑每个案件不同的事实。例如,在国际贸易中的商品买卖就经常可以逃避纳税,导致了不需要考虑税费的扣减。

在 Burmah SS Co v. IRC 的苏格兰先例,案情涉及船公司派遣一个船舶去修理厂进行修理,但修理厂的工程延误导致了船东向它索赔延误带来的营运损失(也就是如果准时完成船舶的修理工程,船东可以在市场营运并赚取租金/收入)。该先例最终双方庭外和解,但法院有针对如果损失赔偿是用来弥补船东的营运损失,并会记载在公司的账目里,就表示公司将来还是要纳税,条件二就不能满足。针对这一个方面,Clyde 勋爵是这样说:“Suppose someone who chartered one of the appellant's vessels breached the charter and exposed himself to a claim of damages at the appellant's instance, there could, I imagine, be no doubt that the damages recovered would properly enter the appellant's profit and loss account for the year. The reason would be that the breach of the charter was an injury inflicted in the appellant's trading, making (so to speak) a hole in the appellant's profits, and the damages recovered could not therefore be reasonably or appropriately put by the appellant – in accordance with the principles of sound commercial accounting – to any other purpose than to fill that hole.”

同样的看法也在 British Transport Commission v. Gourley (1956) AC185 先例后的判例中出现,例如在 Diamond v. Campbell-Jones (1961) Ch 22 先例,案情涉及发展商

向违约/毁约的卖方索赔损失，因为房子交易失败导致他蒙受利润损失。但即使发展商成功索赔，将来也会涉及纳税。所以法院拒绝从损失计算中扣减税费，Buckley 大法官是这样说："If the damages would be taxable in the hands of the plaintiff, in order to give him the degree of indemnity to which he is entitled, I must, I think, award him a gross sum in damages equal to the gross amount of the profit which he would be likely to have made had there been no breach of contract."

4.4　商业案件通常不考虑税务问题

在商业关系下，上文已经提到过如果涉及公司法人，税务的问题就比个人更加复杂。所以假设在商业中，公司如果赚取利润固然是要纳税，而通过损失赔偿取回来的钱也是要纳税，就可以不考虑税务的问题，让这两笔税费互相抵销。这在 Parsons v. BNM Laboratories Ltd（1964）1 QB 95 先例中，上诉庭的 Harman 大法官是这样说：

"On the whole I incline to view that this conclusion of his Lordship, though logical, is impracticable, and that it is better, where the Crown has taken a hand and actually taxed the damages in recipient's hands, to leave the two taxes to set themselves off one against the other. There may be some roughness in this justice but it does at least make an end of the matter. The law, as Lord Wright said in Liesbosch Dredger v. Edison SS, cannot take account of everything.

On the whole, therefore, I would incline to the view that, as seems to be the practice in commercial loss of profit cases, no account should be taken of tax at either end. This may be a matter largely dictated by expediency but it strikes me as preferable in an imperfect world to an over-assiduous search after perfection. To make the punishment fit the crime is no doubt a sublime object but it may land the searcher at the end in the ridiculous."

以上所说的也解释了为什么涉及到商业利润损失就不考虑税务，就算有税务问题也为了节省诉讼的时间与费用而只进行粗略的计算，不可能做到十全十美。即使受害方在取回损失与需要纳税之间会有时间上的差距，或者是针对利润与取回的损失税率并不完全一样，但法院为了省钱与省时间，通常不愿意计算得太细。这可节录在同一个上诉庭先例中的 Pearson 大法官所说："Both the lost profits and the damages to be awarded have the character of taxable subject matter, and rough justice is done and a great expenditure of time and costs is saved by ignoring the tax on both sides so that in effect the tax on the lost earnings is set off against and cancelled out by the tax on the damages. The actual amounts of the tax (if any) to be paid on the one side and the other would depend on the special circumstances of the particular case and might differ widely, but no attempt is made to ascertain the actual difference and adjust the damages accordingly."

在 Julien Praet et Cie., S/A v. H. G. Poland, Ltd（1962）1 Lloyd's Rep 566 先例，涉及比利时的税务，它与英国是有 1% ~2% 的差别，Mocatta 大法官决定不加以考虑，说："In my judgment, these conclusions are sufficient to dispose of the Belgian tax point in this case and constitute an alternative ground for disregarding such tax in assessing damages. Even if I be wrong in the conclusion stated earlier in this judgment on the ambit of *British Transport Commision v. Gourley*, I cannot think it to be part of the English law of damages that a Court here, if satisfied that a tax demand is likely to be made in respect of the damages awarded which it would be reasonable to pay and which would be the same as the tax leviable had there been no breach, must go further into the matter and form a view of what would be the final outcome in foreign litigation on a difficult point of fiscal law."

本小段所讲的考虑与判决或裁决中胜诉方成功索赔的利息大同小异,也就是把它"一般的"或"划一的"对待(general approach),即不论谁是胜诉方,也不管他公司大小,有钱没钱,通常都在最优利率的基础上再加1% ~2%。除非在订约时胜诉方曾经就有关"特别损失"(special damage)告知败诉方,法院或仲裁庭才能作出特殊赔偿,这就是本书第三章第2段提到的 Hadley v. Baxendale (1854) 9 Ex. 341 先例中的第二种做法,即订约之前受害方已将会产生特别损失的后果告诉了违约方。划一的对待利息也是现实的做法,否则计算胜诉方实际因为败诉方延误支付赔偿或债务的真正损失是完全不成比例与艰巨的工作,涉及大量的文件披露、专家证人与争议。例如,胜诉方会是资金困难需要借高利贷、胜诉方资金充足并且暂时找不到投资门路而需要存放在银行、胜诉方是一个大集团可以相互之间以某一个利息作出借贷等。

4.4.1　损失计算考虑税务问题案例之一:Finley v. Connell Associates

但在商业的范畴,损失计算还是有个别案例会与税务的问题扯上关系,这显示了这一个问题的处理还是不肯定。这可先介绍 Finley v. Connell Associates (2002) Lloyd's Rep. P. N. 62 的先例,虽然提到"被告承认在一般的情况下,损失计算与税务扯不上关系,在损失赔偿中扣减税费只是在一些能够满足 British Transport Commission v. Gourley 先例中规定的两个先决条件的例外情况下"(The Defendants recognised that the normal rule is that awards of damages are not reduced because of the incidence of taxation. They submit that there are exceptional circumstances however in which taxation has to be taken into account; those factors are to be found in the case of British Transport Commission v. Gourley [1956] A. C. 185)。该先例的案情涉及原告管理的公司在开发一个地产项目的过程中,公司的律师(被告)疏忽提供了错误的法律意见,导致公司在将这个地产项目的发展方案由建造宾馆改为住宅时,向当地政府多支付了一笔额外的费用。但是根据建造许可条文的规定,当地政府允许该公司改变土地用途而不需要支付费用。为了筹措和交付这笔高昂的费用,原告的公司陷入经济困难并推迟了这个地产项目的开发。因此原告的公司起诉律师违约并要求被告赔偿因此造成的损失。法院最后判是被告疏忽提供法律意见的行为构成违约,根据建造许可的规定,原告本来不需要在改变发展项目用途时给政府支付额外的费用,因此原告有权获得这笔赔偿。

在举证责任方面,是由被告来举证证明满足以上列举的这两个先决条件,因为是由被告提出就税务问题适用 British Transport Commission v. Gourley 先例的例外规定。这也在 Stoke-on-Trent City Council v. Wood Mitchell & Co.（1980）1 WLR 254（CA）先例中被肯定，法院判是被告有责任证明案情符合这两个先决条件，尤其针对第二个，只有在证明原告获得这笔损失赔偿后毫无疑问是不需要缴纳税费的情况下，British Transport Commission v. Gourley 先例中的例外情况才可以被适用把损失金额扣减税费。

在这个先例中针对税务问题，法院判是应该从损失赔偿中扣减 25% 的税费，也就是被告需要承担的赔偿金额从 445,000 减至 333,750 英镑。因为被告的律师成功举证证明原告的公司已经进入破产清算程序，所以获得这笔赔偿后不可能再缴纳税费，而如果当时被告给予正确的法律意见，原告的公司就可以获得这笔利润而需要缴纳税费。同时，被告的律师也成功举证证明，这种营业利润的税率是 25%。这可以节录 Ouseley 大法官的判词如下："I accept the principle of the point which Mr. Brunner（被告的代表律师）makes, namely, that the profits which Forthville（原告公司）would have made in the course of its trading, had it received competent advice, would have been taxable and that those profits would not now be taxable because Forthville was in an insolvent liquidation. Accordingly, in principle, the two limbs of Gourley's case were satisfied. I do not consider that the effect of the Stoke-on-Trent C. C. case is that a detailed reconstruction of a company's tax position is necessary for Gourley's rule to be applied. There may have been some scope, of course, for losses to be carried forward from Phases 1 and 2 and for the receipt of profits to have been delayed. However, I do not consider that uncertainty over what some of the finer points of the tax calculation should mean that no deduction at all falls to be made. Once the principle has been established that taxation falls to be deducted through the application of Gourley's rule, I consider that it is insufficient to defeat it for the Claimant to speculate as to what the possibility or extent of those finer adjustments might have been. There is no evidence from either party as to what those finer adjustments might be and I consider that it would be inappropriate for the Claimant thereby to frustrate the application of a rule which was clearly applicable in principle. Accordingly, in my judgment, a deduction from the damages of 25 per cent has to be made. The figure of £ 445,000 needs to be reduced to £ 333,750."

4.4.2 损失计算考虑税务问题案例之二：Amstrad plc v. Seagate Technology Inc

接下去介绍 Amstrad plc v. Seagate Technology Inc（1998）86 BLR 34 先例。案情涉及受害方（Amstrad）生产与销售低端的私人电脑，为了加强面对 IBM 的竞争力，受害方决定新推出一批安装了性能提高的硬盘的高档机型，所以在 1988/89 年受害方向被告购买了 56,000 个硬盘，价值 17,700,000 美元。但最终这批新机型的推出并不成功，因为用户将数据存储到硬盘上以后不能恢复这些数据。尽管受害方和被告对硬盘进行了补救和研究，但问题依然存在，而且如果电脑开机后待机一个小时左右就会出故障。这些问题导致原告的电脑滞销并蒙受严重的损失,这些损失包括由于推迟上市而被迫降价所蒙受的收益损失,还未出售电脑的利润损失,市场份额的损失与浪费的使费。原告以违约与违反供应符合买卖质量的硬盘的默示保证(这是1979年英国《货物销售法》之 Section 14.2 的保证)为由向被告起诉,要求被告赔偿大约218,000,000 英镑。法院判是原告胜诉,因为证据显示,被告出售的硬盘确实不符合他们在产品说明中对产品质量的描述,这批硬盘会随机产生不可预料的故障,也不符合通常的质量要求。因此,原告有权获得57,000,000 英镑的收益损失与2,166,291 英镑的浪费费用的赔偿。针对税务的问题,本先例的 Humphrey Lloyd 大法官并不追随 Deeny v. Gooda Walker (1995) STC 439 先例的判法,他认为要把税务的好处考虑在内。这好处是在有关的时间赚取的正常利润是会面对34% ~35% 的税率,但到了审理的时候损失赔偿就改为会面对33% 的税率。虽然这个税率看来是差别不大,如果粗略处理的话可以把他们忽略掉。但由于该案件的损失赔偿金额很大,所以实际上还是涉及100 万英镑的数额。针对这一个先例,《McGregor on Damages》(18th edn, 2009 年)之14 -019 段是这样说:"While it would of course simplify the position if the courts could adopt the rough and ready assumption that the effects of taxation cancel out, the facts of a particular case may make such an assumption entirely unjustified. The most obvious cause of tax on damages being lower than tax on loss is falling tax rates between the time of the loss and the time of the award. This was the position in the forward-looking and important, but ill-reported, decision in *Amstrad plc v. Seagate Technology Inc*. Damages had been awarded for the loss of profits which would have been made from the sale in 1989 and 1990 of some 50,000 computers. The tax on damages when received would be at a rate of 33 percent but the tax on the profits had they been received at the proper times would have been at rates of 34 and 35 percent. H. H. Judge Humphrey Lloyd held that the damages, as he put it, 'should be adjusted to take into account the incidence of taxation'. In other words, *Gourley* was applied to the difference between the tax rates which, although small as a matter of rates, was large as a matter of amount, making a difference of about £ 1 million to the claimants. Here was a sensible shift away from the *Praet* and *Parsons* for the rule which was there approved are all neatly and fully answered in H. H. Judge Humphrey Lloyd's extensive and excellent judgment. In the end he found no reason, as he put it, 'why expediency and pragmatism should override logic and justice'."

4.4.3 损失计算考虑税务问题案例之三:BSkyB Ltd v. HP Enterprise Services UK Ltd

最后一个要介绍的在损失计算时把税务问题也考虑在内的商业案例是 BSkyB Ltd v. HP Enterprise Services UK Ltd (2010) EWHC 862 (TCC)先例。案情是涉及原告(卫星广播公司)经过竞标后选择了被告(信息技术公司)为他们设计、建立、管理、执行和整合一套新的顾客关系管理系统。被告在谈判时声称他们经过仔细分析完成这套系统所需要的时间,认为他们能够按照合约要求的时间完成这个项目。最终这个项目并没有按期完成,导致原告接替了被告的系统整合工作。原告在蒙受严重的损失后向被告提出索赔,声称在谈判时被告向原告的受害方做出了欺诈性误述,导致原告签署了有关的合约。原告要求被告赔付延迟完成项目增加的费用及利润损失。在较早的审理中法院判是原告胜诉,有权取回高达2.7亿英镑的损失赔偿。这显然是个非常庞大的损失赔偿,仅是胜诉的原告想取回的律师费用就已经高达4900万英镑。在这一个先例,主要是针对费用的分摊与根据哪一个基础(标准基础或是补偿基础)核算有关的律师费用。

但与本章相关的是该先例也要考虑税务的问题,被告争辩说原告的利润损失应该减掉公司所得税。被告的专家证人说是这套顾客关系管理系统如果顺利推出,时间上应是在2003年2月1日。当时会涉及的税率是大概每年30%(这是从2003年到2007年的财政年度)。但期间税率有改变,当时的损失赔偿所要面对的税率只是在28%。被告的专家计算出一个简单的税率差别,就是2.8%。显然原告的专家证人反对,认为损失赔偿金额根本不应该改变或做出扣减。原告也说到真正找出税务的准确地位是非常复杂,也需要进一步的分析包括额外的文书请求,专家证人与事实证人。对原告的公司而言,找出它的税务地位是非常复杂,因为这是一个跨国的集团,要查询就必须对整个Sky集团的税务进行调查,这也根本不是本案所聘用的专家证人所能胜任。原告的专家证人也提到原告公司在2005到2006年度的业务有亏损,所以根本不存在支付公司所得税。而在2006到2007年度原告公司所支付的平均所得税也只是在14%。

Ramsey大法官看来主要也是受到本先例损失金额庞大的影响,认为应该与Amstrad plc v. Seagate Technology Inc (1998) 86 BLR 34先例判法一致,说:

"Whilst I accept that the assessment of the impact of taxation on damages may require further documentation, expert evidence and submissions, that is not something which should prevent the Court from making an assessment if, in principle, taxation should be taken into account. The passages cited above from the speeches in Gourley make it clear that the approach may have to be broad brush and the range of issues to be taken into account in making the calculation may be wide. That did not prevent the assessment being made in Gourley and the position is similar here. I also bear in mind that, on the current expert evidence, Richard Boulton's(原告的专家证人) view is that the impact of the change in Corporation Tax rates would be less, possibly very much less, than Timothy Hart's (被告的专家证人) 2.8%. However, given the overall sums in issue in this case, the potential sum resulting from the change in Corporation Tax is substantial.

This is therefore a case where I see no obstacle to being able to make the necessary calculation and the potential sum in dispute appears sufficient to justify the issue being considered, because there must always be consideration of proportionality in the approach to assessing damages."

总结而言,商业案件不涉及税务的问题应该是一般的做法。在笔者涉及的大量国际商品买卖与航运仲裁中,绝少有双方代表律师提出这一个问题。这可以想得到,因为在这一个行业中的大环境不涉及利润或损失需要缴税。但即使会涉及,也通常可以把它视为抵销。也就是本来可以赚取的利润需要缴税,而取回来的损失赔偿也需要缴税,所以可抵销掉,即使两者之间并非是完全一致的抵销。但由于今天的诉讼涉及越来越大的赔偿金额,加上在今天讲起来税率都很高昂,这就导致类似 Amstrad plc v. Seagate Technology Inc 与 BSkyB Ltd v. HP Enterprise Services UK Ltd 等的先例,在不能完全一致做出抵销的情况下,法院还是会要回去把税务问题考虑在内,目的就是符合赔偿的大原则,计算损失金额只是为了复原,"no less but also no more"。

5. 利息的问题

利息的问题在上面的4.4段已有提到,并在笔者所著的《仲裁法——从开庭审理到裁决书的做出与执行》一书第二章有详论,不重复。在这里只针对另一方面的小问题,就是损失计算如果考虑税务问题,也往往要面对利息的问题。这是因为受害方本来可以赚取的利润与需要缴纳的所得税在时间上不会与取回来的损失赔偿所要缴纳的所得税一致。本来在许多商业案件这也是一些小差别,可以"粗略"(broad brush)对待或是漠视。而针对利息的问题,也有同样的说法是可粗略对待。但还是有案件会涉及比较大的金额,法院会加以考虑。

有关这个说法的第一个先例是 Tate & Lyle v. GLC (1982) 1 WLR 149,其中 Forbes 大法官是这样说:"The award of interest in these cases is a discretionary matter and, in approaching the task of deciding upon such an award, I think judges are entitled to and do adopt **a very broad approach.** Attempting to do so I would look at this matter in this way. The plaintiff's accounting year runs from October 1 to September 30. For tax purposes, therefore, in order to arrive at an average, it must be assumed that all the invoices were paid halfway through the accounting year, i. e. on March 1. But the plaintiffs' corporation tax liability did not have to be paid until January 1, not of the next year but of the year after. As an example, the invoices for the year ending September 1967 would have been notionally paid in March 1, 1967, and those expenses would have to be paid on January 1, 1969. There was thus a period of 21 months relating successively to each year's invoices. The plaintiffs have thus been kept out of the whole sum of damages for only part of the time (the precise period I shall have to look at later). For the remaining period they have been kept out of £ 550,000 less £ 239,000. It seems to me that one cannot ignore this on the principle that one does not look at the particular borrowing position of a plaintiff; and the fact the plaintiffs may have to pay more in corporation tax (because it is at a higher rate) when they are paid the damages than they saved by charging the dredging costs as an expense is unfortunate but, as Lord Denning MR said in Jefford v. Gee (1970) 2 QB 130 at 149: '... that cannot be helped. The tax man must collect all he can.' The plaintiffs must, in some way, bring into account in the interest computation the amount of corporation tax they saved. The problem is: how? The answer is, I am sure, to look at the problem **broadly** and avoid a lot of complicatcd mathcmatics."(加黑部分是笔者的强调)

接下去的先例是 Deeny v. Gooda Walker (No. 3) (1996) LRLR 168, Phillips 大法官是这样说:"If the Court proceeds on the artificial premise that the plaintiff has been deprived of the use of the whole of the damages notwithstanding the effect of taxation the interest awarded will provide the plaintiff with a substantial unjustified windfall at the expense of the defendant. In my judgment the Court should approach each claim to interest on its own merits, placing a sensible pragmatic restraint on attempts to conduct a detailed investigation of a plaintiff's tax position but, at the same time refraining from awarding interest for loss of use of money if it appears that the plaintiff is unlikely to have suffered the loss of use in question."

在上面所介绍的两个先例 Amstrad plc v. Seagate Technology Inc 与 BSkyB Ltd v. HP Enterprise Services UK Ltd 中,法官也同意按照 Deeny v. Gooda Walker (No. 3)先例认为要考虑利息的问题。在 BSkyB Ltd v. HP Enterprise Services UK Ltd 先例中,Ramsey 大法官对利息做出的命令如下:"(4) In awarding interest pursuant to s. 35A of the Senior Courts Act 1981, such interest should be based on the net amount of the lost benefits, after the deduction of tax."

在今天的零利率环境下,很多案件看来关系不大,即使是赚取利润与取回来的损失赔偿在给税务局缴纳税费的时间上会有一些差别。但如果涉及的损失金额庞大,再加上如果利率攀升(在 80 年代曾经是年利率超出 20%),涉及的利息金额就会是很大一笔。

第十章　避免超额赔偿之二:计算损失以违约方最低合约责任为准原则

1. 以违约方最低合约责任为准的原则

1.1　序言

在进一步探讨这一个"以违约方最低合约责任为准的原则"(minimum performance/contractual obligation/least onerous obligation principle)之前,先重复一次在本书多章有提到的最基本损失赔偿的大原则,也就是复原大原则,这就是在 Robinson v. Harman (1848) 1 Exch 850 先例中,Parke B 大法官所说的:"The rule of the common law is that where a party sustains a loss by reason of a breach of contract he is so far as money can do it to be placed in the same situation as if the contract had been performed."(普通法的规定就是一方当事人如果因为对方违约而蒙受损失,计算的方法就是用金钱来令受害方回到一个合约被履行的经济地位)。

这就表示几乎在每一次的损失计算都需要估计有关合约如果被履行将会是怎么样的经济地位与可能发生的事实,特别是"预期违约"(anticipatory breach)或拒绝履行合约的"违约/毁约"(repudiatory breach)。估计合约会被怎样履行,其中一个考虑因素就是违约方不需要承担比有关合约强加在他身上更多的责任。这一个因素完全可以理解,也符合人性。举一个简单的例子,违约的卖方如果没有按照买卖合约提供货物,原因很可能就是市场价格或成本大幅上升,导致卖方不想做亏本生意。而有关合约的货物数量是"100~120 吨",这表示卖方可以提供 100 吨或 120 吨或任何中间数量的货物都完全是履行了合约。这一来,如果违约的卖方要对买方做出违约/毁约的赔偿,不论是通过双方和解或由法院/仲裁庭做出判决,都应该以 100 吨为准,把赔偿的金额降至最低。这是一个合理与符合人性的估计,可以从另一个角度来看,就是有关货物如果是属于"独一无二"(unique),而法院或仲裁庭在卖方拒绝提供货物时,很快在买方的申请下做出一个"履约指令"(specific performance),表示卖方在强制下非要履行这一个买卖合约。这一来,很简单的人性就可以几乎肯定卖方只会提供 100 吨货物,否则还会多亏一点。所以,在这种情况下计算金钱损失的赔偿,假设违约的卖方如果履行合约,也只会提供 100 吨货物是完全说得通。

这是英国法律的一个原则,甚至是十分重要的原则,但近年来受到批评与处于不肯定的地位，也变得越来越复杂。

1.2 有关“以违约方最低合约责任为准”原则的权威说法

这原则有很多权威说法，先节录《McGregor on Damages》（18th edn，2009 年）一书之8－093段有关这一个原则：“**Damages to be based upon defendant's least onerous obligation**... That principle is that where the defendant has the option of performing a contract in alternative ways, damages for breach by him must be assessed on the assumption that he will perform it in the way most beneficial to himself and not in that most beneficial to the claimant. This was well settled in the 19th century, but finds its main applications in the 20th, being illustrated by a number of miscellaneous cases.”（这是说原则针对被告的违约方如果有一个选择可以以不同方法履行合约，这一来如果发生违约，损失计算就应该假设被告会以一种对他最有利的方法履行，而不是以一种对原告最有利的方法。这个原则在19 世纪就已经出现与被肯定，但在 20 世纪在许多先例有更广泛的适用。）

正如在上述的节录所提到，这一个原则在 19 世纪就已经出现。这可节录早期的Cockburn v. Alexander (1848) 6 CB 791 先例中 Maule 大法官说：“Where there are several ways in which the contract might be performed, that mode is adopted which is the least profitable to the plaintiff and the least burdensome to the defendant.”（如果合约可以有几种不同的履行方法，就要以一种对原告产生最低利润与对被告带来最轻责任的方法计算损失。）

另在 Robinson v. Robinson (1851) 1 De G M & G 247 先例，Cranworth 大法官说：“... in ordinary cases, every wrongdoer is bound to put the party injured, so far as the nature of the case allows, in the same situation in which he would have stood if the wrong had not been done... When a man is bound by convenants to do one of two things, and does neither, there in an action by the convenantee, the measure of damage is in general the loss arising by reason of the convenantor having failed to do that which is least, not that which is most, beneficial to the convenantee: and the same principle may be applied by analogy to the case of a trustee failing to invest in either of the two modes equally lawful by the term of the trust.”

到了 20 世纪，有更多的先例涉及这一个原则。随意节录部分先例的说法，在 Lavarack v. Woods of Colchester Ltd. (1967) 1 QB 278 先例，上诉庭的 Diplock 大法官说：“The general rule as stated by Scrutton L. J. in Abrahams v. Reiach (1922) 1 KB 477 that in an action for breach of contract a defendant is not liable for not doing that which he is not bound to do, has been generally accepted as correct, and in my experience at the Bar and on the Bench has been repeatedly applied in subsequent cases. The law is concerned with legal obligations only and the law of contract only deals with legal obligations created by mutual agreement between contractors - not with expectations, however reasonable, of one contractor that the other will do something that he has assumed no legal obligation to

do. And so if the contract is broken or wrongly repudiated, the first task of the of the assessor of damages is to estimate at best he can what the plaintiff would have gained in money or money's worth if the defendant had fulfilled his legal obligations and had done no more."（Diplock 大法官认同这一个原则的正确性，法律是针对双方在合约中约定的法律责任，不是针对期望，即使是十分合理的期望。在加黑的强调部分 Diplock 大法官是说合约如果被违反并需要计算损失，第一件要做的事情是估计如果被告履行了他合约中的法律责任，而且他不要求多做，那么原告会得到什么经济利益。）

另在 The "Mihalis Angelos"（1970）2 Lloyd's Rep. 43 中，上诉庭的 Denning 勋爵也明确说出了这一假设或原则："that if the defendant has under the contract an option which would reduce or extinguish the loss it will be assumed he will exercise it."（如果被告在合约中有一个选择权可以减少或免除损失赔偿，应该假设他会行使这一权利。）

另 Megaw 大法官也说了同样的话如下："if the contractual rights which he has lost were capable by the terms of the contract of being rendered either less valuable or valueless in certain events, and if it can be shown that those events were at the date of acceptance of the repudiation, predestined to happen, then in my view the damages which he can recover are not more than the true value, if any, of the rights which he has lost, having regard to those predestined events."

在 The "Mihalis Angelos"（1970）2 Lloyd's Rep 43 先例，仲裁庭也有同样的说法（并获得上诉庭的支持）："We think the right view is that when a contract is repudiated, the repudiation accepted, the innocent party can surely say the contract is at an end: its performance is no longer binding: but it (or its ghost) must survive as the datum line for measuring the damages: the innocent party is entitled to be put, financially, in the same position as, but in no better position than, that in which he would have been if the contract had not been repudiated but had come on for performance: and **his claim for damages must be based on that method of performing the contract which would have been least profitable to him.**"（黑体是笔者的强调）

在 21 世纪更近期的先例中，只简单节录贵族院先例 The "Golden Victory"（2007）2 Lloyd's Rep 164，Scott 勋爵说："The lodestar is that the damages should represent the value of the contractual benefits of which the claimant had been deprived by the breach of the contract, **no less but also no more.**"（加黑部分是笔者的强调）

1.3 估计将来合约的履行

大部分适用这一个原则的情况都会涉及对将来"事实"的估计，道理很简单，因为违约方拒绝履行合约，就表示合约的履行根本没有发生过。

这会带来两个困难：一是订约自由会带来千变万化的合约规定，每一个合约都会有它特殊的规定，这包括各种"变数"（contingency），包括给违约方的选择权或弹性的做法。这表示要估计如果合约被履行会是怎样的光景,就必须先对有关合约做出解释:Duffen v. Frabo (2000) 1 Lloyd's Rep 180 先例。这需要对合约条文有正确、合理与整体性的解释,而合约解释本身是一个大学问,可参阅笔者所著的《合约的解释》(法律出版社 2007 年版)。这第一个困难会接下去在本章的第 2 段讨论。二是针对从来没有发生过的"事实"做出假设性的估计,这个估计的过程会涉及很多变数,其中包括来自受害方、违约方与第三人等对履约的选择(这在本书第六章有详论)。法律是要求对这一个将来"事实"必须是根据一些可信的证据(通常是专家意见证据)得出的有一定合理肯定程度的估计,而不能是毫无根据的"凭空臆猜"(pure guesswork)。而在本章以违约方最低合约责任为准的原则下,主要针对的是违约方自己的变数,如行使合约选择权或在合约允许下的弹性做法以一种对他最有利也即是赔偿金额最低的做法为准。

1.4 原则对过去的事实也适用的先例 The "World Navigator"

以违约方最低合约责任为准的原则也适用在过去或已经发生了的事实,这可以在 The "World Navigator" (1991) 2 Lloyd's Rep 23 先例中看到,案情涉及以 FOB 出售的 3 万吨玉米,分三批付运。在 1985 年 6 月 13 日 FOB 买方派船抵达了南美 Rosario 港的外锚地 Zona Comun,由于卖方还没准备好文件,导致船舶延期靠泊装货,延误是从 1985 年 6 月 13 日至 7 月 11 日。买方于是索赔这段延误期间的损失,而在责任方面英国法院判是卖方违反了一条默示条文,即卖方需要合作让买方派遣的船舶尽快靠泊装货。但在损失计算方面就有更大争议。卖方认为,在买卖合约中有条文针对在靠泊后装货率是 500 吨一个"好天气工作天"(weather working day),这一来,针对该批 1.2 万吨玉米的装货就需要 24 天。所以,即使没有违反默示条文,船舶在靠泊后卖方也大可以慢慢装货用尽这 24 天,而不是以实际快速得多的装货率装货(由于有实际履行,所以是知道船舶在 7 月 18 日至 22 日的 4 天内装完)。从而令总的停留在装港时间是差不多,所以买方没有损失。

在第一审的时候,Phillips 大法官不同意卖方的说法,他认为有关的合约没有给予卖方对这方面怎样履行合约的选择权,而以往的先例主要是针对违约方有选择权。所以,判卖方败诉说:"When assessing damages, the board (GAFTA 的上诉仲裁庭) should not have proceeded on the premise that, had the vessel berthed promptly, the sellers would have loaded so slowly that they would have used all the available laytime. The board's task was to ask how long loading would have taken had World Navigator berthed promptly without losing her place in the queue. If sellers were in a position to influence the loading rate, then the board should have considered how they would have done so. , The question fell to be answered, not by assuming that the sellers would have loaded at the slowest permissible rate, but by considering all the factors that would have been likely to influence their conduct."(在计算损失,仲裁庭应该考虑船舶如果很快可以靠泊装货,违约的卖方会否慢慢装,把所有允许的装货时间用尽。仲裁庭应该查问船舶如果很快靠

泊,会使用多少装货时间。如果卖方真的可以影响装货率,仲裁庭应该考虑他们会怎样做。需要回答的问题是,考虑所有会可能影响卖方的做法,而不是只假设卖方为了减少赔偿较早发生的违约损失,可以最慢的速度装货。)

到了上诉庭,高院的判决被推翻,判是卖方胜诉,其中,上诉庭的 Staughton 大法官是这样说:“The principle itself is beyond dispute, although its precise formulation and rationale have varied: see the judgment of Mr. Justice Mustill in Paula Lee Ltd. v. Robert Zehil & Co. Ltd. (1983) 2 All E. R. 390. We have not been referred to any case where (i) the term broken by the defendant (承租人) did not itself contain any choice or option, but was followed by another term which contained a choice or option for subsequent performance, or (ii) it is known how that subsequent term was in fact performed, because breach of the prior term was not treated as a repudiation, and performance continued. But I see no reason why the principle should not apply equally in those circumstances. Thus the sellers may say in this case: ‘true we broke our contract in failing to facilitate the entry of the vessel into a berth; but once she did reach a berth we loaded much faster than the minimum contract rate. If we had not broken our contract we might still have used just as much time, overall, in loading. So the buyers have suffered no loss’.”(大致上是说这一个先例特别的地方是合约中没有给违约方选择权的条文,而是有另一个条文针对在违约后的履行中违约方有一个弹性的做法。另是在本先例,违约后的实际履行[在 4 天内装完货]是知道结果。但 Staughton 大法官认为这对适用以违约方最低合约责任为准的原则不应有什么区别,违约方可以对受害方说:“我破坏了合约,但当船舶靠泊的时候,我会尽快装货。但如果我没有破坏合约,我就会慢慢来。反正从最后的结果来看你不会有时间上的损失。”)

另上诉庭的 Parker 大法官是这样说:“One would . . . consider what are the consequences to the plaintiff of that breach and what is required to put him in the same position as if the breach had not occurred. In that event laytime would have begun to run on June 26. That being so, the sellers’ obligation would have been to load in the number of counting days arrived at the application of the [contract] terms but no more. They did in fact do so. Despite the breach, the buyers therefore got that to which they would have been entitled had there been no breach.”

Parker 大法官同意一审的判决就是有关卖方的违约是“单一的责任”(single obligation),但卖方的履行还是可以有两种弹性的做法。一种就是以租约规定的装货率装货,另一种就是按照实际装货的速度,在许可的装货时间届满前早已经装完了货。反正在这两种做法下,都不会对买方造成实际的损失,因为花在装港的时间都是在买卖合约允许的装货时间内。Parker 大法官是这样说:“. . . I should mention that although I agree that the assumed obligation and breach was single, the sellers were left, in effect, with the option of alternative modes of performing their obligation. They could load when berthed at the minimum rate prescribed by the formula, in which case damages would occur, or they could load at whatever minimum rate was necessary in order just to use up the laytime available under the formula but no more, or they could, as in fact they did, load at such a rate that the vessel was free before the time when they would have been no breach. In the second and third case no damage is suffered."

在这里只简单一提,这一个先例十分有争议性,认为是太善待了违约方。这一个先例的事实如果在今天再度审理,会否有同样的结果会有疑问。这方面稍后在本章之7段会详论。

2. 什么是违约方在合约的责任与承诺

已经在本章1.3段提到过是在计算损失时,第一个困难是首先要看看有关合约中违约方到底有什么责任与承诺,这也包括了他最低的责任。在缔约自由下,责任与承诺会是千变万化,经常作出解释也不容易。其中会影响损失计算特别在以违约方最低合约责任为准的原则方面,可以有以下段节介绍的不同类别责任与承诺,虽然在不同的案件中要区分也不是容易。

2.1　第一种责任与承诺:违约方拥有绝对或无限制的选择权

这是针对有关合约明示给违约方一个特定的"绝对或无限制的选择权"(absolute or unrestricted option)履行他的责任与承诺。在这种情况下,很早就已经有了先例说是计算损失时,估计违约方会行使对他有利的选择或做法,务求将他的损失赔偿减到最低,根本不必理会受害方的利益。有关这种合约的选择权可先节录 Tharsis Sulphur and Copper Co Ltd v. Morel Brother & Co and Others (1891) 2 QB 647 先例,Bowen 大法官是这样说:"The option is given for the benefit of the person who has to exercise it. He is bound to exercise it in a reasonable time, but is not bound in exercising it to consider the benefit or otherwise of the other party."(合约选择权是让有权的当事人得益,他不会行使选择权让对方得益。换言之,有权的一方行使选择权是不存在合理与否的考验。)

Atkins 大法官也早在 Abrahams v. Herbert Reiach Ltd (1922) 1 KB 477 先例提到这一个说法,就是违约方如果在有关的合约中有一个无限制的选择权,以最低合约责任为准计算损失的原则就适用,说:"If a merchant makes a contract to deliver goods to a shipowner to be carried by him for reward, and the merchant fails to provide the goods, the Court must first find what is the contract which has been broken; and if it was to carry the goods to one of two **alternative** ports at different distances from the port of loading at rates of freight differing according to the distance, the only contract on which the shipowner can sue is the contract for carriage to the nearer port. The plaintiff cannot provide a contract for performance of the more onerous obligation. This explains why in cases of this kind the Court regards only the lesser of two alternative obligations." His Lordship referred to three such cases in Thomas v. Clarke (1818) 2 Stark 450; Capper v. Forster (1837) 3 Bing NC 938; Cockburn v. Alexander (1848) 6 CB 791. (如果一位商人以承租人的身份与船东订立一份程租合约,但事后承租人不能提供货物,法院需要先看到底哪些程租合约条文被违反。如果程租合约是明示允许承租人可以在两个不同卸港中自由选择一个,而两个卸港与装港的距离不同并且运费是根据不同的距离来厘定。这样一来,在计算损失的时候显然会选择距离装港较近的那个卸港,而厘定的运费也会是相应降低,从而令损失较少。)

另在 Kaye Steam Navigation Company Ltd v. Barnett Ltd (1932) 43 Lloyd's Rep. 166 先例,也有类似的争议。但这有关的合约选择权从来没有被行使过,因为违约的承租人拒绝装货,所以有关程租租约根本没有履行。法院判是由于运费是固定的一笔钱,所以损失计算要根据承租人可选择港口中最远的一个港口来计算,表示船东如果履行是要花费更多的时间与燃油去该港,导致索赔的利润相应减少。这方面也可看 Roderick Angus Erskine Stuart v. Telecom Sevives Centres Ltd (2004) Scot (D) 22/12 先例。

这种案件还有很多,另介绍的是在 Re Thornett Febr and Yuills Ltd. (1921) 1 KB 219 DC 先例,卖方承诺货物供应是"200 吨,允许 5% 上下的浮动"(200 tons, 5% more or less),违约/毁约的卖方被判只要赔偿 190 吨的损失。

在另一个已经在第六章 3.2.4 段提到的先例 Johnson Matthey Banking v. The State Trading Corporation of India (1984) 1 Lloyd's Rep. 427,涉及白银的买卖,但由于印度政府下禁令阻止白银的出口而导致了卖方(也就是被判是违约方的被告)无法履行,买方接受了违约/毁约并提出索赔损失。简单说就是英国法院判买方胜诉,但所能成功索赔的损失是根据合约价格与市场价格在违约一天的差价,但要减掉卖方有1.5%货量的伸缩性。Staughton 大法官是这样说:"No silver was delivered. On Mar. 31, 1980, the buyers treated the sellers as in default. In my judgement the buyers are entitled to damages from the sellers under the Sale of Goods Act. It is not suggested that Indian law provided any different measure of damages from English law. They are entitled to the difference between the contract prices and the market price on Mar. 31, 1980. That produces a figure of 1,175,675.75 pounds. From it must be deducted a tolerance of 1.5%. (see the buyers' letter of Aug. 15, 1977) Since the sellers might lawfully have made use of that tolerance in performing their contracts. That leaves 1,158,040.50 pounds."(其中提到的 1977 年 8 月 15 日的信中就涉及卖方有 1.5% 的伸缩性。)

撇开上述介绍的笔者熟悉的航运与外贸的例子,同样的原则也适用在其他的领域。在 Withers v. General Theatre Corpn Ltd (1933) 2 KB 536 (CA) 先例,涉及雇主非法解雇一位演员,受害的演员部分索赔是根据他被剥夺了一个著名歌剧院表演的好机会所带来的损失计算，但这被法院拒绝，因为有关雇佣合约中，违约的雇主是有一个绝对或无限制的选择权挑选在哪里表演。

在 Lavarack v. Woods of Colchester Ltd. (1967) 1 QB 278; Beach v. Reed Corrugated Cases (1956) 2 All ER 652; Warman International Ltd. v. Wilson (2002) All ER (D) 93 (Mar), EAT 等一连串先例，都涉及非法解雇后有关加薪、奖金、费用或解雇费等的支付是否可以作为损失的一部分，但支付都涉及雇主的明示选择权/裁量权，所以被判是不能成功索赔。但注意是这方面的先例会有所改变，换言之雇主再也不是有一个绝对与无限制的裁量权：Bold v. Brough Nicholson & Hall Ltd. (1964) 1 WLR 201; Clark v. Nomura plc (2000) IRLR 766。

在 Mulvenna v. Royal Bank of Scotland (2003) EWCA Civ. 1112 先例，涉及一家银行被客户起诉，指称银行没有及时归还一笔钱，而这笔钱是用来发展地产项目，所以银行的违约导致了该项目的利润损失。但这一个索赔被法院拒绝，因为发展项目是需要银行作出进一步的贷款，但银行完全是有权利不同意贷款。

2.2 第二种责任与承诺：违约方有明示或默示限制的选择权或弹性做法

这第二种责任与承诺是有关的合约通常涉及一个针对违约方的选择或弹性做法，而单方面做出的选择或做法会影响合约双方的利益。这一来法律会有一个默示限制，这种默示会要求违约方必须真诚、合理、理性与善意做出选择或裁量。做出这个默示也很有必要，因为订约双方在同意给其中一方做出选择或弹性做法的权利，被动的另一方应该有订约意图不能让对方乱来严重影响他将来的利益。这默示的限制通常是需要满足五个条件，正如 Simon 勋爵在 BP Refinery (Westernport) Pty Ltd v. Shire of Hastings (1978) 52 A. L. J. R. 20 先例中所说："In their [贵族院的大法官] view, for a term to be implied, the following condition (which may overlap) must be satisfied: (1) it must be reasonable and equitable; (2) it must be necessary to give business efficacy to the contract, so that no term will be implied if the contract is effective without it; (3) it must be so obvious that 'it goes without saying'; (4) it must be capable of clear expression; (5) it must not contradict any express term of the contract." [默示的五个条件是：(1)合理与公平；(2)是合约的商业效力所必需，如果缺少此条文合约仍能运作则不会默示；(3)在订约时可以假设双方会理所当然或异口同声地同意这个说法；(4)可以被清楚地表达；(5)不能与合约明示条文起冲突。]

其中默示的一个先例是上诉庭的 Cantor Fitzgerald International v. Horkulak (2004) EWCA Civ. 1287，该先例是涉及雇员被错误解雇，向违约的雇主索赔损失赔偿，其中包括了一笔他本来会获得的奖金，但这是涉及雇主的裁量权。Potter 大法官说："While, in any such situation, the parties are likely to have conflicting interests and the provisions of the contract effectively place the resolution of that conflict in the hands of the party exercising the discretion, it is presumed to be the reasonable expectation and therefore the common intention of the parties that there should be a genuine and rational, as opposed to an empty or irrational, exercise of discretion."(有一种情况是双方当事人很可能有利益冲突,但合约条文把这一个利益冲突的决定权交出给一方当事人,让他行使裁量权。这一来就可以解释双方订约时的共同想法与合理期望是该有权选择的一方当事人在行使裁量权时必须是真诚与理性,而不是空头与不理性)。

在该先例,Potter 大法官也提到了在这种情况下,法律是越来越倾向去对雇主的裁量权加上一个默示的限制要求裁量权的行使是需要真诚与善意,说:"there should be no automatic implication in every instance of a contractual provision 'putting one party at the mercy of another's exercise of a discretion' but that there was an increasing willingness ... to read into a discretion the requirement ... that 'Not only must the discretion be exercised honestly and in good faith but, having regard to the provisions of the contract by which it is conferred, it must not be exercised arbitrarily, capriciously or unreasonably'."

在接下去的另一个先例 Socimer International Bank Ltd v. Standard Bank London Ltd (2008) 1 Lloyd's Rep. 558,案情涉及银行之间的新兴市场远期买卖,其中有条文针对买方如果违约,卖方的渣打银行就可以"单方面与全权在任何时间、任何形式以他认为合理与恰当的价格出售有关资产"(opt to sell the designated assets in its sole and absolute discretion... at such time, in such manner and at such price as it deems reasonable and appropriate...)。上诉庭的 Rix 大法官也说:"When a contract allocated only to one party a power to make decisions under the contract which might have an effect on both parties, the following principles applied. (a) A decision maker's discretion was limited, as a matter of necessary implication, by concepts of honesty, good faith, and genuineness, and the need for the absence of arbitrariness, capriciousness, perversity and irrationality. The concern is that the discretion should not be abused. Reasonableness and unreasonableness were also concepts deployed in this context, but not in the sense when speaking of a duty to take reasonable care. (b) If a contractual discretion ought to have been exercised but was not, the court's task was to put itself in the shoes of the decision maker and to consider what decision, acting rationally, and not arbitrarily or perversely, he would have reached."

这种默示要求与估计违约方的履行即使是有弹性或裁量权,必须达到一个最低的合理标准,实际上在较早前就已经有先例,其中包括本书第六章之 3.4.1 段与 3.4.2段的上诉庭 Abrahams v. Herbert Reiach Ltd (1922) 1 KB 477 先例与 Paula Lee Ltd v. Robert Zehil Ltd (1983) 2 All ER 390 先例。

在较近期的 The "Product Star" (No. 2) (1993) 1 Lloyd's Rep. 397 先例,Leggatt 大法官也有提到对有关合约裁量权应该默示一个合理的要求,说:"... with caution to the assessment of whether a contractual discretion has been properly exercised. The essential question always is whether the relevant power has been abused. Where A and B contract with each other to confer a discretion on A, that does not render B subject to A's uninhibited whim. In my judgment, the authorities show that not only must the discretion be exercised honestly and in good faith, but, having regard to the provisions of the contract by which it is conferred, it must not be exercised arbitrarily, capriciously or unreasonably..." (应该小心估计一个合约裁量权是否被恰当行使,有裁量权的A并非是可以无限制的想到哪里就决定去哪里。已经有不少先例显示了这种裁量权的行使必须是诚实、善意,并根据合约的有关条文不能独断独行、恶意与不合理。)

2.3　第三种责任与承诺:违约方单一的履行责任

这是针对合约明示或默示要求违约方履行一个责任或承诺,不存在有任何其他的选择。例如在1.4段介绍The "World Navigator" (1991) 2 Lloyd's Rep. 23 (CA)先例,涉及FOB卖方因为装货的文件没有及时备妥,导致了买方派遣的船舶不能及时靠泊装货而产生延误。英国法律是默示在一个FOB买卖合约,卖方是有责任把货物与装货文件在船舶抵达装港时备妥,不得耽误船舶靠泊装货。这里卖方是不存在有其他的选择,所以可称为是"单一履行责任"(single obligation)。另一个有关的单一履行责任是在买卖合约允许的装货时间内,卖方把货物装完。卖方只要不超出这一个装货时间,就不存在违约(虽然针对这种违约双方经常会同意一个议定赔偿,也就是滞期费)。但卖方这一个单一履行责任还是有一定的弹性,他可以有两种做法:一种就是以租约规定的装货率装货(如果情况允许,如港口当局不催促尽快装完货),另一种就是以较快的速度装货,在许可的装货时间届满前就已经装完了货(这会是有千变万化的原因,如卖方由于买卖合约中的付运期即将届满所以尽快与加班完成装货)。在后者的情况,买卖合约(或是租约)可能会约定速遣费的支付,鼓励卖方提前装完货,让船舶早日开航,为买方节省时间与费用。但双方除非明示约定,英国法律是没有支付速遣费的默示。这表示卖方提前装完货,还有未用完的装货时间,也只能表示他完全按照合约履行在租约规定装货日期内完成。

有了上述的简单介绍后,读者更加理解在本章1.4段已经介绍过的案情与上诉庭的判决。

只重复说是上诉庭接受违约的卖方的抗辩是就算船舶可以很快在6月26日靠泊装货,不存在有任何违约所造成的延误,卖方还是有24天买卖合约许可的装货时间可让卖方弹性使用。卖方完全可以慢慢装货,把这24天充分利用,令船舶在7月22日才装完货。这是卖方的合约权利,所以从这一个角度看,就算卖方没有尽快让船舶靠泊装货,这一个违约并没有延误买方的船舶从而买方根本没有损失。

这一个上诉庭判决可以说是令这一个以违约方最低合约责任计算损失的原则达到顶峰,被视为是太偏袒违约方而受到批评,如Michael Ashcroft御用大律师提出说法认同第一审Phillips大法官的判决,这会在稍后的结论进一步解释。

另一个近期的先例Durham Tees Valley Airport Ltd v. BMI Baby Ltd. (2011) 1 Lloyd's Rep 68有不同的说法。该先例涉及一个英国中部的飞机场为了吸引旅客与航班,与英国British Midland Airways Ltd集团下的一家廉价航空公司签订了10年的使用权合约,但每年的航班与乘客多少就没有规定。随着营运的亏损,该廉价航空公司在不久后终止使用该机场。这导致机场的所有人向航空公司提出索赔,问题是损失如何计算,因为这是与余下没有履行的8、9年时间内会有多少航班与乘客有关系。如果以航空公司最低的合约责任为准(实际上是还没有确定),损失金额就会变得很低。在该先例,上诉庭推翻了一审的判决,认为这是一个单一责任而不是违约方有权利选择怎样履行,所以不适用最低合约责任为准的原则。法院需要做的就是尽量估计与推算该合约如果获得履行会是怎样的合理履行。Patten大法官是这样说:"There was clearly a consensus between the members of the court that, in relation to alternative methods of performance, the claimant will be unable to rely upon the defendant performing the contract in the more onerous of the two or more ways permitted. But that was not the type of contract under consideration in Abrahams v. Herbert Reiach Ltd (1922) 1 KB 477 and it is not the type of contract which we have to deal with in this case. Where there is only a single obligation to be performed it is clear that the majority view was that an assessment of damages should not, as a matter of law, be limited strictly to what was the minimum level of performance permitted under the contract but should extend to a calculation of how the contract would have been performed at the relevant time had it not been repudiated. This will take into account the likely profitability of the contract and any other relevant facts that would have influenced the method of performance."(法院一致认为在合约有不同的履行方法时,原告是不能依赖被告会以最苛刻的履行方法,但这一合约与Abrahams v. Herbert Reiach先例是不一样性质的合约,这一合约只有一个单一责任履行。上诉庭的多数意见认为计算损失是不应该只看怎样严格在合约允许的最低的履行责任,而是应该看合约如果没有发生违约/毁约而真的是被履行,会是怎样。这表示要把所有有关的因素考虑在内,包括可能有的合约预期利润以及其他会影响履行合约的事实。)

很明显在Durham Tees Valley Airport Ltd v. BMI Baby Ltd.先例,上诉庭的多数判决已经偏离了The "World Navigator"先例的判决,虽然两个先例都是针对单一责任与承诺。在The "World Navigator",上诉庭只考虑违约方最低的合约履行责任是什么,但另一个近期的上诉庭先例,就更持平的对待受害方与违约方,更加愿意考虑违约方如果真的履行合约,会采取怎样的履行方法。这一方面的转变笔者稍后会进一步探讨。

3. 合约涉及违约方有选择或裁量权的进一步细分

在计算损失时,有关合约的条文即使是给了违约方选择或裁量权,它还可以进一步解释与细分并会导致不一样的损失计算结果。这可以细分为四种,其中部分的类别已经在上一段节提到。

(1)合约要求违约方履行 X 或者 Y(给违约方有两个或更多的选择)。这种选择或裁量权会是 2.1 段所介绍的情况。

(2) 合约要求违约方在如果没有履行 X 的情况下,就必须替代履行 Y。

这种情况的案例不多,可以介绍的是 Deverill v. Burnell (1873) LR 8 CP 475 先例。案情涉及原告委托给了被告一些远期汇票,要求稍后如果没有获得承兑与支付,就必须把这些汇票退还给原告。但如果没有退还,被告就必须支付原告这些汇票的金额。但被告后来既没有退还汇票也没有支付汇票的金额。事实上这些汇票事后被证明是毫无价值。所以被告提出抗辩说是即使合约获得履行,退还的汇票也是毫无价值,这等于原告没有蒙受损失。但法院的多数意见认为被告必须支付这些汇票的金额,因为被告既然没有退还有关汇票,合约的规定就是支付汇票的金额,而被告没有这样做也就是要赔后者不履行的损失。从另一个角度看,由于合约有了这一个替代的履行,原来退还汇票的履行即使没有做也不算是违约,而违约的是双方同意的替代也不履行,所以被告应该赔付的损失就是这些汇票的金额。

Bovill 大法官是这样说:“If the contract . . . is simply in the alternative, to do one of two things, it would be satisfied by the performance of either, and the damages would be the loss occasioned by non-performance of that alternative which would be least beneficial to the plaintiff. If the true construction be that of the two things to be done one depended upon the non-performance of the other, that is, if the defendant did not return the bills, then he should pay the amount of them. The damage would be the non-payment of that amount. The rule of law is clear, that, in the case of alternative contracts, the person who has to perform the contract has the right to elect which branch of the alternative he will perform. On the other hand, it is equally clear, if the contract is to do a thing, and if not to pay a sum of money, then the damages for not doing the thing are the sum of money.”

(3)合约要求违约方履行 X,但受害的原告有合理的期望是他会履行 Y。

这方面的先例是 Lavarack v. Woods of Colchester Ltd (1967) 1 QB 278。在该案中有一句名言是:“无论合约一方对另一方会如何履行合约有多么合理的期望,只要该期望并非是另一方的法律义务则都不能够作为其损失计算的依据(it can not take account of “the expectations, however reasonable, of one contractor that the other will do something that he has assumed no legal obligation to do.”)。换言之,合理的期望是没有法律的基础可以强加在违约方。

该案例中,雇主违约提前解雇了一名雇员。该雇员随后入禀法院要求雇主赔偿他在原雇佣期余下时间本来应得收入的损失。雇佣合约中包括一项奖金津贴的规定,但在该雇员起诉之前,这项奖金制度已合法中止,不过绝大部分在职雇员通过雇主的加薪均维持了他们在原有制度下的收入水平。由于原有那项奖金制度是合法中止的，原告索赔时自然不能再将奖金方面的损失作为索赔的项目。因为即使他未被解雇也不能获得这方面的收入。于是原告就提出要依当时其他雇员加薪后的工资水平来计算他的收入损失，理由是如果他被继续雇佣，同样也会加薪。结果法院判定，原告无权将这项加薪额纳入损失赔偿中。因为他的索赔只能严格基于原告雇主在被违反合约中有责任履行的事项，而不能依赖雇主如果没有违约的情况下估计与期望日后可能会做的（也就是加薪），自愿增加雇佣合约责任的事项。其实道理也很简单，如果被非法解雇的雇员索赔说："你雇主当时如果没有违约/毁约，之后很可能会给我加薪，因为我工作出色，公司缺人或通货膨胀你要稳定人心等，所以我索赔的收入损失要按加薪后的数额计算。"这显然只是一种一厢情愿的想法，也就是雇主不履行 X（合法终断奖金制度），就会履行 Y（加薪），因为法律上讲不通。这里介绍的先例可以与在本章 2.2 段介绍表面看来是同性质但结果不一样的先例 Cantor Fitzgerald International v. Horkulak（2004）EWCA Civ. 1287 进行比较与区分。

（4）合约要求违约方履行 X，但允许他有一个选择权/裁量权决定怎么样履行并会影响双方利益。

这方面也已经在较早的 2.2 段提到，就是在法律可以做出默示的情况下，英国法院是越来越倾向对违约方行使裁量权做出合理的限制以计算损失赔偿，再也不是一面倒让违约方可以根据最低的责任计算损失。

4. 其他最低合约责任为准原则的例外情况

一直以来在以违约方最低合约责任为准的原则下，法院变为更加愿意"默示"（imply）违约方的选择或裁量权有一定的限制。还有其他一些比较次要的例外情况，可在这里简单介绍，大致上是有四种。

第一种例外情况是，如果争议中的合约责任是非严格规定的，最低合约责任的原则并不适用。典型的例子就是在合约约定要求一方承担"小心谨慎的义务"（duty to take care）。如被告（如测量师或者是估价师）违反了合约中约定做出评估并给出谨慎建议的义务，他需要承担的赔偿责任是以法院认为的合理性评估为标准，即使被告能证明可以接受的最低评估准则会造成的损失，也不能以此来计算损失赔偿的金额：Lion Nathan Ltd v. C-C Bottlers Ltd（1996）1 WLR 1438；Scotlife Homeloans v. Kenneth James & Co（1995）EGCS 70；South Australia Asset Management Corp v. York Montague Ltd（1997）AC 191 等先例。

第二种例外情况是，遥远的偶然性事件也不会被考虑在内，即使理论上说这是在被告自由裁量权范围内的。例如在 Bold v. Brough Nicholson & Hall Ltd.（1964）1 WLR 201 先例，一位被错误解雇的公司董事（原告）要求他的雇主（被告）赔偿他的养老金损失（除了其他多项请求之外）。被告提出，理论上它有权随时取消整个养老金计划，让所有的员工都没有这项福利的保障。法院最后判是原告胜诉，他有权获得养老金损失的赔偿。另一个例子是在本章6.9段将会详述的 TCN Channel 9 Pty Ltd v. Hayden Enterprises Pty Ltd (1989) 16 NSWLR 130 先例，原告（电视台）提出它有权随时放弃争议涉及的非常受欢迎的电视节目，所以损失赔偿应该减少到以最低的提前3个月通知来计算。同样的，这个理由也被法院拒绝了，因为一个很遥远的偶然性事件的实现几率实际上是很小的，不应该被考虑在内。

第三种例外情况是，以违约方最低合约责任为准的原则只适用于在违约时（或预期违约被接受时）被告仍然有能力选择履行方式的情况。例如，如果出售一批大豆的CIF卖方有权选择在8月或者9月付运，但是他必须在7月之前对买方做出不可反悔的“选择”（election）。假设他在7月做出选择，是要在8月份付运，但结果他做不到（可以是各种原因如供应不了大豆，或租不到适合的船舶，或是大豆市场或航运市场高涨导致卖方犹豫不决），损失的计算就应该以8月的价格为准。违约的卖方不能在诉讼时看到9月份的大豆价格比8月份更低要求损失计算以9月份价格为准，声称毕竟他在合约下有权9月付运。卖方的违约不论是预期违约（如在选择8月份付运后过不了几天就拒绝履行）或是真正违约（错过8月份没有做出付运），结果都应该是一样的，就是以8月的价格为准计算损失。因为他在7月做出选择后，就是把9月履行合约的选择权放弃，合约的承诺变为只是在8月履行，损失赔偿也应该以8月的标准来计算。

第四种例外情况是，只有被告才能援引以违约方最低合约责任为准的原则。如果合约履行方式的选择权是在原告，他不能适用相反的假设来支持他的请求。例如在 Sudan Import & Export Co (Khartoum) v. Societe Generale de Compensation (1958) 1 Lloyd's Rep 310 先例，案情涉及2000吨“落花生”（groundnuts）的买卖合约，卖方（原告）有出售货物数量10%上下浮动的选择权。之后买方违约/毁约，上诉庭判是损失计算应该假设在实际情况下卖方估计会付运的货物数量为准（从卖方发给买方的发票显示，卖方是估计付运2000吨货物），并非以合约允许的最多或最少数量为准。

5. 违约方对可以减少损失的将来变数举证需要达到何种程度？

损失的举证责任是在受害方的原告身上是无可置疑，但举证的责任要达到何种程度曾经有不同的说法。一个说法就是“命中注定会发生”（predestined to happen）: The “Mihalis Angelos” (1970) 2 Lloyd's Rep. 43; North Sea Energy Holdings v. Petroleum Authority of Thailand (1997) 2 Lloyd's Rep. 418。

另一个说法就是只要是合理会发生，发生的可能性只是需要满足平衡的可能性。

这在其他许多先例中都有提到,在 Jill Poole 教授的《Loss of chance and the evaluation of hypotheticals in contractual claims》一文(在 2007 年 2 月的《Lloyd's Commercial & Maritime Law Quarterly》刊登)中,也有提到这种会否发生的变数还是要看平衡的可能性,说:"The probabilities test determines liability in relation to events turning on past facts. It also determines liability where the event turns on a hypothetical which necessitates action by the claimant or defendant, who can generally be predicted to act in their own interests. It follows that, where this is the applicable test, a (say) 55% change will become a certainty and full damages will be recoverable, whereas there can be no liability for a 45%."

在 The "World Navigator" (1991) 2 Lloyd's Rep 23 先例中,Staughton 大法官有针对这方面的争议,并认为首先提到"命中注定会发生"举证标准的 The "Mihalis Angelos"先例(案情请看本章之 6.5 段)只是针对有关事情,就是船舶会否错过销约期会否发生,但并非是针对违约方的承租人会否行使终断合约的权利方面,而只需要假设违约方会选择对他有利的方式(就是减少或排除了任何对船东的损失赔偿)行使,说:

"But I cannot find any suggestion in the judgments of the Court of Appeal that it was also an essential step to prove that the charterers would beyond doubt have exercised the right to cancel, rather than that they could have exercised it. On the contrary Lord Denning, M. R. said: 'if the defendant has under the contract an option which would reduce or extinguish the loss, it will be assumed that he would exercise it.'

Lord Justice Davies said: 'the assumption has to be made that, had there been no anticipatory breach, the defendant would have performed his legal obligation and no more.'...

That does not in my opinion impinge in any way on the general principle that a defendant, in performing his contractual obligations, is assumed to have chosen to perform them in the way least beneficial to the plaintiff where the contract gave him that choice. It is only in connection with the possible occurrence of events extraneous to the contract, whether in the control of the defendant or anyone else, that probability has to be considered."(这最后一段说是 Denning 勋爵与 Davies 大法官在 The "Mihalis Angelos" 先例的说法在我[Staughton 大法官]看来并没有侵犯这一个原则,就是被告如果履行合约并且合约给被告一个选择权,那么被告是被假设会去选择一种对原告最不利的做法[对原告最不利也就表示对被告最有利,他们是相对立的]。只有在这一个选择权会受到来自合约以外的事件的影响[不论被告或第三人可否控制],这时才需要考虑选择的可能性)

6. 重要先例的介绍

6.1 先例之一:Thomas v. Clarke

以下介绍有关损失计算以违约方最低合约责任为准原则的重要或著名先例,首先介绍一个很早期的 Thomas v. Clarke (1818) 2 Stark 450 先例。案情涉及承租人没有提供货物给船舶付运,导致了船东索赔利润/运费损失。但问题是怎样决定金额,因为承租人是可以提供很多不同种类的货物,每种货物都涉及不同的运价。承租人的争辩是运费应该按照船舶付运一些运价最低的货物种类,但船东不同意并提供证据说明在以往的同类航次该船舶可以赚取的运费。Abbott 大法官(后来升职为 Tenterden 勋爵)是这样说:"In an action for not supplying a cargo under a charterparty, according to the terms of which different articles of freight are to be paid for at different rates by weight, and the freighter is at liberty to supply which articles he pleases, an average value of freight, calculated upon the various rates of freight in the proportion of different articles usually carried on such a voyage, is the proper measure of damages."这样看来,这一个很早的先例已经没有严格适用损失计算以违约方最低合约责任为准的原则。

6.2 先例之二:Abrahams v. Herbert Reiach Ltd

这是一个十分重要的先例,也是第一个先例对已经存在的损失计算以违约方"最低合约责任为准原则"(minimum performance principle)作出限制,名为 Abrahams v. Herbert Reiach Ltd (1922) 1 KB 477。案情涉及出版社与作家之间的协议,其中包括了支付给作家每一本将来出售书籍的版权费。但协议并没有针对出版或印刷的数量与价格,这些都是属于出版社的裁量权或决定。但后来出版社没有把该书籍出版就违约/毁约,责任方面是明确不过,问题是损失怎样计算。出版社的争议是按照有关的协议,即使他只出版 1 本书籍并支付给作家大约 4 便士的版权费,就严格履行了协议的承诺。但这一来,对作家就很不公平,因为真履行的话肯定不会是这个样子。在英国的诉讼之中,出版社作为被告曾经存放法院 25 英镑的赔偿,这是假设出版 1500 本书籍。但在高院,作出的假设是 3 万本,赔偿是在 500 英镑。高院的考虑是如果该协议获得履行,怎样才是合理与现实。这是包括考虑许多其他的因素,包括出版的成本、将来估计的书价、作家的名誉、时间与时机等方面。但上诉去了上诉庭,这 500 英镑的赔偿被减少为 100 英镑。从这些不同的判决也可以看到这种估计将来事实的不肯定与困难。但显然是上诉庭与高院都假设出版社如果履行协议,什么才是一个合理与现实的做法,虽然"合理"本身就很大的幅度与不肯定。

上诉庭的三个著名大法官都有作出判决与解释,其中 Bankes 大法官与 Atkins 大法官的看法是一致,可节录如下:

Bankes 大法官是这样说:"This contract only imposes one obligation upon the appellants, namely to publish. The question is what will satisfy that obligation? The appellants (出版社) have wide discretion; the time of publication, the number of copies to be printed, the price at which they are to be offered, and the form the book is to take are all left to their judgment. That however does not dispose of the case, because they have repudiated their obligation altogether, and the difficult question we have to decide is in what position the respondents would have stood if the appellants had performed their obligation. To answer this question the Court must come to some conclusion on matters on which there is no evidence; how the appellants would have exercised their discretion; what number of copies they would have published; how many editions would be reasonable."(最后的一句是说在这种情况下,法院是要在毫无证据地考虑出版社会怎样合理履行协议。Bankes 大法官也说到这一份合约只是针对单一的履行,就是出版书籍。)

Atkins 大法官说:"If a merchant makes a contract to deliver goods to a shipowner to be carried by him for reward, and the merchant fails to provide the goods, the Court must first find what is the contract which has been broken; and if it was to carry the goods to one of two **alternative** ports at different distances from the port of loading at rates of freight differing according to the distance, the only contract on which the shipowner can sue is the contract for carriage to the nearer port. The plaintiff cannot provide a contract for performance of the more onerous obligation. This explains why in cases of this kind the Court regards only the lesser of two alternative obligations. But in the present case there are **no alternatives**, and to adjust the rights of the parties the only method is to form a reasonable estimate of the amount the respondents would be in pocket if the appellant had kept his promise. Everything likely to affect the amount of the profit must be considered: the nature and popularity of the subject matter, the reputation of the authors, the cost of producing a book on that subject, the price at which it would command a sale, the business capacity of the publishers and the chances of earning a profit by the sale of the book. On the other hand the publishers are not bound to run risks contrary to their judgment; they would naturally and properly allow for fluctuation in the public taste for literature of this kind. An analogous calculation has to be made when a man having engaged to take another into his service for a time and to pay him a share in the profit of his business, refuses to employ him at all. In assessing the damages for the breach of this contract the question is not how the employer could carry on his business so as to make the least possible profit and so involve himself in the least possible obligation towards the plaintiff. Apart from his contract, he need not carry on business at all. The proper method of assessment is quite different; it is to make a reasonable computation of the amount the respondents would have received had the contract been fulfilled."(Atkins 大法官大致上是区分有关合约如果有两个选择履行,根据许多的先例是说明违约方就可以要求损失以最低合约责任为准做出计算。但这一个合约不

存在有两个选择,所以对将来履行的估计或推测要以合理会出版的数量为准,什么是合理就要对所有有关因素做出考虑)

最后 Scrutton 大法官是这样说:"C(出版社) contended that if one copy was published that would satisfy the appellant's(出版社) obligation. That cannot be laid down as a proposition of law. I think the appellants were bound to make such a publication as could be considered reasonable in the circumstances. Having done that they are not bound to do anything further. Provided that they make a reasonable publication the number and price of the copies are left to them. They broke their contract, and now what is the measure of damages? There are two principles which may seem to clash. One of these is stated by Lord Selborne in Wilson v. Northampton and Banbury Junction Ry Co (1) 'In the case of damages, as it appears to me, the plaintiff will be entitled to the benefit of such presumptions as, according to the rule of law, are made in Courts both of law and equity against persons who are wrongdoers in the sense of refusing to perform, and not performing their agreements. We know it to be an established maxim, that in assessing damages every reasonable presumption may be made as to the benefits which the other parties might have been obtained by the bona fide performance of the agreement'. I am not inclined to be strict in limiting the damages recoverable against wrongdoers, but if their obligation is left so much to their discretion that there are several ways of performing it, I have always understood that the Court assesses damages on the basis that 'if the contract could have been performed by the performance of the alternative least beneficial to the plaintiff, the measure of damages would be regulated by the loss occasioned by non-performance of that alternative: Deverill v. Burnell, per Bovill CJ. The simple reason for this is that a defendant is not liable in damages for not doing that which he is not bound to do. In assessing the damages in this case I try to ascertain what edition of the contract: I do not forget that the respondents cannot recover more than they have suffered if they themselves acted reasonably; I bear in mind also that the appellants are wrongdoers; and acting on these lines I do not dissent from an assessment of Pds. 100 though I think myself the plaintiffs might have got considerably less."(Scrutton 大法官虽然没有反对 100 英镑的损失赔偿,但他看来是不情愿并认为金额应该是少得多)

6.3 先例之三:Withers v. General Theatre Corp.

在较早的本章 2.1 段已经简单提到的 Withers v. General Theatre Corp. (1933) 2 KB 536 (CA)先例,案情涉及一个演出合约。原告是一位职业艺人,他与被告一家剧场营运公司签订了一份合约,约定原告可以连续 3 个星期在著名的 London Palladium 大剧院演出他的幽默短剧,每星期的报酬是 300 英镑。合约中有一条文规定,被告可以根据自己的意愿,将原告的演出转移到被告所拥有的、掌控的或合伙经营的位于伦敦或同省的其他剧院。原告首先在朴茨茅斯市(Portsmouth)试演了一星期,结果被告看了之后决定不给原告在 London Palladium 大剧院表演的机会了。原告就以违约起诉被告，索赔失去"宣传自己的机会"（loss of publicity）的损失以及"名誉损失"（damage to reputation）。一审法院指引陪审团说原告因此受到名誉上的损害，但没有指引陪审团考虑合约中被告对履行方式的选择。陪审团判原告胜诉，要求被告赔偿薪酬损失 600 英镑以及失去宣传机会的损失 1000 英镑。但上诉庭将一审判决推翻，Bankes 大法官认为一审法官在认定损害赔偿数额的问题上指引陪审团考虑对原告的名誉损害是错误的，因为原告作为一位职业艺人已经拥有了他的名誉，法官应该指引陪审团考虑原告在 London Palladium 大剧院的演出会不会使原告更加出名。Scrutton 大法官和 Romer 大法官进一步指出，在这份演出合约下，原告在 Palladium 大剧院表演的权利"不是绝对的"（no absolute right）。被告在合约中有权选择让原告在哪个剧院进行表演。法院在裁定损害赔偿数额时，应考虑违约的被告会在合约允许的履约选项里选择那个对他自己最有利而不是对原告最有利的一个剧院。

Scrutton 大法官说："Now where a defendant has alternative ways of performing a contract at his option, there is a well settled rule as to how the damages for breach of such a contract are to be assessed... A very common instance explaining how that works is this: A undertakes to sell to B 800 to 1,200 tons of certain commodity; he does not supply B with any commodity. On what basis are the damages to be fixed? They are fixed in this way. A would perform his contract if he supplied 800 tons, and the damages must therefore be assessed on the basis that he has not supplied 800 tons, and not on the basis that he has not supplied 1,200 tons, nor on the basis that he has not supplied the average, 1,000 tons, and not on the basis that he might reasonably be expected, whatever the contract was, to supply more than 800 tons. The damages are assessed ... on the basis the defendant will perform the contract in a way most beneficial to himself and not in the way that is most beneficial to the plaintiff."

接下去 Scrutton 大法官针对该案例的案情说："The plaintiff had under the contract no absolute right to appear at the Palladium ... The defendants had an option as to the halls at which he should appear ... where a defendant has alternative ways of performing a contract at his option, there is a well settled rule as to how the damages for breach of such a contract are to be assessed."

Romer 大法官说："It must be observed that at the time the defendants repudiated the contract on July 2, they had not lost the right of exercising the option which in my opinion they had under the contract of directing the plaintiff to appear, not at the Palladium but at one of the other halls belonging to or under the control of the defendants; and the jury ought to have taken into consideration the possibility, and I think the probability, that if the defendants instead of repudiating the contract on July 2 had elected to go on with the performance they would have sent the plaintiff to perform somewhere else than at the Palladium."

6.4 先例之四:Kaye Steam Navigation Company Ltd v. Barnett Ltd

Kaye Steam Navigation Company Ltd v. Barnett Ltd(1932) 43 Lloyd's Rep. 166 的先例在较早的2.1段已经有简单提到,案情涉及一个航次租约,但船舶到了装港承租人拒绝提供货物,这是清楚不过的违约/毁约。但在损失的计算就有了两方面的争议,第一方面就是承租人说他是有权可以有33天的时间在Rosario装港装货,这根据租约第13条的许可装货时间是他如果支付运费或赔偿运费所应该取得的好处,这时间必须减去,并相应减低了船东的利润损失索赔。受害的船东在这一方面是争辩说在Rosario装货33天是完全不合理与不现实。第二方面的争议是承租人说他有权去卸港范围中最远的港口,也就是英国的伊普斯威奇(Ipswich)。承租人这一个争议也是为了加重船东履约的成本并同时减少索赔的利润损失。

英国法院同意承租人的抗辩,Branson大法官是这样说:"I think the decisive clause is Clause 13. There it states in terms that the obligation upon the charterers is to load the ship at the rate of 225 tons per running day up to the first 3,000 tons and at the rate of 400 tons per running day for any quantity above the first 3,000 tons. That makes it perfectly plain that these charterers could have fulfilled their contract under their charter-party by putting on board the ship 225 tons a day and no more until they had completed the cargo. Calculating the time that the loading would have taken at those rates per diem, the ship would have taken 33 days to load, and it seems to me quite plain, as a matter of legal right as between the charterers and the shipowners, that the charterers could have discharged their obligations under this charter-party by loading at those specified rates per day. Had they chosen to do so, the ship would have had to lie alongside the wharf and incur wharfage dues for the 33 days, which are arrived at by applying those figures to the amount of cargo that the ship could carry. It is said that no reasonable man at Rosario would load a ship in that way. I do not think that that alters the position. It may very well be that no one has yet been in such a position with regard to the collection and the carriage of his cargo that it was convenient to him to do it in that way; but it does not follow that, either because of a railway breakdown or because of strikes in this very agitated port, the shipper might not well have found it impossible to get more than a dribble of the volume of the cargo coming in. If he succeeded in keeping up his loading to the amount of 225 tons a day and 400 tons a day, the shipowner could not complain; and I think therefore, in calculating the damage, the ship must give credit for the wharfage dues which would have been incurred had her obligations to lie at the wharf and receive cargo at these rates been imposed upon her ...

The same principle exactly applies to the question of the port of discharge. It is perfectly plain upon the charter-party that this ship might have been ordered toIpswich. That being so, I think on the principle referred that the charterers were entitled to say: 'You must calculate your damages upon the assumption that we did order you to Ipswich as we might have done;many ships are ordered to Ipswich in this grain trade'."

换言之这一个先例是严格适用损失计算以违约方最低合约责任为准的原则,毕竟有关租约是涉及违约承租人的选择。这种情况在笔者经历或支持的仲裁裁决中经常会出现,就是在一个程租合约,承租人没有履行,在损害赔偿上通常是以对受害的船东最不利的履行方法来计算。例如承租人有权去三个港口,加上每个港口可以使用多达三个泊位。虽然如果真正履行,承租人通常不会要全部使用三个港口加上三个泊位。但在损失计算上,就做出这样的估计或推断,以加大船东为赚取同一笔金额的运费所要承担的费用与时间,进而减少利润损失金额。或在另一种情况是程租租约给予承租人选择权在两个卸港中选择其中一个,但两个卸港的使费一昂贵一便宜,或一远一近,耗油量明显不一样,亦会以更昂贵或更遥远的卸港来计算船东如果获得履行的损失。

6.5 先例之五:The "Mihalis Angelos"

在这一个著名的The "Mihalis Angelos" (1970) 2 Lloyd's Rep. 43先例,已经在本书第六章3.2.2段有详尽的介绍,在此尽量不重复。案情涉及一艘希腊船舶程租给当时的北越政府(承租人)去海防装货,但由于船舶延误而赶不上销约期之前抵达海防港装货。但承租人却先告知船东他没有货可装,给了船东一个机会先接受承租人的违约/毁约并事后向承租人索赔损失。但实际上船东如果履约只会多花费用如燃油费用把船舶开去海防港,然后被承租人以错过销约期取消租约。高等法院先是判违约/毁约的承租人要赔偿船东损失,但去了上诉庭,Denning勋爵等大法官判违约/毁约的承租人只需要赔偿"名义损失"(nominal damage)。因为损害赔偿的大原则是要让无辜的希腊船东"复原"。但由于船舶到海防港的时候肯定是会错过销约期,而在承租人没有货物可装的情况下也肯定会取消合约,所以船东不会有损失。Denning勋爵是这样说:"... the damages must be measured by compensating the injured party for the loss he has suffered by reason of the renunciation. You must take into account all contingencies which might have reduced or extinguished the loss... It follows that if the defendant(承租人)has under the contract an option which would reduce or extinguish the loss,it will be assumed that he would exercise it ... Seeing that the charterers would,beyond doubt,have cancelled,I am clearly of opinion that the shipowners suffered no loss;and would be entitled at most to nominal damages."

另一个上诉庭的Edmund Davies大法官同样说:"In the light of the arbitrators' finding,it is beyond dispute that,on the belated arrival of the Mihalis Angelos at Haiphong, the charterers not only could have elected to cancel the charter-party but would actually have done so. The rights lost to the owners by reason of the assumed anticipatory breach were thus certain to be rendered valueless."

这一个重要的先例表示在计算违约/毁约后的损失时,对之后很有可能会发生的事情(将来"事实")也要做出一个合理的估计或推算。毕竟这就是找出合约如果被履行,受害方会是怎样的经济地位。这先例带来一个"Mihalis Angelos 原则",就是在违约/毁约后很有可能甚至是命中注定会发生的事情,而合约中约定出现这种事情违约方就有权利可终断,这在损失计算中必须加以考虑。往往带来的结果就是违约方不必赔偿受害方的损失或只赔偿名义损失,反正该合约会被终断。这一个 Mihalis Angelos 原则也延伸去受害方自己不能履行合约或被证明没有意图履行合约(这可以说受害方本人也是违约/毁约或预期违约,只是还没有被违约方的被告接受),也会在损失计算方面有同样的结果。

在笔者最近作为仲裁员审理的一个新加坡仲裁案件,涉及一份租约要求船舶必须是没有任何在甲板凸起的障碍物,否则收货人有权拒绝接受该船舶。这是由于该租约是用来装运煤炭,在卸货的码头是有自动卸货设备。该设备必须能够在有关船舶的甲板自由移动,不会受到障碍物的妨碍,甚至造成该昂贵设备的损坏。但船东指定的一艘船舶实际上是已经过时的油矿两用船舶,在甲板的中间部分是有吊杆(装油的时候用作吊岸上的油管)与灯桅,导致该船舶在装港被发觉甲板的障碍物后被拒绝。船东向承租人提出索赔,有关责任方面涉及各种的争议,包括该船舶并没有障碍物与承租人不应该在装港提早拒绝该船舶(因为有关租约的约定是卸港可拒绝),承租人是构成违约/毁约。在该仲裁案件中,代表承租人(是南亚一家大公司)委任的国际律师所竟然漏了提出这一个 Mihalis Angelos 原则,否则会是大大提高胜诉机会。幸亏包括笔者在内的多数意见在其他责任方面判承租人胜诉。

6.6 先例之六:The "Rijn"

在 The "Rijn" (1981) 2 Lloyd's Rep. 267 先例,涉及一个期租合约,还船地点是约定在亚洲的多个港口,说"at a safe port South Japan (not north of Tokyo Bay)/Singapore range excluding North and South Vietnam, Cambodia, North Korea." 本来承租人的计划是在美国装一票散粮去日本,卸完了货就可以按照租约还船。但由于船舶严重延误(包括了主机出问题,但这不一定涉及船东违约),导致了分租约的销约期错过,令承租人的如意算盘打不响,失去了这一票在美国装散粮去日本的航次。估计由于找不到其他适合的替代租约,承租人硬了头皮在美国 Galveston 港把船舶交还给船东。由于该港并非是租约允许的还船地点,承租人这样做显然是违约/毁约。而针对损失的计算船东是索赔替代租约所赚取的利润与原来从美国 Galveston 港装散粮去日本卸下后还船会赚取的利润(租金收入)的差价。但承租人抗辩说在以租约最低合约责任为准原则下,也就是在亚洲港口还船,他是可以让船舶从美国 Galveston 港空放去日本横滨(最近的港口)然后还船。承租人的计算办法与船东的计算办法不同之处就是如果只是空放方式,履行时间上就短得多,按日支付的租金收入自然也减少。空放方式能省下的时间包括在美国 Galveston 港停留的装货时间与在日本横滨卸货的时间。在高院,Mustill 大法官同意承租人的说法,因为承租人在期租下完全有权决定怎么样营运,他是完全可以改变主意并要求船舶空放去日本横滨以履行租约,就谈不上是违约了,这也是复原大原则下把受害的船东放回到一个合约被履行的经

济地位。Mustill 大法官是这样说:

"Apart from any express agreement as to the nature of the voyage, there is little room for doubt. It is quite clear that where a promisor(承租人) has the choice of how this promise shall be performed, it is presumed for the purchase of calculating damages that he would have chosen the way which would have brought least benefit to the promisee(船东). This principle, that an option is presumed to have been exercised in the way which reduces damages to a minimum, is too well established to require citation in support. Applying this approach to the present case yields the conclusion that the loss should be assessed in terms of the voyage which would have yielded the least hire. This was a voyage to the nearest safe port within the redelivery range, namely, Yokohama; and it would have been a voyage in ballast, because this would have saved time which would otherwise have been occupied in loading and discharge...

The owners can argue that there was a course of conduct between themselves and the charterers which makes it inequitable to assess the damages otherwise than on the basis of a laden voyage to Japan. I do not think that it greatly matters how this argument is expressed in legal terms: as a variation of the contract, or as an election or an estoppel. The question is simply this, would the charterers have been entitled to change their minds, when the sub-charter fell through, and say that after all they did not want the ship to carry a cargo of grain toJapan? From a commercial point of view, there is no problem with an affirmative answer to this question. Indeed, any other answer would make little sense. Why should not the charterers have been entitled to change their minds and order the ship to carry grain to Singapore, or coal to Japan, or nothing at all to any port within the range? What commercial reason could there be to hold that the charterers were permanently locked into an obligation to ship grain to Japan, merely because this was what they have said they were going to do; and to go on to say that they would have been compelled to keep the ship idle at Galveston, for no matter how long, until they could find a cargo of grain (and nothing else) to be carried to Japan (and nowhere else)."

这先例看来也是严格适用损失计算以违约方最低合约责任为准的原则,不考虑承租人合理履行的话会否跑一个空放航次从美国去横滨。

6.7　先例之七:Paula Lee Ltd v. Robert Zehil Ltd

接下去是介绍一个已经在第六章 3.3.2 中提到的非航运但著名的先例,可以说是对损失计算以违约方"最低合约责任为准原则"作出限制的第二个重要先例:Paula Lee Ltd v. Robert Zehil Ltd (1983) 2 All ER 390。这是与 Abrahams v. Herbert Reiach Ltd (1922) 1 KB 477 先例的判法一致,认为法律默示违约方的裁量权是有合理的限制,所以在 The "World Navigator" (1991) 2 Lloyd's Rep 23 先例中,Staughton 大法官把这两个先例串在一起并称为是"The Abrahams and Paula Lee doctrine"。

Paula Lee Ltd v. Robert Zehil Ltd 先例是涉及一个供应商与特许分销商的合约，后者承诺要向前者每季度买 1.6 万套各种不同衣服，但没有履行。分销商违约/毁约后在计算要付出的损失赔偿时，指称应以他的最低合约责任为准做出计算，也就是以 1.6 万套最便宜的衣服为准。但 Mustill 大法官判在该合约条文下，分销商不能如此履行，也完全不合理，因为 1.6 万套同样的衣服会把有关分销的服装市场拖垮，也卖不出去，这不会是双方想履行的做法。合约要求是不同种类衣服有一个合理选购，但在计算上仍是以这"合理选购"下被告会支付的最低价格为准(in terms of that reasonable selection which would yield the lowest price)。

Mustill 大法官是这样说："I believe that at least some of the difficulties which arise in this branch of the law can be minimized if it is kept in mind that inquiry always involves a comparison between the plaintiff's(供应商) actual position in face of the breach, and the position which he would have occupied if the contract had been performed. This must involve an identification of the promise, followed by a valuation of its promised worth to the promise. Each part of the inquiry may involve considering a choice which would have been open to the promisor(分销商). Thus,

1. The promisor may have a right of the election which fixes the content of his obligation. This can take more than one form. It may, for example, give the vendor the option to deliver 1500 to 2000 tons of goods. Here, in accordance with the dictum of Scrutton L. J., the damages are assessed on the basis that the quantity delivered would have been 1500 tons, for the seller could not have been compelled to deliver more than this amount. Where the obligation is to deliver at A or B, the dictum does not always work so well, for it cannot necessarily be said that A represents more of an obligation than B. So here the presumption is explained in different terms, by looking for the obligation which would have been least detrimental to perform.

2. Even where the obligation has been fixed in advance, or determined by election, the value of it to the promise, and hence the amount which he has lost through non-performance, may be determined by contingencies. Sometimes, it is possible to be sure what would have happened if the contract had been performed, and (if so) this finding is used to estimate the worth of the promise. More often, the fact that the repudiation has prevented the time for performance from arising means that the best that can be done is to make an estimate of the likelihood that the contingent event would occur, and adjust the damages accordingly. For this purpose it makes no difference that the contingency is one which is under the control of the defendant. Although it is not legitimate to look at what the promisor would have done, but only what he could have done, when **identifying** the promise, the position is different when, as in The "Mihalis Angelos" and Bold v. Brough Nicholson & Hall Ltd., the inquiry concerns the valuation of the promise itself."(黑字部分是笔者的强调)

Mustill 大法官在这一个先例中表示,不同合约的明示的选择或裁量权会带来不同的计算。Mustill 大法官也把"确定"(identification)什么是有关合约的承诺与该承诺的"价值"(valuation)做出区分,后者应查询什么是最可能合理的履行,才知道什么是真正的价值。有关这一方面,在本章的结论部分会进一步探讨。

6.8 先例之八:The"Briton"

第八个先例是 The "Briton" (1975) 1 Lloyd's Rep. 319,案情涉及该原告的疏浚船以光租合约出租给被告,租期为第一条文:"Owners agree to let and Charterers agree to hire the plant for a period of approximately sixteen months from the date of delivery hereunder Charterers shall use months of 1969 and 1970 for two more or less equally divided periods totalling not less than 12 weeks and not more than 52 weeks (Hereinafter called 'the dredging periods')."(条文大致上是约定承租人使用该疏浚船的期间为 1969 年与 1970 年的两年中差不多的时间,而总共的使用时间是不能低于 12 周但不能超过 52 周)。规定承租人使用的时间是因为租金有不同的规定,就是船舶在使用或疏浚期间为每周 500 英镑,但在抛老锚期间(不使用的抛锚期间)则为每周 25 英镑。交船在 1969 年 6 月 5 日,并在当天就开始了疏浚工作,一直到了 10 月 7 日,在 1969 年是总共使用了 17 周 5 天,之后船舶就抛老锚直到还船。被告支付给原告的租金为在 6 月 5 日到 10 月 7 日的疏浚期间每周 500 英镑,在之后的期间每周 25 英镑,但原告指在 1970 年,船舶一直在抛老锚,根本没有满足条文中这两年内都要用差不多的时间让该船舶进行疏浚作用的要求。这表示在 1970 年被告也应该使用该疏浚船并支付每周 500 英镑,为期至少 15 周(这才是与 1969 年的 17 周 5 天使用期差不多)。由于被告没有这样做,导致原告损失了大约 7600 英镑。而被告的抗辩是即使他违约/毁约,原告也没有损失,因为根据第一条文,他只需要使用该船舶疏浚总共不少于 12 周就可以满足条文的要求。事实上仅是在 1969 年,他已经使用了 17 周 5 天。英国高院与上诉庭都判原告只能取得 2 英镑的名义损失赔偿,因为原告没有真正的损失。Denning 勋爵是这样说:

"The problem is one of construction. It seems to me that the main operative clause is that which prescribes the minimum and maximum. The dredging period is to be not less than 12 weeks and not more than 52 weeks. The words 'two more or less equally divided periods' are words of expectation. They must give way to the rest of the contract. If the expectation is not fulfilled, they must be discarded. Let me illustrate it in a simple way. Supposing the plant was only used for six weeks in the year 1969: could it be suggested that the plant should be limited to six weeks or thereabouts in 1970, simply because the clause said 'for two more or less equally divided periods'? That would be absurd. Obviously in 1970 the plant could be used for such time as was considered reasonable, so long as the 52 weeks maximum was not exceeded. Take another illustration. Supposing the plant was used for 14 weeks in the first season and two weeks in the second, or alternatively for two weeks in the first season and 14 weeks in the second: could anyone suppose that the total payment would be any different?（这是一个解释合约条文的问题。关键性的部分是最低与最高的使用期限，也就是 12 周与 52 周。接下去的文字要求“1969 年与 1970 年使用差不多的时间”只代表双方的期望。这期望如果达不到的话就可以不理会，与最低和最高的使用期限的文字相比只是次要。举一个简单例子，如果该疏浚船在 1969 年只被使用了 6 周，难道说因为有两年要使用差不多的时间的文字，在 1970 年被告就只能使用 6 周而不是更长的时间［只要总共不超过 52 周］？再假设，如果在 1969 年使用了 14 周但在 1970 年只有 2 周，或倒过来在 1969 年使用了 2 周但在 1970 年使用了 14 周，被告需要作出的租金支付会有什么不同吗？）

In order to ascertain the total payment due, you have to look at the position at the end of the two seasons and see whether or not the minimum has been fulfilled. If it has been, then you calculate the payment due, irrespective of whether the two years are equally divided or not.

I think the Judge was right. The damages have to be assessed by looking at the two years as a whole. There is really no damage having regard to the fact that the minimum has been exceeded. I therefore would dismiss the appeal.”（我同意一审大法官是判得正确，原告的损失是要把两年一并看待。如果总共使用的时间是超出了最低期限的 12 周，原告就根本没有损失）

6.9 先例之九：TCN Channel 9 Pty Ltd v. Hayden Enterprises Pty Ltd

在 TCN Channel 9 Pty Ltd v. Hayden Enterprises Pty Ltd（1989）16 NSWLR 130 先例，案情涉及一个电视节目制作播出合约，TCN 是一家澳洲非常著名的电视台，它与 Hayden 合作制作并播出的节目“The Midday Show”很受欢迎。后来合约被 TCN 单方面终断，并被 Hayden 接受违约/毁约。合约中约定 TCN 在提前 3 个月通知的情况下，有权终断合约。TCN 声称损失赔偿的计算应该以这 3 个月来计算。这意味着 3 个月后 TCN 需要放弃这一个当时非常受欢迎的电视节目。法院根据双方提供的证据，认为现实中 TCN 不大可能放弃，也表示不会做出这 3 个月的通知。因此法院判是损失的计算不应该以这 3 个月为限。

从这一个先例可比较 The“Mihalis Angelos”（1970）2 Lloyd's Rep. 43 先例（认定将来违约方行使选择权是“命中注定”［predestined］会发生），The“Seaflower”（2000）2 Lloyd's Rep 37 先例（从证据显示将来会发生的失去 MOBIL 的批准最终会让违约方有权终断租约）与 Automotive Latch Systems Ltd v. Honeywell International Inc（2008）EWHC 2171（Comm）先例（从证据显示将来会发生的商业上变得不可行让违约方有权终断合约），可以看到法院不是严格以违约方最低合约责任为准计算损失，而是合理的估计或推测可能会发生的“事情”。

6.10 先例之十：The“Seaflower”

在 The“Seaflower”（2000）2 Lloyd's Rep 37 先例，涉及一个租期 11～12 个月的

期租合约,该油轮租约有一条今天经常会见到的条文,就是该船舶必须得到一些主要石油公司的许可或批准,因为这样承租人才能营运该油轮,如转租给主要石油公司,运他们的油并使用它们的泊位与设施。该先例租约的条文如下:"Vessel is presently MOBIL (expiring 27/1/98) CONOCO (expiring 28/1/98) and SHELL (expiring 14/1/98) acceptable. Owners guarantee to obtain within 60 days (sixty) days EXXON approval in addition to present approvals. On delivery date hire rate will be discounted USD 250 ... for each approval missing, i. e. MOBIL, CONOCO, BP, SHELL, EXXON ... If for any reason, Owners would lose even one of such acceptances they must advise charterers at once and they must reinstate same within 30 (thirty) days from such occurrence failing with Charterers will be at liberty to cancel charter party."

从上述条文可以看到,在交船的一天船东实际上还没有取得 EXXON 这一家世界上最大的石油公司的批准,但做出承诺会在 60 天内取得。要取得批准是要 EXXON 派验船师上船检查并满意船舶的安全与状况。该条文措辞的拟定也不是太好,它首先针对是在交船时如果其中一家石油公司的批准欠缺,每天的租金要减 250 美元,这只是大概 3% 的减租,显示不出这一方面的重要性。可以说,如果交船的时候五大石油公司的批准都欠缺,后果也只是减租 1250 美元,可以说是微不足道,但承租人想营运该油轮就变得十分困难。在该先例,由于该油轮在交船时还没有取得 EXXON 的批准,租金要减少 250 美元是没有争议。但该条文接下去的一句是说在租约期间如果该油轮失去任何一家石油公司的批准,并在 30 天内不能再度取得,承租人就可以终断租约。

该油轮交船后,起初的航次是没有涉及 EXXON。但在一个半月之后,承租人准备装一票属于 EXXON 的燃油,这是需要 EXXON 批准,所以承租人向船东查询到底船舶能否在交船后 60 天内取得 EXXON 批准,赶得及装这票燃油。但船东回答说是需要更多的时间,这导致了承租人回应说船东违反了租约的条件条文,所以终断租约。这表示还有 9~10 个月的租期没有获得履行,租约就被终断。

法院判有关的争议是涉及船东没有准时在承诺的 60 天内取得 EXXON 批准,这与条文最后的一句允许承租人终断合约无关。因为不存在失去 EXXON 批准,而且前一句话是专门针对 EXXON 批准,应该是超越后一句话。而船东违反了这个有关 EXXON 的承诺,既然只涉及减租 3%,显然是不重要,所以承租人无权终断租约,反而自己构成违约/毁约。

但在损失计算方面还涉及另外一个问题,就是在审理时已经明确了该油轮在 1998 年 1 月 27 日(这大约是在承租人违约/毁约后不到一个月的时间)也失去了 MOBIL 的批准,这显然是上述有关条文最后的一句就是船东如果不能在 30 天内再度取得批准,承租人就有权终断租约。这表示如果承租人的争议是站得住脚的话,损失计算就会是少多了,大约是 2 个月的损失而不是 9~10 个月的损失,两者之间涉及金额约 100 万美元。船东的争议是由于被承租人错误终断租约,所以就任由失去

MOBIL 批准,并且没有采取行动再度取得。但法院不接受,根据专家意见的证据与船舶在期间曾经被其他油公司(AGIP)拒绝、船舶的状况与设备、向 MOBIL 再度取得批准所需要的时间等,得出的结论是船东不可能及时再度取得 MOBIL 批准,承租人可以按照合约终断租约。

这一个先例的判法与较早所介绍的 The "Mihalis Angelos" (1970) 2 Lloyd's Rep. 43 先例基本上一样,区分只在 The "Mihalis Angelos"涉及的违约是"预期违约"(anticipatory breach)与说法上是北越承租人假设会以错过销约期的理由选择终断租约。在本案例看来,不需要肯定但只要根据提供的证据与平衡的可能性得出结论是会发生的事实,也可以在损失计算的时候加以考虑。这一个判法与另一个重要的贵族院先例 The "Golden Victory" (2007) 2 Lloyd's Rep 164 基本上是一致,该富争议性的先例在本书第十三章第 6 段有详细介绍。案情涉及期租合约被错误提早终断后,计算将来的利润损失是以余下的 4 年租期或是 14 个月,因为在违约/毁约后的 14 个月发生了海湾战争,违约的承租人按照租约的明示条文是有权终断合约。贵族院的多数是判损失计算只是 14 个月。

总结而言,本先例与 The "Golden Victory"都涉及其他重要的方面就是损失计算的日期,所以后者先例是在本书第十三章介绍。但与针对本章所针对的方面,也就是计算损失"以违约方最低合约责任为准"(Minimum Performance Principle),显然也是有密切的关系,并且会估计或推测有关合约如果被履行可能会发生什么事情。

6.11 先例之十一:And So To Bed v. Dixon

And So To Bed v. Dixon (2001) FSR 935 先例涉及一个特许经营合约。原告是一个专门经营"And so to Bed"品牌的床、卧室家具、床单以及其他床上用品的公司。被告在 1994 年 2 月 28 日起和原告公司签署了一份长达十年的特许经营权合约,约定被告(特许经营人)只可以从原告(特许经营权人)处购买与出售原告同意的产品。任何一方如果想终断合约,需要提前 12 个月书面通知。另如果被告违反合约不支付特许经营权费用,或者每年没有从原告处购买最低数量的产品,在原告通知后 14 天内没有改正,原告有权终断合约。

在 1999 年 2 月,被告告知原告由于合约中约定的特许经营权费用过高,他们打算从 1999 年 4 月 30 日起转变经营方向,也就是要终断特许经营合约。原告提醒被告如果终断合约需要提前 12 个月通知。但被告的律师声称由于原告的误述所以可以导致该份合约无效,因此提前 12 个月通知的要求也不适用于被告。1999 年 3 月 30 日,原告通知被告他违反了合约,因为他没有提供季度账目,支付特许使用费的金额,与储存未经原告同意的竞争品牌的产品。由于被告没有依照合约改正这些违约行为,1999 年 5 月 17 日,原告依照合约权利终断合约。原告要求被告支付剩余的特许使用费,并赔偿从合约终断之日起 12 个月的特许使用费。

法院判是该特许经营权合约有效,被告的行为已经构成违约并在 14 天内没有改正,因此原告有权依照合约权利终断合约,并要求被告支付剩余的特许使用费。至于损失赔偿中的从合约终断之日起12个月的特许使用费，法院认定原告有权获得这笔赔偿，因为合约要求终断合约需要提前12个月通知。依照合约特许使用费是营业额的3.5%。问题是如何确定合约终断后12个月的假设营业额。被告提出应该按照合约第13.5条文来确定，被告应该承担的最低合约责任应该是以这个条文中的4万英镑为标准，该条文如下："If the Licensee shall fail to purchase at least £ 40,000 of goods at cost excluding VAT from the Licensor or Deptich Designs Limited and any other suppliers the Licensor may nominate from time to time during the first calendar year or such sum as is equal to this sum plus inflation at the same rate as the cost of living index in each subsequent year."但法院判是，被告应该承担的责任数额应该按照最类似的两个特许零售点的平均销售额来计算，因为被告有义务合理和真诚的履行特许经营合约，积极地招揽顾客和进行正常的零售交易。而被告提出的第13.5条文，只是说明在被告没有达到这个最低交易量时原告有权终断合约，并没有给被告设定最低或最高的交易责任，所以不应该适用。David Donaldson 大法官是说："This Clause does not target retail turnover, and there might be difficulty in establishing more than the roughest of correlations between the purchases and the downstream sales in any year. The clause did not impose even a minimum purchase obligation, still less a maximum purchase obligation, but only a right to terminate if a minimum level were not achieved, a situation which might in theory arise even if the Licensee scrupulously fulfilled all its obligations as to the operation of the franchised outlets."

6.12 先例之十二：Automotive Latch Systems Ltd v. Honeywell International Inc

在 Automotive Latch Systems Ltd v. Honeywell International Inc (2008) EWHC 2171 (Comm)先例，案情涉及一个"合作协议"(Joint Collaboration Agreement)的争议。原告发明了一种新型汽车门闩，他与被告签订了继续开发这种产品并投入生产的合作协议。但28个月后原告取消了该合作协议，理由是被告没有合理履行他的合约责任去以一个有竞争力的成本、且在不造成不合理延误的前提下生产这种汽车门闩。原告还具体指出了被告的一些不合理做法，如缺乏财力，未经授权进行毫无意义的设计修改而浪费大量时间，没有进行适当的监督管理，以及生产原告竞争对手的电子门闩而对原告的产品造成损害等。原告以"机会损失"(loss of a chance)的名义向被告索赔利润损失，理由是如果被告恰当地履行他的合约责任，原告就有机会赚取这些利润。被告抗辩说他没有违约，反而是他在合作协议的条文下有权取消合作协议，只要是继续履行协议在"商业上变得不可行"(no longer commercially viable)，而且原告以"机会损失"索赔是投机和不现实的。

高院的 Flaux 大法官判是被告胜诉。首先，原告取消合约的时候实际上并没有发生被告违约的情况。虽然原告主张在该案件争议发生的半年前，被告曾有3个月的延误履行合约，但这个延误并不是持续性的及没有补救，不算是被告违约/毁约，所以原告无权以此为理由在合约条文下取消合作协议。

其次,假设原告确实有权以被告违约/毁约为由取消合作协议,那么在考虑给原告的赔偿时就要以“复原”的原则看如果合作协议被履行会有什么结果。法院根据案情认定,原告在取消合约之前已经决定改变产品设计,假设合约没有被取消而是继续履行,原告作出的这个改变也会使履行延误3个月,这与实际中被告延误了3个月没有区别,所以被告先前的延误即使被认定为违约/毁约,也不会对原告造成损失。另外在合作协议约定下,如果原告的行动造成延误,被告有一个是否取消该协议的裁量权,他可自行决定是否取消合约。那么,如果被告以一个合理商人的角度判断,会不会认为这个合约已经变得没有商业上的可行性?高院认为,如果原告的行动导致延误,被告行使合作协议赋予的裁量权取消合作协议是完全正当合理的做法。高院也驳回了原告索赔“机会损失”的请求,因为双方没有对利润分配做出约定,而且原告对汽车门闩市场的设想是不现实的,他所说的“机会损失”完全是臆猜出来的,这无法使他证明他有任何实际的损失。

Flaux大法官是这样说:“Even if C(原告)had been entitled to terminate by reason of delay, it would have had insuperable difficulties in establishing that that breach had caused loss, because of the decision before termination to develop a smaller version of the latch which was always going to cause at least three months delay to the project because of the need to build soft tooled prototypes and validate the design. Further any case that C had suffered any substantial recoverable loss as a consequence of breach caused by delay would face another formidable obstacle in the form of art. 10.3 of the agreement which permitted H(被告)to terminate if it determined, in its sole discretion, that the continued performance of the agreement was not commercially viable. Article 10.3 was a provision which gave H an option in certain circumstances to terminate the contract, not merely a power to make a determination in good faith, Lavarack v. Woods of Colchester (1967) 1 Q. B. 278 and Maredelanto Compania Naviera SA v. Bergbau-Handel GmbH (The Mihalis Angelos) (1971) 1 Q. B. 164 considered. The court had to assess the extent to which the contract was no longer commercially viable at the date of termination or would have become commercially unviable soon thereafter. That was not the same thing as H having to establish that on a balance of probabilities it would have exercised the right to terminate under art. 10.3(这一条文给了被告是否取消合约的裁量权). Rather what had to be considered was whether the circumstances of the collaboration were such that, due to matters other than H's own breach of contract, H could have formed the view, without acting arbitrarily or perversely or irrationally, that the contract was no longer commercially viable. The circumstances of the collaboration as it stood at the date of termination were such as would have fully justified H in determining that the continued performance of the agreement was not commercially viable.”

换言之，Flaux 大法官在针对损失计算的违约方最低合约责任为准的原则下，认为被告是会行使他这一个选择权以商业上变得不可行为由终断合约，而且这样选择根据提供的证据与争辩来看应该不是武断的、荒谬的或者是不合理的。

7. 英国法院更愿意默示违约方的裁量权有限制

从上述的先例看来，这一个看似简单的原则适用在不同的案情还是不容易。这困难就是是否严格适用以违约方"最低合约责任为准的原则"（minimum performance principle），不论这一个最低合约责任如果实际履行是多么不合理、不现实与不大可能会发生？或是客观看如果有关合约获得顺利履行，估计或推测怎么样才算是一个合理与现实的履行？从介绍的案例看来，在以前比较严格以违约方最低合约责任为准，最高峰的就是 The "World Navigator" (1991) 2 Lloyd's Rep. 23 (CA) 先例，但较近期的先例法院有趋势更多的考虑如果合约被履行。特别是针对在本章 2.2 与 2.3 段提到的合约责任或承诺类别，考虑违约方的合理与现实做法会是什么。

另一个发展是以违约方最低合约责任为准的原则计算损失看来越来越不受欢迎，被认为是偏袒违约方，如果真正履行有关合约的话是不会只做最低的合约要求。所以，已经介绍了不少先例显示了法院更加愿意"默示"（imply）违约方的选择或裁量权是必须有各种限制，包括合理、真诚与善意等，除非违约方像本章 2.1 段所讲的明示有绝对或无限制的裁量权而且不必让对方得益。这些先例有早期的 Abrahams v. Herbert Reiach Ltd (1922) 1 KB 477 与更近期的 Paula Lee Ltd v. Robert Zehil Ltd (1983) 2 All ER 390；TCN Channel 9 Pty Ltd v. Hayden Enterprises Pty Ltd (1989) 16 NSWLR 130；The "Seaflower" (2000) 2 Lloyd's Rep 37；Clark v. Nomura plc (2000) IRLR 766；And So To Bed v. Dixon (2001) FSR 935；Cantor Fitzgerald International v. Horkulak (2004) EWCA Civ. 1287；Automotive Latch Systems Ltd v. Honeywell International Inc (2008) EWHC 2171 (Comm)；Durham Tees Valley Airport Ltd v. BMI Baby Ltd. (2011) 1 Lloyd's Rep 68 等。在早期的先例有在本章 6.7 段介绍过的 Paula Lee Ltd v. Robert Zehil Ltd (1983) 2 All ER 390，案情涉及买卖合约，买方（原告）在合约中购买批发服装的选择权被视为是买方选择合理服装的承诺，而不是统一购买廉价部分的产品。另在本章 6.2 段详细介绍过的 Abrahams v. Herbert Reiach Ltd (1922) 1 KB 477 先例中，对不履行出版合约的损失赔偿计算要以合理会出版的书籍数量为准。尽管从合约条文来看出版社对出版书籍的形式和数量有完全的自由裁量权，但法院拒绝以出版社有权印制最低数量（1 本）计算损失，否则就不能称之为"出版"（publication）。

较近期的先例是更多是这种考虑，较早所提到先例的有关案情都已经在本章介绍过，除了 Clark v. Nomura plc (2000) IRLR 766 先例。该先例简单的案情是被错误解雇的高级雇员有权要求雇主赔偿他的奖金损失,因为虽然雇主有不受限制的取消奖金制度的权利,但他也有义务合理对待雇员。

即使合约中不存在选择或裁量权,而是要求违约方单一的履行(这在本章2.3段有介绍),以违约方最低合约责任为准的原则计算损失也不令人满意,其中可节录Michael Ashcroft御用大律师在2007年伦敦的国际海事仲裁员大会(International Congress of Maritime Arbitrators)的发言中对The"World Navigator"(1991)2 Lloyd's Rep. 23(CA)先例做出的批评,认为太偏袒违约的承租人,说:

"In my view, the way in which the so-called principle was applied by the Court of Appeal in The "World Navigator" represents a harsh result which favours the wrongdoer in a way that departs from commercial reality. As I see it, the Court of Appeal paid too much attention to the side of the coin marked 'performance least beneficial to the innocent party', it virtually ignored the other side of the coin marked 'performance most beneficial/least burdensome to the guilty party', exemplified by the passage from McGregor.

If one asks the question: but for the breach, how would the guilty party have performed so as to gain maximum benefit for himself, the answer would *prima facie* be: by loading with customary speed. To put in at its lowest, in the case of a seller, the more quickly the vessel is loaded, the earlier he will be able to present documents to his buyer and to get payment. Thus, in the absence of market movements which might mean that it is in the seller's interest to delay loading, it will ordinarily be in his interest to ship the goods as soon as possible....

To revert toThe "World Navigator", if the vessel had been able to berth earlier, she would in all likelihood have been loaded within a fraction of the laydays. Why in such circumstances should one artificially give credit to the wrongdoing for time which the vessel would never have occupied? The rhetorical question can be presented even more forcefully if it can be shown that commercially it was to the seller's advantage to load the vessel as fast as possible. Why could it not be said that, to approach the issue on the basis that the seller would have detained the vessel to the full extent of the laydays, would indeed be to assume that he would 'cut off his nose to spite his face'?"

还有其他原因或理由支持认为违约方即使是涉及单一的履行合约责任,也应该估计或推测怎样才是将来可能会发生的"事情",如果有关合约被顺利履行,而不是机械性地以最低合约责任为准。这些理由是如下:

(1)贵族院在The"Golden Victory"(2007)2 Lloyd's Rep 164先例以多数意见判是违约的承租人只需要以变数(海湾战争)发生后会导致合约终断的责任计算损失,换言之是估计或推测违约方会怎样合理履行与反应。这一来,即使是没有发生变数的情况下,也应该估计或推测违约方会怎样合理与实际的履行,否则就会针对两种情况有不一致的考虑。这就不是像The"World Navigator"那样漠视已经发生了的事实,还是一面倒只以违约方的履行会是以最低赔偿责任为准。

(2)对不肯定的事实如将来的“事实”,无法有明确的证据证明,英国法律有一个说法是“假设是要去针对违约方/侵权方”(presumption against a wrongdoer [拉丁文的 *omnia praesumuntur contra spoliatorem*])。这一个说法早在 Coldman v. Hill (1919) 1 KB 443 (CA)先例中上诉庭的 Scrutton 大法官就有说:“The House of Lords held that the man who had, by breaking his contract, destroyed the possibility of any evidence on the subject, could not be heard to say that there was no evidence that his breach of contract caused the loss. It was his duty as bailee to prove that his breach of duty did not cause the loss, not the plaintiff' s duty to show that it did. This appears to be merely an application of the principle *omnia praesumuntur contra spoliatorem*, under which a man who, having converted property, refuses to produce it that its exact value may be known, is liable for the greatest value that such article could have.”

这一个说法的使用当然也是要掌握好轻重,否则就会把受害方对他蒙受损失的举证责任转移给了违约方。但这说法显然是有损失计算不应该善待违约方的味道,也表示损失计算以违约方最低合约责任为准的原则有商榷的余地。

总结说严格适用以违约方最低合约责任为准的原则计算损失只局限在合约条文明确给予违约方一个绝对与没有限制的选择权,特别是有明示约定如合约规定了违约方有一个“绝对裁量权”(absolute discretion)等措辞。也就不存在可以默示违约方行使裁量权会有合理的限制。特别是违约方如果真的履行合约,选择行使这一个裁量权下的最低责任的确有可能会发生。

8. 违约/毁约后外来事件或变数带来对合约承诺价值的影响

在一个没有被履行的合约承诺的价值,看来在一连串的有关先例是接受在估计或推测将来如果履行会发生的“外来事件或变数”(extraneous event or contingency),甚至在审理时已经发生了的外来事件或变数,是要从违约方最低合约责任的角度加以考虑并调整或减少损失的计算。这些先例有 The “Mihalis Angelos” (1970) 2 Lloyd' s Rep. 43; The “Seaflower” (2000) 2 Lloyd' s Rep 37; The “Golden Victory” (2007) 2 Lloyd' s Rep 164 等。至于一些权威的说法也可以节录,如在 Lavarack v. Woods of Colchester Ltd. (1967) 1 QB 278 先例,Diplock 大法官说:“The assumption to be made is that the defendant has performed or will perform his legal obligations under his contract with the plaintiff and nothing more. What these legal obligations are and what is their *value* to the plaintiff may depend upon the occurrence of events extraneous to the contract itself and, where this is so, the probability of their occurrence is relevant to the estimate.”

另在 The “Golden Victory” (2005) 2 Lloyd' s Rep. 747 (CA)先例,上诉庭的

Mance 勋爵说："account might have to be taken of the contingency . . . or chance . . . that a war might occur, and consideration would then also have to be given to whether or not charterers would in that event probably cancel."

在估计或推测将来如果履行会有什么外来事件或变数,这显然是以合理性与是否很可能会发生为准。例如在 Lavarak v. Woods of Colchester Ltd. 先例,案情涉及被错误解雇的雇员向雇主索赔如果雇佣合约被履行可能会发放的奖金,但这一个机会因为雇主违约而失去。其中谈到一个变数是雇主会否将来把公司清盘导致不可能发放奖金,Diplock 大法官认为是不应该加以考虑,因为不合理,雇主是不会搬起石头砸自己的脚,为了避免向雇员发放奖金自动清盘令自己蒙受更大的损失。Diplock 大法官是这样说："The events extraneous to the contract, upon the occurrence of which the legal obligations of the defendant to the plaintiff thereunder are dependent, may include events which are within the control of the defendant: for instance, his continuing to carry on business even though he has not assumed by his contract a direct legal obligation to the plaintiff to do so. Where this is so, one must not assume that **he will cut off his nose to spite his face** and so control these events as to reduce his obligations to the plaintiff by incurring greater loss in other respects."(加黑部分是笔者的强调)

9."Mihalis Angelos"原则对损失计算影响的延伸

众所周知,The "Golden Victory" (2007) 2 Lloyd's Rep 164 是很富争议的先例,因为它冲击了英国引以为傲的 Breach Date Rule 与 Market Rule。其中持这种批评看法可以看本书第十三章之 6.3 段前大法官 Anthony Colman 先生所说的："This has to be the worst decision on any aspect of English Commercial Law and certainly shipping law that has come out of the House of Lords in my entire career in the legal profession."但毕竟这就是当今英国普通法的地位。对笔者来说,这是更早的 The "Mihalis Angelos" (1970) 2 Lloyd's Rep. 43 先例或 Mihalis Angelos 原则的延伸。这方面的延伸在本章之 6.10 段的 The "Seaflower" (2000) 2 Lloyd's Rep 37 先例已经有显示,在 The "Golden Victory"先例更是进一步的延伸。这些延伸都反映了针对损失计算,是以违约方最低合约责任为准的原则。

这方面可节录《McGregor on Damages》(18th edn, 2009 年)一书之 8－098 与 8－099段提到 The "Seaflower"先例所说："This case shows that the principle in The 'Mihalis Angelos' is not confined to anticipatory breaches or to predestined events. Where the charterers' right to cancel is neither predestined to happen, as in The 'Mihalis Angelos', nor anticipated in certain events, as in The 'Seaflower', but at the time of breach lies in the mists of the future and yet by the time of trial events have come about which would have given the charterers the right to cancel, the question arises as to whether the court, in assessing the shipowners' damages, is entitled to take into account that the charterers could and would eventually have rightfully cancelled. This issue arose in the 'Golden Victory' where there was a repudiatory, though not anticipatory, breach of a charterparty by the charterers. The charter was a time charter for a seven-year period and at repudiation had nearly four more years to run. The owners claimed the normal measure of damages based upon the difference between the charter rate and the lower market rate for the four years but, because the contract would have entitled the charterers to cancel on the outbreak of the Second Gulf War between the UK and Iraq some 14 months after the repudiation, it was held by a bare majority of the House of Lords, affirming the unanimous courts below, that the owners' claim for damages ran only for this shorter period. It was said that the point at issue had never been considered by the House and remained open for decision, there being no definitive previous authority."

但这三个重要的先例都涉及违约方在合约中有一个终断合约的"选择权"(option),只要发生某些事情。这一来,只要能够证明这些事情将来"命中注定会发生"(predestined to happen)或是在审理的时候已经发生,法律就可以假设违约方会行使他的权利选择终断合约以减少或排除赔偿责任。注意的是,合约的选择权与违约/毁约不必要有任何关系,如在 The "Mihalis Angelos"先例船舶赶不及在租约销约期前到装港并不一定会涉及船东的过错,另在 The "Golden Victory"先例更是涉及海湾战争给了违约方的承租人一个终断合约的选择,更加是与船东(承租人)的过错无关。

但看来,这一个 Mihalis Angelos 原则也在延伸去其他方面,如受害方事后被发觉与证明无法或无意履行他的合约责任,或是违反了合约的"条件条文"(condition)等"违约/毁约"(repudiatory breach)。这种情况非常普遍,如在货物买卖,买方拒绝开出信用证或是接受货物,这构成了违约/毁约,并且被受害方接受终断买卖合约。看来责任是明确,但在损失计算会否在违约方的买方如果能够事后发觉并证明卖方没有能力提供合约约定的货物或是付运了有缺陷的货物的情况下可以避免赔付任何卖方的损失?这种案件不少,如在 Taylor v. Oakes, Roncoroni & Co. (1922) 127 L. T. 267 先例中,Scrutton 大法官提到违约方的买方可以说:"Oh, but if I had not repudiated, you would not have been able to deliver the goods according to the contract."在这种情况下,在以下的段节会进一步探讨在责任方面与损失方面的影响。

9.1　违约/毁约有否被受害方接受或拒绝接受在责任方面的探讨

这方面的法律对大部分读者应该十分了解。只是简单说,如果 A 做出了"违约/毁约"(repudiatory breach)的语言或者行为,B 作为受害方就有两个选择。第一个选择就是接受违约/毁约终断有关的合约,第二个选择就是确认合约的存在,也就是拒绝接受 A 的违约/毁约(这包括了预期违约),并坚持合约的有效存在。B 是没有第三个选择,正如 Ackner 勋爵在 The "Simona" (1988) 2 Lloyd's Rep 199 先例所说:"When A wrongfully repudiates his contractual obligations in anticipation of the time for their performance, he presents the innocent party B with two choices. He may either affirm the contract by treating it as still in force or he may treat is as finally had conclusively discharged. There is no third choice..."

当然,如果 B 坚持合约的有效存在,这会导致 A 有可能回心转意继续履行,这就等于什么事情都没有发生过一样。但如果在之后的履行发生了变数导致合约受阻或合法被终断,无辜方就会后悔没有接受较早时的违约/毁约,因为他可以索赔损失,但合约受阻或合约被合法终断就要自己承受损失了。这方面的说法在《Chitty on Contracts》(30th edn, 2008 年)之 24-024 段介绍的 Avery v. Bowden (1856) 6 E & B 953 先例明确了这方面,但由于本书篇幅有限,所以不在此多谈。

重要的是如果 B 拒绝接受 A 的违约/毁约,等于什么事情都没有发生过,就带来一个问题是 B 不能指称 A 是违约方,更加不会有任何诉因向 A 索赔损失。这也是很明确地显示在 Ackner 勋爵在 The "Simona" 先例的判决:"If an unaccepted repudiation has no legal effect ('a thing writ in water and of no value to anybody'-per Lord Justice Asquith in Howard v. Pickford Tool Co [1951] 1 KB 417 at p. 421) how can the unaccepted acts of repudiation by the charterers in this case provide the owners with any cause of action?"

这就带来一个做法就是合约双方都在互相指责对方拒绝履行合约,或是其中一方知道自己将来没有办法履行合约,就会掌握机会先一步接受对方的违约/毁约。这一来,先一步的合约方 B 就变为受害方,而慢一步的合约方 A 就变为违约方。这种看谁动得快先击中对方的"击剑"(swordplay)经常会出现。例如在造船合约,船厂自己知道将来无法在死亡日期或销约期之前把船舶完成建造与交船给买方,甚至是各种原因(如资金问题)根本无法完成建造,但碰巧买方无法按照造船合约准时支付其中一期的预付船价,这就会给船厂一个机会先一步接受买方的违约/毁约(或按照合约的选择权终断)。这一来,船厂就变为受害方,在责任方面他也不需要证明他能够履行有关的合约。毕竟这造船合约已经终断,船厂能否履行已经是变为无关,也没有必要追究。

这方面的说法可看《Chitty on Contracts》(30th edn, 2008 年)之 24-023 段:"If the breach is accepted, the innocent party is relieved from further performance of his obligations under the contract. He is likewise relived from proving, in any action against the party in default, that he was ready and willing at the date of the renunciation to perform the contract in accordance with its terms. It follows that it is no defence to liability in such an action to show that, if the contract had not been renounced, the innocent party would not at the time fixed for performance have been able to perform it, although proof of such inability to perform might possibly be material in the assessment of damages."

9.2 违约/毁约有否被受害方接受或拒绝接受在损失方面的探讨

9.2.1 没有被接受的违约/毁约会在损失计算加以考虑的法律地位

但在针对损失方面的计算,与上一段所讲的责任方面就看来很不一样。简单的原因是“击剑”(swordplay)的情况下谁先动得快会是变为无关,因为在 Mihalis Angelos 原则的持续延伸下,B 作为受害方如果向 A 的违约方索赔损失,A 就会可以指出 B 也有违约/毁约(这包括是证明 B 根本无法或无意履行),只是 A 慢了一步或是不知道而没有接受。但在损失计算方面,就应该假设 A 作为违约方会接受并终断合约,以减轻他的赔偿责任。

在这种情况下,针对责任与损失方面有不同的对待,早在 Esmail v. J. Rosenthal & Sons Ltd (1964) 2 Lloyd' s Rep 447 先例,Salmon 大法官说:“It was at this stage that the sellers'(受害方) accepted the buyers'(违约方) wrongful repudiation and the contract was rescinded. Accordingly the contract came to an end before the sellers' had committed any breach. There was no question of the buyers' bringing the contract to an end after a fundamental breach by the sellers. What might or might not have occurred had there been no total breach by the buyers accepted by the sellers could not affect the issue of liability **but it might be most material on the issue of damage**.”(加黑部分是笔者的强调)

另在上一段所节录的《Chitty on Contract》(30th edn,2008 年)之 24－023 段也在最后一句清楚说明责任与损失计算在受害方自已也无法或无意履行合约时会有不同的对待,这与 Salmon 大法官的说法是一致的。

对应以上所讲的不明确法律地位,在杨大志律师所撰写的第十九章有关衍生品工具有以明示条文针对。这是因为在 2008 年全球金融危机后,许多银行都陷入朝不保夕的困境,很容易带来一个争议就是胜诉方也没有办法证明它能够履行有关的合约,所以损失计算应该加以考虑。针对 1992 年 ISDA 主协议下提前终止的付款金额,在第十九章之 5.3.1.2.2 段提到 Briggs 大法官在 Anthracite Rated Investments (Jersey) Ltd v. Lehman Brothers Finance SA (in liquidation) (2011) EWHC 1822 (Ch) 先例中明确非违约方因衍生交易终止而产生的交易损失需要一个对所丧失交易“纯粹的”(clear)而不是“非纯粹的”(dirty)市场估值过程。这意味着交易损失的计算会基于下述假定情况发生,而其可实现的利益,即假定交易没有终止,交易会顺利履行直到结束,并且双方全部履行的所有条件都已满足。也就是说违约方在计算损失时不能考虑非违约方的资信状况与有否能力顺利履行。

9.2.2 有关先例之一:Samsung Hong Kong Ltd v. Keen Time Trading Ltd

这方面近期的先例有不少,笔者在接下去只会简单介绍两个先例,一个是香港上诉庭的 Samsung Hong Kong Ltd v. Keen Time Trading Ltd (Civil Appeal No. 240 of 1998),另一个是英国上诉庭近期的 De Montfort Fine Art v. Acre 1127 (in liquidation) (2011) EWCA Civ. 87 先例。

首先是 Samsung Hong Kong Ltd v. Keen Time Trading Ltd 先例,案情十分类似在本

章 9 段介绍的买卖合约例子，并提到 Taylor v. Oakes, Roncoroni & Co.（1922）127 L.T. 267 先例的情况。被告的买方拒绝开出信用证，于是原告的卖方向法院提起索赔诉讼。但被告事后发现原告的聚酯纤维只有 1.4 纤度而不是合约描述的 1.5 纤度，根据香港《Sale of Goods Ordinance》，这是违反了默示的条件条文，被告可以拒货。法院最后是判原告只能获得名义赔偿。而其中上诉庭的刘大法官说："The law would presume that the defendant here, having an option to reject delivery on account of wrong description, would exercise it to its best to reject delivery on account of wrong description, would exercise it to its best advantage so as to reduce or extinguish any claim for loss by the plaintiff... The law recognizes the reality that whenever possible a buyer in default would elect to take a position where he could look to minimum performance."（这是说法律应该假设被告如果有权利拒绝接受这批不符合描述的货物，他就会这样做减少他要对原告作出的赔偿。这就是说以违约方最低合约责任为准的原则适用。）

另陈兆恺大法官说："I do not think that the Court of Appeal there went so far as to require that a defendant must prove that he would have accepted the plaintiff's breach or that he had to prove that beyond a reasonable doubt."（在举证方面，陈大法官并不要求被告证明他必定会终断合约，拒收这票不符合描述的货物。换言之，法律只是假设被告有这一个法律的权利，如同合约的选择权，他是会行使以减少赔偿的金额。）

9.2.3 有关先例之二：De Montfort Fine Art v. Acre 1127（in liquidation）

De Montfort Fine Art v. Acre 1127（in liquidation）（2011）EWCA Civ. 87 先例涉及被告的买方承诺每季度向原告的卖方购买最低数量的当代商业艺术品。反正这也是一个常见的双方互指对方违约的案例，而对笔者重要的是上诉庭的 Tomlinson 大法官所作出的判词（在 51 段）："It is equally clear in my judgment that Castle（被告的买方）can recover no damages from De Montfort（原告的卖方）consequent upon De Montfort's repudiatory breach of the agreement. Whilst Castle was did not immediately terminate the contract on account of De Montfort's repudiatory breach, Castle was neither ready nor willing to perform the contract itself and it did not seek further performance from De Montfort. In such circumstances Castle can in my judgment maintain no claim against De Montfort. The situation is analogous to that discussed in cases such as Braithwaite v. Foreign Hardwood Company（1905）2KB 543, British and Beningtons Ltd v. North Western Cachar Tea Co（1923）AC 48 and Cooper, Ewing & Co Ltd v. Hamel & Horley Ltd（1923）13 Ll L Rep 590. Cases such as these establish the principle that a repudiating party has a defence to a claim in respect of that breach by the innocent party if he can establish that, at the time of the repudiation, **the innocent party was already irremediably disabled from performance**, provided that that inability to perform on the part of the innocent party is not itself attributable to the repudiatory breach. The same result must in my view follow if it can be shown not that the innocent party was disabled from performance, but that **he had no in-**

tention of performing. Castle's unwillingness to perform was not a consequence of De Montfort's repudiatory breach, it long pre-dated it. The problem of course more usually arises in a case where the repudiation is immediately accepted as terminating the contract."(加黑部分是笔者的强调)

9.2.4 总结

总结而言,看来英国法律在这方面的发展显示在损失计算方面就是"击剑"(swordplay)做法下谁先接受对方的违约/毁约已经是区别不大。有区别的只是在责任方面,这还是有一定的作用,因为英国法律的另一个大原则是违约方不能向受害方取回他的任何损失。这可以造船合约案件为例,就是假设船厂明知道自己不能按照合约完成建造有关的船舶,甚至工程已经开始处于半停顿状态。但在之前有了一个机会是买方拒绝准时支付预付船价,或是威胁船厂如果不大幅度减价就不再要这艘船舶。这会是违约/毁约或预期违约,船厂可以接受并终断造船合约。这一来船厂就变为是受害方的原告,但在索赔损失方面会面临上述所讲的问题,就是违约方的买方会能够说服仲裁庭船厂自己也不能或不愿履行合约,或"命中注定"(predestined to happen)不能在死亡日期前交船,所以不存在有任何实质的损失。但买方作为违约方也恐怕十分困难向船厂反索赔并取回已经支付了的预付船价。

最后一提的是笔者的感觉英国法律对这方面好像在放宽,但相比本章之7段讲的收紧是有区别,虽然在本质上在针对违约方只需要以最低合约责任计算损失。

第十一章　债务与损失的区别

1. 序言

了解"债务"(debt)与"损失"(damages)的区别,在很多方面十分重要。简单说,如果在合约中一方当事人(可称为违约方)承诺支付一笔金钱但他没有做到,这就会带来债务的索赔。但如果合约中一方当事人(也可称为是违约方)承诺做一点事情但他没有做到,这就会带来损失的索赔,因为需要把这一个承诺量化为一笔金钱(或变为判决债务)。合约中其他的条文如对某一些事实作出保证但被违反,这也会带来损失,因为违约方在这些条文并非承诺支付一笔金钱。损失通常是"非议定"(unliquidated),所以要通过计算与证明。而所有针对损失的限制如"遥远性"(remoteness)的"因果关系"(causation)与可否"合理预见"(reasonably foreseeable),受害方有否"合理减少损失"(reasonable mitigation)等全部适用。所以,损失计算的争议经常带来漫长与昂贵的诉讼。读者只要看本书所涉及的内容就可以知道计算损失是一个非常复杂的课题,这都不是一笔债务所需要面对的,即使债务有争议(如在计算方面,有没有符合先决条件或是抵销等问题)。债务与损失的不同或被视为是两码事可介绍英国有关损失计算的权威书籍《McGregor on Damages》(18th edn,2009 年)并没有针对债务,只是在 1-005 段简单地说:"Actions claiming money payable by the terms of a contract and for money which the defendant has promised by the contract to pay and therefore are not actions for damages. Illustrations are provided by actions for the price of goods sold and delivered, actions for salary or wages for services rendered, actions for rent, actions for freight and actions to recover money payable under insurance policies. In traditional terminology the contrast is between actions of debt and actions for damages. Actions of debt are to be distinguished from actions for damages for breach of a contract and are outside the scope of this textbook."

有关债务与损失之间的分别,可进一步简单介绍如下。

1.1　区别之一:债务是首要合约义务的违反,损失只是次要合约义务的违反

先简单介绍什么是合约中的"首要合约义务"(primary obligation)与"次要合约义务"(secondary obligation)。首要合约义务在所有的商业合约中都会有,就是其中一方承诺做一些事情。这可以是承诺把财产/货物的所有权转移以交换对方支付货价

的承诺;承诺把货物从一个地方运去另一个地方;承诺按照图纸建造一栋房子或一座桥梁等。承诺首要合约义务的内容与程度完全是订约自由,是要做出承诺的人自己控制自己合约的命运。一份订得好的商业合约会对双方做出的首要合约义务承诺规定得很细,但通常还是无法包罗万有。所以英国法律还会在没有明示条文针对的情况下默示一些合理的首要合约义务,如双方必须给予协助/合作以让对方顺利履行合约:Mona Oil Equipment & Supply Co Ltd v. Rhodesia Railways Ltd (1949) 2 All ER 1014先例。例如事先通知对方银行账户以利对方可以准时按照合约做出支付,这合约不说明也是有默示责任。

而次要合约义务就是指做出承诺的合约方违反了他做出的首要合约义务承诺,这会是拒绝履行或是有缺陷履行首要合约义务,就会带来法律默示的次要合约义务,就是对这一个违约产生的损失向受害方做出金钱上的赔偿。这一个默示的次要合约义务通常也会在订约自由下有明示条文针对,如对赔偿的金额有一个限制。但现实中不会有明示条文完全排除这一默示的次要合约义务,如约定双方违约也不必做出任何赔偿。

有关首要合约义务与次要合约义务的说法在许多先例中有提及,笔者只随便节录,首先是Diplock勋爵在Photo Production v. Securicor (1980) 1 Lloyd's Rep 545先例中的著名说法如下:

"Leaving aside those comparatively rare cases in which the Court is able to enforce a primary obligation by decreeing specific performance of it, breaches of primary obligations give rise to substituted or secondary obligations on the part of the party in default, and, in some cases, may entitle the other party to be relieved from further performance of his own primary obligations. These secondary obligations of the contract breaker and any concomitant relief of the other party from his own primary obligations also arise by implication of law – generally common law, but sometimes statute, as in the case of codifying statutes passed at the turn of the century, notably the Sale of Goods Act 1893. The contract, however, is just as much the source of secondary obligations as it is of primary obligations; and like primary obligations that are implied by law, secondary obligations too can be modified by agreement between the parties, although, for reasons to be mentioned later, they cannot, in my view, be totally excluded. In the instant case, the only secondary obligations and concomitant reliefs that are applicable arise by implication of the common law as modified by the express words of the contract... Every failure to perform a primary obligation is a breach of contract. The secondary obligation on the part of the contract breaker to which it gives rise by implication of the common law is to pay monetary compensation to the other party for the loss sustained by him in consequence of the breach..."

事实上Diplock勋爵较早已经在Moschi v. Lep Air Services Ltd (1973) AC 331先例讲到违约方在违反了他的首要合约义务后,就有了次要合约义务,说:"But for his primary obligations there is substituted by operation of law a secondary obligation to pay to the other party a sum of money to compensate him for the loss he has sustained as a result of the failure to perform the primary obligations. This secondary obligation is just as much an obligation arising from the contract as are the primary obligations that it replaces: see R. V. Ward Ltd. v. Bignall [1967] 1 Q. B. 534,548."

这就可以说明债务与损失的区别,首先是债务的产生完全取决于合约中明示或默示的约定,这不像损失是来自一般的法律。而且损失赔偿是违约方在合约下的次要合约义务,所以必须先有一个合约中的首要合约义务被违反才会有次要合约义务的产生。换言之,必须先有一个违约才会有损失赔偿这一回事。例如在买卖合约中卖方没有履行他要提供货物的首要合约义务,才会带来赔偿金钱损失的次要合约义务。但债务不需要证明对方违约,往往只需要看合约的条文就可以明确到底有没有这个债务的产生与存在。

简单地说,较早的介绍提到合约承诺把财产/货物的所有权转移以交换对方的承诺支付货价,这是一个典型的买卖合约。卖方如果不把财产/货物所有权转让,这是违反首要合约义务并且有了赔偿损失的次要合约义务。但如果卖方履行了他的承诺,反过来是买方没有支付货价,由于支付是合约中明示的规定,就表示买方违反了首要合约义务。由于首要合约义务就是做出支付,所以这是一笔债务,与损失没有关系。

1.2 区别之二:债务通常可以通过法院的简易判决追偿

由于债务不需要受害人提供证明与计算金额(除了有关的一份合约与没有按照合约条文收到承诺支付的钱),所以受害人通常会喜欢索赔债务而不喜欢索赔损失。这可以在诉讼中快速与省钱地取得法院判决(如果是英国法院的管辖就通常可以取得"简易判决"[summary judgment])或在仲裁庭可能是很快的裁决:The "Kostas Melas" [1981] 1 Lloyd's Rep 18)。

随便举一个例子,在造船合约中就有一些著名的有关先例如 Hyundai Heavy Industries Co Ltd v. Papadopoulos (1980) 2 Lloyd's Rep 1 与 Stocznia Gdanska SA v. Latvian Shipping Co (2002) 2 Lloyd's Rep 436。造船合约支付船价的办法一般是按照造船的进度做出分期付款,如果买方没有做出支付,通常合约条文会允许船厂终断合约。对这笔欠下的价款,船厂是可以向买方以债务提出索赔。但如果船厂是要以损失索赔(如买方明确告诉船厂他不会支付下一期即将届临的分期付款,并被船厂接受这一个预期违约,但当时下一期价款的支付日期还没有届临),就会要船厂经过漫长与复杂的事后处理与合理减少损失才能明确船东的违约/毁约到底带来什么损失并与买方结算总账,包括把有关的船舶完成或改装,然后在市场转售。还有是在造船合约,买方通常会为支付船价的分期付款提供担保(如让他的融资银行或母公司作为担保人),但担保的范围就不一定包括非议定的损失赔偿。显然,尤其是对付皮包公司的买方,船厂都会希望索赔债务,或者先走一步尽快把这笔资金取回来,以免花多年的时间在明确与能够证明损失后,向皮包公司的买方提出索赔,落得最后可能是胜诉也没有实质结果,除了船厂要花一大笔律师费用。所以在 Hyundai Heavy Industries Co Ltd v. Papadopoulos 先例,涉及由于航运市场下跌,船东与担保人都没有支付第二期的船价。船厂也就根据造船合约终断合约,并接受了船东的违约/毁约。之后船厂向担保人在英国法院以简易判决索赔已经到期的第二期船价,但担保人作为被告声称造船合约在船厂作出告票之前已经失效。担保人争辩说在作出告票的一天,就再也不可以为分期付款的船价提出债务的索赔,剩下的只是船厂向船东索赔损失的权利。但这不被贵族院接受。另在 Stocznia Gdanska SA v. Latvian Shipping Co 先例,由于案情比较复杂,所以不详细介绍,但本质上船厂的做法也是一样,以债务索赔第二期的船价。

这里可以简单介绍有关简易判决的做法。在英国法院,繁琐的程序规则往往导致漫长与昂贵的诉讼,为了解决这个问题,《民事诉讼规则》(Civil Procedure Rules)第 24 章规定,在适当情况下,原告或被告可以申请法院做出简易判决来避免繁琐的诉讼程序,也可以根据《民事诉讼规则》第 25 章申请"中间付款"(interim payment)。

《民事诉讼规则》第 24.2 条规定,法院可以针对整个诉讼请求或其中任何一个争论点对原告或被告做出简易判决。其中有以下的针对:

(1)给予简易判决的尺度:如果法院认为原告在他所提出的诉讼请求或争论点上没有"真正胜诉的可能性"(real prospect of succeeding),法院就会对原告做出败诉的简易判决。同样,如果法院认为被告在他所提出的抗辩或争论点上没有"真正胜诉的可能性",就会对被告做出简易判决,并要求被告支付索赔的金钱。另外,法院必须确定没有任何其他理由需要继续审理(包括是开庭)这个案件或争论点,才能对此做出简易判决。《民事诉讼规则》第 24 章的"实践指引"(Practice Direction)的第 4 段规定,如果法院认为某个诉讼请求或抗辩有机会胜诉但可能性不大,法院可以做出"有条件的命令"(conditional order)。第 5 段列举了法院可以在当事人申请下做出的命令,包括:针对诉讼请求的判决(a judgment on the claim);驳回或不受理诉讼请求(the striking out or dismissal of the claim);驳回申请(the dismissal of the application);有条件的命令(conditional order)。有条件的命令是法院让一方当事人或者交给法院一笔钱,或者采取与他的诉讼请求或抗辩有关的行动(这会根据具体案件事实来决定),否则他的诉讼请求就会被驳回或者他的案件陈述就不会被法院受理。

有说法是简易判决现在的标准比以前的标准范围更广,以前的测试标准是看针对诉讼请求是否有一个"可争辩的抗辩"(arguable defence)。所以即使某个争论点是可争辩的,如果法院认为在审理中这个争论点确实没有真正胜诉的可能性,法院依然会做出简易判决。

但对于在什么情况下法院会做出有条件的命令却很难预测,因为从它的定义来看,只有法院认为某个诉讼请求或抗辩有真正胜诉的可能性,但胜诉机会不大,才会做出有条件的命令。这可能会出现在案件审理的中间阶段,当时法院很难判断这个诉讼请求或抗辩会败诉,但是根据该案件的诉讼请求或抗辩,法院对能否胜诉的机会有怀疑。

(2)申请简易判决的证据要求:根据《民事诉讼规则》第 24 章,申请简易判决的步骤,基本证据要求和时间要求规定在第 24 章的补充性实践指引中。由于这是民事诉讼改革之后介绍的新规则和新要求,关于它的举证责任和证明标准的早期先例只能提供有限的指引。

(3)法律观点:在民事诉讼改革之前,如果被告提出了一个可争辩的法律观点,通常实践是如果法院认为被告提出的抗辩"站不住脚"(bad),即使是可争辩的,法院仍然会做出简易判决,而不考虑有争议的事实(因为认定事实是需要证据,涉及口头证据就免不了开庭)。但如果被告提出的法律观点导致了法院有"一个严肃的问题要审理"(serious question to be tried),需要详细的论证和成熟的考虑,这个法律观点就不适合以简易判决来处理。从理论上说在新的制度下也不应该有什么实质上的不同。所以《民事诉讼规则》第 24 章规定的简易判决是适用于仅存在一个简单的法律观点,才可以简易处理:Crown Hourse Engineering v. Amec Projects (1989) 48 BLR 32。如果被告的抗辩涉及一个可争辩的问题,既包含法律问题也包含事实问题,并且有真正胜诉的可能性,那么原告申请简易判决就会被驳回。

所以,如果某个争议不需要经过完整的审理/开庭来解决,法院有权决定一个法律争议或者对一份文件做出解释。这种简易的程序可以由当事人申请来适用也可以由法院自己决定来适用。但如果有任何实质的事实争议,简易判决的程序就不适用了。

英国法院这种简易判决的做法在其他国家的法院不一定有,即使有这种简易判决,在做法上也很不一样。反正这套做法在某些商业领域很受欢迎,如银行作出担保经常喜欢加上一条英国法院管辖的"排外管辖权条文"(exclusive jurisdiction clause)。因为银行的担保不会涉及事实的争议(不需要内行人例如仲裁员去认定),对担保的金额也往往以适当的措辞/文字定性为一笔债务,所以银行只需要关心有一种省时与省钱的强制执行救济办法。银行担保通常也很少会有一条仲裁条文,因为在仲裁中没有类似法院简易判决的做法。比较接近的仲裁做法是海事仲裁员会不通过开庭对一笔在文书请求中显示被告(或原告)欠下了一笔"最起码欠的钱"(minimum sum due)很快对这笔金钱做出一个中间裁决书:The "Kostas Melas" (1981) 1 Lloyd's Rep 18。但这种做法恐怕还是比法院的简易判决慢与不肯定,毕竟在有一些仲裁案件,仅是花在成立仲裁庭的时间就已经与取得简易判决的时间差不多。

至于"中间付款"(interim payment)是法院拥有的法定权力(《The Supreme Court Act 1981》之 Section 32)针对被告很可能将来会被判要支付损失、债务或其他金额(除了诉讼费用)时先做出部分的支付。特别在法院估计将来被判要支付的金钱是金额比较庞大,或是已经没有责任的争议而只存在对损失的核算,法院就会更愿意做出中间付款的命令。至于中间付款的金额是多少,法院会有一个更大的责任小心考虑案件是否涉及原告申请人的共同疏忽、有否抵销或反索赔等方面：Shearson Lehman v. Maclain Watson & Co（1987）1 WLR 480；British Holdings v. Quadrex（1989）QB 842；Brian Breeze v. McKennon & Son（1985）32 BLR 41；Imodco v. Wimpey and Taylor Woodrow（1987）40 BLR 1。也会有情况是要考虑到底把一笔金钱根据"有条件的命令"（conditional order）存放进法院或是根据"中间付款"的命令支付给原告申请人：British Holdings v. Quadrex（1989）QB 842；Schott Kem Ltd v. Bentley（1991）1 QB 61；A Ltd v. B Ltd（1991）29 Con LR 53。

1.3　区别之三：债务不要求债权人减少损失，损失的受害人才有减损义务

债务的索赔是不要求原告债权人减少损失，债务纯粹就是按照合约的规定要求违约方支付这笔钱，这是合约履行的"首要合约义务"（primary obligation），不像其他合约条文针对其他方面的履行，如果违约方违反了首要合约义务，才会出现"次要合约义务"（secondary obligation）做出金钱上的赔偿并让受害人回到合约被履行的经济地位。这债务首要合约义务的履行是不存在受害人要合理减少损失，反正就是按照合约的规定严格履行。

这一方面在贵族院 White & Carter（Councils）Ltd v. McGregor（1962）AC 413 先例有针对。该著名先例的原告为当地议会长期提供垃圾箱，他与被告签约在垃圾箱上为被告的修车场业务做广告牌，为期 3 年。被告于签约当日即反悔并且说明他不需要这一个服务，这显然是构成"预期违约"（anticipatory breach）。笔者猜背后的原因会是被告的想法有了改变或是认为这样做广告效益不显著，有其他更好的办法。反正是被告在合约墨迹未干时就要反悔。可是原告并不接受被告的预期违约，继续按照合约为被告做这广告（也真够损的），整整 3 年！最后原告按照合约向被告索赔他履行应得的收费（广告费），这是一笔债务。而如果原告一开始就接受了被告的预期违约，他只能索赔损失。在该先例，上诉庭以多数意见判定原告可全数取回其履约应得的收费，因为是原告根据合约所赚取。原告本来可以在一开始选择接受被告的预期违约终止合约，并索赔违约/毁约的损失赔偿，而这笔损失肯定比这笔债务少，因为原告不用浪费这三年所花费的工作与成本。由于该合约一直没有终止，原告只是按照合约继续履行，所以不存在有减少损失"责任"的说法。该先例中也有少数法官认为，原告本来应该接受被告的预期违约并索赔有关损失，这会是将来估计的纯利润（合约广告费减掉估计要花费的成本），但原告却选择了花费更多的钱执行一个被告不再需要的合约。这虽然没有违反合理减少损失的大原则，但整体说是一种无谓的浪费，这正是违反了"有效益违约"（efficient breach）的说法。这听来也不无道理，但毕竟这个判例更倾向于支持另一种大原则，即无辜方有权选择是否接受对方的预期违约。其中 Reid 勋爵就提出一个说法，就是受害人如果没有一个"合法利益"（legitimate interest）就不能坚持继续履行合约，造成浪费。有关这一个可以说是对债务产生与扩大的限制，会稍后在本章第 4 段详解。

针对同一个问题的另一个先例有 Abrahams v. Performing Rights Society Ltd

(1995) ICR 1028,案情涉及一个长达5年的雇佣合约,合约内有条文约定可以提前2年做出终断雇佣的通知,但这2年也可以以支付工资作为替代。双方的争议是在这长达2年内被解雇的雇员是否有合理减少损失的责任,如另找替代工作并把赚回来的钱在这笔替代工资中扣减。这就关系到这笔替代工资到底是债务或者是损失。该先例判是这笔额外工资是属于债务,上诉庭判是雇主解雇这一位雇员并付出这2年替代工资不属于是违约,这笔钱只是合约约定要支付的钱。就算这笔钱是"议定赔偿"(liquidated damage),也在本质上不需要受害方减少损失。

同样问题另可举比较近期的先例 Codemasters Software Co Ltd v. Automobile Club de l'Ouest (No.2) (2009) EWHC 3194,原告是一家电子游戏制作公司,被告则是著名赛车比赛"勒芒24小时"的组织者,他与原告签订许可合约允许原告将这项赛事改编成游戏。合约中的第10.1条文(保证条文)约定,被告向原告提供的一切许可和资料都不会侵犯任何第三人的权利;第10.3条文约定,"任何一方(补偿方)如果因违反该许可合约中的任何协议或保证而导致另一方(受害方)被第三人索赔,补偿方应对受害方进行补偿"(each party was to indemnify the other in respect of claims arising out of any "breach or alleged breach of any agreement or warranty" made by the indemnifying party "pursuant to this agreement")。原告根据被告提供的资料,在游戏中加入了法拉利、兰博基尼和保时捷这三家名车的车型,但实际上被告并没有这三家车厂的知识产权许可。结果原告被这三家车厂起诉侵犯知识产权,后来达成和解,结果是原告从游戏中移除法拉利车型(因为法拉利对知识产权要价太高),但会保留兰博基尼和保时捷车型,不过需要向他们取得知识产权许可。原告于是根据10.3条文要求被告补偿向兰博尼基、保时捷申请知识产权许可的费用。被告则辩称,原告为了获得这两家公司的知识产权许可所花掉的费用太高,是没有合理减少损失,他不应该为原告这种行为负责。为此被告在第二次开庭时申请加入专家证人意见来评价原告有没有合理减少损失。高院的 Warren 大法官认为,第10.3条文是补偿协议,是债务的性质,不涉及原告要减少损失的问题。但第10.1条文是一个保证条文,它的违反只是对首要合约义务的违反,违约带来的损失索赔就需要面对合理减少损失的问题了,所以被告还是有一个可以争辩的理由,并在该案例中允许被告引进专家意见证据,因为该案例并非是最终的审理。

针对程租合约或国际货物买卖合约的"滞期费"(demurrage)也曾经有过这一方面的争议,就是双方议定金额的滞期费的支付,是债务还是损失。这已经是在 Moor Lind Ltd v. Distillers Co Ltd, 1912 SC 514 先例中有明确的答案,Salvesen 勋爵是说:"The more correct view is that demurrage is 'agreed damages to be paid for delay of the ship in loading or unloading beyond an agreed period.' In other words, the distinction between 'demurrage' and damages for detention is that the one is liquidated damages and the other unliquidated. A claim under either head is a claim in respect of detention, and is in the nature of a claim of damages."所以针对滞期费这个问题,也有说法是受害船东会

有合理减少损失的义务，这一点会在本章2.1段详解。

1.4 区别之四：延误支付债务可以索赔损失，但延误支付损失就只能获得利息的补偿

债务如果是晚了支付，债权人除了可以索赔立法(《Late Payment of Commercial Debts Act 1998》)规定的利息外，还可以索赔延误支付所带来的损失。这些损失的类别可以是千变万化，如延误支付所导致的受害人对其他投资机会损失或需要多做出利息的支付等。但当然这些损失都是受到了损失计算的限制，如"遥远性"(remoteness)。

但针对损失，由于它本身就是属于合约履行的次要合约义务，不存在还有一个第三个合约责任的说法。所以，对违约方延误支付损失有完全不同的对待。就是除了有权为这笔延误支付的损失取得利息外(在仲裁中这笔利息就是在仲裁庭的裁量权内，仲裁庭还可以根据1996年英国《仲裁法》之Section 49做出单息或者复息的裁决，但英国法院只能做出单息的判决)，不存在可索赔额外的损失。在贵族院的The "Lips" (1987) 2 Lloyd's Rep. 311先例中，Brandon勋爵是说："There is no such thing as a cause of action in damages for late payment of damages. The only remedy which the law affords for delay in paying damages is the discretionary award of interest pursuant to statute."

这一个区别对有一些商业活动非常重要，如保险赔偿的延误经常会给受保人带来很大困难。受保人能否索赔这些延误赔付的损失就取决于保险赔偿到底是一笔债务还是一笔损失，这一个问题稍后在本章2.3段会详细介绍。

1.5 区别之五：债务与损失的转让

十分简单地介绍是英国法律对"转让"(assignment)的限制一直以来就受到"帮讼"(champerty)或"包揽诉讼"(maintenance)的影响和困扰，这就是禁止把一个索赔的诉讼当做一般商品的买卖，让一些讼棍把索赔权以转让的方式买过来，然后以"受让人"(assignee)的身份向债务人提出诉讼。帮讼有许多著名的说法，如"Champerty is about interfering without good reason in the enforcement of **other people's** claim"，或是"trafficking in litigation or selling lawsuits as articles of commerce"。包揽诉讼曾经是一种犯罪的行为，也是一种侵权，反正是英国法律有很长的历史大力禁止。但有说法是英国法律在Trendtex Ltd v. Credit Suisse (1982) AC 679先例后已经有一定程度的放宽，但还是对一些非商业的转让如人身伤亡的索赔的自由转让有很大的抗拒。

在英国法律下，债务是完全可以自由让债权人"转让"(assign)给第三人，这第三人也变为"受让人"(assignee)：Fitzroy v. Cave (1905) 1 KB 564；Norglen Ltd v. Reeds Rains Prudential Ltd (1999) 2 AC 1；Camdex International Ltd v. Bank of Zambia (1998) QB 22；M. Smith，《The Law of Assignment》(Oxford University Press, 2007年)之12-88—12-94段。在一些很早的先例，如在Fizroy v. Cave，是把债务视为是一种"财产/货物"(property)，可以自由转让，与包揽诉讼无关。在一个更早的先例Comfort v. Betts (1891) 1 QB 737,判是一个收账人可以合法受让一笔债务,然后向债务人提出诉讼并把追回来的金钱与转让人平分。

但这一个说法也曾经有过质疑,在 Laurent v. Sale & Co (1963) 1 WLR 829 先例,Megaw 大法官就判一个债务的转让无效,转让给一个做出资助的第三人,并约定分摊取回来的钱。但之后一个上诉庭的先例 Levy v. Horesh (27 March 1985)判是一个完全无关的第三人把一家公司的债务买回来(或转让过来)是有效。上诉庭在该先例与 Laurent v. Sale & Co 先例判法不一致所做出的区分只是在后一个先例在转让的时候就已经想到要向债务人提出诉讼。O' Connor 大法官对 Laurent v. Sale & Co 先例的案情是这样说:"the assignee there knew full well that the debt was not going to be paid unless it was forced out of the debtor by action and it was a term of the agreement that the assignee was going to bring the action, finance it, and the consideration for the assignment was to be paid out of the proceeds."

到了 Camdex International Ltd v. Bank of Zambia 先例,上诉庭完全不反对 Zambia 银行的债务被转让人 Kuwait 银行以相对低廉的代价卖给第三人,这第三人的买方除了想从中赚取一大笔利润外,根本没有其他原因接受转让。在该先例,也应该有清楚的迹象是非要通过诉讼才能够取回这一笔债务。但上诉庭完全不理会 Laurent v. Sale & Co 先例。Hobhouse 大法官有这样的判决:"An assignment of a debt is not invalid even if the necessity for litigation to recover it is contemplated. Provided that there is a bona fide debt, it does not become unassignable merely because the debtor chooses to dispute it. Suing on an assigned debt is not contrary to public policy even if the assignor retains an interest. What is contrary to public policy and ineffective is an agreement which has maintenance or champerty as its object; such a consequence will not be avoided by dressing up a transaction which has that character and intent as an assignment of a debt. But, because the assignment of a debt itself includes no element of maintenance and is sanctioned by statute, any objectionable element alleged to invalidate the assignment has to be proved independently and distinctly in the same way as any other alleged illegality has to be proved in relation to a contract which is on its face valid.

The defendant has been unable to show any arguable case that the assignment of the debt by the Central Bank of Kuwait(转让人) to the plaintiff (受让人的原告) was anything other than a bona fide purchase of a debt."

所以总结说,只要是一笔债务(不论债务人是否提出抗辩),都可以不受限制的转让,也一般不会受到包揽诉讼的质疑。

而损失的转让就会受到较多局限,这种限制在早期的先例也很混乱,如可以合法转让一个"权利产权"(chose in action)但不可以转让一个"单纯的索赔权利"(bare right to litigation):Glegg v. Bromley (1912) 3 KB 474。可以合法转让一个实质的权利与它的救济办法(显然是指诉讼的救济办法)但不能只转让救济办法:Prosser v. Edmonds（1835）1 Y & C Ex 481；Torkington v. Magee（1902）2 KB 427。简单说，对这种区别在现实中也很难分得开。贵族院之后把握 Trendtex Ltd v. Credit Suisse（1982）AC 679 先例的机会澄清这一方面的法律。该先例涉及原告（Trendtex）作为贸易商一直是受到被告（Credit Suisse 银行）的资助，原告向尼日利亚公司出售了大批的水泥，支付办法是以尼日利亚银行开出的信用证。但由于尼日利亚的经济崩溃，尼日利亚公司也就倒闭，同时尼日利亚银行拒绝做出 1400 万美元货价的支付。这一来，导致了 Trendtex 也发生经济困难，无法偿还 Credit Suisse 银行 150 万美元的贷款，也无力向尼日利亚银行提起诉讼。这导致了双方的协议，就是把 Trendtex 向尼日利亚银行的诉权转让或卖给 Credit Suisse 银行。但 Credit Suisse 银行并没有作为受让人提出诉讼，而是把这一诉权又卖给了第三人，代价只是 100 万多一点。这表示 Credit Suisse银行只想取回它的一笔贷款，无意赚取任何利润。第三人最后向尼日利亚银行提出诉讼，并通过庭外和解取得 800 万美元的赔偿，显然第三人成功在很短时间内赚取了一笔暴利。之后，Trendtex 或它的债权人反悔，向 Credit Suisse 银行索赔这 800 万美元，理由是他们之间的协议与转让因为包揽诉讼的原因而无效。在该先例，上诉庭的 Denning 勋爵主张大力放宽转让任何的权利包括索赔损失的权利，只要这一个权利并非是属于转让人个人所拥有（如诽谤或个人伤亡）与整体看是合理。但 Oliver 大法官认为还是需要包揽诉讼的限制，但可以放宽，包括允许包揽诉讼（与转让）如果受让人能够指出一个宽松的合法利益接受转让并参与转让人的诉讼。这也在贵族院被接受，带来了一个"真正与重大利益"（genuine and substantial interest）的说法。在该先例，贵族院也认为 Credit Suisse 银行是有一个真正与重大利益接受转让，因为它融资给 Trendtex 并被欠下贷款等原因。

在 Trendtex 先例后有许多案例涉及这一个真正与重大利益考验测试一个损失索赔的转让是否合法的问题，这些案例的判法看来是有很大程度的放宽，如：

（1）Total Liban SA v. Vitol SA（1999）2 Lloyd's Rep 700 先例（涉及买方因为货物质量有缺陷而向卖方索赔，但由于卖方破产，所以买方说服卖方把他向上一个卖方［供应商］的同一个索赔的权利转让给买方）。同样原因与做法的先例也在加拿大被判是合法：Fredrickson v. Ins Corp of BC（1988）28 DLR（4th）414（针对没有钱赔偿的被告转让他向责任保险人的索赔的权利）；Ontario Inc v. White（1984）42 CPC 209（针对没有钱赔偿的被告转让他向经纪人的索赔的权利）。

（2）The "Kelo"（1985）1 Lloyd's Rep 85 先例（涉及一个 CIF 买卖在卸港发生货损，买方把他向船东索赔的权利转让给代理人）。

（3）Offer – Hoar v. Larkstore Ltd（2006）1 WLR 2926 先例（涉及一个建造合约出了问题，受到损失的发展商从上一个发展商［也是他的卖方］取得了他向顾问工程师索赔的权利，因为问题是出在该工程师所出的报告。法院认为受到损害的发展商也就是受让人有参与这一个项目的发展就已经是真正与重大的利益）。

（4）Seven Utility Services Ltd v. Rosekey Ltd（2003）EWHC 3415（QB）（涉及侵权

索赔的转让,在以前曾经一度认为侵权的转让是不合法。在 Defries v. Milne (1913) 1 Ch 98 先例,上诉庭的 Farwell 大法官是这样说:"a right of action in tort was never assignable at law, and no case has been cited to us, nor do I think it is possible to find any case, where it has ever been held to be assignable in equity.")

反正这种先例还有很多,如 Brownton Ltd v. Edward Moore Inbucon Ltd (1985) 3 All ER 499; Oseco Inc v. Hansen (1989) 71 OR (2d) 151; Commonwealth v. Ling (1993) 118 ALR 309(澳大利亚先例); Norglen Ltd v. Reeds Rains Prudential Ltd (3 February 1994) Unreported; Massai Aviation Services Ltd v. Att Gen of the Bahamas (2007) UKPC 12; Simpson v. Norfolk & Norwich University Hospital, NHS Trust (2011) EWCA Civ. 1149;等。

但还是有看法说这一个受让人的真正与重大利益考验并不够明确,这说法可看 A. Tettenborn 教授之《Assignment of Rights to Compensation》(2007) LMCLQ 392 一文。简单说,这一个考验并没有考虑转让人的真正与重大利益,如转让人没有财力或能力提出损失索赔的诉讼,能够让他把这一个诉权通过转让出售,取回部分金钱总比什么都没有强。该文章也提到了一些公共政策不应该允许转让的例子,如把人身伤亡的诉权转让给律师。但由于本章不是主要针对转让的问题,所以略过。

1.6 区别之六:债务的抵销与损失的抵销

1.6.1 英国法律下的抵销

"抵销"(set-off)一词在英国法律下是没有一个统一的定义,并且有一定程度的混乱。从字面的解释就是把两笔不同(如不同合约)的钱(可以是债务,也可以是非议定赔偿),一笔是 A 欠 B,另一笔是 B 欠 A 互相扣减,而剩下来的一笔余额就由 A 支付 B 或 B 支付 A(看谁欠谁的一笔钱更大)。在英国的普通法,是不存在抵销的权利。换言之,A 与 B 对他们互相欠下的两笔不同的钱(即使是债务)是分别要向对方提起索赔与诉讼。在订约自由下,合约方也可以针对抵销的权利作出明示规定,如在租船合约就经常有条文针对承租人可以对到期支付的租金作出某一些的扣减(如停租、耗油、佣金、使费等)。此外在程序法下有允许法院在审理时对索赔或反索赔进行抵销,这是在《民事诉讼规则》之 r 40.13。在清盘的程序中,也有立法允许抵销。目前在英国法律下,只有两种抵销:一是"立法抵销"(legal or statutory set-off),二是"衡平法抵销"(equitable set-off)。它们分别在接下去的段节会简单介绍。

1.6.2 立法抵销

早在 1729 年就通过一个名为《Insolvent Debtors Relief Acts》的立法,出现了"立法抵销"(legal or statutory set-off)。有关的条文是:"mutual debts between the plaintiff and the defendant... one debt may be set against the other."这个立法的地位在之后延续了下去,体现在《Senior Courts Act 1981》之 Section 49(2)与《民事诉讼规则》之 r 16.6,这方面可看 Re Kaupthing Singer & Friedlander Ltd (2009) 2 Lloyd's Rep 154 先例与 Fearns t/a Autopaint International v. Anglo-Dutch Paint & Chemical Co. (2010)

EWHC 2366（Ch）先例。

有关立法抵销的进一步解释，可节录 Hoffman 勋爵在 Stein v. Blake（1996）AC 243 先例所说："Legal set-off does not affect the substantive rights[1] of the parties against each other, at any rate until both causes of action have been merged in a judgment of the court. It addresses questions of procedure and cash flow. As a matter of procedure, it enables a defendant to require his cross-claim（even if based upon a wholly different subject matter）be tried together with the plaintiff's claim instead of having to be the subject of a separate action. In this way it ensures that judgment will be given simultaneously on claim and cross-claim and thereby relieves the defendant from having to find the cash to satisfy a judgment in favour of the plaintiff（or, in the 18th century, go to a debtor's prison[2]）before his cross-claim has been determined."

但立法抵销十分局限，条文中允许的抵销只是"双方相互债务"（mutual debts），这两笔债务必须是不需要进一步的评估或者核算：Axel Johnson Petroleum AB v. MG Mineral Group AG（1992）1 WLR 270 先例与 Stein v. Blake（1996）AC 243 先例。如 B 对 A 提出诉讼索赔一笔债务，但较早前 A 对 B 有一个还没有获得支付的裁决书或判决金额，A 就可以在这一个诉讼中把这笔欠下的"判决债务"（judgment debt）要求做出抵销或用作抗辩：Ronly Holding v. JSC Zestafoni. G. Nikoladze Ferroalloy Plant（2004）EWHC 1354（Comm）先例。

但这不包括损失，因为损失以及它的金额还需要法院或仲裁庭的审理与判定：Stooke v. Taylor（1880）5 QBD 569；Hargreaves v. Action 2000（1992）62 BLR 72, CA；Aectra Refining v. Exmar（1994）1 WLR 1634, CA 等先例。

这使得英国法律进一步放宽抵销，特别是在"非议定赔偿"（unliquidated damage）方面。这方面的放宽体现在两个方面。一个方面是普通法有了一个说法是在货物买卖与提供服务的合约，如果货物或服务有缺陷，买方或接受服务方可以在支付的货价或费用（这是属于债务）中作出"减少"（abatement）。这减少显然不是一笔明确的债务，不能依赖立法抵销。但只要是买方或接受服务方能够说明与合理估计出债权人的违约令有关债务所针对的货物/服务价值有所贬低，法律就允许债务人在面对债权人索赔这笔债务时做出减少。有关这一个课题，稍后在本章 3.3.2 段有进一步探讨。

---

〔1〕 立法抵销是一个程序做法，并非实体权利。这表示立法抵销的权利只能在一个诉讼中出现，要抵销两笔不同的债务的人士（通常是被告）必须在抗辩请求中提出。而直到法院作出最后判决把两笔不同债务混在一起，这两笔不同的债务还是分别与独立的存在。

〔2〕 这一句是指在 18 世纪，民事债务会令债务人由于无法偿还而要坐牢，但这种做法已经是很早被摒弃了，因为大家接受因为穷困无法还债并非等同于犯罪。但在 18 世纪的时候，如果两笔债务不能抵销，就会导致 A 向 B 索赔一笔债务，而 B 要在一个不同的诉讼向 A 索赔另一笔不同的债务。但 A 提起的诉讼动得快，判了下来，B 无法支付而导致要坐牢。直到 B 向 A 的债务判了下来，并且在金额上完全抵销了欠 A 的钱，B 才能被释放。这可以看到立法抵销的重要性。

1.6.3 衡平法抵销

第二方面的放宽是出现了“衡平法抵销”(equitable set-off)。最早的做法是衡平法院对普通法院在审理中的一笔债务(如A向B提起的诉讼)或是作出的一笔判决债务(判B要支付A的债务)作出禁令,阻止诉讼的进行或判决债务的执行,直到进一步的命令。这进一步的命令显然就是等待B向A的索赔(显然这不是一笔明确的债务,否则B可以依赖立法抵销)也有了结果后才允许继续诉讼或执行。但到了《JudicatureAct 1870》,这种申请禁令的做法再也不需要。只要能满足以前衡平法院作出这种禁令的条件,B就可以在A向他提起的诉讼中要求衡平法抵销他的一笔损失。

但必须注意的是B(或是其他债务人)并非任何的损失都可以要求衡平法抵销,进而不支付他欠A(或其他债权人)的债务。可否抵销主要的考验就是被告的反索赔“是否与原告的索赔有一个紧密的关系,不把这一个反索赔一并考虑就判索赔成功会带来明显不公平”(whether it is so closely connected with the claim that it would be manifestly unjust to allow the claim without taking into account the cross-claim):Hanak v. Green (1958) 2 QB 9, CA; Henriksens A/S v. Rolimpex THZ (1974) 1 QB 233; The “Nanfri” (1979) 1 Lloyd's Rep 201; Cathery v. Lithodomus (1987) 41 BLR 76; Guinness plc v. Saunders (1988) 1 WLR 863, CA; Dole Dried Fruit v. Trustin Kerwood (1990) 2 Lloyd's Rep 309, CA等先例。这方面可参考R. Derham所著的《Derham on the Law of Set-off》(4th edn, Oxford University, 2010年)。

衡平法抵销这一个课题不会在本章进一步探讨,只是最后节录Goff大法官在The “Kostas Melas” (1981) 1 Lloyd's Rep 18先例中的判词,说:“although a right of set-off is a defence, with all the legal consequences which follow from it, in practice the exercise of a right of deduction or set-off is essentially a provisional act. It decides nothing finally. Its exercise simply operates as a temporary retention of an economic asset by the party exercising the right, and the temporary deprivation of the other party of that asset. For the exercise of the right does not prevent either party from subsequently proving his claim or cross-claim, and so does not affect the final resolution of the fundamental dispute... Even so, bearing in mind the characteristics of the right, it is in my judgment implicit in its very nature that it should only be exercised in good faith on reasonable grounds...”(衡平法抵销的权利是一个针对债务索赔的拒付与抗辩理由。这拒付只能是暂时性的,不会明确与最后决定双方最后的权利。行使这个权利并不妨碍双方事后通过诉讼或仲裁明确他们之间的索赔与反索赔。但必须要理解这一权利的本质就是被告的拒付与抗辩必须是善意而且有合理根据,毕竟这是衡平法。这表示债务人如果作出非善意与没有合理根据的抵销,如拒赔的金额过大,就会有严重的法律后果。)

这种衡平法抵销的争议经常在租船业务中出现,承租人对他欠下的租金作出所谓的衡平法抵销,理由会是各式各样,常见理由是船速慢或是货损货差。这些都是属于损失,需要进一步的确定,所以这是与立法抵销无关。但期租合约通常有明示规定承租人如果延误或不足数地支付租金,船东可以撤船。而经常在航运高涨时会发生承租人作出衡平法抵销,船东就会趁机撤船。而事后船东的撤船到底是否正确,往往就是依据承租人作出的衡平法抵销是否是被允许,而如果被允许是否在金额上是善意与有合理根据。例如货损货差是不被允许作为衡平法抵销,承租人如果这样做,不支付租金或不足额支付租金就会有很大危险。但船速慢是被允许作为衡平法抵销,只是在金额上还是需要是善意与有合理根据。

1.6.4 针对能否作出抵销的一个实例

能否面对原告一个债务的索赔做出抵销,会是对被告十分重要。这可看贵族院的 The "Aries" (1977) 1 Lloyd's Rep 334 先例,会稍后在3.3.2 段介绍。这里只举一个实例,以显示这方面了解的重要性。在笔者涉及的一个造船合约的伦敦仲裁,简单的案情是外国船东作为买方没有支付第三与第四期的分阶段船价,情况拖了接近一年,最终导致了中国船厂终断造船合约并把该船舶完成建造与出售,并做出"最后的结算"(final accounting)与向买方提出索赔。但买方提出各种反索赔并抗辩说他不支付第三与第四期的分阶段船价是因为该船舶建造得不好,有严重缺陷,因为主机的底板太高。中国船厂由于估计买方提出这一个反索赔并需要时间处理,加上会是看到买方的财力有问题,所以提出了申请要求买方提供反索赔的费用担保(这是针对要抗辩反索赔所估计要使用的诉讼费用)。由于诉讼费用昂贵,所以要求提供费用担保的当事人往往要掏出一大笔钱,如好几十万美元不等。如果是一个复杂与涉及漫长开庭处理的索赔或反索赔要为他提供费用担保,在金额上更加是动辄四五百万美元不等。所以费用担保的命令一做出,往往会令提出索赔的原告或是提出反索赔的被告打退堂鼓,如让步做出和解。

回去继续谈这一个伦敦仲裁,只说买方的律师非常精明,他在抗辩与反索赔请求中把这一个技术性的争议(主机的底板太高)同时加在抗辩与反索赔的部分。这导致中国船厂要求费用担保,买方的抗辩就是即使他不提出这个反索赔,同样的争议也会在抗辩出现以及要处理。但在自然公正下是永远不能剥夺抗辩的权利,所以不存在要提供费用担保以保障抗辩的权利。这一来,主要的问题就是这一个技术性的争议到底能否作为抗辩或抵销中国船厂索赔的债务。笔者认为这一个技术性的争议只能作为一个反索赔(也就是完全独立,不能用来抵销或抗辩中国船厂的债务索赔),不是一个抗辩。简单的原因就是本段所讲的,这一个反索赔不是"双方相互债务"(mutual liquidated debts),谈不上可立法抵销。也因为船舶从来没有交付给买方,所以不会是"减少"(abatement)。而衡平法抵销是更加扯不上关系,被告也没有提出这一个请求。以下就是笔者向伦敦共同仲裁员所做出的部分解释:

"Whether the mis-dimensioning of the main engine bedplate is a defence *or* counter-claim to warrant an order to put up security for costs?

My understanding of English law (subject to your kind guidance): 1) The nature of the Sellers' claim is very much a debt, whether it is the overdue 3rd & 4th instalments, *or* the final accounting. 2) In order to set-off (or becoming a defence proper) to a claim for debt, I believe it has to be either a mutual liquidated debt or by way of abatement. I do not see the alleged damage of mis-dimensioning of the main engine bedplate can be a liquidated debt. I equally doubt there can be an abatement because the Vessel was never delivered to the Buyers. It is not a case of chasing for the price of the goods or Vessel. Therefore, I have difficulty in accepting my (3) above in that the Buyers' defended on the grounds of 'reduction (in value)' and/or 'set-off'. 3) I have greater doubt in whether or not an equitable set-off will be applicable here. In any event, this has not been pleaded. 4) I think I got a lot of guidance in our C/P cases in that an alleged cargo claim cannot set-off freight and/or unpaid hire. But kindly advise your views as I believe this point is most important. 5) I also think the fact that the Vessel was not delivered worth commenting. That means the alleged technical issue, even if valid and of crucial importance, had yet to constitute a breach. Anything can happen prior to delivery. The Vessel may be destroyed at the shipyard by fire or other misfortunes, and the whole case turns to an insurance problem under Article XII of SBC. There will never be a question of abatement or set-off. 6) If my analysis is right, then the technical issue of 'mis-dimensioning of the main engine bedplate' should only be validly pleaded as a counterclaim, but not as a defence. If the Buyers withdraw as a counterclaim and merely plead as a defence, it would not go very far and will be summarily dismissed."

只是简单说,笔者这一个电文说服了伦敦共同仲裁员并最后对买方的外国船东做出了提供费用担保的命令。只是在伦敦共同仲裁员的坚持下,大幅度把费用担保的金额减少,但这是题外话。

1.7 区别之七:债务与损失在债务人公司清盘中的不同影响

如果被告经济有问题,债权人在债务的情况下,可以马上做出“法定的支付要求”(statutory demand for payment)并在没有取得支付时开始把债务人公司清盘的程序。但如果涉及的是一笔损失,通常是必须等待判决或是裁决之后,把损失变为“判决债务”(judgment debt)才能够成功申请把债务人公司清盘。

2. 一些不明确是债务或是损失的双方协议

介绍了以上债务与损失的不同之处,以下介绍一些不同类别与有争议的协议是否属于债务或属于损失。

2.1 协议类别之一:议定赔偿

“议定赔偿”(liquidated damage)到底是一种“有条件的债务”(conditional debt)(什么是“有条件”在本章之3.1段有详解)或是损失赔偿有不明朗之处。这包括是议定赔偿少了一种损失索赔最重要的特征,就是受害人必须证明他的损失。在赔偿金额被约定的情况下,根本不需要走这一步。在较早时有提到的上诉庭先例 Abrahams v. Performing Rights Society Ltd (1995) ICR 1028,就认为议定赔偿下的受害人不需要减少损失,这是接近说议定赔偿是一种债务,上诉庭是这样说:"Even if a payment in lieu of wages was properly categorized as liquidated damages, there would still be no duty on a plaintiff to mitigate his loss. The whole object of a liquidated damages provision in a contract was to fix a certain sum to be paid irrespective of the actual damage suffered by reason of the breach. The concept of a duty to mitigate was entirely foreign to such a claim; it only applied where damages were at large."

但作为国际外贸与航运最常见的议定赔偿类别,也就是"滞期费"(demurrage),受害的船东会面对有否合理减少损失的争辩。这种争议很少听到,但不是没有。例如在一个纽约仲裁的案件 The "Antalya" (NY Arb), LMLN 291, 29 December 1990 中,涉及承租人要求改港,因为原来的卸港太拥挤,如果换了另一个附近的替代港口就可以缩短 25 天。但船东同意改港的条件太苛刻,这恐怕是一些精明的船东遇上承租人有要求改变租约经常会有的态度,就是敲一笔。反正最后改港失败,所以承租人提出了船东没有减少损失的争辩。这一个案件判承租人败诉,但仲裁庭曾经提到如果承租人只是要求船东做一些比较轻微的事情而不是更改卸港的重大决定,而船东拒绝做,就有可能被视为是没有合理减少损失,弄不好就会导致 25 天的滞期费泡汤。反正针对这一个仲裁案件以及伦敦仲裁员的取向(因为伦敦还没有这方面的仲裁案件或先例),John Schofield 在《Laytime and Demurrage》(6th edn, 2011 年)一书之 6.52 段说:"This argument was rejected by the tribunal, who held that, whilst there might be some circumstances in which, from a commercial point of view, it would be unreasonable for the owners to sit stubbornly and earn demurrage when they could take some trifling step which would expedite the discharge, the present case did not come within that category. It is likely that London arbitrators would adopt the same approach."

2.2 协议类别之二:补偿协议

"补偿协议"(indemnity contract)下的补偿是属于债务或是损失赔偿也是富争议,这种文件中一般的措辞/文字可被解释为"补偿人"(indemnifier)的 A 对"被补偿人"的 B 做出了一个承诺,就是 B 如果蒙受损失或要承担责任,A 就会做出补偿,这是有一个债务的意味。但也可以被解释为 A 担保 B 不会蒙受损失,或是在 B 要做出赔偿的时候补偿,这是一个损失计算的意味。可以说,有关的判例一般认为补偿协议是损失而不是债务。其中是 Golf 勋爵在 Firma C-Trade SA v. Newcastle Protection & Indemnity Assn (1991) 2 AC 1 先例说:"A promise of indemnity is simply a promise to hold the indemnified person harmless against a specified loss or expense. On this basis, no debt can arise before the loss is suffered or the expense incurred; however, once the loss is suffered or the expense incurred, the indemnifier is in breach of contract for having failed to hold the indemnified person harmless against the relevant loss or expense."

有关补偿协议与另一种类似的"担保合约"(contract of guarantee)会稍后在2.4段进一步详解。

2.3 协议类别之三:保险合约

"保险合约"(insurance contract)与补偿协议性质上差不多,被视为是损失而不是债务。Donaldson大法官在Forney v. Dominion Insurance Co Ltd (1969) 1 WLR 928先例中就已经明确地说:"All actions against insurers under indemnity policies sound in unliquidated damages rather than debt."这种案例其实有很多,包括早期的Luckie v. Bushby (1853) 13 CB 864以及之后的Post Office v. Norwich Union Fire Insurance Society Ltd (1967) 2 QB 363;The "Italia Express" (No.2) (1992) 2 Lloyd's Rep 281(高院)与Sprung v. Royal Insurance (UK) Ltd (1999) Lloyd's Rep IR 111等。

这就带来一个很大的问题,就是保险人的延误做出赔偿,即使是明确不过的"定额保险"(valued policy)下的全损赔付,都会带来受保人极大的困难以及额外的损失。这种不幸的情况看来经常在发生,这导致了英国法律委员会在针对保险法的改革中专门为这一个问题在2010年3月作出一个报告名为《Insurance Contract Law: Issues Paper 6: Damages for Late Payment and the Insurer's Duty of Good Faith》。这一个问题的严重性可以很容易想得到,投保就是为了出事后有赔偿。但如果保险人拖延赔付,甚至是1、2年之久,会对受保人带来极大的困难,甚至会因此倒闭或破产,期间更加会是丧失很多机会。在Sprung v. Royal Insurance (UK) Ltd. (1999) 1 Lloyd's Rep. 111先例就是这种情况,Sprung先生的厂房被承保风险摧毁,但保险人在3年半之后并且是在诉讼的期间才作出赔付,但Sprung先生的业务已经因为拿不到赔付而无财力再经营下去。在现实中,即使最后还是赔付,受保人失去的业务还是回不来。在该先例中,Sprung先生向保险人索赔延误赔付的损失,但是败诉。看来,这与美国的法院经常对这种延误作出赔付的保险人作出"惩罚性赔偿"(punitive damage),作为警戒,是十分不一样。在英国法律地位是受害的受保人根本不能向保险人索赔损失,唯一只能有利息的补偿,这一个法律地位在好几个重要的先例中被明确。

曾经有受保人试图指责保险人延误做出赔付是违反了另一个保险合约的首要合约义务,这一个首要合约义务就是法律默示的,也在1906年英国《海上保险法》之Section 17有规定的"绝对善意"(utmost good faith)。所以违反了这一个首要合约义务就带来了次要合约义务赔偿受保人的损失。这种先例有Banque Financiere de la Cite SA v. Watergate Insurance Co. Ltd (1990) 2 Lloyd's Rep 377与贵族院的The "Star Sea" (2001) 1 Lloyd's Rep. 389,但判决的结果是根据该立法规定,违反绝对善意的唯一救济就是"回避"(avoid)保险合约。这一个救济看来只有是保险人可以得益,在受保人投保前没有作出全面的披露或误述,或在投保后作出虚假索赔等的情况下,保险人可以回避而拒赔。但保险人对受保人违反绝对善意,如拖延作出赔付,受保人是不会回避保险合约。另一个重要的先例是 The“Italia Express”(No.2)(1992)2 Lloyd's Rep 281,Hirst 大法官也是解释 1906 年英国《海上保险法》之 Section 67 与 Section 68,在保险标的发生全损的时候,在一个定额保单,保险人唯一需要支付就是保单中约定的投保金额。Section 67(1)是这样说:“The sum which the assured can recover of a loss on a policy by which he is insured... in the case of a valued policy to the full extent of the value fixed by the policy is called the measure of indemnity.”看来,问题是出在:(1)1906 年《海上保险法》条文的解释,而立法是超越普通法。(2)英国法律把保险合约的赔偿视为是损失赔偿,不是一笔债务。但针对损失的赔偿,就不存在延误支付,除了利息外还能够索赔其他的损失。即使受保人胜诉,也只能加上利息(可能包括复息)向保险人取回:The“Lips”(1987)2 Lloyd's Rep. 311。一般的保险赔付是不被视为支付债务,所以延误支付也不会带来利息以外的其他损失赔偿。

所以在目前的法律地位是保险人拖上二三年后才做出赔付,赔付的金额还是保单中投保的金额,顶多加上了在今天很低的利息。而受保人不论是根据保险人违反绝对善意,或是根据保险人违反一般法律默示要求在合理时间内支付/赔付,看来都不会成功索赔他所蒙受的损失。

这导致部分保险人为了表示善意,在保单中加上了针对性的条文,这种条文可被称为“time for payment”条文。作用就是为自己加上了一个首要合约义务,如果违反就会带来一个次要合约义务的损失赔偿。其中在 2003 年版本的《国际船舶保险条文》第 46.7 条就是典型的例子,可节录如下:“The Leading Underwriter(s) shall make a decision in respect of any claim within 28 days of receipt by them of the appointed average adjuster's final adjustment or, if no adjuster is appointed, a fully documented claim presentation sufficient to enable the Underwriters to determine their liability in relation to coverage and quantum. If the Leading Underwriter(s) request additional documentation or information to make a decision, they shall make a decision within a reasonable time after receipt of the additional documents or information requested, or of a satisfactory explanation as to why such documents and information are not available.”

这明示条文虽然没有讲清楚延误赔付会带来什么救济,但应该是可以在保险人违约延误赔付的情况下,给了受保人一个独立的诉因提出索赔延误所导致的损失。这赔偿损失的次要合约义务是法律默示,不必再明示。这方面可看 Tonkin v. UK Insurance Ltd (2006) EWHC 1120 先例。最后可节录《Insurance Contract Law: Issues Paper 6: Damages for Late Payment and the Insurer's Duty of Good Faith》报告中的建议,说:“9.42.... the insurer's primary obligation (would be) not to prevent a loss from occurring, but to pay valid claims, after the opportunity for a reasonable investigation. If an insurer fails to carry out this obligation, it should be liable for damages for actual loss caused by the breach provided that loss was foreseeable; that the policyholder acted reasonably to mitigate their loss; and that the loss was not excluded by a contract term.”

2.4 协议类别之四:担保合约

“担保合约”(suretyship or contract of guarantee)通常不如保险合约那么直接。担保合约的具体条文有部分的措辞/文字可以被解释为“担保人”(guarantor or surety)的A同意对“被担保人”(debtor or principal)的B向“债权人”(creditor)的C做出一个承诺,就是在B没有偿还债务时A会代为偿还这一笔债务,这就有一个债务的意味,不需要证明损失。但也有缺陷是这会局限在《Statute of Frauds 1677》的管辖下,而且这笔债务的有效性取决于主债务(这是B欠C的钱)的有效性。但个别担保合约的写法也可以被解释为在B没有偿还债务时A依据合约会补偿债权人,这就不会受以上提到的立法限制。因为这个担保合约不是对债务的承诺,而是在B没有偿还债务时对C带来损失做出保证。

在这里不妨对补偿协议(这在较早的2.2段已经详及)与担保合约之间的区别稍微解释一下。它们之间会是不容易区分,因为一般的商业人士也不会懂得或关心它们的区别,反正就把它们视为是担保的一种。至于这种文件的称呼,也往往不会细分,经常会有补偿协议被称为是担保合约,的确在广义上补偿协议也包括了担保合约。反正文件的名称解释起来也并不重要,更重要的还是内容。经常有文件使用的部分措辞/文字适用在补偿协议,但部分适用在担保合约,导致出了争议解释的困难。但很简单的说,在补偿协议下,A作为“补偿人”(indemnifier)被视为是对债务的“主负责人”(principal)。但在担保合约下,A作为“担保人”(guarantor)只在被担保人B明确欠下债务的时候才需要负责,B才是债务的“主负责人”(principal)。所以,在措辞/文字上会是说明A只是在B证明有责任后才需要做出支付。这表示有争议的情况下往往先要诉讼做出判决或裁决后,才会知道B是否有责任(不论是首要或次要合约义务)。

在Sir Roy Goode教授的著作《Guide to ICC Uniform Rules for Demand Guarantees URDG 758》(2011年版)中,对担保合约的定义或解释是:“A suretyship guarantee (also called an accessory guarantee), a suretyship or simply a guarantee is an undertaking by the surety (i. e. the issuer of the guarantee) to pay sums due from the applicant by way of debt or damages (as opposed to the guarantor's own primary obligation under a demand guarantee). It is payable on actual default and the measure of the surety's liability is that of the applicant debtor. This entitles the surety to assert all defences to the guaranteed debt that are available to the applicant and only to pay the amount that the beneficiary establishes as being owed by the applicant under the underlying relationship.”

而针对补偿协议,该书是讲:“Under English law, an indemnity ... is a primary liability not dependent on another party's default. However, it differs from a demand guarantee in that it is not an undertaking to pay a specified sum or maximum sum but simply an undertaking to hold another party harmless against loss, the amount of which therefore has to be ascertained.”

补偿协议与担保合约有两处重要的不同要求，就是立法的要求与是否要与主合约共存的问题。以下进一步介绍：

（1）关于立法的要求，有一个十分古老的立法名为《Statute of Frauds 1677》针对担保合约，要求担保合约必须是文书形式，同时A作为担保人必须签字才有效。该立法之Section 4是说“no action shall be brought ... whereby to charge the defendant upon any special promise to answer for the **debt** default or miscarriages of another person ... unless the agreement upon which such action shall be brought or some memorandum or note thereof shall be in writing and **signed by the party** to be charged therewith or some other person thereunto by him lawfully authorised.”（加黑部分是笔者的强调）。

简单地说由于立法中说明是承诺针对“另一位人士的债务”（debt of another person），所以立法是针对担保合约，因为在这种合约下，担保人的A不是“主债务人”（principal debtor），被担保的B才是主债务人。但如果是补偿协议，补偿人的A是主债务人，这表示A不是承诺针对另一位人士的债务。所以立法不适用，也表示补偿协议不需要文书记录与签字。这一区分对国际商业社会看来并不是太重要，因为不论是哪种类型的担保，多数会以文书形式并有签字。但这在日常社会中就会有关键性作用，因为担保人只是做出一些口头的担保。如果有争议，这一个担保的有效性就取决于本质上是担保合约或是补偿协议，这会是在个别案件中不容易区分。例如在Harburg India Rubber Comb Co v. Martin（1902）1 KB 778（CA）先例，案情涉及一位公司董事（也是公司的股东之一）在公司发生财政困难的时候，曾经在一个公司债权人大会中做出口头承诺说明他会为公司的债务承担责任。这被判是口头协议而无效，因为这本质上是担保合约，是承诺为第三人也就是公司的债务承担责任，所以受到立法的管制。

但在Guild & Co v. Conrad（1894）2 QB 885（CA）先例，案情涉及孩子的生意陷入困境而导致了债权人拒绝接受他的汇票，而父亲向债权人做出口头承诺是他会想办法找钱兑现这些汇票。这个承诺被视为是有效，因为它本质上是补偿协议。父亲并非是为孩子的一笔债务做出保证，所以不必受到立法的管制。这样看来，很多时候区分补偿协议或是担保合约的确是不容易且是富争论性。

最后一提的是有关担保合约必须是文书形式并有担保人签字的立法要求，看来在英国法律下有放宽的趋势。在最新的上诉庭案例Golden Ocean v. Salgaocar Mining（2012）EWCA Civ. 265已经明确担保合约在形式上并不用拘泥于一份经过签署的文件。在本案中原告是船东，被告是担保人。被告是一家在印度的大型私人家族公司，他通过他在新加坡的租船公司Trustworth Shipping Pte Ltd（以下称“Trustworth”）与原告签署了一份长达10年的租船合约，而被告自己则作为这份10年租船合约的担保人。后来Trustworth在租船合约下违约/毁约，原告在担保合约的基础上向被告索赔。本案争议的焦点主要有两方面：第一，原告所依赖的担保合约并没有一份传统意义上经过签字的文件，而是经过一系列的邮件往来而最终达成的，那么这一系列邮件往来与被声称是担保合约最终形成的那封邮件是否能够满足立法中文书形式的要求？第二，在邮件中“经纪人”（broker）的电子署名（并非全名，仅有名字，没有姓氏）是否满足签署的要求？

上诉庭的判决对于上述两个争议均持肯定的意见，即一系列的邮件满足文书的要求以及在邮件中经纪人的署名构成签署。被告的大律师有以下的抗辩理由：第一，邮件中经纪人在邮件末尾写上自己的名字“Guy”只是礼貌与在惯常的通讯中的做法，而不能被视为是对于担保合约的签署；第二，一系列的邮件并不是一份文书记录形式的担保合约；第三，签署的经纪人虽然有授权代表 Trustworth 签署租船合约，但不能被视为有足够的授权代表被告签署担保合约。

上诉庭的大法官不同意以上的抗辩，对于第一点，他们是说：“It was common ground both before the judge and before us that an electronic signature is sufficient and that a first name, initials, or perhaps a nickname will suffice. . . . Chartering brokers may communicate with one another in a familiar manner but that does not detract from the seriousness of the business they are conducting. In my judgment Mr Hindley put his name, Guy, on the email so as to indicate that it came with his authority and that he took responsibility for the contents. It is an assent to its terms. I have no doubt that that is a sufficient authentication.”（在电子邮件中的电子署名，不论是名字，全名的首字母缩写，甚至是昵称都足够能构成签署。经纪人用他们之间熟悉的签署方式并不会减损他们对所从事生意行为的严肃性。所以本案经纪人 Hindley 先生的署名“Guy”是表示他同意邮件的内容并会对其负责，真实性是不用质疑的。）

（2）另一个重要的不同要求是担保合约必须与主合约共存。显然，补偿协议下的补偿人 A 是主债务人，所以是不必理会被补偿人 B 所欠的债务是否可以执行或有法律上的缺陷。但担保合约由于只是“附带”（accessory），所以有说法就是必须与主合约共存亡。这表示担保合约所针对的债务，如果作为主债务人的 B 因为各种合法理由不必负责，作为担保人的 A 也不必负责。这可以 Yeoman Credit Ltd v. Latter (1961) 1 WLR 828 (CA)先例为例，案情涉及父亲为他未成年的孩子的一笔贷款做担保人，但这笔贷款实际上在《Infants Relief Act 1874》立法下是无效。这表示该父亲是否有责任主要是看有关文件的措辞/文字到底是补偿协议还是担保合约。法院判是补偿协议，也就是不受到有关债务无效的影响，所以父亲要负责。这种贷款给子女并由父亲做出担保的案件当年有很多，如果是以担保合约的形式，就变为一场空，正如在 Wauthier v. Wilson (1912) 28 TLR 239 (CA)先例，Farwell 大法官所说：“It would follow that these three parties ie [the creditor, principal and surety], enter into an arrangement under which money was to be advanced on [a contract] under which no one was liable at all, there being no one liable as principal and therefore no one liable as surety.”

在同样的道理下，主合约如果事后在没有担保人同意下被改动，担保人也可以抗拒说：“我担保的是建造桥梁，不是担保你们改动过的建造马路。”

所以,一种安全的做法就是把有关的文件加上文字说明本质上是补偿协议,这种措辞/文字在银行的标准担保格式都会见到,如说"The security hereby created shall not be discharged nor shall the irregularity, defect or informality in any security given by or on behalf of the Debtor in respect of the monies or liabilities hereby secured nor by any legal limitation, disability, incapacity or want of any borrowing powers of or by the Debtor or want or authority of any director, manager, official or other person appearing to be acting for the Debtor in any matter in respect of the monies or liabilities hereby secured and such monies or liabilities will be recoverable by the Bank from the Guarantor as sole or principal Debtor."

另在 McGuinness v. Norwich & Peterborough Building Society (2010) EWHC 2989 (Ch)先例,涉及担保人为他兄弟的贷款向银行做出了担保,也有这种措辞/文字说明他是主债务人,而不是担保合约的次债务人,说:"2.2 You guarantee that all money and liabilities owing, or becoming owing to us in the future, by the borrower (whether actual or contingent, whether incurred alone or jointly with another and whether as principal or surety) will be paid and satisfied when due...4.2 Your obligations under this guarantee are those of principal, not just as surety. We will not be obliged to make any demand on, or take any steps against, the borrower or any other person before enforcing this guarantee."

至于担保合约下的担保人承诺替被担保人支付的情况究竟是属于债务还是损失这一个问题,在订约自由下也是取决于对担保合约内容的解释。如果这份文件是单纯承诺会支付被担保人的债务,或是在第三人要求时直接支付债务,这就仅仅会产生债务上的责任。例如在 Moschi v. Lep Air Services Ltd (1973) AC 331 先例,担保人的承诺是针对被担保人要分期付款的一笔债务。但如果担保人承诺在被担保人不履行的时候,支付第三人的非议定损失,就会产生损失的责任。

担保人到底是对债务或是损失承诺,主要是在债权人作为担保合约的受益人向担保人提出要求支付时,他是否要先向被担保人确定损失金额而去面对可能是漫长与昂贵的诉讼,或是可以省钱与省时地通过简易判决向担保人取回一笔债务。如果是后者,这担保合约就好像是"见索即付的担保"(on demand guarantee),对担保人而言是承诺支付一笔债务。这种诉讼的案例很多,如 Moschi v. Lep Air Services Ltd (1973) AC 331; Hampton v. Minns (2002) 1 WLR 1; IIG Capital LLC v. Van Der Merwe (2008) 2 Lloyd's Rep 187; TS & T Global Ltd v. Fithian-Franks (2008) 1 BCLC 277; McGuinness v. Norwich & Peterborough Building Society (2010) EWHC 2989 (Ch) 等。

简单介绍 McGuinness v. Norwich & Peterborough Building Society 先例,Briggs 大法官在解释该份担保文件(有措辞/文字把文件写作见索即付担保,也有把它写作补偿协议,令担保人成为主债务人)说:

"20 For my part, I doubt whether the issue is necessarily an either/or question as between debt and damages. Some guarantees, and in particular that which was the subject of the TS & S Global case, may create both. For present purposes, the critical question is whether the guarantee includes, rather than necessarily consists of, a debt obligation.

21 In my judgment the guarantee does include a debt obligation. My main reason for that conclusion is that, by the principal debtor provision in the first sentence of clause 4.2 of the guarantee, the guarantor thereby made his brother's debts his own, as occurred in MS Fashions Ltd v. Bank of Credit and Commerce International SA [1993] Ch 425."

在这个案例中,银行是要将担保人清盘。但根据《Insolvency Act 1986》之 Section 267(2)(b),将担保人清盘必须满足的条件之一是这笔"债务"(debt)必须是一个可以确定的"议定金额"(liquidated sum)。所以,如果担保人是对债权人的"损失赔偿"(damages)承担责任,变成非议定损失赔偿的诉讼,债权人就不能依上述立法直接将担保人清盘,而是需要先向法院取得对担保人的胜诉判决,才能依判决中确定的损失赔偿金额申请将担保人清盘,这样一来是费时费力,也不好说中途会有什么变数。所以在该先例,银行是采用一种技术上的手法,说服法院认定担保人的责任是在补偿协议下的"债务"而不是"损失赔偿",就可以直接将担保人清盘了。

在该先例看来,如果在担保合约清楚写明担保人必须是见索即付,不需要先向被担保人提出索赔,与担保人在这一个担保合约下的责任是作为"主债务人"(principal debtor),不仅是"担保人"(surety)等,就可以有把握向担保人索赔的是债务而不是损失。

2.5 协议类别之五:汇票

"汇票"(bill of exchange)在《Bills of Exchange Act 1882》的定义是"an unconditional order in writing addressed by one person to another, signed by the person giving it, requiring the person to whom it is addressed to pay on demand or at a fixed or determinable future time a sum certain in money to or to the order of a specified person or to bearer."在这个定义下,普遍使用的银行支票也是汇票的一种,是"a bill of exchange drawn on a banker payable on demand",也就是说银行就是受票人。

表面上看,在汇票上签字或背书的"出票人"(issuer/drawer)、"受票人"(drawee)或"背书人"(endorser),面对汇票"持有人"(holder/bearer)要求付款的诉讼中是有一个简单明了的付款责任,这看似是债务。但实际上,出票人/受票人这一责任一直以来都被视为是"损失赔偿"之责。原本这是普通法的法律地位:Browne v. London (1670) 1 Mod 285 先例,后来被《Bills of Exchange Act 1882》之 Section 57 以立法的形式确定下来。这条立法是说汇票的受票人如果没有付款,他的责任是"议定的损失赔偿"(liquidated damages)。而对汇票也负有责任的当事人,如出票人或背书人,他们对持有人的责任也是一样。

3. 合约怎么样产生债务?

已经在本章一开始就提到过,合约中承诺是支付一笔金钱但没有做到,这就会带来债务。这在几乎所有的合约都会有这样的承诺,如买卖合约的明示或默示承诺就是买方在取得货物后需要支付货价;造船合约买方承诺分期付款支付船价;服务性的合约如租船合约下承租人要支付运费或租金;建造合约下发展商支付工程费给承包商或承包商给分承包商等。这些承诺会有条件,如造船合约的船价支付先要取得船级验船师证明建造已经完成某一个阶段的工序(如船舶下水或是主机的安装)、工程费的支付是先要取得建筑工程师的证明等。这一来,只要满足了这个条件,债务也就产生。

合约债务可以根据合约中千变万化的约定产生,如在程租合约下的运费,英国法律默示的地位是要航次完毕,船东把货物付运到卸港并完成托运服务,才能赚取运费。正如 Donaldson 大法官在 The "Lorna I" (1983) 1 Lloyd's Rep 373 先例中所讲:"Freight is the consideration payable for the carriage of the goods to and their delivery at the destination. In the absence of special contractual provisions, it is earned only upon the delivery of the goods at their destination. Forms of words appropriate to alter this position are well known, e. g. 'Freight to be considered earned on shipment'."

许多程租合约今天都会约定在装港装完货或提单一签发后很短的时间内就要承租人支付部分或全数的运费,这明示的约定显然是超越法律默示的地位。由于在国际上做出支付需要时间,所以通常的约定是运费在货物一装船就赚取,但支付会在几天后。如果在这几天内发生了意外如船舶沉没导致程租合约受阻,承租人就不会肯做出支付了。但承租人这样做法是对还是不对就是看有没有清楚约定运费在较早前已经赚取,如果有这样的条文,就表示赚取了的运费是一笔债务,不受事后船舶发生意外的影响,承租人还是要支付。但如果没有这样的条文,就表示合约约定支付的一天一直没有来到就已经发生合约受阻,而由于运费在默示法律下是要到了卸港把货物交出的时候才赚取,也表示船东根本还没有赚取,不存在船东可以向承租人索赔这一笔债务。又比如该船舶的沉没是涉及承租人装运的货物不安全,这显然是承租人违反了首要合约承诺,这就带来了次要合约责任对受害的船东作出损失的赔偿。这损失会是包括如果合约被履行船东在卸港把货物交付之时所能赚取的运费,但要扣减将会要花费的使费(如卸港的代理与港口费用)。但估计船东损失远远是不止这一笔运费,马上可以想得到的就是船舶的全损与船上的燃油等。希望从这一个介绍可以看得出债务与损失的区别。

这种先例也有不少,包括没有约定运费在货物装船就赚取的贵族院的 The "LornaI" (1983) 1 Lloyd's Rep 373 与高院的 The "Samos Glory" (1986) 2 Lloyd's

Rep 603 先例。另有约定“运费在货物装船或签发提单就已经赚取”(Freight deemed earned upon loading/on signing bills of lading)的先例有上诉庭的 The “Karin Vatis” (1988) 2 Lloyd's Rep 330 与贵族院的 The “Dominique” (1989) 1 Lloyd's Rep 431。以 The “Karin Vatis”先例为例,双方约定支付运费是分两笔,余下运费是要到卸港卸了货之后与滞期费一并计算。但由于船舶还没有到卸港就沉没,所以支付的一天永远不会来临。上诉庭推翻了一审的判决,认为余下运费是一笔已经赚取的债务,支付的日程表只是中性,并非是承租人的抗辩说是支付的一个先决条件。所以这一笔债务还是需要偿还,而支付的时间就变为合理时间,就是估计什么时候船舶到卸港与卸货完成并应结算的一天。

3.1 合约中对债务支付的先决条件

在订约自由下,双方可以对债务的产生与支付约定许多不同的先决条件。那么,这些先决条件必须被满足才能让债务产生。

如针对货物买卖,1979 年的英国《货物销售法》之 Section 49 针对两种情况卖方可以向买方追讨货价的债务,或者换另一个角度说,在这两种情况下才可以产生债务。第一种是货物所有权已经转移给了买方。第二种就是双方约定需要支付货款的“明确的一天”(on a date certain)届临,不论在该天货物所有权是否有转移给买方。这两种情况都是涉及买卖双方的订约意图与谈判结果。而其中在第二种情况更加是涉及合约的规定。例如在 Shell-Mex Ltd v. Elton Cop Dyeing Co Ltd (1928) 34 Com Cas 39 先例中,“明确的一天”被解释为“合约规定支付并且没有其他附加条文或变数的时间”(a time specified in the contract not depending on a future or contingent event)。在该先例中,买卖合约中有条文说:“... sellers have the right at any time to invoice to buyers the due quantities of oil not taken up, and to demand payment of the invoice amounts.”这在法院判是没有明确规定支付的一天,所以卖方只能索赔损失。Wright 大法官是这样说:“... not in terms say that the buyers have to pay the invoice price as a debt at any specified time, or on delivery of the invoice, or at any specified time after delivery. What is invoiced under Clause 15 is still the price payable under the contract, which includes the sellers' services in actually delivering the goods to the buyers' works.”

Stein, Forbes & Co v. County Tailoring Co (1916) 86 LJKB 448 先例涉及一个 CIF 买卖。买卖合约中的支付条文是说:“在船舶抵达卸港时以现金交换付运单证”(net cash against documents on arrival of the steamer)。在船舶抵达时,买方拒绝做出支付以交换付运单证,所以财产/货物所有权也没有转让给买方。法院判卖方只能索赔损失而不能索赔货款,因为该条文并非是明确规定支付的一天,而是有其他附带条件或者变数,就是交出与交换付运单证。Atkin 大法官说:“On the contrary, it is payable expressly against delivery (of the documents)”。

最后介绍的是一个苏格兰先例名为 Henderson and Keay Ltd v. AM Carmichael Ltd, 1956 SLT (Notes) 58,有关货物买卖支付货款的条文是:“见发票以现金马上支付”(prompt cash against invoice)。法院也是判不属于“明确的一天”条文,说:“... must mean something of the nature of a fixed date ... The date of the receipt of the invoice leaves it open to the seller to make the price payable at any time either before or after delivery of the goods. The buyer under such a stipulation can have no certainty as to when the price is to be required of him.”

以上的判决主要是针对1979年英国《货物销售法》条文的解释,条文订得比较死,判法也只能依从。但许多其他的情况是针对双方合约的解释,这就带来或紧或松的不同答案。在许多的案件中只挑一个比较近期的上诉庭先例:Euro London Appointments v. Claessens International (2006) 2 Lloyd's Rep 436,案情涉及被告聘请原告(猎头公司)为他们寻找合适的雇员。原告的标准合约第3.1(c)条文约定如果原告成功为被告介绍雇员,被告需要在发票日期7天之内支付介绍费。同时合约第4条文规定,如果被告和该雇员在12周之内解除雇佣合约,这笔介绍费可以被部分退还给被告。这笔可以退还的费用比例是会根据雇员工作时间的长短来确定。同时合约第4.1条文还规定,如果要获得退款,被告必须要在发票日期7天内支付介绍费,并且要在雇佣关系解除7天内通知原告。这个条文可以节录如下:“In order to qualify for the following refund, the Client must pay the Agency's fee within 7 days of the date of invoice and must notify the Agency in writing of the termination of the Engagement within 7 days of its termination.”

原告给被告介绍了两名雇员,他们与被告签署了雇佣合约,但都没有工作到12周。被告要求根据标准合约第4条文退还介绍费。而原告声称由于被告没有在发票日期7天内付款,所以他们拒绝退款,并向被告起诉要求支付欠下的全额介绍费的债务。被告承认他欠原告一笔介绍费,但应该扣除或抵销依据第4条文的退款。之后原告向法院申请简易判决,但被告又抗辩说第4条文是一个惩罚性条文而无效。地区法院判是原告有权获得被告承认的部分介绍费,也就是需要扣除依据第4条文被告可以获得的退款,因为第4.1条文是一个“变相的惩罚性条文”(disguised penalty clause)而无效。但最终上诉庭支持了原告的上诉,认为第4.1条文只不过是一个先决条件,它并没有为被告设定义务也没有要求被告支付金钱。第4.1条文规定的先决条件背后的主要合约目的并不是威慑被告。所以是判原告可以通过简易判决取得全额介绍费这一笔债务,但可以抵销的退款就由于没有满足先决条件而不会产生。

3.2　不得妨碍对方产生债权的先决条件

即使对债权产生是有一些先决条件,对方不得做一些事情(或者不做一些事情)妨碍这一个先决条件的满足。这一个默示要求就是笔者所著的《合约的解释》一书中第七章13段所讲的法律规定的默示条文规定“双方必须给予协助/合作以让对方顺利履行合约”。这就带来很早的一个先例 Mackay v. Dick (1880 - 1881) LR 6 App Cas 251,案情涉及卖方交付了一台挖掘机给买方,但双方约定如果这一个挖掘机在测试之后不合格,买方可以退货。但买方不合作,这导致挖掘机没有办法进行测试。

贵族院判是买方还是必须要支付这一笔货价作为债务。

这一个所谓的 Mackay v. Dick 原则也适用在后来其他的案件，如在 Tiberghien Draperie S. a R. L. v. Greenberg & Sons（Mantles），Ltd（1953）2 Lloyd's Rep 739 先例，涉及一票布料的 CIF 买卖，但约定在伦敦交货。买方在订约后不久就反悔不想要这票布料，所以没有向海关缴纳进口税，导致货物在伦敦码头仓库无法提取。根据双方的约定，货款是要在发票开出后的 30 天支付。但买方没有做出支付，并争辩说是卖方必须要在伦敦交货这一个先决条件还没有满足。Devlin 大法官判是买方败诉并要支付这一笔债务，因为即使有这一个先决条件，也因为买方的不合作或妨碍而没有满足。Devlin 大法官根据 Mackay v. Dick 原则，判说："That leads me then to the matters which are raised in the amended defence, and I am not at all sure that it is a good defence in law. As Mr. Whitworth（原告代表大律师）put the matter in his closing speech for the plaintiffs, his case is this: he is suing for payment. Payment under the contract which I have found was made was due 30 days after invoice. The delivery of the invoice is not disputed, and 30 days have elapsed. Therefore, *prima facie*, his case for payment can proceed. If the only answer that can be made to that is for the defendants to set up some condition precedent to payment which the plaintiffs have failed to fulfil, the only condition precedent which they can set up is that the goods had not been delivered. Whether that is a condition precedent or not, I need not determine, but assuming that it is, for the reasons I have already given it is not open to them now to set up that condition, the non-fulfilment of that condition. Therefore this point fails. In short, by waiving delivery, because that is what it amounts to, they waived their right to inspect and reject the goods."

同样判法的案例还有 Oricon Waren-Handelsgeschellshaft mbH v. Intergraan NV（1967）2 Lloyd's Rep 82 与 General Trading Co（Holdings）Ltd v. Richmond Corp'n Ltd（2008）2 Lloyd's Rep 475 等。

除了货物买卖合约，在其他的合约也是有同样的道理。如在 Leyland & Co（Russel & Co）v. Cia Panamena Europea Navegacion, Ltda（1943）76 Lloyd's List Law Rep 113 先例，涉及一个修理船舶的合约，修理费是要在船东的验船师做出证明有关的修理是满意后才支付。但船东的验船师不合作，所以修理厂没有这份证明。英国法院判是修理厂有权索赔修理费用这一笔债务，即使没有船东验船师的证明。

另在 Ministry of Sound（Ireland）Ltd v. World Online Ltd（2003）EWHC 2178 先例，案情涉及原告与被告签订的长达 2 年的合作协议。被告是一家网络服务供应商，他想要利用原告的品牌来宣传自己的产品。这份合作协议约定，原告负责包装和发行被告生产的压缩光盘。但在 2000 年 8 月之后，被告停止向原告提供他们制造的光盘，这导致原告不能继续履行合约责任包装和发行被告的光盘。之后被告也没有支付最后一笔分期付款，辩称原告没有继续推广的行为构成违约。但法院判是原告有权获得这一笔到期的分期付款，因为被告不能基于他自己的违约行为而排除原告要求立即支付债务的权利,而且这笔到期的付款是要求在合约规定的明确一天支付,并不涉及合约其他条文的履行与否,不能指称违约造成的损失作为抗辩或抵销。

但以上所举的例子都必须要证明债务已经产生,只是支付这笔债务有一些先决条件要满足,但遭到对方的不合作或是阻碍,这样才会适用本段所介绍的法律默示地位。如果债务并没有产生,但对方已经是不合作或是阻碍,导致合约没办法履行,这一来能够向对方索赔的往往还是一笔非议定损失而不是债务,这里最好的例子就是货物买卖。例如,买方拒绝接受货物令卖方无法做出付运(如在 FOB 买卖下买方拒绝派船),这也是可以广义的说买方不合作或是阻碍,令这票货物无法付运与交出。但卖方的损失是永远变不成债务,因为卖方无法把货物所有权转让给买方以赚取货价。这一来,无辜的卖方能够向买方索赔的并非是货价的债务,而只能是一笔需要证明的损失。如果卖方没有损失(因为市场上涨),卖方就没有损失能够证明。这是在1979 年英国《货物销售法》之 Section 50(1)有清楚的规定,如下:"**Damages for non-acceptance** (1) Where the buyer wrongfully neglects or refuses to accept and pay for the goods, the seller may maintain an action against him for damages for non-acceptance."

在其他的合约也是同样的地位,如在一个期租合约下承租人提前拒绝履行合约的 The "Alaskan Trader" (No.2) (1983) 2 Lloyd's Rep 645 先例中,Lloyd 大法官说:"You cannot claim remuneration under a contract if you have not earned it; if you are prevented from earning it, your only remedy is in damages."(船东不能索赔没有赚取的酬金,如果他根本没有履行。如果船东是被承租人妨碍而没有办法履行并赚取酬金,船东只能索赔损失。)

3.3　服务性合约必须完成服务才会产生债务

英国普通法的默示地位是服务性合约必须完成服务才会产生债务,也就是接受服务的合约方需要支付有关的费用: Cutter v. Powell (1795) 6 Term. Rep. 320; O'Driscoll v. Manchester Insurance Committee (1915) 3 KB 499; Bolton v. Mahadeva (1972) 1 WLR 1009; Miles v. Wakefield MBC (1987) AC 539。这一方面在较早时谈到程租合约的运费时已经有介绍过,并讲到双方可以以明确的条文约定改变这一个法律默示地位,最通常的就是约定还没有作出服务就需要支付部分或全部的费用。

3.3.1　没有完成服务的例外:十分轻微

这一个必须完成服务的法律要求曾经是非常严格,如涉及程租合约的运费就有先例判船舶到了卸港外面发生意外,只差"一步路"而完成不了航次,也不能赚取运费,也没有"按比例运费"(pro rata freight)的说法: Thomas v. Horrowing SS Co. (1915) AC 58。当然,运费最主要就是把货物付运,所以能够把货物以其他办法安排转运去卸港做出交付,还是可以赚取运费。但如果船舶与船上的货物在卸港外发生的意外是全损,根本没有救捞与转运的机会,船东也就赚取不了任何运费。

但看来这一方面的法律有所放宽,有一些比较近期的法律规定服务如果不完全完成,只差一点点,也可以被接受是已经产生债务,即"十分轻微"(de minimis)。这经常出现在涉及建筑工程的案件中，因为在一个庞大的建筑工程经常会留下一些未完成的工作，如在一个建筑中的某个房间油漆少了一层。这种权威的说法可节录上诉庭的 Denning 大法官在 Hoenig v. Isaacs (1952) 2 All ER 176 先例中是说："Unless the breach does go to the root of the matter, the employer cannot resist payment of the price."

3.3.2 提供的服务有缺陷

另一种是如果服务已经完成，明确不过是债务已经产生（除非有关合约有不同的明示约定），但完成的服务并不令人满意或者有缺陷，这在英国法律下还是不足够抗辩对债务的索赔。在 Dakin & Co Ltd v. Lee (1916) 1 KB 566 先例中上诉庭的 Pickford 大法官是说："What the plaintiffs have done is to perform the work which they had contracted to do, but they have done some part of it insufficiently and badly; and that does not disentitle them to be paid."

但这一个说法是有两个例外，第一个例外是服务的缺陷是十分严重，第二个就是"抵销"(set-off)。

在第一个例外可举先例 Bolton v. Mahadeva (1972) 1 WLR 1009 为例，涉及中央发热系统的安装，合约价格是 560 英镑，但由于严重与危险的缺陷，被告需要花 175 英镑改善。上诉庭的 Cairns 大法官在考虑"缺陷的本质与合约价格以及改善的费用"(both the nature of the defects and the proportion between the cost of rectifying them and the contract price)后，拒绝了原告索赔的合约价格或是债务。另在一个 Vigers v. Cook (1919) 2 KB 475 先例中，Lush 大法官是说："the work done by the plaintiff was entirely different from what was contracted for."

在第二个例外是普通法对货物买卖与建造合约承认有一个对债务索赔的抵销，只要是债务人能够说明与合理估计债权人的违约构成了对有关债务所针对的货物/服务价值有所贬低。这一个说法在 Mondel v. Steel (1841) 8 M & W 858 先例被提出，并被 Diplock 勋爵在 Modern Engineering v. Gilbert - Ash (1974) AC 689 先例中重复，说："It is competent for the defendant ... not to set off, by a proceeding in the nature of a cross-action, the amount of damages which he has sustained by breach of the contract, but simply to defend himself by showing how much less the subject-matter of the action was worth, by reason of the breach."

这就表示在货物买卖，如果交出给买方的货物有缺陷或是次货，即使买方不拒货，在卖方索赔货价作为债务的诉讼中，买方也可以估计这票次货的贬值并对合约中的货价作为抵销。在建造合约，如果完成的工程有缺陷，做出支付建造费用的业主也可以在这笔债务中做出抵销与扣减。这种权利可被称为是"减少"(abatement)，也就是去减少支付货价。而可以减少的金额是"how much less the subject - matter of the action [is] worth by reason of the breach"。显然，"减少"(abatement)是不可能超出受害人应该支付的债务：Duquemin v. Raymond Slater (1993) 65 BLR 124 先例。但受害人如果是反索赔损失，就不受到限制，因为损失完全可以超出了有关合约的对价。这种做法的重要性是如果不能抵销债务,受害人就必须按照合约支付全数的货价(买卖合约)或建造费用(建造合约)。至于受害人面对的次货或工程缺陷,是要分开向卖方或建造商提出损失的索赔,这显然是无可避免会带来延误与可能是昂贵的诉讼,运气不好的话违约方甚至会在诉讼的期间倒闭。

这可以贵族院的 The“Aires”(1977) 1 Lloyd's Rep 334 为例,案情涉及一个程租合约。在该航次,船舶在 Rotterdam 卸港短交了货,这表示作为收货人的承租人可以向船东索赔货损货差。由于该程租合约是合并了 1924 年的《海牙规则》,表示针对货损货差的索赔,船东是可以享有 1 年的时效。在该先例,承租人并没有提出货损货差的索赔,他只是通过一个简单的做法即把欠下的运费扣减了这笔估计的货损货差,自以为事情就了结了。在卸货后 1 年届满,船东向承租人索赔这笔扣减的运费,这一笔债务是与《海牙规则》没有关系,所以有时效的话也只是法定的 6 年时效,所以时间还多得很。在同一个诉讼中,承租人就提出反索赔这一笔差不多同样金额的货损货差,但船东就以《海牙规则》1 年时效已经届满作为抗辩。这一来主要的争议就是这笔货损货差能否抵销运费的这一笔债务,或作为“减少”做出扣减。如果可以,承租人大可以避免支付任何欠下的运费,否则就会败诉。在该先例,承租人败诉,贵族院不接受运费的债务可以抵销。

这种抵销的权利也在个别其他的服务性合约中被承认,如针对专业人士:涉及设计师的 Turner Page Music Ltd v. Torres Design Associates Ltd (1997) CILL 1263 先例。

4. 受害人对债务的产生与扩大的限制

4.1 White & Carter 先例的两个限制

在本章 1.3 段曾经提到过的贵族院 White & Carter (Councils) Ltd v. McGregor (1962) AC 413 先例会带来一种不令人满意的危险,就是受害人有机会扩大债务并造成浪费。当然这也不是在所有的合约关系都做得到,如买卖合约,违约的买方拒绝接受货物,受害的卖方就不可能单方面履行把货物付运与交出。如果是雇员被无理解雇,受害的雇员也不可以继续上班赚取工资,因为公司或工厂的大门恐怕都进不去。这可以说是 White & Carter 先例说法下的第一个限制,包括在该先例后的两个有关案例:Decro-Wall International SA v. Practitioners in Marketing Ltd (1971) 1 WLR 361 (案情有关一个建造合约,业主终断合约,承建商拒绝接受违约/毁约,但承建商不能在没有业主合作下单方面履行);Hounslow London Borough Council v. Twickenham Garden Developments (1971) 1 Ch 233(案情有关一个独家代理协议,法国生产商终断合约)。

但毕竟还是有一些类似 White & Carter 先例的合约,受害人可以一意孤行履行合约,提供一些违约方根本不再需要的服务而造成浪费。所以在该先例,Reid 勋爵就提出了第二个限制就是如果欠缺“合法利益”(legitimate interest)受害方就不能拒绝接受违约/毁约并继续履行合约,说:“It may well be that,if it can be shown that a person has no legitimate interest,financial or otherwise,in performing the contract rather than claiming damages,he ought not to be allowed to saddle the other party with an additional burden with no benefit to himself. If a party has no interest to enforce a stipulation,he cannot in general enforce it: so it might be said that,if a party has no interest to insist on a particular remedy,he ought not to be allowed to insist on it.”

但 Reid 勋爵并没有对将合法利益作为对受害人有权选择不接受对方“预期违约”(anticipatory breach)或是“违约/毁约”(repudiation)并扩大债务产生的限制有进一步的解释。在 White & Carter 先例后,有好几个海事的案件对这一方面有进一步的探讨,可做出介绍。

4.2 White & Carter 后先例之一:The “Puerto Buitrago”

首先在 The “Puerto Buitrago” (1976) 1 Lloyd's Rep 250 先例,案情涉及一个 17 个月的光船租约,该船舶是一艘老船而且状况并不是太好。有关的事故是船舶主机发生严重问题并要拖带去基辅(Kiev),在该港进行了一个检验并发觉修理费用高达 200 万美元。而当时该船舶即使是修理好后的市场价格也只有 100 万美元,这看来是个典型的推定全损。承租人认为是不值得进行修理,而最好的办法还是船东自己把船舶接过来当做废钢出售,估计有 50 万美元。所以承租人拒绝把船舶修妥(这是在光租租约下违约)就坚持还船,并承认赔偿修理费用 40 万美元。但船东拒绝并坚持承租人必须修妥后才能还船,看来如果光船租约的租金高,这是船东最希望的结果。在第一审的 Mocatta 大法官判是承租人必须把船舶修妥才能还船,而在这个期间由于还不了船租金还是要继续支付,等于把租金的债务不断扩大。但去了上诉庭,第一审的判决被推翻,认为针对承租人拒绝还船前把船舶修妥的违约,金钱的赔偿就已经足够。如果金钱赔偿足够弥补违约损失的情况下,法院是不会做出“履约指令”(specific performance)(这在本书第十二章有详论)。但如果判是船东可以坚持承租人必须修妥船舶才能还船,而期间租金的债务不断在扩大,这等于是法院作出履约指令。针对船东依赖的 White & Carter 先例,Denning 勋爵是这样说:“It has no application whatever in a case where the plaintiff ought,in all reason,to accept the repudiation and sue for damages - provided that damages would provide an adequate remedy for any loss suffered by him. The reason is because,by suing for the money,the plaintiff is seeking to enforce specific performance of the contract - and he should not be allowed to do so when damages would be an adequate remedy. Take a servant,who has a contract for six months certain,but is dismissed after one month. He cannot sue for his wages for each of the six months by alleging that he was ready and willing to serve. His only remedy is damages. Take a finance company which lets a machine for motor-car on hire purchase,but the hirer refuses to accept it. The finance company cannot sue each month for the instalments. Its only remedy is in damages: see National Cash Register Co v. Stanley (1921) 3 KB 292; Karsales (Harrow) v. Wallis, (1956) 1 WLR 936 (2nd point). So here, when the charterers tendered redelivery at the end of the period of the charter – in breach of the contract to repair – the shipowners ought in all reason to have accepted it. They cannot sue for specific performance – either of the promise to pay the charter hire, or of the promise to do the repairs – becausedamages are an adequate remedy for the breach."

4.3　White & Carter 后先例之二:The "Odenfeld"

下一个先例是 The "Odenfeld" (1978) 2 Lloyd's Rep 357,案情涉及一个10年的期租。但在交船后2年,运费市场暴跌,这导致了承租人坚持还船与拒绝继续支付租金。船东已经把租金转让,该先例是受让人向承租人索赔租金,因为船东一直拒绝接受违约/毁约,并在德国港口抛老锚等待承租人做出营运的指令。在高院,一个重要的争议是受害的船东是否有权拒绝接受违约/毁约。在针对 White & Carter 先例以及之后的判例,Kerr 大法官认为 The "Puerto Buitrago" 先例有不同判法是因为它涉及一个极端的案情/事实,但 Kerr 大法官没有说该案例是判对还是判错,只说"... a presently binding authority on this Court in limiting or qualifying the generality of the principle of a virtually unfettered right of election in favour of the innocent party." Kerr 大法官接下去总结英国法律的地位就是只有在极端情况并且受害人坚持履行租约是完全不合理的情况下,才会限制受害人选择不接受对方违约/毁约的权利,说:"... any fetter on the innocent party's right of election whether or not to accept a repudiation will only be applied in extreme case, viz. where damages would be an adequate remedy and where an election to keep the contract alive would be wholly unreasonable." 最后在该先例,Kerr 大法官判是船东有权拒绝接受承租人的违约/毁约去提早还船。

4.4　White & Carter 后先例之三:The "Alaskan Trader"

在另一个先例 The "Alaskan Trader" (No. 2) (1983) 2 Lloyd's Rep 645,案情也是与 The "Odenfeld" 先例类似,就是在船舶发生主机事故后需要好几个月修理,期租承租人就要求提早还船。结果在1981年4月船舶修妥后,船东要求承租人继续履行并做出营运指令,但承租人拒绝。这导致船舶一直在希腊比雷埃夫斯(Piraeus)港外抛老锚,一抛抛了大半年直到12月租期完毕。在事后的仲裁中,仲裁庭判船东没有合法利益不接受承租人的违约/毁约,所以要把承租人在1981年4月至12月多支付的租金退还。在高院,Lloyd 大法官支持裁决书,不认为在法律上仲裁庭有错判。而针对仲裁庭在双方提供证据后得出船东没有合法利益拒绝接受承租人的违约,Lloyd 大法官认为这一个事实的认定是有约束性与最终性。

4.5　White & Carter 后先例之四:The "Dynamic"

再接下去要介绍的先例是 The "Dynamic" (2003) 2 Lloyd's Rep 693,这也是涉及期租合约。案情涉及承租人在最后的卸港卸货后把船舶通过当地法院扣押要求船东提供担保,这导致船舶的延误长达半个月。由于船舶还没有到还船地点(是要在卸港外领航员离船)承租人就提前还船,这导致了船舶被扣押所延误的半个月到底是否有赚取租金成为争议,船东说是他可以不接受承租人的违约/毁约,拒绝提早还船,所以租金在扣押期间一直在赚取。但承租人认为船东必须接受违约/毁约,即使是承租人扣船导致延误是一种违约,船东的救济也只能是索赔损失。仲裁庭判是船东需要接受承租人的违约/毁约,但在裁决书中没有把原因说得很清楚,所以高院决定把裁决书发还给仲裁庭考虑与针对这一个问题。但 Simon 大法官有针对 White & Carter 先例并列举了受害人选择是否接受违约的限制,说:"The authorities established the following exception to the general rule that the innocent party had an option whether or not to accept a repudiation:(i) the burden was on the contract-breaker to show that the innocent party had no legitimate interest in performing the contract rather than claiming damages;(ii) that burden was not discharged merely by showing that the benefit to the other party was small in comparison to the loss to the contract breaker;(iii) the exception to the general rule applied only in extreme cases;where damages would be an adequate remedy and where an election to keep the contract alive would be unreasonable."

4.6 笔者的仲裁案件简介

这种争议在仲裁案件也很多,如在笔者所著的《国际商务游戏规则—英国合约法》(2000 年)之 14 章就有介绍笔者经历过的其中一个仲裁案件。案情涉及一个程租合约,装港是印度。但在租约订立后不久,船舶还在新加坡没有开始空放航次去印度的时候,就知道了印度发生大水灾导致根本没有货物可装。承租人告诉船东船舶不要去印度装港因为不会有货装,并要求船东另找替代租约减少损失。但船东拒绝接受这一个预期违约,并空放去印度装港,结果在印度装港等待了一段时间才接受违约。之后船舶还是要回航去新加坡附近才找到替代航次。可见,船东选择不接受承租人的预期违约造成了很大的损失,客观看来是完全不必要与浪费。

最近,笔者作为仲裁员也有处理一个案件,就是一个在 2008 年年底的金融海啸之前订立的长期期租合约,显然租金是十分高昂,比起现在的市场租金简直是天上地下。显然,中国承租人起初支付部分租金,但后来停付租金。船东开始了伦敦仲裁,笔者被承租人指定为仲裁员。但承租人事后没有在仲裁中自己作出抗辩,这导致了很长一段时间,船东不断来申请一个接一个的欠下租金的裁决书。而包括笔者在内的仲裁庭对这种债务的裁决也是很快与很简单,因为没有抗辩的余地。结果仲裁庭断断续续做出了 5 个中间裁决书,每一个裁决书都针对两三期的租金(每一期是 15 天的租金),反正承租人一欠下一定数额的租金船东就申请一个裁决书。笔者曾经有怀疑,但最后还是没有澄清,有关:(1)承租人为什么不拒绝履行,坚持还船?但估计可能是有这样做但船东不接受,这就可能涉及合法利益的问题。(2)船东不接受并且断断续续花钱(虽然是小钱)申请与取得中间裁决书,显然对承租人最后还是要付出这笔钱有信心。这可能是该承租人本身是中国一家大公司,赖不掉。或是该租约另有担保人。否则如果船东对承租人完全失去信心,如承租人是光棍,船东就只能尽早接受违约/毁约并去市场另寻找替代租约，即使是租金低得多，但总比最后一场空要强。(3)笔者也曾经与伦敦共同仲裁员讨论过是否要船东提供证据说明他在被欠下租金期间，并向仲裁庭申请裁决书的一天，船舶的确是在为承租人提供服务，等待承租人做出营运指令，才能去赚取租金。

4.7　合法利益的不明朗

可以说有关受害人有否“合法利益”(legitimate interest)坚持合约的存在，继续单方面履行并扩大债务，英国法律是肯定有这个说法。但问题是每一个案件事实都不同，加上有或者没有的分水线也不明朗，所以还是有很多不明朗之处。就算是 White & Carter 先例，受害人也可以说是他需要履行，因为他已经雇佣了有关的员工。对承租人提前还船，受害的船东或二船东也会可以说他已经订立了同样的长期分租约把船舶租进来。对承租人明确告知装港没有货装，受害的船东也会可以说他已经为下一个航次订下了租约，而交船的地点与时间就是该有关程租合约的卸港卸完货。反正在这些争辩与事实下，都很难掌握受害人是否有合法利益坚持合约的存在。这可以节录近期的一本 Andrew Tettenborn 教授等所著的《Contractual Duties: Performance, Breach, Termination, and Remedies》(2011 年)之 19 - 036 段如下：“Unfortunately, Lord Reid did not expatiate on what ‘legitimate interest’ was present in White & Carter but not in the case of the consultant. But two things are worth noting. First, the disproportion between the expense of performance and any benefit to the defendant was small in White & Carter. And secondly, the pursuers presumably had some legitimate interest in obtaining the wherewithal to pay their staff. Moreover, it is not difficult to think of other factors that might well justify a claimant in performing: for instance, the fact that he had himself entered into commitments with third parties. But if factors such as these are not present, it is suggested that a court will be more amenable to a plea of ‘no legitimate interest’.

Nevertheless, it must be admitted that the practical application of the rule has been and still remains somewhat uncertain. Claims have been allowed without much question in cases where there has clearly been a tangibleinterest for the claimant in performing: for example, where a confirming house, having made all necessary arrangements with third parties, shipped goods despite a purported countermand by the buyer, and where carriers insisted on carrying goods to the contractual destination in order to cement their lien for carriage charges against an insolvent client. In more debatable cases, such as time charters where owners faced with a charterer's repudiation sought simply to claim monthly hire notwithstanding, the approach has varied: but the position today seems to be that presumptively a claim should be allowed unless the defendant can demonstrate that the case is ‘extreme’.”

4.8　针对合法利益的近期先例：Isabella Shipowner SA v. Shagang Shipping Co Ltd

但在 2012 年有另一个关于期租合约的重要判例，名为 Isabella Shipowner SA v.

Shagang Shipping Co Ltd（2010）EWHC 1077（Comm）。案情涉及中国沙钢船务在2006年年底签订了一份5年的期租合约租进Aquafaith轮。在2008年年底金融海啸导致运费市场大跌。结果是捱到了2011年7月，承租人的沙钢船务告知船东在本航次完毕后就提早还船。但船东拒绝接受这一个违约/毁约，结果导致船舶在中国卸港抛老锚直到2011年年底租约期届满。承租人认为他在抛老锚期间早已经是违约/毁约，船东只能索赔损失。船东也必须减少损失，也就是去市场寻找替代租约并赚取运费或租金以减少向承租人索赔的损失，显然船东并没有这样做。而船东认为抛老锚期间租约还是继续有效，船舶只是在等待承租人的营运指令，因为船东并没有接受承租人的违约/毁约去终断租约。所以，在期间所赚取的租金，船东完全可以简易索赔这一笔债务。

显然，这带来的主要争议就是船东是否有"合法利益"（legitimate interest）可以拒绝接受违约/毁约。在伦敦仲裁中，仲裁庭是判船东必须接受承租人的违约/毁约，并减少他的损失。换言之，船东只能索赔他的损失，仲裁庭认为The "Alaskan Trader"（No. 2）（1983）2 Lloyd's Rep 645先例有约束性而且本质与本案件是一致。

但这一个案件上诉去了法院，被Cooke大法官改变过来，认为White & Carter先例的两个限制都不适用在本案例（本章第4.1段有详述）。

这两个限制的第一个是受害方可以单方面履行合约，不需要违约/毁约方的合作。Cooke大法官认为期租合约并不像光船租约，船东完全可以单方面履行合约，就是把船舶停在那里等待承租人的营运指令。Cooke大法官是这样说："The question, to my mind, is very simple. Could the owners claim from the charterers under this time charter without the need for the charterers to do anything under the charter? The answer is yes. If the charterers failed to give any orders, the vessel would simply stay where it was, awaiting orders but earning hire. Although the master is under the orders of the charterers, the master and crew are the servants of the owners and the ship is available to the charterers for any order they wish to give. Hire continues to be earned. Although the charterers are obliged under the terms of the charter to provide and pay for fuel, should the bunkers run out whilst awaiting orders, it is open to the owners to stem the vessel and to charge that to the charterers' account. In order to complete their side of the bargain, the owners do not need the charterers to do anything in order for them to earn the hire in question. The earning of hire after purported redelivery was not dependent on any performance by the charterers of their obligations."

第二个限制是如果欠缺合法利益受害方就不能拒绝接受违约/毁约并继续履行合约，Cooke大法官认为是违约方需要证明损失赔偿是一个完全足够的救济而且受害方拒绝接受违约/毁约的行为是完全不合理，甚至是不通情理的（the need for the contract breaker to show that the damages were entirely adequate remedy and that the conduct on the part of the innocent party was beyond all reason, wholly unreasonable or, to use my expression perverse)。

而在本案例 Cooke 大法官指出,沙钢船务经济很困难,这表示船东在将来向他提出索赔损失会有很大的难度。甚至时间隔了一久,承租人可能会倒闭,而船东也没有办法为这笔损失取得诉前担保。这表示根本证明不了受害方的船东可以依赖损失赔偿作为一个完全足够的救济。至于受害的船东拒绝接受违约/毁约的行为是完全不合理,Cooke 大法官也是不同意。因为当时是一个非常困难的航运市场,要求船东终断合约并在市场中寻找替代租约并非是易事。而且没有理由承租人自己不能这样做,就是在市场中把该船舶转租出去。至于说承租人多番坚持终断合约,看来是不可扭转,Cooke 大法官认为这一点根本不应考虑,如果考虑是一个法律上的错误。

在本先例看来在一个期租合约下承租人如果想终断也不是一件容易的事情。会是承租人要向船东为将来的损失赔偿提供银行担保,另加上承租人要指出他可能只是一个钢厂只会走特定航线,对航运市场不了解不容易转租,甚至可能在期租合约中写明了承租人不能转租等,在这种条件下,可能会造成船东没有合法利益拒绝接受承租人的违约/毁约。

第十二章　履约指令

1. 概述

合约的一方当事人拒绝、延迟或者不履行合约(这是指“首要合约义务”[primary contractual obligation])时,无辜的另一方主要会从以下两方面寻求救济:(1)受害方会迫使或是促使另一方履行合约;(2)受害方会希望可以从金钱上得到相应的赔偿(这是指违约方的“次要合约义务”[secondary contractual obligation])。

1.1　受害方在金钱赔偿或履约指令之间的选择

受害方会有不少情况希望迫使或是促使另一方履行合约,而不满足于将来可能是时间较长与胜算难卜的金钱上的索赔,而且还有危险是赔偿会是不足够,因为部分的损失会是无法预见、因果关系中断与其他原因。在某一些违约如很难证明实际损失或是被告不履行会导致原告无法履行他与其他人的合约而严重影响他的商誉等的情况下尤其是显著,可以说金钱赔偿的救济在个别情况下会是不完善与不完整。这种情况随手举例是 The“Anwar Al Sabar”(1980)2 Lloyd's Rep. 261,案情涉及装货后船长拒绝签发提单,这会产生一连串的连锁反应包括信用证无法结汇,买卖合约无法履行等。另是在股票的买卖,也是在金钱损失索赔的计算会是太麻烦,所以尽量避免这种救济办法。这就会导致受害方(在 The “Anwar Al Sabar”先例就是承租人)可以考虑用另一个特殊的途径寻求救济,这就是衡平法上的“履约指令”(specific performance)或是“禁令”(injunction)。

在理论上,履约指令应该是最完善与令人满意的救济。道理很简单,违约方拒绝履行或错误履行(甚至只是做出威胁将会不履约),迫使他按照合约履行应该就是完全说的通,受害方也得到他所要的结果。但由于有其他的更重要的原因(后详),导致了英国法律下履约指令并不被视为是“首选的救济”(primary remedy)。而事实上,英国以前的普通法院针对违约的救济是只有做出金钱的赔偿,没有履约指令的做法。这导致了衡平法院(当时是独立的法院)在普通法下作出金钱补偿是不足够的情况才会插手进来给受害方一个针对违约/毁约方必须履行合约的指令。而且给不给这种救济还要是看衡平法院的裁量权,而不像普通法院只要是证明违约所导致的金钱损失就一定可以取得救济。

在这里可以介绍一下履约指令与禁令的区别,它们在本质上都是为了迫使违约方履行合约。它们的区别只是在履约指令是迫使违约方履行他在合约中作出的“作为的承诺”(positive promise),而禁令是迫使违约方履行合约,特别其中有“不作为的承诺”(negative pledge/covenant)。但很多时候,它们就是同一码事,特别是一些为了“保持现状”(maintain *status quo*)而作出的“中间禁令”(interim injunction),根本就是一个“暂时性的履约指令”(temporary specific performance)。比方说在租船合约下作出一个中间禁令禁止船东撤船,直到针对有关该撤船是否正确作出判决或者裁决为止,就等于是一个暂时性的指令要求船东必须先履行租约直到有了判决或裁决。而衡平法法院强制违约方严格执行的主要甚至唯一的武器就是如果不遵守就构成“藐视法院”(contempt of court)的刑事罪行。这一来,就演变出一个情况是向法院申请履约指令会比申请禁令困难得多。这是因为法院在作出前者的命令,总先要想想被命令的被告是否真的可以履行。如果做不到(如被告没有钱履行),向他作出履约指令就等于是将他逼上梁山,法院显然是不应该这样做。早在 Forrer v. Nash(1865)35 Beav. 167 先例法院就明确说:“The court does not compel a person to do what is impossible”。但这种考虑在对违约方作出禁令就可以漠视了,因为法院的命令只是要求被告不准做什么。这表示即使是没有钱或者没有能力,也不会影响被告不做什么的能力。所以有一个说法是申请一个禁令的成功机会比一个履约指令高得多。但这里也要是注意就是禁令有时候在本质上就是一个履约指令,在面对该类禁令的申请时,批准与否所要考虑的因素就要与履约指令类似了。以笔者熟悉的航运为例,在一个期租合约,如果船东撤船(在航运市场好的时候通常的一个原因就是承租人晚了支付租金),承租人会去法院申请禁令阻止船东撤船。但在本质上它是一个履约指令,因为不准撤船也就是要船东履行租约。毕竟船东也没有在租约内作出任何不作为的承诺,就是承诺不会在租约期内撤船。反正是法院通常是不会作出这种禁令与履约指令:The “Scaptrade”(1983)2 Lloyd's Rep 253。但针对租约,法院会愿意作出一种不同措辞的禁令,稍后在本章 7.2 段有详及。

1.2 两种救济谁是优先之争

英国通过 1875 年《Supreme Court of Judicature Act》将普通法院与衡平法院进行合并。这样一来,原先以普通法院的救济为首而衡平法院的救济为辅的区分就不再存在。但是同一法院在判决的时候仍会首先考虑普通法下的救济,而只在普通法下的救济不足够补偿受害方时才会考虑衡平法下的救济手段,如履约指令。这带来了一些问题,就是历史上把普通法下的救济作为优先,而衡平法的救济只是为了补救普通法救济的不足,是由于衡平法院本来就是为了弥补普通法院的不足而产生。但是两个法院合并之后就不再存在这种区分,那为什么能够最完整弥补受害方损失的履约指令仍然不能作为“首选的救济”(primary remedy)呢?这里可以节录一本权威书籍的说法,就是 Fry 大法官在《Specific Performance》(6th edn,1921 年)之 21 页所说如下:“If a contract be made and one party to it make default in performance, there appears to result to the other party a right at his election either to insist on the actual performance of the contract, or to obtain satisfaction for the non - performance of it. It may be suggested from this that it follows... that it ought to be assumed that every contract is specifically enforceable until the contrary be shown. But so broad proposition has never, it is believed, being asserted by the judges of the Court of Chancery or their successors in the High Court of Justice, though if prophecy were the function of law writer, it might be suggested that they will more and more approximate to such a rule."

另也可节录 Andrew Burrows 教授的《Remedies for Torts and Breach of Contract》(2nd edn, 1994 年)中第336 页也提到了这方面,就是履约指令被英国法院更宽松的做出,看来有一点与大陆法接近(大陆法的国家也有履约指令的做法,并把它当做是一般性的违约救济),说:"Finally, a commonly drawn contrast is between English law's regard of specific performance as secondary remedy to damages and the allegedly reverse situation on the civil law systems. What does this mean? It cannot mean that specific performance is as freely available in civil law systems as damages for this plainly not true. It could mean that the bars to specific performance as primary remedy. It seems rather that the contrast is based on the fact that, deriving from the historical role of equitable remedies as supplementary to those of the common law, a plaintiff in English law will not be awarded specific performance unless he has shown that damages are inadequate whereas in civil law systems there is no such major hurdle. Some recent cases indicate a weakening of this bar, and it has even been argued that specific performance is now the primary remedy in England. This seems exaggerated, but a fascinating theme throughout this chapter is the recent apparent weakening not only of this, but of several other of the traditional bars, so that specific performance may be more freely available now than it was in the past."

但以上的期望或者说法,到了贵族院的 Co - operative Insurance Society Ltd v. Argyll Stores (Holdings) Ltd (1998) A. C. 1 先例,明显是受到了打击。在该先例,贵族院推翻了上诉庭的大多数意见,拒绝做出履约指令。案情涉及一个 35 年的商场店铺租约,被告是租客,经营一间食品超市,其面积占整间商场的 30%。在经营了 16 年后因为亏本而感觉难以经营下去。于是该租客决定停止超市的营业并终断租约。但对于商场的业主而言,仅是对租客作出金钱上的索赔是一个很不如意的救济办法,因为其中有很多损失是没办法估计也更没办法向租客提出的。其中,商场的人流将会由于该食品超市的关门而受到很大影响。业主也会因为这一原因无法向其他租客提高租金,而这一切都不可能向超市的租客进行索赔。所以商场的业主向法院申请要求该租客继续该租约的履约指令。贵族院平衡了各种利弊之后拒绝作出履约指令,其中最重要的原因是衡平法的原因,如不能逼使被告继续一个亏本的生意,被告亏本的损失或许会超过商场业主的损失。这里就涉及一个很重要的原则:不可以漠视违约方选择违约的自由,毕竟履约指令是一种"heavy handed nature of the enforcement mechanism",会造成不公正。还有一个很重要的原因则是法院难以监督该履约指令的执行，难以监督也包括很难将这样一个履约指令写的清楚详细，如在余下的19年，该超市应该如何履约才不构成藐视法院。相比另一种违约救济的金钱赔偿，处理起来就干净利落得多。不论是已经产生的损失或是估计将来的损失，反正就一次过作出判决了事。在这一先例中，也表示了不可以要求被告继续活动（to carry on an activity），而只能是要求达到一个结果（to achieve a result）。在这一个重要的贵族院先例后，可以看到履约指令这一救济还是有很多的局限，谈不上可以把它视为一种首选的违约救济。

1.3　履约指令是在法院监督下履行或被撤销

受害方向法院申请作出履约指令，他等于在完全不同的两个救济办法，即一个是履约指令一个是金钱赔偿之间作出选择前者的救济，也是把该合约的履行交付给法院监督。这会有情况是法院会作出与合约不同的指令，如向法院申请时，合约的最后期限已经过去（如房屋交割日期或交船日期），也是这一方面构成了违约/毁约，这就要求法院必须定一个新的日期履行。在 Johnson v. Agnew（1980）A. C. 367 先例，也明确了如果履约指令没有办法获得执行或者受害方自己也不要求对方执行（可能是受害方自己改变主意），是需要向法院申请把履约指令撤销并宣布合约终断。否则，一天履约指令还在，受害方即使有机会减少损失，如有第三者出好价钱买有关的标的，受害方还是不能这样做，因为在履约指令下对受害方也是有合约的约束。而受害方一天不能这样做，他也无法计算金钱上的损失。Wilberforce 勋爵在 Johnson v. Agnew 先例是这样说："... if the order for enforcement of the order, or may apply to the court to dissolve the order and ask the court to put an end to the contract. This proposition is as stated in Austins of East Ham Ltd. v. Macey（1941）Ch. 338（and see Singh [Sudagar] v. Nazeer [1979] Ch. 474, 480, per Megarry V. – C）and is in my opinion undoubted law, both on principle and authority. It follows, indeed, automatically from the facts that the contract remains in force after the order for specific performance and that the purchaser（毁约方）has committed a breach of it of a repudiatory character which he has not remedied. ..."

1.4　履约指令撤销后可否索赔金钱损失

这一问题直到 Johnson v. Agnew（1980）A. C. 367 才有了定论。带来这一问题是由于受害方是在两种不同的救济之中作出了履约指令的"选择"（election），这方面已经有很多的案例说明有权作出选择的一方在作出后，就是"终局与不可反悔的"（final and irrevocable）。这就带来一个说法是选择了履约指令并成功获得法院的颁布，就不存在走回头路接受违约/毁约方的违约/毁约并重新选择金钱上的索赔，因为一作出履约指令就等于把之前发生的违约/毁约一笔勾销了。这个说法是没有太明确的先例的，曾经在 Henty v. Schr™der（1879）12 Ch. D. 666 先例与 Capital and Suburban Properties Ltd v. Swycher（1976）Ch. 319 先例有涉及。但更明确的还是节录《Vendor and Purchaser》（4th edn, 1936 年）一书之 1025 页如下："And if he obtains an order for specific performance of the contract, that will be a bar to his recovering damages for the breach; for in equity the plaintiff suing on a breach of contract, was required, as a rule, to elect which remedy he would pursue; and a man entitled to alternative remedies is barred, after judgement on the one, from asserting the other."

但问题是履约指令在作出后没有办法有效向被告执行的情况还是经常会有,这就带来了一个问题是受害方事后获得法院把履约指令撤销后能否向违约方提出金钱损失的赔偿。在 Johnson v. Agnew 案情是双方订了一个买卖房屋的合约,时间是1973年1月1日。当时的售价是足够卖方(受害方)支付欠银行的抵押并且再买入另一套房屋。但买方没有办法在合约的限期内,也就是1973年12月21日,完成交易或交割。到了延期后的1974年1月21日,买方还是没有办法履约。不完成交割通常是被视为违约/毁约,但到了1974年3月8日,卖方向法院申请履约指令(或金钱损失,或宣告卖方不再需要履行合约以及可以有进一步的救济)。到了1974年6月27日,履约指令作出。但卖方没有自己要求履约指令的执行,其间估计由于卖方没有准时支付银行贷款,房屋被银行收回并在市场拍卖。这一个拍卖的价格比较低,根本不够归还银行的贷款。这一来,卖方在要求法院把原先的履约指令撤销外,能否向买方提出金钱损失的索赔就有了争议。贵族院判是受害方如果选择接受违约并提出金钱损失的索赔,这的确是一个终局与不可反悔的选择。但如果受害方选择向法院申请履约指令,这只能说是一个暂时性与有条件的选择。所以在履约指令没有办法获得执行并被法院撤销后,受害方是可以提出金钱损失的索赔的。Wilberforce 勋爵是这样说:"In my opinion, the argument based on irrevocable election, strongly pressed by the appellant's(违约/毁约方) counsel in the present appeal, is unsound. Election, though the subject of much learning and refinement, is in the end a doctrine based on simple considerations of common sense and equity. It is easy to see that a party who has chosen to put an end to a contract by accepting the other party's repudiation cannot afterwards seek specific performance. This is simply because the contract has gone – what is dead is dead. But it is no more difficult to agree that a party, who has chosen to seek specific performance, may quite well thereafter, if specific performance fails to be realised, say, "Very well, then, the contract should be regarded as terminated." It is quite consistent with a decision provisionally to keep alive, to say, "Well, this is no use – let us now end the contract's life." A vendor who seeks (and gets) specific performance is merely electing for a course which may or may not lead to implementation of the contract – what elects for is not eternal and unconditional affirmation, but a continuous of the contract under control of the court which control involves the power, in certain events, to terminated it. If he makes an election at all, he does so when he decides not to proceed under the order for specific performance, but to ask the court to terminate the contract..."

1.5 履约指令撤销后索赔金钱损失的计算日期

由于市场的波动,以哪一天作为索赔金钱损失的计算日期至关重要。即使是败诉,违约/毁约方要赔100万美元或是1000万美元是有很大差别的。市场的波动可以2008年年底的金融海啸为例,世界的股票市场在这之前和之后相差了一倍,但在2009年年初之后就慢慢复原,直到11月份,当Dubai World发生经济困难的消息传出时,一天就下跌了3%~4%。相比股票市场,其他的市场如航运市场,波动的幅度更加大。所以,计算金钱损失(通常以合约的价格相比计算日期的市场价格之间的差额)定在哪一天就有很大关系了。在法律而言,起点是计算金钱损失的日期就是违约/毁约的那一天,也就是有诉因的一天。这方面在本章第4段有详尽的介绍,就是受害方一接受了违约/毁约,并就此终断了合约,他就有责任去市场转售或者买入有关的货物。而损失的计算就是以接受违约/毁约这一天的市场价格作为与合约价格相比的差额为准。至于受害方有没有这样做,甚至根本没有这样做(比方说从来没有在市场买入替代商品),不影响损失的计算。

但现在有了履约指令的选择,就会带来变数。因为向法院申请履约指令就表示受害方不选择接受违约/毁约,并确定了损失计算的日期与金额事后向违约/毁约方提出。这一来,如果最终还是没有履约,变成以金钱损失作为替代,就存在是哪一天作为金钱损失的计算日期。这在Johnson v. Agnew(1980)A. C. 367一案中,贵族院判是受害方如果合理提出履约指令的申请,并合理要求对方履约,这一来损失的计算就是以该合约最终被法院终断的一天为准。这表示受害方如果是不合理延长合约的寿命,法院就会有权力以另外的一天作为计算损失的日期。

这里不妨简单介绍受害方可以怎样操纵损失计算的日期,以提高索赔的金额。比方合约价格约定为100元,在违约/毁约(假设是卖方拒绝履行合约)的一天市场价格变成150元。如果无辜的买方接受违约/毁约,他索赔的差额就等于是150元减去100元的差额即50元。但如果买方坚持要对方履行合约并去法院申请履约指令,这就延长了合约的寿命。在过了3个月之后,即使履约指令还尚没有作出,市场发生逆转,一下子价格变成80元。这一来,卖方马上快一步同意履约,这导致原来的违约/毁约由于没有被买方接受,等于违约/毁约从未发生过。但买方就吃了大亏,他应该掌握机会,在卖方一违约/毁约的时候就接受并索赔差价。至于在履约指令已经作出的情况下,卖方要履行更加是理所当然,就是交出只有价值80元的货物并同时收取合约价格的100元。

再把上述的例子稍作改变,就是在违约后3个月履约指令作出,市场价格从150元涨到160元,但市场的走势看来还要往上。这表示无辜的买方再多等3个月或更长时间才向法院撤销履约指令,因为履约指令无法执行。这一来,如果法院把合约终断并以该天作为损失计算的日期,有可能市场价格变成200元,这就令索赔的差额是200元减去100元的100元,相比违约/毁约一天的差额50元多了一倍。

这显示在一定程度上,如果无辜的买方预计市场会下跌,则最好马上接受违约/毁约并把金钱的损失确定下来,不会受后来的市场下跌而减少损失索赔的影响。相反,如果买方预计市场会继续上涨,就最好拒绝接受违约/毁约,甚至去法院申请履约指令。这一来即使后来仍旧没法履行合约，买方仍可以扩大最终索赔的金额。但这些说法可能会被认为是理论多于实际，因为没有人可以准确的预计市场的波动。但这也说不定，特别预计的只是一个相对短期的市场波动。

这表示法律，特别是衡平法在计算损失的日期时是需要区分原告合理与不合理的延长合约寿命。这里首先要说明1858年《Lord Cairns Act》或《Chancery Amendment Act》给了当时的衡平法院给予金钱损失的赔偿的权力，而这本来只是普通法院的权力。该立法在损失计算是给了衡平法院看来是颇大的权力，在section 2说："In all cases in which the court of Chancery has jurisdiction to entertain an application... for the specific performance of any covenant, contract, or agreement, it shall be lawful for the same court, if it shall think fit, to award damages to the party injured, either in addition to or in substitution for such... specific performance, and **such damages may be assessed in such manner as the court shall direct**"（加黑部分是笔者的强调）。这就带来了一个说法与做法，就是衡平法的损失计算日期与普通法不一致。在衡平法院，如果拒绝作出履约指令，就会在拒绝的同时计算损失，并给予受害方救济。显然这一天会是与普通法根据违约/毁约的一天不一样，甚至会相隔很长一段时间，而由于市场的急剧变化，最后会带来很不一样的结果。

这一方面在贵族院的Johnson v. Agnew（1980）A. C. 367先例有了明确，就是选择衡平法或是普通法索赔损失，计算应该是一致的。上诉庭判是损失计算应该以1974年11月26日（法院以简易判决作出履约指令）为准。但贵族院改了是判损失计算是以1975年4月3日（卖方的房屋被银行收回拍卖）为准，Wilberforce勋爵认为"The day on which specific performance became aborted（not by the vendor's fault）should logically be fixed as the day on which damages should be assessed... the same day（3 April 1975）should be used for the purpose of limiting the plaintiff's right to interest on damages"。

至于受害方的原告不合理要求对被告作出履约指令与造成延误，这一来，原告到底在期间有否减损的责任不扩大损失（这课题请看本书第五章）？这方面是有一些案例说是原告有这个责任，如一种不合理的情况就是原告不断及延误地申请履约指令，这就相等于受害方在没有"合法利益"（legitimate interest）下仍拒绝接受违约的道理一样，这会带来一个时间，法院认为原告此时不能再拖延，必须终断合约并减损。首先可以节录Johnson v. Agnew（1980）A. C. 367，Wilberforce勋爵说："In cases where a breach of a contract for sale has occurred, and the innocent party reasonably continues to try to have the contract completed, it would to me appear more logical and just rather than tie him to the date of the original breach to assess damages as at the date when（otherwise by his default）the contract is lost."这句话显示了原告如果不合理申请履约指令，损失计算的一天不一定会押后，也表示原告在申请的期间就已经会有减损的责任。在加拿大与新西兰都有过类似的案件。在加拿大的一些先例有Domowicz v. Orsa Investment

Ltd(1994)20 OR(3d)722;Asamera Oil Corpn Ltd v. Sea Oil & General Corpn(1979)1 SCR 633 at 667 - 68;Lawrie v. Gentry Developments Inc(1989)72 OR(2d)512,涉及买方被拒绝作出履约指令,期间由于房价急升,买方不合理地在市场买入替代的房屋(他是用来投资自用),被判是损失计算不能以开庭审理的一天为准。在另一个加拿大的 Garbens v. Khayami(1994)17 OR(3d)162 先例,涉及卖方坚持与不合理延误的申请履约指令(违约与开庭审理相隔接近4年之久),而当时市场明显在下跌,买方应该尽早把房屋推出市场另找其他买方以减少损失,所以是没有尽到减损的责任而不能获得房屋价格下跌的所有损失。看来在这种情况下,如果有十分合理与明确的减损机会,受害方即使还在申请履约指令,也应该考虑减损,并在法院的履约指令申请改变为金钱损失的索赔:Donb v. Isoz(1980)Ch. 548(CA)先例。

在新西兰的先例是 Hickey v. Bruhns(1977)2 NZLR 71,法院判是原告因为怠慢申请履约指令而被拒绝,金钱损失的计算日期是以如果原告合理尽快作出申请(并且有机会可以取得)的一天为准,而不是在实际被拒绝的一天。

2. 履约指令的阻吓力

已经简单地提到过,履约指令或禁令的主要甚至是唯一的阻吓力就是"藐视法院"(contempt of court)的刑事后果。这相比金钱损失的赔偿,虽然会有各种执行办法(这些办法可看笔者所著的《仲裁法——从开庭审理到裁决书的作出与执行》之第十四章)把"判决债务人"(judgment debtor)的金钱或是资产榨出来,但至少不会涉及刑事后果。顺带一提,即使法院针对被告明显欠下一笔固定金额的索赔(如交货后买方欠下了货款,业主欠下建筑商工程费用或是承租人欠下船东运费),通常会很快作出一个即时的"简易判决"(summary judgment),但这也不是一个履约指令,被告不支付也不涉及刑事的后果。除了藐视法院,也有其他的后果,如"扣押令"(Sequestration Order),这是把被告的财产扣押,因为被告没有依照法院命令与藐视法院。

针对被告没有严格按照法院作出的履约指令或禁令的藐视法院后果,可节录 Hoffmann 勋爵在 Co - operative Insurance Society Ltd v. Argyll Stores (Holdings) Ltd (1998)A. C. 1 先例所说如下:

"... the only means available to the court to enforce its order is the quasi - criminal procedure of punishment for contempt. This is a powerful weapon;so powerful, in fact, as often to be unsuitable as an instrument for adjudicating upon the disputes which may arise over whether a business is being run in accordance with the terms of the court's order. The heavy - handed nature of the enforcement mechanism is a consideration which may go to the exercise of the court's discretion in other cases as well, but its use is to compel the running of the business is perhaps the paradigm case of its disadvantages and it is in this context then I shall discuss them.

The prospect of a committal or even a fine, with the damage to commercial reputation which will be caused by a finding of contempt of court, is likely to have at least two undesirable consequences. First, the defendant who*ex hypothesi* did not think that it was in his economic interest to run the business at all, now has to make decisions under a sword of Damocles which may descend if the way the business is run does not conform to the terms of the order. This, as one might say, no way to run a business. In this case, the court of appeal made light of the point because it assumed that, once the defendant had been ordered to run the business, self - interest and compliance with the order would thereafter go hand - in - hand. But, as I shall explain, this is not necessarily true.

Secondly, the seriousness of a finding of contempt for the defendant means that any application to enforce the order is likely to be a heavy and expensive piece of litigation. The possibility of repeated applications over a period of time means that, in comparison with a once - and - for - all inquiry as to damages, the enforcement of the remedy is likely to be expensive in terms of cost to the parties and the resources of the judicial system. "

以上 Hoffmann 勋爵所讲的是法院作出履约指令,唯一的阻吓力就是违反该命令会构成藐视法院,而这是一个非常强而有力的阻吓,甚至是对于商业社会来说制裁的强度过大。其中,以履约指令强制继续做生意就是看到这方面不妥之处的一个典型例子。

对商业人士犯了刑事罪会对他的商业信誉带来重大的损害,Hoffmann 勋爵还没有提到有刑事记录会导致的其他伤害,包括像一些社会地位崇高的职位会被排斥,或是会被拒绝进入美国或澳大利亚的境内等。但 Hoffmann 勋爵接下去提到两个方面对被告有很大的影响。第一个方面就是假设被告是不想继续做生意或营运,因为亏本。但有了这个履约指令就等于迫使他必须要严格按照法院的命令继续营运。上诉庭(多数意见是作出了履约指令)认为被告的自身利益与按照法院的命令是一致的,但 Hoffmann 勋爵不认为这一个假设是正确。第二个方面是按照法院命令继续营运会是十分昂贵,因为稍有不符履约指令的做法双方当事人就会不断要去法院作出各种申请与争辩,这对双方当事人与法院都造成了庞大的浪费。

例如在 Co - operative Insurance Society Ltd v. Argyll Stores (Holdings) Ltd 先例,上诉庭的履约指令的式样如下:"Keep the demised premises open for retail trade during the usual hours of business in the locality and the display windows properly dressed in a suitable manner, in keeping with a good class parade of shops."在履约指令的期限(还有 19 年),会有各式各样的争议。例如,被告因为家里有丧事或者喜事需要停业一天,就为了避免藐视法院,是要委任律师向法院取得批准改变该履约指令不需要在该天的营业时间开业。或是双方会有争议是橱窗没有好好地摆设,特别是圣诞假期马上就要到了,原告业主不满意,认为是没有严格按照履约指令,这就会涉及法院要解释什么是"properly dressed in a suitable manner"。

总结这一个小段,可以说履约指令的阻吓力也是这种救济的缺点,这迫使法院在作出履约指令时必须格外小心考虑不要失去平衡而产生把被告逼上梁山的阻吓。毕竟,在一个商业合约中发生各式各样的违约是常见的,这也导致履约指令无法实现其作为首选的救济方式。而且履约指令或禁令通常是被称为是"例外的救济"(exceptional remedy),纯粹让法院或仲裁庭根据"裁量权"(discretionary)作出或拒绝作出履约指令,而且是要考虑作出履约指令的利弊以及对被告的影响,并且要考虑整体的公平与否(这毕竟是衡平法的救济)。履约指令也可以在法院加上附带或先决条件下作出:Langen & Wind Ltd v. Bell(1972) Ch 685;Harvela Investments Ltd v. Royal Trust Company of Canada Ltd(1985)2 All ER 966(HL)先例。

以上简单地介绍是可以看到履约指令与金钱损失赔偿的救济是截然不同。在下文会进一步介绍一些英国法院会拒绝或不善待一个履约指令申请的情况。

3. 履约指令不针对没有约束力的承诺,不肯定的合约或已经终断的合约

3.1　没有约因或对价的合约不会作出履约指令

针对一些没有约束力的承诺或所谓的单方面"自愿的协议"(voluntary agreement),法院是不愿意作出履约指令。这种承诺或者协议另一种角度看待就是没有"对价/约因"(consideration),在法律上是不被承认的。这种承诺或者合约大量存在,特别是在家庭成员之间,或是一个富商向慈善机构承诺捐赠多少钱。这种违约既没有金钱赔偿的救济,也不会有履约指令的救济:Morris v. Burrough(1737)1 Atk 399 at 401;Wycherley v. Wycherley(1763)2 Eden 175 at 177;Mountford v. Scott(1975) Ch 258 先例。

在同样的道理下,如果对价或者约因是已经过去(past consideration),这种合约也等于是没有对价或者约因,同样不存在作出履约指令:Robertson v. St John(1786)2 Bro CC 140 先例。

但在一个对价或者约因完全是不成比例或只是象征性,这种合约还是可以取得履约指令,毕竟这本来就是一个法律上承认的有效合约。在 Mountford v. Scott 先例中,上诉庭作出了履约指令,案情是有关一个选择权让买方以 1 英镑的对价买下一栋价值 1 万英镑的房屋。但是在这种情况下会有更大可能履约指令的申请会被拒绝,如有迹象这一个约定以 1 英镑这么低的代价买下,其中有古怪。比方说拣到这一个便宜是涉及误述(即使是误述不足以让被告终断合约)、取巧或不大公平之处,这都会导致衡平法下不予协助。这是在《Chitty on Contracts》(30th edn,2008 年)之 27－033 段所说:"The best view seems to be that specific performance may be refused where inadequacy of consideration is coupled with some other factors not necessarily amounting to fraud or other invalidating cause at law – for example, surprise or unfair advantage taken by the claimant of his superior knowledge or bargaining position, even though such other circumstances do not justify rescission of the contract.”。

3.2 不肯定或太含糊的合约条文不会作出履约指令

接下去讲的是另一种情况，就是在一个法律有效的合约下，有关的条文会太含糊。这导致了受害方可以请求其他违约的救济，如索赔金钱上的损失，但就是没有办法成功申请一个履约指令。毕竟会有情况是法院在这种条文下根本没有办法明确说明怎样履约才不会构成藐视法院，法院想作出履约指令也不知道如何写，而写得含糊就导致被告不知道怎样做才不会犯法。一个简单的例子就是条文说双方必须“尽可能”或“善意”履行某一个合约责任，正如在 C. H. Giles Co v. Morris (1972) 1 WLR 307 先例中 Megarry 大法官所说：“It is true that the ground on which specific performance was resisted in that case was... that it was too indefinite in its obligations, requiring a contracting party to use a particular railway ‘in preference to all others’, ‘whenever reasonably practicable’, and ‘for the longest distance it is reasonably capable of use’.”

这方面的先例有很多，随便举一个有关价格的不肯定或难以肯定，导致无法作出履约指令的例子，是 Courtney and Fairbairn Ltd v. Tolaini Bros (Hotels) Ltd (1975) 1 WLR 297，有关价格条文是说：“based upon agreed estimates of the net cost of works, and general overheads with the margin for profit of 5%”。

在另一个较近期的先例 Posner v. Scott – Lewis (1986) 3 All ER 513 中，Mervyn Davies 大法官在谈到是否作出履约指令的三个考虑因素的第一个就是法院的履约指令可否明确与足够说明要被告做什么，说：“Whether or not an order for specific performance should be made seems to me to depend on the following considerations: (a) is there a sufficient definition of what has to be done in order to comply with the order of the court; (b) will enforcing compliance involve superintendence by the court to an unacceptable degree; and (c) what are the respective prejudices or hardships that will be suffered by the parties if the order is made or not made?”

这方面最后可节录《Chitty on Contracts》(30th edn, 2008 年)之 27 – 042 段：“An agreement may be so vague that it cannot be enforced at all, even by an action for damages. But although an agreement is definite enough to be enforced in some form of legal proceedings, it may still be too vague to be enforced specifically. Thus specific performance has been refused of a contract to publish an article as to the exact text of which the parties disagreed. The reason for refusing specific performance in these cases appears to be that the court would find it difficult or impossible to state in its order precisely what the defendant was bound to do in obedience to the order; and precision is essential since failure to comply with the court’s order may lead to attachment for contempt.”

3.3 允许被告选择终断的合约不会作出履约指令

一个法律有效的合约，如果是有明示说明可让被告选择终断，在这种情况下，法院也是不应该向被告作出履约指令。毕竟作出履约指令也不能剥夺被告在合约中所拥有的权利。这可节录《Chitty on Contracts》(30th edn,2008 年)之 27 - 038 段:"If a contract is expressed to be revocable by the party against whom an order of specific performance is sought, the order will be refused as the defendant could render it nugatory by exercising his power to terminate. On this ground a contract to enter into a partnership at will is not specifically enforceable. The same is true of a contract for a lease which by virtue of the contract itself would contain a stipulation enabling the defendant to determine the lease as soon as it was executed, but a tenancy from year to year, determinable by either party by half a year's notice to quit, is specifically enforceable."

3.4 违约/毁约或预期违约，合约受阻或轻微违约下的履约指令

已经在本章第 1.5 段提及过并可以在这里进一步分析，如果涉及一方当事人"违约/毁约"(repudiation)或"预期违约"(anticipatory breach)，受害方有两个选择，他可以坚持违约方必须履行，或可以接受违约/毁约并终断有关的合约，并向违约方索赔金钱损失。一般的说法就是受害方一旦做出了选择就是"终局性"(final)与"不可反悔"(irrevocable)的。正如 Wilberforce 勋爵在 Johnson v. Agnew (1980) A. C. 367 先例所说:"... if the vendor(受害方) treats the purchaser(违约方) as having repudiated the contract and accepts the repudiation, he cannot thereafter seek specific performance."

可以维持这一个选择权直到法院作出判决的一天，在做法上会是申请一个履约指令(这显然是坚持违约方必须履行)，但也可以在作出判决之前受害方放弃申请而改为是请求金钱损失的赔偿(这显然是接受违约/毁约)。在这个期间，是有危险违约方改变主意或情况有变，导致受害方失去这个选择。如卖方在有关商品的市场猛涨的时候拒绝交货，这是违约/毁约行为，而卖方一直拒绝也属于是一种持续性的违约/毁约。但在买方不作出选择，并等待法院作出判决的期间，市场突然改变方向，从猛涨变为猛跌。这一来，如果改变主意的卖方反应比无辜的买方快，马上表示愿意履行，买方就会失去这个选择的机会，如一早接受违约/毁约终断合约，并向卖方提出索赔。另外，在合约已经被受害方接受毁约而终断，事后就再也不会存在可向法院申请履约指令，要求毁约方履行。道理很简单，因为这样做受害方已经是作出了选择。另是受害方的行动或语言终断合约后，就不存在法院可以通过履约指令令一个已经不存在的合约获得重生。以下可节录 Jones 与 Goodhart 的《Specific Performance》(2nd edn,1996 年)一书之 14 页:

"The plaintiff may then claim either that the contract is terminated or ask for specific performance. But he must elect between them at the trial if he has not done so previously. A person pursuing a claim for specific performance is treating the contract as still on foot, despite the existence of his alternative claim. Hence, the plaintiff cannot elect to terminate the contract after the defendant has remedied his breach and has become able and willing to perform his part of the contract. A plaintiff having the right to terminate the contract may of course do so at any time prior to the trial by communicating his election to the defendant or by other acts demonstrating an unequivocal election to terminate, such as a demand for repayment of a deposit or(in the case of repudiation by the purchaser) a sale of the property by the vendor to a third party. However, it appears that the right to elect can only be kept open if the repudiatory breach is a continuing one(such as a failure or refusal to complete). If the breach is not a continuing nature, the innocent party will be treated as having affirmed the contract if after acquiring full knowledge of the breach he takes steps which indicate an intention to proceed with the contract, or delays in exercising the right to terminate the contract.

Where a claim that a contract is terminated(or 'rescinded') is included in the prayer for relief, the claimant is in fact asking for a declaration that the contracts has been effectively terminated by him. It is not the order of the court which terminates the contract but the act of the innocent party in accepting the repudiation..."

在同样的道理下,如果遇上了"合约受阻"(frustration),也表示有关的合约已经没有办法履行,法院是不会作出履约指令。而即使是还没有达到合约受阻的程度,但情况有了重大改变,导致履行非常困难,法院也会认为作出履约指令会是对被告太苛刻与压迫而拒绝。这方面可以节录 Jones 与 Goodhart 的《Specific Performance》(2nd edn, 1996 年)一书之 15 页:"A radical change of circumstances, making performance very difficult but not impossible, may not be enough to discharge at law a contract but the same circumstances may persuade a court that it would be too harsh and oppressive to grant specific performance."

如果涉及一些轻微的违约,法院会是不愿意作出履约指令。但如果是连续性的违反,即使都涉及轻微的违约,法院还是有可能作出履约指令:Mehmet v. Benson (1965)113 CLR 295 先例。

4. 履约指令不针对金钱损失赔偿已经是足够的救济

这是一个对履约指令最主要的限制,也等于把金钱补偿的救济视为是"首选的救济"(primary remedy),只要法院认为金钱赔偿可让受害方回到合约被履行的同样经济地位。这一个限制以前更加是绝对,特别在普通法院与衡平法院是分开操作的年代。但即使到了近期,说是履约指令的救济已经宽松得多,但这一个限制还是被重视,就是金钱损失补偿看来是足够的救济,法院通常不愿意作出履约指令。这里首先可节录 Flake v. Gray(1859)4 Drew 651 先例,Kindersley 大法官是说:"Upon what principle does the court decree specific performance of a contract whatever? A Court of law gives damages from non - performance, but a Court of Equity says 'that is not sufficient - justice is not satisfied by that remedy', and therefore a Court of Equity will decree specific performance, because a mere compensation in damages is not a sufficient remedy and satisfaction for the loss of the performance of the contract."。

在 Price v. Strange(1987) Ch 337 先例,上诉庭的 Buckley 大法官提到了法院面对履约指令的申请是应该分四个步骤按部就班地作出考虑,其中第二个就是看金钱损失赔偿是否是足够的救济。如果是,法院就不需要进一步考虑第三与第四步。他是这样说的:"... it would seem that the questions which should be asked by any court which is invited to enforce specific performance of a contractual obligation should be: (1) Is the plaintiff entitled to a remedy of some kind in respect of the alleged breach of contract? (2) If so, would damages be an adequate remedy? (3) If not, would specific performance be a more adequate remedy for the plaintiff? (4) If so, would it be fair to the defendant to order him to perform his part of the contract specifically? The first question goes to the validity and enforceability of the contract. Only if it is answered affirmatively do the subsequent questions arise. If the second question is answered affirmatively there is no occasion for equity to interfere, so that again the subsequent questions do not arise. If the second question is answered in the negative it will not necessarily follow that the third question must be answered affirmatively. For instance, the circumstances may not be such as to admit of specific performance, as where the subject matter of the contract no longer exists. Only in the event of the third question arising and being answered in the affirmative can the fourth question arise. It is here, as it seems to me that the alleged principle of mutuality comes in."

但近年来,针对这一方面是有一定程度的放宽,毕竟在今天英国都是由一个法院处理普通法的损失赔偿以及衡平法的履约指令。现在的法院是更倾向考虑在选择金钱损失赔偿的救济或履约指令的救济,哪一种会是更完善与公平,而再也不是只问到底金钱损失赔偿是否已是足够。这方面可节录《Chitty on Contracts》(30th edn, 2008 年)之 27 - 005 段,所说如下:"The historical foundation of the equitable jurisdiction to order specific performance of a contract is that the claimant cannot obtain a sufficient remedy by the common law judgment for damages. Hence the traditional view was that specific performance would not be ordered where damages were an 'adequate' remedy. Typically, this would be the case where the claimant could readily make a substitute contract for performance equivalent to that promised by the defendant: the claimant would than be adequately compensated by damages based on the difference between the cost (or market price) of the substitute, and the contract price. Indeed, an award of specific performance in such a case would conflict with the mitigation requirement and be oppressive to the defendant. Some of the earlier authorities approach this problem by asking whether damages would in fact adequately compensate the claimant. At latest days in the development of the subject, the courts tend rather to ask whether damages were likely to be an adequate remedy for breach of the type of contract before the court. But more recently the courts had reverted to the earlier approach, by asking whether specific performance was the most appropriate remedy in the circumstances of each case. The position is not whether damages are an 'adequate' remedy, whether specific performance will 'do more perfect and complete justice than an award of damages'. The point was well put in a case (Evans Marshall & Co. Ltd v. Bertola [1973] 1 Lloyd's Rep. 453) in which an interim injunction was sought: The standard question 'Are damages an adequate remedy?' might perhaps, in light of the authorities in recent years, be rewritten: 'Is it just, in all the circumstances, that a plaintiff should be confined to his remedy in damages?'"

以下进一步分析较早前所提到或涉及的一贯的说法是如果受害方可以在其他渠道如在市场上找到"替代履行"(substitute performance),就不应该命令被告履行合约。因为既然有替代,受害方的损失就可以通过金钱的赔偿作出救济。这种赔偿通常就是替代履行所付出的代价(通常会比较高)相比合约的价格之间的差价。其中在货物买卖就可以给一个很典型的例子,如果是卖方没有或不想履约交货,而有关的货物是到处都买得到。这就表示根本没有必要强制卖方履行合约(毕竟他可能有其他的困难导致违约/毁约)。买方大可以接受违约/毁约终断买卖合约后,尽快从其他渠道购买替代货物,然后向违约/毁约的卖方索赔差价的金钱损失。可以说,在以前法院的考虑,由于在这种情况金钱赔偿是完全足够的救济,所以根本不会考虑履约指令的救济。即使到了今天,法院会更加注意整个案件的公平与恰当,而不是只考虑金钱赔偿是否足够,恐怕在这种情况下还是会认为向违约/毁约的卖方索赔差价还是会比履约指令更加公平与恰当。这是因为要求买方购买替代货物,会同时要求买方"减少损失"(mitigation of loss),否则多出来的损失部分是不能向卖方成功索赔。另外,也会考虑到卖方会有情况是一种"有效益违约"(efficient breach)。反正是这两方面的考虑都会带来经济效益,整体的是值得鼓励,而不应该以履约指令去干预。

4.1 有效益违约

违约/毁约会在有些情况下是值得鼓励的,因为是整体而言更加有效益或节省。举一个简单的例子,也是笔者经历过,就是一家大的国内船公司因为内部协调出了问题,导致了同一艘船舶出租了给两个不同的承租人,租期一长一短。显然该船公司是必须对其中一个租约违约/毁约(除非其中一个承租人愿意放船东一马同意终断租约,而且不会乱敲竹竿),因为不能一船两用。而有效的违约显然是应该拒绝履行租期短的租约,因为造成的损失较少,赔偿也赔得较少。但如果很容易取得履约指令的救济,就会导致该承租人通过这个途径迫使该船公司不能作出有效益的选择。而且如果两位一长一短租约的承租人都能够在他们不同的仲裁庭或法院取得履约指令的救济,就会迫使该船公司非要犯法不可,这正是逼上梁山。可见,金钱赔偿的救济会是对船公司合理得多了。这种“乌龙”的事也不止中国船公司会发生，西方船公司也会发生这种情况：The “Stena Nautica”(No.2)(1982)2 Lloyd's Rep.336 先例。针对上述的货物买卖例子，卖方不想履约交货，也可能会涉及有效益违约，他宁可赔钱也比履行合约更划算。一种情况会是与上述的租船一样，卖方把同样一批货一货两卖。另一种情况会是卖方自己也需要这种货物，突然发生了货物短缺而导致了自己主要的业务因为没有这种货物的供应而要蒙受庞大的损失，所以他决定不履约交货，宁可赔货物的差价。这种千变万化的例子可以不断数下去，反正就可以看到违约/毁约的合理性与有效性。

有关有效益违约的课题可参见笔者所著的《国际商务游戏规则——英国合约法》第十四章之第12.7段。

4.2 减少损失

受害方如果向违约方索赔损失，他是有“责任”减少损失（减损）（mitigation of loss）。如果他没有这样做，并不代表他违反责任，只代表他不能把本来可以通过合理减损而省回的损失部分成功向违约方索赔。有关这一个课题，在本书第五章有详述。在上一小段也已经多处提到了减损与有效益违约之间的关系。因为对违约方没有强加减损的义务，就不会有有效益的违约。等于在较早时介绍的例子有关租房屋2年在1年后违约/毁约，如果房东没有减损的责任，让房屋空置1年，反正可以向违约方索赔，这就不会带来有效益违约的说法。

为了不重复，在这里只会探讨这个减损与履约指令之间的关系。这两个说法之间也是有一定的矛盾，因为履约指令就是受害方拒绝接受以金钱作为赔偿的救济办法，而是要求违约方履行合约。如果这是违约/毁约（特别是预期违约），也表示受害方拒绝接受违约/毁约，坚持违约方必须履行的做法。这一来，是有一个说法，在这个期间受害方是没有减损的责任。毕竟，这种矛盾是显然可见。因为受害方如果能够在市场上找到其他合理的替代（假设是商品），并为减少损失而这样做，岂非与拒绝接受违约方的违约/毁约或申请履约指令有严重的矛盾？试想，如果违约方真的履行并交出合约中约定的商品，受害方岂非是会有两批同样的商品，而他只需要一批。这一个说法可看 Oliver 大法官在 Radford v. De Froberville(1978)1 All ER 33 先例所说：“It is difficult to see how, assuming that it is reasonable for a plaintiff to seek specific performance, he can be under a duty to mitigate by acquiring equivalent property until he knows whether or not the court is going to give him his decree.”

另也可看贵族院的先例 Carter(Councils)Ltd v. McGregor(1962)A.C.413，它的概述可节录《Chitty on Contracts》(30th edn，2008年)之26－122段：“... the plaintiff refused to accept defendant's anticipatory repudiation of the contract and was able thereafter to complete the performance of his side of the contract without the co－operation of the defendant; the majority of their Lordships held that the plaintiff could recover the full amount due for his performance: he was under no obligation to terminate the contract on the ground of the defendant's anticipatory breach and sue for damages. The two of their Lordships in the minority thought the plaintiff should have mitigated his loss by discontinuing his performance of the contract, but the majority held (by implication) that in the special circumstances of the case there was no such duty on the plaintiff to act reasonably."(最后的一句显示了贵族院的多数与少数意见,他们的分歧显然就是在原告是否有合法利益拒绝接受被告的预期违约,这里涉及原告在做法与说法的合理性。)

由于减损的责任只是与受害方索赔金钱损失作为救济才有关系,这就涉及"损失计算"(assess damage)应该是以哪一天为准。在普通法,计算损失是以违约/毁约的一天为准,所以在货物买卖就表示受害方必须在该天在市场试图减损。而如果在后来开庭审理时,受害方索赔更大的一笔金钱损失,就会存在多出来的部分损失可能是他没有减损而造成的。

这表示了受害方如果合理不接受违约/毁约或是进一步向法院申请履约指令,他是不存在有减损的责任的。但如果受害方是不合理延长合约的寿命,要不是在没有"合法利益"(legitimate interest)下还是拒绝接受违约/毁约终断合约,或是去法院申请履约指令,这都会导致损失计算的日期被提前,因为扩大了的损失是由于受害方的不合理(包括没有减损)而造成。这方面已经在本章之1.5段有详细介绍,不重复,除了一提 Hickey v. Bruhns(1977)2 NZLR 71 的先例有关原告怠慢申请履约指令而被拒绝后,金钱损失的计算日子是以原告合理尽快作出申请(并且有机会可以取得法院去作出)的一天为准,而不是在实际被拒绝的一天。

4.3 可以买到替代商品时金钱赔偿通常被视为是更佳的救济

已经解释过在受害方可以从其他渠道找到"替代履行"(substitute performance),就表示通常可以通过金钱赔偿作为救济。不少商业合约涉及货物买卖,如果买卖的货物是在市场上可以随时买到替代的货物,法院通常是不会作出履约指令的:Cohen v. Roche(1927)1 KB 169。但如果一样东西是不能在市场另找合理的替代,法院是会下履约指令。这特别是在岸上的房屋与土地买卖的情况:Meng Long Development v. Jip Hong Trading Co. Pte. Ltd(1985)AC 511;Amec Properties v. Planning Research & Systems(1992)EGLR 70 等先例。还有就是像航运的船舶买卖涉及一艘特别用途的船舶,是买方不能在市场另找合理替代的,也应会有机会成功申请法院或仲裁庭下履约指令,迫使卖方不能转售他人:The "Oro Chief"(1983)2 Lloyd's Rep. 509 先例。

在股票买卖或转让的合约,如果在市场上随时可以买得到这种股票,履约指令也不会被考虑:Cud v. Rutter(1719)1 P Wms 570 先例(这一个古老的先例是涉及价值1000 英镑投机性的南海股票的转让)。但如果不是在市场上可以买到的股票,如是私人公司,法院就会很愿意作出履约指令:O'Neill v. Ryan(No. 3)(1992)1 IR 166 先例;或是合约是针对购买新股:New Brunswick & Canada Railway & Land Co Ltd v. Muggeridge(1859)4 Drew 686;ANZ Executors & Trustees Ltd v. Humes Ltd(1990)VR 6155 等先例。如果涉及上市公司的股票,虽然可以在市场上买到,但会有例外情况,如在市场上很难买得到的一些股票:Re Schwabacher(1908)98 LT 127 先例;或是合约涉及购买一家上市公司的控制性股票:Dobell v. Cowichan Copper Co. Ltd. (1967) 65 DLR (2d) 440;Chinn v. Hochstrasser(1979) CH 447 等先例。

针对货物买卖,在 1979 年英国《货物销售法》是有立法的履约指令的做法,这是在 section 52,如下:“(1) In any action for breach of contract to deliver specific or ascertained goods the court may, if it thinks fit, on the plaintiff's application, by its judgement or decree direct that the contract shall be performed specifically, without giving the defendant the option of retaining the goods on payment of damages. (2) The plaintiff's application may be made at any time before judgement or decree. (3) The judgement or decree may be unconditional, or on such terms and conditions as to damages, payment of the price and otherwise as seem just to the court. . . . ”

立法条文的文字上只针对“特定货物”(specific or ascertained goods)。这一个定义肯定是包括一艘双方约定船名的船舶,或一头名驹,或一幅名画等。但这通常不包括一些“非特定货物”(unascertained goods),这通常就是指一般商品(如散货,如钢材或棉花),这种商品通常有市场可以买入替代商品。如果是在订约时还没有生产或存在的货物,这也应该是非特定货物。针对前者的特定货物,立法条文规定了法院可以作出履约指令的救济,虽然条文在措辞上没有剥夺法院的裁量权。

这特定货物的新定义在 1995 年英国《货物销售法》扩大为:“goods identified and agreed on at the time a contract of sale is made and includes an undelivered share, specified as a faction or percentage, of goods identified and agreed on as aforesaid. ”这一来,在这定义下可能带来了一些微妙的差异,如一般的煤炭买卖曾被枢密院拒绝作出履约指令:Dominion Coal Co. Ltd v. Dominion Iron and Steel Co. Ltd(1909) AC 293 先例。但如果是同样的商品(煤炭)在订立买卖合约时说明了是什么商品(如说明是“长江轮”上所装载的 15,000 吨煤炭),这变为买卖一批特定货物,在新的立法定义下可以有机会取得一个履约指令。但买卖合约换了一个稍微不同的写法,如说是“长江轮”上所装载的其中 5000 吨,就不是特定货物了。这里在 Benjamin 所著的《Benjamin's Sale of Goods》(8th edn, 2010 年)一书之 17 - 097 段有介绍,如下:“But the 1995 extension of the definition means that if a bulk (such as the cargo of a ship) was identified and agreed upon when the contract was made, an order of specific performance may be made under section 52 in respect of a fraction or percentage of the bulk. But where the part sold is a specified quantity to be taken from an identified bulk (e. g. 500 tons out of a cargo of 1,000 tons) it appears that no order can be made, because the goods are not ‘specific’ in terms of the new definition, and they remain unascertained. ”

上述看来是非常细微的区分也不必太关注,因为履约指令涉及法院的裁量权,加上稍后会介绍是特定货物与非特定货物的不同对待不再明显。虽然有说法是 1979 年英国《货物销售法》是一套完整的法典,不应该再加以补充:Re Wait(1927) 1 Ch

606(CA);The "Aliakmon"(1986)2 Lloyd's Rep. 1 等先例。加上解释立法(或合约)条文的原则"特别针对一件事情但不提其他同类事情"(*Expessio Unius*)下,既然只针对特定货物才可以作出履约指令,就显示了立法的意图是非特定货物就不这样做。但近年来也有了案例去针对一些非特定货物与市场上可以买到替代的商品,也会作出履约指令强制买卖合约的执行,如 Sky Petroleum v. VIP Petroleum(1974)1 WLR 576 的汽油与 Howard E Perry Ltd v. British Railways Board(1980)1 WLR 1375 的钢材。在前一个先例,由于当时的市场汽油严重短缺,原告要买替代的汽油不容易,法院作出禁令不允许油公司中断汽油供应给一个车行(有关的禁令在本质上就是相等于履约指令)。在后一个先例,法院下令必须交货,除了是买方很难从市场买入替代钢材外,还有其他原因是 Megarry 大法官所提到的,说:"Damages will be a poor consolation if the failure of supplies forces a trader to lay off staffs and disappoint his customers(whose affections may be transferred to others)and ultimately force him into insolvency."

较近期的先例是 Thames Valley Power Ltd v. Total Gas & Power Ltd(2006)1 Lloyd's Rep. 441,案情涉及 Total 与 Thames Valley 订了一份长达 15 年的提供燃气的协议。Thames Valley 是一个合伙公司,其成立的目标是为了取得为期 15 年的为伦敦希斯罗机场提供暖气与电力的合约。在履行了 10 年左右,Total 说是根据合约的一条不可抗力条文终断合约。Christopher Clarke 大法官判是 Total 不能终断合约,并同时提到可以对 Total 作出履约指令。虽然,在该先例中是不必这样做,因为 Total 明确表示如果是败诉,即不能以不可抗力终断合约,他会继续履行下去。Christopher Clarke 大法官看来是有两个理由支持履约指令。第一个理由是 Thames Valley 找不到替代履行,但照理说燃气应该在市场上买得到,但估计这么大的数量与一个肯定的供应来源就难以替代。他针对该合约的基础是这样说:"to assure a source of supply from a first - rate supplier for 15 - year term ",所以光是作出损失赔偿就会是剥夺了"substantially the whole benefit that the contract was intended to give them"。第二个原因是认为金钱赔偿并非是一个足够的救济,计算接下去 5 年的损失几乎是不可能,因为燃气市场价格的波动。

看来,即使有了立法规定,法院对货物买卖合约作出履约指令或禁令在新的趋势下主要还是考虑在选择金钱损失赔偿的救济或履约指令的救济,哪一种会是更完善与公平,而再也不是只问到底金钱损失赔偿是否已是足够:Evans Marshall & Co. Ltd v. Bertola(1973)1 Lloyd's Rep. 453 先例。

但还是有一些不明朗的先例,会否在新的趋势下法院有不同的裁量权,更愿意作出履约指令。在 Societe des Industries Metallurgiques SA v. The Bronx Engineering Co Ltd(1975)1 Lloyd's Rep. 465 先例,有关的货物是一台"Bronx combined driver and pull through slitting machine"。但被告卖方拒绝提供,紧急需要这一台机器的原告向法院申请履约指令,并提供证据证明虽然在市场上可以找到替代,但需要的时间长达 9 至 12 个月其他的生产商才能够提供。但上诉庭拒绝作出履约指令。这判决看来是受到批评，在 Jones 与 Goodhart 的《Specific Performance》(2nd edn，1996 年)一书之 145 页说："This conclusion ignored the commercial reality that it was impossible to mitigate within a reasonable period of time; it was particularly harsh because the court accepted that the plaintiff would have had difficulty in calculating his loss since the machine was to be used in Tunis."

这种能够在市场找到替代的情况其实经常会有，只不过有时候不容易，如耗时过长。照说，考虑哪一种救济办法比较说是更完善与公平，也应该把这个因素考虑在内。毕竟它在本质上与 Sky Petroleum v. VIP Petroleum 先例和 Howard E Perry Ltd v. British Railways Board 先例没有什么不同，就是在当时的市场找替代不容易，因为有短缺。另是如果再过半年会否市场就不再短缺，而双方争议还是持续，可让被告回来向法院申请更改或取消履约指令？

4.4　不可以买到替代商品通常被视为金钱赔偿是不足够的救济

没有办法在市场上买到替代商品通常是涉及稀有商品，这种商品有说法是属于或接近"独一无二"(uniqueness)，如买卖古董或名画。在这种情况下的违约，往往也表示了对受害方而言光是将来金钱的赔偿并不足够，他无法在市场上买入替代商品或转售给其他买家，再向违约方索赔差价。这稀有商品也不一定需要到独一无二的程度，虽然对独一无二的买卖法院几乎肯定会作出履约指令，如涉及名画"蒙娜丽莎"(Mona Lisa)的买卖。一般而言，越是稀有的商品，就越有机会能够说服法院作出履约指令。这表示较有名气的画家作品也很有机会能够成功取得履约指令，但一些廉价与充斥市场的一些作品，由不知名的街头艺术家所制作的就不会有机会了。同样道理下，曾经成功取得履约指令的先例有：涉及古牛角买卖的 Pusey v. Pusey(1684)1 Vern 273；涉及一个古老烛台买卖的 Duke of Somerset v. Cookson (1735)3 P Wms 390。而在 Cohen v. Roche(1927)1 KB 169 先例中，Hepplewhite 制作的椅子被认为是没有什么特别价值的商品，因此法院拒绝作出履约指令。这表示涉及名牌商品也不会容易取得履约指令，毕竟名牌商品在今天也是大量充斥在市场。

如果涉及的商品有一个感情上的原因，则也会成为一个重要的因素说服法院作出履约指令：Morris v. Sparrow 287 SW 2d 583(1956)先例。

到底是否是市场上买不到替代品也往往涉及证据，如在 The "Oro Chief"(1983)2 Lloyd's Rep. 509 先例，这是关于一艘油矿两用船舶的二手船买卖，这种船舶市场上不多，而在有争议的时候市场上更是没有同类船舶出售。申请履约指令的第一位买方声称他对该船舶有了特殊用途的安排，所以必须强制交船。但他无法说服法院，因为法院认为针对同样的用途可以由一艘一般性的油轮作为替代，而当时这种油轮市场上是有在出售。Staughton 大法官是这样说：

"It is an enquiry whether the charterer of the chattel itself is such that it is unique, or cannot for the time being be replaced by the purchase of a substitute in the market.

That test is plainly satisfied in the present case. Oro Chief is an ore/oil carrier. She has certain advantages of flexibility in trading. Only a limited number of such vessels of similar size exist. At present none is available for sale in the market....

Eximenco(第一买方)sought to prove that they had a particular need for vessel as an ore/oil carrier. The attempt failed. An ordinary tanker would have suited them just as well for the time being. And ordinary tankers of similar size are available."

这一个先例相比另一个较早的涉及二手船买卖的先例,法院就认为船舶是独一无二并作出履约指令。该先例是 The "City"(1927)27 Lloyd's Rep. 24,Wright 大法官是这样说:"... in the present case there is evidence that the 'City' was of peculiar and practically unique value to the plaintiff. She was a cheap vessel, being old, having been built in 1892, but her engines and boilers were practically new and such as to satisfy the German regulations, and hence the plaintiff could, as a German shipowner, have her at once put on the German register. A very experienced ship valuer has said that he knew of only one other comparable ship, but that could now have been sold. The plaintiff wants the ship for immediate use, and I do not think damages would be an adequate compensation."

4.5 独一无二的土地买卖通常被视为金钱赔偿是不足够的救济

在英国法下,土地通常被视为是独一无二(uniqueness),换言之就是无法在市场上买到相同的替代。这是因为土地或房屋会有对个别人士的不同感情、环境或独立因素。所以涉及土地买卖或有关的合约通常都可以向法院取得履约指令,而许多在这方面的先例都涉及土地买卖。即使所买的土地纯粹是为了投资或这买方是想尽快转售以牟利,不是为了自住,也不影响法院的做法:Pianta v. National Finance and Trustee Co Ltd(1964)180 CLR 146(High Ct of Australia)先例。

但看来针对香港许多大厦的楼层,同类房屋在市场上有大量的供应,独一无二的说法站不住脚:Centex Homes Corp v. Boag 128 NJ Super 385(New Jersey)先例。

这方面的说法可节录《Chitty on Contracts》(30th edn,2008 年)之 27-007 段所说:"The law takes the view that the purchaser of a particular piece of land or of a particular house(however ordinary) cannot, on the vendor's breach, obtain a satisfactory substitute, so that specific performance is available to the purchaser. It seems that this is so even though the purchaser has bought for resale. Even a contractual license to occupy land, though creating no interest in the land can be specifically enforced. A vendor of land, too, can get specific performance; for damages will not adequately compensate him if he cannot easily find another purchaser or if he is anxious to rid himself of burdens attached to the land. It seems to make no difference that the land is readily saleable to a third party; or even that after contract but before completion a compulsory purchase order is made in respect of it. Yet in such cases damages(based on the difference between the contract price and the resale price, of the compensation payable on the compulsory acquisition) would seem normally to be an adequate(in the sense of an entirely appropriate) remedy."

4.6 损失很难计算也通常被视为金钱赔偿是不足够的救济

损失很难计算是法院作出履约指令考虑的因素之一,这在较早的4.3段介绍的Sky Petroleum v. VIP Petroleum(1974)1 WLR 576先例已经有涉及。这种案例有很多,可简单节录《Chitty on Contracts》(30th edn,2008年)之27-008段所说:"**Difficulty of quantifying damages.** In a number of other situations damages are considered to be an inadequate remedy because of the difficulty of quantifying them. For this reason specific performance may be ordered of a contract to execute a mortgage in consideration of money advanced at or before the time of the contract(Swiss Bank Corp. v. Lloyds Bank Ltd [1982] A. C. 584,595),and of a term of a contract of loan giving the creditor the right to have the loan repaid out of specific property(Swiss Bank Corp. v. Lloyds Bank Ltd [1982] A. C. 584;Kingcroft Insurance Co Ltd v. H. S. Weaver [Underwriting] Agencies Ltd [1993] 1 Lloyd's Rep. 187):the value to the creditor of obtaining security for a debt cannot be precisely quantified. For the same reason,specific performance can be ordered of a contract to pay(or to sell)an annuity(Beswick v. Beswick [1968] A. C. 58),of a contract to indemnify(Ascherson v. Tredegar Dry Dock & Wharf Co Ltd [1909] 2 Ch. 401),of a sale of debts proved in bankruptcy(Adderley v. Disxon [1824] 1 S. & S. 607)and of a promise in a letter of indemnity to secure the release of a ship in the event of her being arrested by reason of the shipowner's delivering the goods without production of the bill of lading(The "Laemthong Glory" [2005] 1 Lloyd's Rep. 632). Damages may also be an inadequate remedy because the claimant's loss is difficult to prove(Thames Valley Power Ltd v. Total Gas & Power Ltd [2006] 1 Lloyd's Rep. 441)or because certain items of loss(Malik v. B. C. C. I. [1998] A. C. 20)are not or may not be,legally recoverable,because of the difficulty of enforcing a judgment for damages in a foreign country(The "Laemthong Glory"),because of the delays which may occur(even in domestic case)in securing the actual payment of damages(Thames Valley Power Ltd v. Total Gas & Power Ltd [2006] 1 Lloyd's Rep. 441),or quite simply because the defendant may not be 'good for the money'(The "Oro Chief" [1983] 2 Lloyd's Rep. 509;Themehelp Ltd v. West [1996] Q. B. 84)."

以上提到了很多个先例,接下来对其中三个作进一步介绍:Beswick v. Beswick, The "Laemthong Glory"与The "Oro Chief"。

Beswick v. Beswick先例在本书第七章多段有详细介绍,这里主要是针对金钱赔偿是否是足够的救济的问题。案情涉及的是一位老先生把他的一个商店交了给他的侄子打理(估计是老先生年事已高),作为双方约定的交换条件,他的侄子承诺在他死后照顾他的妻子(侄子的伯母),每星期给伯母5英镑作为生活费。但在该老先生死后,侄子拒绝履行合约,之后伯母以死去丈夫的"遗产执行人"(administratrix)的名义向法院申请履约指令,法院也作出了履约指令。当时还没有1999年《Contracts (Rights of Third Parties) Act》,所以不存在伯母以自己的名义起诉她的侄子,因为合约只是老先生与侄子之间,他们才是有“合约相互性”(privity of contract),伯母只是合约的第三人。在这个案例中,原告(作为老先生的遗产执行人)并没有实质上的损失,只有“名义损失”(nominal damage)。在这种情况下,履约指令是比金钱赔偿更完善与公平的救济。

The“Laemthong Glory”先例也在本书第七章之6.1.2.2.4段有介绍,案例涉及的是航运经常面对的无单放货问题,就是船舶在卸港没有正本提单(这是代表货物的所有权)把货物卸下并交付,根据的只是自称是拥有货物所有权的收货人所作出的一封保函。这种保函通常在第一段就会说明会补偿船东将来因为无单放货而要面对第三人(也就是真正的货物所有人)以误交货物索赔所导致的所有损失。有关的案例涉及一批14,000吨的食糖去也门的亚丁港,船东无单放货。而保函是由也门的收货人签发给了承租人,承租人另签发一份给船东。收货人提取了食糖后,再也不向他的银行赎单。这导致了货物的所有权一直没有转让给也门的收货人,船舶也随即被持有正本提单的银行以误交货物提出索赔,并把船舶扣押,要求船东提供索赔担保才放船。船东直接向也门的收货人提起诉讼并要求履行保函的承诺,虽然他签发的保函只是给承租人,但船东作为受益的第三人可以根据已经生效的1999年《Contracts (Rights of Third Parties) Act》提出索赔。在第一审的Cooke大法官看来是同意作出履约指令强制收货人提供担保以利放船,说:

“I turn then to the question of specific performance, if it is necessary for security to be put up in order to secure the release of the vessel. It was contended, both by the charterers and the receivers, that damages are an adequate remedy for the owners here. There is evidence before me that enforcement of judgments in the Yemen is a matter of some difficulty, a matter upon which I would not have required evidence in any event. That in itself means that damages against the receivers would not be an adequate remedy.

So far as the charterers are concerned, they are a French company against whom any judgment is enforceable under the European Convention. But cl. 3 has a particular purpose behind it, namely to ensure the release of the vessel so that issues of damages for detention do not arise. Whilst damages for detention are capable of evaluation by expert evidence and the like, this is never an entirely straightforward matter, and particularly so in the context of a rising market. The point at which contracts might be made is one of some debate.

I consider that the owners are right here in saying that a failure to arrange the provision of security by either receivers or charterers in accordance with their letter of indemnity obligations so negates the object of the letters of indemnity that the Court ought to grant specific performance. The very purpose of the letter of indemnity was to avoid the detention which has actuallyoccurred. This clause is of a different nature therefore from those which constitute the ordinary, primary obligations to be found in most contracts.

Whilst Mr. Lewis(承租人的代表大律师) is right in saying that contracts provide for primary obligations, and this is a primary obligation and therefore it is not right simply to look at the clause and say that it made provision for a certain result and therefore damages are not an adequate remedy (as performance of a secondary liability) this particular clause does fall into a different category from most.

Whereas damages may constitute an adequate remedy for failure to perform many primary obligations, the whole point of the letters of indemnity was to replace secondary liability under any suit for damages for detention by the primary performance of the obligation to ensure release of the vessel, so that such a suit was unnecessary. It would, in such circumstances, be inequitable not to grant specific performance to require fulfilment of that obligation and then to leave the owners to a remedy in damages for detention, or even damages for the loss of the ship, which was the very thing that the letters of indemnity were intended to avoid."。

至于在 The "Oro Chief"(将在本章12.1段进一步介绍),案情涉及的是另一种经常会出现的问题,就是如果很明显被告将无力赔偿违约带来的金钱损失,会否更适合对他(如一家财力不足的小公司)作出一个履约指令,迫使他不能违约。在该先例 Staughton 大法官是说:"... it may be that in special circumstances, such as when the seller is insolvent and can pay no damages, (the buyer) will still obtain an order for specific performance."

但这里也是有不同的看法,在 Anders Utkilens Rederi A/S v. Lovisa Stevedoring Co A/B(1985)2 All ER 669 先例,Goulding 大法官说:"Commercial life would be subject to new and unjust hazards if the court were to decree specific performance of contracts normally sounding only in damages simply because of a party's threatened insolvency."(如果仅凭一方当事人没有财力这个理由就以履约指令对付他,会给商业活动带来新的不公平与风险)

5. 履约指令不针对自己违反合约或有过错的原告

通常作为申请人的原告在申请履约指令时是要向法院证明他有履行所有的合约责任,而且也能够与愿意履行合约下将来的责任:Measures Bros Ltd v. Measures (1910)2 Ch 248;Chappall v. Times Newspapers Ltd(1975)1 WLR 482 等先例。通常如果原告在法院作出判决前发觉自己由于被告违约而导致他没有办法履行自己的责任,他可以改为金钱损失的索赔:Johnson v. Agnew(1980)AC 367 先例。

这里有一个著名的合约解释默示条件就是假设订约方不能从他自己错误的行为中获利(请看笔者的《合约的解释》一书之第197页)。所以对于自己犯错的原告,是不会针对被告作出履约指令,毕竟履约指令是衡平法的救济,一直有著名的说法是前来要求衡平救济的人自己必须是“手脚干净”(clean hand)。这里节录 Jones 与 Goodhart 的《Specific Performance》(2nd edn,1996 年)一书之 84 页:“Similarly there is a well - known rule of construction that a party in breach cannot be permitted to take advantage of his own wrong against the other party to the contract; as has been seen, a wrong doer will be denied an order for specific performance for the reason. ‘A party who seeks to obtain a benefit and a continuing contract on account of his breach is just as much taking advantage of his own wrong as is a party who relies on his breach to avoid a contract and thereby escape his obligations’ (Alghussein Establishment v. Eton College [1988] 1 WLR 587). That presumption is rebutted only in ‘the unlikely case that the contract contains clear express provisions to the contrary...’ (Cheall v. Association of Professional Executive Clerical and Computer Staff [1983] 2 AC 180).”

6. 履约指令必须考虑被告的地位(不剥夺他个人自由,不会给他带来过度的困境)

一直有一个说法是针对自然人提供服务的合约是不会作出履约指令,原因正是考虑不能剥夺被告的个人自由。当然还有其他的原因就是如果涉及特别技能的合约关系是没有办法强制,如在强制下提供服务的被告会十分不情愿地作出服务,肯定是不会令原告满意。

这种类型的合约最明显的就是雇佣合约,这在普通法十分明确是不会作出履约指令。这方面还有了立法更明确的规定。比较近期的普通法先例是 Powell v. London Borough of Brent (1987) IRLR 466, Roger Ormrod 大法官说:“Nobody would willingly grant an injunction forcing either an employer on an employee or an employee on an employer, simply on the basis that it would not work.”

至于在立法方面,可节录 1992 年《Trade Union and Labour Relations (Consolidation) Act》之 section 236:“no court shall, whether by way of (a) an order for specific performance... of a contract of an employment, or (b) an injunction... restraining a breach or threatened breach of contract, compel an employee to do any work or attend at any place for the doing of any work.”

另在 1996 年《Employment Rights Act》,也是有同样的条文。它以金钱赔偿作为被无理解雇的雇员的主要救济。

针对不能剥夺被告的个人自由,在很早以前的先例,De Francesco v. Barnum (1890) 45 Ch D 430, Fry 大法官就已经针对这一方面说不可以将被告从一个服务合约变为奴隶合约(The courts are bound to be jealous, least they should turn contracts of service into contracts of slavery)。

针对强制履行这种涉及个别自然人的“特殊技能”(special skill and talent)的合约关系不会有好结果,可举 C. H. Giles Co v. Morris(1972)1 WLR 307 先例中 Megarry 大法官所说:“The reasons why the court is reluctant to decree specific performance of a contract for personal services(and I would regard it as a strong reluctance rather than a rule) are, I think, more complex and more firmly bottomed on human nature. If a singer contracts to sing, there could be no doubt be proceedings for committal if, ordered to sing, the singer remained obstinately dumb. But if instead the singer sang flat, or sharp, or too fast, or too slowly, or too loudly, or too quietly, or resorted to a dozen of the manifestations of temperament traditionally associated with some singers, the threat of committal would reveal itself as a most unsatisfactory weapon: for who could say whether the imperfections of performance were natural or self - induced?”(法院抗拒在个人服务合约作出履约指令,但这不是一成不变的硬性规定,而主要是为了考虑人性的自然反应。以一个歌手签约演唱为例,对她/他下履约指令,她/他仍不肯演唱显然是藐视法院,犯了刑法甚至导致坐牢。但如果歌手只是在演唱不卖力,唱得或平或尖、或快或慢、或过高声或过低声,又如何处理呢? 毕竟不涉及履约指令的问题,在正常情况该歌手也不是场场演出都是满意的。这一来,如何区分这种“失误”可能是歌手阳奉阴违,会构成藐视法院或只是正常的演出免不了有好坏的波动?)

针对自然人的服务合约,英国法院都是比较愿意作出禁令,只要禁令不是间接迫使被告履行合约的“作为承诺”(positive obligation),因为这一来本质就变成了履约指令。如果有关的合约有一条所谓“限制商贸/就业”(restraint of trade)条文。例如雇主申请禁令阻止离职的高级雇员马上去另一家主要竞争对手的公司就业,因为在雇佣合约有一条“不作为承诺”(negative pledge),该雇员明示同意在离职后的一段短暂的合理时间内不会这样做。禁令等于是迫使该雇员履行他的不作为承诺。有关这一方面的问题在笔者与杨大明律师合著的《禁令》一书之第二章有详论。

但如果作出这种禁令会在实质上等同履约指令,这是不应该与必须谨慎的。这里可举两个先例作为进一步解释,第一个就是 Lumley v. Wagner(1852)1 De G. M. & G. 604,案情涉及 Wagner 女士同意了为原告的歌剧院演唱 3 个月,其间不为任何其他歌剧院演唱,以免分薄观众。但 Wagner 女士(被告)违约,为 Covent Garden 的 Gye 先生(是原告的竞争对手)演唱。法院作出最后禁令,不准被告在这三个月内为任何人(原告除外)演唱,说:“It was objected that the operation of the injunction in the present case was mischievous, excluding the defendant... from performing at any other theatre while this Court had no power to compel her to perform at Her Majestic's Theatre(原告的歌剧院). It is true, that I complaint, ‘if I compel her to abstain from the commission of an act which she has bound herself not to do... in continuing the injunction. I disclaim doing indirectly what I cannot do directly.”(法院不同意是在玩手段,利用最后禁令做本来不应该做的事,就是对 Wagner 女士作出一个履约指令。)

另一个先例是 Warner Brothers Pictures Inc v. Nelson(1937)1 KB 209,案情涉及当时的红星比提戴维斯(Bette Davis)。她答应了为原告华纳电影公司拍片 3 年,并不为其他公司或人士去拍片,但她事后违约。原告成功向法院申请作出最后禁令,不准她在 3 年内为其他公司或人士拍片。这显然是为了逼她履行合约,会是要向华纳电影公司委曲求全,因为其间是没有其他的生计(除非不再做演员)。Branson 大法官看来是想区分这一个禁令并不等同于履约指令,他是这样说:"It was also urged that the difference between what the defendant can earn as a film artist and what she might expect to earn by any other form of activity is so great that she will in effect be driven to perform her contract... but no evidence was addressed to show that, if enjoined from doing the specified acts otherwise than for the plaintiffs, she will not be able to employ herself both usefully and remuneratively in other spheres of activity... She will not be driven, although she may be tempted, to perform the contract, and the fact that she may be so tempted is no objection to the grant of an injunction."

上诉的两个先例看起来是相近的,但在现实中 Lumley v. Wagner 先例的禁令就说得过去,因为 Wagner 女士顶多为了遵守最后禁令,宁可失业 3 个月也不向原告委曲求全。但在 Warner Brothers Pictures Inc v. Nelson 先例,禁令长达 3 年,就有很强的感觉是等于履约指令。比提戴维斯小姐是没有办法失业 3 年,除了坐吃山空外,演员生活也就此完结。这禁令就等于迫使她向华纳电影公司求饶,在这三年内,该服务合约就有很大危险变为一个奴隶合约。所以,在后来的先例 Warren v. Mendy(1989)All ER 103 中(涉及一个拳手的经理人合约),Nourse 大法官认为这种禁令要考虑长短的期限,如果长过 2 年就会变质为履约指令。他是这样说:"Although it is impossible to state in general terms where the line between short and long term engagements ought to be drawn it is obvious that an injunction lasting for two years or more (the period applicable in the present case) may practically compel performance of the contract."

这种同类的案例最后可一提的是较近期的 Page One Records v. Britton(1968)1 WLR 157,案情涉及一支名为"The Troggs"的流行乐队。该乐队雇用原告作为代理人及经理人,为期 5 年,并在合约内作出一个不作为的承诺,即在期间不会为其他人录音。但是该乐队事后违约/毁约,与他人签订了另一个经理人协议,这导致了原告向法院申请禁令阻止乐队这样做。Stamp 大法官认为作出这种禁令等于是履约指令,所以拒绝申请,并说:"... it was said in this case, that if an injunction is granted, The Troggs could without employing of a different nature... I think that I can and should take judicial notice of the fact that these groups, if they are to have any great success, must have managers. As a practical matter... I entertain no doubt that they would be compelled, if the injunction were granted... to continue to employ the plaintiff as their manager and agent... I should if I granted the injunction, be enforcing a contract for personal services, in which personal services are to be performed by the plaintiff."

7. 履约指令不针对难以监督与持续性的合约

7.1 持续性监督对法院带来的困难

一贯的说法就是法院不会对一些难以监督，特别是要持续履行的合约作出履约指令。原因是因为这样做的话会对法院带来沉重的压力，如在履行的期间双方当事人不断要回来法院要求作出决定。被告或被指令的一方当事人会是要去法院申请对履约指令作出宽免或改变，如因为身体或家庭等无法控制的原因导致他没有办法在某一段时间严格履行法院命令。原告会是需要去法院投诉被告阳奉阴违，要求制裁，背后可能是希望对被告加压而达到某一些目的，但也有可能是被告的确是没有严格执行法院的命令。这方面的考虑早在 Ryan v. Mutual Tontine Westminster Chambers Association(1893)1 Ch 116 的古老先例(案情涉及一个酒店式公寓，被告在租约中承诺提供 24 小时的管家服务，但被告没有提供而导致了原告租客申请履约指令。)Esher 勋爵是这样说的："The contract is that these services shall be performed during the whole term of the tenancy: it is therefore a long – continuing contract to be performed from day to day and under which the circumstances of non – performance might vary from day to day. I apprehend, therefore, that the execution of it would require that constant superintendence by the court, which the court in such cases has always declined to give."

同样地，Lopes 大法官也在同一先例说道："... it is clear that it is such a contract, that, in order to give effect to it by an order for specific performance, the court would have to watch over and supervise its execution. But it is recognised rule that the court cannot enforce a contract by compelling specific performance where the execution of the contract requires such watching over and supervision by the court."

也是由于这一个理由而导致了不少先例拒绝作出履约指令：Powell Duffryn Steam Coal Co v. Taff Vale Railway(1874)L. R. 9 Ch. App. 331(指令一个铁路公司操作信号灯与提供发动机动力)；Dowty Boulton Paul Ltd v. Wolverhampton Corp. (1971)1 W. L. R. 204(指令履行一个 60 年合约让机场跑道继续开放)；De Mattos v. Gibson(1858)4 D. & J. 276(指令船东履行航次租约)；Braddon Towers Ltd v. International Stores Ltd (1987)E. G. L. R. 209(早在 1959 年作出的判决)与 Co – operative Insurance Society Ltd v. Argyll Stores(Holdings)Ltd(1998)A. C. 1(指令被告开店营业，不管赚钱或亏本)；Dominion Coal Co v. Dominion Iron & Steel Co(1909)A. C. 293(指令按期提供货物)。

在较近期的先例 Vertex Data Science Ltd v. Powergen Retail Ltd(2006)2 Lloyd's Rep. 591，案情涉及原告向被告提供所有管理账目的服务，为期 7 年(从 2005 年 4 月至 2012 年 5 月)。但双方的关系在合约生效后很快就恶化，导致被告在 2006 年 3 月

24日就通知原告终断合约,指称原告违约/毁约。原告向英国法院申请禁令,阻止被告这样做(有关的合约包括了一条仲裁条文,但明确允许双方向法院申请履约指令或禁令)。高院的 Tomlinson 大法官拒绝作出禁令或履约指令,其中最主要的原因是无法持续地作出监督,因为该合约是需要双方紧密的合作,在双方关系变坏的情况下,这种服务合约的履行也根本没有办法以准确的语言说明要求被告做什么或不准做什么。

7.2 租船合约不作出履约指令会是因为难以监督

以上 De Mattos v. Gibson(1858)4 D. & J. 276 的古老先例提到法院是不会在航次租约作出履约指令,主要的原因是该航次租约的条文"太不肯定"(uncertain and indefinite)可让法院作出履约指令并监督它的执行。该航次是从英国装煤炭到苏伊士,在上诉庭有看法是让其他船舶运载这票煤炭可能会更好,以金钱损失作为赔偿会是更佳的救济办法。这种考虑也包括了期租合约,除了这些合约会需要持续履行(特别是一个较长期的期租合约),笔者认为还涉及涉外因素会让英国法院更加难以监督。租约也涉及只属于一个提供服务的合约,需要双方合作,通常法院不愿意强制。以下可节录贵族院在 The "Scaptrade"(1983)2 Lloyd's Rep. 253 先例中 Diplock 勋爵所说如下:"A time charter, unless it is a charter by demise, with which your Lordships are not here concerned, transfers to the charter no interest in or right to possession of the vessel; it is a contract for services to be rendered to the charterer by the shipowner through the use of the vessel by the shipowner's own servants, the master and the crew, acting in accordance with such directions as to the cargoes to be loaded and the voyages to be undertaken as by the terms of charter – party the charterer is entitled to give to them. Being a contract for services it is thus the very prototype of a contract of which before the fusion of law and equity a Court would never grant specific performance, Clarke v. Price (1819) 2 Wils. Ch. 157; Lumley v. Wagner (1852) 1 De G. M. & G. 604. In the event of failure to render the promised services, the party to whom they were to be rendered would be left to pursue such remedies in damages for breach of contract as he might have at law."

在《Chitty on Contracts》(30th edn, 2008年)之 27 – 025 段,有提到"... Thus specific performance can be ordered of a contract to publish a piece of music, and sometimes of contracts to build. It has, indeed, been suggested that a time charterparty cannot be specifically enforced against the shipowner because it is a contract for services; but the services that the shipowner undertakes to provide under such a contract will often be no more personal than those to be rendered by a builder under a building contract. Denial of specific performance in the case of time charters is best explained on other ground."(这是说有人认为不能针对期租合约作出履约指令,因为它是服务性合约。但是该书作者认为期租合约不属于自然人的个人服务合约,法院拒绝对期租合约作出履约指令会是其他的原因更说得过去。最后一句的脚注中说到,该原因就是要法院太多的监督。笔者还想到

一个期租合约的履行通常是在国外[英国外],这就令英国法院持续作出监督会是更加困难。)

但涉及租约倒是有好几个法院作出禁令的先例,不允许船舶在租约期内做出一些与租约不一致的用途。这看来是与履约指令的本质是一致的,现实中也往往会在经济上迫使被告船东履行原来的租约。唯一对法院的好处就是禁令的措辞会是简单,但要拟定一份紧密的履约指令要求被告明确履行他在租约内的所有"作为承诺"(positive obligation)就恐怕是不容易。而且作出这种禁令在理论上船东的被告还是有一定的选择,如在禁令期间,不作出与租约不一致的用途,但也不必履行原来的租约,就是把有关的船舶短暂抛老锚,什么都不干。

第一个先例 Lord Strathcona Streamship Co Ltd v. Dominion Coal Co Ltd(1926)A. C. 108 中,枢密院作出的禁令内容如下:"employing or using or allowing to be employed or used the sail steamship... in any way inconsistent with or different from the employment and use provided for it in said time charter – party during the existence of said time charter – party."

在第二个先例 The "Georgios C"(1971)1 Lloyd's Rep. 7 中,案情涉及长达 20 至 30 个月的期租,但船东在履行了几个月之后,以承租人没有准时支付租金撤船。Donaldson 大法官在承租人单方面申请下对被告船东作出了一个禁令,内容如下:"restraining the defendants from employing the vessel in a manner which was inconsistent with the charter – party."

第三个先例 The "Oakworth"(1975)1 Lloyd's Rep. 581,案情涉及多个航次并持续 2 年的程租合约,二船东的一家挪威公司在履行了 7 个航次后,把他们期租进来的"Oakworth"轮以更高的运费转租给其他的承租人作其他航次的用途,但还没有开始履行。承租人紧急向法院申请禁令,这在上诉庭也作出。Denning 勋爵说:"It is concede that damages would be no adequate remedy. The Norwegian company has no assets and no means except insofar as the vessel can obtain freight from injunction would seem to be the proper remedy.... So the charter, being still in existence and binding, should be performed by the stances of the case, on the undertaking being given, I think the defendants should be restrained from using in any way inconsistent with or different from the employment and use provided in the charter – party."

第四个先例 LauritzenCool A. B. v. Lady Navigation Inc. (2005)1 Lloyd's Rep. 260,案情涉及一个冷藏船舶的"经营集团"(Operation Pool)。这就是多个不同的船东把他们拥有的一些冷藏船期租给一个承租人,让承租人统筹营运。至于租约的租金就是一条公式,该公式是根据承租人整个船队每个年度所赚取的利润摊分给整个船队的个别船东。这种做法在某些船型是很普遍的,如冷藏船和化学品船。这导致大量这种船舶都租给少数几个承租人,导致他们与货方有很强的议价能力。这个经营集团有其中两艘名为"Lady Racisce"与"Lady Norcula"的冷藏船的船东与承租人发生争执，船东指称承租人是非法垄断集团，并且威胁要把船舶撤走。这导致承租人向船东开始伦敦仲裁，并向英国法院申请禁令（是一个中间禁令）禁止船东撤船，直到仲裁完毕。显然，如果船东撤船，会对承租人带来很大麻烦。例如，他与许多不同货方订下的合约会有困难履行，因为船队少了两艘船舶就会带来调度上的困难，而且这两艘冷藏船是非常特殊，根本无法在市场找到类似的船舶。这会进一步损害承运人在冷藏货运输建立起来的信誉。船东的抗辩就是这种禁令等于是履约指令，不应该针对一个租约作出。这种服务性的合约需要双方的合作与信任。Cooke 大法官认为在这一个案例中作出禁令不允许船东作出与租约不一致的用途应该是不成问题，说："An order restraining a party from exercising a contractual right, whether justifiably or not, is, both in form and substance, different from an order which restrains an owner from employing the vessel outside the time charter does not in itself compel performance of the charter even though in practice, if the defendant is restrained from other gainful employment for the vessel, it is likely that performance under the charter will continue. . . . (4) any order which the Court might make would not be a mandatory order since it would be framed to restrain the owners from use of the vessel outside the charter - party contracts into which they freely entered; the orders would be negative in form and negative in substance and there would be no compulsion to perform the charters—only a financial incentive to do so in the absence of any other legitimate available employment; any injunction grant would perpetuate the *status quo* and would not require some new positive step to be done by anyone."

7.3 服务合约不作出履约指令会是因为难以监督与合约本质不适合

在本章第 6 段有提到自然人的个人服务合约不作出履约指令的原因，但即使是非个人服务合约（一家公司为其他公司提供服务），英国法院也通常不愿意作出履约指令。先节录《Chitty on Contracts》（30th edn，2008 年）之 27 - 025 段："**Services not of a 'personal nature'.** Specific performance is refused in the above cases because the courts are reluctant to force the parties to enter into, or to continue in, a personal relationship against the will of one of the parties. It follows that the refusal of specific performance on this ground is limited to cases in which the services are personal in nature. Specific enforcement of a contract for the supply of services which are not of this nature may, indeed, be refused on some other ground, e. g. because 'mutual confidence [has] broken down' between the person to whom the services were to be provided and their provider. But there is no general rule against the specific enforcement of a contract merely because one party has contracted to provide service. . . "

看来提供服务合约即使是公司法人的非自然人，除了法院难以监督持续性的履行外，这种合约在本质上与本章第 4 段主要介绍的货物买卖合约很不一样，提供服务合约是需要双方当事人的互信，否则是很难以法院一纸命令把两个人的合约关系扯在一起。所以在较早前之 7.1 段介绍的 Vertex Data Science Ltd v. Powergen Retail Ltd

(2006)2 Lloyd's Rep. 591 先例中,Tomlinson 大法官说这种救济办法是“不恰当”(inappropriate)与“不可行”(unworkable)。

7.4　建造合约不作出履约指令会是因为难以监督

一般的说法是,英国法院不愿意对建造合约作出履约指令。这在 Jones 与 Goodhart 的《Specific Performance》(2nd edn,1996 年)一书之 184 页有关建造合约的第一句是说明这一点:“It is commonly said that an English court will not normally grant specific performance of an 'ordinary building or engineering contract'.”在这一句的注脚有说明权威来源,如下:“4(2)Halsbury's Laws(4th edn, reissue) para 470. There are board judicial statements which deny the very possibility of specific performance; for example, Lucas v. Commerford(1790)3 Bro CC 166 at 167, per Lord Thurlow; Merchants' Trading Co v. Banner(1871)LR 12 Eq 18; Cubitt v. Smith(1864)11 LT 298; Wilkinson v. Clements(1872)8 Ch App 96. But these must be weighed against the cases cited below, nn 9 and 10 and p 185, n 2.”

看来原因是与本章 7.1 段所讲的问题是一样,就是建造合约涉及持续性的、繁重与细微的工程,法院是很难监督直到工程完毕。这可以介绍一个先例,即 Gyllenhammer & Partners International Ltd v. Sour Brodogradevna Split(1989)2 Lloyd's Rep. 403,案情涉及造船合约(本质上是建造合约)的履约指令申请被法院拒绝的情况。Hirst 大法官在该先例说道:“... a very complex contract requiring extensive co - operation between the parties on a number of matters, particularly modifications, optional variations, and, perhaps most importantly of all, matters of detail(some by no means unimportant) left undefined in the specification.”

这方面的法律地位的总结可节录《Chitty on Contracts》(30th edn,2008 年)之 27 - 028 段所说如下:“**Building contracts: specific enforcement against builder.** The general rule is that a contract to erect a building cannot be specifically enforced against the builder. There seem to be three reasons for this rule. First, damages may be an adequate remedy if another builder can be engaged to do the work. Secondly, the contract may be too vague to be specifically enforced if it fails to describe the work to be done under it with sufficient certainty. And thirdly, specific enforcement of the contract may require more supervision than the court is willing to provide. But where the first two reasons do not apply, the third has not been allowed to prevail. Specific performance of a contract to erect or to repair buildings can therefore be ordered if(i) the work is precisely defined; (ii) damages will not adequately compensate the claimant; and(iii) the defendant is in possession of the land on which the work is to be done so that the claimant cannot get the work done by another builder.”(建造合约:针对建筑商的履约指令。一个大原则即是一份建造合约不能针对建筑商作出特定履行。原因有三点:第一,如果能让另一个替代建筑商完成该项工程,则对雇主的金钱损失赔偿可以是足够的救济。第二,如果该建造合约没有足够确

定地阐述建筑商的履约内容及义务,则该合约会因意思过于模糊而无法作出履约指令。第三,对于履约指令,往往可能需要超出法院愿意承担的监督。但是,当前两个原因不适用的时候,不能仅仅靠第三个原因作出决定性的考虑。要在建造或修葺大楼的合约下作出履约指令,应符合以下情况:一是对于合约下的工程有足够精确的定义,即有明示条文说明建造什么与达至什么样的结果;二是损害赔偿不足以补偿原告的损失;三是该工程所在的土地属于被告建筑商,以致原告无法让另一个建筑商完成该项工程。)

看来,一般的说法是英国法院通常不会对建造与工程合约作出履约指令,并不完全正确或绝对。针对一些在建造合约中比较确定阐述的建筑商义务,作出履约指令的先例还有不少,如:Hepburn v. Leather(1884)50 LT 660(承诺造一堵特定高度与厚度的墙);Jeune v. Queen's Cross Properties Ltd(1974)Ch 97(房东要求修妥倒塌的阳台);Barrett v. Lounava(1990)1 QB 348;Tustian v. Johnson(1993)2 All ER 675;Rainbow Estates Ltd v. Tokenhold Ltd(1999)Ch 64 等。

在 Wolverhampton Corpn v. Emmons(1901)1 KB 515 先例中,Collins 大法官说:"could order specific performance in certain cases in which the works were specified by the contract in a sufficiently definite manner."

另在 Tito v. Waddell(No. 2)(1977)Ch 106 先例,Megarry 大法官说:"The real question is whether there is a sufficient definition of what has to be done in order to comply with the order of the court. That definition may be provided by the contract itself, or it may be supplied by the terms of the order, in which case there is the further question whether the court considers that the terms of the contract sufficiently support, by implication or otherwise, the terms of the proposed order."

笔者比较少接触岸上建造合约,但经常会处理造船合约的案件。这种造船合约近年来有大量的争议,也经常有买方,也就是船东向仲裁庭申请履约指令的救济。这方面在笔者所著的《造船合约》一书之第 352 ~ 354 页也有简单提及,不重复。这一来,造船合约中是否有足够确定的条文的问题会是一个重要的考虑。如果有,比方说有条文说明买方的总管有权参与船舶交船前的试航,但船厂拒绝让买方参与。又或是船厂拒绝按照造船合约把建造完毕的船舶交给买方,除非买方愿意提高船价。这一来,应该可以明确与针对性地作出履约指令。但相反,如果造船合约中有条文说明买方在交船前有权不受到限制的在船舶与船厂观察(unrestricted access on board the vessel and in the shipyard)或说明买方在建造期间可以参与所有的测试与工程,这看来就不够确定。即使作出履约指令,措辞上也不好掌握。例如买方的人数、时间、不得妨碍船厂的工程、怎样观察、什么测试(如否包括一些船厂外的测试?)等。在《造船合约》一书之 354 页,笔者也有同样的说法是:"在造船合约的情况下,仅在很有限的情况才适用履约指令。如在船舶已经造好,船厂拒绝交船给船东,法院就比较愿意下令要船厂交船。但如果船舶还没开始建造或只是建造了一半,船东向法院申请作出履约指令要求船厂完成建造该船舶,成功机会应该就是十分渺茫了。"

这应该是符合近期的一个重要的贵族院先例 Co - operative Insurance Society Ltd v. Argyll Stores(Holdings)Ltd(1998)A. C. 1,Hoffmann 勋爵区分了"持续性的活动"(to carry on an activity)与"达至一个结果"(to achieve a result),前者应该避免作出履约指令,但后者就没有问题。这可节录《Chitty on Contracts》(30th edn,2008 年)之 27 - 027 段部分所说如下:"The main reason given by the House of Lords for refusing to order specific performance was the difficulty of supervising the enforcement of the order since the question whether it was being complied with might require frequent reference to the court. For that purpose, Lord Hoffmann distinguished between orders(such as that suit here) to carry on an activity and orders to achieve a result. In the later case,'the court only has to examine the finished work' so that compliance with the order could be judged *ex post facto*: it was on this ground that the cases in which building contracts have been specifically enforced were to be explained."(注意最后一句话是针对建造合约。)

从相反的角度,向雇主作出履约指令允许建筑商完成一个建造合约的可能性,可节录《Chitty on Contracts》(30th edn,2008 年)之 27 - 029 段所说如下:"**Building contracts: specific enforcement against owner.** The converse question may also arise whether the builder can, in effect, compel the owner to allow him to complete the work. In Hounslow (London Borough) v. Twickenham Gardens Ltd(1971) Ch. 223 a building contract gave a builder a contractual licence to enter the owner's land to execute the agreed work. The licence was held to be irrevocable till the work had been done, but the owner wrongfully purported to terminate it and sought an injunction to restrain the builder from entering the land, and damages for trespass. These claims failed as the purported termination was wrongful and ineffective. It seems, however, that if the licence had not been irrevocable, or if the owner's active co - operation had been required for the completion of the work, the builder's sole remedy would have been in damages."

7.5 难以监督的替代办法

有说法是这一个难以监督的困难会是夸大其词,特别是英国法院后来发展到可以找到其他的替代做法。在《Chitty on Contracts》(30th edn,2008 年)之 27 - 026 段所说:"... This suggestion that the 'difficult' of supervision has been somewhat exaggerated; and various devices at the court's disposal can be used to overcome it. The court can, for example, appoint a receiver to perform the acts specified in the order(Gibbs v. David [1870] L. R. 20 Eq 373), or appoint an expert to act as officer of the court for the purpose, or it can authorise the claimant to appoint a person to act as agent of the defendant for the purpose to be done by the defendant personally, the court can order him simply to enter into a contract to procure those acts to be done. From this point of view, Ryan v. Mutual Tontine Westminster Chambers Association(1893)1 Ch 116 may be contrasted with Posner v.

Scott – Lewis(1986)3 All ER 513 where the lessor of a block of luxury flats covenanted, so far as lay in his power, to employ a resident porter to perform a number of specified tasks. It was held that the covenant was specifically enforceable in the sense that the lessor could be ordered to appoint a resident porter for the performance of those tasks."

在上述节录,可介绍其中的一些替代办法以减轻或避免法院的监督。第一种提到的办法是法院委任一个接管人,把被告的合约履行接管过来。在 Gibbs v. David 先例,法院就委任接管人把矿场接管过来继续营运。有关委任接管人,在笔者所著的《仲裁法——从开庭准备到裁决书的作出与执行》一书之第 841 ~ 846 页有涉及,并提到全球接管的 Marsi v. Consolidated Contractors International Co SAL(2008)2 Lloyd's Rep 128 先例。第二种办法是委任一个独立专家作为是法院的官员监督履约指令的执行,这就可以解决本章 7.4 段的建造合约问题。该独立专家可以每天在建造现场监督履行,不按照他的决定就会构成藐视法院。第三种办法是授权原告自己委任一位被告的代理人履行合约,并举了 Posner v. Scott – Lewis 先例。

其他的办法也显示在 The "Messiniaki Tolmi"(1986)1 Lloyd's Rep. 455 先例,案情涉及一艘二手船买卖,该船是卖去台湾作为拆废钢之用。估计是由于市场下跌,台湾买方拒绝签发"备妥通知书"(notice of readiness),这等于是拒绝履行合约。该买卖是通过信用证支付船价,而一份有效的备妥通知书是结汇的文件。信用证是适用英国法,卖方船东向英国法院申请履约指令。英国法院除了作出履约指令外,还指示如果买方拒签,该文件就可以让英国最高院的"聆案官"(Master)代签(这是根据 1981 年《Supreme Court Act》之 section 39),效力与买方自己签收一样,银行必须接受结汇。看来,这种情况本来是作出了履约指令也很难监督,因为台湾买方根本不在英国法院的管辖权内。但通过这个做法就可以避免了这方面的困难。

7.6 涉外(除了欧盟国家)的服务合约或者建造合约更加难以监督

在本章 7.2 段已经有提到过在租船合约中有这个考虑导致法院不愿意作出履约指令。造船合约也是有这样的考虑,如在本章 7.4 段所介绍的先例 Gyllenhammer & Partners International Ltd v. Sour Brodogradevna Split(1989)2 Lloyd's Rep. 403, Hirst 大法官就有考虑这一个因素,说:"... a very complex contract requiring extensive co – operation between the parties on a number of matters. ... In my judgment these factors, coupled with the consideration that the work take place in a foreign yard, outside the Court's jurisdiction, would tell strongly against an order for specific performance being in principle appropriate in the present case."(造船合约是一个十分复杂的合约,需要双方大量的合作,特别是在船舶的修改、选择权下的改变或可能是最重要的是一些没有在造船合约的规范说明中明确规定的地方。上述的因素加上考虑外国船厂并非在本法院的管辖下,可以说是很不适宜作出履约指令。)

这里的原因就是没有办法强制完全涉外的当事人(被告)或者合约的履行。只有当被告或者合约的履行是在英国法院管辖权范围内,才有可能作出有效的履约指令。没有办法强制的原因可介绍一个上诉庭的先例 The "Sea Hawk"(1986)1 Lloyd's Rep. 317,案情涉及一票 C&F 去罗马尼亚的黄豆粕。但船东有严重的经济问题,欠下了不少债务,导致在航次中不断延误与被其他债权人扣船。罗马尼亚的收货人为了取得这票货,最后只能对船东作出经济援助,为数 500,000 美元。该先例的原告是有关船舶的抵押权人,他与资助的收货人,也就是该案的被告,事先达成了约定,就是不在罗马尼亚卸货的时候扣船。由于船东没有办法很快的归还 500,000 美元,令收货人没有办法归还这笔钱给融资给他的另一家罗马尼亚政府单位(名为 TIMIS),最终导致在罗马尼亚的 Constanza 卸港把船舶扣押。这导致了船舶抵押权人作为原告向英国法院申请禁令(相等于履约指令要求履行不扣船的承诺),不让收货人扣船。这被英国上诉庭拒绝,认为救济办法应该是金钱损失赔偿而不是禁令。其中,Mustill 大法官就谈到其中一个主要原因是英国法院的禁令或者指令根本没有办法执行。收货人自己不在英国,也没有任何资产在英国。Mustill 大法官是这样说:"Secondly, I am oppressive by the consideration that is the injunction were allowed to stand, it is not susceptible of enforcement by this court. After all, if the evidence adduced on behalf of the defendants is true – and no application has been made to cross – examine the deponents on their affidavits – the defendants cannot pay TIMIS forthwith. What, then, is to happen if an injunction is granted? It seems that the defendants will inevitably be in breach. But this Court would then be powerless to enforce its own order; there is no official of the defendants here who could be the subject of an application to commit for contempt. On the plaintiff's own evidence, Agroexport have no assets within the jurisdiction which could be made the subject of a sequestration order. it is a general principle of the law as to injunction that the Court should not put itself in the position of making an order which it cannot enforce, and that seems to me to be exactly the position in which may find itself if this injunction is granted."

今天受英国法院管辖或伦敦仲裁的涉外服务合约或建造合约为数很多,估计英国法院在今天会是更加愿意对涉外的被告与在外国履约作出履约指令,除非是有关的案件还涉及其他不利作出履约指令的因素。毕竟英国法院已经在一些禁令这样做了,如"全球冻结令"(worldwide freezing injunction):Babanaft International Co SA v. Bassatne(1990) Ch 13; Republic of Haiti v. Duvalier(1990)1 QB 202; Derby v. Weldon(No. 1)(1990) Ch 48; Polly Peck v. Nadir(1992)4 All ER 769 等先例。虽然在全球冻结令,情况不同的是主要履行的对象是银行,他们还是在英国法院的管辖范围内。另一种著名的"止诉禁令"(anti – suit injunction),更是大部分都是外国的被告。

8. 履约指令不针对无法完整履行的合约

在早期的一些先例，曾经有一个说法就是履约指令必须针对整个合约的履行。如果其中有部分没有办法作出履约指令，如有个别的合约承诺是来自自然人，就不会作出履约指令。这里可先举一个早期的先例：Merchants' Trading Co v. Banner(1871) LR 12 Eq 18，Romilly 勋爵说："where the stipulation sought to be enforced is really a part of the contract itself, this court cannot specifically perform the contract piecemeal, but it must be performed in its entirety if perform at all; and where the court cannot perform it in its entirety, neither can it perform any particular portion of it."

但这一个局限在后来有了放宽，其中是在 C. H. Giles Co v. Morris(1972) 1 WLR 307 先例，Megarry 大法官说："The obligation to enter into a service agreement is merely one part of a contract which deals with many other matters; and that obligation is the only part of that complex which is set not to be specifically enforceable. Now there is authority for saying that the mere presence in a contract of one provision which by itself would not be specifically enforceable(because, for example, it requires the performance of personal services) does not prevent the contract as a whole from being specifically enforced..."

最后可以节录《Chitty on Contracts》(30th edn，2008 年)之 27 - 044 段部分所说："This does not mean that the court cannot order specific performance of one individual obligation out of a number imposed by contract: it means only that it will not make such an order in relation to one such obligation if it cannot so enforce the rest of the contract(Odessa Tramways Co v. Mendel [1878] 8 Ch D 235; Rainbow Estates Ltd v. Tokenhold Ltd [1999] Ch 64; Internet Trading Club Ltd v. Freeserve Investments Ltd [2001] EBLR 142). Even in this restricted sense, the rule is by no means an absolute one. Does where an monetary adjustment can be made in respect of the unperformable part the court may order specific performance with compensation."

9. 履约指令的申请不得怠慢

履约指令与禁令的申请通常都需要尽快(特别是禁令更加要动得快)，因为一旦怠慢了就会被认为有可能为被告带来不公平与损害。怠慢申请也会被法院视为是原告对被告违约/毁约的"默许"(acquiescence)。另一个说法就是原告申请履约指令，他本身就应该向法院证明他自己是准备、希望、尽快与迫切地想履行。这可节录 Jones 与 Goodhart 的《Specific Performance》(2nd edn，1996 年)一书之 110 页："A party cannot call upon the court for specific performance unless he has shown himself 'ready, desirous, prompt and eager' to discharge his own obligations under the contract and has used 'such diligence as the nature of the case demands'. In the case of a contract for the sale of business property with a fluctuating value, a delay of a few months may be sufficient to exclude the remedy. In other cases, whether the contract is executed or executory, a delay of a year or so will not normally exclude specific performance. In the case of exucutory contracts, unjustifiable delay for anything much more than a year is likely to be a ground for refusing an order for specific performance, though in one case specific performance of an executory contract was ordered after 12 years (partly attributable to war)."

1980年《Limitation Act》之section 36说明6年的时效不适用在这一种救济办法。即只要原告被视为"怠慢"(guilty of laches),法院就会拒绝作出履约指令。虽然是不适用,但如果是超过了金钱损失索赔的6年时效,法院通常还是会拒绝作出履约指令:Firth v. Slingsby(1888)58 LT 481先例。实际上,即使是比6年时效短得多,原告也可能已经被视为是怠慢,再作出履约指令对被告不公平而被拒绝。此类案例有:Watson v. Reid(1830)1 Russ M 236(1年的延误);Lehmann v. McArthur(1868)3 Ch App 496(15个月的延误);Rich v. Galt(1871)24 LT 745(17个月的延误);Lloyd v. Wilkes(1854)2 Eq Rep 1081(股票买卖,21个月的延误)等。

但如果延误对双方并没有造成不公平,会有不同的判决。在Mehmet v. Benson(1965)113 CLR 295先例与Lazard Bros & Co Ltd v. Fairfield Properties Co(Mayfair)Ltd(1977)121 Sol Jo 793先例,都涉及2年的延误,但法院依然作出了履约指令。

10. 履约指令对相互性原则的要求

"相互性"(mutuality)曾经是履约指令的一个非常重要的原则,就是说在双方都可以取得履约指令的前提下,法院才会作出该救济。判断是否符合相互性的原则的时间点是法院作出判决的时候。

这原则是保障被告在法院的履约指令下,不敢在履约中有任何行差踏错。但倒过来原告不受法院任何指令/禁令约束,不必怕乱来,这对被告并不公平。所以,法院想为被告争取一点保障,防止将来原告会违约/毁约的"风险"(risk)。而真的发生,如在租约的原告/承租人不支付租金,被告的船东却因有法院的履约指令在身,只能一面倒履约,直到成功向法院申请把指令撤销或修改。

这原则是Buckley大法官在Price v. Strange(1978)Ch. 337先例所讲的:"The court will not compel a defendant to perform his obligation specifically, if it cannot at the same time ensure that any unperformed obligations of the plaintiff will be perfectly performed, unless, perhaps, damages would be adequate remedy to the defendant for any default on the plaintiffs part."

在这说法下也免不了有例外的情况与法院作出担心的做法，如：

(1)未成年人的原告，不能成功申请履约指令，因为被告将来无法向原告获得同样保障：Flight v. Bolland(1828)4 Russ. 298；Lumley v. Ravenscroft(1895)1Q. B. 683 等先例。但看来，如果原告申请时已是成年，则合约虽在小孩时订立，是一个"可令无效"(voidable)的合约，仍会做出履约指令(因为已经提到过相互性原则是在作出判决时考虑)：Clayton v. Ashdown(1714)9 Vin. Abr. 393(G. 4)1 先例。关于"无效"(void)与"可令无效"(voidable)合约的区别，可参阅笔者的《国际商务游戏规则——英国合约法》一书之 203 页。

(2)一般情况下，在一个由自然人和公司法人签订的合约下，是不可以作出履约指令的。因为通常公司法人不能以履约指令强迫自然人提供个人服务：Stocker v. Wedderburn(1867)3 K & J 393 先例。

(3)在《Chitty on Contracts》(30th edn，2008 年)之 27 - 047 段说："There are, however, many cases in which specific performance can be ordered in favour of a party even though it could not at the time of contracting have been ordered against him. If A promises to grant a lease of land to B who in return undertakes to build on the land, B's promise to build may not be specifically enforceable, but if he actually does perform that promise he can get specific performance of A's promise to grant the lease. Specific performance cannot be ordered against a person who sells land which he does not own and cannot force the owner to convey to him, but if he becomes owner before the purchaser repudiates he can get specific performance. Conversely, a vendor with defective title may be compelled to convey at a reduced price although he could not himself have got specific performance of a voidable contract made during minority even though he could elected to repudiate the contract. And a victim of fraud or innocent misrepresentation can get specific performance although he may be entitled to rescind the contract, so that it could not be enforced against him."(以上是说有许多例外情况的情况下法院作出履约指令会是一面倒。例如，A 答应了租借一块地给 B 建造房屋，A 是不能向法院取得针对 B 的履约指令。但如果 B 履约建造房屋，而是 A 不履约，B 可以从法院取得针对 A 的履约指令。这种情况就变成一面倒。最后一句是举一个欺诈或无辜误述而导致订立合约的受害方也是可以取得履约指令，如强制对方履行合约，虽然在这种情况下受害方自己不一定需要履行，法院也无法强制他履行，因为他可以根据误述终断有关的合约。)

(4)在 Jones 与 Goodhart 的《Specific Performance》(2nd edn，1996 年)一书之 43 页，关于"担保合约"(contract of guarantee)有讲到："Contracts of guarantee are only enforceable against, a defendant if there is a memorandum in writing signed by him. If the defendant has signed a memorandum, the contract may be specifically enforceable against him even though the plaintiff has not signed a memorandum and cannot be sued."

(5)另一种例外情况是原告自己的经济情况不稳(plaintiff was doubtful solvency),将来如果对被告违约/毁约会赔不出钱。这一来,如果根据原告的申请向被告作出履约指令也会是一面倒。但法院会可以灵活处理在“有条件下作出指令”(conditional specific performance)。正如 Burrows 教授在《Remedies for Torts and Breach of Contract》一书(2nd edn,1994 年)之 370 页说,“法院可要原告提供一定数额的金钱上的担保,以交换作出履约指令”(... The court could grant it [指履约指令] on terms that insure adequate monetary security to the defendant or otherwise provide an incentive for the plaintiff to perform)。

总言之,这相互性的原则有很多例外,法院看来在放松,甚至有说法是法院不必为被告担心将来顶多是一个“风险”(risk)原告可能会违约/毁约。

11. 不作出履约指令的其他考虑

涉及履约指令的其他考虑会有很多,如在《Chitty on Contracts》(30th edn,2008 年)之 27-010 段,就提到了考虑言论自由,说:“Specific performance may be ordered on grounds unconnected with the question whether the claimant has suffered or is likely to suffer material or financial loss for which he could be satisfactorily compensated by damages. Specific performance has, for example, been ordered of a contract to grant a licence to use a hall for a political meeting; and one reason for making the order was said to be that this form of relief would promote freedom of speech and assembly.”

另外,在 Channel Tunnel v. Balfour Beatty(1993)1 Lloyd's Rep. 291,贵族院不作出类似履约指令的禁令是为了不影响双方同意在布鲁塞尔仲裁的仲裁庭权力。

履约指令如果对被告会造成“极大困难”(severe hardship),也是考虑之一。在 Patel v. Ali(1984)Ch 283 先例,被告(一个巴基斯坦女移民)在出售她的房屋时经济情况尚可,可之后急转直下:被告的丈夫被抓去坐牢、被告多生了两个小孩、自己生病等。如果法院作出履约指令,她将会走投无路,所以拒绝了申请。但如果原告(房屋的买方)只能是有金钱赔偿的救济,如房屋涨了价的差价,这救济会是不灵光,很难相信这位赤穷的女被告会赔得出钱。这导致原告在金钱损失索赔胜诉后仍有一连串的事要做,但求能够执行判决。例如,申请被告“破产”(bankruptcy),或针对她的房屋申请一个“抵债令”(charging order)等做法。但这些做法都是费时失事,代价昂贵,也会经常无法收回全部欠下的债务。例如,在破产中原告即使有了胜诉判决,仍是一个“无抵押债权人”(unsecured creditor),恐怕不会分到什么钱。所以,怎比得上法院一早就作出履约指令的救济,把女被告与两个孩子逼走,管她们沦落街头,(对原告而言)干脆利落。

法院拒绝作出履约指令的另一个考虑在本章较早的 7.4 段提到,是有关建造合约内没有足够确定地阐述建筑商的履约内容及义务，条文过于模糊而无法作出履约指令的措辞让被告严格执行。这一个考虑也会在其他情况出现，如在 Bozon v. Farlow (1816) 1 Mer 459 先例，案情涉及买卖一家公司的"商誉"(goodwill)，反正整个买卖不涉及实质财产，如办公楼或货物。这一来，针对履约指令，法院感觉到没有办法找到适当的措辞。上诉庭的 William Grant MR 大法官说："In what way is the court to decree the transfer of such a business?"

如果履约指令会是涉及犯罪、侵权或是不道德，这也导致英国法院拒绝作出履约指令，等于强制被告作出这种事。这里有公共政策的因素，在 Hope v. Hope (1857) 8 De GM & G 731 先例，Turner 大法官说："The question to be considered is not merely whether the contract sought to be enforced is valid according to the laws of the country in which it was entered into, but whether it is consistent with the laws and policy of the country in which it is sought to be enforced. A contract may be good by the law of another country, but if it be in breach, fraud or evasion of the law of this country, or contrary to its policy, the courts of this country cannot... be called upon to enforce it."

另是在 Co – operative Insurance Society Ltd v. Argyll Stores (Holdings) Ltd (1998) A. C. 1 先例，贵族院拒绝作出履约指令的许多考虑的其中一个是强制被告继续亏本营业是不道德的，而且也不知道后果会是怎样。毕竟，会有可能是被告的损失会比被告违约/毁约带给原告的损失更加高昂，造成整体经济上的浪费。

总结而言，履约指令的作出与否要考虑的因素实在数不胜数，而在个别的案件里也会很多。这就导致履约指令的申请本身就可能是个昂贵的诉讼，更不用说是在作出履约指令后涉及监督合约的执行。至于在法院的考虑，就会是把所有的这些因素平衡后作出整体的考虑。可以说这里也涉及了一定程度的不肯定，毕竟每一位法官在同样的事实下会作出不一样的裁量权。也会是这些原因，看来履约指令是没有办法替代金钱损失赔偿的救济办法作为"首要救济"(primary remedy)。

12. 一个以上受害方/原告要求履约指令的考虑

这种情况会出现在一货两卖或一船两租的情况，导致有两位甚至更多的原告同时申请履约指令。这一来，就涉及法院或者仲裁庭怎样作出取舍的问题。这方面可介绍两个著名的先例。

12.1 案例之一：The "Oro Chief"

这种情况在 The "Oro Chief" (1983) 2 Lloyd's Rep. 509 先例中出现，就是一船两卖，前后出售给了两个买方。如果他们都是受害方并都要求履约指令，这就涉及法院或仲裁庭在行使裁量权时要考虑应该指令履行哪一份买卖合约。在该先例，The "Oro Chief" 是由一家挪威公司先出售给一家土耳其背景名为 Eximenco 的公司(第一买方)。但 Eximenco 被卖方指称没有在最后交接的一天支付船价,卖方于是终断买卖合约。之后,卖方把“Oro Chief”轮转售给另一家名为 Levantes 的葡萄牙公司(第二买方)。但之后第一买方先是在英国法院单方面申请了禁令阻止卖方转售船舶,并随即在葡萄牙里斯本把“Oro Chief”扣押。这导致英国法院在三方当事方(第一买方是原告,卖方与第二买方是第一与第二被告)同意下,针对第一买方的买卖合约下卖方可否终断合约作为一个先决问题。如果是不可以,也就涉及法院应否作出履约指令强制卖方把船舶交给第一买方。但如果这样做,又会涉及应否顾及第二被告利益的考虑。注意这些行动是在三方当事方同意下进行,否则就会存在卖方与第一买方要仲裁,因为他们之间的挪威格式买卖合约有一条伦敦仲裁条文。这一来,变成要仲裁庭考虑这些争议了,不论是第二买方能否加进来作为当事人之一。

注意是这种争议在二手船买卖经常会发生,而一种情况会是二手船市场在当时急涨,这导致了卖方借一些可能站得住脚或可能站不住脚的理由把第一个买卖合约终断,而把船舶以更高价格转售给第二买方。而不甘损失的第一买方插手进来,要求强制卖方履行第一个买卖合约。

在 The“Oro Chief”先例,法院在先决问题判是卖方有权终断第一个买卖合约,所以不存在卖方仍有合约责任必须交船给第一买方 Eximenco,虽然卖方无可置疑也有合约责任交船给第二买方 Levantes。这一来,法院是不需要考虑选择把“Oro Chief”轮交给第一或者是第二买方。但 Staughton 大法官也考虑了如果卖方对第一与第二买方都有合约责任交船,这履约指令应该怎样考虑。看来,考虑的因素涉及两位买方之间谁比较方便(test of convenience),其中包括了谁对该船舶更加需要,谁的手续麻烦,谁先谁后订立合约等方面。Staughton 大法官是这样说:

“Eximenco sought to prove that they had a particular need for the vessel as an ore/oil carrier. The attempt failed. An ordinary tanker would have suited them just as well for the time being. And ordinary tankers of similar size are available. Levantes, on the other hand, made somewhat more of a case that they had a special need for this vessel. They – or rather the group of which they formed part – evidently very much wanted the vessel, for good commercial reasons.

Against that, the investments which Eximenco have made in the project of buyingthis vessel is considerable. There is not only the deposit, and similar payments which they have made, and the liabilities which they have incurred to the suppliers of goods and services. There is also the commission on the opening of a letter of credit, and the trouble and expense generally of procuring the Turkish Government machine to finance and authorize the purchase of the vessel. For all this loss and expense they will be left to prove in the liquidation of the owners, if they do not obtain an order for specific performance.

Levantes, on the other hand, entered the field much later. They will have incurred far less trouble and expense. Their deposit is apparently in a joint account, unlike that of Eximenco, and so may well be more easily recoverable.

Those factors can be taken to balance each other. What remains is that Eximenco were firstin the field; and that Levantes came later with their eyes open, knowing that there was a risk that they might lose the vessel to Eximenco. If I had held that there was a subsisting contract to sell to Eximenco, I would have ordered it to be specifically performed.

As it is, I declare that the owners are under no obligation to deliver the vessel to Eximenco. In the event of my reaching that conclusion, no other remedy was sought, so I grant none."

12.2 案例之二:The "Stena Nautica" (No. 2)

The "Stena Nautica" (No. 2) (1982) 1 Lloyd's Rep. 336 先例也是涉及一个以上受害方作出履约指令的考虑因素。该船舶(原名"Stena Nordica"轮)的瑞典船东在1976年5月把船舶出租了5年给加拿大承租人(第一承租人),该租约还给了承租人两个选择权把租约延长1年与"购买船舶"(option to purchase)。事实上,第一承租人行使与打算行使这两个选择权,即在选择了把租约延长1年至1982年,并在1982年底行使选择权把该船舶买下。

该租约是一个比较罕见的安排,就是它不是连续性的5年期租,而只是在每年夏季的4月至10月租用,总共是108天。而其余的时间即长达257天,是把船舶交还给瑞典船东自己营运。所以,在这5年至6年的租约期间不断要交船还船。这种安排对于一些旅游船舶或者是行走美加大湖区的干货轮,由于只在夏季能够营运船舶,就经常会作这种安排,如像著名的 The "Nema" (1981) 2 Lloyd's Rep. 239 先例就是这种安排。

在1981年11月至1982年2月期间,当时船舶是在瑞典船东自己的营运下,他与另一位比利时承租人(第二承租人)谈判并订立了一份两年的光船租约,而且给了他一个买下船舶的选择权。显然,这是因为第二份租约的租金与买下船舶的价钱很吸引。这个做法是严重违反了第一份租约,因为瑞典船东再也无法在1982年的夏季开始时(4月)把船舶交给加拿大承租人,更不用说能让他行使买下船舶的选择权。

在1982年2月28日,瑞典船东把船舶交了给比利时承租人。比利时承租人为了把船舶用在横渡英伦海峡的营运而进行了大量的改装,并把船名改为"Stena Nautica"轮。

两位承租人都是无辜与不知情,比利时承租人固然是不知道第一份租约,加拿大承租人也不知道第二份光船租约。到了1982年3月2日,加拿大承租人行使买下船舶的选择权,并在3月6日派了代表去船坞检查船舶,这才导致整件事情曝光。之后,瑞典船东曾经想以其他船舶替代"Stena Nordica"轮(租给加拿大承租人的原名),但由于替代的船舶完全不适合导致双方谈不拢。

在3月12日,加拿大承租人以"一面之词"(*ex parte*)向英国法院申请了一个中间禁令,禁止船东出售、出租、改装或处理掉"Stena Nautica"(或"Stena Nordica")轮。

在获得中间禁令后,加拿大承租人并送达了一份给比利时承租人,令他不敢协助或参与藐视法院。

在4月6日,上诉庭同意了“权宜安排”,是让船舶继续在北海营运,以减少在“保持现状”(*status quo*)情况下的不必要损失/不便:The “Nema”(1982)2 Lloyd's Rep.323先例。而三位当事人中的两位(船东与加拿大承租人),也同意放弃期租中的仲裁,而让英国法院尽快一次过审理这个争议(包括了第三位当事人的比利时承租人各自的法律权利)。

总之是,争议后约两个月不到,法院便作出判决。高院的Parker大法官判加拿大承租人有权买这艘船,但比利时承租人的两年光船租约优先。换言之加拿大承租人两年后才能买得这艘“Stena Nautica”轮,而1982年4月要船舶去大湖区营运,是要另外在市场租用其他船舶替代。但去了上诉庭,否定了这个好像是“和稀泥”的履约指令,如May大法官质疑:“I confess that where I see an order for specific performance, even in respect of a ship, made subject, as it were, to a stay for two years, I am immediately put on inquiry whether, with respect, that constitutes a proper exercise by the learned judge of his discretion.”

关键是,既然“Stena Nautica”轮不是“真正独一无二”(actual uniqueness),表示金钱赔偿对加拿大承租人业已是足够救济。加上,船东Stena line是瑞典大公司,将来赔得起。故此,上诉庭完全拒绝加拿大承租人的履约指令申请。相反,作出了要履行比利时承租人的两年光船租约(加上有选择权多加一年租约以及购买船舶)的履约指令。

笔者进一步探讨,在The “Stena Nautica”先例,如果当时市场上或加拿大承租人没有替代船舶,这混乱情况又如何解决?笔者看来,这可见Societe des Industries Metallurgiques SA v. The Bronx Engineering Co Ltd(1975)1 Lloyd's Rep.465先例(它涉及中间禁令),受害方要等待6至12个月才会另有替代。看来,加拿大承租人总会在这么长的时间找到替代船舶吧。反正是对两位或以上的受害方/原告的困境作出一个平衡,看看谁应该获得履约指令的救济,谁只能获得金钱赔偿的救济。毕竟只能是有一个受害方/原告能够获得履行。

13. 国际仲裁与履约指令

在这里也可以探讨一下在国际仲裁中的履约指令。仲裁员作出履约指令的权力一早就已经有,在1934年英国《仲裁法》就有section 7:“the arbitrators or umpire shall have the same power as the court to order specific performance of any contract other than any contract relating to land or any interest in land.”接着在1950年英国《仲裁法》,同样一条出现在section 15。而到了1996年英国《仲裁法》,类似的条文出现在section 48

(5)(b):"the tribunal has the same power as the court to order specific performance of a contract(other than any contract relating to land)."给予仲裁员履约指令的权力是完全可以理解的,因为它是其中一种违约的救济方法。既然仲裁员的任务是解决争议,判谁是谁非并给予救济,就没理由只是给他一半的权力作出金钱赔偿的救济,却不给另一半的作出履约指令的权力。毕竟在很多时候这两个救济是替代性的,在法院就会在拒绝给予履约指令的救济下以金钱赔偿作出替代。

在《仲裁法——从开庭审理到仲裁书的作出与执行》之443页,有讲到在1996年英国《仲裁法》,除了section 48(5)(b)条文外,还有其他的有关条文针对禁令以及怎样强制执行由仲裁员作出的指令或裁决书。针对作出禁令裁决书(injunctive award),仲裁员的权力是来自1996年英国《仲裁法》之Section 48(5)(a),如下:"48.(5)(a)to order a party to do or refrain from doing anything."

13.1　怎样强制执行仲裁员作出的指令与禁令

至于怎样让仲裁员作出这一些有阻吓力的指令与禁令,这就是根据1996年英国《仲裁法》之Section 42(1),如下:"42.(1)Unless otherwise agreed by the parties, the court may make an order requiring a party to comply with a peremptory order made by the tribunal."

另外,1996年英国《仲裁法》之section 66规定了可以把仲裁庭的命令与裁决书变为法院的命令或判决:"(1)An award made by the tribunal pursuant to an arbitration agreement may, by leave of the court, be enforced in the same manner as a judgment or order of the court to the same effect."

《香港仲裁条例》section 2GG也有与英国《仲裁法》类似条文可以把仲裁庭的命令与裁决书变为法院的命令或判决,所以仲裁员作出的履约指令或履约裁决书也就是等于法院所作出,效力是一样,违反的被告同样是有藐视法院的危险。至于在外国或中国内地的仲裁庭所作出的履约裁决书,他们也可以前来香港或英国根据1958年《纽约公约》取得承认与执行:Xiamen Xinjingdi Group Ltd(厦门新景地集团公司)v. Eton Properties Ltd(Civil Appeal Nos 106 and 197 of 2008)(请看《仲裁法——从开庭审理到仲裁书的作出与执行》之第763页)。问题是国际仲裁的"履约裁决书"(performance award)会是在全球各地执行,主要的执行地显然就是在被告的所在地。这会带来比"金钱裁决书"(monetary award)困难得多的问题,因为败诉的被告会在许多地方有资产可供执行,包括在一些金融中心。除了机会多了很多,执行起来也相对容易与有经验。

例如,针对中国船厂所作出的一个履约裁决书(这在今天造船合约争议十分之多的情况下经常发生),执行就必须是通过中国法院根据《纽约公约》或与香港相互承认裁决书的协议。但有不少大陆法的国家(如德国或者法国)虽然也有"履约指令"(enforced performance)的做法,但就没有藐视法院的说法,只是作为违约救济的其中一种选择。即使是有强制的做法,严厉程度也不一样。如德国,在Treitel教授在

《Remedies for Breach of Contract - A Comparative Account》(1991 年版)之第 54 ~ 55 页就提到了德国法院通常不愿意针对债务人或被告本人,说:"The first noteworthy feature of this scheme of enforcement is the great variety of means of execution provided by the law. The exercise of physical force against the person of the debtor(which is usually considered to be an argument against enforced performance) is a comparative rarity. Generally, the method of enforcement of is specially tailored to the needs of the judgment to be enforced; the exception is the use of penal sanctions to enforce a judgment that the debtor should suffer, or forbear from doing something."

该书也举了很多例子,其中针对"服务合约"(service contract),是根本不会强制履行,说:"Where the judgment is for an act which cannot be vicariously performed, execution is by means of fines and imprisonment, but this method of execution is not available for the enforcement of a judgment to render services under a contract of service and in a large number of other cases... The result is that these judgments for services cannot be enforced at all; the only effective remedy is a claim for damages."

与香港关系更密切的中国内地,也是同样地位,根本没有藐视法院的概念。虽然不执行法院命令也会有如拘禁 15 天不等的惩罚,但有时不这么做。而且各地法院的做法也不一致,导致大量法院的指令或禁令不被履行或执行。反正是相比英国或者香港地区的严格性相差很远。

这表示仲裁庭作出的履约指令如果是在这些国家或地区执行,根本就没有英国或香港地区针对这种救济最严厉与最有效的威慑力,效果就会很有疑问。这一来,原告如果事后前来仲裁庭申诉,履约指令或履约裁决书被阳奉阴违,甚至被漠视,仲裁庭能够做什么,改为是金钱损失赔偿?但如果没有金钱损失或损失很难计算又该怎么办?如被漠视的履约指令是允许被告作出检查?笔者还没有答案,但手头已经有案件面对这种问题。

这样看来,估计仲裁庭应该对其作出履约指令或履约裁决书要有保留。除了上述所讲的有效性问题,也包括了公平对待双方当事人的考虑。例如,针对两个来自不同地方的当事人,他们的所在地法律显示了不同严厉程度的执行。针对被告所在地的法院会严厉执行包括了藐视法院,但作为申请人的原告所在地的法院就不会严厉执行,甚至不会执行这种命令或者裁决书。这一来,会否是违反了"相互性原则"(want of mutuality)?而且为了公平对待双方当事人,应否对可以严厉执行的一方当事人(如一家香港公司),也避免作出履约指令,因为另一方当事人是一家中国内地的公司,不能与不会严厉执行一个香港仲裁庭的履约指令的命令或者裁决书?

除了执行外,国际仲裁中还会更早出现的问题就是拥有不同法律背景的仲裁员在决定是否能够作出履约指令或履约裁决书的"思维过程"(mental exercise)不同。如果涉及仲裁员是来自中国内地或德国,他们只会把履约指令视为与金钱赔偿的救济没有区分的违约救济手段,估计不会像英国或香港的仲裁员在作决定时会对所有上述介绍过的是否作出履约指令的因素衡量过之后才作出取舍。这一来,仲裁庭如果由这两种不同背景仲裁员组成,就会面对沟通上的困难。而这种由不同思维过程的仲裁庭所作出的履约裁决书在执行时应否被不同对待,在 Xiamen Xinjingdi Group Ltd(厦门新景地集团公司) v. Eton Properties Ltd(Civil Appeal Nos 106 and 197 of 2008)先例中据说有争论过,但香港法院拒绝作出区分。

13.2 "土地例外"

笔者曾经感觉到奇怪的就是在英国的仲裁法的有关授权仲裁员作出履约指令,为什么只是针对土地不能作出。毕竟,由于土地是属于"独一无二"(uniqueness),通常以履约指令迫使违约方是被视为更恰当的救济做法。这一来,等于是不鼓励土地争议去仲裁。笔者曾经怀疑一个原因是土地的转让与争议是非常本地化的,不适宜让仲裁员特别是外国的仲裁员作出履约指令这种强制性的命令。但这也解释不了为什么早在 1934 年的立法就已经有了这一个"土地例外"(land exception),因为当时英国也不会有外国仲裁员与国际仲裁这种考虑。笔者这一个疑问在 2008 年《Interest, Auxiliary and Alternative Remedies in International Arbitration》一书,Johnny Veeder 御用大律师发表了一篇文章,其中涉及他的猜测是在 80 多年前,英国普遍对仲裁员的水平与操守抱有怀疑,根本不会把他们与法官相提并论,所以给仲裁员作出履约指令的权力抱有怀疑。在当时的英国,绝大部分的仲裁员都不是律师,更加谈不上是资深的律师(而法官正是由国家委任的资深律师担任)。至于为什么只针对土地,该文的解释是在那个年代,土地是一个非常敏感的课题,英国议员刚通过了重要的 1925 年《财产法》(《Law of Property Act 1925》),带来对土地有关的法律与土地的登记一些重大改革。这显然不是一个恰当的时机给私人的仲裁员一个与高高在上的法官拥有同等的作出履约指令权利。但问题是到了今天,仲裁员已经有权而且经常在金额十分庞大的商业合约中作出履约指令,为什么偏偏针对土地就在救济方面缺了一大块的权力?毕竟不少土地的争议涉及的金额并非是十分庞大。唯一可以说的是,1996 年英国《仲裁法》之 section 48(针对履约指令的权限)并非是"强制性"(mandatory),允许订约自由作出改变。这表示涉及土地的合约,可以明示规定仲裁庭有权作出履约指令,但现实中会有这种警觉性的做法就从来没有听说过。

13.3 仲裁庭作出的履约指令或者履约裁决书不被执行的情况

国际仲裁庭如果作出履约指令,或者"履约裁决书"(performance award),不被执行或无法执行的情况会比法院作出履约指令的机会更高,这一来就存在仲裁庭能够做什么的问题。这种情况如果发生在法院,在本章 1.3 与 1.4 段就已经有解释过,是可以向法院申请把法院的履约指令撤销并改以金钱损失的索赔作为救济。这是否表示仲裁庭遇到这样的情况也可以这样做呢?这会带来的问题是如仲裁庭能否自己撤销一个裁决书,即使只是一个履约的裁决书?还会有其他的问题如较早前作出的履约指令或者是履约裁决书根据《香港仲裁条例》之 Section 61 变成法院的履约指令或履约判决,是否表示向仲裁庭申请撤销并且成功后还要向法院做同样的事情?这种实际操作的问题解决不是困难,但毕竟还没有类似的案例或做法。

13.4 英国仲裁是否还可以让英国法院作出履约指令或禁令?

这一个问题是由于1996年英国《仲裁法》生效之后,加强对仲裁的支持,排除法院对于仲裁的干涉,特别是在实质争议方面。显然履约指令针对的都是实质争议,权力是在 Section 48(5)(b)明确的赋予仲裁员。另在 Section 1(c),也说明法院在1996年立法没有特别规定的情况下是不能干预仲裁。虽然 Section 48 是属于非强制性条文,双方可以订约自由明确把作出履约指令或禁令的权力同时或任由原告选择交给英国法院,而且也确实在实践中见到过此类条文,但应该是不多。但在上诉庭 Cetelem SA v. Roust Holdings Ltd(2005)2 Lloyd's Rep 494 的先例,看来英国法院还是在这方面有一个角色。这一个先例在笔者所著的《仲裁法——从开庭准备到裁决书的作出与执行》一书第三章1.5.1段有简单介绍,但并不够详尽,在此再补充一下。该先例涉及一个控股股权转让的买卖,合约内有一条 ICC 仲裁条文,仲裁地点是伦敦。重要之处是该合约对于股权转让有一条先决条件就是卖方必须在2005年1月31日之前取得俄罗斯中央银行的批准。要在这个限期内取得批准就所有的文件必须在2004年12月10日之前交给俄罗斯中央银行,虽然这一个时间表并没有在双方的合约内明确规定。有规定的明示条文只有两条:第一条是3.3条文说:"The parties will make their best efforts and provide mutual assistance so that the principal and other conditions precedent are satisfied as rapidly as practicable."另一条有关条文是6.8条说:"The parties hereto shall sign up and deliver all the documents, provide all information and take all reasonable and lawful measures that may be necessary or appropriate to the achievement of the purpose of this agreement."

估计是原告的 Cetelem 害怕被告的 Roust Holdings Ltd(简称 RHL)拖延向俄罗斯中央银行提出申请批准,利用先决条件没有完成把合约赖掉,所以向英国法院提出一个类似履约指令的申请。至于 Cetelem 为什么没有向仲裁庭申请,估计原因是仲裁庭还没有成立,而成立时需要一段时间,在紧急的情况下是等不了。申请的履约指令只要求 RHL 在2004年12月29日(这已经是过了12月10日)前递交所有的文件给俄罗斯中央银行申请批准,文字上是如下:"A with notice application pursuant to Section 44 for an order requiring RHL by 1600 GMT on 29 Dec 2004 to procure that: (1) all documents to be produced by RHL or on its behalf necessary to accompany the application for the authorisation of the Central Bank of the Russian Federation of: (a) the transfer by RTL of all its shares in RSC to RCL; and (b) the acquisition by Cetelem and sale by RHL of 499,500 shares in RCL representing 49.5% of the outstanding share capital and voting rights in RCL, and deliver to the office of ... (2) the application is signed by it or on its behalf by its duly authorised representative and also delivered to the office of ..."(上述英文中出现的 RTL、RSC 与 RCL 是属于同一个集团的公司)

Cetelem 向英国法院申请是根据1996年英国《仲裁法》之 Section 44(3),该条文是允许英国法院在紧急的时候做出中间措施的命令为了保存证据与财产(If the case is one of urgency, the court may, on the application of a party or proposed party to the arbitral proceedings, make such orders as it thinks necessary for the purpose of preserving evidence or assets)。

英国上诉庭同意作出这一个履约指令,认为该条文的"财产"(asset)一词是包括了合约的权利。Clarke 大法官是这样说:"Mr Dunning(RHL 代表律师)correctly accepts that 'assets' are not limited to tangible assets but include, for example, choses in action. This is evident, both because section 44(2) refers to 'property' and 'goods', so that the 'assets' must be wider than both .... It seems to me that, once it is accepted that 'assets' includes 'choses in action', there is no reason to limit them to particular types of chose in action. There may be some other reason for limiting the operation of section 44(3) but I do not see any reason why a contractual right should not be an 'asset' within the meaning of the subsection... It is evidence that the purpose of the order must be to facilitate the arbitration or the enforcement of an award and not to usurp the functions of the arbitral process. However, as I observed earlier, there is nothing in the subsection to limit the power of the court to orders which do not involve a preliminary determination of a contractual right of the parties. I see nothing in the subsection of the Act which provides that the court has no power to make an order which it thinks necessary for the purpose of preserving evidence or assets because it also involve forming a view on the merits of the dispute which the parties have agreed to submit to arbitration or because it involves directing a party to take a step which the contract provides that it must take...."

看来在这一个先例,法院通过它在 1996 年英国《仲裁法》中 Section 44 的"中间措施"(interim measure)权利作出类似履约指令的决定,根据的理由是将合约权利作为财产的一种类别,使得法院可以作出保存的中间措施。但照理说,履约指令作为"救济"(remedy)的一种,也在 1996 年立法下之 Section 48(5)(b)是应该由仲裁员作出,除非是涉及土地的履约指令,这请看上面的 13.2 段。

13.5　有关履约指令仲裁案件例子之一

笔者在实际的仲裁业务中也经常遇到履约指令的申请,本段节与接下去的段节介绍一些近期遇到的例子以及面对的问题。

这是一个中国内地的仲裁案件,案情涉及一个 FOB 买卖,买卖合约本身是涉及多个航次的付运,其中也有条文规定在每次付运前中国买方要向外国卖方开出信用证以及派船。在前 10 个航次基本上都算是顺利履行,到了第 11 个航次就开始出问题,因为刚好在那个时候碰上了 2008 年的金融海啸。这令买方不开信用证,当然也不会派船,而买方的抗辩是"不可抗力"(*force majeure*)导致无法履行。外国卖方在多次督促买方履约不果后,作出了一个仲裁庭看来相对奇怪的决定,就是把存放在外国产地的货物自己安排船舶付运到中国港口,也就是买方本来要卸货的港口。卖方的理由是外国的仓库费用很高,而中国相对便宜得多。结果该批货物在中国港口放了1年之久,其间该货物的市场价格也有过很大的波动,包括在某些时间市场价格比该买卖合约的价格还要高。但由于卖方没有提供任何证据或陈述,而买方也没有追查(如要求披露或盘问证人),所以仲裁庭是不会知道在这一个期间卖方对这批货物做了些什么。例如,是否有试图向其他的买方出售该批货物,但没有结果。仲裁庭在开庭的时候虽然曾经主动问卖方,他的简单回复是由于存放在中国港口的货物打上了买方公司的唛头,所以很难出售。加上开始了仲裁程序,卖方认为不应该随意动这票货。

在该仲裁,卖方作为原告或申诉人向仲裁庭提出唯一的一个救济请求就是向买方作出履约指令,要求接收存放在中国港口的该批货物,并马上支付货价以及赔偿有关的损失(这包括了两个港口的仓库费用以及把货物付运至中国港口的运费等)。

反正笔者看来(也就是仲裁庭的看法),这是一个很奇怪的做法,也认为卖方有很多的错误理解。仲裁庭判是在责任方面,中国买方的确是违约/毁约,因为全球金融海啸不足以令所有的商业合约全部无法履行,这也包括了该买卖合约,所以不可抗力的抗辩理由被否定。但接下去仲裁庭也认为卖方有很多奇怪的做法与错误的理解,包括:(1)卖方作为违约/毁约的受害人是有权向买方提出索赔,由于该种货物(有市场的商品)可以随意在市场上买卖,卖方理应减少损失,而不是增加损失。而他没有减少损失所带来的后果是要自己承担的。而即使开始了仲裁也不影响卖方有减少损失的责任,包括在市场高价的时候转售。(2)如果卖方说货物是因为有了买方的唛头而无法再在中国港口出售给其他买方,就更加应该一早在外国装港就安排出售给第三人,以减少损失,并向买方提出索赔差价。毕竟在装港卖方改变该批货物的唛头就相对容易。(3)最莫名其妙的是卖方自己安排把货物付运到中国港口,这好像是非要把这票货卖给该违约/毁约的买方,这同时把原来的FOB买卖从根本上变为了CIF买卖。在笔者看来,卖方一这样做,就应该视为是从行动上接受了买方的违约/毁约,而原来的FOB买卖合约也就终断。

但仲裁庭包括笔者最不能接受的就是卖方所提出的履约指令救济以及支付货价。显然,这一个案件以金钱赔偿作出救济的做法是完全恰当,甚至是唯一的。因为在买卖合约终断后,接近1年的时间,哪里还有买卖合约履行并作出指令?再说,履约指令只能针对原来的FOB买卖,而不能针对卖方一厢情愿改变为的CIF买卖。这一来,即使买方履约,开出信用证与派船去外国装港,哪里还有一批货物等待装船。仲裁庭一致的意见否定了卖方的请求。但接下来就出现了笔者与其他两位仲裁员的不同意见,这就是涉及接下去的程序。本来整个仲裁庭都一致认为是中国买方违约/毁约,理应作出赔偿或承担后果。只是因为卖方所提出的救济办法不恰当,导致了败诉。本来在这一个案件要求履约指令的救济明显是不恰当,因为对笔者而言是有太多的理由,如本章第4段的金钱损失赔偿应是足够救济,第9段的怠慢申请等。而更大的原因笔者是认为该FOB买卖合约根本无法重生去全面履行。但即使这样提出,也可以同时请求一个替代的救济,就是金钱赔偿的救济。这一来,在审理时,仲裁庭否定了履约指令的救济就可以马上作出对金钱损失的赔偿,一次审理就可以终局。但在这一个案件,已经是提到过卖方只提出履约指令的救济,虽然也有涉及金钱损失如两个港口的仓库费用,但并不完整而且最大的一项也就是买方违约/毁约所带来的货价损失(通常是市场价格与买卖合约价格的区别)也根本没有提到或提供任何证据(如有关时段的市场价格)。

这里就带出了一种在中国内地与国际上是非常不一致的做法或理念,而且是十分危险的。该做法或理念就是在每一个案件中不能提出“替代请求”(alternative case),原因是提出替代请求,在部分法官与仲裁员的眼中是一种示弱的行为,显示了申诉人对他的“主要请求”(primary case)没有信心。笔者完全不能接受这种说法,并认为所说的原因是非常片面与站不住脚。笔者认为提出一个主要的请求再加上其他5个或10个替代请求,等于是为自己多设下几道防线,没理由不值得鼓励。这样做更加说得通的理由是提出多个替代请求(如果有的话)不代表提出的一方当事人对他的主要请求没信心,而没有绝对信心的反而是可能有太多的变数,如诉讼风险下部分法官或仲裁员会犯错与判错。再举一个更说得通的理由是,法官与仲裁员作出判决或裁决,根据的是有关案件的法律地位与相关证据的强弱,至于双方当事人有没有信心根本就不是一个作出判决或裁决考虑的因素。再说当事人有没有信心也是与他的水平有关。此外也要看这对整个社会来说是不是一个好的做法,答案显然是否定的。因为允许申诉人对同一个案件一次又一次地提出不同的请求,如先提出的违约请求失败后,又重新申请仲裁提出一个侵权的请求,这样的做法会使案件没完没了,显然是非常劳民伤财。

笔者也经常会见到案件在所有的请求都被否定,但只有一个看来比较次要的替代请求被法院或仲裁庭接纳而获得最后的胜诉。有关这一个课题在笔者《仲裁法——从开庭审理到裁决书的作出与执行》一书的第十章有详述。该书的第一章之5.3.3.3.2段也提到了英国律师的做法就是任何替代请求都提出,千万不要遗漏任何一个,即使是被法院或仲裁庭接纳的希望很渺茫。所以,英国律师如果漏了一些说得过去的替代请求,则会是一种典型的专业疏忽并会被当事人追究责任。在英国新的《民事诉讼规则》中,就引入了一种希望减少诉讼费用的做法,这就是一方当事人如果提出一些法院看来是无望的替代请求,而且最终是没有发生奇迹地败诉,他是要承担花费在该替代请求的诉讼费用,即使他在整个案件中是胜诉方。这样的规定显然是不鼓励双方当事人与他的律师把诉讼搞得太大,导致费用相应地增加。

笔者在否定了外国卖方的履约指令请求后,建议在该裁决书是以中间或部分裁决书的形式作出,以保留权力审理金钱损失赔偿的救济,毕竟在责任方面是已经判了中国买方违约/毁约。但其他两位仲裁员认为应该作出终局的审理,至于卖方将来如果要提出金钱损失赔偿的救济,可以重新提出仲裁申请,甚至组成另一个仲裁庭。这最终导致了笔者针对这一个方面给了一个不同的意见,如下:“本人杨良宜是完全同意本裁决书,唯一的异议是本裁决书应否属于一份部分裁决书,或是整个仲裁的最后裁决书。本人是认为应该是一份部分裁决书,所以本仲裁庭应该明示保留权力处理本案其他的争议,但不影响在本裁决书已经作出裁决的部分是属于终局。主要的原因是:申请人的主要甚至是唯一的请求是要被申请人接受合约争议的货物,换言之,是要求一个实际履行的救济。这被本仲裁庭视为是不合适而否定,虽然是裁决被申请人拒绝按买卖合约规定受领货物是重大违约。但实际履行的救济本质上只是一种次要救济,所以被否定也就表示首要救济的金钱赔偿才是合理的救济方式。这一来,本人认为仲裁庭应该保留这方面的权力处理本案件其他余下的争议,包括根据首要救济计算金钱损失赔偿。"

13.6 有关履约指令仲裁案件例子之二

这是一个在香港的"临时仲裁"(*ad hoc* arbitration),案情涉及一票印度煤炭的CIF买卖,印度卖方将煤炭运到中国港口,经卸货港的中国出入境检验检疫局(CIQ)检验后,说是显示该票煤炭指标严重偏离合约质量的要求,则中国买方以货不对版为由拒绝接收该票货物。在印度卖方多次要求接收货物但遭到拒绝后,也就以书面确认接受买方的违约/毁约。可以说,到了这个时候,该买卖合约已经终断。其他一些重要的细节是虽然该买卖合约约定以信用证付款,但不知道什么原因没有这样做。这导致卖方一直没有获得货价的支付,而一套正本提单也是继续由卖方持有。但船舶到了中国港口,卖方估计是为了避免昂贵的船期损失,还是安排把煤炭卸下,放置在最终中国买方(一家发电厂)的码头。这些双方都确认的事实看来,笔者是认为煤炭的所有权明显还是在卖方。除了正本提单是他所持有(提单就是对货物所有权的证明),也明显可以看到卖方在没有获得货价的支付下是不会愿意把煤炭的所有权转让给买方。反正是双方就僵持,卖方说是煤炭没有问题,买方必须接受,但买方就坚持货不对版,并且合法拒货。这种争议在国际货物买卖也经常会发生,这导致双方很难心平气和地减少损失,如把这批双方都拒绝要的一票货物尽快出售给第三人以减少仓库费用或避免货物进一步腐烂(如果涉及的是易腐货物)。这会或迟或早导致其中一个当事人(可能是比较明智的或是当时承担主要损失的一方)前来向仲裁庭申请在不损害双方权利的情况下命令出售该票货物以减少损失。而法院或仲裁庭这方面的权力是属于"中间措施"(interim measure)的权力,在1996年英国《仲裁法》之section 44(2)(d)有针对。而在《香港仲裁条例》,是在Section 35。

但在该香港仲裁,印度卖方十分紧急地向包括了笔者的三人仲裁庭提出一个履约指令的请求。这一个履约指令也不是要求买方必须接收货物与不能拒绝接收,而是要求指令中国买方尽快在限期之前缴付中国海关征收的进口税,以避免货物被海关充公。印度卖方的律师不断地以邮件轰炸的策略以要求尽快作出履约指令,而代表中国买方的律师则对卖方这一方面的请求不置可否,反而只针对管辖权的质疑。但这可能是影响了笔者以外的其他两位仲裁员,同意针对支付进口税作出一个中间或部分裁决书,而且根据的是买卖合约中的一条条文说明该票煤炭的进口税是由买方承担。该两位仲裁员(其中有一位是首席)甚至把该“履约裁决书”(performance award)也已经草拟好,要求笔者同意与签字。但笔者对这种做法持完全相反的看法,要求如果该两位执意以多数意见作出这份裁决书,则允许笔者作出一个“不同意见”(dissenting opinion)。事实上笔者也把这个不同意见草拟好,其中提到了笔者反对的理由。这些理由是很多,但笔者只挑二三个重要的作出介绍。

第一个原因是在这一个仲裁案件与上一小段所介绍的中国大陆的仲裁案件是一致的,这就是有关的买卖合约是双方都已经以文书或者行动接受了合约终断(在本案件是卖方已经文书接受买方的违约/毁约)。这一来,仲裁庭怎样可以作出履约指令,等于令该终断的合约重生。如果合约能够重生,这也只是双方当事人能够做的事情,不是仲裁庭的权力。在履约指令的“局限”(limitation),其中一个著名的情况是如果一个合约可以让被告有权终断,也不应该作出履约指令。因为一作出,被告就可以行使权利终断合约令该履约指令变成一纸空文。但法院或仲裁庭作出履约指令,是没有权力剥夺被告的合约权利终断合约,所以就干脆在这种情况下根本不应该这样做。这方面笔者可节录《Chitty on Contracts》(30th edn,2008 年)之 27 - 038 段所说如下:“**Contracts expressed to be terminable.** If a contract is expressed to be revocable by the party against whom an order of specific performance is sought, the order will be refused as the defendant could render it nugatory by exercising his power to terminate. On this ground a contract to enter into a partnership at will is not specifically enforceable. The same is true of a contract for a lease which by virtue of the contract itself would contain a stipulation enabling the defendant to determine the lease as soon as it was executed; but a tenancy from year to year, determinable by either party by half a year's notice to quit, is specifically enforceable.”

第二个原因是整个履约指令会带来的不公平与不合理,这与履约指令本身是属于一个衡平法的救济方法可以说是相互矛盾的。多数仲裁员是认为十分公平与合理,因为印度卖方至今一毛钱的货价都没有到手,再要支付中国的进口税会带来非常沉重的负担。这可以说是一种角度看待,而且是非常暂时性的。会是相等于在一个争议,其中原告蒙受庞大的损失且损失还在继续,仲裁庭在没有分清楚责任之前就命令被告要支付一半的损失以减轻原告的负担。或者这是在商业的角度看来是公平合理,但法律却没有这种说法。原告可以把他最终蒙受的所有损失向被告索赔,如果责任上原告胜诉,并且能够证明所有的损失,原告应该可以向被告成功把所有的损失加上期间的利息要回来。如果原告担心被告将来会赖皮不支付,原告可以考虑采取中间措施的做法如“冻结令”(freezing injunction)。如果原告担心冻结令也不会有成效,反正就是没有钱。这一来要求履约指令的申请也岂非是开玩笑,因为指令被告支付一大笔进口税根本就是不可能,而不可能本来就是决定是否作出履约指令的主要考虑之一。反正就没有一个说法可以要被告在责任没有分清楚之前要分担原告的部分损失。更重要的是笔者认为整个履约指令不公平与不合理是在要求中国买方为印度卖方所拥有的这票煤炭支付庞大的进口税，而最终这票煤炭的命运会是怎么样买方是没有办法控制。这里的变数会有：(1)印度卖方可能把这票煤炭转卖如去越南，这种可能的发展是仲裁庭不会知道，因为他们没有这方面的商业知识。如果真有这个发展，被指令的买方所支付掉的进口税可能就是白付了。至于买方能否在这种情况下获得中国海关退还全部或部分的进口税，由于案件连"文书请求"(pleadings)也没有开始，笔者作为仲裁员就根本无法得知了。(2)印尼卖方也有可能会把这票煤炭运回印尼，这也会带来同一种后果，就是进口税可能是白付了。表面看，煤炭这种相对低价的货物不值得这么做。但笔者作为仲裁员即没有双方的陈述，更加没有证据说明这样做的运费是多少以及当时煤炭市场这票货物的实际货价是多少，以作出估计是否值得这么做。(3)也会是该票在中国港口的煤炭已经是不太值钱(原因可能会是煤炭的市场大幅下跌或放置的过程中该票煤炭遭受到意外而令货价下挫)，导致一种情况就是这票货的实际价值比进口税还要低。(4)也很可能会发生是印度卖方最后在中国找到了这票煤炭的其他买方，甚至会与原来的最后买方(发电厂)作出了另外的协议。这一来进口税还是需要作出支付，但这一份新的合约就有可能说明是由该新的买方承担。

反正笔者认为，最公平的做法还是不要下这种"半桶水"或"和稀泥"的履约指令。如果必须支付这笔进口税，最佳的支付人选还是该票煤炭的所有人，也就是印度卖方。在支付的同时，他可以平衡一下他将会怎样处置该票煤炭，然后作出明智的取舍。而所有这些损失，卖方是可以向买方提出金钱损失的索赔。如果买方不合法拒绝该票煤炭，买方就会要承担所有的损失。相反，如果卖方败诉，也表示他自己要承担所有的损失，谁叫他的煤炭货不对版。总之，笔者看来以金钱作出赔偿是本案件最佳的也最适合的救济办法，没有理由作出一个要求中国买方支付进口税的履约指令。

13.7　有关履约指令仲裁案件例子之三

在 2008 年全球金融海啸后，众所周知，下挫得最厉害的不是股市而是航运市场，它曾经一度下挫高达 90% 以上。这无可避免地导致了大量的诉讼，其中到了 2009 年至 2010 年更是主要涉及造船合约。造船曾经经历过一段很长时间的好日子，作为全球主要的造船国家(特别是建造散货船)的中国，显然取得了大量的高价造船合约在手，但船舶还没有建造好。这一来，在航运市场崩溃后，外国的买方或船东就会想尽办法在该高价的造船合约中脱身。当然懂法律的外国船东是不会贸然对中国船厂说"造船合约不合理，我会亏大本，所以我不干了"。这是一个明显不过的违约/毁约行为，这样脱身也是非常愚蠢的办法，而且要面对中国船厂索赔所有的损失。但如果买方或船东能够找出一个说的过去的合法理由从造船合约脱身，他的地位就是好得多。他非但可以昂首挺胸地脱身，自称是完全遵守合约办事外，还可以把预付的船价要回来。至于合法的理由，其中一个最主要也最常见的就是以货不对版拒绝接受交船。这一个做法与一般的货物买卖道理是一样，如在 13.4 段所介绍的煤炭被指称质量不合格而不予接受的理由一样。毕竟造船合约在本质上与其他的货物买卖是一样，同样适用1979年英国《货物销售法》。但在该立法，现在是有加了条文防止买方以很轻微违反货不对版作为借口拒绝货物，实质上是由于有关货物的市场价格下跌而想取巧。该条文是15A名为"Modification of remedies for breach of condition in non - consumer cases"，主要内容节录如下："...(1)(b) the breach is so slight that it would be unreasonable for him to reject them, then, if the seller does not deal as consumer, the breach is not to be treated as a breach of condition but may be treated as a breach of warranty..."

很简单说明，就是在法律的地位下，买方如果要拒绝接受这一艘高价订购的船舶，他必须挑出货不对版的毛病，而且必须是严重的。这才会构成是1979年英国《货物销售法》下的默示条件，可以合法拒绝。但如果这货不对版的毛病只是鸡毛蒜皮，这在上一条节录的条文可以看到，即使是违反也被视为是一个保证条文，买方还是必须接受船舶，而后再索赔该货不对版造成的金钱损失。既然是鸡毛蒜皮，所以造成的损失金钱金额上也不会大，根本不能满足买方希望借这个借口从造船合约中脱身。当然，能够挑得出货不对版的毛病，即使不算是太严重，但真的打官司还是会有风险。所以买方还是希望能够这样做，至少给了他借口可以跟船厂讨价还价，把原来造船合约的高价减低。这总比什么都不做而把高价的船舶接受下来，眼看着要亏大本来得好。

针对中国船厂而言，也知道在这样的市场下，买方在交船前肯定想挑毛病。所以双方的关系不会十分友好，并且对对方的一切行动都会严加防范。其中一个经常会做的是严格限制买方总管在船上的活动，在传递消息上也尽量不透明，这明显是可以减少机会让买方挑得出将来拒绝接收船舶的货不对版借口。

以上很简单地把这方面的"争议背景"(factual matrix)作出了介绍。接下去就谈到了在这种情况下仲裁庭所面对的履约指令申请。申请人通常来自买方，也就是船东。这种申请会是各式各样，有时候会是十分广泛(如要求指令中国船厂必须允许买方的总管去船舶的所有地方进行检查，或是指令中国船厂必须在递交通知书之前向买方的总管证明该船舶的确是已经备妥交船)，也有时候比较局限与有针对性(如要求指令中国船厂必须允许买方的总管或有多少人参与试航或对某一个买方能证明是有问题的地方修妥才能交船)。

面对这种申请，仲裁庭所要考虑的是有多方面。首先，是要考虑到造船合约既是一个货物买卖合约亦是一个建造合约：McDougall v. Aeromarine of Emsworth Ltd (1958) 2 Lloyd's Rep. 345先例。这一来，从建造合约是否作出履约指令的一系列考虑中(请看本章7.4段)，也可以看到造船合约难以监督，除了因为它是一个建造工程外，而且更是一个在外国(英国以外)的工程，有涉外的因素，导致英国法院更加难以监督。这方面可以再度节录Gyllenhammer & Partners International Ltd v. Sour Brodogradevna Split (1989) 2 Lloyd's Rep. 403先例，Hirst大法官拒绝作出履约指令，说："... a very complex contract requiring extensive co - operation between the parties on a number of matters, particularly modifications, optional variations, and, perhaps most importantly of all, matters of detail (some by no means unimportant) left undefined in the specification. In my judgment these factors, coupled with the consideration that the work take place in a foreign yard, outside the Court's jurisdiction, would tell strongly against an order for specific performance being in principle appropriate in the present case."(造船合约是一个十分复杂的合约,需要双方大量的合作,特别是在船舶的修改,选择权下的改变或可能是最重要的是一些没有在造船合约的规范说明中明确规定的地方。上述的因素,加上考虑外国船厂并非在英国法院的管辖下,可以说是很不适宜作出履约指令。)

在笔者近年来审理的大量有关造船合约的仲裁案件中,就可以随意挑两个案件作为介绍,就是买方作出履约指令申请,内容是要求中国船厂允许买方(或仲裁庭)委任的检验师对船舶作出检查与测试。

第一个是伦敦仲裁,涉及6艘散装货船。笔者是被中国船厂委任为仲裁员,另外两位仲裁员包括买方(希腊船东)委任与首席仲裁员都是英国退休的大法官。该造船合约中有很详细的条文针对船舶在建造中的"检查"(inspection)、"测试"(tests)与"试航"(trials)如何进行与买方的参与,有关的条文稍后会节录。反正是该仲裁由买方的船东所提出,并且推进的很快,很快就在伦敦定下了开庭去审理一个履约指令与宣示裁决的申请。买方提出有关船舶的缺陷与没有按照有关条文作出检查与测试的地方足足有40项之多,买方提出履约指令是要求仲裁庭下令船厂重新在买方的监督下进行检查与测试,否则作出宣示是船厂违约/毁约。

由于内容太多,所以本书只挑其中一项买方投诉的缺陷作进一步探讨,并结合上述7.4段中《Chitty on Contracts》(30th edn, 2008年)之27-028段所讲的三个不作出履约指令的原因以及履约指令会在符合三个条件下(合约下的工程有足够精确的定义;损害赔偿不足以补偿原告的损失;工程所在地属于建筑商)作出。该项缺陷就是船舶的焊接,买方指船厂提供的有关焊接的X光照片弄虚作假,没有按照造船合约以及船级社的要求做。根据船级社的要求(所谓的Non-destructive Tests Plan),焊接测试必须包括船舶170多个重要的连接点与船级社的验船师随机另外抽取的70多个连接点。买方的指控是没有理由170多个重要的连接点的焊接测试是一点问题都没有,买方也在英国找专家在该报告中挑出一些问题与遗漏。反正买方向仲裁庭所提出的救济是如下:"1) The Buyer seeks an order pursuant to section 48(5)(b)(这一条文就是针对履约指令) and/or section 38(4)(这一条文就是针对保存证据) of the Arbitration Act 1996 that: (a) The Yard carries out the radiograph tests and ultrasonic tests required by the approved Non-destructive Tests Plan; (b) The Yard carries out additional radiographs and ultrasonic tests as are reasonably required to verify that the Vessel is in a safe condition. In particular: (ⅰ) Radiographs must be taken of all shell and deck cross-over welds (including bottom-plate), all hatch coaming plate and web transverse butt welds, all internal inner skin and tank to cross-over welds and the main engine bearer weldments(where accessible).(ⅱ) All erection, butt and seam welds in midships half length must be ultrasound tested. (b) The Yard carries out the said tests using an internationally recognised independent company nominated by the Buyer and acceptable to the Tribunal; (c) If the tests reveal the presence of unacceptable indications, then the Yard must repair the welds and submit the same for further tests by an internationally recognised independent company nominated by the Buyer and acceptable to the Tribunal. 2) Further or alternatively, the Buyer seeks a declaration(宣示裁决) that it is entitled to refuse to take delivery of the Vessel unless and until the Yard has carried out the full extent of the Non – destructive Tests of the welds set out above."

从上述的救济表面看来是符合损害赔偿不足以补偿原告的损失(因为在买方的救济申请中提到了船舶安全)与工程所在地属于建筑商(船舶由被告的船厂建造,买方也不可能找其他的建筑商作为替代完成船舶的建造)这两个条件。这剩下来最主要就是看是否符合合约下的工程有足够精确的定义这个条件,这就要节录造船合约的条文如下:

"Tests of Constructions and Installations

All tests for hull structure and installations to be conducted in accordance with the requirements of the Classification Society Rules...

Hull Structures

... X – ray photographs or ultrasonic to be taken mainly at cross – points of seams and butts joints of block assemblies of bottom shell, bilge strake, main deck and sheer strake as required by the Rule. Additional X – ray photographs or ultrasonic to be provided according to the CLASS requirements....

Welding

In order to ascertain the soundness of welding, suitable number of X – ray photograph to be taken for the important members according to the Rule requirement..

All such X – ray photographs to be presented and checked by the Classification surveyor and Buyer's representative."

从上述节录的条文可以十分清楚地看到船厂的确是同意焊接的 X 光照片要符合船级社的要求并不得有遗漏。这变为在开庭审理后,如果笔者的确是被买方说服是船厂提供的 X 光照片是不真实与有遗漏(笔者也不一定会被说服,因为船厂有他的抗辩),那么是有倾向针对这方面作出履约指令。剩下来另一个重要的考虑就是履约指令能否在中国大陆执行(这在本章 13.1 段有详论)。但买方也很精明,他已经提出了一个替代请求,就是在第 2 段的救济申请,要求仲裁庭同时作出一个宣示裁决,就是买方可以拒绝接受船舶直到船厂全部与严格履行后。

但在笔者准备出发去伦敦开庭的前两天收到当事人的通知说他们就此问题达成了和解,所以笔者没有办法进一步的告诉大家仲裁庭最后会对此申请作出什么决定。

至于双方达成了什么和解,仲裁庭也不得而知,这可能是船厂答应降低船价或者进行一些工作以满足买方等。只说在该案件中,买方在文书上的请求与有关证据做的很好也很细针对提出的40项缺陷并要求仲裁庭作出履约指令,表面是完全针对了本章7.4段对建造合约会作出履约指令的条件或要求。

第二个是香港仲裁,涉及3艘船舶的建造。但有关的合约并非是一份完整的造船合约,而是一份二手船买卖的 Memorandum of Agreement(或简称 MOA)。这种做法在现在的中国造船业也越来越多,就是船厂与外国船东中间隔了一个卖方。会是MOA的卖方和船厂关系十分密切,但毕竟是两个不同的法人。纯粹是针对履约指令的方面,就已经对买方不利,因为不符合上述提到的三个条件之一的工程所在地属于被告的卖方所拥有。换言之,仲裁庭即使想做出履约指令也不能针对第三人的船厂,而履约就是靠他。MOA在另一个也不利于买方申请履约指令的地方是在合约本身对于船舶的状况不会规定的好像造船合约一样详细。这一来也不符合"合约下的工程有足够精确的定义"这一条件。而且即使仲裁庭决定要给履约指令,也不知道该怎样写才可以得到实际执行。在这一个香港仲裁,买方是非常粗略的提出了在接船前必须允许买方的总管或者由仲裁庭委任的验船师(费用先由买方垫付)进行非常广泛的检查与测试要求,而根据的是一条在MOA中简短的条文,就是买方的总管有权参加建造船舶测试与试航。这导致笔者许多的考虑,甚至包括了对中国船厂会造成极大的困难(这在本章第11段有提及),因为这样广泛的检查与测试恐怕在时间上就会带来很长的延误,交船会要押后或者由仲裁庭作出履约指令的同时去押后。毕竟,在香港法律而言履约指令是衡平法的范畴。反正结果是仲裁庭(包括笔者在内)拒绝了这一个履约指令的申请。

第十三章　Breach Date Rule 之一：违约一天计算损失与市场价格规则

1. 简介

所有的商业合约如果发生违约/毁约而受害方提出损失索赔，都会涉及第一个最基本的大原则就是在本书第一章就已经提到的"复原原则"（*restitutio in integrum* 或 compensatory principle），也就是著名先例 Robinson v. Harman（1848）1 Exch 850 中 Parke B 大法官所说的："The rule of the common law is, that where a party sustains a loss by reason of a breach of contract, he is, so far as money can do it, to be placed in the same situation, with respect to damages, as if the contract had been performed."（以金钱作为赔偿去让受害方恢复到合约被履行的地位）

1.1　可供选择的一天计算损失与金额上的差异

这带来一个计算损失的问题，也就是受害方的损失以哪一天计算为准。这方面至少会有三个不同的日期作出计算：(1)违约的一天；(2)审理或判决的一天；(3)期间对受害方最有利、最不利、实际采取行动减少损失或补救的任何一天。这里还会有其他的选择，如把违约后的一段时间内的不同损失数字平均计算。但反正选择任何的一天计算损失，都会有它的问题。

在现实中，受害方往往不会在违约/毁约后马上采取补救行动，以"减少损失"（mitigate damage）。背后的原因可以是千变万化，如受害方没有钱做出补救、受害方没有紧急的需要做出补救、受害方对违约方抱有幻想并希望他回心转意、当时情况不需要受害方马上做出补救、受害方想做出补救也有其他方面的困难等。而在期间，受害方很可能就已经向违约方提起了诉讼，而诉讼是需要时间的。而在这一个时间段内（可能是长达三四年不等），受害方会有可能在任何的时间内或在开庭审理前不久才做出补救。但这相比在违约/毁约后马上采取补救行动的情况，金额上几乎一定会存在差异。这一差异也是来自各种不同的原因，其中最为人所熟知的就是通货膨胀，这会影响某些类别的违约造成的损失金额，如工程合约。另一个重要的原因就是市场波动，这会影响另外一些类别的合约，如货物/房屋买卖等。其中市场价格波动十分厉害的商品，受害方（以买方为例）会在违约的一两后才买进，指称这是他买进的替代商品，损失金额应该以它的价格作为比较。但在违约后三四年的审理时可以明确回头看,这真正买进替代商品的一天是这一段长达三四年时段中对受害方最不利的一天(替代商品价格最高的一天)。换言之,受害方做了“蠢事”或投资错误。但会否受害方可以以该天的损失计算向违约方索赔,把他的蠢事或错误转嫁给后者?也会有其他的原因造成不同时间计算损失会有很大的差异,如货币汇率的变化、做出补救当时经济的兴衰、受害方没有合理减少损失等。这一来就存在应该是以哪一天的损失计算为准的问题了。以 Dodd Properties (Kent) Ltd v. Canterbury City Council (1980) 1 WLR 433 先例为例,错误/疏忽(涉及侵权造成建筑物损坏并需要修理)是发生在 1968 年。如果当时做出修理,费用估计是 10,817 英镑。但实际可以合理做出修理是在 1970 年,费用已经超过了 11,000 英镑。这两笔费用相比还是相差不远的,但之后就发生全球严重的通货膨胀。所以到了开庭审理的 1978 年,同样的修理费用变成 30,327 英镑。这就存在一个问题是到底判原告胜诉获得的救济应该是哪一笔费用。

曾经有一个说法是损失计算应该以开庭审理时为准(在人身伤亡的案件就采取这一时间),但要受害方证明在等待审理的期间他没有不合理减少损失。这一说法不被英国法院接受,如在 Dodd Properties (Kent) Ltd v. Canterbury City Council 先例。被英国法院所接受的损失计算,在时间上起点就是在违约/毁约的一天,当然还要加上利息直到做出判决的一天,这就是著名的“违约一天损失规则”(Breach Date Rule)。在正常的情况下,由于针对开庭审理与作出判决所带来的延误有利息给予救济,所以计算损失以违约一天或开庭审理一天应该不会有很大区别。但事实经常不是这样,如在现在,通货膨胀率超越了利率,而这种情况在历史上也经常出现。这就会导致在开庭审理的一天计算损失就会与以违约一天计算损失很不一样。

1.2 不同日期计算损失的利弊

1.2.1 选择违约一天的利弊

总结而言,不同日期计算损失的利弊比较,英国法律还是认为以“违约一天损失规则”(Breach Date Rule)较为合理与妥善。它的弊端在上一小段已经提到过,就是受害方很少会在违约后马上采取行动作出补救,把他的真正损失尽早“凝结”(crystalize)下来。这导致了以该天计算损失,往往只能是“假设损失”(presume loss),如违约一天的同样替代品市场价格,但这也往往不是受害方真正损失。这一条规则也需要有许多例外情况针对受害方无法(即使在理论上)在违约后马上采取行动减少损失,或当时根本没有办法这样做。但总的说,这一条规则还是被视为是好处多过坏处,特别是违约一天有“可供买卖市场”(available market)可出售或买进同样的替代货物,让受害方可以马上采取行动作出补救。简单说,这些好处包括是在有关财产/货物有市场的可供比较会是很容易计算损失,可以节省大量的诉讼费用与时间。其他的好处包括是尽早让受害方摆脱需要合理减少损失的责任(在一定程度上对违约方也有同样的好处),自由决定如何处理他们的业务,如对将来市场价格的走势作出估计与商业决定。这也可以缩短双方需要争议的一段时间,如受害方有否在违约后的一段较长时间内采取合理与减少损失的行动。加上由于不少市场价格是公开资料,所以双方一明确了责任,对损失的计算就很容易获得肯定,这往往带来争议双方很快的和解。

在笔者大量涉及的商业合约如商品/货物买卖,固定了某一天计算受害方在违约/毁约的损失有很大好处,特别加上了这些商品/货物往往有可供买卖的市场价格,计算损失就变得十分简单与明确。有很多商品(石油、主要的农产品、矿石、食糖、化肥、钢材、煤炭)都会有市场报道每天的价格。一明确了以哪一天(通常是违约/毁约被接受的一天)的市场报道价格为准,再比较买卖合约的价格,马上可以得出损失的数字。以上所讲可节录 Scott 勋爵在 The "Golden Victory"(2007)2 Lloyd's Rep 164 先例中所说如下作为支持:"The assessment at the date of breach rule is particularly apt to cater for cases where a contract for the sale of goods in respect of which there is a market has been repudiated. The loss caused by the breach to the seller or the buyer, as the case may be, can be measured by the difference between the contract price and the market price at the time of the breach. The seller can re - sell his goods in the market. The buyer can buy substitute goods in the market. Thereby the loss caused by the breach can be fixed."

其他重要的好处就是避免将来争议受害方应该"减少损失的义务"(obligation to mitigate damage)以及损失应该是与违约/毁约有直接的"因果关系"(causation)等方面的损失计算的限制。这特别在"预期违约"(anticipatory breach)更是重要,如买方一早订立买卖合约是购入 9 月的期货,但卖方在 5 月就拒绝交货。这一来,如果受害方买方随即接受违约/毁约而终断买卖合约后,但迟迟不在可供买卖的市场上买进 9 月份的期货作为"替代货物"(substitute goods),最终因为市场出乎意料或是意料中的上涨而买了昂贵的替代货物,导致是比预料中大得多(或比违约一天计算损失大)的损失都要违约/毁约的卖方承担就在因果关系或合理减少损失义务上有很大疑问了。涉及因果关系的争议会是因为受害方的买方迟迟不在市场买进替代货物往往会有各种人为的原因,而这些原因是可以打断因果关系的,导致后来更大的损失与原来的违约/毁约再也扯不上关系。这会有主要的因素是受害方的买方看错了市场走势,以为市场会进一步下挫但实际上出乎意料的上涨。另也可能是受害方因为经济原因没有办法在市场买进替代货物。或是受害方由于不懂、无能或公司结构僵化而迟迟下不了决定等。反正这里的原因数之不尽,而且违约方的卖方对背后真正的原因调查取证也不容易,这反正是受害方自己心里在想什么只有他自己知道。

涉及减少损失的争议会是因为买方迟迟不在市场买进替代货物,如违约方的卖方声称买方应该在 5 月到 9 月之间选择市场价格最低的一天计算违约/毁约的损失(这在市场价格波动很大的情况下很可能其中有一两天的市场价格相比买卖合约价格根本没有实际的损失),所以受害方应该在该天买进替代货物。但这对受害方的买方不公道,因为他不是神仙,无法预见该天(可能是在 7 月又或者是在 8 月的某一天)的市场价格会是在这一段时间中最低。这减少损失的义务只要求合理,程度相对宽松,不可能有这种不合情理的要求。

所以把这些可能是复杂的争议“一刀切”,Breach Date Rule 与 Market Rule 就是假设没有这种外来的因素下,受害方的买方一旦面对卖方拒绝供应货物的违约/毁约并接受后,就可以去市场马上或尽早买进(通常以更高的价格买进才会有损失)同样的替代货物以解决燃眉之急。然后,在稍后的诉讼把合约价格与市场价格的差价作为损失向卖方索赔。至于买方到底有没有这样做就不必理会了,因为在理论上,买方能够这样做就应该做并把握这一个可以马上合理减少损失的机会,不论这批替代货物是为了履行分销/转售合约或是自己使用。反正,这就是一般性损失计算的起点或是“表面计算规则”(*prima facie* rule)。至于以这种办法计算而显示不了有任何损失,就是市场价格在违约/毁约的时候比合约价格还要低,这表示受害方的买方实际上是没有损失的。所以卖方即使违约/毁约,责任明确,赔偿也只会是象征性赔偿。这种情况下,照理说是卖方不会也不应该违约/毁约,因为这样做对他一点好处也没有。但由于水平或者误解,这种情况不是没有可能发生。这种案件在 The “Mamola Challenger”(2011)1 Lloyd’s Rep 47 先例就有出现,期租承租人违约/毁约终断租约,当时市场高涨,受害方的船东在撤船后转租给其他人赚了大钱。

市场规则另一个显著的好处是在一些较长期的合约,这种合约较少会在货物买卖中发生,但也不是没有一些合约涉及了长期的供货。中/长期合约经常在其他相关的合约如租约中发生。这一来,如果是涉及一个 5 年或 7 年的期租合约,但在第一年就已经被承租人违约/毁约而终断。如果计算与证明真正损失,会是要等多 4 年或 6 年,直到原期租合约的租期届满,才会知道真正损失。但这会涉及大量的文件与争议,包括受害方船东在期间每一个行动都会受到违约方的承租人的质疑是否是明智与合理的决定减少损失。所以,真正损失作为长期合约的计算并不可取,更简单与公平是根据违约/毁约的一天看租船市场价格,这市场必须是对等,剩下 4 年或 6 年的期租,就需要在市场中找到雷同船舶如果以 4 年或 6 年的租期会是有多少钱的租金,然后把原租约的租金比较市场租金的差价,这就是按照 Breach Date Rule 与 Market Rule 计算的损失赔偿的金额。

上述讲的都是好处,但 Breach Date Rule 与 Market Rule 也有弊端,主要就是以违约一天的市场价格计算的损失只能是假设,与受害方真实的损失不一定扯得上关系。现实中,绝大部分的受害方不会在违约一天去市场买进或卖出,马上采取行动减少损失。这一来,如果受害方是在 10 天后才采取行动,这对受害方而言已经算是尽快减少损失,但市场价格已经与违约一天有了变化与波动。这会是对受害方有利,如他是买方可买进比违约一天市场价格更便宜的货物(但还是比合约价格高,所以还是有损失)。如果在这种情况下,买方还是能够以违约一天的市场价格减去合约价格作为 Breach Date Rule 与 Market Rule 计算出来的假设损失向违约的卖方索赔,取回来的赔偿就会比他真正损失多。

此外,这 Breach Date Rule 与 Market Rule 也有许多例外情况,稍后会进一步介绍。

1.2.2 选择审理或判决一天的利弊

如果以"审理或判决一天"(judgment date)计算损失,这一天会是在违约后很长的一段时间。这会带来昂贵的诉讼,因为会涉及这一段漫长时间内受害方是否有合理减少损失或受害方在期间已经作出的补救是否满足各种针对损失的限制性说法,如损失遥远性与因果关系。这也会带来其他的坏处,如在有关标的的市场价格在不断上升,受害方就会有诱因拖延诉讼,包括上诉,以增加赔偿金额。这也会带来双方更加没有办法达成和解协议,因为损失金额说不准,而这是违反大政策鼓励诉讼双方尽量达成和解。另是,这样计算损失也会让受害方在市场投机,但投机的风险却是由违约方承担。例如,受害方的买方迟迟不去市场买进替代货物,认为市场价格会进一步下跌,但结果是相反导致审理一天还没有买进替代货物,可是受害方可把市场价格高涨的严重后果全数转嫁给违约方的卖方。

另在 SM Waddams 著的《The Law of Damages》一书之 1.760 段有提到了其他方面的坏处,说:"There is another point. If judgment date assessment is supported on the theory that the buyer has been deprived of the opportunity of owning goods at present (that is, at the date of judgment), and of receiving the increase in their value, insuperable difficulties arise where the buyer has in fact purchased a substitute on the seller's default, and holds it at the date of judgment. If the buyer is still to be entitled to the judgment date value of the goods promised, he will receive twice over the rise in value between the two dates, and the theory just mentioned does not support such double compensation. If on the other hand he is to be deprived of judgment date assessment on the ground that he has in fact mitigated his loss, distinctions will have to be drawn between cases where he has bought identical goods to those promised, and cases where he has simply made a successful investment of money. It will also become relevant to discover whether the plaintiff would or could have purchased such goods even if the defendant had not defaulted. Intractable problems will arise where the buyer has bought goods similar but not identical to those promised. Gains to the innocent party that she could have made whether the wrong occurred or not are generally treated as collateral gains that do not reduce damages. This approach also suggests the undesirability of establishing a rule which requires substitute purchases to be bought into account."(这是说以审理/判决一天计算损失,理论上就是受害方被剥夺了在该天可以拥有有关涨了价的财产/货物。但如果受害的买方事实上在卖方违约后就买进了替代货物,并且一直持有直到审理或判决一天,就会带来很大困难。如买卖合约价格是 10 块钱,受害方后来买进替代货物也是 10 块钱,但在审理或判决一天有关货物价格涨至 20 块钱,难道判受害方还是可以索赔 10 块钱的差价?如果在这种情况把受害方视为是成功减少损失至零,不赔给他审理/判决一天的价格,又会带来其他十分困难的争议。这争议是受害方在违约后买进的"替代"货物是否是为了替代,因为卖方违约?或是受

害方看准了市场为自己买进或投资?这涉及一些大型跨国贸易商更加是难以说得清,因为他们每天都进行许多同类型货物的买卖,可以随便他们说哪一票货才是与违约有关买进的替代货物)

以上主要是针对财产/货物的损失,如被侵占或卖方拒绝交货等的情况。但针对其他类别的违约或侵权,也适用同样道理就是审理或判决一天计算损失并不恰当。如财产的部分损坏,这也是经常会遇到的争议,受害方的损失计算办法一种是根据财产没有被损坏的价格与被损坏后的价格之间的差异,所谓的"贬值"(diminution of value);另一种是被损坏的财产所需要的修理费用,所谓的"修复费用"(reinstatement costs)。这两种计算往往会得出不一样的金额,有关的问题稍后在本书第十五章会针对。在这里,只说是不论以哪一个办法计算损失,都是以违约一天为准。以一栋房屋受到损坏为例,以贬值计算损失,也就是一栋同样的好房屋与损坏后变了坏房屋的差价(虽然这坏房屋的市场价格会是不容易确定,因为损坏程度会有很大差异),显然是以违约一天为准。否则等了好几年之后的审理与判决时才以该天计算贬值,会带来上述所讲的各种弊端。但涉及财产的部分损坏,更常见的就是受害方索赔修理费用。这种情况很多,也不一定能够证明贬值,如一幢历史建筑物,看来合理修理费用就是相等贬值。修复费用是包括了估计修理费用,因为受害方至少到了审理/判决一天还没有真正进行修理。

表面看来,在估计修理费用的情况下,以审理/判决一天作出估计有一定的公平,就是看来给受害方一个更完整的赔偿。受害方其中一个可以合理化的原因就是违约方或侵权方不把钱赔了给他,他就不能也不愿意进行真正的修理或者是没有钱修理,如在 Dodd Properties(Kent)Ltd v. Canterbury City Council(1980)1 WLR 433 先例有这种争议,Megaw 大法官有提到说:"If there had been no money problem . . . he would still not have spent money on the building before he was sure of recovering the cost from the defendant."但照理说,这种说法不是法律会接受的理由,正如在稍后会提到的 Startup v. Cortazzi(1835)2 C. M. & R. 165 先例。

但以审理/判决一天估计修理费用会造成更大的不公平,除了上述所讲的弊端,还可以一提是在许多情况下违约方或侵权方明知道责任难逃,会是希望尽早进行修理,这特别是在通货膨胀厉害的时候或/与诉讼会带来昂贵的费用,违约方想避免。但由于违约方或侵权方不是控制有关财产的所有人,所以修不修理不是他能决定,而是受害方的决定。另一个坏处是有关的财产如一幢被损坏的房屋在审理之前已经被受害方出售,这就明确了受害方是不会进行修理。这一来会是本来准备根据审理/判决一天估计修理费用的做法改为以违约一天为准的贬值,这显然不是一个好事,把损失的计算改来改任由受害方的行为摆布。

1.2.3 选择违约或侵权至审理期间其中一天的利弊

1.2.3.1 一般违约的损失计算不适用

至于在期间对受害方最有利的一天计算损失,问题与"审理或判决一天"计算损失基本上是一致。但如果在期间以受害方最不利的一天(受害方如果是买方在违约一天至审理一天最不利时市场价格最低的一天,这价格会有可能比合约价格还要低)计算损失,就有很大的可能他根本没有损失而言。例如,受害方可争辩是以违约一天直到开庭审理一天中市场的最高点或最低点,因为理论上他可以把货物或股票在该天买进或出售。这种说法也不是没有支持,如在少数的19世纪英国先例:Archer v. Williams(1846)2 Car. & K. 26,175 ER 11。但普遍认为是这样计算损失不被接受,会让受害方获得不合理的利益,因为他不可能会能够在市场最高峰(或最低潮)的时候采取补救行动,如果碰巧也纯粹是运气。在有关美国法律的《McCormick on Damages》(St. Paul, West Publishing Co., 1935)一书说:"it is in the highest degree improbable that the plaintiff with uncanny prescience would have waited until the market had reached its summit and would have sold at that moment"。这一个说法也会让一些每天进行同样货物买卖的国际贸易商带来取巧的机会,就是如果他们属受害方,就可以随便挑一个对他最有利索赔损失计算的买卖说是这就是他作为减少损失出售或买进的货物。

1.2.3.2 侵占财产/货物的例外

但也不是没有例外情况会是让受害方选择违约或侵权一天至审理期间一天这一段可能是颇长的时间中其中一天作为损失的计算,这就是在财产/货物的"侵占"(conversion)。在英国,侵占是严格责任,所以在责任方面是没有什么好争议,富争议的还是损失的计算。而针对侵占的救济有了立法,是在《Tort (Interference with Goods) Act 1977》之 Section 3 订明如下:"(2) The relief is -(a) an order for delivery of goods, and for payment of any consequential damages, or (b) an order for delivery of the goods, but giving the defendant the alternative of payment damages by reference to the value of the goods, together in either alternative with payment of any consequential damages, or (c) damages."

而根据该立法之 Section 3(3),受害方针对侵占方的法律救济只能是在这三种做法中选一种。而这三种救济的第一种是法院的裁量权决定是否给予。但余下的两种救济却是完全由受害方自己决定选用哪种:"(3) Subject to rules of court -(a) relief shall be given under only one of the paragraphs (a), (b) and (c) of subsection (2), (b) relief under paragraph (a) of subsection (2) is at the discretion of the court, and the claimant may choose between the others."

在选择余下的两种救济时,侵占赔偿的起点是看被侵占货物的市场价格,这在早期的先例如 Mercer v. Jones (1813) 3 Camp. 477; Henderson v. Williams (1895) 1 QB 521 CA; Solloway v. McLaughlin (1938) AC 247;或近期的 BBMM Finance (Hong Kong) v. Eda Holdings (1991) 2 All ER 129 等都有明确。

在 Mercer v. Jones 先例,案情涉及一张汇票的侵占,法院判损失赔偿的计算,应该是以侵占一天的价格为准,这相等于 Breach Date Rule。Ellenborough 勋爵说:"In trover the rule is, that the plaintiff is entitled to damages equal to the value of the article converted at the time of the conversion."

另在 Hall v. Barclay(1937)3 All ER 620 先例,有说明如下:"Where you are dealing with goods which can be readily bought in the market, a man whose rights have been interfered with is never entitled to more than what he would have to pay to buy a similar article in the market."

但这里也很早就有不同的看法,其中在 Greening v. Wilkinson(1825)1 C & P 625 先例,不认同 Mercer v. Jones 先例的说法,认为在侵占后如果市场上涨,就应该是以更高的价格计算损失,因为受害方会有可能选择在之后的最高点把财产/货物出售,但由于被侵占,令受害方无法及时出售或处理这票财产/货物。Abbott 大法官是这样说:"may give the value at the time of the convertion, or at any subsequent time, in their discretion, because the plaintiff might have had a good opportunity of selling the goods if they had not been detained."这一个说法也在 Caxton Publishing Co v. Sutherland Publishing Co(1939)AC 178 先例得到支持。而在稍后期的 Sachs v. Miklos(1948)2 KB 23 CA 与 Munro v. Willmott(1949)1 KB 295 先例看来是倾向以审理/判决一天的财产/货物价格作为被侵权的受害方损失为准。

在 Sachs v. Miklos 先例,上诉庭说:"The value of the goods converted, at the time of their conversion, is one thing ... but it does not follow that sum is the measure of the plaintiff's(受害方)loss. The question is what is the plaintiff's loss, what damage he has suffered, by the wrongful act of the defendants(侵占方)"。在该先例,看来是以侵占一天的市场价格比较作为损失,但之后直到审理/判决一天的价格上涨是作为"间接损失"(consequential damages)向侵占方索赔,因为这才是受害方的损失。

在近期的 Trafigura Beheer BV v. Mediterranean Shipping Co SA(2007)2 All ER 149 先例,涉及船东在上海卸港向持有假提单的骗子做出了交货单,导致真正收货人或提单持有人提不到货。期间该票货物(装在集装箱的铜)一直被放置在上海港的集装箱码头,等待上海海事法院判谁拥有这票货物。期间,铜的市场价格有十分严重的波动,所以真正收货人事后在英国法院向船东索赔侵占他的货物的损失就涉及以哪一天的市场价格作为损失计算。法院判是应该以审理/判决一天的市场价格为准,因为当时在等待上海海事法院判决的情况下,虽然在侵占一天有可供买卖市场买入替代的铜,但收货人不会这样做,而且十分合理。在被侵占的铜的命运还没有被决定的情况下,收货人买入另一票替代的铜,就会有危险如果上海海事法院判决胜诉,收货人就会一下子手中有了两票铜,并且没有把握可转售。在上诉庭是支持这一个判决,Longmore 大法官提到说也可以根据 Sachs v. Miklos 先例的侵占一天市场价格加上"间接损失"的损失计算办法达致同样结果。

看来是如果财产/货物的市场价格在被侵占后下跌,侵占方仍然需要赔偿侵占一天的市场价格。这在 BBMM Finance(Hong Kong)v. Eda Holdings(1991)2 All ER 129

先例被 Templeman 大法官强调说:“The general rule is that a plaintiff whose property is irreversibly converted has vested in him a right to damages for conversion measured by the value of the property at the date of conversion . . . The inexplicable failure by the defendant to collect the sale price cannot mitigate or reduce the damages recoverable by the plaintiffs and cannot alter the measure of damages.”这表示如果财产/货物被侵占后市场下跌,而即使是受害方不会有眼光或机会在市场下跌前出售,但有了侵占赔偿的 Breach Date Rule,他可索赔市场价格,进而把以后市场下跌的风险与损失转嫁给侵占方。

在这方面也可节录 Solloway v. McLaughlin(1938)AC 247 先例。案情涉及股票经纪把寄存在他手中的股票侵占出售。之后在市场以便宜得多的价格再购进,及时归还给股票主人。这一来,股票经纪赚了一大笔钱,但股票主人也谈不上有什么损失。股票主人发觉后以侵占损失向股票经纪索赔,并且成功,判是原告的股票主人有权获得股票被侵占一天的市场价格,减去他接受替代股票当日的市场价格。被告的股票经纪抗辩说只应该赔偿给原告名义上的损失,因为原告只想拿回他原来的股票,这些股票在之后价格下跌并被原告重新买回,所以原告没有损失。但该抗辩被贵族院拒绝。因为贵族院认为侵权一方不能在侵权中得利。如果有,这好处也要归还受害方(account for profits)。这种有关“返还性损失”(restitutionary damages)的救济在本书第一章之第 7 段有详细介绍。

至于在财产/货物被侵占后,如果市场价格不是下挫而是上升,岂非以 Breach Date Rule 计算损失是不会对侵占方不利,而且还会让他赚钱? 因为他会可选择第二种救济办法,赔付侵占一天的市场价格,而不归还已经市场价格大涨的财产/货物。但侵占方不必妄想,英国法律应对他十分严厉与不利。在 Greening v. Wilkinson (1825)1 C & P 625 先例,法院判是在侵占直至法院审判期间货物市场上扬,陪审团有自由裁量权决定以侵占一天之后的任何一天市场价格做出赔偿。另在 Sachs v. Miklos 先例,也有间接损失的说法可以向侵权方索赔。

但在 The “Playa Larga”(1983)2 Lloyd’s Rep. 171 先例,上诉庭认为侵占货物后市场价格上涨,不表示受害方可随意拣市场最高一天作为比较,与合约价格的差价算是“间接损失”。上诉庭认为受害方一定要证明(虽然这个证明只是平衡的可能性)他或是侵占方会在市场最高点转售/出售该票货物。上诉庭的 Ackner 大法官是这样说:

“Mr. Rix(受害方代表大律师),in his cross – appeal,argued that the damages recoverable by Iansa(受害方的买方)in contract should be related to the highest price prevailing at any time between the date of the breach and the date of the award. Mr. Justice Mustill rejected this submission and has set out his reasons most fully, which we are happy to adopt. We would,however,venture to suggest that the matter can be put more simply. Iansa, as complainants,must establish what damage they have suffered. Mr. Rix had to accept:a) That after the date when Iansa could have sold at the highest price. On the contrary,the reasonable inference was that the goods would have been resold for domestic or other consumption in Chile. (b) Although theoretically Cubazucar(侵权方的卖方)was capable of selling the sugar at the highest price, there is no evidence that it did so.

Accordingly, to the plaintiffs' contention that Cubazucar should not profit from its own wrong comes the simple reply: they have not shown that Cubazucar have done so. We cannot, therefore, see any basis upon which Iansa can seek to achieve a windfall in the form of an extra $1,200 per tonne over and above the price which was prevailing when they should have bought in the market."

总结而言,在侵占计算损失赔偿的一般规则还是以货物被侵占一天的市场价格为准,也就是适用 Breach Date Rule,这与违约的大原则一致。但会进一步考虑在侵占发生一天之后直到做出审理/判决前货物市场价格的变化做出调整。如果在期间被侵占的财产/货物价格的上涨又会被区分为不同的情况来处理。这可以节录《McGregor on Damages》(18th edn, 2009 年)之 33 - 013 段:"It is submitted that the soundest approach is to start off with the value at the time of conversion as the *prima facie* measure; this is in accord with the general principle that damages are to be assessed as at the date of the wrong. The effect upon this measure of damages of increases or decreases in the value between wrong and judgment must then be considered. Increase must be divided into those that would have happened without intervention by the defendant, i. e. rises in the market value, and those due to acts done or expenses incurred by the defendant in relation to the goods"。毕竟,即使在侵占的侵权,受害方必须合理减少损失的大原则还是适用:Uzinterimpex JSC v. Standard Bank plc(2008)2 Lloyd's Rep 456 先例。

2. 英国法律支持违约一天损失规则的权威说法

在许多的先例中有明确或重复不论是违约或侵权都适用"违约/侵权一天损失规则"(Breach Date Rule),特别是有关的标的是有市场可马上买进卖出替代标的以减少损失,这带来了"市场规则"(Market Rule 或 Market Value Rule)的说法。首先是在 Gainsford v. Carroll(1824)2 B&C 624,107 ER 516 先例,案情是有关买卖合约,法院说:"Here the plaintiff had his money in his possession and he might have purchased other bacon of the like quality **the very day after the contract was broken**, and if he has sustained any loss, by neglecting to do so, it is his own fault."(加黑部分是笔者的强调)

至于在一个侵权的先例名为 The "Volturno"(1921)8 Lloyd's Rep 449, Wrenbury 勋爵说:"If the plaintiff had been damaged by the defendant tortiously depriving him of three cows the judgment would be: Declare that on January 1 the plaintiff suffered by the defendant's tort a loss of three cows. Declare that on January 1 the plaintiff would have been entitled to go into the market and buy three similar cows and charge the defendant with the price. Declare that the cost would have been £ 150. Adjudge that the plaintiff recover from the defendant £ 150. It would be *nihil ad rem* to say that in July similar cows would have cost in the market £ 300. The defendant is not bound to supply the plaintiff with cows.... The defendant is liable to pay the plaintiff damages, that is to say, money to same amount for the loss of the cows: the only question is, how much? The answer is, **such sum as represents the market value at the date of the tort of the goods of which the plaintiff was tortiously deprived.**"(加黑部分是笔者的强调)

另在贵族院的 Johnson v. Agnew(1980) AC 367 先例，Wilberforce 勋爵说到计算损失的"一般性规则"(general rule):"The general principle for the assessment of damages is compensatory, i. e., that the innocent party is to be placed, so far as money can do so, in the same position as if the contract had been performed. Where the contract is one of sale, **this principle normaly leads to assessment of damages as at the date of the breach** – a principle recognized and embodied in section 51 of the Sale of Goods Act 1893."(加黑部分是笔者的强调)

上述 Wilberforce 勋爵有提到了 1893 年的英国《货物销售法》之 section 51，这也是英国唯一的立法规定了 Breach Date Rule 并加上了 Market Rule 作为计算货物买卖违约的损失。在后来的 1979 年版本，也是有同样的规定。无论违约的是买方(不合理拒绝接收货物)或是卖方(不合理拒绝提供与交出货物)，都是以同样的计算办法针对损失。这是在 Section 50(3) 与 Section 51(3)，如下：

Section 50(3):"Where there is an available market for the goods in question the measure of damages is *prima facie* to be ascertained by the difference between the contract price and the market or current price at the time or times when the goods ought to have been accepted or (if no time was fixed for acceptance) at the time of the refusal to accept."(这是针对买方违约/毁约拒绝接收货物，卖方计算他的损失应使用的市场规则)

Section 51(3):"Where there is an available market for the goods in question the measure of damages is *prima facie* to be ascertained by the difference between the contract price and the market or current price of the goods at the time or times when they ought to have been delivered or (if no time was fixed) at the time of the refusal to deliver."(这是针对卖方违约/毁约拒绝交付货物，买方计算他的损失应使用的市场规则)

由于涉及货物买卖的争议很多，所以在这一个 Breach Date Rule 与 Market Rule 就建立了大量的先例与"法理"(jurisprudence)可供其他类别的案件参考。

3. 违约一天计算损失最适用的情况:受害方可以马上在市场找到补救

再重复,如果在违约一天,受害方是可以在市场找到同样的替代,这损失计算就会更加容易与说的过去。所以,与"违约一天损失规则"(Breach Date Rule)走在一起的是另一条"市场规则"(Market Rule)。这就是假设受害方为了减少损失,可以或应该(因为受害方需要合理减少损失)马上在市场寻找同样替代,而这一个市场价格如果与合约价格不一致,这一个差异就是受害方的损失。而如果受害方在市场找到的替代比合约价格更便宜或没有差异,就代表受害方没有损失,诉讼也只能成功取得名义上的损失赔偿。这对于许多"商品"(commodity)的买卖会是特别适合,因为大部分的商品如石油、农产品、矿石、煤炭、食糖、化肥、钢材等都有权威性的市场价格可作为证据,变成受害方证明损失是非常容易的事情。所以有说法是在有"可供买卖市场"(available market)的情况下,通常是很难说服法院或仲裁庭偏离 Breach Date Rule 与 Market Rule 的计算办法。

而事实上,已经有很多明确的先例是受害方能够证明他真正的损失是更大,而且没有任何不合理之处,但法院还是拒绝偏离。在贵族院的 Williams v. Agius(1914) AC 510 先例,原告向被告购买了一船的煤炭,付运去意大利的热那亚港。原告在货物交付之前已经把它转售给第三人的分买方,转售的价格是比原告与被告之间的买卖合约价格为高(表示原告有差价的利润),但比货物交付一天的市场价格为低。贵族院是判被告违约应该赔偿的损失计算还是按照原告与被告之间的合约价格比较货物交付时的市场价格找出差价,换言之是让原告多"赚取"了损失,因为他的转售合约并没有这么大的差额。贵族院认为原告实际在转售合约的价格是没有关系。这样的判法当然也可以解释,就是原告如果不想在转售合约去违约,不交付货物,就需要在市场以更高的价格买进替代货物以满足分买方,所以原告向被告索赔损失还是应该以市场价格作为比较找出差价。至于原告有没有这样做是另一码事。

另在 Mouat v. Betts Motors(1959) AC 71 PC 先例,涉及原告作为经销商出售一部新的汽车给被告,但价格并非是市场价格而是受到控制的优惠价格。所以,在协议中有规定被告不能在市场把该汽车在 2 年内出售,除非他先让原告有选择以优惠价格减掉折旧去回购。但被告违约,在 2 年期限内以很高的市场价格把该汽车出售。这导致了原告向被告索赔损失,而损失的计算是违约时的市场价格相比原告可以选择回购的价格之间的差价。但被告认为是不应该以这一个办法计算损失,因为即使被告是没有违反合约,原告也只能把汽车回购然后按照当地的规定,同样要以优惠价格出售给第三人。所以损失只能是受控制的优惠价格与回购选择价格之间的差价,这显然是很低的金额,主要就是汽车的折旧。但在英国枢密院,被告的抗辩被驳回,认为违约一天的市场价格大原则还是不能偏离。Denning 勋爵说:"It does not lie in Mouat's(被告)mouth to say that, if he had fulfilled his covenant, the dealers(原告)would only resell the car [at the controlled price]. That was a matter peculiar to the dealers which was no concern of his. The dealers were entitled in law to be put into as good a position as if he had fulfilled his covenant: and to do this they were entitled to go into the market and buy a similar car at the market price."

如果受害方(以买方为例)由于好运气能够从第三人或者他的母亲免费或半价给他替代货物,这不表示卖方可以相应减低他的损失赔偿或只需要赔名义损失。这方面可节录《McGregor on Damages》(18th edn, 2009 年)之 21 - 012 段:"What is important here is that it does not follow... that, where the buyer makes a straightforward claim for market price less contract price, the seller could maintain that the damages were nominal because by some good fortune the buyer had acquired equivalent goods, as by gift from a third party. This would be *res inter alios acta*.(这拉丁文是指受害方与他母亲的馈赠是他们之间的约定,第三人不得受惠)"这等于是受害方买了保险由保险公司赔付他的损失道理一样,违约方或侵权方不能以受害方最后没有受到实际损失作为抗辩。涉及保险是有"代位求偿"(subrogation)的说法,受害方也可以把他向违约方或侵权方索赔的权利"转让"(assign)给他的保险人或是他的母亲。

也曾经有过年代久远的先例如 Startup v. Cortazzi(1835)2 C. M. & R. 165 针对受害的买方争辩说是他预付了货价给违约的卖方,所以影响了他的经济能力在违约一天在市场买进替代货物。但英国法院拒绝偏离 Breach Date Rule 与 Market Rule,认为受害方预付了的货价只能是以利息作出补偿。Alderson B 大法官是这样说:"The more correct criterion is the price at the time when the cargo would have arrived in due course according to the contract; when, if it had been delivered, the plaintiffs would have been enabled to resell it. Another criterion is, to consider the loss of the gain which the party would have made, if the contract had been complied with. In the present case, the loss which the plaintiffs have sustained arises from their having been kept out of their money. That is a matter to be calculated by the interest of the money up to the time when, by the course of practice, the money could have been obtained out of Court."

4. 适用 Breach Date Rule 与 Market Rule 可偏离的例外情况

4.1 主要与最终的目的是必须做到复原

这可节录 Wilberforce 勋爵在 Miliangos v. Frank(Textiles)Ltd(1976)1 Lloyd's Rep 201 先例中提到 Breach Date Rule 是计算损失的"一般性规则"(general rule)后,另

说："it is for the courts, or for arbitrators, to work out a solution in each case best adapted to giving the injured plaintiff that amount in damages which will most fairly compensate him for the wrong which he has suffered."

这 Wilberforce 勋爵的另外说法就显示最关键与最基本的还是"复原大原则"(*restitutio in integrum*)，而由于每一个案件的事实都不一样，但计算损失本身是对事实的认定，所以在考虑是否适用违约一天损失规则或其他的计算损失规则，都不要忘了大原则，即让受害方"复原"回复到没有被侵权或合约被履行的地位。

这在 1979 年《货物销售法》的有关条文，也说明只属于"表面规则"(*prima facie* rule)，不是"结论性规则"(conclusive rule)。换言之，如果 Breach Date Rule 与 Market Rule 在个别案情看来不合理，对受害方做不到复原，就可偏离。

如果在个别的案件，即使是有市场价格，但以"市场规则"(Market Rule)的违约一天损失规则是做不到让受害方复原，这些规则就要靠边站了。这里可以节录 Radford v. De Froberville(1977) 1 WLR 1262 先例中，Oliver 大法官在介绍了一些案例后，说："These cases merely underline what Lord Haldane said, namely, that the quantum of damage is a question of fact and the general principle merely a guide to the approach to each particular case."

但重复是在一些涉及了很成熟与十分容易进行买卖市场的标的如商品或股票，法院与仲裁庭是不愿意也不应该轻易偏离或作出例外情况。这是为了法律的肯定性与可预测性。

4.2　Breach Date Rule 与 Market Rule 可偏离的三大类例外情况

这一条 Breach Date Rule 还是有不少例外，如较早就提到了人身伤亡的案件类别。其中涉及了商业合约，如货物买卖合约，就会有三大类以上的例外情况，如下：

(1)"受害方无法及时觉察违约"(Breach not discoverable with reasonable diligence)：简单说，如果受害方无法觉察违约，而是在后来使用时或是转卖给了第三人的时候才发觉违约，就不再适用 Breach Date Rule。这种情况在货物买卖经常会发生，特别是涉及货物质量有缺陷的违约。如果涉及是卖方拒绝提供货物或延误交货，又或是买方拒绝接受货物，这种违约是马上可以觉察，所以完全适用 Breach Date Rule 要求受害方减少损失。而如果有关货物/商品是有可供买卖市场，也就会加上了 Market Rule 一并使用以计算损失。但如果违约是涉及货物质量的缺陷，特别是不容易觉察的缺陷，就会可能导致了受害方的买方之后才会觉察。所以为了公平，会以后来的一天去计算损失。例如，受害方的买方在没有检查货物下把有关货物分销/转售给了分买方，就会以分买方觉察缺陷的一天为准：Saunt v. Belcher(1920) 26 Com Cas 115 先例；Van den Hurk v. Martens & Co Ltd(1920) 1 KB 850 先例。

(2)"受害方无法减少损失"(Inability to mitigate)：这种例外情况也有不少，其中包括了受害方的"穷困"(impecuniosity)导致了没有财力减少损失。这在货物买卖也有这种情况，即使在违约的一天有可供买卖市场可减少损失。如在 Patrick v. Russo -

British Grain Export Co(1927)2 KB 535 先例中所提到的两种情况。在这里只简单介绍 Wroth v. Tyler(1974) Ch 30 先例,案情涉及了一个房屋的买卖,价格是6000 英镑。在卖方拒绝完成交易的情况下,买方向法院申请作出“履约指令”(specific performance),或作为替代的救济要求卖方赔偿损失。法院拒绝了履约指令的申请,但判卖方必须赔偿金钱的损失。但计算损失的一天是以作出审理与判决的一天的同样房屋价格为准,这是 11,500 英镑。这比卖方违约拒绝完成交易一天的房屋价格的 7500 英镑高的多。至于法院为什么偏离 Breach Date Rule,Megarry 大法官的解释是受害方的买方由于没有办法向银行取得高于 6000 英镑的抵押,所以在违约一天没有办法减少损失,买进另一栋 7500 英镑的替代房屋。

房屋或土地买卖 1970 年开始在英国就不断上涨,经常导致在违约一天,买方无法马上买进替代的房屋,因为该天房价已经比订约的一天涨了。但等下去,房屋价格也就越来越贵直到审理的一天也无法买进。期间,甚至有可能买方曾经合理申请“履约指令”(specific performance)但由于技术原因没有成功。反正在这种情况下,在房屋/土地买卖,只要买方能够说得出与证明合理的原因不能在违约一天或很快买进替代,法院就会以更后的时间甚至在审理一天的房屋/土地价值为准。如在 Malhotra v. Choudhury(1980) Ch 32 CA 先例中,法院判是以判决当天 1 年前的房屋价值为准计算损失,因为原告自己延误了起诉。

(3)“合理坚持违约方必须履约”(Reasonable insistence on performance):经常会发生是受害方不断坚持违约方履行合约,这种坚持也会涉及违约方拖拖拉拉,造成了受害方以为履行合约还会有一线希望。这就会导致了时间上的延误,变成在一个波动的市场失去了减少损失的最佳机会。例如,受害方的买方在违约一天去市场买进替代货物只需要比合约价格多付出 10 美元/吨,但拖拖拉拉过了一个月,由于市场急升,买方才去市场买进替代货物,就需要比合约价格多付出 50 美元/吨。在这种涉及了有衡平法下“禁止反供”(estoppel)味道的情况下,也会需要偏离 Breach Date Rule。这种案例可以 Toprak v. Finagrain(1979)2 Lloyd's Rep 98 为例,买方在一个美国小麦的 CFR 买卖中违约,没有在最后时限的 3 月 31 日前开出信用证,但一直给卖方一个假象是会开出。这拖拖拉拉到了 4 月 30 日,卖方接受违约并开始伦敦仲裁,也另在第二天的 5 月 1 日把终断船舶的租约并赔偿了上百万美元给船东作为和解。在仲裁庭与法院,判是计算损失的一天不是违约的一天,也不是该天的美国小麦市场价格作为比较。赔偿是卖方真正的损失,而计算损失的一天是 4 月 30 日。Denning 勋爵说:“since the conduct of the buyers led the sellers to believe that the contract was still open and that they were hoping all the time to get the letter of credit issued there was ample ground to infer that there was an extension of time until such time as the sellers determined the contract; and the date of default was Apr. 30, 1975.”

4.3 货物买卖合约可偏离的其他例外情况与有关先例

除了上述的三大类例外情况,还会有其他比较次要的偏离的例外情况。以货物买卖合约为例,受害的买方后来才觉察货物的潜在缺陷就是一种例外情况可偏离 Breach Date Rule 与 Market Rule。这方面有很多的先例,而比较近期一点的有 Bence Graphics International Ltd. v. Fasson U. K. Ltd(C. A.)(1998)QB 87;Britvic Soft Drinks Ltd v. Messer UK Ltd(2002)1 Lloyd's Rep 20 与 Bacardi - Martini Beverages LTd v. Thomas Hardy Packaging Ltd(2002)1 Lloyd's Rep 62。但这是属于上一小段所介绍的三大类例外情况之一的"受害方无法及时觉察违约"(Breach not discoverable with reasonable diligence)。

其他次要的例外情况会是受害买方的分销/转售合约中交货日期与违约合约的交货日期一致,因为后果是在原买卖合约的卖方如果违约/毁约去拒绝提供货物,受害的买方在同一时间也对分买方违约/毁约。作为中间商的买方即使可以并且十分愿意马上去市场买进替代货物,也在时间上来不及。即使在第二天交出同样的替代货物,分买方也可以拒绝接受。在这种情况下,买方是可以向违约的原卖方索赔分销/转售合约与其他真正的损失,所以 Breach Date Rule 与 Market Rule 不适用。

再一个次要的例外情况是针对丧失销售额的受害卖方,如买方拒绝接受货物或不开出信用证,导致了受害方的卖方要在可供买卖的市场把有关被拒货物转售给其他买方以减少损失。如果当时市场稳定,会出现的情况是卖方并没有蒙受真正的损失或合约价格与违约时市场价格的差价并不多。这看来买卖双方都是运气,违约导致终断买卖合约并没有造成双方任何的损失。但会有情况是卖方实际上是蒙受损失,因为他丧失了销售额。他虽然找到了另一个替代买方肯以同样的价格购买这一票被拒绝的货物,但如果没有这一次违约,卖方当时手中有大量同样的货物,可以多做一票买卖并多赚一次利润,这就是卖方的损失。这在 WL Thompson Ltd v. Robinson (Gunmakers) Ltd(1955)Ch 177 先例,案情有关买方违约,他拒绝接受一辆汽车,导致了卖方把该辆汽车转售给第三人,但价格是一样。法院判是 Breach Date Rule 与 Market Rule,也就是 1979 年《货物销售法》之 Section 53(3)在这种情况下不适用,卖方的真正损失是丧失了多一次买卖的额外利润。

4.4 Breach Date Rule 与 Market Rule 另可偏离的例外情况:违约后"必然会发生的事情"

还有一种例外情况可偏离 Breach Date Rule 与 Market Rule 是在 The "Mihalis Angelos"(CA)(1970)2 Lloyd's Rep 43 先例所发展出来的违约/毁约后"必然会发生的事情"(predestinated to happen)是应该在计算损失时加以考虑。这个著名先例在本书第六章之 3.2.2 段与第十章之 6.5 段也有介绍,但有不同侧重。案情是有关该船舶由于在香港卸货发生延误,导致无法在下一个租约销约期前到下一个租约的装港,就是越南的海防港。但当时正值越战时期,去海防港的铁路被美军飞机轰炸,导致无法把要装的货物"磷灰石矿"(apatite ore)运到海防港。结果是在 1965 年 7 月 17 日,越南承租人通知船东租约被取消,因为发生了不可抗力的事件。而当时离开销约期的7月20日还差几天，而且船舶仍在香港，根本还没有开航去海防港，船舶是在7月23日才在香港卸完货。反正船东也就接受了承租人取消租约的违约/毁约。在该租约内，并没有这种所谓不可抗力的免责条款，加上这种战争行为也不能说是不可抗力的事件。反正是，承租人违约/毁约的责任是赖不掉了。但看来不像有什么损失，因为船东即使把船舶开去海防港也早已错过了销约期，承租人是有权取消租约，也一定会这样做（这也是裁决书中所认定的），反而令船舶白跑一趟，浪费时间与燃油。良心好一点的船东应该感激越南承租人也来不及，怎会向他提出索赔，损失计算以违约/毁约一天的航运市场租金为准。但商人还是商人，无所谓良心好坏。在上诉庭就涉及了是否应该考虑这在违约/毁约后必然会发生的事情，就是错过了销约期并肯定被承租人取消的事实？如果一并考虑，船东就根本没有任何损失可言。这正是上诉庭所作出的判决，其中上诉庭的 Megaw 大法官是这样说："In my view, where there is an anticipatory breach of contract, the breach is the repudiation once it has been accepted, and the other party is entitled to recover by way of damages the true value of the contractual rights that he has lost, subject to his duty to mitigate. If the contractual rights that he has lost were capable by the terms of the contract of being rendered either less valuable or valueless in certain events, and if can be shown that those events were, at the date of acceptance of the repudiation, predestined to happen, then in my view the damges which he can recover are not more than the true value, if any, of the rights which he has lost, having regard to those events."

结果是受害方的船东如果根据 Breach Date Rule 与 Market Rule 计算的损失是4000英镑，但由于这违约后必然会发生的事情，最后只能获得"名义损失"（nominal damage）的赔偿，这等于是败诉。

与 The "Mihalis Angelos"先例后有同样判法的是 The "Seaflower"（2000）2 Lloyd's Rep. 37先例，案情涉及承租人错误终断一个长达一年的期租合约，这构成违约/毁约。但在该租约中有条文说明有关的船舶是取得了美孚石油公司的批准（这包括是可以被美孚石油租用与使用美孚的泊位），但将会在1998年1月27日届满，而届时需要让美孚石油公司另作出检验以保证船舶状况良好才会获得另一个批准。条文也说到如果在30天内不能获得美孚石油公司的批准，承租人可以终断合约。这种条文的目的是可以想象得到，因为如果船东没有取得主要石油公司的批准，承租人的营运困难就会严重增加。该条文的英文版本是："Vessel is presently MOBIL（expiring 27/1/98）CONOCO（expiring 3/2/98）BP（expiring 28/1/98）and SHELL（expiring 14/1/98）acceptable ... If for any reason, Owners would lose even one of such acceptances they must advise Charterers at once and they must reinstate same within 30（thirty）days from such occurrence failing which Charterers will be at liberty to cancel charter party ..."

而承租人面对损失金额的计算，指称并提供证据说明船舶在美孚石油公司的批准将在1998年1月27日届满，并且船东是必然不会获得另一个批准。这表示到了

1998 年 2 月 26 日,承租人就有权终断合约。这被法院所接受,导致了本来的损失是 966,212 美元(计算到租约履行完毕的 1998 年 10 月 5 日)减少至 363,587.48 美元(计算到 1998 年 2 月 26 日)。Timothy Walker 大法官是这样说:

"I therefore ask myself the simple question, would this contract inevitably have come to an end on Feb. 26, 1998, because the owners would have lost (and been unable to regain in time) the Mobil approval? It of course goes without saying in this context that had the charterers acquired a liberty to cancel under the major approvals clause, they would have used it.

As to whether the owners would have lost the Mobil approval on Jan. 27, 1998, the evidence is strong. It is apparent that the owners had no arrangements of any kind in place to obtain the approvals required, and had not even begun by Dec. 30, 1997 or at all to address the significant logistical problem which would arise with four approvals becoming due for renewal within a few weeks of each other. Not a single document was produced to show any advance preparations, in particular of any notice being given to any oil major of any inspection being required in the near future. Thus Mr. Magliveras'(船东) telex of reassurance on Dec. 30, 1997 was simply a disingenuous attempt to allay the charterers' fears, and thus keep an advantageous time charter in being for the owners. The impression given of a 'proper schedule of vetting inspections' was without foundation ..."

笔者也遇到过类似的案件,如在一个 3 年的期租合约中,起租后约半年运费市场下跌,估计承租人想找理由终断租约。结果在一个欧洲装港该船舶被拒绝装一种十分清洁的尿素(urea),但由于船舱情况很坏,加上船龄高,船东委任的一位船舶检验师告诉船东要求该船舶修理至一个可装这种货的程度是不现实,而船东就把检验师这句话转告给承租人,说是修理不现实。承租人也就趁机指称船东违约/毁约,拒绝维修保养船舶而终断租约。这一方面的争议最后被仲裁庭否定,认为船东并没有明确无误地拒绝修理船舶,不构成违约/毁约。这一来,剩下的是怎样计算提早还船的损失了。该租约有一条文是说明船舶如果停租超过 25 天,承租人就有权终断租约。这一来,双方所争议的就是该船舶要把船舱修好以装这租约允许的尿素的估计时间。由于这个事情根本没有发生过,所以双方都是以专家意见作出估计。显然船东的专家是认为只要不惜代价抓紧时间 20 天就可修理完毕,所以该租约会被承租人以该条文终断并非是"必然会发生"(predestined)。当然这估计的 20 天是要大批修船工人日夜超时赶工的情况下最乐观的估计,至于船东真正会否这样做也是天知道。而承租人的专家认为是要 40 天以上才能修理完毕。但最终仲裁庭还是接受了船东的估计,认为停租超过 25 天让承租人有权选择终断合约并非是必然会发生,结果承租人要赔偿一大笔损失给船东。

4.5 Breach Date Rule 与 Market Rule 另可偏离的例外情况:损失金额币种的兑换

这在本书第十四章有详细针对这一个问题,就是针对损失金额币种的兑换,英国法律已经从违约一天做出计算的 Breach Date Rule 有了改变。在 Miliangos v. Frank (Textiles) Ltd (1976) 1 Lloyd's Rep 201 先例,英国普通法已经从 Breach Date Rule 变了是 Payment Date Rule,在支付一天才把损失金额的币种做出兑换,以避免受害方因为在违约后因为审理造成延误的期间币值兑换的波动导致了赔不足。其他详细的内容,不再重复。

4.6 Breach Date Rule 与 Market Rule 另可偏离的例外情况:买方已支付货款

众所周知,这两条规则是假设在有可供买卖的市场情况下,受害的买方应该在违约的一天尽快去市场买进替代品,以减少损失或避免影响其他相关的合约(分销/转售合约),不至于在间接损失方面产生"多米诺效应"(domino principle)。但问题是如果买方已经支付货款,而违约的卖方还没有把这笔钱退还,买方就会在有可供买卖市场的情况下,也只能眼睁睁地看着市场上涨而无能为力。这种情况在商品的国际货物买卖其实经常会发生,因为买方需要预先做出货款的支付(如通过信用证的结汇)。如果卖方的违约/毁约是拒绝提供/付运货物,这就不涉及买方支付了货款,应该有足够财力可以在市场买进替代商品。但如果是另类违约,如在支付后货物抵达卸港的时候被发觉货不对版,导致买方拒绝接受货物。这种违约/毁约就会导致了买方财货两失,甚至还要支付昂贵的律师费,直到诉讼告一段落。这一来,除非买方是财雄势大的公司如国际贸易商,他就往往不能够很快利用可供买卖的市场以减少损失。而如果买方需要一段时间后才能买进甚至一直无法买进替代货物,这一个延误是不涉及买方自己的选择而是完全被迫要这样做,这在一个不断上涨的市场下是否能够网开一面,让买方的损失可以根据后来一天的市场价格,甚至在判决一天的市场价格计算损失?这在一定程度上也会涉及买方的穷困,这个问题在本书第四章 9.2.2 段有详细的介绍,但 The "Liesbosch"先例中所建立的受害方贫穷可以中断因果链的说法在近期的 Lagden v. O'Connor (2003) UKHL 64 贵族院先例也受到质疑。但很多情况笔者也不认为是穷困的问题,毕竟一船的商品涉及的金额会是非常庞大,动不动就上千万甚至上亿美元。所以 Breach Date Rule 与 Market Rule 针对货物/商品买卖会不会针对受害的买方有否支付了货款给违约的卖方在适用方面有不同对待?答案是目前的法律地位,根据 Startup v. Cortazzi (1835) 2 CM & R 165 先例,法院是拒绝买方以判决一天的市场价格为准进行索赔的要求。但在 Aronson v. Mologa Holzindustrie (1927) 32 Com Cas. 276 先例,上诉庭的 Atkin 大法官认为这一个方面还是没有定论。会否在近期的 Lagden v. O'Connor 贵族院先例有了定论?但在《McGregor on Damages》(18th edn, 2009 年)之 20-014 段,对这一个方面也没有什么补充,只说到货物买卖在这一个方面或问题已经是与其他的领域有所偏离。

4.7 Breach Date Rule 与 Market Rule 另可偏离的例外情况:股票买卖

另一个有所偏离的领域可以是股票买卖,这方面可以节录《McGregor on Damages》(18th edn, 2009 年)之 24-005 段如下:"The time at which the market price is to be taken is the contractual time for delivery. In general the principles worked out in the sale of goods cases apply here: of the several possible situations few have been adjudicated upon in relation to the sale of shares, but the cases that there are indicate an application of common principles while at the same time bringing out small differences. (1) Where the market price has risen between the date of breach and the date of judgment in the action, it was held in Shaw v. Holland(1846) 15 M & W 136 that the time of judgment was not to be taken in preference to the time of breach by not delivering. Parke B. said that the action was more akin to one for non-delivery of goods than to one for not replacing stock, since 'the plaintiff had his money in his own possession, and might have gone into the market and bought other shares as soon as the contract was broken'. This rationale disappears where the purchase price has been paid in advance; and it has been submitted that in the case of goods the buyer should then be entitled to recover for any increase in the market price between breach and judgment ..."(这大致上是说在股票买卖下的损失计算基本上也是与货物买卖一样,如在 Shaw v. Holland(1846) 15 M & W 136 先例,案情涉及卖方没有交出买卖的股票,法院就拒绝损失按照判决一天的市场价格计算。Parke B 大法官认为案情与卖方拒绝交出买卖的货物一样,原告的买方有钱在手中可以在违约一天去市场买进替代的股票。但这个道理看来是不适用在原告的买方已经把购买股票的钱预付给了违约的卖方的情况。在这种情况下,原告应该可以索赔违约一天到判决一天市场上升的价格。)

5. 违约一天计算损失的批评与其他更佳计算办法的探讨

违约一天计算损失的大原则看来在英国法律下已经是明确不过,但还是存在对它的批评。一个原因就是在上一小段所介绍的 Breach Date Rule 与 Market Rule 可以在许多例外情况下偏离,导致适用的情况只局限在相对少数的情况是受害的买方可以马上去市场买进同类替代货物以减少损失。这也是受害方应该做的事情以减少损失,即使是因为受害方自己的原因(不论合理与否)没有这样做,也假设他是这样做了作为损失的计算。但损失计算还有一个重要的大原则,就是在审理/判决的时候,如果有一些明确的事实在期间已经发生了并严重影响(不论是扩大或是减少)受害方真正损失的金额,法院是很难置之不理。正如 Macnaughten 勋爵在 Bwllfa & Merthyr Dare Steam Collieries(1891), Ltd v. Pontryprid Waterworks Co(1903) AC 426 先例中所讲:"Why should he [the arbitrator] listen to conjecture on a matter which has become an accomplished fact? Why should he guess when he can calculate? With the light before him why should he shut his eyes and grope in the dark?"另 Scrutton 大法官在 The Kingsway (1918) P. 344 CA. 先例也说到开庭审理应该把已经发生的事实一并考虑。这一个说法可称为是"Bwllfa 大原则"(Bwllfa principle)。这大原则在人身伤亡的案件就已经适用，就是一审法院在审理/判决的时候看看侵权或者违约所造成的人身伤亡直到审理这一段时间中所发生的情况变化考虑损失的金额。毕竟许多人身伤害会造成的中期或长期结果很难在一开始就做出准确的判断，如一位严重伤害看来一生残废的受害方会在1、2年后的审理期间变了健步如飞，或是一位受害方所蒙受的潜在伤害在后来才表露出来，损失就没有理由以侵权或违约一天的计算为准。这可节录《McGregor on Damages》(18th edn，2009年)之35－036段："There is today universal acceptance of the sensible and realistic rule that trial courts must look at the position at the time of their judgments and take accounts of any changes of circumstances which may have taken place since the injury was inflicted. This applies both to change which increases the claimant's loss and to change which diminishes it."

但如果是根据这"Bwllfa大原则"考虑商业合约的损失赔偿，这又好像接近以审理或判决一天计算损失了，不再适用Breach Date Rule与Market Rule了。

总结而言，可节录Andrew Burrows教授在《Tom Bingham and the Transformation of the Law》(2009年)一书的文章中提到Breach Date Rule的不肯定，如下：

"It is usually taken to be a trite statement of law that，in general，the date for the assessment of contractual compensatory damages is the date of the breach of contract. Yet this is a surprisingly ambiguous and ultimately misleading proposition for at least two reasons. (经常有一个无可质疑的说法，就是合约的损失赔偿计算是以违约一天为准。但这是十分模糊甚至是误导的说法，其中有两个以上的原因。)

First，a contract is clearlybound to take into account consequential losses or consequential gains，provided they are not ruled out by limiting principles such as remoteness and causation，even though these have occurred after the date of breach. So，for example，if as a consequence of a carrier's delay in delivering a broken crank－shaft to manufacturers for a replacement，the claimant's mill is kept at a standstill for several days longer than it otherwise would have been，the number assessing damages for the breach of the carriage contracts. It does not matter that those days of standstill occurred after the date of breach. (第一个原因就是损失计算肯定要考虑违约后的间接损失或间接好处，除非是受到其它方面的限制如损失的遥远性或因果关系中断。)

Secondly，even if one confines the proposition to being concerned with the assessment of the claimant's basic，as opposed to consequential，loss，it is riddled with exceptions. Say，for example，the contract in question was one for the sale of goods and that the vendor has broken the contract by failing to supply the goods. One's starting point for assessing the purchaser's damages may very well be the market value of the goods at the date of the breach. But where the market value has fluctuated，whether by reason of ordinary market movements or changes in the internal or external value of money，a court will take those fluctuations into account subject to the important limiting principles of the duty to mitigate and actual mitigation. The so – called date of breach rule, even when confined to the assessment of basic loss, turns out on close inspection merely to reflect the starting point that a claimant's duty to mitigate is triggered as soon as a breach occurs. Assessment by the market values at the date of breach is accurate only insofar as it is reasonable for a purchaser to mitigate its loss by straightaway going into the market to buy substitute goods. As sometimes a claimant acts reasonably by not immediately going into the market for a replacement, so sometimes a later valuation date is appropriate."(第二个原因就是违约一天计算损失原则是有许多的例外。可以说,这一个原则变成只是一个计算损失的起点。根据违约一天的市场价格计算损失只能是可以肯定适用在要求一位受害买方马上在市场买进替代货物以合理减少他的损失是完全合理的情况。但如果要求买方马上买进替代货物是不合理,那么法院就会认定一个稍后的日期作为计算损失的一天。)

所以有说法是更佳的计算损失日期还是在审理或判决的一天,除非能够提出与证明在更早的时间受害方就已经应该减少损失。例如在违约一天受害方就可以在可供买卖市场马上出售或买入,就会把计算损失日期提前至违约的一天,也就是受害方应该减少损失的一天。这一个说法在 Radford v. De Froberville(1977)1 WLR 1262 先例中 Oliver 大法官有提到说:"... The proper approach is to assess the damages at the date of the hearing unless it can be said that the plaintiff ought reasonably to have mitigated by seeking an alternative performance at an earlier date."

6. 争议性的 The "Golden Victory"先例

虽然是 Breach Date Rule 与 Market Rule 的损失赔偿计算大原则在英国法下已经非常明确,但还是有太多不肯定并与其他的大原则(如"Bwllfa 大原则")混淆在一起。例如,在审理时(重复这会是在违约的多年后)是否应该把所有已经发生了的事情加以考虑以调整违约一天市场价格计算出来的损失?而已经发生的事情是不需要做出估计的,估计只是针对将来的事情。

这一个问题可以简单例子解释,如果一个还有 10 年履行期的合约因为违约/毁约被终断,根据 Breach Date Rule 与 Market Rule 的计算,得出的损失金额是 1000 万美元。但由于各种诉讼的延误导致了违约/毁约后 3 年才能开庭审理,而那个时候刚发生了一些事情(如合约受阻或法律改变),导致了无可争议的该合约会提早终断。这一来,损失的计算应该是按 Breach Date Rule 与 Market Rule 的 10 年还是在审理时刚发生的事情导致合约如果被履行的话也肯定被终断的 3 年?这一难题也带来了一个非常有争议性的著名贵族院先例 The "Golden Victory"(2007)2 Lloyd's Rep 164 以及之后的一些判例 Multiplex Constructions(UK) Ltd v. Cleveland Bridge UK Ltd(2008) EWHC 2220(TCC), Force India Formula One Team Ltd v. Etihad Airways PJSC(2009)

EWHC 2768(QB)等。这些问题在接下去会进一步解释。

6.1 The "Golden Victory"先例的案情与判法

现在探讨这一个重要先例 The "Golden Victory" (2007)2 Lloyd's Rep 164,这一个先例是首次出现 Breach Date Rule/Market Rule 与"Bwllfa 大原则"正面发生冲突。换言之,在以前适用"Bwllfa 大原则"计算损失赔偿的先例都没有出现在违约时候有一个可供买卖的市场可马上让受害方减少损失,而 The "Golden Victory"先例恰恰就是这个情况。

在这个先例,它是涉及船东把该船舶期租了 7 年给日本著名船公司 NYKK。由于市场下跌,NYKK 在租约还剩下 4 年就提早还船。这是明确不过的违约/毁约,责任方面没有什么好争议。船东也就向 NYKK 提出了这 4 年的索赔,而根据的就是违约/毁约一天的航运市场租金与租约租金的差价乘以 4 年尚未完成的租约期。

在该租约中另有第 33 条文,是一条"战争能取消租约条文"(War Cancellation Clause)明示说明如果在有一些列明的国家之间发生战争,船东与承租人均有权终断合约,条文如下:"If war or hostilities break out between any two or more of the following countries:USA,former USSR,PRC,UK,Netherlands,Liberia,Japan,Iran,Kuwait,Saudi Arabia,Qatar,Iraq,both Owners and Charterers shall have the right to cancel this charter . . ."

在 NYKK 违约/毁约后的 14 个月,也就是在 2003 年 3 月份爆发了第二次海湾战争。这被仲裁庭认定为一个美国、英国与伊拉克之间的战争。换言之,NYKK 可根据第 33 条文终断租约。这一来,如果违约损失还是算足 4 年与只算 14 个月金额上就会有极大差别。另是第二次海湾战争并非是"必然会发生的事情"(predestinated to happen),所以 The "Mihalis Angelos"(CA)(1970)2 Lloyd's Rep 43 先例的说法不适用。但另一个角度看公平合理就是船东的真正损失也应该只有 14 个月,因为如果租约被履行,NYKK 抓到了这个机会不会不合法终断租约。公平合理也可以从另一个角度探讨,就是在 NYKK 违约/毁约后的半个月或更短的时间,就爆发了第二次海湾战争。这一来,难道还是计算 4 年的损失,只因为违约/毁约时有市场,而不理会在几天后发生的第二次海湾战争可让租约合法被终断?难道违约的承租人只因为没有多等几天的耐心或运气不好,就要承担这么严重的后果?而作为受害方的船东,是否可以归咎于他运气好,所以差这几天就让他大大地赚了一笔?

结果在仲裁、一审法院与上诉庭都认为应该根据 Bwllfa 大原则计算损失。虽然以违约/毁约一天的市场租金计算损失可带来肯定性与容易计算,但更重要的原则是针对船东真正蒙受的损失。其中上诉庭的 Mance 大法官是这样说:". . . Although certainty,finality and ease of settlement were important general considerations,they would have,so far as necessary,to yield to the greater importance of achieving an assessment of damages and compensation which more accurately reflected the actual loss which the owners could now be seen to have suffered as a result of the charterers' repudiation."

在2007年3月28日,贵族院给了最后的判决,结果还是支持上诉庭。但这是以3:2的多数意见,其中Bingham勋爵与Walker勋爵做出了十分强烈的不同意见。不同意见是认为这个Breach Date Rule与Market Rule是简单与肯定,而这是对商业活动十分重要。其中Bingham勋爵说:"The decision [of the majority] undermines the quality of certainty which is a traditional strength and major selling point of English commercial law, and involves an unfortunate departure from principle."(多数贵族院的意见破坏英国商业法律传统以来的强项与卖点,就是对法律的肯定。但多数意见是偏离了这一个大原则。)而多数意见是认为Breach Date Rule与Market Rule只是一个表面的计算规则,它必须让步给更重要的损失赔偿大原则,就是尽量也不多也不少地补偿受害方的损失,让他回到违约根本没有发生,也就是租约被履行同样的地位。正如Atkinson勋爵在Wertheim v. Chicoutimi Pulp Co. (1911) AC 301.先例所说如下:"... the general intention of the law that, in giving damages for breach of contract, the party complaining should, so far as it can be done by money, be placed in the same position as he would have been in if the contract had been performed."

6.2 The "Golden Victory"先例的影响

这个重要判决的影响也不光是租约的违约/毁约,而是任何其他合约的违约/毁约怎样计算损失。两者比较,根据违约/毁约一天或尽量接近违约/毁约一天的市场(只要有买卖或者租船市场)价格或者租金作比较,带来肯定与容易计算外,也利于双方当事人可尽快达成庭外和解,因为双方都知道在损失金额没什么好争的,这显然是有利公共政策去避免或减少诉讼。这也代表不必要等原租约全部完结才能算得出损失,毕竟像The "Golden Victory"租约是长达7年之久,而违约/毁约后还有4年未完成的租约期。在这4年中市场肯定有波动,受害方的船东如果只短期经营/出租可赚可亏,4年下来可能发了大财,亦可能破产。但这些都是船东自己的选择(如比较乐观,相信航运市场明天会更好),与较早前违约/毁约所带来的损失计算无关,"因果关系"(causation)已经被打断。也有可能船东在违约/毁约后马上就出租了另一个长达4年的期租(这在市场上找得到)。反正,上述的两种情况以违约/毁约时的市场租金为准,可以允许损失马上计算得到。

以违约/毁约一天或尽量接近的市场(只要有市场)价格或者租金作为起点,但要加上看实质违约/毁约后所发生的事情,以找出受害方真正的损失,这符合公平的大原则,也是损失赔偿最基本的"复原原则"(*restitutio in integrum*)。但这也会带来了不肯定与过多的诉讼,包括像违约/毁约受害方有否减少损失等。还有一个弊病是在The "Golden Victory"先例中也有提到,这就是违约方会尽量拖延诉讼,但求出现变数,如发生了第二次海湾战争带来一个可终断原租约的机会。固然,这在大部分的提早还船案件都不是问题,因为通常提早还船不会像The "Golden Victory"是还剩长达4年的租约期。通常也只会是几天至最多一二个月,特别在承租人找不到适合剩下租约期长短的最后航次就干脆硬把船舶归还给船东。这一来,去仲裁的中途,剩下的短暂租约期应早已过去。即使要把违约/毁约后发生的事情一并考虑损失,问题也不大。怕的就是剩下的租约期还有很长的一段时间,违约方就会希望拖延去看变数了。如有关的船舶是一艘老船,拖延下去会有机会发生沉船或者海难等事故。又或者该老船不是全损,但发生海难后甚至不大的事故也要修理一段长时间,而发生违约/毁约而终断了的原租约中却有一条文说明修理多过 15 天或 20 天承租人可终断租约。在 The "Golden Victory",上诉庭的 Mance 大法官不认为这是问题,说:"As to the suggestion that guilty parties might be encouraged to delay in the hope of some event occurring to reducing their liability, guilty parties may seek to delay for many reasons, but, unless an event was already probable, they would, if they delayed on its account, be just as, if not more, vulnerable to its not materializing as they would be likely to benefit by its occurring."

笔者认为这危险的确是存在,因为在正常情况下,类似提早还船的对错在责任上太明显,赔偿金额也容易计算,称职的律师在一般情况下也不建议承租人客户去诉讼,不值得浪费律师费,尽快和解就了事。但现在有了 The "Golden Victory",情况有些不同。在长期租约并且仍剩下很长一段尚未完成的时间,而租约中有类似第 33 条文或其他可让承租人有选择权提早终断租约的条文,又或者有关船舶老龄残旧,违约/毁约的承租人就会有一线生机,在金额大的索赔情况下值得拖延,即使要多花律师费用也在所不惜。等待违约/毁约后会发生的突发事件,虽然这可能只是一个赌博,但对违约/毁约承租人的风险是绝少或者是零,因为真发生了也只会减少损失的计算,而不会增加以违约一天市场租金计算出来的损失金额。相反如果他不拖延诉讼,而在裁决或判决告终后,即使是不久后发生了沉船事故,或者是第二次海湾战争,也不能重来审理一次,因为已经是"一事不再审"(*res judicata*)。

6.3 部分权威人士对 The "Golden Victory"的评论

首先,节录在伦敦海事仲裁协会的 2007 年秋季报刊中在 42 至 45 页有著名前大法官 Anthony Colman 先生在他所写的文章《London Maritime Arbitration: The view from the Commercial Court》中谈到对于贵族院在 The "Golden Victory" 中的有关损失赔偿的判决与笔者持类似的看法,如下:

"I am bound to say that I find this reasoning absolutely dire. Like the Court of Appeal the majority in the HL seem to have been mesmerized by a cascade of previous authority (none of it binding on the HL and none of it determinative of the issue) into ignoring the conceptual foundations of the methodology for calculating recoverable loss in the simplest of contract termination situations. The factual reality of The "Golden Victory" situation was clearly identified by your learned President(当时伦敦海事仲裁协会的主席就是 The "Golden Victory"的仲裁员) when he said in his award: 'if the second Gulf War was no more than a possibility on 17 December 2001, it cannot be doubted that what the owners lost at that date was a charterparty with slightly less than four years to run. For example, had the charterers not repudiated the charterparty but the owners had sold the vessel with her charter on that day, the value they would have received would surely have been calculated on that basis.'

One asks why it could not be assumed at the hearing of the arbitration that the owner had indeed taken that course? That would be the kind ofassumption to be made if the Owners had wrongfully withdrawn the vessel before the end of the charter period, as held by no less a commercial judge than Robert Goff J in The Elena d' Amico(1980)1 Lloyd's Rep. 75 (Colman 先生提到的这个先例也将在本书十五章 2.3.6 段有详细介绍,这是针对租约最重要的先例,判只要在违约时有市场可供寻找替代, Breach Date Rule 与 Market Rule 就适用). In such a case the normal measure of damages, if there is an available market at the day of the breach, will be the difference between the contract rate and the market rate of hire for chartering a substitute vessel for the remainder of the charter period. The reference to available market is not the consequence of an unprincipled mantra. Quite the contrary. It expressed a key consideration in such a case just as it does under the Common Law as codified in the Sale of Goods Act 1893. What matters is for what purpose the market is available. The answer is and always has been: Available to enable the innocent party (in this case the owners) to mitigate their loss by re – letting the vessel on similar terms save as to hire rate. Their loss would be based on the difference between the contract rate and the market rate until the end of the original period of hire. Why does one make this fictional assumption? Simply because justice requires that the Owner recovers no more than he would lose if he had mitigated his loss at or reasonably soon after the date of the breach. That is why the prospective value of the availability of the vessel has to be measured at that time by reference to the available market from about the date of the breach up to the end of the charter period. That would be the course of conduct which justice required from the innocent party and which the party in breach could be taken reasonably to foresee. What he could not normally be taken to foresee would be that ages after the date of the breach some catastrophic after – event would interfere with the operation of the charter so as to cause its subsequent premature termination.

So I agree with the minority – Lord Bingham – the only commercial judge amongst the five – and Lord Walker – that serious violence had been done by this decision to what has long been regarded as a relatively certain area of English Law. With the greatest respect to your President, his instinctive inclination was the right one, though in terms of causation I suspect of the ultimate result could have been the same! **This has to be the worst decision on any aspect of English Commercial Law and certainly shipping law that has come out of the House of Lords in my entire career in the legal profession.**"(加黑部分是笔者的强调,第一句话 Colman 先生同意 Bingham 勋爵的少数不同意见,并指出他是贵族院 5 位大法官之中唯一的一位懂得商法的大

法官。Colman 先生指出 Golden Victory 这一个先例对英国一贯以来是相对肯定的市场规则的法律地位造成了严重的冲击。后一句话是 Colman 先生认为是在他法律生涯中贵族院做出的最坏商业判例,这可以说是一句非常重的话。)

在英国著名的法律学者之间,也是各持不同的意见。其中 Treitel 教授在他的《The Law of Contract》(12th edn,2007 年)一书之 20 - 071 段是持与 Colman 先生一致的意见,但 Andrew Burrows 教授在《Tom Bingham and the Transformation of the Law》(2009 年)一书的文章中是持相反意见,说:

"Such concerns have also been voiced against the majority's approach by Edwin Peel and Guenter Treitel and more generally as regards the date for assessment by Stephen Waddams. However, it is hard to see why Oliver J's formulation(这是在本章第 5 段所提到的 Radford v. De Froberville [1977] 1 WLR 1262 先例所说) is any less certain or predictable or final than a general rule of assessment at the date of breach which is then qualified by exceptions. The correct message, which is a clear and certain one, is that, provided claimants act reasonably to minimize loss, they are entitled to their full non - remote loss taking into account all facts known at trial. Even if their reasonable efforts, viewed in retrospect, augment rather than reduce their loss, it is recoverable. Furthermore, courts are not going to be astute to hold that innocent parties have acted unreasonably; and the burden of proof in relation to a failure to mitigate is firmly on the defendant. (Andrew Burrows 教授认为根据违约一天计算损失,而同时有许多的例外情况[请看本章之第 4 段],本身也谈不上是肯定或可预测。相反,Golden Victory 的贵族院多数判例带出的信息是十分明确与肯定,这就是受害的原告只要合理减少损失,他就可以根据开庭审理一天所知道的事实取回所有的损失,只要这个损失并非是遥远[即损失并非不可预见与因果关系没有中断]。而如果事后看来原告采取合理措施但反而增加而不是减少了他的损失,这也可以向被告取回。此外,法院不会轻易判无辜的受害方没有合理减少损失,而举证责任也是在被告。)

In the latest edition of Treitel, The Law of Contract, Edwin Peel suggests that the majority's approach has the drawback of potentially encouraging repudiating parties to delay the assessment of damages to see if a suspensory condition might come into operation. With respect, this seems a spurious concern. This is because a delay might equally well lead to an increase of damages payable by the repudiating party. So, for example, had the prospect of the second Iraq war disappeared altogether 15 months after breach, the need to reduce the owners' damges to reflect the possibility of the outbreak of war would have been removed."

同样的争议也可多举一个例子是 Harry Street 教授在《Supervening Events and the Quantum of Damages》(1962)78 LQR 中的建议是合约在违约/毁约终断后,如果后来发生了一些是不能预见或不大可能会发生的事情,就不在审理/判决一天的损失计算加以考虑。换言之,如果后来发生的事情是可能会发生,特别是"必然会发生的事情”(predestinated to happen)就不同对待:The “Mihalis Angelos”(CA)(1970)2 Lloyd's Rep 43 先例。Harry Street 教授是这样说:“if an event were so unlikely that it ought not to be a significant factor in valuation, it seems plain that it should not be considered although it did happened later.”

根据 Harry Street 教授的说法,一个不应该在审理/判决一天的损失计算加以考虑的例子是,原告的房屋因被告的错误而导致损坏,这损失在违约一天是算得出来。但后来在审理前不久该房屋在一场大火中全损,如果损失计算是以审理/判决一天的事实为准,原告就不会有损失了,而已经花费了的律师费用也是浪费。另一个相同例子是,在审理前发生了一场战争而导致该房屋的市场价格降了 20%,那么该场战争对房屋的影响就不应该在计算损失赔偿的时候被加进去考虑。在 Harry Street 教授看来,以上例子的后来发生的大火或者是战争都是预见不到与十分间接的事故,故不应被考虑在内,而应该以违约的一天来计算损失。

就计算损失的办法,即以违约的一天来计算而不考虑后来发生的事件/事故,Michael Howard 御用大律师在他所写的一篇文章《Another Golden Victory》中持不同于 Harry Street 教授的看法,如下:“... those two approaches to the quantification of damages, assessment as at the wrong and the ignoring of some subsequent events, can be seen as being mutually supportive. But while they may be mutually supportive, they are also mutually dependent. If damages are assessed as at the date of wrong (or, ... as at the somewhat later when the owners could have re – chartered their ship in the available market), then it follows that subsequent events will be ignored. But if the strait – jacket solution of assessing damages as at the date of the wrong gives way to more flexible approach, **where fairness and better justice is preferred to certainty for its own sake, then it is clear that subsequent events may be taken into account.** ... Inevitably, there is a significant interval between the cause of action arising and damages being assessed by the court or arbitral tribunal. In that period often, perhaps ordinarily, events will occur which impact on the quantum of the loss suffered by the innocent party or the certainty with which it can be calculated.” (黑字部分是笔者的强调)

Michael Howard 御用大律师的说法也正是 The “Golden Victory”(2007)2 Lloyd's Rep 164 先例的上诉庭判决所说的那样,就是如今有一个趋势是在一些涉及人身伤亡或不动产的损失索赔中,往往会采取一些更加灵活的损失计算办法以求做到公平公正。Wilberforce 勋爵在他的两个案例中持相同的看法,该两个案例是:Miliangos v. Frank (Textiles) Ltd (1976) 1 Lloyd's Rep 201 与 The Owners of the Motor Vessel Eleftherotria v. Owners of the Motor Vessel Despina R (1979) AC 685。从这两个案例中可以看出来 Wilberforce 勋爵非常倾向于公平原则为先的做法,即使这样会带来很大的不肯定。这导致 Scott 勋爵在 The “Golden Victory”的贵族院先例中也对 Wilberforce 勋爵在 Miliangos v. Frank (Textiles) Ltd 先例中的看法持同意态度,也就是说,为了达致公平的结果而偏离了所谓的 Breach Date Rule 与 Market Rule。他说:"The argued justification for offending the compensatory principle is that priority should be given to the so - called principle of certainty. My Lords there is, in my opinion, no such principle. Certainty is a desideratum and a very important one, particularly in commercial contracts. But it is not a principle and must give way to principles. Otherwise incoherence of principle is the likely result."

6.4 The "Golden Victory"先例后的一些发展

在 The "Golden Victory" (2007) 2 Lloyd's Rep 164 的贵族院判决后,马上就有案件受到它的影响,在此可介绍两宗。第一宗是有关一艘新船在高价时长期租入,但之后市场下跌而导致承租人以一个很难站得住脚的理由提早终断合约,这看来是一个违约/毁约。由于租约期还是很长而且损失索赔金额很大,所以在 The "Golden Victory" 先例后,承租人是值得去拖时间,希望有"奇迹"出现。但在该租约下,承案律师感到矛盾。因为该租约的条文订得对承租人不利,能够从租约条文脱身的机会(即使是租约终断后才会出现的机会)不多。在一条"战争能取消租约条文"(War Cancellation Clause),内容订得十分局限,是要发生像中美大战才会允许承租人合法脱身,这当然是应该不会发生。另有一条是针对停租过久可让承租人脱身的条文,通常在其他的同类租约会是 30 ~ 40 天不等。但该租约订的是 85 天之久,显然这么长的停租,特别在航运市场下跌但租约租金相对高昂时,船东即使船舶出意外而受严重损坏也会努力尽快修船,是不大可能会发生。所以承案律师的矛盾是应否劝承租人尽早以违约/毁约时的市场租金作为比较向船东提出和解提议,因为拖下去不像会有"奇迹"发生,而拖延的最起码代价就是律师费用,这笔钱也不会少。如果提出和解协议,在 The "Golden Victory" 先例的影响下,会多少增加受害方船东的压力做出一些让步,避免拖延下去会出现的变数。

第二宗是有关一个香港仲裁,涉及一个台湾船东的违约/毁约,因为他在没有等到"反技术取巧通知"(anti - technicality notice)(这通知是针对承租人没有准时与足数支付租金,船东必须先给通知才能合法撤船)。反技术取巧的条文是要求船东做出预先 3 日银行工作日的通知,可是船东急不可待地撤了船。但在违约/毁约的时候,租约期只剩下了 15 日,而承租人也给了 15 日的还船通知。承租人针对船东违约/毁约提出损失索赔,这损失说是承租人真正蒙受的损失,就是他要另安排两艘替代船舶履行被撤船舶所安排的航次。这所谓真正损失计算出来是大约 20 万美元,而根据市场租金的比较再乘以 15 天,估计损失大不了也只不过是 2、3 万美元,可以说两个数字相差甚远。仲裁庭认为这所谓的真正损失有许多对船东来说是遥远或非真正损失。如替代船舶过了销约期到装港而要支付一笔延误罚款,但即使这是可以接受,被撤的船舶如果履行也一样会是赶不及销约期,只是早了一点点。仲裁庭无法接受承租人空口的解释说分承租人如果延误少是不会罚款与会无条件延长销约期的。仲裁庭也认为剩下的 15 天只是能走一个航次而不是两个,因为替代船舶的第一艘就已经要花了接近10天才完成。但最重要导致仲裁庭决定适用 Breach Date Rule 与 Market Rule 的是因为在这种租约期所剩无几的违约/毁约情况下,到了审理的时候可以说是都已经履行完毕了。如果还是要看真正的损失,也就是看真正的履行,作出违约/毁约的损失计算,就会涉及大量的工作。受害方会是在真正的履行中直接损失是比 Breach Date Rule 与 Market Rule 的计算更高或更低,但这一来,今后对绝大部分的案件再也没有 Breach Date Rule 了,只有像 The "Golden Victory"这样违约/毁约后仍有很长未履行租约期,到审理时还没有完结,才存在需要估计损失。该仲裁庭也认为 The "Golden Victory"虽然把第二次海湾战争考虑在内,但没有把其他在违约/毁约后发生的事情加以考虑,如 The "Golden Victory"在违约/毁约后至第二次海湾战争爆发的16个月的营运情况,是赚多还是亏多了。而且也没有把2003年6月航运市场开始上涨与几个月后开始猛涨的事实加以考虑,因为这是要进一步看 Golden Victory 轮有没有被转卖或低价长期出租。如果 Golden Victory 轮仍是在市场短期营运,可以说承租人提早4年还船的违约/毁约(时于2001年12月14日)会是算总账根本没有对船东造成任何损失。所以该香港仲裁的结果是判 Breach Date Rule 与 Market Rule 适用在这个15天提早还船的违约/毁约。

最后总结是 The "Golden Victory"先例虽然富争议性,但贵族院多数的判决还是有约束性。这代表有关案件的标的即使有可供买卖的市场,也不代表 Breach Date Rule 与 Market Rule 一定会适用在损失计算,除非到了审理/判决的一天没有会严重影响损失赔偿金额的重大变化。看来,除了货物买卖的损失计算是受到英国《货物销售法》的规定(因为立法的地位是超越普通法),英国法律目前的地位还是以审理/判决的一天看怎么样的损失计算会更好让受害方复原,这也会是 Oliver 大法官在 Radford v. De Froberville(1977)1 WLR 1262 先例中说的:"... The proper approach is to assess the damages at the date of the hearing unless it can be said that the plaintiff ought reasonably to have mitigated by seeking an alternative performance at an earlier date."

7. 笔者涉及的中国造船合约仲裁

另一个就是笔者早期处理的一个涉及造船的伦敦仲裁案件,涉及中国船厂违约/毁约后对原告希腊船东会带来的利润损失,这看来是与 The "Golden Victory"一样的案件。这方面的争议是希腊船东声称在中国船厂违约/毁约的情况下,去了韩国建造替代的船舶,但交船日期不一样,韩国的船舶迟了9个月交付,希腊船东便索赔这9个月的营运损失。碰巧这9个月的期间刚好就是航运市场最疯狂的时候,所以希腊船东索赔的金额非常庞大(因为涉及了4艘船舶)。笔者作为仲裁庭成员之一,就感觉到有夸大损失的可能性。其中,笔者向其他两位共同仲裁员(他们是英国的退休大法官)提出的疑问是造船合约中,中国船厂是有权把合约约定的交船日期免费延长30天。之后,如果发生工程延误而无法交船,且延误不属于“不可抗力”(*force majuere*)的事件,船厂就要每天赔偿给船东约1万美元。此外,还有条文说明如果这种工程延误长达180天,就到了所谓的“死亡日期”(drop - dead day),希腊船东有权取消造船合约。这些都是造船合约的一些典型条文与安排,只说该造船合约订约时航运市场还不算高,所以每天要赔偿的工程延误的1万美元,这与希腊船东根据航运市场最疯狂的7万美元一天作为索赔损失的计算是相差了一大截。所以笔者的疑问就是希腊船东声称的2个造船合约交船日期相差的9个月利润损失应否减去30天的免费延长,且剩下的8个月利润损失是否应该以1万美元一天计算?这相比以7万美元一天计算9个月得出来的损失是天渊之别。

但笔者倒也不是根据The“Golden Victory”中贵族院多数意见的说法,就是在审理当天要考虑所有的情况后作出复原的赔偿。因为这一个案件不像The“Golden Victory”,事实上发生了海湾战争,而是根据“平衡的可能性”(balance of probabilities)考虑中国船厂会否延误交船(表示要享用合约中的30天免费延长期与在剩下的延误赔偿1万美元一天)。笔者认为这种会延误交船的情况出现的可能性是大于不出现。这一来,就应该考虑另一条有关损失的大原则,即损失赔偿应该以违约方最低的合约责任为准(本书第十章)。这方面只节录Megaw大法官在The“Mihalis Angelos”(1970)2 Lloyd's Rep 43先例所说:“If the contractual rights which he has lost were capable by the terms of the contract of being rendered either less valuable or valueless in certain events, and if it can be shown that those events were, at the date of acceptance of the repudiation, predestined to happen, then in my view the damages which he can recover are not more than the true value, if any, of the rights which he has lost, having regard to those predestined events.”

Megaw大法官也同意仲裁庭在裁决书所陈述的大原则,就是在违约/毁约被接受终断合约后再也不存在履行的问题,但针对损失的计算还是要估计合约如果持续被履行会是怎么样的结果,因为这是复原大原则。裁决书是这样说:“We think the right view is that when a contract is repudiated, the repudiation accepted, the innocent party can surely say the contract is at an end: its performance is no longer binding: but it (or its ghost) must survive as the datum line for measuring the damages: the innocent party is entitled to be put, financially, in the same position as, but in no better position than, that in which he would have been if the contract had not been repudiated but had come on for performance: and his claim for damages must be based on that method of performing the contract which would have been least profitable to him.”

另笔者也考虑到在本书第三章之第9段所介绍的North Sea Energy Holdings v. Petroleum Authority of Thailand(1997)2 Lloyd's Rep. 418先例(并提到一连串先例,如:D. H. Bain v. Field & Co. Fruit Merchants Ltd. [1920] 5 Lloyd's Rep. 16; British and Benningtons LTd. v. North Western Cachar Tea Co. Ltd. [1922] 13 Lloyd's Rep. 67; Continental Contractors Ltd. v. Medway Oil and Storage Co. [1925] 23 Lloyd's Rep. 124; Bulk Oil [Zug] A. G. v. Sun International Ltd., [1984] 1 Lloyd's Rep. 531),案情不重复,只一提的是 Thomes 大法官说是如果原告是根据违约/毁约时的市场损失(Breach Date Rule 与 Market Rule)提出索赔,就不必再理会违约/毁约导致合约终断后可能出现的事实。但如果原告是根据他与他的供应商的合约计算损失(也就是实际损失),就有必要证明如果没有被告的违约/毁约,供应商是能够在这5年内履行合约以保证原告也能够履行该合约。否则,就代表原告没有办法证明他有损失或这么高的损失。Thomes 大法官是这样说:"There was no evidence on which to make an assessment of a reasonable profit on this long term supply contract for Arabian crude; on the basis of the evidence it was impossible to conclude that MSH(原告)would have made a reasonable profit unless they could have made the profit they had contended for by reference to the Magoil (供应商) offer; MSH were not entitled to substantial damages."

但其他两位共同仲裁员坚持认为在违约/毁约后的损失根据 Breach Date Rule 是不应该考虑如果履行造船合约的话会有怎么样的情况。他们也没有给笔者太多的解释,但更大的问题就是中国船厂根本没有作出任何抗辩。这导致了笔者作为一位仲裁员,不会也不应为任何一方当事人争辩。在提出问题后,不论有无进一步的解释与答案,反正共同仲裁员不接受,笔者也就算了。结果显然是判中国败诉,要赔偿一笔笔者认为极大可能是夸大了的损失。

当然还有不同看法是在事实的认定,就是两位共同仲裁员认为中国船厂如果履行合约,是会按时交船,不会有延误。这就表示不必存在"最低的合约责任为准"的说法。原因在裁决书中有提及说:"Firstly, if the tribunal asks itself the question: 'When, but for the repudiation, would(中国船厂)have delivered the vessels?', in point of law, it has to be assumed that(中国船厂)would diligently have performed the obligations undertaken by them under the respective contracts. Secondly, while, of course, there might have been events by way of force majuere which served to delay timely delivery of the vessels by(中国船厂), we consider that, if there were such events, it was for(中国船厂) to put them in issue."

总结而言,在这个案件也可以看到中国船厂(或任何作为被告的中国公司)不抗辩的危险。如果他作出抗辩并提供一些在期间已经发生了会导致延误交船的不可抗力事件,或是提供他为其他买方在期间造船也都发生延误的证据,并证明他延误比提早交船的可能性超出50%,都很可能会带来不同结果。而这些证据的提供估计不会很困难,因为都是掌握在中国船厂的手中。

第十四章　Breach Date Rule 之二：损失币种的兑换日期

1. Forum – Currency Rule 与 Breach Date Rule 的概述

"违约一天损失规则"(Breach Date Rule)下在本章要介绍另一个问题，就是有关损失"币种的兑换规则"(Date of Conversion Rule)，这里重大的影响就是有关损失应该是以哪一种币种作出计算与兑换。首先简单介绍一下为什么这是一个重大的问题，这是根据损失计算大原则的"复原原则"(*restitutio in integrum*)，即以金钱把受害方恢复到合约被履行的地位。这也在逻辑上带出了这一条 Breach Date Rule，即金钱的损失应该是以违约/毁约一天的计算为准。接下去的问题就是损失计算的金钱到底是什么币种？要知道损失在国际案件中可以是任何国家的币种，甚至多于一种的币种。这一来如果判决只能以一种币种作出(如作出判决国家的币种)，就涉及了兑换的问题，而兑换用的汇率根据 Breach Date Rule 就应该为违约或侵权一天的汇率作为计算。

这里就带来了另一个方面的问题，就是绝大多数国家的法院与法律都要求本国的法院判决必须以本国的币种作出。这一来，如果有关的损失计算所针对的纯粹是一个本土的案件，就不应该有什么问题。至于诉讼所带来的延误，就以利息作出补偿，反正都是为了达到复原的效果。

现在就可以看到涉及国际案件的问题，因为有关的合约会以其他币种结算，如以美元、法郎、日元、人民币，实际的情况是受害方蒙受了其他币种的损失。例如，承租人的违约是造成了受害方船东的船舶损坏，导致修理是在新加坡进行，支付的修理费是新加坡元，购买零件是日元，计算损失就复杂了。如果这些争议是同意了去英国法院，或是中国法院，带来了一个问题是损失计算到底应该是以什么币种为准。如果是以英镑或人民币，就涉及新加坡元与日元的兑换时采用的哪一天的汇率问题。或是另一种做法是英国或中国法院能否根据当地的法律有选择可以本土以外的币种对损失作出判决？这些问题涉及法律需要"肯定性"(certainty)与为了追求每一个不同案件的公平而必须要有"伸缩性"(flexibility)两个理念之间的冲突。

欧共体的欧元看来是一个创举，但近年来的经济危机也可以看到是困难重重。其他还有极少数的例外情况，如南美的萨尔瓦多(El Salvador)就以美元作为国家的币种，也没有自己的中央银行。在这一个现实情况下，就无可避免带来币种之间汇率的波动，这尤其是在经济动荡与严重通货膨胀的时候波动更为剧烈。历史上，在1914年放弃了“黄金标准”（gold standard）后，直到1945年的“布雷顿森林体系”（Bretton Woods Regime），国与国之间的币值波动是不得了。自从1961年开始，特别是在1971年8月美国单方面宣布美元与黄金脱钩之后，币值波动又趋向严重。各种不同的币种再也不会有稳定的汇率，甚至每天都会有波动。光是看近年来的人民币升值，与美元之间的兑换也导致了许多问题。反正是汇率的问题将会长期存在下去，这无可避免所有国际性的商业活动以及其他事项（包括了诉讼）都会受到影响，正如在 The “Volturno”（1921）8 Lloyd’s Rep 449 先例，Sumner 勋爵所说：“fluctuations in foreign exchanges inevitably introduce a speculative element into all transactions and affairs.”

在英国法院（也包括伦敦仲裁），直到1975年之前的法律地位（程序法地位）是作出的判决或裁决必须是以英镑作为币种。这种做法当时与其他国家法院（特别是普通法体系的国家）的做法基本上没有什么不同，如美国法院判决就是以美元作为币种。这在上诉庭的 Manners v. Pearson & Son（1898）1 Ch 581 先例有提到，说：“if the defendants were within the jurisdiction of any other civilized State and were sued there, as they might be, the courts of that State would have to deal with precisely the same problem, and to express in the currency of that State, the amount payable by the defendants instead of expressing it, in the money of the contract.”

这可以被称为是“诉讼地点币种规则”（Forum - Currency Rule）。在 Manners v. Pearson & Son 先例，更加说到英国法院是没有管辖权对英镑以外的币种作出任何命令。这就更加提升到英国法院根本不存在有一个裁量权可以适用外国币种，即使在个别案件中觉得是更加公平。

判决是以英镑作为币种已经解释过，而针对损失计算的币种根据 Breach Date Rule 也是以英镑作为币种，就是在违约/毁约的一天，如果合约的币种或是蒙受的损失是外币，也根据该天的汇率转换为英镑。如果原告提出索赔，告票或索赔请求中的损失金额就必须是这一笔转换后的英镑。

理论上把不同币种的损失转换为英镑也可以使用其他较后日期的汇率，如在审理的一天，或是作出判决的一天，或是真正支付或者执行的一天。但无论是以哪一天的汇率作为转换，都会有问题。显然是在 Breach Date Rule 下，还是违约/毁约的一天是最符合这一规则的做法。这就是英国在1976年以前的法律地位，正如 Denning 大法官在 Cummings v. London Bullion Company（1952）1 KB 327 先例所说：“I take it to be clear law that when a creditor comes to the courts to enforce a debt payable in a foreign currency the creditor is entitled to be put into as good a position as if the debtor had done his duty under the contract and had paid the debt in the foreign currency without the intervention of the courts. To do this, judgment must be given for the creditor for the debt turned into sterling at the rate of exchange ruling at the date when it should have been paid.”

Denning勋爵也在另一个贵族院先例 Re United Railways of Havana and Regla Warehouses(1961)AC 1007说:"if there is one thing that is clear in our law, it is that the claim must be made in sterling and the judgment given in sterling. We do not give judgment in dollars any more than the United States courts give judgments in sterling."

2. Forum – Currency Rule 与 Breach Date Rule 带来的问题

这一个做法很容易就看出问题,就是在造成损失的违约/毁约如果币种是英镑,在几年后受害方胜诉,并向违约方取回这一笔英镑的损失,加上利息,就应该可以做到复原。但如果造成真正损失的是其他币种,但必须马上转换为英镑并在将来根据英镑判决书向违约方取回这一笔损失,但审理期间英镑相比真正损失的币种贬值,受害方可要亏了。当然,如果英镑在审理期间升值,受害方就可以赚了。但两种情况实际上都不应该发生,可现实中就经常会出现。例如在 Di Feidinando v. Simon, Smits & Co(1920)3 KB 409(CA)先例,就涉及意大利原告的真正损失是意大利里拉,其间由于里拉贬值,导致了最后判决的英镑金额是原告原来损失的双倍。

英国法律这一个问题在很长一段时间可以被商业社会所接受,原因是在大英帝国的年代,英镑相对稳定。这里可以节录一些说法,如在 The Baarn(1933)P 251(CA)先例,Scrutton大法官说:"a pound in England is a pound whatever its international purchasing power."另在 Treseder – Griffin v. Co – operative Insurance Society(1956)2 QB 127 CA先例,Denning大法官也说同样的话:"Sterling is the constant unit of value by which in the eye of the law everything else is measured. Prices of commodities may go up or down, other currencies may go up and down, but sterling remains the same."

到了1960年,贵族院在 Re United Railways of Havana and Regla Warehouses(1961)AC 1007先例曾经有机会针对 Forum – Currency Rule 与 Breach Date Rule 作出检讨,但贵族院包括 Denning勋爵拒绝作出改变。该先例涉及一个复杂的争议是有关古巴建造铁路的融资,但卡斯特罗当权之后把该铁路收归国有并作出不足够的赔偿,这导致了被告欠下原告融资债务。而在1947年到1949年,英镑相对美元大幅贬值,这严重影响了该先例而原告试图说服英国法院对这一个 Forum – Currency Rule 与 Breach Date Rule 作出改变。但贵族院拒绝,其中 Denning勋爵是这样说:"it may be said that in this conditions the rule is apt to produce an injustice to a creditor in the United States who is owed money in dollars; because, if he comes to our courts after devaluation, he does not recover sufficient sterling to compensate him for his loss. But I am afraid that, if he chooses to sue in our courts instead of his own, he must put up with the consequences ... coming here, it must accept the rule of our law that we can only give judgment in sterling."

而另有提到在有些情况下为了防止这种危险,受害方是可以在违约/毁约的一天对有关的币种与英镑作出"对冲"(hedge),Reid 勋爵是这样说:"... the original reason for the rule has no application in such a case... dollars lent in America are not a commodity, and if they are not repaid at the due date there can be no question of an American going into the market and buying dollars to replace those which the debtor failed to deliver."

3. 这方面问题对伦敦仲裁的影响与有关先例

但在这一个 1960 年 Re United Railways of Havana and Regla Warehouses(1961) AC 1007 先例之后,由于汇率的波动更趋严重,其中包括了英镑的贬值与波动,导致了英国法院有了不同的看法。这里最明显的就是 Denning 勋爵,他在之后的几个判决显示了他有了与 Re United Railways of Havana and Regla Warehouses 完全不同的看法。第一个是在 The "Teh Hu"(1969)2 Lloyd's Rep 365 先例,案情涉及一个 Lloyd's Open Form 的船舶救助之后对报酬所作出的伦敦仲裁裁决书。原告是日本的 Nippon Salvage 救助公司,他经营的成本是当时在升值的日元,而国际航运在当时通用的币种是美元,但偏偏裁决书按照英国法律所作出的裁决下报酬是以贬值的英镑为准。该案例到了上诉庭,Denning 勋爵认为国际救助与仲裁都不必受到普通法下在这方面的约束,判是仲裁员有权以外币计算救助人的费用并以外币作出裁决书;或者作为替代的计算办法,裁决书以英镑为准,但把英镑贬值的影响对赔偿金额作出相应的提高(that arbitrator had power to calculate salvors' expenses and award in foreign currency and make his award in that currency; alternatively, salvage award should be calculated in sterling figures at time services will conclude and arbitrator should uplift those figures after devaluation)。

Denning 勋爵也提到了当时的金融与仲裁环境,英国普通法必须作出改变并希望不要影响伦敦仲裁一贯受到国际支持的地位,说:"I am afraid that the common - law rule on this subject is most unsatisfactory. It was fixed at the time when the sterling was a stable currency 'of whose true fixed and constant quality there is no fellow in the firmament'. But that enviable state of affairs is gone. Sterling is no longer the most stable currency in the world. It has been devalued more than once. We ought to recognize this. We should modify the common law to meet the new situation."

但上诉庭的多数意见并不同意,换言之,Denning 勋爵只是少数意见。其中 Salmon 大法官是这样说:"For myself I am afraid that if a foreign creditor chooses to enter into a contract governed by English law which obliges him to come to this country seeking payment in sterling, he also must put up with the consequences. For these reasons I would reluctantly dismiss the appeal. I only add that, like Mr Justice Brandon, I am very conscious that in the monetary conditions of today this view of the law may well prejudice the international acceptability of the Lloyd's Form of Salvage Agreement. This is something that I too deplore. The difficulty can, however, easily be overcome for the future, as already indicated, by a fairly simple amendment of the present Lloyd's Form of Salvage Agreement. I cannot agree that the confidence of foreign salvors and owners in the justice administered by our Courts can be shaken by the fact that in this particular case the decision of the Court is in accordance with the established rule of English law."(Salmon 大法官不同意的原因是这一个问题很容易解决,就是在 Lloyd's Open Form 的救助合约中加上一条明示条文,如说明兑换救助人真正损失的币种是要根据在判决或真正支付的一天的汇率作出计算。这一来,明示条文就可以超越普通法的默示地位,根本没有必要对英国法律在这个问题的立场作出改变。)

但过了 4 年后,在另一个先例 The "Kozara"(1973)2 Lloyd's Rep 1,Denning 勋爵的运气就好多了。该先例涉及一个期租合约的争议,租约的币种是美元,双方有了争议去伦敦仲裁并被裁定承租人败诉并要支付金额 62,245.75 美元。但承租人并没有支付,这带来了强制执行的问题。在第一审的高院,Kerr 大法官判是以美元作出的伦敦裁决书是不能被承认与执行的,即使事后把裁决书转换为英镑也不能接受,说:"an award made in England and expressed in a foreign currency was not enforceable in the same manner as a judgment even when that currency was the money of account or even where it was the one with which the transaction had its closest connection ... Nor could such an award be enforced upon conversion of the amount awarded into sterling."

但到了上诉庭,这被改变过来,判是仲裁庭有管辖权作出外币币种的裁决书,只要该币种是与有关合约有最密切与真正的关系,说:"the arbitrators did have jurisdiction to make an award in a foreign currency whenever that was the proper currency of the contract i. e. the currency with which the payment under contract had the closest and most real connection; accordingly, in this case, the arbitrators were entitled to make their award in United States dollars and their award was valid."

以上两个先例是针对伦敦仲裁,笔者还记得当时伦敦海事仲裁员包括"伦敦海事仲裁员协会"(London Maritime Arbitrators Association,简称 LMAA)都对英镑不断贬值,但因为租约或其他海事合约都是以美元计算,造成外国原告前来伦敦仲裁都得不到足够的赔偿而深表忧虑,担心会严重影响伦敦仲裁在国际航运的受欢迎度。

4. 这方面问题与欧共体《罗马公约》的先例

接下去另一个先例是 Denning 勋爵以欧共体法律作为理由回避这一条 Forum – Currency Rule 与 Breach Date Rule,名为 Schorsch Meier v. Hennin (1975) 1 Lloyd's

Rep 1。案情涉及德国的原告索赔一笔供应汽车零件但没有收到的货款,原告要求英国法院以德国马克作为损失计算与判决,并提到了根据《罗马公约》106 条,欧共体国家的成员是可以以英镑以外的其他币种作出判决。该 106 条其实与这一问题关系不大,说:"Each Member State undertakes to authorise, in the currency of the Member State in which the creditor or the beneficiary resides, any payments connected with the movement of goods, services or capital, and any transfers of capital and earnings, to the extent that the movement of goods, services, capital and persons between Member States has been liberalized pursuant to this Treaty."

反正是 Denning 勋爵判是原告胜诉,说:"This is the first case in which we have had actually to apply the Treaty of Rome in these courts. It shows its great effect. It has brought about a fundamental change. Hitherto our English courts have only been able to give judgment in sterling. In future when a debt is incurred by an English debtor to a creditor in one of the Member States— payable in the currency of that state — the English court can give judgment for the amount in that money. This change will have effects to, beyond the Common Market. It has already made us think about of our own laws. As a result, it is my opinion, that, whatever the foreign currency, be US Dollars or Japanese Yen, or any other, the English courts can give judgment in that money where it is the currency of the contract."

但在该上诉庭,也不能说是所有的大法官都是一致的看法。其中 Foster 大法官只给了一个简短的判词说他同意 Denning 勋爵。至于 Lawton 大法官说他感觉关于 Forum - Currency Rule 与 Breach Date Rule,他必须依从一直以来的先例,就算要作出改变也不是他的责任或权力,说:"it is disturbing to find that a rule which does injustice to a foreign trader is found on archaic legal nonsense of this kind. It is however my duty to apply the law, not to reform it."

针对这一条 Forum - Currency Rule 与 Breach Date Rule 的改变,到此只是停留在伦敦仲裁与《罗马公约》的说法。真正在普通法作出改变还是需要在贵族院作出决定,毕竟一直以来的先例(包括 Re United Railways of Havana and Regla Warehouses [1961] AC 1007 先例)是在贵族院作出的。

5. 作出根本性改变的贵族院先例:Miliangos v. Frank(Textiles)

这一机会终于在 Miliangos v. Frank(Textiles)(1976)1 Lloyd's Rep 201 先例到来。该先例的案情涉及瑞士的原告出售了一些布料给英国的被告,但被告没有作出货价的支付,这导致原告在英国法院(也就是被告的所在地)作出诉讼,而索赔的金额是以瑞士法郎为准的。贵族院以多数意见同意作出对 15 年前在 Re United Railways of

Havana and Regla Warehouses 的判决的改变，其中 Wilberforce 勋爵与另外三位大法官的总结判决是："The rule adopted by the House of Lords in Re United Railways of Havana and Regla Warehouses to the effect that an English Court could not give judgment for payment of a sum of foreign currency could not now be justified in view of the change which had come over the 'foreign exchange rate' situation generally and the position of sterling in particular in the course of the last 15 years, and must be abandoned."

针对一直以来的 Breach Date Rule, Miliangos v. Frank (Textiles) 先例也把币种的兑换日期改为了所谓的 Payment - Date Rule，也就是支付一天。这可以节录《McGregor on Damages》(18th edn, 2009 年) 之 16 - 029 段：

"In fact, it was not the date of judgment that was chosen by their Lordships but the date of payment in the sense of the date when the court authorizes the claimant to enforce the judgment by levying execution for a sum expressed in sterling. The choice, said Lord Wilberforce, 'is between (i) the date of action brought, (ii) the date of judgment, (iii) the date of payment' in the sense indicated. Of these the date of payment undoubtedly 'gets nearest to securing to the creditor exactly what he bargained for'. Lord Fraser put the matter thus: 'Any conversion date earlier than the date of payment would, in my opinion, be open to the same objection as the breach date, namely that it would necessarily leave a considerable interval of time between the conversion date and the date of payment. During that interval currency fluctuations might cause the sterling award to vary appreciably from the sum in foreign currency to which the creditor was entitled. In my opinion, it would not be justifiable to disturb the existing rule of taking the breach date, merely to substitute for it some other date rather nearer to the date of payment but still more or less distant from it. If the date of raising an action in this country were taken for conversion, a period of a year or more might easily elapse, allowing for appeals, before payment was made. The date of judgment would be better but there seems no reason why one should stop short of the latest practicable date, which seems to be the date when the court authorizes enforcement of the judgment.'

Lord Fraser indeed rightly pointed out that the conversion date should theoretically be at the still later point in time of the date of actual payment of the debt by the defendant as this would give to the claimant exactly the cost in sterling of buying the foreign currency, 'but theory must yield to practical necessity to this extent that, if the judgment has to be enforced in this country, it must be converted before enforcement.'"

贵族院唯一持不同意见的是 Simon 勋爵，他认为汇率波动的问题已经存在了很长的一段时间，其中在 Re United Railways of Havana and Regla Warehouses 的先例中，贵族院也有考虑到，所以这不足为一个作出改变的原因。此外，Simon 勋爵认为更重要的原因是这方面的改变应该留待议会立法改变，说："The main ground of my dissent from the opinion of my noble and learned friends is that this type of issue is unsuitable for law reform by judiciary. It is the sort of case where, in my view, a wide range of advice, official especially but also commercial, is required. The training and experience of a Judge is unsuitable for this type of decision – making unaided: his circumspection is too narrow; his very qualities of keen perception of his immediate problem tend to mitigate against sound judgment of the wider and more general issues involved. But if Courts are to undertake legislative responsibilities, something might be done to equip them better for the type of decision – making which is involved. Official advice and a balanced executive view might be made available by a law officer or his counsel acting as *amicus curiae*. I venture to suggest consideration of some such machinery."

这一个重要的先例在后来的枢密院也有提到,在 Trinidad Homes Developers Ltd v. IMH Investments Ltd(2003) UKPC 85, Hoffman 勋爵是这样说:"The writ ... asked simply for payment in United States currency. Judgments in this form have been possible since Miliangos v. George Frank(Textiles) Ltd, a decision of the House of Lords which has been followed in Trinidad and Tobago. The fact that the judgment may express the obligation in US Dollars does not necessarily mean that a defendant has to pay in that currency. It means that US Dollars are the unit of account for measuring the sum which has to be paid. If the defendant pays in the different currency(e. g. dollars of Trinidad and Tobago) they must be the equivalent of the US Dollar debt at the time of payment."

由于在 Miliangos 先例中容许判决以外币作出,推翻了 Forum – Currency Rule, 自然存在利息的问题,因为每一种币种都会有不同的利率。这一点也被明确下来是要按照外币或被认定币种的利率为准。法院是这样说:"A Swiss creditor, kept out of money he ought to get in Swiss francs, would reasonably borrow in Switzerland his replacement Swiss francs pending judgment. What he would have to pay to borrow them would have nothing whatever to do with the English sterling bank rate or the basic English lending rate ... The approach of English law should be: if you opt for a judgment in foreign currency, for better or worse you commit yourself to whatever rate of interest obtains in the context of the currency."在 The "Texaco Melbourne"(1994)1 Lloyd's Rep 473 先例,上诉庭就因为认定了损失计算的币种是加纳塞地(cedis),所以利息也是加纳塞地的利率。在一定程度上,一个币种如果在下跌,它的利率会相应提高。这可能会对冲部分损失,但这并不是一定的。例如,在 2010 年人民币相对港币是强势,但反而是人民银行在加息而由于港币是与低息甚至零息的美元挂钩,所以不存在加息的可能。

6. 侵权在 Miliangos 先例前的法律地位

针对侵权,在贵族院的 Miliangos v. Frank(Textiles)(1976)1 Lloyd's Rep 201 先例

之前的法律地位,也是根据同样的大原则。但这种案子相比合约方面少得多,加上会涉及币种与汇率的问题,通常是国际性的侵权。这种案件在以前的年代也不多,有的话往往也是涉及船舶,如船舶碰撞。在船舶碰撞,如果受害方船舶没办法修理,如全损。这一来侵权与造成损失的一天就是 Breach Date Rule 下的一天,把外国币种的损失转换为英镑也就是该天为准。这在 The "Volturno" (1921) 8 Lloyd's Rep 449 的船舶碰撞先例中,Sumner 勋爵说:"if the damages were such as need not be repaired at all, the whole loss might have been measured by the immediate depreciation of the ship . . . if there was any conversion into sterling, it would have been calculated at the rate current at the time of the collision."

但如果船舶的损坏要进行修理,这一来就表示受害方船舶的损失是指支付修理费的时候,因为这才是造成损失的一天。这方面的先例是 The "Baarn" (1933) P 251 (CA)。

虽然船舶碰撞的一天与后来作出修理的一天肯定有不同,甚至会隔了很长一段时间,但在 Breach Date Rule 下,没有有关的先例表明是以哪一天 Breach Date 的汇率为准。估计是因为国际侵权的案例不多,或两个不同日子的汇率差别并不显著,不值得诉讼。

7. Miliangos 先例后的进一步问题

重要的贵族院先例 Miliangos v. Frank (Textiles) (1976) 1 Lloyd's Rep 201 把 Breach Date Rule 改变为 Payment - Date Rule,但还是没有解决太多的问题或者又带来了新的问题。如在该先例,案情是针对债务,所以在违约或侵权的损失索赔案件是否适用,还是会有争议(有关债务与损失的不同请看本书第十一章)。虽然在 Miliangos 先例中贵族院表示了也应该延伸去违约与侵权的案例,但这也只是"说说而已"(*obiter*),并不能作为约束性的判决,因为根本在该案件下没有需要针对。所以,在该先例中 Simon 勋爵认为这一个大问题不应该通过案例解决而是应该立法,有他的道理。通过案例只能针对案情作出有约束力的判决,与案情无关法院即使有说法也只是没有约束力的 *obiter*。但通过立法,就可以全面考虑还会有什么问题,而好的立法是可以非常全面地针对,而且有针对的全部是有约束性的法律地位。

其他 Miliangos 先例没有解决的问题是在该先例下,原告是瑞士公司,合约适用法是瑞士法,应支付的钱是瑞士法郎,而合约结算的钱也是瑞士法郎。这一来,Miliangos 先例判是以瑞士法郎作为币种作出支付而不是转换为英镑看来是合情合理得多。但许多国际性的争议,不会是这么一面倒指向一个国家。例如,原告是中国公司,合约结算的钱是美元,这一来,Miliangos 先例的 Payment - Date Rule 是否适用就还是不肯定。

再下一个没有解决的问题是到底以英镑或是其他币种作出索赔与判决是否是原

告的选择权,或是被告也可以坚持某一个币种? 如果在某一个币种被认定后,法院或者仲裁员是否可以强制性适用,不理会原告同意与否? 这里涉及的问题是在其间英镑贬值时,外国的原告就不喜欢这一 Forum - Currency Rule 与 Breach Date Rule 了,认为他的损失得不到充分的赔偿了。但反过来如果其间英镑增值,就轮到原告喜欢 Forum - Currency Rule 与 Breach Date Rule 了,但被告就不喜欢了。

在下一个更大的问题,就是根据 Miliangos 先例可以摒弃英镑的转换与判决并改为使用外国的币种,那应该是什么币种? 较早已经提到,在 Miliangos 先例的话显然这一币种就应该为瑞士法郎,但其他的案件就不会这么简单了。在一个普通的违约案件,就往往会涉及至少三种不同的币种。第一个情况是合约结算的币种,这里更会有情况是合约是有多过一种的币种作为结算。如 Lesotho Highland Development Authority v. Impreglio SpA(2005)UKHL 43 先例,案情涉及非洲建造最大的水坝工程,合约约定的币种是意大利里拉、英镑、法郎与马克的一揽子货币。第二种情况是原告或者受害方真正作出支付的币种。而第三种就是原告或者受害方自己的币种,如中国公司就会是人民币,日本公司就会是日元。这第三种与第二种情况不同之处就是中国公司会在违约或者侵权造成损失时以其他币种作出支付,但还是会通过人民币来转换为外币。所以,中国公司作为原告还是可以说是他蒙受的真正损失是人民币。选择哪一个币种作为索赔与判决的重要性就是在不同币种之间也是有很大的汇率波动的,不仅是在英镑与其他币种之间。这一个由 Miliangos 先例带来的问题带来了一连串的案例,其中有两个著名先例先后去到贵族院:The "Despina R" and "Folias"(1979)1 Lloyd's Rep 1 与 The "Texaco Melbourne"(1994)1 Lloyd's Rep 473。

8. Miliangos 先例后的发展

8.1　Miliangos 先例中的 Payment - Date Rule 是否适用在违约与侵权?

在 Miliangos v. Frank(Textiles)(1976)1 Lloyd's Rep 201 先例后不久,很快的 6 个星期后就有了一个违约的案例,名为 Jean Kraut AG v. Albany Fabrics Ltd(1976)2 Lloyd's Rep 350。案情涉及货物买卖合约,涉及瑞士法郎,而且瑞士法郎相比英镑在违约到审理期间汇率上涨。在原来的索赔请求中,原告按照一直以来的 Breach Date Rule 把该笔瑞士法郎按违约一天的汇率转换为英镑进行索赔。当原告代表律师知道了 Miliangos 先例的判决后,马上申请修改索赔请求,从英镑改为瑞士法郎。被告的抗辩显然是说 Miliangos 先例只能针对债务,而不是违约的损失。高院的 Eveleigh 大法官判是 Miliangos 先例完全适用。但这里还是有一点不明朗之处,就是该合约是适用瑞士法律而不是英国法律。

可以说这方面是一直到了 The "Maratha Envoy"(1977)1 Lloyd's Rep 217 的上诉庭先例才有了明确,该著名先例涉及滞期费的赔付是否以美元计算与判决,而租约是适用英国法。这是 Denning 勋爵所说的:"in contracts where the currency of the contract is a foreign currency, but the proper law of the contract is English law, the Court can and should give judgment in the foreign currency: and this is both when it is for a debt due under the contract ... or damages for breach of contract."

至于 Payment - Date Rule 在侵权案件的适用,这稍后在贵族院的 The "Despina R" and "Folias" (1979) 1 Lloyd's Rep 1 先例有明确适用,这在本章的 8.3.1 段有介绍。

8.2 Payment - Date Rule 是原告的选择权或是强制性适用?

在 Miliangos v. Frank (Textiles) (1976) 1 Lloyd's Rep 201 先例也没有明确的另一个问题就是 Payment - Date Rule 是否只是原告的选择权。在后来的一个先例 Barclays Bank International Ltd v. Levin Bros (Bradford) Ltd (1977) 1 Lloyd's Rep 51 中,看来 Mocatta 大法官认为是原告的选择权。但在 The "Maratha Envoy" (1977) 1 Lloyd's Rep 217 的上诉庭先例被 Denning 勋爵所明确了 Payment - Date Rule 是强制性的,否则会对被告不公平,说:"Once it is recognized that a judgment can be given in a foreign currency, justice requires that it should be given in every case where the currency of the contract is a foreign currency: otherwise one side or the other will suffer unfairly by the fluctuation of the exchange."

这一个说法也是被著名的 Sir Roy Goode 教授所认同:《Payment Obligations in Commercial and Financial Transactions》(London, Sweet & Maxwell, 1983 年)。

8.3 损失支付以何种币种作出?

在 Miliangos v. Frank (Textiles) (1976) 1 Lloyd's Rep 201 先例并没有明确的问题也在 The "Maratha Envoy" (1977) 1 Lloyd's Rep 217 的先例中被 Denning 勋爵认为是应该以合约中被双方同意结算的币种为准来进行支付。但这一问题也不能就这么说死,如合约会是没有双方同意结算的币种,如实物交换的合约或是双方同意以一揽子货币的结算。所以在 The "Maratha Envoy" 先例后,虽然有了依从的先例如 The "Pearl Merchant" (1979) 1 Lloyd's Rep 123 与 The "Doric Chariot" (1979) 1 Lloyd's Rep 123,最后还是要贵族院的 The "Despina R" and "Folias" (1979) 1 Lloyd's Rep 1 先例中明确。该贵族院先例是两个不同案件同时上诉去贵族院,因为针对的都是同一个问题,也就是关系到 Miliangos 先例的适用。

8.3.1 侵权损失的币种

针对 The "Despina R",是一个侵权案件,涉及两艘希腊船舶在上海港外碰撞。针对责任方面,双方同意了责任的分摊是由 Despina R 轮承担 15%,Eleftherotria 轮承担 85%。至于在损失方面,由于原告 Despina R 轮所花的修理费用以及修理期间的延误(也就是侵权所造成的损失)涉及人民币、日元与美元,这就涉及侵权是否适用 Payment - Date Rule 的问题。在贵族院,明确了 Payment - Date Rule 也适用在侵权案件并摒弃了 Breach Date Rule。至于侵权案件的币种,在一定程度上比违约案件的币种更加难以决定。因为在违约案件，至少会有一个双方同意的币种作为起点的考虑。贵族院的 Wilberforce 勋爵认为侵权损失计算的币种一般是以受害方营运所用的币种为准，而即使他要花费其他币种（如支付人民币的修理费用），他也会以他所营运的币种进行兑换，说："My Lords, in my opinion, this question can be solved by applying the normal principles which govern the assessment of damages in cases of tort (I shall deal with contract cases in the second appeal). These are the principles of *restitutio in integrum* and that of the reasonable foreseeability of the damage sustained. It appears to me that a plaintiff, who normally conducts his business through a particular currency, and who, when other currencies are immediately involved, uses his own currency to obtain those currencies, can reasonably say that the loss he sustains is to be measured not by the immediate currencies in which the loss first emerges but by the amount of his own currency, which in the normal course of operation, he uses to obtain those currencies. This is the currency in which his loss is felt, and is the currency which it is reasonably foreseeable he will have to spend."

但接下去的案件表示这一方面还是有不明确，首先要介绍的先例是 The "Lash Atlantico" (1987) 2 Lloyd's Rep. 114。案情涉及 Lash Atlantico 轮撞了一艘挂靠在泊位的 Manina III 轮并导致后者严重损坏，责任方面非常清楚，但争议是在损失计算。受害方的希腊船东（Manina III Shipping Company）要求计算损失的币种是美元，这是可以理解的，毕竟在国际航运中都习惯以美元结算。但被告 Lash Atlantico 轮船东抗辩指币种应该是希腊的德拉克马（drachmas），而在其间德拉克马贬值。该船舶是交给希腊公司作为船舶代理人管理的，并且在被告要求原告所交出的文件披露中显示了该公司的营运与资产负债表全部是以德拉克马作为币种。这就带来了不肯定的审理，在高院，Sheen 大法官判决计算损失的币种应当是德拉克马。但去了上诉庭，多数意见判决以美元为准，说："it was impossible and would be quite unrealistic to conclude that the plaintiffs did not feel this loss in dollars simply because they did not manage the vessel themselves but had it managed through their managing agents; the reality was that the plaintiffs' trading venture in the form of this vessel was conducted exclusively in U. S. dollars; it was irrelevant in what currency the resulting accounts were draw up, in order to give a trading picture of the vessel during a particular year when that currency had no viable commercial significance whatever; everything pointed to U. S. dollars as the appropriate currency and the appeal would be allowed."

但上诉庭持不同意见的 Croom－Johnson 大法官说：

"The collision was on Feb. 23 1979; the plaintiffs' loss took place then. The quantification would clearly take some time, and it was met in several different currencies, the agents buying with dollars in the local currencies, which needed to be used in order to discharge liabilities in, say, Rumania ... The payment of all the losses incurred as a result of this collision would first be met by the managing agents in the way that I have described. The dollars were the agents' dollars and not the plaintiffs'.

But I think one can test the position of the plaintiffs in this way. If, for example, there had been a theoretical settling up between them and the plaintiffs needed to reimburse the managing agents for any expenditure which they had made in the course of the year for the various losses, repairs and incidental expenses caused by this collision, they could not have made them in dollars because they did not have any. If they had wanted to reimburse the managing agents in dollars, they would have had to have bought them, and they would have had to have bought them with drachmas; that would have represented the loss which the shipping company in fact incurred."

另一个要介绍的先例是 The "Transoceanica Francesca" and "Nicos V"(1987)2 Lloyd's Rep. 155,也是涉及船舶的碰撞。原告的 Transoceanica Francesca 轮船东是意大利公司,起初索赔请求的币种是意大利里拉(lire)。但在 3 年半后,原告申请修改请求,变为以美元索赔。显然,在其间里拉贬值。国际航运与美元的关系十分紧密,这包括在碰撞的时候,该船舶是正在履行租约的,租金收入是美元。但从原告披露的文件看来有许多证据显示了与里拉的密切关系,包括银行账户只允许持有美元进账最高额度为 110 万美元,超过的部分需要自动转为意大利里拉。这方面看来是重要的,正如对方大律师指出:"the dollar accounts have the appearance of being used merely as a matter of convenience and that sums were being converted into lire. For example, the 1976 accounts how that at the end of the year the balance was transferred out of dollars into a lire account, but in truth the plaintiffs 'felt their loss' in their own currency, namely lire. Their ships where insured against loss in lire. Those ships were regarded as lire assets. There were frequent conversions from dollars into lire and, save for the balance in hand in the dollar account, the plaintiffs regarded lire as the currency of their own accounts."

另外,看来重要之处是原告原来提出的索赔请求是里拉,隔了很久才修改为美元。高院的 Sheen 大法官是这样说:"It is, indeed, significant that the claim was advanced in lire in 1982. At that time the decision of the House of Lords in the Despina R, (1979)1 Lloyd's Rep. 1 was well in the mind of all those practicing in this field. Furthermore, as the Admiralty Registrar pointed out, one asks oneself whether a commercial organization such as the plaintiffs would have put forward their claim in lire if their true operating currency was U. S. dollars."

最后高院的判决是以原告的损失币种应当以里拉来支付。

8.3.2 违约损失的币种

至于在另一个案例 The "Folias",是一个期租租约(租期为一个从地中海去南美洲包括巴西的回程航次)的案例,并在伦敦仲裁作出裁决。案情是由于船舶冷藏机坏了(这涉及不适航,是船东的责任),导致货物(洋葱)的损坏。最后导致了承租人要对货方作出赔偿，货方（巴西收货人）索赔的损失有关的币种是巴西雷亚尔（Brazilian cruzeiros）。在承租人赔付之后，再向船东通过伦敦仲裁要求补偿。由于原告承租人是一家法国公司，他认为自己真正的损失币种是法郎，至于赔付巴西收货人的币种也是以法郎去兑换。可以说，法郎就是原告的“本土货币”（home currency）。这一来，案例涉及的币种就有三个：一个是租约的美元，另一个是赔付给巴西收货人的巴西雷亚尔，还有一个就是原告索赔的法郎。在伦敦仲裁，仲裁庭判是以法郎作为裁决书的币种。显然在其间由于汇率波动，以哪一种币种作出裁决是有实质区别的。

在 The “Folias”，贵族院支持了仲裁庭的裁决以法郎作为币种。贵族院没有说较早前判的两个先例说主要考虑的币种应该是合约中双方同意结算的币种是错误的：Jean Kraut AG v. Albany Fabrics Ltd（1976）2 Lloyd's Rep 350 与 The “Maratha Envoy”（1977）1 Lloyd's Rep 217。但贵族院的 Wilberforce 勋爵认为针对这一问题是要有弹性，反正就要找出最能够代表原告感觉到损失的一种货币。这也不一定是原告“马上面对的损失币种”（Immediate Loss Currency）（在该案例中为巴西雷亚尔）的币种。Wilberforce 勋爵是这样说：“a flexible rule in which account must be taken of the circumstances in which the loss arose, in which the loss was converted into a money sum, and in which it was felt by the plaintiff.”可以说，贵族院明确下来适用的币种就是原告感觉到损失的币种，这带出了“Loss Felt Currency Rule”的规则。

针对巴西雷亚尔与法郎，选择后者的原因也可以节录 Wilberforce 勋爵所说如下：“I think it must follow from this that their loss, which they claim as damages, was the discharge of the receivers' claim, together with the legal and other expenses they incurred. They discharged all these by providing francs – until they provided the francs to meet the receivers' claim they suffered no loss. Then secondly was this loss the kind of loss which, under the contract, they were entitled to recover against the owners? The answer to this is provided by the arbitrators' finding that it was reasonable to contemplate that the charterers, being a French corporation and having their place of business of Paris, would have to use French francs to purchase other currencies to settle cargo claims arising under the bills of lading. So in my opinion the charterers' loss was, according to normal principle, the sum of French francs which they paid.”

8.4　代表原告感觉到损失的规则带来的进一步问题

The“Despina R” and “Folias”（1979）1 Lloyd's Rep 1 先例又带来了进一步的问题，主要有两个方面。第一个方面就是不像以前的 Breach Date Rule，最终的判决或裁决会以何种币种作出失去了肯定性。即使原告提出的索赔是根据一个币种，但如果被告提出抗辩，最后会是怎么样判决或者裁决也难以肯定，因为这一规则本身就不肯定。如在 The “Folias”（1979）1 Lloyd's Rep 1 先例，因为原告是一家法国公司，判是最感觉到的损失是法郎。但如果原告是一家跨国公司，这就不好说了。第二个方面的进一步问题是看来对原告有所偏袒，这在一些后来的案例中也可以看到最后的判决多数就是接受了原告提出的币种。这里也可以想得到,因为到底哪一种币种最能代表他所感觉到的损失只有听原告的一面之词。被告虽然可以通过要求原告作出文件披露,希望从中能够找到一些资料抗辩原告索赔的币种。但这做法毕竟还是不容易,除了会涉及大量的文件披露而导致诉讼的昂贵与延误,也要同时考虑到特别是在今天的国际仲裁甚至法院都在大力压制文件披露的申请。

反正是在 The "Folias"先例后,还是有源源不断的案例,如 The "Dione"(1980)2 Lloyd's Rep 577;The "Federal Huron"(1985)2 Lloyd's Rep 189;The "Kefalonia Wind"(1986)1 Lloyd's Rep. 273;Metallhandel JA Magnus BV v. Ardfields Transport Ltd(1988)1 Lloyd's Rep 197;The "Texaco Melbourne"(1994)1 Lloyd's Rep 473;The "Mosconici"(2001)2 Lloyd's Rep 313;Barings plc v. Coopers & Lybrand(2003)EWHC 2371(Ch);Nomura International plc v. Credit Suisse First Boston International(2003)EWHC 160;Virani Ltd v. Manuel Revert y Cia SA(2004)2 Lloyd's Rep 14 等,其中不少就是针对这方面进一步的问题。

8.5 倾向原告选择币种作为索赔的有关先例

在上小段所举的案例中许多都是根据原告所要求的币种作出判决。例如,在 The "Dione"(1980)2 Lloyd's Rep 577 先例,船东作为原告向承租人提出索赔。承租人认为币种应该是阿根廷比索(pesos),这对承租人有利因为在有关的期间比索大幅度贬值。但船东是要求美元作为币种,虽然美元也并非是他的本土货币(原告是希腊船东)。理由是起初的损失(阿根廷小工的超时工资)船东是以美元购买比索作出支付。结果是法院支持原告船东的请求。

另在 The "Federal Huron"(1985)2 Lloyd's Rep 189 先例,案情涉及一批大豆的 C&F 买卖,在法国卸港被发现货损,这导致收货人(是一家法国公司)向船东提出索赔。原告收货人是要求以美元作为币种计算损失,因为这是他买卖大豆业务所结算的货币。但船东认为法国法郎才是收货人真正感觉到的损失币种。其间,美元对法国法郎升值,所以带来了争议。Bingham 大法官支持原告收货人的请求,说:"I conclude that the cargo receivers' main claim for damage to the cargo can only be fairly expressed in dollars. They had paid dollars to buy the cargo. I have no reason to suppose that they sold francs to finance this payment, although they may have done so. But the evidence is overwhelming that the cargo receivers treated soya beans as a dollar commodity. In purchases of raw beans the dollar was always the money of account."

另介绍的是 Virani Ltd v. Manuel Revert y Cia SA(2004)2 Lloyd's Rep 14 先例,案情涉及一个买卖合约的违约索赔。原告卖方是一家英国公司,而被告是一家西班牙公司,双方的合约是以西班牙比塞塔(pesetas)结算(买卖的布料是 285 比塞塔一米)。原告提供证据说明他是以美元作为营运的币种,包括这批布料是向巴基斯坦购买后转售给被告,支付的是美元。但被告认为西班牙比塞塔才是最能代表原告感觉到损失的币种,毕竟这也是合约结算的币种。但法院支持原告,认为双方订约的时

候应该料想到在国际贸易中美元才是有最紧密与真正的关联,其中上诉庭 Ward 大法官说:

"The Judge's finding that the defendant company would in all probability know that anyone who ventured into the Pakistan market would be dealing in dollars and not in rupees in a conclusion which cannot be challenged and, to be fair to Mr. Pickering(被告代表大律师), he did not seek to challenge that part of the judgment. It is then a matter of inference from that finding of fact as to whether it was reasonably within the contemplation of the parties that this international trader would have protected itself by ventures into the exchange market to buy forward and protect against fluctuating exchange currencies.

The fact is that the defendant is a large dealerin this cloth and is as familiar as the claimant with the vagaries of exchange rates rising and falling. It must be within the reasonable contemplation of anyone engaged in foreign transactions to expect that steps will be taken to protect the value of the particular transaction by covering it in the way the claimant did. It thus seems to me to be an irresistible inference that it was within the contemplation of the parties that dollars would be the currency which most closely and truly would express any loss suffered by the seller if the buyer did not complete."

可以说在这一方面少有的是对原告不利的著名先例就是 The "Texaco Melbourne"(1994)1 Lloyd's Rep 473,但它涉及非常特殊的事实(在本章 8.7 段有详细介绍),不大可能在其他违约案件中出现,所以改变不了这一个最能代表受害人感觉到损失的币种问题对原告有利。另也有一些案例是原告在诉讼期间把原来索赔的币种作出修改,看来也会带来一定程度的不良影响:The "Transoceanica Francesca" and "Nicos V"(1987)2 Lloyd's Rep. 155; Barings plc v. Coopers & Lybrand(2003) EWHC 2371(Ch)。

8.6 其他有关原告感觉到损失的币种的先例介绍

首先介绍的是 Ozalid Group (Export) Ltd v. African Continental Bank (1979) 2 Lloyd's Rep 231 先例,它是在 The "Folias"先例之后 4 个月作出决定,判是原告"正常营运的币种"(normal operating currency)就是判决所采用的币种。但在另一个先例 Metallhandel JA Magnus BV v. Ardfields Transport Ltd,虽然原告是要求以正常营业币种作为损失的计算,但也没有被法院接受。Gatehouse 大法官是这样说:

"The questions then seem to be, as far as I can see, first, in what currency will an award of damages 'most truly express the plaintiffs loss?' and, secondly, whether the parties must be taken reasonably to have had such other currency in contemplation.

The fact that a foreign plaintiff will necessarily have his bank accounts in, keep his financial books in, and fund his purchases of other currencies from the currency of his own country cannot automatically result in an award of damages in our Courts in that currency. It must depend on the particular circumstances of the case.

The facts in The "Folias" which led the House of Lords to decide that French francs, not Brazilian cruzeiros, still less US dollars(which was the currency of the charter – party), was the appropriate currency for the award in that case are set out in particular at pp. 8 and 430e – g. They are very different, of course, from the facts here, which are essentially simple.

In my judgment, the parties to this contract cannot be said to have had in contemplation that damages payable by the first defendants to the plaintiffs, if damage or loss of the goods should occur for which they were responsible, should be measured in guilders. I accordingly make an award in sterling. . ."

在 Barings plc v. Coopers & Lybrand(2003)EWHC 2371(Ch)先例,案情涉及著名的金融事件导致了百年老店的霸菱银行倒闭。起因是 1995 年 2 月因新加坡霸菱期货公司的总裁兼首席交易员尼克李森(Nick Lesson)预期经济萧条已久的日本股市将自谷底反弹,便在 1994 年期间陆续持有高达 4 万个新加坡国际金融交易所(SIMEX)即大阪证券交易所(OSE)的日经指数期货契约的多头部位[投资人手上持有金融商品(股票、债券等)称为多头部位。此意味投资人看好商品未来行情(上涨),因此会在市场建立多头部位(购买金融商品)],以及日本长期公债(JGB)与欧洲日元期货契约。但日本经济却因遭逢阪神大地震及金融机构超贷倒闭事件而继续疲惫不振,终于在 1 年内暴跌近 4000 点。该事件爆发后,当天日经下跌 1000 点,激发了机构法人的停损性卖盘,而日经更是一蹶不振。这个案例涉及新加坡霸菱期货公司起诉他的会计师索赔金额庞大的损失,理由是会计师应该可以在更早的时间觉察到尼克李森这种没有授权与危险的交易,从而让新加坡霸菱期货公司上层的董事局可以及时采取保障措施。显然,新加坡霸菱期货公司作出的损失支付是日元,所以在原来的索赔请求中的损失币种也是日元。但在诉讼期间日元下挫,这导致了原告申请修改索赔请求为新加坡元。理由是新加坡霸菱期货公司是一家新加坡的公司,所有正常营运的币种是新加坡元,包括支付员工的工资以及目前在清盘的币种。但法院判决以日元为准,这看来与下一个介绍的先例 The "Texaco Melbourne"(1994)1 Lloyd's Rep 473 也有一点不一致。

8.7 对原告不利的贵族院先例:The "Texaco Melbourne"

现在介绍另一个针对这方面的非常重要的贵族院先例,就是 The "C Melbourne"(1994)1 Lloyd's Rep 473。案情涉及原告(加纳共和国政府)买了一船燃油,由被告拥有的 Texaco Melbourne 轮来承运。该批燃油准备从加纳一个港口的炼油厂运到加纳另一个卸港后分批转售给其他的油公司。但这批燃油并没有最终运到该卸港,这导致了加纳政府向船东提出索赔。这方面的责任是明确的,唯一有争议的就是损失的计算。特别是到底计算的币种是以美元或者以加纳的塞地(cedis)。在有关期间(1982 年的违约到 1991 年的审理,长达 9 年),塞地的币值有了灾难性的下跌。在 1982 年违约发生的时候,汇率为 2. 75 塞地折合 1 美元,加纳政府的损失就高达

2,886,178 美元。但到了审理的一天,根据塞地兑美元的汇率,得出的美元金额只是 21,165 美元。所以,加纳政府希望是以 Breach Date Rule 来计算它的损失,但被告船东显然希望以 Payment - Date Rule。加纳政府的索赔请求是美元,这显然不是原告的“本土货币”(home currency)或正常营运币种,而在该案例唯一扯得上美元关系的就是如果要为该批燃油在市场上购买一批替代燃油,最近与最可能的市场是在意大利,支付的价格必须是以美元。而被告的抗辩是指加纳的塞地才是“原告感觉到的损失”(loss felt by the plaintiff)。结果在该案例,大法官之间也有不同的看法。在高院的第一审,Webster 大法官判决以美元为准。到了上诉庭,以多数意见把该判决推翻,但其中的 Hirst 大法官持相反意见。最后到了贵族院,以一致的意见支持上诉庭的多数判决。换言之,加纳政府只能取回 21,165 美元的损失,这笔钱恐怕远不足以支付自己与对方的律师费。

在该先例中,Goff 勋爵把这一方面英国法律的演变作出简单的介绍,十分值得细看,这里节录如下:

“Before the decision of your Lordships' House in Miliangos v. George Frank, (Textiles) Ltd., (1976) 1 Lloyd's Rep. 201, it was accepted that a money judgment could in this country only be expressed in sterling. It followed that if, for example, an action was brought in this country to recover a debt which was expressed to be in a foreign currency, the amount of the debt in that currency had to be converted into sterling as at the date when it fell due, and judgment was then entered in the sterling sum so ascertained (see In re United Railways of Havana and Regla Warehouses Ltd., [1961] A. C. 1007). Likewise as award of damages had to be assessed in sterling as at the date of breach, so the judgment could be entered in sterling. This became known as the **breach date conversion rule**. However, as currencies began to float in the middle of this century, sterling itself began to depreciate against other important currencies, notably against the U. S. dollar. In the result, not only did parties (notably those engaged in shipping) tend to contract with reference to the U. S. dollar instead of the pound sterling, but it also began to be perceived, by arbitrators and lawyers practicing on the City of London, that the effect of the breach date conversion rule was to render the English jurisdiction increasingly unattractive to businessmen. In consequence, arbitrators responded by making their awards in foreign currencies, a practice which was upheld by the Court of Appeal (see Jugoslavenska Oceanska Plovidba v. Castle Investment Co. Inc., [1973] 2 Lloyd's Rep. 1); and in the end, as is well known, in the Miliangos case (1976) 1 Lloyd's Rep. 201, this House decided to depart from the Havana Railways case (1961) A. C. 1007, and to hold that it was open to an English Court to give judgment for a sum of money expressed in a foreign currency fell to be identified. Appeals in two cases, one concerned with damages in tort (Owners of M. V. Eleftherotria v. Owners of M. V. Despina R. [The “Despina R.”]) and one with damages in contract (Services Europe

Atlantique Sud(SEAS) of Paris v. Stockholms Rederiaktiebolag Svea of Stockholm [The "Folias"]),were heard together by your Lordships' House(1979)1 Lloyd's Rep. 1. It is the second of these cases which is most relevant to the problem facing your Lordships in the present appeal. In that case, Lord Wilberforce expressed the applicable principles as follows. First, it is necessary to ascertain whether there is an intention, to be derived from the terms of the contract that damages for breach of contract should be awarded in any particular currency or currencies. In the absence of any such intention, 'the damage should be calculated in the currency in which the loss was felt by the plaintiff or' (adopting the words of Lord Denning, M. R. in the Court of Appeal [1978] 1 Lloyd's Rep. 535) **'which most truly expresses his loss'**. The application of that principle in The "Folias" itself is revealing, and indeed is of considerable relevance to the present case. The claim in that case arose under a charterparty, under which Swedish shipowners chartered their vessel to French charterers for a round voyage from the Mediterranean to the East Coast of South America. The charterers shipped a cargo of onions at Valencia in Spain for carriage to Brazilian ports, and issued bills of lading in respect of the shipment. The cargo was delivered damaged in Brazil, and the charterers settled with the Brazilian receivers; claim in Brazilian cruzeiros, which they purchased with French francs, the currency in which they carried on their business. They then claimed to be indemnified by the shipowners under the terms of the charter - party, their claim taking the form of one for damages for breach of contract. The Judge at first instance(myself,即 Goff 大法官是该先例的一审大法官)held, reversing the arbitrators, that cruzeiros were the appropriate currency for the award of damages to the charterers. In so holding, I was influenced by previous authority(The Canadian Transport, [1932] 43 Lloyd's Rep. 409), and by practical difficulties involved in identifying a currency, other than the currency in which the charterers' liability to the receivers was in fact discharged. My decision was reversed by the Court of Appeal, whose decision was in turn affirmed by your Lordships' House. It is instructive for present purposes to refer to the reasoning which led Lord Wilberforce to reach this conclusion. He said: 'The essential question is what was the loss suffered by the respondents. I do not find this to be identical with that suffered by the cargo receivers: the charterers' claim against the owners is not one for indemnity in respect of expenditure sustained but is one for damages for breach of contract ... I think it must follow from this that their loss, which they claim as damages, was the discharge of the receivers' claim, together with the legal and other expenses they incurred. They discharged all these by providing francs to meet the receivers' claim they suffered no loss. Then secondly was this loss the kind of loss which under the contract, they were entitled to recover against the owners? The answer to this is provided by the arbitrators' finding that it was reasonable to contemplate that the charterers, being a French francs to purchase other currencies to settle cargo claims arising under the bills of lading. So in my opinion the charterers; recoverable loss was, according to normal principle, the sum of French francs which they paid.'

I turn to the facts of thepresent case. There are a number of facts which point to the Ghanaian cedi as the currency in which the department felt its loss. First of all, the currency in which the department carried on business within the Ghana was at the material time the cedi. Consistently with this, the department's bank accounts were maintained in cedis, as were its books and accounts. In particular, had the cargo been delivered by the shipowners at Takoradi(加纳卸港), the department could and would have sold it on the market there to Ghanaian companies, and would have recovered payment in cedis. Second, by virtue of Ghana's stringent exchange control legislation, no person other than the Bank of Ghana(a separate entity with its own legal personality, distinct from the State of Ghana and its government departments, including the department) was or is permitted to receive or own foreign currency. Accordingly, when the department wanted to purchase crude oil from overseas for use in the refining process at its refinery, the bank would provide the necessary foreign currency for this purpose, debiting the department's account(or the account of its buying agents) with the amount in cedis equivalent to the sum in foreign currency required, and itself paying the foreign currency to the seller out of its own foreign currency holdings. Likewise, in the absence of a right of set-off, the bank would provide the foreign exchange for the payment of freight in foreign currency. This procedure did not, however, apply to the fuel oil in the present case, which was the product of the department's own refinery, and was being supplied to Ghanaian companies. This sale was, as is usually the case in such circumstances, being carried out in the domestic currency in question, here the cedi.

It was these circumstances(with others) which persuaded Mr. Justice Webster(1992)1 Lloyd's Rep. 303 to reach the conclusion "without much hesitation" that, when the shipowners failed to deliver the cargo at Takoradi, the department felt its loss in cedis. *Prima facie*, in my opinion, it is impossible to fault that conclusion."

这一个先例看来是对原告不利,但正如已经提到过,原因是它涉及非常特殊的事实,不大可能在其他的案件中会出现。该批燃油是从加纳一个港口的炼油厂提炼后再以 Texaco Melbourne 轮运去加纳另一个卸港,然后分批转售给其他的加纳油公司。换言之,所有涉及的币种只有加纳塞地,与美元(或任何其他币种)是一点关系都没有。至于加纳政府争辩说最近的市场是在意大利,购买替代燃油需要是以美元作出支付,这已经被高院认定是当时在加纳卸港没有一个可供买卖的市场。至于去意大利市场,则被视为是不现实,而加纳政府也的确没有这样做,否则至少可以争辩"马上面对的损失的币种"(Immediate Loss Currency)是美元。另一个重要的事实就是原告由于加纳的外汇管制根本不持有或者不能持有美元。所以在该先例是没有办法与美元扯得上任何关系,可以让原告争辩美元才是他感觉到的损失。显然,如果这批燃油是来自外国,好像在 Virani Ltd v. Manuel Revert y Cia SA(2004)2 Lloyd's Rep 14 先例的布料是原告从巴基斯坦以美元购买,这一个重要的先例结果就会不一样了。仅是看结果,该先例的确是得出对原告受害人很不公平的判决,这方面可节录在 Lloyd's Maritime and Commercial Law Quarterly(1994)p. 314,《The Currency of Damages in Contract》一文中所说"Surely it is not a satisfactory outcome of a dispute under English law that a party who is entitled to compensation for the loss of valuable goods which he was about to sell should, over 10 years after that loss, be awarded a sum which(even including interest)then had a purchasing power of about 2% of the purchasing power he would have obtained 10 years earlier if he had not been deprived of his goods."

9. 总结英国法律对损失计算的币种

目前英国法律对损失计算的币种是可以总结如下:

(1)损失可以根据任何外国的币种,败诉的被告是可以以被认定的外国币种作出支付,或者根据支付当天的英镑汇率来以英镑支付。

(2)如果有关的合约默示或者明示表达了双方的订约意图是损失以某一种币种作出支付,就必须以该种货币为准。这种约定会是针对所有的损失或是个别的损失,如在买卖合约或租约中就经常对船舶的延误会同意以美元作为币种的议定损失,也就是"滞期费"。一般合约都会有针对"结算的币种"(money of account),但也会有针对"支付的币种"(money of payment)。通常这两种币种都会是一样的,如在租约内,有条文约定租金是美元,另有条文约定支付是针对船东某一个银行账号。这两种不同的约定或条文可以节录 Denning 勋爵在 Woodhouse A. C. Israel Cocoa Ltd. S. A. v. Nigerian Produce Marketing Co. Ltd(1971)1 Lloyd's Rep. 25 先例说:"The money of account is currently in which an obligation is measured. It tells the debtor how much he has to pay. The money of payment is the currency in which the obligation has to be discharged. It tells the debtor by what means he has to pay."但如果这两种币种是不一样的,就会带来不稳定,这在 The "Agenor"(1985)1 Lloyd's Rep. 155 先例中出现。案情涉及很大的一笔滞期费,到底是应该以美元支付还是英镑支付。租约的条文第 9 条针对滞期费率是以美元为准,但另一条文第 30 条针对运费的支付是以英镑为准。还有第 40 条约定汇率是根据提单的一天为准,并有依据说:"Demurrage/Despatch and any other payments, under this Charter Party shall also be made in British External Sterling"。换言之,针对滞期费结算的币种是美元,但针对支付滞期费的币种是英镑。高院的 Staughton 大法官不同意裁决书的决定,判以英镑为准,原因是:"as a general rule the judgment of award should be in the money of account but a different solution was appropriate where the contract provided,as it did here,an agreed exchange rate between the money of account and the money of payment;in such cases the judgment or award should *prima facie* be in the money of payment;that was what the creditor had lost if payment had not been made;that was what the debtor might have tendered and the creditor would have been bound to accept at any time at least up to the commencement of proceedings;and there was no suggestion or finding in the award which would displace that *prima facie* rule here."

Staughton 大法官也另提到如果以原告船东感觉到损失的币种而言,也应该是英镑。

(3)如果找不出在合约中有这方面的订约意图(通常合约只会有明示针对结算币种,没有针对支付损失的币种),下一步看哪一种币种最能代表原告所"感觉到的损失币种"(Loss Felt Currency)。这里会有三种可能的币种:一是"合约结算的币种"(Currency of the Contract);二是"原告的币种"(Plaintiffs'/Claimants' Currency),也就是他在营运中使用的币种;三是真正"支出的币种"(Expenditure Currency),这也是在发生损失时马上会面对的币种,如损坏后在韩国修理要支付韩元或中国内地修理要支付人民币。这第三个币种也可以当作是"马上面对的损失的币种"(Immediate Loss Currency)。

10. Miliangos 先例对其他方面的适用或影响

以上已经详细介绍了 Miliangos v. Frank(Textiles)(1976)1 Lloyd's Rep 201 先例在违约方面以及侵权方面的适用,在其他方面该先例也有很大程度但不完全是一致的影响,可以简单做出介绍。

10.1 复原

针对复原(Restitution),在 BP Exploration Co v. Hunt(No. 2)(1979)1 WLR 783 QB 先例也明确了 Breach Date Rule 被摒弃,但针对复原的案件,主要的问题不是原告的损失而是被告的不当得利。所以针对的币种,并非是 Miliangos 先例的原告"感觉到损失的币种"(loss felt currency),而是"被告感觉到得利的币种"(the money in which the defendant felt its gain)。这方面比较近期的先例还有 Gloyne v. Richardson(2002) EWCA Civ. 166(CA);Papamichael v. National Westminster Bank plc(2003)1 Lloyd's Rep 341(QB);Niru Battery Manufacturing Co v. Milestone Trading Ltd(No. 2)(2004)2 Lloyd's Rep 319 等。

10.2 破产

针对破产(Insolvency),Breach Date Rule 也是被明确摒弃了,但也并非是依从 Miliangos v. Frank(Textiles)(1976)1 Lloyd's Rep 201 先例的 Payment - Date Rule。这是因为破产要面对许多债权人,要对破产人的资产平均分摊。这些债权人的债权可能是有许多不同的币种，追究他们所感觉到损失的币种也会是太过复杂。所以在 Re Lines Bros Ltd(1983)Ch D 1(CA)先例，认为只应该有一个汇率兑换的日期针对所有的债权人，即正式开始清盘的一天。这方面也有立法针对，在《Insolvency Act 1986》，c 45，s 322 与《Insolvency Rules 1986》，r 4.91 与 r 6.111。

10.3 抵销

针对抵销(Set – off)，可参阅 Fearns t/a Autopaint International v. Anglo – Dutch Paint & Chemical Co. (2010) EWHC 2366(Ch)先例，案情涉及侵犯商标、"骗卖"(passing off)与违约的争议。而最后的判决是原告的损失索赔胜诉，赔偿金额是 438,569 英镑。但被告的有关货款的反索赔也胜诉，赔偿金额是 594,696 欧元。由于索赔与反索赔都胜诉，就涉及两笔"判决债务"(judgment debt)抵销的问题。由于两笔判决债务是不同的币种，也存在以哪一天的汇率为准，因为在期间英镑对欧元大幅度贬值。

该先例很大的篇幅是针对抵销(包括立法抵销与衡平法抵销，这不在本章的讨论范围)。只针对有关以哪一天的汇率为准，George Leggatt 大法官是说：

"... Suppose further that at the time when the right of set – off arises and is asserted the exchange rate is such that B's(被告)liability, correctly calculated, exceeds the amount of A's(原告)debt. However, the claim is disputed, and by the time its amount has been determined by the court, the exchange rate has fluctuated so that, when converted into the same currency, A's claim is now worth significantly less than the amount of the debt. It may be said that it is unfair if the conversion is made at the exchange rate current at the date of judgment so that A has to bear a liability which has only arisen because of the time taken to resolve the dispute. Moreover, these facts are, in essence, the facts of the present case. (这是说本案的案情看来对原告有一定的不公平，就是在原来抵销的一天，原告欠被告的货款/债务少于被告对原告违约所造成的损失，也表示原告根本不必作出支付。但由于违约的被告质疑原告的损失赔偿，导致了诉讼。这导致了延误与到了判决作出一天，由于汇率的波动，判下来的原告的损失[英镑作为币种]不足抵销原告欠下的货款[欧元作为币种]。这显然是对原告不公平，因为诉讼的延误并非是原告的过错或责任。)

I do not think that the law is defective in this regard because I do not think that it is necessarily the case that on these facts A will have to bear the liability resulting from the movement in the exchange rate. The reason is that the movement in the exchange rate may result in a corresponding increase in the amount of A's claim. Just as a party may in principle recover damages for a currency exchange loss caused by late payment of a debt(see e. g. President of India v. Lips Maritime Corpn [1988] AC 395), so too may such a loss form part of the damage caused by the other party's tort or breach of contract. (George Leggatt 大法官不认为法律有缺陷，也不认为一定是原告要承担汇率变动的风险，因为汇率的变

动是可上可下,会有可能提升了原告损失赔偿的实际价值。)

The basic object of an award of damages in contract or tort is of course to put the injured party in the same financial position as he would have been in if the breach of contract or tortious act had not occurred. Thus, if A would but for the existence of the claim on which he relied by way of set - off have paid the debt, he can in principle (subject to considerations of remoteness etc) add the loss flowing from the movement in the exchange rate to the amount of his claim. If on the other hand he would not have paid the debt anyway—for example, because he disputed the debt on other, invalid grounds and relied on set - off only as an alternative basis for non - payment—then I can see no injustice in A bearing the loss resulting from the fall in the value of the currency of his claim. (损失计算的基本大原则是复原。所以,原告如果选择不依赖任何抵销并马上把欠下的货款/债务支付了,原告可以根据复原原则把汇率波动而带来的额外损失[除了要考虑损失遥远性的方面]加在他的索赔。但如果原告选择质疑欠下的货款[即使是站不住脚的质疑]或是选择抵销作为拒绝支付货款/债务的替代理由,这看来要原告承担诉讼期间汇率对原告不利波动的风险也没有什么不公平之处。)

Accordingly, in the present case the fact that the date of currency conversion is the date of the court's order does not mean that Mr Fearns(原告) must necessarily bear the loss caused by the fall of sterling against the euro since 2005. If on the facts Mr Fearns would have used the profits of which he was deprived by the defendants' wrongful acts of trade mark infringement and passing off to pay off part of his debt to De Beer, he could in principle have claimed the additional loss which he has suffered because sterling has depreciated before the damages were paid as a further head of damages."

所以总结,该先例是判:"... that when ordering such a set - off between amounts payable in different currencies the court should assess and add to each principal amount any interest accruing up to the date of the set - off, convert the smaller amount into the currency of the larger amount at the exchange rate prevailing at that date and order payment of the balance; and that, therefore, the date at which the damages payable to the claimant and the sum which he owed to the defendant fell to be converted into a common currency and netted off against each other was the date on which the amounts of those liabilities were finally determined."(这是说以判决的一天为准,因为在该天明确了损失赔偿的金额,并把两笔索赔与反索赔的判决债务可以抵销。这两笔判决债务必须加上不同的利息[因为欠下或应该支付的日期不一样],然后把金额较小的一笔判决债务以该天的汇率兑换为金额较大的一笔判决债务,剩余的金额也就是要作出支付的一笔钱。)

11. 汇率损失的索赔

与违约损失计算的币种有一定程度关系的是"汇率损失的索赔"(damage for currency loss)。这种争议会是原告指称被告违约,如延误做出支付,导致他没有及时把支付的币种兑换为另一种在升值的币种而蒙受损失。这种索赔案件也曾经与 Miliangos v. Frank(Textiles)(1976)1 Lloyd's Rep 201 先例扯上关系。第一个要介绍的先例是 Ozalid Group(Export)Ltd v. African Continental Bank(1979)2 Lloyd's Rep 231,涉及原告英国公司以 C&F 出售一批机器给被告尼日利亚公司,但后者延误支付货款。原告在事后提出汇率损失的索赔,声称如果他能够及时收到美元货款,他就会按照当时的外汇规定兑换为英镑。但由于被告延误支付 9 个星期,而其间英镑兑美元的汇率上升,令原告蒙受损失。表明看来这不像是 Miliangos 先例的案件类别,因为欠下的货款已经作出支付,不需要考虑哪一种是最能代表原告感觉到损失的币种。但在该先例,Donaldson 大法官还是大篇幅与 Miliangos 先例扯上了关系,说:"The law on claims which involve foreign currencies was revolutionized by the decision of the House of Lords in Miliangos v. Frank(Textiles)(1976)1 Lloyd's Rep 201. Previously the law had been that all claims had to be made in sterling, any necessary conversion into sterling being made at the rate of exchange prevailing at the date of breach of contract or duty... These cases decide that it is for the plaintiff to select the currency in which to make his claim and it is for him to prove that an award or judgment in that currency will most truly express his loss and accordingly most fully and exactly compensate him for that loss ... Notwithstanding that in the present case the price of the goods was agreed to be paid in US dollars, it is clear that the plaintiffs' loss was incurred in sterling and that this was foreseeable by the defendants."

结果是 Donaldson 判原告索赔汇率损失胜诉,说:"Once it is proved that the plaintiff's true loss is to be measured in sterling, any payment made on account in a different currency falls to be credited against that sterling loss at the rate of exchange ruling at the date of payment."

看来这一判决的理由是因为法律在 Miliangos 先例与 The "Despina R" and "Folias"(1979)1 Lloyd's Rep 1 先例有了发展,所以在原告感觉到的损失币种为英镑的前提下成功索赔汇率损失。

接下来的是 International Minerals & Chemical Corp v. Karl O Helm AG(1986)1 Lloyd's Rep 81 先例,案情涉及原告美国公司把一家在卢森堡的子公司出售给被告,合约约定的币种为比利时法郎。诉讼涉及原告对延误支付的索赔,这被高院判是胜诉并命令被告以法郎作出支付。但原告另有一项额外的索赔,就是在期间美元上涨,如果被告准时支付的话原告会马上把法郎转换为美元,但延误支付就导致了汇率损失。原告也指称被告是知道他会是这样做的,这表示在订约时被告是可以预料到会有这种损失类别的。在这一先例中,Hobhouse 大法官不是以 Miliangos 先例与 The "Despina R" and "Folias"先例作为理由,而是根据本书第三章所介绍的损失"遥远性"(remoteness)的 Hadley v. Baxendale(1854)9 Ex. 341 著名先例,说:"... the late payment of money... is justified by the fact that the usual loss is an interest loss and that compensation for this has been provided for and limited by statute. It follows that a plaintiff, where he is seeing to recover damages for the late payment of money, must prove not only that he has suffered the alleged additional special loss and that it was caused by the defendant's default, but also that the defendant had knowledge of the facts or circumstances which make such a loss a not unlikely consequence of such a default. In the eyes of the law, those facts or circumstances are deemed to be special, whether in truth they are or not, and knowledge of them must be proved. Where, as in the present case, the relevant facts or circumstances are commonplace, the burden of proof will be easy to discharge and the Courts may well be willing to draw inferences of knowledge; in other case, there may be a question which would, in any event, have had to be dealt with under the second rule in Hadley v. Baxendale, and then the burden of proof will be more significant. **I do not see it as any objection to the recovery of the damages claimed in the present case that in very many other international transactions similar damages would be recoverable in the event of default.**"(加黑部分是笔者的强调)

接下去的 The "Lips"(1987)2 Lloyd's Rep 311 贵族院先例与 International Minerals & Chemical Corp v. Karl O Helm AG 先例的判法一致,没有与 Miliangos 先例与 The "Despina R" and "Folias"先例扯在一起。值得一提的是在上诉庭,Neill 大法官说要根据 Hadley v. Baxendale 的第二条损失规则针对这一问题。这表示要成功索赔,原告必须证明在订约前有通知被告而且被告知道会有这种损失。另在诉讼或仲裁的时候,也必须在文书的索赔请求中特别提出这个"特别损失"(special damage)。

而最后介绍针对这方面的先例是 Travelers Casualty and Surety Co of Canada v. Sun Life Assurance Co of Canada(UK)(2006)EWHC 2716,案情涉及再保险人延误赔付给原告的受保人。延误直到作出判决期间美元(赔付的币种)兑换英镑(受保人的币种)从弱变强,导致了汇率损失高达 500 万美元。

12. Miliangos 先例对其他国家或地区的影响

英国 Miliangos v. Frank(Textiles)(1976)1 Lloyd's Rep 201 先例对其他普通法国家或地区都带来深远的影响,因为只要诉讼涉及这些国家的外国币种,就难免要涉及这一问题。在受英国法律影响的国家,包括美国,普遍认同 Miliangos 先例,认为英国贵族院能够摆脱以前 Breach Date Rule 针对损失兑换的时间是一种进步与现实的做法。但许多国家接下去的发展都有了一定的差异,导致了今天还是在这一方面并不肯定。这显然不是一件好事,特别是针对国家法院的诉讼,会多了一个因素或考虑需要进行"择地行诉"(forum shopping)。以下简单介绍一些笔者看来是与中国内地关系更密切的普通法国家与地区针对这个问题的法律地位。

12.1 香港地区

香港地区一直以来都是紧密地跟从英国的法律,这包括在损失的计算一直是根据 Forum - Currency Rule 与 Breach Date Rule。到英国贵族院判决了 Miliangos v. Frank(Textiles)(1976)1 Lloyd's Rep 201 先例后,第一个先例并没有依照。这一个先例是地方法院的判例 Stibbe(Burtotex)Ltd v. Bayman(1975)unreported DCCJ005215/1976(DC HK),认为 Miliangos 先例是涉及英镑,而英镑在不断的贬值,所以该先例与港币是没有关系的,Breach Date Rule 并没有对原告有任何不利的影响,所以可以不必理会该贵族院的先例。看来,这样区别 Miliangos 先例的不同事实有一点奇怪,也没有掌握到该重要先例所带来的重大改变。

但接下去的先例就很快紧跟了英国法院的判决。而第一个跟从 The "Despina R" and "Folias"(1979)1 Lloyd's Rep 1 的香港先例就是 Sabah Shipbuilding, Repairing & Engineering Sdn Bhd v. Houston Engineering and Equipment Ltd(1978)HCA001810/1976(CFI HK)。在该先例中香港法院认为选择哪一个币种是"非常难于决定的事情"(an extremely difficult matter to decide)。最后香港法院决定以有关合约支付或结算的币种为准,而不是根据原告认为是"最自然与恰当的币种"(natural and proper currency)。

接下去紧跟了英国法律作出同样有关币种的先例有 Balasing Guring v. Ng Lay(1986)unreported HCA004587/1985(HC HK);Chak Kak v. Pacrim International Capital Inc(2008)unreported CACV 366/2007(CA HK)。另也有香港的判例是有关的利息,也是以判决的币种利率为准:Fargo Shipping Co v. Hwa Haur Trading(Hong Kong)Co(1976)unreported HCA0011959/1978(HC HK)。此外香港高院的程序也特别有了这方面特定的《执行指引》(Practice Direction),好像英国法院的做法,针对外国币种的判决:Practice Direction of the Government of Hong Kong Special Administrative Region of the Peoples Republic of China, PD 162。而有关的命令是以这样的措辞:"It is adjudged that the Defendant to pay to the Plaintiff(state the sum in foreign currency for which Judgment has been order)or the Hong Kong dollar equivalent at the time of payment."

12.2 新加坡

新加坡与香港的情况有一点一致,就是在 Miliangos v. Frank(Textiles)(1976)1 Lloyd's Rep 201 先例作出之后的 14 年,期间新加坡法院的判决根据新加坡的宪法都可以上诉去英国枢密院。所以,新加坡法院紧跟 Miliangos 先例的判决是可以预料到的。这些先例有：Sarathi Co v. The Vishva Pratibha(1980)2 MLJ 265(High Ct Sing)；Ooi Han Sun v. Bee Han Meng(1991 SLR 824),(1991)3 MLJ 219(High Ct)；Tatung Electronics(S)Pte Ltd v. Binatone International Ltd(1991)1 SLR 204,(1991)3 MLJ 212(CA)；Wardley Ltd v. Tunku Adnan(1991)1 SLR 721(HC)724；Indo Commercial Society(Pte)Ltd v. Ebrahim(1992)2 SLR 1041,(1992)SGHC 230(HC)；Chinsim Trading(Pte) Ltd v. Indian Bank(1993)2 SLR 144(HC)153－54；Thai Kenaf Co v. Keck Seng(1993)2 SLR 92(HC)；TKM(Singapore)Pre Ltd v. Export Credit Insurance Corp of Singapore(1993)1 SLR1041(High Ct Sing),aff'd(1994)2 SLR 137(CA)；Re Mohamed Yunus Valibhoy,ex p Bank of Credit and Commerce Hong Kong(1995)1 SLR 601 等。

其中稍作介绍的是 Wardley Ltd v. Tunku Adnan 先例，新加坡高院跟从 Miliangos 先例的判决作出瑞士法郎的判决。法院认同 Breach Date Rule 并不现实，因为在现代的世界，兑换每天甚至每个小时都有很大的波动。此外，判利息也是根据瑞士法郎的利率为准。

另在 Sarathi Co v. The Vishva Pratibha 先例中，它是 Miliangos 先例判决 4 年后作出的。该先例重要的地方就是认同找出原告感觉到的损失的币种，但并非是让原告得利，让他选择，而是强制性的。该先例，根据新的 Payment－Date Rule，事实上是相比 Breach Date Rule 对原告不利，但法院认为还是要强制使用，原告不能在这一问题上输打赢要。12 年后，在 Indo Commercial Society(Pte)Ltd v. Ebrahim 先例也作出了同样的判决，并引申了 Wilberforce 勋爵在 Miliangos 先例所说："(creditor)has no concern with pounds sterling；for him what matters is that a Swiss franc **for good or ill** should remain a Swiss franc." 作出判决说："that some plaintiffs may suffer loss from the strict application of Miliangos should not be allowed to detract from its logic."

新加坡法院在双方并没有对损失与判决的币种作出争辩的情况下，也会以法院认为是恰当的外国币种作出判决，这是在 Chinsim Trading(Pte)Ltd v. Indian Bank 先例，案情是有关一个美元的信用证，法院这样说："the parties focused their energies on the issues of liability and left the issue of the proper currency and sum of claim unaddressed. I will not go into the issue beyond referring to the House of Lords' decision in Miliangos v. Frank(Textiles)Ltd ... and say that the proper currency for this judgment should be the American currency."同样的判决也出现在 Thai Kenaf Co v. Keck Seng。

可以总结说，新加坡在这一个问题上的法律地位是基本上与英国一致。

12.3　马来西亚

马来西亚在 Miliangos v. Frank(Textiles)(1976)1 Lloyd's Rep 201 先例前是强制性使用 Forum－Currency Rule 与 Breach Date Rule：Overseas Chinese Banking Corp v. Firm of Yaik Joo Ann(1936)MLF 88(HC)先例。在 Miliangos 先例后，马来西亚法院很快就全面接受。在 Den Norske Bank Asa v. Owners of the Ship "Forum Alaska"(1998)MLJU 55(High Ct [Johor Bahru])先例，法院提到 Miliangos 先例并说马来西

亚法院一定要勇敢作出外国币种的判决，如下："The realization that currency stability is a thing of the past prompted the English Court of appeal and the House of Lords to change the English jurisprudence as early as 1975. We in Malaysia must not be left behind ... The English judges were bold enough to hold that if an amount due under a contract was in a foreign currency, the courts have the power to give judgment in that foreign currency. In Malaysia the time has come to be progressive and pragmatic in thought and action. Malaysian judges must be bold and be brave enough to hand out judgments in foreign currencies."

另在 Owners of Cargo Carried in the Ship Gang Chen v. The ship Gang Chen(1998)6 MLF 492 先例中，原来的审理双方都没有针对损失计算币种的问题。但到了要求作出判决命令之前，马来西亚令吉(ringgit)币值严重下挫，这导致原告回去法院要求把判决改变为美元。法院根据 Miliangos 先例与 The "Despina R" and "Folias"(1979)1 Lloyd's Rep 1 先例，把判决改为美元，并认为美元才是合约结算的币种以及最能代表原告感觉到损失的币种。至于原告没有在较早的诉讼中作出请求与争辩，看来并不影响法院的做法。

12.4 南非

南非也是基本上跟随了 Miliangos v. Frank(Textiles)(1976)1 Lloyd's Rep 201 先例。这里只介绍在 Miliangos 先例后第一个南非最高院的案例，名为 Standard Chartered Bank of Cananda v. Nedpern Bank Ltd 1994(4)SA 747(AD)。这是一个侵权(涉及疏忽误诉)案件，最高院的多数同意 Miliangos 先例与 The "Despina R" and "Folias"(1979)1 Lloyd's Rep 1 先例，作出了美元的判决。但值得一提的是有一个反对的声音，Harms 大法官批评这一个原告感觉到损失币种的规则太不肯定，不应当跟从，说："I fail to see why, simply because the plaintiff is a foreign plaintiff, these basic principles (这是指按照 Forum - Currency Rule) do not apply and why he should be treated differently. The argument that to do otherwise would mean that the plaintiff may be denied the amount of his actual loss ... misses the point - it is inherent in the law of delict and the principle of nominalism that a plaintiff may, at the end of the day, be out of pocket. In any event, any loss flowing from the depreciation of the local currency is not caused by the wrong ..."

本案中 Harms 大法官对 Miliangos 先例的批评意见在其他国家法院与南非法院是绝无仅有的，这显示了 Miliangos 先例带来的重大改变得到了普遍认同，认为它带来的好处(对受害方的公平)还是超越了它带来的弊端(对损失计算币种的不肯定)。

12.5 美国

美国在这方面的问题起点是在 1792 年的《Coinage Act》，在 20 段时说明法院的判决必须是以美元为准，节录如下："The money of account of the United States shall be expressed in dollars ... and all accounts in the public offices and all proceedings in the courts shall be kept and had in conformity to this regulation. ”

至于在美元以外的外国币种,美国法律也是与英国 Breach Date Rule 一致,也就是在违约或侵权发生的一天把外国币种的债务或者损失金额兑换为美元后作出索赔。这在纽约上诉庭的先例 Hoppe v. Russo – Asiatic Bank 138 NE 497(NYCA 1923)(Hoppe)有明确的判决,说明是不论针对合约还是侵权,不论是债务或损失,也不论当事人是否是美国人或外国人,Forum – Currency Rule 与 Breach Date Rule 都适用。但美国法院把这一问题视为是“实体法”(substantive law),而不是“程序法”(procedural law),这可以从一些早期的最高院先例中显示出来:Guinness v. Miller 299 US 71(1925)80;Deutsche Bank Filiale Nurnberg v. Humphrey 272 US 517,47 S Ct 46(1926)与 Zimmermann v. Sutherland 274 US 253(1927)。这些先例都是涉及美元与德国马克的兑换日期,因为期间德国在第一次世界大战后经济崩溃,马克币值下降。在 Guinness v. Miller 先例,最高院是支持上诉庭的著名 Learned Hand 大法官,认为 Breach Date Rule 适用,也就是违约一天把损失兑换的日期。但后来的两个先例,却适用“判决日期的兑换率”(Judgment – Date Conversion),而理由是 Guinness v. Miller 的合约适用法是美国法,但后来两个先例的合约适用法是德国法。这可以从 Zimmermann v. Sutherland 先例的判词中其中一句显示:“The distinction between Deutche Bank and Hicks v. Guinness is not ... that the plaintiff in Hicks v. Guinness was in the United States, but that, as the court understood the facts, the debt was payable in New York and subject to American law, so that upon a breach of the contract there arose a present liability in dollars.”

这种说法是与英国法律有所偏离的,毕竟在英国这个问题是被认为是程序法。这方面也可以看“美国法律学会”(American Law Institute 或简称 ALI)在 1969 年作出的《The Restatement of the Law Second, Conflict of Laws》(这可被称为是 the Second Restatement)针对这一方面的说法。这里也不妨简单一提有关 Restatement 的作用,它并非是立法,而目的只是为了鼓励美国各级的法院,不论是联邦法院或者是地方法院,作为参考并作出尽量统一的判决。

在 The Second Restatement,首先是说明美国法院必须以美元作出判决:“the rule of this Section owes its existence to the fact that an Anglo – American court may only render a judgment for money damages in its own local currency. ”但针对索赔的外国币种的兑换问题,在另外的段节名为“Time for Converting Foreign Currency into Local Currency”,就说明如果适用法是美国法,Breach Date Rule 适用。但如果有关的诉因是适用外国法,就会是不一样,说:“ § 144. When in a suit for the recovery of money damages the cause of action is governed by the local law of another state, the forum will convert the currency in which recovery would have been granted in the other state into the local currency as of the date of the award. ”

这种情况一路维持到英国贵族院的 Miliangos v. Frank (Textiles) (1976) 1 Lloyd's

Rep 201 先例后接近 10 年才重新在美国成为一个热点问题。之所以隔了这段时间，是因为期间美元比起外币一路升值，所以对原告更有利，但被告对此也并不警觉，以致没有太多的人提出这一问题。直到 20 世纪 80 年代中期，美元开始对其他外币下跌，问题才再度浮现。基本上美国做出的针对可以分三个方面探讨，以下作出简单的介绍。

美国第一方面的针对可以看 1986 年 ALI 作出的 The Third Restatement，它基本上就是跟从了 Miliangos 先例的判决。其中在"Time for Converting Foreign Currency into Local Currency"，它再也不是像在 The Second Restatement 中那样，而是说："§823(1) Courts in the United States ordinarily give judgment on causes of action arising in another state, or denominated in a foreign currency, in United States dollars, but they are not precluded from giving judgment in the currency in which the obligation is denominated or the loss was incurred. (2) If, in a case arising out of a foreign currency obligation, the court gives judgment in dollars, the conversion from foreign currency to dollars is to be made at such rate as to make the creditor whole and to avoid rewarding a debtor who has delayed in carrying out the obligation."

从这两条规定的文字看来，第一条文改变了 Forum - Currency Rule，第二条文改变了 Breach Date Rule，但实际上与 Miliangos 先例有区别，其中一个比较重要的区别是可以看 The Third Restatement 针对第二条文的评述，如下："If the Court gives judgment in United States dollars ... the date used for conversion should depend on whether the currency of obligation has appreciated or depreciated relative to the dollar. In general, if the foreign currency has depreciated since the injury or breach, judgment should be given at the rate of exchange applicable on the date of injury or breach; if the foreign currency has appreciated since the injury or breach, judgment should be given at the rate of exchange applicable on the date of judgment or the date of payment."

The Third Restatement 与 Miliangos 先例不同的地方是后者并不考虑币值升降与否，而是以原告最能感觉到损失的币种为准，至于这一个币种对原告是好是坏，就不予考虑，正如 Wilberforce 勋爵在 Miliangos 先例所说的"for good or ill"。但 The Third Restatement 则考虑损失发生后至判决这一段时间的币值升降情形，如果损失发生后，该币种升值，则适用 Payment - Date Rule。如果该币种贬值，则适用 Breach Date Rule。这样规定将对原告太偏袒，也令双方当事人太晚(在最后作出判决时)才会知道判决结果。依照 The Third Restatement 作出判决的先例有 El Universal, Compania Periodistica Nacional SA de CV v. Phoenician Imports, Inc 802 SW 2d 799，法院选择了 Breach Date Rule，因为外国原告的"本土货币"(home currency)在违约与判决期间下跌。

美国第二方面的针对是由 the National Conference of Commissioners on Uniform State Laws(NCCUSL)这一组织所草拟的立法。该组织是针对美国各州立法的统一，而不是好像 ALI 那样针对法院判决的统一。NCCUSL 草拟的立法是《Uniform Foreign - Money Claims Act》，这好像是"示范法"(model law)一样，要求各州根据其立法。其中

Section 4 针对“索赔的恰当币种”(proper money of the claim)说:“(a)The money in which the parties to a transaction have agreed that payment is to be made is the proper money of the claim for payment. (b)If the parties to transaction have not otherwise agreed, the proper money of the claim, as in each case may be appropriate, is the money:(1)regularly used between the parties as a matter of usage or course of dealings;(2)used at the time of a transaction in international trade, by trade usage or common practice, for valuing or settling transactions in the particular commodity or service involved;or(3)in which the loss was ultimately felt or will be incurred by the party claimant.”

上述的规定看来是非常接近英国的 Miliangos 先例。到了 2009 年中,美国的 50 个州份只有 22 个接受。

美国第三方面的针对是来自纽约州的立法。这立法虽然只针对一个州,但对国际商业合约非常重要,因为有不少合约的适用法会是规定为纽约州法律。在 Miliangos 先例后的 10 年左右,在 1985 年纽约律师协会作出了一份针对外国币种判决的报告,名为《Report on Foreign Currency Judgments(City Bar Report)》。内容对英国之 Miliangos 先例之后的发展推崇备至,其中也提到 Breach Date Rule 会影响纽约作为国际金融与贸易的中心(adversely affects New York's status as a leading center of international finance and commerce)。在 2 年后,纽约州也立法摒弃了 Breach Date Rule:《New York State Chapter Law》(20 July 1987, Ch326)。但该立法也是与 Miliangos 先例及 The Third Restatement 有区别,如针对转换汇率,它采用了 Judgment Date Rule,说:“Such judgment or decree shall be converted into currency of the United States at the rate of exchange prevailing on the date of entry of the judgment or decree.”另也有说法是立法只针对“责任指定为外国币种”(obligation denominated in a foreign currency),这被视为是太局限,立法只适用在一些外国币种的债务与议定损失索赔。至于在其他不少类别的案件,如侵犯商标,原告与被告之间往往就没有合约关系,更谈不上会指定一个币种了。

总结说,美国目前的地位是非常混乱的,特别是在兑换外国币种的日期方面。在纽约州与其他没有跟从《Uniform Foreign - Money Claims Act》立法的州份,法院还是根据普通法针对这一方面的问题。其中有判例是按照 Breach Date Rule:Gathercrest Ltd v. First American Bank and Trust 805 F 2d 995(11th Cir 1986);Middle East Banking Co v. State Street Bank Int'l 821 F 2d 897 (2d Cir 1987); Gonzalez v. Banco de Santander - Puerto Rico 932 F 2d 999(1st Cir 1991);Delchi Carrier SpA v. Rotorex Corp 88 - CV - 1078, Lexis 12820(N D NY 1994);Reliastar Life Insurance Co v. IOA Inc 303 F 3d 874(8TH Cir 2002);Elite Entertainment Corp v. Khela Brothers Entertainment Inc 396 f Supp 2d 680 (ED Virginia 2005); Ligas v. IPD Sales & Marketing LLC 2007 WL 29008893(ED Missouri 2007)。

也有判例是跟从 The Third Restatement,在一定程度是给法院裁量权善待原告:

Nikimha Securities Ltd v. The Trend Group 646 F Supp 1211(ED Penn 1986);Nimrod Marketing(Overseas)Ltd v. Texas Energy Investment Corp 769 F 2d 1076(5th Cir 1980);Sunrise Shipping Ltd v. M/V American Chemist 1999 AMC 2906(ED Louisiana 1999)。

更加有一些判例是跟从 The First Restatement 与 The Second Restatement 的法律冲突去对待:Laminoirs - Treffileries - Cableries De Lens SA v. Southwire Co(ND Georgia 1980);Black Sea & Baltic General Insurance Co v. Al Nisr Insurance Co 575 F Supp 685(SDNY 1983);Cronel Watch SA v. Peterson State Bank 565 F Supp(ND Ill 1983);Seguros Banvenez SA v. S/S Oliver Drescher 761 F 2d 855(2d Cir 1985);Fils et Cables D'Acier de Lens v. Midland Metals Corp 584 F Supp 240(SDNY 1984);La Societe de Diffusion Vinecole SA v. Peartree Imports Inc 1984 US Dist Lexis 17891(SD NY 1984);Ingersoll Milling Machine Co v. Granger 833 F 2d 680(7th Cir 1987)(applying Illionois law);Pecaflor Construction Inc v. Landes 198 Cal App 3d 342,243 Cal Rpt 605(1st Dist 1988);Budejovicky Budvar NP v. Czech Beer Importers Inc 2006 WL 1980308(D Conn 2006);Levis Strauss & Co v. Aetna Casualty and Surety Co 184 Cal App 3d 1479,237 Cal Rptr 473(Ct App Cal 1986);Sembawang Shipyard Ltd v.(MD Penn 2007);Societe Civile Succession Richard Guino v. Redstar Corp 153 Cal App 4th 697,63 Cal Rptr 3d 224(Ct App Cal 2007).

统一解决这个问题,看来是要国会立法或是最高院作出判决,但这种发展不像会很快发生。

12.6 加拿大

加拿大的法律地位也是混乱的,原因是来自几个方面。一个重要的方面是在加拿大立国之后 4 年所通过的一个立法,就是 1871 年的《Currency Act》,其中 section 12 说:"all public accounts established or maintained in Canada shall be in the currency of Canada,and any reference to money or monetary value in any indictment or other legal proceedings shall be stated in the currency of Canada."这立法显然是为了保护当时还非常脆弱的加拿大元,但显然在措辞上太过强硬。如果严格按照这条规定的文字,在加拿大法院进行的诉讼就不能在请求中提到"我丢了钱包,钱包里有 10 美元"这样的事实。所以在以前按照 Breach Date Rule 就没有问题,因为在违约或侵权的一天就已经把外币转换为加拿大元,然后在加拿大法院的诉讼中提出。但一跟从 Miliangos v. Frank(Textiles)(1976)1 Lloyd's Rep 201 先例中的 Payment - Date Rule,就会违反《Currency Act》的立法,因为索赔请求显然不再会以加拿大元提出。这种案例有不少,只先举一个较早的先例 Baumgartner v. Carsley Silk Co(1971)23 DLR(3d)225(Que CA),在第一审是以美元做出判决,但这在上诉庭被推翻,认为是违反了《Currency Act》。但有其他州份做出美元的判例,显然是没有理会《Currency Act》:Sandy Frank Film Syndication Inc v. CFQC Broadcasting Ltd(1983)23 Sask R 241(CA);Trans North Turbo Air Ltd v. North 60 Petro Ltd(2003)YJ No 60(SC)。更重要的是在 Miliangos 先

例后第一个在加拿大法院判决的案例 Batavia Times Publishing Co v. Davis(1978)20 OR(2d)437。案情是执行一个美国法院的判决,判决显然是以美元做出。安大略省的法院表示希望按照 Miliangos 先例,但受到《Currency Act》的局限,说:"I do not believe that the Courts of Canada are able to move to the date of effective payment as providing the rate of exchange as the English Courts have now done in cases involving circumstances similar to those outlined in Miliangos . . . If I could be satisfied that there are no procedural or practical problems and that the Currency and Exchange Act either did not apply to judgments or did not prevent a judgment being given for a sum of foreign currency and its equivalent inCanadian dollars, as the English Courts are now doing, I would adopt the effective date of payment as being the date for determining the rate of exchange. Because I am not certain that there are no problems and because I assume that the Currency and Exchange Act does not permit judgments to be given as they are now being given in England, I will use the rate of exchange as prevailing at the date of the second judgment herein, the date of my judgment . . . "

加拿大的 10 个州份其中有三个(Ontario, British Columbia 与 Prince Edward Island)立法跟从 Miliangos 先例的 Payment – Date Rule,如在 1984 年安大略省的立法《Courts of Justice Act》规定:"Where a person obtains an order to enforce an obligation in a foreign currency, the order shall require payment of an amount in Canadian currency sufficient to purchase the amount of the obligation in the foreign currency at a bank in Ontario listed in Schedule I to the Bank Act(Canada) at the close of business on the first day on which the bank quotes a Canadian dollar rate for purchase of the foreign currency before the day payment of the obligation is received by the creditor."

以上的措辞也显示了各州份的立法怎样绕过《Currency Act》,因为如果两个立法有直接的冲突,联邦法律的《Currency Act》还是超越了州立法的效力。所以在措辞上是要求败诉方支付一笔加拿大元的金额足够或相等于另一笔判决的外国币种根据支付日期的汇率(The defendant shall pay the plaintiff the amount in Canadian dollars equivalent to X amount of [the relevant foreign currency] at the date the payment is eventually made)。

另在 British Columbia 州,在 1996 年也有这方面的立法,名为《Foreign Money Claims Act》规定说:"1(1) If, before making an order for the payment of money arising out of a claim or loss, the court considers that the person in whose favour the order will be made will truly and exactly compensated if all or party of the money payable under the order is measured in a currency other than the currency of Canada, the court must order that the money payable under the order will be that amount of Canadian currency that is necessary to purchase the equivalent amount of the other currency at a chartered bank located in British Columbia at the close of business on the conversion date. (2) The conversion date is the last day, before the day on which a payment under the order is made by the judgment debtor to the judgment creditor, that the bank referred to in subsection (1) quotes a Canadian dollar equivalent to the other currency."

除了《Currency Act》以及加拿大的三个州份有自己的立法所带来的混乱外，还有的原因是加拿大法院对普通法也有不同的看法。部分法院认为还是直到早期最高院判是根据 Breach Date Rule 的先例（Custodian v. Blucher [1927] SCR 420 与 Gatineau Power Co v. Crown Life Insurance Co [1945] SCR 655）被最高院自己推翻，下级法院还是受到 Breach Date Rule 的约束。但另有部分法院认为并没有受到约束，以前最高院的先例可以做出区分，因为时代已经变了。其中针对以哪一天外国币种与加元的汇率为准，就已经是每一个法院各说各的，有很大的裁量权。

例如继续适用 Breach Date Rule 的汇率先例有：NV Bocimar SA v. Century Insurance of Canada 53 NR 383; Dollina Enterprises Ltd v. Wilson Haffenden (1977) 1 FC 169 (TD); Schweizeriche Metallwerke Selve & Co v. Atlantic Container Line (1985) 63 NR 104 (CA); Capitol Life Insurance Co v. Canada (1988) 2 CTC 101; Kruger Inc v. Baltic Shipping Co (1988) 1 FC 262 (Fed Ct); Lee S Wilbur & Co v. The Martha Ingraham (1989) FCJ No 427 (TD); Shibamoto & Co v. Western Fish Producers Inc (1991), 48 FTR 176 (TD); Kiat v. Ng (1992) 128 NBR (2d) 374 (QB)。

另也有先例是针对受害方对违约做出补救一天的汇率：Santa Marina Shipping Co SA v. Madeg Holdings Inc (1986) 6 FTR 269 (Fed Ct Can)。或是受害方原告提出诉讼一天的汇率：Airtemp Corp v. Chrysler Airtemp Ltd (1981) 121 DLR (3d) 236 (Ont High Ct); Clinton v. Ford (1982) 137 DLR (3rd) 281 (Ont Ct Ap); Equipments Stosik Inc v. Hock Seng Lee Heavy Industries Sdn Bhd (2007) QCCA 1531; Armetc Ltd v. Canada Export Development Corp (2007) QCCA 99 等先例。或是被告作出抗辩一天的汇率：Promech Sorting Systems BV v. Branco Rentals & Leasing Ltd (1994) 93 Man R (2d) 36 (QB) 等先例。或是开庭的一天的汇率：Ripulone v. Pontecorvo (1989), 98 NBR (2d) 267 (QB), var'd 104 NBR (2d) 56 (CA) 等先例。或是判决一天的汇率：Alliedsignal Inc v. Dupont Canada Inc (1999) FCJ No 38, 86 Carswells Practice Cases (3d) 324 (Fed Ct App); PLB Holdings v. Gehring 2002 ABQB 594, 322 AR 205 (QB); Proctor v. Schellenberg 2002 MBQB 135, aff'd without reference to this point, 2002 MBCA 170, 30 CPC (5th) 89 (Man Ct App); PLB holdings Corp v. Gehring, 2002 ABQB 594, 322 AR 205 (Alta QB); Lloyd's v. Berezowski 2006 AMQM 625, 63 Alta L R (4th) 169 (QB) 等先例。或是根据判决的一个指定日期（如判决后 3 个月内做出支付）：Skaggs Companies Inc v. Mega Technical Holdings Inc (2001) 1 WWR 359 (Alta QB) 等先例。或是做出支付一天的汇率：Ferris v. Welsh (1985) BCJ No 128 (Co Ct) (QL) 等先例。更或是判有不同的币种与汇率：Grex SA v. Canadian Dairy Commission (1984) 24 BLR 206 (Fed Ct); McCutcheon v. McCutcheon (1989) 102 NBR 271 (QB); Reading and Bates Construction Co

v. Baker Energy Resources(1995)1 FC 483(CA)506 等先例。

还有其他类似加拿大情况的英联邦国家,包括澳大利亚与新西兰,但此处不多讲。

13. 国际性和地区性的公约或规定

接下去是简单介绍有部分国际公约及地区性规定或协议(不论是否生效)已经有条文片面针对兑换币种日期的问题。第一个是《华沙公约》(Warsaw Convention [1929 as amended at The Hague in 1955]),它针对责任限制(金额是以 SDR 的一揽子货币),是要求根据 Judgment Date Rule 兑换为诉讼地点法院的币种。这是在 Article 22(6)说:"The sums mentioned in terms of the Special Drawing Right in this Article shall be deemed to refer to the Special Drawing Right as defined by the International Monetary Fund. Conversion of the sums into national currencies shall, in case of judicial proceedings, be made according to the value of such currencies in terms of the Special Drawing Right at the date of judgment."同样的规定也出现在针对船舶碰撞的责任限制公约。

另在一个尚未生效(也不像是会有足够国家承认令它生效)的《Convention on International Bills of Exchange and International Promissory Notes》(1989)中,有一些条文针对本章所讲的一些问题。其中在 Article 75(4),说明不排除汇率损失的索赔:"Nothing in this Article prevents a court from awarding damages for loss caused to the holder by reason of fluctuation in rates of exchange if such loss is caused by dishonor for non - acceptance or by non - payment." 更重要的是 Article 75(3)(d),它说明原告受害方有权针对损失币种兑换的日期选择 Breach Date Rule 或 Payment - Date Rule:"If such an instrument is dishonored by non - payment, the amount payable is to be calculated . . . If no rate of exchange is indicated in the instrument, at the option of the holder, according to the rate of exchange on the date of maturity or on the date of actual payment."

在 2004 年的《UNIDROIT's Principles of International Commercial Contracts》Article 7.4.12 有一条文是说:"Damages are to be assessed either in the currency in which the monetary obligation was expressed or in the currency in which the harm was suffered, whichever is more appropriate."

美国与英国曾经在 1977 年有一个没有生效的双边协议草案,名为《The United Kingdom - United States Convention on the Reciprocal Recognition and Enforcement of Judgments in Civil Matters》,这是在 Miliangos v. Frank (Textiles) (1976) 1 Lloyd's Rep 201 先例后 1 年,其中 Article 17(5)说:"Money judgments entitled to enforcement under this convention may be enforced by the court addressed either in the currency specified in the judgment or in the local currency at the buying rate in the place where and on the date when enforcement is granted . . . ”

在 Miliangos 先例的 20 年前“国际法协会”(International Law Association 或简称 ILA)就已经预测到这方面的问题,这是在 1952 年的年会中所作出的报告《Report of the Forty – Fifth Conference Held at Lucerne August 31 to September 6 1952》并在 1956 年年会上拟定了一个国际公约草案名为《Payment of Foreign Money Liabilities, revised Draft Convention》,它虽然没有生效,但有一些条文针对 20 年后 Miliangos 先例才解决的问题。其中在 Article 6 是说:“In a case of proceedings instituted to recover a sum of money expressed in a currency which is different from that of the forum, the creditor shall claim the sum of money so expressed . . . ”

针对这一 Article 6,该公约草案在评论说明是英美等国家特有的问题:“Art. 6 is the first of a series of provisions dealing with the peculiar difficulties arising in those cases in which proceedings become necessary. These difficulties exist mainly in the Anglo – American countries by reason of the fact that, in these countries, the plaintiff cannot claim and the Court cannot award any sum of money other than a sum of *moneta fori.* ”

此外,它也有 2 条条文针对违约至判决期间的贬值问题,要求被告作出额外的赔偿。这是 Article 4:“If the debtor does not pay at the date of maturity and if after such date the currency in which the sum of money is due depreciates in relation to the currency of the place of payment, the debtor. . . shall pay an additional amount equivalent to the difference between the rate of exchange at the date of maturity and the date of payment, unless the debtor shall prove that his failure to pay results from ‘*force majeure*’ or default of the creditor or that the creditor has not suffered any damage resulting from the delay. ”(这方面的问题在本章第 11 段有介绍)

另一条条文更是针对判决后直到执行期间的贬值问题,是在 Article 8:“in the event of the depreciation, between the date of judgment and satisfaction of the judgment, of the currency in which the sum of money is due in relation to the currency of the forum, the provision in Article 4 shall apply and the judgment shall not preclude the creditor from pursuing the claim so arising. ”

14. 结论

以上所探讨的问题与中国内地的关系显然是人民币汇率相对美元,港币甚至其他外国币种的上升。这一问题可以说是影响到商业,生活与政治的每一个层面,不限于诉讼。显然中国已经面临着许多这种问题,包括在外国法院的诉讼或要择地行诉到外国法院向外国公司提出索赔。以上探讨的问题恐怕都应该将这些行动考虑在内。

对笔者而言,就想到有不少在香港仲裁的案件(主要是一些非海事的案件),案情会涉及多年前港商或外商在中国内地的投资争议,金额往往不是小的数目,动不动就数以千万或上亿人民币。但短短几年来,恐怕人民币相对港币的升值幅度不低于25%~30%,而且仍然在升值。这一来在香港仲裁,如果几年前索赔的金额是以人民币或港币作为币种,其中的一方当事人(到底是原告还是被告要看不同的案件而言)就可能可以提出人民币(或港币)不是原告"感觉到损失的币种"(loss felt currency),而这是"强制性"(mandatory)的。例如,港商或外商在多年前的投资是以港币在当时对人民币的兑换比率,而当时的法律地位是港商或外商根本不能够持有人民币,所以恰当的损失币种应当是港币。或是港商作为一家香港公司,它日常营运的币种是港币。但坚持以人民币作为币种的另一方当事人会有不同的争辩,如有关合约的结算或支付的币种是人民币。反正只要认定了一个币种是原告感觉到损失的币种,也轮不到原告或被告选择。由于原告感觉到损失币种的规则的不肯定性与富争论性,双方都有话可以说。到目前在笔者作为仲裁员的案件还没有遇到这一方面的争辩或申请修改请求(只有一个仲裁案件曾经提出过,但没有跟进),这可能是当事人或律师尚不警觉或金额上的差别还没有很显著吸引这一方面的关注。

第十五章　市场规则之一

1. 序言

在本书第二章中介绍了违约/侵权损失的类别，其中在第 13 段提到损失赔偿的基本原则是让受害方恢复到合约获得履行或没有发生侵权的经济地位。这表示经常要找出有关财产/货物或服务的“价值”(value)，比较合约被履行的价值与合约不被履行的价值(受害方在合理减少损失的义务下)后，才能找出损失的金额。在不同的案件找出这一个价值会是有千变万化的情况，正如 Brandon 大法官在 Brandeis Goldschmidt & Co. Ltd v. Western Transport Ltd(1981) QB 864 先例中所说的：“Looking at the matter from the point of view of principle first, I cannot see why there should be any universally applicable rule for assessing damages for wrongful detention of goods, whether it be the rule contended for by the plaintiffs or any other rule. Damages in tort are awarded by way of monetary compensation for a loss or losses which a plaintiff has actually sustained, and the measure of damages awarded on this basis may vary infinitely according to the circumstances of any particular case. It is for the plaintiffs to prove what loss, if any, they have suffered by reason of a tort.”

在第二章也提到了任何东西的价值是有人愿意付出某一个价格买进才能显示出来，所以真正的交易价格是对价值的一个好的证明。但如果是仅凭个别交易价格(不论是受害方或违约方/侵权方所提供)来证明，就会有买低卖高或买高卖低的可能性。可以说，个别交易总免不了有一定程度的主观性与受其他外来因素的影响。这主观性可能是来自卖方(认为最少值多少钱)也会是来自买方(认为最多出得起多少钱)。而外来因素更是数之不尽，如卖方急需要现金或买方对有关的财产/货物有特殊感情等。有一个说法是“价值并不是一个客观的事实，只是在特定时间对有关东西价值的一个看法”(value is never a fact but always an opinion of the worth of property at a given time)。

所以，如果有关的财产/货物或服务在违约或侵权时有一个“可供买卖市场”(available market)可买进或卖出，英国法律就倾向将这一个市场所订立的价格作为一个客观、快捷、相对准确与避免其他方面争议(如损失遥远性或减少损失义务)的准则，这就带来著名的“市场规则”(Market Rule)。可以说，如果真有一个市场，就表示在同一时间内有许多交易在进行。虽然个别交易有它的主观性与受其他外来因素的影响,但如果个别交易的数量够大,在主观性与外来因素的相互抵销下,就可以得出一个相对客观的价值,这就是"市场价格"(market price)。

"可供买卖市场"的定义在本书的第十六章会有更详尽的针对,在此只挑选一个比较经典的权威定义,这是 Webster 大法官在 Shearson Lehman Hutton Inc v. Maclaine Watson & Co Ltd(No. 2)(1990)1 Lloyd's Rep 441 先例总结如下:"What, in the light of these decisions, is the meaning of 'available market'? ... Approached in this way, the answer seems to me to be: that if the seller actually offers the goods for sale there is no available market unless there is one actual buyer on that day at a fair price; and that if there is no actual offer for sale, but only a notional or hypothetical sale for the purposes of s 50(3), there is no available market unless on that day there are in the market sufficient traders potentially in touch with each other to evidence a market in which the actual or notional seller could if he wished to sell the goods; see Lord Justice Sellers in ABD(Metals & Waste) and Charter v. Sullivan sup."

市场规则只是损失赔偿大原则"复原"(*restitutio in integrum*)下的一条"分规则"(sub-rule),显然分规则还是必须遵从大原则,如果市场规则在个别案件中做不到令受害方能够复原,那么它还是需要向大原则作出让步。

本章进一步探讨在有"可供买卖市场"(available market)的情况下,怎样计算在不同违约类别(包括不履行合约、延误履行合约与有缺陷履行合约)下的"基本或直接金钱损失"(basic or direct pecuniary losses)。已经在第二章提到过,在这一个商业的社会或世界,大部分的商业活动都会涉及市场,所以英国法律下的"市场规则"(Market Rule)针对"财产/货物的损失"(loss of property)计算基本损失是十分普遍与常见的做法。其中尤其是在货物买卖,更是在立法明确规定这是计算损失的"表面规则"(*prima facie* rule)。在 1979 年英国《货物销售法》之 Section 50(3)与 Section 51(3)有如下的规定:

"50 **Damages for non-acceptance**. (3) Where there is an available market for the goods in question the measure of damages is *prima facie* to be ascertained by the difference between the contract price and the market or current price at the time or times when the goods ought to have been accepted or(if no time was fixed for acceptance) at the time of the refusal to accept.

51 **Damages for non-delivery**. (3) Where there is an available market for the goods in question the measure of damages is *prima facie* to be ascertained by the difference between the contract price and the market or current price of the goods at the time or times when they ought to have been delivered or(if no time was fixed) at the time of the refusal to deliver."

由于货物买卖的频繁,所以许多有关市场规则的先例都涉及这一方面的商业活动，这些重要的先例会在接下去的段节中介绍。大部分的财产/货物都会有可供买卖的市场（如船舶买卖、房屋买卖与租赁、造船合约、汽车买卖、股票买卖等），并且针对这些买卖完全适用市场规则。只有少部分的货物才会是没有可供买卖的市场，如独一无二的货物或是特别制造的货物。这会涉及古董或名画的买卖，或是特别制造的防弹汽车或机器。这一来，由于市场规则无法适用，就会按照真正损失的价值来计算赔偿金额。而由于真正损失的价值（如无价之宝的古董）有时候也不容易计算，所以英国法律会更加倾向于适用金钱赔偿以外的另一种救济办法，也就是做出“履约指令”（specific performance），这方面在本书第十二章已经有详细的介绍。但如果买卖只是涉及一般的汽车（即使是名牌）或是一般的机器（如家电），毫无疑问是这些货物都会有可供买卖的市场，所以市场规则完全适用。而针对“商品”（commodity）的买卖，更是绝大部分商品都会有可供买卖的市场。

与市场规则计算基本损失有最密切关系的就是受害方需要合理“减少损失”（mitigate damage）。这就是假设在违约一天如果有一个可供买卖的市场，如果卖方违约/毁约（典型的违约就是市场上涨或其他原因卖方拒绝交货或交不出货物），受害的买方就可以马上去市场买进“替代货物”（substitute goods），不论是作为自己使用或是履行分售合约。所以在理论上受害的买方再也不应该索赔“使用/利润损失”（loss of user profits）或分售合约下的利润损失/分买方的索赔。受害的买方唯一会损失的就是在违约一天市场价格与买卖合约价格之间的差价。而如果市场价格比买卖合约价格还要便宜，就表示违约的卖方只需要赔偿“名义损失”（nominal damage）或换言之，受害的买方根本没有蒙受金钱上的损失。

如果倒过来是买方违约/毁约（典型的违约就是拒绝接受货物，不开出信用证，FOB 买方不派船去装港等），受害的卖方也同样适用市场规则，理论上可以在违约一天可供买卖市场出售/转售有关货物，基本损失应该只局限在市场价格与买卖合约价格之间的差价。而如果在市场出售/转售的价格比买卖合约价格还要高，就表示违约的买方只需要赔偿名义损失或换言之，受害的卖方没有金钱上的损失甚至是赚了一点差价。

从以上的解释可以感受到市场规则与合理减少损失的密切关系，就是受害方应该去可供买卖市场马上采取行动，这可以避免进一步扩大损失。市场规则也带来其他的好处，其中最重要的就是不必再考虑复杂的“损失遥远性”（remoteness of damages）限制。毕竟受害方在可供买卖市场马上买进或出售，这带来的市场差价是违约方在订约时完全可以合理预见到的，与违约的因果关系也是直接与明显，所以不会有损失遥远性的争议。这表示在损失计算这一个复杂的课题，市场规则是被公认为“简单”（simple）与“肯定”（certain）的计算办法。这方面可看本书第十三章之 6.3 段中 Anthony Colman 先生或大法官对市场规则的肯定性推崇备至。

2. Market Rule 适用在不履行合约

2.1　Market Rule 适用在不履行财产/货物的转让、交出或接受

许多违约或侵权是涉及受害方的原告蒙受"财产损失"(loss of property),其中经常见到的是侵权方的疏忽导致财产/货物的损失、货物被侵占、卖方违约拒绝交付货物、承运人或托管人交不出货物等。这类案件都涉及一个问题,就是怎样以金钱赔偿原告蒙受的财产/货物损失?只要有关的财产/货物有市场,就经常会适用 Breach Date Rule 与 Market Rule 作为计算损失的办法。毫无疑问在国际货物买卖,最经常会发生的争议是卖方拒绝交货或买方拒绝收货,其中一个主要的原因是市场的波动,特别在国际商品市场更是暴升暴跌不停在发生。这一来,市场变为对自己严重不利,卖方或买方都会扯皮,拒绝交货或收货,并同时试图与对方讨价还价,希望抬高或减低原来买卖合约的价格。这种买卖双方的争议也会演变为对货物的侵占,如买卖涉及"特定货物"(specific goods),1979 年《货物销售法》之 Section 18,rule 1 说明是双方一订立了买卖合约,有关特定货物的财产权就从卖方转让给了买方。所以,如果卖方事后拒绝交出货物,这就不只是违约这么简单,还会涉及"侵占"(conversion)买方的财产/货物。

在较早的段节已经提到了英国《货物销售法》在这些年来针对上述的损失计算条文已经建立了它自己的法理或相关案例,但也同时给许多其他按照 Breach Date Rule 与 Market Rule 计算损失的不同业务(如租船,股票买卖等)提供了指引,只要这些业务也有市场。

2.1.1　卖方违约拒绝交出货物

在货物买卖,针对"损失遥远性"(remoteness)的 Hadley v. Baxendale(1854)9 Ex. 341 先例两条损失规则(第一种是"一般性损失"[ordinary damage]与第二种"特别损失"[special damage])套用在 Market Rule,合约价格与违约时的市场价格的差价就是属于"一般性损失",被视为是"通常损失计算"(normal measure)。这可以节录《McGregor on Damages》(18th edn,2009 年)之 20 - 004 段有关卖方违约拒绝交付货物下受害方的买方如何计算损失:"The normal measure of damages, as stated in section 51 (3) thereby incorporating the common law as stated in Barrow v. Armaud(1846)8 QB 595, is the market price of the goods at the contractual time for delivery less the contract price, since this represents the amount that the buyer must obtain to put himself in the position he would have been in had the contract been carried out. For, to put himself in such a position, he must go into the market and buy equivalent goods; and even if he does not choose to re-buy in the market his loss will remain the same. If, therefore, there is no difference between the contract and the market prices the buyer will have lost nothing and the damage will be nominal."

但如果受害的买方在卖方违约时没有可供买卖市场或其他情况下不能适用 Market Rule，由于无法确定"通常损失计算"(normal measure)，买方才能索赔他真正的损失。这种损失在《McGregor on Damages》一书是名为"间接损失"(Consequential losses)，其中在 20－022 段是这样说："In case of non－delivery consequential losses are not likely to arise where there is a market available in which the buyer can buy equivalent goods against his use or resale. But in the absence of an available market consequential losses are frequent."

这些间接损失是包括了买方因为卖方拒绝交付货物(或延误交付货物)导致了"使用/利润损失"(loss of user profits)、"分销/转售的损失"(loss on a resale)、其他额外的使费损失等。

这种间接损失都需要满足对损失赔偿的限制如损失遥远性。以损失使用并可赚取的利润为例，如果买卖的货物是一台投入生产的机器就是一个明显的例子。如果违约的卖方拒绝交付货物(或延误交付)，会令买方蒙受这一方面的损失。由于机器没有市场可买进替代，所以是不能以通常损失计算的 Market Rule 来计算买方的损失。但索赔这方面的损失，就涉及如损失遥远性的争辩。有关损失计算的最著名的两个先例 Hadley v. Baxendale(1854)9 Ex. 341 与 Victoria Laundry v. Newman Industries (1949)2 K. B. 528 针对的就是这方面的争议。首先在 Hadley v. Baxendale 先例，案情已经在本书第三章之第 2 段详细介绍，在此简单重复说案情涉及原告的工厂因蒸汽机曲轴断裂造成停产，原告急忙委托被告承运人将断轴运送给某地的厂家供其依样再做一根新的。结果被告违约(运输合约)延迟了交付，造成新轴比原计划晚了好几天才交到原告厂里。为此，原告向被告索赔若没有这几天延迟工厂本可早点复工而赚取到的生产利润。法院判定这是被告无法合理预见到的，被告订约当时的全部认知就是为原告工厂这一条断轴进行运输，他并不知道原告没有任何备用轴可供应急，更不知道延误会带来停产。结果是受害方的原告败诉。这一个著名的先例是涉及承运人的延误付运，但如果涉及买卖合约，违约的卖方拒绝交付(或延误交付)这一根蒸汽机曲轴，在损失计算方面也会面对同样的损失遥远性的争议。

而另一个 Victoria Laundry v. Newman Industries 先例更是贴切，因为它就是涉及一个买卖合约。这在本书第三章之第 3 段也有详细介绍，只简单重复案情是原告洗衣馆向被告工程公司订购了一个锅炉，被告迟交货达 5 个月之久，原告诉称被告若按期交货，原告除了因使用锅炉可赚取正常利润之外，还应可获得并完成几项来自政府方面的合约，赚取极高额的利润，因此，被告要赔偿所有这些盈利损失。法庭判定被告在订约前已知晓原告是从事洗衣、印染行业，而且该锅炉是原告急待投入使用以扩大业务量的。因此对原告本可赚取的正常利润的损失，被告必须赔偿，因这是他在订约当时可以合理预见的一般损失。至于那几份获利极高合约的盈利损失，则被告无须负责。因为在原告没有特别知会的情况下，被告不可能预见到原告会有这么值钱的几份合约在手。这些合约本可带来的异常利润的损失客观上对被告来说,是遥不可及的"特别损失"(special damage)。

另一种常见的间接损失"分销/转售的损失"(loss on a resale),会涉及受害方的买方在"分合约"(sub - sale)的利润损失、买方赔付给分买方的合理和解金额或裁决金额(这是因为违约的卖方拒绝交付货物给买方,而由于没有可供买卖市场,导致买方也是无可避免的向分买方违约而要作出赔偿)、有关费用如诉讼费用等。同样的是索赔这方面的损失,也要考虑损失遥远性、因果关系甚至是有否合理减少损失等的争辩。其中会有争议的就是违约的卖方对分合约一无所知,所以不应该要他负责赔偿买方在分合约下可赚取的利润或需要负责的赔偿(如分合约有一条议定赔偿条文)。这里涉及的损失遥远性的争议是买卖双方在订立合约时,违约的卖方是否可以合理预见买方会把有关的这批货物分销/转售?这方面有不少的先例,如在 Kwei Tek Chao v. British Traders and Shippers Ltd(1954)1 Lloyd's Rep 16;Hall v. Pim(1928) 33 Com. Cas. 324 HL;Patrick v. Russo - British Grain Export Co(1927)2 KB 535 等先例,会稍后在本章与第十六章多处有介绍。

2.1.2 买方违约拒绝接受货物

这种违约的损失计算大原则与卖方违约基本上是一样的,就是根据 Market Rule,合约价格与违约时的市场价格的差价就是属于"一般性损失",被视为是"通常损失计算"(normal measure),也就是受害方的卖方可以向买方索赔的损失。这可以节录《McGregor on Damages》(18th edn,2009 年)之 20 - 112 段:"The normal measure of damages, as stated in section 50(3) thereby incorporating the common law as stated in Barrow v. Arnaud(1846)8 QB 595, is the contract price less the market price at the contractual time for acceptance. This represents an amount the seller must obtain to put himself in the position he would have been in had the contract been carried out, since he can sell the goods in the market. If, however, there is clearly no available market, then, consequential losses apart, the damages will be assessed at the contract price less the value of the goods to the claimant at the time of breach, which value is likely to be based, as in Harlow and Jones v. Panex(International)(1967)2 Lloyd's Rep 509, upon the price at which they are eventually sold by the claimant."

另可节录 Treitel 教授在他所著的《The Law of Contract》(10th edn,1999 年)之 896 页有针对(虽然在以下节录的未加黑部分是针对预期违约,但这也是违约的一种),如下:"Where the injured party does accept the breach, he can start his action before the time fixed for performance; but the principle of assessment by reference to that time applies even in this type of case. If the action comes to trial before the time fixed for performance, the damages will therefore necessarily be speculative, as they will be based on forecasts or guesses as to future market movements. But where the injured party accepts the breach, the principle of assessment by reference to the time fixed for performance is subject to an important qualification: his damages will be reduced if, after accepting the breach, he fails to take reasonable steps to mitigate his loss. Under this rule, the injured party may, and if there is a market generally will, be required to make a substitute contract; and his damages will be assessed by reference to the time when the contract should have been made. This will usually be the time of acceptance of the breach (or such reasonable time thereafter as may be allowed under the rules stated above)..."(在这个损失规则下,如果有一个市场的存在,受害方是被要求另外订立替代合约,而他的损失就会根据该替代合约与原合约之间的差价来确定。而在时间上就是在受害方接受违约/毁约而令合约终断的一天或者在接下去合理时间内的一天。)

但如果受害的卖方在违约时没有可供买卖市场或其他情况下不能适用 Market Rule,由于无法确定"通常损失计算"(normal measure),卖方会要索赔他的"间接损失"(consequential losses)。在这种情况下,通常卖方不会产生间接损失,因为有关的货物还是在受害的卖方的手中,货物价值没有失去。另一种情况甚至会是卖方还没有收购或生产有关的货物,所以也不会产生任何间接损失。这可节录《McGregor on Damages》(18th edn,2009 年)之 20 - 123 段:"Consequential losses are as infrequent in actions by the seller for non - acceptance as they are common in actions by the buyer for non - delivery, delayed delivery or breach of warranty. This is because a person is less likely to incur consequential loss where goods are not taken off his hands under a contract than where he does not receive goods as contracted. Illustrations are however to be found."

但产生间接损失的情况还是有,如在 Harlow and Jones v. Panex (International) (1967) 2 Lloyds' Rep 509 先例,由于卖方需要一段时间才能成功把有关货物转售给第三人,产生了仓储费用,这被判是可以向违约的买方索赔。

另在 The "Selda" (1999) 1 Lloyds' Rep 729 先例,涉及的间接损失是 CFR 卖方租了船舶付运有关的货物,但买方违约不开出信用证。这导致卖方作为托运人必须与船东达成和解协议并赔了 65,000 美元,否则会面对不履行租约的索赔。卖方向买方索赔这笔钱,但买方认为卖方不能索赔这笔钱。买方在法院的争辩是仲裁庭在裁决书中没有针对货物(木薯片)有无可供买卖的市场作出任何认定,所以不能排除 Market Rule 的适用,也等于是不能排除 1979 年《货物销售法》之 section 53(3) 的表面规则,就是在有可供买卖的市场的情况下,损失是以买卖合约价格与违约一天的市场价格的差价为准。买方认为必须是在这"通常损失计算"(normal measure)不适用时,才可以根据 section 53(2) 索赔间接损失(但这要满足有关损失计算的限制,如损失遥远性原则中的可预见性与因果关系)。而 section 53(2) 基本上就是以立法的形式说明 Hadley v. Baxendale (1854) 9 Ex 341 先例下的第一类损失类别,说:"(2) The measure of damages is the essential loss directly and naturally resulting in the ordinary course of events, from the buyer's breach of contract."但买方的争辩不被接受,其中上诉庭的 Hirst 大法官是说:

"The first question for consideration is the common law rule.

Miss Ambrose(买方代表大律师)submitted that s. 50(3) is the governing principle, and that it is incumbent on the buyer positively to establish that there is no available market before he can invoke the more general rule in s. 50(2).

To my mind this is putting the cart before the horse, since sub - s. (2) lays down the general rule, and sub - s. (3) is expressed to apply '*prima facie*'.

As Mr. Justice Robert Goff(as he then was) put it in The Elenad'Amico, (1980) 1 Lloyd's Rep. 75 at p. 87:

Of course, the normal measure set out in sub - s. (3) of the Act is only a*prima facie* rule. The principle set out in sub - s. (2) remains the governing principle.

A similar view was expressed by the majority in the Court of Appeal(Lord Justice Otton and Lord Justice Auld, Lord Justice Thorpe dissenting) in Bence Graphics International LTd v. Fasson UK Ltd(1998) QB87 in a case concerning the comparable provison of s. 53 of the Sales of Goods Act, 1979(see particularly per Lord Justice Auld at p. 102)."

2.2　Market Rule 适用在租赁或服务性合约被违约终断与不履行的情况

相比有关财产/货物合约的不履行,服务性合约对"市场规则"(Market Rule)的适用就比较不明确。毕竟有许多种类的服务性合约不涉及市场。但也有与市场规则有非常密切关系的服务性合约,笔者熟悉的租船业务就是与市场规则计算违约损失有紧密的关系。

2.2.1　服务性合约的主要三种损失计算办法

先做一个一般的介绍,服务性合约会包括十分广泛的商业活动,这从一个简单的雇用合约到一个复杂的工程承建合约或长期租约都是属于这一类别的合约。如果这种合约不被履行,损失计算也是比较合约被履行的价值(所谓的预期损失[expectation loss])与不被履行的经济地位的差别,其中包括要考虑受害方要合理减少损失的义务。

2.2.1.1　第一种损失计算办法——替代服务

在计算与厘定损失时,可以得出如果按照第一种通常损失计算的办法来计算服务性合约下的损失,就是受害方在市场取得"替代服务"(substitute service)所支付的代价与原合约下价格的差价即为可以索赔的损失。在 Richards v. Hayward(1841) 133 ER 875 先例,就是涉及原告要额外支付金钱雇用另一位船医,以替代违约的被告(也是一位船医)。

这种取得替代服务的例子在租船合约(不论是程租或期租)被违反的情况下更是普遍。而也正如货物买卖一样,Market Rule 也同样适用,即只要违约一天有一个可租进租出的市场,就假设受害方必须马上采取行动减少损失,在市场取得替代服务。而损失也就是原租约的运费或租金与替代租约的运费或租金之间的差价。这种案例多不胜数 The "Elena d'Amico"(1980) 1 Lloyd's Rep 75; The "Concordia C"(1985)

2 Lloyd's Rep 55；The "Noel Bay"(1989)1 Lloyd's Rep 361；The "Golden Victory"(2007)2 Lloyd's Rep 164；The "Sylvia"(2010)2 Lloyd's Rep 81 等。

2.2.1.2 第二种损失计算办法——利润损失

第二种计算的办法就是受害方索赔违约方不提供服务而给其带来的利润损失。但这种损失不容易成功索赔，因为如果找得到同样的替代服务，受害方就应该减少损失这样做。此外，这利润损失与违约的因果关系不容易成立。还有就是损失遥远性的限制，也就是在订约时双方特别是违约方能够合理预见该损失。这一方面可介绍著名的 Anglia Television Ltd v. Reed(1972)1 QB 60 先例，案情涉及被告的演员拒绝履行他在一部电视剧担当主角的合约承诺。这最终导致原告的电视台取消拍摄该电视剧并向被告索赔为该电视剧拍摄做出准备所支付的费用。原告没有索赔利润损失的主要原因是没有办法证明如果电视剧顺利拍摄与推出，会否卖座而赚到钱。上诉庭的 Denning 勋爵是这样说："Anglia Television(原告)do not claim their profit. They cannot say what their profit would have been on this contract if Mr. Reed(被告)had come here and performed it."而即使原告能够证明损失，也会在因果关系与减少损失方面出问题。就是如果该电视剧会赚钱，为什么原告不转聘其他的演员(甚至是更受欢迎的)来完成该电视剧的拍摄？

租约这种服务性合约在本书第三章多段(包括第 3 段、第 3.1 段等)有提到。承运人对业务与运输货物的用途的了解程度比不上买卖双方，所以承运人如果违约(如延误把货物运到卸港)，对买方的利润损失是被视为不可预见，在没有预先通知的情况下不必负责任。另在 The "Achilleas"(2008)2 Lloyd's Rep 275 先例，针对船东与承租人之间，违约的承租人也不必对延误还船所导致的船东在下一个租约的损失或利润减少而负责。

但针对租船合约其中一种违约，就是船舶不去装港装货(这可以是船东拒绝履行合约或是船舶不适航等原因导致不能及时装港)，承租人作为 CIF/CFR 卖方又找不到替代船舶而令整批货物无法付运进而交易告吹。在这种情况下，有不少著名先例明确了承租人可向船东索赔交易告吹带来的损失。该计算办法是假设租约没有被违反，承租人就会有一票货物安全抵达卸港。所以承租人的损失就是这票货物在卸港的实际价值(减掉运输的费用与保险费)减掉该票货物留在装港运不出去的价值(会是 FOB 价格)，得出的金额就是他的损失。通过这一个途径，有一定程度上是让受害的承租人索赔这一个交易的利润损失。这方面的说法，可节录 Moore - Bick 大法官在 The "Kriti Rex"(1996)2 Lloyd's Rep. 171 先例中所说："... damages for failure to carry a cargo may be measured *either* by the difference between market and charter rates of freight *or* by reference to the value of the goods at the port of discharge(with appropriate deductions). Both measures of damage must be taken to have been within the contemplation of the parties because they are different ways of measuring the loss which a charterer suffers by not having his goods carried to the contractual destination. Which will be the appropriate measure in any given case will no doubt depend on the circumstances of the case, given that the plaintiff is under a duty to act reasonably to mitigate his loss ... in many cases alternative shipping space will be available and, if it is, it will probably be incumbent on the charterer to mitigate his loss by making use of it. I do not accept therefore, that the charterer must be able to show that alternative space was not available before he can recover damages measured by reference to the value of the goods at the port of discharge ... This does not, however, prevent the shipowner from seeking to establish that the charterer failed to act properly in mitigation."

这方面可介绍一个早期的贵族院先例 The "Eugenie Livanos"(1941) Vol. 69 Lloyd's Rep 125,案情涉及一个航次租约,从苏丹港装食盐去日本。由于船舶在上一个航次的卸货被延误,所以赶不及履行这一个租约而导致违约。双方的争议基本上就是在损失的计算,而去贵族院要求最后判决是以哪一种算法为准。损失有三种计算办法,第一种就是另一艘替代船舶的市场运费与租约运费的差价;第二种就是承租人因为无法履行这一个航次而失去了这一个交易的利润损失;第三种就是在日本同样一批食盐在船舶应该运抵一天的价格,减去运费、保险费比较在苏丹港这一票食盐的价格的差价。显然,这三种不同计算办法所得出的金额都很不一样。在贵族院,判是第一种计算办法不适用,原因是当时日本对进口的每一票货与每一艘船,都涉及批文,换了一艘船转让批文并不容易。所以,不存在可找一艘同样的替代船舶履行这一个航次。至于第二种办法,贵族院判是根据 Hadley v. Baxendale(1854)9 Ex. 341 先例,针对承运人而言索赔利润损失是属于第二种的"特别损失"(special damage),承租人在订约前没有给船东通知的情况下是不能索赔的。这剩下了第三种办法,贵族院认为是可以接受的损失计算办法,也认为是双方在订约时可以合理预见到的。

这方面还有其他的先例,如 Stroms Bruks Aktie Bolag v. Hutchison(1905) A. C. 515 (HL); The "Heron II"(1967) Lloyd's Rep 457 等。

2.2.1.3 第三种损失计算办法——浪费的费用

第三种计算的办法就是受害方索赔浪费的费用,这也是在本书第二章所讲到的"依赖损失"(reliance loss)。在 Anglia Television Ltd v. Reed(1972) 1 QB 60 先例,原告索赔成功的也就是这一笔金钱的救济。

2.2.2 服务性合约在预期违约的损失计算办法

在这里先简单介绍"预期违约"(anticipatory breach),同样的课题已经在本书第五章之 10 段有详细介绍,并会稍后在本章之 6.2 段继续针对。预期违约就是在承诺的履行还没有到期,违约方就提前向受害方说明他将来是不会履行有关的合约,受害方在英国法律下是有两个选择。他可以选择坚持违约方将来必须履行合约,而在这种坚持的情况下,合约还是有效。而违约方可能在受害方的压力下(受害方可能会开始仲裁或警告违约方将来会面对的庞大索赔)而回心转意履行合约,这就等于较早的预期违约根本没有发生过。但受害方另有一个选择就是接受预期违约,而这样做就是令有关合约终断。这方面可以节录《Benjamin's Sale of Goods》(8th edn,2010年)之17－013段有关卖方违约下买方的救济(倒过来是买方违约,卖方的救济也是同一个道理)如下:"**The seller's anticipatory repudiation.** The rules for the seller's anticipatory repudiation correspond with those for the buyer's anticipatory repudiation. Where the seller, before the date fixed for delivery of the goods, repudiates his liability under the contract, the buyer has a choice: he may either accepts the repudiation as a breach and immediately sue for damages, or he may refuse to accept the repudiation and continue to treat the seller as bound by his contractual obligations."

至于在损失计算方面,如果"市场规则"(Market Rule)适用,也就是指有关的服务可以在市场找到替代,针对预期违约被受害方提前接受就会偏离了本书第十三章介绍的Breach Date Rule,即损失是以该合约应该被履行的一天的市场价格与合约价格作出比较与计算,但受害方有一个合理减少损失的"责任"或义务。而如果预期违约没有被受害方提前接受,有关合约就会持续有效。而到了真正应该被履行的一天仍是被拒绝履行,这就构成了违约/毁约,往往令受害方别无选择接受终断合约。这一来,就完全可以适用Breach Date Rule与Market Rule。有关这一方面稍后在本章之6.2段会进一步介绍有关的先例。

2.2.3 服务性合约在违约/毁约的损失计算办法

在一个中长期的服务性合约的履行中途,如果违约方拒绝继续履行,这构成了类似[1]预期违约的"违约/毁约"(repudiation),受害方可以坚持违约方继续履行或接受违约/毁约,除非好像本书第十一章之4.1段所提到的情况就是受害方不能单方面履行与没有合法利益坚持合约必须继续履行。这一来,如果受害方接受违约/毁约,把一个中长期合约终断,就马上存在Breach Date Rule与Market Rule的适用,只要是有关的服务有替代市场。这种情况在租船合约经常发生,如在2008年金融海啸之后航运市场暴跌,但由于在不久前航运市场的好景维持了一段颇长的时间而使许多承租人过分乐观而签下了不少中长期的期租合约,这令他们在市场暴跌后面对严重亏损而拒绝继续履行租约。这一来,由于租约还有一段需要履行的时间,很多事情还没有发生,所以适用复原原则就会在时间上存在两种不同损失计算办法。第一种就是

---

〔1〕 在《Chitty on Contracts》(13th edn,2008年)之20－017段提到了三种违约可以造成合约的终断,说:"The three sets of circumstances giving rise to a discharge of contract are tabulated by Anson as(1)renunciation by a party of his liabilities under it;(2)impossibility created by his own act;and(3)total or partial failure of performance. In the case of the first two, the renuniciation may occur or the impossibility be created either before or at the time for performance. In the case of the third it can occur only at the time or during the course of performance. Moreover, if the third be partial, the failure must occur in a matter which goes to the root of the contract. All these acts may be compendiously described as repudiation, though that expression is more particularly used of renunciation before the time for performance has arrived."显然,上述三种的"违约/毁约"(repudiatory breach)是包括了"预期违约"(anticipatory breach)。

等到合约如果被履行而实际应该履行完毕的日期,这通常是一个不现实的做法。如在违约/毁约被接受后,有关的合约还有10年的有效期,这就要等到10年后才对实际损失作出计算。如在一个期租合约中,就要看在这10年里,受害方船东实际在"替代营运"(substitute employment)中所赚取的利润或租金,然后去比较被终断的合约如果被履行的情况下能够赚取的利润或租金,两者之间的差别就是受害方的损失(或者没有损失)。这一种计算损失的不妥之处很明显,最主要的就会是迫使受害方要等到10年后才能提出索赔。另是受害方对他的损失会有很多复杂与说不清的举证责任,而违约方也会有许多"事后诸葛亮"的说法提出争辩。例如,受害方没有在某一个替代航次中合理减少损失,因果关系的中断等。反正在漫长的10年的替代营运中,肯定会有许多受害方所作出的商业决定是说不清楚的。例如,在市场曾经一度飙升的时候,违约方质疑受害方为什么不长期出租,可赚取的租金会比终断的租约还要高,就不会有损失了。可以说这一种计算损失的办法由于太麻烦是不被接受的,而且要求受害方为了核算真正损失而需要漫长的等待是不合理。而第二种计算损失的办法就是在违约一天尽量估计受害方将来的损失,但也会是有太多的猜测。对租船合约这一类的服务性合约而言,通常会有市场的同类性质租赁或服务性合约的租金/收费,然后比较合约的租金/收费并找出差价,也就是适用 Market Rule。这显然是被英国法律接受的损失计算办法,只要在违约时有可供租用或替代的市场。

在很大程度上,市场规则计算损失也显示了简单与肯定之外的好处,就是在上述的例子不必要受害方等到10年后才能提出索赔,也不需要依赖专家意见对将来估计的损失作出臆猜。受害的船东(或承租人)可以在违约一天按照市场规则马上租出(租进)同类的船舶如散装船或油轮,替代租约也相同是长达10年,这替代租约与原合约之间的差价也就是受害方的损失。至于该替代租约将来会面对的困难,如新的承租人违约或延误/拒绝支付租金,这些损失与原来承租人的违约已经是在因果关系上完全中断了。

这方面可以航运最常见的期租合约作为例子介绍,毕竟这种合约就是典型的租赁或服务性合约。如果这种合约提前被违约终断与不履行,损失计算方面最权威的先例是 The "Elena d'Amico"(1980)1 Lloyd's Rep 75。案情涉及船东在一个3年期租中只履行了14个月就违约/毁约,提早撤船。Goff 大法官是这样说:"If, at the date of the breach, there is an available market, the normal measure of damages will be the difference between the contract rate and the market rate for chartering in a substitute ship for the balance of the charter period. If however the time charterer decides not to take advantage of that market, then, generally speaking, that will be his own business decision independent of the wrong; and the consequences of that decision are his. If he judges the market correctly, he reaps the benefit; if he judges it incorrectly, then the extra cost falls on him."

Bingham 勋爵在 The "Golden Victory"(2007)2 Lloyd's Rep 164 先例有提到该先例,并说明在这方面是权威性,说:"That case concerned the measure of damages recoverable by a charterer for breach of a time charter during its currency by an owner. While taking care to avoid laying down an inflexible or invariable rule, the judge held, at p. 89, col. 2, that if, at the date of breach, there is an available market, the normal measure of damages will be the difference between the contract rate and the market rate for chartering in a substitute ship for the balance of the charter period. An analogy was drawn, at p. 87, with section 51(3) of the Sale of Goods Act 1893 (56 & 57 Vict c 71). Neither party challenged this decision, which has always been regarded as authoritative."

但上述的解释还是不解决所有的困难,如在2008年年底的金融海啸后,航运市场暴跌超过90%,导致大量的承租人违约/毁约把长期租约(不论是期租还是海上货物运输合约COA)终断。而在当时,市场上根本没有这么长期的替代租约,即使租金是低无可低。这种情况一直持续了几个月,市场才慢慢恢复信心有了长期租约的出现。这一来在计算长期租约下受害船东的损失,不少仲裁员是分两部分计算。第一部分是违约后直到长期租约在市场上出现的一段时间,根据船东实际营运的利润或租金比较长期租约下的利润或租金找出真正损失。第二部分是市场出现长期的替代租约后,根据Market Rule计算剩下租约期的损失。但在近期的The "Kildare" (2011) 2 Lloyd's Rep 360先例与The "Wren" (2011) 2 Lloyd's Rep 370先例,这种混合计算的办法不被接受,也认为是不可以将违约后相隔好几个月才出现的市场价格作为Market Rule中的用作比较的市场价格。这一个问题会在本书第十六章之6.5段探讨并详细介绍有关先例。

2.3 不履行合约适用Market Rule的一些著名先例与说法

已经提到过这一个主要来自货物买卖的违约损失计算规则在1979年英国《货物销售法》已经被明确规定,这也是普通法地位。即使是侵权造成财产/货物的损失,也适用这一个市场价格的计算损失办法,如侵占货物。这方面权威说法可节录《McGregor on Damages》(18th edn, 2009年)之33-006段所说如下:"**The normal measure of damages for conversion is the market value of the goods converted**. This is well settled and is based upon the ground that, as Greer LJ put it in Hall v. Barclay (1937) 3 All ER 620 CA, 'where you are dealing with goods which can be readily bought in the market, a man whose rights have been interfered with is never entitled to more than what he would have to pay to buy a similar article in the market'."(被侵占的货物如果有可供买卖的市场,法律已经明确是损失计算通常就是购入替代货物的市场价格。在Hall v. Barclay先例,Greer大法官说是如果侵权的对象是在市场可以买进替代的货物,损失就不应该超出受害方可以在市场买进替代货物的价格。)

适用违约一天计算将来损失的所谓Breach Date Rule与Market Rule有数不尽的先例,如Johnson v. Agnew (1980) AC 367(房屋买卖);The "Wave" (1981) 1 Lloyd's Rep 521.(租约);The "Noel Bay" (1989) 1 Lloyd's Rep 361.(租约);North Sea Energy Holding NV v. Petroleum Authority of Thailand (1999) 1 Lloyd's Rep 483.(原油买卖);The

"Sea Flower"(2000)2 Lloyd's Rep 37.(租约);Kaines(UK)Ltd v. Osterreichische Warrenhandelsgesellschaft Austrowaren Gesellschaft m. b. H.(1993)2 Lloyd's Rep 1(原油买卖);Jamal v. Dawood(1916)1 AC 175;Bear Sterns Bank plc v. Forum Global Equity Ltd.(2007)EWHC 1575(Comm)(股票买卖);Norden v. Andre(2003)1 Lloyd's Rep 287.(衍生工具)等。因此,Breach Date Rule 与 Market Rule 不是只适用在货物买卖(因为有立法规定)。这些涉及各种不同商业活动的著名先例会在接下去的段节进一步介绍。

2.3.1 案例之一:Jamal v. Dawood

Jamal v. Dawood(1916)1 AC 175 是一个有关股票买卖的枢密院先例,买方在1911 年4~8 月间的6 个不同的合约中承诺以不同的价格购买原告公司的23,500 份股票,约定最迟在1911 年12 月30 日交出股票以交换买方付出的对价。合约中有一个条文是说如果买方没有付款,卖方有权把股票卖给别人,这明示条文看来也就是法律默示的地位。在1911 年12 月30 日,卖方交出了股票,但买方拒绝付款,而当时市场的股票价格在下跌。当天该股票的市场价格为4s. 3d 每股,这23,500 份股票的市场总价比合约规定的价格少了109,218 英镑。卖方书面告知买方他打算把这些股票转售给第三人以减少损失。但是一直等到1912 年2 月28 日,卖方才开始出售这批股票,直到1912 年8 月才通过几次不同交易把这些股票卖尽。而卖方获得的转售股票价格的总数只比原合约价格少了79,862 英镑。在诉讼中,卖方要求违约的买方依据1911 年12 月30 日股票市场价格与合约价格的差价赔偿给他109,218 英镑,而买方认为卖方在后来真正的转售中减少了一些损失,因此只需要赔偿给卖方实际损失的79,862 英镑。法院最后判是受害的卖方有权获得109,218 英镑的损失赔偿,也就是1911 年12 月30 日买方违约/毁约当天股票市场价格与合约价格的差价。尽管卖方有减少损失的义务,但"市场规则"(Market Rule)的适用就已经排除了受害方的卖方事后有否合理减少损失的考虑。枢密院的 Wrenbury 勋爵是这样说:

"The question therefore is the general question and may be stated thus: in a contract of sale of negotiable securities, is the measure of damages for breach the difference between the contract price and the market price at the date of the breach – with an obligation on the part of the seller to mitigate the damages by getting the best price he can at the date of the breach – – or is the seller bound to reduce the damages, if he can, by subsequent sales at better prices? If he is, and if the purchaser is entitled to the benefit of subsequent sales, it must also be true that he must bear the burden of subsequent losses. The latter proposition is in their Lordships' opinion impossible, and the former is equally unsound. If the seller retains the shares after the breach, the speculation as to the way the market will subsequently go is the speculation of the seller, not of the buyer; the seller cannot recover from the buyer the loss below the market price at the date of the breach if the market falls, nor is he liable to the purchaser for the profit if the market rises.

It is undoubted law that a plaintiff who sues for damages owes the duty of taking all reasonable steps to mitigate the loss consequent upon the breach and cannot claim as damages any sum which is due to his own neglect. But the loss to be ascertained is the loss at the date of the breach. If at that date the plaintiff could do something or did something which mitigate the damage, the defendant is entitled to the benefit of it. Staniforth v. Lyall(1830) 7 Bing. 169 is an illustration of this. But the fact that by reason of the loss of the contract which the defendant has failed to perform the plaintiff obtains the benefit of another contract which is of value to him does not entitle the defendant to the benefit of the latter contract: Yates v. Whyte(1838)4 Bing. N. C 272; Bradburn v. Great Western Railway(1874) LR 10 Ex. 1; Jebsen v. East and West India Dock Co(1875) LR 10 CP. 300."

2.3.2 案例之二:Norden v. Andre

在介绍 Norden v. Andre(2003)1 Lloyd's Rep 287 先例之前,先对该先例中会涉及的金融"衍生工具"(derivative)作一些简单的介绍。在1992年左右金融市场开始发展起来的一个有关运费期货市场的"衍生工具"(derivative),作用就是打赌将来某一航次或某一些指定航线的时段运费会比一个固定的价格更高或者是更低。这表示会有两个价格:一个就是"固定价格"(fixed price),也就是双方对赌约定的。另一个叫"浮动价格"(floating price),这是根据市场的机制或波动而变化。对赌赢的一方可以收取这两个价格之间的差价。会对赌,显然对将来的市场存在不同的看法,需要一方认为市场会下跌,而另一方会认为市场会上涨。赌将来市场会上涨的一方,可被称作为"买方"(buyer),而赌市场下跌的一方,可被称作为"卖方"(seller)。显然,这所谓的"买方"与"卖方"与真正的财产/货物买卖是没有关系的。对赌双方会签订一份合约,名为"远期运费协议"(forward freight swap agreement 或简称 FFA)。这种运费期货市场就像其他所有的衍生工具一样,是没有"双赢"的局面,完全是"零和游戏"(zero sum game)。它的作用也和其他衍生工具一样,可以纯粹是用来"投机"(pure speculation)、"套利交易"(arbitrage)或者"对冲"(hedging)。

大致上,如果对赌是因为背后有实质的生意,但害怕因航运市场起变化而令预算可以赚取的利润落空,才利用这个方法对冲,那么这是一个健康的做法。例如,刚刚签订的一份20万吨的CIF散粮买卖合约,是从美湾运去日本。由于要在3~6个月后才分3个航次付运,而当时运费市场高涨与波动十分大。这一来卖方就会怕本来约定的CIF价格可以赚取10%利润,但由于运费市场上涨,导致这个CIF价格中预算的运费远远不足支付实际的运费而变为亏本。那么卖方就可以作为买方签订一份FFA,等到运费市场到时真的上涨,虽然要支付比预算更高的运费,但这差价可以在FFA中得到抵销。

再举一个在FFA做法上的例子是:"At any given time ABC will have chartered in vessels for X days and secured fixtures for Y days. X is likely to be greater than Y, but it could be less. Suppose that X is 1,000 days and Y is 500 days. ABC's 'cargo cover' is therefore 50 per cent. Depending on how ABC perceives that the market is likely to move, it might want to use the forward freight market to ‘sell’ freight. If it sold 365 days, this would give it a cargo cover of 86.5 per cent.”(如果 ABC 长期租进一艘船舶,长达 1000 天。但他手中只有长达 500 天的 COA,他等于只有 50% 的货运保证。如果 ABC 估计市场会下跌,他就可以通过 FFA 出售剩余 500 天的货运能力。如果有买方愿意接受签订一个 12 个月的 FFA,则会使 ABC 的货运保证提高到 86.5%。这货运保证不代表真正有货物运输,只是在金钱上的一个对赌。)

至于不健康的做法就当然是纯粹的投机,也就是根本没有生意在背后,就大量签订这一类的合约与其他公司或金融机构对赌。如果遇上市场突然逆转,要输的话可以说是个无底洞,是很容易导致倾家荡产的。光是这个针对航运市场的 FFA,这些年来已经听说过不少很具规模的公司因为赌输了导致倾家荡产,如早期的 Continental Grain 与较近期的 North American Shipping Co. 等。

在这里可以介绍两个近期的 FFA 先例与法院做出的解释。第一个是 Pioneer Freight Futures Co Ltd v. TMT Asia Ltd(2011)2 Lloyd's Rep 96 先例,Gloster 大法官说:“In essence, an FFA is a ‘bet’ as to the future movements of the fright market. The product can be used as a hedge by parties involved in shipping freight to protect themselves against fluctuation in shipping rates, or as a means of trading in futures.”

第二个是 Pioneer Freight Futures Co Ltd v. Cosco Bulk Carrier(2011)2 Lloyd's Rep 409 先例,Flaux 大法官说:“An FFA is a cash - settled contract for differences referenced to the Index rate or rates published by the Baltic Exchange, as selected by the parties. A ‘Settlement Sum’ is calculated for each FFA and each Contract Month from the ‘Contract Rate’ agreed between the parties, the ‘Settlement Rate’ for that Contract Month derived from the Baltic Exchange indices, and the number of days in the month.”

至于“套利交易”(arbitrage)的做法又可以举一个简单的例子来说明,就是过去一段很长的时期,日元的银行利息几乎是零,但相比有不少其他国家的货币如澳元年利率是 5% ~6%。这一来,如果去向日本银行大量借入日元,然后兑换澳元就可以很稳当的赚取这 5% ~6% 的利息。但这里有个最大的风险就是日元相对澳元会升值,而这些风险是很难预测的,因为如一个国家的政局变动、国家热钱的动向或者甚至是澳洲发现一个大油田等的因素都会造成这些波动。所以针对这个风险,就可以签订一份对冲合约,在日元升值的时候有保障。这一来,只要这个息差如 5% 所能赚取的钱,减去对冲的佣金,剩下所能赚取的就是套利交易。这个可以说是万无一失稳赚的生意,唯一剩下来的风险就是对赌的一方破产,但这种对赌通常是跟一些跨国的大银行进行,所以这种风险是微乎其微的。由于这个世界上有很多这种不平衡的情况存在,特别是在制度上或法规上,这些就是国际上搞金融的人士无时无刻不在等待的机会。

本先例的案情是,有一家名为 Norden 的丹麦老牌船公司,老板希望进入巴拿马运河型散装船的期货市场，而在2000年10月有这么一个机会租入一艘名为Talisman轮的巴拿马运河型散装船，为期16个月，每日租金为11,100美元。但又怕市场下跌而有损失，所以Norden想以一个从2001年1月1日开始为期12个月的FFA作出对冲。结果通过Clarksons作为经纪人与被告Andre订了一个FFA去对赌，而Norden有了这个FFA之后就确认了这个Talisman轮的期租合约。Norden与Andre之间的FFA有以下的条文：

"(1) The contract route was to be the average of four routes (Transatlantic Round Timecharter, Continent to U. S. Gulf to Fareast Timecharter, Transpacific Round Timecharter and Fareast to Nopac to Continent Timecharter) of the Baltic Panamax Index (BPI), known for short as the 4 BPI TC routes.（FFA合约的航线是以4条波罗的交易所巴拿马型散货船指数上的主要航线作为根据）

(2) The fixed rate was to be U. S. $10,675 per day.（固定价格，也就是Talisman租入的每天净租金）

(3) The contract quantity was to be 365 days.（FFA的合约天数是365天，即每天都对赌）

(4) The contract period was to be from Jan. 1 to Dec. 31, 2001.（FFA为期2001年的一整年）

(5) Settlement dates were to be the last day of each month.（结算的时间是每一个月的最后一天）

(6) The floating rate was to be determined monthly as the average of the rates for the 4 BPI TC routes published by the Baltic Exchange during each month（浮动的价格就是根据波罗的交易所每个月公布的有关4条巴拿马型散货船的主要航线每天租金的平均指数）

(7) The settlement sum was to be the difference between the fixed rate and the floating rate multiplied by the contract quantity. If the settlement rate was greater than the fixed rate, the seller was to pay the buyer the settlement sum; and vice versa if the settlement rate was less than the fixed rate.（结算的金额就是固定价格与浮动价格之间的差价再乘以合约天数）

(8) Payment of the settlement sum was to be made within five days after the settlement date.（要在结算后的5天内支付）"

在这份FFA签订当时，Andre是一个国际主要的"粮商"（grain trader）。而在2001年的1月与2月，浮动的价格是比固定价格高的。等于说Norden赌输了，需要在这两个月的结算时支付给Andre。但理论上由于市场好了，Norden可以在营运Talisman轮中赚取该差价。但到了2001年的3月9日，Andre宣布经济困难，并且由瑞士的法院委任接管人接管这间公司并作出破产保护令。这个消息很快在市场传开来，而Norden在3月16日给Andre一份电邮要求他澄清公司的状况，如下："We have learned from press reports that, much to our concern, Andre have filed Chapter 11 proceedings before the Courts in Switzerland, are shutting many of their operations, and that 43 banks have stopped all credit lines to your organisation. Given our present commercial relationship, we would much appreciate it if you could urgently advise by return whether the above mentioned information is correct or not."

虽然 Andre 没有回复,但 Norden 也经过他的互保协会得到 Andre 公司清盘的确认。这样一来,Norden 决定终断这个 FFA,因为继续下去就会对 Norden 很不利,原因是接下来的每个月即使 Norden 赌赢了也收不到钱,因为他只是 Andre 的一个普通债权人,但如果赌输了就要在 5 天内付钱给 Andre,否则就是违约。Norden 是在 3 月 19 日给 Andre 通知终断合约,因为他违反了 FFA 的保证。本来,合约一方发生经济困难并获得法院作出破产保护令并不是终断合约的理由,但 FFA 这个标准格式合约是要十分小心的,它有明示条文规定双方有一个持续保持自己经济状况良好的保证("[9] Each party gave a continuing warranty to the other that it was solvent and in good standing.")。

案情再发展下去,Andre 曾经提议过双方可否达致一个和解协议,就是在这个接管人与瑞士清盘法院同意之下,允许这个 FFA 继续有效。期间运费市场一直下跌,直到 6 月份才开始上涨。这样一来,2001 年 3、4 与 5 月结算时都是由 Andre 支付给 Norden,但到了 6 月就变为是 Norden 要支付给 Andre。到了 2001 年 11 月 2 日,Norden 正式向 Andre 索赔违约的损失,而 Andre 起初否认有任何违约,但在开庭前不久就不再对责任方面有任何抗辩,并接受在 3 月 19 日 Norden 有权终断合约,剩下的就是损失怎样计算的问题。

Norden 索赔 757,385.96 美元,这是根据他与 Andre 之间签订的 FFA 一直没有终断的情况下,每个月结算直到 2001 年 12 月底。这是根据 Hadley v. Baxendale(1854) 9 Ex. 341 先例的一般损失计算规则,即合约如果被履行的情况下的计算办法。也就是 FFA 没有被终断 Norden 应该得到的合约利益。Norden 针对为什么他没有去市场上签订其他的 FFA 作为替代也作出了许多解释,为什么他没有去市场上签订其他的 FFA 作为替代。

Andre 认为损失应该在 3 月 30 日,Norden 一终断 FFA 就应该在市场上签订另一份 2001 年 4 月到 12 月的 FFA,而当时的平均价格是每天 10,000 美元。这样一来,Norden 的损失就是 185,625 美元(即 10,675 美元 - 10,000 美元 × 275 日)

而 Toulson 大法官判计算办法仍然是 Norden 应该在 3 月 19 日进入市场签订替代的 FFA,以当时的市场计算,Norden 可以以 9975 美元的固定价格入市,结果损失的是 192,500 美元,所以是以违约一天的市场价格来计算损失。

2.3.3　案例之三:Diamond Cutting Works Federation Ltd v. Triefus & Co. Ltd

Diamond Cutting Works Federation Ltd v. Triefus & Co. Ltd(1956)1 Lloyd's Rep 216 先例涉及一个一般的买卖,但有关的财产/货物是工业用钻石,原告的买方本身是一个非营利机构,他买进的钻石是以成本价加一个百分比的佣金转售或供应给他的会员。由于期间钻石价格上涨,卖方违约不交货。这导致受害的买方提出索赔,而损失是根据买卖合约的价格与违约时的市场价格之间的差价。但卖方对损失计算提出抗辩,认为买方作为非营利机构根本没有损失。而由于市场价格上涨,买方按更高价格的百分比可赚取更高的佣金。但法院不同意卖方的抗辩,认为损失计算没有理由偏离"市场规则"(Market Rule)的表面规则,偏离反而会造成不公平。Barry 大法官是这样说:"... merely because an individual or company does not propose to make a profit out of goods which he purchases, it cannot, I think, be said that they are not involved in a loss if they have to pay more for goods which they intend either to give away or pass on at cost price to others. I refuse to accede to this argument and I think that here the true measure of damage is the one stated to be the *prima facie* measure, namely, the difference between the contract and the market price of these goods."

上述的判决是完全可以理解,英国法律是不理会受害的买方在收到有关的财产/货物后会怎样处理。即使是准备赠送给第三人,也不表示买方在卖方的不履行违约下,没有任何损失。早在 Williams v. Agius(1914) AC 510 先例,贵族院的 Moulton 勋爵已经说:"it is immaterial what the buyer is intending to do with the purchased goods. He is entitled to recover the expense of putting himself into the position of having those goods." 另 Dunedin 勋爵也在该案例说:"The buyer ... is entitled to be put in the position in which he would have stood if he had got [the goods] at the due date. That position is the position of a man who has goods at the market price of the day."

2.3.4 案例之四:Sudan Import v. Societe Generale de Compensation

Sudan Import v. Societe Generale de Compensation(1958) 1 Lloyd's Rep 310 先例涉及一个 FOB 买卖,付运日期是 1955 年 9 月。在 8 月中,买方知悉这是一宗亏本生意,于是在 8 月 17 日向卖方书面要求终断合约,并请卖方转卖/出售手上货物。卖方在 8 月 22 日拒绝该终断合约的要求。买方在 8 月 29 日明确拒货,这构成了"预期违约"(anticipatory breach)。双方之后另有电文来往,其中卖方在 9 月 10 日发出电文说已备妥货物在装港并问有没有派船。这电文显示了卖方不接受买方的预期违约,坚持买卖合约的有效性并要求买方履行。但到了 9 月 20 日,卖方终于面对现实"接受"(accept)买方在 8 月 29 日的预期违约并终断合约。

在赔偿损失方面,其中最主要的争议是以哪一天的市场价格计算损失,因为市场的波动导致不同日期的价格相差很远。这一天到底是:8 月 17 日(买方要求终断合约)? 8 月 29 日(预期违约)? 9 月 10 日(卖方坚持履约)? 9 月 20 日(卖方接受 8 月 29 日的预期违约)? 9 月 30 日(买卖合约的最后付运一天)? 显然不应该是 8 月 17 日,因为当时买方只不过是提出要求。也显然不应该是 8 月 29 日与 9 月 10 日,因为已经解释过买卖合约还是存在,所以没有法律上要求合理减少损失的义务。那么,作为比较的要不是 9 月 20 日的市场价格要不是 9 月 30 日的市场价格。法律上,在 9 月 20 日受害的卖方选择终断买卖合约就已经是有了合理减少损失的义务。但有关买卖合约的付运期最后一天是在9月30日，理论上违约的FOB买方可以派遣船舶让货物在付运期最后一天装船，如果他没有这样做才会在这一天被视为是违约。所以，如果不涉及预期违约，或是预期违约一直没有被受害的卖方所接受，该买卖合约也就会在9月30日由于FOB买方没有派遣船舶而变为一个真正的拒绝履行合约行为或是“违约/毁约”(repudiation of contract)而终断。所以，在这一个预期违约，根据Market Rule应是以9月30日的市场价格比较合约价格。事实上，上诉庭判是以9月30日一天的市场价格为准。但由于在9月20日卖方接受了买方的预期违约而终断了买卖合约，所以从9月20日到9月30日这一段时间还要看卖方作为受害方是否曾经有过合理机会可减少损失，如有证据显示该票有关的货物曾经另有机会可以高价转售给第三人，甚至违约的买方给卖方做出了一个“新要约”(reoffer)购买这票货物，但卖方没有合理对待。当然，这种有机会减少损失的可能性是由违约的买方提出与证明，而且不会是容易。本先例中，贵族院的Evershed勋爵说：“In my judgment, it is impossible to go back, for the purpose of mitigating the damage, any earlier than Sept. 20, that being the date on which the contract was put to an end by the sellers´ acceptance of the buyers´ repudiation; but it is, I think, right to say that you arrive at the sum of damage by ascertaining what the loss would be to the sellers by non-performance on the performance date, Sept 30, looking back, however, to Sept. 20 to see whether that loss ought to be reduced by steps which the sellers could reasonably have taken, from and after the last-mentioned date, in mitigation.”

有关预期违约下，对Breach Date Rule与Market Rule的适用，将会在本章6.2段进一步去探讨。

2.3.5　案例之五：Kaines v. Ostereichische Warrenhandelsgesellschaft

Kaines v. Ostereichische Warrenhandelsgesellschaft (1993) 2 Lloyd's Rep 1先例在本章2.1.2段有简单提及，案情涉及的是1987年9月的60万桶Brent原油期货买卖。责任方面在这里就长话短说，就是英国法院判卖方违约/毁约，卖方是在6月17日告诉买方他们之间没有订立买卖合约，所以不存在履行的责任。而买方在6月18日接受了卖方的违约/毁约把该合约终断。在后来的诉讼，法院根据证据判双方已经订立了买卖合约，这一来，卖方说没有买卖合约并且不履行很明显就是违约/毁约了。

但这一个先例双方的另一个重要争议是有关损失怎样计算，也是在这一方面要上诉去上诉庭。这里可以介绍当时价格波动非常大的Brent原油市场。首先双方买卖合约的价格是每桶18.48美元，到了6月18日，9月期货的市场价格变了是18.72美元，涨了24美分。到了6月19日，再涨了2美分，平均的市场价格变了是18.74美元。之后的市场价格每天有涨有跌，到了6月25日是有一个“石油出口国”(OPEC)的会议，这一个会议的结果会影响市场价格。当天，Brent原油的9月期货下跌至18.38美元。第二天，即6月26日，市场又上涨了38美分而变为是18.76美元。这之后是周末，没有市场。到了6月29日，油价上涨至平均价格的19.23美元。在同一天，买方在市场买进了60万桶的9月期货，价格是19.30美元。

在上述的事实下，买方希望索赔的金额显然就是19.30美元减去合约价格的18.48美元，等于0.82美分，再乘以60万桶，损失等于599,981.52美元。但卖方认为买方只能获得名义损失的赔偿，因为既然买方没有在6月18或者19日买进9月期货，而选择等待，最后的损失就与违约/毁约不存在有直接因果关系。而如果买方是在6月25日的市场价格18.38美元时买进，这就比买卖合约的价格更低了，根本没有金钱上的损失。

在高院，Steyn大法官判是卖方与买方的损失计算都是错误的，因为这是把违约/毁约后其他的因素加了进来，包括像买方的等待至6月29日才买进9月期货及卖方以6月25日的市场价格为准是完全事后的考虑。Steyn大法官认为计算损失的时间，应该还是根据Breach Date Rule的违约一天或最多第二天，也就是买方接受违约/毁约后在6月18日还有5个小时剩下的市场交易时间至最晚的6月19日，受害的买方就应该在可供买卖市场买进替代货物。如果是在更后的日期，就往往掺进了其他会中断因果关系的因素，如买方对市场走向的看法。在上诉庭，Steyn大法官的判决得到支持，Bingham大法官是这样说："The Judge's conclusion that a reasonable prudent oil trader would have bought in a substitute cargo on June 19 in my opinion fixes the level of the plaintiffs' damages on the facts of this case irrespective of what the plaintiffs did or failed to do at the time. Had the market price risen steadily after June 19, their failure to buy could not have increased the damages payable by the defendants. Had the price fallen steadily after June 19, their failure to buy would not have reduced the damages. It is, as I think, a somewhat unreal exercise to look at the trend of market prices with the benefit of hindsight, seize on June 25 as the one occasion before the plaintiffs actually bought when the market price dropped below the contract price and postulate that the plaintiffs should have bought then. The Judge rightly held that the plaintiffs were speculators (no doubt quite as anxious to make a profit for themselves as to protect the defendants against loss) they may well have stayed out of the market on June 25 in the hope that prices would sink lower. What a reasonable trader would have done is, in my view, a sounder basis for assessing damages than the subjective judgement of any particular player in the market."

2.3.6 案例之六：The "Elena d' Aminco"

在著名的The "Elena d' Aminco" (1980) 1 Lloyds Rep. 75先例中，涉及一个从1972年1月10日开始的长达3年的期租合约，原告将Elena d' Aminco轮出租给作为承租人的被告。承租人公司所在的集团中有其他联营公司经营原油及其产品，承租人租下该Elena d' Aminco轮是为了运输联营公司的原油与履行长期运输合约。

当时意大利沿海的贸易只能由挂有意大利国旗的船舶运营，因此比起那些不能进入意大利沿海的同类船舶，意大利船舶的市场租金更高。尽管承租人没有明确的意图要把这艘船用在意大利沿海贸易运输，但他们意识到Elena d' Aminco轮有挂意大利旗这个优势，如果有机会的话他们也会经营意大利沿海运输来盈利。而船东并不知道承租人经营活动的具体细节但是也意识到，如果承租人愿意，他完全可以用这艘船来开展这项利润高的业务。

在3月2日，Elena d' Aminco 轮被发现需要彻底的修理，但船东决定不修理。3月6日船东通知承租人这艘船舶已经不可能修复至恢复运营的状态，在3月29日又再次通知承租人说 Elena d' Aminco 轮已经不可能进行维修并恢复营运。在3月30日承租人认为船东拒绝修理船舶是违约/毁约并终断租约。之后承租人没有再去租进其他替代船舶，船东给承租人介绍的另一艘挂有意大利国旗的船舶作为替代也被承租人拒绝。承租人在本案例中要求船东赔偿因违约/毁约造成的损失，船东承认了违约/毁约的责任，唯一的争议就是损失赔偿的金额。法院认为如果在期租合约终断时有可供买卖的市场能够租到一艘替代船舶，在期租合约中违约/毁约的船东所应承担的一般损失赔偿应该是在期租租约剩余期限内租金和替代船舶市场租金的差价。根据损失遥远性的因果关系大原则，承租人只能获得因为船东的错误而造成的损失。在船东的违约和承租人的减少损失的行为之间必须存在因果关系。而承租人决定不利用当时可供买卖的市场是他独立于船东违约的决定。在本案中，船东在1973年3月末终断合约时存在可供买卖的市场允许承租人租到替代船舶，而承租人决定不寻找替代船舶是基于他的公司商业利益的独立考虑。由于承租人不行动的结果并不是因为船东的违约/毁约，法院在计算损失赔偿时，仍然应该依照市场规则，也就是合约价格与市场价格的差价，在本案中一般损失赔偿的金额就应该是在违约一天，期租 Elena d' Aminco 轮的租金与在市场上期租一艘类似船舶的租金差价。

2.3.7 案例之七：The “Wave”

在 The “Wave”(1981)1 Lloyd's Rep 521 先例，案情涉及一个24个月 +/-3个月由承租人选择租约期的期租合约，但船东拒绝履行不肯交船，原因是航运市场上涨令期租合约的租金比市场价格偏低。Mustill 大法官在计算承租人因此带来的损失，除了是使用违约/毁约一天(或接近的时间)的市场租金外，只肯以24个月或2年租约期计算，而拒绝加上3个月的额外租约期，因为这涉及对两年后航运市场会涨会跌的预测，而承租人只会在航运市场上涨时才行使这3个月的选择权，所以是不肯定。这一个针对将来不能肯定会发生的事实在本书第六章之2段也有详细介绍。在本先例 Mustill 大法官是这样说：“... In principle the applicable measure of damages is the difference between the hire which would have been payable in accordance with the fixture and the hire which the plaintiffs would have had to pay if they had entered into a kindred fixture on or shortly after the date when the contract was repudiated. I add the gloss ‘or shortly after’ to the principle adopted in The ‘Elena d’ Aminco’(1980)1 Lloyds Rep. 75, because in practice it would not have been possible to obtain a replacement fixture immediately after the repudiation took place. One is therefore looking for a market rate in the early days of September 1979, for a vessel of the same characteristics as Wave available spot for a time charter of two years. This is not an assessment which can be performed with any pretension to accuracy. The plaintiff assert that a rate of ＄16 per deadweight ton per month would have had to be paid in order to secure a replacement vessel. The evidence of Mr. Templeman and Mr. Morton(这两位是有关市场价格的专家证人),an independent expert witness,has not satisfied me that a rate as high as this would have been called for. In my judgment,on the available evidence,the appropriate figure to be used as the basis for computation would be ＄15.25. The difference between this fixture and the contractual rate is ＄6.75 per ton. In the present instance the period was not fixed but was subject to an option of three months more or less. Since it is impossible to predict what the market will be in September 1979,there is no means of knowing how the plaintiffs would have exercised their option if the vessel had been delivered in accordance with the contract. In these circumstances the only fair course is to compute the damages by reference to the basic charter period of two years ...”

2.3.8 案例之八:AS Nordlandsbanken v. Nederkoorn

这是一个新加坡案例名为 AS Nordlandsbanken v. Nederkoorn(2001)1 Singapore L. R. 466,案情涉及被告集团下的一家百慕大公司作为承租人向船东期租了两艘油轮,而被告作为租约的担保人。后来,承租人拒绝接收第一艘油轮“Tamar Song”,并在3个月后拒绝继续租用第二艘油轮“Tamar Summer”,这显然是航运市场下跌的结果。船东认为承租人的行为已经构成了违约/毁约。但是受害的船东没有在违约后去市场寻找替代的期租,而是在现货市场上以程租与收取运费方式营运这两艘船舶,因为船东认为这样会获得更大的收益,估计是看好航运市场会短期内上涨。但最终船东的收益很差劲,甚至不能够偿还银行的欠款而导致有关的油轮被银行没收/占有并出售抵债。但出售油轮的船价依然不足够偿还借款,这导致原告(贷款给船东的银行)向作为租约担保人的被告要求赔偿剩余不足的借款,因为受害的船东已经把被告的担保利益“转让”(assign)给了原告。被告对担保人的责任没有异议(估计没有好的抗辩),但对赔偿金额提出反驳。法院判是损失赔偿的金额应该是违约/毁约一天比较航运市场价格/租金与租约价格/租金之间的差价(如果市场租金低于租约租金的话)。在本先例中,法院认为原告没有合理减少损失,船东自己选择在现货市场上营运该油轮,而不是期租出去。这种高风险与最终的不利结果必须由船东自己承担,因为他完全可以把该油轮在违约后尽快期租出去,就保证了每天租金的收入。Judith Prakash 大法官是这样说:

“1. It was held by the High Court that in a straightforward situation, the measure of damages recoverable by the owner or charterer where there is wrongful repudiation is the difference between the contract rate and the market rate at the time of breach provided the latter is lower.

2. In assessing damages the court must bear in mind two other principles. The first is

the rule of minimum legal obligation or otherwise known as the rule of least benefit to the plaintiff.

3. The other principle is the principle of proportionality. Damages that are disproportionate to the loss will not be awarded.

4. The rationale for these two principles is that the function of damages is to compensate the person wronged on a just and fair basis. It is not to punish the contract breaker. The plaintiff is not entitled to a windfall. This is based on the public policy principle that litigation must not be turned into a lottery.

5. When the owner has a choice of two or more reasonable methods of damage control upon charterer's repudiation, damages will be awarded on the basis of minimum legal obligation that is to say the method least onerous to the defendant and the least beneficial to the plaintiff.

6. It is the plaintiff's duty to mitigate loss, and the plaintiff is required only to act reasonably. Whether or not he has done so is a question of fact in the circumstances of each case, and not a question of law. He must act not only in his own interest but also in the interest of the defendant and keep down the damages, so far as it is reasonable and proper, by acting in a reasonable manner.

7. In this case, the Court found that the plaintiffs had failed to act reasonably in the circumstances. The Judge accepted the position that when assessing damages, courts should take the facts as they stand and not shut their eyes and plug their ears to post injury events. The shipowners themselves chose the disastrous decision of operating the ships on the spot market instead of chartering them out. This high risk act did not mitigate their losses and the consequence must therefore be theirs. Trading on the spot market was risky business, and the shipowners embarked on it at risk to themselves because they could have easily chartered out the ship with a guaranteed hire revenue. Time - charters and spot contracts traverse different terrains. To deduct spot market earnings was inappropriate as it was the imposition of the least favourable method on the charterers."

2.4 违约/毁约后受害方合理希望合约得以履行

前面已经介绍过,通常是以违约/毁约的一天或受害方接受去终断合约的一天的市场价格来计算损失。原因是该合约已经被终断,没有可能再继续履行。而针对受害方而言,比较合理的补救办法或减少损失做法就是走进"可供买卖的市场"(available market)买进/卖出替代财产/货物。然而,当减少损失变得并不现实或者是并不恰当时,计算损失的时间就会被延后。毕竟,市场规则只是一个表面规则或做为损失计算的起点,可以偏离,而最重要的大原则还是在复原。比方说:(1)在货物的所有权有争议的情况下,受害的卖方想进入市场出售该货物的时间就会被延后:Dampskibsselskabet "Norden" A/S v. Andre & Cie SA(2003)1 Lloyd's Rep. 287 先例;(2)当受害方合理希望合约得以履行：Johnson v. Agnew(1980) AC 367 先例；(3) 如股票买卖或某些比较稀有的货物/商品，会难以很快的在市场上买进大量股票作为替代，这样做也会令市场价格被推高至完全不合理的程度：Asamera Oil Corporation Ltd v. Sea Oil & General Corporation and Baud Corporation, NV(1979) 89 DLR(3d) 1 先例。在这些情况下，Breach Date Rule 并不适用在 Market Rule。以下的 Bear Sterns Bank plc v. Forum Global Equity Ltd. (2007) EWHC 1575(Comm) 先例是当受害方合理希望合约得以履行时如何判断计算损失赔偿的一天。

这一个先例是在贵族院的 The "Golden Victory" (2007) 2 Lloyd's Rep 164 先例判下来后不久(这个先例在本书第十三章之 6 段中有详细介绍)，Andrew Smith 大法官在 Bear Sterns Bank plc v. Forum Global Equity Ltd. 先例中又一次的偏离了 Breach Date Rule。

Bear Sterns Bank plc v. Forum Global Equity Ltd. 先例就是属于以违约/毁约的时间来计算损失并不恰当的情况。该先例的案情是，被告 Forum 购入大量由一家德国公司与意大利公司发行的票据，该票交易由 Parmalat Group 担保。然而，在 2003 年 Parmalat Group 由于涉及欺诈与贪污而倒闭。后来由于法律的不确定，Forum 作为该票据债权人的有效性直到 2004 年 12 月 16 日才被确认。在 2005 年 7 月 4 日，原告 Bear Stearns 与 Forum 以电话形式完成以 290 万欧元购买这些票据的交易。在 2005 年 10 月初，这些以票据形式代表的债务转为另一家公司的净资产，并于同月的 6 日在米兰股票市场上市，上市价为 3.175 欧元。在 2005 年 10 月 21 日，Forum 提出拒绝与 Bear Stearns 完成这票交易，这可以说是"违约/毁约"(repudiation)的行为。期间，Bear Stearns 与 Morgan Stanley 达成一个共识/交易，就是 Morgan Stanley 向 Bear Stearns 买进该票据利息的一半。

同年 11 月在该诉讼前，Bear Stearns 向 Forum 发了一封信函提出要求"特定履行"(specific performance)该交易或者是要赔偿损失。但这些票据已经被转换为股票，持有人为 Forum。在 2006 年 7 月 28 日，Forum 将该些股票出售给了第三人，这也是 Forum 再度的违约/毁约，因为这一个行为令合约再也无法去履行。在 2006 年 8 月 23 日，Bear Stearns 通过他的律师向 Forum 提出由于这些股票已经被出售，特定履行已经是无法做到，因而救济只能限制在金钱损失的赔偿，并在 24 日以信件的形式说明。

该案例备受争议的是如何计算 Bear Stearns 的损失赔偿：(1) 在计算损失赔偿的时候是否要把 Bear Stearns 与 Morgan Stanley 之间的合约即 Morgan Stanley 向 Bear Stearns 购买该票据利息的一半考虑在内？(2) 他们是否应该以 Forum 拒绝与 Bear Stearns 完成交易的一天(即 2005 年 10 月 21 日)，也就是违约/毁约的一天的市场价格(当时股票的价格是 2.35 欧元)还是以往后日期，也就是以 Bear Stearns 知悉 Forum 把股票卖给了第三人，知道是即使 Forum 回心转意也无法再履行的一天(即 2006 年 8 月 24 日)的市场价格(当时价格是 2.67 欧元)来计算损失？

1979年英国《货物销售法》Section 51规定:"Where the seller wrongfully neglects or refuses to deliver the goods to the buyer ... the measure of damages is the estimated loss directly and naturally resulting, in the ordinary course of events, from the seller's breach of contract.... Where there is **an available market** for the goods in question, the measure of damages is *prima facie* to be ascertained by the difference between the contract price and the market or current price of the goods at the time or times when they ought to have been delivered or (if no time was fixed) at the time of the refusal to deliver."

该案例涉及的股票并不包括在1979年英国《货物销售法》对"货物"(goods)作出的定义中。但毫无疑问的是Section 51计算损失的起点是只要有关的标的是有一个可供买卖的市场,Breach Date Rule与Market Rule都适合,正如Brown勋爵在The "Golden Victory"(2007)2 Lloyd's Rep 164先例中所说的,如下:"... the rule is by no means confined to the sale of goods context and ... has been applied by analogy to a variety of other situations. Essentially, it applies whenever there is an available market for whatever has been lost and its explanation is that the injured party should ordinarily go out into that market to make a substitute contract to mitigate (and generally thereby crystallize) his loss."(加黑部分是笔者的强调)

然而,双方都不同意根据1979年英国《货物销售法》的Section 51来进行损失赔偿。Forum争辩说在计算损失赔偿时应该把Bear Stearns出售一半的票据予Morgan Stanley的这个交易也考虑在内,这等于是追究实际损失而不是适用Market Rule。而Bear Stearns则说损失赔偿时不应该以2005年10月21日,即Forum违约/毁约或预期违约(拒绝完成交易)的一天计算,而应该以之后的日期,如Bear Stearns知悉Forum把股票卖给了第三人的一天(即2006年8月24日)的市场价格来计算。

到底由哪一天的市场价格来计算损失成为该案例的焦点。Andrew Smith大法官认为应该以2006年8月24日的市场价格来计算,他认为Breach Date Rule只是计算损失的表面规则,不是一条绝对的规则。也就是说法院或仲裁庭在可以根据实际情况来界定一个合适的日期来计算损失,不一定是违约方拒绝履行合约的一天。在违约/毁约的情况下,如果受害方在"合理"(reasonable)的前提下试图把合约履行到底,那么计算损失的一天就应该是合约终断的那天而不应该是之前的违约/毁约一天。

该观点与Wilberforce勋爵在Johnson v. Agnew(1980)AC 367先例中所持的观点相同,如下:"In the present case if it is accepted, as I would accept, that the vendors acted reasonably in pursuing the remedy of specific performance, the date on which that remedy became aborted (not by the vendors' fault) should logically be fixed as the date on which damages should be assessed. Choice of this date would be in accordance both with common law principle, as indicated in the authorities I have mentioned, and with the wording of the Act 'in substitution for ... specific performance.' The date which emerges from this is April 3, 1975 – the first date on which mortgages contracted to sell a portion of the property. I would vary the order of the Court of Appeal by substituting this date for that fixed by them – viz November 26,1974. The same date(April 3,1975) should be used for the purpose of limiting the respondents' right to interest on damages. Subject to these modifications I would dismiss the appeal."

在本案例中,Andrew Smith 大法官认为,只要 Bear Stearns 一天没有选择接受 Forum 的违约/毁约去终断合约,并继续合理希望该合约获得履行,他们都冒着该股票价格下跌的风险。正是由于 Forum 的错误行为导致 Bear Stearns 要决定如何保护他们的利益,因而法院或仲裁庭不会很轻易就怪责 Bear Stearns 的决定。

在违约/毁约的情况下,Breach Date Rule 中的"breach date"应该是受害方接受违约/毁约也就是合约终断的一天。因此,Andrew Smith 大法官判 Bear Stearns 选择在 Forum 违约/毁约的时候没有在市场买进替代股票,而是在 2006 年 8 月 24 日也就是在知悉 Forum 把股票卖给了第三人的一天才选择终断合约是合理的行为,因此损失赔偿应该以该天来计算。

3. Market Rule 适用在合约履行与其他的延误

即使财产/货物不是受到"真正与实体的损坏/损失"(actual and physical loss)而是涉及"经济损失"(economic loss)的产生,如延误交出有关财产/货物(不论是谁造成的延误,如卖方、承运人、侵占方等),只要该财产/货物有可供买卖的市场,也同样会涉及 Breach Date Rule 与 Market Rule 计算损失。损失是根据有关合约约定交付时间当天的市场价格与实际交付一天的市场价格的差价,这使受害的买方能够回复到合约被履行的地位,也就是有关财产/货物按合约准时交付。因为在有可供买卖市场时,受害的买方应该或可以在卖方没有依照合约按时交货后马上去市场上买进替代货物。虽然在实际情况中,买方通常不会这样做。例如,买方知道有关延误交付的货物再等 3 天就会到手,所以就不在市场买进同样的替代货物,以免麻烦。但这也表示买方如果在这 3 天或更长的延误期间产生了使用或利润损失(如需要有关货物作为生产原料),那么他只能按照市场规则索赔合约规定交货一天合约价格与市场价格的差价,因为他可以在市场买进同样的替代货物(数量上可以足够这三天使用而不会让生产停顿),就可以避免出现生产受到干扰而产生的使用或利润的损失,这也是买方合理减少损失应该做的事。

这方面的权威说法可以节录《McGregor on Damages》(18th edn,2009 年)之 20–037 段所说:"The normal measure of damages ... is the market value at the contractual time for delivery less the market value at the time of actual delivery, since this represents the amount that will put the buyer into the position he would have been in had the contract been carried out."

另可以节录《Benjamin's Sale of Goods》(8th edn,2010 年)之 17 - 038 段关于卖方延迟交货时买方的救济如下:"Where there is an available market for the goods, the usual measure of the buyer's damages is the difference between: (a) their market value at the time and place fixed by the terms of the contract for delivery: and (b) their market value at the time when (and the place where) the goods are in fact delivered to the buyer. Apart from consequential losses, such as extra expenses or loss of profits, this sum should put the buyer into the financial position he would have been in if the seller had fulfilled his contractual obligation. The buyer will, of course, be liable to pay the agreed price for the goods, and if he has not paid it before or upon delivery, his claim for damages will be by way of counter-claim. Where there is an available market for the goods within s. 51 (3) (这是指 1979 年英国《货物销售法》), that subsection and the rules of mitigation would normally require the buyer to repurchase in the market immediately following the date of the seller's breach in failing to deliver in accordance with the contract ..."

延误履行的损失计算在不同的商业领域还会有不同的特定问题,这些计算有许多与 Market Rule 谈不上有关系,笔者在接下去的段节会拣部分课题做进一步的介绍。

3.1 Market Rule 适用在卖方延误付运与倒签提单

在货物运输,特别是涉及海上运输,还经常出现延误交货的违约事件,而且会是由于承运人的违约(如不合理绕航或者船舶不适航)而引起。一些有关损失的著名先例,如 Hadley v. Baxendale (1854) 9 Ex. 341 与 The "Heron II" (1967) 2 Lloyd's Rep 457 都是属于这种违约的案件。在货物买卖合约,卖方延误交货也是经常在发生,只是违约方变为卖方而不是承运人。例如,外贸与航运人士非常熟悉的"倒签提单"(back - dated Bill of Lading)的不法行为,就是为了掩盖延误付运与交货的违约。反正在这种类别的违约,英国法律的地位十分明确,都会是根据合约价格与违约当天的市场价格找出差价作为损失的计算,而不会理会买方可能已经分销/转售有关货物并因交货延误而导致的损失。这方面可节录部分重要的先例,如在 Slater v. Hoyle (1920) 2 KB 11 先例,上诉庭的 Scrutton 大法官说:"It is well settled that damages for non - delivery or **delay in delivery of goods**, where there is a market price, do not include damages for the loss of any particular contract unless that contract has been in contemplation of the parties to the original contract."(加黑部分是笔者的强调)

Breach Date Rule 与 Market Rule 的规定适用在承运人或卖方违约延误交货,收货人或买方的损失就会要根据 Breach Date Rule 以违约当天的市场价格计算损失。这价格要比较货物如果准时按照合约交付时的市场价格与延误交付时的市场价格,它们之间的差价就是受害方的损失。否则,如果以另一种办法计算损失,也就是延误交货的几天所造成的货价利息损失(这在今天利息低迷的情况下金额会是不多),就没有什么好索赔。但如果是以市场价格计算,就会有情况是市场暴升暴跌,相差几天的延误就会有很大一笔的差价。至于这是否是受害方的买方所蒙受的真正损失,会是没有办法说的准,要按照个别案件的事实而定。如有关的货物是买来作为长期储存之用,就感觉到赔偿延误期间的利息损失就已经是足够。但换了是 Hadley v. Baxendale 先例中的曲轴,延误付运就会导致了整个工厂生产停顿而蒙受严重损失。但 Breach Date Rule 与 Market Rule 是不理会这些不同案件的枝节。

显然是在该货物的市场价格下跌的情况下延误交付,这样的计算才会有金钱的损失。反之,如果市场价格上涨,则不会有损失,在责任上"胜诉"的话也只会获得"名义赔偿"(nominal damage)。这可以节录 Taylor v. Bank of Athens(1922)27 Com Cas 142 先例,该案涉及一个 CIF 买卖,货物是"蚕豆"(locust bean),付运的时间是 7 月或者 8 月(July/August shipment),这表示提单签发的日期最后一天是 8 月 31 日。事实上的确是出了这一天的一套提单,买方也在稍后根据"提货单"(delivery order)作出了支付。但后来买方发现了提单被倒签了 4 天,由于该批货物已经被转售,所以只能向 CIF 卖方提出延误交货的索赔,不存在拒绝接受货物。由于是市场持续下跌,如果是以合约价格与货物到达目的港(塞浦路斯)的市场价格相比,买方是应该有更大的损失。但偏偏在 8 月底到 9 月初(实际付运的日期)所延误的 4 天,市场价格没有太大差别。所以英国高院的 McCardie 大法官判受害的买方只能取得名义赔偿,这就代表了该 4 天延误交货市场价格的零差异。这样看来,针对倒签提单的计算损失对买方不利,毕竟倒签的日期不会太长,市场的波动也不一定会是太大,或是波动很大但碰巧不在涉及倒签的几天。McCardie 大法官在该先例是这样说:"It is vital to observe that the loss must result from the breach of warranty, as distinguished into the contract. It does not extend, I think to a case where the loss results not from the breach of warranty but from an unfortunate or improvident bargain which the buyer may have made. Market falls are not general due to a vendor's default. A buyer cannot, I think, save perhaps in very exceptional circumstances, attribute to his seller a loss which, in substance and in fact, arises not from the seller's breach, but from a fall in market values. To impose the burden of such a loss on the seller would be to saddle him with something for which he is wholly free from blame."(大致上说市场下跌与卖方延误付运是没有直接的因果关系,买方不能以卖方延误付运的违约,把市场波动的风险也转嫁给卖方,卖方对市场下跌是没有可被怪责之处。)

而这样看来,针对卖方延误付运货物并倒签提单的违约,以 Breach Date Rule 与 Market Rule 计算损失会有不少情况是不足够赔偿受害的买方损失或承受的不利。这一方面有进一步的发展,会在接下去的案例做进一步的介绍。

3.1.1 针对卖方延误付运与倒签提单先例之一:Finlay(James) & Co v. Kwik Hoo Tong Handel Maatschappij

倒签提单的损失计算办法很快有了改变,这是在 Finlay(James) & Co v. Kwik Hoo Tong Handel Maatschappij(1929)1 KB 400 先例。案情涉及食糖的 CIF 买卖,目的地是

印度的孟买,买卖合约也规定了付运时间是9月。但货物实际上在10月才付运,只是提单倒签为9月30日。但这倒签并不是该先例的被告(也就是CIF卖方,但他不是发货人)所知道的。反正是受害方的买方接受了该套单证并作出了支付,但之后买方向"分买方"(sub - buyer)要求支付却被拒绝并指该套提单是倒签提单。这最后导致了受害方把该票食糖根据12月下跌了的市场价格以拍卖方式转售。受害方之后向卖方提出索赔,并提出除了延误交货的违约外,加上了另一项诉因的违约,也就是这一套倒签提单令受害方本来可以拒绝接受这一套单证的权利被剥夺了。这被英国高院与上诉庭所接受,根据这一个新的诉因判,受害方可以向违约的卖方取回买卖合约价格与货物被分买方拒绝后被迫在卸港孟买拍卖的价格(被视为是当天的市场价格)之间的差价作为损失赔偿。(这票食糖是于11月9日抵达孟买,卖方交单是在11月12日,船舶在11月15日完成卸货,受害方的买方在12月10日把这票食糖以拍卖方式转售。但由于市场价格在11月9日至12月10日这段时间没有什么波动,只是比较合约价格下跌很大,所以双方没有刻意针对市场价格应该是以卖方违约交出虚假/有缺陷单证的一天或是以实际到达的一天或其他任何一天为准。)最重要的是,受害方的买方较早前以相对高涨的买卖合约价格购买这票货物,现在可以成功把订约后所有市场下跌的风险都转嫁给卖方。换言之,这才是拒绝单证权利被剥夺所造成的真正损失,不再是倒签这一两天的市场价格差异。

3.1.2 针对卖方延误付运与倒签提单先例之二:Kwei Tek Chao v. British Traders and Shippers Ltd

Kwei Tek Chao v. British Traders and Shippers Ltd(1954)1 Lloyd's Rep 16先例的案情也是涉及倒签提单(这是由于被告所委任的货运代理人所签发的提单弄虚作假)。在这一个CIF买卖,在信用证结汇前与货物到达前,提单被倒签的事实已经曝光。换句话说,在买方有权拒绝这套单证或这票货物之前已经被通知了倒签的事实,但买方迟迟没有采取行动。至于买方为什么不拒绝,这会有千变万化的原因,如在有关的时间刚好是市场还没有下挫,而且普遍市场对有关货物的价格平稳还是很有信心。另一个原因可以是买方不懂,不知道自己的权利,还以为在国际贸易中签发倒签提单是理所当然的事。再另一个原因会是买方已经把这票货转售给了分买方,导致了买方漠不关心,只要这套有缺陷的单证与这票货物被分买方接受。看来在这一个先例正是最后的原因,但在这票货物事后被分买方拒绝后,夹在当中的买方也试图向违约的卖方拒货,并要求卖方退还以信用证支付了的货款。

Devlin勋爵判是受害的买方在知道了提单倒签,还有机会及时拒绝这一套单证与有关货物,但没有这样做时就构成了弃权或禁止反供。所以,买方要求违约的卖方退还货款不被支持。但这不表示买方对索赔损失的权利有所放弃,而这一个损失计算也不是10月(合约付运的日期)与11月(实际付运的日期)之间市场价格的差异,而是根据Finlay(James) & Co v. Kwik Hoo Tong Handel Maatschappij(1929)1 KB 400先例,也就是买卖合约价格与违约一天"市场价格"之间的差价就是买方的损失。在本案违约的一天是指受害方的买方转售或应该出售该票货物的一天,Devlin 勋爵说:"In other words, the measure is the difference between the contract price and the price at which the buyer has sold the goods. Whether that is put as the price which the buyer actually gets for the goods, or whether it is put as the market price obtainable for the goods on the day when the buyer should sell them, I do not think matters very much."

3.1.3 针对卖方延误付运与倒签提单先例之三:Kleinjan & Holst NV Rotterdam v. Bremer Handels

在 Kleinjan & Holst NV Rotterdam v. Bremer Handels(1972)2 Lloyd's Rep 11 先例中,Cooke 大法官也是跟从了 Finlay(James)& Co v. Kwik Hoo Tong Handel Maatschappij(1929)1 KB 400 先例的判决,并指出:"Finlay 先例是为卖方违反合约的条件条文未能提供准确的付运单证,同时买方未终断这一合约并可索赔违约损失的情况提供了一个计算损失的'普遍规则'(general rule)"。买方有权索赔合约价格与违约一天[1]市场价格的差价,而不管买方作为受害方是否被误导或者在知悉全部事实的情况下并没有拒绝单证并终断合约。Cooke 大法官是这样说:"What then is the measure of damages appropriate to that breach? In my view, it is the difference between the contract price of the goods and their market price at the date of the breach. In Finlay(James)& Co v. Kwik Hoo Tong Handel Maatschappij(1929)1 KB 400, the sellers under a c. i. f contract tendered to the buyers a bill of lading which stated, not fraudulently but contrary to the fact, that shipment had taken place in the contract month. In the belief that the bill of lading was correctly dated, the buyers paid the contract price. Subsequently the buyer learned that the goods had not been shipped during the contract month. It was held by the Court of Appeal, affirming the judgment of Mr. Justice Wright([1928] 2 KB 604), that the buyers were entitled to recover damages for the breach by the sellers of their obligation to deliver a bill of lading correctly stating the date of shipment and that the measure of such damages was the difference between the market price and the contract price of the goods. Now it is true that in Finlay's case the buyers were misled by a wrongly - dated bill of lading and accepted the shipment on the basis that the bill of lading was correctly dated. In the present case it cannot be said that the buyers were misled into believing that the documents tendered were in accordance with the contract, for indeed at the very time when the documents were tendered the buyers were maintaining that they were not in accordance with the contract. But by accepting the documents while reserving their rights the buyers must be taken

[1] Cooke 大法官认为违约的一天市场价格是违约的卖方把有缺陷单证向买方交单的一天。然而 Devlin 勋爵在 Kwei Tek Chao v. British Traders and Shippers Ltd 先例的判决中说:"It is quite clear that it never occurred to anybody to take the date of tender as being the relevant date."可以看出到底是以哪一天的市场价格作为比较还是不肯定。

to have reserved their right to take the point that the documents were not in accordance with the contract and to recover damages on that basis. **In my view, the decision in Finlay's case lays down a general rule as to the measure of damages in cases where the sellers have broken a condition of the contract by failing to tender proper documents and the buyers, not having rescinded, are entitled to recover damages for the breach. The reasons why the buyers have not rescinded are immaterial.** Whether they have been misled or have elected not to rescind with full knowledge of the facts the position is the same, namely, that if they had rescinded, they would not have had to pay a price (viz. the contract price) in excess of the market price of the goods at the time of the breach."(加黑部分是笔者的强调,大致上 Cooke 大法官是认为只要涉及倒签提单,即使受害的买方没有在较早前拒绝接受单证,损失计算还是以 Finlay 先例为准)

3.1.4 针对卖方延误付运与倒签提单先例之四:Louis Dreyfus Trading Ltd v. Reliance Trading Ltd

再接下去要介绍的先例是 Louis Dreyfus Trading Ltd v. Reliance Trading Ltd(2004) 2 Lloyd's Rep 243,案情涉及 Louis Dreyfus("LD")作为"CFR Banjul"(在非洲甘比亚的一个港口)买卖合约的卖方,在 2001 年 8 月 10 日同意出售 7000 吨食糖给 Reliance Trading,价格是 257.43 美元一吨。付运为"Dawn 轮船上装载的食糖,当时在 Banjul 卸货"(per m. v. Dawn currently discharging at Banjul)。这买卖看来是出售一批"浮动"(floating)与"特定"(specific)的货物,这种货物通常是不会有可供买卖的市场。较早的时候,Reliance Trading 通过联营公司已经同意把这批食糖的 5000 吨转售给名为 Boule 的一家公司,价格是 290 美元一吨。后来,Boule 在一个附加协议中同意把其余的 2000 吨同时买下,但要以一个优惠的价格,即 253 美元一吨。到了 8 月 17 日,Boule 支付货款给了 Reliance Trading,而 Reliance Trading 也支付给了 LD 3000 吨货物的价款。而迟至 10 月 12 日才把 3000 吨食糖在 Banjul 卸下与交货,卸货的严重延误是由于 LD 的原因所导致。LD 的责任涉及在 8 月 29 日,Dawn 轮在 Banjul 卸货中受到干扰,因为有一位第三人名为 Madi 向甘比亚法院成功取得一个禁令阻止继续卸货,原因是 LD 被指违约,该批食糖应该只能卖给 Madi。该禁令是直到 2001 年 9 月 27 日才被撤销。不论是 LD 与 Madi 之间谁对谁错,面对 Reliance Trading,LD 显然是要对这一延误负责。反正是在 10 月 12 日,把 3000 吨食糖卸下后,LD 继续向 Reliance Trading 要求支付余下的 4000 吨的货价。但由于到了该时,食糖市场下挫,市场价格只在 224 美元一吨。这使 Reliance Trading 向 LD 要求减价(重复原来的合约价格是在 257.43 美元一吨),但被 LD 拒绝并接受违约/毁约(因为拒绝支付货款)而令买卖合约终断。LD 接下去向 Reliance Trading 开始仲裁,索赔有关的损失(就是 4000 吨食糖的价格与 Dawn 轮的滞期费)。而 Reliance Trading 的反索赔的诉因则是该批食糖有债务与无法享有货物的"宁静占用"(quiet possession),这违反了 1979 年英国《货物销售法》之 Section 12(2)(a)。另外,Reliance Trading 也索赔货物延误的损失,也就是根据合约价格的257.43美元与食糖实际卸下当天的市场价格224美元之间的差价。LD对这一反索赔的抗辩是Reliance Trading根本没有真正的损失，因为在分销合约的5000吨是在290美元，而剩下的2000吨是253美元。实际卸下与交付的3000吨，Reliance Trading应该从Boule取得的货款是290美元。但在仲裁庭，裁定Reliance Trading的损失计算正确。这里是涉及在计算延误损失时，不应将“分售合约”(sub - sale)一并的考虑(但这正是LD的说法)，而只是考虑市场价格，这才是“市场规则”(Market Rule)。

在高院，Andrew Smith大法官认为买方在分售或转售合约中的盈亏是通常不能用来计算买方损失的，除非在订约时双方已经预先知道了某一个特定分售或转售，说：

“Profit or loss made by a buyer on a sub - sale is generally irrelevant to the assessment of his damages for breach by a seller of a warranty of quality or a failure to deliver(except, it may be, as evidence of market price). This is an application of general principles governing remoteness of damage, and not an exception to them. If a particular sub - sale is not within the contemplation of the parties when the contract of sale is made, damages are to be assessed without regard to it, and it makes no difference that the parties were aware that the buyer was a merchant dealing in and re - selling such goods: Kwei Tek Chao v. British Traders and Shippers Ltd(1954)2 Lloyd's Rep 114.

However, if the parties to a sale contract had within their contemplation when making their contract a particular sub - sale[1], different considerations can arise. In these circumstances, the buyer might be entitled to have the sub - sale brought into account to increase his damages. Equally, the seller might be entitled to have it brought into account in order to reduce the award against him. As it was put by Mr. Justice Devlin in Biggin & Co. Ltd v. Permanite Ltd, (1951)1 KB 422 at page 436.”

3.2 航运方面期租合约下的延误还船

对期租合约下的延误(或提早)还船，已经有过不少先例说明了损失计算的办法就是在租约中规定的最后日期直到真正还船日期(或提早还船日期直到租约约定最早还船日期)，也就是延误(或提早)的这段时间，把较高的市场同类船舶的租金与较低的租约租金之间的差价乘以延误(提早)的时间，可以说这方法是非常容易计算。这种损失计算办法适用在船东或承租人的违约。

3.2.1 有关先例的介绍

这些先例有：Watson Steamship Co v. Merryweather & Co(1913)18 Com Cas 294；

---

[1] 同样的理由也出现在本章之6.2.3段所介绍的另一个案件是有关造船合约在伦敦的仲裁，这方面涉及本书第三章提到的Hadley v. Baxendale(1854)9 Ex. 341先例针对“特别损失”(special damage)的第二条规则，即订约当时或之前受害方已将会产生特别损失的后果告诉了违约方。

Meyer v. Sanderson(1913)108 LT 428;The "London Explorer"(1971)1 Lloyd's Rep 523; The "Dione"(1975)1 Lloyd's Rep 115;The "Johnny"(1977)2 Lloyd's Rep 1;The "Peonia"(1991)1 Lloyd's Rep 100;The "Black Falcon"(1991)1 Lloyd's Rep 77 与 The "Gregos"(1992)2 Lloyd's Rep 40, The "Golden Victory"(2007)2 Lloyd's Rep 164, The "Achilleas"(2008)2 Lloyd's Rep 275 等。以下节录其中小部分上述先例中法院的有关说法:在 The "London Explorer"先例,Morris 勋爵说:"A charterer would be liable to pay hire at the contractual rate to the time of actual redelivery and in addition(if the current rate exceeded the contractual rate)to pay damages in respect of his failure to redeliver within a reasonable time."

在 The "Dione"先例,Denning 勋爵说:"If he does not do so – and the market has gone up – he will be bound to pay the extra. That is to say he will be bound to pay the charter rate up to the end of the stated period and the market rate thereafter, see Watson v. Merryweather."

在 The "Peonia"先例,Bingham 大法官说:"... was entitled to payment of hire at the charter – party rate until redelivery of the vessel and to damages(being the difference between the charter rate and the market rate if the market rate is higher than the charter rate)for the period between the final terminal date and redelivery."

在 The "Gregos"先例,一审的 Evans 大法官说:"The charterer does commit a breach of contract by failing to redeliver at the end of the charter period and is liable in damages, if the market rate exceeds the charter rate, as well as for hire until redelivery takes place."

在 The "Golden Victory"先例,Bingham 勋爵说(虽然他在该贵族院的先例是持少数不同意见,但这不涉及他提到的期租合约下过早[或延误]还船的损失计算办法): "An injured party such as the owners may not, generally speaking, recover damages against a repudiator such as the charterers for loss which he could reasonably have avoided by taking reasonable commercial steps to mitigate his loss. Thus chartering of vessels, the injured party's loss will be calculated on the assumption that he has, on or within a reasonable time of accepting the repudiation, taken reasonable commercial steps to obtain alternative employment for the vessel for the best consideration reasonably obtainable. This is the ordinary rule whether in fact the injured party acts in that way or, for whatever reasons, does not. The actual facts are ordinarily irrelevant. The rationale of the rule is one of simple commercial fairness. The injured party owes no duty to the repudiator, but fairness requires that he should not ordinarily be permitted to rely on his own unreasonable and uncommercial conduct to increase the loss failing on the repudiator. I take this summary to reflect the ruling of Robert Goff J in Koch Marine Inc v. D'Amica Societa di Navigazione ARL(The Elena d'Amico)(1980)1 Lloyd's Rep 75. That case concerned the measure of damages recoverable by a charterer for breach of a time charter during its currency by an owner. While taking care to avoid laying down an inflexible or invariable rule, the judge held(page 89, col 2) that if, at the date of breach, there is an available market, the normal measure of damages will be the difference between the contract rate and the market rate for chartering in a substitute ship for the balance of the charter period. An analogy was drawn with section 51(3) of the Sale of Goods Act 1893. Neither party challenged this decision, which has always been regarded as authoritative."

3.2.2 有关延误还船的 The "Achilleas"先例

3.2.2.1 期租合约经常发生延误或提早还船违约的原因

在介绍与探讨 The "Achilleas"(2008)2 Lloyd's Rep 275 先例前,可以先简单介绍这种在期租合约经常发生的违约与长期以来被接受的计算损失办法。

期租合约好像房屋的租赁,总会有一个双方同意的"租约期"(charter period),租约期一届满(不论是否加上明示或默示的宽限期),承租人必须归还船舶给船东。期租合约的租约期通常会比岸上房屋租赁期约定的复杂,这是因为租约期的最后一天通常不好准确掌握,船舶最后的航次会因许多承租人无法控制的因素而被延误(或提早)。所以不像房屋租赁,1 年就是 1 年。期租合约通常会约定一些明示的宽限期用类似"大约"(about)或者"多于或少于 10 天"(ten days more or less)的用词赋于租约期一定的灵活性,而还船日期也变为在一段时间内的任何一天。在这种情况下就要找出一个"还船的最早日期"(earliest redelivery date)与"还船的最后日期"(terminal redelivery date)。承租人早于最早日期还船或晚于最后日期还船都构成违约,而且好像其他合约的承诺与责任一样,这是绝对与严格的责任,就算由于不可抗力的原因如坏天气而延长了最后的航次,导致还船超出了最后日期,承租人还是要赔偿船东的损失,问题只是怎样计算。在现实中,即使是有一定程度的宽限期,往往还是避免不了这种类别的违约经常在发生。

这里也加上了航运市场波动的因素,如果在接近还船日期,市场租金高于租约的租金,承租人就会想尽办法安排一个较长的航次务求能够把船舶使用至最后日期,一分一秒都不浪费。这包括在估计最后的航次所需要的时间,对每一方面(包括是航程的长短与在装卸港停留的时间)都打如意算盘,不留任何空间或保留。但人生在世不如意之事十之八九,最后航次也是一样,结果造成延误还船的机会就会很高。相反,在接近还船日期,市场租金低于租约的租金,承租人就会想尽早还船,不必再支付较高的租金。做法就会是安排尽量短的航次,而结果还是差一点时间才会到最早的还船日期,也就只能硬了头皮把船舶还给船东,并要求船东合理减少损失。这种情况是无时无刻不在航运市场发生。

3.2.2.2 船东因延误还船蒙受的其他损失可否索赔

在航运市场高涨,往往也是延误还船争议发生最多的时候。这种延误,经常时间不是太长,最后航次只超出租约期几天会是司空见惯。但对受害的船东所造成的损失可能会是很大,根本不是赔偿延误几天的租约租金与市场租金的差价就可以足够。原因在市场高涨的环境下,船东通常会在较早时约定下一个租约与约定紧凑的"销约期”(cancellation day),以免在一个租约完结与另一个接下去的租约之间有空档。由于在高涨的市场船期是非常昂贵,必须分秒必争。这一来,遇上航运市场在真正还船的时候稍微下挫(这会只是正常的波动),就会因延误几天而导致下一个租约的销约期被错过,船东也就会面临下一个承租人的扣减租金要求(就如 The “Achilleas”先例案情一样)或被取消租约而蒙受可能是庞大的损失。举例说在一个案件中的期租每天租金是 20,000 美元,最后还船日期是 2007 年 3 月 4 日,承租人给了还船通知说是在 3 月 1 日至 4 日之间还船。于是船东就在市场订下一个 6 个月的期租,租金是 40,000 美元,而 laycan(这是指船东可以交船最早与最后的日期)是 3 月 4 日至 6 日,表示销约期是 3 月 6 日。如果承租人准时还船,船东可以正好在 laycan 内在还船地点附近交船给下一位承租人。但如果承租人是在 3 月 7 日才能还船(把最后航次的货物卸清)给船东,延误还船的时间是 3 天,也就是错过了下一个租约的销约期。而在承租人延误还船的这段时间里,由于市场下挫,船东被下一家承租人取消租约而被迫另订下一个为期 4 个月的期租,租金被压到 30,000 美元(这也是市场价格)。

那么在这种情况下,船东因为承租人的延误还船每天的损失看来应该是原来订下的但因为延误还船而被取消的 6 个月每天 40,000 美元租金的期租,减去后来订下的另一个 4 个月每天 30,000 美元租金的期租,等于每天有 10,000 美元的损失。而且,船东与承租人之间会有另一个争辩就是这每天 10,000 美元的损失是应该再乘以 4 个月的天数还是乘以 6 个月的天数。照理说,船东损失是一个价值 40,000 美元一天的 6 个月期租,表面看来应该乘以 6 个月。但一直以来的许多先例是说延误还船的损失计算只是用真正延误还船的天数(租约最后应该还船的日期与真正还船日期的比较)乘以还船时较高的市场租金与较低的租约租金之间的差价。可以说这方法是非常容易计算,而且计算出来的金额不会太高,在一定程度上鼓励了承租人更加安心在航运市场高涨的时候延误还船。比方说,延误还船是 3 天,期间同类船舶与同样长短租约的市场租金上升为原租约 20,000 美元的一倍,这表示损失也只有是 20,000 美元乘以 3 天等于 60,000 美元。这相比把船东可能因为被延误还船 3 天而失去了下一个利润高昂的长期租约所蒙受的真正损失,可以说是微不足道。一直以来,也把船东因为原租约的延误还船而错过了下一个租约的销约期所蒙受的损失是认为“遥远”(remote),也就是本书第三章介绍的 Hadley v. Baxendale(1854)9 Exch 341 先例中提到的特别损失。毕竟承租人与船东是在订约的时候预见不到还船时下一个租约与它的销约期、租约期与租金高低等的问题。

3.2.2.3　The “Achilleas”先例的案情与判决

这在第一审的 The “Achilleas”(2006)1 Lloyd’s Rep 106. 先例终于面对延误还船的损失除了考虑市场价格/租金的 Market Rule 外,是否要考虑受害的船东在下一个租约所蒙受的损失的问题。该著名的先例在本书第三章之 8 段有详细的介绍,在这里尽量避免重复。它涉及在一个期租下,承租人延误了 9 天才还船。这就导致船东错过了订下的下一个 4 至 6 个月的期租合约的销约期。这令受害方的船东蒙受

1,364,584.37 美元的损失,远远超出了这 9 天延误还船的市场租金与合约租金的差价。

在伦敦仲裁、高院与上诉庭都判船东可以索赔这一笔 1,364,584.37 美元的损失。主要原因是这种损失一般船东与承租人约定期租合约的时候都可以预见或料想到,所以是属于 Hadley v. Baxendale(1854)9 Exch 341. 先例中的“一般损失”(ordinary damage)。这一个结果也等于是摒弃了一贯以来法院以 Market Rule 计算延误还船损失的做法(这在本章 3.2.1 段有介绍)。

后来英国贵族院把较早的判决推翻,将延误还船的损失计算恢复到一贯以来的地位,这方面的原因笔者在本书第三章有详述。对笔者而言这方面是有惊无险,因为笔者也是支持不要把经常发生的延误还船把可以索赔的损失进一步扩大。毕竟一打开了“大水门”(flood gate),就难保将来不会把其他因为延误还船所造成的损失算进来,变为没完没了。例如,在该先例中有提到过的船东因为延误还船而错过了预订好的干坞进行年修或者错过了把船舶高价出售的买卖合约中的销约期。这种情况会带来可能是更大的损失索赔,而且也难说这种情况不可能会发生,顶多会发生的频率是低于错过下一个租约的销约期。

笔者觉得最危险的还是对法律精通与狡猾的小部分欧洲船东很容易做手脚。如没有订下下一个租约(甚至已经订下但没有在市场被报道)的情况下遇到延误还船,就借机会与不为外人所知的联营公司或者手中的皮包公司自导自演订一份租约,租金尽量订得偏高(但也不完全与市场脱节,否则这真可能是不可预见了),而销约期是订在船舶延误还船,刚好错过的一天。另外,当然是租约期也尽量订得长。这一来,船东就有机会可向承租人敲诈了,甚至最后能够在仲裁庭取得胜利也不足为奇。这危险被在 The “Achilleas”中持不同意见的仲裁员指出,说:“As we all know, fixtures are concluded so informally these days that it would not be difficult for an owner and a charterer to concoct a ‘fixture’ which never in fact existed just to prove a claim for damages.”

最后一提的是,贵族院的判法看来是与本章 3.1.4 段介绍的 Louis Dreyfus Trading Ltd v. Reliance Trading Ltd(2004)2 Lloyd’s Rep 243 先例与将在 6.2.3 段介绍的造船合约在伦敦仲裁的说法一致。就是,双方在订约时只是笼统地知道可能会有下一个租约的存在并不足够。必须要在订约时或之前双方特别是违约方已经知道这一个特定租约的存在(包括租期、租金、销约期等),才能满足 Hadley v. Baxendale (1854)9 Ex. 341 先例对特别损失的要求。这一来,知情的承租人如果延误还船,导致错过下一个特定租约的销约期而带来的损失,承租人就会要负责赔偿。

3.3 保险赔付下保险人延误作出赔付的损失计算

这种违约在现实中经常发生,违约是保险人或保险公司在发生了受保的意外事故后,延误向受保人作出赔付,令受保人陷入困境或蒙受不必要的额外损失。这会是一个严重与对社会影响大的违约(保险合约)行为,因为保险会影响到方方面面。但在英国法律由于受到 1906 年《海上保险法》的限制而无法对受害方的受保人作出损失赔偿的救济,这在本书第十一章之2.3段有详细介绍,这里不重复。这使得英国法律委员会在针对保险法的改革中专门为这一个问题在2010年3月作出一个报告名为《Insurance Contract Law:Issues Paper 6:Damages for Late Payment and the Insurer's Duty of Good Faith》。该报告的建议是:

"9.42.... the insurer's primary obligation(would be)not to prevent a loss from occurring,but to pay valid claims,after the opportunity for a reasonable investigation. If an insurer fails to carry out this obligation,it should be liable for damages for actual loss caused by the breach provided that loss was foreseeable;that the policyholder acted reasonably to mitigate their loss;and that the loss was not excluded by a contract term. [保险人首要责任不是防止意外事故的发生(他也管不了),而是在合理调查有关意外事故后支付受保人的有效索赔。如果保险人违反了这一个首要责任,保险人就应该对受保人因为延误赔付而蒙受的实际损失(只要是可以预见的损失类别,受保人有合理减损与保单条文没有排除)作出赔偿。]

9.43. We accept that insurers need to be able to refuse invalid claims. Every so often, an insurer will act reasonably in deciding a claim is invalid,but later be found to be wrong. In these circumstances,should the loss lie with the insurer or the insured? We think that in commercial insurance,this question is best left to the parties themselves. The default position in contract law should be that the insurer bears the risk,following its failure to perform its contractual obligation. However, the parties should be free to exclude this liability through a contract term."(法律委员会接受保险人能够对无效索赔作出拒赔。但通常保险人是需要时间调查或/与咨询法律意见才能初步决定索赔是否有效。而如果合理决定索赔是无效,但最后的判决是保险人的决定是错误并需要赔付给受保人。这一来,延误赔付的损失应该是在保险人或是受保人?法律委员会认为在商业的保险合约,这一个问题最好还是让双方当事人自己决定。但如果双方没有明示决定,那么法律地位应该是要保险人承担这一延误赔付带来额外损失的风险,但双方当事人可以根据合约条文改变这一个风险。)

最后一提的是英国保险市场已经开始在保险合约中加上了针对准时作出赔付的条文,名为"time for payment"条文。其中2003年版本的《国际船舶保险条文》第46.7条就是典型的例子,条文的内容在本书第十一章之2.3段,不重复。这条文的作用显然是针对保险人如果延误赔付,受保人就有了一个独立的诉因(违反该条文)去针对延误导致的损失提出索赔:Tonkin v. UK Insurance Ltd(2006)EWHC 1120先例。

3.4　房屋买卖或租用下延误履行的损失计算

当买卖合约中涉及的财产/货物是土地或房屋时,如果卖方延误交付导致买方有权终止合约并拒绝接受该房屋,他就根本不会获得该处房屋,那么损失赔偿的计算方法就和不履行合约时损失赔偿的计算方法一致。但大多数情况买方最后都会获得该房屋,虽然会有延误,要么因为延误并没有导致合约终断,或者买方选择接受延误而继续履行合约,要么就是买方成功请求法院下达"履约指令"(specific performance)而迫使卖方履行合约交付房屋。在这种延误交付的情况下,损失赔偿的通常计算应该是土地或房屋根据买卖合约计算应该交付日期至实际交付日期这段时间的使用价值,也就是这段时间的土地或房屋的租金。这可以节录《McGregor on Damages》(18th edn,2009 年)之 22-011 段所说:"The normal measure of damages is the value of the user of the land, which will generally be taken as its rental value, for the period from the contractual time for completion to the date of actual completion. This is so whether the delay is brought to an end by the voluntary action of an indolent seller or by a decree of specific performance against a recalcitrant seller."

这个原则也同样适用于房屋租赁合约。在 Royal Bristol Permanent Building Society v. Bomash(1887)35 Ch. D 390 先例中,原告作为两处房屋的抵押权人,在获得房屋出售权后,将这两幢房屋拍卖给了被告的买方。但房屋的抵押人 Fleming 先生因为破产依然住在房屋里。买卖双方约定在 1885 年 11 月 11 日完成交易,之后房屋就会交付给买方。但 Fleming 先生一直住在这房屋中,直到 1 个多月之后的 12 月 15 日才被治安官驱逐出房屋。在买下这两幢房屋后,买方将它们以 85 英镑一年的价格出租给了 Wilson 先生,并约定这个长达 14 年的租约从 1885 年 11 月 16 日开始。但买方的房客 Wilson 先生发现在租约开始后他一直不能入住,因此拒绝继续履行租约,之后房屋一直是空闲的。法院判是卖方违反了交付空屋的合约义务,因为在本应履行买卖合约交付房屋的时候 Fleming 先生依然住在房屋里,买方并没有获得合约中约定的空屋的占有。因此买方有权获得合约如果按时被履行他可以在租约下取得的租金,这是从合约如果被履行并出租时直到本案判决时的粗略估计 15 个月的房租损失,也就是 110 英镑。

3.5 建造工程合约(包括造船合约)延误履行的损失计算

在建造合约中,如果承建商没有在合约约定的时间内完成建筑工程,通常损失计算就是在延误工程的这段时间内该建筑物的使用价值,也即这段延误的时间内的租金或使用/利润损失。这可以节录《McGregor on Damages》(18th edn,2009 年)之 26-008 段所说:"If the builder fails to complete the building by the time required by the contract the normal measure of damages should be the value of the use of the building during the period of delay, the value generally being taken as the rental value."

由于一个复杂或庞大的工程会由于各种因素而导致延误,所以在建造合约中经常会有详细的条文针对延误所造成的损失。例如,首先双方会约定一个工程完毕的最后日期(在造船合约中就会是交船日期)。接下去雇主与承建商会约定一条通常名为"可允许延误条文"(permissable delay clause),列明在哪一些情况下承建商可以被允许延长最后日期。而这些情况往往是针对一些承建商不可控制的事件,如坏天气或当局的干预导致了工程不能进行。所以,这条文也经常名为"不可抗力条文"(*force majeure* clause)。在订约自由下,有多少情况可以被列明为不可抗力事件还是看双方的谈判水平与力量,显然越多就对承建商越好,因为可以合法延长工期。至于由于不在条文中列明的事件所造成的工程延误就要由承建商承担后果。毕竟,合约的承诺是绝对或严格责任,所以承诺工程完毕的最后日期是一个严格的责任,承建商必须要做到,否则就是违约。而违约的后果就是要承担上述所讲的对该建筑物的使用价值的损失进行赔偿。但由于一个复杂或庞大的工程不能及时完成会造成什么损失或损失什么使用价值不好计算,所以在这种合约中也经常会双方预先约定一个每天延误要赔偿给雇主的固定金额,这也就是一条“议定赔偿条文”(liquidated damage clause)。这种议定赔偿在工程合约中通常都会被法律支持,即使是订得金额偏高。

4. Breach Date Rule 与 Market Rule 适用在缺陷履行的情况

4.1 财产/货物损坏的两种救济——贬值或修复与对它们的取选

货物买卖如果涉及货物损坏,如卖方交付的货物有缺陷,但买方没有因此拒货,这又会涉及怎么样才是让受害方的买方复原的恰当救济。大致上,它是涉及了“贬值”(diminution of value)与“修复”(reinstatement)两种救济。由于国际货物买卖主要是为了分销/转售,所以在大部分的情况下都采用贬值的救济办法最为恰当。只会在少数的情况下,如买卖的货物涉及了特定的机器或配件,是买方自用,也不存在有市场买卖,才会是适用修复的救济。

针对货物损坏或货不对版的救济在 1979 年《英国货物销售法》之 Section 53 中有作出规定如下:“(1) Where there is a breach of warranty by the seller, or where the buyer elects (or is compelled) to treat any breach of a condition on the part of the seller as a breach of warranty, the buyer is not by reason only of such breach of warranty entitled to reject the goods; but he may – (a) set up against the seller the breach of warranty in diminution or extinction of the price, or (b) maintain an action against the seller for damages for the breach of warranty. (2) The measure of damages for breach of warranty is the estimated loss directly and naturally resulting, in the ordinary course of events, from the breach of warranty. (3) In the case of breach of warranty of quality such loss is *prima facie* the difference between the value of the goods at the time of delivery to the buyer and the value they would have had if they had fulfilled the warranty. (4) The fact that the buyer has set up the breach of warranty in diminution or extinction of the price does not prevent him from maintaining an action for the same breach of warranty if he has suffered further damage.”

针对“贬值”(diminution of value),它涉及在违约一天根据市场确定两个不同的价值。第一个价值就是完全按照买卖合约规定,没有缺陷的货物在交付一天与交付地点的市场价格,这也是复原原则下应该让受害方回复的经济地位,也就是 Market Rule 的适用。如果这一方面的证据欠缺(如有关货物没有市场),就会以其他的办法确定有关货物的真正"价值"(value)。这可节录《Benjamin's Sale of Goods》(8th edn, 2010年)之17-052段所说:"In the absence of other evidence as to the market value of goods which comply with the contractual description and quality, some courts have taken the contract price as evidence of the 'value' of the goods. But the correct measure according to s. 53(3) is the value 'at the time of delivery to the buyer', which should be taken when it is shown to be different from the contract price. The price at which the buyer had previsouly resold the goods is normally irrelevant to the ascertainment of their value at the time of delivery to the buyer; but, in the absence of other evidence, the price at which a sub-buyer had agreed to buy the goods from the buyer before the defect was discovered may be some evidence of their market value, as may the price at which an offer for the goods was made by a third person."

第二个价值就是实际交付的有缺陷货物的价值。通常是有缺陷的货物(看严重程度与怎样的缺陷)不会有市场价格,所以法院往往根据其他的证据确定该批实际交付的有缺陷货物的价值。这方面可以节录《Benjamin's Sale of Goods》(8th edn, 2010年)之17-053段:"**Ascertaining the value of the goods actually delivered.** The second value to be ascertained is that of the defective goods which were actually delivered by the seller. Normally, there is no market in the ordinary sense for damaged or defective goods, and thus other evidence is frequently needed to fix the value of the goods at the time and place of delivery. This value may be evidenced by the price at which the buyer has been able to resell the goods to a sub-buyer who has knowledge of their defective condition. 'If the actual damaged goods are sold with all faults, good evidence can be obtained of the difference in value ...'. But the court is unlikely to place reliance on the evidence of third persons ('hypothetical buyers') as to what they would have paid for goods 'which they never saw and of whose defects they have learnt only at secondhand'. The value of defective goods will depend on the nature of the defect, or the extent of the damage to the goods: 'It is a common practice in the commercial world to deal with this type of case by way of a price allowance; and claims for damaged goods are constantly met to the satisfaction of both parties by the fixing of an allowance by an adjuster or some person skilled in the trade. I think that that is a method which can legitimately be followed by the court where no more precise method of calculation presents itself'."

以上两个不同的价值或市场价值被确定后,它们之间的差价就是违约的卖方应该赔偿的损失,让受害方的买方复原到没有违约下的经济地位。这可节录《Benjamin's Sale of Goods》(8th edn, 2010年)之17-051段:"... the usual or '*prima facie*' measure of damages for breach of the seller's contractual undertaking as to the quality or condition of the goods is the difference between: (a) the value of the goods if they complied with the undertaking, measured at the time and place of delivery; and (b) the actual value of the goods, in their actual condition, at the same time and place. With the sum of money which amounts to this difference, the buyer should (so far as the value of the defective goods is concerned) be put into the financial position he would have been in if the seller had complied with his undertaking."

但如果贬值的救济办法并不恰当,如根本没有办法确定"市场价值"(market value),这就要考虑"修复"(reinstatement)的救济了。这方面可以节录《Benjamin's Sale of Goods》(8th edn,2010 年)之 17 -055 段:"**Cost of remedying the defect.** Where the market value of the defective goods cannot be ascertained, because there was no market in which they could be disposed of, damages may be awarded on the basis of the cost of bringing the goods up to the contractual standard which would make them saleable. This is similar to the position where the seller fails to deliver the goods, and there is no available market in which to buy substitute goods: the buyer may buy the nearest equivalent goods which are available, and recover as damages both the cost of procuring them and the cost of adapting them to meet the contractual standards."这些修复的费用包括像 Mondel v. Steel (1841) 8 M & W 858 先例中有关船舶修理的费用;Minster Trust Ltd v. Traps Tractors Ltd (1954) 3 All ER 136 先例中机器大修与修理期间的利润损失;Zuvela v. Geiger (2007) WASCA 138 先例中修理的费用等。

总结而言,如果违约或侵权令财产/货物被"损坏"(damaged),一般做出的救济有两种,根据不同情况而定。一种是根据财产/货物没有被损坏的价值与被损坏后的价值之间的差异(所谓的"diminution of value"),另一种是被损坏的财产所需要的修理费用(所谓的"reinstatement cost",也可被称为"cost of cure"或"cost of remedial works")。一般而言,进行修理也代表了修理妥的财产就不会再有价格的差异,也就是以修复弥补了贬值。这可以节录《McGregor on Damages》(18th edn,2009 年)之 32 - 004 段所说:"The cost of repair is expected to reflect the diminution in the value of the ship or other chattel ... "但会有个别情况是损失既包括了修复,也同时包括贬值,等于说是财产/货物修妥后依然有所贬值。这一来为了对受害方做到复原,也会有情况可以同时接受两种做法作为损失的赔偿。这方面稍后在本章 4.2 段会进一步探讨。

决定以哪一种救济来计算损失,除了要看个别案件的事实外(包括合理与否),还要客观的看受害方的"意图"(intention)是什么。这里可以节录 Donaldson 大法官在 Dodd Properties (Kent) Ltd v. Canterbury City Council (1980) 1 WLR 433 先例中所说:"The general object underlying the rules for the assessment of damages is, so far as is possible by means of a monetary award, to place the plaintiff in the position which he would have occupied if he had not suffered the wrong complained of, be that wrong a tort or a breach of contract. In the case of a tort causing damage to real property, this object is achieved by the application of one or other of two quite different measures of damage, or, occasionally, a combination of the two. The first is to take the capital value of the property in an undamaged state and to compare it with its value in a damaged state. The second is to take the cost of repair or reinstatement. Which is appropriate will depend upon a number of factors, such as the plaintiff's future intentions as to the use of the property and the reasonableness of those intentions. If he reasonably intends to sell the property in its damaged state, clearly the diminution in capital value is the true measure of damage. If he reasonably intends to continue to occupy it and to repair the damage, clearly the cost of repairs is the true measure. And there may be in – between situations. ”(不论是侵权或违约,赔偿大原则是复原。针对财产的损坏,可以有两种办法计算赔偿。第一种是比较有关财产没有损坏与损坏后的价值,然后找出差价。第二种就是找出该财产被恢复原状的修理费用。以哪一种办法计算在一定程度上是看受害方的意图,并找出最公平合理的办法。会有情况是两种计算办法要混合适用。)

以上的说法可以举个简单的例子,就是在一个房屋租赁中,租客把租赁的两栋房屋做出非法改装,这显然是违约。但受害方的房东在把两栋房屋收回后,有不同的打算或意图。一栋房屋打算自住,这就可能涉及修理费用,计算损失显然是以修复为恰当。但另一栋房屋就打算出售,这就可能涉及价值差异,计算损失显然是以贬值为恰当。

4.2　贬值与修复同时适用的情况

会有情况是两种救济都同时适用,如在损坏的财产/货物修理后,还是相比没有损坏的财产/货物有一定程度的价格差异。这一来为了让受害方复原,就会要把两种不同的救济同时适用。这方面可节录《McGregor on Damages》(18th edn, 2009 年)之 32 – 003 段:“Moreover if, despite the repairs, the market value of the goods is less than before, the claimant should be entitled to such diminution in value in addition to the cost of repair. Thus in Payton v. Brooks (1974) RTR 169 CA Roskill LJ said: ‘There are many cases ... where the cost of repairs is a *prima facie* method of ascertaining the diminution in value. It is not, however, the only method of ascertaining the loss. In a case where the evidence justifies a finding that there has been, on top of the cost of repairs, some diminution in market value ... I can see no reason why the plaintiff should be deprived of recovery under that head of damages also. ’”

在 Payton v. Brooks 先例中,由于被告的疏忽,原告刚刚买了 4 个星期的汽车在与被告汽车碰撞后受到损坏。被告承认自己的过失并承诺赔偿修理费用以及其他附带的费用。除此之外,原告还要求被告赔偿 100 英镑,因为原告发现他的汽车经过修理后,虽然修复得很好,但是在经历过车祸之后,它的价值已经降低了。对于一个购买者来说,遭遇过车祸的汽车价值肯定和一部只用过 4 个星期的新车的价值是不同的。一审法院判是原告没有权利要求赔偿这笔关于汽车价值降低的 100 英镑。而在上诉庭,法院不同意一审法院的看法。上诉庭认为,就算原告通常买车是为了自己用,但这并不排除原告可能会在这辆汽车修理好以后决定卖给别人。如果某天原告想要将这辆修理好的车再出售给别人，他能获得的价格肯定比市场上同类的没有遭遇过车祸的汽车价格要低。所以除了修理的费用，如果有证据证明原告的财产市场价格降低，他也有权获得赔偿。但原告有责任举证证明他的汽车贬值的具体金额，由于在这个先例中，原告没有提出充分的证据证明贬值的具体金额，所以上诉庭最终没有判给原告他所请求的100英镑。

4.3　受害方选择修复必须合理

针对贬值或修复的两种救济，它们的金额都不会一样。而在许多情况，修复会是更大的一笔钱，因为根据常识也会知道有许多东西损坏后与其修好，倒不如买一个新的会更便宜。但如果在比较少见的情况是修理费用比贬值更便宜，受害方在合理减少损失的义务下应该选择修复，而不能索赔更高的贬值：Pacific Blasting Ltd v. D. J. Byrne Construction Co Ltd（1977）2 WWR 505先例。

由于修复会比较昂贵，所以有不少争议是受害方想取巧（他实际上不想也不会修理），要求违约或侵权方赔偿估计的高昂修理费用。本来受害方选择修理他受到违约或侵权损坏的财产是完全可以被接受的救济，特别是在审理时受害方已经修理妥或在修理中。在Darbishire v. Warran（1963）1 WLR 1067 CA先例，Harman大法官曾经说："it has come to be settled that in general the measure of damage is the cost of reparing the damaged article."如果受害方已经修妥，他索赔的就是真正修理费用。他会面对的抗辩就是一般大家熟悉的损失计算限制如可预见性，因果关系或/与有否合理减少损失的大原则。但受害方有权索赔真正修理费用是没有什么可质疑的。

在本章4.1与4.4段提到修复是否是恰当的救济在一定程度上是看受害方的意图，但这等于是由受害方自说自话，作出选择，因为他的意图只有他自己知道，意图也可以在作出判决后改变。加上受害方向违约或侵权方索赔时，是不必真正进行修理并产生费用。毕竟，根据Breach Date Rule在违约或侵权一天计算损失，往往也不可能做到能有真正修理的费用，只能是一个估计。至于受害方取得了这一笔在违约或侵权一天得出的估计修理费用会怎么样做，法院就管不了。受害方可能会在几年后才决定进行修理，但由于通货膨胀令索赔成功所得的一笔钱完全不足够支付真正修理费用，受害方仍无法避免要自己支付多出来的金额。受害方也可能稍后决定把损坏的财产（假设是一栋房屋）出售，而买方由于这一个损坏要求减价或受害方需要承担估计的修理费用。这一来，受害方原先索赔成功所得的一笔钱就代表了这一栋损坏房屋的贬值或价格差异。受害方也有可能不进行修理，也不出售，这看来他是"赚"了这笔索赔成功的估计修理费用。但这是受害方自己的选择，不能说他没有损失或多赔了钱给他，他的损失会是房屋损坏所带来的不便与贬值。

但有一个说法在较早时已经提到，就是受害方选择修复是必须合理。如有关损坏的财产/货物，进行修理的费用是要比贬值高得多，而有关财产/货物是可以马上在"可供买卖市场"（available market）卖出买进。这一来，何必不去市场出售损坏财产/货物并同时买进良好的替代品，而花费更加高昂的修理费用？这可节录《McGregor on Damages》(18th edn,2009 年)之 32 - 004 段:"The cost of repair is, however, appropriate only if in the circumstances it is reasonable for the claimant to effect the repair; it might be cheaper to buy a replacement on the market and sell the damaged item for what it will fetch.... if it can be shown that the diminution in value is below, possibly well below, the cost of repair, then it may be appropriate to award the cost of repair. This appears to have been the view which the Court of Appeal took of the damaged ship in Meredith Jones v. Vangemar Shipping Co, The Apostolis, No. 2(2000)2 Lloyd's Rep. 337, a decision based in contract but equally relevant here. On the other hand, in Aerospace Publishing Ltd v. Thames Water Utilities Ltd(2007)110 Con. LR 1 CA where archives utilized in a business had been damaged by flooding, the cost of restoration rather than the lesser diminution in value was to be awarded since the claimant had a genuine, and reasonable, intention of reinstating the damaged collection. The test is whether it is reasonable or not for the person whose item of personal property has been damaged to decide to repair it. If so, the cost of repair is recoverable. If not, only the diminution in value is to be awarded."

另也可节录SM Waddams 先生著的《The Law of Damages》一书在 1.2340 段提到有关土地/房屋方面的争议,如租赁期届满但租用人不按照合约把损坏或破坏的地方修理妥,受害的房东如何计算损失说是:"如果一位符合常理的房东应该会修理妥[如不修理妥没有办法再使用或出租给第三人],违约方应该赔偿的贬值也就是估计的修理费用(If a rational owner would carry out the repairs, the diminution in value will be measured by their cost)。"该书接下去说是:"但如果一位符合常理的房东不会修理,违约方应赔偿的金额就局限在贬值,即使这是零(But if no rational person would carry out the repairs, then the leassee's liability is limited to the diminution in capital value)。"

这可以另举一个简单的例子说明,如违约方把房屋的颜色在租赁期间从黄色变成蓝色,但没有恢复原状归还给房东,这是很明确的违约。但恢复原状是要花很大一笔钱,而且看不出有什么必要,特别是房东准备把该房屋继续租给第三人,而第三人估计是不会计较黄色或蓝色。这一来就会有可能是计算损失不能以修复,而只能是以贬值,但后者的救济是零。但会有可能是房东能够证明与说服法院或仲裁庭他是准备自住,而他本人或家人喜欢黄色或/与对蓝色有抗拒。而如果房东能提供证据是已经在进行恢复原状或向承建商要求报价,这都会是有可能成功索赔修复的费用。

这一方面可接下去介绍一些有关的先例,会把这一个问题讲的更加清楚。

4.3.1 有关先例之一:The "Puerto Buitrago"

在 The "Puerto Buitrago"(1976)1 Lloyd's Rep 250 先例,涉及有关的船舶被光租 1.5 年的时间。期间,船舶主机发生严重故障,估计修理的费用高达 200 万美元。但即使修理妥,这一艘老船(船龄高达 15 年)的市场价值也只有 100 万美元。换言之,从保险的角度而言,这一艘船舶就已经是推定全损,以商业的角度来看是根本不会花这笔钱修理。案情发展下去是光租承租人把船舶退还给船东,但拒绝进行修理。船东不接受还船,并坚持要求光船承租人把船舶修理妥(这也是光租租约中的要求)才能还船,而期间必须继续支付租金。在英国法院第一审,Mocatta 大法官同意船东的要求,认为光租承租人必须这样做。但去了上诉庭,一审判决被推翻。上诉庭把船东的要求视为是类似"履约指令"(specific performance),也就是强迫光船承租人一定要把船舶修妥,否则要承担漫无止境的延误与支付租金,而这一个修理又是完全不合理与浪费金钱。但如果在本案例金钱赔偿是一个足够的救济,法院是不会作出履约指令的。换言之,即使是针对损失的计算,也只会判船东能够索赔贬值的 100 万美元,而不是修复的 200 万美元。

其中 Denning 勋爵是这样说:"The reason is because, by suing for the money, the plaintiff is seeking to enforce specific performance of the contract – and he should not be allowed to do so when damages would be an adequate remedy. Take a servant, who has a contract for six months certain, but is dismissed after one month. He cannot sue for his wages for each of the six months by alleging that he was ready and willing to serve. His only remedy is damages. Take a finance company which lets a machine or motor – car on hire purchase, but the hirer refuses to accept it. The finance company cannot sue each month for instalments. Its only remedy is in damages... So here, when the charterers tendered redelivery at the end of the period of the charter – in breach of the contract to repair – the shipowners ought in all reason to have accepted it. They cannot sue for specific performance – either of the promise to pay the charter hire, or of the promise to do the repairs – because damages are an adequate remedy for the breach. What is the alternative which the shipowners present to the charterers? Either the charterers must pay the charter hire for years to come, whilst the vessel lies idle and useless for want of repair. Or the charterers must do repairs which would cost twice as much as the ship would be worth when repaired – after which the shipowners might sell it as scrap, making the repairs a useless waste of money. In short, on either alternative, the shipowners seek to compel specific performance of one or other of the provisions of the charter – with most unjust and unreasonable consequences – when damages would be an adequate remedy, I do not think the law allows them to do this."

4.3.2 有关先例之二:The "Alecos M"

在 The "Alecos M"(1991)1 Lloyd's Rep 120 先例,涉及一艘二手船的买卖,船龄已经高达 14 年,所以买卖的价格也不高,只有 245 万美元。有关的买卖合约中包括了船上有一个备用螺旋桨,但实际上该船舶欠缺,所以卖方违约的责任是十分明确,争议只是在损失计算。船舶备用螺旋桨是以前的做法,今天的船舶就很少会有,船级社也没有要求。备用螺旋桨通常是以生铁铸造,安放在船上甲板主要是万一船舶的螺旋桨(这是以铜铸造)遇上事故而掉落,在另铸造新的螺旋桨期间可以备用螺旋桨暂时替代,让船舶继续营运。这种事故显然是很少会发生,加上今天的技术先进与运输便利,也可以很快生产与提供另一个新的螺旋桨。所以,今天是不会有船东愿意花钱给船舶配备一个备用螺旋桨。

在这一个事实背景下,就存在受害方的买方可以索赔什么损失？如果是以贬值,可以说是一艘船舶有否备用螺旋桨根本对船价没有影响。顶多是该相对老龄的船舶出售拆废钢,该备用螺旋桨的废钢价格对船价会有影响,但也只是1100美元。此外,由于备用螺旋桨的用途极少,根本也没有一个可供买卖的市场,所以也无法对贬值作出估计,只能是以修复的救济为准。而修复的费用,根据受害方的买方提供的证据是总共高达20万美元,其中15万美元是估计铸造备用螺旋桨的费用,另加上5万美元的运输与安装费用。

仲裁庭判是受害方所要求的修复费用并不合理,也不相信他会这样做,所以判违约的卖方只需要赔偿备用螺旋桨的废钢价格。该先例上诉去了高院,裁决书被推翻。Steyn大法官认为仲裁庭不应该考虑这一个救济是否合理以及受害方有否意图这样做,认为这方面的先例如 Radford v. De Froberville (1977) 1 WLR 1262 与 Tito v. Waddell (No. 2) (1977) Ch. 106 是主要针对土地买卖而不适用在本案件的货物买卖。之后该先例上诉去了上诉庭,又再度被推翻并支持了仲裁庭原先的裁决。其中Neill大法官在分析了有关先例后说:

"It seems to me that in the light of these authorities it is legitimate to ask: what damage did the buyers really suffer as a result of the non-delivery of the spare propeller? Furthermore, it also seems to me that this was the question which the arbitrator addressed when he considered whether the buyers were likely to or needed to obtain a replacement for the missing spare propeller and whether it was reasonable to order one to be specially manufactured.

With all due respect to the Judge, I do not think that the arbitrator did ignore the interest of the buyers in having the spare properller for potential use if the occasion arose. It may sound surprising to hear that a spare propeller has no more than scrap value, but, as I understand the award, the arbitrator reached this conclusion as to its value not because he applied some wrong principle of law but because he decided as a matter of fact that in the particular circumstances of this case the commercial value of this spare propeller on this ship was no more than its scrap value."

4.3.3 有关先例之三:Ruxley Electronics & Construction Ltd v. Forsyth

接下去介绍著名的 Ruxley Electronics & Construction Ltd v. Forsyth (1995) All ER 1936 先例。案情涉及 Forsyth 先生雇用原告在他家里建造一个游泳池,造价是约1.8万英镑。建造合约说明水池的深度是6尺6寸,但后来在 Forsyth 先生的要求下,原告的承建商同意不加钱将泳池加深至7尺6寸。合约并没有其他要求如安装跳水板。但后来的工作不完善,游泳池底部有裂缝。原告同意免费重建,并赔偿 Forsyth 先生雇用测量师的费用。游泳池在1988年6月重建完毕,原告在11月要求付钱。

Forsyth 先生坚持要减掉1万英镑,因为他受到重建的干扰。原告在不情愿下同意,但余数仍不被付清。在1989年3月,Forsyth 先生发现游泳池深度不是7尺6寸,而只有6尺9寸。这一来,争议扩大,原告最终被迫在1990年1月在法院起诉余数约1万英镑。

在一审的高院,Diamond 大法官认定的事实是:(1)水深6尺已足够有余来"潜水"(diving),所以6尺9寸的深度不妨碍 Forsyth 先生在这方面的使用。(2)水深不够7尺6寸不影响该游泳池的使用价值,更加不会影响该房屋的价格。(3)如要去加深该现有游泳池的水深达7尺6寸,这必须重建,总费用会是2.1万英镑。(4)Forsyth 先生并无意重建或修复。(5)花2.1万英镑重建,只为了从6尺9寸加深至7尺6寸是完全不合理,因为经济效益与所花的钱完全不成比例。

结果是 Diamond 大法官认为若判给 Forsyth 先生一个免费游泳池,另加2.1万英镑估计复原重建的赔偿,并不公平,所以判承建商的原告胜诉。该先例上诉去贵族院,被指是一般的建造工程合约违约后赔偿是修复的费用,特别是在修复的费用低于贬值或是价值上没有差异或是价值差异无法肯定(如有关财产/货物没有市场)的情况。但这不表示可完全罔顾修复估计的费用是否合理,而在这一点上,贵族院不同意上诉庭的 Staughton 大法官判是合理与否只针对"减少损失"(mitigation)的"责任"。

Lloyd 勋爵首先依赖美国纽约上诉庭的 Jacob & Youngs Inc v. Kend(1921)230 NY 239 先例并指该判决非常重要,因为:"... it establishes two principles which I believe to be correct and which are directly relevant to the present case: first, the case of reinstatement is not the appropriate measure of damages if the expenditure would be out of all proportion to the good to be obtained, and secondly, the appropriate measure of damages in such a case is the difference in value, even though it would result in a nominal award."

Lloyd 勋爵接着依赖澳大利亚的 Bellgrove v. Eldridge(1954)90 CLR 613 先例并指出如下:"Once again one finds the court emphasizing the central importance of reasonableness in selecting the appropriate measure of damages. If reinstatement is not the reasonable way of dealing with the situation, then diminution in value, if any, is the true measure of the plaintiff's loss. If there is no diminution in value, the plaintiff has suffered no loss. His damages will be nominal."

而英国本身也有先例说明这修复的费用必须合理:East Ham BC v. Bernard Sunlay & Sons Ltd(1965)3 All ER 619; GW Atkins Ltd v. Scott(1980)7 Const. LJ 215; Darlington BC v. Wiltshier Northern LTd(1995)1 WLR 68。

在该先例,可以说是 Forsyth 先生败诉,无法索赔这2万多英镑估计的修复费用。但因为游泳池深度并不符合合约规定,这是违约,所以贵族院支持 Diamond 大法官所判的2500英镑是给予"失去满足"(loss of amenity)的赔偿,可以说 Forsyth 先生总算得到一个安慰奖。而如果有关的标的不是游泳池而是屋内其他与享受无关的设施,就恐怕这一个失去满足的安慰奖也不会有,Forsyth 先生有的只会是一个名义损失的赔偿,可以说是完完全全的败诉了。关于失去满足的赔偿在本书第二章之15.4.2与15.4.3段有详细的介绍。

4.3.4 有关先例之四:The "Apostolis"(No.2)

The "Apostolis"(No.2)(2000)2 Lloyd's Rep. 337先例的案情涉及一艘老龄(高达20年)的船舶在希腊的Salonica港装一票棉花去巴西时发生火灾,装载棉花的第四与第五舱损坏。起火的原因,货方指是船舶烧焊引起火灾,船方指是货方小工抽烟引起火灾。最后,根据提供的证据,法院认为最大可能性是货方小工抽烟所导致,这表示货方要承担船东的损失。但问题是怎样计算损失才能够令船东复原,到底是以修复或是贬值?因为两种不同的算法会带来很不一样的金额。如果船舶在发生火灾后很快在希腊或在巴西卸完货后进行修理(或即使是部分修理),案件到了审理的时候就可以根据这一个已经发生的事实判船东的救济可以是根据修复计算,也就是合理修理费用以及加上其他相关损失(如干坞与港口费用、船期延误等)。但在该先例中的船舶根本没有进行修理,因为火灾带来的损坏并没有影响船舶继续营运,变为船东即使是进行永久修理,也会在3年后船级特检时一并在干坞进行,从而减少损失(因为可以省下干坞费用与船期损失)。事实上,在审理的时候已经明确,该船舶在船级特检前就已经被出售。换言之,受害方的船东从来没有进行过修理。至于把船舶出售给第三人,这么老的船又会涉及第三人买方的买入用途是否是用来拆废钢。如果是拆废钢,这一来该船舶损坏或不损坏都不会影响有多少吨的废钢,换言之,不应该会有真正的损失。这就表示判受害方船东可以向货方取回修复费用或贬值的金额(如果有)都是让船东获利,两种救济办法都不恰当。但如果第三人的买方是计划把该老船买入继续营运,就有很大的可能在船舶买卖的谈判中,要求受害方的船东对船价作出扣减或承担估计修理费用,这一来船东就会蒙受损失并可向造成火灾的货方索赔。这些千变万化的不同事实是不容易认定,而认定也只能是看证据,如在买卖该船舶时谈判的文件证据。在该先例还有一点是后来运费市场上扬,而第三人的买方的确是买入该老船继续营运,而受害方船东也在出售的价格中作出据说是高达30万美元的扣减或贬值。但问题是估计损失是以Breach Date Rule为准,在违约的一天是没有办法合理预计到几年后出售该老船继续营运与运费市场的上扬,所以在审理的时候不能加以考虑。在以上的解释下,可节录第一审的Longmore大法官怎样判有关损失的计算,如下:

"The vessel undoubtedly suffered damage as a result of the fire. The damage was examined at Salonica and ABS(这是美国船级社) reported that the damage did not impair the vessel's trading capability, and that repairs could be done at the next drydocking, which was not due until December, 1995. The shipowners in fact sold the vessel in June, 1995, and repair was thus not effected by the defendants(船东). The new owners say that the sale price was reduced by US $300,000 to reflect the need for repair. The parties agreed that if repair had been effected at Brazil on completion of discharge they would have cost in the region of US $ 250,000, whereas if they had been effected in Greece or Bulgaira/Romania they would have cost US $ 140,000 or US $ 80,000 respectively. My task is to assess the diminution in value of the vessel at the time of the breach. It is axiomatic that the fact that repairs were not done does not mean the diminution in value cannot be recovered. See The London Corporation, (1935) 51 LL. L. Rep 67; (1935) P70.

Basing himself on the expert valuation evidence of Mr. Wilcox(专家证人) to the effect that the vessel was 20 years old, and only had a scrap value of US $ 1,050,000, and that the sound value of the vessel was US $ 1,225,000, Mr. Milligan(货方代表大律师) said it was uneconomic to repair(whatever the repair costs), and the diminution in value was nil. That seems to me altogether too artificial in a case where the vessel was not sold for scrap but as a going concern.

I do not, however, think it right to assess the diminution in value by reference to notional repairs inBrazil. Any reasonable owner would wait for dry – docking, as these owners presumably intended to do, until they decided to sell the vessel. They would probably have drydocked in Greece, and thus spent US $ 140,000 rather than US $ 80,000 at what would be a less convenient location. I see no reason why that should not be the diminution in the value of the vessel which was still a going concern. Mr. Glen(货方专家证人), the plaintiffs' expert, said that the repairs would not extend the time for drydocking for more than eight days, and that additional expenses for that period would be in the region of US $ 15,000. So I would award US $ 155,000 under this head."

换言之,Longmore 大法官判是该船舶既然继续营运而不是拆废钢,它的修理费用就最能代表贬值。这修理费用是以在出事地点希腊的估计金额为准,也就是 14 万美元。再加上估计修理所带来的其他使费 1.5 万美元,总共货方要赔给船东的钱就是 15.5 万美元。但该先例去了上诉庭,因为货方不认为该有关的老船花这笔钱修理是一种合理的做法,货方并提供证据说明这种损坏对这一艘老船只会带来约 2.5 万美元至 5 万美元之间的船价贬值。在上诉庭,货方的争辩得到支持,并认为在违约一天作出损失估计,是不会合理认为要修理。在违约一天也不能预见后来的运费市场上扬,第三人买入船舶继续营运。所以恰当的救济办法还是根据贬值的赔偿,在 2.5 万美元至 5 万美元之间的金额。Waller 大法官是这样说:"There was no challenge to the proposition that the owners could recover although the repairs had not been done, and no reliance was placed on the decision of the House of Lords in Ruxley Electronics & Construction Ltd v. Forsyth(1996) AC 344. The question then is whether, at the time when the damages fell to be measured, it was reasonable to repair the vessel. All the evidence was one way on that point, if one paid no regard to the possibility that freight rates might take a turn for the better in the future. Our provisional view is that the diminution in value was no more than US $ 25K or US $ 50K."

4.4　受害方选择修复需要说服法院或仲裁庭他有意图进行修理

这也是一个很重要的因素说明受害方选择修复是否合理：Tito v. Waddell(No. 2)(1977)Ch 106；Radford v. De Froberville(1977)1 WLR 1262；Hospitality Investments Ltd v. Everett Lord Building Construction Ltd (1993) 166 NBR (2d) 241 (CA)；Chase v. deGroot(1994)1 NZLR 613(HC)；Ruxley Electronics & Construction Ltd v. Forsyth (1995)All ER 1936 等先例。

在 Chase v. deGroot 的新西兰先例，有关房屋在审理前已经出售，法院拒绝了受害方原告要求的修复费用，但同时说到原告如果“能够证明有一个真正的意图修理”(had demonstrated a genuine interest in having such work done)那他的索赔会成功。

另在 Tito v. Waddell 先例，Robert Megarry 大法官是说：“*Per contra*, if the plaintiff has suffered little or no monetary loss in the reduction of value of his land, and **he has no intention of applying any damages towards carrying out the work contracted for**, or its equivalent, I cannot see why he should recover the cost of doing work which will never be done. It would be a mere pretence to say that this cost was a loss and so should be recoverable as damages.”

在 Radford v. De Froberville 先例，案情涉及原告将自己土地的一部分出售给被告，条件是被告要在这块土地上建造合约规定的房屋，并修建一堵墙来把这块土地和原告自己剩余的那块土地分开，被告还要负责这堵墙的维修，这个前提条件也是原告与被告的买卖合约中的部分对价。在原告自己剩余的那块土地上，原告将他自己的房屋分隔成单元房并出租给几个租客。虽然原告自己并不住在那里，但是他和租客约定可以共用这幢房屋的公共部分。但之后被告没有在这块土地上建造房屋也没有修墙，而是把这块土地转让给了第三人，并将被告与原告合约中的义务(包括建造房屋和修墙)都转让给了第三人。但是第三人最后也没有修建房屋和围墙。原告向法院请求被告赔偿修建围墙的费用，而第三人抗辩认为，虽然没有修建围墙，但是原告土地的价值没有任何减损，所以被告和第三人不应该赔偿原告这笔费用。但法院最后判是被告应该赔偿给原告在这块土地上修建围墙的费用。原因是原告的土地并不是用来投资，所以被告需要赔偿的损失并不是没有围墙而会产生的土地价值的差异或贬值(这会是不多甚至是零)。原告的意图就是要修建围墙来防止他的土地上长杂草或有入侵者，而不是为了出售这块土地，所以贬值的考虑在这里是没有关系。证据也显示由于被告没有修建围墙，原告有意图自己修建，所以被告应该承担的赔偿数额是关于这项修建围墙的工程的费用，而不是原告土地的贬值。

另在本章4.3.3段介绍过的 Ruxley Electronics & Construction Ltd v. Forsyth 先例，贵族院的 Lloyd 勋爵讲到有关受害方是否有意图进行修理的重要性以及修复是否合理救济的考虑，说：

“I fully accept that the courts are not normally concerned with what a plaintiff does with his damages. But it does not follow that intention is not relevant to reasonableness, at least in those cases where the plaintiff does not intend to reinstate. Suppose in the present case Mr Forsyth had died, and the action had been continued by his executors. Is it to be supposed that they would be able to recover the cost of reinstatement, even though they intended to put the property on the market without delay?

There is, as Staughton LJ observed, a good deal of authority to the effect that intention may be relevant to a claim for damages based on cost of reinstatement. The clearest decisions on the point are those of Sir Rober Megarry V – C in Tito v. Waddell (No. 2) (1977) Ch 106 and Oliver J in Radford v. DeFroberville (1977) 1 WLR 1262. One of the many questions in the former case was whether the plaintiffs could recover the cost of replanting the plots of land in question, or whether the recovery of damages was limited to the difference in the market value of the land by reason of the work not having been done ...

In the present case the judge found as a fact that Mr Forsyth's stated intention of rebuilding the pool would not persist for long after the litigation had been concluded. In these circumstances it would be mere pretence to say that the cost of rebuilding the pool is the loss which he has in fact suffered."

4.5　贬值与修复都以违约一天作出估计

根据 Breach Date Rule 计算损失的大原则,无论是贬值还是修复的救济,损失计算或估计都是以违约一天的损失为准。这也是在 Dodd Properties (Kent) Ltd v. Canterbury City Council (1980) 1 WLR 433 先例的一审中 Cantley 大法官所说:

"In the case of destruction of a chattel, the normal measure of the damage is its market value at the time of the loss. That was the measure of damage applied in The 'Liesbosch' (1933) A. C. 449. I do not suppose that it would have made any difference in that case if the unfortunate owners of that elderly dredger had done nothing to replace it for 10 years except to go on trying to save up enough money to buy another similar dredger and had then claimed the current cost of one on a risen market. **They would, I suppose, have recovered the market value at the time of loss.** If they also were given interest on the money that they ought to have received 10 years before, that might have bought them another similar dredger. As ... has pointed out, it is when the rate of inflation exceeds the rate of interest that it becomes important to have your damages assessed at the date of hearing. [在财产/货物的毁灭,通常的损失计算是在毁灭时的市场价值。这一个损失计算的大原则适用在 The "Liesbosch" (1933) 45 Ll. L. Rep. 123 先例(这个先例在本书第二章之13.2.6.4 段有详细介绍)。Cantley 大法官不认为案情变化会给损失计算带来什么区别,如该先例中穷困的受害方等了 10 年才积蓄足够的金钱买进另一艘替代疏浚船,并索赔当时已经大幅度上升的市场价格。**但 Cantley 大法官认为能够取回的是侵权造成损失时的市场价格**。受害方也可以索赔在 10 年前就应该做出赔偿的市场价格在 10 年间所损失的利息。只是在通货膨胀率比利率更高时,在什么日期(侵权造成

损失一天或开庭审理一天)厘定市场价格才变得十分重要,因为开庭审理一天的市场价格由于通货膨胀会大幅度超出侵权一天]

A similar rule as to the measure of damage applies where chattels are damaged as opposed to be destroyed and it is reasonable to deal with the damage by way of repair.(同样道理适用在财产/货物被损坏,损失计算是以修理费用计算为合理)

Philips v. Ward(1956)1 W. L. R. 471 was an action for damages against a surveyor who had made a negligent report about the condition of a house which was bought by the plaintiff on his advice. The measure of damages claimed for the plaintiff in that action was the cost of repairing the house **at prices ruling at the date of hearing**. In the event, the plaintiff was **not** awarded damages on that basis but on the basis of the difference between the value of the house in its actual condition when he had bought it and the price that he had then paid for it. But the court made some observations on the claim for the cost of repairs which find of assistance.(Philips v. Ward 先例涉及一个测量师对一栋房屋的情况提供给原告有疏忽的意见,而根据该错误的意见原告购买了该房屋而蒙受损失。原告要求的损失是开庭一天对该房屋的修理费用。但原告并没有被判是可取回这一笔钱,而只是能够取回该房屋贬值的价值,也就是原告付出的房价相比该房屋实际的市场价格。在该先例中,法院针对修理费用的计算应该根据哪一天有一些看法,在以下节录。)

Denning L. J. said, at p. 474:'Another point arose about the time at which the damages should be assessed. The cost of repair has risen considerably since the house was bought, and it will cost Mr. Philips a good deal more than £ 7,000 now to put his house right. The £ 7,000 is based on 1952 costs, not 1956 costs ... I think that it is right to assess the damages as at 1952 prices. The general principle of English law is that**damages must be assessed as at the date when the damage occurs**, which is usually the same day as the cause of action arises, but may be later: see Cummings v. London Bullion Co. Ltd. (1952)1 K. B. 327 . A fall thereafter in the value of money does not in law affect the figure, for the simple reason that sterling is taken Market Rule to be constant in value: see Di Ferdinando v. Simon, Smits & Co. Ltd. (1920)3 K. B. 409 ... S. S. Celia(Owners) v. S. S. Volturno(Owners)(The "Volturno")(1921)2 A. C. 544 ... Bishop v. Cunard White Star Co. Ltd. (1950)P. 240 ... In the case of continuing damage...'"(上述是 Denning 大法官说明英国法律的大原则是损失以违约一天计算,这也是受害方的原告有了诉因的一天,但这里会有一些伸缩性以稍后的日期作出计算,如果这才能够更加满足复原的大原则。)

5. Breach Date Rule 与 Market Rule 所带来的争议

这个 Breach Date Rule 与 Market Rule 计算损失虽然是相对简单与快捷，但基于不同的案件涉及千变万化的不同事实，它仍然有不少的争议。而比较常见的是如：(1)“一般违约”(ordinary breach)与“预期违约”(anticipatory breach)计算上的区别。(2)受害方能否通过不接受预期违约(这导致有关的买卖或其他类别的合约依然有效)而延后计算市场损失的一天？(3)受害方如果向法院或仲裁庭申请作出“履约指令”(specific performance)会带来什么影响？(4)违约/侵权的一天与地点到底有没有一个可供买卖的市场？(5)如果受害方是在稍后才真正在市场买进或转售，价格比违约/侵权一天高或低，这额外的损失(或节省)应否也由违约方承担(或享有)？(6)虽然是有市场，但由于供不应求或供过于求而令受害的买方或卖方在尽全力的情况下也无法在违约/毁约一天买进或转售的损失计算。(7)其他方面。

6. 一般性违约与预期违约在损失计算的差异

导致以 Breach Date Rule 与 Market Rule 来计算损失会发生在两种情况：(1)“一般性违约”(ordinary breach)；(2)“预期违约”(anticipatory breach)(有关预期违约在本书第五章之 10 段与本章 2.2.2 段已经有介绍)。

6.1　一般性违约的损失计算

一般性违约可以很简单，经常会发生的例子就是卖方应该提供货物的最后日期到了，但没有提供；或者是买方应该接受货物的日期到了，但没有接受；或者是货不对版。这个违约可以是违反一个“条件条文”(condition)或者是违反“保证条文”(warranty)，它们两者的差别只是可否让受害方终断合约，而在损失计算方面是毫无区别的。例如，在一个 10 年的供货合约下，卖方在其中一次交付中没有及时供货或是供应的货物货不对版，违反了保证条文。这使得买方需要在市场上购买替代货物并蒙受损失。于是就存在向卖方索赔损失的计算是根据 Breach Date Rule 与 Market Rule，但是对于该 10 年合约能否终断是没有影响的。

6.2　预期违约的损失计算

6.2.1　预期违约被提前接受去终断合约，损失计算以合约应该被履行的一天为准

预期违约就比较复杂，如 9 月才需要付运的买卖合约，但在 5 月卖方已经明言说不会履行，因为市场上涨或他提供不了货物。这一来，受害方的买方有两个选择，而他一作出选择就会是最终与无法改变的。第一个选择就是接受预期违约把合约终

断,这一来,受害方马上就有了减少损失的"责任"或义务,即在5月尽快去市场购买9月的商品(如果合理的情况下,如当时的市场明显在上涨)。第二个选择就是坚持卖方必须履行,毕竟5月距离要履行的9月还是有一段时间,卖方回心转意的情况经常会出现。这会是市场的波动导致了卖方从不想履行变为愿意履行,也可以是买方坚持要求履行的同时用其他的办法施压,如开始仲裁或者是施加其他的压力(如威胁冻结卖方的财产或是商业压力)。反正如果没有把合约终断的情况下,卖方回心转意结果把合约履行了,就等于什么事情都没有发生过一样。由于没有被接受的预期违约相等于合约一直是有效存在,所以如果有突发事件如出口国家对有关商品/货物作出禁令,令本来不想履行的卖方可以有机会合法根据买卖合约的免责条文、不可抗力条文或合约受阻为由脱身,买方就会失去了较早接受预期违约终断合约并索赔损失的机会。

如果买方选择了坚持卖方必须履行,这是回不了头的。买方之后再想终断合约(如对卖方会履行的可能感觉到无望或者突然有了其他更好的替代生意或者市场逆转),就必须是有另一个卖方新的预期违约才会给买方提供另一个终断合约的机会。例如,买方在持续坚持卖方必须履行交货,卖方一直没有表态。但过了一个星期,买方由于自己的原因而再也不想要这票货,就不能突然改变想法去终断合约了。正确的做法就是试探卖方问他到底交不交货,如果卖方重复他的预期违约说是不会履行,买方就可以借此新的预期违约接受与终断合约。这不但是合理与正确的做法,而且保留了索赔损失的权利,如根据 Breach Date Rule 与 Market Rule 计算出来的损失。

6.2.2 《McGregor on Damages》权威书籍的说法

这方面可节录《McGregor on Damages》(18th edn,2009 年)之 20－017 段如下:"The fact that the seller has repudiated the contract before the time fixed for delivery does not affect the *prima facie* rule that the market price at the time so fixed is the relevant one. In the first place, if the seller's repudiation is not accepted by the buyer it is a nullity and there is no breach till there is non－performance, i. e. at the time fixed for deliver, and the buyer, with no duty to mitigate, is entitled to sit back on a rising market, and then claim the normal measure based on the market price at the time fixed for delivery: the authorities for this proposition are Leigh v. Paterson(1818)8 Taunt 540 and Brown v. Muller(1872) LR 7 Ex 319. The buyer is not holding the seller to ransom here: the sanction is that the contract is still open and not only may the seller still perform but subsequent events may even, unexpectedly, relieve him of the necessity to perform. In the second place, if the seller's repudiation is accepted by the buyer so that there is then a breach, the damages are still *prima facie* calculated at the time fixed for delivery, a point settled by Roper v. Johnson(1873) LR 8 CP 167, and confirmed by the House of Lords in Garnac Grain Co v. Faure & Fairclough (1967)1 Lloyd's Rep. 495, but the buyer is now under a duty to mitigate and cannot therefore sit back with impunity on a rising market. It is indeed the seller's onus to prove that the buyer has failed to mitigate by not going into the rising market and repurchasing, so that in the absence of any such evidence from the seller the *prima facie* rule will still be applied in the buyer's favour, as in Roper v. Johnson and again in Garnac Grain Co v. Faure & Fairclough. If the seller discharges this onus and shows that the buyer could in the interim between the acceptance of the repudiation and the time fixed for delivery have repurchased in the market at a price lower than that prevailing at the time fixed for deliver, he is entitled to have the damages assessed by reference to this lower price. Where the buyer fails to repurchase when he ought to have done, the market price at the date fixed for delivery will be taken against him where it proves to be lower that the market price at the date when he could and should have repurchased. This was the position in Melachrino v. Nickoll (1920) 1 KB 693 where the market price was above the contract price at the time of the acceptance of the repudiation but below the contract price at the time fixed for delivery: only nominal damages were awarded. Where the buyer fails to repurchase when he ought to have done and no evidence is tendered as to the price prevailing at the time fixed for delivery, the price at which the buyer subsequently, but again before the delivery time, did purchase. All of this is illustrated by Kaines v. Osterreichische Warrenhandelsgesellschaft (1993) 1 Lloyd's Rep. 1. Finally, if the buyer repurchases, in a reasonable attempt to mitigate, at a market price which in the event turns out to be higher than that at the time fixed for delivery, he is entitled, on general principles of mitigation, to have the damages assessed with reference to his repurchase price."

另在第16－081段，说：

"**Acceptance of the buyer's anticipatory repudiation**. If the seller accepts the buyer's anticipatory repudiation, he may sue immediately for damages for breach of contract; but in those situations in which there is an available market for the goods, the relevant date for ascertaining the market price remains *prima facie* (and subject to any requirement of mitigation) the date fixed for delivery, since that is when the contract ought to be performed. If the action is heard before the date for delivery arrives, the court should attempt to estimate what the market price is likely to be at that future date. The seller cannot advance the relevant date for ascertaining the market price merely by exercising his option to accept the anticipatory breach: a lower market price at the time of repudiation should not increase the damages. Thus, it is submitted that the provision in s. 50 (3) [这是指1979年英国《货物销售法》) that, when no time is fixed for acceptance, damages should be assessed by reference to the market price 'at the time of the refusal to accept' should not apply to an anticipatory breach by the buyer. (如果预期违约的是CFR买方，他在货物应该交出的一天(假设是8月31日)之前3个月对卖方说他不会接受这票货物，所以卖方不必租船与装船，因为是白费心机。这显然就是一个典型的预期违约，如果受害的卖方接受，合

约就终断。卖方也可以马上向买方索赔损失,但如果涉及市场规则适用,计算损失的一天是合约规定要履行的一天,也就是 8 月 31 日,因为买方还是持续不接受有关货物就构成了违约,损失也是以该天的市场价格作出比较。换言之,损失计算是不会以买方在 3 个月前的 5 月 31 日作出预期违约一天的市场价格为准。可以说在预期违约的情况下,损失计算是偏离了“违约一天计算损失规则”(Breach Date Rule)。而即使是受害的卖方在预期违约的 1 个月后,也就是 6 月 30 日接受了预期违约,这令买卖合约终断,但计算损失还是不能以该天的市场价格为准。适用的还是以买方需要履行接受货物的最后一天,也就是 8 月 31 日的市场价格为准。如果诉讼进行的很快,在 8 月 31 日前的 7 月底审理,就表示法院或仲裁庭需要估计将来在 8 月 31 日的市场价格会是多少,这往往需要靠专家意见证据。总结说,Breach Date Rule 与 Market Rule 是不会因为预期违约被或迟或早的接受令合约终断而有所改变,否则损失的金额就会在一定程度上被受害方操纵。]

But the rules of mitigation may override this rule. If the seller does accept the buyer's anticipatory repudiation, his damages will be assessed on the basis that he took reasonable steps to mitigate his loss. Where the seller should have mitigated by the reselling, the relevant market price is that existing at the date he ought reasonably to have resold, not that at the date of the repudiation, not that at the date when the repudiation is accepted. If the market price is falling after the time the seller accepted the repudiation, it will normally be reasonable for the seller to resell immediately, so that he will be unable to recover the difference between the price on the date he ought to have resold and the price on the date when he actually resold."[但在上述的情况下,提前接受了买方的预期违约终断买卖合约,由于合约不再存在与违约已经是有了定论,受害方的卖方就马上有了一个减少损失的义务。而如果感觉当时市场上有关货物价格会持续下跌,就表示卖方有一个合理减少损失的责任马上把货物在市场上转售。如果他没有这样做,虽然不影响 Breach Date Rule 与 Market Rule 对损失的计算,也就是以 8 月 31 日的市场价格为准,但卖方没有合理减少损失就会导致他需要承担这部分的损失。笔者可以多举一些变化,如在期间违约的买方曾经给过卖方一个“新要约”(reoffer)要买这票同样的货物或是买方有证据说明卖方曾经在期间把有关货物出售给第三人,而这些价格都比 8 月 31 日的市场价格高,也会使卖方不能要买方承担这 8 月 31 日市场价格与合约价格的全部差价]

6.2.3 一个造船合约的伦敦仲裁有关争议

笔者举一个近期的造船合约仲裁进一步说明这方面的争议。案情涉及欧洲买方指中国船厂在 2007 年年底以语言与行动构成了预期违约,并且被买方接受终断造船合约。这种预期违约的语言与行动的确在当时航运市场高涨时也经常在发生,部分中国船厂会很笨拙与毫不掩饰地以文书对外国买方说:“除非你加多少船价,否则我不会在稍后交船给你。”这是典型的预期违约,受害的买方可以拒绝接受并坚持中国船厂必须履行造船合约。也会有买方在抗议下接受船价的增加,务求能够顺利接船。但也会有买方选择接受预期违约去终断造船合约,并向中国船厂提出索赔。如果有关的船舶是有市场,这就会适用 Market Rule 与 Breach date rule,即损失是在有关造船合约下中国船厂应该交船的一天的市场价格与合约价格之间的差价。但在有关先例,该造船合约的交船日期是在 2009 年年底,也就是在 2008 年年底的金融海啸后。这一来很明显可以看到以哪一天的市场适用 Market Rule 关系十分重大,因为以 Breach Date Rule,也就是 2007 年年底买方接受中国船厂预期违约一天为准,当时该船舶的市场价格十分高涨,相比合约价格高很多,这损失就有上千万美元。但如果是按照合约应该交船一天的市场价格,也就是 2009 年年底,当时航运市场已经暴跌,买方就根本没有损失了,因为当天的市场价格比合约价格低。

众所周知,造船合约也属于是货物买卖,受到 1979 年英国《货物销售法》约束。其中 Section 51(3)是针对卖方(也就是中国船厂)拒绝交付货物(船舶)的损失计算,说:"Damages for non – delivery.... (3) where there is an available market for the goods in question the measure of damages is *prima facie* to be ascertained by the difference between the contract price and the market or current price of the goods at the time or times when they ought to have been delivered or(if no time was fixed) at the time of the refusal to deliver."

显然在该仲裁案件,欧洲买方主张以预期违约被接受的一天适用 Market Rule,而中国船厂的主张是以造船合约承诺交船的一天为准。买方指出 Section 51(3)只是表面规则,仲裁庭只要是认为买方的确是蒙受了真正的损失就可以偏离。买方也大力主张英国的法律是越来越倾向于赔偿受害方真正的损失,如像 The "Golden Victory"(2007)2 Lloyd's Rep 164 等先例。而在这一个案件中,显然买方蒙受的真正损失会是金额十分庞大。原因是当时船价不断上涨,不少买方都会在船舶建造的中途把有关的造船合约或船舶在市场转售。这可以通过"转让"(assignment)、"合约变更"(novation)或是把订立造船合约的单船公司转售。而事实上,买方声称他有很大的可能会在 2008 年底金融海啸之前把该建造中的船舶转售,并赚取一笔庞大的利润。买方声称他不会想等到 2009 年年底接船,所以在 2008 年年底的金融海啸导致航运市场暴跌,对他不会有影响。

中国船厂的代表大律师同意 Section 51(3)的表面规则是可以在两种情况下被排除:(1)没有可供买卖的市场(这显然不适用在本案件,毕竟所建造的船舶只是散货船,有很明确与蓬勃的可供买卖的市场);(2)受害方蒙受"特别损失"(special damage)并且是双方在订约时预见或料想到的。

显然,欧洲买方要在这方面胜诉必须是说服仲裁庭他蒙受的是特别损失,而且是双方订约时可以预见。事实上,中国船厂也很难争辩说他不能预见到该造船合约下的船舶不会在建造中被买方转售,毕竟这种活动非常频密。而有关的合约中甚至也没有一条禁止转让条文。

但最后仲裁庭的多数判中国船厂胜诉(这是一个极少数中国船厂在伦敦或香港

仲裁胜诉的案件），认为双方订约时预见或料想到建造中的船舶有可能被转售并不足够。多数仲裁员认为这一个预见或料想必须是更有针对性，如有一个双方都知道的特定转售。仲裁庭是这样说："We conclude that if the loss of the ability to resell the contracts was factually established, then the Yard, if liable, was bound to compensate for the loss caused thereby. But it is necessary to identify clearly what was in the contemplation of the parties. That was only the ***possibility*** of a future assignment agreement whereby the contracts were resold. If a ***particular*** resale has been in contemplation at the time of contracting, that would be enough for the Buyers to succeed under this part of their claim. But that certainly was not the case. It does not follow from the fact that possible resales were in contemplation that the loss actually occurred. The burden of proof would still lie on the Buyers to establish that they would in fact have flipped the contracts. To show that they might have done so would not be enough."

6.3 申请过履约指令的损失计算

违约方如果"违约/毁约"（repudiatory breach），这包括"预期违约"（anticipatory breach），受害方特别要小心的一种情况是，他曾经向法院或仲裁庭取得"履约指令"（specific performance）。这是明显不过地作出了一种选择，就是要违约方履行合约。同样地，选择一经作出，受害方再也没有终断合约的权利了。当然，也不是每一种违约都会有履约指令的救济，但一种经常会遇到的而且与社会密切相关的就是房屋买卖合约。如房价下跌，买方不肯在约定的一天完成交易。受害的卖方就会有两个选择：(1)向买方索赔损失，也就是买方违约/毁约一天的估计市场价格与合约价格的差价；(2)向法院申请履约指令，决定另一个完成交易的一天，并希望法院的命令有阻吓力能够迫使买方履约。但这一来，受害的卖方要知道他是受到买卖合约的约束，变成如果在等待履约指令最后期限届临期间，另有一个出更优越价格的买方出现，卖方也不能接受以免夹在两个合约中间。受害的卖方看来也不能去法院申请把原来的履约指令取消，以便终断合约。原因之一是法院不会接受出尔反尔改变主意的做法，而且也违反了受害方对违约/毁约或预期违约一作出选择就是最终的原则。看来正确的做法是等到履约指令的最后一天，但买方还是不履行，受害的卖方才能向法院申请把指令"撤销"（discharge），而损失的计算也就是在履约指令"无效"（abortive）的一天适用市场规则。这种情况在贵族院的先例 Johnson v. Agnew (1979) 2 WLR 487 中有介绍。

第十六章　市场规则之二

1. Market Rule 计算损失

在本书第十五章的“市场规则之一”，已经谈到了“基本金钱损失”（basic pecuniary loss）在涉及了有市场的情况下，通常就是以合约被履行的价值相比不履行的价值（或市场价格）之间的差价计算违约/毁约所带来的“利润损失”（loss of profit）作为一种简单、快捷与相对准确的计算办法。但是“市场规则”（Market Rule）与其他一些规则如“违约一天损失规则”（Breach Date Rule）只属于损失计算的“分规则”（sub－rule），而在主要政策或大原则仍是“复原”（*restitutio in integrum*）。如果这些分规则是做不到复原对受害方做出充分的损失赔偿，这些分规则就要靠边站。所以，市场规则或违约一天损失规则也不是这么简单，经常会要做出改变与“有弹性”（flexible）以尽量配合每一个案件中不同的案情，务求能够做到复原。这也是符合 1979 年英国《货物销售法》中所讲到的市场规则只是一个“表面规则”（*prima facie* rule）。

这可节录贵族院在 Admiralty Com'rs v. S. S. Chekiang（1926）AC 637 与 The“Liesbosch”（1933）45 Ll. L. Rep. 123 先例中说到：“... the dominant rule of law is the principle of *restitutio in integrum*, and subsidiary rules can only be justified if they give effect to that rule.”

市场规则的适用最重要也是最常见是在货物买卖，这已经在立法中早有了规定（在 1893 年英国《货物销售法》）。在 1979 年英国《货物销售法》，Section 50（3）针对买方违约/毁约，损失的计算是：“Where there is an available market for the goods in question the measure of damages is *prima facie* to be ascertained by the difference between the contract price and the market or current price at the time or times when goods ought to have been accepted or（if no time was fixed for acceptance）at the time of the refusal to accept.”

另是 Section 51（3）针对卖方违约/毁约，损失的计算是：“Where there is an available market for the goods in question the measure of damages is *prima facie* to be ascertained by the difference between the contract price and the market or current price of the goods at the time or times when they ought to have been delivered or（if no time was fixed）at the time of the refusal to deliver.”

虽然没有立法规定，同样的理念下，Breach Date Rule 与 Market Rule 也适用在所有其他拥有市场的业务与相关合约下的违约/毁约所造成的损失计算。其中最著名与经常有先例针对的几类业务可作为介绍是股票买卖合约：Jamal v. Moolla Dawood (1916) 1 AC 175 先例（涉及买方违约/毁约）；“衍生工具”（derivative）合约：Norden v. Andre (2003) 1 Lloyd's Rep 287 先例与租船合约：The“Elena d'Amico”(1980) 1 Lloyd's Rep 75 先例。Breach Date Rule 与 Market Rule 的理念或合理性可节录 Goff 大法官在 The“Elena d'Amico”先例中著名的说法如下：“In considering the submission that these lost profits are recoverable from the owners as damages, in my judgment guidance is provided ... by cases concerned with the sale of goods. Taking ... the case of non-delivery, where goods are not delivered on the due date, or the contract is repudiated, the buyer is placed in a situation where he has to decide whether or not to buy in and, if he is going to buy in, whether he should buy in immediately or wait for a time and buy in later. The position in law appears to be that, generally speaking, if there is an available market for the goods in question at the time when they ought to have been delivered, then if the buyer decides not to buy in on that date, which he is fully entitled to do, he cannot visit the consequences of that decision upon the seller. If he buys in later he may, of course, either buy in ... at a higher price or at a lower price than the available market price at the date when they ought to have been delivered. But if he has to buy at the higher price he cannot, generally speaking, claim the extra cost from the seller; and if he makes a saving then that saving is not, generally speaking, to be brought into account to reduce the damages which are recoverable from the seller.”

简单重复，英国《货物销售法》或普通法在 Market Rule 下就假设受害方（不论是卖方还是买方，船东或是承租人）在违约的一天有一个可供买卖的市场情况下，就应该在该市场寻找同样或接近的替代。如果这替代与原来合约的价格有差别导致受害方蒙受损失，这就是他可向违约方索赔的金额。换言之，Market Rule 适用的话，就把违约一天的市场价格作为一个损失计算的分水岭或基准线。这一个理念是主要结合了“减少损失”（mitigation）与“因果关系”（causation）。在减少损失下，就假设受害方应该尽快去市场寻找替代。在因果关系下，就假设受害方在违约/毁约后更后的时间寻找替代而导致了真正蒙受的损失更大或是更小，就会涉及其他的原因，如受害方看错了市场的走势或是其他本人的问题导致太晚才采取减少损失的行动。所以这种好处或是坏处都是受害方自己享有或承担，与违约的关系中断。

1.1 何谓“可供买卖市场”

“市场规则”（Market Rule）适用在计算违约或侵权的损失首先就要求有一个可供买卖的市场（available market）针对有关的财产/货物。可供买卖的市场的基本定义在《Benjamin's Sale of Goods》(8th edn, 2010 年）一书中 16－063 段是这样说：“An early view was that an available market is some place (e. g. an exchange) where the goods in question can be sold; a later view was that it 'means a particular level of trade' in a particular locality; another that it refers to a sufficient demand for the goods 'to absorb readily all the goods that were thrust on it'; another that it means a situation where the current price for the goods may fluctuate according to supply and demand (which rules out the situation 'where the goods can only be sold at a fixed retail price'); and another that '... there must be sufficient traders who are in touch with each other'."[早期的看法是市场必须在一些地方,如交易所对有关的商品进行买卖。现代的看法比较有弹性,可以是指在某一个有关的地方有足够数量的交易;另一个定义是指一些商品/货物有足够的需求可以吸收所有的供应;再另一个定义是指有关商品/货物的价格根据供求关系浮动,这表示不包括一些商品/货物以固定零售价格或"管制价格"(controlled price)出售:British Motor Trade Association v. Gilbert (1951) 2 All E. R. 641; Mouat v. Betts Motors (1959) A. C. 71 PC 等先例;再另一个定义是指有足够的贸易商互相接触与进行买卖。]

另一本权威书籍《McGregor On Damages》(18th edn,2009 年)在针对受害方的买方要买进"替代商品/货物"(substitute property/goods),是否当时有一个可供买卖的市场主要的考验是买方能否买到替代品。这是在 20-006 段所说:"The essential requirement is that the buyer should be able to go out and buy equivalent goods. If he can do this, then the court awards damages on the basis of the price at which he can buy, either by way of 'available market' and an application of section 51(3) or, despite a holding of no 'available market' within the meaning of the subsection, but still regarding the price at which the buyer can buy as the market price."

如果受害方是卖方,如买方不合理拒货,何谓可供买卖的市场有三个重要先例,分别为: Dunkirk Colliery Co v. Lever (1878) 9 Ch. D. 20 CA; Thompson v. Robinson (1955) Ch. 177 与 Charter v. Sullivan (1957) 2 Q. B. 117 CA。这三个先例在最近的 Shearson Lehman Hutton v. Maclaine Watson & Co Ltd. (No. 2) (1990) 1 Lloyd's Rep 441 先例中被 Webster 大法官分析后,说:"The answer seems to me to be: that if the seller actually offers the goods for sale there is no available market unless there is one actual buyer on that day at a fair price; that if there is no actual offer for sale, but only a notional or hypothetical sale for the purposes of s. 50(3), there is no available market unless on that day there are in the market sufficient traders potentially in touch with each other to evidence a market in which the actual or notional seller could if he wished to sell the goods."[在 Webster 大法官看来,如果卖方实际上出售有关货物,除非有一个真正的买方愿意出合理价格,否则不算是有可供买卖的市场。如果没有这样的一个买方,只有名义或假设的价格,这不算是有英国《货物销售法》之 Section 50(3)下的一个可供买卖的市场。除非,在当时有证据证明有足够的贸易商在互相接触与谈判,使得卖方有机会在他愿意时出售货物。]

1.2 有关货物买卖是否有可供买卖市场的先例介绍

虽然 Market Rule 也广泛适用在其他的商业活动中,但以下分段进一步介绍的有关先例,大部分是涉及了货物买卖。已经提到过,货物买卖是商业活动最频繁的类别。再加上 1979 年英国《货物销售法》对货物买卖的违约损失有立法规定是以 Market Rule 作为表面规则或计算的起点。所以在过去上百年,不断有先例对什么是"可供买卖的市场"做出解释与进一步澄清。在以下的先例,即使是有关货物买卖,同样的道理与原则也适用在任何其他有市场的商业活动。

1.2.1 有关案例之一:Bulkhaul Ltd v. Rhodia Organique Fine Ltd

总的说,法院或仲裁庭看来是宽松对待是否有一个可供买卖的市场,这大概是因为倾向于用 Breach Date Rule 与 Market Rule 作为计算损失的办法。会有案件表面看来有些商品不像是有可供买卖市场的一般商品,但也会被视为是有市场。在 Bulkhaul Ltd v. Rhodia Organique Fine Ltd(2009)1 Lloyd's Rep 353 上诉庭先例,涉及 18 个油柜,专门设计用于装载一种名为 hydrofluoric acid(HF)具强烈腐蚀性的化学品。有关的合约涉及 Bulkhaul 把这 18 个油柜出租 10 年给 Rhodia,预计在 10 年后这 18 个油柜也将报废。该 10 年租约过了一半时间,Rhodia 就因减少生产 HF 而拒绝继续租用,这也被 Bulkhaul 视为是违约/毁约并且接受终断租约。在损失计算,涉及 Rhodia 指称 Bulkhaul 没有合理减少损失,因为 Bulkhaul 可以在合约终断后的 3 年内把这 18 个油柜在市场出售,每一个油柜可以卖得 20,000 英镑。Rhodia 认为应该把这笔钱(20,000×18)从 Bulkhaul 在余下租期中的利润损失中扣除。这一个争议就涉及这 18 个油柜是否有可供买卖的市场,而不像一般的商品会有报道有关的市场价格,在这种特殊的货物则需要考虑不同案件的情况。Rhodia 能够提供证据证明当时 Bulkhaul 的老板要价过高,其中,在 2004 年 10 月中(违约/毁约发生是在当月月底),有另一家名为 Lanxess 的公司想购买这 18 个油柜,并出价 20,000 英镑。但 Bulkhaul 拒绝,要价是 26,000 英镑。结果 Lanxess 就向其他人购买同样的油柜。到了 2005 年 7 月,Rhodia 发觉泰国有一个买方并介绍给 Bulkhaul,但交易没有成功。再到了 2005 年 8 月,Rhodia 又介绍一家西班牙公司给 Bulkhaul,该公司有兴趣租用 6 个月。到了 2007 年 8 月,Rhodia 再介绍一个有兴趣购买的阿根廷买方,但当时已经要开庭审理。

对这些 Rhodia 介绍过来的生意,虽然都没有成事,但 Bulkhaul 的老板在开庭审理时被迫解释他没有接受这些生意以减少损失的原因。这些原因有部分被接受,如针对西班牙公司,如果把 18 个油柜运至西班牙出租 6 个月,在整体经济上根本是不划算。至于泰国买方,实际上连一个发盘都没有作出,根本就是很空泛。但针对 Lanxess 与阿根廷买方,就显示了这 18 个油柜是有价值与有市场的。看来 Bulkhaul 就不被法院所接受为有合理减少损失了。在第一审判决的有关部分,上诉庭是这样说:"The judge rejected Bulkhaul's submission that the tanks had no residual value and were in effect unsaleable. In giving his reasons for rejecting that submission, at para 117 of his judgment, he said: First, a third party, Lanxess offered £ 20,000 for each of the tanks in late 2004. Second the tanks were manufactured with a life expectancy of 10 years and thus in the autumn of 2004 would be expected to have a further 5 to 6 years of use before they were scrapped. Third, I accept the evidence of Mr Merfield as to the state and extent of the HF market. Fourth, it appears from the 2004 discussions that the cost of new tanks had increased since 1999 thus increasing the potential value of second hand tanks. Fifth, the approaches that have been made between 2004 and 2008 are to my mind an indication that the tanks are not valueness. Sixth, although Bulkhaul has reacted to introductions made by Rhodia they have not been pro – active in attempting to sell the tanks. Indeed, the 2005 (I think he may have meant 2004) correspondence indicated that Bulkhaul are reluctant to sell the tanks. It would appear that on at least one occasion, Addlestone Keane(Bulkhaul 的律师) advised Bulkhaul that they did not need to sell the tanks. As already noted, Bulkhaul is a large company with many connections in the industry. Indeed, the recent evidence in relation to the Argentine company demonstrates that Bulkhaul are not making stringent efforts to sell the tanks. They were informed on 19 September 2007 that the invitation to view the tanks had not been received, yet they seem to have made no effort to follow this up between September 2007 and February 2008."

总而言之,这 18 个油柜被视为有可供买卖的市场。

1.2.2 有关案例之二:ABD(Metals & Waste) Ltd v. Anglo Chemical

在 ABD(Metals & Waste) Ltd. v. Anglo Chemical & Ore Co Ltd. (1955) 2 Lloyd's Rep 456 先例,案情涉及一个"CIF Lisbon"的买卖,货物是一种高等级的"电镀锌"(electrolytic zinc),共 200 吨。在该先例,只有损失计算的争议,因为在责任方面卖方已接受不交付货物的违约责任。

受害方的买方说这批货物已经转售,所以不交付货物给他带来的"利润损失"(loss of profit)约 400 英镑,另加上赔偿给分买方的 2311 英镑。但卖方说应是根据 1893 年《货物销售法》的 Section 50(3),即损失计算以违约一天的市场价格与合约价格的差价为准,损失赔偿的金额是低得多了。

照说伦敦有一个"金属交易所"(Metal Exchange),也有锌的买卖,怎会是没有市场?但证据显示,交易所对这种高等级的电镀锌(纯度达 99.97%)并没有买卖进行。只有一般的锌,纯度在 98%,才有买卖。这种高等级的电镀锌也会有在交易所内外以私下方式进行买卖,而且间中会在"The Metal Bulletin"刊登有关交易的价格。

Sellers 大法官判是有市场可供比较,并说:"It is not necessary to establish a market that it should have a fixed place or building, but there must be sufficient traders who are in touch with each other to evidence a market, and I think that is so here."

当然作出比较还必须是各重要方面对等(与买卖合约价格看齐),在伦敦成交的市场买卖价格是"ex ship London",故此需要调整为"CIF Lisbon"。这是要调整高等级/纯度的"溢价"(premium),运去 Lisbon 的运费与保费。反正 Sellers 大法官最后计算出来的差价是 7 镑 16 先令一吨,而 200 吨的总损失应是 1560 英镑,也是买方胜诉所得的赔偿。

1.3 时间上的考虑

接下去是探讨"可供买卖"(available)一词需要给予"时间上"(temporal)与"地域上"(geographical)两层意思,也就是说受害方的卖方或买方可以在离发生违约的地方合理的距离内马上接触到有关的市场。

因为不少货物/商品的市场价格每天不同,会是大起大落,一两天内已是面目全非,如在 Alfred C. Toepfer v. Peter Cremer(1975)2 Lloyd's Rep 118 先例。所以,有必要找出哪一天的价格才可作为进一步估计应比较的市场货价。在 Petrotrade v. Stinnes(1995)1 Lloyd's Rep 142 先例,已可见这日子是违约/毁约后的两个星期内市场平均价格。因为涉及大批货物,最快也需要两个星期分批出售。在 SHV Gas Supply & Trading SAS v. Naftomar Shipping & Trading Co Ltd Inc(The Azur Gaz)(2006)1 Lloyd's Rep 163 先例,这段日子可以超过一个月。另在 Carbopego - Abastecimento de Combustiveis SA v. Amci Export Court(2006)1 Lloyd's Rep 736 先例,更是涉及买卖合约中最后交货一天后的几个月的市场价格。这些先例看来都有一定程度上与"违约一天损失规则"(Breach Date Rule)有偏差,但显然是有关法院或仲裁庭认为是这样才能符合复原的大原则。反正是有许多国际货物买卖的先例都为了针对以哪一天的市场价格为准与合约价格作出比较找出差价,以下会进一步探讨。但可一提的是在涉及租约的近期两个先例:The"Kildare"(2011)2 Lloyd's Rep 360 与 The"Wren"(2011)2 Lloyd's Rep 370,针对在 2008 年底金融海啸后的一段时间内都没有市场可把船舶租出同样期限的期租,而要过了好几个月甚至一年才重新有这个市场,但判是不能适用 Market Rule 来计算损失。这方面会在本章 6.5 段详及。

1.3.1 以买卖合约履行期限最后一天的市场价格为准

Breach Date Rule 与 Market Rule 是通常走在一起的两条规则。如果涉及卖方的违约,就是在应该交货的一天没有交货,或者延误交货,或者交的货是货不对版等,就以该天的市场价格为准。在买卖合约中,通常会有一段交货的时间,如 9 月,这一来市场价格就以 9 月 30 日为准,原因是他有权在付运期间最后一天做出付运。如果过了这一天不付运,才能算是卖方违约。如果约定是分批交货,损失的计算就按照每一批货应该交付但没有交付的日期确定几个不同的市场价格。这可以节录《McGregor On Damages》(18th edn,2009 年)20 - 016 段说:"**Where a specific period or a succession of times is fixed for delivery.** The last possible moment within a specific period fixed for delivery is the time to be taken, since the seller is entitled to tender a delivery up till that moment. Where delivery is to be by instalments so that there is a number of successive time fixed for delivery, each fixed time is taken as to each instalment."

1.3.2 预期违约的差异

在上述的例子还会存在有其他的争议,如在一个8月份作出的“预期违约”(anticipatory breach)被受害方的买方接受而终断合约,而在买卖合约允许交货期的9月,该商品/货物市场价格波动很大,在9月30日市场价格很高,但9月有一两天价格却很低。如果以很低的市场价格比较合约价格会令损失降的很低或是零。这一来,违约的卖方就会抗辩不应该以9月30日的市场价格为准,毕竟大道理是卖方有权在9月任何一天交货,而损失计算就应该以违约方最低的合约责任或最有利的履行为准。但预期违约并不影响计算损失是以违约一天的9月30日市场价格为准,唯一的要求就是受害方在接受了预期违约与终断合约后,有一个合理减少损失的“责任”。这方面的先例有不少,如:Roper v. Johnson(1873)LR 8 CP 167;Melachrino v. Nickoll(1920)1 KB 693;Garnac Grain Co v. Faure & Fairclough(1967)1 Lloyd's Rep 495;Kaines v. Ostereichische(1993)2 Lloyd's Rep. 1 等。在 Melachrino v. Nickoll 先例,接受了预期违约的受害方合理在市场买进,但市场后来的波动与发展说明他买进的价格比买卖合约规定了交货最后日期一天的市场价格更高,法院判是根据受害方已经合理减少损失,不管结果是好是坏,他还是可以按照他买进的价格作为标准计算他的损失。这方面的问题在本书第十五章之6.2段有更详尽的介绍,不重复。

1.3.3 违约方拖拖拉拉的情况

这里还有其他千变万化的情况,其中一种是在现实中经常会发生,就是违约方不会一下子拒绝履行合约,而是会拖拖拉拉,这就涉及另一个衡平法的说法就是“弃权与禁止反供”(waiver and estoppel)。以货物买卖合约为例,在市场一路上扬的时候,卖方往往就是要求买方允许他延误把货物付运或交货,而买方虽然不情愿但为了不想失去这票便宜货而同意或默许。但市场继续上扬一点也没有逆转导致卖方在稍后的日子干脆明言不会履行。这一来又涉及以哪一天的市场价格为准。以买卖合约本来应该交货的一天或是买方后来同意的一天或是卖方明确拒绝履行合约的一天都会得出不一样的损失金额。Ogle v. Vane(1868)LR 3 QB 272 先例涉及一批钢材的买卖,交货日期是7月,但在卖方的要求下,买方一路等到第二年的2月。到了2月,买方再也不肯无限期等候交货,终断合约后去市场买进了替代钢材,但那个时候市场价格比7月上涨。这就带来了争议到底以哪一天的市场价格为准,Kelly CB 大法官以2月的价格为准,说:“It would be contrary to common sense and justice, when there has been a series of proposals by the defendant(违约方的卖方)involving delay for his own benefit, and acquiescence on the part of the plaintiff(受害方的买方), that because there may be no binding contract, varying the terms of the former contract, the plaintiff is to be tied down to the strict letter of the rule as to the measure of damage for the non - delivery of goods, and not to be entitled to the damages consequent upon the delay.”

这一方面在更近期的 Johnson Matthey Bankers v. The State Trading Corp of India(1984)1 Lloyd's Rep. 427 先例,Staughton 大法官这样说:“in cases where a breach of a contract for sale has occurred, and the innocent party reasonably continues to try to have the contract completed, it would to me appear more logical and just rather than tie him to the date of the original breach, to assess damages as at the date when (otherwise than by his default) the contract is lost."

1.3.4 受害方要求延误履行的情况

再讲一种就是延误交货不像是上一段的例子(要求是来自违约方),而是来自受害方的买方。买方要求延误交货会是各种原因(如自己的方便与安排),如买卖合约的9月交货被买方要求押后至12月交货,而卖方也同意。要在这里一提的是这种双方同意延误交货通常是不足够构成合约的"更改"(variation),没有约束性,因为没有"对价"(consideration)。所以,卖方是可以撤回他的同意,如在10月向买方做出通知要求买方在合理时间内接受货物。但也可能发生的情况是卖方在10月不想履行合约,对买方说我不会在现在或任何时间(包括12月)交货。这一来又存在是以哪一天的市场价格为准的问题。显然是不应该按照买卖合约的9月,但也不应该是按照12月,因为这一个日期并没有任何法律效力,不代表是一个新的交货日期。考虑到Market Rule的市场价格是为了针对受害方应该马上进入市场采取行动减少损失的大精神,看来市场价格应该是在10月卖方向买方拒绝履行合约的一天为准。这方面可部分节录《McGregor On Damages》(18th edn, 2009年)之20-019段:"Where the request to postpone delivery comes from the buyer and the seller at first concurs, but subsequently refuses to deliver on the basis of the buyer's unpreparedness to accept at the date originally fixed by the contract, the matter is more complex. The general rule as to liability evolved by the courts is that the seller cannot suddenly retract his forbearance but must give reasonable notice to the buyer, thereby placing the buyer under an obligation to accept the goods within a reasonable time of the retraction. On the seller's peremptory refusal to deliver, it would seem that this will constitute the breach and the damages will be assessed with reference to the market price at that date."

1.3.5 买卖合约没有约定哪一天交货的情况

再介绍一种情况是在买卖合约没有约定交货日期情况下的违约应该是以哪一天的市场价格为准。这种情况在现实中应该不多,但还是有而且笔者也见到过。英国《货物销售法》之Section 51(3),针对没有约定交货日期的情况,交货日期为"货物应当交付的日期"(at the times when they ought to have been delivered)。这里法律并不完全明确是哪一天,正如《McGregor On Damages》(18th edn, 2009年)之20-020段所述:"It is not, however, settled whether the case is one in which no time is fixed within section 51(3) should the contract provide expressly or by implication for delivery at a time fixed by the happening of a certain event, such as the arrival of a ship as in Melachrino v. Nickoll (1920) 1 KB 693, or within a reasonable time of the making of the contract, or combining the two, within a reasonable time of the happening of an event, as in Millett v. Van Heek

(1921)2 KB 369 CA which provided for delivery within a reasonable time of the removal of a Government embargo."

这一问题在违约的卖方拒绝履行的情况下应该很容易解释,就是在该天被卖方视为是应该把货物交付的一天,但他拒绝履行。所以该天也应该被视为是买卖合约应当交货的一天,市场价格以该天为准。这在英国《货物销售法》之 Section 51(3)的最后一句也有说明为"or(if no time was fixed)at the time of the refusal to deliver"。

比较困难的是预期违约,因为这就需要认定在该合约下将来应该交货的一天,但合约偏偏就没有作出约定。这一个方面有在 Millett v. Van Heek 先例与 Tai Hing Cotton Mill v. Kamsing Knitting Factory(1979)AC 91 PC 先例有针对。这两个先例是判决 Section 51(3)的条文不适用在预期违约,这里可节录《McGregor On Damages》(18th edn,2009 年)之 20-021 段所说:"The correctness of Millet v. Van Heek(1921)1 K. B. 369 CA was unsuccessfully challenged in Tai Hing Cotton Mill v. Kamsing Knitting Factory (1979)A. C. 91 PC where the Judicial Committee of the Privy Council 'affirmed the principle that the second limb of section 51(3) does not apply in any case of anticipatory breach of contract'. While recognizing that 'there may be great difficulty in determining when the contract ought to have been performed, and that there could be much convenience in assessing damages as at the date of repudiation by the seller assuming the buyer accepts it', their Lordships were nevertheless persuaded that Millett v. Van Heek should be upheld as 'it would be surprising if the first limb of one and the same subsection were intended to be a specific application of the general principle in the proceeding subsection, and the second limb to be a radical departure from it.'"

1.3.6 需要长时间或分批转售/买进有关货物的情况

由于不是所有商品/货物都可以很快在市场上出售或是买进,特别是一些比较罕见的,所以就存在时间上的考虑。这也会带来额外的争议,如在有关的时间根本不存在有可供买卖的市场,或市场太窄而无法很快把商品/货物出售或是买进。但由于法律对所谓可供买卖的市场有一个十分宽松的解释,所以即使是需要较长时间才能出售(不论是一次性还是分批)或是买进也可以认为是有一个可供买卖的市场。在进一步介绍先例说明这一问题之前,可先节录《Benjamin's Sale of Goods》(8th edn,2010 年)一书中 16-067 段如下:"**The temporal test of availability**. The 'ready' or 'immediate' accessibility to substitute buyers or sellers should not be taken too literally. In Charter v. Sullivan(1957)2 QB 117 the Court of Appeal found that the demand for the goods exceeded the supply, but(apart from the question of a fixed retail price) Sellers LJ held that the fact that the resale of a car was made some seven to ten days after the breach prevented there being an available market: 'there was no immediate buyer'. It is submitted that the temporal test should be one of a reasonable time after the breach, given the nature of the goods in question and the business situation of the claimant; and that the option of Sellers

LJ is wrong on this point. With many types of goods there would need to be the possibility of immediate resale flexibility in the particular circumstances. In the case(Petrotrade Inc v. Stinnes Handel GmbH [1995] 1 Lloyd's Rep 142) of the sale of 10,000 tons of gasoline the judge held that there could be an available market where the seller could have disposed of the gasoline in smaller cargo loads of 1,000 to 3,000 tons over a period of about two weeks from the buyer's breach. With some types(or quantities) of goods, negotiations with potential buyers would take several days to achieve a sale: in these circumstances, the market price should be fixed on the assumption that the hypothetical seller had begun to negotiate sufficiently far ahead to enable a sale to be made on the day in question. It is most unlikely that there will be an available market where the goods in question have been(or were to be) specially manufactured to suit the particular requirements of the buyer: the chance of resale of such goods within a reasonable time after the breach is too limited and fortuitous."

另在《McGregor On Damages》(18th edn, 2009 年)一书的 20 - 115 段, 在提到 Shearson Lehman Hutton v. Maclaine Watson & Co Ltd. (No. 2)(1990) 1 Lloyd's Rep 441 先例中的有关商品是 7.5 吨的锡, 在违约的一天是没有市场, 但几天后就有市场, 这不影响该货物被判决有一个可供买卖的市场。"Webster J. went on to hold that, since it could be reasonable or sensible for the seller to have waited before going into the market and selling the goods, in this case some seven - and - a - half tons of standard grade tin, the market price could take into account the price which might have been negotiated within a few days of the breach with other potential buyers who earlier were not part of the market because of the difficulties of communication. There is thus a temporal aspect to 'available market'; the market does not necessarily have to be available on the date of breach itself."

但如果与违约的相隔时间是长达几个月才出现可供买卖的市场, 这就有不同的判法, 会被视为是在违约时根本没有市场。这种情况在 2008 年底的金融海啸后曾经出现, 导致了租船市场根本没有中长期租约, 无法与被承租人违反的期租合约做出比较。这些先例有 The "Kildare" (2011) 2 Lloyd's Rep 360 与 The "Wren" (2011) 2 Lloyd's Rep 370 等。这会在本章稍后的 6.5 段介绍。

上述所讲可举以下的例子来说明。

1.3.6.1 案例之一: Petrotrade v. Stinnes

Petrotrade v. Stinnes(1995) 1 Lloyd's Rep 142 先例是一个"FOB 安特卫普"(卖方在安特卫普交货上船)的有关"加铅汽油"(leaded gasoline)的买卖合约。该批 1 万吨的汽油是准备运去德国转卖给 Exxon。在买卖合约签订前几天, 德国为了减少污染通过法律规定在德国出售的汽油必须没有"氯化物"(chloride)与"溴"(bromine)的杂质, 而这种杂质是在加铅的过程中会带进去。如果汽油处理过把这两种杂质排出的话, 该汽油就被称为"scavenger free"。当时, 欧洲也只有德国首先通过法律这样规定。而该买卖合约规定了这 1 万吨汽油必须是 scavenger free。但在买方派出的船舶

Rava 轮抵达安特卫普要装货前，检察员确定该批汽油并不是 scavenger free。这一来，买方 Stinnes 在 1992 年 7 月 20 日早上发出传真给卖方 Petrotrade 要求在中午之前提供另一批 scavenger free 的汽油。

事实上，Petrotrade 成功向 Total 买到 1 万吨 scavenger free 的汽油可交付给 Stinnes，但装货的地点是在荷兰的 Flushing。照理说，Flushing 是比安特卫普离船舶停留的锚地更近。Petrotrade 也可以安排在安特卫普交货，但付运时间需要延长（如其中一个方法就是把 Flushing 的 1 万吨汽油从 Flushing 转运过来）。但 Stinnes 要求减价才肯接受（估计当时汽油市场下跌，所以 Stinnes 借这个要求改港或延长付运期的机会减价），结果大家谈不拢而 Stinnes 也在 7 月 20 日当天接受违约/毁约而终断买卖合约。

这先例涉及许多的争议，其中包括了非常重要与先例不多的争议，就是有关 FOB 买卖合约的交货地点或港口是否是合约的条件条文。在本先例的案情是买卖合约同意的就是"FOB 安特卫普"，但可否单方面变成是"FOB Flushing"。看来是没有什么分别，因为两地十分接近。但考虑到如果 FOB 买方以程租合约的形式而不是期租合约的形式租船，装港只是约定了安特卫普。这一来，FOB 买方作为承租人要求船东改港去邻近的 Flushing 会被拒绝或敲竹杠，因为船东按照租约根本无需同意。所以，Colman 大法官判这交货地点与交货日期一样，都属于货物的"描述"（description）的一部分，属于"条件条文"（condition）。也就是说如果 Petrotrade 违约，Stinnes 有理与有权终断买卖合约。

但本书在此提到该先例更为关注的是如果 Stinnes 无权终断买卖合约，Petrotrade 的损失如何计算，这损失就是来自他向 Total 买进 1 万吨 scavenger free 的汽油，但不被 Stinnes 接受。由于这种汽油只有德国市场需要，而其他欧洲国家是不会多付钱买这种汽油的，这导致市场很窄。加上 Stinnes 是德国市场主要的一个买方，所以 Petrotrade 面对找不到买方的苦恼，而把 1 万吨的这种汽油在德国市场很快的出售会令市场价格崩溃。所以，Petrotrade 索赔的损失是在之后的 3 个月，把该 1 万吨汽油分成 10 批货物以不同价格出售所带来的损失，另加上仓储费与运费。

但带来争议的是损失计算应该是上述在 3 个月内分 10 批转卖带来的损失，还是 Stinnes 应该接受该批货物一天的市场价格与买卖合约价格之间的差价。显然，这两个计算办法带来的损失并不相同。Petrotrade 认为他所提出的索赔是他真正的损失，而他也尽力处理该批被拒绝接受的 1 万吨 scavenger free 的汽油，而事实上当时不能称为有一个可供买卖的市场可一次性转售。

在听了双方专家证人关于这个市场的证言后，Colman 大法官认为当时是存在这样的一个可供买卖的市场，而在做法上是在两个星期内把这票汽油分批成 1000 或 3000 吨陆续出售，这应该对市场价格带来的影响不会超过 5%。至于 Petrotrade 足足花了 3 个月才分批出售，而不是在 2 个星期内，Colman 大法官认为 Petrotrade 是自己把该批汽油扣在手中，估计以后市场会上涨，但结果价格下降得更厉害，看来这部分的额外损失就是与 Stinnes 的违约/毁约中断了因果关系，说："Petrotrade's failure to dispose of it as rapidly as that, was, I infer, more likely the consequence of their holding out for prices which were not obtainable because of the general level of demand in the market or for a general rise in market prices which did not occur. No doubt they had perfectly good reasons for wanting to maximize the overall resale recovery and genuinely believed that, having regard to the state and movements of the market, they were marketing the gasoline so as to achieve the most advantageous prices, even having regard to the cost of being out of their money and of the storage of the unsold material."

Colman大法官根据专家意见证据认为只需要短短两个星期就可以成功出售,并不影响是有可供买卖的市场,而损失也必须以这个市场计算,即把这两个星期内估计分批出售会在当天市场得到的价格,然后取它们的平均数作为计算卖方损失的基准。他是这样说:"There can be no doubt that the starting point is to ask whether there was an available market. On the facts which I have found, the limited demand for this product which meant that it would take two weeks to sell all of it does not mean, in my judgement, that the market was not 'available' within s. 50(3)(这是指1979年英国《货物销售法》). It was indeed 'available' because the price of the product was regulated by supply and demand at the material time and because a seller acting with reasonable determination could have disposed of at least some of the gasoline at that time and of the balance within a mere two weeks. It is perfectly true that one could not arrive at the final loss figure until the whole parcel had been sold, perhaps at differing prices, over that period and so one could not appropriately identify as the market price for this quantity of produce the price ruling on July 20 - the day when, on Petrotrade's case, the gasoline ought to have been accepted - but the words '*prima facie*', in my judgement, introduce sufficient flexibility into the test under s. 50(3) to justify calculation of the loss in a case such as this by taking a weighted average of the prices that would have been obtained during the minimum period that it would have taken a reasonable oil dealer acting with reasonable expedition to sell the entire parcel as the relevant market or current price which would provide the yardstick under s. 50(3). To the extent that such price is below the contract price, that is the measure of damages. . . . Once it is accepted that the entire parcel could have been sold in approximately two weeks, there can be no basis for adopting as the basis for the calculation of damages the resale prices actually achieved over the ensuing three months. The seller's genuine belief that by holding the parcel for a much longer period he would be able to recover a larger return on resale does not justify departing from the market price obtainable at and immediately after the buyer's non-acceptance."

1.3.6.2 案例之二:The"Baltic Surveyor"

The"Baltic Surveyor"(2001) 1 Lloyd's Rep 739是一个有关侵权的先例,涉及一艘大型游艇的市场价格。事故本身是非常罕见的,就是普利茅斯(Plymouth)的港内有一个“浮桥”(pontoon),它是靠铁链连接海底的两大块水泥块将其固定。而浮桥边就停靠了该游艇,浮桥与该游艇属于同一拥有者。她在出事当时也允许另外一艘游艇名为 Timbuktu 停靠于该浮桥,但后来遇上非常坏的天气,导致 Timbuktu 左边与浮桥的边碰撞而穿了个洞导致沉没。在沉没的过程中,她的一条主桅杆又把 Baltic Surveyor 的船旁穿了一个洞导致入水而沉没。由于 Baltic Surveyor 比较大,下沉的时候也同时把浮桥拖了下去,导致全部全损。Timbuktu 的船东承认疏忽责任,问题只是损失怎样计算。

对 Baltic Surveyor 这艘游艇而言,Colman 大法官认为应该是以出事时的市场价格作为基准,说:“There can be no doubt that this is based on the presumption that the owner will try to mitigate his loss by replacing the vessel as soon as practicable after the loss. For this purpose, it is assumed that he will explore the market for a vessel comparable in size, speed and other characteristics to those of the lost vessel. The market value of such a vessel at the time and place of the loss will be the starting point in this exercise, but, beyond that, it may be necessary to take account of pecuniary loss arising from the fact that the vessel may not be immediately replaceable and that money may have to be spent to create a replacement sufficiently similar to that lost. In such a case the owner is entitled also to be compensated for trading losses during the period from the loss of the vessel up to the time when it would be expected that she would be replaced.”

原告打算索赔 25 万英镑,认为这就是市场价格。但决定 Baltic Surveyor 的市场价格十分不容易,因为她是一艘罕见的游艇。她本身长 29.5 米,是在“二战”期间于德国汉堡建造的一艘鱼雷快艇,所以速度很快,达到 18 节。另是她的船壳是木制的,这会导致维修保养费用很高。该鱼雷快艇是在 1976 年买进,而且经过大幅度改装后变为现在的游艇。改建期间因为经济的理由一再延误,结果工程在 1987 年才完成。

这游艇也尝试过要出售但卖不出去,在 1991 年 4 月,Baltic Surveyor 在市场放手出售的要价是 32.5 万英镑,而专家证人认为该游艇价值高达 35 万英镑。但该游艇乏人问津,因为当时经济还是非常低迷。到了 1991 年 7 月该游艇的船东减价至 25 万英镑,但仍然乏人问津。到了 1992 年 6 月中旬该游艇减价到 19.5 万英镑。到了 1993 年 4 月,要价更是降到 15 万英镑,虽然当时市场与经济状况正在恢复,但仍然是没有买方。

在这期间有少数的游艇买卖交易,但很难作出比较。其中比较接近的是一艘有历史价值属 Malcolm Campbell 爵士所拥有的名为 Bluebird 的游艇。她是 103 尺,比 Baltic Surveyor 稍长,在 1938 年建造,船身是由钢板建造,并且也是经过改装。该游艇的速度是 12.5 节,船上有 5 间套房。在 1991 年,Bluebird 在市场求售,要价是 25 万英镑。但最终要到 1996 年才成功出售,售价只是 12.78 万英镑。

被告的专家证人对 Bluebird 的交易认为是最接近,因为她与 Baltic Surveyor 吸引同一类的买方。对于 Bluebird 只能以叫价的一半才能成功出售,他不感到奇怪,因为这些有历史的经典船舶只有一个很小的市场，而在1985年开始价钱根本没有什么变化，其中一个原因是更大与马力更强的游艇可以在市场上以10万英镑买到。而原告的专家证人当然是强调 Baltic Surveyor 是很好的游艇，如 Bluebird 是一艘没有什么特色的游艇，而且太慢，加上原告准备在1996年为 Baltic Surveyor 装修令她更加容易在市场上出售，毕竟当时经济环境在不断变好。

最后 Colman 大法官不接受原告的25万英镑的损失索赔，认为该价格很离谱，而只判12万英镑，说："I am bound to say that I find it difficult to accept Mr. Berwick's(原告的专家证人) evidence on basic value. If this vessel attracted no buyers at £ 150,000 from April, 1993 for over three years, even though she was not specially marketed and even though she was at Plymouth and not at a more attractive marketing venue, I find it quite inconceivable that she could have fetched £ 250,000 anywhere. No doubt her refurbishment in 1996 would have rendered her significantly more marketable. No doubt if she had been moved to Lymington more possible purchasers might have noticed her, and given the improved economic climate, might have shown interest in her. However, the notion that anyone would have been prepared to pay £ 250,000 or anything like that amount is, I find, quite unsustainable."

这估计12万英镑的市场价格是根据 Baltic Surveyor 在状况良好的情况下作出的，所以还要扣减游艇如果在出售前所必须花费的装修与维修，其中也包括专家证人检查沉了进海底游艇的状况，被告专家认为要针对船壳的龙骨翼板所作出3.5万英镑的估计修理费用。但原告专家本来是接受估计修理费用为3万英镑，但后来改变主意认为只要4千英镑。这当然不为 Colman 大法官所相信，而最后认定的总数是3.8万英镑要从发生事故时的市场价格的12万英镑中扣除，最后应该赔偿的市场价格就只有8.2万英镑，与原告索赔的25万英镑大相径庭。

从上述先例可以见到是怎样确定这些"市场价格"(market price)或侵权时的"价值"(value)，包括通过文件披露与专家证人的意见。有一些商品市场价格是十分容易确定，特别是有交易所去发表各种指数，如股票、石油、农产品、食糖等。但只要有买卖，存在有意向的买方与有意向的卖方，就会有市场价格。如在中国市场，奥迪轿车固然是有十分明确的市场价格，但比较少有交易的劳斯莱斯或古董轿车，一样可确定市场价格，如 Baltic Surveyor 这一艘游艇。还有有关的商品/货物相比市场的同类商品/货物，是不需要完全一致，只要是达到接近即可。同样道理也适用在房屋买卖，正如 Colman 大法官所说的如下："A similar exercise is familiar to those concerned with the valuation of residential or commercial real property. However, it is an exercise which, although capable of producing relatively clear evidence of value in the case of a house or other property having characteristics which are commonly found in a particular locality, may give rise to acute problems of comparison where the house or property is highly unusual or has some special features not ordinarily found in the neighbourhood. In such a case it may be extremely difficult to find comparables having sufficiently similar characteristics to enable any evidence indicative of the market value of the property in question to be derived from them; see, for example, Living Waters Christian Centres Ltd v. Henry George Fetherstonhaugh, (1999) CA. Transcript QBCMF 98/0304/3 where the problems of evidence derived from comparables having dissimilar characteristics are more fully discussed."

1.3.6.3 案例之三:Garnac Grain Co. Inc. v. H. M. F. Faure and Fairclough Ltd

第三个是贵族院的 Garnac Grain Co. Inc. v. H. M. F. Faure and Fairclough Ltd (1967) 1 Lloyd's Rep 495 先例,案情涉及"CIF Bromborough/Purfleet"买卖(这是英国港口),货物是15,000吨的美国猪油,而价格是每吨195美元。付运日期是1963年12月或1964年1月。但卖方违约,他并没有作出付运。在第一审,Megaw 大法官认为在1964年2月4日会有买方可以买进替代货物的市场并估计市场价格应该是每吨242.50美元。但在后来上诉到贵族院,才提出该批货物数量庞大,必须要分批买进才不会把市场抬高。但由于这一点没有包括在上诉通知,所以不予处理。Pearson 勋爵是这样说:"... it was contended that no assessment could properly be made on the basis of the difference between the contract price and the market price on Feb 4, 1964 (or any other date that might be material) because there was then no market in the United Kingdom for 15,000 tons of lard for immediate delivery, and the evidence did not reveal any other basis for assessing damages. There was evidence that all material times (towards the end of January and early February 1964) you could not buy that quantity for immediate delivery in the United Kingdom. There was, however, evidence that you could buy smaller quantities - up to 2,000 tons at a time - in the USA for delivery to ports for shipments to the United Kingdom; and there was a market price, given by one witness as $243.60 per ton, for such purchases on Feb 4. If you wished to buy 15,000 tons at those prices you could have to do so over a period. According to one witness, if you were able to buy 15,000 tons of lard at a time you could have to pay a higher price. There was thus some evidence on which Mr. Justice Megaw could find that there was a market price and that it was $242.50 per ton on Feb 4. No arrangement to the effect that there was no market price proved was presented at the trial of the action. No such point was included in the respondents' notice given by Garnac to the Court of Appeal. It may have been raised in the Court of Appeal but it is not mentioned in the judgment. In these circumstances I do not think the finding of fact of Mr. Justice Megaw on this point can be successfully challenged."

1.4 地域上的考虑

Breach Date Rule 与 Market Rule 是假设受害方会在违约后马上到市场上寻找同类替代货物,而这也是在合理减少损失的原则下,受害方的一项义务。这带来的一个问题是替代货物的市场价格应以何地的市场价格为准。相对有一些标的,有关的市场或价格相对简单。如涉及香港股票的市场价格,这个地域就很容易确定。但如果涉及跨国的交易,地域这一问题就不这么简单了,因为可能会有几个地域的市场都扯的上关系。例如,在CIF买卖下,照理说对受害方的买方而言,替代货物的市场价格应当以同类货物在卸港的市场价格为准。FOB贸易下,替代货物的市场价格则以同类货物在装港的市场价格为准。但如果有关合约特定的交货地点(装港或卸港)没有可供买卖的市场,只是在临近港口或地点才会有。比方说某一种货物的卸港或交货地点是舟山,但这一种货物的市场能买进替代货物的地点是在宁波,这显然是不影响找出在宁波的市场价格作为比较。而如果这种市场价格也存在在其他较远的地方,甚至是更加活跃,如日本东京,显然就改变不了是以宁波的市场价格为准。这是因为宁波对买方而言是最近与最合理的市场。这里的一个先例是Lesters Leather and Skin Co v. Home and Overseas Brokers(1948)64 T. LR. 569 CA,案情涉及买方向被告的卖方购买一批蛇皮,在英国港口交货。但货物运到的时候,因为质量问题被买方拒货,上诉庭判买方胜诉并可取回他的利润损失,并否定了被告所作出的抗辩说原告应该在印度市场购买蛇皮以减少损失。Goddard大法官说:"I cannot say that the buyers are bound to go hunting the globe to find out where they can get skins."(我不能要求买方必须全世界寻找蛇皮)。这表示太远与不现实的市场价格是不能作为依据的,反正就是根据合理与否作出决定。

在The"Texaco Melbourne"(1994)1 Lloyd's Rep 473先例,主要针对是在本书第十四章之8.7段,因为受害的买方(加纳政府)如果按照事故后贬值的加纳的"塞地"(cedis)向船东索赔,折合美金只赔得到21,165美元。但如果按照一直稳定的美元做出赔付,船东就要支付买方的损失高达2,886,178美元。该批有关的燃油是从加纳一个港口(Tema)的炼油厂运到加纳另一个卸港(Takoradi)后分批转售给其他的油公司,但这批燃油并没有最终运到该卸港,这导致买方向船东提出索赔。而整个交易与其他环节(如把该批原油在卸港转售或买方自己持有的存款)所涉及的币种都只有塞地,与美元没有关系,所以买方就扯上了远在意大利的市场,因为最近与最合理的同类货物(燃油)市场是意大利,而去该市场买进替代货物就必须是以美元支付。在第一审,其中一个争议是如果多过一个可供买卖的市场如何做出选择。Webster大法官说是如果在最近的意大利或加纳卸港都有市场,就显然是以卸港的市场为准,说:"If there was an available market both in Takoradi and in Italy then for the reasons I have just given I would conclude that the relevant market would be that at the place of delivery, namely Takoradi; but if there was no available market in Takoriadi, it would follow that the only available market was that in Italy, since the evidence that, if there was no market at Takoradi, the nearest market was in Italy was not challenged. Even if fuel oil of the particular specification of this cargo('the goods in question') could not have been bought in Italy, it was common ground that oil of a similar specification could have been bought and processed so as to produce fuel oil of an identical specification."但Webster大法官最终是认定卸港没有一个可供买卖的市场,因为这一个市场必须是一个"自由市场"(free market),该加纳的卸港虽然可让买方转售这票燃油,但这并不足够。所以,意大利才是最近与最合理的市场。但在当时的现实中,买方(加纳政府)要动用外汇去意大利进口燃油在程序上并不现实,所以即使是可供买卖市场在意大利也帮不了买方的原告可以美元向船东索赔损失,因为这 Market Rule 只是假设,所以美元一直不是买方损失所感受到的币种,这方面在本书第十四章有详论。

地域方面考虑可供买卖市场也从上述举的少数先例可以感受到不同市场的价格有很大的差异,如在上述 The"Baltic Surveyor"(2001)1 Lloyd's Rep 739 先例中的 Baltic Surveyor 游艇在普利茅斯卖不到好的价钱,但在地中海的其他地区如 Lymington 因为有较多的有钱买方聚居就可以卖到好的价钱。又如在中国内地的轿车的市场价格就肯定比美国贵得多。但考虑到可供买卖的市场价格的说法主要是针对要求受害方要去市场中出售或者是购入以减少损失,针对的市场应该指的是违约/毁约或者是侵权的所在地,顶多是临近但必须合理(包括买卖时间、费用与麻烦)的市场,而不是要求受害方可能是十分遥远的市场。毕竟,Market Rule 主要的考虑是受害方合理减少损失,而这一个"责任"或义务在合理与否是最重要的考虑。

最后可以节录《Benjamin's Sale of Goods》(8th edn,2010 年)一书之 16-068 段:"**The extent of the market area.** Since an innocent party's damages, following a breach of contract, are assessed on the basis that he should have taken reasonable steps to mitigate his loss, the question arises whether the concept of 'market' extends to places other than the place of delivery. James LJ in discussing the meaning of 'available market' in a case (Dunkirk Colliery Co v. Lever [1878] 9 Ch. D 20) where the buyer refused to accept coal he had bought, said that the sellers: '... might have sent it in wagons somewhere else, where they could sell it, just as they sell corn on the Exchange, or cotton at Liverpool: that is to say, that there was a fair market where they could have found a purchaser either by themselves or through some agent at some particular place'. Thus, it has been assumed that where the sellers' business area was the East Riding of Yorkshire, that was the area in which he should seek a substitute buyer. It is submitted that the test is one of reasonableness, in the light of the time, expense and trouble involved."(什么是可供买卖市场主要的考虑是合理,这包括了所需要做出替代买卖的时间、费用与麻烦)

1.5 市场必须是合约描述的货物

针对货物买卖,由于不少货物(如石油产品)对货物的描述或特殊要求的重视,所以可供买卖市场必须是合约描述之货物,不能是差不多作为替代的货物。

这里首先可节录 Coastal International v. Maroil(1988)1 Lloyd's Rep 92 先例,是一个 CFR 买卖,涉及的燃油是"July/August Rumanian bunker C 3.5% straight-run atmospheric"。照说,燃油的市场会是很大,没有理由买不进替代货物。但法律要求针对的是买卖合约约定的货物。在该先例中,卖方没有提供货物,而针对违约当天是否有市场,Leggatt 大法官是这样说:

"The contract description of the fuel oil in the instant case was 'July/August Rumanian bunker C 3.5% straight - run atmospheric'. As the defendants' own unavailing attempts amply testify, there was an embargo on the export of Rumanian bunker C fuel oil from Rumania from mid - July to the end of September, 1982. A certificate from Petrolexport of Oct 12, 1982, declares this to have been due to a shortage of deliveries of crude to Rumania.

For the plaintiffs, Mr. Van Gemerden(受害方的买方证人)also searched in vain for a replacement cargo, as did their broker, Mr. Been(经纪人)of Stardust International Ltd. Unsurprisingly, the defendants(违约方的卖方)did not adduce any evidence that any cargoes were available of fuel oils answering to the contract description. I am quite satisfied, and I find, that in these circumstances there was no market, available or otherwise, in late August or September, 1982 for goods of the contract description."

另可介绍 Mance 大法官在 Coastal(Bermuda)v VTT(1994)2 Lloyd's Rep. 629 先例的 633 页说:"The delivery date under the present contract was in my judgment port of the contract description of the goods agreed to be sold: Benjamin's Sale of Goods(4th ed.) pars. 18 - 116/118. On this basis the notion of a 'market' for replacement goods is here a restricted one, and could only be met if the plaintiffs(受害方的买方)were able to buy in replacement goods for delivery at Aruba in the bracket of Aug. 4 to 10, 1991: Benjamin par. 19 - 153; re Bourgeois and Wilson Holgatel(1920)25 Com. Cas. 260 at P. 281."

显然,该先例涉及的货物"Russian E4 straight run fuel oil ex Black sea for delivery CIF basis Aruba 4 - 10 August 1991"被判是没有同样货物的市场。

这种先例还有 Obaseki Bros v. Reif & Son Ltd(1952)2 Lloyd's Rep 364 与 The "Golden Rio"(1990)2 Lloyd's Rep 273。

可见货物描述越细,交货日期越短暂,加上如卖方很接近付运或交货期才违约/毁约,就会让受害方的买方越不容易有市场可以买进替代货物。

另是针对 CIF/CFR 买卖,也会是局限。如涉及"浮动货物"(floating cargo),针对是装在某一艘船舶已经在付运中的货物,就不可能有市场买进替代货物。这方面可节录《Benjamin's Sale of Goods》(8th edn,2010 年)之 19 - 185 段说:"The first is whether there is a 'market' for goods sold by reference to a particular set of shipping documents. Where the sale is of goods afloat and en route to a particular port or range of ports, this requirement will be satisfied only if there is a market in which such goods can be bought and 'it is not sufficient to show that there was a market for goods which belong to the same genus, but which were not of the contract description'. As the description may include the date of shipment and other statement about the ship the notion of the market in relation to c. i. f. contracts can be a restricted one. Thus Scrutton L. J. has said that, where the goods were sold by reference to a bill of lading bearing a particular date, there was no market for goods of the contract description and that therefore the ‘market’ rule did not apply. It seems that there can similarly be no ‘market’ for goods sold afloat on a named ship, though such a transaction has been said now to be a ‘rare phenomenon’. If there is no market, damages may be assessed by reference to an actual sub - sale, so long as this contract no unusual features which make the loss, or part of it, too remote.”

估计这方面的法律相对严格是因为英国法律一直以来对以货物描述进行买卖这方面的重视，一旦货不对版，买方就可以根据所谓的“perfect tender rule”拒绝接收货物，如 Re North Western, Rubber Co. Ltd and Huttenbach & Co(1908)2 K. B. 907; Toepfer v. Continental Grain Co(1974)1 Lloyd's Rep. 11; Toepfer v. Warinco A. G. (1978)2 Lloyd's Rep. 569 等先例。加上 1979 年的英国《货物销售法》下“市场”一词是局限的概念，因为 Section 50(3)与 Section 51(3)都说明是“可供买卖市场是针对有关货物”(an available market for the goods in question)。

在其他的合约涉及 Market Rule 计算损失，会有一定的伸缩性。如租船市场，如果一个期租合约在船东违约下终断，承租人就可以根据 Market Rule 向船东提出索赔，也就是在租船市场中同类型船舶的租金比较原租约的租金以找出损失：The“Elena d'Amico”(1980)1 Lloyd's Rep 75; The“Wave”(1981)1 Lloyd's Rep 521; The “Product Star”(No. 2)(1991)2 Lloyd's Rep 468 等先例。但如果租船市场的同类型船舶是必须要与原租约的船舶描述一模一样的姐妹船，就变为几乎没有可能适用 Market Rule。例如，原租约是 65,432 载重吨位或 1999 年 6 月建造，就不可能在当时的租船市场中会有一艘这样的替代船舶可供租用。会是只要是一艘能够起到同样作用的同类型的船舶，如“巴拿马型”(panamax)船舶的市场就可以用来作为比较，即使同类型船舶会是更大或更小，更新或更旧。换言之，这只需要是“最接近”(the nearest equivalent)的替代货物。毕竟是即使考虑合理减少损失的“责任”或义务，受害方也应该这样做。

1.6 以合约条文肯定哪一天的市场价格计算损失

以哪一天的市场价格计算损失会根据不同案件的案情而有相当大的弹性，情况会是：(1)来自受害方在预期违约的情况下不接受而导致合约并没有终断，而受害方没有“责任”在市场购入或出售减少损失，受害方只有履行他份内的合约责任；(2)法院或者仲裁庭在适用 Breach Date Rule 与 Market Rule 的同时，不认为是以违约/毁约那天的市场价格为准，而是稍后的时间。

所以，有些合约为了肯定市场价格计算损失，会硬性约定以哪一天的市场价格为准。这除了可以方便计算之外，也可以避免昂贵的诉讼。这种明示条文最出名的就是在买卖粮油经常使用的 GAFTA 或者是 FOSFA 的标准合约中，其中 FOSFA 的第 27 条就是这种条文，如下：

“27. **DEFAULT**: In default of fulfillment of this contract by either party, the other party at his discretion shall, after giving notice, have the right either to cancel the contract, or in the right to sell or purchase, as the case may be, against the defaulter who shall on demand make good the loss, if any, on such sale or purchase. If the party liable to pay shall be dissatisfied with the price of such sale or purchase, or if neither of the settlement, be determined by arbitration. The damages awarded against the defaulter **shall be limited to the difference between the contract price and the actual or estimated market price on the day of default**. Damages to be computed on the mean contract quantity. If the arbitrators consider the circumstances of the default justify it they may, at their absolute discretion, award damages on a different quantity and/or award additional damages.

Prior to the last day for making a declaration of shipment a Seller may notify his Buyer of his inability to ship but the date of such notice shall not become the default date without the agreement of the Buyer. If, for any other reason, either party fails to fulfill the contract and is declared to be in default by the other party and default is either agreed between the parties or subsequently found by arbitrators to haveoccurred, then the day of the default shall, failing amicable settlement, be decided by arbitration."

在一个香港仲裁案件,涉及的是在2004年中国发生的巴西大豆/红豆的大量案件中的其中一宗,该38,000吨巴西大豆合约是一个C&F买卖合约,合约日期是2004年4月1日。根据合约中国买方应该在4月22日开出信用证,但是在4月16日,中国发现第一宗巴西毒豆的事件,这些毒豆是被发现停泊在厦门的一艘Bunga Saga Tujuh轮上,这一个负面的消息会是导致中国买方在4月22日没有开出信用证的主要原因。中国买方是想拖时间看看有关巴西毒豆事件的发展,所以他向卖方要求延期到4月30日才开出信用证,卖方也答应了。到了2004年5月10日开始,中国政府就开始禁止为数达23个大豆进口商(包括本仲裁案件的卖方)进口巴西大豆,这演变成为一宗国际事件与巴西大豆市场价格崩溃。在中国政府出禁令之前,该中国买方显然已经收到消息,所以并没有在延长的4月30日或之后的任何时间中开出信用证。但显然卖方希望买方开出信用证(即使很明显是妄想),因为除了大豆市场崩溃之外,卖方已经把货物装了上船与前往中国卸港的那票货物没方法转售。这种拖拖拉拉的情况一直维持到9月15日,卖方因为找到另一个中国买方才接受原买方的违约/毁约(就是拒绝开出信用证)而告终。这里涉及损失的计算问题,因为巴西大豆的市场价格在2004年3、4月的时候是非常高与平稳。例如,在4月15日,C&F North China Port价格是每吨393美元,而到了5月3日,就微升变成396美元,而价格暴跌是发生在6月3日之后的,一直到了9月15日更加是非常低微。

在以上的事实下,卖方的损失计算最佳的显然是以他在9月15日转售给另一中国买方的低微价格(每吨285美元),或者当时的市场价格。但中国买方就依赖上述的FOSFA条文,应该以4月22日或者是4月30日没有开出信用证当天的市场价格为准,因为如果他违约/毁约,就是在那天发生。这一来中国买方需要赔偿的损失就少得多。

关于这条文中所谓的"date of default"(违约/毁约的一天)是有先例针对过:Topark v. Finagrain(1979)2 Lloyd's Rep 98 与 Fleming v. Sanofi(2003)2 Lloyd's Rep. 473。其中 Topark v. Finagrain 正是买方没有开出信用证的先例,Goff 大法官判的就是以买方没有开出信用证那天计算,而不是受害方可以通过坚持要买方履行合约而可以拖延,说:"If the contractual date for performance comes and goes, the innocent party may not immediately treat the other party as in default. He has an election whether to do so or not; he may, for a variety of reasons, decide to wait for a time, and while he waits the contract remains open to performance. But the mere fact that he waits and does not treat the other party as in default until a later date, does not mean that, for the purpose of the clause, the 'date of default' is changed; that date remains the day when the time for performance came and went without due performance."

所以,包括笔者在内的香港仲裁庭判这个巴西大豆的案件中违约/毁约的一天是在 4 月 30 日(这是因为买方自己要求延长,而延长之后又没有履行的一天),但在那一天的市场价格根本不能显示任何的损失,所以卖方在这一项的索赔中(本来是大约 450 万美元)败诉,裁决书说:"While the Tribunal notes that the international pricing for Brazilian soybeans began to drop shortly after 30 April 2004, the evidence which the Claimant itself has relied upon in showing the market conditions over the disputed period indicates that the actual or estimated market price on the date of default, 30 April 2004, was most likely equal to or even slightly higher than that of the Contract. Accordingly, under the calculation method that is contemplated by the FOSFA Default Clause, the Tribunal finds, that there is no damage amount owing to the Claimant..."

这里特别要强调的是,由于合约是这样规定的,就不存在普通法上只是把这个 Breach Date Rule 与 Market Rule 当成是表面规则,可以有裁量权在造成很大的不公正与做不到复原的情况下不适用。因为如果以公正与不公正的角度来说,笔者就记得在那个案件中,卖方是想尽方法都不能转售船舶上的那票巴西大豆的,蒙受很大损失(包括间接损失)。所以把卖方的损失局限在以违约/毁约一天的市场价格为准来计算损失肯定是不足够的,但这是合约条文的规定。

另一个是在同期发生的关于巴西大豆争议的同类案件,也是关于以哪一天的市场价格来计算损失起着关键性的作用。案情当然不是完全一样,它涉及的是四个买卖合约,付运的时间是 2004 年 6 月 15 日到 8 月底。但正如上述的同类案件也已经提到的在 2004 年 5 月 10 日中国政府对巴西大豆进行禁运,市场已经开始有波动,而在 6 月 3 日市场已经开始暴跌,虽然在这个案件中的巴西大豆还没有开始付运。当然,在那时就中国买方来看,卖方(一个著名的国际粮商)可以履行在 6 月 15 日付运第一个买卖合约的巴西大豆机会是微乎其微,因为该卖方也是被中国政府列入黑名单的一国际粮商。当然,大豆价格跌到这么低,中国买方也不会希望合约可以被履行。反正就是由于大豆价格在中国禁运之后虽然没有马上暴跌,因为大家还处于观察阶段,但价格已经有了上下的波动。所以卖方就在5月11日根据合约条文的规定,要求中国买方提供一个市场价格下跌的履约保证,就是在2个银行工作日内支付约300万美元的担保金。但由于市场波动越来越大,卖方到了5月26日已经把担保金提升到1200万美元。中国买方当然没有支付这笔钱,也没有表态,而卖方就在6月4日声称接受中国买方的违约/毁约而终断合约。之后,卖方提出的索赔金额高达2700万美元,而根据的就是合约价格与6月4日大豆市场中最低的价格的差价,再乘以四个买卖合约的货量所得出。

在这里进一步解释一下担保金,它是在这四个买卖合约里面有一条条文针对在付运之前,如果市场价格比合约价格下挫5%以上,卖方有权要求中国买方在两个银行工作日内以人民币支付这5%的货价给该卖方在中国北京的公司作为保证金。由于这一个买卖没有涉及信用证,所以卖方需要这条文作出保障,因为如果在订约后与付运前的一段时间内市场价格大幅度下挫,中国买方会扯皮的机会就增加。如果卖方在这种情况下还是要履行合约把大豆付运,就变为十分被动与可能面对庞大损失,所以有了条文强制中国买方支付的保证金就可以避免这一个风险。条文是这样的:"Once pricing begins if market moves down 5% or more, Buyer must remit additional 5% of cargo value that have bought by the Buyer at the pre – payment default penalty in RMB to Seller's office in Beijing within 2 working days according to seller's instruction. The Seller should remit the above pre – payment default penalty to the Buyer within 2 banking days after payment for full cargo value is received by Seller according to the Buyer's instruction."

在仲裁中,双方有很多争议,包括这卖方要求的保证金是否计算正确,还是刁难中国买方来找借口终断合约,并提出索赔。中国买方也提出其他对责任方面的抗辩,包括:(1)上述条文要求给保证金但在没有准时支付的情况下是否属于违反了条件条文而让卖方终断合约;(2)是否违反默示条件不得因为他的错误(被中国列入黑名单)导致买方无法履行合约。但在这里笔者还是主要针对损失的计算,就是如果卖方在5月11日要求这笔保证金,而中国买方在2个银行工作日内并没有作出支付,这就等于说违约的一天就应该是5月13日,所以根据FOSFA的第27条文,就应该以这一天的市场价格计算损失。而如果以那一天的市场价格来计算损失是只有550万美元,而当时在中国买方与卖方之间的长期累计(主要是以前多年的买卖)下"往来的账目"(running account)中,卖方仍然持有属于中国买方的600万美元,这等于说,即使是中国买方在责任方面是全部败诉,中国买方也根本就不用掏钱。

在一连串斗争之后,笔者知悉双方就是以大家"罢手达成和解"(drop hand settlement),但那600万美元的累积金额就归卖方。可见,以哪一天的市场价格为准所得出来的结果是天壤之别。而GAFTA与FOSFA标准合约中规定与局限以违约一天的市场价格计算损失是有它的好处的,但在一些情况下会与实际损失相差太大而有失公平,当然Breach Date Rule与Market Rule本身就有这个矛盾。

2. Breach Date Rule 与 Market Rule 只是表面规则，有弹性与可以偏离

正如本章开头所讲，Breach Date Rule 与 Market Rule 只是表面或作为起点的计算损失规则，这在 1979 年英国《货物销售法》中十分明确，但已经有很多权威的先例说明这一个规则是有很大的"弹性"（flexibility）。这表示配合不同案件的事实，为了达到公正的结果与不偏离复原原则，法院或仲裁庭是可以灵活适用 Breach Date Rule 与 Market Rule 的。但为了法律的肯定，要偏离是需要有被法律认可的原因。受害方应该可以有一段必要的时间来安排替代的买进或卖出，而不是必须严格地在违约/毁约被接受导致合约终断的一天。毕竟不是所有的替代货物/商品受害方的买方要买就马上买得到或受害方的卖方可以把买方拒绝的货物马上转售，或是适合的替代船舶受害的承租人要租就租得到（即使在理论上）。

这个问题已经在本书第十三章之 4 段有针对可以偏离 Breach Date Rule 的例外情况。在本章，会在这一方面进一步探讨这一个重要的损失计算规则。

这里的权威说法也有不少，如 Wilberforce 勋爵在 Miliangos v. George Frank (Textiles) Ltd (1976) 1 Lloyd's Rep 201 先例中在提到以违约一天的 Breach Date Rule 去计算损失是"一般性规则"（general rule）后，说："it is for the courts, or for arbitrators, to work out a solution in each case best adapted to giving the injured plaintiff that amount in damages which will most fairly compensate him for the wrong which he has suffered."

另 Wilberforce 勋爵也在 Johnson v. Agnew (1980) AC 367 先例中说："but this is not an absolute rule; if to follow it, would give rise to injustice, the court has power to fix such other date as may be appropriate in the circumstances."

另在 Norden v. Andre (2003) 1 Lloyd's Rep 287 先例中，Toulson 大法官说："... Mr. Justice Robert Goff similarly stressed in measure of damages applied by him in that case was (as in sale of goods cases under s. 50 [3] and s. 51 [3] of the Sale of Goods Act, 1979) only a *prima facie* rule. Mr. Gruder, Q. C. for Norden（原告代表大律师）accepted (rightly in my view) that he could not distinguish the present case from The Elena d'Amico by reference to the nature of the contract. But he submitted that there were particular reasons on the facts of this case which would make it unjust to apply the normal measure of damages which I have been considering."

可以明显看到，以违约一天计算损失，也只能以当时市场价格的差价为准找出损失金额。所以，Breach Date Rule 与 Market Rule 是走在一起的。如果是以受害方真正损失为准，就不能以违约一天作出计算，因为受害方是需要时间善后，如受害的卖方把买方错误拒绝的货物处置掉才会知道真正损失的金额。

由于 Breach Date Rule 与 Market Rule 有很大的弹性，就表示法院或者仲裁庭认为适用这个表面规则进行损失计算会带来不公平，就会改用其他的方法计算受害方真正的损失。它的弹性也包括法院或者仲裁庭即使是适用这个表面规则，也会有所偏离。其中一个主要的偏离是不以违约一天的市场价格为准，而是会采用隔一二星期后的市场价格计算，又或者是用一段时间内的平均市场价格（Petrotrade v. Stinnes [1995] 1 Lloyd's Rep 142 先例）。但为了法律的肯定，只要是有市场，法院或仲裁庭应该也会尽量适用 Breach Date Rule 与 Market Rule，避免偏离。反正这又是追求法律肯定与个别案件的公平之间所产生的矛盾做出平衡。在现实中，受害方会在对方违约/毁约一天马上就去市场购入或者是出售，并且成功完成交易，机会会是十中无一。绝大多数的情况，受害方是会拖拖拉拉，即使会买进替代货物或者是出售给其他买方，也会隔一段时间，甚至从来没有这样做。这就表示看市场的走势是升还是跌，受害方真正的损失会比假设性的 Breach Date Rule 与 Market Rule 计算出来的损失或多或少，所以产生很多这方面的争议。而受害方如果蒙受更大金额的真正损失，想避开 Breach Date Rule 与 Market Rule，最惯常用的争辩是他在违约后的行为是怎样的合理与所导致的真正损失是如何的难以避免，务求说服法院或者仲裁庭会偏离这个 Breach Date Rule 与 Market Rule，判他更大的一笔真正损失。但这些争辩通常不是一个好的理由避开 Breach Date Rule 与 Market Rule 的适用，管用的理由可在接下去的段节做进一步的介绍。

这里也可以节录 Bingham 勋爵在 The "Golden Victory" (2007) 2 Lloyd's Rep 164 先例所提到的一些情况是法院会偏离这 Breach Date Rule 与 Market Rule 如在人身伤亡的损失计算，说："The charterers further submit that even if, as a general rule, damages for breach of contract... are assessed as at the date of the breach... the court has shown itself willing to depart from this rule where it judges it necessary or just to do so in order to give effect to the compensatory principle. I accept that this is so. But it is necessary to consider the cases in which the court departs from the general rule. Some are personal injury claims... The court has also departed from the general rule in cases where, on particular facts, it was held to be reasonable for the injured party to defer taking steps to mitigate his loss and so reasonable to defer the assessment of damage. Radford v. De Froberville (1977) 1 WLR 1262 and Dodd Properties (Kent) Ltd v. Canterbury City Council (1980) 1 WLR 433 are examples. In both cases the general rule was acknowledged and reasons given for departing from it. Country Personnel (Employment Agency) Ltd v. Alan R Pulver & Co (1987) 1 WLR 916 was a claim against solicitors whose negligent advice had saddled the plaintiffs with a ruinous underlease, from which the plaintiffs had had to buy themselves out. The ordinary diminution in value measure of damage was held to be wholly inapt on the particular facts. Again, reasons were given for departing from the normal rule. In Miliangos v. George Frank (Textiles) Ltd (1976) 1 Lloyd's Rep 201 the effect of inflation led the House to sanction a departure from the rule that losses sustained in a foreign currency must be converted into sterling at the date of breach... None of these cases, as is evident, involves the accepted repudiation of a commercial contract such as a charterparty. It is necessary to consider some cases more similar to the present case to which the House was referred."

以下分别介绍在货物买卖可偏离 Breach Date Rule 与 Market Rule 的情况。

2.1　不适用 Breach Date Rule 与 Market Rule 情况之一：独一无二的货物

"独一无二"(unique)的货物一般就不会有市场，如没有人会说名画《蒙娜丽莎》会有一个可供买卖的市场或是在 Times Newspapers Ltd v. George Weidenfeld & Nicolson Ltd(2002)FSR 463 先例中的首相回忆录版权。在《Benjamin's Sale of Goods》(8th edn, 2010 年)一书之 16－067 段说："It is most unlikely that there will be an available market where the goods in question have been(or were to be) specially manufactured to suit the particular requirements of the buyer: the chance of resale of such goods within a reasonable time after the breach is too limited and fortuitous."

在本章 1.3.6.2 段介绍的 The"Baltic Surveyor"(2001)1 Lloyd's Rep 739 先例中，与 Baltic Surveyor 游艇同时沉没的浮桥显然是独一无二而没有可供买卖的市场的。这一来，就要计算它在被侵权摧毁时的实际"价值"(value)了。估计这个浮桥重新建造要 6 万英镑，而这些浮桥估计寿命是 50 年。至于出事的浮桥已经是很残旧并有严重的腐蚀，需要塞入塑料填充物来帮助浮起。Colman 大法官接受这沉没的浮桥顶多只剩 8 年寿命，而估计一个新的浮桥，50 年寿命太长，30 年寿命的话就比较接近。所以，Colman 大法官这样折旧，从 6 万英镑的建造价格减少为 1.6 万英镑，也就是要赔付的金额。

在这里顺便一提，针对独一无二货物与有可供买卖的市场的货物在法律上的救济很不一样。针对独一无二货物，由于计算真正损失不容易以及法院认为金钱赔偿往往是不足够，受害方也无法在市场找到替代，所以是十分愿意作出"履约指令"(specific performance)的救济的。但相对有可供买卖的市场的货物，法院是不愿意作出履约指令的，认为受害方可以去市场买进替代货物或卖给替代买方来解决问题，然后将来以金钱去作出赔偿。

2.2　不适用 Breach Date Rule 与 Market Rule 情况之二：违约太晚导致可供买卖的市场欠缺

如果违约方的卖方太晚才拒绝交货，会导致可供买卖的市场欠缺。原因是可供买卖市场是为了要求受害方在市场尽快买进替代商品/货物，以减少损失。但该替代商品/货物显然是要与有关合约的商品/货物是一致的，或是尽量接近的。这一来，由于商品的付运日期或交货日期(如果有的话)也是货物描述的重要部分，就变为违约太晚就根本找不到符合要求的替代货物了。因为再去装港付运同样的货物去卸港也赶不上付运日期或交货日期。这一来能够做到买进替代商品/货物，就会是在卸港有否合约约定的商品/货物的市场。如果没有，另一个可能是某一些商品/货物可以符合付运日期或交货日期的要求,因为是已经装在其他船舶上,而这种“浮动货物”(floating cargo)也可能买得到作为替代货物。但一般而言这种机会不会太高,因为已经装在船舶上的货物往往是已经有了其他的买卖合约。所以,卖方如果违约太晚就会造成根本没有雷同的替代货物可以买进。以下介绍有关的一些先例。

2.2.1 案例之一:Contigroup Companies,Inc v. Glencore A. G.

在 Contigroup Companies,Inc v. Glencore A. G. (2005)1 Lloyd' s Rep 241 先例中,涉及的是丁烷(butane)与丙烷(propane)以 CFR 卖给中石油,卖方就是 Glencore,交货地点是中国的温州,时间是 2002 年 6 月 7 日至 12 日。而 Glencore 就是在较早前向 Contigroup 买进一批丙烷并装在一艘名为 Sunway 的船上。由于 Sunway 轮受到延误,所以根本赶不上交货日期。在 5 月 31 日,中石油才被告知交油的日期要比约定的日期晚 3 天(6 月 15 日才会抵达温州),而当时中石油是急于要货的。在之后的 6 月 5 日,中石油终于被告知 Sunway 轮只有丁烷但没有丙烷。期间,Glencore 想尽方法找其他的替代的丙烷,只要是能够在 6 月 15 日之前到达温州,但没有成功。由于 Glencore 在两方面毁约:没有丙烷与延误交货,最后与中石油在 6 月 10 日达成和解协议,赔偿 172,899.67 美元给中石油或每吨减价 8 美元。而最终 Sunway 轮也在 6 月 15 日到达温州卸货。

Glencore 后来向 Contigroup 索赔这笔钱的损失,因为 Sunway 轮的延误是来自 Contigroup 的。这里涉及两个争议,因为和解协议中的 172,899.67 美元肯定是和可供买卖的市场价格(如果有的话)不一样。Ian Click 大法官最后判是认为在当时的情况下是没有可供买卖的市场的,说:

“Could Glencore have gone into the market and acquired a substitute for Lot 2 on June 10,2002,the date of breach,or,indeed,at any time between learning on May 29 that Sunway would be late and June? For if it could,it would be difficult to argue that Glencore' s loss could have been any more than the additional cost(if any)of obtaining that substitute.

Glencore was entitled to receive a cargo of between 21,000 and 22,000 metrictones of butane at Wenzhou not later than June 10,2002. It knew by May 29 that Sunway could not arrive by that date. Moreover,despite requests by Glencore,Contichem never showed any sign of itself finding a substitute cargo to enable the sale contract to be performed on time.

I have already indicated that I accept that between May 29 and June 4 Glencore and Glencore International made strenuous efforts through Mr. DuPay(石油气买卖的经纪人) to find a substitute cargo on a vessel able to reach Wenzhou,by June 10,or at least earlier than Sunway. They also,mostly through Mr. Schneider,tried to find smaller cargoes to keep Petrochina supplied. The former efforts failed altogether. The later only produced one,unsuitable,cargo.

Moreover,the expert evidence called by Contichem entirely failed to establish that at the end of May or in early June,2002 there were available butane for purchase or exchange, and that could have been re – directed to Wenzhou to arrive there earlier than Sunway. Mr. Hoare(Contichem 或 Contigroup 的专家证人)listed eight vessels carrying large cargoes of butane,or butane and propane,that could have arrived at Wenzhou between June 6 and 12, 2002. That is,they were so positioned that,had they been ordered so to do,they could have reached Wenzhou at some time within that period. These include apparently,a vessel Mr. Delia suggests might have been diverted to Wenzhou. Mr. Hoare accepted that none of those cargoes was for sale and that all were committed to other parties. Possibly,he said,they could have been exchanged for other cargoes. He was not,however,saying there was such a cargo available for purchase or exchange. He was saying it is possible that there was such a cargo available.

It is,of course,to be observed that if such a cargo did exist,then between May 29 and June 4,Mr. DuPay,who did had every incentive to find it,did not do so. Indeed,it was not even possible to find much smaller cargoes of suitable butane. Moreover,the closer in time to June 10,the less chance there was that cargo found would have been able to reach-Wenzhou by then. Nor was it suggested that there was any sufficient butane already at Wenzhou available to be acquired.

In my judgement,on the evidenceconsidered as a whole,it is fanciful to suppose that Glencore,or Petrochina for that matter,could have gone out into the market and acquired substitute butane for delivery at Wenzhou before Sunway arrived,whether at the date of breach(June 10 or 12)or between learning Sunway would be late and that date. It is in my judgement plain that there was no relevant available market for butane."

由于在该先例判是不适用 Breach Date Rule 与 Market Rule,所以 Glencore 是可以向 Contigroup 成功索赔他真正的损失,也就是与中石油达成和解协议中所赔偿的 172,899.67 美元,这笔钱可以从 Glencore 欠下的货款中扣除。

2.2.2 案例之二:Coastal(Bermuda)v. VTT

在 Coastal(Bermuda)v. VTT(1994)2 Lloyd's Rep. 629 先例中,案情也是相对简单的。原告是一个庞大的石油产品贸易与炼油集团,而被告是一家瑞士的石油产品贸易公司。他们订了一个"CIF Aruba"买卖合约,是被告卖给原告 50,000 到 55,000 吨的燃油。这批燃油实际上是原告为他在 Aruba 的一家集团公司(名为 Coastal Aruba Refining N. V.)购买的。在订约的几天后,被告指定了一艘名为 Marine Star 的油轮,而原告也接受了。但很快被告就把该油轮撤回,承诺会另找一艘替代的油轮。但被告这样做也没有得到原告的接受,而事实上被告再也没有指定任何一艘替代的油轮。过了大概一星期的时间,原告接受被告的违约/毁约并终断买卖合约。看来,这是一个明显的卖方拒绝提供货物的例子,而通常的原因就是市场价格上涨。事实上,该先例责任明确,主要的争议是在损失的计算。在该先例受害的买方的损失主要分两个部分，第一部分是分销或者转售的利润损失，第二部分是对分买方 Coastal Aruba Refining N. V. 的责任。要成功索赔这两个部分的真正损失，必须是在不适用 Breach Date Rule 与 Market Rule 的情况下。否则受害方的买方理论上应该马上在市场中买进同样的燃油向分买方交货。在本小段所要针对的只是在当时是否有一个可供买卖的市场，如果有，这两部分的损失就站不住脚了。在高院，Mance 大法官判是没有一个可供买卖的市场，因为"多重原因"(combination reasons)结合所造成，包括原买卖合约的交货时间非常局限以及违约是在很晚才发生，说：

"I turn therefore to the plaintiffs' claim to have suffered loss of the profit of 25 cents per tonne which the plaintiffs say that they would have earned by delivering the Marine Star cargo to Coastal Aruba under their contract of sale with Coastal Aruba. The first issue is whether there was an 'available market' in which, following the defendants' breach, the plaintiffs could have acquired replacement cargo: cf. Sale of Goods Act, 1979 s. 51(3). If there was, then the defendants say that loss of profit is irrecoverable - and no claim has been presented on the basis that, if there was a market, it would have been more expensive to buy in replacement cargo on it. **The delivery date under the present contract was in my judgement part of the contract description of the goods agreed to be sold** . . . On this basis the notion of a '**market**' for replacement goods is here a **restricted** one, and could only be met if the plaintiffs were able to buy in replacement goods for delivery at Aruba in the bracket of Aug. 4 to 10, 1991. . . (加黑部分是笔者的强调，Mance 大法官是说交货日期是货物的描述部分，所以有关货物的市场就变得非常局限，因为找替代货物是需要有同样的对交货日期的描述与特征)

The existence of an available market operates as a restraint on recovery; its presence or absence does not have specifically to be contemplated. An available market is a means of mitigating any loss otherwise contemplated which had become incorporated into the general measure of recovery. . . The formulation in ss. 50 and 51 of the Sale of Goods Act in effect proceeds on the basis that there may not always be an available market for a replacement purchase or sale. In parenthesis, that itself seems to me unsurprising when, as the present case shows, the lack of an available market may result not from any particular intervening event, but, from a combination of market forces, **a tight contractual delivery date and a late repudiation by the defendants leading to a situation in which no replacement goods are available.** (在本先例没有一个可供买卖的市场是由于各种因素加起来如一个很紧的交货日期与被告很晚的违约/毁约，这导致一种情况就是当时根本没有方法能在市场找到同样替代货物)

. . . I find that there was at the end of July and in early August, 1991 no available market for the purchase by the plaintiffs (or indeed Coastal Aruba) of a cargo of E4 of the contractual description for delivery to Aruba in the period Aug. 4 - 10, 1991."

2.2.3 案例之三:The"Ile Aux Moines"

在 The"Ile Aux Moines"(1974)2 Lloyd's Rep 502 先例,涉及一艘二手船的买卖,但由于在交船的时候船舶市场急升,卖方拒绝交船,结果是受害方的买方在相隔两个月后才以更高的价格买进了一艘同样的姊妹船作为替代。买方之后向违约方的卖方提出了两项主要的索赔,第一项就是在违约当天(1972 年 12 月 15 日)有关船舶的合约价格与市场价格差别的 26 万美元。第二项就是在违约日期直到在 1973 年 2 月 16 日买进替代船舶(姐妹船)并在 1973 年的 7 月才真正交船,这相隔好几个月的营运利润损失。

在仲裁庭,认定的事实是在违约时没有同船龄、航速、载重与容积,并加上交船日子接近的替代船舶可供买进。受害方的买方最早是在两个月后才首次有机会买进 Ile Aux Moines 轮的另一艘姐妹船(总共有 6 艘同类船舶)作为合理的替代,但交船要多等 5 个月之久。换言之,违约一天是没有可供买卖市场,所以法院认为买方是可以索赔这额外的营运利润损失。但由于他没有在仲裁的时候向仲裁庭提出这一个请求,所以错过了机会。

2.3 不适用 Breach Date Rule 与 Market Rule 情况之三:有缺陷货物后来才被觉察

这种情况经常出现在货物买卖,在进一步分析前可先介绍一个比较近期与富争议性的先例。在 Bence Graphics International Ltd. v. Fasson U. K. Ltd(C. A.)(1998)QB 87(Reliance case P247)先例,案情涉及原告 Bence Graphics(买方)向法院要求判被告 Fasson(卖方)把买卖合约的货款退还,因为该货物完全是货不对版,不值钱。该案例的案情是,Fasson 把有瑕疵的"乙烯基薄膜"(vinyl film)提供给 Bence Graphics,而这种瑕疵是 Bence Graphics 在采用乙烯基薄膜制造辨认集装箱的贴纸时才能被发现的。看来如果货不对版要在后来才被发现,就会不适用 Breach Date Rule 与 Market Rule,因为在发现的时候去市场买进替代的时机已经过去。在该先例,Bence Graphics 事实上只面对一个最终采用该贴纸的集装箱用户的有限索赔,而其他用户就没有提出索赔。换言之,如果把分销合约考虑在内,Bence Graphics 的真正损失就很有限。但如果 Bence Graphics 能够根据市场价格(因为货不对版不值钱)成功要求把货价要回来,他就可以赚一笔。第一审的高院判 Bence Graphics 的损失应该以 1979 年英国《货物销售法》之 Section 51(3)的表面规则,也就是 Breach Date Rule 与 Market Rule 来计算。但高院的判决被上诉庭推翻,上诉庭的大部分意见是 Bence Graphics 的损失应该把他要面对第三人的责任(这里的责任不大)也计算在内。Auld 勋爵说:"Would have contemplated that, in the event of a breach by the seller discovered only after the decals had been in use, the buyer might wish to pass on to it claims for damages from dissatisfied customers."

Michael Furmston 教授在他所著的《Law of Contract》(4th edn, 2010 年)一书之第 766 页也有讨论这一个先例,说:"In Bence Graphics International Ltd. v. Fasson U. K.

Ltd the defendants were suppliers of cast vinyl film and supplied film to the value of £ 564,328 to the plaintiffs. The plaintiffs, to the defendants' knowledge, intended to use the film to manufacture decals which were used in the shipping industry to identify bulk containers. It was a term of the contract that the film would last in good legible condition for five years. In fact the film was defective and degraded prematurely. The plaintiffs argued that the film was worthless at the time of delivery and that they should get their money back. This view appeared to be supported an earlier Court of Appeal decision on Slater v. Hoyle and Smith Ltd and was accepted by the trial judge and by Thorpe LJ, but the majority of the Court of Appeal disagreed. They attached decisive weight to the fact that nearly all the film had been sub – sold but that very few customers has pursued claims. In their view, therefore, the buyers had in practice suffered little loss and an inquiry should be directed as to how much."

以下对这一个问题做进一步分析，涉及货物缺陷，主要考虑 Breach Date Rule 与 Market Rule 是否适用是要看这一缺陷是否"表面化"(patent)。如果是，就表示 Breach Date Rule 与 Market Rule 适用，这也在 1979 年英国《货物销售法》之 Section 53(3)有说明。

如果缺陷是表面化或受害的买方可以合理觉察并找出毛病，但买方疏忽或是错误不加以理会，进一步把货物分销/转售或加以使用。这一来就涉及了买方没有减少损失，而这进一步的真正损失(不论是赔偿给分买方或使用有缺陷货物带来的严重后果)，是由于买方自己的疏忽或错误所引致，与卖方提供有缺陷货物没有直接因果关系，也不能偏离 Breach Date Rule 与 Market Rule 的适用。这方面可节录 Devlin 大法官在 Biggin v. Permanite(1951)1 KB 422 先例中所讲的："A claimant cannot pass on his liability to an outside party for bad quality if, before the sale to the outside party, he had notice of the defect in quality.... Similarly, if the knowledge of the defects comes to the claimant after the sale to the outside party, and if, by passing on that knowledge to the outside party, he can diminish his liability to that party, he is bound to do so."另在更早的 British Oil and Cake Co v. Burstall(1923)39 TLR 406 先例，Rowlatt 大法官也说："If a buyer received from his seller an article which was 'patently' not the article contracted for, he could not use it at the risk of the seller."

但还是有不少的情况是货物缺陷是隐蔽，但隐蔽还是能够检查到，只是买方没有这样做。这样看来，如果买方不检查是属于合理，英国法院还是会允许买方依赖卖方对货物描述的承诺或保证，不必进行检查就分销/转售或使用。这一个方面的有关先例有三个，买方都成功向卖方索赔了赔偿给分买方的损失与费用：Pinnock v. Lewis (1923)1 KB 690；British Oil and Cake Co v. Burstall(1923)39 TLR 406；Dobell v. Barber (1931)1 KB219 CA。

至于隐蔽的货物缺陷是在使用时才觉察的案例也不少，如在 Wagstaff v. Shorthorn

Dairy Co(1884)Cab & Ell 324 先例,有关货物是有缺陷的种子,这一个缺陷在收成的时候才觉察,判卖方要赔偿的损失是按照买卖合约的健康种子所种出来的谷物与有缺陷种子所种出来的的谷物收成之间的差价。另在 Holden v. Bostock(1902)18 TLR 317 CA 先例,有关货物是食糖,但食糖中有砒霜。结果买方把食糖使用在酿啤酒并最后导致了买方把所有酿造的有毒啤酒全部销毁。受害的买方事后向卖方索赔这一笔真正的损失,并被法院支持。在 The"Ocean Dynamic"(1982)2 Lloyd's Rep 88 先例,有关货物是樱桃,但樱桃中有碎玻璃,在买方生产果酱的时候才发现,导致严重损失。

在较近期的 Britvic Soft Drinks Ltd v. Messer UK Ltd(2002)1 Lloyd's Rep 20 与 Bacardi - Martini Beverages Ltd v. Thomas Hardy Packaging Ltd(2002)1 Lloyd's Rep 62 的两个先例,涉及有关货物(二氧化碳)的缺陷在使用时才被觉察,损失计算也是按照买方的真正损失,包括把生产了的饮料销毁。这货物的缺陷涉及二氧化碳内受到苯的污染,这种缺陷会带来极严重的后果,一个活生生的例子就是法国著名的毕雷矿泉水。在 1998 年左右,也是涉及它使用的二氧化碳受到苯的污染。估计是由于管理不善,导致这一个消息最初传出来的时候法国公司采取回避与暧昧的态度。拖拖拉拉过了一段时间后才采取行动,把全球共 1.6 亿瓶的毕雷矿泉水回收,损失共达 1.5 亿英镑。但估计为时太晚,已经对商誉造成严重创伤,导致了毕雷矿泉水的销售大幅度下跌。在大约两年后,他也失去了自主权,被雀巢公司收购。显然,计算真正损失也并非是易事,总不能把这些致命的损失都算在提供缺陷二氧化碳的卖方,其中会涉及因果关系与损失遥远性的考虑。

这种争议笔者在近期的一个仲裁中也有遇到,案情涉及中国制造的摩托车出口去美国,买卖合约中对货物的描述与保证是必须符合美国环保当局的要求,这包括了车辆的排放方面。该批车辆在运抵美国后被买方分销/转售,是在事后的使用才被美国环保当局发觉并提出起诉。最后美国买方与美国环保当局达成和解协议,但还是要付出一大笔钱。美国买方是向中国卖方索赔或要求补偿这一笔支出,作为货物质量问题的损失。双方其中的一个争议是买卖合约中有条文说到货物抵达后 3、4 天内买方有对货物进行检查的权利,并向卖方提出任何货物短缺或质量问题。中国卖方的争辩就是美国买方如果进行了这一个检查,就不会导致后来被美国环保当局处罚。笔者作为仲裁员之一根据专家证据是认为排放的缺陷是隐藏性的缺陷,美国买方看不出来就分销/转售没有不合理之处,他也可以依赖在买卖合约中对符合美国环保当局要求的保证。这一来,美国买方是可以索赔真正损失,只要是质量缺陷所导致的损失,因果关系没有中断与买方没有不合理减少损失(这方面包括与美国环保当局的诉讼与和解),都可以向卖方索赔或要求补偿买方的真正损失。

在这种隐蔽的货物质量问题,如果不适用 Breach Date Rule 与 Market Rule 而是适用真正损失的计算,再重复与强调是对"损失限制"(limitation of damages)都会需要考虑,如"损失的遥远性"(remoteness of damages),这包括了损失类别是在订约时可以“合理预见”(reasonably foreseeable)或“料想得到“(within reasonable contemplation)与满足“因果关系”(causation)。另外,受害方的买方也要证明与满足他有合理“减少损失”(mitigation)。例如,在 Bunting v. Tory(1948)64 TLR 353 先例,在公开拍卖中买进的公牛事后被发觉用作配种的精力不足够,但买方向卖方索赔这方面的损失败诉,因为公牛的买卖可以有其他的用途,用作配种只是其中之一。买方没有在订立买卖合约之前告知卖方公牛的用途,更没有在合约中对这方面作出任何承诺或保证,这种损失是属于 Hadley v. Baxendale(1854)9 Ex 341 先例下的第二种损失类别的“特别损失”(special damages)。

2.4 不适用 Breach Date Rule 与 Market Rule 情况之四:特定货物或买方的分销/转售合约与违约合约的交货日期一致

这种情况与较早所介绍的不适用情况看来有一定程度的重叠/重复,如此段提到的“特定货物”与 2.1 段介绍的“独一无二”的货物相对接近,都是指没有可供买卖的市场的货物。另在有关买卖合约与分合约的交货日期一致也与 2.2 段所介绍的情况十分接近。在这种情况下即使在违约/毁约当天有可供买卖的市场,Market Rule 计算受害的买方的损失也不适用。这方面可先节录《McGregor on Damages》(18th edn, 2009 年)之 20 - 026 段:“**Loss on a resale.** Loss on a resale, like damage through loss of use, is most likely to arise where there is no market in which similar goods can be bought. But, in addition, loss can arise here despite the existence of a market generally, because this market is not available to the buyer himself. As Salter J pointed out in Patrick v. Russo - British Grain Export Co(1927)2 KB 535, there are two such cases. ‘One is when the sale is of specific goods, and the buyer has resold the same goods. The other is where the contract of resale has the same delivery date as the contract of sale.’... ”

本来如果是有关货物可以让受害方的买方在市场买进,他的损失应该仍是适用 Breach Date Rule 与 Market Rule 计算损失。大道理就是受害方的买方可以甚至应该马上在市场买进同样的替代货物,履行对分买方的责任。一这样做,就不会有分销/转售合约的间接损失,也不会有无法使用货物(如作为生产的原料)的损失或其他真正损失。例外的情况是即使在违约时候有市场,受害的买方无法在市场买进(不论他是否有意图这样做)。这在上述的节录中提到 Patrick v. Russo - British Grain Export Co 先例说是两种情况会导致违约时有市场但受害的买方还是不能去市场买进以减少损失。

2.4.1 特定货物

第一种情况是买卖涉及“特定货物”(specific goods),这特定货物也不一定是独一无二的货物,而是违约方的卖方知道受害方的买方非要依赖他的履行才能向分买方提供该特定的货物。这种情况会是即使涉及了市场有买卖的商品,如食糖或小麦,但买方分销/转售给分买方所约定的货物就是卖方所提供的一票货物。这种情况会出现在“一连串买卖合约”(string contracts)或是两份买卖合约所针对的都是已经装在某一艘船舶上的一票“浮动货物”(floating cargo)。比方说在本书第十五章之3.1.4段介绍的 Louis Dreyfus Trading v. Reliance Trading Ltd(2004)2 Lloyd's Rep 243先例,涉及食糖,但有关买卖合约中约定是装在 Dawn 轮的食糖,这就变成有关货物不是随便在市场能够买进替代货物的食糖。而卖方如果预计到买方要分销/转售,就知道他不提供这特定的货物,买方也不能提供给分买方。在 Patrick v. Russo – British Grain Export Co 先例中有关的货物是小麦,Salter 大法官说:“that the seller should have known, when he sold, that the buyer was buying to implement a contract already made or that the buyer would certainly resell; it is enough if both parties contemplate that the buyer will probably resell and the seller is content to take the risk. I think, therefore, that the arbitrators' finding(that the probability of resale was contemplated) is sufficient to support a claim for loss of profit on a resale”Salter 大法官这一段话与本书第十五章之3.1.4段、3.2.2.3段与6.2.3段的内容与注脚所提到的有关索赔特别损失必须是双方订约前可以预见或料想得到是完全吻合。

另在 Kwei Tek Chao v. British Traders and Shippers Ltd(1954)1 Lloyd's Rep 16先例中,Devlin 大法官是这样说:“There are, of course, cases where that *prima facie* measure of damage is not applicable because something different is contemplated. If, for example, a man sells goods of a special manufacture and it is known that they are to be re – sold, it must also be known that they cannot be bought in the market, being specially manufactured by the seller. In such a case the loss of profit becomes the appropriate measure of damage. Similarly, it may very well be that in the case of string contracts, if the seller knows that the merchant is not buying merely for re – sale generally, but upon a string contract where he will re – sell those **specific goods** and where he could only honour his contract by delivering those goods and no others, the measure of loss or profit on re – sale is the right measure.”

2.4.2 买方的分销/转售合约与违约合约的交货日期一致

第二种情况就是分销/转售合约的交货日期与原买卖合约的日期是一致。这会带来的后果是在原买卖合约的卖方很迟才违约/毁约,买方在同一时间也对分买方违约/毁约。作为中间商的买方即使可以并愿意马上去市场买进替代货物,在时间上也来不及。即使在第二天交出同样的替代货物,分买方也可以拒绝接受。在这种情况下,买方是会可以向违约方的卖方索赔分销/转售合约与其他真正的间接损失。另可多介绍在《Chitty On Contracts》(30th edn, 2008年)一书之43 – 428段的同样说法:“**Loss of profits under sub – sale.** Where a market price at the date of the seller's breach is ascertainable, a higher or lower price at which the buyer has resold the goods to a sub – buyer is generally irrelevant to the assessment of damage of the fact that the buyer, following the seller's failure to deliver. Thus, the seller cannot take advantage of the fact that the buyer, following the seller's failure to deliver, fulfilled his obligations under a resale by using other goods, and thereby made a greater profit on the resale than he would have done if the seller had not broken the contract. In the exceptional cases where the seller is liable for loss of profits or expenses under the sub - sale, his liability is based on the parties' reasonable contemplation of the consequences of a breach of the contract. The buyer may have contracted to sell to his sub - buyer the very same goods as he bought from the seller(这是指第一种例外情况), or he may have fixed the same delivery date in the contract of resale as in the original contract(这是指第二种例外情况). In these situations, when the seller fails to deliver on the due date, the buyer cannot, despite the presence of an available market, avoid loss under the contract of resale: but the buyer can recover damages for that loss only where the seller should have contemplated, at the time the original contract was made, both that the buyer was, or was probably, buying for resale, and that the buyer could perform his obligations under a contract of resale only by delivering the same goods. Thus, in the leading case of Hall v. Pim(1928)33 Com. Case 324, the buyers bought a cargo under a c. i. f. contract, which expressly contemplated that the buyer might resell during the voyage, and that any resale would be of the identifiable or named cargo, which meant that the buyers would necessarily be in default under the sub - contract if the sellers failed to deliver under the original contract. The buyers were able to recover the difference between the contract price and the resale price since 'the seller in such a case contracted to put the buyer in a position to fulfil his sub - contracts if he entered into them.' But the actual loss of the profits on a resale will be awarded only if the terms of the resale were reasonable and usual. Although the decision in Hall v. Pim has been criticised, it is submitted that it is sound in principle . . ."

2.5 不适用 Breach Date Rule 与 Market Rule 情况之五:丧失销售额的卖方

这又是另一种例外情况,针对的是买方拒绝接受货物或不开出信用证,导致受害方的卖方要去把有关货物转售给其他买方。如果当时市场稳定,会造成的情况是卖方并没有蒙受真正的损失或是按照合约价格比较违约时市场价格的差价计算。这看来是买卖双方都是运气,违约/毁约并终断买卖合约并没有造成双方任何的损失。但会有情况是卖方实际上是蒙受损失,因为他丧失了销售额。他虽然找到了另一个替代买方肯以同样或更高的价格购买这一票被拒绝的货物,但如果没有这一次违约,卖方手中有大量同样的货物,可以多做一票买卖并多赚一次利润,这就是卖方的损失。这在 WL Thompson Ltd v. Robinson(Gunmakers)Ltd(1955)Ch 177 先例,案情涉及买方违约,他拒绝接受一辆汽车,导致卖方把该辆汽车转售给第三人,但价格是一样。法院判是 Breach Date Rule 与 Market Rule,也就是 1979 年英国《货物销售法》之 Section 53(3)在这种情况下不适用,卖方的真正损失是丧失了多一次买卖的利润。

但几乎是同样的情况下在另一个先例,Charter v. Sullivan(1957)2 QB 117,受害方的卖方就败诉。这两个看来是一样案情的先例有一个重要的区别,就是在 WL Thompson Ltd v. Robinson(Gunmakers)Ltd 先例,违约的时候市场是供过于求,但在

Charter v. Sullivan 先例，当时市场是供不应求。在后者的先例，卖方只要是有货物（汽车），是不愁没有买家，所以违约并没有令他丧失一次买卖的利润。

3. 没有可供买卖的市场的情况

3.1　情况之一：固定价格的市场

当相关的货物价格是固定价格的时候，在决定是否存在一个可供买卖的市场的时候就会产生问题。有两个相关的先例针对这个问题，它们分别是：WL Thompson Ltd v. Robinson（Gunmakers）Ltd（1955）Ch 177 与 Charter v. Sullivan（1957）2 QB 117。这两个先例都是买方违约/毁约，而卖方只能以与合约价格相同的固定价格再出售该商品。在这两个先例中，法院判在货物价格是固定的情况下，有没有可供买卖的市场是无关紧要，因为得出来的结果都会是一样。判决是在供过于求或者是供需平衡的情况下，卖方只要根据平衡的可能性证明有可能与机会从他能找到的每一位买方身上赚取利润，他是可以从违约方的买方身上拿回该相应的利润，这到底已经在本章的 2.5 段有详及。但如果供不应求，在这种情况下，卖方是可以把手上的商品全都销售出去，那么当他在替代的交易中取得相同的利润时，是不能从违约方的买方拿回这些利润。

3.1.1　供过于求的情况

这种情况发生在 WL Thompson Ltd v. Robinson（Gunmakers）Ltd（1955）Ch 177 先例中。案情涉及原告答应以制造商所定下的固定价格出售一辆 Vanguard 轿车给被告，但被告拒绝买下。虽然在该交易中的市场价格与合约价格没有差别，但法院判违约/毁约的被告要承担原告在该买卖下损失的利润。由于在该地区 Vanguard 轿车并不缺货，替代的买方不能马上找到，因此法院判是没有可供买卖的市场。Upjohn 大法官说："Has the matter been *res integra* I think that I should have found that an 'available market' merely means that the situation in the particular trade in the particular area was such that the particular goods could freely be sold, and that there was a demand sufficient to absorb readily all the goods that were thrust on it, so that if a purchaser defaulted, the goods in question could readily be disposed of."

但似乎也有不同看法的案例，如供过于求极度严重或当违约/毁约时（如货不对版），虽然在市场上该货物还是存在名义上的报价，但受害方的卖方是很难再把该货物转售出去。那么，在这种情况下，是否存在一个可供买卖的市场而适用 Breach Date Rule 计算损失？在 Kwei Tek Chao v. British Traders and Shippers Ltd（1954）2 Lloyd's Rep 114 先例中，Devlin 大法官的看法是这种情况下是存在可供买卖的市场的，他说："But 'virtually unsaleable' of course does not mean that the goods have no value for the purpose of the calculation of damages. They have not been sold yet, and it is possible that they may never be sold, but it is also possible that trade may revive and that some sort of a market may be found for them if they are held on to for long enough. They therefore have some value, although it may be a speculative one, but that possibility in itself is something that must be valued."

不管怎样, Breach Date Rule［1979 年英国《货物销售法》之 Section 50(3)与 51(3)］只是一条表面规则,如果该规则不足以赔偿受害方的利润损失时,该规则就不适用。在原买方违约/毁约而卖方所找的下一个买方是额外的而不是替代的买方的情况下,卖方本来是有能力与机会做成两单交易,因此对于在原买方违约/毁约的交易中的利润损失,卖方可以获得这笔赔偿,即使替代的买卖价格与原来合约价格相比并没有差异。

3.1.2 供不应求的情况

这种情况发生在 Charter v. Sullivan (1957) 2 QB 117 先例中。案情是被告拒绝接受他原本答应以固定价格买下的 Hillman Minx 轿车。后来卖方以同一价格把该汽车卖给了另外一个买方,证据证明该卖方可以在任何时候找到 Hillman Minx 轿车的买方。因此,法院只是判给了卖方名义损失,理由是即使是原买方没有违约/毁约,该卖方也只能达成相同数目的交易,也就是说获取相同数目的利润。因此,后来找到的买方是一种替代而不是额外的买方。该先例中,法院认为在这种情况下有没有可供买卖的市场是无关紧要的,如 Jenkins 大法官所说的,如下:"I doubt if there can be an available market for particular goods in any sense relevant to section 50(3) of the Sale of Goods Act 1893, unless those goods are available for sale in the market at the market or current price in the sense of the price, whatever it may be, fixed by reference to supply and demand as the price at which a purchaser for the goods in question can be found, be it greater or less than or equal to the contract price. The language of section 50(3) seems to me to postulate that in the cases to which it appears there will, or may, be a difference between the contract price and the market or current price, which cannot be so where the goods can only be sold at a fixed retail price."

4. 当事人不理解 Breach Date Rule 与 Market Rule 而蒙受损失的案件介绍

笔者曾经处理过的一个案件,时隔多年还是记忆犹新,该案件在本书第二章之 10 段已经有详细介绍,所以不重复有关的案情。只进一步提有关本章市场规则这一个课题的方面,就是作出预期违约的美国公司(也是该 4 万吨食糖的 CFR 买卖合约中的卖方)因为食糖市场急升而拒绝向中国买方付运食糖。结果在合约终断后,中国买方向美国公司索赔损失,但损失是根据中国买方自己认为蒙受的真正损失,也就是在第一个航次为2万吨食糖开出了信用证后所浪费了的使费，加上4万吨食糖中国买方在分合约下转售给中国没有外贸权的分买方可以每吨赚5美元的利润损失等，总共约70万美金。但实际上在该CFR买卖合约约定的付运期一天的食糖市场价格由于急剧上涨，相比4万吨食糖的买卖合约价格，差价是1000万美元以上，这才是根据Breach Date Rule与Market Rule中国买方可以向美国卖方索赔的损失。但如第二章之10段有谈到，笔者最终没有办法说服中国买方允许笔者通过伦敦仲裁向美国卖方索赔这一笔1000万美元的损失。理由是根本没有蒙受这笔损失，因为他并没有意图在市场买进替代货物，所以没有蒙受这一笔损失。反正笔者就认为中国买方失去了一个公平、合理、合法与相对十分简单的索赔机会。

在这个例子还可以见到是如果以70万美元的"真正"损失索赔，对证据的要求反而会很高，因为美国卖方要求中国买方提供证据给这70万美元的每一项损失，这包括在分买卖合约的赔偿责任，开出信用证与作出修改等的费用。反而，以Breach Date Rule与Market Rule来计算，就只需根据报道的当天市场价格，这样就简单多了。

笔者多举一个近期的香港仲裁案件，涉及中国买方把一批钢材出售去南美洲一个国家，但货物在卸港被检查发觉比买卖合约的有关钢板厚度的描述有所偏差，是薄了一点。这带来了一个200多万美元的索赔。造成这一个相对货价算是庞大损失的另一个理由是外国买方声称在订立买卖合约前的一天，曾经通过电话告诉了中国卖方有关这批钢材的特殊用途，是用作机器建造，所以对质量的描述要求得特别严格。包括笔者的仲裁庭是不接受外国买方这一个说法，因为即使接受有电话通知，也认为通知内容不够明确与详细让中国卖方知道这一个要求并愿意接受订立买卖合约。所以，中国卖方是不需要承担Hadley v. Baxendale(1854)9 Ex. 341先例中的"特别损失"(special damages)。但由于中国卖方的确是违约，也就是钢板厚度比合约规定薄了一点，中国卖方还是需要赔偿"一般损失"(ordinary damages)。这一来，针对一般损失在钢材这种市场上肯定有买卖的商品，就完全适用Breach Date Rule与Market Rule。这也是香港《货物销售法》中所规定的损失计算表面规则。但可惜的是，中方代表律师没有对这方面做出争辩，更提不上是提供这方面的证据（更加没有专家证人），导致了仲裁庭没有办法计算违约的一般损失。结果仲裁庭是根据外国买方与分买方所达成的和解协议粗略的做出折扣，作为是从特别损失调整为一般损失后中国卖方应该赔偿的金额。但根据笔者对钢材市场的了解，如果中国律师提出了市场价格的差价，应该会是比裁定的损失金额低得多。以下可部分节录裁决书在这方面的内容，也显示了仲裁庭的为难之处：

"With regard to the normal measure of damages in defective goods, in Sale Of Goods Ordinance, Section 55(3) provided for the well-established "Market Rule", as follows:... Based on the Tribunal's general knowledge of the market, there should or would be market price for different thickness of steel at any given time. But neither party had made any submissions regarding market price, let alone adducing evidence, the Tribunal has to treat it as the agreement of both parties that the *prima facie* rule in the measure of damages does not apply in this instance....

In that case, having decided that the Buyer is only entitled to claim general or normal damages against the Seller for the defective Steel in terms of thickness, this Tribunal is in a difficult position to determine the difference in actual monetary value between special damages and normal damages (whether by way of market price or a reliable estimate of the diminution or reduction of value of the Steel by reason of thickness) in this case.

The Tribunal can exercise its discretion by issuing a Partial Award, leaving aside the exact measure of damages or quantum in this case to be determined by a Final Award. But this is against the wishes of the parties to save costs and obtain a speedy final award. It may also trigger the parties to re-argue the case, such as, in bringing in the Market Rule, which have not been raised in this Award and should not in all fairness be allowed to come back.

The Tribunal can also act inquisitorially by inviting parties for additional submissions over this issue. But this is also problematic in that the outcome of this Award may be revealed prematurely. It may also inadvertently aid one party to the detriment of another party. As Coulson J. in F Ltd. v M Ltd. (2009) 1 Lloyd's Rep. 537 has said: 'It is not, I think, for the arbitral tribunal to hunt through the contract and find other ways in which the claimant's claim might be put, and then offer the claimant a further opportunity to make submissions on any provision thereby identified. In an adversarial system it is for the claimant to identify the ways in which it puts its case.'

The Tribunal has ultimately came to a decision after some protracted deliberations and based on the best estimation it can made on the facts and evidence of this case, together with the general knowledge of the steel market, by reducing 40% from the claimed amount put forward by the Buyer. That is, the Buyer is entitled to recover from the Seller a sum of: US \$ 2.1 million × 60% = US \$ 1.26 million."

5.《联合国国际货物销售公约》不同的规定

英国法律这一个 Breach Date Rule 与 Market Rule 是与 1980 年《联合国国际货物销售公约》(United Nations Convention on Contracts for the International Sale of Goods 或简称 CISG)并不一样,CISG 之 Article 75 规定在违约/毁约的情况下计算受害方损失起点是看转售或买进替代货物的差价为准,如下:"If the contract is avoided and if, in a reasonable manner and within a reasonable time after avoidance, the buyer has bought goods in replacement or the seller has resold the goods, the party claiming damages may recover the difference between the contract price and the price in the substitute transaction as well as any further damages recoverable under article 74."

而根据市场价格只是适用在没有在合理时间内真正转售或在市场买进的情况下，这就是 Article 76 所说的："(1) If the contract is avoided and there is a current price for the goods, the party claiming damages may, **if he has not made a purchase or resale under article 75**, recover the difference between the price fixed by the contract and the current price at the time of avoidance as well as any further damages recoverable under article 74. If, however, the party claiming damages has avoided the contract after taking over the goods, the current price at the time of such taking over shall be applied instead of the current price at the time of avoidance. (2) For the purposes of the preceding paragraph, the current price is the price prevailing at the place where delivery of the goods should have been made or, if there is no current price at that place, the price at such other place as serves as a reasonable substitute, making due allowance for differences in the cost of transporting the goods."（加黑部分是笔者的强调）

在美国 UCC Article 2 – 706 与 2 – 712 也有与 CISG 相似的规定，即只有在替代买卖或交易没有发生的时候才适用 Market Rule 来计算损失。

其中原因之一估计会是 CISG 比较适用在机器/设备等独一无二或特定的货物，因为这种货物往往没有一个可供买卖的市场。而英国《货物销售法》则更适用在"商品买卖"(commodity sale) 如一船的矿砂、石油、煤炭、食糖等，因为这种货物通常都会有市场，只有在没有市场时才根据真正损失来计算赔偿金额。而真正损失在英国法律而言，是被视为是"间接损失"(consequential losses)，"直接损失"(direct losses) 则为比较市场差价的损失。有关这一方面，可参考杨大明律师的《国际货物买卖》（法律出版社 2011 年版）一书第八章。

6. 租船业务与可供租用市场

6.1　航运的争议与损失计算是否会涉及可供买卖/租用市场的简介

航运争议经常会涉及市场价格（市场运费或租金）针对损失计算，如船舶买卖就是与一般的货物买卖没有本质上的区别，而大部分船舶（不论是新旧船）都会有它的市场价格与相近的替代。货损货差也经常会涉及市场价格计算损失，因为有关的货物会有市场买进替代。而争议最多的还是租船业务，其中一种经常出现的争议类别是船东或承租人违约不完成租约，这可以是一个"期租合约"(time charter) 的租期没有完成，也可以是一个"程租合约"(voyage charter) 的航次没有履行，甚至是一个两种租约的混合体即"航次期租"(time – charter – trip, TCT) 没有被履行。造成的原因可以是千变万化，经常会与航运市场波动有关系。如市场上涨，船东就有诱因不想履行原来租金或运费定得偏低的租约（特别是在较长期的期租或多航次运输合约

[COA])。船东很可能会找一些理由拒绝履行,如期租就经常以承租人晚了支付租金为由撤船,在程租就会以各种理由如装港不安全、待装货物并非是合约约定等拒绝履行。这些理由如果站得住脚,船东就可以从收益偏低的租约中脱身,另找市场上更赚钱的替代租约甚至把船舶高价出售。否则,就变为船东违约/毁约,并要对承租人的损失做出赔偿。这一个损失通常就是船东如果履行租约,承租人将会赚取的利润,也就是受害方的"利润损失"(loss of profit)。以上简单的例子也可以反过来是承租人因为市场下跌而有了诱因不想履行原来租金或运费定得偏高的租约(特别是较长期的期租),但也可以是其他原因造成承租人的违约/毁约。例如,经常发生货物供应有了问题,导致 CIF 卖方或是 FOB 买方作为承租人租进了船舶,但到了装港没有货可装。这一来,受害方变成船东要提出利润损失的索赔。

如果针对利润损失的计算,就会想到"市场规则"(Market Rule)。通常船舶都会有一个"可供租用的市场"(available market)有其他同类型的船舶出租给其他的承租人的报道。报道的内容会包括如期租合约的租期长短与租金,或是程租合约的装卸港与运费等。这些报道的成交租约如果有一定的数量,就很容易作出比较并找出违约/毁约一天的市场运费或租金,并计算出"客观的"(objective)"推断损失"(presumed loss)。

针对同类型的船舶,一般会是比货物买卖的同类型要求没有这么高,基本上只要是能够做到同样的营运要求,都会可以当作是同类型船舶比较。即使同类型船舶有较大与重要的差别,如在船龄或耗油量,一般船舶经纪作为专家证人还是可以为这些差别做出金钱上的折让。

但也不难想象到会有情况是在违约的时候,实际上是没有一个可供租用的市场可找到相关的市场价格,估计这种情况会在程租更多出现,而期租合约(尤其是较长期与全球可营运的期租)就相对比较容易了。但在程租的情况下,如在承租人违约/毁约(通常会发生的情况就是在装港没有货可装)的情况下,而有关的装港与货物并非是在一些热门的航线("热门"表示有大量同类的货物与同样装卸港的生意可让船东寻找替代租约),就很难想象到船东能找到同样的替代航次的市场运费,可以比较原程租的运费,并假设两者之间的差别就是船东的损失。受害的船东通常能够减少损失而采取的措施就是另找替代租约(这可以是程租或期租),然后向原承租人提出索赔损失,而损失的计算就只能是根据复原大原则了。但反过来如果船东违约/毁约(通常会发生的情况是船东因为各种不按照租约要求把船舶开去装港),受害的承租人由于手中的货物还在装港,在不少情况下需要很快另找替代船舶把货物运走。这一来如果能够做到,就表示有一个可供租用的市场,承租人的损失就可以根据替代船舶的运费与原租约的运费的差额作为索赔。但如果找不到替代船舶,也表示在违约/毁约的时候没有合理的可供租用的市场,承租人的损失就要根据复原大原则了。这方面的先例有很多,包括近期一点的 The"Kriti Rex"(1996)2 Lloyd's Rep 171 先例(这在本书第三章之 11.4 段有介绍)。

遇到没有可供租用的市场的情况，损失的计算就只能针对真正的损失了。这就会相比以市场价格做出比较的计算办法复杂的多与变化无穷了，因为每一个案件的事实都不一样。简单的例子会是原来违约/毁约的租约时间不长，如只是一个维持15天的程租或航次期租，在受害的船东接受违约/毁约后（假设是船舶到了装港承租人无法提供货物）的15天内都找不到替代租约，可以说船东尽了很大的努力也只能让船舶在装港停留待命。这一来，损失计算会是最容易，只要计算原租约如果履行，船东会赚多少钱就可以了，因为根本不存在合理减损的利益可以在“利润损失”（loss of profit）做出扣减。如果是一个TCT，船东就可以赚取15天的净租金（net hire，通常要扣除佣金），这就是损失金额。如果是一个程租合约，就要把估计能够赚取的运费扣减履行这一短航次的费用与燃油，这也是损失金额。这里可节录Bingham大法官在The“Concordia C”（1985）2 Lloyd's Rep 55先例中所说如下：“Had the owners been unable to find any employment for the vessel during the period which the Rheinoel charter（原租约）would have taken to perform, their loss would *prima facie* have been the net revenue under that charter which they lost, assessed by the arbitrators at USD225,143.00. Had the charter been performed the owners would at 0800 hours on Feb. 16 have had a net profit in their pocket of this sum, plus a free ship.”

但通常情况不会这么简单，真正损失的计算也就会变得困难与不肯定。一个极端的例子会是在一个很赚钱的长期期租合约或多航次运输合约被承租人违约/毁约，船东如果把船舶继续在市场营运或转租会带来损失，倒不如把船舶出售或拆废钢。在市场暴跌后租约被终断的情况下，船东是经常会做出这样的决定。但这一来，真正的损失也就更加难以计算，特别是船舶出售或拆废钢卖的价钱还不错。

但撇开这种极端的例子，受害的船东继续营运与在市场寻找替代租约也会有千变万化的情况。例如，在违约/毁约被接受后的15天的确没有找到替代租约，但船舶并非只是停航在等待替代租约，而是空放去了一个可以赚取相对高租金或运费的地区。如果原租约被履行，船舶在完成15天的短航次之后是会在一个不易找到高利润后续租约的地区。这种情况在航运市场经常会发生，可以赚取高租金或运费的地区往往就是货多船少，如散粮船的情况下会是美湾，如果是油轮就会是波斯湾。至于找不到利润高的后续租约地区，显然就是货少船多，如非洲或是波斯湾（针对散货船）。所以，这一因素也必须考虑在内才能做到真正的复原，而计算起来就往往要靠船舶经纪人的专家意见了。这一方面可节录Staughton大法官在The“Noel Bay”（1989）1 Lloyd's Rep 361先例中所说有关这方面的计算：“Another problem is that the vessel may have been better - or worse - placed for future employment at the end of one voyage than at the end of the other. That is commonly a factor which is said to be relevant.”

这种现象可以举The“Johnny”（1977）2 Lloyd's Rep 1为例，案情涉及欧洲去巴基斯坦Karachi的航次，而在同一时间，如果是从欧洲去Karachi之后还船，每天的租金是6875美元。但如果Karachi去欧洲、美湾或者日本每天的租金只是4800美元。

接下去是假设在受害的船东接受违约/毁约后，船东马上找到并开始履行替代租约（替代租约也是类似的短航次），中间根本没有任何时间损失。这一来，计算损失应该不太难，只要把原租约的预期利润（运费减去履行所要花费的估计费用）减去替代租约的实际利润相比较就是损失的金额了。反过来如果是没有方法减，因为替代租约的利润更高，则船东就没有实际损失，虽然责任是明确的，受害的船东也只能获得名义损失赔偿。如果原租约与替代租约都属于TCT，每天有一笔固定的租金，这就更加容易计算了。例如，原租约租金是15,000美元一天，替代租约（会长过15天）租金为10,000美元一天，则它们之间的差额5000美元一天乘以这段期间的天数（如15天），就是受害的船东的损失。如果原租约与替代租约是属于程租而且履约时间长短不完全一样，也可以通过在两个程租合约中，运费减去履行估计所要花费的费用得出的利润，分别除以两个程租合约所需的不同履行时间，得到的两个租约的每天"同等期租费率"（time charter equivalent，简称TCE）来进行比较，得到的费率差额乘以原租约的天数，就可以得到受害的船东的损失。如果原租约是一个程租，但替代租约为TCT，难度也不会增加多少。只要把原租约的运费减去估计所要花费的费用再除以原租约估计履行的天数，同样找出每天的TCE，就可以与替代租约作出比较了。

但情况千变万化，损失计算也会变得困难与不肯定。除了上述已经介绍过的不同还船或卸货地区会带来很大的影响外，还有另一个重要变数就是替代租约的长短与性质，因为这可能严重影响租金或运费的高低。可以说如果替代租约跟原租约的长短与性质差不多，比方说原租约有15天，替代租约为20天，就可以根据它们每天的租金或TCE的差别作出比较，因为这是所谓"苹果对苹果的比较"（apple to apple comparison）。但如果替代租约是长达3年或5年，就很难与原租约的15天作出比较了，因为变为"苹果对梨子的比较"。至于替代租约为什么订得这样长，有很多商业上与现实上的原因。例如，只有这一种可以找到的替代租约，或者租金相对吸引，或者替代租约的承租人是受害方的船东乐意合作的对象，或者受害方的船东对中长期航运市场不乐观等。反正如果是合理且船东认为对自己有利，就没有理由为了考虑在原租约的索赔中损失计算容易而一定要寻找一个与原租约类似的租约。以The "Johnny"（1977）2 Lloyd's Rep 1先例为例，已经介绍过，TCT的租金为6875美元（从欧洲去Karachi），但如果出租不是TCT而是12个月，每天的租金就变为4800美元了。但这还是要看市场普遍对航运前景的展望，相信是如果普遍认为市场会上涨，恐怕12个月的租金就不会是4800美元而可能比TCT的6875美元还要高。这一来，也会导致原租约的15天不能与替代租约的3年或5年之间的租金差异来直接做出比较，而需要调整。但除非是能够证明替代租约带来很明显的利益，通常是不加以理会。

6.2 期租合约的不履行通常以Market Rule计算损失

说到没有完成或履行的期租与程租，针对受害方提出的利润损失在适用"市场规则"（Market Rule）计算损失的做法有很大不同。这是因为期租经常是针对广泛的航区与可以装运多种货物，反正就是给承租人一个广泛的权利把该船舶营运，导致了不论是中期或长期的租期，所针对的都会是差不多的合约条文与做法。所以在一些比较常见的船型如散装船或油轮，市场上经常有其他同类船舶订下的租金可以做出"苹果对苹果的比较"。所以，一般期租合约涉及将来的利润损失，找出市场价格或租金与原租约的租金比较都不会是太困难。一般而言，市场的租金仅是看一些著名的船舶经纪人所刊登的市场报告都已经有所依据。如果有争议，通常会是船东与承租人各自聘用船舶经纪人作为专家证人，企图说服法院或仲裁庭接受对他们有利的较高或较低的市场租金。例如，针对市场报告中偏高（或偏低）的同类船舶租金，会解释为因该船舶比较省油（或耗油）或是其他原因所造成。笔者估计在很多这种争议，仲裁员会找一个中间的数字做出这方面的事实认定。

6.2.1 适用 Market Rule 计算损失的先例

根据 Market Rule 计算损失相对容易可以看几个在这方面最著名的先例，其中的 The Elena d' Amico（1980）1 Lloyd' s Rep 75 与 The"Wave"（1981）1 Lloyd' s Rep 521 已经分别在本书第十五章之 2.3.6 段与 2.3.7 段介绍过，不重复。在这里只先介绍 The"Product Star"（No.2）（1991）2 Lloyd' s Rep 468 先例，案情涉及该油轮的一个 6 个月加 6 个月的 1 年期租合约，当时是两伊战争期间。船舶在交船后走了 4 个短航次，从阿联酋的 Ruwais 港装运原油去孟加拉吉大港。但到了第五个航次，船长认为太危险拒绝再回去 Ruwais 港口，这最终导致双方各指对方违约/毁约，并接受与终断租约。在英国法院，被判违约方是船东，因为船长拒绝走这个航次的战争风险并没有比订立租约的时候有任何显著的增加。至于损失的计算 Diamond 大法官是这样说："In these circumstances, ADNATCO（承租人）claimed that they were entitled to recover damages based on the difference in October, 1987 between the contract rate and the market rate for the time charter of a vessel to perform the Ruwais - Chittagong voyages for the balance of the charter period. It was rightly submitted that the fact that ADNATCO had not, in fact, chartered in a substitute vessel could not, in principle, affect their right to damages, see *The Elena d' Amico*, (1980) 1 *Lloyd' s Rep* 75 in which it was held by Mr. Justice Robert Goff, as he then was, following ealier cases, that the normal measure of damages in the case of a wrongful repudiation of a time charter by owners was the difference between the contract rate for the balance of the charter - party period and the market rate for the chartering in of a substitute vessel for that period. ADNATCO relied on the financial terms on which they could have chartered *Grazia*（另一艘同类船舶，是承租人考虑租进但没有这样做）as the best evidence of the market rate for the chartering in of a substitute vessel for the balance of the charter period... Having taken into account all the material put in evidence before me, including the figures relating to *Grazia*, as well as those relating *Brilliant* and *Purity*, I find that ADNATCO have established that the market rate for the chartering in of a substitute vessel for *Product Star* was not less than \$ 7,855 per day, made up as follows: \$ 7,600 per day hire, less 1.25 per cent. commission, plus $ 350 per day in respect of war risks premium. I therefore assess ADNATCO's damages for the balance of the charter period at $ 774.65 a day. Appying this figure to the remaining 159.39 days of the charter period, I arrive at the result that ADNATCO's damages in respect of his item of claim amount to $ 123,471.46."

另一个要提到的是 The"Mamola Challenger"(2010)(2011)1 Lloyd's Rep 47 先例,它已经在本书第二章之7段有介绍。在这里只一提是在该长达5年的期租合约,承租人从来没有履行。但承租人的违约/毁约并没有为受害的船东带来任何利润的损失,因为当时市场上涨,船东把该船舶在市场出租,但替代租约可以租到更高的租金。Teare 大法官是这样说:"The rate of hire under the charterparty was US $ 13,700 per day whereas the market rate of hire was US $ 21,347. Thus a result of the termination of the charterparty the owners were able to earn about US $ 7,500 per day more than they would have earned under the charterparty."

所以,根据 Market Rule 的计算是不存在有否真正损失与多寡,根本不需要等待5年才能看该船舶真正营运的经济后果与知道有没有与有多少的真正损失。

6.2.2 期租合约的不履行没有可供租用市场而需要找出真正损失的先例

但也会有一些特殊的案件,是不能适用 Market Rule 而要找出真正损失,这就会导致更麻烦与更富争议性的计算。如在 The"Elbrus"(2010)2 Lloyd's Rep 31 先例,案情涉及一个5个月到7个月的期租,并加上了同一个期限的选择权可以延长,而承租人也的确行使了这一选择权。但在2005年4月4日,承租人违约/毁约并提早把船舶交还。而当时船舶所在地是在西非的安哥拉,比租约中最早还船的时间早了39天。本来按照租约计划还船的地点在美国的休斯顿,时间为2005年5月13日。由于在西非安哥拉是没有"可供租用市场"(available market),也就是根本没有方法为船舶找到替代的租约从西非的安哥拉或附近的地区到美国休斯顿或美湾其他的港口。这一来就要找出真正的损失了,而通过大量的文件披露与调查取证,说明受害方的船东曾经在违约/毁约前成功出租给另一个承租人名为 Navimed,销约期为2005年5月1日到20日(因为没有估计到原租约的承租人会提早还船),租金订的非常高,是每天18,000美元。而原租约只有10,800美元一天。Navimed 租约的交船地点是在地中海,是 TCT,估计要到2005年的6月中才能完结。Navimed 租约还有一个特殊的要求,就是船舶在交船前必须进干坞(freshly drydocked)清洁船底。

受害方的船东在原租约的承租人违约/毁约后,由于西非没有可供租用市场,所以做出决定提早把船舶安排进坞,干坞是葡萄牙的 Setubal。由于当时船舶在地中海的期租市场在下跌,可以说原租约的承租人违约/毁约反而是挽救了 Navimed 租约。原因是原租约如果履行,并在休斯顿按时在5月13日还船,船舶是无论如何也赶不及进干坞清洁船底并及时交船给 Navimed 的。从休斯顿去 Setubal 是要比安哥拉去 Setubal 航程至少要多1天,也没有更近的港口可以进坞。由于地中海的期租市场下跌,而Elbrus类型的船舶在地中海很容易可以找到替代船舶,所以估计Navimed不可能会延长5月20日的销约期。所以,在伦敦的仲裁中,仲裁庭认为原租约承租人的违约/毁约并没有对船东造成实际损失,反而带来好处。裁决书对损失计算的法律观点是作出以下的认定:"1. The normal measure of damages for early redelivery under a time charter is the difference between contract and market rates of hire as at the date of the breach.(提早还船的违约/毁约通常的损失计算是租约与市场租金的差别)2. There was however no available market.(但没有可供租用的市场)3. In those circumstances the measure of damages is 'the sum which would put the Owners in the same financial position as if the charter had been performed'.(在这种情况下损失计算就是把受害的船东复原回到在租约被履行的情况下的经济地位)4. The owners acted reasonably in sailing the vessel to dry dock and delivering her to Navimed, thereby ensuring that that fixture was not lost and earning the high rate of hire under the Navimed fixture earlier than would otherwise have been the case.(船东合理地把船舶安排进坞后并交船给Navimed,保证了这一租约不会失去并赚取比原租约更高的租金,并且提前起租)5. The various permutations and schedules provided by the charterers showed that the owners did not lose as a result of the cancellation of the charterparty but made a gain to a greater or lesser extent.(无论如何计算,船东都没有蒙受经济损失)"

针对期租合约提早还船的损失计算,由于变数多,比房屋的租客提早退租的情况复杂的多。租客违约提早退租,房东作为受害方就有了减少损失的义务。但如果市场太坏没有其他租客有兴趣,或涉及的房子十分古怪,地点十分荒僻,都表示会没有一个可供出租的市场,也就令受害方的房东无法合理减少损失,这计算就相对简单了。

在The"Elbrus"先例中,主要争议是船东真正损失以什么期限做出计算。对船东最有利的计算是从原租约承租人违约/毁约的一天(4月4日)计算到船舶进干坞的一天(4月18日),因为在这一期间中没有一天是有过任何收入的,可以向承租人索赔每天10,800美元的租金而不需要做出任何扣减。

另一个计算是从违约/毁约一天(4月4日)计算到原租约中船舶应还船的一天(5月13日),总共是39天。这一来,这一段时间所赚取的Navimed的高额租金有7天(从5月6日到5月13日)就需要被扣减了。

还有的一种就是违约/毁约一天(4月4日)计算到Navimed租约中更后的一天(6月13日),这会是所谓的"time equalisation"计算办法。这样计算的话显然船东就不会有损失了,正如Teare大法官所说的金额是:"Had the charterparty not been prematurely terminated, the owners would have earned US $ 421,200(that is US $ 10,800 per day from 4 April to 13 May 2005). But as a result of the premature termination the owners were able to earn the higher rate under the Navimed charter of US $ 18,100 per day from 6 May to 13 June 2005. This meant that they earned US $ 226,000 more between 4 April and 13 June than they would have done had the charter been prematurely terminated."

这里就涉及这方面的计算,其中一个大问题就是替代期租通常是不会与原期租的期间是一样的,变成不能做出"苹果对苹果的比较"。所以一贯的做法是在原租约能够赚取的利润中,扣减在原租约履行时间内由替代租约赚取的利润,也就是上述第二种计算办法。这也可以节录将在本章之6.3.5段介绍的The"Noel Bay"(1989)1 Lloyd's Rep 361先例,Staughton大法官所说:"The solution commonly adopted is to take a proportion of the profits on the substitute voyage to set off against the profits lost on oringinal voyage; otherwise one would be involved in calculations to the end of the ship's working life."

这就表示只是把替代租约的部分收入拿出来做出扣减,也就是提早还船这段时间,而不是把整个替代租约会赚取的利润一并考虑。毕竟替代租约的期间长短、装货种类、还船地点等许多因素都会影响到租金的高低。仅是还船地点,就会影响到替代租约后的另一个替代租约将会赚取的租金高低。都加以考虑,做出损失计算,就会像Staughton大法官所说,要等到船舶使用寿命结束才能算得清楚。

但会有情况是这样的计算并不足够,如替代租约的交船或还船地点是好是坏(这会很大程度影响租金或运费高低),这一来在复原的大原则下,是有说法这些证据显示明显有利益的情况下要做出扣减。在这方面Teare大法官是这样说:"It is to be noted that Staughton LJ makes reference to an invariable problem, namely, that the subtitute voyage lasts longer than the original voyage. He refers to the solution commonly adopted in such a case, namely, to take a proportion of the profits on the substitute voyage to set off against the profits lost on the original voyage. That proportion was not identified but was no doubt the proportion referable to the period of time during which the original voyage would have been performed, as stated by Bingham J in The Concordia C. He identified another problem, namely, that the vessel may have been better placed for future employment at the end of the substitute voyage than she would have been at the end of the original voyage. He did not say how this problem could be solved but presumably such benefit would go to depress recoverable damages as suggested by Bingham J in the Concordia C."

6.3 程租合约的不履行通常需要计算真正损失

涉及单航次的程租合约(或是在个别短期的航次期租),由于每一个合约所针对的货物品种、货量、装卸港、航线或其他方面都会是独特,所以很难适用"市场规则"(Market Rule)比较原租约的运费以找出客观的推断损失,也就是它们之间的差价。因为在违约/毁约的时候通常不会有市场可以找到同类船舶行走同一航次的运费,可以与原租约的运费做出比较以计算损失。这导致在程租合约,如果计算租约不被履行的利润损失,比较少会涉及Market Rule,而是看受害方真正蒙受的损失。

特别是在受害方是船东的情况下,除了是在少数特殊的船舶行走同样主要的航线,几乎可以肯定大部分船东寻找替代租约会是在本质上都不会一样。针对以上所讲,可节录《Voyage Charter》(3rd edn,2007年)一书之21.89段:"The measure of damages recoverable by owners, where a charterer's breach deprives them of the opportunity to earn the chartered freight, is sometimes defined as the difference between the contract and the market rates of freight, thus reflecting the measure of damages recoverable in the case of failure to accept and pay for goods for which there is an available market. In practice, however, there is rarely an available market in substitute charters, in the sense of sufficient cargoes to create a market and available for carriage from the same loading port, to the same destination and the same time as the original chartered voyage..."

反过来受害方是承租人,如果能够找到替代船舶履行有关的航次,也往往看他到底是否在合理减损的情况下租进了该替代船舶的真正损失。而如果承租人事后没有租进替代船舶,往往不可以以 Market Rule 计算损失,因为同样的航次往往不会有市场可以比较(除非涉及的航次是一个主要航线如美湾去日本的65,000吨散粮但如上海去印尼苏门答腊的3500吨钢管就不会有市场)。这带来 Breach Date Rule 与 Market Rule 以外的损失计算办法,在这一方面的问题会在接下去的段节介绍。

6.3.1 船东不履行,受害的承租人怎样计算真正损失

这方面在本书第十五章之2.2.1.2段有提到,包括了介绍 The"Eugenie Livanos"(1941) Vol 69 Lloyd's Rep 125 的贵族院先例。该先例提到程租合约如果不履行,损失计算有三种办法。

第一种计算办法就是另一艘替代船舶的市场运费与租约运费的差价,这是适用 Breach Date Rule 与 Market Rule。但如果没有市场运费,就要考虑其他计算办法。第一种办法的市场与原租约运费的差价已经解释过,就是除了一些热门的航线与货物品种外,通常很少会有市场价格可供比较找出一个客观推断的运费。而如果受害的承租人真正租进另一艘替代船舶,这就有了承租人的真正损失,就是多支付给了替代船舶的运费差价。如果真的是有市场涉及其他可供租用的同类型船舶,会有违约/毁约的船东指称承租人实际租进的替代船舶不恰当与支付太高的运费,并以市场报道其他船舶在同样的程租下与个别承租人约定的运费作为依据。笔者认为这不严格是 Market Rule 的适用,而是根据市场其他船舶所报道的运费质疑承租人真正租进替代船舶的运费。笔者认为主要还是看承租人租进的替代船舶与所支付的运费是否合理(毕竟会与其他在市场上的船舶都会有个别不同之处,如承租人需要尽快在付运期之前找到替代船舶把货物运走),而不会理会其他船舶所报道的运费。毕竟承租人已经租进了替代船舶,并且是履行了,有了已经产生了的损失(多支付的运费)的证据,就没有理由再猜测与推断市场价格。正如在本书第十三章之5段提到的 Macnaughten 勋爵在 Bwllfa & Merthyr Dare Steam Collieries(1891), Ltd v. Pontryprid Waterworks Co(1903) AC 426 先例确定的"Bwllfa 大原则",即开庭审理时应该把已经发生的事实一并考虑。

第二种计算办法就是承租人因为无法履行这一个航次而失去了这一个交易的利

润损失,但这个办法涉及订约双方是否在订约时可以合理预见或料想到的测试。针对程约这种服务性合约,已在本书第三章多段(包括第3段、第3.1段等)有提到,船东作为承运人比不上买卖双方对有关货物买卖的业务与运输货物的用途有足够的了解。所以船东如果不履行,对承租人的交易所带来的利润损失往往会被视为不可预见,在承租人没有预先告知的情况下船东不必负责任。

而第三种计算办法就是货物在船舶"应该"(这算得出来)运抵卸港一天的市场价格,减去运费与保险费,再比较在装港这一票货物价格(FOB价格)的差价。这种计算损失办法会对承租人也是货方特别讲的通,因为船东如果没有违约/毁约并履行该租约的航次,承租人就会顺利把有关货物运到卸港。如果运气好,就可以享有抵达后市场价格如果上升的好处。而显然如果那一天的市场价格是下挫,就表示以这一个办法计算就没有损失。但要注意的是如果第三种计算办法得出的损失金额是比较高昂,承租人就会受到船东的质疑就是如果可以找到替代船舶作出付运,为什么承租人不这样做减少损失。所以,承租人就必须要有充分理由支持他为什么不采取行动减少损失。

6.3.2 承租人不履行,受害的船东怎样计算真正损失

船东如果在原来的程租合约不被承租人履行(通常就是承租人无法提供货物),事后找不到替代租约,甚至在原租约的航次估计完成的15天内还是找不到,导致船舶一直在停泊待命。这种情况下的损失计算十分简单,已在本章6.1段提到。

但比较多的情况是船东会在较早的时间找到替代航次并有了收益可以抵销或者扣减原租约的利润损失,这也是他应该做的事情,就是减少损失。这一来,由于替代租约与原租约的航次往往有本质上的差别,所以真正损失计算会是复杂与富争议性,其中会涉及所有有关损失计算的限制如遥远性(包括损失是否可以预见与因果关系),减少损失(这针对船东作为受害方就是寻找替代租约所获得的好处要做出扣减)等。这计算的困难部分已经在本章6.1段有提到,在这里会加以补充。这些损失计算的复杂性可以在几个比较著名的先例中看到,如 The"Concordia C"(1985)2 Lloyd's Rep 55;The"Noel Bay"(1989)1 Lloyd's Rep 361等。这些先例会稍后进一步介绍,在这里先谈谈为什么单航次的程租合约在船东计算"利润损失"(loss of profit)时会在很多情况下十分困难。因为主要的精神就是复原,把船东放回到原租约被履行的经济地位。这就表示原来的航次如果被履行,除了会收到原租约的运费外,还会有其他原租约带来的一些不容易以金钱量化的好处(或坏处)。这些好处包括是卸港将会是十分临近下一个航次交船地点,或是船东已经安排好船舶进干坞修理的地点,或原租约的卸货地点是在一个非常容易找到下一票货物的地区(货多船少),或原租约卸完货就可以在下一个租约交船,或在一个二手船买卖合约下交船给新船东等。如果原租约不被履行,受害船东在需要合理减少损失的"责任"下找到另一票替代航次。但由于每一个程租合约的独特性,替代航次几乎肯定不会是与原租约的航次一样。这种并非是"苹果对苹果的比较"肯定会带来很多困难,如航次的不同长短

(影响耗油、需要行走两个短的替代航次才足够原航次的估计天数等)、装卸港(港口费用就已经会有很大不同)、货物品种与它的装卸率(也会影响航次的长短)等。这一来会导致了船东在原租约本来有的好处受到影响,如替代租约的卸货地点离开船东原先安排卸货后进干坞或下一租约交船的地点更遥远,导致了需要多花时间与燃油才能到。在复原的大原则下,船东会提出索赔,但承租人也有很多抗辩的理由,其中包括了这种损失(进干坞或下一个租约/船舶买卖合约)是在订约时不可以预见,除非船东事前告知。

而面对船东提出这些原租约如果获得履行会带来的好处,精明的承租人也会挑出一些坏处或不利之处,需要在计算损失的时候做出调整。反正最后就会带来很多的争议与计算的困难,因为原程租合约航次与替代租约航次的许多不同之处会带来一个"苹果对梨子的比较",双方会从许多方面可以争议,如它们的糖分、水分、纤维、营养、市场占有量、当事人的喜好等不同之处,最后怎么样以金钱做出调整,务求使他们达到对等。此外,在替代租约的履行也经常不会是一帆风顺,导致了一些履行中的意外如延误,经常会带来这些额外的损失到底与原租约的违约/毁约是否有因果关系。

6.3.3 程租合约通常计算真正损失的办法

最常见的情况是一般受害的船东接受违约/毁约后不是马上就能找到并开始履行替代租约(替代租约也是类似的短航次),中间会有一段船舶闲置的时间。比方说,原租约本来需要15天完成,但船舶去了装港,承租人无法提供货物,受害方的船东接受违约/毁约并在市场寻找替代租约。船东是在5天后找到替代租约,装港是在附近约1天航程的另一个港口。而替代租约的履行在20天内完成。这一来,就可以带来几种不同计算损失的办法,而且结果都不会一样。第一种办法就是把替代租约所赚取的利润(运费减去使费)除以26天(5天+1天+20天)找出每天的"同等期租费率"(TCE)。第二种办法就是5天等待替代租约的时间不包括在内,每天以原租约的"滞期费率"(demurrage rate)作为"延误损失"(detention damage)。但其余的21天(1天+20天)才是履行替代租约的时间(其中第1天是空放航次的时间,道理是一般做法会把船舶空放的时间算入替代租约的航次中,因为没有这票生意就不会浪费时间与金钱去有关的装港,所以要一并计算这一个航次的TCE,这也是所谓的常见"ballast - laden"计算办法[1]),然后把替代租约的运费减去使费再除以21天找出TCE。第三种计算办法是把1天的空放航次也算在闲置或延误时间,变成总共是6天,而替代航次的TCE就只是根据20天来计算。显然,这样计算的话,TCE会比较

---

〔1〕 有关ballast - laden与另一种名为time equalisation计算办法的不同之处,在本章之6.3.9段的The"Vicky 1"(2008)2 Lloyd's Rep 45先例会介绍。后者的计算是在更长的替代航次下,把船舶估计失去的利润在时间上算到替代航次完成的一天,理由是该替代航次的进一步损失也是由于承租人违约/毁约所导致。这种计算办法得出的损失金额肯定是与"ballast - laden"计算办法不一样。

高,肯定会比第一种计算办法高得多。上述所讲或许假设一些数字会更容易说清楚,第一个假设是净运费(减去了佣金或回扣等)是100万美元;第二个假设是该航次的使费(这包括了许多项目,其中最主要的会是该航次的空放与满载航次估计所要消耗的燃油价值、装卸港的港口使费、代理费、气象导航等与该航次有关的费用)是70万美元;这表示运费减掉使费剩下的利润只有30万美元。如果这30万美元除以26天等于11,538.46美元,这就是该航次的TCE。但如果这30万美元是除以20天,该航次的TCE就上升为15,000美元。

但在这里要探讨的是另一个问题,就是替代租约的20天恐怕只有9天的TCE是需要拿出来作为比较,因为9天加上原来闲置/延误与空放的6天,就等于原租约所需要的15天。至于替代租约余下的11天的TCE,就可以不理会。但以这样的办法计算,也会按不同的情况对承租人或船东有利,反正肯定是不同的计算办法会带来不同的结果,所以双方也往往会有争议。英国法律目前的地位是,原租约与替代租约的比较只算到原租约估计的终结时间。如果要把替代租约余下的时间也计算在内,这计算就会很困难并且是没完没了的。这方面可节录Staughton大法官在The"Noel Bay"(1989)1 Lloyd's Rep 361先例中所说:"... one problem that almost invariably arises, and does in this case, is that the substitute voyage lasts for longer than the voyage under the original charterparty. The solution commonly adopted is to take a proportion of the profits on the substitute voyage to set off against the profits lost on the original voyage; otherwise one would be involved in calculations to the end of the ship's working life."[替代航次如果比原租约航次需要更长的时间,计算办法就只把替代航次所赚取的部分利润抵销原租约失去的利润(运费减去履行航次的使费)。否则就会是计算起来没完没了,直到船舶拆废钢的一天。]

同一说法也可以节录《Scrutton on Charterparties》(21st edn,2008年)之193段:"In an action against a charterer for not loading a cargo, the measure of damage is the amount of freight which would have been earned under the charter after deducting the expenses of earning it and any net profit the ship may, or might have earned during the period of the charter on a substitute voyage... Where the substitute voyage is of a longer duration than the charter voyage, no attempt will normally be made to determine the relative positions of the shipowner in a period after the date on which the charter voyage would have been completed, unless there is clear evidence that the shipowner has obtained a benefit by reason of the longer duration of the substitute voyage."

最后是节录《Voyage Charter》(3rd edn,2007年)之21.89、21.90段:"... the ship will frequently have to proceed to a different loading port, and the substitute voyage will usually commence later than the original chartered voyage, and will finish later, and at a different port of destination.(这是指替代航次通常与原租约不会是一样。) In these circumstances, the damages are normally calculated by making a comparison between the gross profit(namely freight, demurrage and other charges, less voyage expenses) which the owner would have derived from the broken charterparty, and the gross profit which he has earned under the substitute charter or charters, the latter being apportioned so as to reflect the amount earned up to the date when performance of the original charter would have been completed..."[一般计算损失的办法是在两方面做出一个比较,一方面是因为违约/毁约而终断的原租约估计能够赚取的毛利润[就是把原租约的运费、滞期费与其他收费如空放航次奖金等减掉该航次的使费];另一方面是替代航次实际能够赚取的毛利润。然后两方面做出一个比较。如果替代航次时间上比较长,就需要把毛利润除以航次的天数找出 TCE,然后看原租约估计履行天数与替代航次天数之重叠部分的天数,再乘以这个替代租约的 TCE,得出的就是在计算受害的船东的损失时要扣减的金额了。]

接下去的段节介绍一些有关的先例,第一个是 The"Concordia C"(1985)2 Lloyd's Rep 55,第二个是 The"Noel Bay"(1989)1 Lloyd's Rep 361。介绍先例后也会介绍几个伦敦仲裁裁决,反正就是显示计算程租合约没有被履行的真正损失的困难与复杂性。

6.3.4 案例之一:The"Concordia C"

The"Concordia C"(1985)2 Lloyd's Rep 55 先例的案情涉及一个程租合约从西非(尼日利亚/加蓬)去欧洲、地中海、加勒比海、美国西岸与美湾。这看来是一个很特殊的程租合约,一般是不会有这么广泛地域的卸港的。Concordia C 轮是一艘油轮,承租人在该程租合约下要求船舶去尼日利亚的 Forcados 装原油去欧洲。当船舶在1982 年1 月25 日抵达并递交通知书后,发货人宣告他因为技术或设备的问题不能提供原油。这导致承租人对船东宣告程租合约因为受阻而终断。而船东就接受了承租人的违约/毁约(这一方面的责任也是被仲裁庭与法院所认定)。之后船东就找一个替代的租约,是从喀麦隆(Cameroons)装货去美湾。在时间上是 Concordia C 轮抵达喀麦隆装港是在2 月13 日,装货开始是在2 月15 日,最后在美湾卸货完毕是在3 月10 日。而如果原租约没有违约/毁约,估计在尼日利亚装货后去欧洲卸货完毕的时间应该是2 月16 日。

船东之后根据复原大原则向承租人提出索赔。这就分开三个部分的损失:第一部分就是运费的差价,第二部分就是船期的延误,第三部分就是多花的费用,主要是从尼日利亚装港绕航去喀麦隆装港的费用。而仲裁庭作出的判决是如下:

第一部分:在运费的差异方面,取18.33 天,也就是在原租约在尼日利亚的 Forcados 的装货时间开始起算的1 月29 日(注意通知书是在1 月25 日递交的)一直到如果程租合约正常履行的情况下船舶应该在欧洲卸港离开并完成整个航次的2 月16 日。在原租约如果履行的18.33 天中,TCE 应为12,281 美元一天。而在替代租约中,从2 月13 日到3 月10 日,TCE 为9,368 美元一天。将每天 TCE 的差额,即2913 美元一天,乘以18.33 天,得出的53,395.29 美元就应当作为运费收入的差额或利润损失。

第二部分：关于滞期的索赔，仲裁员取了从原租约下装货时间完结（也就是滞期费起算的时间）的2月1日开始到2月15日（也就是船舶在替代租约下装货完成的时间，并请注意这一段时间与第一部分有重叠，因为第一部分计算到2月16日），共计14.33天。用原租约下的滞期费率乘以14.33天，得出的159,430美元就是滞期的赔偿。[实际上仲裁员认为正确的滞期时间应该是15天，从1月29日（这是原租约开始起算装货时间）到2月13日（这是船舶在替代租约下开始装货的一天），但是由于这一点没有被受害方的船东提出，所以仲裁庭也不私自做出裁决。]

第三部分：关于绕航费用，仲裁员判在Forcados的港口费用有3000美元，从Forcados到Kole的耗油有7399美元，这一项共计10,399美元，双方对这一点没有争议。

因此，三个部分加起来裁决的赔偿是共计223,224.29美元。

Bingham大法官认为，仲裁庭在计算损失中应用的原则是正确的，但在计算中出现了重复（在2月1日开始到2月15日的14.33天中重复计算了滞期费与运费差异）。Bingham大法官认为应该有更简单的算法，就是如果船东在原租约的期间内找不到任何替代租约，那么船东的表面损失（即原租约如果被履行承租人应支付的运费减去使费）应是225,143美元。这表示到了2月16日（船舶在原租约下应在该天完成卸货，原租约履行完毕），船东拥有的是该笔净运费的收入与一艘没有租约约束并可马上出租的船舶。但实际情况是，船东在原租约期间临界之前找到了替代租约，该替代租约的装货时间由2月13日的0点开始。所以将船东复原到原租约被履行的经济地位，必须要把船东仍在原租约期间内从替代租约中赚取的利润/好处减去。在该先例中，替代租约占去的好处就是在2月13日0点至2月16日08:00时的一段时间，这3.3天是原租约与替代租约的重叠。在这段时间，替代租约的利润/好处是31,195.44美元（替代租约的TCE乘以3.3天），要从船东的表面损失的225,143美元中扣除。但绕航的费用10,399美元仍然是船东应获得的赔偿部分，这样船东一共可获得的赔偿应该为204,346.56美元。

6.3.5 案例之二：The“Noel Bay”

The“Noel Bay”（1989）1 Lloyd's Rep 361先例涉及船东于1987年5月8日将Noel Bay轮租给承租人运输“汽油”（gas oil），装港为意大利西岸港口，而卸港为广泛的欧洲港口。租约规定装卸时间连续共计72小时，滞期费为8500美元一天。其中租约第4条文规定承租人应在船舶离开上一挂靠港（通常是前一个租约的卸港）之前宣告装港名字。

船舶于5月29日在马耳他卸货完毕，完成上一个租约。这是承租人应当指定装港的最后时刻，但承租人未能这样做。同一天，船舶在马耳他抛锚，等待承租人对装港的指定。在5月30日，船舶驶向意大利西西里的Augusta。到了6月1日，承租人通知说取消租约。船东于6月3日接受违约/毁约并很快找到了一个替代租约。替代租约是从黑海东海岸的Tuapse去叙利亚的Banias。船舶于6月7日到达Tuapse，并于6月17日在Banias完成卸货。

船东向承租人索赔损失,计算是根据好几个不同的“假设”(assumptions)。首先是假设在原租约下,承租人指示船舶在意大利的Augusta装货,然后到法国南部的Lavera卸货。这样一个航次应于6月3日开始至6月9日结束,在6.17天内可完成。船东索赔可以在这一航次中获得的净利润35,543美元,消耗的72小时的装卸时间与4天半(5月29日至6月3日)等待指示的时间的滞期费27,766美元,与从Augusta(原租约待命的意大利港口)到Tuapse(替代租约的装港)的空放航次的使费(主要是燃油)。

受害方的船东索赔分为四个部分。

第一部分:假设原租约航程为从Augusta到Lavera(原租约假设的法国卸港),该航次预计需要6.17天,于6月9日结束,预计可赚取运费为90,350美元,估计花费的使费为54,806美元。因此,预计该原租约下可获得净利润35,543美元。

第二部分:这是最具有争议的部分,船东索赔27,766美元的滞期费或滞期损失。理由是如果承租人没有违反租约第4条文并准时宣告装港名字,船舶就可以提前到达Augusta的装港,并在5月30日凌晨递交通知书与开始起算72小时的装卸时间。这72小时装卸时间应在6月3日08:00时终结,之后的时间包括原租约如果履行会需要估计3天的装卸,显示了船舶会有3.266天的滞期。把这一个滞期的时间乘以租约滞期费的8500美元就得出了27,766美元的滞期费。船东认为这是第一部分损失外的另一笔真正损失。

第三部分:从Augusta到Tuapse的空放航次共花费17,444美元,船东声称这笔使费是用来减少损失以取得下一个替代租约的。

第四部分:船东同意扣减替代租约的部分利润。该期间由船舶抵达Tuapse开始,到6月17日在Banias卸货完成结束,共9.77天。所以,从运费收入的125,019美元减去使费56,618美元,净运费是68,480美元,或7000美元一天的TCE。这一部分的计算有错误,因为船东应当扣减的利润部分应该截止到6月9日,也就是原租约下假设从Augusta去Lavera港的航次结束的一天,共计12,538美元。

承租人接受了35,543美元的利润损失(第一部分),但是拒绝了船东索赔的滞期费(第二部分)与空放航次的使费(第三部分)。承租人指出从Augusta到Tuapse的空放航次应当被视为是Tuapse到Banias航次的部分,而这航次中船东应有3606美元一天的利润。承租人称他只需赔付给船东假设从Augusta到Lavera的原航次(在6月9日结束)与Augusta经Tuapse至Banias的实际替代航次在日期上重叠部分的TCE差价即可。

至于最富争议的第二部分的船东索赔,被高院与上诉庭拒绝。船东索赔的滞期费或滞期损失基本上是以承租人违反租约第4条文没有准时宣告装港名字,所以带来在6月3日接受违约/毁约并终断合约前的3.266天延误。而承租人的抗辩是在这种没有履行的程租合约下计算损失,就是假设原租约航次(notional voyage)如果被履行会带来什么经济后果。所以在本先例中的假设航次,应该从5月29日在马耳他就开始计算,之后去Augusta装货,最后在Lavara卸货,假设航次终结的时间是在6月5日。这样的计算船东只损失35,543美元,船东不能分拆多加一个第4条文的违约,因为计算假设航次的损失,就不应该加上假设航次有任何违约。

承租人的说法看来被上诉庭接受,例如Balcombe大法官说:"The owners do not have two separate claims for damages, to be viewed in isolation, but a single claim for the damage flowing from the Charterers' total failure of performance."但看来更重要船东败诉的原因是他没有在索赔请求中加上这一项损失,是事后想出来的。这是因为在劳合法律报告的总结中把上诉庭拒绝请求的原因单独显示了出来,说:"that at no time was it ever pleaded that there had been a breach of cl. 4 of the charter which gave rise to a right to damages for detention which had accrued before the charter was terminated by the owners' acceptance of the charterers' repudiation, as well as to general damages for loss of freight; the claim as pleaded was simply for damages for repudiation of the charter and the learned Judge was right to say that the owners had suffered no loss beyond the $ 35,543 for loss of freight; the appeal would be dismissed."

至于船东第三部分索赔的损失,上诉庭也支持了承租人的抗辩,判是船东不可以索赔空放航次使费的17,444美元。从Augusta到Tuapse的空放航次应视为替代租约的一部分,该航次使费应当计入接下去从Tuapse到Banias的使费中,然后在计算替代租约的整体收入时,把这些使费从运费中减去。船东只可以索赔2份租约在日期上重叠部分的TCE差价,而不能单独索赔17,444美元的空放航次使费。

简单但希望是可以让读者明了的介绍本先例后,可以看到这种损失的准确计算的复杂性与重要性。在The"Noel Bay"先例,船东曾提出另一个计算办法是:(a)所有船东航次使费自5月29日(在马耳他卸完货)至6月17日(替代租约下在Banias卸完货),共花:237,658.38美元;(b)替代租约下的运费:125,000.00美元;(c)应可索赔的损失是:112,658.38美元。可见,这笔钱与最后船东被判决只能获得的35,543美元是有很大的差别。

在此先例,可总结它在几个疑难的解答如下:

(1)船东不能用这另一种算法索赔112,658.38美元,主要道理是损失计算只应针对如果原租约获得履行的经济地位,而不是针对船东在履行替代租约后的经济地位。否则如果替代租约是很长时间,岂非要漫无止境算下去?而且,它也不符合赔偿的所谓"复原"(*restitutio in integrum*)的大原则。故此船东算至6月17日,而不是只算至6月9日(估计原租约完结的时间),并不正确。

(2)如果在地理环境上,替代租约比原租约有额外好处,如令船舶去了一个在下一航次会赚取极高利润的地区(end up in profitable area),这好处应可折算,虽然The"Noel Bay"先例与这问题无关。

(3)在计算航次利润(如替代航次),空放航次也应算是该航次一部分,不能独立出来。这也公道,可防止船东取巧。例如,在原租约的上海去广州的航次,估计共需10天,但被承租人违约/毁约。船东在哀求承租人履约不果后,在上海滞留5天后才接受违约/毁约,并空放前往新加坡履行一个替代租约。该替代租约是一个"航次期租"(TCT),承租人可在上海开航后接船,每天租金4000美元,或船舶抵达新加坡才接船,则每天租金可以是7000美元。因为空放去新加坡有5天时间是重叠了原租约的时间,船东会想:如果一离开上海马上有租金收入岂非这收益要从损失计算中减除,为数是4000美元乘5天等于2万美元?所以,船东即使是稍不划算仍接受替代租约下抵达新加坡才开始有7000美元租金的收益。这令空放去新加坡的5天看来是毫无收益,不必向原租约的承租人索赔损失时打任何折扣。而且,还可像The"Noel Bay"先例一样多加一笔这空放航次所花的燃油费用。这肯定是不对,索赔损失不能让船东任意摆布。看来,如果替代航次利润一定要包括空放航次在内,则这个不妥的地方可就解决了。这也是在本章之6.3.3段所提到的"ballast - laden"计算办法。

(4)在接受违约/毁约前已产生的延误,船东可在与替代租约比较损失的同时,追加这方面损失。如果同类船舶在当时市场能赚取的收益不好决定,也有先例允许适用原租约内同意的滞期费:Zim Isreal Navigation Ltd. v. Tradax Export S. A. (1971) 2 Lloyd's Rep. 91。

6.3.6 伦敦仲裁之一

伦敦仲裁有很多这种案件,要计算程租合约后的真正损失。接下去段节要介绍的仲裁案件是在笔者的《国际商务游戏规则——英国合约法》第十四章"损害赔偿"中有提到,第一个是原程租合约约定从新奥尔良装货去土耳其,船舶在新奥尔良待装货时被承租人违约/毁约。之后,船东找了一替代租约是在新奥尔良装货去爱尔兰,在爱尔兰之后,船舶空放去比利时的安特卫普交船跑一航次去阿尔及利亚的亚尔吉尔(Algiers)。

有专家证据说明如果原租约被履行,在土耳其卸完货后,最有可能的下一票生意是土耳其装货去阿尔及利亚。

船东说损失计算应是简单的比较:原租约去土耳其与替代租约去爱尔兰的每天TCE收益的差异比较。

承租人说不对,因为爱尔兰是一上佳还船/卸空地点,附近有很多机会可以找下一票生意,而且运费或租金相对其他地区市场会更高。所以去爱尔兰卸货的运费肯定低,所有船东都抢,不能简单的与土耳其的原租约航次比较。承租人认为原租约的假设航次与实际替代租约的航次都应该以阿尔及利亚卸完货为准,之后才比较,这才公平。

承租人也指出船舶在开往爱尔兰时慢速(这些事实估计是在船东披露的航海日志中有记录),导致抵达爱尔兰时碰上长假期带来时间损失,这部分损失要扣除,因为因果关系并非是来自他的违约/毁约。

仲裁庭判的结果是:(1)与土耳其比较爱尔兰确是上佳还船/卸空地点,地理环境的优越确应打折扣。(2)所以,承租人提出的计算办法可以接受,即算至阿尔及利亚为止,来看每天的平均 TCE 收益差异,然后乘以原租约估计所需"期限"(duration)。(3)船东虽要尽合理减少损失义务,但事后攻击船东的商业决定(开往爱尔兰慢速),又说不出什么严重错误,并不被接受。

6.3.7 伦敦仲裁之二

第二个仲裁案例是原租约约定从新奥尔良装货去肯尼亚的蒙巴萨(Mombasa),也是在新奥尔良待装货时被承租人违约/毁约。在等待了一段时间后找不到替代租约,船东只能把船舶空放去巴西。之后总算找到了一票替代航次是巴西装货去印度洋港口。

仲裁庭判的结果是:(1)船东损失应是原租约运费减除:(a)应要花费的估计航次使费,否则不花这些钱是赚不到这笔运费。(b)替代租约所占用了原租约的时间,所带来的额外收益,这是船东成功合理减少损失所获得的利益/好处。(2)在估计原租约(如完成履约需时多久),可/应参考船舶在替代租约的实际履行情况。例如,航速只有 10 节而非是租约做出承诺的 13 节。(3)在替代航次中船舶主机在海上损坏,带来时间损失,这要扣除,船东自己负责,与承租人的违约/毁约也没有因果关系。(4)在替代航次中途的加油港,船舶因文件不妥被港口当局延误,这时间损失也要扣除,船东自己负责,也是与承租人的违约/毁约没有因果关系。(5)在替代航次中曾遇上其他船舶碰撞,但因为这意外是"完全天意"(purely fortuitous),没有任何人为的错误,所以不中断因果链,时间损失不扣除。

6.3.8 伦敦仲裁之三

第三个仲裁案例,涉及一艘油轮的原租约是从尼日利亚装原油去美湾的 LOOP (Louisiana Offshore Oil Platform)卸货。船舶在 3 月 27 日到了尼日利亚装港,但一直没有货装。到了接近两个月后的 5 月 20 日,船东被迫接受违约/毁约。之后,船舶空放去了波斯湾/阿拉伯湾,在海湾口的 Fujairah 港等待下一票生意,由 6 月 15 日等待至 7 月 2 日才总算找到了生意,是从科威特装原油去红海。

仲裁庭判是船东可获得从尼日利亚装港"装卸时间届满"(laytime expired)时开始至租约终断的 5 月 20 日止所有的滞期费赔偿。这会是很大的一笔钱,因为延误时间很长。但 5 月 20 日后船东的运费损失可不易计算。本案件有以下特点:(1)仲裁庭看到有可能的替代生意,几乎都出自波斯湾才有货装。(2)即使原租约的航次有履行,并估计在 5 月 20 日开始(3 月 27 日至 5 月 20 日这一段时间就算是装货与滞期时间),也应该在 6 月 14 日在 LOOP 完成卸货。但这时候,科威特去红海的替代航次仍未找到(7 月 2 日才找到),所以原租约与替代租约根本没有重叠的日子或时间。这一来,带来疑问是替代航次有否额外 TCE 收益要在原租约的损失中做出扣减?(3)去红海的替代航次对船东十分有利,只需要看空放回波斯湾(主要装货与可以赚取高运费的地区市场)的路程:红海去波斯湾口有 2569 海里,尼日利亚去波斯湾口有 6994 海里,LOOP 去波斯湾口有 9628 海里。

仲裁庭认为仅是计算原租约的运费(尼日利亚去 LOOP),再减去这航次在 5 月 20 日如果履行必须支付的航次使费(如燃油、港口费等),这损失结果会让船东赚了经济上的“好处”。所以,即使替代租约是往后才开始,不存在占用原租约时间,仲裁庭仍认为要给一个折扣。

仲裁庭多数成员认为要减去在 LOOP 卸完货之后估计要空放回去波斯湾,与船舶真正在这航次从尼日利亚空放去波斯湾,这两者之间在耗油的区别。

另一位不同意见的仲裁员则是找该船舶在替代航次(尼日利亚至 Fujairah 港等待,再至科威特装货,最后至红海卸货)这整段时间的真正平均的每天 TCE 收益,这应是只有科威特至红海的运费收益然后减去所有这段期间航次使费(燃油、港口费等),再除以所有加起来的天数。这平均的每天 TCE 收益也不会高,如 1000 美元。然后乘以原租约如果在 5 月 20 日能履行至 6 月 14 日在 LOOP 完成的 24 天,等于 2.4 万美元。这笔钱算是替代租约的折扣,要扣减后才是船东的运费损失。

6.3.9　利润损失两种不同计算办法的先例:The“Vicky 1”

The“Vicky 1”(2008)2 Lloyd's Rep 45 先例在本书第六章之 7 段已经有介绍,但涉及的重点不一样。在该章节,针对的是对将来利润损失是否要为“机会损失”(loss of chance)打折扣,但在这里是想介绍计算利润损失的困难与较早 6.3.3 段的脚注中已经提到过的两种不同办法。在本先例以“time equalisation”计算所得出的利润损失是高达 2,360,496 美元。但以另一种“ballast - laden”计算办法,得出的利润损失就只有 850,000 美元。这两个数字是相差很远,虽然是针对同样已经发生了的事实。另一提的是该先例针对船舶碰撞后有责任的一方如何赔偿船舶的利润损失,但在计算损失这方面的道理是与本章所针对的违约/毁约完全一样。所以,需要进一步解释这两种计算办法。

有关的案情是在 2002 年 12 月 12 日,船舶(是一艘 VLCC 的超级油轮)在印尼与另一艘船舶 Front Ace 轮发生碰撞,Vicky 1 轮对碰撞没有责任,但蒙受损失并需要去一个新加坡临近的港口进行修理。在早一天的 12 月 11 日,Vicky 1 轮的船东定下了一个程租合约,承租人是一家大石油公司 Chevron,航次是去波斯湾装原油然后去新加坡或泰国或菲律宾卸货,运费是 World Scale 125。这是一个相当高的运费,而市场在碰撞发生后下挫。由于碰撞必须进行修理,就导致了去装港的销约期赶不上而在 12 月 26 日被 Chevron 取消。船东之后在 12 月 30 日订下了一个替代租约,承租人是另一家大石油公司 Vitol,航次是去西非装货然后去新加坡或日本卸货,但运费只是 World Scale 90。看来,这两个程租合约的卸货地点都比较一致,但想做出“苹果对苹果的比较”还是有重要的差异。其中重要的是航程的长短,Chevron 租约的航次是估计在 2003 年 1 月 20 日就可以完成,但 Vitol 的航次就要在 3 月 18 日才完成。

侵权人的 Front Ace 轮船东说是根据 The“Argentino”(1889)14 App Cas 519 先例,应该是以“ballast - laden”计算损失。根据这一个计算办法,是把没有履行的 Chevron 航次假设被履行,也就是在印尼的 Cilacap 港卸完上一个航次的货物,假设没有碰撞事故就开始履行并在 1 月 20 日完成,计算出每天的 TCE。这也就是 Chevron 租约的运费减去航次的使费,然后除以航次所需要的天数。换言之这就是合约获得履行的经济地位。然后,把真正履行的 Vitol 航次假设也是在 Cilacap 港卸完货物后就马上开往西非,然后把 Vitol 租约所赚取的运费减掉使费并除以该航次所需要的天数找出 TCE。而总共利润的损失就是从开始履行一天至 Chevron 租约完成的一天与 Vitol 租约重叠的同一天得出的天数乘以他们之间 TCE 的差额。反正以这个算法,就是能够把两个租约的空放航次与装运货物的航次(在 Vitol 租约应该只是部分的航次)都能做出计算并找出 TCE。这方面可节录上诉庭 Clarke 大法官有关的判词:"Under the ballast/laden method both the theoretical Chevron voyage and the actual Vitol voyage are defined as starting on completion of discharge at Cilacap and finishing on discharge of Chevron cargo. In this way each voyage has a ballast leg followed by a laden leg and (as set out above) the time charter equivalent is calculated for actual time charter equivalent achieved on the Vitol fixture for the period over which the voyage dates coincide."

这样以"ballast - laden"的计算办法得出的损失就只有 850,000 美元。

但 Vicky 1 轮船东是要求以"time equalisation"的计算办法,这一个办法主要是计算到 3 月 18 日 Vitol 租约完成的一天,毕竟两个租约都在卸港范围是比较一致。在这一个算法下,估计 Chevron 租约在完成的一天是在 1 月 20 日并会带来利润 1,987,765美元(这笔钱如果除以该航次估计的完成天数,就变为 TCE)。而在 1 月 20 日到3 月 18 日,就假设 Vicky 1 轮在当时的市场中随便租出去,估计会赚取的平均利润是 3,553,622 美元。这一笔估计的利润是根据 Vicky 1 轮在 1 月 20 日的油轮市场可以找到的不同程租合约所能够赚取的市场运费减掉这不同航次的使费。而这一段时间,总共有 57 天,是足够完成两个从波斯湾装货去新加坡的航次或一个从波斯湾装货去欧洲的航次。根据这些航次所能赚取的利润,平均数就是 3,553,622 美元,再加上 1,987,765 美元,但减掉 Vicky 1 轮船东实际赚取的 Vitol 租约运费的净利润 3,180,891 美元,就得出了他索赔损失的 2,360,496 美元。

在上诉庭,判是应该以"time equalisation"办法为准。Clarke 大法官对这两种不同计算办法的优劣是这样说:"While this method(这是指"ballast - laden"计算办法)is much used for some purposes in the industry, as the Registrar recognized it has some flaws. First, it is unsuitable for VLCCs which have one major loading area, namely the AG(波斯湾/阿拉伯湾), because it does not reflect the commercial importance to an owner of discharging as closely as possible to the AG. Secondly, it does not take account of different voyage lengths. It is not possible satisfactorily to compare the Chevron voyage which would have ended on 20 January with the Vitol fixture which did not end until 18 March, whereas the time/equalisation method does take account of the overall position until the end of the substitute charterparty, which was entered into as a direct result of the collision."(这是说

"ballast - laden"计算办法在航运市场中经常被使用计算损失，但不适合本案件。本案件涉及超级油轮，她只有一个主要的装货地点就是波斯湾，所以能够在波斯湾附近营运十分重要。笔者估计指 Vitol 租约的航次是去西非，而且是远离波斯湾并加长了这个 Vitol 航次。另是 Vitol 租约的订立也是因为船舶碰撞所引起，就应该把损失计算延伸至替代租约完成的一天）

Clarke 大法官也强调以什么办法计算利润损失没有单一的办法，还是要看每一个不同案件的事实，而主要的目的还是做到复原。

6.4　同一时间的市场有不同租金的选择

上述的 6.3 段是针对程租合约对真正利润损失的计算办法，以下有回去针对期租合约的计算可能会有的问题或争议。已经多次提到过，如果能够以"市场规则"（market rule）计算违约/毁约后带来的利润损失虽然是一个相对简单与快捷的计算办法，但大前提是在违约的一天有可供租用的市场，有市场就表示有其他船东与承租人达成协议的租约与双方可以接受的租金，并在市场被报道。以这种办法计算利润损失虽然是比较简单与快捷，但也不是毫无难度，其中什么才是市场租金？市场租金会根据不同的交船与还船地点与/或期租的长短而在同一时间有不一样的金额。例如，在 The"Johnny"（1977）2 Lloyd's Rep 1 先例，就说到在同一个时间有三个不同的市场租金（数字是假设）：（1）从英国到印度的 TCT，租金高达每天 35,000 美元；（2）英国—印度—英国的"往返期租"（round - voyage time charter），租金每天 30,000 美元；（3）两年的期租合约，租金是每天 27,000 美元。

而原来发生违约/毁约的 2 年期租合约的租金是每天 15,000 美元。法院认为应该采用市场同样是 2 年的期租合约，也就是 27,000 美元减去 15,000 美元等于 12,000美元（重复数字是假设）再乘以延误的天数即可得出损失数额。法院的理由是根据一个"对等比较原则"（like must be compared with like），换言之，原来的租金是根据一个 2 年期租合约条件而订立的，而所谓的市场租金亦只能采取一个对等条件（即是同样 2 年期租合约）为标准。船东当然哇哇大叫，因为若承租人不坚持要多走此超时的"非法航次"（illegitimate last voyage），而在英国就还船给船东，他就可以自己缔结那一个租金高达每天 35,000 美元的租约去印度。但现在的情况，船舶到了印度却只能拿 27,000 美元租金，还船时已大大超出租约最后日期，岂非每天损失 8000 美元？事实就是这样，若船东任由承租人多走一次"非法航次"，到头来损失的是船东，表面上承租人会赔偿超出日期的损失，但这赔偿却很可能不足。

注意的是，The"Johnny"先例只是上诉庭的多数意见，而 Denning 勋爵是认为承租人赔偿应该是比较市场上 TCT 的 35,000 美元租金，说："In either case the amount would be assessed at the market rate then ruling for a time charter trip for a voyage at that time. That is for a time charter for the period of time occupied by such a voyage based on spot rates for the voyage charter but adjusted to a time charter basis. That would be obviously fair and just. The charterer by sending her on that last illegitimate voyage would have received the high market rate then prevailing and should pay damages based on that rate for that voyage."

The"Johnny"先例树立的大道理在一个伦敦仲裁 LMLN No. 557 被依从。虽然在这个案件,期租的租约期很短(所以"对等"的租金相当高)而船舶迟了 80 天还船,但仲裁庭照样容许船东索赔以这一高租金计算出的整个 80 天的差价。

6.5 金融海啸后暂时没有市场对损失计算的困扰

6.5.1 混合计算可否被法院接受

什么是市场租金的问题也出现在 2008 年年底金融海啸之后,当时航运市场一度暴跌超过了 90%,许多高租金的长期期租合约或高运费的多航次运输合约被承租人拒绝履行而终断。笔者见到有部分期租合约还有长达 5 ~7 年不等的时间需要履行,但面对严重甚至致命的亏损,承租人还是硬了头皮终断租约,很多时候甚至不给任何理由或是找一些很牵强的理由。这种违约/毁约一般而言是责任非常明确,虽然也有个别的一两个案件会被违约方承租人提出一些牵强的抗辩,如金融海啸属于不可抗力事件导致合约受阻,但这种抗辩在英国法律下一般不会成功:Classic Maritime Inc v. Lion Diversified Holding Berhad(2010)1 Lloyd's Rep 59 先例。在责任明确后,针对损失的计算并不容易,因为在当时违约/毁约的一天,根本在国际航运市场是没有这么长租期的期租合约被其他船东或承租人达成协议,可以以这些被报道的同样或接近条件的租约与原租约作出比较,并希望这是一个"苹果对苹果的比较"。虽然短航次的活动还是有,但短航次的市场租金不能用作与长期期租的对等比较。但如果不按照 Breach Date Rule 与 Market Rule,船东损失的计算恐怕就要按照真正的损失了。虽然不是要船东营运 5 ~7 年后才能提出真正损失的索赔,但涉及很长期的合约(不论是否是租约),要做出估计将来会真正蒙受的利润损失会是涉及许多更加不肯定的臆猜,结果肯定不准甚至会是天差地别。如果受害方的船东干脆把船舶出售或拆废钢,省的继续亏本营运,真正损失更加是难以计算。有部分仲裁员以其他的办法处理。一种办法是在稍后作出审理的时候,市场已经开始渐渐恢复,虽然数量不多,但已经开始有一些长期的租约可以提供市场价格。但那个时候离开违约/毁约的一天可能已经长达 1 年,照理说那时候的市场价格不能符合 Breach Date Rule 与 Market Rule 视为是违约一天的市场价格作为比较。但没有办法的情况下,有不少仲裁员以这一个晚来的市场价格比较原租约的租金找出将来的利润损失,再加上在这 1 年里的真正损失(这在审理的时候会是已经明确,如有关船舶没有替代租约而抛了 1 年老锚)。这种计算办法可被称为是"混合计算"(hybrid basis)。这在法律上是否可以被接受到了现在已经开始有先例针对,就是 The"Kildare"(2011)2 Lloyd's Rep 360 与 The"Wren"(2011)2 Lloyd's Rep 370。

6.5.2 案例之一:The"Kildare"

在第一个先例 The"Kildare"(2011)2 Lloyd's Rep 360,涉及一个多航次运输合约,而承租人在金融海啸后的 2009 年 1 月拒绝履行。这一来,还剩下了大约 4.5 年的时间才能完成该运输合约的履行。在违约/毁约的时候,市场根本没有这么长期的租约可供比较。双方当事人接受是到了1年后的2010年2月才开始有3~3.5年的同类租约,换言之,是到了那个时候才会有市场价格可以作出比较。受害方的船东的计算办法是"混合计算",但承租人认为后来才出现的市场价格与损失计算无关,除了在证明真正损失的时候看船东是否有合理减少损失,如否应该接受一个长期租约而不应该继续短航次的营运。David Steel大法官同意承租人的说法,认为Market Rule下去根据违约一天的市场计算损失是可以肯定说该损失是违约/毁约直接引起。但如果隔了1年后的市场价格重现,比较作出损失计算就在很大程度涉及船东自己的商业决定,如他估计航运市场会否继续上涨而决定是否长期出租。如果船东订立了一个长期租约,包括了原来承租人违约/毁约的租约的余下租期,该长期租约的租金也就代表了船东的真正损失,不必争议Market Rule是否适用。所以,David Steel大法官认为混合计算的办法是不能接受,说:"The decision in The Elena d'Amico (1980)1 Lloyd's Rep. 75 was to the effect that the normal measure of recovery in cases of premature termination of a charterparty is the difference between the contractual rate for the balance of the charter period and the market rate. But where there is no market at the time of termination, this measure does not and cannot arise. It is common ground that the spot fixtures entered into by Zodiac(船东)at that stage could not be the outcome of an independent decision since no alternative form of mitigation was available. As explained Zodiac submits however that, where a market emerges at some later date on which a term charter covering the residual balance of the period could be fixed, damages for that remaining period should be assessed on the same basis since any alternative employment would constitute independent speculation. The fact that a term market thereafter emerges for the (yet shorter) outstanding balance of the charter period does not in my judgment import with it the proposition that a decision not to take advantage of that market at that later stage becomes a business decision independent of the wrongful termination. The rationale is that acceptance of the market rate at the date of breach is deemed to constitute reasonable mitigation."

6.5.3 案例之二:The"Wren"

这一个判法在接下去的第二个先例The"Wren"(2011)2 Lloyd's Rep 370也被Blair大法官接受。案情涉及一艘新造船舶租约,租期是36~38个月,交船日期是2008年6月21日。在不久后就碰上了金融海啸,而承租人在2008年11月违约/毁约并终断了租约。双方对责任方面是没有争议,承租人承认了他的违约/毁约,剩下的争议是在损失的计算。在违约/毁约当天,市场没有这么长期的租约,这导致了船东只能断断续续在市场上营运,这方面的真正损失可计算出来。到了2009年7月,市场开始恢复以及有了同样租期的市场价格可以作出比较。而船东就以这种混合计算算出两部分的损失,从违约/毁约一天到2009年7月是真正损失,之后直到原租约还船是以Market Rule计算。这被仲裁庭所接受并判承租人败诉要赔偿

22,823,858.90美元。承租人之后向英国法院根据1996年《仲裁法》之Section 69申请上诉,有关的法律观点就是针对第二部分的赔偿金额的15,698,591.45美元是否站得住脚,也就是能否适用在后来才出现的市场价格计算损失?正如上述提到,Blair大法官接受David Steel大法官的判决,认为后来才出现的市场并不能作为Market Rule计算损失。

看来,如果不能适用相对简单的Market Rule计算长期租约的损失,就要考虑其他的应对办法,这会在接下去的段节介绍。

6.5.4　应对办法之一:分开审理(分段核算)将来的利润损失做法

在英国法律下,民事诉讼的起点就是审理一次,而做出的赔偿也是针对所有原告蒙受或将会面对的损失,并要求败诉的被告"马上、一次过与无条件"(immediate unconditional lumpsum award)做出支付。可以说在普通法院,这是唯一的一种救济。在Fournier v. Canadian National Railway(1927) AC 167 PC先例,枢密院明确是英国法院不允许与不合法按年计算与支付损失。正如Pearce勋爵在Murphy v. Stone - Wallwork Ltd(1969)2 All ER 949先例所说:"our courts have adopted the principle that damages are assessed at the trial once and for all."另在Mulholland v. Mitchell(1971) AC 666先例中,Hodson勋爵说:"Damages are accordingly assessed once and for all at the time of the trial notwithstanding that in many cases . . . undetermined matters have to be taken into account."

这带来长期合约(包括长期租约)计算损失的困难,受害方是否需要等到长期合约最后一天届满才能算出真正损失并向违约方提出索赔?如果这是50年的长期合约会否要等50年或45年之久(看违约/毁约的一天),而届时恐怕时效也早已届满。再说,针对将来(特别是时间隔了很久的)实际损失做出准确的预测是非常困难,甚至是不可能的。正如Scarman勋爵在Lim Poh Choo v. Camden and Islington Area Health Authority(1980) AC 174先例所说:"there is really only one certainty: the future will prove the award to be either too high or too low."照说,更好的做法是分多次提出索赔,如过了半年或1年就先以第一个裁决书或判决索赔已经产生了的真正损失,然后再等半年或1年申请第二个裁决书或判决。但这显然是劳民伤财,而且违约方的被告在20、30年后会变成怎样的经济状况也是天知道,变成受害方如果没有取得诉前保全在手,恐怕也不会这样做。再说,这在普通法的领域已经被枢密院的Fournier v. Canadian National Railway先例与其他先例所否定,要改变恐怕是需要通过立法。

这种所谓"分开审理"(split trial)的做法在1996年《Damages Act》之Section 2(1)已经是合法存在,并被2003年《Courts Act》之Section 100所替代。针对侵权案件中的人身伤亡,如果对将来损失赔偿的估计太困难的案件,就可以适用。另在违约的案件也会这样做是在劳合社成员起诉他的承保代理人案件的Deeny v. Gooda Walker Ltd (in liquidation) (No. 3) (1995) 4 All ER 289先例,Phillips大法官认为在RSC Ord 33, rr 3 & 4.2(在民事诉讼改革后是CPR 27.4、27.6、28.6、29.2 & 29.3),法院是有权分开审理将来的损失,因为案件要准确计算将来的损失有很大的困难,如将来会要对第三人的受保人做出的赔付是多少还没有底。但这种分开审理笔者还没有在租约的领域听说过(即使对将来损失的估计是十分困难,如在金融海啸后违约/毁约下被终断的长期租约)。所奉行的做法还是一贯的一次过审理。

最后,可节录《McGregor on Damages》(18th edn,2009 年)之 1 – 015 段所说如下:"In Trans Trust SPRL v. Danubian Trading Co. (1952)2 QB 297 CA, the CA spoke *obiter* of the wisdom of deferring dealing with a head of damage until the extent of the defendant's liability for it became known. This idea was eventually taken up by Phillips J. in Deeny v. Gooda Walker(1995)1 WLR 1206 where he awarded a lumpsum for some items of loss and postpone adjudication on the others. And today there is included within the court's general powers of management the power to direct that part of any proceedings be dealt with as separate proceedings and the power to stay part of the proceedings generally or until a specified date or event(CPR, r. 3. 1[2][e] and [f]). Here then is a further illustration of a detraction from the immediacy of a damages award. However, the possibility of allowing a further award in the future has not been taken too far. Thus, in Firth v. Geo. Ackroyd Junior Ltd. (2001) PIQR Q27, the court was not prepared to give the claimant an indemnity against the risk of having to meet future care costs as this would involve a liability on the defendant to top up the lumpsum at a later stage."

这方面 Andrew Baker 御用大律师在《LMAA Law Review 2010 – 2012》一文中也有提到说仲裁员在 1996 年英国《仲裁法》也没有这种权利,除非是双方当事人同意,说:"Arbitrators under English law have no power, absent agreement, to award payments on account pending some later, final assessment. That is a form of provisional relief, power to grant which the parties are entitled to confer on the arbitrators under section 39(1) of the 1996 Act, but which in the absence of such agreement arbitrators do not enjoy (section 39 [4]). Given arbitrators' general duty to avoid unnecessary delay (section 33[1][b]), and whilst it will not be appropriate to defer the resolution of a dispute that is otherwise ready for final determination on the ground that the repudiated period is still running. Proof on the balance of probabilities, and the concept of the burden of proof, are legal tools sufficient to enable arbitrators to reach a final decision; delaying because of a concern that an assessment made now, as the best estimate arbitrators feel able to make on the evidence presented to them, may in due course compare poorly against what actually happens, is **not necessary** for the governing arbitral purpose of finally resolving the dispute following a fair procedure."(加黑部分是笔者的强调)

6.5.5 应对办法之二:一次过审理并尽量准确估计将来真正的利润损失

一次过审理就带来另一种做法是让法院或仲裁庭对将来(也就是长期合约余下的时间)会蒙受的利润损失作出估计,这种估计经常在一些不涉及有市场的国际工程合约或投资合约中出现。例如，外国公司投资了发电厂，有关合约有50年之久，但过不了二三年就给当局非法没收或充公，这一来对外国投资者的损失就需要估计将来漫长的45～50年每年会赚取的利润，然后再以“贴现现金流”(Discount Cash Flow)为多年后估计的利润打折计算判决或裁决书的赔偿金额。[1] 显然，这种计算办法不会太科学，不见得会比混合计算的办法准确。而且估计一个租约下船东将来会蒙受的真正损失会是比估计一个发电厂的利润更困难，毕竟船舶不会有固定航线或固定货物，不会好像长期投资发电厂会对将来收取的电费与成本在合约有规定或算得出来。但这是目前英国法律的地位，除非这一个法律问题能够上诉去更高的法院，并作出改变。

至于仲裁庭应该怎么样估计将来的利润损失，Andrew Baker 御用大律师在《LMAA Law Review 2010－2012》一文中说：

“The general point to make is the same: this is a fact－finding exercise, to be conducted by reference to evidence. All that has changed is the target: it is not now to find what has happened in the past; but to make a finding as to what will happen in the future. The arbitrators must consider, and make a finding as to, what the parties' evidence has persuaded them will probably occur.

The first stage in the enquiry will normally be to decide what employment the vessel will probably take for the remaining duration. Arbitrators will expect to have evidence of the vessel's actual employment since the repudiation, with associated evidence of the owners' reasons and trading intentions/preferences that led to any choices they have made between different types of available employment. There should also be expert evidence providing the arbitrators with informed, independent, views of the types of employment likely to be available to the vessel for the remaining duration: the arbitrators should consider what that evidence persuades them the vessel is likely to do and make a finding accordingly.（第一步仲裁庭是考虑有关船舶在余下的租期很可能会怎样营运，这会是根据船舶在违约/毁约后直到审理的一段时间中实际的营运。仲裁庭也会有专家证人提供有关该船舶在余下租期会怎样营运的意见。最后仲裁庭会是根据他认为该船舶最可能会做的，并做出认定为将来会发生的事实。这样看来，笔者认为仲裁庭虽然不能以后来才出现的中长期租约市场作为 Market Rule 计算损失，但可以认定有关的船东会在中长期租约市场一但出现，就会很愿意马上出租。）

Such a finding having been made, the arbitrators can move to consider what the vessel will probably earn, as to which they will need assistance from the experts, they will undoubtedlyrecognize that no expert prediction can be truly reliable, and they can only do the best they can on the material presented to them.”（在仲裁庭认定船东将来最可能会怎样营

---

[1] 针对这方面的介绍，可参阅本书第十八章。

运后，他可以进一步从专家证人的意见找出该船舶可能会赚取的利润。专家证人的意见不是真正可靠，但仲裁庭只能根据提供给他最好的资料或证据做出判断。）

Andrew Baker 御用大律师也提到是否有可能在 2008 年金融海啸后虽然在国际航运市场没有中长期的期租合约成交，也就是没有实际的市场可以 Breach Date Rule 与 Market Rule 简单地计算损失，但会有"远期运费协议"（forward freight swap agreement 或简称 FFA）的市场。问题是可否以 FFA 的市场差价计算损失或作为参考？有关 FFA 市场在本书第十五章之 2.3.2 段有详述，另也可参见本书第三章之 10.3 段有关"对冲市场"（hedging market）。只说 Andrew Baker 御用大律师认为以对冲市场计算损失有关的英国法律还在发展，说："English law is still developing its thoughts on what to do with hedging transactions, actual or available, in damages assessments." 只说，对 Market Rule 做出立法的 1979 年《货物销售法》，在 Section 50（3）与 Section 51（3）所针对的"可供买卖市场"（available market）所针对的是实质市场，不是对冲交易市场。

6.5.6　Market Rule 的弹性到什么程度不明确

笔者要指出在介绍过的 The "Wren"（2011）2 Lloyd's Rep 370 先例，船东也有争议说在 2008 年 11 月违约/毁约后没有市场（因为金融海啸的关系），根本没有办法减少损失。而等到了 2009 年 7 月，市场恢复的时候才是他"尽早"（as soon as possible）适用 Market Rule 的一天。至于船东届时是否有订立同样租期的长期期租合约，这在 Market Rule 下是不理会受害方真正的决定。但这一个说法也被 Blair 大法官简单地拒绝，说："Further, I do not think that in the present case the arbitrators 'effectively' assessed loss on the basis of a replacement charter obtained 'as soon as reasonably possible'. That was clearly not the basis of their decision." 看来，如果再碰上好像 2008 年金融海啸的不幸事故，但市场重新出现是要相隔较长的时间，是几个月而不是一两个星期，法律就没有这一个"弹性"（flexibility）了，这 Breach Date Rule 与 Market Rule 的弹性到什么程度也是说不清。

这可重复本章第 1.3.6.1 段提到的 Petrotrade v. Stinnes（1995）1 Lloyd's 142 先例，在长达违约/毁约后的两个星期，也被 Colman 大法官接受可以适用 Market Rule，不严格要求违约的一天。但在 The "Kildare" 与 The "Wren" 先例，看来可供买卖或可供租用市场是在违约/毁约后的大半年或以上才出现，Market Rule 就不适用。估计是这晚来的市场即使有，也只会被作为参考之用让法院对审理将来利润损失时作出估计与认定。

第十七章　索赔损失的诉讼时效

1. 序言

"时效"(limitation of actions)的说法在英国普通法下不存在,但显然允许民事诉讼(不论是侵权还是违约)无限期的拖延不是好事。第一个不好之处是扰民,特别对被告,会是要在心理上与实质上承担一个可能是遥遥无期的索赔。第二个考虑就是虽然要尊重任何有权提出诉讼以保护权利的原告,但如果原告由于自己的延误不尽快执行他的权利,就应该失去。第三个也是很重要的不好之处是时间的逝去令证据流失以及当事人记忆模糊而导致不可能有一个公平的审理。

这方面还涉及举证责任就是在刑事案件(特别是严重的刑事罪行如杀人放火),作为被告是没有任何责任举证他是无辜的,他完全可以保持沉默。举证的责任完全是在提起诉讼的原告,也就是检察院。在检察院提出的证据,如果有任何不完整或疑点,利益都是归被告。被告可以说是根本不必关心保留证据,以保证对自己将来有一个公平的审理。所以,时效并不重要。但涉及民事诉讼,由于总是有一方需要胜诉,所以举证责任变为"平衡的可能性"(balance of probability)。原告提出索赔的诉讼,被告也有必要提供证据以支持他的抗辩。如果被告没有保留任何证据,原告只要有一张纸(文件证据),会是断章取义或片面地记录一些事情,被告就已经有很大的败诉可能性,因为法院或仲裁庭根据唯一的证据认定原告的指控有51%的可能性而胜诉。这表示民事诉讼的时效就完全有必要。

由于以上三个重大原因,所以英国有不少立法规定时效。而针对这方面的大原则,也有不少著名的先例有提到。第一个就是Best大法官在A'Court v. Cross(1825) 2 Bing 329先例所说:"It has been supposed that the Legislature only meant to protect persons who had paid their debt, but from length of time had destroyed the proof of payment... Long dormant claims have often more of cruelty than of justice in them. Christianity forbids us to attempt enforcing the payment of a debt which time and misfortune have rendered the debtor unable to discharge. The Legislature thought that if a demand was not attempted to be enforced within six years, some good excuse for non-payment might be presumed, and took away the legal power of recovering it."

另在Board of Trade v. Cayzer, Irvine & Co(1927) AC 610先例,Atkinson勋爵说:

"The whole purpose of the Limitation Act(民事诉讼时效的立法)is to apply to persons who have good causes of action which they could, if so disposed, enforce, and to deprive them of the power of enforcing them after they have lain for a number of years respectively and omitted to enforce them. They are thus deprived of the remedy which they have omitted to use."

所以英国很早就有立法针对时效的问题,在1623年,就有了第一个立法名为《Statute of Limitation》。之后,又有了许多针对不同方面的立法针对时效,如《Civil Procedure Act 1833》、《Real Property Limitation Acts 1833》、《Real Property Limitation Acts 1874》与《Public Authorities Protection Act 1893》。这些立法之后都被合并在《Limitation Act 1939》,后来这部1939年立法与它后来被修改的立法如1963与1975年的《Limitation Act》都被《Limitation Act 1980》所代替,这也是关于时效目前的立法。

在1980年的立法中,它针对各种不同"诉因"(cause of action)规定了不同的时效,它可以短至1年或长达60年。其中的一些比较常见的诉因与它的时效是:(a)侵权是6年——Section 2;(b)诽谤是1年——Section 4A;(c)"一般合约"(simple contract)是6年——Section 5;(d)执行仲裁裁决书是6年——Section 7;(e)盖印的契约是12年——Section 8;(f)依据法规可取回的钱是6年——Section 9;(g)针对判决书进行的诉讼是6年——Section 24。

总的来说,各种不同的时效期限是在缩短。在1980年立法后也有针对其他方面不同的立法改变或针对时效,如《Latent Damage Act 1986》、《Consumer Protection Act 1987》、《Administration of Justice Act 1985》与《Defamation Act 1996》。

英国在这方面的法律也受到了欧共体的法律影响,如针对人权的《Human Rights Act 1998》。可以说在过去30年,时效的课题是变得越来越复杂。所以,也有不少针对性的书籍探讨,如Ruth Redmond - Cooper所著的《Limitation of Actions》(1992年),Terry Prime与Gary Scanlan所著的《The Modern Law of Limitation》(2nd edn,2001年),Rodney Nelson - Jones与Frank Burton所著的《Personal Injury Limitation Law》(1994年),R. D. James所著的《Limitation》(1996年),David Oughton所著的《Limitation of Actions》(1998年),与Andrew McGee所著的《Limitation Periods》(2010年)。

笔者不会深入探讨各种不同诉因下不同的时效,只一提与商贸关系最密切的违约/毁约时效是规定在《Limitation Act 1980》之Section 5,如下:"**Time limit for actions founded on simple contract**. An action founded on simple contract shall not be brought after the expiration of six years from the date on which the cause of action accrued."其他与商贸关系密切的规定还包括Section 33关于人身伤亡时效,Section 34关于仲裁裁决时效,以及Section 35关于反诉与第三人诉讼的时效。

2. 时效的开始计算与如何保护时效

2.1 什么是诉因?

"诉因"(cause of action)在《Limitation Act 1980》并没有一个法定的定义,该立法只针对"诉讼"(action)有一个定义,就是在 Section 38(1)说明是法院的程序,另在 Section 34(1)包括了仲裁。所以,诉讼是包括了仲裁与法院,而 1980 年立法的时效也同样适用在这两种的诉讼程序。

而虽然在立法没有定义,但普通法对什么是诉因有过定义,其中著名的是在 Coburn v. Colledge(1897)1 QB 702 先例中,Esher 勋爵所说:"Every fact which it would be necessary for the plaintiff to prove, if traversed, in order to support his right to the judgment of the court."换言之,原告必须证明被告欠他一个责任(不论是合约责任或是侵权下的谨慎义务),但被告违反了这一个责任,这就是诉因。

对民事诉讼而言,开始计算时效的起点是假设原告有了诉因,就可以让原告去法院或仲裁庭提起诉讼。这一个起点的一天可称为"date of accrual",这是一个非常复杂的问题,会在下一段详细介绍。

2.2 哪一天开始计算时效

2.2.1 产生诉因一天

"产生诉因一天"(date of accrual),也是时效起算的日子对于时效的长短显然会是很重要,只有原告知道哪一天开始计算时效,才能警觉与及时采取措施保护时效。显然,受害方或原告有了上一小段所讲的诉因,就应该开始计算时效并尽早提起诉讼。在 19 世纪,已经有与合约有关的案例判是 date of accrual 是违约/毁约的一天,并开始计算时效,即使是有关的违约/毁约并没有造成实际的损失。在 Gibbs v. Guild (1882)8 QBD 296 先例中,Field 大法官说:"It was well settled that in actions on assumption the time ran from the breach of the contract, for that was the gist of the action, and the subsequent damage, though happening within six years next before the suit, did not prevent the application of the Statute."

一般而言,合约关系的诉因的产生是有了违约但不要求原告蒙受损失。毕竟违约即使不带来真正的损失还是可以提起诉讼并获得赔偿"名义损失"(nominal damage)。但针对侵权,诉因的产生是需要蒙受了损失,而不仅是侵权方有了疏忽。所以,侵权的 date of accrual 是在受害方或原告蒙受损失的一天。

在贵族院的一个著名先例 Pirelli General Cable Works v. Oscar Faber & Partners (1983)2 AC 1 中,判是一般民事诉讼(包括侵权)都适用诉因一产生就开始计算时效的原则,也就是以 date of accrual 为准。

侵权经常会造成人身伤亡,在另一个贵族院的先例 Cartledge v. E. Jopling Ltd

(1963) AC 758,也判是时效的开始是从伤害发生的一天,即使受害人并不能合理知道他蒙受了什么伤害。但显然如果针对一些潜在的伤害,如受害人的症状在多年之后才显现出来,会是带来不令人满意的情况。

这两个贵族院先例都是针对1939年的立法,所以为了防止可能会造成受害人或原告的不公平,就有了1963年的立法针对人身伤害的时效,并引进了一个"发现原则"(principle of discovery)。

2.2.2 损失被发现一天

在上述提到的1963年《Limitation Act》,针对人身伤亡有了一个新的发现原则,就是在"法院的许可"(leave of the court)下可把时效的计算延长到伤害被发现的一天才开始。这一天可被称为是"损失被发现一天"(date of discoverability)。

由于1963年立法的复杂性,这部立法后来被废除并被1975年立法所取代。现在适用的是1980年立法,在针对人身伤亡的索赔基本上是一致,时效期限仍旧是3年。但是诉讼时效是从诉因产生一天或者原告发现伤害一天开始计算(time begins to run *either* from when the cause of action accures, *or* from the date of the claimant's knowledge),此外是法院也有一个广泛的自由裁量权延长时效。

另是《Latent Damage Act 1986》的立法扩大了针对疏忽的侵权诉因,时效的计算只会从潜在损失被发现后才开始,但加了一个最高15年的时效期限。同样的理念也在《Consumer Protection Act 1987》的立法出现。可以说针对侵权,Pirelli General Cable Works v. Oscar Faber & Partners先例的原则已经很少适用。

针对以上所讲,可节录《McGregor on Damages》(18th edn, 2009年)之9-020段如下:"The current position is that under the provisions of section 11 of the Limitation Act 1980 the limitation period for such claims – from the accrual of the cause of action or, if later, three years from the date of the claimant's knowledge, as defined, and that under the provisions of section 14A, as inserted by section 1 of the Latent Damage Act 1986, the limitation period in actions for negligence in respect of latent damage not concerning personal injury expires six years – which is the normal limitation period for negligence actions generally – from the accrual of the cause of action or, if later, three years from the date of the claimant's knowledge, as defined. This latter statutory change can assist not only property owners suing the damage to their buildings but also clients claiming for economic loss against their professional advisers where, as in Forster v. Outred & Co (1982) 1 WLR 86 CFA, the loss is held to have occurred, long before the client was aware of it, at a time when he acted on the advice. A noval feature of the Latent Damage Act 1986 is that it provides, by way of the insertion of a new section 14B in the Limitation Act 1980, that an action for negligence which is not in respect of personal injury will be barred after 15 years from the negligent act or omission even thought there has by then been neither accrual of the cause of action – by virtue of the occurrence of damage – nor knowledge, as defined, by the claimant. . . ."

2.2.3 侵权与违约开始计算时效一天的不同所带来的问题

已经提到过,在合约关系下诉因的产生是一旦有了违约但不必需要蒙受损失就开始计算时效。但这会产生一些问题,因为在合约关系中,违约发生与蒙受损失或损失被发现之间会有一段时间。即使从技术上说有违约发生,但如果原告没有蒙受损失或者还没有发现损失,他通常就不会起诉索赔。在 Howell v. Young(1826)5 B&C 259 先例,案情涉及原告起诉他的律师(被告),因为在原告与他人签署抵押合约时,他的律师提供了疏忽的建议,导致后来证明这笔抵押不足够为借款提供充分的担保。但从被告提供疏忽的建议导致原告同意抵押直到原告发现这个不充分的担保已经超过了 6 年的时间。最后法院判是这个针对律师的诉讼已经错过了时效,因为开始计算时效的一天是抵押生效的一天。

这种看来对受害人不公平的案件会大量在专业人士向客户疏忽提供意见或服务中出现,就是违约发生的早,但损失在很久以后才出现。可是受害人作为原告提出索赔,就面对错过时效的抗辩。

2.2.4 同步责任可以解决或减轻这方面问题

在法院允许侵权与合约的"同步责任"(concurrent liability)[1]之后,这个方面的问题正在逐渐减少。在同步责任,原告是可以以违约与侵权同时提起诉讼,典型的情况就是涉及专业人士疏忽提供意见或服务造成损失的案件。

这方面可介绍两个重要的先例,首先在 Midland Bank v. Hett, Stubbs & Kemp (1979) Ch. 384 先例中,案情涉及 Walter 先生在 1961 年给予 Geoffrey 先生一个选择权可以在未来 10 年内的任何时候购买他的农场,他们一起请了一位律师(被告)来帮他们完成这笔交易,而被告也为他们草拟了协议。但被告由于疏忽,一直没有依据《Land Charges Act 1925》登记这个不动产契约,之后 Geoffrey 先生也曾经多次向被告咨询过这个购买选择权但没有结果。直到 1967 年 Walter 先生发现他与 Geoffrey 先生之间的不动产契约还没有登记,便把这个农场转让给了他的妻子,使 Geoffrey 先生的选择权不能再行使。之后 Geoffrey 先生起诉 Walter 先生及 Walter 夫人的遗产执行人并败诉。在 1972 年 Geoffrey 先生去世后,他的遗产执行人开始起诉被告所在的律师事务所,要求赔偿由于被告疏忽登记不动产契约给 Geoffrey 先生造成的损失。针对诉讼时效问题,法院判是 Geoffrey 先生的起诉并没有超过诉讼时效。首先对于侵权责任,由于被告的律师与他的客户之间的关系导致律师有一个小心谨慎的义务,被告违反这个小心谨慎义务的行为就构成侵权。由于侵权的诉讼时效是从损失发生一天开始计算,也就是土地被登记在 Walter 夫人名下的 1967 年 8 月 17 日,所以起诉时并没有错过 6 年的侵权诉讼时效。法院判即使是违约责任,原告也没有错过 6 年的违约诉讼时效,因为被告有一个"持续性合约义务"(continuous contractual obligation)登记,也就是每一天可以补救做出登记但没有做都是一个违约的新诉因,直到 1967

[1] 这同步/竞合责任的课题在本书第八章有详论。

年8月17日这个义务不能履行,被告的行为才不再有持续的责任,也就开始计算诉讼时效。

而在涉及同步责任的 Henderson v. Merrett Syndicates Ltd.（1994）3 All ER 506（HL）贵族院先例,时效的问题也得到了更好的解决。案情涉及一些劳合社保险小组的成员（原告）起诉管理这些小组的保险代理人（被告）,称被告的管理行为有疏忽并给他们造成了损失。法院判是他们之间存在的关系导致被告有一个小心谨慎义务,而被告违反小心谨慎义务的行为就构成侵权,时效是从损失发现一日开始计算,原告起诉时没有错过6年的诉讼时效。显然在该先例,部分原告如果通过违约的索赔并不能获得成功,因为已经错过时效。在诉讼时效方面同步责任在该先例所带来的好处可以节录 Goff 勋爵的判词如下:"I think it is desirable to stress at this stage that the question of concurrent liability is by no means only of academic significance. Practical issues, which can be of great importance to the parties, are at stake. Foremost among these is perhaps the question of limitation of actions. If concurrent liability in tort is not recognised, a claimant may find his claim barred at a time when he is unaware of its existence. This must moreover be a real possibility in the case of claims against professional men, such as solicitors or architects, since the consequences of their negligence may well not come to light until long after the lapse of six years from the date when the relevant breach of contract occurred. Moreover the benefits of the Latent Damage Act 1986, under which the time of the accrual of the cause of action may be postponed until after the plaintiff has the relevant knowledge, are limited to actions in tortious negligence. **This leads to the startling possibility that a client who has had the benefit of gratuitous advice from his solicitor may in this respect be better off than a client who has paid a fee.**"（加黑部分是笔者的强调）

2.2.5　合约产生诉因一天

在本书2.2.2段提到过,《Latent Damage Act 1986》与《Limitation Act 1980》都是规定了疏忽的侵权与人身伤亡的诉讼时效是从损失被发现一天开始计算,而针对合约关系,关于诉讼时效起算的产生诉因一天是指违约发生的一天,不需要证明蒙受损失。但合约的情况是千变万化的,什么才构成违约并导致了有诉因产生也有很多变化,所以问题比侵权会更加复杂。由于合约是本书主要针对的课题,所以在接下去的段节会详细介绍不同合约的产生诉因一天。

2.2.5.1　违约何时发生是一个事实问题

违约何时发生并产生诉因通常是一个事实问题,需要根据具体的案情来决定。这可以介绍一个著名的海事先例 The"Mary Lou"（1981）2 Lloyd's Rep 272,案情涉及一个程租合约中要求承租人指定一个"安全港口"（safe port）来让船舶抵达。但事后证明他们选择的港口并不安全而导致船舶遭受损坏。问题是承租人指定不安全港口的违约诉因何时产生的？Mustill 大法官认为并没有严格规定说承租人指定港口的时候就是违约的诉因产生的时候。如果承租人指定的时候港口是安全的，但后来某个时候港口突然变得不安全，违约的诉因就应该从这个不安全的时候开始产生。

2.2.5.2 持续性合约义务

如果被告有一个“持续性合约义务”(continuous contractual obligation)履行某种行为，而被告一直没有履行，就会带来争议到底是在第一天没有履行或是最后一天没有履行去开始计算时效。如果这个持续性义务本应履行的最早或最迟日期很难确定，问题就会更加复杂。在 Shaw v. Shaw(1954)2 QB 429(CA)先例，案情涉及被告因为重婚而违反了婚姻的承诺，因为一个已婚人士对第三人的婚姻承诺是违反公共政策而无效。被告 1938 年与原告结婚，而直到被告的法定妻子 1950 年死亡，被告也在 1952 年死亡后，原告才发现被告在与她结婚前已经有一段合法婚姻。这表示被告在生前一直没有告知原告这一段婚姻，可以说是隐瞒了原告 24 年之久，这是违反了对原告婚姻的承诺。因此原告起诉要求从被告的遗产中获得金钱赔偿，这马上涉及是否已经错过诉讼时效的问题。上诉庭判是没有错过时效，原因是这个违反婚姻承诺的诉因一直持续到 1950 年还是每天在产生一个新的诉因。从 1938 年起被告就一直有对原告持续性地承诺他可以结婚，每天被告都有机会告知原告他以前有一段合法婚姻，但被告没有这样做而构成了违约。直到 1950 年被告以前的合法妻子去世，被告在法律上是的确可以再次结婚，对原告这个承诺才开始不存在违约。但由于被告的这种行为属于欺诈，这也是属于侵权行为，直到 1952 年被告死亡后原告才能够知道这个隐藏的欺诈与她蒙受的损失(损失就是她不是被告的合法遗孀，无法继承被告的财产)。所以立法时效的 6 年是从 1952 年才开始起算，诉讼还没有错过。关于这方面的问题在接下去的 3.4.2.2 段有针对。Denning 勋爵说：“Every man who proposes marriage to a woman impliedly warrants that he is in a position to marry her, and that he is not himself a married man; and he reaffirms that warranty when he afterwards goes through a form of marriage with her — whether in church or in a registry office. To take the familiar words of the banns of marriage, he warrants that there is no“cause or just impediment”why he should not marry her. Every day of their married life he continues the warranty; he warrants that their marriage was valid and that there was no impediment to it. In the present case the law imports that Percy Shaw(被告，也就是重婚与后来死亡的人)gave such a warranty to the plaintiff.... In my judgment Shaw broke his warranty at every point. He broke it when he proposed marriage; he broke it when he married the plaintiff; and he broke it throughout their married life. That breach continued all the time. The most important breach of all was at the moment of his death, because when he died she was not his widow as she thought she was. She was in law a stranger. That is the breach for which, in my judgment, damages can be recovered.”

在另一个先例 Vai Industriess(UK)Ltd v. Bostock & Bramley and others(2003)EWCA Civ 1069 中，案情涉及卖方向买方提供一套设备，并在合约中约定了 2 年的“保证

条文"(warranty)说这套设备不会有任何设计缺陷,并保证在买方接受这套设备后3年内出现的潜在缺陷都由卖方来采取补救措施。这个保证条文是设备根据FOB买卖在1995年7月28日"交付"(delivery)给买方的时候生效。后来设备出现故障,卖方在1999年2月又提供了替代的配件,替代配件也在2000年11月之后出现问题。所以原告2002年2月起诉向被告索赔损失。一审法院判是违约的诉讼时效从交付设备一天开始计算,所以原告已经错过了诉讼时效。去了上诉庭以后,法院认为有关先例导致合约中的保证条文有三种可能的解释:(1)这个条文是一个"持续性承诺保证条文"(continuous promissory warranty),保证该设备在这2年内的每一天都没有设计缺陷并且符合描述;(2)这24个月的期限只是表明在设备交付后的合理期间内该设备具备合适的质量;(3)这2年的期限是为了限制保证的有效期,也就是说,买方必须在这2年提出任何质量不符的投诉。

上诉庭的多数判决是认为这24个月的保证条文是属于第二种解释,即保证在设备交付后的合理期限内该设备具备合适的质量,而不能解释为是保证该设备在这2年内的每一天都不会有设计缺陷并且符合描述。所以违约是在交付时(1995年7月28日)已经产生,而原告起诉时就错过了诉讼时效。但法院认为合约中有一个默示的条文规定任何替代的配件也必须符合原设备的质量要求,被告提供不符合质量要求的替代配件(在1999年2月)的违约行为并没有错过诉讼时效。而针对原告提出的持续性合约保证的问题,法院判是类似Shaw v. Shaw先例中这种夫妻之间的持续性保证具有特殊性,并不适用在货物买卖的商业合约中,这可以节录Newman大法官所说如下:"The relationship of landlord and tenant(Bell v. Peter Browne & Co [1990] 2 QB 495) and husband and wife(Shaw v. Shaw [1954] 2 QB 429) have a continuing quality and character giving rise to an"exceptional"obligation and, in my judgment, are of no assistance when considering a commercial contract for the supply of goods."

2.2.5.3 补偿协议

不少商业合约都会涉及了"补偿协议"(indemnity contract),通常会针对合约一方为另一方做出一些服务但带来对第三人的责任或蒙受损失,就会要他做出这一笔损失的补偿。以笔者熟悉的期租合约而言,就会有许多这种补偿协议。例如,承租人可以要求船长签发提单,而船东因为提单带来的对货方/提单持有人的额外责任(通常针对货损货差)而蒙受损失,承租人要补偿给船东。另一个例子是安全港口/安全泊位,如果该港口或泊位是在承租人的营运命令下挂靠,不安全港口导致船舶损坏与对第三人造成责任(如损坏导致油污或把码头碰坏)也是需要承租人做出补偿。这种补偿协议通常是以明示条文做出,但会有法律认为在这种情况下是理所当然应该做出补偿,就会在没有明示条文的情况下也默示,如针对安全港口:The Evaggelos TH (1971)2 Lloyd's Rep 200先例。如果补偿协议是针对第三人的责任,就经常会在时效方面带来问题。原因是被补偿一方会先要面对第三人的诉讼,如果在有机会胜诉的情况下,是不会想到需要根据补偿协议要求承诺补偿方做出补偿,毕竟要补偿的责任与金额还没有定论,甚至有可能是零。但如果面对第三人的诉讼是败诉,被补偿方再向承诺补偿方要求补偿,这往往会是相隔一段时间。如果在有关的合约有一个短暂的合约时效,就经常会发生错过时效的情况。这一来,在补偿协议下诉因是在什么时候产生,并开始计算时效就变得十分重要。这方面有许多先例,只说在 The "Caroline P"(1984)2 Lloyd's Rep. 466 先例,Neill 大法官考虑了以前的多个先例后,做出了不同补偿协议(明示或默示)的产生诉因与起算时效一天的一般性指引。

该先例案情涉及一个 1974 年的船舶期租合约,合约中的第 8 条文规定"承租人在船长的监督下负责装卸、配载、整理和卸载所运货物并承担相应的费用"(... Charterers are to load, stow, trim and discharge the cargo at their expense under the supervision of the Captain ...)。在 1974 年 11 月,承租人又将这艘船舶转租给了其他承租人。船舶在 Houston 装了 14,600 吨大米后,分别于 1974 年 12 月 13 日与 1975 年 1 月 12 日签发了 2 份提单。船舶在 3 月 31 日抵达最终的卸港也就是伊拉克的 Basrah 港,并在 4 月 21 日完成卸货。但在卸货的过程中收货人发现许多货物被损坏,因此在伊拉克法院向船东提起诉讼要求赔偿。最终伊拉克上诉法院是判船东要赔偿 79,341.412 伊拉克第纳尔币。船东为了向承租人取回这笔赔偿,在 1981 年 3 月 30 日启动了仲裁程序并任命了独任仲裁员。在仲裁中,承租人以船东错过时效作为抗辩,声称:"Further the Charterers received notice of the appointment of the Owners' arbitrator on 9th April 1981. As discharge of the cargo at Basrah took place in March 1975 the appointment was made more than six years after the claim arose. In the premises the Owners' claim is time-barred."

只说在关于诉讼时效的争议,法院判是船东向承租人要求补偿的诉因最早产生于 Basrah 港所在的伊拉克一审法院确定船东对收货人责任的一天,所以船东在 1981 年 3 月 30 日任命仲裁员(并非是承租人最早说的 4 月 9 日)并没有错过诉讼时效。另也提到是,即使诉讼时效在船东需要对收货人承担赔偿责任时开始计算,收货人也只能在完成卸货后或者最早也只能在开始卸货时发现货损才能提起诉讼索赔。由于卸货是在 1975 年 4 月 2 日开始,所以船东也没有错过诉讼时效。

而 Neill 大法官针对不同合约下的补偿协议(明示或默示)的产生诉因一天的一般性指引是如下:

"From a consideration of these cases and other authorities to which my attention was directed it seems to me that it is possible to identify at least three ways in which a person (A) who has become liable to (B) may be able to obtain redress from (C).

The first way is by an action for damages for breach of contract (or warranty). In such a case (A) will be in a position to claim that the incurring of his liability to (B) flowed directly from an act of (C) which constituted a breach of a contract between (A) and (C) or of a warranty given by (C) to (A). The damages will be assessed in accordance with Hadley v. Baxendale principles. The cause of action will date from the date of breach. (第一种是根

据违约索赔损失,这就与补偿没有直接关系。例如,承租人签发的提单不但为船东带来对货方/提单持有人额外责任,而且根据租约条文下承租人无权签发这种提单。这一来,承租人的签发本身构成了违约,船东如果根据违约索赔损失,产生诉因的一天就是承租人违约的一天,也就是不合法签发提单的一天)

The second way is by a claim on an express indemnity. In such a case the extent of the indemnity and the time at which the cause of action arises will depend on the construction of the contract. If the indemnity is an indemnity against liability, as it was held to be in Bosma v. Larsen(1966)1 Lloyds' Rep. 22, the cause of action will come into existence when (A) incurs a liability to (B). It may be that in certain circumstances a liability may be incurred for this purpose when the liability is still merely contingent: see Foirster v. Outred & Co. (1982)1 WLR 86. If, however, the indemnity is a general indemnity, as the relevant clause was held to be in R. H. Green & Sillet Weir Ltd. V. British Railways Board and Kavanagh(Third Party)(1980)17 BLR 94, then time will not begin to run against (A) for the purpose of pursuing his indemnity against (C) until (A)'s liability to (B) has been established and ascertained.... [第二种是根据明示补偿协议,诉因产生的一天需要根据补偿协议的用字/措辞来决定,毕竟明示是超越普通法的默示地位。其中提到的 Bosma v. Larsen 先例也是涉及租约,明示补偿协议是补偿'所有的后果或责任'(all consequences or liabilities)。McNair 大法官判是文字针对责任,就表示诉因的产生是在船东对第三人有了责任的一天。这会是较早的一天,因为就算是船东与第三人有否责任是有争议而需要诉讼,判下来如果船东有责任也不会改变船东对第三人有了责任的一天。在该先例货物抵达意大利港口卸货但有损坏,这是在 1956 年 7 月。意大利法院在 1962 年 3 月判船东要对货方或代位保险人作出赔付。船东在 1965 年 3 月向承租人要求补偿。承租人承认责任,但以错过时效作为唯一的抗辩。法院判承租人胜诉指租约中 6 年的时效是从 1956 年 7 月起算,所以船东错过时效。这一个先例显示了明示补偿协议在用字/措辞上的重要性。举例说,如果明示补偿协议是说明"补偿所有的损失"(indemnify against all losses),这就会不一样了,诉因的产生会是船东对第三人的损失被确立与明确后一天。所以在另一个 County and District Properties Ltd. v. C Jenner & Son Ltd. [1976] 2 Lloyd 's Rep. 728 建筑合约的先例,有关的明示条文是说明分承建商要对承建商作出广泛的一般性补偿(to indemnify and save harmless the contractors against and from any breach, non – observance or non – performance of the provision of the main contract, or any act or omission of the sub – contractor which involved the contractor in any liability and any claim, damage, loss or expense resulting from any breach of duty on the part of the sub – contractor)。Swanwick 大法官判是诉因在承建商的责任被明确后才开始计算时效,所以时效并没有错过。这一个判法显然与 Bosma v. Larsen 先例不一样,Swanwick 大法官认为是明示补偿条文的用字不一样。接下去的 R. H. Green & Sillet Weir Ltd. 先例,Dillon 大法官在两个不同的先例下选择 County and District Properties Ltd. 的先例并说明在‘一般性补偿’(general indemnity)的明示条文,就会需要根据普通法的默示地位在对第三人的责任确立后(通过诉讼或合理和解),才有诉因向作出补偿承诺方提出补偿要求。]

The third way in which(A)may claim against(C)in respect of sums which he has had to pay to(B)is under an implied indemnity. As I understand the matter, such an implied indemnity would *prima facie* be a general indemnity of the kind recognized by the common law. The rules relating to what I have described as a general indemnity were explained by Lord Justice Fletcher Moulton in Re Richardson(1911)2 KB 705 at p. 712 as follows:

If, for instance, B was bound to pay a sum to A and C was bound to indemnify B... then B could not sue C unless he could aver payment to A. It was the same thing whether it was a case of suretytship, indemnity, or contribution. In all cases before you can make a guarantor pay you must prove that you have actually paid the money .... You could file a bill against the principal debtor to make him pay the debt so that you would not be called upon to pay it, and then you obtained a declaration that you were entitled to an indemnity. You could in certain cases have a fund set aside in order that you might be indemnified, to avoid the necessity of your having to pay and then to sue for the money you had paid, which perhaps would not repair your loss and credit even if it discharged the debt. But I do not think that equity ever compelled a surety to pay money to the person to whom he was surety before the latter had actually paid. He might be ordered to set a fund aside, but I do not think that he could be ordered to pay."[第三种是默示协议,诉因的产生是与一般性补偿一样,就是对第三人的责任被确立后的一天。上文也提到它的法律地位是与“担保”(suretyship)、“补偿”(indemnity)或者“分摊”(contribution)一样,也就是原告自己先要作出了支付才能向被告的担保人取回这一笔钱。]

由以上看来,补偿的时效问题并不简单。笔者在这方面处理过与作为仲裁员见过不少处理办法。这种问题特别会出现在航运中的货损货差案件,因为根据1924年的《海牙规则》,索赔的时效只有卸货/交货后的1年,而这个很短的时效通常是强制性适用在提单与通过明示条文(所谓的首要条文)合并在租约。船东一旦面对货方的货损货差索赔,就会需要考虑向承租人要求补偿。但货方的货损货差需要时间通过诉讼或仲裁才能决定,而到了责任确立与赔偿金额明确下来船东再找承租人就往往会面对错过时效的抗辩。为了保护时效,船东与互保协会在遇上这样的危险会有一种做法,这就是面对货方的索赔即使是十分有信心可以抗辩成功,也会先告知承租人。如要求承租人接手对货方的抗辩(这通常受到拒绝)或同意延长时效。如果承租人不合作,船东就会开始仲裁。而如果仲裁需要推进,就可以要求仲裁庭作出一个“宣告裁决”(declaratory award)判承租人在租约下必须补偿船东对货方将会被确定的货损货差责任。

这样做还有一点不肯定,但笔者很少见到有这种争议。就是船东向承租人要求的补偿如果是属于上述 Neill 大法官所讲的第一类(根据违反租约)或第二类(租约有明示补偿条文,用字类似 Bosma v. Larsen 先例),诉因是在对货方产生责任的一天就出现,所以向承租人马上开始仲裁是不成问题。但如果船东向承租人要求的补偿是属于第二类的一般性补偿条文或普通法地位适用,就表示船东对货方的货损货差责任没有被确定前是没有诉因,时效也没有开始起算。这就带来一个疑问是到底能否有效向承租人开始仲裁,即使只是要求一个宣告裁决?笔者看来是不成问题,因为有争议才能开始仲裁,而“争议”(dispute)的定义是十分宽松。所以笔者认为承租人不接受或不吭声有关租约下对船东的补偿责任,这已经是一个争议。另是,诉因的出现针对时效的起算会与衡平法下可以提起补偿的诉讼会有一点不同。看来,衡平法相比普通法会是更加宽松。这可节录在 Re Richardson, Ex parte Governors of St Thomas's Hospital(1911)2 K. B. 705, Cozens - Hardy M. R. 勋爵在第 709 ~ 710 页说:“It is settled at common law that, given a contract of indemnity, no action could be maintained until actual loss had been incurred. The common law view was first pay and then come to the court under your agreement to indemnify. In equity that was not the view taken. Equity has always recognised the existence of a larger and wider right in the person entitled to indemnity. He was entitled, in a court of equity, if he was a surety whose liability to pay had become absolute, to maintain an action against the principal debtor and to obtain an order that he should pay off the creditor and relieve the surety. So that in the view of the court of equity it was not necessary for the person entitled to the indemnity to be ruined by having to pay the full amount in the first instance. He had full power to take proceedings under which that fate might be averted, and he might substantially protect himself and secure his position by coming to the court.”

2.2.5.4 保险合约

有关海上货物“保险合约”(insurance contract)向保险人提出索赔的时效在笔者所著的《海上货物保险》(法律出版社 2010 年版)一书第 12 章第 7 段有详细的介绍。

至于其他类别的“non - marine”保险也有同样的有趣先例针对保险合约的诉因是哪一天产生。在 Lefevre v. White(1990)1 Lloyd's Rep 569 先例,案情涉及一个在 1972 年发生的交通意外,受害人(原告)是发生意外车子上的一个乘客,该车子是由一个司机在酒后驾驶并疏忽造成事故,而事故令该车子失控并猛烈撞向一个金属电线杆,这导致了原告受伤。在 1977 年,原告向该疏忽司机提起诉讼,并最后获得 275,000英镑赔偿的法院判决。但由于没有获得支付,原告需要向英国法院申请把该疏忽司机宣告破产。而由于破产,也导致原告可以根据《Third Party(Rights against Insurers)Act 1930》的立法直接向该疏忽司机的保险人要求赔付。在这立法下,是允许第三人在原来的被告如果死亡或是破产的情况下,可以直接向被告所投保的第三人责任的保险人要求赔付。简单说,这立法除了避免英国法下合同相对性问题(因为保险合约的关系只属于被告的受保人与他的责任保险人,第三人是没有关系),也避免在被告破产的情况下会涉及其他债权人一起分享这一笔责任保险人的赔付。这一方面也可看本书第七章之3.7段。

原告是在1987年向责任保险人发出告票,而保险人作为被告的其中一个主要抗辩是时效已经错过。如果从事故的一天算起来,原告必须提起诉讼或发出告票的最后一天应该是1981年12月16日。而原告在1987年12月7日才发出告票,显然是错过了时效。但原告声称是应该从该疏忽司机破产的一天起算,这一来时效还没有错过。而事实上,直到该疏忽司机被宣告破产,原告在1930年立法下是不会有诉因可以直接向责任保险人索赔。但英国高院判是1930年立法只是把原来受保人向责任保险人索赔的权利转移给第三人,所以原告受保人的时效期限也同样适用在第三人。这表示在这一个先例下,原告败诉,因为时效已经错过。Popplewell 大法官是这样说:

"I accept Mr. Pardoe's(原告的代表大律师)argument that the 1930 Act transfers the assured's rights to the third party. But that does not answer the question in the instant case, which is the nature of the rights transferred to the third party. He has his own cause of action direct against the insurance company, namely to exercise his right to claim all the benefits which attached to the insured... to do so, he must issue proceedings within six years of the cause of the action arising, namely Dec. 16, 1981.

(有关计算时效从疏忽司机破产一天开始的说法), I confess that I find neither logic nor sense in that argument. It would enable a plaintiff to bring an action under the 1930 Act years outside any limitation period contemplated by the Limitation Acts. It would undermine totally the concept that liability under the policy is the starting point for determining when the cause of action arises. Finally, it gets no support that I can see from the wording of the Act - indeed, such authorities as there are and the terminology of the Act itself are to the contrary sense."

另在 Universities Superannuation Scheme Ltd. v. Royal Insurance(2000)1 All ER(Comm)266 先例,涉及"雇员诚信保险"(fidelity insurance policy),判是诉因产生的一天是从不诚实雇员偷钱的一天,并开始计算时效。至于对公司的损失是后来才被发现,这不在考虑之内。换言之,在本章2.2.2段的"发现原则"(principle of discovery)并不适用在这种保险合约关系。

再接下去介绍的是 Virk v. Gan Life Holdings(2000)52 BMLR 207 先例,案情涉及原告投保了一个"重大疾病保险"(critical illness policy)。在该保险合约下,如果原告发生了中风,并继续生存30天,就可以获得22,000英镑的赔付。这被判是继续能够生存30天是原告可以向保险人索赔的先决条件,所以诉因产生的一天是中风之后的30天。这一个先例又可以看到在合约下,条文怎么样拟定会决定诉因何时产生。

最后介绍是 British Credit Trust Holdings v. UK Insurance Ltd.(2003)EWHC 2404(Comm)All ER(D)412(Oct)先例,案情涉及一个保险合约,承保的是原告的汽车融

资租赁业务所蒙受的损失。在保险合约中是有一条时效条文,要求原告在蒙受损失后的一年内提起诉讼。原告在 2001 年 7 月在有关的保单中停止投保,并知道蒙受损失。它在 2002 年 2 月去法院向被告(保险人)发出告票,并在 1 个月之后做出索赔请求,要求赔付投保损失。但在索赔请求中原告漏了一项索赔,就是要求法院做出一个宣告有关原告在提起诉讼后的损失也要被告承担。原告是到了 2003 年 7 月才发觉错漏并做出修改,但被告指这一个修改已经错过了时效。在这里只说法院是判诉因产生的一天是在原告的损失能够被确定的一天,也就是汽车融资租赁下租赁人没有支付租金导致租赁权人(原告)要把汽车收回并在出售后取回多少钱才能够算得出损失。

2.2.5.5 账户

如果双方当事人(他们不一定是银行与客户,而可以是任何的商业或其他关系人士)是在一个"账户"(account)的基础上进行交易的结算,那么就要考虑债权人要求偿还的权利是从账户中有未偿还的款项一天开始还是从做出一个正式的"偿还要求"(notice of demand)一天开始。在 Lloyds Bank v. Margolis(1954)1 WLR 644 先例中,案情涉及 Lyster 先生(第三被告)将自己的农场抵押给银行(原告),银行在抵押合约中允许它的客户通过账户透支,该抵押合约规定客户需要在银行"做出要求"(on demand)后偿还到期的欠款。原告银行在 1938 年 12 月 19 日书面通知第三被告偿还他账户中的到期欠款。1944 年这个农场以及农场的抵押被合法转让给 Morris Margolis 先生。1950 年 11 月 29 日原告向法院要求行使赎回权或者出售这个农场来实现银行的抵押权。原告认为 12 年的诉讼时效应该从它 1938 年做出还款要求开始计算,所以它的赎回权请求刚好没有错过诉讼时效。但被告认为时效是应该从出现欠款一天开始计算。法院最后支持了银行(原告)的观点,认为由于抵押合约中约定做出要求是还款的"先决条件"(condition precedent),所以诉讼时效应该从银行提出还款要求的一天开始计算。银行行使赎回权并没有错过诉讼时效的期限。Upjohn 大法官是说:

"In my judgment, where there is the relationship of banker and customer and the banker permits his customer to overdraw on the terms of entering into a legal charge which provides that the money which is then due or is thereafter to become due is to be paid 'on demand' that means what it says. As between the customer and banker, who are dealing on a running account, it seems to me impossible to assume that the bank were to be entitled to sue on the deed on the very day after it was executed without making a demand and giving the customer a reasonable time to pay. It is, indeed, a nearly correlative case to that decided in Joachimson v. Swiss Bank Corp (1921) 3 KB 110 where the headnote was this: 'Where money is standing to the credit of a customer on current account with a banker, in the absence of a special agreement a demand by the customer is a necessary ingredient in the cause of action against the banker for money lent.'

In this case the agreement has provided quite clearly what is to be done before the bank can sue. They must demand the money."

2.2.5.6 银行账户

有关"银行账户"(bank account),在 Joachimson v. Swiss Bank Corporation(1921)3 KB 110(CA)先例中,法院判不论是存款账户还是往来账户,"还款要求"(demand for repayment)都是起诉的先决条件,所以诉讼时效要从做出还款要求一天开始计算。

但是对于"透支"(overdraft)账户这个规则可能就不适用。在 Parr's Banking Co. v. Yates(1898)2 WB 460 先例,法院判是不管针对主债务、利息、佣金或者其他的银行费用,都是在它到期未还的一天产生诉因,诉讼时效也应该从这一天开始计算。Vaughan Williams 大法官说:"My view is that the cause of action on the guarantee arose as to each item of the account, whether principal, interest, commission, or other banking charge, as soon as that item became due and was not paid, and, consequently, the Statute of Limitations began to run in favour of the defendant in respect of each item from that date.... I think that the interest stands on the same footing as any other item to the debit of the party guaranteed in the account; and that the defendant continues liable as guarantor in respect of interest which has accrued within six years before action, and does not get rid of that liability because his liability to be sued on the guarantee with regard to the principal has become barred by the Statute of Limitations."

2.2.5.7 错误的提取款项

关于"错误提取款项"(wrong debits)的时效问题,可介绍在 National Bank of Commerce v. National Westminster Bank(1990)2 Lloyd's Rep. 514 先例中,案情涉及被告银行错误地在 1978 年 12 月 5 日至 1980 年 3 月 24 日期间从原告的银行往来账户中转账共达 8 次,涉及约 30 万英镑。这些转账命令被被告执行是因为有原告表面授权负责人的签名,但这被事后发觉为伪造签名。原告因此委托他的律师在 1987 年 11 月 30 日、1988 年 5 月 4 日、8 月 1 日与 8 月 31 日分别发信给被告,要求归还这些没有授权的转账。到了 1988 年 9 月 13 日,原告在英国法院提起诉讼,要求法院做出一个宣告是被告没有权转账并需要归还原告这笔损失。被告提出的抗辩其中是包括了原告已经错过时效,因为在每一次错误转账时(重复第一次是发生在 1978 年 12 月 5 日),有关的金钱就已经被提取了,原告的诉因也就产生。

但原告根据上一小段所提到的 Joachimson v. Swiss Bank Corporation(1921)3 KB 110(CA)先例,诉因的产生是原告向被告提出还款要求的一天。这显然是较晚的一天即 1988 年 8 月 31 日(或较早的信函),原告没有错过时效。

英国法院是支持原告的说法,认为只有在原告做出还款要求时,关于偿还错误提取款项的诉因才会产生。Webster 大法官说:

"... If a customer suffers damage as a result of an unauthorized debit, it seems not likely, subject to the precise terms of the agreement between banker and customer, that he has in principle a claim for damages for breach of contract(if only a claim for nominal damages) which arises when the breach occurs.

But the question still remains whether the debits had any effect on the defendant bank's debt to its customer. Merely to plead that they were ineffective, as a matter of fact, is not conclusive in the plaintiff's favour because the question of their effectiveness, though involving question of fact, primarily raises a question of law. Even upon that basis, however, there is authority to support Mr. Donaldson's(原告的代表大律师) submission that as a matter of law the debits are ineffective and that the customer can disregard them and claim as money owed to it by its bank the balance remaining when those debits are left out of account.

... In my view, the plaintiff's claim ... is a claim in debt in respect of which the cause of action arose, since the parties were in the relationship of banker to customer, when the demand was made."

2.2.5.8　汇票

关于拒绝承兑"汇票"(bill of exchange)的时效起算日期问题，是在 Englehill Ltd. v. J. Needham(Builders) Ltd. (1973) AC 992(HL)先例中得到了答案。在该先例，贵族院判是诉讼时效应该从"不予承兑通知"(notice of dishonour)实际收到一天开始计算，或者在正常商业活动下应该收到通知的一天起算。即使当事人很早就知道不予承兑是不可避免的，这也不影响诉因产生并开始计算时效的一天。

2.2.5.9　本票/期票

在 Allendale Ltd v. Mousalem(2004) EWCA Civ 915 先例，案情涉及一个 1988 年 6 月 30 日"发出"(executed)的"本票"(promissory note)。上诉庭判是诉讼时效从本票发出的一天开始计算，而不是做出支付要求但被拒绝的一天，即使它明示写明是"见索即付"(payable on demand)。Buxton 大法官是说："The facts of the matter can be stated extremely shortly. The case concerned a promissory note executed on 30 June 1988, payable on demand. The promissory note was executed as a deed and therefore was a speciality falling under section 8 of the Limitation Act 1980, with a limitation period of 12 years. No demand was made for payment under the note within the period of 12 years. It is, and has been recognised for nearly 200 years as the law, that a promissory note payable on demand is enforceable from the date of its execution, and not from the date of any demand. That was made clear by the high authority of Mr Baron Parke in Norton v. Ellam(1837) 2 M & W 461, where he said at page 464 of that report: 'It is quite clear that a promissory note, payable on demand, is a present debt, and is payable without any demand, and the statute begins to run from the date of it.'"

2.2.6　法律的改变不影响产生诉因一天

开始计算时效的日子也会有其他的争议，如法律的改变导致本来认为是没有诉因的案件变了有了诉因。看来,这不会对开始计算日子有改变,正如 Hoffmann 勋爵在 Kleinwort Benson Ltd v. Lincoln City Council(1999)2 AC 349 先例所说:"the Limitation Act ... as presently drafted is inadequate to deal with the problem of retrospective changes in law by judicial decision."

这种影响可举 Awoyomi v. Radford(2007)EWHC 1671(Admin)先例为例,案情涉及较早的贵族院先例名为 Hall v. Simons(2000)3 All ER 673,判一位出庭大律师再也不能对他的疏忽责任有豁免,这是改变了以前的法律。在 Awoyomi v. Radford 先例,被指控的大律师疏忽是发生在 1995 年,但原告是到了 2000 年才因为法律的改变而知道他可以有一个诉因去向被告(曾经在 1995 年代表他并有疏忽导致原告败诉的大律师)提出损失索赔。问题是计算时效的日子如果是从 1995 年开始,时效已经错过,但如果是从 2000 年开始就没有这个问题。在该先例,被判是从 1995 年就应该开始计算时效。

而这种法律的改变也出现在专家证人方面,这是在 Jones v. Kaney(2011)UKSC 13,30 March 2011,unreported 先例。在英国法律,已经有 400 年的历史给出庭的专家证人豁免疏忽责任。背后的原因是鼓励专家证人为了帮助法院了解专业,尽量坦率陈述他的意见。会出现的情况是专家证人在对方大律师的盘问下,承认他以前做出的专家报告有部分错误或遗漏。但如果这一个承认是导致他的委任方败诉,有危险是他的委任方会事后向他索赔损失,这损失主要就是较早时败诉的诉讼费用,这可能是一大笔钱。委任方会说是这笔损失由于专家证人所引起,因为如果不是他给了一个相当乐观的(但是错误的)专家意见与报告,委任方是不会提起或继续这一个诉讼。但现在已经有了 Jones v. Kaney 的最高院先例,表示专家证人如果有错误或遗漏,再也不能豁免他的疏忽责任,地位与出庭大律师是一致的。这会带来什么后果还要拭目以待,会否是专家证人在出庭时再也不会太坦率,虽然在盘问下明知道他以前提交的专家报告有部分错误或遗漏,也要坚持到底。这至少不会令他的疏忽责任太明确,毕竟任何事情都会有不同意见。但针对本小段而言,这一个法律改变就可能带来许多以前看来是没有诉因的案件有了诉因,让以前败诉的当事人考虑向他的专家证人(如果该专家证人在开庭时改变说法)提出损失索赔。但要小心的是,诉因的产生是在该专家证人疏忽的一天,不是在 2011 年 Jones v. Kaney 先例判决的一天,时效就已经开始计算。

这在普通法的精神而言,也是无可厚非。法院的判决成为先例,表面看来是"改变"法律地位或创造了新的法律,但有说法是法院只是针对每一种不同的情况或事实"发现"(discover)与解释一直存在的普通法地位。如果后来的法院把较早的一个判例视为是错误,不依从,这是因为较早的法院错误理解了普通法地位。这一个名为"declaratory theory of judicial decision"的说法在 Kleinwort Benson Ltd v. Lincoln City Council(1999)2 AC 349 先例被贵族院否定,但这不影响后来的判决"改变"(不仅是"发现")法律地位,是有追溯性的。这也表示英国的法律地位一直是最后的法院所做出的权威性判决,不受较早的错误判决影响。

2.2.7　怎样计算

计算开始时效的日子,通常在诉因产生的第一天中的部分时间是不予理会。换言之,在出现诉因的一天如果剩下了部分时间(但不构成一整天)是不必加在时效的期限内。以一个简单的人身伤害的3年时效为例,由于诉因产生当天不计入时效期限内,但诉讼开始当天是包含在时效期限内的。所以,假设原告是在1995年11月8日受伤,那么他可以在1998年11月8日之前的任何一天起诉,包括1998年11月8日的一整天。

这方面的先例是Gelmini v. Moriggia(1913)2 KB 549,案情是原告手中的本票规定最后支付日期是1906年9月22日但显然是没有作出支付。Channell大法官判是1906年9月23日才是开始计算的日子,这是原告可以提出诉讼的最早的一天。

另可举Marren v. Dawson Bentley & Co(1961)2 QB 135先例,案情涉及原告是在1954年11月8日的下午1点半受到伤害。原告发出的告票是在1957年11月8日。问题是3年的时效是否应在1957年11月7日已经届满,在11月8日才做出的告票已经错过了时效?Havers大法官判是原告没有错过时效,原因是诉因产生的一天不计算在内,也就是1954年11月8日不计算在内,开始的一天是11月9日。

如果时效期限届满的最后一天是周末或者法院不工作的一天(如公众假期),原告必须要在法院开始工作后的第一天"发出告票"(issue his writ)才能保护时效,这方面也在Gelmini v. Moriggia先例有针对。

2.3　如何及时保护时效

2.3.1　立法要求保护时效必须要提起诉讼

及时保护时效,不论是立法或者是合约条文通常是规定要在时效期限内必须开始提起诉讼(包括有管辖权的法院或仲裁庭)。如针对一般合约下的索赔,针对时效的立法《Limitation Act 1980》之Section 5是规定"**An action** founded on simple contract **shall not be brought** after the expiration of six years from the date on which the cause of action accrued."(加黑部分是笔者的强调,它的用字/措辞是6年时效一旦错过,原告就不能提起一个诉讼)。另在笔者熟悉的1971年《海上货物运输法》(Carriage of Goods by Sea Act 1971)之Article 3(6)是规定"the carrier and the ship shall in any event be discharged from all liability whatsoever in respect of the goods, **unless suit is brought within one year of their delivery** or of the date when they should have been delivered."(加黑部分是笔者的强调,它的用字/措辞是交货后1年时效错过,针对承运人与船舶的有关货物诉权就被排除)。在1980年立法,对"action"的定义是一个法院诉讼,但在立法多处会涉及仲裁协议是说明"any action or arbitration"。而在1971年《海上货物运输法》,早已明确"suit"是包括法院诉讼或是仲裁(如果双方有仲裁协议)。在The"Merak"(1964)2 Lloyd's Rep 527先例,上诉庭的Sellers大法官说:"I can see no good reason for giving the word 'suit' in this context the limited meaning which has been advanced. The Hague Rules are of international application, arbitration has long been a method of settling disputes agreed by parties to contracts for carriage by sea, and while it was agreed that there should be a period of limitation there is nothing to indicate that a step in an arbitration would not be as effective as a writ in an action unless 'suit' can only have the meaning in our Courts of an action. I do not find any authority which requires us so to hold. In that context I think the words mean 'unless proceedings are brought within one year', and that the commencement of arbitration proceedings would meet the requirement."

关于在法院何时开始诉讼的问题,英国法院根据《民事诉讼规则》(Civil Procedure Rules)是要求原告向法院递交"索赔申请表"(claim form)与相关费用的支票,然后由法院盖章并记录完成"签发"(issue)这份表格。以上所说在《Chitty on Contracts》(30th edn, 2008 年)之 28 - 116 段有说明如下:"**Legal proceedings.** A cause of action will be barred unless legal proceedings in respect of that cause of action are commenced by the claimant within the limitation period. Proceedings are started when the court issues a claim form at the claimant's request or on the day on which the form was received by the court office (if earlier). The claim form must normally be served within four months after the date of its issue. But the claimant may apply within that period for an order extending the period within which the form must be served. The court has a discretion whether or not to make the order. Under the old Rules of the Supreme Court, however, the court would not exercise its power to grant an extension if the relevant period of limitation had expired, unless good reason existed for doing so. That approach can still be illuminating, albeit not binding, under the Civil Procedure Rules. An application may even be made after the four month period has expired. But the court may then make an order only if the court has been unable to serve the claim form or the claimant has taken all reasonable steps to serve the form but has been unable to do so, and in either case the claimant has acted promptly in making the application. If the claim form is served, but not within the four months or the extended period specified in the court order, the defendant should file an acknowledgment of service and make an application under Pt 11 of the Civil Procedure Rules. This must be done within the period for filing a defence."

2.3.2 什么是仲裁的提起/开始

而仲裁的开始就比较复杂,何谓"开始"(commencement)有时不易确定。这在笔者所著的《仲裁法——从 1996 年英国仲裁法到国际商务仲裁》一书第三章有针对,在 3.2.3 段提到的《UNCITRAL Arbitration Rules》之 Article 3 所要求的严格仲裁通知必须包括的内容,而少了其中任何一项都会使仲裁通知变得无效,进而保护不了时效。由于内容太多,所以不在本章多介绍。本章只在 2.3.5 段针对英国法院能否去延长英国仲裁经常会面对"合约时效"(contractual time - bar)的问题,因为在订约自由下经常会有很短的合约时效在某一些类别的合约如租约或买卖合约中出现。

2.3.3 什么是有管辖权法院的提起诉讼

在本章已经多处有说到，如果在时效届满之前没有开始一个"恰当管辖"(competent jurisdiction)的诉讼，诉权就完蛋。恰当管辖的诉讼有两方面的考虑，第一方面就是针对原告必须是有诉权的当事人：Compania Colombiana de Seguros v. Pacific Steam Navigation(1965)1 QB 101 先例与 The"Leni"(1992)2 Lloyd's Rep 92 先例。这方面也涉及不同国家会有不同的法律，如英国法律下做出了赔付的保险人代位求偿向责任方提出索赔，必须还是以受保人的名义作为原告。这与中国内地(或美国)的法律不一样，所以是如果保险人以自己名义在时效期间内在英国法院提起诉讼，这不是一个恰当管辖的诉讼可以保护时效。在同样的考虑下，提起的诉讼所针对的被告也必须是一个准确与有责任的当事人，否则也是保护不了时效。

第二方面的考虑是开始起诉的有关法院即使对有关的案件(不论是合约或侵权关系)有管辖权，这还是不一定足够。特别在合约下，双方会同意一条"排外管辖权条文"(exclusive jurisdiction clause)或一条"仲裁条文"(arbitration clause)，如果原告漠视这些条文的规定另向其他原因拥有管辖权的法院(如在扣船地点的法院)在时效期限内开始诉讼，这还是保护不了时效：The"Havhelt"(1993)1 Lloyd's Rep 523 先例与 The"Markos N"(2000)2 Lloyd's Rep 243 先例。

2.3.4 英国法院诉讼的提起如果错过时效是无法延长

一旦错过了时效就导致了"诉权的排除"(barring of right)，这方面是不存在公道不公道的问题，如不是原告的过错所导致。这是涉及本章一开始就介绍过的一些关于时效的大原则。但法律总是有例外，除了下一段节会介绍的五种例外情况，还会在非常罕见的情况下错过时效是由于法院的问题。

这方面有近期在民事诉讼改革后的先例，是上诉庭的 St Helens Metropolitan BC v. Barnes(2006)EWCA Civ 1372。首先可节录在《民事诉讼规则》下的保护时效做法，这是在 para. 5 of CPR 7PD，有关的条文是：

"5.1 Proceedings are started when the court issues a claim form at the request of the Claimant(see r. 7.2) but where the claim form as issued was received in the court office on a date earlier than the date on which it was issued by the court, the claim is 'brought' for the purposes of the Limitation Act 1980 and any other relevant statutes on that earlier date.

5.2 The date on which the claim form was received by the court will be recorded by a date stamp either on the claim form held on the court file or on the letter that accompanied the claim form when it was received by the court."

在该先例，原告的律师及时在时效最后一天之前的法院办公时间内递交了索赔申请表与相关费用的支票。但在第二天(星期五)，由于法院的职工罢工，所以没有理会这一份索赔申请表。原告的律师在这天向法院查问，但被告知法院没有人工作，要等到下周一才能"签发"(issue)索赔申请表。这导致该索赔申请表是错过了时效 3

天之久。上诉庭判是在《Limitation Act 1980》的立法下与上述节录的 para. 5 of CPR 7PD，索赔申请表“被带去”（brought）的一天是原告向法院递交的一天，而不是索赔申请表签发的一天。

2.3.5　英国仲裁的提起如果错过合约时效的延长问题

众所周知，仲裁的开始如果已经是错过了时效，被告就可以以这个理由作为抗辩，而且会是万无一失的抗辩。针对笔者有关的业务中（航运与国际货物买卖），这种情况并不少见。而错过时效的时效类别，主要是在“合约时效”（contractual time bar）。这是因为在笔者的航运业务中，当事人（特别是承租人）十分喜欢在合约中加上一条短暂的时效条文，如程租合约中的 Centrocon arbitration clause。

由于订约自由，所以“合约时效”喜欢订多久就多久，国际航运与国际货物买卖也不会受到针对消费者立法的保护。由于 Centrocon arbitration clause 原来版本的 3 个月时效（从卸完货起算）经常导致船东在 100 年前左右国际上的通讯还是非常不发达的时候会因为不知道有了诉因（如船舶在远东港口或南美港口因为延误而产生了滞期费，但在英国的船东无法很快知道），结果错过了这 3 个月的时效的情况比比皆是而造成了大面积的不公平。所以，在英国《仲裁法》的 1934 年版本开始有条文允许延长“合约时效”，只要法院认为是允许被告以错过时效作为抗辩会对原告造成“过度困境”（undue hardship）。这立法的起因可以说是不满意 Centrocon arbitration clause 中太短的“合约时效”而否定订约自由，这方面的历史在 The“Angeliki”（1973）2 Lloyd's Rep. 226 先例有介绍。同样的立法条文也搬去 1950 年英国《仲裁法》，是在 Section 27。

“过度困境”在后来一连串的案例中被法院作出十分宽松的解释，其中最重要的是上诉庭的 The“Pegasus”（1967）1 Lloyd's Rep 302 先例。这导致合约时效不一定起到时效的作用，原告错过时效还是可以去英国法院申请延长时效，而在相对宽松的解释过度困境下（如错过的时间不要太久或是索赔金额较大），法院也经常会允许。更重要是英国开始了针对消费者作出保护的立法（其中最重要的是 1977 年英国《不公平合约法》[Unfair Contract Terms Act 1977]），表示英国认为该保护的群体已经有了保护，其他特别是涉及国际业务的非消费者就应该自己小心，包括是否要在合约中做出很短暂时效条文的承诺。这导致在 1996 年的英国《仲裁法》中把法院延长时效的权力大大收紧。在该立法之 Section 12，一开始说明是针对“合约时效”，说：“（1）Where an arbitration agreement to refer future disputes to arbitration provides that a claim shall be barred, or the claimant's right extinguished, unless the claimant takes within a time fixed by the agreement some step...（a）to begin arbitral proceedings, or...”

接下去在 Section 12（3）针对延长时效只在以下两种情况，说：“（a）情况是双方订约时合理预料之外（that the circumstances are such as were outside the reasonable contemplation of the parties when they agreed the provision in question）；或（b）一方当事人的行为导致不公正去强加在另一方当事人严格的时效规定（that the conduct of one party makes it unjust to hold the other party to the strict terms of the provision in question)。"

在上述第一种情况之 Section 12(3)(a),是绝少发生。双方是同意协议中的时效条文,不论是多长多短,怎能说时效错过,这"不在双方合理预料内"(outside the reasonable contemplation)?同样的考验也出现在合约"受阻"(frustration),这是众所周知在英国法下很少会出现或能够成立的情况,就是造成受阻的原因是双方合理预料外。著名伦敦海事仲裁员 Bruce Harris 先生曾参与 1996 年《仲裁法》的立法,他在该立法生效的时候曾经给了一个假设例子:租约内约定有 12 个月的时效条文,而提单也一般有 1 年的法定时效,这是根据《海牙规则》或有关法律。收货人在提单合约起诉船东是在 1 年内,这一来,船东应在租约内同一时效开始仲裁,以保障这 12 个月(1 年)的合约时效,保护自己向承租人对此货损货差要求"补偿"(indemnity)的权利,否则合约时效一过则无法延长。但是,如提单是在 1 年后收货人才提起诉讼[可以是告票在 1 年内"作出"(issue),但在告票的有效期内才送达,如出了告票的三四个月后],这会导致船东一知道被货方索赔但租约下时效已错过。Bruce Harris 先生认为这是 Section 12(3)(b)所包括的,法院会延长时效。但将来实际判例是如何,仍要等着瞧。

不久后果然出了类似先例名为 The"Catherine Helen"(1998)2 Lloyd's Rep. 511。案情涉及一个程租合约中有一条修改过的 Centrocon arbitration clause,时效是在卸货后的 1 年内提起仲裁。货物是在 1996 年 4 月 13 日卸完,但不久后双方因为滞期费与其他额外的费用有了争议,船东在 5 月 24 日向承租人提起仲裁。这显然是在租约有效的时效期限内,不会有任何问题。但同时船东是面对提单持有人根据提单合约下提出的货损货差索赔,只是货损货差通常是由互保协会去处理,所以是到了 10 月 22 日船东才知道,并通知了已经成立的仲裁庭将来会有一个有关货损货差的补偿诉因要加上。这遭到了承租人的抗拒,指仲裁庭对这一个新加的补偿诉因没有管辖权。本来船东还是有时间另成立一个新的仲裁庭(可以设法委任相同成员的仲裁庭),但船东没有这样做而错过了这 1 年的合约时效。本案例涉及船东向英国法院申请一个"宣告"(declaration),说明原告在原来的仲裁庭加上货损货差补偿的诉因是在有效的时效期限内。或是如果法院认为是的确错过了时效,去在 1996 年《仲裁法》下延长时效。但这被英国法院否定与拒绝,其中针对延长时效部分 Brice 大法官是这样说:"It is not possible or reasonable to find in this case that the commencement of arbitration proceedings regarding an indemnity claim was outside the contemplation of the parties when the charter – party was concluded."一提的就是以上所探讨提单与租约的时效问题,已经在本章之 2.2.5.3 有关补偿协议部分有所针对。

另外也有其他被拒绝延长时效的先例,如:(1)在 Fox & Widley v. Guram(1998)3 EG 142 先例,涉及房东/租客之间的合约。内中规定了房东提高租金并给了通知,租客要在 3 个月的时效内提出"反通知"(counter – notice)等。该先例中房东大幅度提高租金,但租客错过了时效。法院判大幅度提高租金并非是订约时不能合理预料。(2)在The"Siki Rolette"(1999)1 WLR 708先例,案情涉及有关合约的时效条文是通过合并才有,但原告不警觉(合约方经常不会细看合并文件的内容),很晚才发觉合约有时效条文而因此错过了。此外,因稍晚了开始仲裁,变成原先是1950年《仲裁法》适用(适用哪一版本的仲裁法以开始仲裁日子为准)但现在是1996年《仲裁法》适用(1996年立法适用在1997年1月31日当天与之后开始的英国仲裁)。已经说过,1950年立法之Section 27对时效延长十分宽松但1996年的立法就十分严格。但法院判这一些事情都不是订约时无法合理预料。(3)在Harbour and General Works Ltd v. The Environment Agency(1999)2 All ER(Comm.)953(CA)先例,判是只要有疏忽遗漏,即使是极轻微的延误,法院仍是无法去与"合理预料之外"的事扯上关系。上诉庭指出了Section 12(3)(a)的作用是:"让法院在双方当事人订约时无法合理预料到时效会适用的一些情况考虑延期。"(to allow the court to consider an extension in relation to circumstances where the parties would not reasonably have contemplated them as being ones where the time bar would apply)

幸亏,也曾经有过一个先例是同意给予延长时效。但知道了案情,可理解到这是"万中无一"的特殊情况,它是Union Trans - Pacific Co Ltd v. Orient Shipping Rotterdam BV(2002)EWHC 1451(Comm)先例。有关仲裁本是在有效期内开始,但半途发觉原告的公司注册在无意中被吊销,令原告再没有任何法人的身份,这意外马上获得补救,仲裁也就重新开始,但时效已错过。Teare大法官认为这情况在订约时无法预料,故同意延长。

至于另一种情况可以延长时效是Section 12(3)(b),同样是适用情况罕见。但被告仅是沉默或不提醒原告有关时效条文(如The"Catherine Helen"(1988)2 Lloyd's Rep 511先例与Harbour and General Works Ltd v. The Environment Agency先例)并不足满足法院会延长时效。

讲到这里,笔者不禁问:既然如此局限,何不干脆取消这1996年《仲裁法》之Section 12(3)对合约时效条文延长的做法,以免对原告带来"美丽的误会"? 对当事人而言,笔者的建议或警告是:

(1)对合约的时效条文,多想想后果/变数才好同意。例如,将来有机会要索赔对方,就必须有足够时间的时效。如会有补偿行动的可能性,在时效条文应分开针对像《海牙-威斯比规则》(Hague - Visby Rules)的国际公约一样多了一句针对补偿的时效是在出了"诉因"(cause of action)后的另一段更长的时间才是时效/时限。

(2)在业务中要警觉,行动/决策要快与习惯仲裁的做法。如"补偿"(indemnity)有可能,即使"原诉讼"(primary action)仍在进行,补偿行动仍未成熟,也要保护时效先在补偿行动申请一个"宣告"(declaration)有关补偿责任,这一点已经在本章2.2.5.3段提到。

最后一提的是,在英国法律,错过时效不表示仲裁庭没有“管辖权”(jurisdiction)。这可以节录 Hobhouse 大法官在 The“World Era”(1992)1 Lloyd’s Rep 45 先例中所说如下:“the character of the time limit was the same in an arbitration as it was in an action;it provided a procedural bar the remedy which had to be raised as a defence in the arbitration;it did not go to the jurisdiction of the Court or the arbitration tribunal;it merely provided the defendant or respondent with a defence to the claim made by the plaintiff or claimant;the time bar relied on was purely a time bar under the Limitation Act 1980;and in so far as Leif Hoegh(仲裁中的被告)founded their attack on the arbitrator’s jurisdiction on the question of time bar that attack was misconceived and failed.”

所以,错过时效的原告不是向法院申请延长时效,而是去法院提起诉讼,而被告要求“中止”(stay),法院仍会同意中止:The“Siki Riolette”(1999)1 WLR 708。反正是在稍后的仲裁程序中,被告可以以合约或法定时效已经错过作为抗辩。

3. 时效中断计算的情况

一开始计算时效,就不会中断:Prideaux v. Webber(1661)1 Lev 31 先例。这显然是为了法律的肯定,否则时效会很难计算外,太容易中断也会导致时效的立法因为有太多的例外情况就失去了意义。所以不管合理与否,6 年的时效是不会变成 6 年零 1 个月。但法律总会是免不了有一些例外,所以在五大种情况下会是可以中断时效的计算。以下会分段进一步介绍。

3.1 第一种例外情况:仲裁

在《Limitation Act 1980》之 Section 34(5),有说明一份裁决书如果被法院“撤销”(set - aside)或者法院判是仲裁协议失效的情况下,法院是可以下令在仲裁开始的一天直到做出命令的一天不计算在时效期限内。这一个规定的需要可以以一个简单例子说明,如在一个合约的争议中诉因是在 2000 年 1 月 1 日出现,原告在 4 年后的 2004 年 1 月 1 日提起仲裁,仲裁程序拖了 2 年并做出了裁决书,但败诉方向法院申请把裁决书撤销,而法院也的确是在 2006 年 7 月 1 日做出命令把裁决书撤销。造成的结果就是双方当事人需要重新仲裁,好像已经被撤销裁决书的仲裁并没有发生过一样。但问题是想提出另一个仲裁的原告会面临时效已经错过,因为撤销裁决书的一天距离诉因出现的一天已经过去了 6.5 年,即使原告马上开始另一个仲裁也要面对时效已经错过的抗辩。所以,《民事诉讼规则》规定了法院可以中断被撤销裁决书的仲裁所花费的时间,也就是从 2004 年 1 月 1 日直到 2006 年 7 月 1 日的这一段时间不算在 6 年的时效内。

3.2 第二种例外情况:失去能力

在《Limitation Act 1980》之 Section 28、28A 与 38,针对原告“失去或没有能力”

(disability)照顾自己,法院有权延长如针对人身伤害的3年时效。法院在行使这方面的权力或选择权时,会考虑原告有了诉因但因为失去或没有能力而错过时效。如受到了伤害的原告由于失忆或者瘫痪而无法及时提起诉讼。

第一种失去或没有能力是尚未成年的小孩,也就是在18岁以下。这在《Family Law Reform Act 1969》之Section 1有规定。这种情况比较少有争议性,因为它会中断时效的期限毕竟是可以算得出来。例如,在Torpador v. D(2010)LRIR 358先例,受到交通事故意外伤害的小孩只有10岁,这表示他可以到了8年后的18岁才提起诉讼索赔他的损失,而3年的时效也是在他满了18岁才开始计算。

第二种失去或没有能力是根据《Mental Health Act 1983》立法下的自然人,由于精神失常而没有办法照顾他自己的事务与财产。在该立法下,有两种情况下有关的自然人被视为是结论性的精神失常:"(a)while he is liable to be detained or subject to guardianship under the Mental Health Act 1959 and(b)while he is receiving treatment as an in-patient in any hospital or mental nursing home within the meaning of that Act, without being liable to be detained under that Act, being treatment which follows without any interval a period during which he was liable to be detained or subject to guardianship under that Act or by virtue of any enactment repealed or excluded by that Act."

以上所讲的一种情况是"监护人"(guardianship),这表示该失去能力的自然人由于失去能力,所以必须把他的事务与财产交给一个监护人托管。这样做,是需要一个法院的命令,向法院申请是可以由任何有关人士做出,而该申请人士必须要有两个英国注册医生证明有关人士由于精神失常或者其他的障碍,需要一个监护人的命令。监护通常是维持6个月,但可以向法院申请延长这一个期限。而针对中断时效计算,就表示一发生监护人的情况下,时效就会中断。直到监护人的做法中止,时效才继续计算。

至于另一种情况的"扣留"(detention)是与监护人的做法差不多,这是需要两位英国注册医生证明有关人士是没有办法给予适当的治疗,除非他被扣留在医院。

在这一方面,《Mental Health Act 1983》立法有很多变化与争议,在本章是没有办法详细介绍。只说在Chagos Islanders v. AG(2003)EWHC 2222先例,曾经有争议说1980年立法下的失去或没有能力应该有更广泛的情况可以包括在内,如原告由于被告的原因而导致身在英国法院管辖权以外的地方,或是原告的贫穷、无知、没有阅读能力等都属于失去或没有能力。但这不被英国法院所接受。这也是较早提到的不能有太多例外,否则就失去了对时效立法的意义。

失去或没有能力的原告或被告在英国民事诉讼规则下(CPR Pt 21)是不可以为自己做出索赔或抗辩。但这不表示他不可以提出诉讼,只是这样做根据CPR Pt 21是需要委任一位"诉讼之友"(litigation friend)代他进行诉讼。至于是小孩,他如果想提出诉讼,也是需要他的父母或者监护人代劳。

反正在以上所讲的情况在时效方面是可以中断计算,直到失去能力的人士恢复能力或是死亡,时效计算才会开始。也表示一位自然人如果永久失去能力(如变成了植物人),他所拥有的诉因就永远不会错过时效。这方面立法的原则在一些先例也有提到,如在 Turner v. WH Malcolm Ltd(1992)Times Law Reports,August 24,上诉庭的 Glidewell 大法官是这样说:"In section 28 and 38 of the 1980 Act Parliament has in effect provided that there is no limitation period for a plaintiff who is under a permanent disability if he,or his solicitor,did not proceed with his action expeditiously. That meant that the maxim that it was in the public interest that there should be an end to litigation had little or no application to an action by such a plaintiff."

另 Mustill 大法官在 Bull v. Devon AHA(1993)4 Med L Rev 23 上诉庭先例中说:"since the unfortunate plaintiff has been under a double disability for almost all of the time since the asserted under statute to delay the institution of proceedings beyond the point at which,as the Judge has rightly said,it would have been unfair to allow his mother to persist. Parliament must therefore have decided that the public interest in requiring factual disputes to be litigated promptly is outweighed,in cases such as this,by the public interest in giving the disadvantaged a long time within which to sue. By making this choice the legislature has imposed heavy burdens on the parties and also on the trial Judge. Heavy as they are,the law requires them to be assumed. And,after all,medical negligence cases are not unique amongst those in which claims are allowed to be brought long after the facts have faded from recollection."

这一个法律地位有合理或公道之处(主要是为了保护失去或没有能力的原告),但也是有令人感到不满意之处。原因是被告可能会在很久以后才面对一个索赔的推进,而由于记忆或其他原因失去了所有可以抗辩的证据。这正是法律设立时效为了避免的情况,正如本章序言中所说的三个原因中最重要的一个。特别是在这一个中断时效计算的时间内,失去或没有能力的原告完全是可以通过他的监护人或是诉讼之友尽早提出诉讼。这种不满意的被告,很多时候是出现在意外事故如经常会出现的交通意外的疏忽驾驶人。而真正不满意的实际上是该驾驶人背后的保险人,他们会要遥遥无期地等待这一个诉讼并做出拨款作为赔付之用,如在 Atkinson v. Oxford HA(1993)Med L Rev 18 先例是诉因出现之后拖了 22 年,在 Alexander Linsey v. National Health Service Litigation Authority(December 21,2000,Unreported)先例是拖了23年。

在这种情况下,也曾经有潜在的被告试图采取行动不让失去或没有能力的原告把诉讼拖得太久。其中一种做法是在 Torpador v. D(2010)LRIR 358 先例,就是被告转为原告向法院申请一个"否定宣示"(negative declaration)。这就是要求法院宣示被告在有关的事故中没有疏忽,所以也没有责任。这实际是迫使失去或没有能力的原告必须通过监护人或是诉讼之友出庭指证被告有疏忽并且要做出赔偿,这也就达到了被告的目的,不让原告拖得太久。英国法律在目前对这一个做法还没有太明确的指引,在 A. McGee 的《Limitation Periods》(6th edn)之 19.023 段是这样总结:"It is submitted that this approach rather understates the difficulties involved in this case. As has been seen above, the law is quite clear that a claimant who is under disability has an extended limitation period. It is for him(or his litigation friend) to decide whether to bring a claim at any point within that period. The decision taken may be to delay the bringing of proceedings. To allow a defendant to force the issue by seeking a negative declaration surely undermines that rule. The point is by no means unimportant. There are many child victims of road accidents, and it does not seem unreasonable to suppose that defendants(in reality their insurers) might often be attracted by the idea of seeking a negative declaration. This is an issue which requires consideration at appellate level, and, if this practice becomes commonplace, it will no doubt receive such consideration before too long."

3.3 第三种例外情况:货物/旅客运输

这种例外情况出现在多个针对货物/旅客运输的立法或公约。例如,在针对公路货物运输的《Carriage of Goods by Road Act 1965》, Article 32(2)有规定是原告向承运人做出文书的索赔要求,即使是没有开始诉讼,期间计算 1 年时效的时间也会被中断,直到承运人回信拒绝索赔要求。这方面可参考 ICI Fibres Ltd and ICI France SA v. MAT Transport Ltd(1987)1 FTLR 145 先例。可节录 Article 32(2)如下:"A written claim shall suspend the period of limitation until such date as the carrier rejects the claim by notification in writing and returns the documents attached thereto. If a part of the claim is admitted the period of limitation shall start to run again only in respect of that part of the claim still in dispute. The burden of proof of the receipt of the claim, or of the reply and of the return of the documents, shall rest with the party relying upon these facts. The running of the period of limitation shall not be suspended by further claims having the same object."

另在针对铁路旅客的《International Transport Conventions Act 1983》与公路旅客的《Carriage of Passenger by Road Act 1974》,也是规定如果旅客向承运人做出文书的索赔要求,计算时效的时间同样会被中断,直到承运人回信拒绝索赔。

其他有同样规定的立法或公约有《Carriage by Railway Act 1972》,《Railway Passenger Convention》与《Railway Freight Convention》。

针对海上货物运输的 1971 年《海牙—维斯比规则》,在 Article Ⅲ, rule 6 要求货方向承运人的索赔必须在交货后的 1 年内提出,是没有好像较早提到有关货物/旅客运输立法的用字/措辞,但可以顺便一提一个有关时效的案例。在 The "Aghia Marina" (1989)1 Lloyd's Rep 62 先例,案情涉及货方及时委任的仲裁员由于后来发生利益冲突而需要退出仲裁。但货方作为原告另委任仲裁员时是已经错过了 1 年的时效,这被承运人(被告)指是时效已经错过。但 Evans 大法官不同意,认为原来委任仲裁员是善意做出,所以可保护 1 年的时效。

3.4 第四种例外情况:欺诈、隐藏与错误

这三种情况是在1980年立法之Section 32所针对,它们都可以导致时效不开始起算,直到欺诈、隐藏与错误被原告的受害方通过“合理谨慎”(reasonable diligence)发现。

首先针对什么是“合理谨慎”,Webster大法官在Peco Arts Inc v. Hazlitt Gallery Ltd(1983)1 WLR 1315先例判是原告不需要采取任何可以采取的行动,所需要的只是在每个不同案子的案情下做一个一般合理谨慎人士所会做的事情就已经是足够。另可以举Paragon Finance Plc v. D. B. Thakara & Co(1999)1 All ER 400先例,上诉庭的Millett大法官说:“The first plaintiffs submit that they acted reasonably throughout. They cannot be criticised for their decision to concentrate on the repossession actions in the first instance, nor for their delay in instructing their present solicitors until October 1991. There was no need for urgency; they had almost six years in which to bring proceedings. In my judgment this reasoning is misconceived. The question is not whether the plaintiffs should have discovered the fraud sooner; but whether they could with reasonable diligence have done so. The burden of proof is on them. They must establish that they could not have discovered the fraud without exceptional measures which they could not reasonably have been expected to take. In this context the length of the applicable period of limitation is irrelevant. In the course of argument May L. J. observed that reasonable diligence must be measured against some standard, but that the six - year limitation period did not provide the relevant standard. He suggested that the test was how a person carrying on a business of the relevant kind would act if he had adequate but not unlimited staff and resources and was motivated by a reasonable but not excessive sense of urgency. I respectfully agree.”

3.4.1 “欺诈”

接下去是在《Limitation Act 1980》之Section 32(1)(a),针对“欺诈”(fraud),这被说是只适用在有限的情况。在Chagos Islanders v. AG(2003)EWHC 2222先例,说是必须是被告的一些行为导致他依赖时效作为抗辩变得是不合理(behaviour which made it unconscionable for a defendant to rely on the lapse of time as a bar to the claim)。另在Barnstaple Boat Co Ltd v. Jones(2007)EWCA Civ 727先例,判是原告知道被告涉及一些不知名的欺诈行为是不足够的,他必须知道有欺诈并且被告的确做出了欺诈的行为。

Section 32(1)(a)只针对原告因为被告的欺诈导致没有办法及时发现诉因,但不适用在可以及时发现只是找不到被告。在R. B. Motor Policies at Lloyd's v. Butler(1950)1 KB 76先例,涉及车辆失窃,原告的保险人在赔付车主之后根据代位求偿向一位无辜第三人(作为涉及车辆的买方)取回有关的车辆。但起诉是在失窃后的12年,并且错过了时效。其中有好几年是花在寻找这辆车上。在英国法院,Streatfield大法官拒绝接受找不到有关车辆的一段时间可以中断时效,也不认为这是属于欺诈

的情况。

最后介绍的是比较早期的 Beaman v. ARTS Ltd(1949)1 KB 550 先例,案情涉及在第二次世界大战期间,被告受到原告的委托照顾一些财产(5 个包裹,笔者估计是艺术品)。期间被告由于害怕财产在德军空袭伦敦的时候受到损坏,就把财产处理掉,也没有告诉原告因为找不到原告。在大战过后,原告重新出现向被告要回这些财产,并在被告无法归还的情况下向被告提出侵占的诉讼。而由于已经是错过了时效,所以原告声称在 1940 年被告非法处理掉财产的时候(也就是产生诉因的时候)直到 1946 年原告向被告取回这些财产时才知道失去的 6 年期间,原告是没有办法发现他的损失,而没有办法发现的原因就是被告的欺诈,所以可以中断计算。但这个说法不被法院所接受,Denning 大法官判是被告诚实地认为他找不到原告取得处置掉财产的批准是不属于欺诈。

3.4.2 "隐藏"

"隐藏"(Concealment)在《Limitation Act 1980》之 Section 32(1)(b),说是"任何有关原告诉因而被告故意隐藏的事实"(any fact relevant to the plaintiff's cause of action has been deliberately concealed from him by the defendant)。换言之,目前立法所针对的是"故意隐藏"(deliberate concealment),与以前的"欺诈性隐藏"(fraudulent concealment)有区别。这种情况以前一直以来被英国法院解释是十分宽松,导致了在 Tito v. Waddell(No. 2)(1977) Ch 106 先例,Megarry 大法官说是上一个 1939 年立法所针对的"欺诈性隐藏"在本先例中既不要求欺诈,也不要求隐藏。例如,在上一小段介绍过的 Beaman v. ARTS Ltd(1949)1 KB 550 先例,法院虽然不接受 1940 年被告非法处理掉财产的时候直到 1946 年原告才发现财产失去的 6 年期间是欺诈,但被判是属于隐藏。虽然在该先例,被告没有做过任何事情向原告隐藏有关财产失去的事实。

另在 Kitchen v. Royal Air Force Association(1958)2 All ER 241 先例,第一被告是对原告造成了伤害,而第二被告本来是原告的代表律师。由于第二被告的疏忽错过了向第一被告索赔的时效,导致第一被告以错过时效作为抗辩。其间,第二被告说服第一被告向原告支付一笔"不承认责任的优惠"(*ex gratia*)金钱,但不向原告说明为什么做出这个支付。原告不愿意接受这一笔金额不足的钱,并把错过时效的代表律师加进诉讼作为第二被告,诉因是他的疏忽。但第二被告把这个时候时效已经错过作为抗辩,而原告就以隐藏作为中断时效计算的理由。照说这一个隐藏只涉及第二被告要求第一被告不告诉原告为什么做出这笔金钱支付,与原告向第二被告的诉因(也就是后者的疏忽导致时效错过)是没有关系。但上诉庭还是允许原告可以中断时效继续诉讼,虽然原因并没有说得太清楚。

3.4.2.1 什么才算是"有关原告诉因"的事情/事实被隐藏

这带来另一个问题,就是什么算是"有关原告诉因"(any fact relevant to the plaintiff's cause of action),因为被告即使隐藏会局限在一些无关重要的事情。在 Johnson v. Chief Constable of Survey(1992) The Times, November 23 先例与 The "Kriti Palm"

(2007)1 Lloyd's 555 先例,判是隐藏的事情必须会令原告无法完整提出他的诉因。也可以说原告所知道的(不论是真正知道或是假设应该知道)事实能否令他足够拟定一份索赔请求？所以,也有说法这是一个"索赔请求考验"(statement of claim test)。如果被告隐藏的事实只是涉及让原告可以增强他的索赔请求,这并不包括在内。

在 The"Kriti Palm"先例,杨大明律师的《国际货物买卖》之269 页有介绍,可节录如下:"案情涉及了一个'FOB Coryton(英国)'的买卖,货物是汽油(gasoline),卖方是美孚石油公司(Mobil),而本案例的原告 AIC 是中间商,他把有关的货物转售给另一家美国公司名为 Galaxy。FOB 买卖合约的条文是说明:'Quality and quantity at load-port:as determined by mutually acceptable independent inspectors,appoint by seller,results to be final and binding for both parties save fraud and manifest error. Costs to be shared 50/50 buyer/seller.'但在转售买卖合约,是没有条文说明检验证明是最终与有约束性。而 Mobil 是后来指定了 ITS Testing Service(UK)Ltd,这也是本案例的被告。在装港,ITS 在测试后作出了一个质量的证明,说明是符合买卖合约的规格(主要是'Reid Vapour Pressure'或简称 RVP 的质量要求是 8.22psi,而买卖合约规定不能超过 9)。但后来船舶抵达纽约的卸港,收货人在测试后认为货物是不符合规格(off specification)。也发觉在装港 ITS 是使用了一个错误的测试方法,就是应该适用 ASTM D5191,但实际使用的是 ASTM D323。在卸港,Galaxy 委任了另一家检验公司 SGS 所得出的 RVP 是 9.3－9.69。这事后带来了一连串的诉讼。而 AIC 就起诉美孚石油公司,但最后双方达成和解,美孚石油公司支付了 20 万美元给 AIC。在这之后 AIC 就开始起诉 ITS,要求赔付其余的损失与瑞士法院的诉讼费用。至于诉因是包括了违约、欺诈、故意隐瞒等方面,因为是涉及了 ITS 的一位负责人在电话中告知 AIC 负责人该测试证明准确,当时是在 AIC 支付货款给 Mobil 前的一天。而 ITS 当时已经做了另一个内部测试发现 RVP 是 9.33 psi,ITS 的负责人应该知道。"

ITS 主要的抗辩是时效已经错过,这导致了法院需要针对欺诈与隐藏这两个方面看看是否可以中断时效的计算。只说法院判是的确存在欺诈或"欺骗"(deceit),所以不严格需要针对隐藏这方面。但 Cresswell 大法官也十分详尽地针对了隐藏这一个方面,以下可部分节录有关的判词:

"In view of the finding of deceit it is not strictly necessary to consider section 32(1)(b) and section 32(2). Nonetheless I add the following for completeness.

I turn to consider the meaning of 'any fact relevant to the plaintiff's right of action.'

In *Johnson v. Chief Constable of Surrey*, *The Times*, 23 November 1992, Court of Appeal (Civil Division) Transcript No 961 of 1992 the plaintiff sought to bring an action for damages for false imprisonment after the expiry of six years from the accrual of the cause of action. He relied on section 32(1)(b) of the Act of 1980. The plaintiff contended that the police had concealed material from him which demonstrated that they did not have reasonable grounds to suspect the relevant offence at the time of the arrest. The court construed the expression 'fact relevant to the plaintiff's right of action' narrowly.

Rose LJ stated:

For my part I accept [the] submission that, in construing the section, there is no middle ground between facts and evidence ... Facts which improve prospects of success are not, as it seems to me, facts relevant to the right of action ... I accept that the construction proposed ... is a narrow one, but unless it is correct it is difficult to see what purpose it served by the special provisions with regard to personal injury actions which are contained in section 33 of the Act.

Rose LJ accepted the statement of claim test, that it is knowledge of the facts which should be pleaded in the statement of claim....

In my judgment ITS by Mr Lucas should have informed AIC about the fact of the re-tests and the results thereof during the telephone conversation on17 April 1996. (It should be remembered that ITS was jointly instructed by Mobil and AIC. Any information given to AIC should equally have been given to Mobil).

I find that Mr Lucas and Mr Chalmers made a deliberate decision not to disclose the fact of the Cooper re-tests and the results thereof to AIC and Mobil in circumstances in which the re-tests and the results thereof should have been disclosed to AIC and Mobil, and Mr Lucas and Mr Chalmers knew that the re-tests and the results thereof should have been disclosed to AIC and Mobil. I further find that Mr Lucas and Mr Chalmers were aware that ITS was under such a duty and that Mr Lucas and Mr Chalmers made a deliberate decision not to disclose the re-tests and the results thereof....

In my judgment ITS (by Mr Lucas and Mr Chalmers) deliberately concealed a fact relevant to AIC's right of action against ITS."

3.4.2.2 被告的沉默是否属于隐藏

被告的沉默会否属于隐藏,在早期的先例判是可以。例如,在本章之2.2.5.2段提到的Shaw v. Shaw(1954)2 QB 429先例,涉及原告指被告破坏了一个婚姻承诺,而被告对他已经有一个合法妻子的事实保持沉默,这属于隐藏令原告错过了时效,这被上诉庭支持。

但最近一些先例看来有一定程度的收紧,在Ayles v. LAH Ayles Ltd, February 8, 1990先例,涉及被告建造的房子(阳台)有缺陷。原告起初的诉因是侵权,但后来被明确是侵权不会成功。这导致原告向法院申请"修改索赔请求"(amendment to statement of claim),把侵权变成是违约。但修改加上一个新的诉因也必须是在时效内,在该先例房子是在1973年竣工,而申请修改是在1989年,这显然是严重错过了时效。所以,原告需要有理由中断时效的计算,这就是指被告曾经在1975年收到建筑师一封信函,承认对阳台的设计有缺陷。但被告没有告诉原告,导致原告不知道是可以有一个违约的诉因，这构成了隐藏。但上诉庭 Lloyd 大法官判是被告没有责任披露这一封信函，所以也不存在隐藏。这先例看来隐藏是需要有一些行动，不仅是沉默。

这也在后来的先例被依从，在 Foreman v. O'Driscoll & Partners(2000)1 Lloyd's P. N. Rep 720 先例，法院是说："Initial negligence by a solicitor, followed by further negligence in not informing his client of that negligence, whether by act or omission initially, does not suffice to constitute deliberate concealment."

但在 Williams Fanshaw Porter & Hazelhurst(2004)EWCA Civ 157 先例，涉及一位律师疏忽但对他的客户故意隐藏这一个事实。上诉庭看来是认为被告律师如果是知道他的疏忽或是违约，不主动告诉他的客户会是构成隐藏。看来，就沉默会构成隐藏还是有一定的危险。现实中，专业人士知道他犯了错可以说是十之八九不会主动向客户交待，让后者在时效内向他提起诉讼。当然也会有专业人士犯了错但不知道，如疏忽的律师由于不知道某一个重要的先例，所以给了他的客户错误的法律意见。这一个疏忽或是违约可能会是维持很久，但律师自己也不知道。

3.4.2.3　近期先例收紧有关故意隐藏的说法

收紧隐藏的说法也在贵族院的先例 Cave v. Robinson, Jarvis and Rolf(2002)1 WLR 581 HL，Millett 勋爵是这样说："In my opinion, section 32 deprives a defendant of a limitation defence in two situations: (i) where he takes active steps to conceal his own breach of duty after he has become aware of it; and(ii) where he is guilty of stances where it is unlikely to be discovered for some time. But it does not deprive a defendant of a limitation defence where he is charged with negligence if, being unaware of his error or that he has failed to take proper care, there has been nothing for him to disclose."

3.4.2.4　诉因出现后被告故意隐藏

这一个问题一直没有先例针对，以前大量的先例所针对的都是在诉因出现之前的隐藏，导致原告没有发现(即使是合理谨慎下)他的诉因。在这种情况下，带来的后果就是《Limitation Act 1980》之 Section 32 所规定的时效"不开始起算"(shall not start to run)。这一个规定针对欺诈与错误也通常不会有问题，因为只会发生在诉因之前。但针对隐藏，就会存在事先或事后的故意隐藏，导致原告不完全知道他的诉因。这一个问题在贵族院的 Sheldon v. Outhwaite(1995)All ER 558 先例中出现，有关的案情涉及在八九十年代出现的劳合社危机，因为大量的美国石棉与其他的案件带来了巨大的再保险索赔，导致不少劳合社的"名字"(names)因为没有限制的做出赔偿而面临破产。有不少这些名字或自然人(他们等于是保险人)事后向劳合社的"保险小组"(syndicates)负责人提出诉讼，指后者的疏忽接受承保导致前者的损失。Sheldon v. Outhwaite 也是其中之一的先例。面对索赔，被告的抗辩之一是 6 年的时效已经错过。而原告指是由于被告的"事后隐藏"(subsequent concealment)，所以可以根据 1980 年立法之 section 32(1)(b) 延长 6 年时效。但问题就是立法的用字/措辞看起来适用于事前隐藏,因为它规定隐藏的情况下时效不开始起算。这变成立法如果适用,就存在事后隐藏怎样中断时效的计算。一种计算办法是比较符合立法的用字/措辞,也就是一有了事后隐藏,就要在隐藏被发现后从零开始计算6年时效。但这会是不合理,因为在诉因开始后,由于不涉及事前隐藏,所以时效期限需要起算。这会是起算了3年后甚至原来时效已经届满后才出现事后隐藏,难道也可以在事后隐藏发现后从零开始?这看来很不合理与拖得太长。另一种计算办法是把已经起算了的3年不等的时间在出现事后隐藏后直到被发现的一段时间停算,然后重新继续启动算够6年时效。这看来是比较合理的计算办法,但问题是它完全不配合1980年立法的用字/措辞。

只说在该先例,上诉庭是判事后隐藏是不适用1980年立法。但去了贵族院,以多数意见(Mustill勋爵与Lloyd勋爵持不同意见)判是被告在诉因出现后故意隐藏一个重要事实的情况下,会令原来的时效重新从零开始计算。

3.4.3　"错误"

在英国普通法下,错误可以分为两类:"双方共同的错误"(common or mutual mistake)或者合约"一方错误"(unilateral mistake)都可以导致合同无效。与合约"受阻"(frustration)的说法一样,错误只是在十分有限的情况下适用令有关的合约无效。关于这两种错误的定义,可以参见笔者所著的《国际商务游戏规则——英国合约法》(中国政法大学出版社2000年版)有关内容。

《Limitation Act 1980》之Section 32规定错误可以中断时效的开始,但并没有对这两种的错误做出区分,它主要的问题还是在原告是否能够发现或通过合理谨慎能够发现有关的错误。而且错误必须涉及有关的诉因。所以在Philips - Higgins v. Harper (1954)1 QB 411先例,原告是被告所雇佣的助理律师,对雇佣期间所赚取的收费,双方同意分摊利润。到了1951年,双方有了争议有关分摊利润的计算办法有错误,而争议的年份早到1938年。显然,针对6年前的年份,时效早已经错过,所以原告根据1939年立法的同一条文,希望根据错误中断时效的开始计算。这被Pearson大法官拒绝,判是错误必须是导致诉因被发现的重要因素才令有关的立法适用。

错误这一个问题也经常被适用在纳税的问题上,往往是一有了先例解释某一方面的税法,就会有多缴纳了税款的纳税人向税务局提出索赔要求退还,如果时效错过了纳税人就根据1980年立法之Section 32要求中断时效的计算,因为涉及一个"法律的错误"(mistake in law),所以没有发现他的诉因。这导致英国需要立法改变这一个普通法的立场,就是《Finance Act 2004》之Section 320,排除1980年立法之Section 32(1)(c)有关法律的错误。

错误这一个问题也适用在其他方面,如在Peco Arts Inc v. Hazlitt Gallery Ltd (1983)1 WLR 1315先例,案情涉及在1970年,原告向被告购买一幅称为是真迹的画。该幅画在1970年与1981年被两度检验过,但只是在后一次的检验中被发现是复制的。原告(买方)向被告提出起诉,诉因是由于错误而导致原来的买卖合约失效。但被告的抗辩是时效已经错过,而有关的先例主要争议是原告能否在1981年之前就应该可以通过合理谨慎发现这一个错误。

3.5 第五种例外情况:敌人与战犯

这是根据《Limitation(Enemies and War Prisoners) Act 1945》,在该立法下如果原告变为敌人或是原告在敌区被作为战犯扣留,时效的期限就中断计算,直到原告不再是英国的敌人或是不再被扣留后的1年。在今天世界相对比较太平时,这种例外情况估计不会太多。

3.6 衡平法下的例外情况

这不像上述所讲的五种例外情况,谈不上是其中的一种或是一大类,而是看个别的案情会出现一种情况就是被告曾经向原告明示或者是默示承诺过不去以错过时效作为抗辩,会是构成一个"承诺性禁止反供"(promissory estoppel):Central London Property Trust Ltd v. High Trees House Ltd(1947) KB 130先例。特别是被告对原告做出的承诺是有"约因"(consideration)支持,这约因通常会是原告不在时效期限内提起诉讼。在这种情况下可以说是法院肯定会以"承诺性禁止反供"的说法禁止被告提出错过时效的抗辩。

4. 重新启动时效的情况:确认与部分支付

在本章3.4.2.4段介绍过的Sheldon v. Outhwaite(1995) All ER 558先例,曾经谈到过事后隐藏会否导致已经开始起算的时效要从零开始重新启动的问题。在《Limitation Act 1980》,的确是有一种情况可以导致已经开始起算时效会被事后发生的事情一笔勾销,重新再启动,而且已经过了几年的时间也不必加上。这种事后发生的情况就是被告对欠下原告债务的"确认"(acknowledgment)或"部分支付"(part payment)。这规定在1980年立法的Section 29 - 31。以下把一些与本章有密切关系的小部分内容节录,并删去其他大部分针对土地与抵押的内容:

"29 Fresh accrual of action on acknowledgment or part payment....

(5) Subject to subsection(6) below, where any right of action has accrued to recover—

(a) any debt or other liquidated pecuniary claim; or ....

and the person liable or accountable for the claim acknowledges the claim or makes any payment in respect of it the right shall be treated as having accrued on and not before the date of the acknowledgment or payment....

(7) Subject to subsection(6) above, a current period of limitation may be repeatedly extended under this section by further acknowledgments or payments, but a right of action, once barred by this Act, shall not be revived by any subsequent acknowledgment or payment.

30 Formal provisions as to acknowledgments and part payments.

(1)To be effective for the purposes of section 29 of this Act, an acknowledgment must be in writing and signed by the person making it.

(2)For the purposes of section 29, any acknowledgment or payment—(a)may be sent by the agent of the person by whom it is required to be made under that section; and(b) shall be made to the person, or to an agent of the person, whose title or claim is being acknowledged or, as the case may be, in respect of whose claim the payment is being made.

31 Effect of acknowledgment or part payment on persons other than the maker or recipient. . . ."

4.1 立法规定的历史背景

这一个立法让时效从零开始重新启动是早在1939年立法中出现,原因是被告如果对合约欠下的债务在原来的6年时效之内做出了确认(也就是承认这一笔债务)或是做出部分支付,被认为继续适用原来的6年时效就不再公平,因为有可能原来的6年只剩下了很短的时间就时效届满。这立法规定的历史背景在Surrendra Overseas Ltd v. Government of Srilanka(1977)1 WLR 565先例中Kerr大法官有针对说:"I must shortly summarize the pre-1939 history. It is fully set out in the speech of Lord Sumner in Spencer v. Hemmerde(1922)2 A. C. 507. The Limitation Act 1623 contained nothing which would permit the recovery of simple contract debts after six years. The pleas of acknowledgment and part-payment were invented by the judges in mitigation of the injustices which this statute could work. The basis of the statute had been to free debtors from liability after the limitation period had expired, because 'long dormant claims have often more of cruelty than of justice in them': per Best C. J. in A'Court v. Cross(1825)3 Bing. 329, 332-333. But where the debtor had acknowledged the debt or made a part-payment on account of it within the limitation period, it was held that in the interests of justice the debtor should then no longer be allowed to invoke the statute. However, in relation to simple contract debts, perhaps because these required consideration moving from the debtor, it was repeatedly held that an acknowledgment must also imply a promise to pay the debt in question. In a large number of decisions the courts accordingly considered, often on highly artificial grounds, whether or not a promise to pay could be implied from the words 'employed by generations of shifty debtors,' to quote Lord Sumner in Spencer v. Hemmerde, at p. 534. The upshot was that almost anything short of a denial of liability was held to be capable of implying a promise to pay; but if the statement was altogether inconsistent with the implication of such a promise, then the acknowledgment was held to be insufficient."

这一个方面也涉及许多的要点可进一步解释,第一方面就是立法规定只针对"债务"(debt)或者"议定赔偿"(liquidated damage),但不针对"非议定赔偿"(un-liquidated damage)。

4.2 立法规定只适用在合约关系,不适用在侵权

这表示针对侵权,几乎肯定是非议定赔偿,本立法规定就不会适用,适用只局限在合约。这方面在近期的一个先例 Dwr Cymru v. Marthenshire CC(2004)EWHC 2991(TCC),Jackson 大法官有针对说:

"1. In all legislation prior to 1939 the doctrine of acknowledgment applied only to claims in contract. If Parliament had intended to extend this doctrine to tortious claims it would have done so expressly. There is no express reference to tort in the subsection.

2. The phrase 'liquidated claim' connotes a claim for a specific sum or, alternatively, for a sum which can be readily and precisely ascertained ... A claim for damages in tort is by definition not a liquidated claim. The assessment of damages in tort involves the application of a set of common law rules to the particular circumstances of the case. The application of those rules may be relatively straightforward in some instances, but that does not make the claim a liquidated one.

3. The global phrase 'any debt or other liquidated pecuniary claim' suggests a sum which is due to be paid pursuant to some contractual or similar obligation. The words on their natural meaning do not connote damages or compensation which the law requires to be paid by someone who has acted in breach of an obligation or duty.

4. In none of the cases cited by counsel or uncovered by my own researches has a claim in tort ever been revived by reason of an acknowledgment."

4.3 什么才算是足够的确认债务或议定赔偿

已经提到过,确认就表示被告承认债务或议定赔偿。由于被告面对原告的追偿会有千变万化的反应,所以有不少先例针对各种不同的反应判到底是否是一个足够的确认,可以从零开始重新启动 6 年的时效。

4.3.1 不足够的确认先例

显然,被告对原告的追偿否认有任何责任,这就明显不是一个确认:Commissioners For Her Majesty's Revenue and Customs v. Benchdollar Ltd(2009)EWHC 1310(Ch)先例。另在 Lia Oil SA v. ERG Petroli SPA(2007)EWHC 505(Comm)先例,涉及被告在一个"无损害"(without prejudice)会议中向原告交出一份有关文件,这被英国法院判是不足够构成确认,因为被告并非表明他的公开立场。以上是比较明显的情况,但会有比较不明确甚至富争议性的案例,如在 Swann v. Sowell(1819)2 B & Ald 759 先例,被告写了信向原告承认一笔债务,但多加了一句说:"我有一个抵销债务,所以你欠我更多的钱"(You owe me more money. I have a set - off against it.),这被法院判是不足够构成确认。

另在 Good v. Parry(1963)2 QB 418 先例,涉及被告说"有关欠下租金的问题可以分开解决"(the question of outstanding rent can be settled in a separate account),上诉庭也是判不足够构成确认。但有说法是这一个上诉庭先例对确认的解释太严格,被视

为是不正确。这与另一个先例涉及几乎是一样的案情但判法不同:Dungate v. Dungate(1965)1 WLR 1447,案情是被告向原告发了一封关于他们之间债务的信,其中一句话是说“请检查我欠你的债务,我们会一直负责”(keep a check on totals and amounts I owe you, and we will have account now and then)。这在第一审与上诉庭都判是一个足够的确认债务,而事后也在另一个贵族院的先例(Bradford & Bingley Plc v. Rashid, The Times 13 July, 2006)被认可。

4.3.2 相隔10年还是可以执行的裁决书先例

最后要介绍的是一个与笔者关系密切的仲裁裁决书,在相隔10年后还是获得英国法院的允许向罗马尼亚执行,虽然裁决书的有效期只有6年。能够拖得这么长还能执行主要是因为债务人曾经“确认”(acknowledgement)这一笔债务,这可以见到确认的危险,因为它会把债务遥遥无期拖下去,令6年的法定时效变为是空的。这一个先例在笔者所著的《仲裁法——从开庭审理到裁决书的作出与执行》(法律出版社2009年版)第14章9.2段有详细介绍。

4.3.3 公司账目显示了债务

有好几个先例针对这一个问题,就是在公司的“资产负债表”(balance sheet)中显示了某一笔债务。如果该公司是私人公司,而债权人是其中一个股东时,他才会获得这一份资产负债表。这几个先例都判这是欠债公司的一个足够的确认,可以重新启动时效:Jones v. Bellgrove Properties(1949)1 All ER 498;Re Gee & Co(Woolwich)Ltd(1975)Ch 52 等先例。

在 Re Transplanters(Holding Company)Ltd(1958)1 WLR 822 先例,也是涉及资产负债表显示了一笔债务,但该表格只是由一位公司董事,加上一位核算师签字。法院判这是不足够,因为在当时的1985年《公司法》之 Section 238 是需要有两位公司董事签字才有效。而原告与核算师在该表格上的签字都不能被视为是公司代理人确认这一笔债务。

4.4 被告的确认可以向原告代理人作出

另一个问题是被告的确认不需要直接向原告做出,向原告的代理人确认就已经是足够。在 Re Compania de Electricidad(1980)Ch 146 先例,Slade 大法官是说:“In my judgment, though no authority has been cited to me which either confirms or rejects such proposition, a written acknowledgment cannot be said to be made to a creditor or his agent, within the meaning of s. 24(2)... [as that section then was] ... unless either(a) it is delivered to the creditor or his agent by or with the authority of the debtor or his agent or (b) it is expressly or implicitly addressed to and is actually received by the creditor or his agent.”

在后来的另一个先例 London Borough of Wandsworth v. Birchwood June 16, 2000, unreported, CA, 涉及在一个法院判决执行的其中一个手段,就是根据有管辖法院作出的“要求提供资料命令”(order to provide information)把判决债务人传召到法院接受有关他经济状况的盘问。其中在申请人(也就是胜诉方的债权人)的代表律师向债务人的盘问中,债务人确认了债务。虽然在当时债权人本人并没有在场,也被判是债务人向债权人律师的确认足够令时效从零开始重新启动。

反过来,被告也不必自己做出确认。在 Section 30(2)(a),被告是可以通过自己的全权代理人向债权人做出确认。

4.5 被告在其他诉讼中的败诉或在文书请求做出过确认

在 Re Flynn(Dec'd)(No.2)(1969)2 Ch 403 先例,原告指称在纽约较早前的一个诉讼中,被告做出的抗辩虽然是否认责任,但最终不被纽约法院所接受。原告认为这就是一个确认,但这说法不被英国法院接受,Buckley 大法官认为没有办法把被告否认责任的抗辩与被告确认债务联系在一起。接下去在 Horner v. Cartwright July 11, 1989(CA)unreported 的上诉庭先例,也是有同样的判法。在该先例,一个重要的地方是他提到了被告在文书请求中如果承认索赔的金额,这会构成是一个确认,而时效重新启动的日子是在请求送达的一天。这看来是一个正确的法律地位,在后来的 Ofulue v. Bossert(2008)EWCA Civ 7 先例也被认可。这方面也可以提及一个较早的先例 Busch v. Stevens(1963)1 QB 1,案情涉及原告提起一个已经错过了时效的债务索赔,而当被告以错过时效作为抗辩,原告指这一个抗辩就是确认债务。这被 Lawton 大法官指原告这样的做法不妥善,债务如果被确认是需要在索赔请求中提出,不是在答辩请求提出。Lawton 大法官指出有这种做法将会被惩罚有关的费用,但没有说明是不准这样做。看来,安全的做法会是在抗辩请求中明示说明是请求的内容不能被视为对债务的确认。

4.6 共同与连带责任的债务

如果有几位被告对同一笔债务有"共同与连带责任"(jointly and severally liable),只要有一位被告或债务人曾经做出过确认,就会导致所有的被告都受到了约束:Whitcomb v. Whiting(1781)2 Doug KB 652;Read v. Price(1909)2 KB 724(CA)等先例。

4.7 做出确认的时间

在《Limitation Act 1980》之 Section 29(7),有规定是做出确认的时间必须是在原来的债务或议定赔偿还是没有错过时效,这才能延长并启动一个新的时效。如果原来债务或议定赔偿已经错过时效,被告做出确认也不会令已经被排除的诉权复活。但什么才是做出确认的时间也会有争议。在 Consolidated Agencies Ltd v. Bertram Ltd(1965)AC 470(PC)的枢密院先例,案情涉及"资产负债表"(balance sheet)中显示了某一笔的债务的一天,原来的时效还没有错过。但该表格隔了一段时间后才被董事签署,而在签署的一天时效已经错过。英国枢密院判是确认以签署的一天为准,所以是无效。但后来的 Re Gee & Co(Woolwich)Ltd(1975)Ch 52 先例有不同的判法,认为后来的签字只是与原来资产负债表的一天联系起来。但后来这一个判决有批评说是混乱与不合理:可参阅 Andrew McGee 所著的《Limitation Periods》(2010 年)之 403 页。

4.8 部分支付

4.8.1 部分支付必须是针对索赔的债务

对债务做出部分支付与确认有同样的后果,就是被假设为被告的债务人对欠下的债务做出承认,则会令时效从零开始重新被启动。部分支付与确认两方面有很多相似之处,疑点也是一样,如怎样才算是做出部分支付与构成足够的支付。在 Surrendra Overseas Ltd v. Government of Srilanka(1977)1 WLR 565 先例,承租人对船东索赔的债务只承认部分(运费与滞期费超出货损的部分),并针对这部分做出了支付。船东指这部分支付对其余的债务也可重新启动时效。但这不被 Kerr 大法官所接受,因为立法的规定是部分支付必须是针对原告要索赔的一笔债务。Kerr 大法官是这样说:

"Since the balance paid by the charterers to the owners stemmed from the fact that the admitted liability for freight and demurrage exceeded the cargo claim, the owners contend that the payment of this balance was a 'payment in respect of' the owners' claim within the wording of section 23(4). But that is not what the payment purported to be. It purported to be, and was, a payment of the only sum which the charterers admitted to be due. It was not on account; nor a part – payment of any kind. In my view this is fatal to the owners' contention for the same reasons as those which define the character of an acknowledgment. A part – payment, like an acknowledgment, can only revive the cause of action and start time running afresh if it provides evidence in the form of an admission by the debtor that the debt remains due despite the passage of time. This is consonant with the authorities. In Cottamv. Partridge(1842)4 Man. & G. 271, 280 the doctrine of part – payment was in my view correctly described in the argument as 'payment of money in part – payment of the whole debt, which is an acknowledgment of a debt being due, not in words, but by an act done.' Tindal C. J. said, at p. 287: 'The ground on which part – payment was previously held to take the case out of(the Limitation Act 1623) was, that a payment of a part was an admission of the rest by inference, and that, from such payment, a jury might conclude that the rest was due.'

In In re Oliver(1927)2 Ch. 323, 331 Tomlin J. said: 'But the common law has always recognised that payment on account of something in respect of which the statute is set up may amount to a fresh promise to pay and found a fresh cause of action. . . . It seems to me plain that any payment which is to have that effect must be a payment made in respect of that which it is sought to recover.'

And in In re Footman Bower & Co. Ltd. (1961) Ch. 443, 449 Buckley J. said: 'For a payment to have this effect it was necessary that it should amount to an acknowledgment of the debt and import a new promise to pay the outstanding balance. The mere act of the creditor appropriating a payment to a statute – barred debt could not have this effect, for such an acknowledgment and promise could only come from the debtor. Since the enactment of the Limitation Act. 1939, the position is different, for section 23(4) now contains a statutory provision applicable to simple contract debts whereby any payment in respect of a debt will make time start to run afresh in respect of that debt. There is no longer need to establish a new promise to pay. In my judgment, however, one must still look at the act and intention of the debtor to see whether the payment is made in respect of the particular debt. Payment is in this subsection dealt with in close conjunction with acknowledgment. Just as an acknowledgment can only acquire that character by the act of the debtor or his agent, so also, I think, a payment can for the purposes of this subsection only acquire the characteristics of being made"in respect of"the debt by the act of the debtor or his agent.'"

如果多笔债务是独立并可以分割,而部分支付是针对某一笔分割的债务,也同样不能把其余债务延长并从零开始重新启动时效。在 Kleinwort Benson v. s. Tyneside MBC(1994)4 All ER 972 先例,被告对部分债务做出了部分支付,但该笔债务因为非法而后来被判无效,原告是不能把收到的部分支付拨归在其他还没有清偿的债务。

4.8.2　往来账户下的部分支付

这方面会经常有原告与被告之间保持一个"往来账户"(running account),如双方是买卖的关系,原告经常向被告按月交付货物,然后双方定期或不定期结账。这一来,如果被告向原告做出部分支付,而且是针对某一笔独立的债务,就也会需要搞清楚,因为有可能部分的债务在往来账户中已经错过时效。这里是有几个方面要注意:

(1)起点是部分支付到底应该拨归给哪一笔债务的选择权是在债务方,他怎样说就怎样算:Re Footman Bower & Co Ltd(1961)Ch 443 先例。如果债务人没有做出选择,就由债权人做出决定:Mills v. Fowkes(1839)5 Bing(N.C.)455 先例。如果双方都没有做出任何选择,法律就假设与默示部分支付是针对一些时效还没有错过的债务:Nash v. Hodgson(1855)6 De GM & G 474 先例。

(2)在 Re Footman Bower & Co Ltd 先例,涉及该公司正在清盘,其中与一个债权人保持一个往来账户。该债权人是供应商,并在过去不断供应货物给清盘中的公司。期间清盘公司过一段时间就会做出部分支付给供应商,而最后的一次支付是在 6 年时效内。问题是这笔部分支付是否要把往来账户所欠下的独立债务分开对待,看看是否有部分债务已经错过时效并不能因部分支付重新启动时效?但法院是判往来账户下应该只有一笔"总欠债"(single balance),所以部分支付在没有说明的情况下应该只是针对这一笔总欠债,所以所有的债务都可重新启动时效。

4.8.3　支付/收取部分支付的是代理人

部分支付也可以由被告的代理人做出,而支付的对象也可以是原告或是他的代理人或是他指定的第三人。这方面可节录 The"Good Challenger"(2004)1 Lloyd's Rep. 67 先例的第一审,Crane 大法官是这样说:"The sole issue in relation to this payment is whether, given the directions by NGM, as the claimants' agent, for payment to the credit of an account in the name of Good Faith Shipping, the part - payment can be said to have been made to the person, or to an agent of the person, whose claim is being acknowledged. The evidence is that Good Faith Shipping were the managers of the vessel *Good Challenger*; but the defendants say that there is no evidence that they received this payment in their capacity as agents of the claimants (the vessel's owners) as distinct from on their own account as creditors of the claimants. For the purpose of the Act I do not think this matters. Even if the correct inference is that Good Faith Shipping received this payment on their own account so as to discharge or reduce a liability incurred to them by the claimants, the payment was made by the defendant (or its agents) as debtor at the direction and request of the claimant (or its agents) as creditor so as to reduce or extinguish a liability owed by the creditor to a third party. This is a payment at the request and for the benefit of the claimant, as creditor, and, therefore, is a payment made to the claimant for the purpose of the Act. If any authority were needed for this conclusion it is to be found in *Worthington v Grimsditch*, 7 QB Reps 478 (ER. Vol. CXV) in which payments made by a defendant to a third party creditor of the plaintiff, at the request of the plaintiff and so as to reduce pro tanto a debt owed by the defendant to the plaintiff, were treated as capable of taking the plaintiff's claim outside the statute of limitation."

5. 错过时效的后果

错过时效的后果可以是十分严重,通常原告不能把一个错过时效的索赔提起诉讼。不论在法院诉讼或是仲裁,错过时效是一个抗辩,被告可以在抗辩一个索赔时提出要求先对时效做出初步审理。如果原告败诉,这个索赔也就完蛋了,根本不必审理其他方面的实质性争议。

不同针对时效(不论是在立法或是合约)的文字或措辞带来的错过时效的后果会有十分微妙与技术性的区别:一种是"排除诉权"(barring the right),另一种涉及抗辩是"排除救济"(barring the remedy)。

简单地说,立法的时效通常是前者,也就是排除诉权。这表示有关的诉因再也没有办法提起诉讼,因为诉权已经被排除与不存在。这种法定时效的用字/措辞可举1924年《海牙规则》为例,Article 3(6)所说如下:"In any event the carrier and the ship shall be discharged from all liability in respect of loss or damage unless suit is brought within one year after delivery of the goods or the date when the goods should have been delivered."

但涉及合约时效(通常会是在仲裁条文中约定),由于订约的自由与当事人经常不警觉,所以经常会带来排除救济的时效。这种条文会约定原告必须在某一个时限内提起仲裁,否则他就再不能提起仲裁。字面看来,这顶多也就是如果错过时效的话只会排除救济,但诉因还在而且并没有被审理。这就会导致有诉权的原告可以通过其他救济办法提出他的诉因,如仲裁的救济被排除就可以去法院。这种仲裁条文在现实中也不多见,许多标准格式合约的仲裁条文都会排除诉权。例如,在著名的Centrocon arbitration clause,它的有关文字就是排除诉权,说:"Any claim must be made in writing and Claimant's Arbitrator appointed within three months of final discharge and where this provision is not complied with **the claim shall be deemed to be waived and absolutely barred**."(加黑部分是笔者的强调)

这方面的问题可节录David St John Sutton,Judith Gill与Matthew Gearing所著的《Russell on Arbitration》(23rd edn,2007年)之5-006段如下:"**Contractual time limits.** A contractual time limit, whether contained in an arbitration agreement or some other provision of the contract, or indeed in arbitration rules referred to in the arbitration agreement, may (1) impose a time limit for commencing arbitration proceedings, and/or (2) provide that a claim shall be barred or extinguished if arbitration is not commenced within the time limit. These provisions are not necessarily found together. The parties' agreement may limit the time for commencing arbitration without barring or extinguishing the claim, so that a party who is out of time loses his right to arbitrate and will be confined to whatever remedy, if any, is available in the courts. Alternatively, and much more commonly, the parties' agreement may make compliance with a time limit a condition of any claim, without limiting the operation of the agreement to arbitrate, so that a claimant who is out of time may still have a right to arbitrate, but the respondent may raise a time bar by way of defence to the claim. If the contract does not make clear which of the above is intended but simply requires notice of a claim to be given or arbitration to be commenced within a certain period of time, then if the notice is not given or the arbitration is not commenced the claim will be barred. It is possible for a respondent to waive any objection to arbitration, while still relying on a limitation clause as barring or extinguishing the claim."

这一问题目前也还停留在高院,会有可能上诉到更高的法院,对这一个问题进行简化与改善。毕竟对这种咬文嚼字地解释仲裁条文的做法,英国的贵族院(目前已改为最高法院)已经在The"Fiona Trust"(2008)1 Lloyd's Rep 254先例予以否定。这一来,很难想象双方当事人会有"定约意图"(contractual intention)约定仲裁条文的时候会定下一个时效,如果错过也不影响诉权的存在,原告可以改去法院提出同样的诉因。这可以节录Sir Michael J. Mustill与Stewart C. Boyd所著的《Commercial Arbitration》(2nd edn,1989年)之203页的注脚13如下:"This distinction is a creature of the lawyers, not of the merchants. It must be very doubtful whether the draftsmen of the various clauses had the point in mind at all, still less intended to give effect to it. As the law stands at present, the distinction must be regarded as valid; but the point is open to review in the

Court of Appeal, and it may yet be that the law will be simplified and improved."

这种争议还是有在发生，如笔者在2010年底所参与的一个造船合约的伦敦仲裁，就涉及这一方面的问题。合约的Article X针对支付船价与还款担保有详细的约定，包括外国买方（外国船东）在什么情况下可以终断合约。这条文其中一段（双方在订立合约的时候加上的）是说对于买方终断合约，卖方（中国船厂）如果根据Article XIII在买方宣称终断合约之日起30天内启动仲裁程序，就有权争议买方这个终断行为。这条文的英文用字/措辞是："The Seller shall have the right to dispute the Buyer's cancellation and/or rescission by instituting arbitration in accordance with Article XIII, if such institution of arbitration is made within thirty(30) days of the Buyer's cancellation and/or rescission."这也是根据银行做出的还款担保中所规定唯一可以保护或延迟做出支付给买方的办法。所以卖方很快开始仲裁并委任了笔者，但已经是错过了30天的时间。而该合约的Article XIII是一个复杂的仲裁条文，规定了什么样的争议该找船级社专家，什么样的争议该去伦敦仲裁，以及其他争议要交给法院判决。卖方声称这30天的时效只是排除救济，错过的后果顶多是不能再去仲裁，但仍有诉权可转而去英国法院。但仲裁庭多数（笔者不同意，但主要不在这一方面）认为这是排除诉权的时效，卖方错过时效就再也不能争议买方的终断合约行为。裁决书的部分内容可节录如下：

"It is true that Article X.2 does not spell out the consequences in the familiar phrase 'failing which such right shall be deemed to be waived and absolutely barred' or similar words. But it was common ground that such words were not critical to that being the effect. There are numerous authorities so holding, the most recent being the judgment of Longmore J(as he then was) Metalimex v. Eugenie(1962) 1 Lloyd's Rep 378 and Hon Ma J in Tommy C. P. Sze v. Li & Fung(Trading) (2002) HKCU 1242. Counsel for the Seller accepted this in terms, as indeed they accepted the prescriptive effect of the phrase following 'if'.

The Majority is in little doubt but that it was intended to beright - barring. Article X.2 is expressed as dealing with the 'right' and the 'if' phrase would therefore fairly to be seen as itself referable to the right. True it is that Article X.2 also refers to the mechanism of challenge (and thus might be regarded as concerned with the remedy) but it does so in terms which can only fairly and sensibly be limiting of the method of protecting the right from the effects of prescription. Thus it reads '*If Buyer's cancellation and/or rescission of this Contract is disputed by the Seller as aforesaid ...*'

No business purpose would be served by saying that a dispute about the cancellation must be referred to arbitration within30 days, but failing that, it may be referred to a court determination at any time within the statutory limitation period of 6 years. Indeed, the business purpose would be wholly frustrated by it. The business purpose is best seen in relation to the period of time chosen, not to matters of jurisdictional choice, especially where the parties expressed their agreement specifically in terms of 'arbitration' of such disputes. The business purpose of the short period would be undermined by the mere fact of the Seller (intentionally or unintentionally) delaying the reference of its dispute until the 30 day period had elapsed. Nothing would be gained by that and pretty much everything would be lost; it would be wholly irreconcilable with the fact that the vessel would herself then remain in limbo until the dispute had been resolved in the succeeding possibly 6 years or so, even though very possibly nearly complete. If the Seller sought to treat the Buyer's cancellation as a repudiation, that dispute would have to be referred to arbitration and so one would then have the unbeguiling prospect of two parallel sets of proceedings all about very similar issues. The Majority cannot think that this is what the parties can possibly have intended."

这一个多数裁决,中国船厂在败诉后曾经向英国法院申请批文上诉这一个法律观点,但被英国法院所拒绝并且被报道,即在 7.2.5 段将介绍的 Nanjing Tianshun Shipbuilding Co Ltd and Jiangsu Skyrun International Group Co Ltd v. Orchard Tankers PTE Ltd(2011)EWHC 164 先例。而其中还款担保所涉及的金额是数千万美元。

6. 衡平法救济的时效与怠慢说法

在上述所讲到的一些普通法的救济(不论是合约或是侵权)的时效问题,也适用在衡平法的救济。这些救济主要包括了"履约指令"(specific performance)、"禁令"(injunction)等。但除了这些法定的时效外,衡平法救济还有另一个"怠慢说法"(doctrine of laches)。这就是原告如果晚了去法院请求衡平法救济,法院就会拒绝给予。这方面重要的先例是 Lindsay Petroleum Co v. Hurd(1874)LR 5 PC 221,贵族院的 Selborne 勋爵说:"Now the doctrine of laches in courts of equity is not an arbitrary or a technical doctrine. Where it would be practicably unjust to give a remedy, either because the party has by his conduct done that which might fairly be regarded as equivalent to a waiver of it, or where by his conduct and neglect he has, though perhaps not waiving that remedy, yet put the other party in a situation in which it would not be reasonable to place him if the remedy were afterwards to be asserted, in either of these cases lapse of time and delay are most material, but in every case if an argument against relief which otherwise would be just is founded upon mere delay, that delay, of course, not amounting to a bar by any statutory limitations, the validity of that defence must be tried upon principles substantially equitable."

在近期的 Fisher v. Brooker(2009)UKHL 41 先例,贵族院的 Neuberger 勋爵根据

Lindsay Petroleum Co v. Hurd 先例说:"... laches is an equitable doctrine, under which delay can bar a claim to equitable relief."

7. 其他种类的时效

除了上述介绍的《Limitation Act 1980》,还会有其他类别的时效会经常面对,是有诉权的原告必须要留心的。这些类别的时效包括:(1)英国承认国际公约而去立法所带来的法律地位;(2)合约的规定;(3)适用外国实体法的争议。以下会针对这些不同类别的时效做进一步的分析。

7.1 英国承认国际公约立法所带来的时效

英国是多项国际公约的缔约国,这些国际公约会针对各种不同的事项,如海上货物运输、空运、油污责任等。这些国际公约中都会有不同的诉讼或仲裁时效,要求原告及时提出诉讼。而由于国际公约是许多成员国经过长期讨论与谈判的产物,所以如果涉及时效条文,经常会出现不同的期限,也很少会与英国法一致。这一来,如果英国(或任何承认与签署国际公约的国家)承认这些国际公约,就必须接受最后确定下来的时效条文,因为对国际公约的承认是不能部分接受。例如,1924 年的《海牙规则》与 1968 年修订的《海牙—维斯比规则》被英国承认就通过立法变为 1971 年《海上货物运输法》,其中 Article 3(6)规定有关货方因为货损货差要向承运人或船舶提出索赔,就必须在交货或估计应该交货后的 1 年内开始诉讼,除非双方同意延长。此外,如果涉及向第三人提起"补偿"(indemnity),就不受到这 1 年时效的局限。这种补偿行动经常在海上货物运输出现,就是货方根据提单向船东(作为承运人)索赔货损货差,船东败诉或者通过和解赔付后,根据租约向承租人要求补偿这一笔损失,因为根据租约条文造成货损货差的责任不在船东,或是租约豁免了船东的责任。在 The"Caroline P"(No. 2)(1984)2 Lloyd's Rep 466 先例,Neill 大法官认为在该先例的补偿行动是要等到船东对货方的责任已经被第一审法院明确下来要负责,才会可以向承租人通过诉讼提出要求。这方面的问题已经在本章2.2.5.3段与 2.3.5 段有详论。所以,补偿行动经常会在很后的时间提出,不能与货方向承运人索赔的 1 年时效相提并论。

涉及空运的《华沙公约》通过 1961 年《航空运输法》(Carriage by Air Act 1961)适用,其中 Article 29(1)规定索赔损失必须在飞机到达目的地后 2 年内提出(The right to damages shall be extinguished if an action is not brought within two years, reckoned from the date of arrival at the destination, or from the date on which the aircraft ought to have arrived, or from the date on which the carriage stopped.)

其他被英国立法的国际公约,涉及各种不同长短的时效,在笔者熟悉的业务范围内包括有针对船舶碰撞索赔时效的国际公约是 1910 年《Brussels Convention》,在英国被立法为1911年《Maritime Convention Act》。它在Section 8是规定了2年的时效,从碰撞造成损失的一天开始计算。但也给了有管辖权法院裁量权延长时效,这在英国法院有关的先例可参考The"Al Tabith"(1995)2 Lloyd's Rep 336。另一提的是1911年《Maritime Convention Act》之Section 8已经被1995年《Merchant Shipping Act》之Section 190所替代。

针对油污损失的国际公约是1969年《International Convention on Civil Liability for Oil Pollution》,并在1992年做出修改提高责任限额。这国际公约的英国立法是1971年的《Merchant Shipping(Oil Pollution)Act》与1995年的《Merchant Shipping Act》。这立法规定的时效是在索赔诉因(造成损失)出现后的3年内,或是在造成责任的油污发生或在一连串事件中的第一次的6年后。后者的情况会出现在一艘沉船慢慢渗出燃油而累积造成损失。这可节录1992年的《International Convention on Civil Liability for Oil Pollution》之Article Ⅷ如下:"Rights of compensation under this Convention shall be extinguished unless an action is brought thereunder within three years from the date when the damage occurred. However, in no case shall an action be brought after six years from the date of the incident which caused the damage. Where this incident consists of a series of occurrences, the six years' period shall run from the date of the first such occurrence."

针对海上旅客的伤亡或是他们的财产损失,如果适用1974年的《雅典公约》(Athens Convention),会是从受害旅客离船的一天算起的3年(针对伤亡)或2年(针对财产损失)内必须提起诉讼。如果有关旅客死亡,就不存在有离船的一天,这就假设他应该离船的一天开始计算。

以上表示涉及这些立法的诉因(不论这立法是由于强制性或双方当事人的约定而适用),都必须按照这些不同的时效期限开始诉讼,以保护索赔权利。好像针对《海牙规则》或《海牙—维斯比规则》(不论是立法的强制适用或是订约自由去适用)的时效届满前有否开始诉讼就涉及有无数先例,如:The"Merak"(1964)2 Lloyd's Rep 527;Compania Colombiana de Seguros v. Pacific Steam Navigation(1965)1 QB 101;The"Angeliki"(1973)2 Lloyd's Rep 226;The"Virgo(1978)2 Lloyd's Rep 167;The"Aiolos"(1983)2 Lloyd's Rep 25;The"World Ares"(1984)2 Lloyd's Rep 481;The"Kapetan Marcos"(1986)1 Lloyd's Rep 211;The"Antares"(1987)1 Lloyd's Rep 424;Sabah Flour and Feedmills v. Comfez Ltd(1987)2 Lloyd's Rep 647;The Nordglimt(1988)QB 183;The"Amazona"(1989)2 Lloyd's Rep 130;The"Jay Bola"(1992)2 Lloyd's Rep 62;The"Leni"(1992)2 Lloyd's Rep 92;The"Havhelt"(1993)1 Lloyd's Rep 523;The"Finnrose(1994)1 Lloyd's Rep 559;The"Pionier(1995)1 Lloyd's Rep 223;Anglos Irish v. Federated Stevedores(1997)1 Lloyd's Rep 207;The"Standard Ardour"(1998)2 Lloyd's Rep 159;The"Markos N"(2000)2 Lloyd's Rep 243;The"Toledo Carrier(2006)EWHC 2054(Comm.);The"Voc Gallant"(2009)1 Lloyd's Rep(Comm)418。

7.2 合约规定的时效

《Limitation Act 1980》的立法并没有禁止双方当事人的订约自由。所以,如果涉及合约关系,就经常会发生双方当事人另约定一条时效条文。这种合约时效通常会比1980年立法的6年时效短或是短得多,但只要是用字/措辞上写得明确,完全有效,并且超越了1980年立法针对一般合约的6年时效。例如,在航次租约中曾经是经常会加入一条很苛刻的时效条文,名为“Centrocon arbitration clause”,要求原告在卸货后3个月内提起诉讼,委任原告的仲裁员。有关这个条文在本章2.3.5有详细的针对,不重复。

7.2.1 合约时效条文的合理性

客观地说,立法的6年时效在分秒必争的今天的确是太长。一家公司有管理人事上的改变、员工的替换等,6年内可能已经发生几轮了。这会导致争议提出太晚,作为被告的当事人会失去了一些重要的证据(特别是重要证人)。再加上很多公司也希望能早日在一宗交易后“结总账”(close account),或是“毁掉档案文件”(dispose documents),不必等6年之久。

所以在合约内订下较短的如1、2年的时效条文完全有必要或是合理。但是,如果订得太短,如买卖合约的交货后1星期内有货物质量问题即要起诉,否则错过时效,就会对潜在的原告(买方)严重不公平,现实中也不一定做得到。但这种情况也不是没有,如多处提到的Centrocon arbitration clause只有在卸完货后的3个月时效,往往令船东(他们是主要的潜在原告)的滞期费索赔或是货损货差的“补偿行动”(indemnity action)等面临时效已过的噩运。但在订约自由的大原则下,只要是写得清楚,合理与否就不是漠视条文明确规定的理由。

这种太短、太不合理的时效条款,在1977年的英国《不公平合约法》(Unfair Contract Terms Act 1977)生效后针对岸上一般“消费者”(consumer)已经站不住脚,条文写得再清楚也没用。这种有关的先例可列举Ocean Chemical Transport Inc and Another v. Exnor Craggs Ltd(2000)1 Lloyd's Rep 446。但《不公平合约法》只是想保护消费者,它不适用在一般与消费者无关的的商业合约。所以,国际商业合约内约定太短时效仍是非常危险,除非自己知道这个合约下对方才是潜在原告,自己不大会向对方索赔。例如,自己是卖方,准备交次货给对方的买方,乐得订一个很短的时效作为一个“圈套”(trap)。

英国法律针对合约时效条文的解释在本质上是看该条文的用字/措辞,而且不会有敌意或涉及公共利益,因为时效条文是有它商业上的合理之处(如上述提到的证据不会流失或早日结总账)。

7.2.2 合约时效条文在英国法律的地位

这一个法律地位可节录Mustill与Boyd的《Commercial Arbitration》(2nd edn,1989年)一书之200至202页所说如下:

“It is common to find in mercantile contracts an express provision to the effect that certain formalities must be performed within a specified time, and that in default of due performance either the claim or the right to assert the claim in arbitration will be barred. A typical example of such a clause, which has featured in several reported case, is the 'Centrocon' arbitration clause, which reads as follows – '... Any claim must be made in writing and claimants' arbitrator appointed within three months of final discharge, and where this provision is not complied with the claim shall be deemed to be waived and absolutely barred ...'

Clauses of this type are variously expressed, both as to the nature of the formality to be performed, and as to the consequence of a failure to perform it. The effect of such a clause is ultimately a matter of construction. There are, however, certain general principles which apply to all provisions of this type.

First, a contractual time – bar is accepted by the Court as intrinsically valid. It was at one time believed that clauses of this type, when coupled with arbitration provisions, involved an ouster of the jurisdiction of the Court. This view was repudiated by the House of Lords, and the courts have during the past five decades repeatedly recognized and enforced such clauses. Indeed, the courts now appear to regard a contractual time limit as a positively beneficial feature of a commercial contract. The objects of such a clause are, it has been stated – (i) to provide some limit to the uncertainties and expense of arbitration and litigation; (ii) to facilitate the obtaining of material evidence; and (iii) to facilitate the settling of accounts for each transaction as and when they fall due.

Second, there is no trace in the authorities of any notion that a short time limit offends against public policy. The three – month time limit fixed by the Centrocon clause has repeatedly been upheld. Moreover, much shorter periods than this have been enforced without comment.

Third, clauses of this type must be construed strictly, and a claim will not be barred by lapse of time unless the provision clearly applies to the claim in question. The Court will, however, be prepared to read a clause as a time – bar provision, even if no barring words are expressed, if this is necessary in order to give some meaning to the contract."

7.2.3 合约时效条文在用字/措辞上需要明确

说到合约时效条文必须是在用字/措辞上写得明确，毕竟条文是剥夺原告的一个重要权利。这在一些先例也有提到过，如在 Bunge v. Deutsche Conti (1980) 1 Lloyd's Rep 352 先例，Donaldson 大法官有说："Applying the general principle that claims are not to be barred, except by clear words."另在 The "Pera" (1985) 2 Lloyd's Rep 103 先例，Staughton 大法官也有说："A time bar clause must be clear and unambiguous if effect was to be given to it and since the clause was prepared and put forward by the charterers for inclusion in the charter – party any ambiguity must be construed against them"。而上诉庭

的 Griffiths 大法官是这样说:"... this clause is, at best, ambiguous, and that being so I return to the fundamental rule that a contractual clause intended to cut down the rights which a party to a contract would otherwise enjoy, must be expressed in clear and unambiguous language."

这种解释严格的先例有 Bunge v. Deutsche Conti,案情是有关一个大豆的 CIF 买卖,买卖合约的时效条文是要求仲裁在合约付运期之后的 3 个月内提起,并接下去有另一条文说明是:"如果不按照合约这样做,有关质量的索赔就被视为是放弃与完全过期"(In the event of non - compliance with any of the preceding provisions of this Rule claims for quality shall be deemed to be waived and absolutely barred unless the ... Board of Appeal ... shall in their absolute discretion, otherwise determine ...)。由于密西西比河大水泛滥的原因,美国立法禁止大豆出口,大豆市场价格也因此暴升,所以卖方没有付运部分货物而导致了买卖双方的争议。这一个争议由于不属于货物质量的索赔,被法院判是不受这 3 个月时效条文的约束。

类似 Bunge v. Deutsche Conti 先例判法也可见上诉庭的 Board of Trade(Minister of Materials) v Steel Brothers & Co Ltd(1952)1 Lloyd's Rep 87 先例。

另在 Odfjfell Seachem A/S v. Continentale des Petroles et d'Investissements and Another(2005)1 Lloyd's Rep 275 先例,案情涉及一个程租合约。船舶到了装港并递交了通知书,但由于承租人没有货物可提供装货,最终导致租约被中断而船东需要另外找替代租约以减少损失。之后船东作为原告向承租人提出索赔,其中承租人的抗辩之一就是索赔时效已经错过,因为从违约/毁约的一天起算,诉讼是在 1 年多之后才提起。但在该程租合约内,有一条文说明是在卸完货之后的 90 天内提出,租约索赔时效条文可节录如下:"20.1 charterers shall be discharged and released from all liability in respect of any claim for demurrage, deviation or detention which owners may have under this charter unless a claim in writing has been presented to charterers, together with all supporting documentation substantiating each and every constituent part of the claim within ninety(90) days of the completion of discharge of the cargo carried hereunder."

由于从来没有装货与卸货,所以承租人的时效抗辩假设如果在装港提供了货物,船舶估计出需要完成航次与卸货的时间,然后再加上 90 天就算作是时效届满。但法院不同意,认为是既然没有卸货,时效届满就无从算起,所以是以 1980 年立法的 6 年时效为准。Teare 大法官是这样说:"... as to the limitation defence, the owners' claim for damages was not within cl. 20 of the charterparty; where there was no discharge of cargo, there was no contractual period within which the claim had to be presented with full supporting documentation; accordingly, the charterers were not entitled to rely on the limitation."

另举一个非航运先例名为 Hancock v. Brazier(Anerley) Ltd. (1966) 1 WLR 1317,

案情涉及一个房屋建造买卖合约。合约中第11条保证条文是说："If the purchaser shall discover any structural defects in the said house and works within six months from the date of completion and shall notify the vendor thereof in writing the vendor shall forthwith make good such structural defects without expense to the purchaser."在订立合约之前，卖方(被告)已经建造好了地基和混凝土楼板，但卖方并不知道他所使用的混凝土中含有硫酸钠的成分，在工程完工的时候也没有出现任何问题。直到该房屋完工2年后，混凝土开始吸水并膨胀，导致混凝土破裂。买方(原告)因此向被告索赔损失。法院判是原告的起诉并不会受到第11条文中6个月的限制，因为第11条文仅针对买方在6个月内发现的房屋缺陷，有权要求卖方维修，但并没有剥夺原告针对房屋的缺陷要求赔偿的权利。

这种争议在笔者的仲裁案件中经常遇到，以一个近期的国际货物买卖的香港仲裁案件为例，有关的FOB买卖合约有一个条文说："Quality discrepancy claim should be filed by the buyer within 45 days after arrival of the goods at the port of discharge. The seller shall, within 10 days after receipt of the notification of the claim, send reply to the buyer."(货物质量问题的索赔在货物抵达卸港的45天内买方应该做出通知。卖方必须在收到该通知后的10天内答复买方。)

在该案件，买方是在船舶抵达卸港后50天才通知中国卖方有关货物质量的问题。买方本人并没有任何拖延，因为他把货物转售后是从分买方得到通知后才能马上转告中国卖方。这一来，在后来的质量问题索赔中，中国卖方一个主要的抗辩就是过了45天的时效。笔者不认为外国买方的索赔是错过了时效，上述节录的条文也不是一条时效条文。但笔者的共同仲裁员坚持这是一条时效条文，并认为在中国法律下(虽然不适用在这一个香港仲裁中)，任何条文如果规定了一个时间就是一种时效条文。所以，在该案件中，中国卖方对外国买方的索赔是有一个完全的抗辩，就是错过了时效。

笔者同意这种条文往往是拟定的不太好，像这上述条文就有许多漏洞。一个就是45天是从货物抵达卸货港的一天开始计算，但这一天不代表货物是从船舶卸下。换言之，遇上卸货港拥挤的情况下，可能过了45天货物还是在船舱内，买方根本没有机会对货物的质量做出检查。另一个漏洞就是明知道货物会转售(尤其是不少商品会多次转售)，所以最后对货物的质量检查往往是来自最终的分买方，因为他才会对货物做出检查，这会带来多长时间的延误是天知道。所以，笔者是觉得上述条文订得并不合理，解释就必须严格针对。如果一条不合理的条文订得明确，解释起来只能得出唯一的一个不合理解释，作为仲裁员也就只能依从，因为他不是订约方。

但在上述条文，笔者并不觉得是订得明确，其中有以下几点：

(1)针对45天所用的文字是"应该"(should)，这一个字并非是足够决绝或肯定。这特别是相对下一句的10天所用的文字是"必须"(shall)有很大的不同。虽然是针对一般商人，他们经常在用字/措辞上不会像有水平的律师这么谨慎，这种不同的用字有可能是随意或不小心。但仲裁员做出解释,就不能做这样的假设,而要假设双方当事人故意选择两个不同的文字在履行同一样性质的事情(就是在规定的时间内做一些事情),就表示了他们有不同的要求。

(2)上述条文针对45天只要求买方做出质量问题的通知,没有要求这45天内提起仲裁等措辞。这种措辞通常会在时效条文中出现。

(3)上述条文也没有说到错过45天会有什么结果。往往在一些常见的时效条文中,会规定如果错过了时效,就再也不能提起索赔或接受责任等的"排除"(barring)文字。这一点在下一个小段会提到并非是关键性,没有这些文字也可以是一个有效的时效条文。但在本案件,这一个因素再配合其他因素,包括是上述的(1)与(2),笔者就感觉不一样。

(4)上述条文还有一个至关重要的地方,就是在第二句话是说明中国卖方"必须"(shall)在10天内答复买方。这一来,如果中国卖方没有在10天内答复(这种情况是经常会出现,包括在本案件),会对中国卖方有什么法律后果?会否是买方不在45天给通知就失去了索赔的权利,但如果卖方不在10天内答复,就失去了抗辩的权利?这可不是开玩笑,因为否定被告的抗辩权利是严重违反自然公正与国际上的公共政策,也不可能以明示条文排除抗辩权利。

还有,笔者并不觉得这种有规定一个时间的条文如果不被解释为时效条文就失去了意义。笔者是觉得可以给它一点意义或解释,如如果买方在450天而不是45天内通知卖方有关货物质量问题,就表示在诉讼中会对买方做出不利推断,因为他晚了通知令卖方没有机会对有关货物做出检查以保留证据作为将来抗辩之用。本来,这种规定一个短时间做出通知的条文主要的原因也是为了让对方或卖方有机会马上去调查取证。另外也可以在利息方面做出考虑,如买方延误做出通知这一段时间否定利息的补偿,因为如果即时做出通知让买方做出检查,有可能这一个索赔很快就能够解决或裁定。这一方面最后是与其他仲裁员达成一致看法。

7.2.4 合约时效条文没有明示说明索赔过期也被默示

相对而言,对时效条文有没有明示的"排除"(barring)文字并不重要,原因是如果条文要求在一个期限内提起诉讼或仲裁,如果错过时效,除了把有关的索赔视为是过期外,不会有其他的意思。所以,认为"排除"不明示也可以默示双方订约的意图。

当然,合约时效条文把错过的后果说清楚明白是最好的,如较早介绍过的 Centrocon arbitration clause,说明是一错过时效就"the claim shall be deemed to be waived and absolutely barred"。这种清楚说明错过时效后果的条文也出现在许多其他先例,如:The"Himmerland"(1965)2 Lloyd's Rep 353;The"Simonburn"(1973)1 Lloyd's Rep 392;Sabah Flour and Feedmills v. Comfez Ltd(1987)2 Lloyd's Rep 647;Ocean Chemical Transport Inc and Another v. Exnor Craggs Ltd(2000)1 Lloyd's Rep 446 等。

但看来有更多的先例是接受不需要明确的错过时效的后果,也可以达到索赔过期并排除诉权的效果。这里可先介绍 Metalimex Foreign Trade Corpn v. Eugenie Maritime Ltd(1962)1 Lloyd's Rep 378 先例,有关的程租合约有条文说是"在卸货后 6 个月内要提起伦敦仲裁"(Arbitration to be in London ... Any Claim arising under this Charter Party has to be made in writing within 6 months after final discharge....)。英国高院的 McNair 大法官判说:"Accordingly, approaching this case from the point of view of the words themselves, and from the point of view of reasonableness, it seems to me that the right construction is that contended for by the defendants here, namely, that unless the claim is made in writing within the time limited then the claim shall be barred or not admissible, or whatever words one cares to choose. I am reinforced in that conclusion by the consideration that, as far as I have been able to understand, if that effect is not given to the clause, no effect is given to it at all."

另在 Metalfer Corporation v. Pan Ocean Shipping Co Ltd(1998)2 Lloyd's Rep 632 先例,有关租约的时效条文可节录如下:"Any dispute arising out of this charterparty to be referred to the London Arbitrators within 30 days of completion of the voyage and English law to apply. One Arbitrator to be appointed by each of the parties thereto and the third by the two so chosen."英国高院的 Longmore 大法官判在航次完结后的 30 天内必须提起伦敦仲裁,否则时效就会错过,说:"unless one reads this provision as a time bar it really has no meaning at all."

7.2.5 合约时效条文的总结

总结而言,合约的时效条文会是十分危险。这些时效条文也不必出现在仲裁条文内或有标题说明是索赔时效条文,让合约的双方当事人警觉。往往时效条文如果加在其他的条文会是更危险。例如,在买卖合约或租约中的"滞期条文"(demurrage clause)中加上一句索赔必须在装卸后的 30 天内向卖方或承租人提起,就会更容易让买方或船东看漏了这一句。这尤其是在今天一些标准格式合约都可以在网上下载与修改后再打印出来,导致了加上这样的一句时效条文并不显著,好像是原来印本格式条文的一部分,有诉权的原告就更加会容易看漏。在本章之 5 段提到的 Nanjing Tianshun Shipbuilding Co Ltd and Jiangsu Skyrun International Group Co Ltd v. Orchard Tankers PTE Ltd(2011)EWHC 164 先例,也涉及一个根据日本造船格式合约的造船合约,买方在 Article X 有关买方终断合约的条文中加上了一条简单的时效条文,说明船厂如果质疑船东的终断,就需要在终断后 30 天内提起仲裁。这时效条文没有加在 Article XIII 的仲裁条文内,导致中国船厂不警觉。而且,加在 Article X 的时效条文是从表面上看不出原来的格式合约中是没有这一句话。结果是错过了二三天时间才提起伦敦仲裁,这被仲裁庭(笔者持不同意见)判是时效已经错过,失去了质疑船东终断合约的合法性,也保护不了还款担保,而涉及的金额高达数以千万美元。

7.3 适用外国法律的时效

这是另一个非常复杂与危险的课题。复杂的原因就是如果一涉及其他国家针对时效的法律(这在侵权与合约关系都有可能,特别是国际性业务),就会是困难重重。

读者只要看本章对英国法律针对时效的方方面面,如果也感觉到掌握起来有困难,就更加不用想掌握外国(可能涉及很多国家)有关时效的法律。这一来,受害方的原告甚至代表他的律师在不了解的情况下错过时效的机会就大大增加。在这里可简单说明不同国家对时效规定有巨大差异,不论是在时间的长短、怎样才能保护时效、有哪些情况可以中断或延长等方面都有不同的规定。笔者记得在30多年前(1982年)曾经阅读过国际海事委员会(CMI)对20多个国家的海商法在时效方面的规定做出过的一个报告,厚度足可以构成一本可观的书籍。这20多个国家对时效的规定有很大差异,如在一般民事索赔的时效,有荷兰的长达30年或葡萄牙的20年之久,但也有西班牙或委内瑞拉的针对运费或滞期费索赔时效短至交货后的6个月。

CMI的报告与大部分的读者恐怕关系不大,特别是不涉及航运的读者。但与香港有最密切关系的中国内地,众所周知是针对一般的民事索赔,有一个2年的时效期限,这就会与接下去笔者要讨论的内容有密切关系了。

至于这一个课题的危险性,可以先简单说是英国法律现在承认并接受外国实体法的适用,包括是在伦敦仲裁,而且会把时效作为是实体法对待。

7.3.1 英国普通法把时效视为是程序问题

英国普通法把时效作为"程序问题"(procedural issue)而不是"实体问题"(substantive issue)。即在英国法院或伦敦仲裁,是要依从英国程序法,所以英国法律的时效仍适用。在Huber v. Steiner(1835)2 Bing N. C. 202先例,案情涉及一批法国的"本票"(promissory note),双方承认实体法是适用法国法律,而根据法国法律时效是已经错过。但这被判在英国法院的诉讼,由于英国的时效还没有错过,所以不能以时效作为抗辩。虽然在Huber v. Steiner先例是有假设法国时效只是"排除救济"(remedy barring)而不是"排除诉权"(right barring)。但可以说在该先例与之后的先例,时效的适用被视为主要是一个程序的问题。

这一个普通法的传统地位,可以节录一个澳大利亚高院的较近期先例作为总结:McKain v. RW Miller & Co(SA)Pty Ltd(1991)174 CLR 1。该先例是说:"It is well-established principle that statutes of limitation, except where title is affected, are rules of procedure only and form part of the *lex fori*. The reason why such statutes are so regarded is that they relate to the remedy and not the right."

把时效视为是程序法的传统地位带来最不好的问题就是鼓励有诉权的原告全球"择地诉讼"(forum-shopping),只要能够找到其他可能有管辖权的国家法院。例如,在最有关国家(如中国)发生的侵权损失或违约已经错过了时效,有诉权的原告就去英国法院提起诉讼,因为英国会判英国的6年时效适用。而如果连英国的6年时效也错过,就可以去荷兰的法院,时效更加会长达30年。这样做显然对被告不公平,他(假设是一家中国公司)认为适用的时效法律是2年,所以会在时效届满把有关的证据与档案销毁,殊不知过了多年后会在外国法院被起诉。这显然也违反了有这个时效规定的本意。

7.3.2　区分时效法律是排除救济或排除诉权所带来的问题

已经提到过是在传统的普通法中,时效问题属于程序问题还是实体问题是要看有关诉讼时效的立法或合约的用字/措辞。如果错过时效会"排除诉权"(right barring),那么这个时效就是实体问题。相反,如果错过时效只"排除救济"(remedy barring),就会是程序问题。在英国的立法中通常使用"可执行性"(enforceability)这一个词,所以时效规定都会被视为程序问题。这种分类方法也适用于解释外国的诉讼时效法律规定。但这种传统的分类方法会导致各种问题,首先是太注重文字的差别,感觉有一点吹毛求疵。另一问题就是在国际私法的理论上可以分以下四种不同的情况并带来不同的时效后果:

(1)如果诉讼地法律与外国法律的时效规定都是程序问题。在这种情况下,只应该适用诉讼地的时效规定。所以就算原告在实体法规定下已经错过了诉讼时效,他还是可以依据诉讼地法律继续诉讼。这就会导致已经提到过的"择地诉讼"问题。

(2)如果诉讼地法律和外国法律的时效都是实体问题,那么就只适用外国法律的时效规定。

(3)如果诉讼地法律的时效是实体问题而外国法律的时效是程序问题,这就会得出结论是两种都不适用。在实践中,普通法国家的法院都不会得出这种结论,但在这种情况下还是没有定论应该适用哪一个法律针对时效。

(4)如果诉讼地的时效法律是程序问题而外国法律的时效是实体问题,就会得出结论是两种都应该适用。在实践中,诉讼地法院在这种情况下通常会决定适用比较短的时效期限。如果诉讼地法律较短的时效已经错过,但外国法律的时效还是有效,原告还是得不到救济。相反是诉讼地法律的时效较长,但外国法律的时效已经错过,原告也是得不到救济。

7.3.3　把时效视为是实体问题的近期看法

这一个更近期的看法,可简单节录新加坡在2011年针对这方面立法所做出的一个法律报告名为《Report of the Law Reform Committee on Limitation Periods in Private International Law》,它在第3、4段是这样说:

"3. The main argument in favour of applying the law of the forum to limitation periods is that it is a reflection of the public policy of shutting out stale claims from the courts. However, the modern view is that the invariable application of the law of the forum is too blunt an instrument to give effect to the fundamental public policies of the forum. A more sophisticated approach, where the forum's public policy is the rear guard, has been the preferred solution in other major jurisdictions.

4. The main reasons for preferring the modern approach are: (a) the distinction in traditional approach between rights and remedy is illusory; (b) the traditional approach with its forum bias encourages forum shopping; and (c) the traditional approach goes against modern notions of international comity underlying choice of law in the somewhat intrusive

and invariable application of forum rules of limitation periods."

这大致上是说传统的英国普通法地位的三个主要反对原因:(1)区分排除诉权与排除救济是虚幻的;(2)鼓励择地诉讼;(3)影响国际友好,因为干预适用外国法律对时效的规定。

该新加坡法律报告的第2段也有提到在这个近期看法下,而做出立法更改的普通法国家包括英国、澳大利亚、加拿大、部分美国法院与最后新加坡自己也在2012年立法。可节录这第2段如下:"Major jurisdictions have moved away from this approach. The United Kingdom departed from the traditional common law approach by statute in 1984. The highest courts in Australia and Canada have moved away from this historical approach. Many courts in the United States have rejected this approach. The European Union has rejected the notion of the invariable application of the law of the forum for limitation periods in two very important instruments regulating choice of law for contractual and non - contractual obligations respectively. Civil law jurisdictions have generally regarded limitation period laws as substantive in the private international law sense (and therefore applicable as part of the substantive law governing the claim). Recent developments in China confirmed this to be its position. Thus, the prevailing modern approach is to apply the limitation period law of the law applicable to the claim as a general rule."

7.3.4 英国的1984年立法把时效视为是实体问题

英国的法律委员会在英国加入了欧共体后就已经开始要面对这一个问题,因为欧洲的大陆法国家与普通法国家不同,一贯是把时效视为"实体问题"(substantive issue)。这可以看欧共体的规定(对英国也适用),如在《Rome Convention on the Law Applicable to Contractual Obligation》(2008年)针对合约的规定如下:"[t]he law applicable to a contract by virtue of this Regulation shall govern in particular ... the various ways of extinguishing obligations, and prescription and limitation of actions; ..."

另在《Rome Ⅱ Regulation on the Law Applicable to Non - Contractual Obligations》(2007年)也有规定针对非合约责任如下:"[t]he law applicable to non - contractual obligations under this Regulation shall govern in particular ... (h) the manner in which an obligation may be extinguished and rules of prescription and limitation, including rules relating to the commencement, interruption and suspension of a period of prescription or limitation."

在1982年英国法律委员会做出了一份报告名为《Classification of Limitation in Private International Law》,建议英国立法改变把所有有关索赔的时效适用实体法,并不再理会有关时效规定的用字/措辞。其中最主要的一个建议是在4.13段与第1(1)条文说:"**Our principal recommendation.** The English rule whereby statutes of limitation, as opposed to rules of prescription, are classed as procedural should be abandoned, and, where under our rules of private international law a foreign law falls to be applied in proceedings in this country, the rule of that foreign law relating to limitation should also be applied, to the exclusion of the law of limitation in force in England and Wales."

法律委员会做出的一些主要建议都在《Foreign Limitation Periods Act 1984》的立法,变得现在在英国法院或仲裁的诉讼如果涉及时效争议,要看有关侵权或违约所适用的外国法律对时效有什么说法。这1984年立法在针对与其他欧共体国家之间的侵权与合约关系已经在《Rome Ⅱ Regulation on the Law Applicable to Non - Contractual Obligations》(2007年)与《Rome Convention on the Law Applicable to Contractual Obligation》(2008年)生效后在一定程度上被边缘化,但还是适用在一些非欧共体国家,如中国公司去伦敦仲裁。

这英国法律的改变可以说是解决了一方面的问题,但重新带来另一方面在本章7.3段开头所讲的全球不同国家有不同时效规定的复杂问题。这导致的结果是时效问题变得更复杂与不肯定。

7.3.5　英国1984年立法的例外情况

在1984年的《Foreign Limitation Periods Act》, Section 2规定了有一种例外的情况,这就是如果违反英国"公共政策"(public policy),就不适用外国实体法的时效规定。另也延伸到一种例外情况,就是适用外国实体法的时效规定会是对原告造成"过度困境"(undue hardship),如外国的时效规定在时间上实在是太短,是英国接受不了。这种情况不足够构成公共政策的例外,正如上诉庭的Bingham大法官在Durham v. T & N plc, 1 May 1996, unreported先例中说:"[it] would in our judgment be wrong to treat a foreign limitation period as contrary to English public policy simply because it is less generous than the comparable English provision in force at the time."所以,立法多加了另一种"过度困境"的例外情况。

以上两种例外的情况也已经有不少的先例做进一步的解释。例如在Gotha City (A Body Corporate) v Sotheby's (An Unlimited Company); Federal Republic of Germany v. Sotheby's, The Times, October 8, 1998先例,案情涉及一幅名画在第二次世界大战中在哥达(在之前的德意志民主共和国西南部城市)的一个博物馆失踪,该名画在1980年左右曾经在莫斯科出现,也短暂于1987年在西柏林出现,然后在1992年通过苏富比拍卖行出售。哥达市政府作为原告要求把该名画归还,这就涉及一个侵占财产的诉讼,在英国法院适用的立法是1977年《Torts (Interference with Goods) Act》。这一个先例涉及几个方面的问题,包括依据德国法律的所有权与时效问题。而如果德国的法律适用并且是错过了时效,英国可否根据公共政策作为例外不适用德国法的时效。只说英国法院判是没有错过时效,而针对公共政策作为例外情况,虽然在该先例不必考虑,但Wright大法官也给了一些指引如下:

"(1) Public policy should be invoked for the purposes of disapplying a foreign limitation period only in exceptional circumstances. Too ready a resort to public policy would frustrate our system of private international law, which 'exists to fulfil foreign rights not destroy them'.

(2) Foreign law should only be disapplied where that law is contrary to a 'fundamental principle of justice'.

(3) The fundamental principle of justice with which it is said foreign law conflicts must be clearly identifiable. The process of identification must not depend upon a judge's individual notion of expediency or fairness but upon the possibility of recognizing with clarity a principle derived from our own law of limitation or some other clearly recognized general principle of public policy. English courts should not invoke public policy save in cases where foreign law is manifestly incompatible with public policy. The Law Commission expected that that approach would be adopted and thus did not recommend the use of the word 'manifestly' in its proposed Bill.

(4) The English law of limitation serves the purpose of providing protection for defendants from stale claims, encouraging claimants to institute proceedings without unreasonable delay and conferring on a potential defendant confidence that after the lapse of a specific period of time he will not face a claim.

(5) A foreign limitation period will not be disapplied as being contrary to public policy merely because it is less generous than the comparable English provision. Some reason other than mere length must be identified for invoking public policy (see Law Commission Report No. 114, paragraph 4.46)."

至于"过度困境"(undue hardship)一词,在本章 2.3.5 段介绍的 1950 年英国《仲裁法》也是有同样的用字/措辞。在 1994 年立法下,如果适用外国实体法的时效规定会是对原告造成过度困境,是另一种可以不适用的情况。这也已经有了一些重要的先例,其中一个较近期与重要的先例是 Harley and Others v. Smith and Another (2009) 1 Lloyd's Rep 359,案情涉及多位原告是职业潜水员,受到被告的聘用在沙特阿拉伯的海上钻井平台工作。他们之间的雇佣合约是适用沙特法律。在工作期间,由于需要在一些有毒化学品排出的水域工作,导致了原告有长期的病患。原告在英国法院提出诉讼,这一个诉讼是在英国《Limitation Act 1980》的时效期限内,但如果适用沙特法律,就已经错过了时效,因为沙特法律的规定时效是 1 年,从事故发生一天或是雇佣合约终结一天起算。这就涉及适用沙特法律会带来对原告的过度困境问题,这被英国法院判是的确会造成这种例外的情况。Foskett 大法官在分析了有关的先例后总结一些原则说:"The following propositions can be deduced from these authorities: (i) That it is not sufficient to cross the 'undue hardship' threshold by reason only of the fact that the foreign limitation period is less generous than that of the English jurisdiction. (ii) That the claimant must satisfy the court that he or she will suffer greater hardship in the particular circumstances than would normally be the case. (iii) That in considering (ii) the focus is on the interests of the individual claimant or claimants and is not upon a balancing exercise between the interests of the claimants on the hand and the defendant on the other."

而在 Harley and Others v. Smith and Another 先例，判是的确对原告会造成过度困境，所以不适用沙特法律的时效。Foskett 大法官是这样说："I would be satisfied that the 'undue hardship' threshold had been crossed in respect of each claimant in this case. On the premise to which I have referred the following factors would persuade me that this is so：(i) Each claimant was impeded in obtaining local advice and representation in the KSA（沙特阿拉伯王国）in the manner I referred to in paras 33 to 35 above. (ii) Had each of them obtained such advice or representation at the time, their respective interests would probably have been protected. (iii) Each sought advice in the UK as soon as it was practicable to do so upon their return. (iv) Each was misled by advice that was received to the effect that the limitation period did not begin until June 2006. (v) Those giving the advice, whether in the UK or in the KSA, were disadvantaged because of the uncertainty of the legal position in the KSA and, as a result, the claimants were victims of that uncertainty. (vi) Through no fault of their own they will be deprived of any opportunity of seeking any kind or redress as a result of the incident unless the limitation period is disapplied."

7.3.6　普通法针对合约的适用法

简单说，英国在 1991 年 8 月 1 日开始，就有了立法针对合约"适用法"(proper/governing law)的问题，该立法名为《Contracts (Applicable Law) Act 1990》。这一个立法是根据 1980 年的《Rome Convention》，适用在所有欧共体的国家。但笔者看来，该立法与英国一贯的普通法地位也相差不远。

普通法针对一个合约的适用法是分三个步骤确定。第一步就是看双方有没有明示条文约定有关合约的适用法。如果没有，第二步就是看其他的合约条文中有没有一个默示的适用法。例如，合约中如果有一条"排外管辖权条文"(exclusive jurisdiction clause)或一条仲裁条文，就会是一个非常强而有力的说明管辖的国家法院或仲裁地点的国家法律就是适用法：Compagnie d'armement Maritime SA Compagnie Tunisienne de Navigation SA (1970) 2 Lloyd's Rep 99 先例。相反是如果合约有一条"非排外管辖权条文"(permissive/non - exclusive jurisdiction clause)，默示适用法的力度就大大降低：Armadora Occidental SA v. Horace Mann Insurance Co (1977) 2 Lloyd's Rep 406；Cantieri Navali Riuniti SpA v. NV Omne Justitia (1985) 2 Lloyd's Rep 428 等先例。而最后也就是第三步，在没有明示或默示条文可找出适用法的情况下，就是考虑所有涉及该案件的情况确定双方会意图适用的法律。在一定的程度上，第三步所要考虑的因素会是包罗万象，而导致最后被法院或仲裁庭所确定的适用法也是最不肯定。有说法是第三步是找出与该有关合约的履行有"最接近最真实联系"(closest and most real connection with the transaction)的法律体系。针对第三步，可简单节录 Merkin 教授所著的《Arbitration Law》(2004 年)一书之 7.10 段如下："... Failing any indication in the contract itself, the court will seek to ascertain on objective grounds the intention of the parties, which is assumed to be that the contract is to be governed by the system of law with which the contract has its closest connection. The factors to be taken into account will vary depending upon the nature of the contract, but will in general include the domicile of the parties, the place in which the contract was made and the place in which the contract is to be performed or administered: where the factors point in different directions, fine choices may have to be made. As far as an arbitration clause is concerned, additional factors may be relevant if the contract itself is silent on law or jurisdiction. In Al Midani v. Al Midani(2000)1 Lloyd's Rep 923 the beneficiaries of two wills entered into what was described as an arbitration agreement so that their dispute as to entitlement could be resolved. The agreement did not provide expressly for an applicable law, but was written in Arabic and provided for the appointment of a named Islamic Saudi Arabian citizen as arbitrator. In those circumstances, Rix J concluded that it was likely that the law applicable to the arbitration agreement was Shari's law, either alone or as modified by Saudi law. In the event this proved immaterial, as Rix J was not convinced that the agreement amounted to one for arbitration."

可以说,在上述的第三步会是最危险,因为它会"意外"把原告没有想适用的实体法带进来,其中包括时效的规定。如果在该适用的法律体系下是一个很短的时效并且已经错过,被告大可以以这一个理由作为一个强而有力的"抗辩理由"(defence)。所以涉及跨国合约,也表示将来出了问题使用什么适用法就会有争议,就必须加上一条明示条文明确合约的适用法律。可以说在国际性的商业活动中,由于英国商法的完整性,所以大部分的合约如果有想到加上一条明示条文,都会选择英国法。

7.3.7 香港仲裁但适用中国法的疑问

最后一提的是近年来前来香港地区仲裁的案件有数量不少的仲裁与适用法条文是约定适用中国内地的法律,也就是适用中国内地的实体法解释双方的争议。有不少有关条文只是简单的一句:"Hong Kong arbitration, PRC law to govern"。这应该被解释为中国内地的法律只是适用在实体法(如有关合约的解释),而仲裁的程序法应该还是香港地区的仲裁法,因为仲裁地点是香港。如果把这个简单条文解释为香港地区仲裁的程序法也必须适用中国内地的法律(仲裁法),就会导致该香港仲裁如果要向法院寻求救济,也必须去中国内地的法院而不是香港法院了。

这就带来一个问题是中国法下的2年索赔时效(以前是更短的1年)是否也适用在香港地区仲裁。这一个问题对中国公司尤其重要,因为笔者长期以来的感觉就是中国公司经常是作为被告,而作为原告向外国公司提起索赔诉讼的几率是寥寥无几。不论是什么原因,中国公司作为被告就会被逼上梁山,要硬着头皮面对,这就带来了面对一个金额庞大的索赔最好不过的是有一个错过时效的抗辩。这表示中国公司可以考虑这一方面,也就是在香港地区开始的仲裁中,经常有外国原告心里只想到6年的香港地区法定时效(因为有不少合约没有规定合约时效),没有顾及中国的2

年法定时效。这表示如果香港地区仲裁把时效问题视为是程序法,6 年时效就会适用。但如果把时效问题视为是实体法,2 年时效就会适用。

但香港地区法律地位还不明确,也不肯定,不像新加坡或英国已经有了立法针对合约适用外国法律时的时效问题。特别是香港仲裁的裁决是终局,不能把法律观点向法院上诉确立一个先例,让所有其他的香港仲裁案件依从,这变为个别仲裁庭可以任意做出裁决。例如,仲裁庭可以认为香港地区虽然还没有立法,但显然近期的国际做法是以合约的适用法为准适用在时效方面的规定,所以应该依从。同样的仲裁庭也可以认为香港地区还没有立法,就表示立法机构还没有做出这方面的打算,并继续把时效问题作为程序问题看待。

第十八章　投资仲裁的损失计算

1. 概述

近年来，根据国际公约如 1965 年《华盛顿公约》(The Washington Convention on the Settlement of Investment Disputes Between States and Nationals of other States)或简称《ICSID 公约》(International Centre for the Settlement of Investment Disputes)，以及该公约下国与国之间所签订的“双边投资协议”(Bilateral Investment Treaty 或简称 BIT)或“多边投资协议”(Multilateral Investment Treaty 或简称 MIT)如“北美自由贸易协议”(North American Free Trade Agreement 或简称 NAFTA)等，带来了大量的投资仲裁案件(基本上都是由外国投资者控告主权国家)，并经常涉及庞大金额的索赔。随手拈来举几个例子，最近一个 ICC 的仲裁案件中判委内瑞拉要赔付 Exxon Mobil 9.09 亿美元。另一个 Yukos Oil Company 与俄罗斯的仲裁案件中，Yukos Oil Company 声称俄罗斯没收其资产的行为违反了《能源许可公约》(Energy Charter Treaty)，俄罗斯被判需要赔偿 300 亿美元。而在另外一个 Generation Ukraine v. Ukraine 的仲裁案件中，赔偿的金额也是高达 94 亿美元。在笔者的网站上也曾经介绍过一个涉及 1000 亿美元的投资仲裁案件，可以说这些金额会是令世界上不少的发展中国家在赔付后会破产，这类案件不论是索赔金额之大还是对败诉国家影响的深远均令人震惊。

根据 SD Franck 在《Empirically Evaluating Claims about Investment Treaty Arbitration》[1]文章中的调查，这种投资仲裁的赔偿金额平均是 3.434 亿美元。可见这种赔偿金额远超出一般的商业仲裁案件，包括在 2008 年金融海啸之后中国船厂在伦敦败诉的仲裁案件。这也是完全可以理解，因为外国投资者是通常不会向主权国家索赔小金额的赔偿。要走到投资仲裁这一步，外国投资者就是准备撤走在该主权国家的业务，而且不准备在短期甚至中期内再回该主权国家进行投资。这表示外国投资者很少敢向美国政府提起索赔，即使美国政府有违反双边投资协议下的责任。但面对一些发展中国家，特别是在发生严重政治或经济上的动荡后，外国投资者通常就不会手软而在撤离之前狠敲一笔。

---

〔1〕 (2007)80 North Carolina Law Review 1(http://ssrn.com/abstract=969257).

就投资仲裁的胜负结果而言，根据调查是38.5%仲裁案件是投资者作为原告胜诉并获得赔偿，而57.7%的仲裁案件是投资者败诉。至于双方在诉讼中途达成和解的比例就不详，因为这种结果往往是机密，不像投资仲裁的裁决书在今天而言是相对透明。

至于败诉的主权国家是否会作出支付，根据V. Lowe所写的文章《Changing Dimensions of International Investment Law》，[1]调查的结果是大部分主权国家在败诉后都肯做出支付（期间可能会有谈判并达成部分支付的和解）。但还是有部分投资仲裁裁决书是需要强制执行，所以在今天的国际仲裁中，如何对败诉主权国家执行也是一个热门的话题。这种裁决书还会在国际市场上被作为"资产"去买卖，并有一些所谓的"秃鹫基金"（vulture funds）或"坏账基金"（distress debt fund）来购买胜诉投资者的裁决书，因为通常这种基金有无限的财力可以向败诉的主权国家执行这一笔高昂的赔偿（这包括调查这些国家的资产，甚至是来自其他国家的援助或投资，如香港著名的涉及"主权豁免"（Sovereign Immunity）的FG Hemisphere Associates LLC v. Democratic Republic of Congo, FACV 5, 6 & 7/2010先例，这是一般的发展中国家都难以抵抗的。

一般而言，投资者会更加喜欢在世界银行下的ICSID去仲裁，这会对作为被告的主权国家有更大的阻吓力，因为世界银行会帮助迫使败诉的主权国家做出支付。但是否是ICSID仲裁，或是根据联合国仲裁规则（UNCITRAL Arbitration Rules）的"随意仲裁"（*ad hoc* arbitration），或是国际商会仲裁（ICC Arbitration）就要看相关国家所订立的双边投资协议，它们有规定以哪一种仲裁方式解决争议。

投资仲裁的裁决书执行，也往往比一般商业仲裁有更强的政治味道。在2012年3月28日，美国总统奥巴马就宣布了终断给阿根廷的贸易优惠，原因是阿根廷不赔付两个投资仲裁裁决书的败诉金额给两家美国公司Azurix与CMS Gas。这一个贸易优惠是来自US Generalized System of Preferences，在这一个优惠计划下，阿根廷向美国出口大量的餐酒、牛肉、橄榄油等都可以免税。在2001年度，阿根廷向美国出口的金额高达4.77亿美元，是上述优惠计划中出口金额排第九的国家。估计阿根廷在此压力下还是会妥协而支付败诉金额给上述两家美国公司。

这两个仲裁案件的案情涉及美国的石油气公司，与阿根廷政府协议约定依据美元来计算关税，以适应美元的浮动，再按照当时的汇率转换成比索。但在1999年阿根廷政府要求用比索来计算关税，而比索之后严重贬值，2000年阿根廷经济崩溃。这导致美国公司的利润与收益急剧下降并提起仲裁，裁决书判决的赔偿金额共是3亿美元。

以阿根廷为代表的发展中国家普遍认为ICSID仲裁过于保护商业投资者的利

---

[1] (2007) University of Oxford Faculty of Law Legal Studies Research Paper Series Working Paper No. 4/2007 (http://papers.ssrn.com/sol3/papers.cfm?abstract_id=970727).

益。因为ICSID仲裁庭的成员通常都是具有商业背景,这些仲裁员往往局限于合约规定,不会更好地平衡被告主权国家广泛利益(如公共健康或环境利益的考虑)并给予保护。这可以引用《经济学家》杂志2012年2月18日版中第38页的文章段落如下:"Argentina(and other developing countries)sees ICSID as too business – friendly,with some justification. According to Jurgen Kurtz, a law professor at the University of Melbourne,its tribunal members often come from commercial arbitration,where disputes are resolved narrowly,on the basis of firm contracts rather than treaties. But many ICSID claims involve investment treaties,which grant governments exceptions for broad interests such as public health or the environment. The arbitrators must determine whether a state's actions meet those criteria."

另外一些发展中国家如玻利维亚、厄瓜多尔与委内瑞拉已经完全退出了ICSID公约。据知,前不久退出ICSID公约的委内瑞拉面对的投资仲裁案件数量与金额已经超越了阿根廷。即使是一些发达国家也开始质疑ICSID仲裁对主权国家不利。在2011年,澳大利亚就表示它不会在未来的贸易协议中约定投资者与国家间的仲裁。当时澳大利亚政府正在新加坡的仲裁中面临Philip Morris(一家美国烟草公司)的起诉,这一个投资仲裁所涉及的是香烟包装的法定标准问题。

毕竟,参加ICSID公约与其他国家签署双边协议是否对吸引外资具有十分重要的作用也有一定的怀疑。例如,巴西与印度都是吸引外资的重要国家,但它们就没有加入ICSID公约。

1.1　损失赔偿

本章的篇幅有限,所以不会针对投资仲裁的各种问题,包括经常会出现的管辖权争议与责任方面(如解释有关的双边投资协议)的争议。针对的只是局限在投资仲裁的损失计算方面,这一个方面也被视为是很难理解与最不肯定。这一个看法可节录Rubbins与Kinsella在《International Investment,Political Risk and Dispute Resolution:A Practitioners' Guide》(Oceana Publications,Oxford,2005)一书中所说:"在国际投资法律中,损失赔偿的金额是最难以理解以及最不可预计的"(the quantum of damages remains one of the least understood and most unpredictable areas of international investment law)。

但问题是它涉及的金额十分庞大,计算十分复杂,导致在一个投资仲裁中经常双方当事人都会花大量的金钱与时间在这一方面的争议。毕竟在不少的投资仲裁,责任方面相对简单明确,剩下来真正值得争议的就是被告的主权国家应该赔偿多少金额。在现实中赔偿30亿美元或3000万美元还是会有天壤之别。

1.2　什么是国际投资

在国际投资争议中,损失赔偿是作为诉讼或仲裁裁决责任问题之后的救济,但前提之一就是相关争议必须涉及外国投资者的"投资"(Investment)行为。

"投资"概念的范围取决于具体投资协议的条文规定。许多条文包含一个"广泛的以资产为基础"(broad asset - based)的投资,这会包括投资者直接或间接所有或控制的各种资产(every kind of asset)。这表明这种广泛的投资概念包含所有具有经济价值的资产,而没有任何限制(这方面可参阅联合国文件之 UNCTAD,Scope and Definition,UNCTAD Series on Issues in International Investment Agreements [United Nations, Geneva,1999] 18.)。

投资的目的通常是赚取金钱/利润,因此与交易有关的资产可以分为以下的类别:(1)传统的不动产权利,如建筑物、工厂、土地等;(2)某一家公司的参与权,如股东持有的股份;(3)货币债权与要求履行的权利;(4)知识产权与工业产权;(5)特许权或其他类似权利。

也会有情况是投资者为他的投资项目成立一家"特殊目的/专设公司"(Special Purpose Vehicle 或简称 SPV),这就涉及该公司的股权价格会是代表该投资的市价。不过以股权的价格计算赔偿的方式也有其限制:如交易的次数不足甚至股份没有在公开市场出售过都使仲裁庭难以计算出一个合理的价格作为赔偿金额。

国际投资仲裁中涉及的投资类别有以下几种,可以列举一些有关每个类别被报道的投资仲裁裁决如下:

(1)直接或间接拥有的公司/企业:MTD v. Chile, Award of 25 May 2004; CME v. The Czech Republic, Final Award of 14 March 2003; Nykomb v. Latvia, Award of 16 December 2003; Tecmed v. Mexico, Award of 29 May 2003; Pope & Talbot v. Canada, Award of Damages of 31 May 2002; Myers v. Canada, Partial Award of 13 November 2000; Metalclad v. Mexico, Award of 30 August 2000。

(2)在某一个公司/企业中参股:Sempra Energy v. Argentina, Award of 28 September 2007; Enron v. Argentine, Award of 22 May 2007; LG&E v. Argentina, Award of 25 July 2007; CMS v. Argentina, Award of 12 May 2005; Maffezini v. Spain, Award of 13 November 2000; AMT v. Zaire, Award of 21 February 1997; SPP(ME) v. Egypt, Award of 20 May 1992, (1997) 106 ILR 502。

(3)动产与不动产,如房子、土地等:Sedelmayer v. Russia, Award of 7 July 1998; Tecmed v. Mexico, Award of 29 May 2003; Middle East Cement v. Egypt, Award of 12 April 2002; Santa Elena v. Costa Rica, Award of 17 February 2000; SwemBalt v. Latvia, Award of 23 October 2000。

(4)商业特许权或其他合约权利:Vivendi v. Argentina, Award of 20 August 2007; Siemens v. Argentina, Award of 6 February 2007; LIAMCO v. Libya, Award of 12 April 1977; Kuwait v. Aminoil, Award of 24 March 1982; Azurix v. Argentina, Final Award of 14 July 2006; Autopista v. Venezuela, Final Award of 23 September 2003; ADC v. Hungary, Final Award of 2 October 2006; Amco v. Indonesia II, Award on the merits of 31 May 1990, (1992) 89 ILR 368。

(5)借贷:SPP(ME) v. Egypt, Award of 20 May 1992; Siemens v. Argentina, Award of 6 February 2007; Sempra Energy v. Argentina, Award of 28 September 2007。

(6)依据合约对金钱的请求权: Nykomb v. Latvia, Award of 16 December 2003; Petrobart v. Kyrgyz Republic, Award of 29 March 2005; CSOB v. Slovak Republic, Final Award of 29 December 2004。

(7)其他金钱请求权(如退税权): Occidental v. Equador, Award of 1 July 2004; Feldman v. Mexico, Award of 16 December 2002。

1.3 主权国家干预行为的类别与具体例子

在国际投资交易中,与投资者订立合约的通常会是主权国家本身或国有企业,但也会是私人公司/企业。投资争议往往是因为主权国家政府合法或是非法干预了外国投资者的权利,导致投资者把主权国家作为被告索赔他蒙受的损失。这些干预的类别会有很多种,以下举少数的几个例子来具体解释。

1.3.1 政府对资产权的干预

在 Santa Elena v. Costa Rica, Award of 17 February 2000 仲裁案件中,外国投资者被政府剥夺了一块长达30公里的海岸线土地的使用权,而投资者原本计划把这块海岸线土地用作开发旅游项目。

在 AMT v. Zaire, Award of 21 February 1997 仲裁案件中,案情涉及扎伊尔武装部队毁坏、运走属于一个美国投资者的制成品、原材料与其他有价值的资产。

在 Asian Agricultural Products v. Sri Lanka, Award of 27 June 1990 仲裁案件中,案情涉及投资者在斯里兰卡成立公司养殖和出口虾,但公司所有的虾养殖场被斯里兰卡武装部队在反叛乱(泰米尔老虎组织的叛乱)行动中破坏。

在 SwenBalt v. Latvia, Award of 23 October 2000 仲裁案件中,案情涉及拉脱维亚当局扣押了投资者的船舶并将她拍卖,但没有给予赔偿。

在 Tecmed v. Mexico, Award of 29 May 2003 仲裁案件中,墨西哥政府非法拒绝更新美国投资者运营垃圾填埋场的许可,导致美国投资者不能继续运营垃圾填埋场,损失包括浪费的建筑、设施和其他资产。

这种政府的各种干预行为在今天还是不断有发生,在2012年6月12日的《Global Arbitration Review Briefing》中,有报道关于玻利维亚采取一连串的行动把资产收归国有,并在不久前宣布把瑞士的 Glencore 拥有的一个矿产公司收归国有。

1.3.2 政府对合约权利的干预

在 ADC v. Hungary, Final Award of 2 October 2006 仲裁案件中,案情涉及匈牙利政府通过法令收回在合约中给予外国投资者运营机场候机楼的权利。

在 Azurix v. Argentina, Final Award of 14 July 2006 与 Vivendi v. Argentina, Award of 20 August 2007 两个仲裁案件中,涉及政府非法干涉特许权合约中分别给予两个外国投资者提供供水服务的权利,并导致合约的终止。

在 Petrobart v. Kyrgyz Republic, Award of 29 March 2005 仲裁案件中,外国投资者

向他的合约合伙人(一个国有公司)提供气体凝析油,但由于政府的干预,导致这个国有公司拒绝付款给投资者。

在 Himpurna v. PLN, Award of 4 May 1999 仲裁案件中,案情涉及资本输入国印尼总统发布法令,导致美国投资者 Himpurna 与一家印尼国有电力公司 PLN 订立的能源买卖合约被推迟履行,并且这个合约之后再也没有被履行。

1.3.3 政府对管理权利的干预

这种干预会导致对商业活动的干扰、临时的损失或对公司的接管。在几个"美国—伊朗索赔仲裁庭"(US - Iran Claims Tribunal)案件中,美国政府委任"临时或暂时管理人"(provisional or temporary managers)来接管外国投资者部分拥有的伊朗公司,这种行为被判是令外国投资者的所有权变得毫无意义,等同于对权利的没收:Tippetts v. Iran, Award of 29 June 1984, 6 Iran - US CTR 219; Payne v. Iran, Award of 8 August 1986, 12 Iran - US CTR 3; Starrett v. Iran, Final Award of 14 August 1987, 16 Iran - US CTA 112; Sedco v. IMICO, Award of 30 March 1989, 21 Iran - US CTR 31; Saghi v. Iran, Award of 22 January 1993, 29 Iran - US CTR 20; Birnbaum v. Iran, Award of 6 July 1993, 29 Iran - US CTR 260; Ebrahimi et al v. Iran, Final Award of 12 October 1994, 30 Iran - US CTR 17 and others.

1.3.4 政府对行政或公共财政权利的干预

这种外国投资者的权利会涉及特许、许可以及税务,政府的干预行为会使投资者的这些权利遭受损害。

在 Feldman v. Mexico, Award of 16 December 2002 仲裁案件中,案情涉及墨西哥税务部门拒绝退还外国投资者出口香烟的特许权税,而墨西哥政府从 1992 年起授予墨西哥香烟出口商这个出口退税权,但从 1997 年起禁止分销商享有这个出口退税权,这包括了本案例中投资者所拥有的公司。

在 Occidental v. Ecudor, Award of 1 July 2004 仲裁案件中,案情涉及美国投资者被厄瓜多尔政府非法拒绝退还"增值税"(value added tax)。

在 MTD v. Chile, Award of 25 May 2004 仲裁案件中,马来西亚投资者以及它的智利分公司被智利政府拒绝授予"土地使用变更许可"(land - rezoning permit),但政府之前保证会授予投资者这项许可,而这个许可对于投资计划的实施十分必要。

在 Amco v. Indonesia II, Award on the merits of 31 May 1990, (1992) 89 ILR 368 仲裁案件中,印尼政府收回给 Amco 的商业许可,导致该投资者在一份合约中失去了管理酒店的权利。

在 Wena Hotels v. Egypt, Award of 8 December 2000 仲裁案件中,投资者 Wena 从一个埃及国有公司租借了酒店运营许可,但埃及旅游部对于酒店运营许可的干预导致 Wena 不能继续运营他的酒店。

在 Tecmed v. Mexico, Award of 29 May 2003 仲裁案件中,墨西哥政府非法拒绝更新美国投资者运营垃圾填埋场的许可,导致投资者不能继续运营。

1.3.5 政府对规章制度的改变

主权国家政府或立法机构有时会对本国的法律或规章制度做出改变,这会涉及环境、健康、消费者保护与经济规定等不同方面。例如,政府会对外国投资者购买股票做出限制,制订新的税收政策,或者设定外币兑换限制等。这些改变可能会影响外国投资者在主权国家商业活动的盈利能力而令其蒙受损失,或者直接导致投资者完全不能继续经营。

在 Myers v. Canada, Partial Award of 13 November 2000 仲裁案件中,原告(美国投资者)在加拿大建立分公司,专门用于从加拿大把一种名为 PCB 的化学复合物出口到美国,然后在他美国的公司进行加工。后来加拿大政府声称为了保护环境,禁止这种化学复合物的进出口。导致原告投资者不能继续出口 PCB 而蒙受损失。

在 Middle East Cement v. Egypt, Award of 12 April 2002 仲裁案件中,原告在埃及建立了买卖水泥的分公司,并获得了一个 10 年的经营许可。但后来埃及政府禁止在埃及进口与出售"灰色硅酸盐水泥"(grey portland cement),这导致原告不能继续经营,并对他的供应商和顾客都构成违约。

在 CMS v. Argentina, Award of 12 May 2005; Enron v. Argentina, Award of 22 May 2007; LG & E v. Argentina, Award of 25 July, 2007 与 Sempra Energy v. Argentina, Award of 28 September 2007 等仲裁案件中,都涉及阿根廷政府对汽油运输与分配征税立法的改变。外国投资者开始在阿根廷投资时,当地税法是规定依据美元来计算税款,再按照当时的汇率转换成比索。每六个月都会调整一次税率,以体现出当时的通货膨胀情况。但是在 2000 年阿根廷经济危机之后,阿根廷终止了以美元计算税款,也停止了根据通货膨胀来调整税率的措施,再加上之后比索严重贬值,导致投资者的公司利润与收益急剧下降。

1.4 赔偿标准

在 1917 年俄罗斯改革以及 20 世纪 30 年代墨西哥国有化之后,把资产没收与国有化在东欧、拉丁美洲、印尼、中东等国家和地区开始兴起,并且在第二次世界大战之后越来越多。大家同意对这种合法没收必须提供一些赔偿,但关键是应该有多少赔偿才足够。可以说,做出赔偿的政府与接受赔偿的受害投资者(不论是外国或者本土)在对赔偿金额方面往往都是各走极端,前者往往是落地还钱,后者往往是漫天要价。

发展中国家特别是拉丁美洲国家依赖"Calvo Doctrine"[1]的说法,认为国际投资者应受到与本国投资者同等的待遇,而且政府要做出的赔偿应该依本国的法律,表示审理的管辖权也应该由本国的法院负责。这说法最明确显示在一个名为《Convention Relative to the Rights of Aliens adopted by the Second International Conference of the

[1] Carlos Calvo 先生(1822-1906)是阿根廷的法学家与外交家。但有说法是他提出的 Calvo Doctrine 在更早的时候已经由委内瑞拉的学者 Andres Bello 在 1832 年提出。

American States(1902)》的国际公约之 Article 1 所说:"First:Aliens shall enjoy all civil rights pertaining to citizens, and make use thereof in substance, form or procedure, and in the recourses which result therform, under exactly the same terms as the said citizens, except as may be otherwise provided by the Constitution of each country."这样一来,显然在 Calvo Doctrine 的说法下发展中国家即使做出对外资不利的行为所需要的赔偿金额自然低很多。

而发达国家认为国际投资者针对他遭受的损失应该获得"全部赔偿"(full reparation),也就是使受害的投资者恢复到错误的行为没有发生过的经济地位。这是以另一个说法名为"赫尔标准"(Hull Formula)为代表。这在 1938 年,墨西哥政府将美国投资者拥有的农用土地国有化之后,负责与墨西哥政府谈判的美国国务卿科德尔·赫尔所提出的,要求墨西哥政府做出"及时"(prompt)、"充分"(adequate)与"有效"(effective)的赔偿。

在 20 世纪的 60、70 年代,资本输出国(以美国为首)与发展中国家之间关于赔偿标准的争论进入白热化。但到了 80 年代后期与 90 年代初,特别是已经坚持了 Calvo Doctrine 将近一个世纪的拉丁美洲国家突然转向,并开始接受与签署 1958 年的《纽约公约》与 1965 年的《ICSID 公约》,也开始了与其他国家签署"双边投资协议"(BIT)。其中作为例子,在 2009 年,阿根廷已经签署了 58 个 BITs,智利签署了 51 个,古巴签署了 59 个等。

可以说到了近期,毫无争议的是赔偿标准还是以西方发达国家提出的"赫尔标准"为准,也几乎没有人再倡议发展中国家的"Calvo Doctrine"。[1] 这个"赫尔标准"也反映在联合国大会在 1962 年 12 月 14 日第 1803 号决议通过的《关于天然资源之永久主权宣言》中,该宣言指出,"采取收归国有、没收或征用等措施以行使其主权的国家,应该根据本国现行法规及国际法,对原有所有权人给予适当的补偿"。(In case of nationalization, expropriation or requisitioning the owner shall be paid appropriate compensation, in accordance with the rules in force in the State taking such measures in the exercise of its sovereignty and in accordance with international law.)

1.5 投资仲裁的损失计算不确定的原因

造成这种结果的通常看法就是认为在计算损失赔偿数额时缺乏连贯系统的方法,导致争议结果的不确定性以及不可预测性。造成这一个局面的原因有几个方面。第一个方面就是一直以来,没有太多的"国际规则"(international rules)针对损失的计算,更谈不上有类似英国法下有数不尽与针对每一方面细节的先例可以依从或参考,甚至对后来的英国法院审判有约束力。

---

〔1〕 这也有一点例外,就是在本章第 1 段提到的玻利维亚已经退出了 ICSID 公约,时为 2007 年 5 月 2 日。接下去玻利维亚在 2009 年 2 月修改宪法,并在 Article 320 加入了 Calvo Doctrine。而在稍后 2007 年 12 月 4 日退出 ICSID 公约的厄瓜多尔也对它的宪法作出同样修改。

涉及国际投资的损失赔偿本来就没有很多的先例可依从或做出指引。从20世纪中期开始直到ICSID公约的生效,外国投资者只能通过与资本输入的主权国家订立的私人投资合约下的争议解决条文,或者去主权国家的法院要求赔偿损失,或者通过国(资本输出国)与国(资本输入国)之间的交涉,如像“美国—伊朗索赔仲裁庭”(US - Iran Claims Tribunal)。

随着ICSID公约下的“双边投资协议”(Bilateral Investment Treaty或简称BIT)以及ICSID仲裁的出现,个人投资者(不论大小的投资者)都可以直接通过国际仲裁庭要求主权国家对他的损失做出赔偿。在解决投资争议的损失赔偿问题时,投资仲裁仲裁员们开始适用传统与有限的国与国之间的国际公法来解决争议与计算损失,也同时参考了国际习惯法。但问题是在国际公法或习惯法,都只是一些很笼统的原则。

国际法的这种“笼统性/概括性”(generality)适用在投资争议中会是一把“双刃剑”,它的好处是会带来针对不同案件事实适用上的灵活性,毕竟国际投资的争议会是千变万化。但它的坏处是会带来法律原则适用的主观性和随意性,而且允许来自不同国家与不同法律背景的国际仲裁员在做出裁决时有太多的主观与随意性,会导致仲裁裁决的判法难以理解、不可预计与不肯定。

由于ICSID的仲裁案件现在大部分都是公开的,会给之后的仲裁员一些指引(虽然也只是自愿性)。另也有一些书籍开始针对这些ICSID仲裁案件与损失计算,也能够提供指引,例如:A Damodaran 的《Investment Valuation》(第三版)(John Wiley & Sons, London, 2012年);Sergey Ripinsky 与 Kevin Williams 的《Damages in International Investment Law》(British Institute of International and Comparative Law, 2008年);Michael E. Schneider 与 Joachim Knoll 的《Performance as a Remedy: Non - Monetary Relief in International Arbitration》(ASA Special Series No. 30, 2011年)等。希望是这些判决和权威书籍可以为国际法条文、法律原则与损失赔偿计算提供更加清晰和精确的解释以及适用方法,这会减少国际投资仲裁中令人感觉不满意与不确定的裁决,也会增强投资者对国际投资仲裁做法的信心。

2. 国际投资争议中损失计算的大原则

2.1　国际投资协议中的损失计算条文

一般来讲,双边投资争议会依据所适用的国际投资仲裁协议中的争议解决条文交由仲裁庭解决,而国际投资协议的条文是解决投资纠纷的主要法律来源。在国际投资协议中,通常有三种条文会针对损失赔偿,分别是:“启动诉讼条文”(claims - enabling clause)、“没收条文”(expropriation clause)与“武装冲突条文”(armed conflict clause)。

2.2　国际习惯法中规定的与其他的损失赔偿原则

但针对其他"违反义务"(breaches of substantive obligations)的行为,如违反"国民待遇"(national treatment)义务,违反"公平公正对待"(fair and equitable treatment)义务与违反"完全保护和安全"(full protection and security)义务,投资协议通常不会规定损失赔偿计算。在这种情况下,针对这些违反义务行为的损失赔偿就会参照国际习惯法的规定。在实践中,仲裁庭会依据以下三种国际习惯法中的损失赔偿规定来做出裁决:(1)"国际法委员会"(International Law Commission)制订的针对国际不法行为的《国家责任条款》;(2)建立了习惯规则的法院判决或仲裁庭裁决,尤其是权威性的"国际常设法院"(Permanent Court of International Justice或简称PCIJ)在The Factory at Chorzow(Germany v. Poland)(Claim for Indemnity)(Merits),(1928)PCIJ Rep, Series A No 17案例中的判决;(3)一些联合国大会的决议。

问题是这三种国际习惯法的损失赔偿在原则上是一致,但只是一些笼统的大原则,没有细节。一适用在每一个不同事实的案件,仅靠大原则是远远不够。这些大原则可以介绍部分。首先在The Factory at Chorzow案例中,国际常设法院有判决如下:"It is a principle of international law that the reparation of a wrong may consist in an indemnity corresponding to the damage which the nationals of the injured State have suffered as a result of the act which is contrary to international law . . . The reparation due by one State to another does not however change its character by reason of the fact that it takes the form of an indemnity for the calculation of which the damage suffered by a private person is taken as the measure. The rules of governing the reparation are the rules of international law in force between the two States concerned, and not the law governing relations between the State which has committed a wrongful act and the individual who has suffered damage."

2.2.1　国际法委员会制订的《国家责任条款》

第一种国际习惯法是在"国际法委员会"制订的《国家责任条款》第二部分,规定了国家做出不法行为后的法律责任,以及对伤害或损失的赔偿。有许多投资仲裁案件都适用或采纳了其中的条文来做出关于损失赔偿的裁决:British Gas v. Argentina, Final Award of 24 December 2007;Siemens v. Argentina, Award of 6 February 2007;ADC v. Hungary, Final Award of 2 October 2006;CME v. Czech Republic, Final Award of 14 March 2003;Nykomb v. Latvia, Award of 16 December 2003等。可以节录《国家责任条款》其中的几个条文如下:

"**Article 31　Reparation**

1. The responsible State is under an obligation to make **full reparation** for the injury caused by the internationally wrongful act.

2. Injury includes any damage, whether material or moral, caused by the internationally wrongful act of a State.

Article 34 Forms of reparation

Full reparation for the injury caused by the internationally wrongful act shall take the form of restitution, compensation and satisfaction, either singly or in combination, in accordance with the provisions of this chapter.

Article 35 Restitution

A State responsible for an internationally wrongful act is under an obligation to make restitution, that is, **to re – establish the situation which existed before the wrongful act was committed**, provided and to the extent that restitution: (a) Is not materially impossible; (b) Does not involve a burden out of all proportion to the benefit deriving from restitution instead of compensation.

Article 36 Compensation

1. The State responsible for an internationally wrongful act is under an obligation to compensate**for the damage caused thereby**, insofar as such damage is not made good by restitution.

2. The compensation shall cover**any financially assessable damage including loss of profits** insofar as it is established.

Article 38 Interest

1. Interest on any principal sum due under this chapter shall be payable when necessary in order to ensure **full reparation**. The interest rate and mode of calculation shall be set so as to achieve that result.

2. Interest runs from the date when the principal sum should have been paid until the date the obligation to pay is fulfilled.

Article 39 Contribution to the injury

In the determination of reparation, account shall be taken of the contribution to the injury by willful or negligent action or omission of the injured State or any person or entity in relation to whom reparation is sought. ”(加黑部分是笔者的强调,强调主要说明是要主权国家做出完全的赔偿、复原、利润损失等)

从以上条文来看,在《国家责任条款》下关于投资的损失计算基本原则就是对损失需要“完全赔偿”(full reparation)以及“复原”(restitution)原则,也就是使受害的投资者恢复到错误的行为没有发生过的经济地位。这实际是与英国法下关于侵权的“复原”(restitution)大原则一致,即把受害方恢复到侵权没有发生过的经济地位。这说法在本书多章(特别是第一章)都有详细的介绍。

2.2.2 国际常设法院判决或仲裁庭裁决认可的国际习惯法

第二种国际习惯法是国际投资领域最著名的国际常设法院案例 The Factory at Chorzow(Germany v. Poland)(Claim for Indemnity)(Merits),(1928)PCIJ Rep, Series A No. 17 中,案情涉及波兰政府非法没收两家德国投资公司的工厂,法院在判决中指出国际法下赔偿的目的以及“恢复原状”(restitution)与“金钱赔偿”(compensation)的基本原则如下:“The essential principle contained in the actual notion of an illegal act – a principle which seems to be established by international practice and in particular by the decisions of arbitral tribunals – is that reparation must, as far as possible, wipe – out all the consequences of the illegal act and re – establish the situation which would, in all probability, have existed if that act had not been committed. Restitution in kind, or, if this is not possible, payment of a sum corresponding to the value which a restitution in kind would bear; the award, if need be, of damages for loss sustained which would not be covered by restitution in kind or payment in place of it – such are the principles which should serve to determine the amount of compensation due for an act contrary to international law.”

该案例中另外也有说:“It is a principle of international law, and even a general conception of law, that any breach of an engagement involves an obligation to make reparation... It is a principle of international law that the reparation of a wrong may consist in an indemnity corresponding to the damage which the nationals of the injured State have suffered as a result of the act which is contrary to international law.”

还有一些在国际投资仲裁案件中建立的其他国际投资习惯法原则可以列举如下:如在 CME v. Czech Republic, Final Award of 14 March 2003 案件中,多数仲裁员认为依据国际投资习惯法,在外国投资者资产被没收后,主权国家应该赔偿给投资者被没收资产的公平市价的全部损失(full compensation equivalent to the fair market value of the expropriated investment)。在该投资仲裁案件中,仲裁庭也重申了国际习惯法不认可依照主权国家的国内法做出赔偿的原则,也就是不适用“Calvo Doctrine”。在另一个投资仲裁案件 Nykomb v. Latvia 中,仲裁庭认为在国际投资习惯法中,损失赔偿的计算需要遵循“因果关系”(causation)、“可预见性”(foreseeability)以及“合理性”(reasonableness)的要求。这些都是英国法律针对损失赔偿计算的原则,分别在本书之前的章节已有详论。由此可以看出,虽然国际投资协议中没有规定适用英国法,但是由于国际投资案件的仲裁员多数都是西方仲裁员,国际投资仲裁案件双方的法律代表也多数是英美的跨国律师所,加上英国法又被认为是西方商业社会普遍所接受的“有组织的常识”(organised common sense),所以英国法律的原则也就自然而然地被接受,这是所有处理国际投资仲裁的人士必须理解的。

2.2.3　联合国大会决议

第三种国际习惯法是根据“国际法院法规”(International Court of Justice Statute)第 38 条,国际机构的决议并不能作为国际法的来源,但可以作为国际惯例的一部分。联合国大会决议对联合国成员只具有建议的效力而没有约束力。但在国际法院近些年的实践中,越来越多开始引用联合国大会决议作为国际习惯法规则的一部分。例如,国际法院针对 Nuclear Weapons 一案给出法律意见说:“General Assembly resolutions, even if they are not binding, may sometimes have normative value. They can, in certain circumstances, provide evidence important for establishing the existence of a rule or the emergence of an *opinion juris*. To establish whether this is true of a given General Assembly resolution, it is necessary to look at its content and the conditions of its adoption; it is also necessary to see whether an *opinion juris* exists as to its normative character. Or a series of resolutions may show the gradual evolution of the *opinion juris* required for the establishment of a new rule."

在 Texaco v. Libya, Award on the Merits on 10 October 1977, 53 ILR 389 仲裁案件中，就涉及联合国大会决议在投资仲裁中被作为国际习惯法的一部分。案情涉及利比亚政府把两家美国公司的资产没收后的损失赔偿计算问题。当事人提出了两份联合国大会决议，可以作为损失计算的根据。第一份是 1803 号决议，要求投资者资产被没收或者国有化的损失要根据"国际法的原则提供适当赔偿"（appropriate compensation in accordance with international law）。而第二份是 1974 年《国家经济权利与义务宪章》，要求损失根据没收国家的法律进行赔偿，而没有提及国际法。仲裁庭最后判是应该按照 1803 号决议计算损失，因为根据投票情况，1974 年的宪章没有获得任何市场经济体制的发达国家的投票支持，而这些国家占据了国际贸易的主导地位，仲裁庭是说："The absence of any connection between the procedure of compensation and international law and the subjection of this procedure solely to municipal law cannot be regarded by this Tribunal except as a *de lege fereda* formulation, which even appears *contra legem* in the eyes of many developed countries."

2.2.4 世界银行关于投资的指引

世界银行在 1992 年发布了《外国直接投资待遇指引》，这份不具有法律约束力的指引对世界银行成员国领域内的外国直接投资的接受和待遇提供了有效界定。在这份指引第四部分建议主权国家如果没收以及单方面改变或终止合约，需要做出赔偿，并提出在主权国家没收后，应该对投资者基于所没收资产的"公平市价"（fair market value）提供"充分、有效以及及时"（adequate, effective and prompt）的赔偿。另外，这份指引还定义了充分、有效、及时、公平市价、"贴现现金流价值"（discounted cash flow value）、"清算价值"（liquidation value）、"账面价值"（book value）等词语，列举和解释了在特殊情况下计算公平市价的具体方法。

但是，尽管世界银行有多达 184 个成员国，这份指引只被 24 个成员国的发展委员会采纳。虽然在这份指引的序言中说，这份指引是经过世界银行组织对其内部以及外部国家广泛的咨询后才做出，但它并不能被视为是所有世界银行组织成员国权威性的一致意见。指引的第一部分也清楚表明，它并不代表国际习惯法的规定。

2.2.5 一次性和解协议

已经在前文提到过，第二次世界大战后许多国家都会通过一些其他方式来解决国民的国际性投资争议，其中就包括通过协商来达成一次性和解协议。大多数情况下，巨大社会变革导致国有化之后，这种一次性和解协议就会产生，用来解决国际性投资争议。

在这种和解协议中，通常被起诉的国家会支付给原告的国家一笔固定数量的赔偿，获得赔偿的国家再依据国内法建立一个诉讼委员会，对自己国家投资者的诉讼进行裁判，然后把这笔赔偿分配给所有胜诉的投资者。但是，通常这种一次性和解协议都只是做出部分赔偿，因为会涉及两个国家之间其他的条件、让步、交换协议甚至是外交妥协等。

因此，一次性和解协议能否被视为国际习惯法的一部分引起了很多争论：Barcelona Traction, Light and Power Company, Limited (Belgium v. Spain), Second Phase (Judgment) (1970) ICJ Rep 3; Sedco Inc v. NIOC & Iran, Interlocutory award of 27 March 1986, 10 Iran – US CTR 180; Kuwait v. Aminoil, Award of 24 March 1982 等诉讼/仲裁案件。总的来说，就是在达成这种协议的过程中，参与的国家在谈判中往往会涉及交换、补偿与其他外交上的因素，而并不必然涉及国际法原则。

2.2.6　双边投资协议(BIT)

双边投资协议的条文中通常会规定对外国投资者的待遇，这会构成或改变国际习惯法中的原则。但问题是双边协议中的条文能否改变国际投资习惯法中对于没收赔偿标准的规定？

针对这个问题有很多不同的观点，一些学者认为在大量双边投资协定中一致的条文可以构成一个国际习惯法规则。例如，SM Schwebel 在《The Influence of Bilateral Investment Treaties on Customary International Law》(Proceedings of the 98th Annual Meeting of the American Society of International Law [31 March – 3 April 2004])的演讲中所说，针对外国投资者待遇与保护的一条同样措辞的条文在超过 2000 个双边投资协定中出现，那么这些规则就可以变成国际投资习惯法的一部分。同样的说法也出现在 M Shaw 所著的《International Law》(5th edn, 2003 年)一书中，可以引用如下："While normally great care has to be taken in inferring the existence of a rule of customary international law from a range of bilateral treaties, the very number and uniformity of such agreements make them significant exemplars."

但是还有一些学者认为双边投资协议不能构成国际习惯法，因为双边投资协议是合约双方(国与国)之间的特别约定，即使这些协议的条文表面上看起来一致，但具体内容还是会有很大不同。而国家之间选择订立双边而非多边投资协议行为，也证明协议双方国家在双边投资协议中约定的内容不应该成为国际习惯法。在国际法院最近的一个案例 Abmadou Sadio Diallo (Republic of Guinea v. Democratic Republic of the Congo), Judgment on Preliminary Objections of 24 May, 2007 中，国际法院也是认为，针对股东保护的一项广泛接受的投资协议约定并不构成国际习惯法的一部分，这里可以引用相关判词如下："The fact invoked by Guinea that various international agreements, such as agreements for the promotion and protection of foreign investments and the Washington Convention, have established special legal regimes governing investment protection, or that provisions in this regard are commonly included in contracts entered into directly between States and foreign investors, is not sufficient to show that there has been a change in the customary rules of diplomatic protection; it could equally show the contrary."

所以,只有在相关投资协议的条文构成持续的国家实践以及法律确认时,它才可以构成国际习惯法的一部分。但不能笼统地说所有的双边投资协议条文都可以成为国际习惯法,必须根据具体的案情来决定。换言之,如果在参考了大量具有代表性的投资协议,这些协议由来自不同区域的资本输出国以及资本输入国的参与,确定在这些协议中的有关条文都是一致的,这个条文才可以被认为是国际习惯法,能够约束非合约的当事国家。

2.3 损失赔偿计算可以被广泛承认的法律体系原则加以补充

作为国际法来源之一的先进国家(或被广泛承认的法律体系)一般的法律原则,通常用来补充国际投资协议与国际习惯法没有规定的部分。这也完全可以理解,本章之2.2.2段提到ICSID仲裁仲裁员通常就是一些西方的国际商业仲裁员,他们不少成员是英美法背景。例如,部分成员是英美法院的退休大法官、大律师或国际律师所的律师。他们的手中可能有几个投资仲裁案件在审理,但同时有几个国际货物买卖的案件。很难想象他们会在处理损失赔偿计算问题时是可以完全泾渭分明,但是在平衡主权国家利益之后计算出来的损失与在根据国际货物买卖案件中完全按照合约规定所计算出来的损失总会有差别吧。对这些国际商业仲裁员而言,在较早前所介绍的一些国际习惯法中,投资仲裁也是强调了完全赔偿、复原、利润损失等与英美商法一致的大原则。这可以节录LIAMCO v. Libya, Award of 12 April 1977, (1981) 20 ILM 1仲裁案件中仲裁庭的相关判词如下:"These general principles are usually embodied in most recognized legal systems ... They are applied by municipal courts and are mainly referred to in international and arbitral case - law. They, thus form a compendium of legal precepts and maxims, universally accepted in theory and practice. Examples include the principle of the sanctity of property and contracts, the respect of acquired vested rights, the prohibition of unjust enrichment, the obligation of compensation in cases of expropriation and wrongful damage, etc."

2.4 总结国际投资损失计算的大原则

总结以上所介绍的来自双边投资协议、国际习惯法与一些被承认法律体系的先进国家法律原则,可以对目前国际投资仲裁中,计算损失赔偿通常会适用的一些基本原则总结如下:(1)"复原"(Resitution)是国际投资仲裁中计算损失的基本原则,这与英国法中的复原大原则是一致的,就是以金钱赔偿让受害方恢复到侵权没有发生或合约被履行的地位。(2)损失赔偿应该用来补偿由于违反国际义务而造成的实质伤害:Myers v. Canada, Partial Award of 13 November 2000, para. 315; SwemBalt v. Latvia, Award of 23 October 200, para. 38; LIAMCO v. Libya, Award of 12 April 1977, (1981) 20 ILM 1, 132。(3)违约的损失赔偿应该只包括直接以及可以预见的损失:Amco v. Indonesia, Award of 20 November 1984, (1992) 89 ILR 368。(4)针对外国投资者所提出的损失,他需要承担举证责任,再由仲裁庭根据平衡的可能性来做出裁决。如果在某些案件中事实的证明极其困难,仲裁庭可能会接受不太令人信服的证据,也就是接受"表面证据"(*prima facie* evidence):Myers v. Canada, Partial Award of 13 November 2000, para. 316; AAPL v. Sri Lanka, Award of 27 June 1990。(5)损失与外国投资者声称被违反的条文之间必须有充分联系,这笔损失才可以获得赔偿。这也是英美法下"因果关系"(causation)的说法:Myers v. Canada, Partial Award of 13 November 2000。(6)受害的外国投资者有"减少损失的义务"(duty to mitigate damage):Middle East Cement v. Egypt, Award of 12 April 2002。

当中所涉及的法律层面与本书其他章节所详论的其实没有什么区别。毕竟,英国法律在国际的影响力是毫无疑问会被相当部分的国际投资仲裁案件中的仲裁员采纳与参考。

3. 收归国有

3.1　合法或非法的收归国有

可以用经常会出现的"收归国有"(expropriation)事件显示国际投资仲裁案件中对损失的计算,商业背景的仲裁员通常是不会平衡其他的政治或主权国家利益的因素。"收归国有"可以分为合法的收归国有与非法的收归国有。两者在理论上对损失赔偿的计算应该有区别,如非法的收归国有应该有更严格的标准。但实际中并不容易区分,因为在目前的说法下他们都强调"完全赔偿"(full reparation)。

3.2　合法的收归国有

首先简单介绍什么是合法的收归国有。在国际法中,如果主权国家将外国投资者拥有的资产(如主权国家要没收一片土地作为其他的发展用途)收归国有的行为是在它权力范围内,就会被视为合法。通常合法的收归国有行为需要满足以下条件:(1)为了公共目的;(2)不存在歧视;(3)依照合法程序实施;(4)对投资者给予赔偿。前三个条件被称为"行为要求"(conduct requirements),而第四个被称为"赔偿要求"(compensation requirement)。

在考虑收归国有是否合法时,赔偿要求是最复杂的一项,也会涉及艰难的谈判,最后做出的赔偿是否是正确与合理也会富争议性。所以一些学者与司法判决认为,主权国家不给予赔偿并不能够使原来属于合法的收归国有行为变为非法。如Mohebi认为:"the non - payment of compensation does not, as such, make a taking *ipso facto* wrongful, rather it is a violation by the expropriating state of an independent duty which applies evenly to both unlawful and lawful taking."欧洲人权法院也采纳了同样的观点。

另在《The Iran - United States Claims Tribunal》(Martinus Nijhoff, The Hague, 1999)

一书中,也是国际仲裁员的作者 C Brower 与 J Brueschke 认为,无数涉及美国—伊朗投资仲裁的裁决承认在国际习惯法下,及时支付“正确”金额的赔偿是决定收归国有是否合法的考虑因素之一。但即使是这样,什么是正确的赔偿,主权国家是否承认有义务支付赔偿,采取支付赔偿的行动是否足够,或主权国家是否在收归国有后很短时间内支付一部分赔偿,这些因素都不确定是否构成合法的收归国有。

但也有说法是如果主权国家在合理期限内不支付任何合理赔偿,就不能视为合法的收归国有。所以主权国家将外国投资者的资产收归国有后在很长时间内都不提供任何赔偿,或者赔偿数额明显不合理,都会被视为是非法收归国有。此外,主权国家如果做出真诚与善意的努力履行它的赔偿责任,如提供赔偿(即使赔偿并不足够,但不是明显地不合理),这个收归国有行为就会被视为合法。

近年来国与国之间签订了大量双边或多边投资协议,这类协议中都会约定收归国有后适用的具体赔偿标准,而不适用其他国际法标准。它们通常会约定给付赔偿是合法收归国有的条件之一,因此这些条文只能适用于合法收归国有的赔偿。

间接的收归国有行为通常也被认为是不合法的,因为从间接收归的定义来看,主权国家根本不会承认收归行为的事实,因此也不会对投资者提供任何赔偿。

3.3　合法收归国有的赔偿标准

关于合法收归国有的赔偿标准在国际习惯法上从 20 世纪初期开始就一直有很大的争议,这在本书 1.4 段关于赔偿标准有介绍。总的来说,早期的赔偿标准为“适当赔偿”(appropriate compensation),这允许法院或仲裁庭在考虑公平的因素后作出部分赔偿的决定。但这种灵活的标准近年来开始转化为“充分”(adequate)或“完全”(full)赔偿,这是基于被收归国有投资的“公平市价”(fair market value)来提供赔偿,除非这种赔偿标准会导致明显不公平的结果,并破坏了公共利益与个人利益之间的平衡。

在国与国之间的投资协议中针对合法收归国有的赔偿标准,固然是要根据有关条文的分析与解释。但在这些条文中,大多数都会要求“充分”(adequate)赔偿[这也是“及时、充分与有效赔偿”(prompt, adequate and effective)标准的一部分],也就是本章 1.4 段提到的赫尔标准。例如,在 75% 的双边投资协议与 70% 的多边投资协议,以及在成员国最多的多边投资协议—《能源宪章条约》(Energy Charter Treaty)中都有同样的规定。其他的投资协议要么只简单规定“赔偿”(compensation),要么规定“公正”(just)、“公平”(fair)或者“公正合理”(just and equitable)的赔偿标准。

投资协议中的收归国有条文通常会进一步规定如何依据这些标准来计算赔偿金额,其中大多数会规定根据被收归国有投资的价值来衡量赔偿的金额。这些协议的条文可能会规定赔偿的金额等于投资的“市价”(market value)、“公平市价”(fair market value)、“实际价值”(actual value)、“真实价值”(genuine value)、“真正价值”(real value)或者“准确价值”(true value)。其中公平市价是最常见的措辞,也为如何计算赔偿金额提供了最多的信息,但其他的文字可能还需要进一步解释来确定具体含义。如在 Siemens v. Argentina, Award of 6 February 2007 仲裁案件中,仲裁庭认为本案所适用的双边投资协议中"价值"(value)一词应该被解释为"完全价值"(full value)或者"公平市价"。类似情况也出现在 Vivendi v. Argentina, Award of 20 August 2007 仲裁案件中,仲裁庭认为所适用的双边投资协议中的"实际价值"也等同于"公平市价"。而被收归国有投资的公平市价被普遍认为是需要达到完全赔偿的标准。

3.4　非法收归国有的赔偿标准

什么是非法的收归国有应该不需要多解释,因为不属于合法的就是非法。在本章 3.1.1 段已经提到过,主权国家是否在收归国有后很短时间内支付赔偿或者是否支付了合理的赔偿金额,这些对于确定收归国有的合法性是极富争议的。但毫无疑问的是,如果一开始主权国家收归国有就不满足合法的行为要求条件,即并非为了公共目的,存在歧视或没有依照合法程序实施,就会构成非法的收归国有。

非法收归国有的赔偿标准通常不是规定在投资协议中,而是规定在有关国际不法行为国家责任的国际习惯法中。这可以节录仲裁庭在 ADC v. Hungary, Final Award of 2 October 2006 中的裁决如下:"Since the BIT does not contain any *lex specialis* rules that govern the issue of the standard for assessing damages in the case of an unlawful expropriation, the Tribunal is required to apply the default standard contained in customary international law in the present case. The customary international law standard for the assessment of damages resulting from an unlawful act is set out in the decision of the PCIJ in the Chorzow Factory case ..."

在国际习惯法中,非法的收归国有行为构成国际不法行为,而令主权国家承担国家责任,这在 The Factory at Chorzow (Germany v. Poland) (Claim for Indemnity) (Merits), (1928) PCIJ Rep, Series A No 17 与"国际法委员会"(International Law Commission)制订的针对国际不法行为的《国家责任条款》都规定,主权国家需要承担完全赔偿责任,这可以节录 The Factory at Chorzow 的判词如下:"Reparation must, as far as possible, wipe out all the consequences of the illegal act and re – establish the situation which would, in all probability, have existed if that act had not been committed. Restitution in kind, or if this is not possible, payment of a sum corresponding to the value which a restitution in kind would bear; the award, if need be, of damages for loss sustained which would not be covered by restitution in kind or payment in place of it – such are the principles which should serve to determine the amount of compensation due for an act contrary to international law."

3.5　合法与非法收归国有存在的区别:何时对资产进行估值

有说法是非法收归国有的主要救济方式是"复原"(restitution),但这与合法收归国有中的完全赔偿或公平市价也没有原则或实质的区别。也有说法是非法收归国有的赔偿还包括"附带费用"(incidental expenses)或者其他间接损失。在这种情况下,投资者可以获得的赔偿就会超过没收资产的公平市价。例如,在 ADC v. Hungary 仲裁案件中,仲裁庭判是主权国家需要赔偿投资者在资产被收归国有后价值上涨的金额。另在 Siemens v. Argentina, Award of 6 February 2007,仲裁庭判是主权国家需要赔偿投资者在资产被收归国有后的花费。

这区别会是来自接下去解释的原因。针对合法收归国有,国际法(国际协议与国际习惯法)都规定了收归国有的一天就是"估值"(valuation)或计算损失的一天,这个道理是和本书第十三章所针对"违约一天计算损失与市场价格规定"介绍的原则一致,就是以违约的一天来计算损失。至于违约一天直到审理的一天由于市场变化或其他原因,导致了受害方的实际损失可能变大或变小,英国法下通常是不予理会,特别是在"市场规则"(market rule)适用的情况下。这在合法收归国有的案件中看来也是同样道理,在 INA v. Iran, Award of 13 August 1985, 8 Iran – US CTR 373 仲裁案件中,仲裁庭说:"... the amount which a willing buyer would have paid a willing seller for the shares of a going concern ... *excluding consideration of events thereafter that might have increased or decreased the value of the shares.*"另在 Phillips Petroleum v. Iran, Award of 29 June 1989, 21 Iran – US CTR 79 仲裁案件中,仲裁庭说:"The Tribunal's objective here is to determine the range of expectations that seemed reasonable in September 1979, not the accuracy of those expectations in fact. The actual course of prices since 1979 to the date of this Award, while relevant to the present value of the property, *is irrelevant to the value of the property in 1979, and it is the 1979 value which the Claimant seeks and to which it is entitled.*"

通常投资协议中的收归国有条文中都会规定适用的估值日期,如在涉及克罗地亚、丹麦、德国、印度、秘鲁、南非、泰国、土耳其与瑞典的双边投资协议中都有条文规定估值的日期应该是收归国有发生的一天。如在 Kuwait v. Aminoil, Award of 24 March 1982, 21 ILM 976 仲裁案件中,仲裁庭就是按照收归国有法令发布的一天来对有关的资产做出估值。

如果收归国有的消息被提前公布,这会导致有关资产的价格降低,所以有说法是这期间的损失也应该由主权国家承担赔偿责任,所以估值日期应该以收归国有消息被公众知晓的一天的价值计算。这种情况也会在一些投资协议中规定,在一些仲裁案件中也出现,如 Azurix v. Argentina, Final Award of 14 July 2006。

如果收归国有是一个渐进的过程,针对估值的日期问题,有一个说法是要根据整个收归国有过程中真正导致外国投资者资产被剥夺的一天来估值(irreversible deprivation test)。这可以节录 Santa Elena v. Costa Rica, Award of 17 February 2000 的仲裁裁决书对这一个方面的说法:"There is ample authority for the proposition that a property has been expropriated when the effect of the measures taken by the state has been to deprive the owner of title, possession or access to the benefit and economic use of his property ... The expropriated property is to be evaluated as of the date on which the governmental 'interference' has deprived the owner of his rights or has made those rights practically useless."

以上讲了有关合法收归国有的估值与计算损失日期,但在非法的收归国有,如果收归国有后投资或资产的价值提高,估值的日期会是后来做出裁决的一天,因为事后的信息会被仲裁庭考虑在内。即使在投资协议中有条文规定估值的日期是收归国有的一天,这也不会被适用在非法的收归国有,因为投资协议只针对合法的收归国有。仲裁庭针对非法收归国有是依据 The Factory at Chorzow(Germany v. Poland)(Claim for Indemnity)(Merits),(1928)PCIJ Rep,Series A No 17 先例的说法,就是判词中所说的"Reparation must ... re – establish the situation which would, in all probability, have existed if that act had not been committed"。这一个说法被视为主权国家在非法收归国有的情况下是永远不准在经济上得益,所以在收归国有后直到裁决的一天如果有关资产升值也不能让有关主权国家获得利益。

总的来说,非法收归国有的赔偿不能低于合法收归国有的赔偿。所以,只有在收归国有之后的情况导致投资的价值增加时,这些事后的信息才会被仲裁庭考虑在内,计算非法收归国有的损失赔偿金额。但除此之外,合法与非法收归国有基本上在损失计算方面没有太大区别,它们都强调全部赔偿。

值得一提的是,这种投资仲裁经常会涉及某些国家经济上非常动荡的时期,这导致不同的估值日期会造成价值上巨大差异,如在 Amoco International Finance v. Iran, Partial Award of 14 July 1987 仲裁案件中,估值的日期相差 10 天,就让计算出来的价值相差 3000 万美元之多。

4. 针对其他非收归国有的违反国际法行为的赔偿

针对与收归国有无关的主权国家违反义务的行为,如果投资协议中没有规定赔偿方式,就会适用国际习惯法来计算赔偿的金额,也就是主权国家需要对投资者提供完全赔偿。这在"国际法委员会"(International Law Commission)制订的针对国际不法行为的《国家责任条款》之 31 条规定,主权国家对国家责任需要提供"完全赔偿"(full reparation);36 条规定,赔偿包含所有经济上可估价的损失以及利润损失。在 The Factory at Chorzow(Germany v. Poland)(Claim for Indemnity)(Merits),(1928)PCIJ Rep,Series A No 17 判决中,"国际常设法院"(Permanent Court of International Justice)也认为针对一般性的违法行为,赔偿必须包含所有违法行为造成的后果,以使投资者的经济地位尽可能恢复到该行为没有发生时的经济地位。

国际习惯法只是原则性地规定投资者遭受的与能够证实的损失都可以获得完全赔偿。这个一般性的原则也为仲裁庭在具体案件中计算赔偿金额提供了灵活性与自由裁量权。例如在 Myers v. Canada, Partial Award of 13 November 2000 仲裁案件中,仲裁庭说:"By not identifying any particular methodology for the assessment of compensation in cases not involving expropriation... the drafters of the NAFTA intended to leave it open to tribunals to determine a measure of compensation appropriate to the specific circumstances of the case, taking into account the principles of both international law and the provisions of the NAFTA."

这会导致仲裁庭采用不同的方法计算损失赔偿的金额,因为仲裁庭需要考虑不同案件中"损失的性质与程度"(nature and extent of the loss)来做出决定,"因果关系"(causation)也是重要的考虑因素之一(这在本书第四章有详论)。这可以节录LG&E v. Argentina, Award of 25 July 2007 仲裁案件中的裁决如下:"The issue that the Tribunal has to address is that of the identification of the '*actual loss*' suffered by the investor '*as a result*' of Argentina's conduct. The question is one of '*causation*': what did the investor loss by reason of the unlawful acts?"

原告投资者的损失类别会取决于具体案件的实际情况,通常会涉及以下几种损失,这些不同类别的损失会涉及不同的计算方法。笔者将在接下去的段节分别探讨。

4.1 投资价值的全部损失

在许多案件中,非收归国有的违法行为可能会产生与收归国有一样的后果,就是导致投资价值的全部损失(full loss of investment's value),如主权国家破坏了投资者的资产或终止特许权。在这种情况下,仲裁庭就会根据投资价值损失的市价来计算赔偿的金额。

例如,在 Asian Agricultural Products v. Sri Lanka, Award of 27 June 1990 仲裁案件中,香港(当时是英国殖民地)投资者公司的活虾养殖场被斯里兰卡武装部队在反叛乱行动中破坏,这导致投资者公司的养殖与出口虾业务不能继续进行。仲裁庭判是斯里兰卡政府违反了它的"恪尽职责"(due diligence)义务,需要赔偿外国投资者这笔"投资损失的完全价值"。

4.2 投资本身价值的贬值

如果违法行为导致一笔投资的价值大幅贬值(diminution in the investment's value),仲裁庭会根据价值的减少来计算赔偿金额。在 CMS v. Argentina, Award of 12 May 2005 仲裁案件中,阿根廷政府的行为违反了公平公正对待义务,导致美国投资者在一家阿根廷石油运输公司的股权利益急剧减少。由于案件涉及的双边投资协议中没有规定有关的赔偿标准,仲裁庭运用了它的自由裁量权找出最适合这种违法行为的赔偿方式。考虑到阿根廷多次违反双边投资协议,以及对投资者造成的长期损失,仲裁庭选择了以公平市价的方式来计算损失。仲裁庭找出了违法行为发生之前这笔投资的价值,以及违法行为发生之后投资的剩余价值,裁决这二者之间的差价就是阿根廷政府需要承担的赔偿金额。

如果主权国家的违法行为令投资的损失是永久性,即投资的价值在裁决作出后也不会反弹,那么这种价值减少的方式就能够计算出恰当的赔偿金额。但如果投资的价值在未来反弹,如政府撤回了损害性行为或者经济情况发生变化,这种计算方式就会导致投资者被过度赔偿。在 Enron v. Argentina, Award of 22 May 2007 仲裁案件中，仲裁庭是以这种价值减少的方式来计算损失，因为外国投资者在仲裁过程中将这笔投资转售给了其他人，所以不会有投资价值在未来反弹的可能性，而转售的价格也被仲裁庭采纳作为损害发生后的较低剩余价值来计算赔偿金额。

另一个避免过度赔偿的考虑因素，就是原告的投资价值减少是否单纯因为政府的违法行为，这是因果关系的考虑。例如，在 British Gas v. Argentina, Final Award of 24 December 2007 仲裁案件中，涉及原告在一家阿根廷公司 MetroGAS 的股权。仲裁庭裁决赔偿的金额是这些股权在阿根廷政府违法行为发生前后的差价。然而仲裁庭并没有考虑到，外国投资者股权利益减少的一部分原因是阿根廷国内的一般经济危机，但在国际法上阿根廷并不需要为此承担责任。换言之，阿根廷做出的部分赔偿的实际近因/主因是阿根廷的经济危机，不是阿根廷政府的违约行为。

4.3 未付的税款

计算投资价值的方式在一些其他类型的案件中可能会不适用，而仲裁庭需要考虑投资者遭受的具体损失。如果外国投资者遭受的单纯经济损失是“未被退还的税款”(unpaid tax refunds/rebates)，这就不需要考虑整体投资的价值损失。

例如，在 Feldman v. Mexico, Award of 16 December 2002 仲裁案件中，涉及墨西哥政府违反 NAFTA 国民待遇条文而没有给外国投资者退税。仲裁庭判是墨西哥政府不需要赔偿原告投资的完全市场价格，只需要赔偿与违约有充分联系的损失部分，也就是原告合法要求退还而被墨西哥政府拒绝的这一部分税款。

4.4 股东的股利损失

原告投资者的身份也会影响损失的类别，如果原告是股东，仲裁庭可能会根据主权国家违法行为导致的股东收益损失(loss of dividends by shareholder)来计算投资者的实际损失。

在 LG&E v. Argentina, Award of 25 July 2007 仲裁案件中，案情涉及阿根廷政府的违法行为导致美国投资者在一家阿根廷公司的股权利益急剧减少，但由于投资者继续拥有股权，公司也在继续运营，投资者的股权价值已经出现了反弹，而且未来有可能会继续反弹，所以仲裁庭没有采纳价值减少的方式来计算赔偿金额。相反，仲裁庭判是阿根廷需要赔偿原告如果没有违法行为原告会获得的股利收益(the amount of dividends that could have been received but for the adoption of the measures)。

4.5 短暂干扰导致的损失

如果主权国家的违法行为对投资者的经营只构成一个短暂的干扰(losses due to temporary interference)，就不能通过衡量价值损失的方式来计算赔偿的金额，因为只有在这段短暂的期间内外国投资者的营运被干扰，之后他还是会继续正常营运。

例如，在 Myers v. Canada, Award on Damages of 31 May 2002 仲裁案件中，涉及加拿大政府关闭边境长达 16 个月，禁止某种化学复合物的进出口，导致原告(美国投资者)在加拿大分公司这段时间内无法营运。在责任方面仲裁庭认定加拿大政府违反了 NAFTA(北美自由贸易协议)的国民待遇与最低国际标准待遇义务，但由于 16 个月后加拿大政府重新开放边境，所以投资者只损失这期间的利润而没有停业。仲裁庭认为不应该适用投资的公平市价来计算损失，而应该依据投资者在这段期间内的收入损失来计算赔偿金额。

5. 投资价值的评估

5.1 公平市价

"公平市价"(fair market value，简称 FMV)是在投资仲裁中计算受损投资项目或资产价值的主要方式，这也是大多数投资协议规定的主要赔偿标准，这在本章3.3段有介绍。在《Black's Law Dictionary》中 FMV 被定义如下："... the price that a seller is willing to accept and a buyer is willing to pay on the open market in an arm's length transaction; the point at which supply and demand intersect."(在一个公开市场，价格完全是根据供求关系，一位愿意出售的卖方与一位愿意购买的买方所订的价格)

另在美国评估师协会发布的《International Glossary of Business Valuation Terms》中也对 FMV 做出了如下定义："... the price, expressed in terms of cash equivalents, at which property would change hands between a hypothetical willing and able buyer and a hypothetical willing and able seller, acting at arm's length in an open and unrestricted market, when neither is under compulsion to buy or sell and when both have reasonable knowledge of the relevant facts."

所以通常来说，仲裁庭在决定公平市场价格时会假设一个理想化的市场，假设在这个市场中只有市场推动力会影响价格的高低，并压制其他因素的影响。公平市场价格的方式可能会涉及太多假设，只有存在完全相同产品的市场时才会比较容易适用。否则就只能适用一些其他的方式来计算赔偿金额，如"账面净值"(net book value)、"重置价值"(replacement value)或"贴现现金流"(Discounted Cash Flow)等方式。这可以节录 Amoco International Finance v. Iran, Partial Award of 14 July 1987 仲裁案件中的裁决如下：

"Market value, on the other hand, is an ambiguous concept, to say the least (it might be more accurate to term it misleading), when an open market does not exist for the expropriated asset or for goods identical or comparable to it.... In such circumstances, referring to market value for the purpose of determining compensation in case of expropriation inevitably leads to a pyramid of hypotheses, since it is necessary to conjecture as to the price on which a hypothetical willing buyer and a hypothetical willing seller negotiating at arms - length would eventually agree. Such conjecture is more especially artificial as the owner of the expropriated asset usually is not a willing seller.

The truth is that the absence of a market giving rise to the fixing of an objective market value compels recourse to alternative methods of valuation ... such as net book value, replacement value, DCF calculation, etc. None of these values can, however, legitimately be labelled 'market value'.... It is impossible to verify that had a free transaction taken place the price would have corresponded to this value.... The Tribunal is therefore of the view that the phrase 'market value' is of no help in the absence of regular transaction in a free market and can too easily be misleading."

5.2　价值评估方式

5.2.1　概述

采用何种价值评估方式取决于投资争议中需要估价的具体对象,这可能会需要区分被政府违法行为损害的是有形资产还是商业利益。如果主权国家的行为导致一个企业的所有有形资产被损毁(如出租车公司的车辆,制造厂的厂房等被收归国有),但这些资产被重置后,投资者还是可以继续在主权国家经营,那么赔偿就应该依据这些有形资产的价值来计算,再加上经营被中断期间的利润损失,而不是按照商业利益的价值来计算。相反,如果投资者在资产损失的同时也被剥夺了继续经营的机会(如出租车公司被吊销营业许可或者制造厂的产品被禁止出售),那么就要根据整个商业利益的损失来计算赔偿金额。而如果投资者的经营是能够盈利的,就会需要按照"贴现现金流"(Discounted Cash Flow 或简称 DCF)的方式来计算赔偿。这可以节录联合国赔偿委员会的报告如下:"Where an income - producing property, ie an asset or a group of assets, such as a business, has been completely destroyed or irreparably damaged, the Discounted Cash Flow method can be used to estimate the cash flows through the end of the property's expected economic life in order to value that property. Where the asset or business can be repaired or resumed, however, the DCF method will not be an appropriate measure of loss to the extent that it takes into account estimated losses beyond the restoration date of the asset or business."

价值评估会是一个复杂的技术问题,往往超过了法律的范畴。这可能会要求法官或仲裁庭具有专业的知识或技能,即使他们会有双方当事人的"价值评估专家"(quantum experts)作为专家证人去协助,所以部分仲裁员被批评在做出赔偿裁决时并不能提供充分透明的经济分析与理据,这可以节录 T Stauffer 的《Valuation of assets in International Takings》[1]一文如下:"Most tribunal awards are parsimonious in the economic detail which is presented. Whatever financial data is offered by the tribunal has been filtered through a jurist's prism and typically is not amenable to economic analysis. The terminology is either too casual - confusing income with cash flow, for example - or the pieces of the financial puzzle are too few."

而在另外一些案件中,仲裁庭被指经常做出一人一半的裁决:James M Saghi v.

---

〔1〕 1996 17 Energy Law Journal 459.

Iran, Award of 22 January 1993, 29 Iran - US CTR 20; AMT v. Zaire, Award of 21 February 1997; Santa Elena v. Costa Rica, Award of 17 February 2000; Middle East Cement v. Egypt, Award of 12 April 2002。

5.2.2 三种价格评估方法

投资争议通常会涉及以商业利益的公平市价去计算损失,这就会要求仲裁庭或法院评估整个企业的价值,或者其中包含的股份利益价值,或者其他可能产生收益的资产或权利,如合约权利的价值。对这些商业价值的评估通常会采用三种方法中的一种或多于一种的方法核算一个投资或资产的实际市价,这三种方法如下:

(1)"基于收入的计算方法"(income - based approach):这是计算一项投资或资产将来会赚取的利润/收入以寻找该投资或资产的价值。这种计算方法最重要的就是表现在不少投资仲裁会适用的"贴现现金流"(Discounted Cash Flow 或简称 DCF),并会在本章第6段作出进一步的分析。

(2)"基于市场的计算方法"(market - based approach):这是根据市场可能会有的买卖一项投资或资产的价值来计算。这可以是很简单,如如果原告的投资或资产已经上市并且有股值可以作出计算。但这种情况不会是太多,就会带来投资或资产需要与公开市场上相似公司的账面价值、股值、收益、盈利能力等的指标做出比较,以估算出该项目的价值。如在本章第9段所介绍的 CME Czech Republic B. V. (The Netherlands) v The Czech Republic 仲裁案件中,有关投资或资产是一家媒体公司/电视台,它的估值方法之一是比较全球29家电视台的"税息折旧及摊销前利润"(EBITDA)。这种方法是在金融与商业市场普遍适用的计算方法,并会在本章第7段做进一步的分析。

另也可以透过该公司和其他买家在股权上的私人交易来比较,如原告被收归国有或被干预的投资或资产曾经在几个月前被第三人出价收购。

(3)"基于资产的计算方法"(asset - based approach):这是计算构成企业的动产与不动产的价值,它们的总和就是这个企业的价值。找出动产的价值,根据它的"重置价值"(replacement value),也可以是根据有关资产的"账面价值"(book value),或是"清算价值"(liquidation value)。严格说,以原告投入的资本计算赔偿金额(valuation by reference to amounts invested)也应该是属于这一种计算方法。

这些不同的计算方法适用在不同的投资都有它们的利弊,这方面会在本章第8段做进一步的分析。

6. 基于收入的计算方法——"贴现现金流"

6.1 贴现现金流的概念

"贴现现金流"(Discounted Cash Flow 或简称 DCF)计算方法是上一段所讲的基

于收入来对商业价值进行评估的一种最主要方式。在投资仲裁中,这也是原告的受害方最经常提出的一种损失项目,也往往涉及庞大的金额。用这种损失计算办法找出"公平市价"(fair market value 或简称 FMV)是因为许多资产(如一项业务、一个许可或一个企业/公司)的价值就是它估计能够赚取的利润,而投资者也是因为这一个估计而做出这一项投资。所以能够计算出投资者本来可以赚取的利润就会是被主权国家干预而失去资产的真正价值。所以有说法是贴现现金流是对一项投资或资产估值时理论性最强的计算方法。

由于估计所得出的利润(这方面的金额已是十分富争议性)是将来才会赚取,而仲裁如果胜诉是要被告的主权国家马上支付,因为裁决书一判下来就把将来的利润变为是马上要支付的判决债务,所以需要把这笔代表将来才会赚取的利润损失变为"现值"(present value)做出"折算"(discount)。这方面在许多著名的说法中有显示,如西方就有说法是"1 只在手中的鸟要好过 10 只在林中的鸟"(a bird in hand is better than ten in the bush)。例如,其中需要折算的好处就是期间的利息,同一笔预计利润如果在 5 年后才能赚取,如果是现在就可以取得,显然这 5 年间的利息就应该折算。但利息还比较好估计,其他的风险则难以预测并给予恰当的折算,如经济下滑、市场占有率减少或新科技发展等风险会导致 5 年后能够赚取的利润根本达不到预计。这种对将来预期利润在考虑各种风险后进行折算的计算就是所谓的"贴现现金流"方法。

世界银行的指引对"贴现现金流"的定义可引用如下:"The cash receipts realistically expected from the enterprise in each future year of its economic life as reasonably projected minus that year's expected cash expenditure, after discounting this net cash flow for each year by a factor which reflects the time value of money, expected inflation, and the risk associated with such cash flow under realistic circumstances. Such discount rate may be measured by examining the rate of return available in the same market or alternative investments of comparable risk on the basis of their present value."

关于"贴现现金流"的计算方法,可以简单节录仲裁庭在 Amoco International Finance v. Iran, Partial Award of 14 July, 15 Iran – US CTR 189 中的判词如下:"The first step in valuing an asset pursuant to the DCF method must be to project from the valuation date onward the most likely revenues and expenses of the on – going concern, year by year. The revenues less the expenses will give the future cash flow. The second step will be to discount the projected net cash flow to its 'present value' as of the valuation date by applying a discount rate."

6.2　贴现现金流的计算方法

简单地说,在计算贴现现金流时,原告需要对损失的将来预期利润提供一个合理的估计(如提供货物生产的成本及售价、市场情况及推算等),仲裁庭便会用原告所损失的"预期收入"(projected revenue)减去将来的"预期成本"(projected costs),然后再“根据通胀/利息与其它风险因素作出折算”(apply a discount rate to reflect the value of those future cash flow at a present date),给原告所损失的未来利润算出一个现值。以上的计算显然是有很多的假设与臆猜,特别是贴现现金流的计算时常是10年或以后的情况。

以这种方法做出计算,原告与被告通过他们的“价值评估专家”(quantum expert),会得出很不一样的结果。这是因为针对将来会赚取的利润,需要折算的并不是期间的利息这么简单(虽然几年后的利息走势到底怎样也是只有天知道)。这里涉及数不清的风险会影响某一项投资将来的利润,需要折算,这方面会稍后详论。特别是投资在一个发展中国家,这种风险也有许多根本不是主权国家的政府可以控制或需要承担。本来在预期利益的损失或将来利润损失就会面对许多不肯定的因素,需要做出估计。但经常会出现好像 Scarman 勋爵在 Lim Poh Choo v. Camden and Islington Area Health Authority(1980) AC 174 所说的情况:“... there is really only one certainty:the future will prove the award to be either too high or too low”(只会有一个方面是肯定,就是将来会证明判决或裁决的预期利益的损失赔偿金额要么太高要么太低)。

6.3 贴现现金流的简单计算公式

首先给一个简单介绍,单纯从数学角度来看,计算贴现现金流的公式是:

$$\text{现值} = \sum_{t=1}^{n} \frac{CF_t}{(1+r)^t}$$

其中,n = 资产收益的期限,CF_t = 在时间 t 内的现金流,r = 折现率或折算。

根据以上的公式,假设有一项投资估计未来5年都会有收益的现金流,代表风险的折现率是15%。

年份	现金流(按年度)
1	\$ 18,000
2	\$ 20,000
3	\$ 21,000
4	\$ 22,000
5	\$ 22,000
总现金流	\$ 103,000

所以这项投资的现值就是把现金流每一年的现值加和:

$$\text{现值} = \frac{(\$\,18{,}000)}{(1+0.15)^1} + \frac{(\$\,20{,}000)}{(1+0.15)^2} + \frac{(\$\,21{,}000)}{(1+0.15)^3} + \frac{(\$\,22{,}000)}{(1+0.15)^4} + \frac{(\$\,22{,}000)}{(1+0.15)^5}$$

$$\text{现值} = \frac{(\$\,18{,}000)}{1.15} + \frac{(\$\,20{,}000)}{1.323} + \frac{(\$\,21{,}000)}{1.521} + \frac{(\$\,22{,}000)}{1.749} + \frac{(\$\,22{,}000)}{2.011}$$

$$\text{现值} = 15{,}652 + 15{,}129 + 13{,}807 + 12{,}579 + 10{,}940$$

$$\text{现值} = \$\,68{,}107$$

在以上简单的例子,可以看到整个计算的根据都是对将来的估计或臆猜。其中

15%的折现率更加是不可靠，在 Amoco International Finance v. Iran, Partial Award of 14 July 1987, 15 Iran - US CTR 189 仲裁案件中，仲裁庭认为在贴现现金流计算中，估计什么是适合的折算是最具有潜在的主观性(the inherent subjectivity of the DCF process was at a peak)。

6.4　计算贴现现金流的期限

对于有固定有效期限的投资(例如，投资合约有效期为 3 年，或者主权国家授予投资者一个 5 年的经营许可)，理论上现金流就要根据这个固定的期限来计算，特别是有效期限是相对短的。也有许多的投资项目不存在确定期限，理论上就要算到有关投资(如厂房或机器)在经济上被使用至最后的期限。在许多这种投资仲裁案件，经常会涉及较长的期限，如 30 年或以上。

对于不确定期限或者是很长有效期限(如 30 年)的商业投资，资产价值的计算会分为两部分：第一部分是投资资产前期所产生的一连串现金流(如首 5 年的现金流)；第二部分便是该资产于第一部分的现金流完结时的剩余价值，又称"终值"(terminal value)。

终值的计算公式为：

$$\frac{\text{Expected Income}_n \text{x}(1 + \text{Terminal Growth})}{(\text{Discount Rate} - \text{Terminal Growth})}$$

这两部分的总和便能得出资产的总预计价值(如把资产的预计首 5 年现金流加上资产第 5 年的终值便能得出该资产的总价值)。至于应该估算多久的现金流，便应按情况而定。一般来说，为了提高计算的精确性，推算未来现金流的年期会尽可能在合理的范围内延长，直至资产所产生的现金流有足够的"稳定增长"(stable growth)。这是因为投资资产于计算终值后的收益(cash flow after the terminal year)越稳定，"终值"的计算公式就越能准确反映资产的真实价值。

至于"终值"的估算方法主要是先假定该投资资产能提供一个"永续"(perpetuity)现金流，然后透过估算第一部分期末(如第 5 年)的现金流，加上长远经济的预期增长率(terminal growth)及折现率(discount rate)等因素(折现率按国家、公司、行业等而有所不同，详见本章6.7 段)，估算出投资资产于"最后一年现金流"(terminal year)时的终值。只要以终值现值再加上前面的现金流现值，便能计算出整个投资资产价值。

但无论如何，由于估算第一部分的现金流涉及太多未知的因素，第一部分的现金流的期限亦难以过份延长。《Lawyer's Business Valuation Handbook》一书认为这个期限一般为 3 ~ 10 年，最普遍的是 5 年。不过实际数字还需要考虑到资产的发展潜力及行业增长等因素。例如，对于规模小但有可能于短期内录得大量盈利(或亏损)的资产，由于要达到收益"稳定增长"(stable growth)的时间较长，估算现金流的年期便应相应延长，并尽可能把终值的估算推迟到较后的年期，不过亦需考虑到过长的期限有可能使评估变得不切实际。同理，由于越远期的现金流越难被合理预计，所以适用此类估算方法的投资资产均为一些拥有一定规模及竞争优势，而且处于竞争不太激烈的行业内的项目,因为这类投资的盈利一般较为稳定,估算出来的终值亦会相对与实际价值相近。事实上,由于在发展中国家的投资项目均涉及各种风险,一般来说营运时间亦未必会太长,所以这种方法对于一般发展中国家的投资仲裁案件未必适用。

对于有特定期限的商业投资,根据年期长短,终值有可能是合约到期的一天(如短期合约)又或是合约的中段(如长期合约)。在短期合约中,一般所有现金流均会被估算,在这情况下亦不一定有太多实质的终值。这是因为特定的机器、厂房等在合约完成后的转售价值可能很低甚至是零,会有机会出现受害方得到过多或重复赔偿的风险(详见本章6.6段)。所以说并非所有的短期合约项目均有一个实质的清算价值。

至于在中长期的合约下要计算的资产总价值,终值便相对重要:资产的总价值除了包括"最后一年现金流"(terminal year)以前的现金流,还要加上终值。在这种情况下的终值可以是资产于"最后一年现金流"(terminal year)的"清算价值"(liquidation value),亦可以是透过其他同类投资资产或公司的各种指标去估算(这一个方面会在本章7.2段作进一步介绍)。

在损失计算中仲裁庭以多长的期限计算现金流会对最终的赔偿金额有很大影响,这里就已经存在很大与很多的裁量权。可以随便举一些例子,在2005年的一个仲裁案件CMS Gas Transmission Company v. The Argentine Republic(ICSID Award, Case No. ARB/01/8)(2005)[1]中,阿根廷政府给原告发了营运天然气运输的牌照,在计算利润损失时,牌照有条文规定于2027年后原告有权续领10年的牌照,仲裁庭把预期利润的损失计算至牌照的终止日期(2027年),这是因为牌照的延长必须要有政府的批准,所以仲裁庭不考虑续领的10年。但是,长达27年的预期利润也已经是足够多。

也有其他类似的案件是不根据整个合约的期限推算预期利润的损失,这可以ICC的Case No. 7006 of 1992, 18 Y. B. COM. ARB. 58(1993)仲裁案件为例。案情同样涉及一个分销的合约,虽然该合约的年期为3年,仲裁庭却只计算了第一年的预期利润损失,但这里涉及另一个不同的理由(会在6.5段会详论),就是仲裁庭认为原告可以在1年后找到相关的替代合约而把损失减少(mitigation of loss)。

6.4.1 贴现现金流计算期限的长短会令赔偿金额有天壤之别

计算损失期限的长短会令最后的赔偿金额有天壤之别,并给整个案件带来不同的结果。可以举一个例子,涉及一家美国公司向一家中国国有公司索赔一笔当时是天文数字的金额,最初的索赔高达近十亿美元。据称这是新中国成立后国有公司面对的最高一笔索赔(在当时而言)。索赔金额这么高是因为双方的"合资合约"(joint venture contract)中没有订下合作的年限或/与双方如何可解约/脱身。当双方合作了

---

[1] 之后阿根廷提起仲裁撤销程序,特别委员会于2007年给出了裁决,撤销关于保护伞条文的适用。

几个月后，中方发觉美方的管理技术没有什么可取之处，估计派几个学生去外国大学学习或邀请哈佛商学院的教授前来中国授课会学得更多，就单方面终断合约。这一来，美国公司就接受中国公司的“违约/毁约”(repudiation)。由于合约中没有约定合作期限，美方索赔预期利润损失的期限由最初的70年改为后来的50年，根据贴现现金流方法计算出的金额就会大得惊人。当时中国公司也曾经在美国律师建议下试图与美国公司达成和解，但美国公司要求的赔偿金额也是上亿美元。笔者在开庭前约3个月被要求提供协助后，做了两件事情把该索赔击退。第一件事已经在笔者所著的《仲裁法》(法律出版社2006年版)第11章第9段中详细介绍过，就是要求该美国公司作为原告提供“费用担保”(security for costs)；第二件事是涉及损失赔偿计算期限。笔者记得英国曾经有贵族院先例针对一些没有规定期限的合约，主要是向一些城市的市政府或者企业提供水电，由于多年来的通货膨胀导致10年或15年前所订下的价格不再切合实际，所以供应水电的机构很希望能够合法脱身。先例是说由于合约中没有明示的期限，法律就可以对这一个期限做出合理的默示。这表示供应水电的机构可以做出合理通知后在合理时间内终断原来订下的合约。笔者建议中国公司马上修改抗辩文书的请求，把损失计算的50年预期利润损失减为最多2年，理由是学习西方管理技术(这订约的意图是双方都知道的)并不需要漫无止境的期限，如果2年学不好也就别学了，毕竟去哈佛商学院读一个MBA也只不过需要这些时间等。这一来根据2年的贴现现金流计算，这预期利益的损失马上大幅度减低至1、2千万美元。这是一笔中国公司能够负担的赔偿金额，更不用说在这1、2千万美元中还有许多地方可以争议，也是把这一损失大幅度减少而且是有理有据。估计这导致美国公司对索赔的灰心，最终不提供费用担保而令整个案件不了了之。可以说这两件事情(一件是在仲裁程序，另一件是在实体争议)需要同时进行，才会最终成功击退索赔。

6.4.2　分段或暂定计算预期利润损失的可能性

还有一种做法是目前在投资仲裁中没有见到过，就是以一个“暂定”(provisional)的方式为受害方提供利润损失估算及赔偿。例如，受害方提出了未来30年如果没有违约/毁约下的利润估算，仲裁庭只会按为首5年的利润作出估算，待5年后再按当时的情况为第6年至第10年的利润再作估算，以此类推。这种分段核算将来利润损失的做法在本书第十六章“市场规则”之6.5.4段有详细的介绍，不重复。笔者认为这种做法也应该在投资仲裁中使用，反正被告主权国也“逃不到哪里去”，以这种计算方法提供一个合理准确的估算，总比动辄要发展中国家一次性赔上数10亿美元来得公平。

6.5　受害投资者应该减少损失的责任

除了上文6.4段所讲的ICC仲裁案件Case No. 7006 of 1992，18 Y. B. COM. ARB. 58(1993)，另在多处提到的Asian Agricultural Products Limited v. Democratic Socialist Republic of Sri Lanka(ICSID Case No. ARB/87/3)(1990)的仲裁庭也认为虽然斯里兰

卡军队的反叛乱军事行动的确损坏了原告的活虾养殖场，但原告需要 2～3 年的时间重新建立业务并继续提供虾给它唯一的市场（日本），而在这一段时间内也不至于失去了原告的商誉，说："... it would be appropriate to ascertain that 'goodwill' requires the prior presence on the market for at least two or three years, which is the minimum period needed in order to establish continuing business connection, and during that period substantial expenses are incurred in supporting the management efforts devoted to create and develop the marketing network of the company's products, particularly in cases like the present one where the Company relies exclusively on one product (shrimps) exportable to a single market (Japan)."

这就带来了一个说法，就是在一些合约期限很长或没有期限的投资，贴现现金流不应该漫无止境地计算下去。这不仅是因为现实中"好景不常在"的道理（这一个方面是受害的投资者应该承担的风险照说是已经折算），也是另一个英美法下的说法，就是受害方必须合理减少损失，这在本书第五章"减少损失"有详细介绍。受害的投资者，作为一个有经验与水平的公司或个人，应该可以用他获得的赔偿做其他投资，包括在另一个国家的投资。举一个简单的例子，在英国的雇佣法律下，如果雇主无理提前解雇受害的雇员，雇员索赔的损失也不是漫无止境或根据长期雇佣合约的期限提出索赔。他是有一个合理减少损失的责任，另寻找工作，索赔只能是新工作与原雇佣合约工资的差价。这可以节录《Halsbury's Laws of England》（Vol. 12[1], 4th edn, 1998）一书如下："In actions for breach of a contract of employment, a plaintiff who has been wrongfully dismissed must take reasonable steps to obtain other suitable employment. He is not entitled to remain idle at the defendant's expense simply because no precisely similar employment can be found, but must accept employment which, having regard to his standing, experience and personal history he can reasonably be expected to accept."

所以在投资仲裁中，也有这一个说法。事实上在 1990 年伊拉克萨达姆政权侵略科威特的战争中，受害方事后要求伊拉克做出赔偿的案件中，联合国的救济委员会（United Nation Compensations Commission）曾经针对计算预期利益做出了以下的规定："In the case of a business which has been, or could have been, rebuilt and resumed, compensation would be awarded for the loss from cessation of trading to the time when trading was, or could have been, resumed. In the case of a business ... which it was not possible to resume, the Commissioners would need to calculate a time limit for compensation for future earnings and profits, taking into account the claimant's duty to mitigate the loss wherever possible."

6.6 "重复计算"的危险

贴现现金流还会有重复计算的危险，特别是在一些期限很长的投资中。因为原告的投资者是在执行裁决书后取回他将来才会赚取的利润（不论是否会赚取，这是风险与应该折算多少的问题），他可以把这笔钱做其他的用途，包括做出更好的投资。这一来,原告就有可能获得重复计算的赔偿。在 L Wells 的《Double Dipping in Arbitration Awards? An Economist Questions Damages Awarded Karaha Bodas Company in Indonesia》(2003 19[4] Arbitration International 471)一文中就有介绍有关重复计算危险的例子,可以节录如下:"Consider an individual saver whose bank account is covered by deposit insurance. Say the saver's bank fails, and deposit insurance pays both the amount of the deposit and foregone interest for 30 years into the future. The large award ... leaves the saver better off with bank failure than without, because it can deposit the principal (and the compensation for foregone interest) elsewhere and earn interest again, ending up with principal plus twice the interest (and interest on the interest, as well)."

在这个说法下,可以说贴现现金流一直计算到合约期限届满的一天或投资项目经济使用的最后一天都会是多赔偿了原告。

6.7 应该折算的各种风险

在上文6.3段已经提到过,在 Amoco International Finance v. Iran, Partial Award of 14 July 1987, 15 Iran – US CTR 189 仲裁案件中,仲裁庭认为在贴现现金流计算中,估计什么是适合的折算是最具有潜在的主观性(the inherent subjectivity of the DCF process was at a peak)。本段将会具体介绍在贴现现金流计算中需要折算的各种不同风险。

一般来说,这些风险在主权国家违约前就已经存在,但要客观找出并计算这些风险却并不容易。通常仲裁庭会在计算出现金流后将现金流乘以一个"折现率"(discount rate)以反映那些有机会影响该项投资回报的风险和变数。在 Glamis Gold Ltd v. United States of America (2009) 中,仲裁庭这样说:"The valuation of an investment ... must take into account ... increases the number and variety of risks that may interfere with the investment and reduce its expected return. This uncertainty is reflected in the discount rate, a rate at which future cash flows are discounted to account for a number of risks, both general and specific, to reflect the investment's specific risk profile."

在贴现现金流下计算出的赔偿数额需要反映出某个特定现金流的风险和不确定性,所以在计算贴现现金流时需要折算各种风险因素,如所投入资本的机会损失。"折现率"(discount rate)越高,根据贴现现金流计算出的整体价值就会越低。折现率会反映出金钱的时间价值,以及在现实中商业投资所涉及的风险。这些风险可能包括会影响整体经济环境的系统性风险,以及只影响相关行业领域的非系统性风险。说到行业领域的风险,简单例子是相比航运或航空等的业务,公共事业如供水或供电的投资所面对的收入现金流就应该比较稳定。

行业领域的风险也可以多举一个目前(2012 年 6 月)十分热门的社群网站 Facebook 在美国上市的新闻。这一个社群网站在这几年快速兴起,2007 年微软用 2.4 亿美元收购 Facebook 1.6% 的股权,使 Facebook 的估值达到 150 亿美元。而 2011 年高盛集团以 5 亿美元购买 Facebook 1% 的股权,导致 Facebook 的估值高达 500 亿美元。

Facebook 的市价估计如此之高,原因就是它现在在全球拥有超过 6 亿使用者,而且每个月也约有 2000 万的新增用户。针对商业风险而言,Facebook 主要是以广告以及其他一些附加收费作为获利来源,但有说法是能够在社群网站上被广告吸引而购买产品的用户应该十分有限,所以通用公司在 2012 年 5 月停止继续在 Facebook 上刊登付费广告的行为也间接证明这种广告的收益是十分有限的。再加上现代网络科技产业每天都会发生翻天覆地的变化与新的竞争,Facebook 社群网站的产业将来估计的收入现金流能够维持多少年与多少利润是值得商榷的。反正是在这一个行业,所涉及的商业风险显然会比其他较稳定的行业大得多。所以在 2012 年 Facebook 上市时估值 1040 亿美元,带来颇大的争议性,但毕竟这一个数字也是经过有说服力与看来是科学的贴现现金流计算与估值。

6.7.1 主要风险的类别

通常在一项投资项目中会涉及投资者需要承担的几个主要的风险:

(1)"商业风险"(Business risk):包括投资错误、价格变动、客户需求降低、生产成本高出预期、购买者破产等风险。尽管这类商业风险会影响任何产业,不论这项投资是在国内还是国外经营,但在大部分发展中国家,由于缺乏基础设施,及大量的低收入消费者等因素,商业风险会更大。

这种风险应该是由投资者自己承担的,毕竟商业环境的改变会给不同行业带来不同的影响,会有少数行业甚至在商业环境变坏时反而可以得利。在 Oscar Chinn affair,(1934)PCIJ Rep,Ser A/B,Case No 63 案件中,国际常设法院是说:"No enterprise ... can escape from the chances and hazards resulting from general economic conditions. Some industries may be able to make large profits during a period of general prosperity, or else by taking advantages of a treaty of commerce or of an alteration in customs duties; but they are also exposed to the danger of ruin or extinction if circumstances change. Where this is the case, no vested rights are violated by the State."

另在美国—伊朗索赔仲裁庭(US - Iran Claims Tribunal)中有许多案件也可以充分理解到伊斯兰革命使商业环境变坏的商业风险,而这种商业风险应该在事后资产被伊朗政府收归国有考虑赔偿金额时被排除,因为这是美国投资者的风险。这在 AIG v. Iran, Award of 19 December 1983, 4 Iran - US CTR 96 仲裁案件中,仲裁庭说:"Prior changes in the general political, social and economic conditions which might have affected the enterprise's business prospects as of the date the enterprise was taken should be considered."

另在 Starrett Housing v. Iran, Interlocutory Award of 19 December 1983, 4 Iran - US CTR 122 仲裁案件中,仲裁庭也是提出了同样的看法,可以节录如下:"Investors in Iran, like investors in all other countries, have to assume a risk that the country might experience strikes, lock - outs, disturbances, changes of the economic and political system and even revolution. That any of these risks materialized does not necessarily mean that property rights affected by such events can be deemed to have been taken. A revolution as such does not entitle investors to compensation under international law. ”(伊朗的投资者,好像其他国家的投资者一样,需要承担风险,如果该主权国家发生罢工、资方停工、骚乱、经济与政治制度的变更,甚至是革命。如果这些风险真的发生,并不代表外国投资者的资产权利被剥夺。在国际法下,革命并不能让外国投资者获得赔偿)

另在几个投资仲裁中,仲裁庭也说双边投资协议并非是投资者商业风险的保险。在 MTD v. Chile, Award of 25 May 2004 仲裁案件中,仲裁庭是说:“The BITs are not an insurance against business risk”。在 Maffezini v. Spain, Award of 13 November 2000,仲裁庭也是说:“Bilateral Investment Treaties are not insurance policies against bad business judgments.”(双边投资协议并非是错误商业决定的保险)

其他针对投资者自己应该承担的商业风险,不能向主权国家提出索赔损失的案件也不少,如 Methanex Corporation v. US, Award of 3 August 2005(损失是来自主权国家的合法管制,不属于收归国有);Waste Management v. Mexico, Award of 2 June 2000(损失是来自投资者自己的计划失败)等。在后一个仲裁案件,仲裁庭说:“In the Tribunal's view, it is not the function of the international law of expropriation as reflected in Article 1110 [of the NAFTA] to eliminate the normal commercial risks of a foreign investor, or to place on Mexico the burden of compensating for the failure of a business plan which was, in the circumstances, founded on too narrow a client base and dependent for its success on unsustainable assumptions about customer uptake and contractual performance.”[在仲裁庭看来,NAFTA 的第 1110 条文中规定的收归国有的国际法原则并非是解除外国投资者要承担的正常商业风险,或是试图把外国投资者错误的商业计划(包括拥有太狭窄的客户群体以及将成功建立在一些不持久的对客户新增数量和对合约履行情况的假设上)的后果要墨西哥政府承担]

在本段开始也介绍过,在发展中国家往往面临巨大的商业风险,所以也有一些案件判是由投资者自己承担这一类的商业风险。这些案件包括了 Alex Genin, Eastern Credit Limited, Inc v. Estonia, Award of 25 June 2001(投资者自己冒险去一个刚刚成立的国家投资);Olguin v. Paraguay, Award of 26 June 2001(投资者明知道巴拉圭的国家与法律制度,自己选择做出一个投机性与不谨慎的投资);Parkerings - Compagniet AS v. Lithuania, Award of 11 September 2007(投资者自己选择去一个刚从苏联分离出来的国家投资,这个国家正处在加入欧共体的过渡阶段,应该可以预见会有法律的改变影响他的投资)等。

(2)“金融风险”(Financial risk):指公司融资方式造成的不确定性,如“股票”(equity)、“债务”(debt)等。这一般也是属于投资者自己要承担的风险。

(3)“资产流动性风险”(Liquidity risk):指二级市场的风险,如投资是否可以容易地出售给其他人套现,这也是属于投资者自己要承担的风险。

(4)“汇兑风险”(Exchange rate risk)与“通货膨胀风险”(Inflation risk):如果外

国投资者以他自己国家的货币进行投资或者获得融资,但在主权国家获得的收益是该国货币,这就有不确定性,因为如果后者货币贬值的话就换不回投资的金额。而投资者本国货币与他所使用货币的兑换率浮动越大,造成的汇兑风险也就越高。至于通货膨胀风险就不必多讲。这些风险通常也是投资者自己承担,但会有特殊情况/安排是主权国家承担。这里可举阿根廷的例子,政府为了在国内的汽油行业吸引外国投资,立法规定对汽油运输和分配的价格表是依据美元来计算,再按照支付当天的汇率转换成比索,以保证外国投资者在比索兑换美元不会遇到贬值风险。相关的立法还规定价格表每半年都会根据"美国生产者物价指数"(US Producer Price Index)调整,同时降低或排除了通货膨胀的风险。但这些对外国投资者的法律保障在2000年阿根廷经济危机之后被取消,这导致了一系列针对阿根廷政府的根据双边投资协议的索赔请求与仲裁:CMS v. Argentina, Award of 12 May 2005; Enron v. Argentina, Award of 22 May 2007; LG&E v. Argentina, Decision on Liability of 3 October 2006 and Award of 25 July 2007; Sempra Energy v. Argentina, Award of 28 September 2007 等。

至于是投资者自己要承担的汇兑风险,可介绍 Biloune v. Ghana, Award on Damages and Costs of 30 June 1990 仲裁案件,仲裁庭拒绝了投资者索赔的因塞地(加纳货币)贬值造成的损失,因为塞地的贬值是发生在投资项目被收归国有之前。仲裁庭最终判是损失赔偿的金额是投资者在该项目上已经投入的金额。投资者辩称这应该按照他在该项目上投入资金的不同日期来把塞地兑换为美元,而不应该按照收归国有发生一天的汇率来兑换。由于在投资与收归国有这段期间内塞地贬值,投资者所提出的计算方式得出的赔偿金额(美元)会是按照收归国有一天计算出的赔偿金额的2倍。仲裁庭驳回了投资者的计算方式,认为被告的主权国家并不应该为外国投资者因货币贬值而遭受的风险提供保险,说"... the Respondents ... did not insure foreign investors against depreciation of the cedi between the date of investment and the date of expropriation."所以,在这段期间内的货币贬值风险应该是由投资者自己承担。

(5)"国家风险或政治风险"(Country risk or political risk):国家政治或者经济环境的变动可能性也会给投资者的收益带来不确定性。而对国家风险的分析会取决于这个国家过去和以前的环境。国际法接受由于国家政治变动的风险所带来的利润减少甚至不再盈利是外国投资者自己的风险,这是与主权国家政府干预带来的风险完全不同。

国家风险通常会被视为是基于多种变量的复合性标志。例如,一家著名的风险评估机构 PRS 集团在评估超过140个国家的国家风险时,就是基于对三大类风险22个变量的评估,这包括政治、经济与金融风险。政治风险涉及国家的政治稳定,包括如国家稳定性、社会经济环境、国家内部冲突、外部冲突、腐败、军事政治情况与官僚情况等。经济风险是评估一个国家现在的经济优势与劣势,包括人均 GDP、实际 GDP 增长、每年的通货膨胀率、平衡预算与往来账户情况等。金融风险是指一个国家的支付能力,包括外国债务、汇兑率稳定性与其他因素。通过对每一个风险变数分配不同分数并衡量得分的结果,PRS 集团计算出了每个国家的综合等级。这可以参考 http://www.prsgroup.com/ICRG_Methodology.aspx。看来,这也是投资者自己选择投资在某一个国家所应该承担的风险。这方面可看较早在商业风险中所提到的 Oscar Chinn affair 与 Starrett Housing v. Iran 仲裁案件中所节录的判词。

至于什么是主权国家干预带来的风险,这通常是指一些国家的行为给投资者预期利润带来不利的影响。这种风险包括了直接或间接的把资产收归国有,货币风险(无法把当地的货币兑换为硬货币或即使能够兑换也会遭遇外汇管制等),政治暴力(战争、动乱、革命等)把资产摧毁(双边投资协议中有"保护及安全"[protection and security]条文)与主权国家违反投资协议行为。这种政治风险通常是会要主权国家承担,也会在投资协议中有说明。

除了以上所列举的各类主要风险外,还有许多其他的风险如主权国家一般保留决定本国货币价值(贬值或升值)的权利,通过或改变财政预算等。这些非商业性风险也是需要由外国投资者承担的。

6.7.2 把主要风险分类为将来利润损失与将来支付金额的不同折算先例

在以上所列举的各类主要风险,还可以进一步把它们分为两大类。第一类是一些风险针对估计将来利润损失的折现,英文可以是"risks associated with future cash - flow"。第二类是针对"金钱本身有时间上的价值"(time value of money),所以"将来支付金额变回现值的折算"(discount for accelerated receipt)。显然在投资仲裁,第一类的风险会有更多与更高,如果分开计算应该会有更大的折现率。上述提到的商业风险、金融风险、汇兑风险、资产流动性风险、国家风险或政治风险都属于这一类。至于是第二类的风险,会是上述所提到的通货膨胀风险以及上述没有提到的将来利息波动的风险。显然,第二类的风险会是不高,特别在近年来低通胀与低利息的环境。但估计将来甚至是 20/30 年后的投资仲裁案件,还是困难、富争议与很可能与真实情况相差很远。

针对这两大类风险的区别,英国倒是有一个近期商业先例名为 Lilly Icos LLC v. 8PM Chemists Ltd(2010)FSR 4。案情涉及在原告的申请下法院较早前向被告做出了多个"中间禁令"(interim injunction)禁止被告使用某商标。而这些禁令摧毁了被告的主要业务与造成他客户的流失。而最后的审理是被告胜诉,也表示原告申请禁令的行为是错误的。于是被告要求用原告申请禁令时所提供的担保赔偿他业务的损失,也就是预期利润的损失。Arnold 大法官在解释了这两大类的风险后,适用三个不同的贴现率。第一个贴现率是第二类风险的 15%,基本上双方也没有什么争议。第二个贴现率是第一类的风险,Arnold 大法官还进一步把估计的时间分为两个部分。第一个部分是开始计算损失的一天(2007 年 11 月 23 日),直到开庭审理的一天,贴现率是 10%。这比较低的贴现率是因为到了审理时已经知道这一段时间发生了什么,包括一些估计的风险并没有出现。但第二部分是将来的利润损失,风险就相应更

多与更高,所以贴现率判是20%。Arnold 大法官是这样说:

"Risk factor for the future(将来的风险与折现率)

237 In projecting the lost profits which the defendants' Turkish fulfilment business(被告的业务)would have made but for the Injunctions,it is necessary to take account of the risks to which that business was subject. These include the risk of the defendants' customers going out of business,the risk that one or more of those customers might transfer their business elsewhere and so on. It is common ground that it is appropriate to allow for this by applying an annual percentage risk factor to the calculation of future profits,representing the risk that the business would come to an end within that year.

238 Mr Bezant(被告的赔偿金额专家证人)considered that the appropriate risk factor to be applied for the future was 10 per cent per annum. He explained in cross - examination that this was not arrived at as a matter of accountancy practice,but through the exercise of professional judgment. He accepted that a higher risk factor might be appropriate, but not as high as 20 per cent per annum.(被告专家证人认为利润损失的风险只是10%,这不是根据科学的会计计算,只是他的专业判断。这百分比也可能会是高一点,但怎么样都不会高达20%。)

239 Ms Gutteridge(原告的赔偿金额专家证人)suggested that a risk factor of 20 - 25 per cent was appropriate based on a list of risks set out in her first report. She was cross - examined at some length both on the individual risks she had taken into account and on the headline figure. In my judgment,the cross - examination demonstrated that she had over - estimated a number of the risks. By way of example,I consider that she overestimated the risks due to the absence of a written contract, illegality under US law(as to which see below)and competition in Turkey. She also looked at the matter from the perspective of a buyer of the business,whereas the defendants were not intending to sell it.(原告专家证人认为风险高达20%~25%,根据一连串列明的风险。Arnold 大法官在反盘问后认为专家证人夸大了一些损失,如美国会是非法与土耳其的竞争。)

240 Nevertheless,considering the evidence as a whole,I think that considerable caution as to the future of the business is required. This is not a business which had been established for a long period of time. Moreover,it was not operating in a well - established market sector. On the contrary,it had been established for a relatively short period of time and was operating in a fairly young and dynamic sector. Furthermore, the business was dependent on one customer for 88 per cent of its business,and as noted above the relationship with that customer was a fragile one in the sense that the customer could decide to go elsewhere at any time. As stated above,I think it is also appropriate to take into account the risk that,even if the business continued,its profitability would decline. Accordingly,I consider that the appropriate risk factor for the future is 20 per cent per annum.(Arnold 大法

官在整体考虑了风险后认为将来的利润损失计算折现率是20%。)

Risk factor for the period from November 23,2007 to date(2007 年 11 月 23 日到审理一天的风险与折现率)

241 Mr Bezant was instructed to assume that the defendants business would have continued down to the date of his report. In his first report, he took this to be December 31, 2008 for convenience. In his second and third reports, he took it to be March 31,2009. He therefore did not apply any risk factor for the period from November 23,2007 until then. Mr Bezant was cross – examined on this assumption, and it was evident that he was uncomfortable with it. As counsel for the claimants pointed out, it amounts to treating the risk that the business would have ceased prior to the trial as a question of fact to be evaluated on the balance of probabilities(i. e. applying the approach laid down in Hotson v. East Berkshire HA [1987] 1 A. C. 750); but treating the risk that the business would cease in the future as a contingency to be reflected in the quantum of compensation. This is inconsistent and over – compensates the defendants.

242 Ms Gutteridge's approach was to take November 23,2007 as the date of assessment and then apply the same risk factor both to the period from then until trial and to the period from trial onwards. As counsel for the defendants pointed out, this involves shutting one's eyes to what has happened since November 23,2007. There are also other problems with this approach: it involves applying a discount rate to this period and then adding interest back, and it has the effect of imposing exchange rate movement losses on the defendants.

243 In my judgment neither approach is correct. As set out above, I consider that the correct approach is to assess the compensation with the benefit of hindsight. Hindsight is not available looking forward, and it is appropriate to reflect the contingencies to which the defendants' business was subject by the application of a risk factor. With regard to the period from November 23,2007 to date, however, the court does have the advantage of hindsight. As a result, it is now known that some of the contingencies did not materialise during that period. In particular, Canada Drugs did not itself go out of business. On the other hand, it is not known whether other contingencies would have materialised or not. [Arnold 大法官认为两位专家证人的意见都不对。将来的利润损失去非要做出预测,无法事后诸葛亮。但针对这一段时间(2007 年 11 月 23 日到审理一天)是完全可以根据事后诸葛亮看看预测的风险到底有没有发生。事实上,有一些风险是没有出现。]

244 Accordingly, I conclude that a lower risk factor should be applied to the period from November 23,2007 to date. In my judgment a risk factor of 10 per cent is appropriate for this period. (所以 Arnold 大法官给了一个较低的贴现率是 10%。)

Discount rate(金钱的时间价值的折现率)

245 In addition to applying a risk factor, it is necessary to calculate the net present

value of the future income stream so as to make allowance for the advantage of accelerated receipt. It was common ground between the experts that it was appropriate to do this by means of a discounted cash flow(DCF) analysis. Mr Bezant used a discount rate of 15 per cent in his DCF analysis. The claimants did not in the end dispute the appropriateness of this rate.(这里是指被告以15%的折现率作为对将来利润损失的贴现现金流的计算,原告并没有反对。笔者估计15%会是相对高,所以要做出支付的原告也没有反对的必要。)

Conclusion on lost profits(总结)

246 For the reasons given above, I conclude that the quantum of the defendants' loss is represented by the sterling equivalent of a figure which is to be calculated by taking the profit calculatedusing Mr Bezant's figures for the profit margin for the base period of the year to September 23, 2007, applying growth rates of 4 per cent and 1.9 per cent, a discount rate of 15 per cent and risk factors of 10 per cent for the period from November 23, 2007 to the date of this judgment and 20 per cent thereafter. I invite the parties to try to agree this calculation."

6.7.3 如何在外国投资者与主权国家间分摊风险来计算出折现率

针对风险分摊的困难,可以先节录国际仲裁员 C Brower 与 J Brueschke 的《The Iran - United States Claims Tribunal》[1]一书谈到伊朗革命与后来资产被收归国有的混乱情况与怎样把风险分摊,说:"Due in large part to the fact that for a taking to be established the expropriatory act must be attributable to the Iranian Government, and the fact that it was the Islamic Revolution which brought the new Government to power, the distinction between the rule excluding from the valuation the effects of the taking and the rule incorporating the effects of changed conditions brought about by the Revolution often has divided the parties."

这是以贴现现金流来计算损失最困难与最不科学的地方,裁量权看来完全是在仲裁庭。他们很多时候都是以一些大概的百分比或者一个总数做出折算,根本不会针对将来会面对的风险以及对这种风险如果发生如何分摊作出进一步科学的解释。

这里先介绍 AMT v. Zaire, Award of 21 February 1997 仲裁案件,案情涉及美国投资者的资产被扎伊尔军队摧毁,这是违反美国与扎伊尔的双边投资协议,需要作出赔偿。仲裁庭认为损失赔偿应该比投资在一个经济与政治稳定的国家(如瑞士或德国)低,因为投资者自己选择了去扎伊尔投资。但最后仲裁庭判的赔偿金额只是一笔总数,看不出他们怎么样计算与分摊有关的风险。该仲裁庭是说:

"The Claimant would have liked to adopt a method of calculating compensation including interests practicable in the normal circumstances prevailing in an ideal country where

[1] Martinus Nijhoff, The Hague, 1999.

the climate of investment is very stable, such asSwitzerland or the Federal Republic of Germany. The Tribunal does not find it possible to accede to this way of evaluating the damages with interests in the circumstances under consideration, in which it is apparent that the situation remains precarious [...] It would neither be practical nor reasonable to apply the method of assessment of compensation in a way so far removed from the striking realities of the current situation.

Preferably, the Tribunal will opt for a method that is more plausible and realistic in the circumstances of the case, while rejecting all other methods of assessment which would serve unjustly to enrich an investor who, rightly or wrongly, has chosen to invest in a country such as Zaire, believing that by so doing the investor is constructing a castle in Spain or a Swiss chalet in Germany without any risk, political or even economic or financial or any risk whatsoever."

在更早的美国—伊朗索赔仲裁中也有不少案件都涉及这方面，如在 Phillips Petroleum v. Iran, Award of 29 June 1989, 21 Iran - US CTR 79，涉及外国投资者与伊朗政府订立合约勘探开采石油，但后来这个合约权利被伊朗政府收归国有，仲裁庭判是投资者有权获得该合约权利的公平市价。但仲裁庭认为投资者在计算贴现现金流方式中提出的折现率过低，不能反映一些潜在的风险，这种风险是这个投资项目潜在的买方在评估它的公平市价会考虑在内的。其中一些风险可以被视为国家风险，这包括伊朗或其他石油输出国组织国家的政策、伊朗国家石油公司的优先权以及金融与产量的限制会阻止投资者取回部分石油（Iranian or OPEC policies and NIOC priorities and financial and production limitations might prevent recovery of some of the oil that otherwise could be recovered）。同时，未来可能会有无法抗拒的压力修改投资者与伊朗的合约，导致合约利益的未来收益大幅度减少（irresistible future pressures to modify the [claimant's contract] in ways that would greatly reduce the anticipated future profitability of those [contractual] interests）。所以仲裁庭最终是允许了投资者三分之一的索赔。

另一个是 Faith Lita Khosrowshahi v. Iran 仲裁案件，美国投资者分别在伊朗两家公司中拥有股份。在美国投资者的股份被收归国有后，仲裁庭判是按照收归国有发生之前 8 个月该公司股票的市场价格来计算损失，也就是股票最后一天在伊朗股票交易所自由交易的市场价格。但由于之后的伊斯兰革命导致这些股票的价格下跌，仲裁庭是按照当时的市场价格分别折算/扣减了 25% 与 30% 作为伊朗政府应该支付给美国投资者的赔偿金额。

接下去介绍的是在 Himpurna v. PLN, Award of 4 May 1999 的仲裁案件中，涉及美国投资者在印尼投资的争议。仲裁庭判是由美国投资者承担而需要折算的国家风险应该是 19%，并非投资者要求的 8%，因为是美国投资者自己冒险选择在风险更高的印尼投资，而不去其他成熟经济体中投资。同样是美元的债券，也同意在期限届满时要绝对做出支付,但发行国是瑞士或是斯威士兰(非洲国家)还是有区别。这可以节录仲裁庭的判词如下:"The fact remains that it is riskier to enter into a 30 – year venture in Indonesia than in more mature economies. And it is no answer to say that the contract has allocated 99 percent of the risk to the Indonesian side. After all, there are documents which by their terms allot 100 percent of the risk to the debtor bonds. Although they may be denominated in US dollars, although they may stipulate absolute obligation to pay, it still makes a difference whether the issuer is Switzerland or Swaziland."

再接下去介绍的案件是 MTD v. Chile, Award of 25 May 2004,仲裁庭判是投资者索赔的损失只能获赔 50%,因为投资者没有对投资涉及的风险尽到充分的注意义务。

还有可以介绍的案件是 Azurix v. Argentina, Final Award of 14 July 2006 仲裁案件,涉及阿根廷政府非法干涉给予外国投资者的供水特许权合约。投资者声称是支付了 4.385 亿美元获得这个供水特许权,但仲裁庭认为投资者做出了错误的商业判断,并过高支付了这笔特许权费用,而其他投标者更是曾经提出比投资者低 10 倍的价格投标。因此仲裁庭判是招标时这个供水特许权的公平市场价格应该只有 6000 万美元。所以对商业风险不充分评估的损失是由投资者自己承担。

笔者作为一个旁观者总结,就感觉到仲裁庭通常在原告与被告之间的贴现现金流计算的折算去中间落墨,甚至是粗糙地分为一人一半,虽然在说法上还是头头是道。例如,在 Himpurna v. PLN, Award of 4 May 1999 的仲裁案件中,仲裁庭在考虑所有的风险后,做出了一个 19% 的折算,并解释说:"The arbitrators make no pretence that this discount rate is the result of precise weighing of the discrete considerations that have influenced the arbitrators, nor do they wish to create an illusion that they have engaged in econometric modeling .... Both the rate and its application reflect a series of adjustments made by the arbitrators in their equitable assessment of the evidence, and, in the circumstances of this case, resolving all doubts in favour of PLN, the debtor."

6.8 投资仲裁中适用"贴现现金流"的案件

从金融角度来看,"贴现现金流"的计算方法比较适用于拥有"正向现金流"(positive cash flow)或者可以比较可信地估计出未来一段时间有正向现金流的投资,而且有未来风险的指标可以估计出折现率。但是越偏离这种理想模式,就越难以利用"贴现现金流"计算损失的数额或是计算出来也是与将来的现实有很大偏差。所以,当有关的投资已经有了一段赚钱的历史,并且原告能够提出强而有力的证明时,仲裁庭愿意适用贴现现金流计算预期利润损失。

在 CMS v. Argentina, Award of 12 May 2005; Enron v. Argentina, Award of 22 May 2007 与 Sempra Energy v. Argentina, Award of 28 September 2007 仲裁案件中都涉及类似的案情,就是阿根廷政府在 2000 年经济危机后立法改变,导致原告分别占股的公司价值急剧下降。仲裁庭裁决阿根廷政府违反了"公平公正对待"(fair and equitable treatment)义务,并根据公平市价的方法判是阿根廷政府需要赔偿投资者的股份价值损失。同时,由于投资者公司争议发生期间持续盈利,并有充分证据证明公司的经济状况。所以仲裁庭采纳贴现现金流方法来计算这部分损失,并列举了适用"贴现现金流"方法计算损失的原因,如下:(1)公司以前以及现在都一直持续经营(the company had been and remained a going concern);(2)"贴现现金流"的计算方法是普遍被接受(包括被大多数仲裁庭接受)为一种计算商业资产价值的恰当方法(DCF techniques had been 'universally adopted, including by numerous tribunals, as an appropriate method for valuing business assets');(3)有充分的数据可以对公司资产做出合理的"贴现现金流"计算(There was 'adequate data to make a rational DCF valuation' of the company);(4)当事人双方的专家都同意适用"贴现现金流"方法计算,即使他们会对怎样具体适用有不一致意见(Experts from both sides agreed that the DCF was a proper method, although they disagreed on the manner of its application)。

可以 Enron v. Argentina 仲裁案件为例详细介绍仲裁庭是怎样按照"贴现现金流"的方法计算损失。案情涉及阿根廷政府在 2000 年经济危机后对汽油运输和销售征税立法的改变,导致原告运输与销售石油的公司(名为 TGS)价值急剧下降。仲裁庭判是应该采用"贴现现金流"的方式来计算原告遭受的损失。首先,TGS 只有石油运输的业务(占公司整个业务的 88%)受到阿根廷立法改变的不良影响,因此仲裁庭只需要衡量这部分业务的价值下降。这样计算下来受影响的业务价值约是 15.74 亿美元,仲裁庭去掉其中的债券价值 9.34 亿美元,这部分业务的股票价值就为 6.40 亿美元。原告在 TGS 公司中占有 35.5% 的股权,所以他所享有的股权价值为 2.23 亿美元。仲裁庭接下去考虑到,原告曾经为他的分公司的借款提供担保,作为出资的一部分,但在一些交易之后,原告不再承担担保义务,所以原告在这部分借款中的责任(共计 0.98 亿美元)应该被扣除,所以根据"贴现现金流"计算出最终原告所拥有 TGS 的股份价值应为 1.29 亿美元。

"贴现现金流"计算方法也可以适用在涉及与主权国家所订立合约(如采矿权利被剥夺)的投资案件中,因为这种合约权利会难以找出其他办法计算它的价值。这可以节录 Phillips Petroleum v. Iran, Award of 29 June 1989, 21 Iran - US CTR 79 中介绍的原因如下:"The property taken is not a manufacturing or processing enterprise, but rather contract rights to continue to exploit natural resources previously discovered pursuant to the contract, and the Tribunal considers the use of the DCF method by the claimant a relevant contribution to the evidence of the value of the Claimants' contract rights ... However, the Tribunal agrees that it is not an exclusive method of analysis and that all relevant considerations must be taken into account."(有关资产并不是一个生产的企业,而是一个可以让原告继续勘探石油的合约权利,仲裁庭认为可以适用贴现现金流计算原告失去合约权利的价值。但仲裁庭也同意这不是计算价值的唯一办法,而且必须把所有有关的因素都一并考虑)

6.9 投资仲裁中不适用"贴现现金流"的案件

"贴现现金流"计算方法在部分投资仲裁案件中不被接受,原因不外是:(1)有关投资没有一段时间显示了有关盈利的记录与证据,或是投资只录得亏损;(2)没有办法证明有关的投资将来会产生利润;(3)投资者没有办法证明他有能力(特别是财力)完成与将来经营有关的投资项目;(4)投资的金额与"贴现现金流"计算出来的估计利润金额相差太远,不像有这么好的投资回报。

这些投资仲裁案件有:Metaclad v. Mexico, Award of 30 August 2000; Wena Hotels v. Egypt, Award of 8 December 2000; Tecmed v. Mexico, Award of 29 May 2003; SPP v. Egypt, Award of 20 May 1992; Vivendi v. Argentina, Award of 20 August 2007; Amoco International Finance v. Iran, Partial Award of 14 July 1987, 15 Iran – US CTR 189。

显然,贴现现金流本身就是一个"高度臆猜"(highly speculative)的计算方法,这个问题在没有充份证据支持该项投资会在未来赚钱的情况下显然特别严重。正如 Biwater Gauff Ltd v. United Republic of Tanzania(2008)的仲裁庭所说:"the DCF method ... is only appropriate where the future profits of the investment can be determined with a degree of certainty, or in other words, when the expropriated entity has had a history of profitable operations."

也有情况就是投资者本来的生意也不太好(甚至录得亏损),或者工程只进行了很小部分,这种情况下一般来说仲裁庭也不愿意判"预期利润损失"给受害方。其中一个 Iran – United States Claims Tribunal 的 Levitt v. Islamic Republic of Iran(15 IRAN – U. S. Claims Tribunal Rep, Award No. 310 – 56 – 3 of 1987)仲裁案件,涉及伊朗房屋委员会因为违反了一个在伊朗发展住房的合约。仲裁庭虽然判伊朗政府违约,不过认为该房地产项目由于只进行了一部分(该范围已被清理及评级,但建筑并未开始),所以只判了"依赖利益损失"(reliance loss)(这在本书第二章第一部分有关预期利益与依赖利益有详细介绍)而未能判给原告任何预期的"利润损失"(loss of profit)。

如果投资项目还没有完成,显然也是不会有一段时间盈利的记录与证据,通常也是一个不以贴现现金流计算损失的理由,因为仲裁庭不会有足够的数据与资料。在 ICC 的案件 SPP(Middle East) v Egypt ICC Award, Case No. 3493, 11 March 1983, 22 ILM 752(1983)中则有提及:在该项投资被没收时,如果还有大部分的工作(如装修)还未完成,那么便难以此作为计算将来利润的基础。

另在 William J. Levitt v. The Government of the Islamic Republic of Iran(1987)的仲裁中也被仲裁庭认为由于建筑工程还未正式开始,所以该项投资是否能带来利润还是未知之数:"By the time the Contract came to an end only initial stages of clearing and grading had been completed, and no construction work had begun on buildings. The project had therefore reached only a very early stage. ... For these reasons the Tribunal finds that the Claimant has not established with a sufficient degree of certainty that the project would have resulted in a profit."

一般来说，如果受害的原告未能提供足够的（特别是赚钱的）营运历史，仲裁庭通常会避免使用贴现现金流这种损失计算方法。在举证方面，营运历史的证据可以是有关投资项目已经营运一段时间的会计记录，再加上其他方面如有证明是有关投资项目（如一个企业）拥有良好的"商誉"（good - will），也可作为一个证明该投资项目拥有良好营运历史与估算将来利润的指标。

在 Metalclad v. Mexico 仲裁案件中，原告是美国的一间废物处理公司，由于墨西哥政府禁止原告的子公司开设一间处理有毒废料的工厂，所以在仲裁中提出了4000多万美元的赔偿。仲裁庭裁决墨西哥政府的行为构成了间接收归国有，而且墨西哥政府后来宣布这片垃圾填埋区域为自然保护区，导致原告被永久排除建立垃圾填埋设施的机会。仲裁庭最后是适用公平市价的方式来计算赔偿金额，而不适用"贴现现金流"计算损失，因为这个垃圾填埋场还没有开始运营，适用"贴现现金流"就会是臆猜而已。这可以节录仲裁庭的判词如下："Normally, the fair market value of a going concern which has a history of profitable operation may be based on an estimate of future profits subject to a discounted cash flow analysis. In contrast, where the enterprise has not operated for a sufficiently long time to establish a performance record or where it has failed to make a profit, future profits cannot be used to determine going concern or fair market value."

在 Wena Hotel v. Egypt 仲裁案件中，原告与埃及政府签订了两份长达 21 年与 25 年的酒店租约，埃及政府后来将这两个酒店收归国有。仲裁庭裁决按照这两个投资项目中已经投入的资本来计算赔偿金额，而拒绝按照"贴现现金流"来计算，因为首先在收归国有发生时，其中一个酒店只经营了 18 个月，另一个酒店甚至连有关的装修工程还没有完成。其次，投资者是否有足够的金钱来继续酒店的装修与运营是有疑问的。最后的一个原因是投资者索赔的金额（4570 万美元）与他实际投资的金额（880 万美元）之间有巨大差异。

在 Tecmed v. Mexico 仲裁案件中，仲裁庭也判是不能适用"贴现现金流"计算损失，因为原告仅有 2 年多的营运历史不足以提供足够的资料计算出将来的利润损失，而且原告索赔的金额（5200 万美元）与他实际投资的金额（400 万美元）之间也存在巨大差异。仲裁庭是这样说："... the non - relevance of the brief history of operation of the Landfill by Cytar - a little more than two years - and the difficulties in obtaining objective data allowing application of the discounted cash flow method on the basis of estimates for a protracted future, not less than 15 years, together with the fact that such future cash flow also depends upon investments to be made - building of seven additional cells - in the long term, lead the Arbitral Tribunal to disregard such methodology to determine the relief to be awarded to the Claimant".

在 Vivendi v. Argentina 仲裁案件中，涉及政府非法收回给予投资者的供水特许权,仲裁庭认为在国际法中可以适用“贴现现金流”来计算投资项目的公平市价,但在这个案件中并不适用,因为原告没有提供充分肯定的证据证明这个特许权合约的未来收益。对仲裁庭来说,只有相关企业是盈利的,而且拥有长时间的营运记录时,才可以适用“贴现现金流”方法。但是即使投资者企业没有持续的盈利,投资者如果提供充分肯定的证据,也可以索赔利润损失,如提供充分的专家证据,或者类似特许权合约的盈利记录。这可以节录仲裁庭的判词如下:“The absence of a history of demonstrated profitability does not absolutely preclude the use of DCF valuation methodology. But to overcome the hurdle of its absence, a claimant must lead convincing evidence of its ability to produce profits in the particular circumstances it faced . . . A claimant which cannot rely on a record of demonstrated profitability requires to present a thoroughly prepared record of its (or others) successes, based on first hand experience (its own or that of qualified experts) or corporate records which establish on the balance of the probabilities it would have produced profits from the concession in question in the face of the particular risks involved, other than those of Treaty violation.”

但上述所介绍在个别投资仲裁中仲裁庭的判法也并非完全一致,这显示了仲裁的不肯定。例如,在 Delagoa Bay and East African Railway Co (United States and Great Britain v. Portugal) (1900) 的仲裁中,即使该铁路项目在没有开始营运前就已经被终止,完全是纸上谈兵,而由此推算出来的利润损失也不会准确,但仲裁庭还是根据专家意见证据判定了预期利润的损失。

6.10 “贴现现金流”计算方法适用在一般的商业仲裁案件

许多商业仲裁案件在计算损失时如果涉及将来的利润损失,也同样采取这种贴现现金流的计算方法。但与国际投资仲裁去比较,商业仲裁会比较简单,如年期通常不会这么长。而且如果针对有可供买卖市场的行业(如商品买卖或租船合约),将来的利润损失根据“市场规则”(Market Rule)可以市场的替代商品或船舶推算。但还是有不少情况争议的标的是不存在可供买卖的市场,这在估算有关合约价值时(也就是将来会带来的利润是多少)需要以贴现现金流计算方法才能做到。这方面商业仲裁也会比国际投资仲裁容易,因为经常是双方已经合作与履行了一段时间,估计将来的利润损失会有较多的依据。

有了将来的利润损失金额,接下去的考虑就是把这笔代表将来才会支付的金额变为现值支付给受害方,这现值是要根据为受害方所带来的好处进行折算,也相当于银行的“贴现率/折现率”(discount rate)。这里考虑的风险就不会好像国际投资仲裁这么多,如在本章 6.7.1 段提到的商业风险、金融风险、资产流动性风险、汇兑风险、国家风险或政治风险等。但也要考虑如通货膨胀或银行利率变动等的风险。

英国法律不像有权威性的先例全面针对“将来支付金额变回现值的折算”(Discount for Accelerated Receipt)这一个问题以及订立一些计算的原则。但也有涉及这方面的案例,可以介绍如下:

（1）Total Spares & Supplies v. Antares SRL（2004）EWHC 2626（Ch）先例，案情是有关一个特许经营的合约被违约/毁约而终止，导致了要计算该合约剩下没有履行的16年的利润损失。这一个先例主要针对还是6.7.2段提到的两大类风险的第一类，也就是折现一些将来利润损失的风险，英文可以是“risks associated with future cash - flow”，而不是第二类的风险。只节录David Richards大法官在他的判词中说：

“219. In assessing Limited's（原告）loss of future profits, both experts first sought to estimate a figure for its maintainable annual profits but then adopted very different approaches to arrive at a capital value. I will consider later the differences in their estimated maintainable profits, and first consider the fundamental difference in their approaches. Mr Cottle（被告的赔偿金额专家证人）correctly took the view that Limited's only significant asset was its rights under the franchise agreement（特许经营合约）, and argued from this that there was no difference between valuing its lost rights under the agreement and valuing Limited itself. On either basis, the task was to estimate the price which a willing buyer would pay on a hypothetical sale of Limited or the rights under the agreement, assuming the estimated level of maintainable annual profits. For this purpose he adopted a price earnings analysis and used a p/e ratio（市盈率）of 4 - 5. As a check, he also conducted a discounted cash flow analysis of those profits over the unexpired term of the agreement, using a discount factor of 22.5% which is within the range which would be required by an equity investor.

220. Mr Thacker（原告的赔偿金额专家证人）explained in his oral evidence that he was not attempting to arrive at a price which an equity investor would pay for Limited or for its future profits under the agreement, but was seeking to estimate the loss to Limited of the profits which it could otherwise have made under the agreement. For this purpose he used a discounted cash flow analysis and used a discount factor of 7%. He chose that factor because the capital of the business was financed by borrowings and a return of 7%, being 3% over base rate at the time of his report, represented a standard bank borrowing rate.

221. In arriving at a net present value of the future profits of a business, there need to be considered both**a discount for accelerated payment** and **the commercial risks associated with the business**.（David Richards大法官是同意被告的赔偿金额专家证人的说法，针对将来的利润损失要考虑将来金额变为现值的折算和有关生意将来的商业风险，这等于在本章6.7.2段提到的两大类风险）Mr Cottle is critical of Mr Thacker's approach on the grounds that it does not sufficiently take account of those commercial risks in relation to a period in excess of 14 years. In particular he referred to the following matters：

“i) a franchise operation has complete dependence on the franchisor for supplies of the product and has only limited control over the pricing and marketing of the product.（有关生意其中的一个商业风险是特许经营是完全依赖特许人供应商品，而且原告自己没有太大的能力控制价格以及推销有关商品。）

ii) The Antares products that Limited sold were prone to substitution and were sold into a mature market where overall market growth was forecast to be relatively stagnant and where growth could only be achieved by increasing market share at the expense of others (原告销售的商品很容易被替代,而且面对的是一个成熟的市场,将来的市场增长会是很有限,并且必须抢竞争者的份额。)

iii) The absence of any significant technological or costs barriers to entry meant that Limited or other less established companies may be vulnerable to prospective competitors. (有关商品并不涉及高科技或高成本,表示原告将来很容易会面对新的竞争者。)

iv) The requirement to purchase in euro; but sell in£ resulted in Limited's profit margin being at risk to exchange rate fluctuations. (原告需要以欧元买进有关商品,但以英镑出售,会面对汇率风险。)

v) The fact that Limited had only been trading within theUK for a period of approximately two years." (原告在英国市场大约只有 2 年的经验。)

I accept these criticisms and consider that Mr Thacker's approach does not give anything like sufficient weight to the many serious uncertainties which would be attached to the franchise over a period of 16 years from 2002. (David Richards 大法官同意这些批评,认为原告的赔偿金额专家证人没有对这些不肯定的因素做出足够份量的估计) Mr Thacker applied the discount rate to his estimate of maintainable profits for the first seven years from April 2004 and to that estimate less a reduction of 20% for the remaining years. He agreed in cross examination that, leaving aside a discount for early payment, his view was that there should be no discount, or at any rate a low discount, for the first seven years and that the 20% reduction in profits for the remaining years sufficiently reflected the commercial risks.

222. An approach which seeks to arrive at the price which a willing third party negotiating at arms – length would pay for Limited or for the benefit of the agreement will fully reflect the uncertainties of the business. (另一个途径可以一位乐意的买方向原告出价购买这一份特许经营合约的利益,也会全面反映了这盘生意将来会面对的不肯定因素) It was for this reason that a similar approach was adopted by the Court of Appeal in Crehan v. Inntrepreneur Pub Co (2004) EWCA Civ 895. (上诉庭的 Crehan v. Inntrepreneur Pub Co 先例也是这个原因适用这一个途径。)

223. In doing so, the Court of Appeal applied the decision in UYB Ltd v. British Railways Board (16 April 1999 unreported), itself affirmed on appeal, which concerned the proper value of a nightclub business over a 25 – year term which was never able to open because of the defendant's tort and breach of contract. In his judgment in that case, HH Judge Raymond Jack QC (as he was then) said: 'The resolution is in my view to take a capital value for the hypothetical business at the time at which it became clear that it could not pro-

ceed, that is, when it was lost. That is the best reflection of what UYB . . . [has] been deprived of. That value should be based on the value which the business would have fetched in the open market at that date. That figure will reflect the fact that the new purchaser would be running the business and taking the risks in place of UYB. It would reflect the market view of the value. It will carry appropriate interest commencing at the date of the valuation.'

After citing that passage, the Court of Appeal in its judgment in Crehan continued: 'Accordingly, the judge held that the loss was to be measured, first, by an assessment of the profits lost between the date the premises would have opened in October 1992 had there been no water problem and 11 November 1993, secondly, by an assessment of the value of the hypothetical business in November 1993 and, thirdly, by the deduction from that value of such loss as should have been avoided by steps taken in mitigation. . .'"

(2)在近期的 The"Kildare"(2011)2 Lloyd's Rep 360 先例,案情涉及一个 5 年的租约被承租人违约/毁约而终止,船东索赔将来利润的损失,也就是这 5 年租约如果被履行可以赚取的利润。这种案件在 2008 年年底金融海啸之后因为航运市场大跌发生了很多宗。许多承租人(不少涉及是中国的钢厂或船东)在金融海啸前雄心万丈以高价长期租进船舶都面临这种困境,部分承租人也选择粗暴地终止租约,毫不掩饰地违约/毁约,所以责任都没有什么好争。但问题是将来才会支付的租金提前了 3/4 年不等做出支付,显然会给受害方的船东带来好处,至少他可以提早使用这笔钱。在 The"Kildare"先例中,双方同意按照 3 年期的美国债券的利率作为折现率。Steel 大法官针对这一方面是这样说:"There remains the question of the appropriate discount for accelerated receipt of income. In part there is no dispute that an allowance reflecting the three - year yield in US Treasury bonds must be made. This amounts to about 1.5 per cent. FMG contends that a further allowance must be made for the risk - free 'investment' thereby created in contrast to the shipping market. Of course some allowance has been made in that respect in regard to downtime. But in my judgment a further discount must be made to reflect what I have earlier categorized as more catastrophic contingencies such as total loss, bankruptcy and so on. I assess this at a further 1.5 per cent."

(3)笔者在近期(2012 年 9 月)也涉及一个伦敦仲裁,案情是有关一个还剩下 6 年的期租合约被中国钢厂违约/毁约而终断,这导致这一仲裁包括开庭主要是针对违约的承租人需要做出赔偿的金额。针对本章之 6.7.2 小段提到的第一种类别的将来利润损失,这种商业案件就比投资仲裁案件简单得多。双方基本上没有什么争议,因为接下去 6 年的租金双方已经约定,如 65,000 美元一天,而在违约/毁约一天的市场租金只有 15,000 美元一天(市场价格基本上双方也没有什么好争议)。所以两个数字的差别 50,000 美元一天就是每天船东的利润损失,这数字乘以 6 年(减去该船舶估计会因为维修保养等原因需要停租的天数)就可以得出索赔的金额,也就是"预期利益”(expectation interest)或“履约利益”(performance interest)的损失。但由于裁决书是马上会做出,也等于很快可以执行并可以向违约的承租人取回这笔钱来,所以存在本章之6.7.2小段提到的“将来支付金额变回现值的折算”(discount for accelerated receipt)。这里涉及的争议是折现率是否应该是“一般的”或“划一的做法”(general approach),好像裁决书的“利息”(interest)一样。或是折现率应该针对个别不同的原告或船东,如原告提早收到一大笔将来才会赚取的利润可以马上用来支付一笔涉及高昂利息的债务,或可以进行一个可以赚取高额利润的投资,这可以称为是“针对原告的做法”(claimant - specific approach)。在该案例,原告的船东说是应该以划一的做法并认为折现率应该是与美元债券的利率一致,也就是0.6%年率。但被告的承租人认为是应该以针对原告的做法找出折现率,因为原告自己的经济状况也不好,所以向银行借贷会需要付出高昂的利息,而这一利率也会包含了这个风险。被告投诉原告没有就他的经济状况做出足够的文件披露,但来自其他方面的资料(包括法院的告票与冻结令等)被告专家证人估计的折现率会是高达12%以上。可以说原告与被告分别提供的折现率的数字是天壤之别,而这两个分别适用在一笔很大的损失金额(接近1亿美元)会有很大区别。

包括笔者的伦敦仲裁庭认为是没有在这一方面的先例,而不论是谁对谁错(仲裁庭是认为双方都没有错),原告披露出来的经济状况文件是不足够做出一个比较科学的针对原告的做法的计算。所以,仲裁庭最后还是选择以划一的做法针对这一有趣的问题,也就是在裁决利息的5%外,多加上了1.5%的“风险”(risk premium),总共是6.5%的折现率。

(4)在一个ICC的仲裁案件中,原告控告美国的买家没有全力推销原告生产的酒,反而专注推销被告自己的品牌,违反了“代理人合约”(agency agreement)的协定。仲裁庭以合约被违反前12个月的营业额为整个代理人合约的年期推算一个现金流。仲裁庭是说:“In the first 20 months of the Agreement, from its signature through termination, respondent ordered a total of 233,124 bottles of ‘Brand X’ wine. This yields an amount of 139,874 bottles for a 12 months period. As was stated above, from the second half of 1983 to the second half of 1984 there was a drop of 34 percent. It can therefore safely be assumed that this diminution of turnover would have continued through the remaining 40 months of the term of the Agreement. Therefore, the calculation of the lost hypothetical profits is as follows: Through the first 20 months of the Agreement, a total of 233,124 bottles of ‘Brand X’ wine was ordered, which yields an average of 139,874 bottles per year. If this amount is discounted at the rate of 34 percent through the remaining 40 months of the term of the Agreement, the following amounts are obtained . . . This amount could have been foreseen when claimant terminated the Agreement . . .”

(5)在笔者所知晓的另一个仲裁案件,涉及位于中国一个大城市的一座高价值的商业大厦,已经有好几年在赚取高昂的租金。由于两个合作投资的合伙人发生争议,被驱逐出去的一方合伙人向另一方提出的索赔也是根据这一个商业大厦在接下去的年份会赚取的租金利润,根据他在投资中占有的股份百分比计算出他应该获得的损失赔偿。这也是采用了"贴现现金流"的计算办法。这一个案件与投资仲裁不同的是,被驱逐出去的一方合伙人不是外国人,而被剥夺权利也不是来自于中国政府的行为,而纯粹是两个合伙人之间发生争议。

(6)另一个笔者涉及的仲裁案件,涉及一家中国大陆的工厂与外商订立了一个生产医学设备的合约,为期10年。但由于一开始大陆工厂延误交货,导致外商终断合约(是否合法需要看合约怎样规定,而在订约这一方面外商水平是高得多),并索赔庞大的损失。外商索赔的主要损失是因为中国工厂延误交货导致他无法在一个国际招标会中投标,这是涉及一个利润高昂的供应有关设备的10年合约,而大陆工厂在订立合约时知道外商有这一个计划。所以,外商索赔的是他如果投标成功可以赚取的10年合约利润。这笔利润显然会涉及许多臆猜与变数,因为所谓的10年利润会是外商支付给大陆工厂的合约造价与招标如果成功的第二份合约价格之间的差价。虽然外商与大陆工厂的合约价格已经在合约中确定,但长达10年的第二份合约价格也会有很多变数,如合约中可能会有价格调整条文或是通货膨胀条文。而其他的数据就更加不确定,如国际招标会如果成功的合约价格会是多少,因为毕竟会有其他竞争者参与投标,而他们会出什么价格也只有天知道。另外招标的国际机构愿意出的价格会是什么底线也是没有人知道。再加上运输与其他的行政费用等,更是需要臆猜。总之,这10年的利润估算就是需要依靠"贴现现金流"的方法计算。此外,由于外商能否成功投标也要看许多其他因素,如已经提到的其他竞争者、招标的条件、招标会否取消等,这就会涉及贴现现金流计算出的利润损失还要适用一个"机会损失"(loss of chance)的计算,这可以参考本书第六章之4段。至于这一个机会损失是多少百分比,看来也是要由双方专家证人各执一词,然后仲裁庭(包括笔者)中间落墨了。

6.11 "贴现现金流"计算方法的好处与坏处

"贴现现金流"计算方法的一个主要好处就是它从概念上说是估算出一个公平市价最正确的方式,即计算出未来利润的现在价值,而许多投资项目就是为了将来赚取利润。

但它的主要坏处就是不确定性,因为在估计时需要做出无数的假设,而且要对未来(特别是多年后)市场情况、技术进步、竞争、重置/替代、出售、成本、增加的资本要求、货币浮动、通货膨胀率与各种风险水平等做出主观的推测,导致对这些因素不同的评估计算出的结果就会相差很大。可以想得到是作为原告的外国投资者,他的"贴现现金流"计算得出的金额会是夸大,类似在股票市场火热的时候,排队上市的公司就会把自己的价值夸大计算。而作为被告的主权国家就会得出偏低的金额。

在他们两个不同的计算中,只要对这些估算的因素如通货膨胀率或市场占有率有一点的差异，都会带来最后金额很大的差异。而且也说不清到底谁的估算比较可以接受，因为他们都有自己的道理与专家证人支持各自的推测，这毕竟是将来的事情。这可以节录 H Weisburg 与 J Ryan 的《Means to Be Made Whole: Damages in the Context of International Investment Arbitration》一文中所说如下："There is no single means by which to determine the future cash flow and profits of a going concern. Rather, parties and tribunals must extrapolate future performance from a company's current financial position, past profitability, market trends and industry analysis. Doing so involves significant assumptions and frequently turns into a battle of multiple experts. Likewise, it is often extremely difficult to calculate an appropriate discount rate ... Finally, it is often difficult to obtain the objective data necessary to allow a tribunal to calculate a company's future stream."

而 T Stauffer 在《Valuation of Assets in International Takings》一文中也有提到，如果原告在按照"贴现现金流"计算时，过高的损失估算可能会产生"灰姑娘效应"（Cinderella effect），也就是"好得难以置信"（too good to be true），好像任何投资在发展中国家都会是最终赚得盆满钵满。

比如在上文 6.7.3 段所介绍的几个案件，可以在很大程度显示贴现现金流计算方法中对折算/折现率的确定有很大的主观性与不肯定性。在裁决书中仲裁庭可以堂而皇之地说他们对所有风险与各方应承担的百分比平衡下所得出的折算已经充分考虑了双方，特别是考虑到主权国家（被告）的利益。但这还是难以找出比较科学的依据，也不能令一些主权国家（特别是发展中国家）感到安心，特别是许多投资仲裁的著名仲裁员都是一些有国际商业背景的西方仲裁员。

难以比较科学地确定折算也导致了一些投资仲裁被拒绝以贴现现金流估值，或只是以贴现现金流作为比较或反证仲裁庭以其他方法所估计的价值。在 Amoco International Finance v. Iran, Partial Award of 14 July 1987, 15 Iran – US CTR 189 仲裁案件中，仲裁员 Mouri 说："... the evaluation of a business in terms of its future cash flow has not been found to be generally practicable, particularly when it comes to the real world, volatile economic realities affected by thousands of various and very complex factors and constant changes of the political and social structure of societies, which all together make the reasonableness of any projection into the future, not only in connection with the cash flow but in relation with the capital expenditure and degree of risk involved highly uncertain and speculative."

经常在较早做出真正投资时，原告就已经有可能对这项投资将来的风险和变数做出多于一个的"预期利润"（projected profit）的估算。如有三个不同的估算（乐观、中庸、保守），这往往也是根据贴现现金流的计算方法。如果这些是披露出来的文件，仲裁庭显然也可以作为参考选择他们认为合适的风险和变数。这个参考可以用来调整在有关的投资已经营运了一段时间并有了实际收益的数据，这些数据由于是针对已经发生了的事实,应该是更加可以信赖的证据。

6.12 法律与商业对将来收益在证据认定方面的差异

这里也可以谈谈英国法律针对过去已经发生事实以及预测将来的"事实"在证据方面是有很大不同的对待。这一区分别对贴现现金流计算方法有一定的影响,甚至导致部分仲裁庭拒绝适用作为对有关投资或资产的估值。这可以先节录 SK Khalilian 的《The Place of Discounted Cash Flow in International Commercial Arbitrations: Awards by Iran – United States Claims Tribunal》(1991,8 Journal of International Arbitration 31)如下:"There is a big difference between an investment decision in the market and a judicial decision in a court ... a businessman can and should accept calculated risks ... based on forecasts of an uncertain future. The juridical organs, however, have a mandate to reduce to the minimum possible the element of uncertainty or risk while deciding on juridical issues."(商业社会与法院对将来的不肯定的态度有很大的差异。商业人士可以并且会接受一定的风险,只根据将来的预测做出投资。但法院就必须减少这一个不肯定才能做出判决。)

6.12.1 对已经发生事实与将来会发生"事实"的不同举证责任

这是探讨损失赔偿的一个"举证责任"(burden of proof)的原则。基本和简单的说法就是提出索赔的受害方有责任证明他所说的损失,但是还有其他重要的细节。其中与本章所探讨的问题有密切关系的一条就是在英国普通法中,举证责任的程度对"过去的事实"与"将来发生的'事实'"是有所不同的。针对"过去的事实",因为已经是有证据可以证明(不论是文件或口头证据),所以在举证的程度只需是"平衡的可能性"(balance of probabilities),也表示原告或受害方证明的程度只需要达到51%的可能性便会成功。涉及这些过去的事实主要是针对"依赖利益损失"(reliance loss),如受害方为这合约或投资项目所作出的损失及所花的费用,按理都会有文件或口头证据可以证明。而这情况也会适用在证明有关资产的"市价"(market value)的损失类别,因为曾经被作出估值或第三人收购的话均会有清楚的文件(与口头)证据留下来。

但针对将来会发生的"事实"由于尚未发生,往往是不可能有文件或口头证据作出证明。即使在法理上依然需要有证据才能作出认定,也只能依赖专家的意见作为证据。不过专家意见永远走不出"说故事"的大毛病。而且当事人委任的专家总是难以洗脱偏坦委任方的嫌疑,但没办法的情况下也只能如此。所以在人身意外的案子中为了估计受害方将来医疗和照顾的费用,往往是要依靠医生等专家证人提出意见作为证据。而在投资仲裁中,估计将来的"预期利益的损失"(expectation loss),也往往离不开会计师等"价值评估专家"(quantum expert)提供意见和证据。

回头说举证责任,要证明将来的"事实",原告或受害方举证的程度在普通法下要求更高。这需要证明将来"事实"的发生有一个"合理的肯定"(reasonable certainty)。为何会有这种举证责任的差别呢?背后的原因并不清楚,但估计是由于将来的"事实”根本还未发生,所以比较容易被夸大甚至弄虚作假。有关这个说法可节录 Michael Furmston 教授的《The Law of Contract》(4th edn,2010 年)之 1703 - 1704 页中所说的:“In order to succeed in an action for breach of contract a claimant must establish liability upon the normal civil burden of proof i. e. the balance of probabilities. By extension it might be thought that the claimant's right to recover substantial damages(where loss must be shown)is dependent upon proof of loss to the same standard. However as Lord Nicholls observes in Gregg v. Scott(2005)2 AC 176:'... common law has drawn a distinction between proof of past facts and proof of future prospects'. A past event either occurred or did not and falls to be established in civil proceedings upon the balance of probabilities. Claims for wasted expenditure will fall within this category. However, where the loss being claimed requires an investigation of future events, a different approach is taken; proof of future possibilities is approached differently. Then damages are only recoverable if the item of loss claimed for can be proven with reasonable certainty. The policy behind the application of different burdens of proof in respect of past facts and future events is unclear. It is possible that the risk of exaggeration and falsification in relation to the latter is thought to justify the imposition of a higher standard of proof.”

6.12.2 损失不肯定的情况下还是需要尽力估计一个尽量接近的损失金额

在笔者看来这种举证责任中的分别常被很多商业仲裁员忽略或轻视。当然还有其他有关举证责任的“次要规则”(sub - rules)也可以在这里提及一下。

第一就是损失的不肯定性并不表示仲裁庭或法院不会尽力估计一个尽量接近的损失数字,特别是在缺乏其他计算损失方法的情况下。但这和“凭空臆猜”(pure guess work)还是有区别的,因为凭空臆猜是法律所不容许的。这里可节录一个有关选美的著名英国先例 Chaplin v. Hicks(1911)2 KB 786:“It was clearly impossible under the facts of that case to estimate with anything approaching to mathematical accuracy the damages sustained by the plaintiffs, but it seems to me to be clearly laid down there by the learned Judges that such an impossibility cannot 'relieve the wrongdoer of the necessity of paying damages for his breach of contract' and that on the other hand the tribunal to estimate them whether jury or judges must under such circumstances to do 'the best it can' and its conclusion will not be set aside even if 'the amount of the verdict is a matter of guess work'.”

当然在这个选美的案子中因为受害方被剥夺了参选的资格蒙受了“机会损失”(loss of chance),所以其“机会损失”的计算方法唯有估计这个机会的价值,是没有其他办法确定损失的金额。关于这方面在本书第六章有关“损失的肯定性:将来的变数与机会损失”有详细介绍。

在 Sapphire International Petroleums Ltd. v. National Iranian Oil Co. ,35 I. L. R. 136 (1967)案件中,被告和一所加拿大公司合作在伊拉克进行石油勘探。而在仲裁开始

时油井还没有开始被勘探(不过原告已经有所支出),变的损失难以证明,因为是否勘探到石油都不确定,更加不会知道能够开采出石油的数量。但也无阻仲裁庭根据"机会损失"(loss of chance/opportunity)为受害方估计损失的利润(这一个方面会在本章10.3段进一步介绍),说:"It is not necessary to prove the exact damage suffered in order to award damages. On the contrary, when such proof is impossible, particularly as a result of the behavior of the author of the damage, it is enough for the judge to be able to admit with sufficient probability the existence and extent of the damage."

6.12.3　被告的主权国家如果阻碍原告的投资者取得有关损失的证据会面对不利的推断

最后要探讨的有关投资仲裁的证据问题是在受害的原告对将来"事实"的认定如果需要很多的假设,而因为被告的原因[这包括是违约/毁约或没收的本质(如Sapphire International Petroleums Ltd. v. National Iranian Oil Co. 案件),或被告阻挠投资者取得证据]导致原告未能提供证据支持这些假设,就有一个说法是所作出的假设要对被告不利,这估计也是一种"不利的推断"(adverse inference)。这其实是和仲裁员惯常为了惩罚违反披露命令的一方当事人的做法是一样。唯一的区别是,这个说法往往是在投资仲裁的一开始就在损失的举证责任方面敌视被告,而这与违反仲裁庭命令的程序并无关系。仲裁庭这样做要非常小心,因为过了火的话便会颠倒举证责任(就是本来要求受害方证明他的损失,但变了是被告的主权国家要证明没有这个损失)。这一方面的说法可参考Scrutton大法官在上诉庭的先例Coldman v. Hill (1919) 1 KB 443中所说的:"The House of Lords held that the man who had, by breaking his contract, destroyed the possibility of any evidence on the subject, could not be heard to say that there was no evidence that his breach of contract caused the loss. It was his duty as bailee to prove that his breach of duty did not cause the loss, not the plaintiff's duty to show that it did. This appears to be merely an application of the principle *Omnia praesumuntur contra spoliatorem*, under which a man who, having converted property, refuses to produce it that its exact value may be known, is liable for the greatest value that such article could have."

6.13　总结贴现现金流计算方法

总的来说,贴现现金流计算方法还是被许多仲裁庭视为一种计算投资利益损失的有效方式,在理论上也是最说得过去。这种计算方法的合理性也被联合国赔偿委员会所接受,这可以节录联合国赔偿委员会在1999年6月24日的报告如下:"... where an income-producing property, ie an asset or a group of assets, such as a business, has been completely destroyed or irreparably damaged, the DCF method can be used to estimate the cash flows through the end of the property's expected economic life in order to value that property."但许多仲裁庭也认为在投资仲裁中应该谨慎使用这个计算方法,以防止对推测性的损失做出过多的赔偿,因为法律要求将未来收益的不确定性风险降到最低，要求原告的举证责任能够满足“合理的肯定”(reasonable certainty)而不只是“平衡的可能性”(balance of probability)。至于这里对举证责任的分水线是否掌握的恰当，这就需要靠个别的国际投资仲裁员。正如一开始就提到过的，很多西方的仲裁员都是有商业背景，会否个别仲裁员比较接近商业人士的想法，更愿意接受有一定风险的预测做出裁决就不得而知了。

至于仲裁庭是否采纳贴现现金流方法来计算投资争议中的损失，以及仲裁庭会采纳哪一方当事人计算出的赔偿金额，还是要看哪一方提交的有关现金流预计的证据更加充分以及更具有说服力。从之前的仲裁裁决来看，大多数仲裁庭都会认为有关投资项目的历史盈利证据是证明未来现金流金额的最有力证据。但总的来说，贴现现金流的计算方法还是给予法官或仲裁庭很大的灵活性，这可以节录 Amco v. Indonesia II, Award on the Merits of 31 May 1990, 89 ILR 368 中的判词如下：“The DCF method itself relies on the application of assumptions which are necessarily judgmental. The DCF method is at once a flexible tool that allows for an application of factors and elements judged as relevant. At the same time, it allows for the application of these judgmental elements to be articulated.”

笔者最近也听一名英国著名的国际商事仲裁员说，在其判过的几个金额庞大的投资仲裁案件中，由于有很多关于有关主权国家前景的臆猜，所以他对这些有关国家的新闻特别感兴趣，所以经常比对现实与之前的臆猜是否接近。

7. 基于市场的计算方法——与相同投资业务作比较

在本章之 5.2.2 段已经有提及，这一种方法是对私人交易(如果比较的公司没有上市)或公开市场(如果有上市)上可供买卖的类似投资/业务、类似商业所有权利益或有价证券/股值作出各种调整后(如一些一般性的变数，如利润、现金流、账面值或收益等)计算一项投资的价值。例如，百事可乐的投资项目可以以可口可乐或其他饮料的业务作出比较，找出它的实际价值。显然可口可乐的价值需要调整各种变数，包括是收益、市场占有率、销路或成本等。这也是在金融与商业市场最普遍适用的计算方法。这种计算方法可以节录 M Kantor 的《Valuation for Arbitration: Compensation Standards, Valuation Methods and Expert Evidence》(Kluwer Law International, 2009 年)一书如下：“If the market values an asset or activity by reference to its future earnings capacity, then the chosen method will incorporate that potential into the valuation. To illustrate, valuation experts may employ the Market - Based Approach to derive the value of the business in dispute by looking at the value placed by the securities markets on publicly traded stock of a second, comparable company. In such a case, the current public stock prices of the comparable company will embody, among other matters, the accumulated views of individual stock market investors about the future earnings prospects of the comparable company. Thus, by relying on the market's stock price quotations for a comparable company, the perception of the second, comparable company's earnings potential becomes embedded in the final valuation of the first company."

7.1　比较要考虑的因素

在《IVSC Business Valuation Guidance Note》中指出，寻找一家或多家公司作为比较是需要考虑以下的因素：(1)进行比较的公司应该属于同一个业务领域内的，或者是对经济变数有相同反应的公司(the businesses should be in the same industry or in an industry that responds to the same economic variables)；(2)在商业特征的质量与数量方面，进行比较公司的业务应该具有相似性(similarity to the subject business in terms of qualitative and quantitative business characteristics)；(3)在相似业务方面应该有足够数量与可证明的数据(amount and verifiability of data on the similar business)；(4)相似业务的价格是否是在公平交易中所体现出来的价格(whether the price of the similar business represents an arm's - length transaction)。

还会有其他的因素需要考虑，如作出比较的公司是否是一家国有公司，而另一家是私人公司？是否它们都为同一个市场提供了同样的服务或产品？它们所在的地理环境是怎样(这包括政治上、当局的规管与税务、汇兑风险等)？它们的公司规模大小？资本结构与"负债比率"(debt - to - equity ratio)如何？

另在计算的时间方面也是十分重要，这是因为作出比较的公司股价会是大升大落。即使是这几天(2012 年 6 月)，笔者就听新闻说房屋价格还是很高，但地产公司的股价就偏低，只有它们资产的 50% 以下，所以购买股票比购买房产划算。更不用说在一些更大的波动，如在 2002 年网络泡沫的破灭导致这些网络公司的股份在 1 年的时间内失去了 99% 的市价。

7.2　计算方法

这种对一个业务或公司作出估值的方法早已在金融与商业的业务中大行其道，这种业务包括公司上市、合并与收购等。方法是拿另一个已知市场价值的类似业务或公司(如通过在市场的股票价值)的指标(如盈利能力)，然后把该指标套用到受害方的投资项目计算出公司的价值。这种估值办法可以称为是"Multiples Method"。例如，以其中一个经常被使用的指标"息税前利润"(Earnings Before Interest and Taxes 或简称 EBIT)为例，如果比较的业务或公司上市的估值是 5000 万美元，而"摊销前利润"(Earnings Before Interest, Taxes, Depreciation and Amortization 或简称 EBITDA)是 500 万美元，它的"企业倍数"(EBITDA Multiple)就是"10X"。只要找出受害投资者的投资项目或业务/公司的 EBITDA(如 50 万美元)，就可以用该行业的"企业倍数"推算出该投资项目的价值(或损失)是 500 万美元。(50 万美元 ×10)。其他指标如"息税折旧"及"摊销前利润"亦常有运用，而且很多时候专家证人会以多个不同的会计指标比较两间公司，务求使评估数字更准确及一致。在 CME v. Czech Republic,

Final Award of 14 March 2003 的仲裁案中，原告是一家媒体公司，并提供了 29 家来自世界各地的媒体公司的 EBITDA 指标，以计算公司价值。

7.3 这种计算方法的利弊

这种计算方法也不是经常可以适用，如有关的投资项目并没有类似的可供比较的业务或公司，又或是可供比较的公司并没有足够的透明度，而且选择何种因素作为比较的基础亦会有很大争议。不过计算方法有好处也有坏处，好处就是计算方法相对简单与实际。但坏处也不少，如这种计算方法也纯粹看将来，不理会有关投资项目的历史可能会提供大量准确的数据。另外，现实中很难找出两个相同的公司作为比较，专家很容易主观选定符合他最终估值的比较对象，导致有偏见的分析。固然，贴现现金流计算方法也免不了有偏见。但在计算起来，"Multiples Method"会更容易对它的一些数据不说明或不做解释。而在贴现现金流，计算与做出的解释就需要更透明与清楚达致最后的金额。

与贴现现金流一样，这种计算方法也需要许多的假设与臆猜，虽然会比贴现现金流计算方法的臆猜性少。

7.4 很少在投资仲裁中被接受与适用

虽然"Multiples Method"在金融与商业市场被普遍适用，但在投资仲裁案件中的适用并不多。如在 CMS v. Argentina, Award of 12 May 2005 中，被告的阿根廷政府建议原告所部分拥有的一家公司的价值可以与其他 4 家上市的公司作比较。但仲裁庭拒绝并接受原告专家证人的说法，在流通性不足的市场如阿根廷，资本市值不适合作为估值之用(market capitalization in illiquid markets such as Argentina is not the most adequate method to value companies)。而且原告有关的公司与其他 4 家公司之间是有很大的差别，包括在资产水平、业务、金融政策与其他方面。

在两个美国—伊朗索赔仲裁庭(US - Iran Claims Tribunal)案件中，也是有同样的命运。第一个仲裁案件是 Thomas Earl Pyane v. Iran, Award of 8 August 1986, 12 Iran - US CTR 3，被拒绝的原因是仲裁庭认为伊朗在 1979 年伊斯兰革命后，整个商业与经济活动有了基本改变，所以有关公司过去的盈利不能作为将来盈利的准则。换言之，估值不能往前看。

另在 Phelps Dodge v. Iran, Award of 19 March 1986, 10 Iran - US CTR 121，原告是以一些在同一个业务的美国公司做为比较，但仲裁庭拒绝，认为美国公司不能与一家在伊朗的公司作比较。

7.5 其他并非与同类业务/公司比较的基于市场计算方法：市场上曾经有过买卖/试图收购

说到以"基于市场的计算方法"(Market - Based Approach)，也可以考虑其他会是更准确与可靠的方法，如有关的业务或公司曾经有第三人试图收购。这严格说不是"Multiples Method"的计算方法，但还是认为市场上有第三人通过公平交易作出的估值，是一个比较可以信赖的赔偿金额，因为可以估计得到第三人出价收购的一个投资项目或为该项目而成立的“特殊目的/专设公司”(Special Purpose Vehicle 或简称 SPV),肯定是作出过各种“恪尽职责”(due diligence)的资料搜集,准确性往往比投资仲裁中的受害方(原告)所依赖的会计师作为专家证人所计算的贴现现金流更为准确。当然,在这种投资仲裁中即使有过这些事情发生,如为公司估价或被第三人收购时反映出一个比贴现现金流更低的金额,是不会主动被披露出来的。这表示抗辩的被告(主权国家)千万别节省调查的费用,虽然这种费用通常不会便宜甚至有可能是会浪费的。

这些仲裁案件也有不少,如在 CME v. Czech Republic, Final Award of 14 March 2003 仲裁案件中(在本章第 9 段会详细介绍),其中一个估值方法是根据原告公司在被捷克政府没收前 1 年出资收购该投资资产 5.8% 股份估算该资产的总价值。但仲裁庭拒绝接受,一个原因是仲裁庭看到证据是在该交易中,卖方制造了一定程度的压力要买方购买,所以价格不能反映一个公平与自由交易所订下的价格标准。再说 5.8% 的小额股份不能反映整个公司的价值。但仲裁庭确实接受了在捷克政府干预前不久曾经有另一个第三人出资收购整个公司,这一价格被仲裁庭所接受。

在 SwemBalt v. Latvia, Award of 23 October 2000 仲裁案件中,仲裁庭也是接受第三人曾经的收购出价作出估值。

但在 SPP(ME) v Egypt, Award of 20 May 1992, (1997) 106 ILR 502 仲裁案件中,仲裁庭就拒绝了以原告在 2 年前的 25% 股份买卖价格作为作出估值的依据。仲裁庭拒绝的理由是:“... there was a very limited number of transactions and there was no market as such for the shares that were sold. The price at which the shares were sold was privately negotiated.”但这一个理由看来有一点疑问,因为他们是认为只有上市公司才能以这种办法估值,但在私人公司就不会有第三人作出完全符合公平市场的出价。这显然是一个有问题的看法,会是错判。

在另外一个美国—伊朗索赔仲裁庭的 James M Saghi v. Iran, Award of 22 January 1993, 29 Iran – US CTR 20 仲裁案件中,伊朗将有关资产收归国有的 5 年之前,曾经有第三人出价 670 万美元收购有关公司 45% 的股份。仲裁庭愿意接受这个出价作为标准或依据,但需要根据这五年来的变化作出调整。这种变化包括了伊朗的通货膨胀导致的收益以美元计算有所增加,与公司也因为伊斯兰革命而前景变得黯淡。如此作出调整后的赔偿金额是 550 万美元。

在 INA v. Iran, Award of 12 August 1985 仲裁案件中,原告投资者在一家伊朗公司中占有股份,这家公司后来被伊朗收归国有。仲裁庭接受原告在 1 年前购买这家公司股份时的出价应该与收归国有时的市场价格差不多,可以作为赔偿的金额。

总结而言,如果有一些过去发生的交易,不论是实际买卖或者是意图买卖,都可以被仲裁庭接受作为估算公平市场价格的标准或依据,但会需要符合以下的条件(或可作出调整的条件):(1)股份的比例必须足够大,因为大额股份与小额股份的价格会相差很远(The shareholding sold is large enough to avoid the danger of magnification of a pricing inaccuracy. However, it would seem possible to rely, where the data is available, on multiple transactions with smaller shareholdings, if they consistently point to the same range of figures)。(2)交易必须是公平合理,出价必须是除了商业因素以外没有其他的压力。换言之,出价的买方是愿意出这个价格,接受的卖方也是愿意出售(The transactions must be at arm's length and the negotiated price must not be affected by non - market considerations or other value - distorting factors)。(3)作为标准或是依据的买卖,发生的时间与后来计算损失的时间之间没有重大的变化会导致有关的市价发生严重变化(Since the time of the transaction, there have been no events or other circumstances that would significantly change the market value)。显然,两者相隔的时间越久,有变化的可能性就越大。

8. 基于资产的计算方法——重置价值、账面价值、清算价值等

这种方法是把构成企业的所有资产的价值计算总和后来计算企业或投资的价值。找出资产的价值,可以根据它的"重置价值"(replacement value)、"账面价值"(book value)或是"清算价值"(liquidation value)。这三种方法的不同之处只是在于计算不同资产采用了不同的标准。但这种计算方法的缺点就是它不会考虑投资或企业中动产与不动产之外的价值,如企业的"商誉"(good - will)。举例说,对于一家著名的咨询公司来说,它的主要资产就是专家与品牌,而并非大楼或办公设备这些有形资产,这家公司的价值就不能简单地通过资产的价值来计算。

另一个问题是这种计算方法没有考虑到一个盈利十分高的投资,这会是投资者的眼光或是运气,反正就是投入的金额可以带来不成比例高昂的利润。这一来,如果按照重置价值计算损失,就好像著名的美国投资仲裁员 C. Brower 在 Amoco International Finance v. Iran, Partial Award of 14 July 1987 仲裁案件中所作的比喻是:"... seems to be saying that one who for the price of a chicken turns out to have acquired the proverbial goose that lays golden eggs can legitimately demand back only the price of a chicken when his goose is taken by his landlord and not the value of the goose". [一位投资者以一只鸡的价格收购了一只会生金蛋的鹅,那么在他的房东(主权国家)没收这一只鹅时,投资者只能索赔一只鸡的价格]

所以比起基于收入(就是贴现现金流)与市场(就是 Multiples method)的计算方法来说,基于资产的计算方法就会得出不太可靠的结果,也只能适用在其他方法并不适用的情况下,如缺少相关的数据,或者有关投资或企业除了动产与不动产之外没有其他的价值。基于资产的计算方法更加适合需要赔偿动产或不动产损失的情况,如

设备、建筑、库存产品与土地等被收归国有或摧毁的损失。

8.1 重置价值

资产的重置价值(replacement value)是指把有关资产替换为类似种类、功能与要件的资产所需要花费的金额。在世界银行指引中,将重置价值定义为"the cash amount required to replace the individual assets of the enterprise in their actual state"。这样计算出的重置价值通常会高于资产的账面价值,因为在账面中资产价值通常会贬值得更快。重置价值也会高于资产的清算价值,因为重置价值中通常不会包括"压力下出售的扣减"(distress discount)。所以市场上类似资产的公平合理价格是重置价值的一个最好的标准。考虑到本章7.2段所提到的"Multiples Method",这种重置价值计算方法的可靠性就取决于重置资产与争议所涉及的受损害资产的可比性。

重置价值的计算方法也可以用来评估一个投资项目的价值,并从中减去这个投资需要承担的责任。与其他基于资产的估值方法一样,重置价值的方法在评估投资价值时也会有一些缺点,这可以节录Weisburg与C Ryan所写的《Means to Be Made Whole: Damages in the Context of International Investment Arbitration》一文如下:"Replacement value assumes that it is possible to reconstruct the value of the entire investment simply by replacing its physical assets. Lost in this methodology is the value that comes from, for example, existing customer relationships, a skilled work force and opportunities in established markets."有可能基于这些缺点,世界银行指引认为重置价值的方法只能适用在评估动产或不动产价值的情况中。

这里可以介绍几个适用重置价值来计算损失的美国—伊朗索赔仲裁庭的案件。在Oil Field of Texas v. Iran, Award of 8 October 1986, 12 Iran – US CTR 308仲裁案件中,仲裁庭判是赔偿的金额应该是相关钻孔设备名为blowout converter的公平市场价格,也就是这个设备在市场中的重置价值,并说:"As Claimant seeks and is entitled to its replacement value, what has to be determined is the amount it would have cost to replace the three blowout converters that had been leased to and were retained by NIOC, based on the market conditions for such equipment at that time."

在另外一个涉及把钻孔设备收归国有的Petrolane v. Iran, Award of 14 October 1986, 12 Iran – US CTR 64仲裁案件中,仲裁庭也判是要赔偿相关设备的重置价值,尽管仲裁庭也认为这个已经被使用过设备的重置价值用一个全新的设备价值来衡量是存在疑问的,但被告并没有提出相反的证据。

在Kuwait v. Aminoil, Award of 24 March 1982, 21 ILM 976仲裁案件中,仲裁庭判是要赔偿被收归国有的投资项目中的固定资产的重置价值,再加上外国投资者的利润损失。换言之,仲裁庭是采用了"混合的方式"(hybrid approach)计算损失。这也是合理,因为取得替代会需要时间,在这一个期间内外国投资者就会遭受"利润损失"(loss of profit)或"机会损失"(loss of opportunity)。所以让原告获得全部赔偿,就需要同时赔偿这两项损失。

8.2 账面价值

账面价值(book value)是指相关资产体现在公司资产负债表上的价值。这可以节录世界银行指引中的定义,账面价值是"the amount at which the taken tangible assets appear on the balance sheet of the enterprise, representing their cost after deducting accumulated depreciation in accordance with generally accepted accounting principles"。在商业估值中,账面价值是公司的价值与公司财务报表中负债金额的差值,也就是公司账面净值。

在购买相关资产时,公司支付的价格通常就是该资产的市价。因此反映在买方公司账面上的当日购买价格就代表相关资产的账面价值与当时的市价。但是,从公司获得该资产开始随着时间的变化,该资产的账面价值与它的市价之间的联系就会越来越少。换言之,账面价值是一个会计学上的概念,它代表了某个资产最初的历史成本,它的价值会随着时间变化开始折旧而逐渐下降。而折旧是该资产价值下降的一个预计观点,这会根据主权国家的会计规则来计算。但问题是这种会计学上计算出的折旧可能与实际情况中的折旧毫不相关。随着时间的流逝,资产的市价可能会高出它的账面价值,尤其在通货膨胀严重的时期。资产的市价也可能会低于账面价值,如由于科学技术的进步导致该资产因为过时而严重贬值。所以,资产的市价与它的账面价值很少会有直接的联系。

为了弥补这种缺陷,在估值时仲裁庭或法院可以适用"调整后账面价值的方式"(adjusted book value method)来计算损失,这是把资产的账面价值进行调整,使它能够反映出资产的市价。通常这是转化为重置价值的计算方法来估算资产的价值,也就是参考市场上可比较的资产后对争议涉及的资产进行估值。

这种账面价值的方式可以适用于对个别资产估值,也可以适用于对整个投资项目估值。但世界银行指引认为账面价值的计算方法只能适用在评估个别资产价值的情况中,而且适用的条件是"such value has been recently assessed or has been determined as of the date of the taking and can therefore be deemed to represent a reasonable replacement value."对于投资项目的估值,账面价值的方法只能适用于一些主要为有形资产,便于销售的公司(如船公司),而不能反应出公司超出有形资产部分的价值。

在 Amoco International Finance v. Iran, Partial Award of 14 July 1987 仲裁案件中,仲裁庭也指出账面价值计算方法的缺陷,可节录如下:"... in the case of a going concern, the value of the enterprise as a whole is greater than the sum of the discrete elements which constitute it."

在 Sedco Inc v. NIOC & Iran, Interlocutory award of 27 March 1986, 10 Iran – US CTR 180 仲裁案件中,仲裁庭也是提出了类似的观点,如下:"The theory that net book value is the appropriate standard of compensation in all cases of lawful expropriation overlooks the fact that a nationalized asset is not only a collection of discrete tangible goods(equipment, stocks and, possibly, grounds and buildings). It can include intangible items as well, such as contractual rights and other valuable assets, such as patents, know – how, goodwill and commercial prospects. To the extent that these various components exist and have economic value, they normally must be compensated, just as tangible goods, even if they are not listed in the books ... The fact that the expropriated assets form a going concern certainly cannot be disregarded at the time of the valuation ..."

也是由于这些不足之处,仲裁庭在 Enron v. Argentine, Award of 22 May 2007 仲裁案件中同样拒绝适用账面价值来计算损失赔偿的金额,因为仲裁庭认为账面价值不能反映公司未来的预期收益等情况。

总结而言,尽管账面价值的计算方法是国际投资案件中的估值方法之一,但它只能适用在一些不需要评估未来收益的赔偿案件中,或者原告只是索赔他已经投入的资本作为赔偿,或者在原告索赔之前有关资产还没有开始盈利的情况。这可以节录 Amco v. Indonesia II, Award on the merits of 31 May 1990, (1992) 89 ILR 368 仲裁案件中仲裁庭的总结如下:"While it is true that the value of the assets has been used as the measure of damages in a number of international claims, it is by no means the prevailing method of valuation of damages ... In fact, the book value basis of valuation seems to have been only used where compensation for prospective earnings was excluded for some reason, either 'in the absence of other evidence', or because a claim for prospective profits was 'not compensable under the Act', or because the claimant himself had requested as damages the reimbursement of his invested capital, or the liquidation value of its equity interest, or again because the claimant's property had never become a 'going concern' before the claim for damages arose."

在另外一个仲裁案件 LIAMCO v. Libya, Award of 12 April 1977 中,仲裁庭虽然采纳了账面价值来计算有关固定资产的价值,但这只是作为赔偿利润损失的补充,所以可以说仲裁庭也是采用了"混合的方式"(hybrid approach)计算损失。

8.3 "清算价值"

清算价值(liquidation value)是指公司或企业的个别资产或所有资产在破产清算时可以出售给自愿买方的价格减去公司应该承担负债的金额。这在世界银行指引中是被定义如下:"the amounts at which individual assets comprising the enterprise or the entire assets of the enterprise could be sold under conditions of liquidation to a willing buyer less any liabilities which the enterprise has to meet."这个估值方法通常适用于陷入严重经济困境的公司或企业,也可以用来评估一个公司或企业的"纯最低价值"(bare bottom value)。

在计算资产的清算价值时,通常在破产清算压力下出售的资产价格都会低于它们的公平市价,所以这部分压力下的价值减少会作出扣减,这也被称为是"distress discount”。而一些有形资产(如土地)的清算价值就会与它的市价很接近。另一方面来讲,企业或公司的库存或可以收回的账目在估值时通常也会低于它们显示在账面上的价值。

通常清算价值的估值方式只适用在投资项目或公司、企业的估值方面,并非个别资产的估值。在破产清算过程中,会计算出公司或企业个别资产的清算价值,再减去这个公司或企业的负债,从而得出这个公司或企业的清算价值。由于清算价值是基于每一个个别资产在破产清算时出售的价格,而不是作为整个资产集合的部分出售,所以该公司或企业的商誉(估计在清算下也不会剩下太多)不会被考虑在内。所以清算价值的估值方式通常不会评估具有商誉价值或正在运营的企业或公司的价值。世界银行指引也是认为清算价值的计算方法只能适用于不再运营并证明为缺乏盈利能力的公司或企业。

许多美国—伊朗索赔仲裁庭案件中都在美国投资者的请求下适用这个清算价值的方法来计算收归国有后的损失,这通常是因为所涉及的公司或企业在主权国家收归国有后没有再继续运营,或者原告根本没有索赔预期利润的损失。但是仲裁庭并不是完全严格按照有关资产破产清算的出售价格来计算清算价值,而是评估资产的完全价值,没有考虑在破产清算出售压力下需要扣减的部分(也就是上段提到的distress discount)。

这可以节录 Sedco Inc v. NIOC & Iran, Award of 2 July 1987, 15 Iran – US CTR 23 仲裁裁决有关解释如下:“Claimant does not use ‘liquidation value’ in the strict accountancy sense, as it does not request that we attempt to reconstruct what it might have recovered had SEDIRAN actually undergone liquidation proceedings in November 1979. Rather it requests that we assume ‘the winding up of Sediran’s affairs and the disposition of its assets . . . on the open market,’ presumably with no discount from the fair market value of the assets as might occur in actual distress liquidation circumstances. We agree that this is a fair measure of value in this Case.”

在这个案件中,评估被收归国有的原告拥有的 Sediran 公司 50% 的股份,以及同时被收归国有的原告拥有的 SISA 子公司价值时,仲裁庭是参考了其他类似的买卖、专家的估价、资产的保险价值、重置价值与现在的账面净值。仲裁庭最终是按照账面净值对存货与可收回的账目估值,并按照类似买卖与保险价值对石油钻塔估值并得出赔偿的金额。

其他适用清算价值来计算损失赔偿金额的案件还包括:Sedco v. IMICO, Award of 30 March 1989, 21 Iran – US CTR 31; Tippetts v. Iran, Award of 29 June 1984, 6 Iran – US CTR 219 与 Harold Birnbaum v. Iran, Award of 22 June 1984, 6 Iran – US CTR 219 等案件。从这些仲裁案件中可以看出,尽管仲裁庭标明是采用清算价值的方法来计算损失,但实际上仲裁庭采用了大量的其他估值方式来对有关资产估值,而没有考虑假设的破产清算结果,或者仲裁庭只是简单地设想一个清算价值,而没有做出有关“压力下出售的扣减”（distress discount）。所以总的来说，在涉及投资协议的国际投资仲裁中，几乎没有仲裁案件是采用了清算价值的估值方式来计算损失。

8.4　根据已经投入的资本来计算赔偿金额

正如本章3.2段提到，仲裁庭或法院通常会根据遭受损失的投资的“公平市价”（fair market value 简称 FMV）来计算赔偿的金额，这在本章5.1段也有详细的介绍。仲裁庭有时也会适用“基于收入的计算方法”（income - based approach），也就是贴现现金流的方式来评估遭受损失投资的市价，这在本章第6段有详述。但是在这些方法不能适用时，仲裁庭就会考虑根据投资项目已经花费的费用来计算赔偿金额。也就是说，如果投资者被终止的投资项目在主权国家做出非法行为时只处于“发展的初级阶段”（early stage of development）而没有开始形成现金流或未来的盈利，仲裁庭一般就不会按照投资本身的价值来计算赔偿的金额，而是按照投资者投入的资本来计算。

在 PSEG v. Turkey, Award of 19 January 2007 仲裁案件中，外国投资者与土耳其政府订立合约，打算在当地建造一个发电站，并在附近开采一个煤矿。投资者进行了可行性研究以及其他准备工作。后来土耳其政府的违法行为导致投资者的投资项目在初期阶段就被终止，因此原告要求土耳其依照这个投资项目的公平市价提供赔偿。但仲裁庭认为，政府的违法行为并不涉及对投资者“生产性资产”（productive assets）造成损失，而是没有进行合理的协商，以及对投资者造成其他干扰，而且投资项目还处于发展的初级阶段。所以仲裁庭最终是依照投资者针对这个项目已经投入的费用来计算赔偿的金额。

另在 Biloune v. Ghana, Award on Damages and Costs of 30 June 1990 仲裁案件，案情涉及一个叙利亚投资者 Biloune 先生在一家加纳公司拥有60%的股份，这家公司是负责建造一个综合性休闲酒店。在酒店的实体工程完工时，Biloune 先生被驱逐出加纳，这个投资项目也被加纳政府收归国有。Biloune 先生在仲裁中要求加纳政府要么赔偿他已经投入的资金，要么根据未来利润的损失做出赔偿，也就是通过贴现现金流方法计算出的市价。仲裁庭判是加纳政府需要赔偿收归国有行为发生时这个投资工程的公平市价或实际价值。但由于在收归国有发生时，这个项目还没有完工也没有开始运营，也就没有足够的理据来证明将来的收益/利润，所以最终还是按照 Biloune 先生实际投入的资金来计算赔偿的金额。

在 Siemens v. Argentina, Award of 6 February 2007 仲裁案件中，涉及外国投资者与阿根廷政府订立合约为政府提供服务。但在投资者开始提供服务之前，投资的项目就被政府收归国有，所以在收归国有发生时这个投资项目还没有开始运营。仲裁庭判是投资者有权获得他投资项目的公平市价，这是他已经投入的“沉没成本”（sunk costs），也就是“投资者企业的账面价值”（book value of Siemens' enterprise），或是“投资者实际投入成本的账面价值”（book value of Siemens' costs actually incurred）。但对于利润的损失，仲裁庭认为由于投资项目还没有营运所以投资者不应该获得未来利润损失的赔偿。

总的来说,这种根据实际投资或已经投入的资本来计算赔偿金额的方式更加确定以及简单,仲裁庭不需要估计未来的利润。但已经投入的资本并不一定能够正确反映投资项目的市价,因为投资就是为了将来可以赚取利润。这可以节录 H Weisburg 与 C Ryan 所写的《Means to Be Made Whole:Damages in the Context of International Investment Arbitration》一文中的解释如下:"Imagine a scenario, in which there are two identical enterprises, both of which have the same capacity to generate identical profits over time. Now, imagine that the owner of the first enterprise paid twice what the owner of the second enterprise paid to establish their facilities. If both owners tried to sell their enterprises, they would each be valued based on their abilities to generate revenues. The fact that one investor paid more for his investment would be irrelevant, since a rational buyer would not be willing to pay more simply because the original owner overpaid. . . . The fair market value of the companies would be tied directly to their abilities to produce revenues, without regard to the amount of money invested."(可以做一个简单的比喻,就是有两家完全一样的企业,大家都有相同的能力为将来提供同样金额的利润,但其中一家企业原来的成本或收购价格比另一家企业贵一倍。如果有一位投资者考虑购买其中一家企业,他愿意支付的价格只会考虑将来可以提供的利润。而如果两家企业的预计利润都是一样,也表示投资者愿意支付的价格也是一样。他是不会考虑其中的一家企业在最早成立或收购的时候支付了高一倍的成本。所以,企业的公平市价只针对盈利的能力,与投资的金额无关。)

所以,这种根据已经投入资本来计算赔偿金额的方法也并非适用于所有的投资争议。在一些失败的投资中,投资者虽然投入了大量资金,但投资项目的价值实际为零,如在勘探开采石油的项目中,投资者可能最终并没有开采出石油,或者在制药的投资项目中,投资者研发的药剂最终没有能够投放市场。在另一些投资争议中,可能投资项目的转售价值远远超过投资者最初投入的资本,尤其对于一些事后证明很成功的投资项目。在这些情况下,赔偿实际投入资本可能就会导致"不足赔偿"(under - compensation)或者"过度赔偿"(over - compensation)。

虽然存在以上的缺点,根据投入资本计算赔偿金额的方法还是可以在投资者与主权国家的利益之间达到平衡。"贴现现金流"方法会涉及未来的现金流,以及长期合约的整个剩余期限,这会给被告的主权国家造成很大经济负担。另外,通过投资者企业的账面净值或者资产的重置价值来评估企业价值的方法可能会对投资者造成不公平,因为这样计算出的价值通常会低于投资者实际投入的资本与努力,只能使投资者恢复到比投资前更差的经济地位。因此根据实际投入资本计算赔偿金额的方法可以在以上提到的两个极端中间达到平衡,从而得出一个看起来公平的结果。

9. CME Czech Republic B. V. (The Netherlands) v. The Czech Republic 仲裁案件

在本章第6至8段介绍了对投资或资产的不同的估值方法，以下会用 CME Czech Republic B. V. (The Netherlands) v. The Czech Republic 一案的简述作为介绍。[1]

原告：CME(一家荷兰从事媒体业务的公司)

被告：捷克共和国

背景："捷克媒体评议会"(Media Council)于1993年批准CNTS公司(由CEDC, CET 21及Czech Savings Bank投资成立的)营运捷克首间全国性私营电视台。该电视台随即成为全国最受欢迎的电视台，于1998年更拥有超过全国50%的观众及每年超过3000万美元的净利润。CME公司于1994年购入了CNTS公司66%的股权，并于1997年再次通过其子公司购入CNTS公司的股权，成为拥有CNTS 99%股权的大股东。

争议：CME声称包括购买CNTS的股权，其总投资额达1.4亿美元，而这些投资是受荷兰/捷克双边投资协定(Netherlands/ Czech Republic Bilateral Investment Treaty)所保护。原本捷克政府只容许CNTS及另一家私营电视台于国内进行播映，捷克的"媒体法"(Media Law)甚至为CNTS自动延续牌照12年。但由于捷克媒体评议会于1996年透过修改法例并迫使CNTS的股东修订其协议备忘录(MoA)，CNTS因而失去该独家经营牌照及其位于捷克的独家经营权，间接导致CNTS于2002年倒闭。(这可能是因为捷克政府不愿意国内最大的电视台受外资控制)原告声称损失超过5亿美元。

公平的市场价值的计算(Fair market value)

由于仲裁庭判已经在较早的裁决(裁决书可于 http://italaw. com/documents/CME - 2001PartialAward. pdf 下载)针对责任判被告违反了双边投资协议，使原告损失了其在捷克的投资项目(CNTS)，所以在这个只针对损失计算的仲裁中要把原告复原到被告违反投资协议前的状态，就必须把CNTS项目的实质价值赔偿给CME。仲裁庭认为被告应该赔偿CNTS于被告违反投资协议(1999年)前的市场价值，并减去CNTS的剩余价值(CNTS的剩余价值为原告在被告违反投资协议后卖出的CNTS的部分资产价值，加上仲裁庭于裁决时CNTS的资产值，减去变卖资产的成本及其他营运的成本。由于厂房及仪器等的变卖价值不高，而且大部分的电视节目亦有附带的版权问题，所以CNTS的剩余价值只有约1000万美元)。至于何谓公平的市场价值

〔1〕 裁决可于 http://italaw. com/documents/CME - 2003 - Final_001. pdf 下载。

(Fair market value),其中一个看法是市场上的买家愿意出的价钱。仲裁庭引用了 Starrett Housing Corp. v. Iran(Final Award),Award No. 314 - 24 - 1(1987),说:"... the price that a willing buyer would pay a willing seller in circumstances in which each had good information, each desired to maximize his financial gain, and neither was under duress or threat."也就是说,公平的市场价值是由买卖双方在拥有充分的资讯及于没有任何威逼的情况下各自为了达至最高利润(profit maximization)所定下的价钱。

以此仲裁案件为例,原告便为这个公平的市场价值提出了四个不同的计算方法(仲裁庭只采纳了首两个方案)。

(1)透过第三方买家的出价来计算项目价值(Value ascribed to CNTS by a Willing, Arms' - Length Purchaser)

在1998年时一家叫 Scandinavian broadcaster and investor Scandinavian Broadcasting System(简称 SBS)的公司与 CME 协商合并,虽然后来 SBS 赔付了违约金并终止了合并(部分原因是对捷克前景不乐观),但 SBS 曾视 CNTS 为 CME 的重要资产并于1999年时对 CNTS 作出了详细的估价。这个估价考虑了 CNTS 的股价、资产及盈收能力等因素。由于这个估值是由第三方的独立估价专家所提供,所以相对会较公平及准确。仲裁庭最后判这个交易客观地反映了 CNTS 当时的价值。虽然这个方法相对准确,却难以经常被运用。主要原因是这个第三方买家必须是认真的提出收购,提出的时间亦不能太过久远。而且在谈判过程当中可能有多于一个的"要约"(offer),以及买家也有可能考虑到其他非金钱的利益(如协同效应或扩大市场占有率等这些因素在会计上未必能充分反映),这些都会增加使用这个估算方法的难度。

(2)透过独立的估价公司计算项目价值

正因如此,仲裁庭亦用由双方委任的针对核算赔偿金额的"价值评估专家"(quantum expert)作出的估价确定/反证上述方法所提供的数据。该公司以"折现现金流"分析及"贸易比较"(trading multiple)分析这两个于公司并购中很常用的方法去估计项目的价值,再以"贸易比较"分析的数据来对照确定"折现现金流"分析所得出的数据之准确性。

a. 折现现金流(Discounted cash flow)

在以折现现金流(Discounted cash flow)来计算 CNTS 的价值前,仲裁庭首先要确定 CNTS 拥有的创造盈利的能力。仲裁庭引用了《World Bank Guidelines on the Treatment of Foreign Direct Investment》,说:"Compensation for taking of 'a going concern with a proven record of profitability' is presumptively reasonable if determined 'on the basis of the discounted cash flow value'."也就是说要使用折现现金流来计算公司价值,仲裁庭便需要参考 CNTS 在被告违反投资协议前的纪录,确定 CNTS 有一个能够被证明的盈利能力(proven record of profitability)。仲裁庭查看 CNTS 于1994年到1999年间的会计纪录,发现 CNTS 于5年间不论是净利润收入(Net Revenue)及税息折旧及摊销前利润(EBITDA)均有稳定的增长。

至于原告所聘用的估价公司在以折现现金流分析前亦先审视了由 CME 及 CNTS 所提供的盈利预测报告,认为 CNTS 有产生盈利的能力(going concern)才使用 DCF 来计算 CNTS 于 1999 年的价值。详细方法是先从捷克政府违约的 1 年(1999 年)起开始计算项目于往后 10 年所产生的现金流(首 7 年使用了 CNTS 对自己的盈利预测),再考虑营运所包含的风险折算成现值,最后再加上 CNTS 于 2009 年的终值(terminal value),计算出 CNTS 于 1999 年的价值约为 5.56 亿美元,(根据该报告,这个估值还得加上估计约值 1 亿美元的"控制权溢价"(Control Premium),以反映大股东出售持股时伴随的经营控制权的移转对价钱的正面影响。所以一般收购人也会以高于市价,对大股东提出收购要约。不过仲裁庭认为不应考虑这个溢价)。

b. 贸易比较分析(Trading Multiple Analysis)

估价公司找来了 29 家来自世界各地的上市媒体公司的税息折旧及摊销前利润(EBITDA)指标,以这 29 家公司的税息折旧及摊销前利润的平均值尝试作为计算 CNTS 价值的基础。估价公司把 29 家公司按地区划分为美国、欧洲及亚洲三大类,发现这三个地区的媒体公司的税息折旧及摊销前利润并没有大区别。当把这个指标(EBITDA multiple)套进 CNTS 的 5500 万美元税息折旧及摊销前利润后,得出 CNTS 的价值约为 5.82 亿美元。不过每个地方的经济亦不一样,很多时不同地区得出来的指标亦不尽相同。这种情况下怎样把地区划分和选用哪个地区的指标也会是另一个大问题。所以这个赔偿专家证人只用了贸易比较分析验证其在折现现金流所得出的数据。

不过同样使用折现现金流的方式计算,被告所聘用的估价公司则认为考虑到 CNTS 将会面对更激烈的市场竞争及节目成本的上涨,CNTS 只值 3.35 亿美元。可见即使是相同的估值方法,只要在假设上有少许不同,亦会带来大相径庭的结果。结果仲裁庭参考双方专家均有引用的一份第三方报告作为一个中立的参考意见,取两份报告间一个大概的数字作为 CNTS 的实际价值(4 亿美元)。不过仲裁庭亦强调由于两个报告的假设有很多不同,所以这个数据只是为仲裁庭在方法一所得的数据作一个参考。"The Tribunal, however, makes clear that the adjusted DCF calculation due to its dependence on disputed assumptions can serve only as a confirmation of the Tribunal's findings in assessment of the SBS offer, which as described above provided a firm value for CNTS at the amount of USD 400 million. The Tribunal does not see any need to review this finding in the light of the parties' DCF valuations, which contain a rather high element of uncertainty and speculation."

c. CME 对 CNTS 的盈利预测报告

可以一提的是上面提到仲裁庭为了决定 CME 对 CNTS 的盈利预测报告是否可信时,亦有把预测报告发表后 CNTS 的实际盈利和预测报告中的数据比对。不过一般来说,由于公平的市场价值是买卖双方在拥有充分的资讯的情况下而定下的(详情可见 Starrett Housing Corp. v. Iran(Final Award), Award No. 314 - 24 - 1(1987)一案）。而所谓充分的资讯，则只限于违反协议时已知的市场状况（因为买卖双方并不能把将来（违反后）的事件计算在该价钱内，这也意味着所谓公平的市场价值也存在了一定的不确定性），所以仲裁庭一般也只会使用于违反以前的估算报告，而不会考虑违反以后发生及不能预见的事件所带来的影响。

另外仲裁庭亦相信这份报告可信程度颇高。因为撰写该份盈利预测报告的CMS雇员知道自己部门未来的工作表现将会按根据该份报告的预测来评估，所以亦应该不会有偏颇的情况出现。事实上仲裁庭发现在1999年及2000年这两年间预测报告稍微低估了CNTS的实际盈利能力，结果裁定该份报告为CNTS于1999年的公司价值提供了一个可具参考的数字，故亦参考原告估价公司以这份报告为基础作出的预测。

（3）透过CME购入项目的价钱计算项目价值

此外，原告还提出了在CME收购CNTS的99%股权的过程中，其中5.8%的股权是CME以28,537,500美元收购Nova Consulting所获得（CNTS 5.8%的股权是Nova Consulting唯一的资产）。只要把这5.8%的股权价值转换成99%便能算出赔偿金额约为5亿美元。不过有指股价除了受股票市场影响外，有时在并购前公司的股价有可能被“战略性”地提高或降低。例如，在本案中被告便提出了有CME的管理层认为该5.8%是明显高于市场当时的合理价格（仲裁庭认为这是因为卖方威胁CME会把股份出售给不知名的第三方买家，给CME造成一定程度的压力去购买）。这种偏差即使再轻微，如果把这5.8%的小额放大成整间公司的价值，计算结果也可以有巨大差别。而事实上仲裁庭亦以此原因拒绝接受这种估算方式。

（4）透过独立的金融市场报告计算项目价值

根据同期（1997~1998年间）8间金融市场分析公司（如Schroder，Prudential Security，DLJ，ING Barings，MSDW，Smith Barney等）对CNTS的股价分析报告，虽然最乐观和最悲观的报告对CNTS的盈利预测相差颇大（分别是8.35亿和3.54亿美元），但所有报告均一致指出CNTS拥有一定的盈利能力。不过如果撇除最乐观和最悲观的报告不算，另外6份报告的结果区分不算太大：他们把CNTS的市场价值定于5.04亿至6.91亿美元间，平均为5.78亿美元。要注意这些股票分析报告一般会假定公司的股价自由流动于一个平稳发展的金融市场，所以遇到金融风暴等风险时这些报告便不会适用。而且由于这些金融市场的分析公司在估算公司的价值或股价时有很多主观的预测，甚至有些估算报告或多或少会有控制股票市场的目的，所以不同的分析公司的数据偏差会很大，难以算出一个准确的价值。因此这类报告一般只能用来验证上面提及过的方法所计算出来的公司价值，而在这一案件中仲裁庭亦认为难以判断这些金融市场分析公司所使用的数据是否全面及准确，而且这些报告并非在仲裁庭的管辖下撰写，准确性未必比其他方法（方法一）更可靠，所以决定不接纳这种由金融市场专家的证据。

以上四个估值的方法都假设了CNTS能一直提供现金流（future cash flow to perpetuity)。而原告的估值方法均得出了一个约为5.6亿美元的数字。不过仲裁庭认为这些数据对于未来的市场增长和节目成本都是过于乐观,况且公司人才的流失,合作伙伴的关系决裂和经济环境转差均会对未来现金流造成难以预测的影响。(其中值得一提的是所有的估值方式均假定CNTS的首席执行官兼CET21的董事长Dr. Zelezny会继续于CNTS内任职,仲裁庭认为其经验和知识价值7200万美元。由于他不再和CNTS合作,所以这个人事因素亦必须考虑在内。)所以仲裁庭以第一个方法(SBS的收购要约)为基础,取了一个较保守的数字,判CNTS于1999年的价值为4亿美元,减去上面提到的人事因素7200万美元及CNTS的剩余价值3850万美元,得出2.89亿美元的数字。(实际赔付金额还得计算CME所占CNTS的股权及加上从被告违约起至被告赔付给原告为止该段时期的利息。)

10. 其他的损失项目

较早的段节针对了最重要的方面,就是对有关的投资或资产做出估值,并要求被告的主权国家做出赔偿。但在全部赔偿的大原则下,投资者会有其他类别的损失项目,这也是可以一并提出索赔。毕竟,主权国家如果违反双边投资协议对外国投资者做出损害,也不会只是令所有的投资与资产失去,而是一个相对轻微的干预,造成的损失也比较有限并不会涉及对资产的估值。但这种情况带来的投资仲裁不会很多,因为外国投资者如果真的向主权国家提出诉讼,一般都是在极端的情况,也往往是做出了心理与实际的准备在诉讼后不论是否能够取得赔偿,外国投资者也会放弃在这一个国家的业务。所以,一般轻微的干预造成有限的损失通常都不会发展成为一个投资仲裁。

言归正传谈谈其他类别的损失项目,这与其他商业案件一样,只要一些法律要求的大原则能够满足,如因果关系(证明有关类别的损失的确是主权国家的不法干预所造成)与可预见性(这会是以侵权的准则)等,都应该可以向被告提出。在这里简单介绍少数几项会在投资仲裁中出现的损失项目。

10.1 投资的费用

投资会涉及各种不同的费用,这会可以作为损失向被告的主权国家提出。这些费用会包括谈判与计划的费用:SPP v. Egypt, Award of 20 May 1992; PSEG v. Turkey, Award of 19 January 2007; Autopista v. Venezuela, Final Award of 23 September 2003;资金投入与贷款:Siemens v. Argentina, Award of 6 February 2007; SPP (ME) v. Egypt, Award of 20 May 1992; MTD v. Chile, Award of 25 May 2004; Starrett v. Iran, Final Award of 14 August 1987, 16 Iran – US CTA 112; Eastman Kodak v. Iran, Award 1 July 1991, 27 Iran – US CTR 3;财务费用(如贷款服务费用或银行担保费用):MTD v. Chile, Award of 25 May 2004; Autopista v. Venezuela, Final Award of 23 September 2003;广告费用:SPP

(ME) v. Egypt, Award of 20 May 1992;把某些资产投入进投资项目的费用:Sedelmayer v. Russia, Award of 7 July 1998; Biloune v. Ghana, Award on Damages and Costs of 30 June 1990; Metalclad v. Mexico, Award of 30 August 2000;招聘与重新部署员工的费用:SPP (ME) v. Egypt, Award of 20 May 1992;旅行与住宿的费用:Biloune v. Ghana, Award on Damages and Costs of 30 June 1990;保险、咨询甚至电话联络的费用:Metalclad v. Mexico, Award of 30 August 2000;以及一些临时性费用。

临时性费用一般是指发生在主权国家违法行为之后,由于该违法行为而造成的使费。仲裁庭有时可能不会把这项费用单独列为一个损失的类别,而是作为投资使费的一部分给予赔偿。例如,在 Vivendi v. Argentina, Award of 20 August 2007 仲裁案件中,就涉及阿根廷政府违法行为发生后,原告为它的当地分公司提供借款以帮助分公司度过困境,这个借款的费用被仲裁庭判是原告投资使费的一部分,所以属于受损害投资公平市价的一部分而获得赔偿。

这一个类别的临时性费用还会包括外国投资者较早时花费的清盘的费用以及聘请律师的费用。如果在主权国家违法行为发生后投资者决定放弃在主权国家的业务,就会涉及清盘的费用、重新部署员工的费用,以及支付给被解雇员工的工资等。在投资者因主权国家行为遭受损害时,他可能会聘请律师提供法律服务,提供意见或为自己的案件向有关部门辩护或索赔等。在 Pope & Talbot v. Canada, Award on Damages of 31 May 2002 仲裁案件中,仲裁庭判是投资者有权获得他因加拿大政府有关部门以前的不合法行为而产生的聘请会计、律师与游说的费用赔偿,因为正是由于加拿大政府违反了公平公正对待义务才导致投资者遭受了这些费用的损失。但对于投资者公司的经理因为处理这些诉讼而花费的时间损失,仲裁庭判是不能给予赔偿,因为这些并非是投资者支付的额外费用。仲裁庭认为,经理的工资是投资者公司的固定成本,不论有没有加拿大政府的违反行为都会产生。

但是,投资者在有关案件之前参加的其他法律程序中的律师费用是不应该在这个正在进行的案件中获赔,因为这些费用是之前法律程序中关于费用的裁决中应该处理的问题,并非正在进行中案件产生的临时性费用。如在 Petrobart v. Kyrgyz Republic, Award of 29 March 2005 仲裁案件中,仲裁庭拒绝了投资者索赔他在之前的国内诉讼与 UNCITRAL 仲裁中支付的律师费用,因为这些费用在之前的法律程序中就应该解决,而与正在进行的仲裁程序有关的支出才应该作为本案诉讼费用而在最后的裁决中加以考虑。但如果在之前的诉讼中,主权国家的国内法院违反国际法,使投资者没有得到公正的裁决,在后来的国际仲裁中就可以把之前不合法的国内诉讼带来的律师费用作为本案中的临时性费用给予赔偿。

10.2 道德或精神损失

这一个损失项目类似于本书第二章之15段介绍过的"非金钱损失"(non - pecuniary loss),这通常在违约的赔偿是不承认的损失类别。但在国际法,这一类的损失是站得住脚的。例如,G Arangio - Ruiz 在国际法委员会(International Law Commission)1989 年年鉴第 2(1)卷的报告《Second Report on State Responsibility》(A/CN. 4/425 & Corr 1 and Add 1 & Corr 1)中所说“... the practice and literature of international law show that moral(or non – patrimonial)losses caused to private parties by an internationally wrongful act are to be compensated as an integral part of the principal damage suffered by the injured State.”国际法委员会在针对国际责任有关条款的评论《ILC Articles on State Responsibility, Commentary to Article 36》中也说:“... no loss than material injury sustained by the injured State, non – material damage is financially assessable and may be the subject of a claim of compensation...”

看来直到目前还没有太多的投资仲裁案件加入这一项损失,但也不是说没有发生过。例如,在 DLP v. Yemen, Award of 6 February 2008 仲裁案件中,案情涉及外国投资者为也门政府修建道路,但没有获得支付以及受到了不公平的对待,包括公司职员受到了来自也门军队的侮辱与威胁。在后来的 ICSID 仲裁中,除了经济上的损失,原告也索赔了道德损失。仲裁庭判原告可以索赔这一种类别的损失,并判了 100 万美元的赔偿。仲裁庭是说:“Even if investment treaties primarily aim at protecting property and economic values, they do not exclude, as such, that a party may, in exceptional circumstances, ask for compensation for moral damages. It is generally accepted in most legal systems that moral damages may also be recovered besides pure economic damages. There are indeed no reasons to exclude them.... The respondent shall be liable to reparation for the injury suffered by the Claimant, whether it be bodily, moral or material in nature.”

另在 Benvenuti and Bonfant v. Congo, Award of 15 August 1980, 67 ILR 345 仲裁案件中,投资者在仲裁中要求刚果索赔道德与精神损失,因为刚果政府强制要求投资者离开刚果,这导致投资者在他的供应商以及银行方面丧失信誉。仲裁庭最后判是刚果政府需要赔付投资者 XAF5,000,000(刚果法郎)作为精神损失的赔偿。

但也有提出这一项索赔失败的案件 Tecmed v. Mexico, Award of 29 May 2003 与 Bogdanov v. Moldova, Award of 22 September 2005。在这两个仲裁案件中,虽然道德或精神损失的索赔请求被驳回,但仲裁庭并没有质疑在投资仲裁中是可以索赔这一类的损失。

10.3 利润损失或机会损失

利润损失(loss of profit)作为损失的一部分是在国际法中普遍接受的,也与投资仲裁的完全赔偿大原则是完全配合的,在较早时候详细介绍的贴现现金流计算方法本身就是针对预期的利润损失。在投资仲裁中会涉及的收归国有案件,与收归国有无关的违反国际法或者双边投资协议的非法行为或是违反合约案件,都经常涉及利润损失的索赔。

至于机会损失(loss of opportunity)会适用在原告无法明确证明他对预期利润的损失,所以提出机会损失希望仲裁庭会接受主权国家的非法行为导致他失去了一些赚钱的机会,可按百分比作出赔偿。这也被国际法完全接受,在《UNIDROIT Principles of International Commercial Contracts》中 Article 7.4.3.(2)也有规定:“... compensation may be due for the loss of a chance in proportion to the probability of its occurrence.”

这方面的案件可以介绍 Sapphire v. NIOC, Award of 15 March 1963, 35 ILR 136 投资仲裁,这先例也已经在本章 6.12.2 段简单提到过。案情涉及一个石油勘探开采合约在勘探的初期就被主权国家违反而终止。仲裁庭判是投资者可以获得利润损失的赔偿,但在利润损失金额方面双方有很大争议,因为石油还没有被开采出来,所以很难计算。仲裁庭认为是可以适用机会损失,并说:“... although in such cases the existence of damage is uncertain, case law has looked at the position at the time when the opportunity was lost and has accepted that this opportunity itself has a value whose loss gives rise to compensation.”仲裁庭最终是根据专家意见,认定在被授予特许权的区域有很大可能存在具有商业价值的石油。原告的专家认为如果主权国家没有违约,外国投资者最多可以赚取 4600 万美元的利润,最坏的情况是根本开采不出石油,这样外国投资者就会损失 800 万美元。仲裁庭最终行使自由裁量权裁决是原告可以获赔的公平合理的机会损失是 200 万美元,再加上原告已经支付的成本 65 万美元,作为赔偿。

另一个案件可以介绍 SPP(ME) v. Egypt, Award of 20 May 1992,案情涉及埃及政府把原告在旅游设施的投资合法收归国有,仲裁庭拒绝以贴现现金流方法来计算损失,因为这个投资还处在初期,没有足够数据计算将来的预计利润。但仲裁庭是接受原告的损失不仅是他投资的金额,结果是判原告可以索赔一个他失去的可以令这项投资变为成功商业投资的机会损失。原告投资的金额是大约 500 万美元,仲裁庭多判了 300 万美元作为这一个机会损失的赔偿。

11. 投资仲裁损失计算的总结与一些看法

综合以上所说,可以说投资仲裁通常提出的赔偿金额是极其庞大和惊人的,因为本质上这是外国投资者对主权国家做出的最后一击。导致这个情况的原因可能是有以下几种:

(1)有很多投资仲裁都涉及不懂行或愚昧的发展中国家乱引进外国投资,其中有相当一部分是国家(或国有公司)与外国投资者签订的合约。即使涉及许可权、批文或是保证,也往往与一些合约有连带关系。这些合约的年期往往非常漫长,如果出问题的话会带来庞大的损失,特别是预期的利润损失。

(2)可以肯定说,外国投资者会向发展中国家提起仲裁的可能性远远比向发达国家多。这在本章第 1 段已经提到过,外国投资者向主权国家提起投资仲裁,通常是准备撤离在这个国家的业务,所以不会手软而希望在撤离之前狠敲一笔。这种情况很少会发生在美国或欧洲的一些发达国家,除了外国投资者不敢这样做的原因之外,他们也很少会想到在美国或欧洲这种市场中撤离他们的业务。中国也是一个庞大的市场，不少外国投资者希望分一杯羹，因此没有人想过要撤离。所以中国虽然是世界上主要的资本输入国，但并没有面对外国投资者的投资仲裁，直到近年来才开始听到。但如果中国经济下滑，外国投资者不见得会手软。

(3)正如许多其他的商业争议，投资仲裁会在责任方面相对简单，复杂的反而会是在损失的计算。但不像英国法院或伦敦/香港仲裁，对将来的预期利润损失计算困难之余还是有比较肯定的计算方法，毕竟还是有一套法律制度的先例可以依从，这也在本书其他章节有涉及。而一旦涉及投资仲裁，如ICSID仲裁，仲裁员就会是各种背景的人士，具有不同的法律背景，也往往熟悉商业社会(特别是西方跨国公司)，对如何计算将来的预期利润损失的臆猜或是对投资项目或资产的估值更加会是百花齐放，导致了计算方法十分不肯定。

(4)另在损失的类别方面，可以看到在投资仲裁中索赔的损失类别非常多样。虽然有类似英国侵权法中将受害方恢复到损害行为没有发生的复原大原则，但是却又超越英国法下针对侵权不可以索赔纯经济损失的原则。另一方面投资仲裁中也会给予非金钱赔偿(如本章10.2段提到的“道德或精神损失”)，这一点又超越了英国合约法下的损失赔偿原则。由此损失类别的多样性可以看出，投资仲裁的危险性以及有感觉是将惩罚主权国家非法干涉外国投资者的行为变为国际公共政策。

(5)投资仲裁对发展中国家特别危险还有另一个近十年来的发展。一般而言，很多时候在发展中国家取得这类致命合约、许可权或是批文都是一些靠关系甚至提供好处的外国中小型公司(大公司往往考虑和受制较多，如受制于西方国家针对国际上贪污受贿行为的立法)。以前这类中小型企业取得这些价值高昂的投资项目时都会找些有实力的大企业一并参与执行，但今天他们或许有些不安好心的打算。以前当这些合约出问题并发生争议时，由这些中小型企业出面向发展中国家提出索赔，往往背后的财力和决心比较有限。发展中国家往往较容易应付，如赔很少的金钱便能使这类原告满足。笔者也曾有处理这类案件的经验：单单通过要求原告提供费用担保(如果是在有这种法律规定的仲裁地点)即可令原告知难而退或大幅度让步和解。但在今天或近十年来已经有很多所谓的“秃鹫基金”(vulture capital)盯着这些合约，愿意付钱收购这些被违反或没收的投资合约或项目并资助诉讼，也愿收购已经胜诉的仲裁裁决书，然后自己接过来寻找败诉主权国家的资产以利执行。例如，在香港著名的有关主权豁免的刚果案FG Hemisphere Associates LLC v. Democratic Republic of Congo, FACV5, 6 & 7/2010中，原告的FG Hemisphere Associates就是这类秃鹫基金。所以在今天这些案件的原告(可能是受让方的vulture capital)会是有无限耐心、决心和财力追溯这笔赔偿金额，这是一般发展中国家难以抵抗的。虽然已经有部分国家说是要对这种行为作出禁止，但如果要全球性禁止，困难还是很大。

(6)在本章一开始的一段就已经有提到国际投资仲裁中有57.7%的仲裁案件是投资者败诉，另加上不知数量的和解，令笔者怀疑有不少是外国投资者针对发展中国家试探性的诉讼,就其本身并没有一个很好的理据,而只想借此机会狠敲一笔。

(7)有很多国际投资仲裁是针对一些新投资项目,因为发展中国家作为资本输入国都是一些新兴市场。这表示外国投资者进入这些市场时对未来的发展前景大多持积极的态度,所根据的数据也是十分乐观的。这一来,如果一出现问题导致仲裁案件,仲裁庭往往是要根据这些乐观但无实质根据的数据估计将来的利润。可以说,即使仲裁庭十分保守,最后得出的结果还是会倾向对外国投资者有利。如果该投资项目在相关主权国家履行下去,会有更大的可能是真正经济效益差很远,因为发展中国家在中长期会有比发达国家更多的不利变数。即使是在一个相对稳定的香港,笔者随便举一个例子,就是在近30年来香港政府只发给两个无线电视台牌照经营。但只有"无线电视"(TVB)能够一直盈利,而"亚洲电视"(ATV)却一直亏本。但如果这两家电视台在投资的早期就已经被香港政府收归国有或是干预,就有可能导致在有关的投资仲裁的案件中,亚洲电视根据当时的数据与臆猜,会得出接近无线电视估计的利润,并获得仲裁庭做出相近金额的赔偿,让亚洲电视的投资者可以扭亏为盈,毕竟他们在做出投资的早期并没有计划与预见到自己会最后把老本也亏掉了。

(8)针对中国而言,有说法是国际投资仲裁也对中国有利,因为中国在近年来已经开始变为一个资本输出国,是需要在这方面建立一些保护的。但这种说法笔者认为不一定站得住脚,因为这需要很多方面的配合。例如,西方的外国投资者就习惯以仲裁主张他们的法律权利,动不动就会向主权国家提起诉讼。但中国公司即使作为外国投资者,也往往不会这样做。原因有很多方面,包括不愿意花律师费用(投资仲裁的律师费用是十分高昂的)、不习惯诉讼、对证据的准备与收集不足以及对投资的主权国家提起诉讼会有很多政治上的考虑等。所以笔者肯定理论与实际上会差很远,就是中国虽然变为资本输出国,不再纯粹是一个资本输入国,但仍然还是在国际投资仲裁中占不到好处,而只是蒙受其害。

第十九章　衍生品合约下的损失赔偿*

1. Introduction to Derivatives

Derivatives are a class of financial instruments whichhave come to form an integral part of the global financial markets. Over the last two decades, derivatives have experienced an exponential rate of growth, with the value of all outstanding over – the – counter("**OTC**") derivatives contracts rising from approximately USD 2.5 trillion in 1998 to nearly USD 20 trillion at the end of 2011.[1] Over the last ten years, the Asia – Pacific region has grown from the third largest derivatives marketin the world to overtaking the Americas and EMEA (Europe, Middle East and Africa) as the region with the most derivatives contracts traded, accounting for approximately 40% of global volumes.[2]

Although derivativesinstruments have existed and have been used for a long time already,[3] the OTC derivatives market as we know it todaywas largely formed in the last twenty years. It should be noted that the International Swaps and Derivatives Association ("**ISDA**") was only formed in 1985, and the first widely used standard form of derivatives contract(the 1992 ISDA Master Agreement) was only published in January 1993.[4]

Following the global financial crisis("**GFC**") in 2007, which is widely considered to be the worst economic recession since the Great Depression of the 1930s, many governments, regulators and market commentators debated the role which OTC derivatives played in the GFC. Although the majority agree that the root causes of the GFC did not lay in the OTC derivatives market, there is general consensus that the widespread usage of OTC derivatives exacerbated the effects of the GFC. Some of the damages associated with OTC deriva-

---

* 如有兴趣，可以在杨良宜的个人网站(www.yangliangyee.com)下载中英文对照版本。

〔1〕 Source: Bank of International Settlements(BIS)(November 2011).

〔2〕 Macquarie Research, May 2012.

〔3〕 For example, forward contracts played a role in creating the Dutch tulip bubble in 1637(one of the first recorded market bubbles in history).

〔4〕 ISDA published a Master Agreement in 1987, but this form of Master Agreement is rarely, if ever, seen in the derivatives market today.

tives were famously outlined by Warren Buffett in his annual report to shareholders of Berkshire Hathaway in 2002,[1] in which he described derivatives as "financial weapons of mass destruction".

Given the importance of the derivatives market to international finance, as well as the increasing role which OTC derivatives plays in the Chinese financial markets, the first half of this chapter will provide some background information on what derivatives are and why they have become so widely used in the global financial markets. The second half of this chapter will describe how the early termination valuation process is conducted for derivatives contracts entered into under the ISDA Master Agreement (the single most important document in the derivatives market).

2. Whatare derivatives?

Despite the technical and complex jargon that is frequently found in the derivatives world, almost all derivatives share the following features: (1) they are bilateral contracts entered into between two parties (and therefore general principles of contract law apply); (2) the contract will involve future performance by one or both parties; (3) the value of the contract (and the rights and obligations of each party under the contract) will be linked to the value of an underlying asset (i. e. the value of the contract is *derived* from the value of the underlying asset); and (4) a derivatives contract is a financial instrument as it has a value which can be traded or sold independently of the underlying asset.

While there is a vast range of different types of derivatives contracts, all derivatives contracts can be categorisedaccording to following three characteristics: (a) Form of derivatives contract; (b) Type of underlying asset; (c) Method of trading.

These three categories are explored infurther detail below.

2.1 *Form of derivatives contract*

Generally speaking, there are three forms of derivatives contracts: (i) forwards,[2] (ii) options and (iii) swaps.

2.1.1 *Forwards*

2.1.1.1 *What is a forward contract?*

---

[1] http://www.berkshirehathaway.com/letters/2002pdf.pdf

[2] Please note that forward contracts and futures contracts are essentially the same, except that futures contracts are standardised contracts which are traded on exchanges and forward contracts are bilaterally negotiated OTC contracts.

A forward contract is a contractwhere a *buyer and seller* agree to the sale and purchase of an *underlying asset* for settlement at an *agreed price* on a *future date*.

The development of forward contracts was a natural extension to the development of agricultural exchanges, where suppliers and purchasers both desired to find a method to hedge the fluctuating price of the commodities being traded. One of the most historic developments in the trading of forward contracts was the establishment of the Chicago Board of Trade in 1848. At that time, Chicago served as a very important hub for the trading of agricultural products in the United States given its central location between the farmlands on the west side of the country and the major cities and ports on the east coast of the United States.

The ability for suppliers and purchasers to "lock in" the price at which an agricultural product would be bought or soldon a future date provided both sides with some degree of predictability and stability.

Forwards can be settled by way of either*physical settlement* or *cash settlement*. With physical settlement, the seller will be obliged to deliver the underlying asset to the buyer on the date specified in the contract against payment by the buyer of the agreed price. Cash settlement, in contrast, involves a payment on the date specified in the contract by either the buyer or seller to the other party, depending on the change in value of the underlying asset during the life of the forward.

2.1.1.2 *Example of a forward contract*

If a Chinese company enters into a contract to import raw materials worth 1 million Australian dollars ("**AUD**") from Australia (which will be delivered and paid for in 3 months time), the Chinese company will need to ensure that it has access to AUD 1 million in three months time. If the current exchange rate between AUD and Renminbi ("**RMB**") is AUD 1 : RMB 6.5, then the Chinese company will need to use RMB 6,500,000 to purchase the raw materials.

However, it is possible that AUD may rise in value in the next 3 months (making it more expensive for the Chinese company to pay for the raw materials). In order to protect itself against a potential rise in the value of AUD, the Chinese company can enter into a foreign exchange ("**FX**") forward with a bank today to "lock – in" the current exchange rate between RMB and AUD.

If the FX forward is physically settled in 3 months time, the Chinese company will receive AUD 1 million from the bank against payment of RMB 6,500,000.

If the FX forward is cash settled, then the exchange rate between RMB and AUD on the date of settlement (i. e. after 3 months) will be compared with the exchange rate agreed between the parties. If the actual rate is higher than the rate agreed by the parties (e. g. the exchange rate has moved from AUD 1 : RMB 6.5 to AUD 1 : RMB 6.7, which represents a rise in the value of AUD), the bank will pay to the Chinese company RMB 200,000 (which represents the additional amount of RMB which the Chinese company would have needed to pay in order to acquire AUD 1 million at the more expensive exchange rate). Conversely, if the actual rate is lower than the rate agreed by the parties (e.g. the exchange rate has moved from AUD 1 : RMB 6.5 to AUD 1 : RMB 6.2, which represents a drop in the value of AUD), the Chinese company will need to pay the bank RMB 300,000. The net effect of the FX forward is that the Chinese company will always need to pay RMB 6,500,000 to acquire AUD 1 million at the time of settlement of the FX forward, regardless of the movement in the exchange rate between AUD and RMB.

2.1.2 *Options*

2.1.2.1 *What is an option contract?*

In contrast to forwards, an option is a contract under which one party has the*right but not the obligation* to buy or sell an underlying asset from or to another party. An option which involves the right to buy an underlying asset is referred to as a *call option*, whereas an option which involves the right to sell an underlying asset is referred to as a *put option*. The parties will agree a price (known as the *strike price*) at the outset which is the price at which the underlying asset will be bought or sold at. The party who has the right to exercise the option (i.e. exercise the right to buy or sell the underlying asset) (known as the *option holder*) will pay an amount as consideration (known as the *premium*) to the other party for the option.

Different names have been given to different types of options depending on when theoption holder can exercise the option: (1) *European options* are exercisable on only one particular date (i.e. the expiration date of the option); (2) *American options* are exercisable on any day until the option expires; (3) *Bermudan options* are exercisable on a number of pre-agreed dates.

The earliest written record of option contracts dates back to the writings of Aristotle,[1] where he described how a fellow philosopher named Thales had predicted that the olive harvest in a particular year would be bountiful. Relying on this prediction, Thales entered into contracts with a number of olive-press[2] owners in the region to purchase the right to use their machines following harvest time. When the olive harvest turned out as Thales had predicted, the demand for olive-presses increased and Thales was able to sell

---

[1] Aristotle, Politics, trans. Benjamin Jowett, vol. 2, The Great Books of the Western World, book 1, chap. 11, p. 453.

[2] A device to extract olive oil from olives.

his optionsto use such olive - presses for a profit.

As an option contract creates a right but not an obligation to perform the contract, the option holder may allow an option contract to expire without exercising the right to require the other party to perform the option contract, depending on the movement in the value of the underlying asset.

2.1.2.2 *Example of an option contract*

An investor taking a positive view on aHong Kong listed company (for the purposes of this paragraph, ABC Limited) may buy a call option in relation to 100 shares of this company with an expiration date of 3 months and a strike price of HKD 125. If the share price of ABC Limited has risen to HKD 150 in 3 months time, the investor will make a profit by exercising the call option. Like forward contracts, option contracts may be physically settled or cash settled.

If the option contract in the above example is physically settled, the investor, upon exercise of the call option, would be required to pay HKD 12,500 (the strike price of HKD 125 multiplied by 100 shares) to the option seller against delivery by the option seller of 100 shares (each worth HKD 150) to the investor (i.e. total value of HKD 15,000).

If the option contract is cash settled instead, upon exercise of the call option by the investor, the option seller would be required to pay to the investor an amount equal to HKD 2,500, which represents the difference between the value of the shares on the expiration date (i.e. HKD 15,000) and the amount which the investor would have been required to pay the option seller if the call option were physically settled (i.e. HKD 12,500).

However, if in the above example, the share price fell to HKD 100 after 3 months (instead of rising to HKD 150), the investor would choose not to exercise the call option at all since it would be cheaper for the investor to purchase 100 shares at the market price than compared to the strike price of the call option.

2.1.2.3 *Development of modern options trading*

Although option contracts have been used for a very long time to help hedge risks or as a method of speculation, it is only recently that the financial markets have developed a quantitative method of measuring how much an option contract is worth. Historically, the pricing of option contracts was done by traders largely on gut instincts and common sense, and the trading of option contracts was limited as parties had difficulty assessing the value of option contracts objectively. The publication of the Black - Scholes formula in 1973[1] became a watershed moment in the history of modern finance since it provided market participants the ability to value option contracts (as well as other complex financial instru-

[1] http://www.bbc.co.uk/news/magazine-17866646.

ments) objectively.

In a nutshell, the Black – Scholes formula is derived through the creation and maintenance of an artificial risk – free portfolio made up of a combination ofthe underlying asset and option contracts in relation to that underlying asset. Since the value of a risk – free portfolio and the underlying asset are known, a formula to calculate the value of the option contract in relation to that underlying asset can be created (which is a function of the future volatility of the underlying asset). [1]

2.1.3 *Swaps*

2.1.3.1 *What is a swaps contract?*

A swap is a bilateral contract under which two parties agree to an exchange of cash flows over a period of time, with each cash flow being determined in a different manner. Out of all the different types of derivatives contracts, the*interest rate swap* ("**IRS**") comprises the largest percentage of the derivatives market when measured by the market value of all outstanding contracts.

Under a typical IRS, the two parties to the contract will agree an amount (known as the*notional amount*), and one party will pay a fixed rate of interest with respect to such notional amount whereas the other party will pay a floating rate of interest with respect to such notional amount.

2.1.3.2 *Example of a swap contract*

A typical example where an IRS may be used is where a Hong Kong company has borrowedHong Kong dollars ("**HKD**") from a bank under a three year loan to invest in a new project. This loan may carry a floating rate of interest which is payable quarterly (i.e. four times a year), in which case it will be a certain percentage (representing the *margin* or the profit which the bank makes) above 3 month HIBOR. [2]

Since HIBORwill fluctuate over the course of the three year loan, the Hong Kong company does not have certainty as to how much its interest payments will cost on a quarterly basis. One method by which the Hong Kong company can deal with such market risk (i.e. the risk inherent in fluctuating interest rates) is to enter into an IRS with a *swap counterparty*.

Under such an IRS, the swap counterparty will make periodic payments to the Hong Kong company which will be equal to the amount of interest which the Hong Kong company needs topay under its three year loan. In return, the Hong Kong company can agree to pay a

[1] For more background information, please see http://www.mayin.org/ajayshah/PDFDOCS/Shah1997_bms.pdf.

[2] HIBOR is the Hong Kong Interbank Offer Rate, which represents the average interest rate at which leading banks in Hong Kong will lend money to each other.

fixed rate of interest on the notional amount of the IRS (which will be equal to the amount outstanding under the three year loan) to the swap counterparty. In this way, the Hong Kong company will have converted the uncertainty related to paying a floating rate of interest under the three year loan into a fixed amount of interest payable every three months.

2.2 *Type of underlying asset*

Due to the flexible nature of derivatives contracts, it is possible to find derivatives transactions entered into in relation to a wide range of underlying assets. As mentioned above, the vast majority of OTC derivatives in existence are IRS (i. e. the underlying asset is interest rates). This is then followed by derivatives transactions over FX, credit, equities and commodities.[1]

In recent years, market participants have developed more 'exotic' types of derivatives such as mortality bonds and catastrophe bonds which don't reference an underlying asset in the traditional sense of the phrase. The 'underlying asset' in relation to mortality bonds is effectively (and somewhat morbidly) the length of people's lives (i. e. the payment under a mortality bond in any year is calculated by reference to the number of people in a selected age group (e. g. 65 year olds) that survive such year). With respect to catastrophe bonds, the 'underlying asset' is a defined natural disaster, meaning that the holder of a catastrophe bond will receive regular coupon payments unless a specific event (such as a hurricane or earthquake) occurs and fulfils specific parameters, in which case the holder of the catastrophe bond will lose his or her principal investment.

One of the more innovative uses of derivatives in recent years is the creation of a 'social impact' bond,[2] where money raised from the sale of the bonds is used for the rehabilitation of prisoners. As the payout to investors under the social impact bond is linked to the level of re – offending by prisoners, it can be said that the 'underlying asset' of the social impact bond is the crime rate attributable to rehabilitated prisoners.

2.3 *Method of Trading*

Derivatives contracts are either exchange traded or OTC. Exchange traded derivatives will be standardised contracts which are bought or sold on an exchange (such as the Shanghai Futures Exchange[3]) and will generally be financial instruments with a high degree of liquidity and transparency. OTC derivatives, on the other hand, can be highly bespoke contracts which are bilaterally negotiated with less transparency as to the value of such contracts. Following the GFC, one of the main objectives of the G20 has been to push for the

---

〔1〕 http://www.bis.org/statistics/otcder/dt1920a.pdf

〔2〕 http://www.bbc.co.uk/news/uk – 11254308

〔3〕 http://www.shfe.com.cn/

standardisation of OTC derivatives to increase liquidity and the reporting of such contracts to trade repositories in order to give greater transparency of the OTC derivatives market to regulators.[1]

3. Why use a derivative?

One of the key attractions of derivatives contracts is their flexibility and ability to be used in a wide range of commercial situations. Some examples of the use of derivatives contracts have already been provided above. In this section we classify their usage into three main categories: (a) Risk Management; (b) Investmen; (c) Arbitrage.

3.1 *Risk management*

While derivatives has becomeassociated with risk – taking and speculation following the GFC, the vast majority of derivatives contracts are entered into for the purposes of reducing or managing financial risk. Examples of how derivatives contracts can be used to manage risk have already been provided above (such as with the Chinese company using a forward contract to manage the exchange rate risk between RMB and AUD as well as the Hong Kong company using an IRS to manage interest rate risk).

However, it should be noted that derivatives cannot eliminate all risk for its users becausethere will always be an inherent risk in every derivatives contract – the risk that the counterparty may not perform its obligations under such derivatives contract (also called *credit risk*). Unlike a standard loan agreement where the lender will be exposed to the creditworthiness of the borrower but not vice versa (following drawdown), under many derivatives contracts, either party may be exposed to the creditworthiness of the other party depending on the change in the value of the underlying asset.

For example, where two parties (*Party A* and *Party B*) enter into a foreign exchange ("**FX**") swap where Party A pays 100 in Currency "X" to Party B in return for Party B paying 200 in Currency "Y" to Party A (i. e. an exchange rate of 1X to 2Y), the value of the FX swap will change depending on the movement in the exchange rate of X and Y in the market.

If the value of Y rises in relation to X during the life of the FX swap (e. g. if 1X can only buy 1.5Y in the market), the FX swap can be said to be*in the money* for Party A since Party A can obtain 2Y for 1X under the FX swap. At this point, Party A becomes exposed to the credit risk of Party B as Party A would suffer the loss of the benefit of the derivatives

---

〔1〕 http://www.sfc.hk/sfcPressRelease/EN/sfcOpenDocServlet? docno = 11PR129.

contract if Party B became insolvent and unable to perform its obligations under the FX swap.

Conversely, if the value of X rises in relation to Y during the life of the FX swap (e. g. if 1X can buy 3Y in the market), Party A would not need to worry about the creditworthiness of Party B since, Party A can obtain a better exchange rate in the market. Party B is now the party which becomes exposed to the credit risk of Party A.

Some of the techniques which the derivatives market has developed for the management of counterparty credit risk (such as close - out netting) will be explored later on in this chapter.

3.2 *Investment*

In contrast to risk management, users can construct investment positions through derivatives contracts in ways which may not be achievable through traditional investment devices. Generally speaking, there are three ways in which derivatives can provide advantages to investors seeking to gain exposure to a certain underlying asset.

3.2.1 *Access*

Derivatives instruments can be used by investors to gain access to underlying assets which they would normally be restricted from buying directly. For example, certain countries may impose limits on the amount of foreign currency denominated assets which its pension funds can invest in.[1] Subject to other regulations being complied with, it may be possible for such pension funds to nevertheless increase its exposure to foreign currency denominated assets through the use of*total return swaps*.

By way of illustration, a pension fund from country A may wish to invest in the government bonds issued by country B, but is unable to buy these bonds directly due to restrictions on its holding of foreign currency denominated assets. The pension fund can enter into a total return swap with a bank under which the pension fund will receive all of the economic performance of the government bonds of country B (including coupon payments and any movement in the value of the bonds), but the payments will be denominated in the currency of country A. In this way, the pension fund will gain exposure to the bonds without breaching the restrictions on its holding of foreign currency denominated assets.

3.2.2 *Leverage*

A prime example of the use of derivatives contracts to create leveraged investment positions is the invention of *contracts for differences* ("**CFDs**"). CFDs were initially devel-

---

[1] For example, see South Africa: http://www.resbank.co.za/RegulationAndSupervision/FinancialSurveillanceAndExchangeControl/Guidelines/Guidelines%20and%20public%20awareness/Guidelines%20-%20South%20African%20Institutional%20Investors.pdf.

oped in London[1] as a form of swap over equity securities with two main benefits: (a) no stamp duty is payable as the swap is synthetic andthere is no physical transfer of the equity securities and (b) the investor does not need to pay the purchase price of the equity securities and only needs to provide the bank counterparty with cash collateral.

CFDs quickly became a very popular tool for investing institutions (such as hedge funds) to build up a leveraged positionin underlying assets such as equity securities or commodities. This is because the initial margin required to maintain a CFD position will normally be a fraction of the notional size of the derivatives contract. For example, equity CFD contracts listed on the Australian Securities Exchange[2] only require an initial margin of AUD 3.75 per contract i. e. if an investor bought 1,000 equity CFD contracts trading at AUD 50.00 (a notional size of AUD 50,000), the investor would only be required to deliver AUD 3,750 (AUD 3.75 x 1,000 contracts) as collateral i. e. 7.5% of the total size of the investor's position (AUD 50,000 divided by AUD 3,750).

3.3 *Arbitrage*

The term "arbitrage" (套利) is used here in a general sense to describe a range of structures set up using derivatives contracts which help users to achieve their objectives in ways that traditional financial structures or transactions cannot.

One example of such a structure is the collateralized mortgage obligation ("**CMO**") created by Salomon Brothers (now part of Citigroup) and First Boston (now part of Credit Suisse) in the early 1980s. Prior to the development of the CMO, if a mortgage lender repackaged the performance (and risk) of a mortgage into a mortgage bond,[3] the mortgage lender would find it difficult to persuade investors to purchase such a bond for various reasons (some of which are described below). This meant that mortgages would remain on the mortgage lender's balance sheet to the detriment of the mortgage lender. If a mortgage lender were able to sell off the performance (and risks) of such mortgages to investors, this would free up space on the mortgage lender's balance sheet and enable the mortgage lender to extend further loans to home purchasers (and profit from such additional activity).

There are several reasons why a mortgage bond would be unattractive to investors. Firstly, since a mortgagor benefits from the equity of redemption, this means that a mortgagor

---

[1] Generally credited to UBS Warburg in the early 1990s.

[2] http://www.asx.com.au/products/initial-margins.htm.

[3] Under the terms of this mortgage bond, the bondholder would be entitled to receive all payments of principal and interest received on the mortgage but would also suffer any consequences associated with a default on the mortgage by the mortgagor.

has the right to pay off the mortgage (which serves as the underlying asset to the mortgage bond) at any point during the life ofthe mortgage. For investors, the uncertainty of when they may receive repayment of the principal amount of their investment is highly unappealing (such risk referred to as prepayment risk). This problem is particularly acute in the case of mortgages, as a mortgagor is most likely to refinance their mortgages when interest rates fall. Therefore, an investor is most likely to receive repayment of the principal amount of their investment in an economic environment where the investor will receive a low rate of return if they reinvested the money repaid by the mortgagor. Secondly, it may be difficult and/or cumbersome for investors to investigate the creditworthiness of a mortgagor to determine the default risk associated with an investment in the relevant mortgage bond. Furthermore, even where such assessment is possible, many institutional investors (such as money market funds and/or pension funds) are often restricted to holding investments with high credit ratings, and therefore would be unable to purchase mortgage bonds.

The solution devised by Salomon Brothers and First Boston was to package hundreds or thousands of mortgages together into one structured product which was then split into several tranches. If any mortgagors prepaid or defaulted on their mortgages, this would only affect the 'lowest' ranking tranche. In return for taking on such risk, investors in the lowest ranking tranche would receive a higher rate of return compared to other tranches of the structured product. The 'highest' ranking tranche received a very high credit rating on the basis that the vast majority of the mortgages (making up the underlying asset of the structured product) would need to be prepaid or be in default before investors in the highest ranking tranche would be affected.

This structure solved both the prepayment risk and credit risk associated with mortgage bonds and therefore, the invention of the CMO opened up a new market for the trading of debt securities over mortgages.

4. Document structure for derivatives contracts

4.1 *History of ISDA and the ISDA Master Agreement*

When the OTC derivatives market first evolved in theUnited States and Europe, parties (usually large international banks) needed to spend significant time and effort in negotiating bespoke derivatives contracts due to the lack of a market standard for key provisions such as the consequences following an "**Event of Default**"[1] by the counterparty.

---

[1] The definition for bolded terms can be found in the 1992 or 2002 ISDA Master Agreement.

As the number of derivatives transactions grew and the profit margin for market participants fell (due to increased competition), there was an increasing demand for legal costs and negotiation time to be reduced. Several different initiatives were launched in the derivatives market in the mid 1980's to develop a set of standard terms for derivatives contracts,[1] andone initiative ultimately led to the publication of the 1992 ISDA Master Agreement which became adopted by the majority of the derivatives market.

As stated by Mr Justice Briggs in the High Court judgment of*Lomas and others v. JFB Firth Rixson Inc and others*:[2] "The ISDA Master Agreement is one of the most widely used forms of agreement in the world. It is probably the most important standard market agreement used in the financial world. English law is one of the two systems of law most commonly chosen for the interpretation of the Master Agreement, the other being New York law."[3]

4.2 *ISDA documentation architecture*

A typical financial transaction between two parties will need contractual terms setting out both (i) the specific rights and obligations of each party under the transaction and (ii) the legal and credit 'framework' within which such transaction takes place.

One of the key reasons why the 1992 ISDA Master Agreement became the mostwidely adopted standard terms was the 'layered' approach of the ISDA Master Agreement. Under the ISDA documentation architecture, the ISDA Master Agreement and Schedule only sets out the framework of the overall trading relationship between two parties. This framework applies to every derivatives transaction entered into under the ISDA Master Agreement[4] (these include contractual terms relating to representations, Events of Default, "**Termination Events**", early termination procedures and governing law).

Where the parties wish to enter into a derivatives transaction (such as an IRS), they would execute a "**Confirmation**" (referencing the relevant ISDA Definitions depending on the relevant type of underlying asset for such derivatives product) which sets out the rights and obligations of each party under each transaction, and each Confirmation will be governed by the terms of the ISDA Master Agreement.

4.3 *Early termination under the ISDA Master Agreement*

While a clause – by – clause examination of the ISDA Master Agreement is beyond the

---

[1] Such as the Recommended Terms for Interest Rate Swaps published by the British Bankers Association (BBAIRS) and ISDA's Code of Standard Wording, Assumptions and Provisions for Swaps (Swaps Code).

[2] [2010] EWHC 3372 (Ch).

[3] *Ibid*, at para 53.

[4] As such, the ISDA Master Agreement is often referred to as an 'umbrella' agreement.

scope of this chapter, it is important toexplain the purpose of and several key provisions in the ISDA Master Agreement in order to understand how 'damages' are calculated in the context of early termination of derivatives contracts governed by the ISDA Master Agreement.

4.3.1 *Key purpose*

The key purpose of the ISDA Master Agreement is to assist market participants in managing the credit risk associated with their derivatives counterparties. The ability to manage credit risk efficiently will directly impact on an institution's profitability (by reducing the amount of regulatory capital required) and losses (arising from defaults by their counterparties). One of the mechanics used in the ISDA Master Agreement to reduce credit risk between parties is to provide for "*close – out netting*" to be available on an early termination of the ISDA Master Agreement.

4.3.2 *What is close – out netting?*

Asstated above, the ISDA Master Agreement is an 'umbrella' agreement under which two parties can enter into hundreds or thousands of derivatives transactions, some of which will be 'in – the – money' and others 'out – of – the – money' from the perspective of one party. The provisions of the ISDA Master Agreement operate to ensure that, on the insolvency of one party, the other party will not be left in the position where the liquidator or other insolvency official of the bankrupt party is able to demand the other party to continue performing transactions which are 'in – the – money' for the insolvent company but refuse to perform under transactions which are 'out – of – the – money' for the insolvent company[1] (a process known generally as "*cherry picking*").

Any derivatives contracts which a liquidator disclaims will effectively be converted into a claim for damages or losses by the solvent counterparty against the insolvent party. Unless the solvent counterparty holds some form of collateral provided by the insolvent party, it will only rank as an unsecured creditor in the insolvent estate and is unlikely to recover the full amount of its damages or losses under the disclaimed derivatives contracts.

The ISDA Master Agreement seeks to avoid this scenario by providing that, an early termination of the ISDA Master Agreement (such as when one party becomes insolvent): [2] (1) the future rights and obligations of both parties under all of the derivatives transactions

---

[1] See section 178 of the Insolvency Act 1986 (United Kingdom), which provides that the liquidator of a company has the power to disclaim unprofitable contracts. Similar powers are often provided to liquidators in other jurisdictions (see section 59 of the Bankruptcy Ordinance (Cap. 6) (Hong Kong)).

[2] An ISDA master Agreement will terminate early if one party designates an "Early Termination Date". A party will have the right to do this if an Event of Default or Termination Event (under which all transactions are "Affected Transactions".) See Sections 5 and 6 of the 1992 ISDA Master Agreement.

entered into under the ISDA Master Agreement are terminated; and(2) a single sum(the "**early termination payment amount**")[1] becomes payable by one party to the other party as compensation for such termination.

This process is known as "*close – out netting*".

4.3.3 *Close – out netting and regulatory capital*

The enforceability of close – out netting is critical to participants in the derivatives market[2] to reduce their exposure to counterparties in the event of the insolvency of such counterparties. However, the availability of close – out netting is also very important during the 'day – to – day' operations of such market participantsas it reduces the amount of regulatory capital required by such parties.

For example, Bank A and Bank B have entered into two IRS transactions. Under the first IRS, Bank A has an exposure of USD 75 to Bank B(i. e. if the IRS were terminated, it would cost Bank A USD 75 to replace the IRS with another counterparty) and under the second IRS, Bank B has an exposure of USD 50 to Bank A.

From Bank A's perspective, the worst case scenario in the event that Bank B becomes insolvent is that Bank B ceases to perform under the first IRS(meaning that Bank A will need to spend USD 75 to find a replacement IRS) while Bank A is still contractually bound to continue performing under the second IRS. However, if close – out netting is enforceable, in the event of Bank B's insolvency, Bank A would be able to terminate both IRSs and claim an amount equal to USD 25(being Bank A's exposure to Bank B(USD 75) less Bank B's exposure to Bank A(USD 50)) from Bank B's estate. Even if Bank A is an unsecured creditor and may be unlikely to recover the full USD25, it is still in a better position than if close – out netting were not available.

For institutions which are governed by regulatory capital rules(such as banks), theyare required to set aside far more capital against exposures to derivatives counterparties if close – out netting is not available. So in the above example, if close – out netting were not available, Bank A would be required to set aside sufficient regulatory capital for an exposure of USD 75 to Bank B(i. e. gross exposure), but such exposure would be reduced to USD 25 if Bank A could demonstrate that close – out netting is legally enforceable against Bank B(i. e. net exposure).

---

[1] The valuation process is explained further below under paragraph 5(*Damages in the context of the ISDA Master Agreement*).

[2] In fact, ISDA has commissioned legal opinions in over 50 different jurisdictions in the world to ensure that close – out netting is available under the laws of such jurisdictions.

5. Damages in the context of the ISDA Master Agreement

5.1 *Distinction between early termination payment amount and damages*

Under the description of the close – out netting process above, the second step of the process requires the early termination payment amount to be determined with respect to the "**Terminated Transactions**". This section explains the determination process under the ISDA Master Agreement.

It is important to highlight at the outset that the provisions in the ISDA Master Agreement governing the determination of the early termination payment amount should not be classified as a liquidated damages clause and therefore will not necessarily be subject to the contractual principles surrounding liquidated damages clauses.

This is because the close – out netting process under the ISDA Master Agreement can be triggeredby a wide variety of events, not all of which will involve a breach of the terms of the ISDA Master Agreement. [1] Furthermore, as will be described below, it is possible for the early termination payment amount to be payable from the 'innocent' party to the party which defaulted under the ISDA Master Agreement, [2] which is very different from the general principle of contractual damages that the party in breach of a contract should not benefit from such breach.

This view was espoused by Mr Justice Flaux in*Britannia Bulk plc v. Pioneer Navigation Ltd and others*, [3] cited with approval by Mr. Justice Briggs in *Anthracite Rated Investments (Jersey) Ltd v. Lehman Brothers Finance SA (in liquidation)* [4] and confirmed by the Court of Appeal in *Lomas and others v. JFB Firth Rixson Inc and others*. [5]

As such, it is more accurate to describe the close – out netting process under the ISDA Master Agreement as the pre – agreed mechanism by which the parties wish to terminate their derivatives transactions on the occurrence of certain events concluding with the determination and payment of the early termination payment amount by one party to the other.

---

[1] For example, tax event (section 5 (b) (ii) of the 1992 ISDA Master Agreement) and insolvency (section 5 (a) (vii) of the 1992 ISDA Master Agreement) does not amount to a breach of contract as there is no obligation on the parties to prevent such events from occurring.

[2] If the Second Method applies with respect to a 1992 ISDA Master Agreement or if the parties entered into the 2002 ISDA Master Agreement.

[3] [2011] EWHC 692 (Ch).

[4] [2011] EWHC 1822 (Ch) at para 116.

[5] [2012] EWCA Civ 419 at para 131.

5.2 *Early termination payment amount as a penalty*?

However, to the extent that the close – out netting process is triggered as a result of a party breaching its obligations under the ISDA Master Agreement (such as failure to pay or deliver[1] or breach of obligation[2]), consideration may need to be given to the question of whether the terms of the ISDA Master Agreement requiring the payment of the early termination payment amount may be void on the grounds that it operates as a penalty.

As set out under Chitty on Contracts (30th edn, 2008) at paragraph 26 – 125: "Where the parties to a contract agree that, in the event of a breach, the contract – breaker shall pay to the other a specified sum of money, the sum fixed may be classified by the courts either as a penalty (which is irrecoverable) or as liquidated damages (which are recoverable)."

The crucial question which needs to be considered in classifying a contractual term as either a liquidated damages provision or a penalty clause is whether "the alleged penalty clause can pass muster as a genuine pre – estimate of loss".[3]

As summarized by Lord Dunedin in *Dunlop Pneumatic Tyre Co Ltd v. New Garage and Motor Co Ltd*,[4] whether a payment stipulated by a contractual provision is a penalty or not is a question of construction. One of the tests suggested for consideration is whether "the sum stipulated for is extravagant and unconscionable in amount in comparison with the greatest loss which could conceivably be proved to have followed from the breach."

As will be explored further in this chapter, the calculation methodology for determining the early termination payment amount under the ISDA Master Agreement (whether under the 1992 version or the 2002 version) is intended to be an amount which reflects the value of both a party's accrued rights under the derivatives transactions governed by the ISDA Master Agreement as well as their future rights and obligations under such contracts. On this basis, it would appear that there is little basis for arguing that the close – outnetting provisions under the ISDA Master Agreement constitute a penalty clause.

This issue has been considered in the English courts before in *BNP Paribas v. Wockhardt EU Operations (Swiss) AG*,[5] which involved the non – payment by the defendant under a series of FX forward transactions governed by the 2002 ISDA Master Agreement. In this case, the defendant attempted to claim that the early termination payment amount determined by the claimant was unenforceable by reason of the doctrine relating to penalties. Mr

---

〔1〕 See section 5(a)(i) of the 1992 ISDA Master Agreement.

〔2〕 See section 5(a)(ii) of the 1992 ISDA Master Agreement.

〔3〕 *Lordsvale Finance Plc v. Bank of Zambia* [1996] Q. B. 752, 762 – 4, cited with approval in *Euro London Appointments Ltd v. Claessens International Ltd* [2006] EWCA Civ 385.

〔4〕 [1915] A. C. 79.

〔5〕 [2009] EWHC 3116.

Justice Christopher Clarke decided against the defendant on the issue of penalties and gave the following reasoning: "The effect of the provisions is not that either party receives a windfall but that both receive the benefit (or disbenefit) of the unperformed transactions comprising their agreement crystallized at an earlier point in time (of the Non Defaulting party's choosing). Whilst the analogy is not exact, since the amount, if any, payable as an Early Termination Amount (and thus the total value of the performance remaining) will change throughout the life of the agreement in line with market fluctuations, there is nothing penal in a provision which requires the acceleration in the event of breach of an amount which, without breach, would become due later."[1]

It should also be noted that under section 6(e)(iv) of the 1992 ISDA Master Agreement, the parties agree that the early termination payment amount represents "a reasonable pre-estimate of loss and not a penalty. Such amount is payable for the loss of bargain and the loss of protection against future risks and except as otherwise provided in this Agreement neither party will be entitled to recover any additional damages as a consequence of such losses."

5.3 *Two versions of the ISDA Master Agreement*

Before proceeding further in this chapter, itshould be highlighted that there are two versions of the ISDA Master Agreement which are generally used in the market: the 1992 ISDA Master Agreement and the 2002 ISDA Master Agreement.[2] For the purposes of this chapter, theearly termination payment mechanics under the 1992 ISDA Master Agreement will first be explored before describing the developments made in the 2002 ISDA Master Agreement.

5.3.1 *Determination of the early termination payment amount under the* 1992 *ISDA Master Agreement*

5.3.1.1 *Designation of Early Termination Date*

Under the 1992 ISDA Master Agreement, the close-out netting process is set out under section 6(*Early Termination*). Sections 6(a) and 6(b) provide that, following the occurrence of an Event of Default[3] or Termination Event[4] under which all transactions are

---

[1] *Ibid*, at paragraph 38.

[2] The 2002 ISDA Master Agreement was developed by ISDA in response to several market shocks (such as the collapse of Long Term Capital Management in 1998 following the default by the Russian government on their government bonds). This version of the ISDA Master Agreement contains some new provisions (such as force majeure and set-off) as well as amendments to certain existing mechanics (such as the early termination payment mechanics to be explained in this chapter).

[3] As set out under section 5(a) of the 1992 ISDA Master Agreement.

[4] As set out under section 5(b) of the 1992 ISDA Master Agreement.

Affected Transactions, the relevant party[1] will have the right to designate an "**Early Termination Date**" with respect to the 1992 ISDA Master Agreement.

Following the designation of an Early Termination Date, each party's obligation to make further payments or deliveries under the derivatives transactions governed by the 1992 ISDA Master Agreement will be terminated. Instead, the early termination payment amount will be determined in accordance with section 6(e) of the 1992 ISDA Master Agreement and becomes payable by one party to the other party shortly following the Early Termination Date.[2]

5.3.1.2 *Section 6(e) calculation of early termination payment amount*

Under section 6(e) of the 1992 ISDA Master Agreement, the method by which the early termination payment amount is calculated will depend on: (1) whether "**First Method**" or "**Second Method**" is applicable; and (2) whether "**Market Quotation**" or "**Loss**" is applicable.[3]

The parties should make their elections when entering into the 1992 ISDA Master Agreement by specifying which combination is applicable in the Schedule to the 1992 ISDA Master Agreement. If the parties do not make any election, then Second Method and Market Quotation will be deemed applicable.[4]

5.3.1.2.1 *Party making the determination*

Before explaining the calculation methodology for determining the early termination payment amount, it is important to first establish which party under the 1992 ISDA Master Agreement is responsible for calculating such amount. This is dependent on the type of event leading to the designation of an Early Termination Date under the 1992 ISDA Master Agreement: (1) if as a result of an Event of Default, the "**Non-defaulting Party**" will determine the early termination payment amount;[5] (2) if as a result of a Termination Event with respect to which there is only one "**Affected Party**", the party which is not the Affected Party (the "**Non-affected Party**") will determine the early termination payment

[1] For an Event of Default, this will be the Non-defaulting Party. For a Termination Event, where there is one "*Affected Party*", this will be Non-affected Party. If both parties are Affected Parties, then this will be either party.

[2] See section 6(c) of the 1992 ISDA Master Agreement.

[3] i.e. there are a total of four different options for the parties to choose from: (a) First Method and Market Quotation, (b) First Method and Loss, (c) Second Method and Market Quotation or (d) Second Method and Loss.

[4] See section 6(e) of the 1992 ISDA Master Agreement.

[5] See section 6(e)(i) of the 1992 ISDA Master Agreement.

amount;[1] and(3) if as a result of a Termination Event with respect to which both parties are Affected Parties, the average of both parties' calculation will be used as the early termination payment amount.[2]

The right for a party to determine the early termination payment amount can be very important as the provisions of the 1992 ISDA Master Agreement are designed to protect the position of the party making the determination(irrespective of whether the Market Quotation or Loss methodology applies). This advantage is described in detail further below.

5.3.1.2.2 *Relevant authorities*

There have been remarkably few judgments on the interpretation of theearly termination payment provisions of the ISDA Master Agreement given that the 1992 version has been published in the market for nearly twenty years now. There could be many potential reasons for this, although it is submitted that one important factor may be the desire of participants in the derivatives market, when faced with a potential dispute or litigation, to settle matters swiftly and carry on business rather than see such matters through to trial.

However, with the turmoil in the financial markets in recent years, there have been several judgments handed down with respect to the close – out valuation methodology under the 1992 ISDA Master Agreement. As set out by Mr Justice Briggs in*Lehman Brothers International(Eurpoe) v. Lehman Brothers Finance SA(in liquidation)*,[3] there are now six authorities on the early termination payment provisions of the 1992 ISDA Master Agreement. They are: (1) *Australia and New Zealand Banking Group Ltd v. Societe Generale* [2000] CLC 833, (2) *Peregrine Fixed Income Ltd(in liquidation) v. Robinson Department Store plc* [2000] CLC 1328, (3) *Britannia Bulk plc(in liquidation) v. Pioneer Navigation Ltd* [2011] 2 Lloyd's Rep 84, (4) *Pioneer Freight Futures Co Ltd v. TMT Asia Ltd* [2011] 2 Lloyd's Rep 96, (5) *Anthracite Rated Investments(Jersey) Ltd v. Lehman Brothers Finance SA(in liquidation)* [2011] 2 Lloyd's Rep 538, and(6) *Lomas & others v. JFB Firth Rixson* [2012] EWCA Civ 419.

The most comprehensive summary of the judicial principles with respect to the early termination payment provisions of the 1992 ISDA Master Agreement was set out by Mr Justice Briggs in *Anthracite Rated Investments(Jersey) Ltd v. Lehman Brothers Finance SA(in liquidation)*.[4] Givenits importance, it is necessary to set out the summary in full here:

---

[1] See section 6(e)(ii)(1) of the 1992 ISDA Master Agreement.

[2] See section 6(e)(ii)(2) of the 1992 ISDA Master Agreement.

[3] [2012] EWHC 1072(Ch) at para 40.

[4] [2011] EWHC 1822(Ch), and affirmed by the Court of Appeal in *Lomas & others v. JFB Firth Rixson* [2012] EWCA Civ 419 at para 131.

"(1) Loss and Market Quotation are, although different formulae, aimed at achieving broadly the same result, so that outcomes derived from one may be usefully tested by way of cross – check by reference to the other: see per Mance LJ in the Australia case at paras 2, 15 and 22. This derived from a concession in that case, but has subsequently been reaffirmed after adversarial argument in the Peregrine case at para 30, in the Britannia Bulk case at paras 44 to 46 and 51, and in the Pioneer case at paras 98 and 105. It is one of those sensible concessions which has hardened into hornbook law.

(2) The identification of the non – defaulting party's loss of bargain arising from the termination of the Derivative Transaction requires a "clean" rather than "dirty" market valuation of the lost transaction. This means that the loss of bargain must be valued on an assumption that, but for termination, the transaction would have proceeded to a conclusion, and that all conditions to its full performance by both sides would have been satisfied, however improbable that assumption may be in the real world: see in the Australia case at paras 5, 22 to 27 and 30 – 31, the Britannia Bulk case at paras 11 to 14 and 34 – 35, and in the Pioneer case at paras 112 to 117.

(3) The termination payment formulae under s 6(e) are not to be equated with, or interpreted rigidly in accordance with, the quantification of damages at common law for breach of contract. They are methods of calculating close – out positions on the termination of a derivative transaction or series of transactions: see the Britannia Bulk case per Flaux J at para 37. This is, in particular, because the Second Method works both ways, and may lead to a close – out payment due to the defaulting party."

The reasoning behind the three principles set out above will be explored in this chapter at the relevant points.

5.3.1.2.3 *Market Quotation methodology*

The definition of Market Quotation under the 1992 ISDA Master Agreement is as follows: "'**Market Quotation**' means, with respect to one or more Terminated Transactions and a party making the determination, an amount determined on the basis of quotations from Reference Market – makers. Each quotation will be for an amount, if any, that would be paid to such party (expressed as a negative number) or by such party (expressed as a positive number) in consideration of an agreement between such party (taking into account any existing Credit Support Document with respect to the obligations of such party) and the quoting Reference Market – maker to enter into a transaction (the "Replacement Transaction") that would have the effect of preserving for such party the economic equivalent of any payment or delivery (whether the underlying obligation was absolute or contingent and assuming the satisfaction of each applicable condition precedent) by the parties under Section 2(a)(i) in respect of such Terminated Transaction or group of Terminated Transactions that would, but for the occurrence of the relevant Early Termination Date, have been required after that date. For this purpose, Unpaid Amounts in respect of the Terminated Transaction or group of Terminated Transactions are to be excluded but, without limitation, any payment or delivery that would, but for the relevant Early Termination Date, have been required (assuming satisfaction of each applicable condition precedent) after that Early Termination Date is to be included. The Replacement Transaction would be subject to such documentation as such party and the Reference Market – maker may, in good faith, agree. The party making the determination (or its agent) will request each Reference Market – maker to provide its quotation to the extent reasonably practicable as of the same day and time (without regard to different time zones) on or as soon as reasonably practicable after the relevant Early Termination Date. The day and time as of which those quotations are to be obtained will be selected in good faith by the party obliged to make a determination under Section 6(e), and, if each party is so obliged, after consultation with the other. If more than three quotations are provided, the Market Quotation will be the arithmetic mean of the quotations, without regard to the quotations having the highest and lowest values. If exactly three such quotations are provided, the Market Quotation will be the quotation remaining after disregarding the highest and lowest quotations. For this purpose, if more than one quotation has the same highest value or lowest value, then one of such quotations shall be disregarded. If fewer than three quotations are provided, it will be deemed that the Market Quotation in respect of such Terminated Transaction or group of Terminated Transactions cannot be determined."

Where the parties have selected the Market Quotation methodology for determining the early termination payment amount, the early termination payment amount will be made up of two components: the "**Settlement Amounts**" and the "**Unpaid Amounts**".

In summary, the early termination payment amount calculated on the basis of the Market Quotation methodology will be made up of: (1) positive Market Quotations (i. e. amounts which the Non – defaulting Party would need to pay to Reference Market – makers to enter into replacement transactions); (2) **plus** negative Market Quotations (i. e. amounts which the Non – defaulting Party would receive from Reference Market – makers for entering into replacement transactions); (3) **plus** Unpaid Amounts which are due from the Defaulting Party to the Non – defaulting Party; (4) **minus** Unpaid Amounts which are due from the Non – defaulting Party to the Defaulting Party. (the first two bullet points take into account the Settlement Amounts and the latter two bullet points take into account the Unpaid Amounts)

The Unpaid Amounts represents the payment and/or delivery obligations which were due prior to the Early Termination Date from either party to the other but were not discharged, together with interest (at the "**Applicable Rate**"[1]) on such amount from the date such obligation was due until the Early Termination Date.

The determination of the Settlement Amounts using Market Quotations is built on the principle of determining the 'replacement value' of all of the outstanding derivatives transactions entered into between the parties under a 1992 ISDA Master Agreement from the point of view of the party making the calculation.

The 'replacement value' of a derivatives transaction is the amount which a party (the "**Determining Party**"[2]) would need to pay to a new counterparty (or receive from such new counterparty) in consideration for such new counterparty to enter into a replacement derivatives transaction with the Determining Party which has" the effect of preserving for such party the economic equivalent of any payment or delivery... that would, but for the occurrence of the relevant Early Termination Date, have been required after that date.[3]

In practice, the Determining Party will be required to obtain, in respect of every derivatives transaction under the ISDA Master Agreement, a set of quotations (reflecting the 'replacement value' as described above) from four "**Reference Market – makers**". Each Reference Market – maker will be selected by the Determining Party in good faith and needs to be a dealer in the relevant derivatives market.[4] For each derivatives transaction (or group of derivatives transactions if the Determining Party decides to obtain quotations in the market in such manner), if more than three quotations are provided by the Reference Market – makers, the arithmetic mean of those prices (ignoring the highest and lowest price) will be the Market Quotation in respect of such derivatives transaction(s). If the Determining Party receives three quotations exactly, the highest and lowest quotation will be ignored and the remaining quotation will be the Market Quotation. If fewer than three quotations are received by the Determining Party, the value of such derivatives transaction will instead be determined by the Loss methodology (as described further below).

(1) Bid/Offer spread

---

[1] The Applicable Rate i. e. the rate at which interest accumulates on obligations which became due prior to an Early Termination Date but were not discharged will depend on whether (a) an Event of Default or Termination Event led to the close – out of the ISDA Master Agreement and (b) the obligation was due from the Defaulting Party or the Non – defaulting Party.

[2] Note that the term "Determining Party" is only defined under the 2002 ISDA Master Agreement and is not used under the 1992 ISDA Master Agreement. In the context of this chapter, the term "Determining Party" is also used in relation to the 1992 ISDA Master Agreement to refer to the party calculating the early termination payment amount payable.

[3] See the definition of "Market Quotation" under section 14 of the 1992 ISDA Master Agreement.

[4] See the definition of "Reference Market – maker" under section 14 of the 1992 ISDA Master Agreement.

When a Reference Market - maker provides a quotation for any derivatives transaction, just as with any foreign currency exchangeservice provider, there will be a bid/offer spread built into the 'price' which reflects the profit to be made by the Reference Market - maker from offering this derivatives product to the market. Generally speaking, the smaller the difference (or "*spread*") between the bid price and the offer price for an asset, the greater the liquidity(流通性) of the asset.

As a result of the bid/offer spread, the Determining Party will, in obtaining quotations from Reference Market - makers for the terminated derivatives transactions, show a larger loss or smaller gain than if the defaulting party had been responsible for obtaining such quotations. This effect is compounded for derivatives transactions which are more bespoke (i. e. less liquid), since the bid/offer spread is likely to be greater.

(2) Creditworthiness of Determining Party

Since the basis of Market Quotation is for Reference Market - makers to provide a 'price' (the quotation) for entering into a replacement derivatives transaction with the Determining Party, this led to the question of whether Reference Market - makers should take into account the creditworthiness of the Determining Party in providing their quotations.

In the case of*Peregrine Fixed Income Ltd v. Robinson Department Store Public Company Ltd*,[1] the High Court determined that Reference Market - makers were entitled to take into account the creditworthiness of the Determining Party when providing quotations for the terminated derivatives transactions. However, the facts of this particular case were very bespoke and therefore the conclusion of the court needs to be carefully considered.

Peregrine and Robinson had entered into one derivatives transaction under a 1992 ISDA Master Agreement (electing Market Quotation, Second Method and "**Automatic Early Termination**"[2]). Unlike most derivatives transactions which involve obligations on both parties, the derivatives transaction in this case was more akin to a loan under which Robinson is required to make periodic payments of a fixed sum to Peregrine. Peregrine 和 Robinson

When Peregrine became insolvent, an Early Termination Date was deemed to be designated on the date of insolvency as a result of the election ofAutomatic Early Termination. As the non - defaulting party, Robinson was responsible for obtaining quotations from Refer-

[1] [2000] C. L. C. 1328.

[2] Automatic Early Termination is switched on by parties under the ISDA Master Agreement in cases where there may be doubts as to the enforceability of close - out netting with respect to one or both parties due to the applicable insolvency laws. The effect of Automatic Early Termination is to designate an Early Termination Date for all derivatives transactions governed by such ISDA Master Agreement immediately prior to the insolvency of the relevant party.

ence Market – makers as per the terms of the 1992 ISDA Master Agreement. However, Robinson did not obtain quotations until nearly two years after the Early Termination Date, by which time Robinson itself had also run into financial difficulties and had entered a restructuring.

When Robinson asked Reference Market – makers to provide quotations for the derivatives transaction between Robinson and Peregrine, the Reference Market – makers were effectively quoting a ' price ' for the right to receive payments from Robinson under the derivatives transaction (which the parties agreed was worth approximately USD 87.3 million in present value[1]). As a result of Robinson's lack of creditworthiness, three Reference Market – makers responded with quotations worthonly USD 750,000, USD 9.5 million and USD 25.5 million. As per the definition of "Market Quotation", the highest and lowest prices were ignored and Robinson determined that according to the Market Quotation methodology, the derivatives transaction was "in – the – money" for Peregrine for an amount equal to USD 9.5 million.

Peregrine contended in court that it was wrong for the Market Quotation methodology of determining the early termination payment amount to reduce what originally was a derivatives transaction worth (in present value terms) USD 87.3 million to Peregrine to an early termination payment amount equal to approximately USD 9.7 million due to the lack of creditworthiness of Robinson. The court agreed with Peregrine's submission and determined that although Reference Market – makers were entitled to take into account Robinson's lack of creditworthiness when providing quotations, the Market Quotation methodology produced a commercially unreasonable result and therefore the early termination payment amount should instead have been determined using the Loss methodology (under which the Determining Party's creditworthiness could not be taken into account). The Loss methodology is discussed further below.

It should be noted that this decision has received criticism from certain market participants[2] and even Mr Justice Moore – Bick acknowledged that "This case is far from being

---

〔1〕 A very interesting point to note is that the derivatives market takes a very different approach to future payment obligations under a contract compared to the loan market. Where a loan facility becomes accelerated as a result of an Event of Default by the borrower, the lender will typically only look to recover the outstanding principal amount of the loan and any accrued interest (see clause 28.20 (*Acceleration*) of the Loan Market Association template for *Senior Multicurrency Term and Revolving Facilities Agreement for Leveraged Acquisition Finance Transactions*). In contrast, under the ISDA Master Agreement, the non – defaulting party will be entitled to recover the present value of all future payments it is owed.

〔2〕 See, for example, the Allen & Overy memorandum to ISDA members (available on the ISDA website at http://www2.isda.org/search?keyword=peregrine).

typical of those to which these provisions are likely to apply. Only one transaction between these two parties has been affected by the Early Termination provisions of Section 6 and that transaction is itself far from being a typical swap transaction." However, the principle that taking into account the Determining Party's creditworthiness will lead to a commercially unreasonable result and should therefore be ignored has been reinforced by subsequent cases on this point (see below).

(3) Commercially reasonable result

Under the definition of Settlement Amount in the 1992 ISDA Master Agreement, paragraph (b) provides that the Loss methodology should be used where "Market Quotation... would not (in the reasonable belief of the party making the determination) produce a commercially reasonable result."

Under New York law, where a procedure is agreed between parties to determine the amount of liquidated damages payable (and there is authority that the Market Quotation methodology constitutes a liquidated damages clause[1]), provided that such procedure was not unconscionable when the parties entered into the agreement, the New York courts will not look at the reasonableness of the outcome of such calculation (on the basis that the party determining the liquidated damages complied with the procedure). Generally, the same approach will be adopted under English law.

However, as a result of the inclusion of the wording set out above under paragraph (b) of the definition of Settlement Amount, it is quite possible that a reasonableness test has been imported into the Market Quotation methodology, as was the case in the *Peregrine* case.

Furthermore, it appears that the reasonableness of the Market Quotation methodology will be determined by reference to the Loss methodology. For example, Mr Justice Flaux has stated that: "Given that the definition of Settlement Amount expressly contemplates that, if a Market Quotation cannot be determined or would not produce a commercially reasonable result, the fallback position will be a calculation of Loss, it would be very odd if the two payment measures were not intended to achieve broadly the same result, in terms of the payments that have to be made either way by way of close out, on the termination of a transaction or series of transactions."[2]

Therefore, regardless of whether the parties to a 1992 ISDA Master Agreement elected for Market Quotation, it will be necessary for the Determining Party to attempt to determine the early termination payment amount by reference to Loss in order to determine whether the

---

[1] *Drexel Financial Products v. Midland Bank Ltd* US Dist LEXIS 21223 (SDNY, 1992).

[2] *Britannia Bulk plc v. Pioneer Navigation Limited* [2011] EWHC 692 (Comm) at para 44.

result provided by the Market Quotation methodology is commercially reasonable.

(4) Indicative quotation vs firm quotation

When Reference Market – makers provide quotations to the Determining Party, it is possible that such quotations are only "indicative quotations" rather than "firm quotations". As the name suggests, an indicative quotation is only a reasonable estimate of the 'price' at which the Reference Market – maker is willing to enter into the derivatives transaction with the Determining Party, whereas with a firm quotation, the Reference Market – makerhas given an offer to the Determining Party and is obliged to enter into the derivatives transaction at the price specified in such firm quotation if the Determining Party elects to accept such an offer.

Since Reference Market – makers will typically know that they have been approached by the Determining Party to provide quotations for derivatives transactions only for the purpose of assisting the Determining Party in calculating the early termination payment amount and that the Determining Party is not genuinely interested in transacting with the Reference Market – makers, the quotations provided by the Reference Market – makers maybe determined with a lower level of due diligence than the Reference Market – makers would normally conduct. Commentators have suggested that the use of indicative quotations to calculate the early termination payment amount may be open to challenge if such quotations did not reflect the true trading price of the derivatives transaction being valued.[1]

5.3.1.2.4 *Loss methodology*

The definition of Loss under the 1992 ISDA Master Agreement is as follows: ""**Loss**" means, with respect to this Agreement or one or more Terminated Transactions, as the case may be, and a party, the Termination Currency Equivalent of an amount that party reasonably determines in good faith to be its total losses and costs (or gain, in which case expressed as a negative number) in connection with this Agreement or that Terminated Transaction or group of Terminated Transactions, as the case may be, including any loss of bargain, cost of funding or, at the election of such party but without duplication, loss or cost incurred as a result of its terminating, liquidating, obtaining or reestablishing any hedge or related trading position (or any gain resulting from any of them). Loss includes losses and costs (or gains) in respect of any payment or delivery required to have been made (assuming satisfaction of each applicable condition precedent) on or before the relevant Early Termination Date and not made, except, so as to avoid duplication, if Section 6(e)(i)(1) or (3) or 6(e)(ii)(2)(A) applies. Loss does not include a party's legal fees and out – of – pocket expenses referred to under Section 11. A party will determine its Loss as of the relevant Early Termina-

[1] See chapter 11 of *Derivatives: Law and Practice* by Simon Firth.

tion Date, or, if that is not reasonably practicable, as of the earliest date thereafter as is reasonably practicable. A party may (but need not) determine its Loss by reference to quotations of relevant rates or prices from one or more leading dealers in the relevant markets."

The Loss methodology is used to determine the early termination payment amount in two situations: when the parties elected to use the Loss methodology in the Schedule to the 1992 ISDA Master Agreement or if the Determining Party decides that the Market Quotation methodology does not produce a commercially reasonable result.

Unlike the Market Quotation methodology, which is intended to produce a early termination payment amount through relatively objective means, the Loss methodology is subjectively determined by the Determining Party.[1] As the name suggests, the Determining Party calculates the total loss incurred or gain received as a result of the termination of the derivatives transactions entered into under the 1992 ISDA Master Agreement. This calculation is to be made as of the Early Termination Date unless it is not reasonably practicable to do so.

In contrast to Market Quotation, which is comprised of Settlement Amounts (representing future rights and obligations under the terminated derivatives transactions) and Unpaid Amounts (representing accrued rights and obligations under the terminated derivatives transactions), both of these elements are taken into account in oneamount representing the Determining Party's losses or gains.

However, as stated above, the generally accepted approach now is for the Market Quotation methodology and the Loss methodology to produce a broadly similar result.[2]

Under the definition of Loss in the 1992 ISDA Master Agreement,[3] the Determining Party can take into account any "loss of bargain, cost of funding or... loss or cost incurred as a result of its terminating, liquidating, obtaining or reestablishing any hedge or related trading position (or any gain resulting from any of them)".

In many ways, the Loss methodology adopts an approach which is very similar to the general principle of contractual damages where "[t]he claimant is, as far as money can do it, to be placed in the same position as if the contract had been performed".[4]

---

[1] Mark Phillips QC has described the Market Quotation measure as providing "*a rigid and mechanistic approach which produces an objectively verifiable result*" (see para 27 of *Britannia Bulk plc v. Pioneer Navigation Limited* [2011] EWHC 692).

[2] See, for example, para 98 of *Pioneer Freight Futures Company Ltd (in liquidation) v. TMT Asia Ltd* [2011] EWHC 778 (Comm).

[3] See the definition of Loss under section 14 of the 1992 ISDA Master Agreement.

[4] See paragraph 26 - 001 of Chitty on Contracts (30th Ed.) and *Golden Strait Corp v. Nippon Yusen Kubishika Kaisha* [2007] 2 A. C. 353.

For example, on the basis that there is an available derivatives market for a Determining Party to enter into a replacement transaction with respect to a terminatedIRS (where the Determining Party was paying the fixed rate of interest), it is submitted that the Loss should be determined by reference to the difference between the fixed rate of interest under the terminated derivatives transaction and the fixed rate of interest which the Determining Party would need to pay under a replacement IRS to achieve the same economic effect as the terminated derivatives transaction.[1]

As explained by Mr Justice Toulson in*Dampski Bsselskabet "Norden" A/S v. Andre & CIE. S. A*[2] at paragraph 41: "The broad principle deducible from the Elena d' Amico and the authorities there considered is that where a contract is discharged by reason of one party's breach, and that party's unperformed obligation is of a kind for which there exists an available market in which the innocent party could obtain a substitute contract, the innocent party's loss will ordinarily he measured by the extent to which his financial position would be worse under the substitute contract than under the original contract."

The advantage of this approach is that "[t]he availability of a substitute market enables a market valuation to be made of what the innocent party has lost, and a line thereby to be drawn under the transaction."[3]

Although this method of determining Loss appears to be similar to Market Quotation, it should be noted that the definition of Loss under the 1992 ISDA Master Agreement provides explicitly that the Determining Party "may (but need not) determine its Loss by reference to quotations of relevant rates or prices from one or more leading dealers in the relevant markets."

(1) Creditworthiness of Determining Party not relevant

In contrast to the Market Quotation methodology, where the judgment in the*Peregrine* case determined that the creditworthiness of the Determining Party could be taken into account when obtaining quotations from Reference Market - makers (although this led to a commercially unreasonable result), under the Loss methodology, it was decided that the opposite was true and the Determining Party's creditworthiness could not be considered in assessing its Loss.

Over time, the requirement for the creditworthiness of the Determining Party to be ig-

---

[1] See *Transfield Shipping Inc v. Mercator Shipping Inc (The Achilleas)* [2008] UKHL 48 in relation to the application of this principle to determining damages for breach of a charterparty.

[2] 2003 EWHC 84 Comm.

[3] See Lord Bingham in *Golden Strait Corp v. Nippon Yusen Kubishika Kaisha* [2007] UKHL 12 at para 20 approving of the dictum provided by Mr Justice Toulsen in *Dampski Bsselskabet "Norden" A/S v. Andre & CIE. S. A* 2003 EWHC 84 Comm.

nored in determining the early termination payment amount under the ISDA Master Agreement has been referred to as the 'clean' valuation process, with the opposite method being dubbed 'dirty'.[1]

Under the general principles applicable to contractual damages, the solvency of the parties is not taken into account when determining the quantum of damages. In the case of *Chiemgauer Membran Und Zeltbau GmbH v. The New Millennium Experience Company Limited*,[2] the claimant was assisting in the construction of the roof for the Millennium Dome in London (managed by the defendant). Under the construction contract, the defendant had the right to terminate the contract at any point provided that the claimant was entitled to recover certain amounts to cover "any direct loss and/or damage caused to [the claimant] by the [termination]". As the claimant became insolvent shortly after the termination of the contract, the defendant contended that the claimant's losses should be discounted by the fact that it would not have been possible for the claimant to perform the construction contract in any event. The court considered that "where a contract is terminated by the acceptance of a repudiation, the repudiating party is not entitled to contend that the innocent party could not or might not have performed the contract according to its terms".[3]

Arguments have been raised for the creditworthiness of the Determining Party to be taken into account when determining Loss under the 1992 ISDA Master Agreement. Under an action for breach of contract, the court will be assessing the consequences of such breach from the 'innocent' party's point of view (i. e. the losses suffered by the innocent party as a result of the breach). Similarly, the Loss methodology requires the Determining Party to assess its losses or gains under the terminated derivatives transactions.

Under the *Peregrine* case, the Non – defaulting Party was Robinson, who (if the Loss methodology was applicable) would need to assess its gain as a result of the insolvency of Peregrine (since under the terminated derivatives transaction, Robinson was under an obligation to make payments to Peregrine). Unfortunately, the effect of the close – out netting mechanism was to create an 'early' payment obligation due from Robinson to Peregrine (since periodic payments from Robinson to Peregrine under the derivatives transaction

〔1〕 See, for example, *Lehman Brothers International (Europe) v. Lehman Brothers Finance S. A.* [2012] EWHC 1072 (Ch) at para 39.

〔2〕 2000 WL 1918504.

〔3〕 Clearly, the case involved a termination in accordance with the terms of the contract rather than a repudiation of the contract. However, the court considered that the analogy with repudiation was apt because in both cases (termination in accordance with the terms of the contract and repudiation), certain causation issues are side – stepped since the contract specifically sets out the types of damage which are recoverable.

which should have been spread out over the remainder of the term of the derivatives transaction were converted into a single lump sum payment(i. e. the early termination payment amount) payable shortly after the Early Termination Date).

The requirement under the close – outnetting mechanism of the 1992 ISDA Master Agreement for Robinson to pay such early termination payment amount to Peregrine can be considered a 'cost' for Robinson, since Robinson needs to secure a source of funds in order to finance the payment of the early termination payment amount to Peregrine. As a result of Robinson's lack of creditworthiness, it is very likely that Robinson would have needed to incur higher than normal costs to secure such funding.

However, it is submitted that given the strong line of judicial authority which has now emerged on the "continuity assumption" (discussed later on in this chapter), the courts are very unlikely allow a Determining Party to take into account its own creditworthiness in assessing Loss under the 1992 ISDA Master Agreement.

It is submitted that there are two important arguments for the adoption of the 'clean' valuation process. Firstly, to take into account the creditworthiness of the Determining Party would introduce a serious risk of 'moral hazard' in the valuation process, since the Determining Party would have a very strong incentive to appear as a party with weak credit in order to reduce the 'value' of any obligations it owes to the other party. This type of behavior would clearly not have formed part of the parties' intention when entering into the1992 ISDA Master Agreement and should be discouraged by the courts.

Secondly, if the Determining Party's creditworthiness were taken into account when determining the value of any obligations it owes to the other party, this could potentially lead to 'double counting' of the Determining Party's weak credit, which would be to the detriment of the Defaulting Party or Affected Party (as the case may be). For example, taking the facts of the *Peregrine* case, if as a result of Robinson's lack of creditworthiness, Reference Market – makers have determined that Robinson will likely only pay 20 cents on the dollar (i. e. Robinson can only pay 20% of each dollar it owes to other parties), the Reference Market – makers will value a right to receive USD 100 from Robinson at USD 20. This would mean that Peregrine would only be entitled to USD 20 from Robinson as the early termination payment under the 1992 ISDA Master Agreement. However, if Robinson did in fact default on its payment obligations as the Reference Market – makers had predicted that Robinson had a high chance of doing, Peregrine (assuming it is an unsecured creditor) would only receive USD 4 (being 20% of the early termination payment amount of USD 20). This would appear to be a grossly unfair result for Peregrine.

(2) Assumption of satisfaction of conditions precedent

In *Pioneer Freight Futures Company Ltd (in liquidation) v. TMT Asia Ltd*,[1] an interesting argument was raised as to whether conditions precedent with respect to future rights and obligations should be assumed to be satisfied for the purposes of determining Loss under the 1992 ISDA Master Agreement.

The facts of the *Pioneer* case involved a series of freight forward agreements entered into between Pioneer and TMT. A freight forward agreement involves a payment due from one party to the other based upon a comparison of the 'final' price (the price published on the Baltic Exchange for certain pre – agreed freight routes at a pre – agreed future date) to the 'fixed' price (a contract price pre – agreed by the parties). In essence, it is a bet by two parties on the future movement of the price of the pre – agreed freight route. The freight forward agreements were governed by the terms of a 1992 ISDA Master Agreement, with the parties selecting Loss and Second Method.

Following the insolvency of Pioneer, the freight forward agreements wereterminated due to the election of Automatic Early Termination, with the freight forward agreements in – the – money for Pioneer and out – of – the – money for TMT. TMT, as the Non – defaulting Party, ought to have determined the early termination payment amount in accordance with the Loss methodology, but did not do so. As a result, Pioneer made the relevant calculations (which showed that a early termination payment amount ought to be due from TMT to Pioneer) and made a claim on such basis.

One of TMT's contentions in defence was that Pioneer's calculation of the early termination payment amount was incorrect since it took into account payment obligations due from TMT to Pioneer following the Early Termination Date. This, in TMT's view, was wrong since such payments from TMT to Pioneer would never arise due to the effect of section 2 (a)(iii) of the 1992 ISDA Master Agreement.

Under the 1992 ISDA Master Agreement, there is a provision (section 2(a)(iii)) which provides that: "(iii) Each obligation of each party under Section 2(a)(i) is subject to (1) the condition precedent that no Event of Default or Potential Event of Default with respect to the other party has occurred and is continuing, (2) the condition precedent that no Early Termination Date in respect of the relevant Transaction has occurred or been effectively designated and (3) each other applicable condition precedent specified in this Agreement."

(the reference to Section 2(a)(i) above is a reference to the obligation of the parties to the ISDA Master Agreement to fulfill their payment and/or delivery obligations under the derivatives transactions entered into between the parties which are governed by the ISDA

[1] [2011] EWHC 778 (Comm).

Master Agreement)

Section 2(a)(iii) of the ISDA Master Agreement is one of the fundamental provisions in the ISDA Master Agreement as it operates as a 'flawed asset' clause. The purpose of this provision is to allow a party, when faced with a counterparty which has defaulted under a derivatives transaction (or is in danger of doing so), to minimize its credit exposure to the counterparty by suspending the obligation to make further payments or deliveries to such counterparty. This means that every right of a party under a derivatives transaction governed by an ISDA Master Agreement to receive a payment or delivery is a 'flawed asset', as it is subject to the condition precedent that there is no Event of Default or "**Potential Event of Default**"[1] occurring to such party.

TMT argued that since Pioneer could never fulfill the condition precedent set out under section 2(a)(iii) of the ISDA Master Agreement, any future payments from TMT to Pioneer should not be taken into account as the payment obligation would never arise due to the 'flawed asset' principle. This point, from TMT's point of view, was strengthened by the fact that the definition of Loss only included the phrase "assuming satisfaction of each applicable condition precedent" in the second sentence which only covers "any payment or delivery required to have been made... on or before the relevant Early Termination Date" (i. e. only retrospective payment obligations).

The court therefore had to consider whether payment obligations owed from the Non-defaulting Party to the Defaulting Party under derivatives transactions following the Early Termination Date should be included in the calculation of the early termination payment amount.

Mr Justice Gloster, in giving judgment, found that the interpretation put forward by TMT was not accurate and that such future payment obligations should be taken into account despite the fact that Pioneer (because of its insolvency) could not fulfill the conditions precedent required for such payment obligations to arise.

In the first sentence of the definition of Loss, it provides that the Determining Party needs to take into account "its total losses and costs (or gain, in which case expressed as a negative number) in connection with this Agreement or that Termination Transaction or group of Terminated Transactions". This, according to Mr Justice Gloster, clearly envisages that the Determining Party needs to account to the Defaulting Party for any "gain", which must include payment obligations under the derivatives transactions in the future. This sentence does not include any language about "assuming satisfaction of each applicable condi-

---

〔1〕 A Potential Event of Default is defined under the ISDA Master Agreement as "*any event which, with the giving of notice or the lapse of time or both, would constitute an Event of Default*".

tion precedent" because the assumption must apply in order for any "gain" to exist for the Determining Party.

If TMT's contention is accurate, and future payment obligations from the Determining Party to the Defaulting Party should be ignored as the conditions precedent cannot be satisfied by the Defaulting Party, there will never be any "gain" for the Determining Party to take into account. The accurate interpretation of the definition of Loss must therefore be that the Determining Party must assume that all conditions precedent for future payment obligations owing from it to the Defaulting Party are satisfied.[1]

(3) Losses under hedging contracts

The definition of Loss allows a Determining Party to take into account "any loss of bargain, cost of funding or, at the election of such party but without duplication, loss or cost incurred as a result of its terminating, liquidating, obtaining or reestablishing any hedge or related trading position (or any gain resulting from any of them)", or in simplified terms, any loss or gain in relation to hedging contracts.

As set out near the beginning of this chapter, many participants in the derivatives market use derivatives transactions to hedge their exposure, which may include exposurearising under another derivatives transaction. This leads to the question of what extent the loss or gain on a hedging contract can be taken into account under the Loss methodology of determining an early termination payment amount.

In the case of*Australia and New Zealand Banking Group Ltd v. Société Générale*,[2] the Court of Appeal had to consider this very question. The *ANZ* case involved two international banks (ANZ and SocGen) who had entered into several non - deliverable foreign exchange forward contracts (a type of FX derivative called a "**NDF**") involving USD and the Russian rouble. In order to hedge its exposure under the NDFs, SocGen had entered into certain hedging contracts with a Russian bank (of which ANZ had no knowledge). The NDFs contained a provision which allowed for early termination of the NDFs on the occurrence of certain events to the Russian financial markets. When Russia declared a banking moratorium in August 1998, SocGen terminated the NDFs and proceeded to determine the early termination payment amount using the Loss methodology (which had been selected by the parties). As a result of the Russian banking moratorium, the Russian bank with which SocGen had entered into hedging contracts was unable to meet its payment obligations to SocGen under such hedging contracts. The dispute between ANZ and SocGen was whether SocGen could take into account the losses on its hedging contracts when determining the

[1] See Mr Justice Gloster at para 116 of the *Pioneer* case [2011] EWHC 778 (Comm).

[2] [2000] 1 All ER (Comm) 682.

early termination payment amount with respect to the NDFs.

It was held by the Court of Appeal that the losses suffered by SocGen on its hedging contracts could not be included for the purpose of determining the early termination payment amount under the NDFs with ANZ. Lord Justice Mance observed that: "(a) it is readily understandable that the parties should agree to share loss or gain arising from the accelerated termination or liquidation or the need to take accelerated steps to obtain or re – establish a hedge, but that (b) it is inherently unlikely that a party in ANZ's position entering into a futures contract with SG would agree to share the risk of the simple collapse in value of a hedge arranged by its counterparty, SG."[1]

Furthermore, the inclusion of such losses on hedging contracts in the calculation would be "adventitious, since it would depend upon the identity and circumstances of any particular counterparty with whom SG chose to hedge their commitments to ANZ, in circumstances where ANZ would not normally and did not here know whether any hedge had been concluded or with whom."[2]

Therefore, the position appears to be that losses on hedging contracts can only be taken into account by the Determining Party if such loss stemmed directly from the termination, liquidation or re – establishment of the hedging contracts. Any losses on hedging contracts which arise otherwise (such as due to the inability of the counterparty to the hedging contract to perform its obligations) will need to be excluded from the calculation of the early termination payment amount by the Determining Party.

The Court of Appeal's restrictive approach to the interpretation of the definition of Loss under the 1992 ISDA Master Agreement in the*ANZ* case raises an interesting question of whether 'inappropriate' hedging contracts entered into by a Determining Party are allowed to be included in the determination of Loss.

For example, if as a result of a Determining Party entering into 'inappropriate' hedging contracts, the losses on such hedging contracts were much greater than if the Determining Party had entered into 'standard' hedging contracts, would the courts limit the Determining Party's ability to take into account all of its losses suffered on its hedging contracts?

It is submitted that the courtsmay apply a test of 'commercial reasonableness' to any determinations under the Loss methodology, and accordingly a Determining Party will need to demonstrate that any losses arising from its hedging contracts are reasonable, including the fact that the hedging contract represents a reasonable method to hedge its exposure under the derivatives transactions which have been terminated.

---

[1] *Ibid*, at para 13.

[2] *Ibid*, at para 12.

(4) Timing of determination

The definition of Loss under the 1992 ISDA Master Agreement provides that: "A party will determine its Loss as of the relevant Early Termination Date, or, if that is not reasonably practicable, as of the earliest date thereafter as is reasonably practicable."

Under normal market circumstances, it is generally not difficult for a Determining Party to calculate the early termination payment amount as of the Early Termination Date. However, as has been seen in recent financial crises (such as following the insolvency of Lehman Brothers), it may be very difficult for a Determining Party to obtain valuations or terminate its hedging contracts during a period of market turmoil.

The 1992 ISDA Master Agreement clearly considers this issue, and therefore provides that the determination of Loss may take place after the Early Termination Date. However, if a Determining Party decides to postpone its calculation to a date falling after the Early Termination Date, this decision will be subject to a test of whether it was commercially reasonable to do so.

Mr Justice Briggs, in relation to the timing of the determination of Loss, has stated that: "The value of being able to draw a line under the transaction by the use of a breach date basis of valuation of the Claimant's loss is that, save in special cases, for example where the Claimant is locked into a disadvantageous position by reason of the breach, it provides a neat and precise distinction between matters relevant to the Claimant's loss of bargain and matters such as his subsequent dealings, which are for his own risk and benefit and therefore in principle irrelevant to the damage flowing from the Defendant's breach... On its face, the determination of Loss is required to be made as at the Early Termination Date, which broadly corresponds with the breach date used by the common law."[1]

There has been little judicial consideration of what circumstances would make it commercially reasonable for a Determining Party to postpone the calculation of its Loss, and any such cases in the futureare likely to be determined on a case - by - case basis. While it is understandable that a Determining Party, when faced with market disruption, would like to adopt a 'wait and see' approach in order to be certain of its losses or gains, as Mr Justice Briggs points out, "there comes a point when a desire to be certain rather than to predict becomes commercially unreasonable".[2]

[1] Mr Justice Briggs in *Anthracite Rated Investments (Jersey) Ltd v. Lehman Brothers Finance SA (in liquidation)* [2011] EWHC 1822 (Ch) at para 118.

[2] *Lehman Brothers International (Europe) v. Lehman Brothers Finance S. A.* [2012] EWHC 1072 (Ch), at para 80. Note that this judgment relates to a close - out under a 2002 ISDA Master Agreement, although the same issue as to timing of determination arises.

An interesting point arises where, following a Determining Party's decision to delay the calculation of its Loss, subsequent event(s) occur which would have affected the rights and obligations of the parties under the Terminated Transactions had they not become the subject of early termination under the ISDA Master Agreement.

In the case of *Golden Strait Corporation v. Nippon Yusen Kubishka Kaisha*,[1] the appellant had chartered a ship to the respondent. The charterparty contained a term providing that if war broke out between certain selected countries, either party would have the right to cancel the charter without penalty. The respondent repudiated the charterparty, and the damages for such breach came to be determined by an arbitrator. However, before the arbitrator determined the damages payable, the second Gulf War broke out. Since it was extremely likely that the respondent would have cancelled the charter if the contract had still been in existence at the time of the second Gulf War, the issue was whether damages for the respondent's breach of charterparty should be limited to the time when the respondent would have had the right to cancel the charter, or should be calculated until the original maturity date of the charterparty.

The House of Lords, by majority (Lord Bingham and Lord Walker dissenting), determined that the calculation of damages should be limited to the time when the respondent would have had the right to cancel the charter. Lord Carswell, in agreement with Lord Justice Mance in the Court of Appeal judgment, states that "considerations of certainty and finality have in this case to yield to the greater importance of achieving an accurate assessment of the damages based on the loss actually incurred".[2]

Although at the time of the repudiation of the contract, there was only a possibility of theout break of war, by the time of the determination of damages, this contingency had crystallised into an actual event. Lord Carswell, in support of the proposition that the arbitrator should be able to take into account the occurrence of this event, cited Lord Macnaghten (from *Bwllfa and Merthyr Dare Steam Collieries* (1891) *Ltd v. Pontypridd Waterworks Co.*[3]), who had commented on a similar circumstance in the following manner: "Why should he listen to conjecture on a matter which has become an accomplished fact? Why should he guess when he can calculate? With the light before him, why should he shut his eyes and grope in the dark?".[4]

This principle could be applicable to the determination of Loss under the ISDA Master

---

[1] [2007] 2 A. C. 353.

[2] *Ibid*, at para 63.

[3] [1903] AC 426.

[4] [2007] 2 A. C. 353 at para 65.

Agreement where the Determining Party delays the calculation of its Loss till after the Early Termination Date. For example, if an event occurs following the Early Termination Date but before the Determining Party calculates its Loss, and such event would have terminated such derivatives transactions before their scheduled maturity, the Determining Party may not be entitled to calculate its Loss on the basis that such derivatives transactions would have continued for the remainder of their entire term.

(5) Other general principles of contractual damages applicable?

It is clear that "[t]he termination payment formulae under s 6(e) are not to be equated with, or interpreted rigidly in accordance with, the quantification of damages at common law for breach of contract."[1] In fact, it has been stated that "the phrase "loss of bargain" has led to common law principles about the use of the cost of obtaining a replacement transaction to become the normal, and indeed expressly available, method of determination of that head of Loss (or gain). But that limited incursion of common law principles is not in my view a warranty for the wholesale dis – application of the close – out formula, in favour of some more general application of the common law."[2]

However, it ispossible that the courts may nevertheless consider certain general principles applicable to the calculation of contractual damages (such as remoteness and mitigation) when determining whether the early termination payment amount according to the Loss methodology is commercially reasonable.

For example, the duty for the Determining Party to mitigate may arise in the context where the Determining Party has entered into certain hedging arrangements with respect to the terminated derivatives transactions. If the Determining Party believes that it will be able to recover the cost of terminating the hedging arrangements from the Defaulting Party under the early termination payment provisions of the 1992 ISDA Master Agreement, then the Determining Party may not have the appropriate incentive to take reasonable care in terminating the hedging arrangements at the market rate. As was set out in Viscount Haldane L. C.'s judgment in*British Westinghouse Electric Co. Ltd v. Underground Electric Railways*:[3] "The fundamental basis is thus compensation for pecuniary loss naturally flowing from the breach; but this first principle is qualified by a second, which imposes on a plaintiff the duty of taking all reasonable steps to mitigate the loss consequent on the breach, and debars him from claiming any part of the damage which is due to his neglect to take such

〔1〕 Mr Justice Briggs in *Anthracite Rated Investments (Jersey) Ltd v. Lehman Brothers Finance SA (in liquidation)* [2011] EWHC 1822 (Ch) at para 116.

〔2〕 Ibid at para 126.

〔3〕 [1912] A. C. 673.

steps."

A Determining Party is likely to be bound by the same requirement to take reasonable steps to mitigate its losses under the Loss methodology for determining the early termination payment amount as it would if such amount were determined in accordance with general principles of contractual damages.

It is also quite possible that in the calculation of the early termination payment amount in accordance with the Loss methodology, the Determining Party may be restricted by the doctrine of remoteness as famously set out in*Hadley v. Baxendale*,[1] where a party should only be entitled to damages "such as may fairly and reasonably be considered either arising naturally, i. e., according to the usual course of things from such breach of contract itself, or such as may reasonably be supposed to have been in the contemplation of both parties, at the time they made the contract, as the probable result of the breach of it."

5.3.1.2.5 *Market Quotation vs Loss*

As has been stated, it is clear from judicial authorities that Market Quotation and Loss should lead to broadly the same result. However, there are still certain considerations in relation to the two calculation methodologies which users of the 1992 ISDA Master Agreement should be aware of.

Firstly, Market Quotation is generally considered the more objective and impartial method for determining the early termination payment amount under the 1992 ISDA Master Agreement. Since a certain degree of discretion is inherent in the determination of Loss, parties may be concerned that a Determining Party will seek to calculate a early termination payment amount which is as beneficial to itself as possible.

Secondly, in a derivatives market which is dominated by a handful of dealers (which make up most of the Reference Market – makers), it is quite possible in the event of a collapse of a large entity that the Reference Market – makers will each be a Determining Party with respect to derivatives transactions entered into with such insolvent entity. In this scenario, there is a certain potential for bias in the Market Quotation methodology since each of the Reference Market – makers will be obtaining quotations from each other with respect to similar derivatives transactions.

Thirdly, the Market Quotation methodology is only suitable for use with derivatives transactions where there is a lot of liquidity in the market. If the parties have agreed to enter into a highly bespoke and/or complex derivatives transaction, it may be the case that a Determining Party may obtain quotations from Reference Market – makers which diverge wildly due to the lack of a transparentand liquid market for such a derivatives transaction (if

[1] (1854)9 Exch. 341.

the Determining Party can obtain quotations at all). In such cases, it is probably preferable for the parties to stipulate that the Loss methodology applies.

Fourthly, although parties have traditionally been hesitant about the application of the Loss methodology given its subjective nature, the spread of industry expertise in derivatives transactions has allowed more participants to delve into the complex pricing systems used by large dealers to calculate the early termination payment amount using the Loss methodology. This has given a certain degree of comfort to market participants and has made the Loss methodology more acceptable in the derivatives world.

5.3.1.2.6 (*VI*) *First Method vs Second Method*

Apart from the election between Market Quotation and Loss, the parties to a 1992 ISDA Master Agreement can elect whether First Method or Second Method applies to derivative transactions between them which are governed by the 1992 ISDA Master Agreement.

Interestingly, the 1992 ISDA Master Agreement does notprovide a definition for First Method and Second Method mean, and does not even explain the difference between them. A person reading the 1992 ISDA Master Agreement must instead infer the difference by reading section 6(e). In essence, the First Method provides that a early termination payment amount is only ever payable from a Defaulting Party to a Non-defaulting Party (or an Affected Party to a Non-affected Party in the case of a Termination Event), whereas with the Second Method, the Determining Party will calculate the early termination payment amount, and such amount will be payable by one party to the other (depending on whether the early termination payment amount is positive or negative).

As explained in Simon Firth's book "Derivatives Law and Practice": "First Method reflects the position that applies at common law, where damages are never payable to the party in breach. In other words, if First Method has been chosen and the calculation has a negative value, no payment is due to either party. Such a provision is often referred to as a walkaway clause because it means that the Defaulting Party forfeits the embedded value of the transactions that have been closed out."[1]

Historically, the First Method was preferred by market participants as it accorded with the general position at common law, as described above. However, this approach could potentially lead to instability or uncertainty as a party, upon insolvency, could find that they are not entitled to any payments in respect of derivatives transactions which were "in-the-money" for such party if the First Method applied.

As a result, the Basel Committee on Banking Supervision amended the capital adequacy rules for financial institutions in July 1994 to state that "contracts containing walkaway

[1] 2010 version, at para 11.157.

clauses will not be eligible for netting for the purpose of calculating capital requirements pursuant to this Accord"[1] (i. e. derivatives transactions governed by a 1992 ISDA Master Agreement applying the First Method would not be eligible for netting, which would worsen the regulatory capital requirements set out under the rules of the Basel Committee on Banking Supervision). Following the amendment to the Basel Accord, very few market participants (if any) elect to apply First Method in their 1992 ISDA Master Agreements and the Second Method is now undoubtedly the market standard.

5.3.2 *Determination of the early termination payment amount under the* 2002 *ISDA Master Agreement*

5.3.2.1 *History of the* 2002 *ISDA Master Agreement*

The idea to 'upgrade' the 1992 version of the ISDA Master Agreement started in 1999 following a series of financial shocks which occurred during the late 1990's. These included: (1) the failure of Peregrine Investments Holding Limited, an investment company incorporated in Hong Kong, in January 1998; (20the banking moratorium imposed by the Russian government in August 1998; and (3) the collapse of Long Term Capital Management, a hedge fund based in Connecticut, United States, in September 1998.

These events provided a stress – test for all of the market standard documentation used by financial institutions and market participants at the time, which included not only the 1992 ISDA Master Agreement but also documentation used for other types of financial transactions (such as the Global Master Repurchase Agreement for repurchase transactions and the Global Master Securities Lending Agreement for securities lending transactions).

The aftermath of the stress – test was considered by the Counterparty Risk Management Policy Group in January 1999, which was made up of international banks as well as other institutions (such as the Federal Reserve Bank ofNew York and The Bond Market Association). The Group published a report in June 1999 titled *Improving Counterparty Risk Management Practices*, of which one section was dedicated to documentation issues in the financial markets. This was one of the factors which led to ISDA identifying several areas for improvement in the 1992 ISDA Master Agreement, which included the need for better provisions relating to the valuation process following early termination of the derivatives transactions.

The first draft of the 2002 ISDA Master Agreement was unveiled to members in November 2001. Following a series of large – scale meetings and revised drafts, the final version of the 2002 ISDA Master Agreement that we know today was published on 8 January 2003.

---

[1] http://www.bis.org/publ/bcbs12a.pdf.

5.3.2.2 *Differences in the determination of the early termination payment amount under the* 2002 *ISDA Master Agreement*

Apart from the changes made to the close – out valuation methodology, the 2002 ISDA Master Agreement also contains certain new features such as the inclusion of provisions relating to force majeure and set – off. However, it is beyond the scope of this chapter to discuss all of the differences between the 1992 ISDA Master Agreement and the 2002 ISDA Master Agreement.

With respect toearly termination under the 2002 ISDA Master Agreement, there is little substantive difference from the 1992 ISDA Master Agreement as far as the mechanisms for triggering the right for a party to select an Early Termination Date with respect to which all derivatives transactions become Terminated Transactions. This has already been covered above with respect to the 1992 ISDA Master Agreement and will not be repeated here.

The crucial amendment made in the 2002 ISDA Master Agreement is the replacement of the Market Quotation and Loss methodologies, as well as the First Method and Second Method election, with a single method for determining the early termination payment amount under section 6(e) of the 2002 ISDA Master Agreement.

The philosophy behind the design of the new valuation methodology is to provide the Determining Party with greater flexibility in determining the early termination payment amount by synthesizing the advantages of the calculation process under Market Quotation and Loss while avoiding the pitfalls of these methodologies (i. e. inability to obtain representative quotations from Reference Market – makers (in the case of Market Quotation) and subjectivity (in the case of Loss)).

Under the 2002 ISDA Master Agreement, the Determining Party needs to calculate the "**Close – out Amounts**" and the Unpaid Amounts. Conceptually, the definition of Unpaid Amounts corresponds quite closely to the definition of Unpaid Amounts under the 1992 ISDA Master Agreement as both definitions cover any amounts due between the parties which have accrued prior to the Early Termination Date but have not been paid, and amounts which (but for the event which led to the designation of an Early Termination Date) should have become payable prior to the Early Termination Date. However, the 2002 ISDA Master Agreement has introduced a more detailed system for calculating the amount of interest which should accrue on such Unpaid Amounts. The major difference under the 2002 ISDA Master Agreement is therefore the introduction of the concept of Close – out Amounts.

5.3.2.2.1 *Close – out Amount*

The definition of Close – out Amount is fairly long, but worth setting out in full here as each part of the definition will be explored in more detail. The first paragraph of the definition of Close – out Amount is as follows: "'Close – out Amount' means, with respect to each Terminated Transaction or each group of Terminated Transactions and a Determining Party, the amount of the losses or costs of the Determining Party that are or would be incurred under then prevailing circumstances (expressed as a positive number) or gains of the Determining Party that are or would be realised under then prevailing circumstances (expressed as a negative number) in replacing, or in providing for the Determining Party the economic equivalent of, (a) the material terms of that Terminated Transaction or group of Terminated Transactions, including the payments and deliveries by the parties under Section 2(a)(i) in respect of that Terminated Transaction or group of Terminated Transactions that would, but for the occurrence of the relevant Early Termination Date, have been required after that date (assuming satisfaction of the conditions precedent in Section 2(a)(iii)) and (b) the option rights of the parties in respect of that Terminated Transaction or group of Terminated Transactions."

The wording in this paragraph is fairly similar to the concept used under the Market Quotation methodology, particularly with respect to the reference that the losses or gains should be determined with respect to replacing or providing the Determining Party with the economic equivalent of the Terminated Transactions.

However, the difference contained in the 2002 ISDA Master Agreement is the reference to "material terms" and "option rights" in respect of the Terminated Transactions. According to the *User's Guide to the* 2002 *ISDA Master Agreement*, the intention in using "material terms" is to restrict the replacement transaction to replicating the direct payment flows or other terms that impact on pricing of the derivatives transaction.

The second paragraph of the definition of Close – out Amount is as follows: "Any Close – out Amount will be determined by the Determining Party (or its agent), which will act in good faith and use commercially reasonable procedures in order to produce a commercially reasonable result. The Determining Party may determine a Close – out Amount for any group of Terminated Transactions or any individual Terminated Transaction but, in the aggregate, for not less than all Terminated Transactions. Each Close – out Amount will be determined as of the Early Termination Date or, if that would not be commercially reasonable, as of the date or dates following the Early Termination Date as would be commercially reasonable."

This paragraph sets out the Determining Party's duty to act in good faith and a commercially reasonable manner. The implications of this standard are explored further below. The timing by which the Determining Party needs to determine the Close – out Amount is similar to the 1992 ISDA Master Agreement in that such determination should take place as of the Early Termination Date if it is commercially reasonable to do so.

The next section of the definition of Close – out Amount is set out below:

"Unpaid Amounts in respect of a Terminated Transaction or group of Terminated Transactions and legal fees and out - of - pocket expenses referred to in Section 11 are to be excluded in all determinations of Close - out Amounts.

In determining a Close - out Amount, the Determining Party may consider any relevant information, including, without limitation, one or more of the following types of information: -

(i) quotations (either firm or indicative) for replacement transactions supplied by one or more third parties that may take into account the creditworthiness of the Determining Party at the time the quotation is provided and the terms of any relevant documentation, including credit support documentation, between the Determining Party and the third party providing the quotation;

(ii) information consisting of relevant market data in the relevant market supplied by one or more third parties including, without limitation, relevant rates, prices, yields, yield curves, volatilities, spreads, correlations or other relevant market data in the relevant market; or

(iii) information of the types described in clause (i) or (ii) above from internal sources (including any of the Determining Party's Affiliates) if that information is of the same type used by the Determining Party in the regular course of its business for the valuation of similar transactions.

The Determining Party will consider, taking into account the standards and procedures described in this definition, quotations pursuant to clause (i) above or relevant market data pursuant to clause (ii) above unless the Determining Party reasonably believes in good faith that such quotations or relevant market data are not readily available or would produce a result that would not satisfy those standards. When considering information described in clause (i), (ii) or (iii) above, the Determining Party may include costs of funding, to the extent costs of funding are not and would not be a component of the other information being utilised. Third parties supplying quotations pursuant to clause (i) above or market data pursuant to clause (ii) above may include, without limitation, dealers in the relevant markets, end - users of the relevant product, information vendors, brokers and other sources of market information."

This section sets out three examples of information which the Determining Party can take into account when determining the Close - out Amount. Note that the list is not exhaustive and the definition specifically says that "one or more" types of information can be used.

In relation to the first type of information, the ability to use either firm or indicative quotations from third parties is designed to provide greater flexibility to the Determining Party compared to the Market Quotation methodology under the 1992 ISDA Master Agreement(which required quotations from Reference Market – makers and was silent on whether indicative quotations could be used). "Third parties" in this context refers to, without limitation, "dealers in the relevant markets, end – users of the relevant product, information vendors, brokers and other sources of market information".

Furthermore, the definition specifically provides that the creditworthiness of the Determining Party can be taken into account to address the dispute which arose in the*Peregrine* case.

In relation to the second and third types of information, this allows the Determining Party even greater flexibility to determine the Close – out Amount by either breaking down derivative transactions into their economic components(i. e. using market data) or their internal pricing models(i. e. using internal sources).

In reality, it is submitted that a Determining Party will prefer to use market quotations from third parties as this provides an objective basis to justify their calculation of the Close – out Amount whichprovides less room for challenge from the other party. However, in cases involving bespoke derivatives transactions or where there is market disruption, the other types of information identified in this definition will provide the Determining Party with other means of determining the Close – out Amount.

The definition of Close – out Amount also includes a paragraph in relation to hedging: "Without duplication of amounts calculated based on information described in clause(i), (ii) or(iii) above, or other relevant information, and when it is commercially reasonable to do so, the Determining Party may in addition consider in calculating a Close – out Amount any loss or cost incurred in connection with its terminating, liquidating or re – establishing any hedge related to a Terminated Transaction or group of Terminated Transactions(or any gain resulting from any of them)."

This paragraph incorporates certain elements of the Loss methodology from the 1992 ISDA Master Agreement in relation to losses or gains arising from hedge positions. It is submitted that the same judicial principles established in relation to the 1992 ISDA Master Agreement relating to loss on hedging contracts(as discussed above) will apply equally to the 2002 ISDA Master Agreement.

The final section of the definition of Close – out Amount is as follows: "Commercially reasonable procedures used in determining a Close – out Amount may include the following: —(1) application to relevant market data from third parties pursuant to clause(ii) above or information from internal sources pursuant to clause(iii) above of pricing or other valuation models that are, at the time of the determination of the Close – out Amount, used by the Determining Party in the regular course of its business in pricing or valuing transactions between the Determining Party and unrelated third parties that are similar to the Terminated

Transaction or group of Terminated Transactions; and(2) application of different valuation methods to Terminated Transactions or groups of Terminated Transactions depending on the type, complexity, size or number of the Terminated Transactions or group of Terminated Transactions."

This final section provides certain parameters for what constitutes commercially reasonable behavior for the Determining Party. For example, in order for a Determining Party to rely on internal sources to calculate the Close – out Amount, it must demonstrate that it has been using such valuation methods for similar derivatives transactions during its regular course of business. However, this section also provides a certain degree of flexibility by stating that valuation methodologies may change depend on the "*type, complexity, size or number*" of derivatives transactions.

5.3.2.2.2 *Standard of good faith and commercially reasonable manner*

The definition of Close – out Amount requires the Determining Party to "act in good faith and use commercially reasonable procedures in order to produce a commercially reasonable result". Similarly, the definition of Loss under the 1992 ISDA Master Agreement stated that this should be an amount that the Determining Party "reasonably determines in good faith to be its total losses and costs".

With respect to this standard, Mr Justice Briggs made several observations. Firstly, the standard contained in the 2002 ISDA Master Agreement imposes two objective standards (both the procedures and the result must be commercially reasonable). Following from this, it appears that there is a range of procedures and results which the Determining Party can elect. However, as the provisions of the 2002 ISDA Master Agreement provide an objective standard which can be applied by the court itself, if the Determining Party fails to determine the Close – out Amount, it is possible for the court to do so on the application of the other party to the 2002 ISDA Master Agreement.[1]

It should be noted, as a side point, that even where the ISDA Master Agreement does not expressly provide a standard of good faith and commercially reasonable manner(such as a discretion to adjust the terms of a derivatives transaction following certain market events), the courts will nevertheless imply standards to prevent abuse by the decision – maker. As a result, any discretion is limited by "concepts of honesty, good faith, and genuineness, and the need for the absence of arbitrariness, capriciousness, perversity and irrationali-

[1] See, for example, *Sudbrook Trading Estate v. Eggleton* [1983] 1 AC 444, where the court stepped in to carry out a valuation procedure which had been agreed by the parties but where one party had refused to co – operate in the valuation process.

ty".[1] Furthermore, although standards of reasonableness and unreasonableness come into play, the courts will only impose the *Wednesbury* rationality test[2] on the decision – maker.

5.3.2.2.3 "*Value clean" principle and the* 2002 *ISDA Master Agreement*

As of the writing of this chapter, there is unfortunately scant judicial authority in relation to the determination of the early termination payment amount under the 2002 ISDA Master Agreement. As was observed by Mr Justice Briggs in*Lehman Brothers International* (*Europe*) *v. Lehman Brothers Finance S. A.*,[3] "[t] here is, so far as counsel are aware, no reported authority on the meaning and effect of the replacement provisions in the 2002 edition"[4] (i. e. the 2002 ISDA Master Agreement).

However, in this case (hereinafter referred to as the*LBIE* case), Mr Justice Briggs offered valuable insight into the scope of what "material terms" and "option rights" includes for the purposes of determining the Close – out Amount with respect to Terminated Transactions.

In the*LBIE* case, LBIE had entered into a series of derivatives transactions with its clients and had separately entered into back – to – back derivatives transactions with LBF. The economic terms of the back – to – back transactions were identical to the derivatives transactions entered into between LBIE and its clients, and the intention between LBIE and LBF was to pass on all economic risks and rewards under the derivatives transactions from LBIE to LBF.

In a side letter (separately documented from the ISDA Master Agreement between LBIE and LBF) (the "**Side Letter**"), it was agreed that if any derivatives transaction between LBIE and a client were closed out, the equivalent back – to – back transaction between LBIE and LBF would also be closed out, and the amount payable between LBIE and LBF would mirror the amount payable between LBIE and its client. In this way, LBIE would neither gain nor lose any money with respect to any close – out of a derivatives transaction between itself and its client.

Unfortunately, the Side Letter only addressed the situation where a derivatives transac-

---

[1] *Socimer International Bank Ltd v. Standard Bank London Ltd* [2008] EWCA Civ 116, at para 66. *Socimer International Bank Ltd v. Standard Bank London Ltd*([2008] EWCA Civ 116,第66段)。

[2] See *Associated Provincial Picture Houses Ltd. v. Wednesbury Corporation* [1947] 1 KB 223. The *Wednesbury* rationality test consists of three questions: (i) did the decision – maker, in making that decision, take into account factors that ought not to have been taken into account; (ii) did the decision – maker fail to take into account factors that ought to have been taken into account; and (iii) is the decision so unreasonable that no reasonable decision – maker would ever consider it.

[3] [2012] EWHC 1072(Ch).

[4] *Ibid*, at para 39.

tion between LBIE and its client closes out prior to the back – to – back transaction between LBIE and LBF, but does not cover the situation where the back – to – back transaction between LBIE and LBF terminates prior to the equivalent derivatives transaction between LBIE and its client.

As a result of Lehman Brothers' insolvency in September 2008, an Early Termination Date was designated with respect to the ISDA Master Agreement between LBIE and LBF[1], with the effect that all back – to – back transactions became Terminated Transactions. The issue which the High Court needed to consider was whether LBIE (as the Determining Party) was entitled to take into account the effect of the Side Letter in determining the early termination payment amount under the ISDA Master Agreement between itself and LBF.

LBIE's contention was that it should be allowed to take into account the terms of the Side Letter, which would then mean that LBIE could determine the early termination payment amount with respect to the amounts it was liable to pay to its clients on the derivatives transactions which the back – to – back transactions were meant to cover. LBF's argument was that the Side Letter should be ignored, with the effect that LBIE would need to calculate the early termination payment amount in accordance with the terms of the 2002 ISDA Master Agreement only (i. e. without reference to the amounts it owed to clients under the close – out of the derivatives transactions with its clients).

Having concluded that the provisions of the Side Letter constitutes terms of the Terminated Transactions (since the Side Letter introduces a new mechanism for the close – out of a back – to – back transaction between LBIE and LBF in the event that a derivatives transaction between LBIE and a client terminates), the court needed to consider whether the terms of the Side Letter could be taken into account when determining the Close – out Amount.

LBIE argued that the inclusion of "material terms" and "option rights" under the definition of Close – out Amount demonstrates that the 2002 ISDA Master Agreement should be interpreted as widening the scope of provisions which can be taken into account when determining the early termination payment amount under the 2002 ISDA Master Agreement when compared to the 1992 ISDA Master Agreement. However, in both cases, the fundamental issue in the eyes of Mr Justice Briggs was that the 'value clean' principle required there to be a "continuity assumption" i. e. "the assumption that the stream of payments and deliveries under [the Terminated Transactions] would run their course [assuming all conditions

---

[1] Automatic Early Termination was applicable.

precedent are fulfilled]" .[1]

Mr Milligan, on behalf of LBIE, submitted that the 2002 ISDA Master Agreement did in fact depart from the 'value clean' principle, such as the fact that the definition of Close – out Amount explicitly provides that the Determining Party can consider third party quotations for replacement transactions which take into account the creditworthiness of the Determining Party (clearly in response to the *Peregrine* case). Since the Determining Party's creditworthiness could only be relevant in relation to the value of future payment obligations from the Determining Party under the Terminated Transactions (by virtue of the fact that a default by a Determining Party to pay such amount would lead to early termination), the determination of Close – out Amount clearly contemplates that future rights and obligations under the Terminated Transactions need to be adjusted or discounted for the risk that such future rights and obligations may not accrue.

Extending this line or argument, Mr Milligan contended that provisions allowing for early termination are an important factor in the valuation of transactions in the commercial world. By implication, to exclude such provisions in the valuation of such transactions would lead to the risk that, if the Determining Party was out – of – the – money under the Terminated Transactions, it would be required to pay a much larger early termination payment amount to the Defaulting Party by virtue of the fact that the Determining Party could not take into account any provisions relating to early termination.

However, Mr Justice Briggs observed that the 'value clean' jurisprudence in relation to the valuation methodology under the 1992 ISDA Master Agreement had been confirmed by the Court of Appeal in *Lomas & others v. JFB Firth Rixson*,[2] which meant that he was now bound by this interpretation when approaching the close – out valuation process under the 2002 ISDA Master Agreement. As such, the Side Letter must be ignored unless "the 2002 edition could be construed as having substantially abandoned that principle [of 'value clean'], or because the unusual purpose of the Intercompany Transactions [the back – to – back transactions] (as a means of transferring risks and benefits undertaken under the Client Transactions) justified some wholly exceptional interpretation with no wider consequences".[3]

In particular, the court considered that the requirement to assume satisfaction of the conditions precedent in section 2(a)(iii) of the ISDA Master Agreement (which is the crucial element of the continuity assumption) under the Market Valuation methodology was in-

[1] [2012] EWHC 1072(Ch), at para 56.

[2] [2012] EWCA Civ 419.

[3] [2012] EWHC 1072(Ch), at para 61.

troduced in verbatim into the definition of Close – out Amount under the 2002 ISDA Master Agreement. Section 2(a)(iii) of the ISDA Master Agreement, as described above, provides that no Event of Default or Potential Event of Default has occurred and no Early Termination Date has been designated. This meant that the Determining Party had to assume that all future payment and delivery rights and obligations under the Terminated Transactions would have been satisfied and any events which could potentially lead to the designation of an Early Termination Date would need to be ignored.

It is interesting to contrast the emerging 'value clean' jurisprudence in relation to close – out valuation under the ISDA Master Agreement with the position at common law. In the *LBIE* case, Mr Justice Briggs comments on LBIE's argument as follows: "Mr Milligan [counsel for LBIE] submitted that the value clean principle required no more than that the Section 2(a)(i) stream of payments and deliveries be valued clean first, before adjustment by reference to other economically relevant terms. If that were the correct analysis of the principle, then it seems to me firstly that the ANZ case would have been differently decided, and the value of the US dollar payment stream heavily discounted by reference to the virtual certainty that Soc Gen would thereafter have elected to make payment by a different method. Secondly it would, to my mind, create a pointlessly circular valuation approach."[1]

It appears that under the 'value clean' approach, there is no ability for the Determining Party to adjust the future payment and delivery rights and obligations to take into account other "*economically relevant terms*" such as additional events leading to early termination.[2]

Comparing this conclusion with the judgment given by Lord Carswell in *Golden Strait Corporation v. Nippon Yusen Kubishka Kaisha*[3] with respect to the impact of a contingency event on the calculation of damages under general common law principles: "The damages can be assessed at the date of repudiation by valuing the chance that the contingency would occur and that the charter would be cancelled... That value might lie anywhere on the scale between extreme unlikelihood, which would give the deduction a minimal value, to virtual certainty, which would mean that it would be assessed at a figure very close to that which would be reached if one made the definite assumption that the contingency would occur.

〔1〕 *Ibid*, at paragraph 65.

〔2〕 Mr Justice Briggs comments at para 60 of the judgment that an early termination triggered by (i) a rate exceeding a stated cap or floor or (ii) the outbreak of war between USA and Iran (examples provided by Mr Milligan (counsel for LBIE)) could not be taken into account due to the 'value clean' principle.

〔3〕 [2007] UKHL 12.

This approach is well known and recognised in other areas of the law. It is commonplace in the assessment of damages for personal injuries to award a sum which reflects the chance that a condition such as osteoarthritis may set in."[1]

It should be acknowledged that, as has been set out by Mr Justice Briggs early on in the judgment on the *LBIE* case, the valuation methodology under the ISDA Master Agreement should not be equated with the calculation of damages under common law contractual principles. As such, any differences between the calculation of the early termination payment amount by a Determining Party under the ISDA Master Agreement and the position under the common law for contractual damages are of general interest only. As the *LBIE* case may potentially go to appeal, it will remain to be seen if any further developments or refinements in the 'value clean' principle will occur.

---

[1] *Ibid*, at para 64.

案 例 目 录

图书在版编目(CIP)数据

损失赔偿与救济 / 杨良宜著. -- 北京 : 法律出版社, 2013.4(2025.6 重印)
研究生教学书系
ISBN 978-7-5118-4767-6

Ⅰ.①损… Ⅱ.①杨… Ⅲ.①国际商法-研究 Ⅳ.①D996.1

中国版本图书馆 CIP 数据核字(2013)第 057565 号

损失赔偿与救济
SUNSHI PEICHANG YU JIUJI

杨良宜 著

责任编辑 吴 昉
装帧设计 凌点工作室

出版发行 法律出版社
编辑统筹 法律教育出版分社
责任校对 郑怡萍
责任印制 刘晓伟
经　　销 新华书店

开本 710 毫米×1000 毫米 1/16
印张 74　**字数** 1480 千
版本 2013 年 4 月第 1 版
印次 2025 年 6 月第 5 次印刷
印刷 永清县金鑫印刷有限公司

地址:北京市丰台区莲花池西里 7 号(100073)
网址:www.lawpress.com.cn
投稿邮箱:info@lawpress.com.cn
举报盗版邮箱:jbwq@lawpress.com.cn
销售电话:010-83938349
客服电话:010-83938350
咨询电话:010-63939796

书号:ISBN 978-7-5118-4767-6
定价:128.00 元

凡购买本社图书,如有印装错误,我社负责退换。电话:010-83938349